Encyclopedia of the American Constitution

Supplement I

Editorial Board

Encyclopedia
of the
American Constitution

Supplement I

LEONARD W. LEVY, Editor-in-Chief
The Claremont Graduate School, Claremont, California

KENNETH L. KARST, Associate Editor
University of California, Los Angeles

JOHN G. WEST, JR., Assistant Editor
The Claremont Graduate School, Claremont, California

MACMILLAN PUBLISHING COMPANY
NEW YORK
MAXWELL MACMILLAN CANADA
TORONTO
MAXWELL MACMILLAN INTERNATIONAL
NEW YORK • OXFORD • SINGAPORE • SYDNEY

Macmillan Publishing Company
866 Third Avenue, New York, NY 10022

Maxwell Macmillan Canada, Inc.
1200 Eglinton Avenue East, Suite 200
Don Mills, Ontario M3C 3N1

Library of Congress Catalog Card No.: 86–3038

Printed in the United States of America

printing number
1 2 3 4 5 6 7 8 9 10

Macmillan, Inc., is part of the Maxwell Communication Group of Companies.

Library of Congress Cataloging-in-Publication Data
(Revised for Supplement I)

Encyclopedia of the American Constitution.

   Supplement I edited by Leonard W. Levy, Kenneth L. Karst, John G. West, Jr.
   Accompanied by: Supplement I, 1991.
   Includes bibliographies and indexes.
   1. United States—Constitutional law—Encyclopedias.
I. Levy, Leonard Williams, 1923–   . II. Karst, Kenneth L.   III. Mahoney, Dennis J.
KF4548.E53 1986   342.73′023′03   86–3038
ISBN 0–02–918610–2   347.3022303
ISBN 0–02–918678–1 (Supplement : red version : $90.00)
ISBN 0–02–918675–7 (Supplement : blue version : $90.00)

Editorial and Production Staff:

Philip Friedman, *Publisher*
Elly Dickason, *Editor in Chief*
Martha Goldstein, *Senior Project Editor*
Lynn Constantinou, *Production Manager*
Karin K. Vanderveer, *Assistant Editor*

The paper used in this publication meets the minimum requirements of American National Standard for Information Sciences—Permanence of Paper for Printed Library Materials. ANSI Z39.48–1984.

Contents

Preface

The continuing deluge of problems and developments concerning the Constitution makes an updating of the *Encyclopedia of the American Constitution* desirable. The Supreme Court decides at least 250 cases annually, about 150 of them with full opinions. Before the bicentennial of the ratification of the Bill of Rights concludes, the Court will have decided about 1500 cases since we finished the manuscript for the four-volume edition in mid-1985. New opinions of the Court are having a substantial impact on most of American constitutional law and the public policies that it reflects.

The Court itself is undergoing major changes in personnel. Chief Justice Warren Burger and Justices Lewis H. Powell, William J. Brennan, and Thurgood Marshall have retired. William H. Rehnquist now sits in the center seat; Antonin Scalia succeeded to Rehnquist's former position; Anthony Kennedy became Powell's successor; David H. Souter holds Brennan's old chair; and Clarence Thomas succeeds Marshall. Changes in personnel herald additional and significant changes in constitutional law. For example, the senate Judiciary Committee hearings on the nomination of Robert H. Bork, in itself a landmark event, reflected a national concern on all sides for the integrity and impartiality of the Court and its interpretation of the Constitution.

As we finished editorial work on the Encyclopedia in 1985, the Department of Justice intensified a broad attack on the "judicial activism" of the Supreme Court, the finality of its decisions, and its incorporation doctrine, which makes the Bill of Rights applicable to the states. Soon after, the protracted Iran-Contra inquiries raised some of the most important constitutional issues since Watergate. New, important, and even sensational developments of concern to the Constitution have become almost common.

This Supplement to the Encyclopedia has enabled us to present many topics that we had originally neglected and to cover all major developments and decisions since 1985; it includes articles on the full range of developments in constitutional law. Because we wanted the Supplement to be a free-standing volume, as well as an additional volume to the original work, we instructed contributors to introduce each article with a short background to its topic and to write as if the Encyclopedia did not exist. In addition to articles on concepts such as abortion, affirmative action, establishment of religion, equal protection, and free speech, we have included analyses of major cases. We have treated new developments conceptually, topically, biographically, historically, and by judicial decision.

We continued our policy of getting a wide range of scholarly opinions. For the sake of variety, generally we did not ask the authors of the original articles to "update" their contributions; we sought different authors, sometimes of differing constitutional persuasions. The Supplement is an independent reference work.

The Supplement enables us to include articles on topics that we had omitted from the four-volume set, either as a result of editorial neglect or because some authors failed to produce the articles and too little time remained to replace them. As comprehensive as the Encyclopedia is, it has gaps that we have sought to close with this Supplement (e.g., Court-packing plans, the Judicial Conference of the United States, original intent, constitutional remedies, special prosecutors, entitlements, constitutional fictions, the civil-rights movement, gender rights, legal culture, law and economic theory, ratifier intent, textualism, unenumerated rights, the Senate Judiciary Committee, and so on). The Supplement also gave us the opportunity to treat at greater length a variety of topics to which we originally allocated insufficient space. Although 1,500,000 words for the four-volume set was a huge amount, we found the publisher's limitations on length to be too constraining. An additional volume of over 400,000 words, which Macmillan approved for the Supplement, gave us space to redo overbrief articles, to repair omissions, and to update the entire work.

For the most part, the Supplement covers wholly fresh topics, not only those omitted from the original set but those that have come to attention since then. When we planned the Encyclopedia in the late 1970s, for example, the subject of original intent was far less discussed than it was a decade later. Other comparatively new topics include the relation of capital punishment to race, the anti-abortion movement, children and the First Amendment, critical legal studies, the right to die, vouchers, independent counsel, the balanced budget amendment, the controversy over creationism, Iran-Contra, ethics in government, criminal justice and technology, political trials, the Gramm–Rudman Act, patenting the creation of life, government as proprietor, the Attorney-General's Commission on Pornography, the Boland Amendment, feminist theories, drug testing, joint-resolutions, constitutional realism, the Bail Reform Act of 1984, recent appointees to the Court, low-value speech, unenumerated rights, private discrimination, visas and free speech, and the Rehnquist Court. The updating of old topics, covering the period since 1985, also, of course, presents new material. We estimate that about 75 percent of the entries in the Supplement consist of new topics. Of the total 320 articles in this volume, 247 present entries not in the original Encyclopedia. Nevertheless, any encyclopedia is merely an epitome of knowledge, and we again labored under practical constraints on word lengths. Space is always limited. We do not mislead ourselves or readers by suggesting that we have managed to cover everything.

The articles in this Supplement, as in the original edition, are intended primarily to be doorways leading to ideas and to additional reading. Thus, all articles in this Supplement are elaborately cross-referenced to other related articles within the same covers and to articles in the original four-volume edition. Cross-references are indicated by words set in SMALL CAPITALS and are followed by a bracket [ ] noting the volume(s) where the cross-referenced entry appears. A roman numeral one within brackets [I] indicates that the cross-referenced entry appears in the present volume, *Supplement I* to the Encyclopedia. Arabic numerals 1, 2, 3, or 4 refer to entries contained in one of the Encyclopedia's four original volumes.

As in the original edition, we believe readers will find any article on almost any topic reasonably conceivable or a cross-reference to related topics. The Supplement contains articles by 178 contributors. Most of the contributors are academic lawyers who teach constitutional law, but other professors of law have made contributions, as well as a few lawyers in private practice and five federal judges. In addition many historians and political scientists are among the contributors, as are ten deans and three associate deans. We sought as much interdisciplinary balance as the entries themselves permitted and, with respect to the location of the contributors, we sought geographical balance by recruiting authors from the whole of the nation, as well as from different sorts of institutions. UCLA continues to be the institution with the largest number of contributors, followed by Harvard, Michigan, Yale, Minnesota, USC, Georgetown, Chicago, NYU, and Stanford, in that order. All together, 85 institutions have been represented.

Every article is signed by its author. We have encouraged the authors to write commentaries in essay form, not merely describing and analyzing their subjects but expressing their own views. Specialists and ordinary citizens alike hold divergent viewpoints on the Constitution. Readers should be alert to the likelihood that a cross-referenced article may discuss similar issues from a different perspective, especially if the issues have been the subject of recent controversy.

October 1991

LEONARD W. LEVY
KENNETH L. KARST
JOHN G. WEST, JR.

Acknowledgments

We are grateful to our authors as well as to the members of the Editorial Board. We acknowledge with utmost appreciation the support given to this project by the Earhart Foundation, by The Claremont Graduate School and University Center and its officers, President John D. Maguire, former Vice President Jerome Spanier, and especially former Vice President Christopher Oberg. Three graduate students of The Claremont Graduate School served, indispensably, as editorial assistants: Mary Bellamy, Dana Whaley, and Jeffrey Schultz. The Macmillan Reference Division, headed by Philip Friedman, his editor in chief, Elly Dickason, and Senior Project Editor Martha Goldstein have done extraordinarily well and generously by us, earning our appreciation.

As before, the grandchildren of the senior editors assisted not a whit, but we acknowledge our pleasure in remembering them and especially in seeing in print the names of those who came into this world since Aaron, Renee, Natalie, and Adam. The new ones are Elon Glucklich, Jacob Harris, and Elijah Dylan Karst. We are pleased, too, to thank our wives, Elyse Levy and Smiley Karst, to whom this work might have been dedicated if a personal dedication page were appropriate for a reference work. Along with their names would be that of John West's sister Janet, a plucky woman who graduated from law school and passed her bar exam during the life of this project despite medical adversities.

List of Articles

List of Contributors

Henry J. Abraham
James Hart Professor of Government and Foreign Affairs
University of Virginia

APPOINTMENTS CLAUSE

Norman Abrams
Professor of Law
University of California, Los Angeles

FEDERAL CRIMINAL LAW

T. Alexander Aleinikoff
Professor of Law
University of Michigan

IMMIGRATION AND ALIENAGE

Ronald J. Allen
Professor of Law
Northwestern University

PROCEDURAL DUE PROCESS OF LAW, CRIMINAL

Albert W. Alschuler
Professor of Law
University of Chicago

BAIL
THIRD-PARTY CONSENT

Akhil Reed Amar
Professor of Law
Yale Law School

AMENDMENT PROCESS (OUTSIDE ARTICLE V)

Alison Grey Anderson
Professor of Law
University of California, Los Angeles

SOBELOFF, SIMON E.

Peter Arenella
Professor of Law
University of California, Los Angeles

FOURTH AMENDMENT

Lance Banning
Professor of History
University of Kentucky

FEDERALISTS

Edward L. Barrett
Professor of Law
University of California, Davis

INTERGOVERNMENTAL TAX IMMUNITIES

Norma Basch
Professor of History
Rutgers University

Woman Suffrage
Women in Constitutional History

Sara Sun Beale
Professor of Law
Duke University

Grand Jury

Michal Belknap
Professor of Law
California Western School of Law

Political Trials

Herman Belz
Professor of History
University of Maryland

Constitutional History, 1980–1989

Robert W. Bennett
Dean and Professor of Law
Northwestern University of Law

Interpretivism
Poverty Law

Walter Berns
John M. Olin University Professor
Georgetown University

Conservatism

Scott H. Bice
Professor and Dean of the Law Center
University of Southern California

Delegation of Power

Lee C. Bollinger
Dean and Professor of Law
University of Michigan

Commercial Speech
Extremist Speech

Richard J. Bonnie
John S. Battle Professor of Law
University of Virginia

Drug Regulation

Craig M. Bradley
Professor of Law and Harry T. Ice Faculty Fellow
Indiana University

Rehnquist, William H.

Harold H. Bruff
John S. Redditt Professor of Law
University of Texas, Austin

Judicial Review of Administrative Acts

David P. Bryden
Professor of Law
University of Minnesota

Judicial Role

Robert A. Burt
Southmayd Professor of Law
Yale University

Mental Illness
Patients' Rights

John O. Calmore
Program Officer, Rights and Social Justice
Ford Foundation

Residential Segregation

Lincoln Caplan
Staff Writer
The New Yorker Magazine Inc.

Solicitor General

Clayborne Carson
Director and Senior Editor
The Martin Luther King Jr., Papers Project
Stanford University

Civil Rights Movement

Stephen L. Carter
Professor of Law
Yale University

RACIAL DISCRIMINATION
SCIENCE, TECHNOLOGY, AND THE CONSTITUTION

Erwin Chemerinsky
Professor of Law
University of Southern California

HABEAS CORPUS

Jesse H. Choper
Dean and Professor of Law
University of California, Berkeley

GOVERNMENT AID TO RELIGIOUS INSTITUTIONS

William Cohen
*C. Wendell and Edith M. Carlsmith Professor
of Law*
Stanford University

ECONOMIC DUE PROCESS
ECONOMIC EQUAL PROTECTION
FOURTEENTH AMENDMENT, SECTION 5 (JUDICIAL
CONSTRUCTION)

Ruth Colker
C. J. Morrow Professor of Law
Tulane University

ABORTION AND THE CONSTITUTION (I)

Daniel O. Conkle
Professor of Law
Indiana University School of Law

ESTABLISHMENT CLAUSE

Kimberlé Crenshaw
Professor of Law
University of California, Los Angeles

ANTIDISCRIMINATION LEGISLATION
CIVIL RIGHTS

Michael Kent Curtis
Associate Professor, School of Law
Wake Forest University

FOURTEENTH AMENDMENT AND SECTION 5
(FRAMING)
INCORPORATION DOCTRINE AND ORIGINAL INTENT

George Dargo
Assistant Professor of Law
Duke University

JEFFERSONIANISM

Walter Dellinger
Professor of Law
Duke University

ARTICLE V CONVENTIONS CLAUSE
ADVICE AND CONSENT TO SUPREME COURT
NOMINATIONS
SCHOOL PRAYERS

George W. Dent
Professor of Law
Case Western University

RELIGION IN PUBLIC SCHOOLS
VOUCHERS

David Dolinko
Professor of Law
University of California, Los Angeles

RIGHT AGAINST SELF-INCRIMINATION

Rochelle C. Dreyfuss
Professor of Law
New York University School of Law

COMPUTERS

Robert F. Drinan, S.J.
Professor of Law
Georgetown University

HOUSE OF REPRESENTATIVES

Donald A. Dripps
Associate Professor of Law
University of Illinois

MIRANDA RULES

Ronald Dworkin
Professor of Law
New York University, and University College,
Oxford

JURISPRUDENCE AND CONSTITUTIONAL LAW

Peter B. Edelman
Associate Dean and Professor of Law
Georgetown University

WELFARE RIGHTS

Theodore Eisenberg
Professor of Law
Cornell University

CONSTITUTIONAL REMEDIES

Richard E. Ellis
Professor of History
State University of New York, Buffalo

JACKSONIANISM

Edward J. Erler
Chair and Professor of Political Science
California State University, San Bernardino

CAPITAL PUNISHMENT AND RACE
RACE-CONSCIOUSNESS

Samuel Estreicher
Professor of Law
New York University

SUBSTANTIVE DUE PROCESS
SUPREME COURT'S WORKLOAD

Julian N. Eule
Professor of Law
University of California, Los Angeles

DIRECT DEMOCRACY
DORMANT COMMERCE CLAUSE
TEMPORAL LIMITS ON LAWMAKING POWERS

Richard Fallon
Professor of Law
Harvard University

POWELL, LEWIS F., JR.

Daniel A. Farber
Henry J. Fletcher Professor of Law
University of Minnesota

ENVIRONMENTAL REGULATION
TAKING OF PROPERTY

Paul Finkelman
Professor of Law
Brooklyn Law School

REPUBLICAN PARTY
WHIG PARTY

Edwin B. Firmage
Professor of Law
University of Utah

CONGRESSIONAL WAR POWERS

Peter Graham Fish
Professor of Political Science and Law
Duke University

JUDICIAL CONFERENCE OF THE UNITED
STATES

Louis Fisher
*Senior Specialist, Congressional Research
Service*
Library of Congress

FEDERALISM AND SHARED POWERS
LINE-ITEM VETO
NONJUDICIAL INTERPRETATION OF THE
CONSTITUTION
SENATE JUDICIARY COMMITTEE

William A. Fletcher
Professor of Law
University of California, Berkeley

ELEVENTH AMENDMENT

William E. Forbath
Professor of Law
University of California, Los Angeles

LABOR MOVEMENT

Richard S. Frase
Professor of Law
University of Minnesota

CRIMINAL JUSTICE SYSTEM

Paul A. Freund
Karl M. Loeb University Professor, Emeritus
Harvard University

WYZANSKI, CHARLES C., JR.

Barry Friedman
Professor of Law
Vanderbilt University

CONDITIONAL SPENDING

Lawrence M. Friedman
Professor of Law
Stanford University

LEGAL CULTURE

Robert Diderot Garcia
Professor of Law
University of California, Los Angeles

RACKETEER INFLUENCED AND CORRUPT
ORGANIZATIONS ACT (RICO)

Tom Gerety
President
Trinity College

RIGHT OF PRIVACY

Michael J. Gerhardt
Associate Professor of Law
Marshall-Wythe School of Law
The College of William and Mary

KENNEDY, ANTHONY M.

Stephen Gillers
Professor of Law
New York University

GOVERNMENT SECRECY

Ruth Bader Ginsberg
United States Circuit Judge
United States Court of Appeals, District of
Columbia Circuit

McGOWAN, CARL

Michael J. Glennon
Professor of Law
University of California, Davis

SENATE AND FOREIGN POLICY

Robert D. Goldstein
Professor of Law
University of California, Los Angeles

BALANCED-BUDGET AMENDMENT
CONFRONTATION, RIGHT OF
DRUG TESTING
BLYEW V. UNITED STATES (1982)

Robert A. Goldwin
Resident Scholar
American Enterprise Institute

GENDER RIGHTS

Gary S. Goodpaster
Professor of Law
University of California, Los Angeles

AUTOMOBILE SEARCH
CRUEL AND UNUSUAL PUNISHMENT
OPEN FIELDS DOCTRINE
RIGHTS OF CRIMINALLY ACCUSED

POSADAS DE PUERTO RICO ASSOCIATES V. TOURISM
COMPANY OF PUERTO RICO (1986)
RICHMOND (CITY OF) V. J.A. CROSON CO.
(1989)
SEXUAL ORIENTATION
THORNBURGH V. AMERICAN COLLEGE OF
OBSTETRICIANS AND GYNECOLOGISTS (1986)
WASHINGTON V. HARPER (1990)
WEBSTER V. REPRODUCTIVE HEALTH SERVICES
(1989)
WYGNANT V. JACKSON BOARD OF EDUCATION
(1986)

Evan J. Kemp, Jr.
*Chairman, United States Equal Employment
Opportunity Commission*
Washington, D.C.

AMERICANS WITH DISABILITIES ACT (1990)

Randall Kennedy
Professor of Law
Harvard University

MARSHALL, THURGOOD

Charles R. Kesler
*Associate Professor of Government
Director, Henry Salvatori Center for the Study
of Freedom in the Modern World*
Claremont McKenna College

REAGAN, RONALD

Kit Kinports
Associate Professor of Law
University of Illinois

BLACKMUN, HARRY A.

Douglas W. Kmiec
Professor of Law
Notre Dame University

ZONING

Neil K. Komesar
*James E. & Ruth B. Doyle-Bascom Professor
of Law*
University of Wisconsin

POLITICS

Alex Kozinski
United States Circuit Judge
United States Court of Appeals, Ninth
Circuit

ADMINISTRATIVE SEARCH

Seth F. Kreimer
Associate Professor of Law
University of Pennsylvania

ENTITLEMENT

James E. Krier
Earl Warren Deland Professor of Law
University of Michigan

EMINENT DOMAIN

Philip B. Kurland
Professor of Law
University of Chicago

IRAN-CONTRA AFFAIR

Philip A. Lacovara
Managing Director & General Counsel
Morgan, Stanley, & Co., Inc.

INDEPENDENT COUNSEL

Wayne LaFave
David C. Baum Professor of Law
University of Champaign

PLAIN VIEW DOCTRINE
REASONABLE EXPECTATION OF PRIVACY

Kenneth Lasson
Professor of Law
University of Baltimore

PATENT

Michael Laurence
Washington, D.C.

CAPITAL PUNISHMENT

David W. Leebron
Professor of Law
Columbia University

COMPUTERS

William E. Leuchtenberg
Professor of History
University of North Carolina, Chapel Hill

COURT-PACKING PLANS

Martin Lyon Levine
*UPS Professor of Law, Gerontology and
    Psychiatry, and the Behavioral Sciences*
University of Southern California

PSYCHIATRY AND CONSTITUTIONAL LAW

Sanford Levinson
Professor of Law
The University of Texas, Austin

CONSTITUTION AS CIVIL RELIGION

Leonard W. Levy
*Andrew W. Mellon All-Claremont Professor of
    the Humanities, Emeritus*
The Claremont Graduate School

ANNAPOLIS CONVENTION
BETHEL SCHOOL DISTRICT v. FRASER (1986)
BOLAND AMENDMENT
BOOTH v. MARYLAND (1987)
BOWEN v. KENDRICK (1988)
BOWSHER v. SYNAR (1986)
BRASWELL v. UNITED STATES (1988)
CALIFORNIA v. GREENWOOD (1988)
COLORADO v. CONNELLY (1986)
FLAG DESECRATION
FORD v. WAINWRIGHT (1986)
FRAZEE v. ILLINOIS DEPARTMENT OF
    EMPLOYMENT SECURITY (1989)
HEATH v. ALABAMA (1985)
HUSTLER MAGAZINE AND LARRY FLYNT v.
    JERRY FALWELL (1988)
ILLINOIS v. PERKINS (1990)
ILLINOIS v. RODRIGUEZ (1990)
MARYLAND v. CRAIG (1990)
MCCLESKEY v. KEMP (1987)

MICHIGAN DEPARTMENT OF STATE POLICE v. SITZ
    (1990)
MILKOVICH v. LORAIN JOURNAL CO. (1990)
NATIONAL TREASURY EMPLOYEES UNION v.
    VONRAAB (1989)
PENRY v. LYNAUGH (1989)
RATIFIER INTENT
SALERNO, UNITED STATES v. (1987)
SKINNER v. RAILWAY LABOR EXECUTIVES
    ASSOCIATION (1989)
STANFORD v. KENTUCKY (1989)
TEXAS MONTHLY, INC. v. BULLOCK (1989)
TEXTUALISM
THOMPSON v. OKLAHOMA (1988)
UNENUMERATED RIGHTS

Hans A. Linde
Herman Phleger Visiting Professor of Law
Stanford University

SPENDING POWER

Christine A. Littleton
Professor of Law
University of California, Los Angeles

COMPARABLE WORTH
FEMINIST THEORY

Charles A. Lofgren
*Crocker Professor of American Politics and
    History*
Claremont McKenna College

VIETNAM WAR
WAR POWERS

Daniel Hays Lowenstein
Professor of Law
University of California, Los Angeles

GERRYMANDER
POLITICAL PARTIES, ELECTIONS, AND
    CONSTITUTIONAL LAWS

Ira C. Lupu
*Professor of Law
    National Law Center*
George Washington University

SEPARATION OF CHURCH AND STATE

Stephen Macedo
Assistant Professor of Government
Harvard University

NEW RIGHT

Paul Marcus
Dean and Professor of Law
University of Arizona

CONSPIRACY LAW

John Marini
Professor of Political Science
University of Nevada, Reno

BUDGET PROCESS

Michael W. McConnell
Professor of Law
University of Chicago

RELIGIOUS LIBERTY

Thomas R. McCoy
Professor of Law
Vanderbilt University

CONDITIONAL SPENDING

Frank I. Michelman
Professor of Law
Harvard University

PROPERTY RIGHTS
REPUBLICANISM AND MODERN CONSTITUTIONAL
    THEORY

Abner J. Mikva
United States Circuit Judge
United States Court of Appeals, District of
    Columbia Circuit

LEGISLATIVE PURPOSES AND MOTIVES

Martha Minow
Professor of Law
Harvard University

DISABILITIES, RIGHTS OF PERSONS WITH

Madeline Morris
Assistant Professor of Law
Duke University

ADVISE AND CONSENT TO SUPREME COURT
NOMINATIONS

Robert P. Mosteller
*Professor of Law and Senior Associate Dean
    for Academic Affairs*
Duke University

DOUBLE JEOPARDY
SPEEDY TRIAL

Paul Murphy
Professor of Law
University of Minnesota

WORLD WAR I

Gene R. Nichol
Dean and Professor of Law
University of Colorado

CIVIL LIBERTIES
DAMAGES CLAIMS

Marlene Arnold Nicholson
Professor of Law
DePaul University

CAMPAIGN FINANCE

John E. Nowak
Professor of Law
University of Illinois

POLICE INTERROGATION AND CONFESSIONS

David M. O'Brien
Professor of Government and Graduate Advisor
University of Virginia

SUPREME COURT AT WORK

Phillip S. Paludan
Professor of History
University of Kansas

CIVIL WAR

Donald J. Pisani
Professor of History
Texas A & M University

ECONOMY
PROGRESSIVISM

Robert C. Post
Professor of Law
University of California, Berkeley

FEDERALISM AND CIVIL RIGHTS
PUBLIC FORUM

L. A. Powe, Jr.
Professor of Law
Anne Regents Chair
University of Texas, Austin

BROADCASTING
FREEDOM OF THE PRESS

Jeremy Rabkin
Professor of Political Science
Cornell University

BUSH, GEORGE
RACIAL PREFERENCE

Jack N. Rakove
Professor of History
Stanford University

ORIGINAL INTENT

Norman Redlich
Judge Weinfeld Professor of Law, Emeritus, and
former Dean
New York University Law School
Counsel, Wachtell, Lipton, Rosen, & Katz
New York City

RELIGIOUS SYMBOLS IN PUBLIC PLACES

Donald H. Regan
Professor of Law
University of Michigan

STATE REGULATION OF COMMERCE

Judith Resnik
Orrin B. Evans Professor of Law
University of Southern California

PROCEDURAL DUE PROCESS OF LAW, CIVIL

Donald A. Ritche
Associate Historian
United States Senate

SENATE
SENATE SUBCOMMITTEE ON CONSTITUTIONAL
RIGHTS

John P. Roche
John M. Olin Distinguished Professor of
American Civilization and Foreign Affairs
Fletcher School of Law and Diplomacy
Tufts University

LIBERAL CONSTITUTIONAL CONSTRUCTION

Ralph A. Rossum
President
Hampden-Sydney College

PRISONERS' RIGHTS

Eugene V. Rostow
Sterling Professor of Law, Emeritus
Yale University
Distinguished Fellow
United States Institute of Peace

CONGRESS AND FOREIGN POLICY
EXECUTIVE POWER

Ronald D. Rotunda
Professor of Law
University of Illinois

WELFARE STATE

Lawrence G. Sager
Professor of Law
New York University

JURISDICTION, FEDERAL

Terrance Sandalow
Edison R. Sunderland Professor of Law
University of Michigan

LOCAL GOVERNMENT
MCCREE, WADE HAMPTION, JR.

Frederick Schauer
Frank Stanton Professor of the First Amendment, John F. Kennedy School of Government
Harvard University

BORK NOMINATION
CHILDREN AND THE FIRST AMENDMENT

Harry N. Scheiber
Associate Dean and Professor of Law
University of California, Berkeley

NEW DEAL

Pierre Schlag
Professor of Law
University of Colorado

FIRST AMENDMENT

Arthur M. Schlesinger
Albert Schweitzer Chair in Humanities
The Graduate School and University Center
The City University of New York

KENNEDY, ROBERT F.

Peter H. Schuck
Simeon E. Baldwin Professor of Law
Yale University

CITIZENSHIP
GOVERNMENT WRONGS

Stephen J. Schulhofer
Frank and Bernice J. Greenberg Professor of Law
University of Chicago

SENTENCING

Jeffrey D. Schultz
Georgetown University

JUDICIAL POWER AND LEGISLATIVE REMEDIES
MEESE COMMISSION

Gary T. Schwartz
Professor of Law
University of California

PUNITIVE DAMAGES
WRIGHT, J. SKELLY

Herman Schwartz
Professor of Law
The American University

CRIMINAL JUSTICE AND TECHNOLOGY

Martin Shapiro
Coffroth Professor of Law
University of California, Berkeley

BUREAUCRACY

Suzanna Sherry
Professor of Law
University of Minnesota

O'CONNOR, SANDRA DAY

Steven H. Shiffrin
Professor of Law
Cornell University

LOW-VALUE SPEECH
O'BRIEN FORMULA
PORNOGRAPHY AND FEMINISM

Larry G. Simon
W.H. Armstrong Professor of Constitutional Law and Associate Dean
The Law Center
University of Southern California

REHNQUIST COURT

David M. Skover
Professor of Law
University of Puget Sound

POLITICAL QUESTION DOCTRINE
STATE ACTION DOCTRINE

Roger M. Smith
Professor of Political Science
Yale University

CONSTITUTION AND CIVIC IDEALS, THE
DECONSTRUCTION

Rodney A. Smolla
*James Gould Cutler Professor of Constitutional
Law*
Director, Institute of Bill of Rights Law
College of William and Mary

PRIVATE DISCRIMINATION

Aviam Soifer
Professor of Law
Boston University

CONSTITUTIONAL FICTIONS
COVER, ROBERT M.

Rayman Soloman
Associate Dean and Professor of Law
Northwestern University

SCALIA, ANTONIN

Frank J. Sorauf
Professor of Political Science
University of Minnesota

POLITICAL ACTION COMMITTEES (PACS)

Theodore J. St. Antoine
Degan Professor of Law
University of Michigan

LABOR

Kate Stith
Professor of Law
Yale University

SEARCH AND SEIZURE
WHITE, BYRON R.

Geoffrey R. Stone
Dean and Professor of Law
University of Chicago

BRENNAN, WILLIAM J.
FREEDOM OF SPEECH

David A. Strauss
Professor of Law
University of Chicago

SOUTER, DAVID H.

Kathleen M. Sullivan
Professor of Law
Harvard University

AFFIRMATIVE ACTION

James L. Sundquist
Senior Fellow Emeritus
The Brookings Institution

CONSTITUTIONAL REFORM

Athan Theoharis
Professor of History
Marquette University

FBI

Phillip R. Trimble
Professor of Law
University of California, Los Angeles

EXECUTIVE PREROGATIVE
PRESIDENT AND THE TREATY POWER

Louise G. Trubek
Clinical Professor of Law
University of Wisconsin

PUBLIC INTEREST LAW

Mark Tushnet
Professor of Law
Georgetown University

CONSTITUTIONAL THEORY
CRITICAL LEGAL STUDIES
INTEREST GROUPS

Gerald F. Uelman
Dean and Professor of Law
Santa Clara University

CONTROLLED-SUBSTANCE ABUSE
ELECTED JUDICIARY

Melvin I. Urofsky
Professor of History
Virginia Commonwealth University

POPULISM
RECONSTRUCTION
WORLD WAR II

William W. Van Alstyne
*William R. and Thomas S. Perkins Professor
of Law*
Duke University

FEDERALISM (CONTEMPORARY PRACTICE)

Jonathan D. Varat
Professor of Law
University of California, Los Angeles

GOVERNMENT AS PROPRIETOR
STEVENS, JOHN PAUL

Joseph Vining
Hawkins Professor of Law
University of Michigan

ADMINISTRATIVE AGENCIES

Silas Wasserstrom
Professor of Law
Georgetown University

TORTS

John G. West, Jr.
Ph.D. Candidate
The Claremont Graduate School

ANTI-ABORTION MOVEMENT
BENDER V. WILLIAMSPORT (1986)
BOWERS V. HARDWICK (1986)
CHILD PORNOGRAPHY
CITY OF RENTON V. PLAYTIME THEATRES
    (1986)
COUNTRY OF ALLEGHENY V. ACLU (1989)
COY V. IOWA (1988)
CREATIONISM
DIAL-A-PORN
EMPLOYMENT DIVISION, DEPARTMENT OF
    HUMAN RESOURCES OF OREGON V. SMITH
    (1990)
EQUAL ACCESS
FREEDOM OF ASSOCIATION
FRISBY V. SCHULTZ (1988)
GOLDMAN V. WEINBERGER (1986)
JIMMY SWAGGART MINISTRIES V. BOARD OF
    EQUALIZATION OF CALIFORNIA (1990)
JOHNSON V. TRANSPORTATION AGENCY (1987)
LEMON TEST
LYNG V. NORTHWEST INDIAN CEMETERY (1988)
O'LONE V. ESTATE OF SHABAZZ (1987)
PARADISE, UNITED STATES V. (1987)
POLITICAL PHILOSOPHY OF THE CONSTITUTION
RELIGIOUS FUNDAMENTALISM
RIGHT TO DIE
RUTAN V. REPUBLICAN PARTY OF ILLINOIS
    (1990)
SPECIAL PROSECUTOR
WITTERS V. WASHINGTON DEPARTMENT OF
    SERVICES FOR THE BLIND (1986)

James Boyd White
Hart Wright Professor of Law
Professor of English
University of Michigan

CONSTITUTION AS LITERATURE

Charles H. Whitebread
George T. Pfleger Professor of Law
University of Southern California

EYEWITNESS IDENTIFICATION

Christina Brooks Whitman
Professor of Law
University of Michigan

SEX DISCRIMINATION

Stephen F. Williams
United States Circuit Judge
United States Court of Appeals, District of
    Columbia Circuit

LAW AND ECONOMICS THEORY

Ralph K. Winter
United States Circuit Judge
United States Court of Appeals, Second Circuit

ORIGINALISM

Woolhandler, Anne
Georgetown University

TORTS

Gordon S. Wood
Professor of History
Brown University

AMERICAN REVOLUTION AND CONSTITUTIONAL
    THEORY
REPUBLICANISM

Mark G. Yudof
*Dean and James A. Elkins Centennial Chair
    in Law*
University of Texas, Austin

EDUCATION

Franklin E. Zimring
Professor of Law
Director, Earl Warren Legal Institute
University of California, Berkeley
Director, Death Penalty Project
American Civil Liberties Union of Northern
    California

CAPITAL PUNISHMENT

ABORTION AND THE CONSTITUTION, I
(Update)

Abortion legislation rarely, if ever, demonstrates concern for the well-being of women. It usually represents the state using coercive measures to persuade women to bear children rather than have abortions. As long as American society treats women and their reproductive capacity with disrespect by not funding prenatal care, postnatal care, paid pregnancy leave, effective and safe forms of BIRTH CONTROL [1], or child care, it is hard to imagine that a legislature that respects the well-being of women could enact restrictions on abortion. Thus, when we read abortion legislation or an abortion decision by the courts, we should ask ourselves whether that legislature or that court could have reached the decision that it reached if it fully respected the well-being of women. Under such a framework, we would have to conclude that the Missouri legislature that enacted the abortion legislation challenged in WEBSTER V. REPRODUCTIVE HEALTH SERVICES (1989) [I] did not respect the well-being of women, especially poor or teenage women. Nevertheless, no member of the Supreme Court in *Webster*, including the dissenters, demonstrated a real grasp of the significance of the Missouri legislation on the lives and well-being of poor women and teenage women.

In *Webster*, the Supreme Court was asked to consider the constitutionality of a Missouri statute that contained four provisions arguably restricting a woman's ability to have an abortion. Two provisions received most of the Court's attention: first, a requirement that a physician ascertain whether a fetus is viable prior to performing an abortion on any woman whom he or she has reason to believe is twenty or more weeks pregnant; and, second, a prohibition against using public employees or facilities to perform or assist an abortion not necessary to save the mother's life.

Chief Justice WILLIAM H. REHNQUIST [3,I] wrote the opinion for the Court. His opinion was joined by four other Justices—BYRON R. WHITE [4,I], SANDRA DAY O'CONNOR [3,I], ANTONIN SCALIA [I], and ANTHONY M. KENNEDY [I]—with respect to the second provision. Rehnquist's conclusion that this part of the statute was constitutional was an extension of the Court's earlier decisions in the Medicaid abortion-funding cases. Rather than apply the more stringent test that had been developed in ROE v. WADE (1973) [3], Rehnquist applied the more lenient standard developed in HARRIS v. McRAE (1980) [2]—asking whether the state legislature had placed any obstacles in the path of a woman who chooses to terminate her pregnancy. Rehnquist concluded that the state's refusal to allow public employees to perform abortions in public hospitals leaves a pregnant woman with the same choices as if the state had chosen not to operate any public hospitals at all. As in *Harris v. McRae*, Rehnquist acknowledged that a state was permitted to make a value judgment favoring childbirth over abortion and to implement that judgment in allocating public funds and facilities.

Justice HARRY BLACKMAN's [1,I] dissent, which was joined by Justices WILLIAM J. BRENNAN [1,I] and THURGOOD MARSHALL [3,I], argued that Missouri's public facility provision could easily be distinguished from *Harris v. McRae* because of the sweeping scope of Missouri's definition of a public facility. (JUSTICE JOHN PAUL STEVENS

1

[4,I] dissented separately.) Under Missouri's broad definition, any institution that was located on property owned, leased, or controlled by the government was considered to be public. Thus, the essentially private Truman Medical Center, which performed ninety-seven percent of abortions in the state after sixteen weeks of pregnancy, would be prohibited from performing abortions under the state statute. Even under the more lenient test developed by the Court in *Harris*, Justice Blackmun concluded that the funding provision should be held unconstitutional.

Justice Blackmun's discussion of the public facility provision comes only in a footnote and is not the primary focus of his decision. In order to understand the full impact of this provision on women's lives and health, it is useful to consider the AMICUS [1] briefs filed on behalf of women of color and teenage women. These briefs noted that poor women and teenage women are more likely than other women to seek abortions at public health facilities because they do not have private physicians. They are also more likely to have second-trimester abortions because they delay having abortions until they save the necessary amount of money or find out how to get an abortion. When Blackmun noted that the health-care provider that performs nearly all of the second-trimester abortions will not be able to do so, he could have observed that poor women and teenagers would be disproportionately unable to procure legal abortions. Given the relationship between teenage pregnancy and the cycle of poverty, the inability to procure an abortion often has dramatic consequences in the life of a poor, teenage woman. Although Justice Blackmun was certainly correct to note that the public facility ban "leaves the pregnant woman with far fewer choices, or, for those too sick or too poor to travel, perhaps no choice at all," it would have been better if he had described the impact of this regulation in the race-, class-, and age-based way in which it is most likely to operate.

Justice Blackmun's discussion of the public facility provision skirted the question whether *Harris v. McRae* should be overturned. He tried to distinguish *Harris* from *Webster* rather than call for its reconsideration. The amicus brief submitted by women of color was not so subtle. They often used exactly the same information that they had provided the Supreme Court in *Harris* to argue that the well-being of poor women cannot be protected unless the government ensures that legal abortions are available to poor women on the same basis as middle-class women. A chart in an amicus brief submitted by an international women's health organization showed that the United States stands alone in the world in permitting abortion to be lawful but not funding any abortions for poor women unless their very lives are endangered. Although not all countries fund "abortion on demand" for poor women,

all countries that make abortion lawful also fund therapeutic abortions for poor women. These comparative data show that the United States stands alone in the world in its disrespect for the lives and well-being of poor women. Unlike other Western countries, the United States fails to fund prenatal care, postnatal care, pregnancy leave, and child care but then tries to tell poor women that it "prefers" childbirth to abortion. The most logical explanation for this position of both the United States government and the state of Missouri is that government officials have not bothered to educate themselves on the impact that funding and public facility restrictions have on the lives of poor women. And, as long as poor women have virtually no political power, it seems unlikely that government officials will focus on their needs.

Both the majority and dissenting opinions in *Webster* did focus on the first provision of the Missouri statute. Chief Justice Rehnquist's discussion of this provision only received the support of Justices White and Kennedy, but the separate concurrences of Justices O'Connor and Scalia made a majority for the conclusion that the provision was constitutional. The provision presented both technical and substantive difficulties. Technically, the provision appeared to require physicians to perform viability tests that were contrary to accepted medical practice, such as performing amniocentesis on a fetus that was under twenty-eight weeks old. If that had been the actual meaning of the statute, most of the Justices would have been compelled to find it unconstitutional even under the most lenient standard of review used by courts—the RATIONAL BASIS [3] test—because the statute would have rationally served no public purpose. In order to avoid that conclusion, Rehnquist offered a somewhat strained interpretation of the statute so that a physician would have the discretion to perform only tests that were medically appropriate.

Having overcome this technical hurdle, Rehnquist then turned to the substantive difficulties posed by the provision. Under the Court's prior doctrine, as articulated in *Roe v. Wade*, a state was permitted to impose abortion restrictions to protect fetal life only in the third trimester of pregnancy. Because the viability-testing requirement took effect as early as twenty weeks, four weeks before the beginning of the third trimester, Rehnquist faced a seeming conflict with *Roe*.

Rehnquist concluded that the *Roe* trimester framework was too rigid and that if the state has an interest in preserving potential human life after viability, it also has an interest in preserving that potential life before viability. Although Rehnquist's statement about preserving potential human life might be read to mean that states could outlaw abortions before the twenty-fourth week and thereby overturn *Roe,* he refrained from reaching that conclusion, because that question was not before the Court.

A fourth vote for the majority position was cast by Justice Scalia. Scalia, unlike Rehnquist, concluded that *Roe* should be overturned and that states should be free to regulate or criminalize abortion at any stage of pregnancy.

The fifth vote for the majority position was cast by Justice O'Connor. Unlike the other members of the majority, she did not argue that *Roe* needed to be overturned, or even modified, to reach the conclusion that the viability provision was constitutional. O'Connor reinterpreted the Court's prior decisions to require that states "not impose an undue burden on a woman's abortion decision." Because she concluded that the viability tests could be performed without markedly increasing the cost of abortion, O'Connor concluded that the undue burden test had been satisfied. O'Connor's framework, unlike that of Rehnquist or Scalia, made it clear that states could not criminalize abortion as they had in the pre-*Roe* era because a criminal penalty certainly would constitute an "undue burden." What other kinds of regulations would impose an undue burden, however, is unclear from O'Connor's opinion.

Justice Blackmun wrote a blistering opinion for the dissenters. He accused Justice Rehnquist of being deceptive in not acknowledging that he was really overturning *Roe.* Moreover, he chided Rehnquist for not giving the Court a usable framework to evaluate future abortion cases. Blackmun said that he feared "for the liberty and equality of the millions of women who have lived and come of age in the sixteen years since *Roe* was decided" and "for the integrity of, and public esteem for, this Court." Substantively, he accused the Court of offering no rationale for its rejection of the trimester framework, saying that the Court used an "it is so because we say so" jurisprudence. The trimester framework, he argued, does make sense because it reflects the developmental view that one is more entitled to the rights of CITIZENSHIP [1] as one increases one's ability to feel pain, to experience pleasure, to survive, and to react to one's environment. Finally, he criticized the test purportedly used by the majority—whether the regulation "permissibly furthers the State's interest in protecting potential human life"— as circular and meaningless. He argued that the standard of whether a regulation "permissibly furthers" the state's interest was itself the *question* before the Court; it therefore could not be the *standard* that the Court applied in resolving the question.

Although Justice Blackmun wrote his dissent in strong language and even mentioned that the majority's opinion would have a dramatic effect on the "liberty and equality" of women's lives, there is no specific discussion of that effect. Blackmun spent most of his opinion explaining why there was no good reason to change the course of using the RIGHT OF PRIVACY [3,I] on which the Court had commenced in his opinion in *Roe.*

One of the most disappointing parts of Blackmun's opinion is his conclusion that if the majority's technical interpretation of the provision were correct, he "would see little or no conflict with *Roe.*" In other words, he appeared to agree with Justice O'Connor that such a provision would not constitute an undue burden on a woman's abortion decision. Blackmun dissented from the majority because he disagreed with its technical interpretation of the viability-testing provision, not because he fundamentally disagreed about the impact that requirement would have on women's lives and well-being.

If Justice Blackmun had truly considered the "liberty and equality" interests of sixteen million women, he would not have been so easily satisfied. As the briefs that were presented to the Court by women of color and teenage women dramatically showed, raising the cost of abortion, even marginally, has a marked impact on the ability of poor women to purchase abortions. And because women of color and teenage women are more likely to delay abortion decisions, they will be hit harder by the viability-testing requirement than are other women. For poor women, even the requirement that they pay for their own abortions is an undue burden on their reproductive decision making. Raising the cost of abortion presents an even greater—and even more undue—burden.

From the perspective of protecting the well-being of women, *Webster* is doubly discouraging. Not only did the majority of the Court not seem to understand the meaning of abortion regulations in women's lives, but even the dissenters did not display much understanding or sensitivity. They seemed more determined to protect the integrity of their prior decisions than to consider the reality of new abortion restrictions on women's lives.

RUTH COLKER

(SEE ALSO: *Abortion and the Constitution I* [I]; *Anti-abortion Movement and the Constitution* [I]; *Feminist Theory* [I]; *Reproductive Autonomy* [3].)

Bibliography

COLKER, RUTH   1989   Abortion and Dialogue. *Tulane Law Review* 63:1363–1403.

JAGGAR, ALISON   1974   Abortion and a Woman's Right to Decide. *Philosophical Forum* 5:347.

JUNG, PATRICIA BEATTIE AND SHANNON, THOMAS A., EDS.   1988   *Abortion and Catholicism: The American Debate.* New York: Crossroad Press.

MCDONNELL, KATHLEEN   1984   *Not An Easy Choice: A Feminist Re-examines Abortion.* Boston: South End Press.

ABORTION AND THE CONSTITUTION, II
(Update)

With President RONALD REAGAN's [3,I] elevation of Justice WILLIAM H. REHNQUIST [3,I] to CHIEF JUSTICE [1] and his appointment of Justices ANTONIN SCALIA [I] and ANTHONY M. KENNEDY [I], many expected the Supreme Court to revisit its decision in ROE V. WADE (1973) [3], which struck down laws against abortion. Tension mounted when the Supreme Court noted probable jurisdiction in WEBSTER V. REPRODUCTIVE HEALTH SERVICES (1989) [I]. Relying on *Roe*, the lower court in *Webster* had held unconstitutional several provisions of a Missouri statute regulating abortions, including a statement from its preamble that human life begins at conception, a requirement that the aborting physician perform a viability test when he or she has reason to believe the woman is at least twenty weeks' pregnant, and a prohibition on the use of public employees or public facilities to perform an abortion that is not necessary to save the mother's life. In its appeal, Missouri, joined by the Department of Justice as AMICUS CURIAE [I], argued not only that the invalidated provisions should be upheld under *Roe* and the Court's subsequent abortion cases but, more significantly, that *Roe* itself should be overruled.

Without passing on the constitutional validity of all the statutory provisions that had been challenged, the Court, in a 5–4 decision, reversed the lower court and gave the prolife movement its first major legal victory since *Roe* was decided. Whether *Webster* will prove a truly significant victory for this movement, however, remains to be seen. First and most encouraging for prochoice advocates, the Court once again found no occasion to revisit *Roe*'s controversial conclusion that the right to an abortion is protected by the Constitution's DUE PROCESS [2] clauses. Second, although the Court's judgment of reversal garnered majority support, portions of Chief Justice Rehnquist's opinion did not obtain five votes. Particularly noteworthy was Justice SANDRA DAY O'CONNOR's [3,I] refusal to join important sections of the opinion. Third, the extraordinary media publicity surrounding *Webster* may have contributed to exaggerated perceptions by both sides of what the Court actually held.

In upholding Missouri's restriction on the use of public employees or facilities to perform abortions, the *Webster* majority relied on the Court's previous abortion-funding cases. The Court emphasized, as it had done before, that as long as the states do not actually restrict the abortion decision, the Constitution allows them to make the value judgment that childbirth is preferable to abortion. In denying the use of public employees and facilities for abortions,

Missouri did not place any obstacles in the path of women who choose to have an abortion; that is, Missouri's restriction left pregnant women with the same choices they would have had if the state had not chosen to operate public hospitals at all. In short, although the Constitution, as interpreted by *Roe*, may not allow the states to prohibit abortions, it does not give either doctors or women a right of access to public facilities for the performance of abortions.

Many prochoice commentators have criticized this aspect of the Court's holding in *Webster* because of its alleged effect on the availability of abortions for certain women. The Court's task, however, was to decide not whether Missouri made a wise or good policy choice but whether anything in the Constitution invalidated the choice that Missouri made through its democratic process. Viewed in this light, *Webster* and the previous abortion-funding cases are consistent with prevailing constitutional doctrine. Few would argue, for example, that because the state may not prohibit parents from sending their children to private schools, the state must fund private education for those parents who cannot afford it.

The statute's viability-testing requirement gave the Court more difficulty. The section of Chief Justice Rehnquist's opinion regarding this requirement, which was joined by only two other Justices, said that the constitutionality of the viability-testing requirement was called into doubt by the rigid trimester system established in *Roe* and followed in the Court's other abortion cases. The Chief Justice reached this conclusion because mandatory testing when the physician reasonably believes the pregnancy is at least in the twentieth week may impose burdens on second-trimester abortions involving fetuses who have not yet become viable. Taking the position that STARE DECISIS has less force in constitutional law than elsewhere, the plurality then abandoned *Roe*'s trimester framework as unsound in principle and unworkable in practice.

The plurality emphasized that the concepts of trimesters and viability are not found in the Constitution's text or in any other place one might expect to find a constitutional principle, thus describing the Court's previous holdings as resembling an intricate code of regulations more than a body of constitutional doctrine. The plurality also questioned why the state's interest in protecting potential human life should come into existence only at the point of viability. Finally, eschewing STRICT SCRUTINY [4], the plurality upheld Missouri's testing requirement by concluding that it permissibly furthers the state's legitimate interest in protecting potential life. Without otherwise purporting to disturb *Roe*, the plurality thus modified and narrowed it.

Justice HARRY A. BLACKMUN [1,I], the author of *Roe*,

wrote a stinging dissent contending that *Roe* could not survive the plurality's analysis. Justice Scalia wrote a concurring opinion agreeing with Justice Blackmun that the plurality's analysis effectively would overrule *Roe*, something he was prepared to do explicitly. Nevertheless, a majority of the Court did not accept Justice Scalia's invitation. Even assuming that the three Justices in the plurality share the view that their anlaysis is devastating to *Roe*—and it is not clear that they do—it requires five votes, not four, to overrule *Roe*. On the fundamental issue of whether *Roe* should be totally overruled, the still unresolved question is where Justice O'Connor stands.

Although she had strongly attacked the trimester system in her dissent in *Akron v. Akron Center for Reproductive Health Services* and had defended the position that the state's interest in protecting potential life exists throughout all the stages of pregnancy, Justice O'Connor did not join the plurality's rejection of the trimester system in *Webster*. Instead, she criticized the plurality for unnecessarily reaching out to modify *Roe*, and insisted that the viability-testing requirement was constitutional even when considered under the Court's previous cases. In her view, the testing requirement did not unduly burden the woman's abortion decision, and only on this ground did she vote to sustain the testing requirement. Prochoice advocates thus may have reason to hope that Justice O'Connor has had a change of heart since *Akron*. In contrast, prolife advocates may take heart that Justice O'Connor indicated that she both continues to view the trimester framework as problematic and would find it appropriate to reexamine *Roe* in a case involving a statute whose constitutionality actually turned on its validity.

Because the plurality's reasoning in *Webster* tracks rather closely Justice O'Connor's dissent in *Akron*, it is fair to question, as Justices Blackmun and Scalia did, whether that reasoning, if explicitly endorsed in the future by a Court majority, would effectively overrule *Roe*. From the standpoint of logic, the position that *Webster* completely undermines *Roe* has considerable force. If the state's interest in protecting potential life exists equally at all stages of pregnancy, it would seem that the state should be able to prohibit abortions not simply in the third trimester, as *Roe* held, but throughout pregnancy. As Justice O'Connor stated in *Akron*, "potential life is no less potential in the first weeks of pregnancy than it is at viability or afterward." In Justice Blackmun's dissenting words, "if the Constitution permits a State to enact any statute that reasonably furthers its interest in potential life, and if that interest arises as of conception," then it is difficult to see why any statute that prohibits abortion is unconstitutional. The Court can escape the force of this reasoning only by repudiating the reasoning in the plurality's opinion in *Webster*.

It is curious that the future of *Roe* might turn on how a Court majority ultimately views the validity of the trimester framework. The fundamental jurisprudential issue in both *Roe* and *Webster*, as Justice Blackmun correctly recognized, is whether the Constitution protects an "unenumerated" general RIGHT OF PRIVACY [3,I] or, at least, whether such an UNENUMERATED RIGHT [I] properly includes the right to terminate a pregnancy. The Court rejected *Roe*'s trimester framework in part because the concepts of trimesters and viability cannot be found in the Constitution's text, but this can equally be said of the right of privacy in general and of the right to terminate a pregnancy in particular. If the Constitution's text must be the source of constitutional rights, more than the trimester system is illegitimate about *Roe*. However, if the Court continues to adhere to the view that the Constitution can protect unenumerated rights and if one of these protected unenumerated rights is the right to terminate a pregnancy, Justice Blackmun would seem correct in finding it irrelevant that the Constitution does not refer to trimesters or viability. How could it, when it does not refer to abortion at all?

The debate about unenumerated rights is important because of its implications for the Court's proper role in constitutional interpretation. Viewed in these terms, the debate about *Roe* is a debate not about abortion as such but about the Court's role and the role of JUDICIAL REVIEW [3,I] under the form of government established by the Constitution. Those who oppose the Court's use of unenumerated rights to invalidate statutes essentially argue that such action constitutes an abuse of authority, one that allows the Court to substitute its own value judgments for those of the politically accountable branches of government. Justice Scalia, who alone in *Webster* was prepared to overrule *Roe*, thus insisted that the Court in *Roe* had entered an area that, because of the Constitution's silence, demands political answers. He observed that both sides had engaged in street demonstrations and letter-writing campaigns to influence the Court's decision—the kind of activity, in his view, that should be directed at elected legislators rather than at judges who hold life tenure and who are sworn to uphold the Constitution even against majority will. From this perspective, *Roe* is no more defensible than the now infamous decision in LOCHNER V. NEW YORK (1905) [3], which invalidated economic reform legislation on the basis of rights that could not be found in the Constitution's text.

Roe has been attacked even by some who defend the existence of unenumerated rights that the judiciary may enforce. One argument contends that *Roe* improperly rejected a natural law position with regard to human existence by permitting the state, through the device of law, to define human life in a way that excludes fetuses. Under this view, laws banning abortions are not simply constitutionally permissible but constitutionally required. Whatever the present Court does regarding the abortion issue, it does not seem prepared to embrace such an argument.

Shortly after deciding *Webster*, the Court agreed to decide cases raising issues concerning abortion statutes in other states. In these cases, the Court upheld parental notification without making further modifications of *Roe*. Whether or not the Court uses future cases to reexamine *Roe*, it is clear that a majority of the Court is now inclined to permit the states greater leeway in regulating abortions. How much additional regulation the states will enact, if so permitted, is not easy to predict. After *Webster*, abortion became a key issue in several political races, and the prochoice side of the debate came away with some resounding political victories. Perhaps these elections have something to say to those who would substitute JUDICIAL ACTIVISM [3] for the political process. At the least, the up-or-down choice presented by *Roe*'s constitutionalization of abortion seems to have precluded the various states from achieving through democratic means the political compromises that many other societies have reached on the abortion question.

JOSEPH D. GRANO

(SEE ALSO: *Abortion and the Constitution* [I]; *Anti-Abortion Movement* [I]; *Reproductive Autonomy* [3].)

Bibliography

BOPP, JAMES, JR. 1989 Will There Be a Constitutional Right to Abortion After Reconsideration of *Roe v. Wade? Journal of Contemporary Law* 15:131–173.

BORK, ROBERT J. 1989 *The Tempting of America*, pages 110–116. New York: Free Press.

FARBER, DANIEL 1989 Abortion After Webster. *Constitutional Commentary* 6:225–230.

GLENDON, MARY ANN 1987 *Abortion and Divorce in Western Law*. Cambridge, Mass.: Harvard University Press.

GRANO, JOSEPH 1981 Judicial Review and a Written Constitution in a Democratic Society. *Wayne Law Review* 28:1–75.

HIRSHMAN, LINDA 1988 Bronte, Bloom and Bork: An Essay on the Moral Education of Judges. *University of Pennsylvania Law Review* 137:177–231.

LOEWY, ARNOLD 1989 Why *Roe v. Wade* Should Be Overruled. *North Carolina Law Review* 67:939–948.

NOONAN, JOHN 1984 The Root and Branch of *Roe v. Wade*, *Nebraska Law Review* 63:668–679.

ADMINISTRATIVE AGENCIES

Administrative agencies, often called the "fourth branch," are entities of government that make decisions within particular substantive fields. Although these fields range over the full spectrum of public concern, the specificity of agencies' focus distinguishes them from other decision-making entities in the constitutional structure—the judiciary, the presidency, the Congress, indeed the individual citizen—each of which can be taken to have a scope of interest as broad as imagination will allow.

Agencies are perceived and known as such virtually without regard to their form or institutional location. They may be independent agencies—that is, not associated with any Article II executive department—which are generally administered by officials protected by law from the President's removal power. The Interstate Commerce Commission is such an agency, established over a century ago to decide entry, rates, and standards of service in the field of transportation. Alternatively, an agency may be found deep within an executive department, as the Food and Drug Administration is found within the Department of Health and Human Services. Or an agency may be identified with a cabinet officer in his or her capacity as administrator of a program. Agencies may have a handful of employees or they may have thousands. Large or small, they may speak through single individuals or through multimember collegial bodies, usually known as commissions.

The Administrative Procedure Act of 1946 serves as a second-level constitution for agencies of the federal government, specifying procedures and structural relations within and among them, and between them and other entities. But agencies are only presumptively subject to the Administrative Procedure Act—the Selective Service system, for example, has been exempted by Congress—and the act itself is in substantial part a restatement of the combination of COMMON LAW [1] and constitutional law known as ADMINISTRATIVE LAW [1], which has been developing virtually since the beginning of the Republic in response to agencies' decision-making and enforcement activities.

Agencies have their origins as alternatives to Article III courts, making decisions in suits between individuals and to executive officials making decisions and seeking to enforce them in court suits. More recently agencies also have been seen as alternatives to decision making by legislative process through Congress and the President under Article I. Agencies have thus presented a difficulty for constitutional thinking under Articles I and III, arguably absorbing functions reserved to Congress, the President, and the judiciary. Agencies present a further difficulty under the due process clause of the Fifth Amendment when DUE PROCESS OF LAW [2] is identified with legislative substance and court process.

The constitutional problem agencies pose has never reached any kind of closure. Instead, it has remained a tension in constitutional thought, unresolved because the creation and the maintenance of agencies have proceeded from inadequacies perceived in both legislative and judicial decision making.

Courts do not investigate or plan. Courts are not thought to display the resourcefulness of decision making committed to the achievement of a particular substantive end, such as workplace safety, nor the expertise of the specialists'. Courts other than the Supreme Court do not take initiative. There is widespread consensus, in fact, that courts should remain neutral and general. Moreover, the making of decisions in very large numbers of cases—those cases produced, for example, by disability benefit claims or the military draft—may be impeded by judicial process to the point that delay alone decides issues and legislated values are imperiled.

Congress also is not equipped to make any great number of particular decisions, and may be able to attend to a field of concern only at long intervals. Furthermore, where the unprecedented is faced, such as the discovery of radio waves or of nuclear energy, Congress often cannot do much more than define the field for decision. But legislators can foresee that failure to create a decision-making agency in the field effectively consigns the decisions of great public concern which will inevitably be made to individuals exercising powers under state laws of contract, property, and corporations.

Thus the existence and activity of agencies is rooted in felt necessity and is not the product of, or subject to, independent development of CONSTITUTIONAL THEORY [I]. Nonetheless, SEPARATION OF POWERS [4], due process, and delegation concerns weave through determinations of internal agency structure and procedure made pursuant to statutes establishing particular agencies or under the Administrative Procedure Act. The same constitutional concerns underlie arrangement and rearrangement of the relations of the Judiciary, Congress, and the President to and through agencies. The concerns become acute and surface as explicit issues when Congress, seeking speed of decision or protection of an agency's initiative or planning, limits access to courts for review of agency decisions—partially or wholly precluding JUDICIAL REVIEW [3]—or when the judiciary, for similar reasons, independently constricts STANDING [4] to challenge an agency's action. The same concerns surface when Congress proves incapable of making even large choices of value within an agency's field of decision and again when the courts or Congress demand deference to agency choices of value—"deference," in this context, consisting of giving weight to what an agency says is the law because the agency says it. Constitutional questions constantly attend agency use of informal procedures in decision making. And constitutional questions both spark and restrain efforts

by units within the office of the President, such as the OFFICE OF MANAGEMENT AND BUDGET [3], and by committees and individual members of Congress to intervene in an agency's consideration of issues. The LEGISLATIVE VETO [2], now disapproved on constitutional grounds, is only one of the means of congressional and executive involvement extending beyond formal participation in agency processes or the processes of judicial review.

The demands on agencies often press them to issue statements, characterized as rules, explicitly limiting the factors to be taken into account in a decision of a particular kind. These rules may govern decisions by the agency itself or by individuals and corporate bodies within the agency's field. In their formation some public participation may be allowed. Rule-making, if not peculiar to agencies, is characteristic of them, and agencies make rules whether or not explicitly authorized by statute to do so. But inasmuch as relevant factors for decision may then be excluded and decisions in particular cases may not be made on their full merits under the governing statutes, constitutional questions of due process are presented when individuals affected by such decisions challenge them. Here, too, justification is grounded in felt necessity, the acceptance of rough justice as preferable to the entire failure of justice. In addition, the crystallization of an agency rule is viewed as facilitating congressional reentry into a field through debate of defined issues leading to focused statutory amendments.

The demands on agencies to do what other governmental bodies are not equipped to do have also led to bureaucratic hierarchies within agencies. BUREAUCRACY [1,I] raises the fundamental question of responsibility in decision making. The constitutional shadow is that of arbitrariness—the making of decisions by individuals within an agency who have not been delegated authority to make them or responsibility for them, and the enforcement of decisions that are not deliberately made but are rather the outcome of contending forces within and outside the agency. Congress and the courts have responded by establishing a body of administrative law judges, by requiring records of evidence and explanations of decisions, by requiring personal decision making (one constitutional formula is "the one who decides must hear"), and by prohibiting various kinds of EX PARTE [2] contacts with agency decision makers. These responses to administrative bureaucracy have led in turn to fears that modern agencies may be overjudicialized as a result of attention to constitutional concerns.

The principal influence of administrative agencies on constitutional law is the impact of the form of legal thought they have generated, which has differed from conventional doctrine over a substantial period of American legal history. "Legality" in agency administration is not the correctness of an outcome but rather the proper taking of factors or values into account in the making of a decision. There is little or no finality in administration: Decisions frequently remain open to revision and to justified reversal. There is no real distinction between agency action and agency inaction. The effects of agency decisions are examined and reexamined far beyond the bipolar limits of the judicial case. Values are routinely recognized—sometimes identified as noneconomic—to which no private claim can be made. In these respects, even though administrative law is evidently molded by constitutional concerns, administrative agencies may be considered seeds of anticonstitutional thought, for standard constitutional doctrine has maintained a markedly different structure of presuppositions and dichotomies. In judicial review of agencies the strong emphasis on the actualities of agency decision making, in contrast to acceptance of formal regularity in constitutional review of other decision-making bodies, contains further fundamental challenge. In large perspective, there is in administrative law a vision of agencies and courts joined with each other and with Congress in pursuit of evolving public values. This vision sits uneasily with an inherited vision, still alive in much constitutional thought, of government as invader of a private sphere of rights that it is the duty of courts to guard. The future of constitutional law will be guided in substantial part by the way these competing visions and modes of thought are integrated.

JOSEPH VINING

(SEE ALSO: *Appointing and Removal Power (Presidential)* [1].)

Bibliography

MASHAW, JERRY L. 1983 *Bureaucratic Justice.* New Haven, Conn.: Yale University Press.

STEWART, RICHARD B. and SUNSTEIN, CASS R. 1982 Public Programs and Private Rights. *Harvard Law Review* 95:1193–1322.

VINING, JOSEPH 1978 *Legal Identity: The Coming of Age of Public Law.* New Haven, Conn.: Yale University Press.

ADMINISTRATIVE SEARCH
(Update)

The Supreme Court has placed fewer checks on government searches pursuant to administrative schemes (health and safety inspections, for example) than it has placed on searches aimed at gathering evidence of criminal wrongdoing. Moreover, under current doctrine, government officials are less likely to need a SEARCH WARRANT [4] for administrative searches of businesses than for similar searches of homes.

It is not at all obvious why this should be so. The FOURTH AMENDMENT [2,I], by its terms, protects people "in their persons, houses, papers, and effects, against unreasonable searches and seizures." The language of the amendment gives no indication that the reasonableness of a search should turn on whether the object of the search is evidence of a crime or of a safety code violation. Nor does it suggest that less protection is due papers and effects that are located in businesses rather than in homes. Nonetheless, the Supreme Court has shown a marked discomfort with the notions that safety inspections are to be subject to the same constitutional standard as criminal investigations and that businesses are entitled to the same protections as homes.

The Court first considered the administrative search in *Frank v. Maryland* (1959), holding that a homeowner could be arrested and fined for refusing a WARRANTLESS SEARCH [4] of his home for health code violations. The majority made the remarkable assertion that the fundamental liberty interest at stake in the Fourth Amendment was the right to be free from searches for evidence to be used in criminal prosecutions, not a general RIGHT OF PRIVACY [3,I] in one's home. The safety inspection, they said, touched "at most upon the peripery" of the interests protected by the Constitution. Justice WILLIAM O. DOUGLAS [2], writing for the four dissenters, argued that the Fourth Amendment was not designed to protect criminals only. He pointed out that, historically, much of the government action to which the Fourth Amendment was directed involved searches for violations of shipping regulations, not criminal investigations.

Justice Douglas was eventually vindicated, at least in part. CAMARA V. MUNICIPAL COURT (1967) [1] held that Fourth Amendment protections do apply to administrative housing inspections and that such inspections require a warrant supported by PROBABLE CAUSE [3]. While this is nominally the same standard as for criminal investigations, the Court explained that probable cause must itself depend upon a balancing of the need to search and the degree of invasion the search entails. To establish probable cause for administrative searches, government officials need satisfy only some reasonable legislative or administrative standard applicable to an entire area; they need not have specific information about a particular dwelling. The area warrant, as it is called, is thus based on a notion of probable cause very different from the traditional concept applicable in criminal cases. There is no probable cause for a search for evidence of a crime unless it is more likely than not that relevant evidence will be found at the specific dwelling searched. *See v. City of Seattle* (1967), the companion case to *Camara*, applied the area warrant requirement to the administrative inspection of businesses.

In arriving at its new balance for administrative searches, the *Camara* Court relied on three factors, none of which is wholly satisfactory. "First, [area inspections] have a long history of judicial and public acceptance." As an empirical matter, this statement was probably incorrect, as few of these cases had been to court, and none had previously made it to the Supreme Court. More important, the Court generally has found such historical justification insufficient to sustain government action that otherwise violates the Constitution.

"Second, the public interest demands that all dangerous conditions be prevented or abated, yet it is doubtful that any other canvassing technique would achieve acceptable results." Is the same not true of criminal law enforcement? Could government officials justify searching an entire block looking for a crack house on the theory that "[no] other canvassing technique would achieve acceptable results"? Surely not.

"Finally, because the inspections are neither personal in nature nor aimed at the discovery of evidence of crime, they involve a relatively limited invasion of the urban citizen's privacy." This reasoning has much in common with the majority's argument in *Frank*. Although the *Camara* language does support a more general right to privacy under the Fourth Amendment than *Frank* recognized, the Court apparently continues to see protection from unwarranted criminal investigation as more central to the amendment. Why this should be so remains a mystery; the individual's right to privacy and property protected by the Fourth Amendment should not vary according to the nature of the government's interest in the intrusion.

Another problem with the administrative search–criminal search distinction is that it is often difficult to tell one from the other. In many instances, health and safety regulations call for criminal penalties against offenders, and much administrative regulation of business is aimed at preventing criminal activity. A case in point is *New York v. Burger* (1987). When two police officers arrived to conduct an administrative inspection of Burger's automobile junkyard, Burger was unable to produce the required license and records. Proceeding without the traditional quantum of probable cause for a criminal investigation, the officers searched the yard and uncovered stolen vehicles, evidence used against Burger in a subsequent criminal prosecution. The Court held that the evidence could be used against Burger as the fruit of a valid administrative search, notwithstanding that the regulatory scheme was directed at deterring criminal behavior. By way of explanation, the Court offered a rather confusing distinction between administrative schemes, which set forth rules for the conduct of a business, on the one hand, and criminal laws, which punish individuals for specific acts of behavior, on the other.

The diminished safeguards applicable to administrative searches have been further eroded in cases involving businesses. Although *See* applied the area warrant requirement equally to searches of businesses and searches of homes, the Court has subsequently elaborated a distinction between the two. *Burger* is the present culmination of that line of cases. In *Burger*, not only was the search conducted with less than traditional probable cause, but the police officers did not have a warrant.

The Court began its move away from the *See* warrant requirement in *Colonnade Catering Corporation v. United States* (1970), where it upheld a conviction for turning away a warrantless inspection of a liquor storeroom. *United States v. Biswell* (1972) allowed a warrantless search of a gun dealer's storeroom. *Biswell* made it clear that the balancing approach of *Camara* and *See* would be applied not only in determining the quantum of probable cause necessary to support a warrant but also in deciding whether a warrant was necessary at all. In *Biswell* the Court argued that the effectiveness (and hence reasonableness) of the firearm inspection scheme depended on "unannounced, even frequent, inspections," which a warrant requirement could frustrate. No doubt we could reduce crime of all sorts if police were allowed to make "unannounced, even frequent, inspections" of everyone's home and business.

In addition to the familiar balancing approach, *Colonnade* and *Biswell* introduced another element into administrative search jurisprudence. The Court excused the warrant requirement, in part because those engaging in "closely regulated businesses," such as liquor vendors and firearms dealers, have a reduced expectation of privacy.

The Court at first seemed to limit the reach of *Colonnade* and *Biswell*, explaining in MARSHALL V. BARLOW'S, INC. (1978) [3] that the closely regulated business exception to the warrant requirement was a narrow one. *Barlow's* established an area warrant requirement for searches pursuant to the federal Occupational Safety and Health Act, which applies to a wide range of businesses not necessarily subject to extensive government regulation.

The closely regulated exception returned, however, in *Donovan v. Dewey* (1981), which allowed warrantless inspection of mines pursuant to the federal Mine Safety and Health Act. The Court also returned to a balancing approach. Quoting *Biswell*, the Court stressed the need for unannounced and frequent inspection of mines, where "serious accidents and unhealthful working conditions" are "notorious."

In *Burger*, the most recent business search case, the Court summarized its case law and brought together the closely regulated and balancing approaches. Administrative searches of closely regulated businesses may be made without a warrant if three criteria are met: (1) there is a substantial government interest that informs the regulatory scheme; (2) warrantless inspections are necessary to further the regulatory scheme; and (3) the inspection program is of sufficient certainty and regularity as to limit the discretion of the inspecting officer and advise the business owner that the search is within the scope of the regulatory law.

Despite this latest attempt to refine the exception to the warrant requirement, the closely regulated distinction remains troubling. In essence, it is a form of implied consent theory: By voluntarily engaging in certain businesses, or seeking government licenses, business owners have agreed to give up a measure of their privacy. This line of reasoning is in apparent conflict with the doctrine of UNCONSTITUTIONAL CONDITIONS [4], where the Court, in other cases, has frowned upon the conditioning of government privileges on the surrendering of a constitutional right. There is indeed something anomalous in the notion that the government, by its own intrusive actions, can create a reduced expectation of privacy.

ALEX KOZINSKI

(SEE ALSO: *Reasonable Expectation of Privacy* [I]; *Search and Seizure* [4,I].)

Bibliography

KRESS, JACK M. and IANNELLI, CAROLE D. 1986 Administrative Search and Seizure: Whither the Warrant? *Villanova Law Review* 31:705–832.

LAFAVE, WAYNE R. 1987 *Search and Seizure: A Treatise on the Fourth Amendment.* St. Paul, Minn.: West Publishing Co.

ADVERSARY TRIAL

See: Rights of the Criminally Accused [I]

ADVERTISING

See: Commercial Speech [1,I]

ADVICE AND CONSENT TO SUPREME COURT NOMINATIONS

The proper scope of the SENATE'S [I] role in confirming Supreme Court nominees has been the subject of recurring and often heated debate. The Constitution provides simply that the President "shall nominate, and by and with the advice and consent of the Senate, shall appoint . . . Judges of the Supreme Court." Although the Senate also has the constitutional responsibility of advising on and consenting to presidential appointments of ambassadors, lower federal court judges, and many executive branch officials, debates over the nature of the Senate's role have generally arisen in the context of Supreme Court nominations.

The central issues of controversy have concerned the criteria the Senate should consider in making confirmation decisions and the appropriate range of questions that may be posed to and answered by a nominee. Debated points regarding appropriate criteria for confirmation have included the degree to which the Senate should defer to the President's preferred choice and whether it is appropriate to take a nominee's political views or judicial philosophy into account. The debate about the scope of questioning has centered on whether it is appropriate for senators to ask and nominees to answer questions about the nominee's political views and judicial philosophy and how these views and philosophy would apply to issues that may come before the Court.

Presidents and some members of the Senate have argued that selecting Justices is the President's prerogative and that, although the President may take a judicial prospect's philosophy into account, the Senate must limit its inquiry to whether the nominee has the basic qualifications for the job. These commentators maintain that the Senate should defer to the President's nomination of any person who is neither corrupt nor professionally incompetent. Others have contested this view and argued that the Senate, when it decides whether to consent to a nomination, is permitted to take into account the same range of considerations open to the President and to make its own independent determination of whether confirmation of a particular nominee is in the best interests of the country.

Presidents have often taken the position that the Senate should defer to the President's choice. President RICHARD M. NIXON [3], for example, claimed in 1971 that the President has "the constitutional responsibility to appoint members of the Court," a responsibility that should not be "frustrated by those who wish to substitute their own philosophy for that of the one person entrusted by the Constitution with the power of appointment." This view was echoed by President RONALD REAGAN [3,I], who asserted that the President has the "right" to "choose federal judges who share his judicial philosophy" and that the Senate should confirm Presidents' nominees "so long as they are qualified by character and competence."

Many of those who agree with Presidents Nixon and Reagan believe that the proper standard for Senate review of Supreme Court nominees is the deferential standard that the Senate has typically accorded to presidential nominations of executive officials, whose confirmation is generally expected unless the nominee is found to lack the character or competence necessary for the job. This analogy between executive and judicial appointments is not wholly apt. Whereas the President is entitled to have in the executive branch officials who share the President's philosophy and will carry out the chief executive's policies, judicial nominees are expected to exercise independent judgment. Those favoring a more active Senate role in the judicial confirmation process suggest that the proper analogy is to the Senate's role in ratifying or rejecting treaties or to the President's decision to sign or veto legislation—instances in which an independent exercise of judgment by each branch is thought appropriate.

The consideration of the APPOINTMENTS CLAUSE [I] by the CONSTITUTIONAL CONVENTION OF 1787 [1] offers some support for the position that senators should exercise their own independent judgment about whether to confirm a nominee. The convention considered the issue of judicial appointments separately from its consideration of the appointment of executive officers. For much of the summer of 1787, the evolving drafts of the Constitution gave the Senate exclusive authority to appoint judges. Suggestions for giving the appointing authority to the President alone rather than to the Senate were soundly defeated.

On May 29, 1787, the convention began its work on the Constitution by taking up the VIRGINIA PLAN [4], which provided "that a National Judiciary be established . . . to be chosen by the National Legislature. . . ." Under this plan, the executive was to have no role at all in the selection of judges. When this provision came before the Convention on June 5, several members expressed concern that the whole legislature might be too numerous a body to select judges. JAMES WILSON's [4] alternative providing that the President be given the power to choose judges found almost no support, however. JOHN RUTLEDGE [3] of South Carolina stated that he "was by no means disposed to grant so great a power to any single person." JAMES MADISON [3] agreed that the legislature was too large a body, but stated that "he was not satisfied with referring the appointment to the Executive." He was "rather inclined to give it to the Senatorial branch" as being "sufficiently stable and independent to follow their deliberate judgments."

One week later on June 13, Madison rendered his inclination into a formal motion that the power of appointing judges be given exclusively to the Senate rather than to the legislature as a whole. This motion was adopted without objection. On July 18 the convention reconsidered and reaffirmed its earlier decision to grant the Senate the exclusive power of appointing judges. James Wilson again moved "that the Judges be appointed by the Executive." His motion was defeated, six states to two, after

delegates offered, as GUNNING BEDFORD [1] of Delaware said, "solid reasons against leaving the appointment to the Executive." LUTHER MARTIN [3] of Maryland, stating that he "was strenuous for an appointment by the 2nd branch," argued that "being taken from all the States [the Senate] would be the best informed of character and most capable of making a fit choice." ROGER SHERMAN [4] of Connecticut concurred, "adding that the Judges ought to be diffused, which would be more likely to be attended to by the 2d branch, than by the Executive." NATHANIEL GORHAM [2] of Massachusetts argued against exclusive appointment by the Senate, stating that "public bodies feel no personal responsibility, and give full play to intrigue and cabal." He offered what was to be the final compromise: appointment by the Executive "by and with the advice and consent" of the Senate. At this point in the convention, however, his motion failed on a tie vote.

The issue was considered once again on July 21. After a debate in which GEORGE MASON [3] attacked the idea of executive appointment as a "dangerous prerogative [because] it might even give him an influence over the Judiciary department itself," the convention once again reaffirmed exclusive Senate appointment of judges of the Supreme Court. Thus the matter stood until the closing days of the convention. On September 4, less than two weeks before the convention's work was done, a committee of five reported out a new draft providing for the first time for a presidential role in the selection of judges: "The President . . . shall nominate and by and with the advice and consent of the Senate shall appoint Judges of the Supreme Court." Giving the President the power to nominate judges was not seen as tantamount to ousting the Senate from a central role. GOUVERNEUR MORRIS [3] of Pennsylvania, a member of the Committee, paraphrased the new provision as one that retained in the Senate the power "to appoint Judges nominated to them by the President." With little discussion and without dissent, the Convention adopted this as the final language of the provision. Considering that the convention had repeatedly and decisively rejected any proposal to give the President exclusive power to select judges, it is unlikely that the drafters contemplated reducing the Senate's role to a ministerial one.

During the nineteenth century, the Senate took a broad view of the appropriate criteria to govern "advice and consent" decisions. During this period, the Senate rejected more than one of every four Supreme Court nominations. The Senate first rejected President GEORGE WASHINGTON's nomination of John Rutledge. The Senate went on to reject five of the nominees proposed by President JOHN TYLER [4] and three of the four nominees put forward by President MILLARD FILLMORE [2]. Since 1900, however, the rate of senatorial rejection of Supreme Court nominees has dropped sharply to a twentieth-century rejection rate of a mere one in thirteen.

Virtually all the parties to the twentieth-century debate on appropriate confirmation criteria agree on two threshold issues. The first is that it is appropriate for senators to consider "judicial fitness." No one contests that adequate judicial competence, ethics, and temperament are necessary conditions for confirmation and, therefore, appropriate criteria for senators to consider. The publicly stated bases of opposition to the nominations of LOUIS D. BRANDEIS [1], Judge Clement F. Haynsworth, and Judge George H. Carswell were presented in terms of these threshold, judicial-fitness criteria.

The unsuccessful opposition to Brandeis, nominated in 1916 by President WOODROW WILSON [4], based its public case against the nominee on alleged breaches of legal ethics. The successful opposition to confirmation of Judge Haynsworth, nominated to the Supreme Court by President Nixon in 1969, was articulated primarily in terms of charges that Haynsworth had violated canons of judicial ethics by sitting on cases involving corporations in which he had small financial interests. In addition to the ethics charges, some opponents raised objections to Haynsworth's CIVIL RIGHTS [1,I] record. Two judicial-fitness objections formed the basis for the successful opposition to confirmation of Judge Carswell, nominated to the Supreme Court by President Nixon in 1970. The primary objection was that Carswell allegedly allowed racial prejudice to affect his judicial behavior. The second theme in the opposition to Carswell was that, as a matter of basic competence, he was at best a mediocre jurist.

Thus, in the Brandeis, Haynsworth, and Carswell nominations, opposition was presented as based on the judicial-fitness criteria of judicial temperament, ethics, and basic competence. In all three of these twentieth-century confirmation controversies, the acceptability of the judicial-fitness criteria went unchallenged.

The second area of general agreement in the debate on appropriate criteria for confirmation decisions is that senators should not base their decisions on the nominee's predicted vote on a particular case or "single issue" likely to come before the Court. Supporters of the nomination of Judge John Parker, nominated to the Supreme Court by President HERBERT HOOVER [2] in 1930, alleged that opposition to the nomination was based on a "single issue" of Parker's position on a particular labor-law question. Parker's opponents took pains to deny that their opposition was based on a single issue and argued that Parker's ruling in a previous case involving the question reflected Parker's own anti-union bias. This accusation—that, as a judge, Parker was biased in his rulings on such matters—was a

way for the opponents of confirmation to frame their objection as one of judicial temperament and, thus, judicial fitness. The premise underlying the positions of both opponents and supporters of Parker was that a rejection based on a result-oriented single-issue criterion would be inappropriate.

Between the margins of agreement that judicial-fitness criteria are appropriate and that single-issue criteria are inappropriate lies the area of controversy. The debated issue is often framed as whether the nominee's "judicial philosophy" should be considered in the decision-making process. The term "judicial philosophy," when used in this context, refers to a range of concerns including the nominee's theory of judging (that is, the degree of judicial interference with legislative and executive decision making the nominee views as appropriate), the nominee's views on the level of generality at which constitutional provisions should be interpreted, and the nominee's interpretation of specific constitutional clauses or doctrines (such as the applicability of the EQUAL PROTECTION [2,I] clause to women or the existence of a constitutional RIGHT OF PRIVACY [3,I].

The bases of opposition to President LYNDON B. JOHNSON's [3] 1968 nomination of Justice ABE FORTAS [2] (to be Chief Justice) and to President Reagan's nomination of Judge Robert Bork to the Supreme Court were framed largely in terms of these controversial "judicial philosophy" criteria. Consequently, the confirmation battles in these cases raged as much around the appropriateness of the criteria applied as around the merits of the nominees themselves.

The attack on Fortas's judicial philosophy was based on charges that he was a "judicial activist" (meaning that his theory of judging envisioned excessive intervention in the discretion of the elected branches) and that his substantive interpretations (of the First, Fifth, Sixth, and Fourteenth amendments) were flawed. Supporters of the Fortas nomination responded both on the merits—defending Fortas's theory of judging and his substantive interpretations—and by assailing the judicial philosophy criterion as inappropriate considerations for advice and consent decisions. (Although some ethics charges were raised during the confirmation proceedings, the very serious ethics charges that resulted in Fortas's resignation did not arise until the spring of 1969, during the Nixon presidency, many months after President Johnson had withdrawn his nomination of Justice Fortas to become Chief Justice.)

Like the Fortas nomination, the nomination of Judge Robert Bork to the Supreme Court was opposed largely on judicial philosophy grounds. (Although some critics raised ethics issues, including Bork's role in the "Saturday

Night Massacre" in which the special prosecutor in the WATERGATE [4] affair was fired, these issues did not form a primary basis of opposition.) Judge Bork's theory of judging was assailed as an inadequate conception of the proper role of the Supreme Court in protecting individual and "unenumerated" constitutional rights. Objections were also presented in terms of Bork's interpretations of specific constitutional clauses and doctrines, including his position on the existence of a constitutional right to privacy, his previous and contemporaneous interpretations of the equal protection clause as regards the protections afforded to women, his interpretations of the FIRST AMENDMENT's [2,I] free speech clause, and his positions on civil rights. Much of the defense of Judge Bork took the form of challenging the acceptability of these controversial criteria.

The contours of the areas of agreement and disagreement on appropriate advice-and-consent criteria are not surprising. The debate on appropriate criteria follows from the constitutional provisions that structure the process of appointments to an independent, principle-oriented, countermajoritarian judiciary in a way that requires the consent of an elected, representative, majoritarian body. Senators' views about the proper role of the judiciary inform their positions on the relevance and propriety of each category of advice-and-consent criteria.

A foundational precept of the role of an independent judiciary is that judges must render decisions based on the rigorous application of principles, not their personal preferences, much less their biases. The broad agreement about this precept underlies and is reflected in the broad consensus that judicial fitness is an acceptable category of criteria for consent decisions. Competence in legal reasoning, high ethical standards, and unbiased judicious temperament are prerequisites to the consistent rendering of rigorously reasoned and principled decisions of law.

The same precept—that the essence of the judicial function is to render decisions based on principles—underlies the broad consensus that single-issue result-oriented criteria are unacceptable. Because of the principle-based nature of the judicial function, a judicial nominee must be evaluated on the basis of the anticipated process of his or her application of principles, regardless of whether that process will produce a senator's preferred outcome in any particular case. The ability of elected Presidents and elected senators to exert some general influence on the future course of the nation's jurisprudence is an appropriate (and appropriately limited) popular check on the exercise of the power of JUDICIAL REVIEW [3], without which this institution might not be acceptable in a constitutional democracy. Nonetheless, for Presidents or senators to demand that the judiciary not render decisions based

on principle but, rather, act as an agent of the legislature furthering particular preferences, and for senators to enforce this demand by the threat or reality of nonconfirmation, would subvert the independence of the judiciary and violate the spirit of the SEPARATION OF POWERS [3].

Rather than a continued focus on the appropriate criteria for advice-and-consent decisions, a different aspect of the debate over the appropriate role of the Senate in the confirmation process came to the fore during consideration of the nomination of Justice DAVID H. SOUTER [I]. Souter's views on controversial judicial and political issues were little known. The prominent questions during the Souter confirmation, therefore, were (1) where relatively little is known about the nominee's thinking, how may the Senate properly learn more about the nominee; and (2) what questions may properly be posed to the nominee during the confirmation hearings? These questions are not merely derivative of the larger question of what decision-making criteria are legitimate. The core objection to direct questions to the nominee—even on issues that might constitute legitimate decision-making criteria, such as substantive interpretation of particular constitutional clauses—is that, by offering an opinion on such issues, the nominee may thereafter feel bound to hold in subsequent cases in a manner consistent with the opinions stated during the confirmation hearings. Thus, the fear is that the nominee who opines on, say, the level of protection afforded to women by the equal protection clause during the confirmation hearing will, in effect, be "committed" to a certain outcome in future cases involving that issue.

But fear of judicial precommitment may be exaggerated. Surely there is no requirement that the individuals nominated to our highest court have never thought about—or reached tentative conclusions on—the important issues of law that face the country. So the only issue is whether sharing those thoughts with the senators during confirmation hearings would constitute a commitment not to change those views or not to be open to the arguments of parties litigating those issues in the future. There is no reason to believe that a statement of opinion during confirmation would constitute such a commitment. It would seem reasonable to suppose that an opinion mentioned during a confirmation hearing would be seen as not binding if it were generally understood that such statements are not binding. It would seem reasonable that a nominee might preface an opinion on such an issue with a statement that "these are my initial views on the issue, but they would certainly be open to change in the context of a case in which persuasive arguments were put forth by the parties." Justices would not be in any way committed to be "consistent" with their confirmation comments if it were understood that confirmation comments constitute nothing more and nothing less than frank statements by nominees of their best thinking on a particular issue to date.

(SEE ALSO: *Appointing and Removal Power (Presidential)* [1].)

MADELINE MORRIS
WALTER DELLINGER

Bibliography

MORRIS, MADELINE 1988–1989 The Grammar of Advice and Consent: Senate Confirmation of Supreme Court Nominees. *Drake Law Review* 38:863–887.

REES, GROVER, III 1983 Questions for Supreme Court Nominees at Confirmation Hearings: Excluding the Constitution. *Georgia Law Review* 17:913–967.

TRIBE, LAURENCE H. 1985 God Save This Honorable Court. New York: Mentor.

AFFIRMATIVE ACTION
(Update)

Do constitutional guarantees of EQUAL PROTECTION [2,I] command that government must be "color-blind" or only that government may not subordinate any group on the basis of race? The Supreme Court's equal protection decisions have long straddled these two different principles. The color-blindness approach deems race morally irrelevant to governmental decision making under all circumstances. The antisubordination approach, by contrast, sees racial distinctions as illegitimate only when used by government as a deliberate basis for disadvantage. The two approaches divide sharply on the permissibility of affirmative action: advocates of color blindness condemn the use of racial distinctions even to benefit previously disadvantaged racial groups, whereas those who view equal protection solely as a ban on racial subordination see affirmative action as constitutionally benign.

Since 1985, the Supreme Court has continued to steer between these two approaches rather than unequivocally embrace either one. In earlier decisions, the Court had upheld a variety of RACIAL PREFERENCES [I], including the use of race as a factor in university admissions (as long as rigid RACIAL QUOTAS [3] were not employed) in REGENTS OF UNIVERSITY OF CALIFORNIA V. BAKKE (1978) [3], the set-aside of places for blacks in an industrial skills-training program in UNITED STEELWORKERS OF AMERICA V. WEBER (1979) [4], and the set-aside of public works construction projects for minority business enterprises in FULLILOVE V. KLUTZNICK (1980) [2]. These cases made clear that affirmative action would not be struck down as readily as laws harming racial minorities, but neither would it be lightly tolerated. Governments could successfully defend affirmative action programs, but only with an especially strong justification.

The affirmative action cases since 1985 have bitterly divided the Court, and their outcomes have signaled a partial retrenchment for affirmative action. With the appointments of Justices SANDRA DAY O'CONNOR [3,I], ANTONIN SCALIA [I], and ANTHONY M. KENNEDY [I], the Court veered off its middle course and more sharply toward the color-blindness pole. Although the Court readily upheld affirmative action as a court-imposed remedy for RACIAL DISCRIMINATION [3,I] against minorities, as in *Local 28, Sheet Metal Workers International Association v. EEOC* (1986), the Court struck down two municipalities' efforts to impose affirmative action on themselves. In WYGANT V. JACKSON BOARD OF EDUCATION (1986) [I] the Court invalidated a school district's plan to protect minority teachers against layoffs ahead of more senior white teachers. And in RICHMOND (CITY OF) V. J. A. CROSON CO. (1989) [I], the Court struck down a city's reservation of a percentage of public works construction for minority business enterprises—a set-aside modeled on the congressional program upheld in *Fullilove*. But METRO BROADCASTING V. F.C.C. (1990) [I], which upheld federal policies preferring minority broadcasters in the allocation of broadcast licenses, confounded those who thought *Croson* had sounded the death knell for affirmative action.

The central conflict in these cases was over what justification for affirmative action would suffice. Up until *Metro*, the Court accepted only narrowly remedial justifications. Affirmative action was upheld only as penance for particularized past sins of discrimination—not as atonement for "societal discrimination" as a whole. The Court treated affirmative action as a matter of corrective rather than distributive justice; minorities might be preferred for jobs, admissions, or contracts not to build a racially integrated future, but only to cure a racially discriminatory past.

The Court's account of affirmative action as a permissible remedy for past discrimination, however, left both sides unsatisfied. Opponents charged that affirmative action was a poor version of corrective justice because (1) unlike standard compensatory justice, affirmative action extends benefits beyond the specific victims of past discrimination; and (2) unlike standard retributive justice, affirmative action demands current sacrifice of persons who were not the actual perpetrators of past discrimination—persons the Court sometimes labels "innocent" whites. In the opponents' view, if affirmative action were truly remedial, neither would nonvictims benefit nor nonsinners pay. In contrast, advocates of affirmative action found the Court's requirements for proving remedial justification far too stringent. Governments are reluctant to confess to past sins of discrimination, advocates argued, and should be permitted to adopt affirmative action plans without official *mea culpas*.

Metro Broadcasting departed from the sin-based approach by accepting a nonremedial justification for the Federal Communications Commission's (FCC) minority-ownership preference policies: increased minority ownership would help diversify broadcast program content. A majority of the Court had never endorsed such a justification before, although Justice LEWIS F. POWELL's [3,I] crucial *Bakke* opinion had defended racial preferences in university admissions as producing diversity in the classroom and Justice JOHN PAUL STEVENS [4,I] had persistently advocated similar diversity-based justifications for affirmative action, for example, in his *Wygant* dissent. Such justifications implicitly adopt the antisubordination rather than the color-blindness approach: using racial distinctions to increase diversity is not a constitutional evil because it does not use race to impose disadvantage. As Justice Stevens wrote in his *Metro* concurrence, "[n]either the favored nor the disfavored class is stigmatized in any way."

When *Wygant*, *Croson*, and *Metro* are considered together, it appears that the Court's affirmative action decisions continue to steer between the color-blindness and antisubordination poles. *Wygant* and *Croson* should not be overstated as victories for color blindness because those decisions left open the possibility that other governments might do better than the Jackson school board or the Richmond city council at tailoring affirmative action narrowly to remedy demonstrable discrimination in their past. After *Wygant* and *Croson*, state and local affirmative action plans face a high but not insurmountable hurdle: the clearer the paper trail of past discrimination, the more flexible or waivable the target, the shorter the plan's duration, and the less entrenched the reliance interests of the displaced whites, the more likely such a plan will be upheld. However, *Metro* should not be overstated as a victory for the antisubordination view because this decision turned heavily on the Court's deference to its coequal branches (Congress and the FCC) and low valuation of broadcasters' rights—two factors especially appealing to Justice BYRON R. WHITE [4,I], who cast the decisive vote despite his earlier negative votes on affirmative action.

The dissenting opinions in *Metro Broadcasting* may well be more portentous for the future of affirmative action than Justice WILLIAM J. BRENNAN's [1,I] majority opinion—the last opinion he wrote before retiring from the Court. The dissenters made thinly veiled reference to the backlash against affirmative action evident in national politics since the 1980 elections. Justice O'Connor's dissent, joined by Chief Justice WILLIAM H. REHNQUIST [3,I] and Justices Scalia and Kennedy, spoke of affirmative action as "contributing to an escalation of racial hostility and conflict," and Justice Kennedy's dissent, joined by Justice Scalia, compared the FCC's policies with those of South Africa and suggested that affirmative action makes

whites feel wrongfully stigmatized. Justice Scalia wrote similarly in his *Croson* concurrence that "[w]hen we depart from" pure meritocracy, "we play with fire, and much more than an occasional DeFunis, Johnson, or Croson burns." To the *Metro* majority, these objections appeared wildly overstated, and affirmative action readily distinguishable from the evils of apartheid or Jim Crow. Which view will prevail in the wake of Justice Brennan's departure from the Court remains to be seen.

KATHLEEN M. SULLIVAN

(SEE ALSO: *Johnson v. Transportation Agency* [I]; *Paradise, United States v.* [I]; *Race-Consciousness* [I].)

Bibliography

SULLIVAN, KATHLEEN M. 1986 Sins of Discrimination: Last Term's Affirmative Action Cases. *Harvard Law Review* 100:78–98.

WILLIAMS, PATRICIA J. 1990 Metro Broadcasting, Inc v. FCC: Regrouping in Singular Times. *Harvard Law Review* 104:525–546.

ALCOHOL ABUSE

See: Punitive Damages [I]

AMENDMENT PROCESS (OUTSIDE ARTICLE V)

Few constitutional rules are as important as those regarding amendment because these rules define the conditions under which all other constitutional norms may be displaced. It is commonly believed that the words of Article V specify with precision the necessary and sufficient conditions for legitimate constitutional change:

The Congress, whenever two thirds of both Houses shall deem it necessary, shall propose Amendments to this Constitution, or, on the Application of the Legislatures of two thirds of the several States, shall call a Convention for proposing Amendments, which, in either Case, shall be valid to all Intents and Purposes, as Part of this Constitution, when ratified by the Legislatures of three fourths of the several states, or by conventions in three fourths thereof, as the one or the other Mode of RATIFICATION may be proposed by the Congress; Provided that . . . no State, without its Consent, shall be deprived of its equal Suffrage in the SENATE.

Yet things are not so simple. First, the procedures seem far less precise than one might expect. Can Congress call for a CONSTITUTIONAL CONVENTION [1] limited by subject matter? Does the President have any PRESENTMENT [3] role? What voting rule must a convention follow? What apportionment ratio must it follow? Who sets the rules as to selection of delegates? The spare words of Article V are not very helpful in answering these and many other key questions. If determinate answers do exist, they lie outside of Article V: in other provisions of the Constitution, in the overall structure of the document, and in the history of its creation and amendment (and perhaps also the history of the creation and amendment of analogous legal documents, such as STATE CONSTITUTIONS [1]).

Second, it is far from clear whether Article V lays down universally sufficient conditions for legitimate amendment. Could an amendment modify the rules of amendment themselves? (If so, the "equal suffrage" rules could easily be evaded by two successive "ordinary" amendments, the first of which repealed the "equal suffrage" rules of Article V and the second of which reapportioned the Senate.) Similarly, could a legitimate amendment generally purport to make itself (or any other random provision of the Constitution) immune from further amendment? But if not, what about an amendment that effectively entrenched itself from further revision by, for instance, outlawing criticism of existing law? For answers, we must once again look beyond the words of Article V to the general structure of the Constitution and its overriding themes of POPULAR SOVEREIGNTY [3] and republican government, which establish the preconditions for Article V itself. Thus, the rest of the document can help us distinguish between true constitutional amendments (changes within the preexisting deep structure of the document) and constitutional repudiations (which may formally seem to fit Article V, but in fact reject the Constitution's essence of deliberative popular sovereignty).

Finally, it is also dubious whether Article V specifies universally necessary conditions for legitimate amendment. Two major theories of non–Article V amendment have recently emerged in legal scholarship. The first, championed by Professor Bruce Ackerman, begins by noting that the Philadelphia "Convention," which drafted Article V, was itself acting (in the name of "We, the People") in ways not expressly contemplated by the spare words of Article XIII of the ARTICLES OF CONFEDERATION [1]. Like Article V, Article XIII at first seemed to specify absolutely necessary conditions for legitimate amendment, but Ackerman argues that the Philadelphia experience itself—the process by which our Constitution was framed and ratified—belies any such simplistic idea. And the same is true for Article V, especially given the Framers' self-referential use of the word "convention" in this article. Ackerman goes on to argue that the most important subsequent additions to our constitutional text, the Reconstruction Amendments, were not in fact adopted in strict compliance with Article V, and thus can only be legitimated

if we properly recognize that "We, the People" may legitimately amend the Constitution by acting beyond the formal rules of Article V, but within the deep structure of popular sovereignty established by the document as a whole.

The second theory, propounded here, resembles Ackerman's, but differs in important respects. Whereas Ackerman focuses on Article XIII of the Articles of Confederation, this second theory begins by looking at state constitutions in effect in 1787. Virtually all the constitutions had amendment clauses similar to Article V, yet in none of these states was the federal Constitution ratified in strict conformity with the clauses. Like Article V, these clauses at first seemed to specify necessary conditions for amendment, but the events of 1787–89 belie such a simplistic reading. Subsequent developments in state constitutional law confirm the nonexclusivity of various amendment clauses; scores of amendments were adopted in the nineteenth century by means of popular ratification nowhere specified in the text of preexisting amendment clauses. These state clauses illuminate Article V. Like its state constitutional counterparts, Article V nowhere explicitly declares itself to be the only legitimate mechanism of constitutional amendment. Rather, Article V is best read as prescribing only the exclusive mechanism by which ordinary governmental entities—Congress and state legislatures—can amend the document that limits their powers. But Article V nowhere qualifies the right of the sovereign people themselves, acting outside of ordinary government in specially convened national conventions, to alter or abolish their governments at their pleasure. This reading of Article V draws support not only from the language of Article VII and the 1787–89 ratification process, but also from the specific words of, and the popular-sovereignty ideology underlying, the PREAMBLE [3] ("We, the People"); the FIRST AMENDMENT [2,I] ("right of the People [collectively] to assemble" in conventions); and the NINTH AMENDMENT [3] and the TENTH AMENDMENT [4] (reserving to "the People" collective right to alter and abolish government). Only if a current majority of deliberate citizens can, if they desire, amend our Constitution, can the document truly be said to derive from "We, the People of the United States," here and now, rather than from the hands of a small group of white men ruling us from their graves. Any contrary reading of Article V would violate the Preamble's promise that the Framers' "posterity" would continue to enjoy "the blessings of liberty"—most importantly, the liberty of popular self-government.

In the end, a narrow clause-bound approach is no more satisfying in the Article V context than elsewhere. The rest of the document and its subsequent history must always be consulted—sometimes with, at first, surprising results.

AKHIL REED AMAR

(SEE ALSO: *Amending Process* [1]; *Republicanism* [I].)

Bibliography

ACKERMAN, BRUCE 1984 The Storrs Lectures: Discovering the Constitution. *Yale Law Journal* 93:1013–1072.

_____ 1989 Constitutional Politics/Constitutional Law. *Yale Law Journal* 99:453–547.

AMAR, AKHIL REED 1987 Philadelphia Revisited: Amending the Constitution Outside Article V. *University of Chicago Law Review* 55:1043–1104.

BLACK, CHARLES 1963 The Proposed Amendment of Article V: A Threatened Disaster. *Yale Law Journal* 72:957–966.

_____ 1972 Amending the Constitution: A Letter to a Congressman. *Yale Law Journal* 82:189–215.

CAPLAN, RUSSELL 1988 *Constitutional Brinksmanship.* New York: Oxford University Press.

DELLINGER, WALTER 1979 The Recurring Question of a "Limited" Constitutional Convention. *Yale Law Journal* 88:1623–1640.

_____ 1983 The Legitimacy of Constitutional Change: Rethinking the Amendment Process. *Harvard Law Review* 97:386–432.

HALLETT, BENJAMIN FRANKLIN 1848 *Argument in the Rhode Island Causes on the Rights of the People.* Boston: Beale and Greene.

HOAR, ROGER SHERMAN 1917 *Constitutional Conventions.* Boston: Little, Brown.

JAMESON, JOHN ALEXANDER 1887 *A Treatise on Constitutional Conventions,* 4th ed. Chicago: Callaghan and Co.

VAN ALSTYNE, WILLIAM 1978 Does Article V Restrict the States to Calling Unlimited Conventions Only?—A Letter to a Colleague. *Duke Law Journal* 1978:1295–1306.

_____ 1979 The Limited Constitutional Convention—The Recurring Answer. *Duke Law Journal* 1979:985–998.

WOOD, GORDON 1969 *The Creation of the American Republic, 1776–1789.* Chapel Hill: North Carolina Press.

AMERICAN REVOLUTION AND CONSTITUTIONAL THEORY

The era of the American Revolution was one of the greatest and most creative periods of CONSTITUTIONALISM [2,I] in modern history. The American revolutionaries virtually established the modern idea of a written CONSTITUTION [1,I]. There had, of course, been written constitutions before in Western history, but the Americans did something new and different. They made written constitutions a practical and everyday part of governmental life. They showed the world how written constitutions could be made truly fundamental and distinguishable from ordinary legislation and how such constitutions could be interpreted on a regular basis and altered when necessary. Further, they offered the world concrete and usable governmental institutions for carrying out these constitutional tasks.

Before the era of the American Revolution a constitution was rarely distinguished from the government and its operations. In the English tradition a constitution referred not only to FUNDAMENTAL RIGHTS [2] but also to the way the government was put together or constituted. "By constitution," wrote Lord Bolingbroke in 1733, "we mean, whenever we speak with propriety and exactness, that assemblage of laws, institutions and customs, derived from certain fixed principles of reason, directed to certain fixed objects of public good, that compose the general system, according to which the community hath agreed to be governed." The English constitution, in other words, included both fundamental principles and rights and the existing arrangement of governmental laws, customs, and institutions.

By the end of the revolutionary era, however, the Americans' idea of a constitution had become very different from that of the English. A constitution was now seen to be no part of the government at all. A constitution was a written document distinct from, and superior to, all the operations of government. It was, as THOMAS PAINE [3] said in 1791, "a thing *antecedent* to a government, and a government is only the creature of a constitution." And, said Paine, it was "not a thing in name only; but in fact." For the Americans a constitution was like a Bible, possessed by every family and every member of government. "It is the body of elements, to which you can refer, and quote article by article; and which contains . . . everything that relates to the complete organization of a civil government, and the principles on which it shall act, and by which it shall be bound." A constitution thus could never be an act of a legislature or of a government; it had to be the act of the people themselves, declared JAMES WILSON [4] in 1790, one of the principal Framers of the federal Constitution in 1787; and "in their hands it is clay in the hands of a potter; they have the right to mould, to preserve, to improve, to refine, and furnish it as they please." If the English thought this new idea of a constitution resembled, as Arthur Young caustically suggested in 1792, "a pudding made by a recipe," the Americans had become convinced the English no longer had a constitution at all.

It was a momentous transformation of meaning in a short period of time. It involved not just a change in the Americans' political vocabulary but an upheaval in their whole political culture.

The colonists began the imperial crisis in the early 1760s thinking about constitutional issues in much the same way as their fellow Britons. Like the English at home, they believed that the principal threat to the people's rights and liberties had always been the prerogative powers of the king, those ancient but vague and discretionary rights of authority that the king possessed in order to carry out his responsibility for governing the realm. Indeed, the whole of English history was seen as a perennial struggle between these two conflicting rights—between a centralizing monarchy trying to fulfill its obligation to govern, on the one hand, and, on the other, local-minded nobles and people, in the House of Lords and the House of Commons, trying to protect their liberties. Each of the great political events of England's past, from the Norman Conquest to the Glorious Revolution, marked a moment defining the proper relationship between these two sets of conflicting rights—between power and liberty.

The eighteenth-century colonists had no reason to think about government much differently. Time and again they had been forced to defend their liberties against the intrusions of royal prerogative power. Relying for their defense on their colonial assemblies, their miniature counterparts to the House of Commons, they invoked their rights as Englishmen and what they called their ancient COLONIAL CHARTERS [1] as devices guaranteeing the rights of the people against their royal governors. In fact, the entire English past was littered with such charters and other written documents to which the English people had repeatedly appealed in defense of their rights against the crown's power. All these documents, from MAGNA CARTA [3] to the BILL OF RIGHTS [1] of 1689, were merely written evidence of those "fixed principles of reason" from which Bolingbroke had said the English constitution was derived.

Although eighteenth-century Englishmen talked about the fixed principles and the fundamental law of the constitution, few of them doubted that Parliament, as the representative of the nobles and people and as the sovereign lawmaking body of the nation, was the supreme guarantor and interpreter of these fixed principles and FUNDAMENTAL LAW [2]. Parliament was in fact the bulwark of the people's liberties against the crown's encroachments; it alone defended and confirmed the people's rights. The PETITION OF RIGHT [3], the HABEAS CORPUS ACT OF 1679 [2], and the Bill of Rights were all acts of Parliament, mere statutes not different in form from other laws.

For Englishmen, therefore, as WILLIAM BLACKSTONE [1], the great eighteenth-century jurist, pointed out, there could be no distinction between the "constitution or frame or government" and "the system of laws." All were of a piece: every act of Parliament was part of the English constitution and all law, customary and statute, was thus constitutional. "Therefore," concluded the British theorist William Paley, "the terms *constitutional* and *unconstitutional* mean *legal* and *illegal*."

Nothing could be more strikingly different from what Americans came to believe. Indeed, it was precisely on this distinction between "legal" and "constitutional" that the American and British constitutional traditions most obviously diverged at the Revolution. During the 1760s and 1770s the colonists came to realize that although acts of Parliament, like the Stamp Act of 1765, might be legal, that is, in accord with the acceptable way of making law, such acts could not thereby be automatically considered constitutional, that is, in accord with the basic rights and principles of justice that made the English constitution the palladium of liberty that it was. It was true that the English Bill of Rights and the Act of Settlement in 1689 were only statutes of Parliament, but surely, the colonists insisted in astonishment, they were of "a nature more sacred than those which established a turnpike road." Under this pressure of events the Americans came to believe that the fundamental principles of the English constitution had to be lifted out of the lawmaking and other processes and institutions of government and set above them. "In all free States," said the revolutionary leader SAMUEL ADAMS [1] in 1768, "the Constitution is fixed; and as the supreme Legislature derives its Powers and Authority from the Constitution, it cannot overleap the Bounds of it without destroying its own foundation." Thus, in 1776, when Americans came to frame their own constitutions for their newly independent states, they inevitably sought to make them fundamental and to write them out explicitly in documents.

It was one thing, however, to define a constitution as fundamental law, different from ordinary legislation and circumscribing the institutions of government; it was quite another to make such a distinction effective. In the years following the DECLARATION OF INDEPENDENCE [2], many Americans paid lip service to the fundamental character of their STATE CONSTITUTIONS [I], but, like eighteenth-century Britons, they continued to believe that their legislatures were the best instruments for interpreting and changing those constitutions. The state legislatures represented the people, and the people, it seemed, could scarcely tyrannize themselves. Thus, in the late 1770s and the early 1780s several state legislatures, acting on behalf of the people, set aside parts of their constitutions by statute and interpreted and altered them, as one American observed, "upon any Occasion to serve a purpose." Time and again, the legislatures interfered with the governor's designated powers, rejected judicial decisions, disregarded individual liberties and PROPERTY RIGHTS [I], and in general, as one victim complained, violated "those fundamental principles which first induced men to come into civil compact."

By the mid-1780s many American leaders had come to believe that the state assemblies, not the governors as they had thought in 1776, were the political authority to be most feared. Legislators were supposedly the representatives of the people who annually elected them; but "173 despots would surely be as oppressive as one," wrote THOMAS JEFFERSON [3]. "An *elective despotism* was not the government we fought for." It increasingly seemed to many that the idea of a constitution as fundamental law had no practical meaning at all. "If it were possible it would be well to define the extent of the Legislative power," concluded a discouraged JAMES MADISON [3] in 1785, "but the nature of it seems in many respects to be indefinite."

No one wrestled more persistently with this problem of distinguishing between statutory and fundamental law than Jefferson. By 1779, Jefferson had learned from experience that assemblies "elected by the people for the ordinary purposes of legislation only have no power to restrain the acts of succeeding assemblies." Thus, he realized that to declare his great VIRGINIA STATUTE OF RELIGIOUS LIBERTY [4] to be "irrevocable would be of no effect in law; yet we are free," he wrote into the bill in frustration, "to declare, and do declare, that the rights hereby asserted are of the natural rights of mankind, and that if any act shall be hereafter passed to repeal the present or to narrow its operation, such act will be an infringement of natural right." But such a paper declaration was obviously not enough; he realized that something more was needed. By the 1780s, both he and Madison were eager "to form a real constitution" for Virginia; the existing one, enacted in 1776, was merely an "ordinance," with no higher authority than the other ordinances of the same session. They wanted a constitution that would be "perpetual" and "unalterable by other legislatures." But how? If the constitution were to be truly fundamental and immune from legislative tampering, somehow it would have to be created, as Jefferson put it, "by a power superior to that of the legislature."

By the time Jefferson came to write his *Notes on the State of Virginia* in the early 1780s, the answer had become clear: "To render a form of government unalterable by ordinary acts of assembly," said Jefferson, "the people must delegate persons with special powers. They have accordingly chosen special conventions to form and fix their governments." The conventions and congresses of 1775–1776 had been legally deficient legislatures made necessary by the refusal of the royal governors to call together the regular and legal representatives of the people. Now, however, these conventions were seen to be special alternative representations of the people temporarily given the exclusive authority to frame or amend constitutions. When Massachusetts and New Hampshire wrote new constitutions in 1780 and 1784, the proper pattern of constitution making and altering was set: constitutions were formed or changed by specially elected conventions

and then placed before the people for ratification. Thus, in 1787 those who wished to change the federal government knew precisely what to do: they called a CONSTITUTIONAL CONVENTION [1] in Philadelphia and sent the resultant document to the states for approval. Even the French in their own revolution several years later followed the American pattern.

With the idea of a constitution as fundamental law immune from legislative encroachment more firmly in hand, some state judges during the 1780s began cautiously moving in isolated cases to impose restraints on what the assemblies were enacting as law. In effect, they said to the legislatures, as GEORGE WYTHE [4], judge of Virginia's highest court did in 1782, "Here is the limit of your authority; and hither shall you go, but no further." These were the hesitant beginnings of what would come to be called JUDICIAL REVIEW [3], that remarkable American practice by which judges in the ordinary courts of law have the authority to determine the constitutionality of acts of the state and federal legislatures.

In just these ways did Americans in the revolutionary era devise regular and everyday constitutional institutions both for controlling government and thereby protecting the rights of individuals and for changing the very framework by which the government operated.

GORDON S. WOOD

(SEE ALSO: *Bill of Rights (United States)* [1]; *Constitutional Convention of 1787* [1]; *Constitutional History Before 1776* [1]; *Constitutional History, 1776–1789* [1]; *Constitutionalism and the American Founding* [2]; *Natural Rights* [3]; *Social Compact Theory* [4].)

Bibliography

CORWIN, EDWARD S. 1955 *The "Higher Law" Background of American Constitutional Law.* Ithaca, N.Y.: Cornell University Press.

McLAUGHLIN, ANDREW C. 1932 *Foundations of American Constitutionalism.* New York: Norton.

WOOD, GORDON S. 1969 *The Creation of the American Republic, 1776–1787.* Chapel Hill: University of North Carolina Press.

AMERICANS WITH DISABILITIES ACT

The Americans with Disabilities Act (ADA) of 1990 is the high-water mark in the expansion of CIVIL RIGHTS [1,I] initiated by the CIVIL RIGHTS ACT OF 1964 [1]. The tactics, language, and libertarian aims of the disability rights movement note this debt, especially in the ADA's references to ending "segregation," "discrete and insular minority" status, and "political powerlessness." Brought about through a remarkable coalition of activists concerned about diverse disabilities, the personal involvement of President GEORGE BUSH [1], and overwhelming support in Congress, the ADA proclaims that "the Nation's proper goals regarding individuals with disabilities are to assure equality of opportunity, full participation, independent living, and economic self-sufficiency for such individuals" with disabilities.

The ADA defines disability as a "mental or physical impairment that substantially limits one or more of the major life activities." The legislation also covers those who have had a disability or are "regarded as having" a disability.

The four major titles of the ADA deal with employment, state and local governmental services (including public transportation), public accommodations, and telecommunications, respectively. The ADA requires that hearing or speech-impaired persons be able to communicate with hearing persons through a telephone relay system. New commercial buildings and alterations to existing ones must be designed and constructed to be fully accessible. However, only "readily achievable" alterations need be made to existing places of public accommodation. Public accommodations include facilities ranging from those specifically covered in the 1964 act, such as restaurants and hotels, to gymnasiums and bowling alleys. As a general rule, people with disabilities must have "the full and equal enjoyment of the goods, services, facilities, privileges, advantages, or accommodations of any place of public accommodation." New buses, trains, and other transportation facilities will also have to be accessible.

The most important provision of the ADA is Title I, which is the analogue of Title VII, the EMPLOYMENT DISCRIMINATION [2,1] section of the 1964 Civil Rights Act. Enforced as well by the U.S. Equal Employment Opportunity Commission, Title I strikes down barriers to employment and promotion found in job qualifications, examinations, and classifications. Particularly noteworthy is the requirement that an employer provide "reasonable accommodation" to an "otherwise qualified" individual with a disability—thus enabling performance of the "essential functions" of the position. An employer cannot, however, be asked to bear an "undue hardship" in accommodating an otherwise qualified person with a disability.

Disputes over the ADA focused largely on the costs it would impose on covered entities and the definition of disability. Proponents argued that most of the required modifications are a minor financial burden, particularly in light of the estimated $169.4 billion spent annually on programs that primarily promote dependency. Supporters predicted that the productivity unleashed by in-

dividuals now able to work would cease their being dependent.

The ADA presents a striking interpretation of the equality of NATURAL RIGHTS [3] on which the Constitution rests. It seeks to halt the slow march toward the nightmare world of perfectly classified types depicted in Aldous Huxley's *Brave New World*. The law relies on the FOURTEENTH AMENDMENT [2,1] and the COMMERCE CLAUSE [1] for its constitutional authority. But it not only affirms the equal civil rights of all persons, including those with severe mental and physical disabilities; it requires as well the elimination of both physical and attitudinal barriers. The enforcement of the ADA should not produce the quotas and preferences that have hitherto plagued civil rights enforcement. Individuals with disabilities need to be accommodated on an individual basis, not treated as a group. In seeking entry into the mainstream of American life the disability rights movement has fought ceaselessly against exactly this thoughtless group classification.

EVAN J. KEMP, JR.

Bibliography
HUXLEY, ALDOUS 1932, 1969 *Brave New World*. New York: Harper & Row.
U.S. COMMISSION ON CIVIL RIGHTS 1983 *Accommodating the Spectrum of Individual Abilities*. Washington, D.C.: U.S. Government Printing Office.

ANNAPOLIS CONVENTION

In 1785 a few nationalists led by JAMES MADISON [3] and ALEXANDER HAMILTON [2] sought desperately to preserve the Union of the states under the ARTICLES OF CONFEDERATION [1]. Congress seemed inept and powerless. The chances that the United States might "Balkanize" seemed likely. As early as 1782 Hamilton had proposed a convention of the states to reassess their union. In 1785 delegates from Maryland and Virginia met in Alexandria to reconcile their mutual interests in Chesapeake Bay and the Potomac River. Madison promoted the plan of a convention of delegates from all of the states to consider augmenting the powers of Congress over commerce. Maryland and Virginia agreed on the call of such a convention in Annapolis in September 1786, and they invited all the states to send delegates.

When the Annapolis Convention met, only five states were in attendance. Undaunted, Hamilton and Madison made the best of the situation by framing a report, which those in attendance unanimously adopted, critical of the inadequacies of the Articles of Confederation and urging still another convention of all the states to assemble in

Philadelphia in May 1787. The purpose of that convention would be to "take into consideration the situation of the United States, to devise such other provisions as shall appear to them necessary to render the constitution of the Federal Government adequate to the exigencies of the Union," and to report recommendations to Congress for confirmation by the states.

Thus, the Annapolis Convention was significant for calling the meeting that became the Philadelphia CONSTITUTIONAL CONVENTION [1] of 1787. SHAYS' REBELLION [4] assisted the Confederation Congress in making up its mind to endorse the work of the Annapolis Convention. Confronted by the fact that the states were already electing delegates to the Philadelphia Convention, Congress saved face by issuing its own call for that convention in the language used by the Annapolis Convention.

LEONARD W. LEVY

ANTI-ABORTION MOVEMENT

After ROE V. WADE (1973) [3], opponents of ABORTION [1,I] scrambled to find restrictions on abortion that the Supreme Court would uphold. These included laws requiring a short "cooling off" period between the request for an abortion and its performance; informed-consent laws requiring disclosure of the medical risks of abortion to women considering the procedure; medical regulations requiring that second-trimester abortions be performed in hospitals or establishing professional standards for those who perform abortions; viability regulations that would establish a uniform definition for viability or that required a doctor to determine whether the unborn child was viable before performing an abortion; and parental and spousal consent provisions. All were invariably struck down in the federal courts, leading law professor Lynn Wardle to conclude in 1981: "The courts have carried the doctrine of abortion privacy to incredible extremes. . . . The abortion industry . . . has wrapped itself in the robes of *Roe v. Wade*, [has] challenged many simple and ordinary state regulations (from record-keeping laws to parental notification requirements) and today claims constitutional immunity from many medical regulations."

Given the judiciary's effective ban on any local abortion regulation during the 1970s, the anti-abortion movement soon sought other methods to achieve its goals, including the constitutional-amendment process. Several constitutional amendments dealing with abortion were introduced in Congress after the Republicans gained control of the Senate in 1980. The first would have defined the term "person" in the Fifth Amendment and the FOURTEENTH AMENDMENT [2,I] as encompassing "unborn offspring at

every stage of development" and provided that "[n]o unborn person shall be deprived of life by any person." Another proposal, dubbed the "Human Life Federalism Amendment," provided that a "right to abortion is not secured by this Constitution" and that "Congress and the several states shall have the concurrent power to restrict and prohibit abortions." The intent of the latter amendment was to restore to the legislative branch the power to enact laws dealing with abortion. Many in the anti-abortion movement were critical of this approach, however, believing that it did not go far enough.

When it became clear that no constitutional amendment dealing with abortion could muster sufficient support, some sought to overturn *Roe* by congressional statute. The "Human Life Statute" was the result; it would have provided a congressional finding of fact that human life begins at conception; it also would have used congressional power to curtail the jurisdiction of the lower federal courts to deal with abortion. The Human Life Statute attracted a great deal of controversy while it lasted, and it received scorching criticism from many in the legal community as an unconstitutional attack on federal JUDICIAL POWER [3]. The statute's defenders included law professors John T. Noonan, Jr. (now a federal appellate judge) and Joseph Witherspoon. Both argued that the right to life guaranteed by the Fourteenth Amendment ought to apply to children in the womb as a matter of proper constitutional interpretation; Witherspoon went to great lengths to show that the Fourteenth Amendment was enacted during a time when stricter abortion laws were sweeping the nation, indicating a general regard for unborn infants as persons with certain rights.

Despite a flurry of hearings and public debate, none of these measures ever had a serious prospect of passing. Once the Republicans lost control of the Senate, even the most zealous members of the anti-abortion movement realized this fact, and so attention turned to executive-branch action. By the late 1980s, many in the movement had decided that their best chance of overturning *Roe v. Wade* lay in new appointments to the Supreme Court. Hence, both RONALD REAGAN [3,I] and GEORGE BUSH [I] received widespread electoral support from abortion opponents, even though neither did much to promote anti-abortion legislation in Congress. Abortion opponents hoped Reagan and Bush would appoint Justices willing to undercut *Roe*. They did not hope in vain. In 1989 the Court finally upheld some minor abortion restrictions in WEBSTER V. REPRODUCTIVE HEALTH SERVICES [I], and Reagan-appointed Justices provided the decisive votes.

For many opponents of abortion, however, the change in the Court's direction came too late. Appalled by over fifteen million abortions since 1973 and alienated by a court system that they felt had disenfranchised them from the political system, a large segment of the anti-abortion movement turned from politics to mass CIVIL DISOBEDIENCE [1] in the mid-1980s. Thousands became involved in a loose-knit organization known as "Operation Rescue," which staged nonviolent sit-ins to shut down abortion clinics. The magnitude of these protests is indicated by the number of protestors arrested, estimated at between twenty-eight and thirty-five thousand during one eighteen-month period. When tried for criminal trespass, members of Operation Rescue commonly invoke the necessity defense, arguing that they are compelled by a HIGHER LAW [3] to engage in civil disobedience in order to save human life. A few courts have acquitted protestors on this basis, most notably one in Missouri that based its decision on a state law declaring that human life begins at conception.

As Operation Rescue protests have grown in size and number, some fairly drastic measures have been taken to stop the organization, including lawsuits based on the RACKETEER INFLUENCED AND CORRUPT ORGANIZATION ACT (RICO) [I]. Operation Rescue protestors have also encountered widespread police brutality. In Buffalo male protestors were handcuffed, beaten with clubs, and dragged face-down down a flight of stairs. In Dobbs Ferry, New York, women protestors were strip-searched and photographed nude by prison guards. In Los Angeles police broke a nonresisting man's arm twice, pounded the faces of other peaceful protestors into the asphalt, and repeatedly inflicted pain on protestors who were trying to comply with police requests. In several cities abusive police have removed their badges and name plates to prevent identification by both protestors and the news media. Reports of police brutality became so widespread that in late 1989 the United States Commission on Civil Rights voted to launch an investigation. William B. Allen, then chairman of the commission, declared: "It is imperative that we as a nation assert our commitment to equal treatment before the law. Nonviolent protestors should all be accorded the same treatment no matter what the subject of protest. To do less is to destroy the most prized achievement of the CIVIL RIGHTS MOVEMENT [I]—the recognition of the rights of everyone." The majority of public officials and members of the media, however, paid scant attention to the protestors' plight, and the brutality continued.

JOHN G. WEST, JR.

(SEE ALSO: *Conservatism* [I]; *Federal Jurisdiction and Congressional Power* [I].)

Bibliography

ALLEN, WILLIAM B.   1989   Police Brutality—But No Outrage. *The Wall Street Journal*, August 18.

SENATE COMMITTEE ON THE JUDICIARY   1982   *The Human Life Bill* (Hearings). 2 volumes. Washington, D.C.: U.S. Government Printing Office.
SENATE COMMITTEE ON THE JUDICIARY   1983   *Constitutional Amendments Relating to Abortion* (Hearings), 2 volumes. Washington, D.C.: U.S. Government Printing Office.
TERRY, RANDALL A.   1988   *Operation Rescue*. Springdale, Penn.: Whitaker House.

ANTIDISCRIMINATION LEGISLATION

Most antidiscrimination legislation forbids RACIAL DISCRIMINATION [3,I] in such contexts as employment, housing, public accommodations, education, and voting. Similar legislation prohibits SEX DISCRIMINATION [4,I] and, more recently, discrimination on the basis of age and handicap.

Enacted in response to racial unrest and mass civil protests, the CIVIL RIGHTS ACT OF 1964 [1] was the first major federal antidiscrimination law in the modern era. Congress subsequently enacted the VOTING RIGHTS ACT OF 1965 [4] and the Fair Housing Act of 1968. Each act has been amended several times.

The most ambitious titles of the 1964 Act—Title VII, prohibiting EMPLOYMENT DISCRIMINATION [2], and Title II, prohibiting discrimination in public accommodations—are now central features of the modern regulatory state. This legislation, however, initially faced stiff opposition. The opponents argued that the law represented undue federal intrusion into both the private sphere and state sovereignty and that the "law could not change what lies in the hearts of men." Modern antidiscrimination legislation rejects both these views. It effectively nationalizes nondiscrimination as a basic right of CITIZENSHIP [1,I], apparently laying to rest the post-Reconstruction view that the task of protecting CIVIL RIGHTS [1,I] lay primarily within the powers of each state. Equally significant, the passage of antidiscrimination legislation seemed to embody a belief that law could significantly alter conduct and, eventually, "the hearts of men."

More recent developments suggest a fraying around the edges of antidiscrimination, both as national policy and as moral imperative. This fraying is suggested by debates over the status of antidiscrimination as a national priority, by judicial decisions limiting the reach of federal regulation, and by continuing racial hostilities that raise questions about the hearts of men and women.

Antidiscrimination law is not self-executing. Rather, its effectiveness is contingent upon the cooperation between the several branches of government and private citizens. Ideally, Congress creates the substantive protections and establishes the broad outlines of the enforcement framework, and the executive branch, ADMINISTRATIVE AGENCIES [I], and the judiciary elaborate these policies and apply them to specific contexts. The system works well when there is a general consensus about the importance of eliminating racial discrimination. In the last decade, however, the various governmental branches have been in conflict as to the scope, content, and priority of the antidiscrimination mandate. These conflicts not only reflect ideological differences with respect to race and racism, but hamper the development of a coherent and effective antidiscrimination law.

In the first seven years of the 1980s, the Civil Rights Division of the Justice Department opposed civil rights plaintiffs more often than it had in the previous two decades combined. A notable example is BOB JONES UNIVERSITY V. UNITED STATES (1982) [1], in which the department, reversing the position of the administration of President JIMMY CARTER [1], argued against the decision of the Internal Revenue Service to deny tax-exempt status to private colleges that practiced racial discrimination. Other evidence of a declining consensus concerning antidiscrimination policy is found in the increase of cases in which the Justice Department has sided against plaintiffs in antidiscrimination suits and others in which it has intervened to support reopening discrimination cases that were believed settled with AFFIRMATIVE ACTION [1,I] consent decrees.

Legislative activity manifesting the growing conflict is represented by the frequency in which Congress has considered overturning Supreme Court decisions narrowing the scope of a number of civil rights acts. In 1982, Congress amended the Voting Rights Act and, in 1988, enacted the Civil Rights Restoration Act, both of which were to overturn Supreme Court decisions. The latter was enacted over a presidential veto. Another bill was introduced to provide a statutory basis for challenging the racially disproportionate distribution of the death penalty, in response to the Court's rejection of an EQUAL PROTECTION [1,I] claim in MCCLESKEY V. KEMP (1987) [I]. Although this bill failed, Congress did strengthen the Fair Housing Act and is currently considering an omnibus bill to overturn several civil rights decisions of 1989.

The clearest evidence of the disintegrating consensus over antidiscrimination policy is apparent in these Supreme Court decisions. The Court's interpretive choices are often of critical importance in facilitating the effective enforcement of basic antidiscrimination principles. In the first decade after the Civil Rights Acts of 1964, the Court frequently interpreted ambiguous provisions in a manner that strengthened the substantive protection of civil rights legislation. Guided by a principle that eliminating racial discrimination "root and branch" was the highest priority,

the Court upheld the constitutionality of civil rights legislation in the face of unfavorable precedent. In JONES V. ALFRED H. MAYER CO. (1968) [3] and RUNYON V. MCCRARY (1976) [3] the Court even resurrected Reconstruction civil rights laws long buried under an interpretation that placed most private discrimination outside the scope of antidiscrimination law.

Recently, however, the Court has been hesitant to take such broad interpretive positions and has even been willing to narrow the reach of antidiscrimination law. *Grove City College v. Bell* (1984) exemplifies this shift. Title IX of the 1972 amendments to Title VI of the 1964 act prohibited sex discrimination in any educational "program or activity" receiving federal financial assistance. President Carter's Justice Department read the words "program and activity" broadly to require a cutoff of funds to an entire institution whenever a single program or activity (for example, a college financial aid office) was in violation of the statute. In 1984, the Supreme Court in *Grove City* took a contrary view, limiting the cutoff of funds to the specific department rather than the entire institution.

PATTERSON V. MCLEAN CREDIT UNION (1989) [I] reflects a similar shift away from expansive readings of the scope of antidiscrimination law. In one of his first opinions for the Court, Justice ANTHONY M. KENNEDY [I] determined that a part of the CIVIL RIGHTS ACT of 1866 (section 1981) prohibiting racial discrimination in the making and enforcement of contracts applied only to the formation of an employment contract and not to subsequent racial harassment by the employer. The dissenters argued that the Court created a false dichotomy between an employer who discloses discriminatory intentions at the time the contract is formed and the employer who conceals those discriminatory intentions until after the plaintiff has accepted the employment. *Patterson*'s holding exemplifies a larger development: a partial deregulation of racial discrimination in employment.

Two primary reasons may explain the breakdown of the civil rights consensus and the increasing conflict over antidiscrimination law. First, the nature of racial discrimination in American society has changed. Antidiscrimination legislation has removed many formal barriers to full societal participation that previously excluded some groups. In one view, the removal of these barriers justifies a presumption of nondiscrimination; hence, claims of discrimination must overcome high burdens of proof. In this view, the removal of formal barriers also gives weight to competing interests, such as the seniority of other employees, STATES' RIGHTS [4], and freedom from governmental oversight. Others argue that antidiscrimination law must seek to eliminate practices that effectively discriminate against traditionally excluded groups, whether such discrimination is formal and intentional or informal and inadvertent.

A second factor increasing the civil rights conflict reflects the relationship between antidiscrimination law and electoral politics. In eight years, President RONALD REAGAN [3,I] not only presided over a major shift in Justice Department enforcement policy, but also appointed three conservative Supreme Court Justices (SANDRA DAY O'CONNOR [3,I], ANTONIN SCALIA [I], and Anthony M. Kennedy, and elevated the most conservative Justice, WILLIAM H. REHNQUIST [3,I], to Chief Justice. In addition, he appointed 370 judges to the federal bench, nearly half the federal judiciary. Many of these jurists interpret laws against a background preference for states' rights and employer autonomy, a preference that readily translates into decisions narrowing the reach of antidiscrimination laws. The demise of formal barriers and the ideological shifts within the judiciary and Justice Department have produced both a more restrictive antidiscrimination jurisprudence and a stagnated enforcement record.

For many critics, the Supreme Court's recent decisions raise the specter of an evisceration of antidiscrimination law comparable to the fate of laws enacted during the first Reconstruction. Congress may yet prevent the full eroding of the antidiscrimination law. However, the persistence of racial discrimination and the reemergence of analytical frameworks and values that have historically blunted the impact of civil rights laws suggest that antidiscrimination victories are, at best, provisional.

KIMBERLÉ CRENSHAW

(SEE ALSO: *Capital Punishment and Race* [I]; *Race-Consciousness* [I]; *Racial Preference* [I].)

Bibliography

AMAKER, NORMAN C. 1988 *Civil Rights and the Reagan Administration*. Washington, D.C.: Urban Institute Press.
FREEMAN, ALAN 1990 Antidiscrimination Law: The View from 1989. *Tulane Law Review* 64:1407–1441.
KARST, KENNETH L. 1989 Private Discrimination and Public Responsibility: *Patterson* in Context. *The Supreme Court Review* 1989:1–51.

APPOINTMENTS CLAUSE

Examining the debates of the CONSTITUTIONAL CONVENTION OF 1787 [1], one finds that Article III, the Constitution's judicial component, proved to be its least controversial and the most readily draftable of all of its provisions. Delegates viewed the judiciary broadly as "the least dangerous branch," in the words of ALEXANDER HAMILTON [2], and such debate as did occur on the range and extent of the judiciary's power was predominantly concerned with the appointment of judges. Under EDMUND RANDOLPH's [3] VIRGINIA PLAN [4], the appointment power would have been granted to Congress as a whole, but the delegates yielded to JAMES MADISON's [3] countersuggestion to vest it in the SENATE [I] alone. Further debate moved the delegates toward vesting the appointment power solely with the President. To resolve the impasse, a special committee of eleven delegates was constituted in late August. Its compromise report, suggesting presidential appointment "by and with the ADVICE AND CONSENT [1,I] of the Senate," was promptly adopted by the convention in early September, and it became part and parcel of Article III, section 2, paragraph two of the Constitution. Unamended, this provision governs today.

Under the terms of the appointments clause, Presidents have nominated and the Senate has confirmed, thousands of federal jurists. Although there have been some rejections of lower federal court nominees, by and large the Senate has been a willing partner in the confirmation process—arguably even playing a perfunctory role at this level. At the apex of the judicial ladder, the Supreme Court of the United States, senators have taken their role far more seriously, rejecting or refusing to take on one-fifth of all nominees to the high court. Thus, of 145 nominations made by thirty-five Presidents from 1789 through 1990, twenty-eight were formally rejected, purposely not acted on, indefinitely postponed, or were withdrawn by the President involved. (Presidents William H. Harrison, ZACHARY TAYLOR [4], and JIMMY CARTER [1] had no opportunity to choose any nominee; ANDREW JOHNSON [3] saw all of his rejected by a hostile Senate.) Of the twenty-eight rejections, all but five occurred in the nineteenth century.

The five rejections of the twentieth century—not counting the never acted on nominations of Homer Thornberry (LYNDON B. JOHNSON [3], 1968) and Douglas H. Ginsburg (RONALD REAGAN [3,I], 1987)—were lower federal court judges John J. Parker (HERBERT C. HOOVER [2], 1930); Clement F. Haynsworth, Jr. (RICHARD M. NIXON [3], 1969); G. Harrold Carswell (Nixon, 1970); the aborted promotion of Justice ABE FORTAS [2] to CHIEF JUSTICE [1] by President Johnson in 1968; and most recently, President Reagan's nomination of United States Court of Appeals Judge Robert H. Bork in 1987, which was rejected by the decisive vote of 58–42.

Inevitably, the Senate's role in judicial appointments has frequently given rise to the questioning of its authority to weigh factors other than pure "competence" in considering a nominee's qualifications. Is it entitled to examine, for instance, political, personal, and ideological factors, or anything else that it may deem appropriate along the road to its ultimate judgment? The answer is clearly "yes," no matter how distasteful certain aspects of the senatorial investigative role in individual cases may seem to both lay and professional observers. That "politics" indubitably plays a role may be regrettable, but it is also natural under our system. It plays a distinct role at both ends of the appointment process.

Although only incumbent Presidents really know why they selected nominees to the Court (or gave the nod to members of their administrations to do the basic selecting for them), history does identify four reasons or motivations governing the selection process: (1) objective merit; (2) personal and political friendship; (3) balancing "representation" or "representativeness" on the Court; and (4) "real" political and ideological compatibility. Obviously, more than just one of these factors may have been present in most nominations, and in some, all four played a role; yet it is not at all impossible to pinpoint one as the overriding motivation. And, more often than not, it has been the fourth reason listed, namely, concern with a nominee's *real*, as opposed to his or her *nominal*, politics. This concern prompted Republican President WILLIAM HOWARD TAFT [4] to give half of his six appointments to Democrats who were kindred political soulmates; it prompted Republican Nixon to appoint Democrat LEWIS F. POWELL, Jr. [3,I]; it spurred Democrat FRANKLIN D. ROOSEVELT [3] to promote Republican HARLAN F. STONE [4] to the Chief Justiceship; and it caused Democrat HARRY S. TRUMAN [4] to appoint Republican HAROLD H. BURTON [1]—to cite just a few illustrations. Yet, as history has also shown, there is no guarantee that what a President perceives as "real" politics will not fade like a mirage. Hence CHARLES WARREN [4], eminent chronicler of the judiciary in general and the Supreme Court in particular, properly observed that "nothing is more striking in the history of the Court than the manner in which the hopes of those who expected a judge to follow the political views of the President appointing him are disappointed."

So why has the Senate chosen to reject or failed to confirm twenty percent of the presidential nominees? The record points to eight reasons: (1) opposition to the nominating President, not necessarily the nominee (for example, all of Andrew Johnson's selectees); (2) opposition to the nominee's perceived jurisprudential or sociopolitical philosophy (for example, Hoover's choice of Parker); (3) opposition to the record of the incumbent court, which, rightly or wrongly, the nominee presumably supported (for example, ANDREW JACKSON's [3] initial nomination of ROGER BROOKE TANEY [4] as Associate Justice; (4) "senatorial courtesy," which is closely linked to the consultative nominating process (for example, GROVER CLEVELAND's

[1] back-to-back unsuccessful nominations of William B. Hornblower and Wheeler H. Peckham); (5) a nominee's perceived "political unreliability" on the part of the political party in power (for example, ULYSSES S. GRANT's [2] selection of Caleb Cushing); (6) the evident lack of qualification or limited ability of the candidate (for example, Nixon's "I'll show the Senate" choice of Judge G. Harrold Carswell); (7) concerted, sustained opposition by interest and pressure groups (for example, the Hoover nomination of Parker and, most recently, Reagan's of Bork); and (8) the fear that the nominee would dramatically alter the Court's jurisprudential "line-up" (for example, the BORK NOMINATION [I]). Judge Bork's professional credentials were not in question; he lost overridingly because of his approach to constitutional law and CONSTITUTIONAL INTERPRETATION [1].

The appointments clause connotes a joint enterprise: informed by the Constitution's seminal provisions and providing for a SEPARATION OF POWERS [4] and CHECKS AND BALANCES [1]. The President selects; the Senate disposes. The Senate's role is second, but not secondary.

Arguably, Presidents' judicial appointments are their biggest "plums." Few if any other posts a President has the authority to fill possess the degree of influence, authority, and constitutionally built-in longevity that characterizes the judicial branch. But there are many other offices to be filled by presidential selection, including, by the language of Article II, section 2, paragraph two, "Ambassadors, other public Ministers and Consuls. . . , and all other Officers of the United States, whose appointments are not herein otherwise provided for and which shall be established by Law. . . ." All such others are to be appointed "by and with the Advice and Consent of the Senate," but the Constitution adds an important caveat: "Congress may by Law vest the Appointment of such inferior Officers, as they think proper, in the President alone, in the Courts of Law, or in the Heads of Departments."

The huge number of federal employees—some 3,500,000 as of mid-1990, not counting the military—has required Congress to provide for appointments as constitutionally authorized in the above-quoted ultimate sentence of the appointment power. In addition to all federal judicial nominations, Congress has retained full "advice and consent" authority over top positions in the military and the diplomatic services; over CABINET [1] and top subordinate cabinet-level selections (it has drawn a line above a certain salary level for other high departmental and agency heads); and over specifically law-designated officials, such as independent regulatory commissioners. However, Congress has vested appointive authority over huge numbers of nominations in the President alone—for example, the bulk of that vast army of civil service employees and almost all of the members of the ARMED FORCES [I] (whose letters of appointment or draft are headed "Greetings"—the butt of many jokes—and are signed by the President in his role of chief executive). Moreover, again in line with the above-noted authority, Congress has by law empowered "Heads of Departments" to make appointments, a necessarily ongoing practice. Finally, on occasion Congress has seen fit to utilize its authority to vest the power at issue in the "Courts of Law."

The latter power became a hotly debated issue when Congress, in the Ethics of Government Act of 1978, created an INDEPENDENT COUNSEL [I] to investigate high-ranking officials in the executive branch. In accordance with the statute's provisions, the ATTORNEY GENERAL [1] must request an independent counsel unless he or she "finds that there are no reasonable grounds to believe that further investigation or prosecution is warranted." The request for an independent counsel must be directed to a panel of three federal judges, who are authorized to appoint the counsel (also called a SPECIAL PROSECUTOR [I]) and to delineate the counsel's JURISDICTION [3]. The act, which provides for removal of a court-appointed counsel by the attorney general only "for cause," was challenged by the President on sundry constitutional grounds, including the doctrine of the separation of powers (the chief executive's duty to see that laws are "faithfully executed") and the presidential APPOINTING AND REMOVAL POWERS [1]. The controversy reached the Supreme Court in its 1987–88 term after a three-member panel of the U.S. Courts of Appeals for the District of Columbia had declared the statute unconstitutional by a 2–1 vote. In a dramatic 1988 opinion by Chief Justice WILLIAM H. REHNQUIST [3,I], for a 7–1 majority in *Morrison v. Olson*, the high tribunal reversed the lower court, ruling that the provisions of the challenged law vesting appointment of independent counsels in the judiciary do not violate the appointments clause, that the powers exercised by the counsel do not violate the judicial article of the Constitution, and that the law does not violate the separation of powers principle by impermissibly interfering with the functions of the executive branch. In a lengthy stinging solo dissent, Justice ANTONIN SCALIA [I] charged his brethren with a misreading and gross violation of the separation of powers.

Aspects of the appointment power will continue to be controversial. It is a joint enterprise, even if the presidency can usually count on having its way. That there are major exceptions, however, was tellingly demonstrated by the Senate's dramatic rejections of President Reagan's Supreme Court nominee Robert H. Bork in 1987 and that by President GEORGE BUSH [I] of John Tower to be his Secretary of Defense in 1989. Even if it is exercised infre-

quently, the Senate's potential check on the presidential prerogative is indeed real.

HENRY J. ABRAHAM

(SEE ALSO: *Appointment of Supreme Court Justices* [I].)

Bibliography

ABRAHAM, HENRY J. 1985 *Justices & Presidents*, 3rd ed. New York: Oxford University Press.

FARBER, DANIEL A. and SHERRY, SUZANNA 1990 *A History of the American Constitution.* St. Paul, Minn.: West Publishing Co.

HARRIS, JOSEPH P. 1953 *The Advice and Consent of the Senate.* Berkeley: University of California Press.

SCHMIDHAUSER, JOHN R. 1979 *Judges and Justices.* Boston: Little, Brown.

SEGAL, JEFFREY 1987 Senate Confirmation of Supreme Court Justices: Partisan and Institutional Politics. *The Journal of Politics* 49:998–1015.

TWENTIETH CENTURY FUND TASK FORCE ON JUDICIAL SELECTION 1988 *Judicial Roulette.* New York: Priority Press.

ARMED FORCES

At the height of the Cold War, a doctor was drafted into the army; he was denied the commission usually afforded doctors because he refused to disclose whether he had been a member of any organization on the ATTORNEY GENERAL'S LIST [1] of subversive organizations. Urging that he had a constitutional privilege to maintain the privacy of his associations, he sought a writ of HABEAS CORPUS [2] in a federal court to compel the army either to discharge him or to award him a commission. The Supreme Court, in *Orloff v. Willoughby* (1953), first rejected his claim to a commission and then held that there was no right to JUDICIAL REVIEW [3] "to revise duty orders as to one lawfully in the service." In discussing the latter point the Court remarked, almost as a throwaway line, "The military constitutes a specialized community governed by a separate discipline from that of the civilian."

The author of the *Orloff* opinion was Justice ROBERT H. JACKSON [3]; one of his clerks that year, who would later become Chief Justice of the United States, was WILLIAM H. REHNQUIST [3,I]. In PARKER V. LEVY (1974) [3] and ROSTKER V. GOLDBERG (1981) [3] Justice Rehnquist, writing for the Court, sought to make the "separate community" idea the foundation for a broad principle of deference—to military authorities and to Congress in military matters—that comes close to creating a "military exception" to the BILL OF RIGHTS.

Parker involved another drafted army doctor who was a bitter opponent of the VIETNAM WAR [4,I] and who counseled enlisted men to refuse to go to Vietnam. He was convicted by a court-martial of "conduct unbecoming an officer" in violation of the Uniform Code of Military Justice (UCMJ). The court of appeals held this statutory language to be unconstitutionally vague in its application to speech, but the Supreme Court reversed. Parker's own speech was plainly beyond the pale, by any stretch of the FIRST AMENDMENT [2,I]. The question was whether the VAGUENESS [4] of the UCMJ entitled him to act, in effect, as a representative of officers not in court who might be deterred by the "conduct unbecoming" provision from engaging in speech that was constitutionally protected. Justice Rehnquist concluded that the answer was No; in applications of the UCMJ, the usual First Amendment standard of vagueness gave way to the looser standard for criminal laws regulating economic affairs. In discussing this issue he wrote at length on the theme of deference to the special needs of the military as a "separate community."

Rostker presented a quite different issue: whether Congress could constitutionally limit registration for the military draft to men, exempting women. Here too, Justice Rehnquist began by announcing an extreme form of deference—not to the judgment of military leadership or the President, both of whom had favored registering women as well as men, but to the judgment of Congress. Speaking of military affairs, Justice Rehnquist said, "perhaps in no other area has the Court accorded such deference to Congress." Furthermore, he said, courts have little competence in this area: "The complex, subtle, and professional decisions as to the composition, training, equipping, and control of a military force are essentially professional military judgments, subject always to civilian control of the Legislative and Executive branches." The rest followed easily for Rehnquist: any future draft would be designed to produce combat troops; women were ineligible for combat; therefore, women and men were "not similarly situated" and need not be treated equally.

Both of these decisions have had influence beyond their immediate concerns. *Parker v. Levy* has been cited in support of the military's power to impose much more far-reaching restrictions on First Amendment claims. Examples are *Greer v. Spock* (1976), holding that the streets of Fort Dix, although open to the public, could constitutionally be closed to a political speaker, and *Brown v. Glines* (1980), upholding an Air Force regulation requiring a service member to get a base commander's approval before circulating a petition on the base. *Rostker v. Goldberg* is routinely cited in political arguments supporting the services' continuing segregation of women to noncombat positions—to their severe disadvantage in the competition for promotion to high leadership positions. Furthermore, *Rostker* has been cited by some lower federal courts in support of service regulations purporting to bar the enlistment or commissioning of lesbians and gay men.

The Constitution explicitly recognizes the existence of a separate system of MILITARY JUSTICE [3]. And no one contends that a private has a First Amendment right to debate with the lieutenant as to whether the platoon should assault an enemy gun emplacement. Plainly, the requirements of military discipline and the military mission demand significant attenuations of constitutional rights that would be protected in analogous civilian contexts. As either Justice Jackson or his clerk wrote in *Orloff*, "judges are not given the task of running the Army." But arguments for judicial abdication lose much of their force when the question is one of equal access to service membership for all citizens. When the issue is the SEGREGATION [4] of the armed forces, the idea of a military exception to the Constitution is deeply offensive to the principle of equal CITIZENSHIP [1,I].

When the military services practice discrimination based on race or sex or SEXUAL ORIENTATION [I], they do not merely reflect patterns in the larger society; they reinforce those patterns in ways both instrumental and expressive. In the United States as in Europe, effective citizenship and eligibility for military service have gone hand in hand. Today the services are major educational institutions, serving as gateways to civilian employment and offering other educational benefits to veterans. Members and former members of the services are seen as having a special authority to speak on some of the most vital questions of national public policy. The services have historically performed a vital function in integrating into American life the members of diverse cultures. (In World War I, for example, some twenty percent of draftees were foreign-born.) In short, the services not only shape the distribution of material and political advantages in our society; they are carriers of the flag, playing a special symbolic role in defining the nation.

Although President HARRY S TRUMAN [4] ordered the armed services (along with the federal civil service) to end racial segregation in 1948, the effective DESEGREGATION [2] of the army was not accomplished until the KOREAN WAR [3]—and then at the instance of battlefield commanders who recognized that their mission was jeopardized by the severe costs of segregation. Until that time, the army's leadership had resisted racial integration on two main grounds. First, they believed, as General George C. Marshall had put it in 1941, that "the level of intelligence and occupational skill of the Negro population is considerably below that of the white." Second, they believed that integration would be harmful to discipline, to morale, and to the mutual trust service members must have if they are to perform their missions successfully. In this view, blacks would make poor combat troops, and so whites would have little confidence in them. Korea proved otherwise; Vietnam proved otherwise. Today thirty percent of the army's enlisted personnel are black, and the army's General Colin Powell chairs the Joint Chiefs of Staff.

Still, the legacy of extreme judicial deference remains—attached not only to military judgments but to congressional judgments about military affairs, even when those judgments plainly are political, or sociological, or both. When the subject is discrimination, this sort of deference has no more justification than did judicial deference to the World War II orders that removed Japanese Americans from their West Coast homes and sent them to camps in the desert. Those orders, like today's discriminations against women and gays in the services, were advertised as a military necessity; the "military" judgment was summed up in the statement of General John DeWitt, who supervised the army's early administration of the program: "A Jap's a Jap."

Today the services have undertaken a massive educational program aimed at reducing racial and ethnic tensions. The myths of white supremacy have been discarded in a segment of American society that is crucial to the definition of equal citizenship. If and when the myths of masculinity are stripped away from the facts of service life and the services' missions in the 1990s, perhaps both Congress and the courts will recognize their responsibilities to end the services' continuing patterns of segregation by gender and sexual orientation. Until then, members of Congress and judges can ponder the comment of Justice HUGO L. BLACK [1], dissenting in *Orloff v. Willoughby*: "This whole episode appears to me to be one . . . to which Americans in a calmer future are not likely to point with much pride."

KENNETH L. KARST

Bibliography

DALFIUME, RICHARD M. 1969 *Desegregation of the Armed Forces: Fighting on Two Fronts, 1939–1953*. Columbia: University of Missouri Press.

HIRSCHHORN, JAMES A. 1984 The Separate Community: Military Uniqueness and Servicemen's Constitutional Rights. *North Carolina Law Review* 62:177–254.

KARST, KENNETH L. 1991 The Pursuit of Manhood and the Desegregation of the Armed Forces. *UCLA Law Review* 38:499–581.

KORNBLUM, LORI S. 1984 Women Warriors in a Men's World: The Combat Exclusion. *Journal of Law and Inequality* 2:351–445.

STIEHM, JUDITH HICKS 1989 *Arms and the Enlisted Woman*. Philadelphia: Temple University Press.

ZILLMAN, DONALD N. and IMWINKELRIED, EDWARD J. 1976 Constitutional Rights and Military Necessity: Reflections on the Society Apart. *Notre Dame Lawyer* 51:396–436.

ARTICLE V CONVENTIONS CLAUSE

Article V provides for two methods of proposing amendments to the Constitution. Congress may propose amendments by a two-thirds vote of both houses or "on the Application of the Legislatures of two thirds of the several States, shall call a Convention for proposing Amendments." Any amendments proposed by a CONSTITUTIONAL CONVENTION [1], like those proposed by Congress, become part of the Constitution upon RATIFICATION [3] by three-fourths of the states. No such convention has been called since the adoption of the Constitution. In the 1980s, however, more than thirty state legislatures applied to Congress for the calling of a "limited" convention restricted to proposing a BALANCED BUDGET AMENDMENT [I] to the Constitution. Proponents claimed to be only a few states short of the thirty-four applications necessary to trigger such a constitutional convention. Other states have in recent years submitted applications for constitutional conventions limited to other single subjects, including ABORTION [1,I], SCHOOL PRAYER [I], and term limitations for members of Congress.

The issue of the validity of these applications has been a subject of sharp debate. Do the state legislatures have the power to control the agenda of a constitutional convention by limiting the convention to considering only one precise amendment or one defined subject? If the state legislatures do not have the authority to limit the convention to a single subject or a particular amendment, should state applications that contemplate a "limited" convention be treated as valid application for a more general convention? Some light is shed on these questions by the debates over the AMENDING PROCESS [1] at the CONSTITUTIONAL CONVENTION OF 1787 [1].

The drafters of the Constitution were generally in agreement that some provision should be made for future amendments and that Congress should be empowered to propose amendments. There was also agreement that Congress should not be the only body empowered to propose amendments. As GEORGE MASON [3] of Virginia noted, exclusive congressional authority to propose amendments would pose a problem if Congress itself were in need of CONSTITUTIONAL REFORM [I]. One alternative—allowing state legislatures to propose amendments—was rejected after ALEXANDER HAMILTON [2] warned that "[t]he State Legislatures will not apply for alterations but with a view to increase their own powers." If state legislatures had the power to propose amendments that would then be returned to those same state legislatures for ratification, those legislatures could enhance their power at the expense of the national government without the active participation of any national forum.

The constitutional convention device created by Article V provided an institution in addition to Congress empowered to propose constitutional amendments. Such a convention would be, like Congress, a deliberative body capable of assessing, from a national perspective, the need for constitutional change and drafting proposals for submission to the states for ratification. At the same time it would *not* be Congress and therefore could not pose the threat of legislative self-interest blocking needed reform of Congress itself.

The essential characteristic of the constitutional convention is that it is free of the control of the existing institutions of government. The convention mode of proposing amendments was seen as avoiding both the problem of congressional obstruction of needed amendments and the problem posed by state legislative self-interest. To be sure, such a convention can be held only upon the petition of state legislatures; once properly convened, however, such a convention, in the view of many scholars, may properly determine its own agenda and submit for ratification the amendments it deems appropriate.

The most contentious question concerning constitutional conventions under Article V is whether state requests for a convention are valid applications if they presume to limit the convention to a single amendment specified in the application. Many of the applications submitted in the 1980s, for example, called for a convention for "the sole and exclusive purpose" of proposing an amendment requiring a balanced federal budget.

Some scholars and members of Congress argued that such "limited" applications were valid and that if a sufficient number of legislatures applied in this fashion Congress should call a "limited" convention. Some of those who consider the applications valid would have Congress limit the convention to the exact wording proposed by the state legislatures; others would have Congress broaden the subject matter to the "federal budget," for example, and limit the convention to this more general subject.

There is a substantial argument, however, that applications for a "limited" convention are simply invalid. The debates of the Framers suggest that any convention was to be free of controlling limits imposed either by Congress or by the state legislatures. Although the applying state legislatures are free, of course, to suggest amendments they desire a convention to consider, the convention itself would have the final authority to determine what kinds of amendments to propose. If the state legislatures were to possess, in addition to the right to summon a convention into existence and to ratify any proposed amendments, the added power to control the convention's deliberations

by specifying the amendment to be proposed, state legislatures would be given more authority over constitutional revision than the Framers contemplated.

The argument that state legislatures lack the power to control a convention's proposals does not preclude an applying state legislature from suggesting the amendment it desires the convention to consider or even from submitting a suggested draft, as long as the application is premised on an understanding that the convention has final control over the decision of what amendments to propose. Many state legislatures that applied in the 1980s made it clear that they opposed the calling of a convention if the convention could not be limited, and some explicitly deemed their applications "null and void" unless "the convention is limited to the subject matter of this Resolution." If it is the case that a "Convention for proposing Amendments" has the final authority under the Constitution to determine what amendments to propose, then state resolutions requesting a convention only if the convention is restricted by constraints that cannot constitutionally be imposed are not valid.

WALTER DELLINGER

(SEE ALSO: *Amendment Process (Outside Article V)* [I].)

Bibliography

CAPLAN, RUSSELL L. 1988 *Constitutional Brinksmanship: Amending the Constitution by National Convention.* New York: Oxford University Press.
DELLINGER, WALTER 1979 The Recurring Question of the "Limited" Constitutional Convention. *Yale Law Journal* 88:1623–1640.
———— 1984 The Legitimacy of Constitutional Change: Rethinking the Amendment Process. *Harvard Law Review* 97:386–432.
GUNTHER, GERALD 1979 The Convention Method of Amending the United States Constitution. *Georgia Law Review* 14:1–25.
VAN ALSTYNE, WILLIAM W. 1979 The Limited Constitutional Convention—The Recurring Answer. *Duke Law Journal* 1979:985–998.

ATTORNEY GENERAL OF NEW YORK v. SOTO-LOPEZ
476 U.S. 898 (1986)

The fragmentation of the Supreme Court in this case offered one more proof of the doctrinal disarray of the RIGHT TO TRAVEL [3]. The Court, 6–3, held invalid a New York law giving military veterans a preference in hiring by the state civil service, but limiting the preference to veterans who had been New York residents when they entered the service. Justice WILLIAM J. BRENNAN, for four Justices, concluded that the law was a "penalty" on the right to free interstate migration and thus subject to the test of STRICT SCRUTINY [4]; under this test, the law failed. Chief Justice WARREN E. BURGER [1] and Justice BYRON R. WHITE [4,I] each concurred separately, following the EQUAL PROTECTION [2,I] rationale of *Zobel v. Williams* (1982) and concluding that the law's discrimination lacked a RATIONAL BASIS [3].

Justice SANDRA DAY O'CONNOR [3,I], for the three dissenters, argued as she had in *Zobel* that there is no "free-floating right to migrate" and that the proper question was whether the law violated the PRIVILEGES AND IMMUNITIES [3,I] clause of Article IV. She answered this question in the negative. The law offered only a one-time preference to a relatively small number of applicants, who were treated the same as the vast majority of New Yorkers in seeking state jobs; the preference was not absolute, but added points to examination scores. Thus, the interest at stake could not be considered "fundamental" to interstate harmony. Addressing Justice Brennan's argument on its own terms, she said the same considerations showed that the discrimination was not a "penalty" on interstate travel.

The Brennan and O'Connor views each have a threshold test that requires some importance for the interest lost when a state prefers its own residents. Once past this threshold, however, Justice O'Connor would measure the law's validity against the privileges and immunities rhetoric of intermediate scrutiny rather than the rhetoric of strict scrutiny. Given that no Justice under eighty years of age joined Justice Brennan's opinion and that three members of the *Soto-Lopez* majority have retired from the Court, Justice O'Connor's view appears to be ascending. There is the embarrassment that the text of the privileges and immunities clause prohibits a state's discrimination, not against its own citizens, but against citizens of another state; however, the Court has confronted more serious textual embarrassments in the past, with only a trace of a blush.

KENNETH L. KARST

ATTORNEY GENERAL'S COMMISSION ON PORNOGRAPHY

See: Meese Commission [I]

AUTOMOBILE SEARCH
(Update)

The Supreme Court has interpreted the FOURTH AMENDMENT [2,I], which protects persons, houses, papers and effects from unreasonable governmental SEARCH AND SEIZURE [4,I], to mean that governments may not conduct unwarranted searches where people have a REASONABLE EXPECTATION OF PRIVACY [I]. In general, to conduct a search invading protected privacy, governmental authorities must obtain a SEARCH WARRANT [4] from a judicial officer, issued after showing there is PROBABLE CAUSE [3] to conclude that EVIDENCE [2] of a crime is discoverable at a certain place. There are some exceptions to this general rule requiring search warrants to conduct a search, and automobile searches constitute one of them.

Obtaining a warrant takes time, and the delay might permit an automobile to leave the JURISDICTION [2] before a warrant was issued or police executed it. All mobile vehicles, including mobile homes capable of ready movement, thus present fleeting search targets. The Supreme Court has also concluded—not without substantial criticism—that because of automobile uses and pervasive governmental regulation of them, persons have a lesser expectation of privacy in automobiles than in homes or offices. Consequently, because of an automobile's mobility and the lesser privacy accorded it, where police have probable cause to believe an automobile is, or contains, evidence of a crime, they may stop it and seize it, or, in the latter case, search it, without a warrant.

Police retain this WARRANTLESS SEARCH [4] authority even when the automobile is not immediately mobile or even likely to be moved. Furthermore, although an automobile is immobilized once seized, thus allowing time to obtain a warrant, the Supreme Court—reasoning that delayed vehicle searches involve no greater privacy invasion than immediate search at the scene—has permitted warrantless automobile searches after immobilization. A rule requiring warrants for delayed searches would incline police to conduct on-scene searches, causing traffic problems or creating other difficulties for the police, particularly in arrest cases involving prisoner transportation. Consequently, when police have probable cause to search an automobile, they may search it immediately on seizure or subsequently.

The nature of the probable cause, and the evidence the police seek, determine the legitimacy and the proper scope of an automobile search. For example, probable cause to believe that a suitcase in a car trunk encloses evidence of crime justifies stopping the car and seizing the suitcase from the trunk, but not a more general car search. By contrast, probable cause to think that an automobile contains marijuana may justify a close search of the entire automobile, including door panels, upholstery, and any containers within the car. Police may thus search any vehicle parts or containers—whether locked, hidden, or generally inaccessible—that may contain the evidence they have probable cause to seek.

Police may stop and search a car when they have probable cause to believe it contains evidence of a crime, whether or not they have probable cause to arrest the driver or passengers. They may also stop a car to arrest the driver or passengers, but probable cause to arrest does not necessarily give rise to probable cause to search the car for evidence of a crime. Arresting automobile occupants for a just-completed convenience-store robbery undoubtedly justifies an extensive search of their car for evidence related to the robbery. Arresting a driver for an outstanding traffic warrant, however, does not justify an automobile search, for the offense is not one involving evidence that might be in the car.

A separate rule governing SEARCHES INCIDENT TO AN ARREST [4], however, comes into play in automobile cases. To protect themselves and others from harm and to prevent the destruction of evidence, officers may, on taking persons into custody upon ARREST [1], search them and any areas the arrestees may immediately reach. In arresting automobile drivers or occupants officers may, at least when those arrested are in or near the automobile, search them and any place in the car they may reach. Generally speaking, this rule authorizes a search of any area within the passenger compartment or open to it.

Police may also search vehicles after impounding them. Police sometimes impound an automobile on arrest of the driver or when the vehicle is found unsafe, illegally parked, or abandoned. To protect the owner's property, and the police from property claims, police may, pursuant to standardized procedures, conduct warrantless inventory searches of impounded vehicles and secure the items found within them. The standardized-procedures requirement is designed to ensure that police do not use their inventory search authority as a pretext to search vehicles when they lack probable cause.

GARY GOODPASTER

Bibliography

LaFave, Wayne R. 1987 *Search and Seizure: A Treatise on the Fourth Amendment.* St. Paul, Minn.: West Publishing Co.

B

BAIL
(Update)

In 1986, when the *Encyclopedia of the American Constitution* was published, some scholars maintained that the Eighth Amendment's prohibition of "excessive bail" implied a right to bail in all noncapital cases. Others argued that the clause afforded no right to bail in any case. According to this second group, the Eighth Amendment imposed no limitation on Congress's power to deny bail; it governed only the amount of bail when bail was permitted.

Strongly supported by the language of the Supreme Court in *Stack v. Boyle* (1951), many scholars also maintained that the only legitimate purpose of bail under the Eighth Amendment (and of detention when an accused could not secure his or her pretrial release) was to prevent flight or else to protect the integrity of the trial process in other ways (notably, by preventing the intimidation of witnesses). Other scholars contended that a court also could lawfully consider the risk that a defendant would commit crimes during the pretrial period in setting bail and, perhaps, in denying pretrial release altogether. The principal unresolved issues posed by the Eighth Amendment were whether the amendment implied a right to bail and what standards, criteria, or objectives a court could consider in determining whether bail was "excessive."

The Supreme Court addressed these issues and the due process issues posed by pretrial PREVENTIVE DETENTION [3,I] in UNITED STATES V. SALERNO (1987) [I]. *Salerno* upheld the constitutionality of the Federal Bail Reform Act of 1984, which permits detention without bond in some federal cases when neither bail nor other conditions of release "will reasonably assure . . . the safety of any other person and the community."

Holding that the Eighth Amendment does not afford a right to bail in all noncapital cases, the Court quoted the suggestion of *Carlson v. Landon* (1952) that the amendment does not create a right to bail in any case. Finding it unnecessary to resolve this issue, however, the Court indicated that the amendment might create a right to bail in some cases and not others, depending on the strength of the government's reasons for denying bail. The defendants had argued that a denial of bail could be regarded as "infinite" bail, and the Court did not reject this contention. It held, however, that infinite bail was not always excessive. The Court also concluded that dangerousness, as well as the risk of flight, could be considered in judging the propriety of pretrial detention.

The Supreme Court resolved the Fifth Amendment due process issues in *Salerno* through the sort of cost-benefit analysis that has characterized much of its recent constitutional jurisprudence. The Court's opinion noted "the individual's strong interest in liberty" and declared that this interest was both "important" and "fundamental." The opinion concluded, however, that "the government's interest in community safety can . . . outweigh an individual's liberty interest."

The phrase "liberty interest" first appeared in a Supreme Court opinion in 1972. Its author, Justice WILLIAM H. REHNQUIST [3,I], later became chief justice and wrote the Salerno opinion. Use of the phrase "liberty interest," which seems to mark liberty as the appropriate subject of a utilitarian trade, has increased greatly in recent years.

Critics of the Supreme Court's cost-benefit analysis

suggest that even the most brutal governmental actions may advance "compelling" interests and that some governmental impositions cannot be justified by countervailing public gains. For example, if psychologists developed the capacity to predict future criminality with substantial accuracy, the detention of people who, unlike the defendants in *Salerno,* had not been charged with any crime might be justified through the same analysis that the Supreme Court used to justify the preventive detention in Salerno. The liberty interests of the people detained for failing the psychologists' predictive tests would not differ from the liberty interests of the people detained under current law, and the governmental interest in preventing future crime would also be identical.

An analysis that balances the burdens imposed by a governmental action against the public gain produced by this action seems to omit traditional considerations of individual responsibility and opportunity. This analysis also departs from a tradition-based "fundamental fairness" approach to the due process clause—an approach that might have been more likely to invalidate the detention in *Salerno.* For more than 300 years following the Pennsylvania Frame of Government in 1682, Americans withheld bail only in capital cases and then only when the proof of guilt was "evident and the presumption great." These Americans apparently chose to run greater risks than cost-benefit analysis could have justified.

The Supreme Court recognized that its cost-benefit analysis would not have justified the detention in *Salerno* if this detention had qualified as punishment. However strong the government's interest in imposing criminal punishment, the Constitution precludes it unless the accused has been afforded a trial at which the government must establish his or her guilt beyond a REASONABLE DOUBT [3] and must comply with other constitutional requirements. Examining Congress's intent, the Court concluded that the objective of the Bail Reform Act was to "prevent danger to the community" and that this objective was "regulatory, not penal."

The Court did suggest that "detention in a particular case might become excessively prolonged, and therefore punitive." It is difficult to envision how Congress's motive could change from regulatory to punitive at some moment in a case of prolonged detention, and the Court offered no hint of when this metamorphosis of LEGISLATIVE INTENT [3] might occur. The Bail Reform Act itself imposes no limit on the length of preventive pretrial detention, and the deadlines of the Federal Speedy Trial Act are flexible. In one recent case, an appellate court declined to find a sixteen-month period of pretrial preventive detention unlawful per se. The Supreme Court's view of retrospectively changing legislative motive may be difficult to understand, but it is likely to save some defendants from detention for a year or more without trial.

Federal courts have made extensive use of the preventive detention provisions of the Bail Reform Act, and both the percentage of defendants detained before trial and the populations of federal pretrial detention facilities have increased substantially. Although many states have enacted preventive detention measures as well, judges and prosecutors appear to have used these state statutes less frequently. One reason may be that the state statutes typically lack a significant provision of the federal act: "The judicial officer may not impose a financial condition that results in the pretrial detention of the person." In state courts, judges and prosecutors may find it easier to set high bail and thereby accomplish preventive detention sub rosa than to comply with the procedural requirements of local preventive detention legislation.

Since the 1960s, bail reform has proceeded from two directions. Judges have released more defendants on recognizance and on nonfinancial conditions, and, especially in the federal courts, judges have detained more defendants without the option of posting bond. Both reforms have made the wealth of defendants less important in determining the probability of their pretrial incarceration, and even the opponents of preventive detention might agree that dangerousness is a less offensive basis for detention than poverty. Both currents of reform move the United States closer to the patterns of pretrial release and detention found in European nations, where bail either is not authorized or has fallen into disuse.

ALBERT W. ALSCHULER

(SEE ALSO: *Compelling State Interest* [1]; *Pennsylvania Colonial Charters* [3]; *Procedural Due Process of Law, Criminal* [3,I].)

Bibliography

ALSCHULER, ALBERT W. 1986 Preventive Pretrial Detention and the Failure of Interest-Balancing Approaches to Due Process. *Michigan Law Review* 85:510–569.

UNITED STATES DEPARTMENT OF JUSTICE, BUREAU OF JUSTICE STATISTICS 1988 *Pretrial Release and Detention: The Bail Reform Act of 1984.* Washington, D.C.: U.S. Department of Justice.

BALANCED-BUDGET AMENDMENT

Since one was first introduced in 1936, various versions of a balanced-budget amendment to the United States Constitution have been proposed in Congress. Such proposals have been introduced regularly since the 1970s. Moreover, since 1975, such an amendment has been the subject of applications (approximately thirty-two by 1990) by state legislatures for a CONSTITUTIONAL CONVENTION [1]. All such proposals seek to encourage or mandate the adoption of a balanced BUDGET [1]. Some of them have additional goals and would more accurately be denominated "balanced-budget and tax limitation," "deficit limitation," or "federal government limitation" amendments.

The only such proposed amendment to have passed either house is S.J. Res. 58, adopted by the Senate in 1982. It provided that Congress must annually adopt (and may subsequently amend as needed) a prospective statement in which anticipated total outlays (other than principal payments) do not exceed anticipated total receipts (other than borrowing), unless such an anticipated deficit is authorized by three-fifths of the whole number of each house. It charged Congress and the President with assuring that actual outlays do not exceed the anticipated outlays provided in the statement, although they may exceed actual receipts. It limited each year's rate of growth of planned receipts to the previous year's rate of growth in the national income, unless otherwise authorized by a majority of the whole number of each house. It also fixed the deficit as of the date of ratification, subject to enlargement by a vote of three-fifths of the whole number of each house. In wartime these requirements could be suspended by a simple majority.

Enforcement of such an amendment could affect the SEPARATION OF POWERS [4]. It could enhance presidential power by justifying the IMPOUNDMENT OF FUNDS [2], for example, or involve the judiciary in overseeing the BUDGET PROCESS [I], an area heretofore at the very center of majoritarian decision making. Whether current doctrines of STANDING [4], JUSTICIABILITY [3], and POLITICAL QUESTION [3,I] would preclude this judicial supervision is uncertain, and was left uncertain in the congressional debates.

Quoting Justice OLIVER WENDELL HOLMES, JR.'s [2] dissent in LOCHNER V. NEW YORK (1905) [3] to the effect that "a constitution is not intended to embody a particular economic theory. . . . It is made for people of fundamentally differing views," critics argue that the proposed amendment does not belong in the Constitution. That charter can endure the ages by defining structures of power within a regime of ordered liberty, rather than by specifying temporary and highly controversial economic policies, especially amendments, such as this one, with profound distributional effects. Moreover, they fear that such an amendment would weaken constitutional government. If effective, it could create paralyzing supermajority hurdles to daily governance. In contrast, the few other constitutional provisions requiring supermajorities (other than the veto override) do not risk interfering with the ongoing functions of government; even a DECLARATION OF WAR [2] requires only a simple majority. Alternatively, critics argue that if the amendment proved a nullity by being either suspended or ignored, the Constitution's authority as positive law could be undermined. A suspension clause is a rarity in the United States Constitution, in contrast to those of other countries with a lesser tradition of CONSTITUTIONALISM [2]. Even if such an amendment were not formally suspended, Congress might evade the amendment through such devices as off-budget federal agencies and CORPORATIONS [2] and costly regulation of the private and state sectors in lieu of spending programs. For example, states with a balanced-budget requirement have resorted to splitting their budgets into a balanced operating budget and a capital budget financed by borrowing.

In response, supporters argue that current deficits are economically, politically, and morally ruinous, and are destructive of the country's future. Further, they contend that such proposed amendments seek not only to enact a particular economic theory but also to cure a flaw, identified by public choice theory, in the constitutional structure. Because of the nature of "concentrated benefits and dispersed costs," no effective constituency exists to oppose spending decisions. In the absence of a mandatory balanced budget, Congress has ceased to be a deliberative body that resolves and transcends factions' competing demands, because deficits allow representatives to respond to their constituents' multiple spending demands without regard to taxing decisions. This structural defect did not appear before 1960, the proponents explain, because an unwritten constitutional principle favoring peacetime balanced budgets and the reduction of debt had prevailed since 1789. But in the past few decades, Keynesian theory and theories of the WELFARE STATE [I] have undermined this principle; and the institutions that had enforced the principle, POLITICAL PARTIES [3] with strong local ties and the congressional seniority system, have been weakened. Moreover, Supreme Court decisions broadly interpreting Congress's ENUMERATED POWERS [2] have eliminated other constitutional restraints that limited spending. It should be noted that this explanation does not account for the President's major role in enlarging and perpetuating deficits.

ROBERT D. GOLDSTEIN

Bibliography

CONGRESSIONAL BUDGET OFFICE 1982 *Balancing the Federal Budget and Limiting Federal Spending: Constitutional and Statutory Approaches.* Washington, D.C.: Government Printing Office.

MOORE, W. S. and PENNER, RUDOLPH G. 1980 *The Constitution and the Budget.* Washington, D.C.: American Enterprise Institute.

WHITE, JOSEPH and WILDAVSKY, AARON 1989 *The Deficit and the Public Interest: The Search for Responsible Budgeting in the 1980's.* Berkeley and Los Angeles: University of California Press.

BALTIMORE CITY DEPARTMENT OF SOCIAL SERVICES v. BOUKNIGHT (1990)

See: Freedom of Association [I]

BATSON v. KENTUCKY
476 U.S. 79 (1986)

This decision made a major change in the law of JURY DISCRIMINATION [3]. In SWAIN V. ALABAMA (1965) [4] the Supreme Court had held that systematic exclusions of black people from criminal trial juries in a series of cases would be a prima facie showing of RACIAL DISCRIMINATION [3,I] in violation of the EQUAL PROTECTION [2,I] clause of the FOURTEENTH AMENDMENT [2,I]. The Court said, however, that a prosecutor's use of peremptory challenges to keep all potential black jurors from serving in a particular case would not be such a showing. In *Batson* the Court, 7–2, overruled *Swain* on the latter point and set out standards for finding an equal protection violation based on a prosecutor's use of peremptory challenges in a single case.

In a Kentucky state court James Batson had been convicted of burglary and receipt of stolen goods. After the trial judge had ruled on challenges of potential jurors for cause, the prosecutor had used peremptory challenges—challenges that need not be justified by a showing of potential bias—to keep all four black members of the jury panel from serving on the trial jury. The Kentucky courts denied the defendant's claims that this use of peremptory challenges violated his Sixth Amendment right to TRIAL BY JURY [4] and his right to equal protection of the laws.

In reversing this decision, the Supreme Court's majority spoke through Justice LEWIS F. POWELL [3,I]. The equal protection clause barred a prosecutor from challenging potential jurors solely on account of their race. *Swain's* narrow evidentiary standard would allow deliberate racial discrimination to go unremedied. Accordingly, the majority ruled that a defendant establishes a prima facie case of racial discrimination by showing that the prosecutor has used peremptory challenges to keep potential jurors of the defendant's race from serving and that the circumstances raise an inference that the prosecutor did so on account of the defendant's race. If the trial court makes these findings, the burden shifts to the prosecution to offer a race-neutral explanation for the challenges. The judge must then decide whether the defendant has established purposeful discrimination. Plainly, *Batson's* evidentiary standard leaves much to the trial judge's discretion.

Justice THURGOOD MARSHALL [3,I] concurred, but said he would hold all peremptory challenges unconstitutional because of their potential for discriminatory use. Justices BYRON R. WHITE [4,I] and SANDRA DAY O'CONNOR [3,I] concurred separately, stating that the new evidentiary standard should be applied only prospectively. Chief Justice WARREN E. BURGER [1] dissented, stating that the longstanding practice of peremptory challenges served the state's interest in jury impartiality and arguing that such challenges were typically made for reasons that could not be articulated on nonarbitrary grounds. Justice WILLIAM H. REHNQUIST [3,I] also dissented, defending the legitimacy of peremptory challenges even when they are based on crude stereotypes.

Peremptory challenges have, indeed, long been based on group stereotypes. If the Supreme Court were to apply the standard to challenges of other groups, the law would be, in practice, much as Justice Marshall said it should be. Even if the new standard is limited to cases of racial discrimination, if trial judges apply it zealously, prosecutors will likely confine their challenges of potential black jurors in cases involving black defendants to challenges for cause.

In *Holland v. Illinois* (1990) the Court rejected, 5–4, a white defendant's claim that the prosecutor's use of peremptory challenges to keep blacks off the trial jury violated the Sixth Amendment right to a jury drawn from a fair cross-section of the community. A majority of the Justices, however, expressed the view that *Batson's* equal protection principle, which in this case the defendant had not raised, would extend to such a case. That view became law in *Powers v. Ohio* (1991).

KENNETH L. KARST

BENDER v. WILLIAMSPORT
475 U.S. 534 (1986)

High-school students in Pennsylvania sought permission to meet together at school for prayer and Bible study during extracurricular periods. School authorities refused permission on the basis of the ESTABLISHMENT CLAUSE [I], despite the fact that the school allowed a wide variety of other student groups to meet on school premises. The students filed suit, claiming violation of their FIRST AMENDMENT [2,I] right to FREEDOM OF SPEECH [2,I].

The district court sided with the students, invoking the doctrine of EQUAL ACCESS [I] enunciated by the Court in WIDMAR V. VINCENT (1981) [4]. However, the appeals court reversed, claiming that allowing the students to meet would violate the establishment clause. The Supreme Court granted certiorari to decide the question, which it subsequently declined to do. A bare majority of the Court's Justices side-stepped the constitutional controversy altogether by holding that the party who appealed the district court ruling lacked STANDING [4].

The four dissenters would have reached the merits of the case and extended the analysis of *Widmar* to secondary schools. According to the dissenters, not only did the establishment clause not forbid religious student groups from meeting on school premises, but schools had an affirmative duty under the First Amendment to allow such groups access to school facilities on the same basis as other groups.

The decision in *Bender* allowed the Court to put off indefinitely the question of whether the Constitution requires equal access in secondary schools. While *Bender* was still in litigation, Congress guaranteed equal access by statute, thus reducing pressure on the Court to resolve the free-speech question.

JOHN G. WEST, JR.

(SEE ALSO: *Religious Fundamentalism* [I]; *Westside Community Schools v. Mergens* [I].)

BETHEL SCHOOL DISTRICT v. FRASER
478 U.S. 675 (1986)

The Supreme Court had previously held that the FIRST AMENDMENT's [2,I] protection of FREEDOM OF SPEECH [2,I] does not stop at school doors. In this case the Court held that a student's freedom of speech is not coextensive with an adult's because school authorities may rightly punish a student for making indecent remarks in a school assembly, which disrupt the educational process. School authorities might constitutionally teach civility and appropriateness of language by disciplining the offensive student. Justice THURGOOD MARSHALL [3,I] agreed with the majority on the obligation of the school to safeguard its educational mission, but believed that the authorities failed to prove that the speech was offensive. Justice JOHN PAUL STEVENS [4,I], also dissenting, claimed that the speech was not offensive. The case is significant as a diminution of free speech by students; they cannot say what can be said constitutionally outside a school.

LEONARD W. LEVY

BLACKMUN, HARRY A.
(Update)

Harry Andrew Blackmun was born in the small town of Nashville, Illinois, on November 12, 1908, but spent most of his childhood in St. Paul, Minnesota. He attended Harvard College on a scholarship, graduating summa cum laude in 1929 with a major in mathematics. Torn between medicine and law, he chose the latter route and attended Harvard Law School, from which he graduated in 1932.

Immediately after graduation Blackmun served as a law clerk to Judge John B. Sanborn of the UNITED STATES COURT OF APPEALS [4] for the Eighth Circuit. He then joined the Minneapolis law firm of Dorsey, Coleman, Barker, Scott, and Barber, where he specialized in tax, civil litigation, and estates. Blackmun left the firm in 1950 to become resident counsel at the Mayo Clinic in Rochester, Minnesota, where he says he enjoyed "the happiest years of my professional experience," with "a foot in both camps, law and medicine."

In 1959 President DWIGHT D. EISENHOWER [2] nominated Blackmun to replace his former employer, Judge Sanborn, on the Eighth Circuit. Blackmun served on that court for eleven years, and then, after the Senate refused to confirm Clement F. Haynsworth, Jr., and G. Harrold Carswell for ABE FORTAS's [2] seat on the Supreme Court, President RICHARD M. NIXON [3] nominated Blackmun, thus accounting for the nickname that Blackmun uses to refer to himself—"Old No. 3." Blackmun was unanimously confirmed by the Senate and was sworn in as the Supreme Court's ninety-ninth Justice on May 12, 1970.

In appointing Blackmun, Nixon was looking for a judge who shared his philosophy of judicial restraint and would work to reverse the liberal, activist rulings of the WARREN COURT [4]. Nixon's hopes for his new appointee, coupled with Blackmun's long-term friendship with Chief Justice WARREN E. BURGER [1], who had known Blackmun since childhood and had asked Blackmun to serve as the best man at his wedding, led the media to refer to Burger and Blackmun as the "Minnesota Twins." The two Justices' similar voting patterns during Blackmun's early years on the Court lent credence to the epithet.

Although Blackmun has generally lived up to Nixon's expectations in criminal procedure cases, he increasingly sided with Justice WILLIAM J. BRENNAN, JR. [1,I], in other controversial cases and is now considered part of the Court's liberal wing. For his part, Blackmun puts little stock in such labels, noting shortly after being nominated to the Supreme Court, "I've been called a liberal and a conservative. Labels are deceiving." He claims that his views have not changed over the years, but that "it's the Court that's changed under me."

Whatever the truth on this issue, Blackmun will likely be best remembered for his controversial and groundbreaking opinion in ROE V. WADE (1973) [3]. *Roe* held that the constitutional RIGHT OF PRIVACY [3,I] protected a woman's right to an ABORTION [1,I], thereby in effect invalidating abortion statutes in forty-six states.

Blackmun has continued to advocate the constitutional right to abortion. He wrote the Court's opinions in PLANNED PARENTHOOD OF CENTRAL MISSOURI V. DANFORTH (1976) [3], invalidating requirements of spousal and parental consent, and in *Akron v. Akron Center for Reproductive Health, Inc.* (1983) and *Thornburgh v. American College of Obstetricians and Gynecologists* (1986), striking down various efforts to impose procedural restrictions limiting the availability of abortions.

More recently, however, Blackmun has found himself in dissent on the abortion issue. In *Webster v. Reproductive Health Services* (1989), Chief Justice WILLIAM H. REHNQUIST [3,I], joined by Justices BYRON R. WHITE [4,I] and ANTHONY M. KENNEDY [I], observed that *Roe*'s "rigid trimester analysis" had proven "unsound in principle and unworkable in practice." Although they did not believe the case required the Court to reconsider the validity of *Roe*'s holding, Justice ANTONIN SCALIA's [I] concurrence indicated that he was ready to overrule *Roe*. Responding in a passionate dissent, Blackmun voiced his "fear for the liberty and equality of the millions of women who have lived and come of age in the 16 years since *Roe* was decided" and concluded that "for today, at least, . . . the women of this Nation still retain the liberty to control their destinies. But the signs are evident and very ominous, and a chill wind blows."

Although Blackmun's position on abortion has remained constant, in other areas he has demonstrated an admirable willingness to reconsider his views. His open-mindedness reflects his belief that the law is "not a rigid animal or a rigid profession," but rather a "constant search for truth," as well as his perception that a Supreme Court Justice "grows constitutionally" while on the bench.

One illustration of Blackmun's evolution is his increased tolerance of nontraditional lifestyles. Dissenting in COHEN V. CALIFORNIA (1971) [1], Blackmun argued that the "absurd and immature antic" of wearing a jacket in court bearing the words "Fuck the draft" was not constitutionally protected. He likewise dissented in *Smith v. Goguen* (1974), concluding that the states may constitutionally prosecute those who "harm[ ] the physical integrity of the flag by wearing it affixed to the seats of [their] pants." More recently, however, he joined the controversial majority opinions in *Texas v. Johnson* (1989) and *United States*

v. Eichman (1990), which held that the FIRST AMENDMENT [2,I] prohibited prosecution of defendants who had burned the American flag during political protests.

Blackmun's growing tolerance of diversity is also obvious in his dissent in BOWERS V. HARDWICK (1986) [I], which upheld the criminalization of sodomy. His stinging dissent observed that "a necessary corollary of giving individuals freedom to choose how to conduct their lives is acceptance of the fact that different individuals will make different choices" and that "depriving individuals of the right to choose for themselves how to conduct their intimate relationships poses a far greater threat to the values most deeply rooted in our Nation's history than tolerance of nonconformity could ever do."

As he has become more accepting of the unconventional, Blackmun has also become more suspicious of institutions. During his early years on the Court, he tended to defer to institutional prerogatives, believing that a judicial policy of noninterference would leave institutions free to exercise their discretion in the public interest. In his first majority opinion, WYMAN V. JAMES (1971) [4], Blackmun rejected a welfare recipient's FOURTH AMENDMENT [2,I] challenge to home visits from the welfare department caseworker, whom Blackmun described as "not a sleuth but rather . . . a friend to one in need." He dissented in BIVENS V. SIX UNKNOWN NAMED AGENTS (1971) [1] because he feared that creating a tort remedy for Fourth Amendment violations by federal agents would "open[ ] the door for another avalanche of new federal cases," thereby tending "to stultify proper law enforcement and to make the day's labor for the honest and conscientious officer even more onerous."

More recently, however, Blackmun has become less trusting of public officials and institutions. In *United States v. Bailey* (1980), for example, his recognition of the "atrocities and inhuman conditions of prison life in America" led him to support a broader duress defense in prison escape cases than the majority was willing to recognize. The picture he painted of prison officials was not a sympathetic one: he described them as indifferent to prisoners' health and safety needs and even as active participants in "the brutalization of inmates."

Given his growing distrust of public officials, Blackmun has increasingly minimized the concerns about the federal courts' caseload expressed in his *Bivens* dissent and instead has opposed limitations on ACCESS TO THE COURTS [1]. He believes that statutes authorizing federal CIVIL RIGHTS [1,I] suits represent "the commitment of our society to be governed by law and to protect the rights of those without power against oppression at the hands of the powerful." Accordingly, in *Allen v. McCurry* (1980) he dissented from the Court's holding that federal courts must give preclusive effect to prior state court adjudications in civil rights suits; in *Rose v. Lundy* (1982) he opposed the strict exhaustion requirement the majority imposed on HABEAS CORPUS [2,I] petitioners; and in ATASCADERO STATE HOSPITAL V. SCANLON (1985) [1] he joined Justice Brennan's dissent, which would have prohibited the states from invoking the ELEVENTH AMENDMENT [2,I] to bar FEDERAL QUESTION [2] suits in federal court.

Another manifestation of Blackmun's increased suspicion of institutions has been his endorsement of more rigorous judicial scrutiny of social and economic legislation under the EQUAL PROTECTION [2,I] clause. Such legislation is upheld so long as it meets the RATIONAL BASIS [3] test—that is, so long as the legislative means are rationally related to a legitimate governmental purpose. Over the years, the Court has given conflicting signals as to how deferential the rational basis test is. In *United States Railroad Retirement Board v. Fritz* (1980) the Court held that the test was satisfied if a judge could think of some plausible, hypothetical reason for the statutory scheme; whether this hypothetical justification bore any relationship to the legislature's actual purpose was, the Court said, "constitutionally irrelevant." Less than three months later, however, Blackmun's majority opinion in *Schweiker v. Wilson* (1981) observed that the rational basis test is "not a toothless one," and upheld the Medicaid provision at issue there only after finding that the statutory classification represented "Congress' deliberate, considered choice." Similarly, in his separate opinion in *Logan v. Zimmerman Brush Company* (1982), Blackmun found a legislative classification irrational, explaining that the justification for statutory classifications "must be something more than the exercise of a strained imagination."

The limitations imposed by FEDERALISM [2,I] on the federal government's powers provide a second illustration of Blackmun's willingness to rethink his views. Blackmun represented the decisive fifth vote in NATIONAL LEAGUE OF CITIES V. USERY (1976) [3], where the Court concluded that the TENTH AMENDMENT [4] prohibited Congress from regulating the wages and hours of state employees. His brief concurring opinion interpreted the majority opinion as adopting a balancing approach that sought to accommodate competing federal and state concerns and that would permit federal regulation in areas where the federal interest was "demonstrably greater." Although this interpretation may have represented wishful thinking on Blackmun's part, he did join the majority opinion in full.

After deserting the other Justices from the *National League of Cities* majority in both *Federal Energy Regulatory Commission v. Mississippi* (1982) and EQUAL EMPLOYMENT OPPORTUNITY COMMISSION V. WYOMING (1983) [2], Blackmun ultimately wrote the opinion overruling

National League of Cities in GARCIA V. SAN ANTONIO METROPOLITAN TRANSIT AUTHROITY (1985) [2]. Blackmun explained that the *National League of Cities* approach had proven unworkable because it had been unable to identify a principled way of defining thoseintegral state functions deserving of Tenth Amendment protection. He likewise renounced his own balancing approachbecause it, too, had not provided a coherent standard capable of consistent application by the lower courts.

Though he ultimately rejected a balancing approach in the Tenth Amendment context, one of Blackmun's judicial trademarks has been his tendency to reach decisions by balancing conflicting interests. He believes that "complex constitutional issues cannot be decided by resort to inflexible rules or predetermined categories." Consequently, he pays close attention to the facts of a case and often makes decisions on a case-by-case basis, rather than a sweeping doctrinal one.

Illustrative of Blackmun's balancing approach are his majority opinions in *Bigelow v. Virginia* (1975), VIRGINIA STATE BOARD OF PHARMACY V. VIRGINIA CONSUMERS COUNCIL (1976) [4], and BATES V. STATE BAR OF ARIZONA (1977) [1], which provided the framework for the Court's modern approach to First Amendment cases involving COMMERCIAL SPEECH [1,I]. Prior to these decisions, the Court considered commercial speech outside the realm of constitutional protection. In each of these three cases, however, Blackmun balanced the First Amendment interests of the advertisers against the public interests served by regulating commercial speech, because, as he explained in *Virginia State Board of Pharmacy*, "the free flow of commercial information is indispensable . . . to the proper allocation of resources in a free enterprise system, . . . [and] to the formation of intelligent opinions as to how that system ought to be regulated or altered." Applying this BALANCING TEST in each case, Blackmun struck down statutes banning advertisements of abortions, prescription drug prices, and legal fees. In each instance, he decided only the narrow issue confronting the Court, expressly declining to consider the extent to which commercial speech might be regulated in other contexts.

Blackmun's commercial speech opinions also illustrate another characteristic of his judicial philosophy—an interest in the real-world impact of the Court's decisions. His opinions often express concern that the Supreme Court operates too frequently from an "ivory tower." In his separate opinion in REGENTS OF UNIVERSITY OF CALIFORNIA V. BAKKE (1978) [3], for example, Blackmun urged his colleagues to "get down the road toward accepting and being a part of the real world, and not shutting it out and away from us." The balancing approach Blackmun adopted in the commercial speech cases likewise avoided abstract generalizations and focused the Court's attention on the concrete results of each case—in *Virginia State Board of Pharmacy*, for example, on the fact that "those whom the suppression of prescription price information hits the hardest are the poor, the sick, and particularly the aged."

Blackmun has written a series of majority opinions in cases discussing the constitutionality of state efforts to tax interstate and foreign commerce that similarly emphasizes the real-world impact of the state tax at issue in each case. In *Complete Auto Transit, Inc. v. Brady* (1977) his opinion overruled prior Supreme Court precedent that held state taxes on the privilege of doing business within the state per se unconstitutional as applied to INTERSTATE COMMERCE [2], and instead adopted a four-part test that stressed the practical effect of the state tax. He followed the same approach in *Department of Revenue v. Association of Washington Stevedoring Companies* (1978) and then in *Japan Line, Ltd. v. County of Los Angeles* (1979), where he adapted the *Complete Auto Transit* test to state taxation of foreign commerce.

Blackmun's emphasis on real-world concerns has often been directed more specifically to the effect of the Court's decisions on the powerless, less fortunate members of society. He strives to do justice to the parties in each case, remarking in one interview, "To me, every case involves people. . . . If we forget the humanity of the litigants before us, . . . we're in trouble, no matter how great our supposed legal philosophy can be." This concern is evident in Blackmun's opinions as well. He concurred only in the result in *O'Bannon v. Town Court Nursing Center* (1980) because he found the majority's approach "heartless." His dissent in *Ford Motor Company v. Equal Employment Opportunity Commission* (1982), an employment discrimination case, criticized the majority's reliance on "abstract and technical concerns" that bore "little resemblance to those that actually motivated" the injured employees or anyone "living in the real world."

Aliens are perhaps the disadvantaged group for whom Blackmun has spoken most forcefully and consistently. In a series of majority opinions during the 1970s beginning with GRAHAM V. RICHARDSON (1971) [2], which held that WELFARE BENEFITS [4] could not be conditioned on citizenship or duration of residence in this country, Blackmun urged that alienage be treated as a suspect classification. His more recent statements on behalf of aliens have come in dissent. In *Cabell v. Chavez-Salido* (1982), which upheld a statute that denied aliens employment in any "peace officer" position, Blackmun's dissent focused on the majority's failure to consider the practical impact of its holding. He objected that the Court's abandonment of strict scrutiny was more than an academic matter; in *Cabell*, for

example, the majority's permissive standard of review might permit the state to exlude aliens from more than seventy jobs, including toll takers, furniture and bedding inspectors, and volunteer fire wardens.

Blackmun has also focused on the impact of the Court's decisions on the poor. Although one of his early opinions, *United States v. Kras* (1973), upheld a fifty-dollar filing fee in bankruptcy cases in part because paying the fee in installments would result in weekly payments "less than the price of a movie and little more than the cost of a pack or two of cigarettes," Blackmun recently has exhibited more understanding of the plight of the poor. In addition to the concerns articulated in the commercial speech cases, he dissented from the Court's decision in *Beal v. Doe* (1977) to approve a ban on the use of Medicaid funds for nontherapeutic abortions, characterizing the majority's assumption that alternative funding sources for abortions are available to indigent women as "disingenuous and alarming, almost reminiscent of: 'Let them eat cake.' " Again, he contrasted the actual impact of the Court's ruling with its abstract, formalistic approach: "There is another world 'out there,' the existence of which the Court, I suspect, either chooses to ignore or fears to recognize."

Finally, Blackmun has spoken on behalf of racial minorities and the institutionalized. He has consistently voted to uphold AFFIRMATIVE ACTION [1] plans, concluding in his separate opinion in *Bakke* that "in order to get beyond racism, we must first take account of race." In *Youngberg v. Romeo* (1982) his concurring opinion argued that involuntarily committed retarded persons are entitled to treatment as well as care. "For many mentally retarded people," he reasoned, "the difference between the capacity to do things for themselves within an institution and total dependence on the institution for all their needs is as much liberty as they ever will know." His dissent in *Bailey* criticized the majority's "impeccable exercise in undisputed general principles and technical legalism" and argued that the scope of the duress defense available in prison escape cases must instead be evaluated in light of the "stark truth" of the "shocking" conditions of prison life.

Although history may best remember Blackmun as the author of *Roe v. Wade*, his contribution to the Court has in fact been much broader. He has thoughtfully balanced conflicting policies, conscientiously and thoroughly digesting the details of each case without reaching out to make decisions based on broad, sweeping generalizations. He has been concerned about the actual impact of the Court's decisions, refusing to permit his place on the Court to allow him to lose compassion for the "little people." He has been receptive to new ideas and exhibited a capacity for growth, in keeping with his recognition that "there is no room in the law for arrogance" and his sense that he, as well as the Supreme Court, has "human limitations and fallibility."

KIT KINPORTS

(SEE ALSO: *Flag Desecration* [2,I]; *Judicial Activism and Judicial Restraint* [3].)

Bibliography

KOBYLKA, JOSEPH F. 1985 The Court, Justice Blackmun, and Federalism: A Subtle Movement with Potentially Great Ramifications. *Creighton Law Review* 19:9–49.
NOTE 1983 The Changing Social Vision of Justice Blackmun. *Harvard Law Review* 96:717–736.
SYMPOSIUM 1985 Dedication to Justice Harry A. Blackmun— Biography; Tributes; Articles. *Hamline Law Review* 8:1–149.
SYMPOSIUM 1987 Justice Harry A. Blackmun: The Supreme Court and the Limits of Medical Privacy. *American Journal of Law and Medicine* 13:153–525.
WASBY, STEPHEN L. 1988 Justice Harry A. Blackmun in the Burger Court. *Hamline Law Review* 11:183–245.

BLYEW v. UNITED STATES
80 U.S. 581 (1872)

The Supreme Court first interpreted the CIVIL RIGHTS ACT of 1866 [1] in April 1872 in *Blyew v. United States*. That case narrowly construed a jurisdictional provision, in the act's Section 3, that granted JURISDICTION [3] to federal trial courts over criminal and civil "causes" that "affect[ed]" persons who "are denied or cannot enforce" in state court the rights of equality secured by the act's Section 1.

The case arose following the ax murder of a black family in rural Kentucky. Because a state statute precluded the testimony by a black person against a white defendant, it appeared probable that a state court would have excluded the dying declaration of the family's teenage son identifying the perpetrators as John Blyew and George Kennard. The federal attorney for Kentucky, Benjamin Bristow (who would soon argue this case as the first SOLICITOR GENERAL [4,I] of the United States), obtained a federal INDICTMENT [2] for the state-law crime of murder against Blyew and Kennard and prosecuted them in federal court. To establish jurisdiction under the 1866 act, the indictment asserted that the defendants' victims were denied or could not enforce the same right to testify in state court as white persons enjoy. This was only one among many criminal and civil cases brought in the Kentucky federal court on such a theory.

Convicted and sentenced to death, the defendants appealed. Exercised by this federal interference with its state courts, Kentucky hired (and the Supreme Court permitted) Judge Jeremiah Black to represent Kentucky at ORAL ARGUMENT [3].

The Court, through Justice WILLIAM STRONG [4], held that in a criminal trial only the government and the defendant, but not the victim, are persons "affected" within the meaning of the 1866 act. Because neither of these parties had been denied rights under Section 1, the federal court lacked jurisdiction.

With its narrow construction of the "affecting" jurisdiction, the Court avoided the constitutional question of whether Congress can enforce the FOURTEENTH AMENDMENT [2,I] by granting federal court jurisdiction over state-law causes of action to avoid the risk of a biased state forum. The Court partially resolved this question in *Strauder v. West Virginia* (1880), which upheld the 1866 act's removal jurisdiction. But by then Congress had eliminated the narrowly interpreted "affecting" jurisdiction in its 1874 codification of United States statutes.

By its HOLDING [2], the Court eliminated the important CIVIL RIGHTS [1,I] remedial tool of providing a nondiscriminatory federal forum to enforce the COMMON LAW [1] of crimes and torts (including common law duties of nondiscrimination). Since *Blyew*, the model for federal civil rights criminal enforcement has primarily involved the adoption of a substantive federal criminal statute, with the attendant constitutional and practical difficulties of defining federal rights under both the SLAUGHTERHOUSE CASES (1873) [4] and the CIVIL RIGHTS CASES (1883) [1]. Effective civil rights enforcement has been hobbled by this limitation, among others, ever since. Moreover, without the counterexample of the "affecting" jurisdiction, the Court has more plausibly developed doctrines restraining federal court intrusion on discriminatory state enforcement of state law.

The *Blyew* decision permits identifying the Supreme Court's hostility to federal civil rights enactments as early as the end of the first administration of ULYSSES S. GRANT [2]. It also suggests that by the time the Court rendered the *Slaughterhouse* decision, it understood the implications that decision would have for federal civil rights enforcement. This precludes treating the Court's subsequent decisions limiting civil rights legislation as merely expressing a consensus of the political branches reached in the waning days of RECONSTRUCTION [I].

Blyew is also noteworthy because Justice JOSEPH P. BRADLEY [1], in dissent, first put forward a theory of a group right to the adequate protection of the law and the "badges and incidents" theory of the THIRTEENTH AMENDMENT [4] found in the *Civil Rights Cases*.

The Court's failure to appreciate a class's cognizable interest in the effective protection of the law continues to the present. *Blyew*, for example, anticipated *Linda R. S. v. Richard D.* (1973) a century later, in which the Court held that a crime victim lacked standing to challenge a prosecutorial decision, because it directly affected only the state and defendant.

ROBERT D. GOLDSTEIN

Bibliography

GOLDSTEIN, ROBERT D.   1989   *Blyew:* Variations on a Jurisdictional Theme. *Stanford Law Review* 41:469–566.
KAZCOROWSKI, ROBERT   1985   *The Politics of Judicial Interpretation: The Federal Courts, Department of Justice and Civil Rights, 1866–1876.* New York: Oceana.

BOARD OF DIRECTORS OF ROTARY INTERNATIONAL v. ROTARY CLUB (1987)

See: Freedom of Association [I]

BOARD OF EDUCATION OF THE WESTSIDE COMMUNITY SCHOOLS v. MERGENS
497 U.S.   (1990)

In WIDMAR V. VINCENT (1981) [4] the Supreme Court held that a state university had denied a student religious group's FREEDOM OF SPEECH [2] by barring the group from holding a worship meeting on campus. Concluding that the university had created a limited PUBLIC FORUM [3], the Court rejected the university's argument that allowing the meeting would amount to an unconstitutional ESTABLISHMENT OF RELIGION [2]. In 1984, Congress adopted the Equal Access Act, prohibiting a public high school that receives federal aid from denying religious, philosophical, or political student groups access to its facilities if it allows access by other "noncurriculum related" student groups. The lower federal courts disagreed about the law's constitutionality, and some commentators expected the Supreme Court's resolution of the conflict to illuminate the future path of ESTABLISHMENT CLAUSE [I] jurisprudence. In the event, the light failed.

In *Mergens* the Supreme Court upheld the act, 8–1, against an establishment clause challenge. Justice SANDRA DAY O'CONNOR [3,I], writing for herself and three other Justices, found the case closely similar to *Widmar*—as far as the establishment clause question was concerned—and applied the three-part LEMON TEST [I]. First, Congress had a secular purpose of preventing discrimination against religious speech. Second, the primary effect of the law was not to advance religion. Neither Congress nor the school district had endorsed or sponsored any religious group's speech. Furthermore, the act had forbidden school officials to participate in religious groups' meetings and required that any such meetings be held during noninstructional time. Third, the school's requirement of a faculty sponsor did not amount to excessive entanglement of the school with religion.

Justice ANTHONY M. KENNEDY [I], joined by Justice ANTONIN SCALIA [I], concurred. Following his opinion in COUNTY OF ALLEGHENY V. AMERICAN CIVIL LIBERTIES UNION (1989) [I], Kennedy rejected the "endorsement" gloss on the LEMON TEST. He would uphold a law against an establishment clause challenge if it did not directly benefit religion to the degree of establishing a state religion, or coerce someone into participating in a religious activity. Here, Congress and the school board had done neither.

Justice THURGOOD MARSHALL [3,I], joined by Justice WILLIAM J. BRENNAN [1,I], also concurred. For him, the law raised more serious establishment clause problems than had *Widmar;* the school had not simply opened a forum, but had treated its after-school clubs as serving educational functions. He concurred on the assumption that the school would be required to redefine its club program to negate the appearance of sponsorship. Justice JOHN PAUL STEVENS [4,I] dissented on statutory grounds, arguing that the school's existing club program was "curriculum related," so that the act did not require access for a religious group.

KENNETH L. KARST

(SEE ALSO: *Bender v. Williamsport* [I]; *Equal Access* [I]; *Religious Fundamentalism* [I].)

BOARD OF TRUSTEES OF STATE UNIVERSITY OF NEW YORK v. FOX
492 U.S.   (1989)

This decision significantly altered the doctrinal formula governing COMMERCIAL SPEECH [1,I]. In CENTRAL HUDSON GAS AND ELECTRIC CORP. V. PUBLIC SERVICE COMMISSION (1980) [1] the Supreme Court had held that a state's regulation of commercial speech must be "no more extensive than necessary" to achieve the regulation's purposes. In *Fox,* a 6–3 majority explicitly disavowed the idea that a state was limited to the LEAST RESTRICTIVE MEANS [3] in regulating commercial advertising. Justice ANTONIN SCALIA [I] wrote for the Court.

A state-university regulation of on-campus business activity effectively prevented a seller of household goods from holding "Tupperware parties" in the dormitories. Although the company's representatives not only sold goods but also made presentations on home economics, the Court concluded that the speech was commercial.

The transactions proposed were lawful, and the advertising was not misleading; thus, the interest-balancing part of the *Central Hudson Gas* formula came into play. Here the university had important interests in preserving a noncommercial atmosphere on campus and tranquillity in the dormitories. Although the regulation did directly advance these interests, other means, less restrictive on speech, would arguably have served just as well. Justice Scalia noted that previous opinions had suggested that regulations of advertising must pass a "least restrictive means" test, but decided that such a formulation was too burdensome on the states. Rather, what is required is "a fit [between means and ends] that is not necessarily perfect, but reasonable; that represents not necessarily the single best disposition but one whose scope is 'in proportion to the interest served' (quoting from *In re R.M.J.* [1980], dealing with lawyer advertising).

Justice HARRY A. BLACKMUN [1,I], who had written the Court's early opinions admitting commercial speech into the shelter of the FIRST AMENDMENT [2,I], wrote for the three dissenters. He argued that the statute was invalid for OVERBREADTH [3], and said he need not discuss the least-restrictive-means question.

KENNETH L. KARST

BODY SEARCH

The term "body search" is limited to strip searches (forcing a suspect to disrobe to enable an officer to observe the naked body), body cavity searches (inserting a finger or instrument into the rectum or vagina), and other penetrations of the body, such as extracting blood. Body searches do not violate the RIGHT AGAINST SELF-INCRIMINATION [3,I], because, as held in SCHMERBER V. CALIFORNIA (1966) [4], they do not result in TESTIMONIAL COMPULSION [4]. Nor do they violate DUE PROCESS OF LAW [2] unless conducted in a shocking manner. The FOURTH AMENDMENT [2,I] is the principal restriction on body searches.

The Supreme Court has, in recent years, balanced competing interests in determining whether a search violates the Fourth Amendment. This approach, which usually results in upholding the search, has been used by courts with devastating effect in situations such as BORDER SEARCHES [1] and prison searches; in the context of both, body searches may occur.

A person who enters the United States may be searched without a SEARCH WARRANT [4], without PROBABLE CAUSE [3], and without even reasonable suspicion. This rule applies to a search of a suspect's outer garments and luggage or other containers. If a border search is more intrusive, it may be governed by more stringent standards. The Supreme Court has never reviewed a strip search case that arose at the border. Although lower courts require neither a warrant nor probable cause for such a search, they do require some justification, often expressed as "real suspicion." This standard approximates the "reasonable suspicion" standard that TERRY V. OHIO (1968) [4] used to justify a STOP-AND-FRISK [4]. Although a strip search is far more intrusive than a stop-and-frisk, its occurrence at the border is said to justify the *Terry* standard.

The Supreme Court has never reviewed a body cavity search case that arose at the border. Lower courts do not require a warrant. Nor do they require probable cause, most choosing a "reasonable suspicion" standard. These are dubious positions. Given the lack of EXIGENT CIRCUMSTANCES [2] and the indignity of an exploration of body cavities, it would be appropriate to require both a warrant and probable cause. Even if constitutional at its inception, a body cavity search might be unreasonable and therefore unconstitutional in its execution. Relevant factors include the place in which the examination occurs, the person making the examination, and the manner in which the examination is made.

The Supreme Court held in *Hudson v. Palmer* that, as a result of the needs of prison security and discipline, "society is not prepared to recognize as legitimate any subjective expectation of privacy that a prisoner might have in his prison cell." This means that a prison cell may be searched without a warrant, probable cause, or even reasonable suspicion. It probably also means that prisoners' outer garments may be searched routinely. *Hudson* does not directly deal with strip searches or body cavity searches.

Five years before *Hudson*, in *Bell v. Wolfish* (1979), a highly debatable 5–4 decision, the Supreme Court relied on the interest in prison security to uphold the strip searching of inmates of a pretrial detention facility whenever they had a contact visit with an outsider. As part of the search, the prisoner had to expose body cavities to visual inspection. The Court required neither probable cause nor reasonable suspicion. *Bell* does not explicitly authorize routine strip searches, however. Nor does it deal with the digital or instrumental exploration of body cavities.

Lower courts have disagreed about the scope of *Hudson* and *Bell*. Most courts wisely have not interpreted these cases to withdraw all Fourth Amendment protection from prison inmates. Although they do not require a warrant or probable cause, these lower courts authorize strip searches and body cavity searches only on reasonable suspicion or after the occurrence of some event such as a contact visit or the leaving and reentering of the prison. These lower courts also recognize that even if a strip search or body cavity search is justified at its inception, its execution may offend the Fourth Amendment. For example, in *Bonitz v. Fair* (1986) the United States Court of Appeals for the Second Circuit held that body cavity searches of female prisoners were unconstitutional when conducted by nonmedical personnel in an unhygienic manner and in the view of male officers.

Courts apply higher standards when the person searched is a prison employee or visitor.

Body searches occur in settings other than the border and prisons, and the Supreme Court has decided several relevant cases. In *Schmerber*, the Court held that the Fourth Amendment did not require a police officer to obtain a warrant before ordering a doctor to withdraw blood from an apparently drunk driver. The alcoholic content of blood is evanescent and might disappear or change in the time it would take to obtain a warrant. If evidence is not evanescent, however, a warrant might well be required unless the officer is entitled to act routinely, as in fingerprinting all arrestees, for example. Even though it did not require a warrant, *Schmerber* did require a "clear indication" that the driver's blood would disclose intoxication. The Court probably meant to require more than probable cause to justify the subcutaneous intrusion, but in subsequent cases it suggested that "clear indication" means no more than probable cause and may mean less.

In *Winston v. Lee* (1985) the Court prohibited the surgical removal of a bullet from a robbery suspect's body. The removal had been ordered by a state court on probable cause to believe that the bullet, fired from the victim's gun, would identify the suspect as the robber. The Supreme Court balanced the state's need for the evidence against the intrusion of surgery under a general anesthetic. It found that the state already had substantial identification evidence and that the operation posed significant risks. *Winston* is one of the rare cases in which the Court has used the balancing approach to increase, rather than lower, the protections of the Fourth Amendment.

LAWRENCE HERMAN

(SEE ALSO: *Prisoners' Rights* [3,I]; *Right of Privacy* [3,I].)

Bibliography

LaFAVE, WAYNE R. 1987 *Search and Seizure*, 2nd ed. St. Paul, Minn.: West Publishing Co.

WHITEBREAD, CHARLES H. and SLOBOGIN, CHRISTOPHER 1986 *Criminal Procedure*, 2nd ed. Mineola, N.Y.: Foundation Press.

BOLAND AMENDMENT

The Boland Amendment featured in the IRAN-CONTRA AFFAIR [I] and implicated President RONALD REAGAN [3,I] in a failure to perform his constitutional duty to execute the laws faithfully.

From 1982 through 1986, Congress annually enacted the Boland Amendment as a rider to Defense Department appropriations. The amendment prohibited military assistance to the Contras, the armed opposition to Nicaragua's communist government. The amendment applied to any agency or entity of the United States "involved in intelligence activities." The President signed the amendment annually, although opposing it on policy grounds. Reagan never intimated his belief that its restrictions were unconstitutional or did not apply to him, to any of his executive officers, or to the National Security Council (NSC). When the Iran-Contra Affair became public, the President made inconsistent statements; only then did his administration take the position that the Boland Amendment did not extend to the NSC.

While the amendment was operative, however, the administration, including the director of the NSC, had consistently declared that it complied with the amendment in letter and spirit. In fact, executive officers in the White House had covertly aided the Contras. Furthermore, all involved acknowledged that the amendment prohibited solicitation of funds from other countries. Yet, while the amendment was operative, funds were solicited from Saudi Arabia and Taiwan for military assistance to the Contras, and monies from Iran were used for the same purpose.

The power to appropriate conditionally would be an empty one if the President could command his subordinates to violate an act of Congress that he had signed. Funds raised by the government must, under Article I, section 9, go through the federal Treasury and be in accord with laws passed by Congress. Otherwise, Congress's power over the purse would be debilitated if not meaningless. President Reagan either failed in his constitutional duty to "take care that the laws be faithfully executed" or participated along with high-ranking subordinates in the clandestine violation of law.

LEONARD W. LEVY

(SEE ALSO: *Constitutional History, 1981–1989*.)

Bibliography

UNITED STATES: PRESIDENT'S SPECIAL REVIEW BOARD 1987 *Tower Commisson Report*. New York: Bantam-Times Books.

BOOTH v. MARYLAND
482 U.S. 496 (1987)

Conflicting views on CAPITAL PUNISHMENT [1,I] emerged in this case dealing with the constitutionality of victim impact statements (VIS). In conformance with state law, the prosecution introduced VIS at the SENTENCING [I] phase of a capital trial. Those statements described the effects of the crime on the victims and their families. Naturally, they were intensely emotional and, according to the majority of the Court, had the effect of prejudicing the sentencing jury. Dividing 5–4, the Court ruled that the VIS provided information irrelevant to a capital-sentencing decision and that the admission of such statements created a constitutionally unacceptable risk that the jury might impose the death penalty arbitrarily or capriciously. Therefore, according to the Court, the VIS conflicted with the Eighth Amendment's CRUEL AND UNUSUAL PUNISHMENT [2,I] clause. How the murderer could have been exposed to cruel and unusual punishment by the jurors' having listened to statements describing the impact of his crime is mystifying.

Justice BYRON R. WHITE [4,I], for the dissenters, believed that VIS are appropriate evidence in capital-sentencing hearings. Punishment can be increased in noncapital cases on the basis of the harm caused and so might be increased in capital cases. VIS reminded the jurors that just as the murderer ought to be regarded as an individual, so too should the victim whose death constituted a unique loss to his family and the community. Justice ANTONIN SCALIA [I], for the same dissenters, contended that the Court's opinion wrongly rested on the principle that the death sentence should be inflicted solely on the basis of moral guilt. He thought the harm done was also relevant. Many people believed that criminal trials favored the accused too much if they did not consider the harm inflicted on the victim and the victim's family. The Court's previous opinions required that all mitigating factors must be placed before the capital-sentencing jury; yet the Court here required the suppression of the suffering caused by the defendant. This muted one side of the debate on the appropriateness of capital punishment.

LEONARD W. LEVY

BORK NOMINATION

On June 26, 1987, Justice LEWIS F. POWELL [3,I] retired from the Supreme Court for reasons of health and age. On July 1, 1987, President RONALD REAGAN [3,I] nominated Judge Robert H. Bork of the United States Court of Appeals for the District of Columbia Circuit, former Solicitor General of the United States and Professor of Law at the Yale Law School, to replace Justice Powell. The nomination was rejected by the Senate on October 23, 1987 by a vote of forty-two for and fifty-eight against. Although any Senate rejection of a presidential nominee for the Supreme Court is noteworthy, the proceedings surrounding the Bork nomination were uniquely important in providing what turned out to be virtually a public referendum on the deepest questions of constitutional-theory. The outcome of this referendum is likely to have long-term effects not only on future nominations, but also on the practice of CONSTITUTIONAL INTERPRETATION [1].

As a prominent academic, public official, and judge with a firmly established reputation as a political and judicial conservative, Judge Bork had been thought of as a potential nominee for some years. When he was nominated in 1987, opposition crystallized immediately, led by groups such as Common Cause, People for the American Way, Planned Parenthood, and the AMERICAN CIVIL LIBERTIES UNION [1], the last of whose opposition to the nomination represented a departure from longstanding practice. This opposition, reflected first in the divided and only qualified endorsement of the American Bar Association Standing Committee on the Federal Judiciary, was manifested in newspaper and television advertisements, extensive lobbying efforts, organization of letter-writing campaigns directed primarily at members of the SENATE JUDICIARY COMMITTEE [I], and in elaborately orchestrated testimony before this Committee (chaired by Senator Joseph Biden of Delaware), testimony featuring a significant number of prominent law school professors.

The public debate and the televised proceedings before the Judiciary Committee focused on five issues, four of which turned out to be much less important than the fifth. First was Judge Bork's role as solicitor general during the administration of President RICHARD M. NIXON [3] and, in particular, his role as the one who as acting attorney general finally implemented the President's order to remove Archibald Cox as SPECIAL PROSECUTOR [I] after both the attorney general (Elliott Richardson) and the deputy attorney general (William Ruckleshaus) had refused. Testimony at the hearings, however, including testimony from Richardson supporting the nomination, established the political and moral plausibility, if not the ultimate correctness, of Bork's action, and quickly removed this issue from center stage.

Second, Judge Bork's writings on ANTITRUST LAW [I] generated some objections based on the possibility that he would be insufficiently supportive of vigorous enforcement of the antitrust laws. Little came of this, however, in part because of the comparative infrequency of antitrust cases in the Supreme Court and, in larger part, because it became clear that Judge Bork's writings in this area, although controversial, were widely respected and well within the mainstream of academic and professional debate.

Third was Bork's view about FREEDOM OF SPEECH [2,I] and FREEDOM OF THE PRESS [2,I] under the FIRST AMENDMENT [2,I], in particular the position articulated in a 1971 article, "Neutral Principles and Some First Amendment

Problems," in the *Indiana Law Journal*. In this article, Bork argued that only explicitly political speech and not art or literature or anything else not directly relating to political argument was protected by the First Amendment. Although this view represented a substantial departure from both the existing case law and the bulk of academic commentary, Bork's testimony before the Judiciary Committee, conjoined with opinions he had written while on the Court of Appeals, like *Ollman v. Evans* (1984), established that he no longer held this view, at least to such an extent, and the issue turned out to be less important than was first expected.

Fourth, Judge Bork had objected both to the Supreme Court's opinion in SHELLEY V. KRAEMER (1948) [4] striking down judicial enforcement of racially restrictive covenants as unconstitutional state action and to the public-accommodation provisions of the CIVIL RIGHTS ACT OF 1964 [1], calling the latter at the time an act of "unsurpassed ugliness." At the hearings, however, Judge Bork made it clear that he was an unqualified supporter of BROWN V. BOARD OF EDUCATION OF TOPEKA (1954) [1] and many other Supreme Court decisions outlawing racial SEGREGATION [4] and that he no longer held the views he had set forth in 1963. Moreover, his record on the Court of Appeals and as solicitor general, although hardly aggressive on questions of discrimination on the basis of race and gender, confirmed that Judge Bork no longer held views as hostile to civil rights as might have been inferred solely from some of his earlier writings. This issue never disappeared from the hearings and represented a significant reason for the opposition of numerous civil rights organizations, but in the final analysis, like Bork's views on the First Amendment, it played a somewhat smaller role than had earlier been anticipated.

Fifth and most important were Judge Bork's views about constitutional interpretation and constitutional theory, particularly as they related to questions about the use of ORIGINAL INTENT [I] and about the existence of UNENUMERATED RIGHTS [I] in general and the RIGHT OF PRIVACY [3,I] in particular. In this context, Judge Bork's views were more consistent over time, as shown in cases like *Dronenburg v. Zech* (1984), representing a view pursuant to which constitutional interpretation was legitimate according to Bork only if restricted to provisions explicitly set forth in the constitutional text, with textual indeterminacies to be resolved by exclusive reference to the original intent of the drafters.

The import of this position was that Judge Bork viewed these Supreme Court decisions finding unenumerated rights in the Constitution as illegitimate judicial usurpation of legislative or majoritarian authority. The discussion of this issue focused largely on the right of privacy, whose recognition Judge Bork viewed as beyond the proper prov-

ince of the Supreme Court, and on the Supreme Court decisions in ROE V. WADE (1973) [3] on ABORTION [1,I] and GRISWOLD V. CONNECTICUT (1965) [2] on contraception, both of which were based on principles of enforcement of unenumerated rights or Fourteenth Amendment SUBSTANTIVE DUE PROCESS [4] that Judge Bork found impermissible.

Although Judge Bork's views in this regard were often characterized during the hearings as outside of the academic or professional mainstream, his skepticism about substantive due process, unenumerated rights, and the right to privacy reflected a commonly articulated academic position throughout the 1970s and early 1980s and a position often articulated by academics whose personal political views would have been sympathetic to the enforcement of privacy and abortion rights as a matter of legislative or political policy. In this regard, the charge that Bork's views were widely divergent from the so-called mainstream was simply factually inaccurate.

That Bork's views did not represent some alleged radical right-wing view (see Ronald Dworkin, "The Bork Nomination," *The New York Review of Books*, August 13, 1987), however, does not entail the conclusion that these views could not permissibly be taken into account by the President in nominating him or by the Senate in deciding whether to give their advice and consent to the nomination. From this perspective, one of the lessons of the entire process was that a prospective Justice's views about questions of constitutional interpretation and substantive constitutional law became more a permissible part of senatorial inquiry than they had previously been. Although the rhetoric at the time inaccurately stressed the "out of the mainstream" character of these views, it does not follow that the senators are obliged to give their ADVICE AND CONSENT [1,I] to every nominee whose views are within the mainstream. The rejection of the Bork nomination represents a change in practice (in part confirmed in subsequent nominations) toward a process in which senators feel more comfortable about critically inquiring into substantive questions of constitutional law than they had in the past.

The rejection of the nomination can therefore also be taken as a virtual public referendum on the right to privacy and perhaps also on the authority of the Supreme Court to enforce unenumerated rights. Although opposition to the abortion decisions was taken to be less "extreme," Bork's opposition to *Griswold* was the focus of the controversy. In their testimony, Bork and his supporters stressed the distinction between the desirability of a right and its existence or historical embodiment in the Constitution, arguing that the desirability of a right, including the right to privacy, was not a sufficient condition for its judicial recognition under a view that recognized majoritarian supremacy and the limited role of JUDICIAL REVIEW [3,I]. And in opposition, Bork's adversaries before the Judiciary Committee focused on the intrinsic desirability of a right to privacy, on the social obsolescence of the contraception prohibition struck down in *Griswold*, on a Lockean tradition of NATURAL RIGHTS [3], on the NINTH AMENDMENT [3], and on a relatively long history of Supreme Court use of substantive due process to encompass unenumerated rights and to invalidate state and federal legislation inconsistent with them.

The final committee vote of five to nine against the nomination (October 6, 1987), as well as the Senate vote consistent with this negative recommendation (both of which included negative votes by Republicans), may well represent a public and legislative endorsement of the authority of the Supreme Court both to interpret the Constitution by use of sources not limited to the original intentions of the Framers and to identify and to enforce rights not explicitly enumerated in the text of the document. Although other factors played a role in the defeat of the nomination, including Bork's views on CIVIL RIGHTS [1,I] and freedom of speech and a personal style more academic than publicly engaging, the centrality of the privacy–unenumerated rights issue has been confirmed by subsequent nominations. During the proceedings leading to the confirmation of Justice DAVID H. SOUTER [I], he consistently avoided expressing his views about *Roe v. Wade*, but made clear that he believed both that it was permissible for the Court to identify and enforce unenumerated rights and that the right to privacy was one of them. Insofar as these statements manifest a shift such that it is no longer plausible for a Supreme Court Justice (or nominee) to deny the existence of unenumerated rights or the right to privacy, the rejection of the Bork nomination must be considered not only as the rejection of a particular nominee, but also and more significantly, as the punctuation mark on a longer term constitutional transformation.

FREDERICK SCHAUER

(SEE ALSO: *Conservatism and the Constitution.*)

Bibliography

ACKERMAN, BRUCE 1990 Robert Bork's Grand Inquisition. *Yale Law Journal* 99:1419–1439.

BORK, ROBERT H. 1990 *The Tempting of America: The Political Seduction of the Law.* New York: Macmillan.

BRONNER, ETHAN 1989 *Battle for Justice: How the Bork Nomination Shook America.* New York: W. W. Norton.

NAGEL, ROBERT F. 1990 Meeting the Enemy. *University of Chicago Law Review* 57:633–656.

PERTSCHUK, MICHAEL and SCHAETZEL, WENDY 1989 *The People Rising: The Campaign Against the Bork Nomination.* New York: Thunder's Mouth Press.

SANDALOW, TERRANCE 1990 The Supreme Court in Politics. *Michigan Law Review* 88:1300–1325.

SYMPOSIUM 1987 The Bork Nomination. *The Cardozo Law Review* 9:1–530.

BOWEN v. KENDRICK
487 U.S. 589 (1988)

In this case the Court sustained the facial constitutionality of Congress's 1981 Adolescent Family Life Act against a claim that it violated the ESTABLISHMENT CLAUSE [2,I] of the FIRST AMENDMENT [2,I]. The statute authorized federal funds for services, publicly or privately administered, that related to adolescent sexuality and pregnancy. A federal district court found that the statute, on its face and as administered, advanced religion by subsidizing and allowing sectarian organizations to preach their message to adolescents; the statute also unduly entangled the government with religion, by requiring official monitoring to ensure that religiously affiliated grantees did not promote their religious missions. The Court, by a 5–4 vote, reversed and remanded the case for a determination whether it was unconstitutionally applied.

Chief Justice WILLIAM H. REHNQUIST [3,I], for the majority, observed that the statute neither required grantees to be religiously affiliated nor suggested that religious institutions were specially qualified to provide the services subsidized by the government. Congress merely assumed that religious organizations as well as nonreligious ones could influence adolescent behavior. Congress impartially made the monies available to achieve secular objectives, regardless whether the funds went to sectarian or secular institutions. This was not a case in which the federal subsidies flowed primarily to pervasively sectarian institutions; moreover, the services provided to adolescents, such as pregnancy testing or child care, were not religious in nature. The majority also held that the government monitoring required by the statute did not necessarily entangle it excessively with sectarianism. Conceding, however, that the act could be administered in such a way as to violate the establishment clause, the Court returned the case to the district court for a factual finding on that issue.

The four dissenters, speaking through Justice HARRY A. BLACKMUN [1,I], may have been influenced by the fact that the statute banned grants to institutions that advocated ABORTION [1,I]. Blackmun, as devoid of doubts as was Rehnquist, confidently deplored a decision that breached the LEMON TEST [3,I] by providing federal monies to religious organizations, thereby enabling them to promote their religious missions in ways that were pervasively sectarian and, contradictorily, requiring intrusive oversight by the government to prevent that objective. The majority, Blackmun reasoned, distorted the Court's precedents and engaged in doctrinal missteps to reach their conclusion, by treating the case as if it merely subsidized a neutral function such as dispensing food or shelter instead of pedagogical services that impermissibly fostered religious beliefs.

LEONARD W. LEVY

BOWEN v. OWENS

See: Sex Discrimination [I]

BOWERS v. HARDWICK
478 U.S. 186 (1986)

Hardwick was charged with engaging in homosexual sodomy in violation of a Georgia statute, but after a preliminary hearing the prosecutor declined to pursue the case. Despite the fact that Hardwick was not going to be prosecuted, he brought suit in federal court to have the Georgia sodomy statute declared unconstitutional. The court of appeals held that the Georgia statute violated Hardwick's FUNDAMENTAL RIGHTS [3] because homosexual activity is protected by the NINTH AMENDMENT [3] and the DUE PROCESS [2] clause of the FOURTEENTH AMENDMENT [2,I].

The Supreme Court disagreed, holding 5–4 that the statute did not violate any fundamental rights protected by the Constitution—in particular, the act did not violate the RIGHT OF PRIVACY [3,I], announced by the Court in previous cases.

Writing for the majority, Justice BYRON R. WHITE [4,I] contended that previous rulings delineating a constitutional right of privacy could not be used to strike down a law against sodomy. Previous precedents in this field focused on "family, marriage or procreation," said White, and neither Hardwick nor the court of appeals had demonstrated a connection between homosexual activity and these areas. In making his argument from precedent, White explicitly denied that the Court had ever announced a general right of private sexual conduct. Precedent aside, White argued that if the Court itself is to remain constitutionally legitimate, it must be wary of creating new rights that have little or no basis in the text or design of the Constitution. Such rights can be adopted by the Court only if they are so implicit in the concept of ordered liberty or so rooted in the nation's history that they mandate protection; homosexual sodomy meets neither requirement. Given White's framework of analysis, the other arguments marshaled by Harwick also had to fail. The argument that since his conduct took place in the privacy of his home it must be protected fails because one has no right to engage in criminal conduct within one's home.

And the argument that the law has no RATIONAL BASIS [3] because it was based solely on the moral views of its supporters fails because "law . . . is constantly based on notions of morality."

Writing for the dissenters, Justice HARRY A. BLACKMUN [2,I] declared what the majority denied—that a general constitutional right of private sexual conduct (or "intimate association") exists. Blackmun thereby shifted the burden of proof from Hardwick to the government. Because intimate association is generally protected by the Constitution, the government must prove that any regulations in this area are valid. Georgia did not do so; hence, the statute was invalid.

The Court's ruling in *Bowers* engendered a great deal of controversy. Many had wanted the Court to use the case to place discrimination on the basis of SEXUAL ORIENTATION [I] in the same category as racial or gender discrimination. Yet it is understandable why the Court did not do so. Gender and race are not clearly analogous to sexual orientation, for neither is defined by conduct in the way that sexual orientation is. Homosexual sodomy has faced public disapproval for centuries because it is *behavior* that society has judged destructive for a variety of reasons, including its effects on public health, safety, and morality. Whether this judgment is correct or not may be debated, but the Court did not wish to resolve the debate by imposition of its own will in the matter.

JOHN G. WEST, JR.

(SEE ALSO: *Freedom of Intimate Association* [3]; *Sexual Preference and the Constitution* [4].)

Bibliography

WELLER, CHRISTOPHER W. 1986 *Bowers v. Hardwick:* Balancing the Interests of the Moral Order and Individual Liberty. *Cumberland Law Review* 16:555–592.

BOWSHER v. SYNAR
478 U.S. 714 (1986)

A 7–2 Supreme Court held that a basic provision of a major act of Congress unconstitutionally violated the principle of SEPARATION OF POWERS [4] because Congress had vested executive authority in an official responsible to Congress. The Balanced Budget and Emergency Deficit Control Act of 1985 (GRAMM-RUDMAN-HOLLINGS [2]) empowered the comptroller general, who is appointed by the President but removable by JOINT RESOLUTION [3] of Congress, to perform executive powers in the enforcement of the statute. In the event of a federal budget deficit, the act requires across-the-board cuts in federal spending. The comptroller general made the final recommendations to the President on how to make the budget cuts.

Five members of the Court, speaking through Chief Justice WARREN E. BURGER [1], applied a severely formalistic view of separation of powers. They sharply distinguished EXECUTIVE POWER [I] from LEGISLATIVE POWER [3]. The comptroller general was removable only at the initiative of Congress for "transgressions of the legislative will." Congress regarded the official as an officer of the legislative branch, and persons holding the office had so regarded themselves. But the powers exercised by the comptroller general were executive in nature, preparing reports on projected federal revenues and expenditures and specifying the reductions necessary to reach target deficit levels. Because the comptroller general was "Congress's man" and was removable by Congress, the assignment of executive powers to the office gave Congress a direct role in the execution of the laws, contrary to the constitutional structure of the government.

Justice JOHN PAUL STEVENS [4,I], joined by Justice THURGOOD MARSHALL [3,I], agreed that the Gramm-Rudman-Hollings provision was unconstitutional, but for wholly different reasons. Stevens too described the comptroller general as a legislative officer, but believed that the removal power was irrelevant. Gramm-Rudman-Hollings was defective because by vesting the officer with important legislative powers over the budget, it subverted the legislative procedures provided by the Constitution. Money matters require consideration and voting by both houses of Congress; this body cannot constitutionally delegate so great a legislative power to an agent.

Justice BYRON R. WHITE [4,I], dissenting, believed that the threat to separation of powers conjured up by the seven-member majority was "wholly chimerical." He believed that the NECESSARY AND PROPER CLAUSE [3] supported vesting some executive authority in the comptroller general. This officer exercised no powers that deprived the President of authority; the official chosen by Congress to implement its policy was nonpartisan and independent. He or she could not be removed by Congress by joint resolution except with the President's approval.

The concurring Justices and the dissenters understood that the Constitution's separation of powers does not make each branch wholly autonomous; each depends on others and exercises the powers of others to a degree. The Constitution mixes powers as well as separates them. The three branches are separate, but their powers are not. Gramm-Rudman-Hollings reflected the modern administrative state. The majority Justices, who could not even agree among themselves whether the comptroller general exercised executive or legislative powers, lacked the flexibility to understand they did not have to choose between labels. The Court, which quoted MONTESQUIEU [3] and misapplied THE FEDERALIST [2], ignored #47 and #48, which warned only against "too great a mixture of powers," but approved of a sharing of powers. Currently, money bills originate in the White House and its Bureau of the Budget, despite the provision in Article I, section 7. The First Congress established the President's CABINET [1] and required the secretary of treasury to report to Congress, and all of ALEXANDER HAMILTON's [2] great reports on the economy were made to Congress, not the President. No Court that cared a fig for ORIGINAL INTENT [I] or that understood the realities of policymaking today would have delivered such simplistic textbookish opinions.

LEONARD W. LEVY

BRASWELL v. UNITED STATES
487 U.S. 99 (1988)

Because the Fifth Amendment's RIGHT AGAINST SELF-INCRIMINATION [3,I] is a personal one that can be exercised only by natural persons, the custodian of a CORPORATION's [2] records may not invoke this right. The contents of corporate records are not privileged either. In this case, however, Braswell, who had been subpoenaed to produce the corporation's records, was its sole shareholder. He claimed that the production of the records, under compulsion, forced him to incriminate himself. Had he been the sole proprietor of a business, the Court would have agreed. But because he had incorporated, he lost the protection of the Fifth Amendment.

Four dissenters strongly maintained that the Court majority, by splitting hairs, had ignored realities. The Court used the fiction that the government did not seek the personal incrimination of Braswell, when it forced him as the head of his solely owned corporation to produce the records. This had the effect of giving the government the evidence needed to convict him. The majority openly conceded that to hold otherwise would hurt the government's efforts to prosecute white collar crime.

LEONARD W. LEVY

BRENNAN, WILLIAM J., JR.
(Update)

After graduating near the top of his Harvard Law School class, William Brennan returned to his hometown, Newark, New Jersey, where he joined a prominent law firm and specialized in labor law. As his practice grew, Brennan, a devoted family man, resented the demands it made on his time and accepted an appointment to the New Jersey Superior Court in order to lessen his work load.

Brennan attracted attention as an efficient and fair-minded judge and was elevated to the New Jersey Supreme Court in 1952. President DWIGHT D. EISENHOWER [2] appointed him to the Supreme Court of the United States in 1956. The appointment was criticized at the time as "political," on the ground that the nomination of a Catholic Democrat on the eve of the 1956 presidential election was intended to win votes for the Republican ticket.

Once on the Court, Brennan firmly established himself as a leader of the "liberal" wing. Often credited with providing critical behind-the-scenes leadership during the WARREN COURT [4] years, Brennan fashioned many of that Court's most important decisions. He continued to play a significant role—although more often as a dissenter, lamenting what he believed to be the evisceration of Warren Court precedents—as the ideological complexion of the Court changed in the 1970s and 1980s.

Brennan was a committed civil libertarian who believed that the Constitution guarantees "freedom and equality of rights and opportunities . . . to all people of this nation." For Brennan, courts were the last resort of the politically disfranchised and the politically powerless, and constitutional litigation was often "the sole practicable avenue open to a minority to petition for redress of grievances." Thus, in Brennan's view, the courts played an indispensable role in the enforcement, interpretation, and implementation of the most cherished guarantees of the United States Constitution. As Brennan observed, the Constitution's "broadly phrased guarantees ensure that [it] need never become an anachronism: The Constitution will endure as a vital charter of human liberty as long as there are those with the courage to defend it, the vision to interpret it, and the fidelity to live by it."

Brennan had an especially influential impact in the areas of EQUAL PROTECTION OF THE LAWS [2,I], DUE PROCESS [2], FREEDOM OF SPEECH [2,I], and CRIMINAL PROCEDURE [2]. In his interpretation of the equal protection clause, Brennan evinced little tolerance for INVIDIOUS DISCRIMINATION [2] by the government. When Brennan joined the Court in 1956, the equal protection clause was high on the Court's agenda, for the Court had just handed down its explosive decisions in BROWN V. BOARD OF EDUCATION OF TOPEKA (1954, 1955) [1]. Despite these decisions, and to the Court's mounting frustration, SEGREGATION [4] of southern schools remained largely intact more than a decade after *Brown*. In GREEN V. COUNTY SCHOOL BOARD OF NEW KENT (1968) [2], however, Brennan's opinion for the Court finally dismantled the last serious barriers to DESEGREGATION [2] by invalidating the "freedom of choice" plans that had been used to forestall desegregation in the rural South. Putting aside the ALL DELIBERATE SPEED [1] formula, Brennan emphatically expressed his own and the Court's impatience at the pace

of desegregation: "The burden on a school board today is to come forward with a plan that promises realistically to work, and promises realistically to work *now*."

When the Court first considered the lawfulness of school segregation in a city that had never expressly mandated racially segregated education by statute, it was again Brennan, writing for a closely divided Court in KEYES V. SCHOOL DISTRICT NO. 1 OF DENVER (1973) [2], who took a strong stand on the issue: "A finding of intentionally segregative school board action in a meaningful portion of a school system . . . creates a presumption that other segregated schooling within the system is not adventitious [and] shifts to school authorities the burden of proving that other segregated schools within the system are not also the result of intentionally segregative actions."

Although Brennan naturally assumed a leadership role in condemning RACIAL DISCRIMINATION [3,I], he sharply distinguished such discrimination from race-conscious AFFIRMATIVE ACTION [1,I] programs designed to protect racial minorities. Brennan explained the distinction in his separate opinion in REGENTS OF UNIVERSITY OF CALIFORNIA V. BAKKE (1978) [3]: "Against the background of our history, claims that law must be 'color-blind' or that the datum of race is no longer relevant to public policy must be seen as aspiration rather than as description of reality. [We] cannot . . . let color blindness become myopia which masks the reality that many 'created equal' have been treated within our lifetimes as inferior both by law and by their fellow citizens." Brennan therefore concluded that the purpose of "remedying the effects of past societal discrimination is . . . sufficiently important to justify the use of race-conscious" affirmative action programs "where there is a sound basis for concluding that minority representation is substantial and chronic and that the handicap of past discrimination is impeding access of minorities to the [field]."

Brennan also played a pivotal role in the evolution of equal protection doctrine in the area of SEX DISCRIMINATION [4,I]. In FRONTIERO V. RICHARDSON (1973) [2] Brennan, writing a PLURALITY OPINION [3] for four Justices, argued that classifications based on sex are inherently suspect and, like racial classifications, must be subjected to STRICT SCRUTINY [4]. Taking a strong stand on the issue, Brennan explained that "our Nation has had a long and unfortunate history of sex discrimination" and that history has traditionally been "rationalized by an attitude of 'romantic paternalism' which, in practical effect, put women, not on a pedestal, but in a cage." Although Brennan never garnered the crucial fifth vote for this position, he did gain a decisive victory in CRAIG V. BOREN (1976) [2], in which he wrote for the Court that gender-based classifications must be subjected to intermediate scrutiny and that "to withstand constitutional analysis" such classifications "must serve important governmental objectives and must be substantially related to achievement of those objectives."

Brennan also opened the door to the Court's REAPPORTIONMENT [3] revolution. Prior to 1962, the Court had consistently declined to consider claims that state laws prescribing legislative districts that were not approximately equal in population violated the Constitution. As Justice Frankfurter explained in COLEGROVE V. GREEN (1946) [1], such controversies concern "matters that bring courts into immediate and active relations with party contests," and "courts ought not to enter this political thicket." In BAKER V. CARR (1962) [1] Brennan rejected this reasoning and held that a claim that the apportionment of the Tennessee General Assembly violated the appellants' rights under the equal protection clause "by virtue of the debasement of their votes" stated "a justiciable cause of action." Brennan explained that "the question here is the consistency of STATE ACTION [4,I] with the Federal Constitution," and such claims are not nonjusticiable merely "because they touch matters of state governmental organization." Brennan's opinion for the Court in *Baker* led the way to REYNOLDS V. SIMS (1964) [3], and its progeny, which articulated and enforced the constitutional principle of ONE PERSON, ONE VOTE [3].

Closely related to the Court's reapportionment decisions was the equal protection doctrine of implied FUNDAMENTAL RIGHTS [2]. Prior to 1969, the Court had hinted on several occasions that the RATIONAL BASIS [3] standard of review might not be applicable to classifications that penalize the exercise of such rights. Building upon these intimations, Brennan held in SHAPIRO V. THOMPSON (1969) [4] that a law that denied WELFARE BENEFITS [4] to residents who had not resided within the JURISDICTION [2] for at least one year immediately prior to their application for assistance penalized the right to interstate travel by denying newcomers "welfare aid upon which may depend the ability of families to subsist." Brennan concluded that because the classification penalized an implied fundamental right it amounted to unconstitutional "invidious discrimination" unless it was "necessary to promote a compelling governmental interest." Brennan's opinion in *Shapiro* crystallized the implied fundamental rights doctrine and thus opened the door to a series of subsequent decisions invalidating classifications that unequally affected VOTING RIGHTS [4], the right to be listed on the ballot, the RIGHT TO TRAVEL [3], and the right to use contraceptives.

Although Brennan played a central role in shaping equal protection doctrine in the 1960s, by the 1970s and 1980s he often found himself fighting rearguard actions in an effort to protect his earlier equal protection decisions, particularly in the areas of reapportionment and implied fundamental rights. Occasionally, however, he won a hard-earned victory. In PLYLER V. DOE (1982) [2], for example, Brennan mustered a five-Justice majority to invalidate a Texas statute that denied free public education to children who had not been legally admitted into the United States. Although conceding that education is not a fundamental right, Brennan nonetheless persuaded four of his brethren that intermediate scrutiny was appropriate because the statute imposed "a lifetime hardship on the discrete class of children not accountable for their disabling status."

As these decisions suggest, Brennan was consistently ready and willing to assert judicial authority to enforce the Constitution's guarantee of "the equal protection of the laws." This same activism was evident in Brennan's due process opinions. GOLDBERG V. KELLY (1970) [2] is perhaps the best example. Traditionally, the Court had defined the "liberty" and "property" interests protected by the due process clause by reference to the COMMON LAW [1]. The Court held that if government took someone's property or invaded his bodily integrity, the due process clause required some kind of hearing; but the Court deemed the clause inapplicable if government denied an individual some public benefit to which he had no common law right, such as public employment, a license, or welfare. This doctrine seemed increasingly formalistic with the twentieth-century expansion of governmental benefit programs and governmental participation in the economy, for while more and more individuals grew increasingly dependent upon government, prevailing doctrine gave no constitutional protection against even the most arbitrary withdrawal of governmental benefits.

In *Goldberg*, Brennan dramatically redefined the scope of the interests protected by the due process clause. Brennan explained that "much of the existing wealth in this country takes the form of rights that do not fall within traditional common law concepts of property," and it is "realistic today to regard welfare entitlements as more like property than a 'gratuity.'" This being so, Brennan held, a state could not constitutionally terminate public assistance benefits without affording the recipient the opportunity for an evidential hearing prior to termination. In this opinion, Brennan launched a new era in the extension of due process rights, and in subsequent decisions, the Court, building upon *Goldberg*, held that the suspension of drivers' licenses, the termination of public employment, the revocation of parole, the termination of food stamps, and similar matters must be undertaken in accordance with the demands of due process.

Despite his extraordinary contributions to the governing principles of American equal protection and due process jurisprudence, Brennan's greatest legacy may be in the area of free expression. When Brennan joined the Court, the country was in the throes of its efforts to suppress communism, and this undoubtedly affected Brennan's views on free expression. Brennan's influence on the Court in this area of the law was felt almost immediately. Two years before Brennan's appointment, the Court, in *Barsky v. Board of Regents* (1954), reaffirmed the RIGHT/PRIVILEGE DISTINCTION [3] in upholding the suspension of a physician's medical license because of events arising out of his communist affiliations. Four years later, in SPEISER V. RANDALL (1958) [4], Brennan's opinion for the Court explicitly rejected the right/privilege distinction. *Speiser* involved a California law that established a special property tax exemption for veterans, but denied the exemption to any veteran who advocated the violent overthrow of the government. Brennan rejected the state's argument that the disqualification was lawful because it merely withheld a "privilege": "To deny an exemption to claimants who engage in certain forms of speech is in effect to penalize them for such speech. Its deterrent effect is the same as if the State were to fine them for this speech. The appellees are plainly mistaken in their argument that, because a tax exemption is a 'privilege'. . . , its denial may not infringe speech."

Brennan's rejection of the right/privilege distinction in *Speiser* was a critical step in the evolution of FIRST AMENDMENT [2,I] doctrine. It did not, however, end the case, and Brennan proceeded to articulate a second—and equally important—principle of First Amendment doctrine. Turning to the procedure mandated by the California law, Brennan held that the law violated the First Amendment because it required the applicant to prove that he had not advocated the violent overthrow of government. Brennan explained that "the vice of the present procedure is that, where particular speech falls close to the line separating the lawful and the unlawful, the possibility of mistaken factfinding—inherent in all litigation—will create the danger that the legitimate utterance will be penalized." Moreover, "the man who knows that he must bring forth proof and persuade another of the lawfulness of his conduct must steer far wider of the unlawful zone than if the State must bear these burdens."

This emphasis on the procedure by which government regulates expression was a hallmark of Brennan's First Amendment jurisprudence. Indeed, Brennan was the principal architect of both the First Amendment VAGUENESS [4] principle and the OVERBREADTH [3] doctrine. Brennan's first full articulation of the vagueness principle came in KEYISHIAN V. BOARD OF REGENTS (1967) [3], which invalidated a New York law prohibiting schoolteachers from uttering "seditious" words. Building upon his opinion in *Speiser*, Brennan grounded the vagueness principle in his observation that "when one must guess what conduct or utterance may lose him his position, one necessarily will 'steer far wider of the unlawful zone.' "

Brennan coined the term "overbreadth" in NAACP V. BUTTON (1963) [3], and he first fully explained the rationale of the doctrine in *Gooding v. Wilson* (1972): "The transcendent value to all society of constitutionally protected expression is deemed to justify allowing 'attacks on overly broad statutes with no requirement that the person making the attack demonstrate that his own conduct could not be regulated by a statute drawn with the requisite narrow specificity.' . . . This is deemed necessary because persons whose expression is constitutionally protected may well refrain from exercising their rights for fear of criminal sanctions provided by a statute susceptible of application to protected expression."

Brennan's views on free expression were influenced not only by governmental efforts to suppress communism but by the CIVIL RIGHTS MOVEMENT [I]. In *NAACP v. Button* (1963), for example, Brennan held that a Virginia law prohibiting any organization to retain a lawyer in connection with litigation to which it was not a party was unconstitutional as applied to the activities of the NAACP and the NAACP LEGAL DEFENSE & EDUCATIONAL FUND [3]. Brennan explained that "in the context of NAACP objectives, litigation is not a technique of resolving private differences; it is a means for [achieving] equality of treatment [for] the members of the Negro Community." In such circumstances, litigation "is a form of political expression," and "groups which find themselves unable to achieve their objectives through the ballot frequently turn to the courts." Indeed, for the group the NAACP "assists, litigation may be the most effective form of political association." By bringing litigation within the ambit of First Amendment protection, Brennan's opinion for the Court in *Button* both highlighted the central role of courts as effective instruments of political and social change and empowered organizations like the NAACP to pursue aggressively the vindication of constitutional rights without obstruction from often hostile state governments.

Perhaps Brennan's most important First Amendment opinion, NEW YORK TIMES V. SULLIVAN (1964) [3], also grew out of the civil rights movement. At issue in *Sullivan* was the Alabama law of libel, which permitted a public official to recover damages for defamatory statements unless the accuser could prove that the statements were true. The case was brought by a Montgomery city commissioner on the basis of several inaccurate statements contained in an advertisement that described the civil rights movement and concluded with an appeal for funds. An Alabama jury found in favor of the commissioner and awarded him damages in the amount of $500,000.

Prior to *Sullivan* it was settled doctrine that libelous utterances were unprotected by the First Amendment and could be regulated without raising "any constitutional problem." With a sensitivity to the history of SEDITIOUS LIBEL [4] and an awareness of the dangers even civil libel actions pose to free and open debate in cases like *Sullivan*, Brennan rejected settled doctrine and held that "libel can claim no talismanic immunity from constitutional limitations." To the contrary, libel "must be measured by standards that satisfy the First Amendment." Moreover, considering the case "against the background of a profound national commitment to the principle that debate on public issues should be uninhibited, robust, and wide-open," Brennan maintained that the "advertisement, as an expression of grievance and protest on one of the major public issues of our time, would seem clearly to qualify for constitutional protection." Balancing the competing interests, Brennan concluded that because "erroneous statement is inevitable in free debate" and "must be protected if the freedoms of expression are to have the 'breathing space' that they 'need . . . to survive,'" the First Amendment must be understood to prohibit any public official to recover damages for libel unless "he proves that the statement was made with 'actual malice'—that is, with knowledge that it was false or with reckless disregard of whether it was false or not."

Brennan also played a central role in the evolution of the law of OBSCENITY [3]. In ROTH V. UNITED STATES (1957) [3], the Court's first confrontation with the obscenity issue, Brennan wrote for the Court that obscenity is "utterly without redeeming social importance" and is thus "not within the area of constitutionally protected speech." Characteristically, however, Brennan emphasized that "sex and obscenity are not synonymous" and that it is "vital that the standards for judging obscenity safeguard the protection of . . . material which does not treat sex in a manner appealing to prurient interest." Sixteen years later, after struggling without success satisfactorily to define "obscenity," Brennan came to the conclusion that the very concept is so inherently vague that it is impossible to "bring stability to this area of the law without jeopardizing fundamental First Amendment values." Brennan therefore concluded in his dissenting opinion in *Paris Adult Theatre I v. Slaton* (1973) that "at least in the absence of distribution to juveniles or obtrusive exposure to unconsenting adults," the First Amendment prohibits the suppression of "sexually oriented materials on the basis of their allegedly 'obscene' contents." Not surprisingly, this analysis once again revealed the essential touchstones of Brennan's First Amendment jurisprudence—a recognition of the need for precision of regulation and a sensitivity to the practical dynamics of governmental efforts to limit expression. As Brennan cautioned in *Paris Adult Theatre*, "in the absence of some very substantial interest" in suppressing even LOW-VALUE SPEECH [I], "we can hardly

condone the ill effects that seem to flow inevitably from the effort."

As in the equal protection area, and as suggested in *Paris Adult Theatre*, Brennan spent most of his energies in free speech cases in the 1970s and 1980s in dissent. This was especially true in cases involving content-neutral regulations of expression, such as HEFFRON V. INTERNATIONAL SOCIETY FOR KRISHNA CONSCIOUSNESS, INC. (1981) [2], and cases involving the regulation of sexually oriented expression, such as FEDERAL COMMUNICATIONS COMMISSION V. PACIFICA FOUNDATION (1978) [2]. As in the equal protection area, however, Brennan won a few notable victories. In *Elrod v. Burns* (1976), for example, Brennan wrote a plurality opinion holding the patronage practice of dismissing public employees on a partisan basis violative of the First Amendment; in BOARD OF EDUCATION V. PICO (1982) [1] he wrote a plurality opinion holding unconstitutional the removal of books from a public school library; and in *Texas v. Johnson* (1989) he wrote the opinion of the Court holding that an individual who burned the American flag as a form of political protest had engaged in constitutionally protected conduct that could not be prohibited under a state FLAG DESECRATION [2,I] statute.

Brennan's opinions in the realm of criminal procedure followed a similar pattern—landmark opinions expanding CIVIL LIBERTIES [1,I] during the Warren Court, vigorous and often bitter dissents during the BURGER COURT [1] and the REHNQUIST COURT [I]. Brennan's earlier opinions are illustrated by FAY V. NOIA (1963) [2], *Davis v. Mississippi* (1969), and UNITED STATES V. WADE (1967) [4]. In *Fay*, Brennan significantly expanded the availability of federal HABEAS CORPUS [2,I], holding the writ available not only to persons challenging the jurisdiction of the convicting court but to any individual who was convicted in a proceeding that was "so fundamentally defective as to make imprisonment . . . constitutionally intolerable." In *Davis*, Brennan limited the use of dragnet investigations and invalidated as an unreasonable SEARCH AND SEIZURE [4,I] the detention of twenty-five black youths for questioning and fingerprinting in connection with a rape investigation where there were no reasonable grounds to believe that any particular individual was the assailant. And in *Wade*, Brennan held that courtroom identifications of an accused must be excluded from evidence where the accused was exhibited to witnesses before trial at a postindictment LINEUP [2] without notice to the accused's counsel. The common theme of these and other Brennan opinions in the area of criminal procedure was that judges must be especially vigilant to protect those individuals whose rights to fair, decent, and equal treatment in the CRIMINAL JUSTICE SYSTEM [I] might too easily be lost to intolerance, indifference, ignorance, or haste.

Brennan also adopted a consistently firm stand against the constitutionality of CAPITAL PUNISHMENT [1,I]. In *Furman v. Georgia*, Brennan maintained that the CRUEL AND UNUSUAL PUNISHMENT [2] clause "must draw its meaning from the evolving standards of decency that mark the progress of a maturing society" and that a punishment is cruel and unusual "if it does not comport with human dignity." Noting that the "uniqueness" of capital punishment is evident in its "pain, in its finality, and in its enormity," Brennan concluded that the death penalty "stands condemned as fatally offensive to human dignity" because it is "degrading" to the individual, "arbitrarily" inflicted, "excessive," and unacceptable to "contemporary society." Although he did not persuade a majority to this point of view, he adhered to this position as a matter of unshakable principle throughout his career.

At the time of his appointment to the Supreme Court, much was made of Brennan's Catholicism. It was thought by many, for better or worse, that he would narrowly represent the interests of a Catholic constituency. Brennan did not meet those expectations. To the contrary, guided by his constitutional philosophy rather than his religion, Brennan frequently angered Catholics on such controversial issues as SCHOOL PRAYER [I], Bible readings, moments of silence, GOVERNMENT AID TO RELIGIOUS INSTITUTIONS [2,I] (including parochial schools), public displays of the crèche, BIRTH CONTROL [1], and ABORTION [1,I]. In this way, as in others, Brennan no doubt surprised many of those who were most responsible for his appointment to the Court.

After serving more than three decades as an Associate Justice, Brennan resigned from the Supreme Court in 1990. He will be remembered as one of the most influential Justices in the history of the Court. Throughout his long and distinguished tenure, Brennan unflinchingly championed the rights of the poor, the unrepresented, and the powerless. There were, of course, those who rejected Brennan's vision of the Constitution and who maintained that he too readily mistook his own preferences for the demands of the Constitution, but there can be no doubt that Brennan expressed his unique and powerful vision of the Constitution as "a vital charter of human liberty" with rare eloquence, intelligence, clarity, and courage.

GEOFFREY R. STONE

Bibliography

BERGER, RAOUL 1988 Justice Brennan vs. the Constitution. *Boston College Law Review* 29:787–801.

BLASI, V. 1982 *The Burger Court: The Counter-Revolution That Wasn't.* New Haven, Conn.: Yale University Press.

BRENNAN, WILLIAM J., JR. 1977 State Constitutions and the Protection of Individual Rights. *Harvard Law Review* 90:489–504.

―――― 1988 Reason, Passion, and the Progress of the Law. *Cardozo Law Review* 10:23–24.

KALVEN, HARRY, JR. 1988 *A Worthy Tradition: Freedom of Speech in America.* New York: Harper & Row.

LEEDS, J. 1986 A Life on the Court. *New York Times Magazine,* October 5, pp. 24–80.

SCHWARTZ, H. 1987 *The Burger Years: Rights and Wrongs in the Supreme Court, 1969–1986.* New York: Viking.

STONE, GEOFFREY R.; SEIDMAN, LOUIS M.; SUNSTEIN, CASS R.; and TUSHNET, MARK V. 1986 *Constitutional Law.* Boston: Little, Brown.

BROADCASTING
(Update)

From its inception in the early days of commercial radio, federal regulation of the broadcast industry has rested on three policies that are not always compatible: (1) competition among broadcasters; (2) a fiduciary duty to serve the public interest; and (3) the promotion of local needs and interests. From the FAIRNESS DOCTRINE [2] to the allocation of television licenses, broadcast regulation represented a conscious effort to maximize the public welfare by providing essential information and to encourage national diversity through the celebration of local uniqueness. In the name of the public interest standard of the COMMUNICATIONS ACT [1] of 1934, broadcasters have been characterized as owing fiduciary obligations to their audiences—with the Federal Communications Commission (FCC) and then the courts as appropriate bodies to enforce the trust. The goal of assuring local, public-interest programming, however, is built on theoretical foundations that weaken significantly when it must confront the economic forces and consumer choices that underlie the policy of relying on competition.

The linchpin of broadcast regulation is limited entry by government license, reinforcing an idea of scarcity that has convinced decision makers that broadcasting is so different from the print media that it may be regulated in ways that would be unconstitutional if applied to a newspaper. From *NBC v. United States* (1943) to RED LION BROADCASTING CO. V. FCC (1969) [3], to CBS, INC. V. FEDERAL COMMUNICATIONS COMMISSION (1981) [1], the Supreme Court has concluded that the broadcast spectrum is an inherently limited resource. Because this conclusion justifies distinguishing broadcasting from print, the Court must implicitly conclude that newsprint, printing presses, and therefore the print media in general, are not inherently limited. Thus, the Court has noted that more people want broadcast licenses than can have them, without ever pausing to note that the reason for excess demand is that broadcast licenses are highly valuable yet given away free. If the facilities for publishing major newspapers were given away free, there would also be more individuals who wish them than could have them. Essentially the Court has seen broadcasters as competing only against other local broadcasters providing the same service, but print outlets as competing against every other print possibility in the world. After being the last bastion for the belief in broadcast scarcity, the Court signaled in *FCC v. League of Women Voters of California* (1984) that if Congress or the FCC would say that broadcasting was no longer scarce, it, too, would agree.

As notions of scarcity were losing their former intellectual force, the FCC ceased a variety of policies that limited direct competition with broadcasting. Beginning with a deregulatory period in the late 1970s, policies brought broadcasters under increasing competition, not only from UHF stations that had been marginal but, more important, from two other sources: (1) an unshackled cable industry that was able to exceed fifty percent household penetration by the late 1980s; and (2) videocassette recorders, which, being outside the jurisdiction of the FCC, rapidly became standard household items in the 1980s. Because of increased competition, broadcasters could no longer assume they could reap monopoly profits and then assert that they would use some of the excess revenues to air the sort of public-interest programming that appeals far more to the FCC than to local audiences. These changes in the marketplace brought many of the key assumptions about broadcasting into question. Nowhere was this more apparent than with the fairness doctrine, the talisman of broadcaster as fiduciary.

The fairness doctrine mandates that broadcasters give adequate coverage to significant public issues and ensure that such coverage fairly presents conflicting views on those issues. Held constitutional in *Red Lion*, the fairness doctrine encapsulates a journalistic code of ethics to which most reporters and publishers in all media profess allegiance. Nevertheless, as the Court unanimously held in MIAMI HERALD PUBLISHING COMPANY V. TORNILLO (1974) [3], in all other media the idea of fairness is enforced internally rather than by the legal system. For the non-broadcast media the FIRST AMENDMENT [2] mandates that the government leave issues of fairness to editors and readers, not to judges.

The fairness doctrine allows legal challenges to broadcasters who present controversial programming. Even if the challenges ultimately fail, the questioning of editorial decisions (where the law mandates that the editor answer) not only imposes time and legal costs but also carries the dim possibility of loss of license. There are no similar costs for avoiding controversy, and everyone agrees that is what some broadcasters do. This is precisely the behavior that the CHILLING EFFECT [1] doctrine would predict. *Red Lion* had denied the existence of a chilling effect

because the fairness doctrine fit so perfectly within the premises of broadcast regulation, but in the years following *Red Lion*, accented by President RICHARD M. NIXON's [3] attitudes toward the networks as the most visible example of the hated media establishment, the chill became so obvious that it was a major part of the FCC's decision to repeal the doctrine in 1985.

The FCC's repeal was attacked on two fronts. Congress passed legislation codifying the fairness doctrine, but President RONALD REAGAN's [3,I] veto, on constitutional grounds, was sustained. Similarly the District of Columbia Circuit Court of Appeals, relying on the alternative that the fairness doctrine no longer served the public interest, affirmed the repeal and the Supreme Court denied CERTIORARI [1] in early 1990. Congressional Democrats, however, remain wedded to the fairness doctrine because they confuse its name with its effects and are pressured by constituency groups that view the potential of acquiring airtime as overriding any adverse effects the doctrine might have. As long as the majority party in Congress holds this position, it is likely that the fairness doctrine will be imposed legislatively and the Supreme Court will be forced to settle the constitutional question.

It is conceivable, although unlikely, that the Supreme Court could cling to scarcity as the explanation for the constitutional distinction between print and broadcasting. More likely, however, the Court would either concede there are no relevant constitutional distinctions or fashion a new one, as it did to sustain the regulation of indecency in FEDERAL COMMUNICATIONS COMMISSION V. PACIFICA FOUNDATION (1978) [2]. *Pacifica* concluded that broadcasting could be regulated differently because its unique pervasiveness made it an uninvited intruder in the home and in any event it was uniquely accessible to children. Pervasiveness could be the Court's echo of the more common, if unexplained, conclusion that broadcasting is too powerful a force not to be regulated. Although this explanation is antithetical to the First Amendment because of its similarities to the rationale for regulating the press under the English COMMON LAW [1], power is nevertheless the most likely surviving rationale for treating broadcasting differently. The rationale might be made more platable by a suggestion that broadcasting had obtained its power because of its privileged monopoly status under federal law, so that continued regulation would be both essential and constitutional.

Whatever may be the answer to the constitutional question of the status of over-the-air broadcasting, the answer's importance, if and when it is given, may be largely historical, given the increasing dominance and penetration of cable with its more numerous viewing options. Once a poor stepchild whose growth was hindered by the FCC to benefit broadcasters, by the 1980s cable had become a major force in communications policy. The Cable Communications Policy Act of 1983, a compromise between the cable industry and the National League of Cities, has set the terms of the current debate by allowing cities to select their own (typically monopolistic) franchisees, but freeing cable from most regulations, especially rate regulation, to which it had formerly been subject. The result has been a predictable escalation in the price for cable service, which too often is accompanied by poor service. This combination has led to increasing calls for reregulation. This development places legislative compromises back at issue and makes it increasingly likely that the Court will have to decide where cable fits into the constitutional scheme of FREEDOM OF THE PRESS [2,1].

Franchising is the key issue in cable. Almost every city has preferred to grant an exclusive franchise to the operator of its choice, which thereafter enjoys a monopoly. Initially perceived as in the cities' interest by guaranteeing service (and as a patronage plum), the monopoly franchise is increasingly recognized as having the attributes of monopolies everywhere: a poor product at an excessive price. Yet fears remain that allowing unlimited entry may allow a cable company to skim the cream from the best areas (typically high-density residential areas with customers who can pay), leaving other areas of the city with little or no service.

The answer to exclusive franchises and to subsidiary issues such as rate regulation or requiring a cable system to dedicate a fixed number of no-user-cost access channels over which it has no program control will probably turn on how the Supreme Court chooses to conceptualize cable. In *Los Angeles v. Preferred Communications* (1986), the Court ducked a constitutional decision on exclusive franchising, but three options seem dominant: the broadcast model, the print model, and a hybrid of the two. The last, in keeping with recent jurisprudence that every medium is "a law unto itself," would allow the Court to make up rules that strike a majority as sensible as each case arises. The Court's confidence in its ability to tailor constitutional doctrine to the needs and attributes of a new medium of mass communication harkens back to similar ill-fated hopes for its constitutional treatment of broadcasting.

L. A. POWE, JR.

Bibliography

KRATTENMAKER, THOMAS G.   1985   The Fairness Doctrine Today. *Duke Law Journal* 1985:151–176.

POWE, LUCAS A., JR.   1987   *American Broadcasting and the First Amendment.* Berkeley: University of California Press.

SPITZER, MATTHEW   1989   The Constitutionality of Broadcast Licensing. *New York University Law Review* 64:990–1071.

BROWNING-FERRIS INDUSTRIES, INC. v. KELCO DISPOSAL, INC. (1989)

See: Punitive Damages [I]

BUDGET PROCESS

Budgeting moved to center stage in American politics in the last quarter of the twentieth century. The budget process, with the TAXING AND SPENDING POWER [4], has become the focal point of the administrative state. It is the place where political institutions have sought to accommodate the various interests seeking a share of the national wealth. The growth of the public sector, which has accompanied the increase in size of both federal and state budgets, has obscured the distinction between the public and private spheres. At one time, governments controlled expenditures, and budgets provided the means of limiting claims on available resources. Budget conflict was contained because of fundamental agreement concerning the ends of government. With the growth of the bureaucratic state, the consensus in support of LIMITED GOVERNMENT [3] has weakened, as has support for limited—or balanced—budgets. The problem of budget control is exacerbated by a failure of the parties and institutions of government to achieve a new consensus, or political realignment, concerning the purposes of public spending. The Constitution, which separates the powers of government, has provided the conditions for budget strife.

The budget, as a formal plan of government in a fiscal year, is a centralizing device, one that presupposes a conception of the state as an active mechanism pursuing positive purposes in the interest of the people it is created to serve. The modern budget system is the concomitant of the administrative state, which, in principle, is an unlimited government. In America the administrative state traces its origins to the Progressive movement. The national executive budget system was among the political reforms demanded by the Progressives. In their view, the presidential budget, along with party reform, would give activist Presidents the ability to pursue the interests of a national majority. The United States was the last modern industrial nation to adopt an executive budget system. Congress was reluctant to give Presidents the power to formulate budgets, because its members thought such authority would undermine the SEPARATION OF POWERS [4].

The growth of federal expenditures during World War I convinced national leaders—including those in Congress—that the legislative body was incapable of effective management of public resources. Thus, in 1921 an executive budget system was established through the BUDGET

AND ACCOUNTING ACT [1]. The President was given the power to formulate a budget and oversee its implementation. At its inception the executive budget was not considered a means of aggrandizing presidential power but a neutral mechanism to ensure economy and efficiency.

In 1939 President FRANKLIN D. ROOSEVELT [3] reorganized the executive branch and placed the Bureau of the Budget at the center of the newly created Executive Office of the President. Roosevelt had become aware of the planning and management capabilities of the budget office. Furthermore, increased government expenditures during the Great Depression and the economic theories of John Maynard Keynes provided the conditions for using the budget to implement federal fiscal policy. The federal budget became an important tool in the presidential attempt to manage the economy. As long as Presidents and Congress agreed on national priorities, there were few unmanageable conflicts concerning economic policy or budget control.

The centralization of administration in Washington during the 1960s and early 1970s began to erode the consensus forged during the New Deal. The new regulatory bureaucracy created during the Great Society tended to polarize society as well as the political institutions. The divergence between the parties led to heightened conflict between the political branches of government. The Democratic Party, which dominated the legislative branch, was committed to the maintenance of an administrative state. The Republican party, increasingly able to capture the executive branch, sought to limit the size of government. The 1972 reelection of RICHARD M. NIXON [3] produced a crisis in the budget process that led to fundamental reform. In Nixon's view, Congress had become so wedded to the interests of the bureaucratic state that it could no longer control its appetite for increased public expenditures. Nixon sought to limit public spending by impounding expenditures that broke the executive budget. Without control of the budget, the Democratic majority in Congress was unable to challenge the President's authority in formulating economic policy or in establishing national priorities. The 1974 CONGRESSIONAL BUDGET AND IMPOUNDMENT CONTROL ACT [2] gave Congress the technical capability and institutional means of controlling the amounts of money spent. Congress was at once a dominant force in the formulation of fiscal policy and a major force in setting the priorities of the nation.

Congress succeeded in challenging presidential control of the budget, but the price of success was an institutional inability to reach agreement on expenditures, except at ever higher levels. The reforms in Congress during the 1970s, which accommodated the growth of the administrative state, had weakened congressional leadership and empowered individual members. Power moved from committee chairs to subcommittee chairs. The links between Congress and the permanent bureaucracy undermined presidential attempts to manage the executive branch. The budget process was dominated by those interests in Congress and the bureaucracy that supported the priorities of the administrative state. The growth of the federal government could not be seriously challenged without control of the levers of public spending.

The election of RONALD REAGAN [3,I] proved to be a serious threat to those committed to the growth of the administrative state. Reagan used the budget process to establish his own priorities, which included a reduction in the size of government. He took advantage of the reconciliation procedure of the Budget Act to force reductions in expenditures, but at the same time reduced tax rates. However, the 1982 recession, coupled with the rapid collapse of inflation, prevented a reduction of expenditures. Instead, the growth of the defense budget and the maintenance of social spending led to an explosion of deficit financing and increased the national debt. Further, the budget process could no longer limit expenditures without fundamental changes in the laws. Nearly half of all federal expenditures now take the form of direct transfer payments to individuals, called ENTITLEMENTS [I]. The political difficulty of raising new revenues, coupled with a mistrust of presidential power, led Congress to attempt to reduce the deficit by procedural devices such as the GRAMM-RUDMAN-HOLLINGS ACT [2]. Congress lacked the will to act, but refused to trust Republican Presidents with the power to cut the few remaining controllable portions of the budget. The result has been stalemate and budget gimmickry.

Until recently, the Constitution of the United States was considered "the instrument and symbol" of politics in America. The Constitution authorized and legitimized the limited character of government and symbolized the notion of a HIGHER LAW [2]. That law was seen to be dictated by nature and reason—not merely legislative majorities—and was the source of legitimate authority. It provided the means by which the various institutions of government and the rights and powers of majorities could be reconciled. It presupposed a structure of government in which the characteristic activity of government—lawmaking by legislative majorities—could culminate in reasonable public law in the interest of all. The primary virtue of the legislative branch is the capacity for such deliberation, or public reasoning. It is by means of such deliberation and reconciliation that the various private interests could be made compatible with the common good.

But Congress no longer functions primarily as a deliberative body, and the constitutional order has readjusted itself accordingly. The courts are now routinely involved in general policymaking, and Congress is excessively concerned with the details of executive administration. Moreover, Congress is less effective today in reconciling particular interests in light of the general interest. Congress has delegated much of its lawmaking authority to administrative bodies, and its primary role has become one of administrative oversight. Since the late 1960s, Congress has maintained an administrative apparatus whose task it is to solve—in a technically rational way, using the methods of science and social science—the social and political problems of industrial or postindustrial society.

The federal budget is in the process of replacing the Constitution as the "instrument and symbol" of American politics. Whereas the powers of government were once thought to be limited, now only resources are limited. The budget is the instrument by which the bureaucratic state is fueled; it is the symbol of the centralization of administration that is the dominant political reality of the American regime. The most important political questions are no longer questions of principle or public right but of money and finance. The Constitution was the embodiment of the principles of republican government. The budget has become the symbol of American pluralism at best and redistributionist politics at worst. The Constitution was concerned with institutions, law, and the common good. The budget is the embodiment of the administrative state. It reflects a concern with administrative detail rather than principle, rulemaking rather than lawmaking, and the attempt to placate every private interest, rather than pursuance of a common good.

JOHN MARINI

(SEE ALSO: *Balanced Budget Amendment* [I]; *Impoundment of Funds* [2]; *Progressive Constitutional Thought* [3]; *Progressivism* [I].)

Bibliography
SCHICK, ALLEN 1980 *Congress and Money*. Washington, D.C.: Urban Institute.
SHUMAN, HOWARD E. 1984 *Politics and the Budget*. Englewood Cliffs, N.J.: Prentice-Hall.
WILDAVSKY, AARON 1988 *The New Politics of the Budgetary Process*. Glenview, Ill.: Scott, Foresman.

BUREAUCRACY
(Update)

The Constitution fails to provide for the largest and one of the most important components of American government, the bureaucracy. The Framers understood that the presidency could not function without a group of persons comparable to the English servants of the crown. The Constitution does provide one specific reference to at least the top level of the bureaucracy: "The President . . . may require the Opinion in writing, of the principal officer in each of the executive Departments" (Article II, section 2). The Constitution also specifies how government officers are to be appointed—some by the President with the ADVICE AND CONSENT [1] of the Senate and some by the President alone. It prohibits members of Congress from holding executive office, thus preventing the creation of cabinet government of the European kind. It specifically authorizes Congress to establish an army, navy, and post office. The Framers could also have specified what other departments, such as Treasury and State, should exist. Indeed, they could have provided a complete organization chart of the whole executive branch. But they did not. Instead, they appear to have deliberately left further evolution of the executive branch to Congress and to the President.

The Supreme Court has on occasion played a major role in shaping the CONSTITUTIONAL THEORY [I] of bureaucracy. From early in the Republic there have been two rival views of the bureaucracy. One, associated with ALEXANDER HAMILTON [2] and later the Progressives, stresses the need for neutrality and expertise. The other emphasizes democratic responsibility. Jacksonian notions of "rotation in office" and "the spoils system" were the expression of this democratic theme. To prevent a gap between the governors and the governed, ordinary citizens were to take their turns in office and then return to private life. The partisans of the party that won one election were to be given government jobs and then turned out in favor of the partisans of whatever party won the next. Such arrangements undercut any vision of an expert bureaucracy reaching "correct" decisions. The Progressive view was eventually embodied in a series of state and federal civil service statutes that gradually incorporated more and more government workers into a system of entry and promotion by technical examinations and GOOD BEHAVIOR [2] tenure.

The Hatch Act of 1939 prohibited federal civil servants from making contributions to, or participating in, election campaigns, in order to protect them from pressure by the President or their politically appointed superiors to actively support the President's party. The Hatch Act was challenged as a violation of the civil servants' FIRST AMENDMENT [2,I] political participation rights. In *U.S. Civil Service Commission v. National Association of Letter Carriers* (1973) the Supreme Court decisively supported the Progressive theory of bureaucracy by holding that the compelling interest in an expert neutral career civil service outweighed the First Amendment claims at issue.

In a subsequent case, the Court directly confronted

one of the last true "rotation in office" systems in the United States. Cook County, Illinois, prosecutors were political appointees. Whenever party control of the elected county executive changed, prosecutors of the winning party replaced those of the losing party. In *Elrod v. Burns* (1979) the prosecutors of the losing party argued that their First Amendment rights were being violated since they were being fired solely because of their political beliefs. Although the Court acknowledged the American tradition of the spoils system, it concentrated on the First Amendment issues and held for the fired prosecutors. Historically, whenever civil service protections were extended to a further category of government positions, those currently holding the positions, even though they owed their appointments to political favor rather than expert qualifications, were "blanketed in"—that is, allowed to keep their jobs. In the Cook County case, the Court in effect blanketed in all the remaining spoils appointees in the United States. The theory of a neutral bureaucracy free of party control has become part of the Constitution, not as a distinct provision but by judicial interpretation of the free speech clause.

The simple schema of the first three articles of the Constitution—Article I, Congress; Article II, presidency; and Article III, judiciary—would seem to place the executive department under the President, who is constitutionally endowed with "the executive power of the United States." Particularly since the New Deal, many commentators have stressed the need for presidential control over the ever-growing and increasingly complex federal bureaucracy. In spite of what would appear to be the clear structure of the Constitution, the federal departments are as much, or more, the creatures of Congress as they are the servants of the President. Precisely because Article II does not itemize the executive departments or specify their organization, they have no independent constitutional status. Instead, every executive agency must be crafted by congressional statute, and all of its powers, programs, and expenditures also must be authorized by statute. Congress may further specify by statute the details of agency organization and procedure.

Beginning in the mid-1970s, with the presidency increasingly in the hands of one party and Congress in that of the other, more attention was given to the potential contradictions between the legal basis of the executive departments as congressional creations and the position of the President as chief executive. Agencies live between the duties imposed on them by statute and the executive authority wielded by the President. Recent Presidents have sought to give substantive content to their constitutional authority to "take care that the Laws be faithfully executed" and to assert that whatever discretion the executive agencies wield in the administration of law ultimately belongs to the President. The President's opponents respond by stressing the degree to which the agencies are bound by statutory duties imposed by Congress and the obligation of the President to obey those statutes. Typically these issues arise in the context of broadly worded or incomplete regulatory statutes that must be fleshed out by agency enacted rules. Because they involve ADMINISTRATIVE LAW [1] and statutory interpretation, these issues often escape the attention of constitutional law specialists. The regulatory statute may be conceived as expressing, however vaguely and incompletely, a single, definite government policy that the agency must discover and embody correctly in its rules. Or such a statute may be seen as setting general goals and outer limits and then delegating to the agency an element of lawmaking discretion in fashioning detailed rules. In this view, although some rules are clearly foreclosed by the statute, the agency is free to choose from among a number of alternatives within the boundaries set by the statute. Agency choice will, and should, vary, depending on the policy views of the President and political appointees to the agencies. The former view tends to isolate the agency from presidential control, and the latter, to maximize such control.

Most immediately the issue is one of the relative policy-making power of the career agency bureaucracy and the politically appointed agency executives. The more we conceive of a single correct rule that most closely corresponds to the dictates of the statute, the greater must be the policy authority of the bureaucracy; it is the administrators who have long experience in dealing with the statute and great expertise in the factual data on which the correctness of a rule must depend. The more the statute is conceived as delegating lawmaking authority to the agency—that is, the discretion to choose from among alternative, equally valid rules—the greater policy authority should be vested in the President and his appointees, for if rule making really is discretionary lawmaking, then it should be done by those held accountable by the electoral process—not by a nonelected technocracy.

When courts reviewing the lawfulness of agency rules choose one of these visions or the other, the judges are deciding the degree to which the agencies belong to Congress or to the President. Depending on the statutory language, the circumstances, and the underlying constitutional theory of the judge, individual decisions go in one direction or the other. The collective impact of these decisions over time will move the federal bureaucracy more toward Article I or toward Article II and thus determine a fundamental aspect of constitutional law, even though those cases do not overtly raise constitutional questions. Such recent Supreme Court decisions as *Chevron U.S.A. v. Natural Resources Defense Council* (1984) and *Motor*

Vehicle Manufacturers Institute v. State Farm Mutual (1983) keep both visions alive.

In a series of decisions on more explicitly constitutional SEPARATION OF POWERS [4] issues, some Justices have sometimes sought to draw bright lines between congressional and presidential control over the bureaucracy. The Court's basic position, however, appears to be that it will seek to maintain a balance between the two without creating a firm boundary. This estimate seems confirmed in such cases as IMMIGRATION AND NATURALIZATION SERVICE V. CHADHA (1983) [2], NIXON V. ADMINISTRATOR OF GENERAL SERVICES (1977) [3], *Bowsher v. Synar* (1986), and *Morrison v. Olson* (1988). One of these cases, *Chadha*, raises the specter of bureaucratic escape from both Congress and the presidency. Congress often passes statutes that vest great lawmaking authority in the agencies. If the bureaucrats in the agencies can use a theory of statutory duty to shield themselves from presidential control, then the agencies may float free of both Article I and Article II and become a "fourth branch" of government unless Congress exercises some continuing control over the agencies after it has made broad delegations of power to them. One congressional attempt to exercise such poststatutory enactment control is the LEGISLATIVE VETO [3]. In some of its delegatory statutes Congress has provided that before an agency promulgates a rule, it must submit the rule for Congress's approval. The Supreme Court ruled the legislative veto unconstitutional in *Chadha*. Congress has a number of other important weapons of administrative oversight, the most important being its appropriation control. It always retains the power to amend the statutes so as to preclude agency action of which it disapproves and ultimately the power to pass new statutes fundamentally altering the programmatic mandates and the organization or even existence of an agency that displeases it. Yet Congress frequently makes broad, vague, or contradictory delegations to the agencies precisely because it cannot muster the political will to specify what it wants. In such circumstances, it also may not muster the will to control the agency's exercise of the lawmaking power delegated to it. Therein lies the appeal to some of enhancing the power over the agencies of another elected official, the President. These grave constitutional questions work themselves out less in major Supreme Court cases than in the detailed language of statutes and the day-to-day practices of such presidential arms as the OFFICE OF MANAGEMENT AND BUDGET [3].

MARTIN SHAPIRO

(SEE ALSO: *Administrative Agencies* [I]; *Appointing and Removal Power (Presidential)* [1]; *Appointments Clause* [I]; *Freedom of Speech* [2,I]; *Hatch Acts* [2]; *Regulatory Agencies* [3].)

Bibliography

FISHER, LOUIS 1988 *Constitutional Dialogues*. Princeton, N.J.: Princeton University Press.
SHAPIRO, MARTIN 1988 *Who Guards the Guardians*. Athens, Ga.: University of Georgia Press.
WOLL, PETER 1963 *American Bureaucracy*. New York: Norton.

BUSH, GEORGE
(1924–   )

George Bush served two terms as vice-president during the presidency of RONALD REAGAN [3,I], who had been his rival for the Republican presidential nomination in 1980. With Reagan's support, Bush was then elected President in 1988. Bush was thus the first President since 1836 to be elected from the VICE-PRESIDENCY [4], an office that does not usually provide much prominence or stature to its incumbent. Bush was also one of the few Presidents in this century to have reached the White House without having previously won a single statewide election (he was defeated in bids to become U.S. senator from Texas in 1966 and 1970). With the exception of the popular leader DWIGHT D. EISENHOWER [2], all the others in this category—WILLIAM HOWARD TAFT [3], HERBERT C. HOOVER [2], and GERALD R. FORD [2]—proved to be one-term Presidents.

Apart from serving two terms in the U.S. HOUSE OF REPRESENTATIVES [I] (1966–1970), Bush owed his political experience before 1980 to a succession of presidential appointments in the administrations of RICHARD M. NIXON [3] and Gerald Ford. He served successively as U.S. ambassador to the United Nations (1971–1973), chief of the U.S. Liaison Office (that is, de facto ambassador) in the People's Republic of China (1974–1975), and director of the Central Intelligence Agency (1976). His performance in these posts made no enemies but also did little to define his political character or to win him a broad popular following.

In the 1988 presidential campaign, Bush courted the conservative constituencies of Ronald Reagan. He attacked his opponent for his affiliation with the AMERICAN CIVIL LIBERTIES UNION [1] and expressed sympathy with several key conservative complaints against the constitutional rulings of both the WARREN COURT [4] and the BURGER COURT [1]. He thus expressed support for constitutional amendments to prohibit ABORTION [1,I] and to reauthorize SCHOOL PRAYER [I]. He also supported a constitutional amendment to require a BALANCED BUDGET [I]. As President, he urged a constitutional amendment to overturn the Supreme Court's ruling that FLAG DESECRATION [2,I] is protected by the FIRST AMENDMENT [2,I]. None of these amendments was pushed with any sustained energy or intensity by the Bush administration, however, and none found majority support in Congress.

Bush's first choice for the Supreme Court when the retirement of Justice WILLIAM J. BRENNAN [1,I] opened a vacancy in the summer of 1990 was characteristic of his nonconfrontational style as President. DAVID H. SOUTER [I], an almost totally unknown New Hampshire state supreme court justice, proved to have taken few public stands on constitutional controversies, and President Bush announced that he, himself, had neither questioned Souter nor learned from others what Souter's views might be on abortion or on other controversial subjects. Bush did, however, emphasize his expectation that Souter would fairly interpret the Constitution instead of "legislating" his own policy preferences. The President was prepared to indicate in general terms that he thought recent Supreme Court Justices had not always properly observed this distinction, but he did not single out any particular decisions for such criticism.

In general, during his first two years in office, President Bush adopted a conciliatory stance toward a Congress dominated by the opposition party. He did assert presidential prerogatives in vetoing congressional measures he thought overly restrictive of the presidency or of the constitutional duties of the executive branch, but he did not make this a major theme either. He conceded before his election that the so-called IRAN–CONTRA AFFAIR [I] in the Reagan administration may have involved significant departures from the law and pledged to observe legal constraints with complete devotion. He did make efforts to consult congressional leaders when he committed U.S. forces to conflict in Panama in 1989 and in the Middle East in 1990, and both efforts generally received broad support in Congress. Like his predecessors, however, President Bush did not acknowledge that he was bound by the 1974 War Powers Resolution; he submitted required reports to Congress, but presented these as voluntary measures of cooperation rather than compliance with binding law.

In the conflict over Iraq's conquest of neighboring Kuwait, President Bush pursued active diplomatic efforts, culminating in a United Nations Security Council Resolution authorizing the use of force to liberate Kuwait. After sending almost half a million American troops to Saudi Arabia, President Bush did finally seek and receive direct congressional authorization for the use of force in this conflict. U.S. air strikes followed within days of this vote in accord with a deadline established in both the U.N. resolution and the congressional resolution. Though the congressional resolution received only a bare majority in the Senate in a largely partisan vote, it was widely accepted as the constitutional equivalent of a DECLARATION OF WAR [2] and essentially put an end to further legal debate about the U.S. military role in the war against Iraq. With the onset of decisive military operations, support for the President in the country rose to record levels.

JEREMY RABKIN

Bibliography

BUSH, GEORGE with DOUGLAS WEAD   1988   *Man of Integrity.* Eugene, Ore.: Harvest House.

BUSH, GEORGE   1989   Statement on Signing the Treasury, Postal Service and General Government Act, 1990 (November 3, 1989) in *Public Papers of the Presidents, Administration of George Bush, 1989.* Washington, D.C.: U.S. Government Printing Office.

CABLE TELEVISION

See: Broadcasting [I]

CALIFORNIA v. GREENWOOD
486 U.S. 35 (1988)

A person's trash if subjected to public scrutiny might reveal intimate matters that could be embarrassing and even expose one to blackmail or criminal prosecution. But anyone throwing away household trash takes the risk of exposure, even if the trash is disposed of in an opaque plastic bag that is sealed. This was the Supreme Court's announcement in this case.

Justice BYRON R. WHITE [4,I], for a 6–2 Court, held that the FOURTH AMENDMENT's [2,I] prohibition against UNREASONABLE SEARCHES [4,I] and seizures does not apply to those who leave their sealed trash outside their curtilage for collection by the trash collector. In this case, an observant policewoman, suspecting Greenwood of dealing in narcotics, obtained the trash collector's cooperation and found enough incriminating EVIDENCE [2] to establish PROBABLE CAUSE [3] for a search of the residence. This evidence was used to convict him. The question was whether the initial WARRANTLESS SEARCH [4] of the trash violated the Fourth Amendment. The Court ruled that those discarding their trash by placing it on the street for collection abandoned any REASONABLE EXPECTATION OF PRIVACY [3] they might otherwise have. The two dissenters believed that the warrantless investigation of the trash constituted an appalling invasion of privacy.

LEONARD W. LEVY

CALIFORNIA FEDERAL SAVINGS AND LOAN v. GUERRA

See: Sex Discrimination [I]

CAMPAIGN FINANCE
(Update)

Criticism of political-funding practices and calls for further reforms increased in the latter half of the 1980s as the cost of campaigns continued to escalate and repeated fund-raising scandals were publicized. Turnover of congressional seats reached an all-time low, in part because challengers found it difficult to compete in expensive media campaigns. The growing number of POLITICAL ACTION COMMITTEES [I] contributed most heavily to congressional incumbents, particularly to those in the majority party, and both parties exploited the loopholes found in the federal funding restrictions.

During this period the Supreme Court again considered the constitutionality of existing campaign-finance restrictions, continuing to grapple with the conflict between FIRST AMENDMENT [2,I] liberties and the concern for political equality, a conflict inherent in attempts to regulate political funding. In the mid-1980s, the Court reiterated and even strengthened principles previously established in BUCKLEY V. VALEO (1976) [1], including the rejection of equalization of political influence as an appropriate rationale for funding restrictions. However, at the end of the 1980s, a majority of the Court for the first time explicitly resolved the conflict by giving preference to equality rather than liberty, possibly signaling that they would view further legislative reforms with greater favor than in the past.

In *Federal Election Commission v. National Conservative Political Action Committee* (1985) the Court invalidated a federal statute that limited independent expenditures by political committees supporting presidential candidates who accepted public subsidies. Writing for the majority, WILLIAM H. REHNQUIST [3,I], then an Associate Justice, asserted that "the only legitimate and compelling government interests thus far identified" were preventing the appearance and reality of corruption. Defining the term "corruption" more explicitly than in previous cases, Justice Rehnquist made clear that he was referring to "quid pro quo" arrangements with office holders.

One year later, in *Federal Election Commission v. Massachusetts Citizens for Life* (*MCFL*) (1986), the Court held that the federal requirement that independent expenditures by CORPORATIONS [2] in federal elections be made through voluntary funds given to political committees was unconstitutional as applied to MCFL. However, a change in the premises of a majority of the Justices was evident in Justice WILLIAM J. BRENNAN's [1,I] opinion both from the narrowness of the HOLDING [2] and from the lengthy explanation, quite unnecessary to the decision, as to why the restriction could be constitutionally applied to most other corporations.

The dicta from *MCFL* became a holding when the Court, in *Austin v. Michigan Chamber of Commerce* (1990), upheld the application of a state statute similar to the one at issue in *MCFL*. According to Justice THURGOOD MARSHALL's [3,I] majority opinion, the Chamber was not the kind of ideological corporation that was entitled to First Amendment protection under the reasoning of *MCFL* because its assets did not necessarily reflect support for its political expression.

The majority in *Austin* asserted that the compelling interest served by the statute was preventing "a different type of corruption in the political arena: the corrosive and distorting effect of immense aggregations of wealth that are accumulated with the help of the corporate form and that have little or no correlation to the public's support for the corporation's political ideas." In dissent, Justice ANTONIN SCALIA [I] scoffingly referred to the majority's rationale as "the New Corruption" and accused them of adopting the approach of "one man, one minute." Indeed, the distinction between the compelling interest found in *Austin* and the interest in equalization of political influence, which had been rejected in *Buckley* and other cases, is not easy to discern.

By limiting the rationale to situations in which the wealth used for expression "was accumulated with the help of the corporate form," the majority purported to avoid a clash with PRECEDENT [3]. Stressing that the state gives corporations the advantages of perpetual life and freedom from personal liability, the Court concluded that it was appropriate to prevent the use of funds amassed with the help of these benefits from unfairly influencing the electoral process. However, Justice ANTHONY M. KENNEDY [I] pointed out in dissent that the majority's analysis was inconsistent with the reasoning in FIRST NATIONAL BANK OF BOSTON V. BELLOTTI (1978) [2], in which the Court had invalidated bans on corporate expenditures in ballot-measure elections. Indeed, the shift in the majority's approach in *MCFL* and *Austin* is illustrated by the fact that the Court's opinions in these cases strongly resemble the DISSENTING OPINIONS [2] in *Bellotti*. Although *Bellotti* is distinguishable from *MCFL* and *Austin* because the burdens on corporate expression were more severe, the broad principles articulated in *Bellotti* are clearly at odds with the basic premises of *Austin*.

The dichotomy between the majority and the dissents in *Austin* is a classic formulation of the tension between equality and liberty that lies behind all the cases in this area. Because *Austin* and *MCFL* represent a shift toward greater attention to political equality, these decisions could open up new possibilities for reform as legislatures in the 1990s struggle with the problems caused by the ever spiraling costs of political campaigns.

MARLENE ARNOLD NICHOLSON

Bibliography

MUTCH, ROBERT E. 1988 *Campaigns, Congress and Courts: The Making of Federal Campaign Law.* Westport, Conn.: Greenwood Press.

NICHOLSON, MARLENE A. 1987 The Supreme Court's Meandering Path in Campaign Finance Regulation and What It Portends for Future Reform. *Journal of Law and Politics* 3:509–565.

CAPITAL PUNISHMENT
(Update)

During the 1980s, a majority of Justices on the Supreme Court struggled without success to disengage the Court from playing an intimate role in the day-to-day administration of capital punishment. As early as 1984, an article on the evolving jurisprudence of capital punishment in the Court could plausibly be titled "Deregulating Death," and the Court continued to reject major challenges to state systems of capital punishment for the rest of the decade. In the wake of *McCleskey v. Kemp*, decided in 1987, scholars could conclude that "nothing appears left of the abolitionist campaign in the courts—nothing but the possibility of small-scale tinkering" (Burt, p. 1741).

Yet conflicts about capital punishment have been a persistent and growing problem for the Court through the 1980s, and there are no indications that the burden will lessen soon. The number of capital cases producing opinions increased during the decade from about five per term in the early 1980s to about ten per term in the late 1980s. Moreover, the level of dispute among the Justices has substantially increased during the course of the decade. In the early 1980s, most challenges to capital punishment were rejected by substantial majorities of the Justices, with a 7–2 vote being the most common outcome during the 1982, 1983, and 1984 terms. Only three of seventeen opinions issued during these three terms were decided by 5–4 margins. Justices WILLIAM J. BRENNAN [1,I] and THURGOOD MARSHALL [3,I] were the isolated dissenters in most of these early cases.

By contrast, in the four terms after October 1985, the Court has been sharply and closely divided. Of the twenty-seven cases decided over this span, fourteen produced 5–4 divisions, with Justices JOHN PAUL STEVENS [4,I] and HARRY A. BLACKMUN [1,I] usually joining Justices Brennan and Marshall in opposition to the deregulatory thrust of the Court majority. We know of no other body of the Supreme Court doctrine in which the majority of cases divide the Court 5–4.

With the Court divided almost to the point of a mathematical law of maximal disagreement, both JURISPRUDENCE [I] and decorum have suffered. Few would suggest that the Court's decisions of the past decade cumulate into a body of doctrine that is even minimally coherent. And close decisions on questions that are literally matters of life and death do not promote good manners among Justices locked in conflict. It is thus no surprise that Court decorum has been put at some risk by the sustained contentiousness of the death penalty cases.

Close and acrimonious division of the Justices may also undermine the degree to which the Supreme Court's decisions confer legitimacy on the practice of execution in the 1990s. Confidence in the fairness of the system is not bolstered when four of nine Justices publicly proclaim that the race of the victim has a discriminatory influence on whether defendants receive death sentences. The result is that the consistent but slim majority support on the Court may not provide much momentum for public acceptance of the equity of capital punishment, much as the Court's leadership toward abolition was undermined by a slim and divided majority on the Court in *Furman v. Georgia* (1972). A 5–4 majority may lack the institutional credibility to help make executions an accepted part of a modern American governmental system.

One other pattern is of special significance when discussing capital punishment in the Supreme Court during the 1980s: The transition from theory to practice of executions has not yet occurred in most of the United States. Despite the Court's attempts to withdraw from close supervision of death cases, the backlog of death cases has increased substantially, and the lower federal courts continue to play an important role in stopping executions. Indeed, over half of federal court of appeals decisions in death penalty cases result in overturning the death sentence.

As of January 1990, although thirty-seven states have legislation authorizing capital punishment (and thirty-four of these have prisoners under death sentence), only thirteen states have executed since the reauthorization of the capital punishment in *Gregg v. Georgia*, in 1976. Nine of the thirteen states with a recent execution are located in the South; only one new state resumed executions during the last four years of the 1980s.

The number of executions has also stayed low throughout the 1980s, with a high of twenty-seven in 1987 and an annual average of about twenty for the last five years of the 1980s. But, although the level of executions remained low and eighty percent of these are clustered in four southern states, the number of prisoners under death sentence had increased by the end of 1989 to about 2,400, a more than one-hundred-year supply at the prevailing rates of execution.

Thus, by the end of the 1980s, the withdrawal of the Supreme Court from regulation of the administration of the death penalty had not yet produced a substantial increase in the number of executing states or the number of executions. But the long involvement of the federal courts had helped produce a death row population four times as great as that which cast a shadow on the Court when *Furman v. Georgia* was decided in 1972.

Against this backdrop, an ad hoc committee chaired by retired Justice LEWIS F. POWELL [3,I] diagnosed the problem that generated these numbers as the delay produced by repetitive and multiple federal APPEALS [1]. The committee suggested the enactment of new statutory procedures for handling death penalty cases in the federal court, which, by and large, would eliminate the filing of successor federal petitions. Under the new procedures, if the state has provided counsel to those sentenced to death through the state appeal and HABEAS CORPUS [2,I] process, absent extraordinary circumstances, a federal court would lack the power to stay an execution of the condemned person upon the filing of a successor federal petition.

Should such procedures be enacted and actually reduce federal appeal time more than they increase state appeal time, further pressure toward increasing numbers of executions will occur just when large numbers of cases will be exhausting currently available federal reviews.

But even if the Powell committee recommendations were to maintain delay at current levels, but shift more of the total procedural load onto state courts, this result might serve one significant objection that motivated the exercise—it would reduce the extent to which the federal courts could be blamed for delay in execution. A persistent fact of American government is that even among institutions and actors that believe twenty-five executions a year is more appropriate in the United States than 250, there is constant pressure to avoid appearing to be responsible for restricting the scale of executions. The politics of capital punishment at all levels in the United States involves passing the apparent responsibility for preventing executions to other actors or institutions. And the Powell committee's work can be understood in part as a public-relations gesture in this tradition of passing the buck away from the federal court system.

In 1989 and 1990, the Supreme Court, by the familiar 5–4 vote, responded to the considerations that had moved the Powell committee. Now, with few exceptions, a federal habeas corpus petition must be denied when it rests on a claim of a "new right"—one that had not yet been recognized by the Supreme Court when the appeals ended in the state courts. Not only has the Court specifically applied this new bar to death penalty cases, but it has also read the idea of a "new right" broadly enough to bar all but a very few claims.

What would be the impact of true federal court withdrawal from restrictions on execution? The potential number of executions that could result is quite high, two or three times as many as the 199 executions that were to date the twentieth-century high recorded in 1935. How many state governors or state court systems would compensate and to what degree remains to be seen. Practices like executive clemency that used to be a statistically important factor in restricting executions atrophied during the twenty-five years of primary federal court intervention in the capital-punishment process. Whether these processes would reappear under the pressure of large numbers of pending executions in northern industrial states cannot be predicted, nor is it possible to project a likely national number of executions that could represent a new level of equilibrium.

The one certainty is that the U.S. Supreme Court will play a central day-to-day role in any substantial increase in executions. Whatever its doctrinal intentions or public-relations ambitions, the Supreme Court will be for the mass media and the public the court of last resort for every scheduled execution in the United States for the foreseeable future. If executions climb to 100 or 150 per year, the continuing role of the Court as the last stop before the gallows will be that element of the Court's work most sharply etched in the public mind. For an institution narrowly divided on fundamental questions, this case-by-case process could increase both the labor and the acrimony of the Court's involvement with capital punishment. To escape this role would call for more than a shift in procedure or court personnel; it would require a different country.

Under these circumstances, will the hands-off doctrine the Court has so recently constructed continue as executions multiply? In the short run, any major shift in doctrine would be regarded as a surprise. This is a matter more of personnel than of precedent. STARE DECISIS [4] has not often been a reliable guide to Supreme Court pronouncements in capital punishment. Instead, doctrine seems more the servant of policy than its master in this field, and this is equally the case for *Gregg v. Georgia* as for *Furman v. Georgia*. But the current majority is apparently firm and includes the four youngest Justices.

In the long run, if the United States is to join the community of Western nations that has abolished capital punishment, the U.S. Supreme Court is the most likely agency of abolition in the national government. The principal flaws in the system of capital punishment are the same as they have been throughout the twentieth century. The doctrinal foundations for reacting to these matters are easily found in the Court's prior work.

No matter the course of the Court's future pronouncements, capital punishment will remain an area of inevitable judicial activism in one important respect: Whatever the substance of American policy toward executions, the U.S. Supreme Court will continue to be the dominant institutional influence of national government on executions in the United States.

FRANKLIN ZIMRING
MICHAEL LAURENCE

(SEE ALSO: *Capital Punishment Cases of 1972* [1]; *Capital Punishment Cases of 1976* [1]; *Capital Punishment and Race* [I].)

Bibliography

AD HOC COMMITTEE ON FEDERAL HABEAS CORPUS IN CAPITAL CASES 1989 *Committee Report and Proposal.* Washington, D.C.: Judicial Conference of the United States.

BURT, ROBERT A. 1987 Disorder in the Court: The Death Penalty and the Constitution. *Michigan Law Review* 85:1741–1819.

WEISBERG, ROBERT 1983 Deregulating Death. In Philip J. Kurland, Gerhard Gasper, and Dennis J. Hutchinson, eds., *Supreme Court Review*, pp. 305–396. Chicago: University of Chicago Press.

ZIMRING, FRANKLIN E. and HAWKINS, GORDON 1986 *Capital*

Punishment and the American Agenda. New York: Cambridge University Press.

CAPITAL PUNISHMENT AND RACE

In MCCLESKEY V. KEMP (1987) [I], the Supreme Court grappled with the difficult issue of race and CAPITAL PUNISHMENT [1,I]. Confronted with statistical studies that indicated potential RACIAL DISCRIMINATION [3,I] in the assignment of death sentences in the state of Georgia, the Court considered Eighth Amendment and EQUAL PROTECTION [2,I] challenges to the application of the Georgia death penalty statute. Whereas no significant disparities existed with respect to the race of defendants, statistical evidence, using sophisticated regression analysis, indicated that blacks were 4.3 times more likely to receive death sentences when they killed whites than when they killed blacks.

McCleskey, a black, had killed a white police officer during an armed robbery. The fact that the race of the victim made it more likely that he would receive the death penalty was, McCleskey argued, a violation of equal protection guarantees and the Eighth Amendment's ban on CRUEL AND UNUSUAL PUNISHMENT [2,I]. The Court, although expressing some reservations about both the credibility and the relevance of the statistical evidence, nevertheless assumed their validity in order to reach the constitutional questions.

Speaking through Justice LEWIS F. POWELL [3,I], the Court's majority of five refused to break new ground in its equal protection jurisprudence. Powell began by noting that it was a settled principle that "a defendant who alleges an equal protection violation has the burden of proving 'the existence of purposeful discrimination'" and that the purposeful discrimination had "a discriminatory effect on him." Therefore, "McCleskey must prove that the decisionmakers in *his* case acted with discriminatory purpose." Statistical inference, the Court ruled, could at best indicate only that there was a risk that racial discrimination had been a factor in McCleskey's sentencing. The Court has in certain contexts—selection of jury venire and Title VII—accepted statistics as prima facie proof of discrimination. Moreover, the statistics (particularly in the jury cases) do not have to present a "stark" pattern in order to be accepted as sole evidence of discriminatory intent.

Yet the Court in *McCleskey* distinguished capital sentencing cases as less amenable to statistical proof because of the "uniqueness" of each capital case and the consequent difficulty of aggregating data. Each jury is unique and "the Constitution requires that its decision rest on consideration of innumerable factors that vary according to the characteristics of the individual defendant and the facts of the particular capital offense." In contrast, the jury-selection and Title VII cases are concerned only with limited ranges of circumstances and are thus more amenable to statistical analysis.

The Court therefore held that for McCleskey's claim of purposeful discrimination to prevail, he "would have to prove that the Georgia Legislature enacted or maintained the death penalty statute *because* of an anticipated racially discriminatory effect." But, as the Court laconically notes, this was a claim that was rejected in *Gregg v. Georgia* (1976). Thus, the Court concluded that "absent far stronger proof, . . . a legitimate and unchallenged explanation" for McCleskey's sentence "is apparent from the record: McCleskey committed an act for which the United States Constitution and Georgia laws permit imposition of the death penalty."

McCleskey also sought to use statistics to support his Eighth Amendment claim that the discretion given to sentencers in the Georgia criminal justice system makes it inevitable that any assignment of the death penalty will be "arbitrary and capricious." The Court has interpreted Eighth Amendment requirements to mean that sentencers must be governed by state laws that contain carefully defined standards that narrow the discretion to impose the death penalty. That is, sentencers must exercise only "guided discretion." But there can be no limits with respect to the sentencer's discretion not to impose the death penalty.

As the Court stated in *Lockett v. Ohio* (1978), "the sentencer" cannot be "precluded from considering, as a mitigating factor, any aspect of a defendant's character or record and any of the circumstances of the offense that the defendant proffers as a basis for a sentence less than death." Discretion that ensures the treatment of all persons as "uniquely individual human beings" is thus an essential ingredient of Eighth Amendment jurisprudence. The Court has ruled that mandatory death sentences are unconstitutional because the "respect for humanity underlying the Eighth Amendment requires consideration of the character and record of the individual offender and the circumstances of the particular offense as a constitutionally indispensable part of the process of inflicting the penalty of death."

The presence of such discretion, however, makes it impossible for actual decisions to result in racial proportionality. And to stipulate racial proportionality as a requirement either of equal protection or the Eighth Amendment would mean that the sentencer's discretion would have to be limited or extinguished. Proportionality requirements also present the daunting prospect that blacks who are convicted of killing blacks will have to receive the death penalty at an accelerated rate. Of course, proponents of the use of statistics as a measure of equal protection and Eighth Amendment rights do not expect any such result. Rather, their ultimate purpose is to abolish capital punishment under the guise that it is impossible to mete out death sentences in any rational or otherwise nonarbitrary manner. The Court, however, remains unwilling to accept statistical evidence as a sufficient proof of capriciousness and irrationality.

Because the existence of discretion will always produce statistical disparities, the "constitutional measure of an unacceptable risk of racial prejudice influencing capital sentencing decisions" cannot be defined in statistical terms. Rather, the constitutional risk must be addressed in terms of the procedural safeguards designed to minimize the influence of racial prejudice in the criminal justice system as a whole. After a thorough review of the Georgia system in *Gregg*, the Court concluded that procedural safeguards against racial discrimination were constitutionally adequate. As the Court rightly said, "where the discretion that is fundamental to our criminal process is involved, we decline to assume that what is unexplained is invidious."

The Eighth Amendment is not limited to capital sentencing but extends to all criminal penalties. Thus, a racial proportionality requirement for capital sentencing would open the possibility that all sentences could be challenged not only on the grounds of race but on the grounds of any irrelevant factor that showed enough of a statistical disparity to indicate that the sentencing was "irrational" or "capricious." Some cynics have described this as a kind of AFFIRMATIVE ACTION [1,I] for sentencing decisions. Such a situation not only would prove unworkable but, by limiting the discretion that remains at the heart of the criminal justice system, would also prove to be unjust. The vast majority of convicted murderers, for example, do not receive death sentences, because the discretionary element of the system spares them. The small percentage who do receive death sentences have thorough and exhaustive procedural protections. Under these circumstances, it would be impossible to argue that statistical disparities based on race indicate systemic racism in the CRIMINAL JUSTICE SYSTEM [I] or that the statistical disparities indicate a fundamentally unjust system.

Moreover, some scholars have questioned the validity of the statistics used in the *McCleskey* case. Interracial murders are more likely to involve aggravating circumstances (e.g., armed robbery, kidnapping, rape, torture, or murder to silence a witness to a crime) than same-race murders, which involve more mitigating factors (e.g., quarrels between friends and relatives). Given the relative rarity of blacks being murdered by whites, the statistics are bound to be skewed, but they do not necessarily prove or even indicate racial discrimination.

Taking into account the different levels of aggravating and mitigating circumstances, one recent study of Georgia sentencing practices concluded that evidence "supports the thesis that blacks who kill whites merit more serious punishment and are not themselves the victims of racial discrimination. By the same token, the same evidence suggests that blacks who kill blacks deserve less punishment and are not being patronized by a criminal justice system because it places less value on a black life."

Given the controversial nature of the statistical evidence proffered in the *McCleskey* case and the doctrine that equal protection and Eighth Amendment rights belong to "uniquely individual human beings" rather than racial groups, the Supreme Court was wise to reject abstract statistical disparities as proof of individual injury.

EDWARD J. ERLER

(SEE ALSO: *Race and Criminal Justice* [I].)

Bibliography

HEILBRUN, ALFRED B., JR.; FOSTER, ALLISON; and GOLDEN, JILL 1989 The Death Sentence in Georgia, 1974–1987: Criminal Justice or Racial Injustice? *Criminal Justice and Behavior* 16:139–154.

KENNEDY, RANDALL L. 1988 *McCleskey v. Kemp*: Race, Capital Punishment, and the Supreme Court. *Harvard Law Review* 101:1388–1443.

CHILD PORNOGRAPHY

Every year, thousands of children are compelled to engage in pornographic acts for the production of films and photographs. Child pornography is one of the most insidious forms of child abuse because the victimization does not stop with the physical acts of abuse. In the words of Justice BYRON R. WHITE [3,I], "the pornography's continued existence causes the child victims continuing harm by haunting the children in years to come." Because child pornography is child abuse, the Supreme Court has held that it is not protected by the FIRST AMENDMENT [2,I]. In NEW YORK V. FERBER (1982) [3] the Court ruled that the production and distribution of child pornography can be prosecuted even if the material does not meet the legal test for OBSCENITY [3] because, even if it is not legally obscene, it is still the product of child abuse and, hence, a proper object of state regulation.

In *Osborne v. Ohio* (1990) the Court extended the doctrine of *Ferber* to cover the private possession of child pornography. Ohio prosecuted Osborne for possessing child pornography in violation of a state statute. Osborne contended that the First Amendment prohibited the state from proscribing private possession, but the Supreme Court disagreed by a vote of 6–3. (Osborne's conviction was nevertheless overturned on procedural grounds.) The

Court noted that much of the production and sale of child pornography has gone underground and is therefore difficult to prosecute. The only effective way to stop the child abuse by pornographers is by banning possession of the material outright.

Writing for the dissenters, Justice WILLIAM J. BRENNAN [2,I] argued that the Ohio statute suffered from OVERBREADTH [3] because of its loose definition of what constituted child pornography. Even if the statute had not been overbroad, however, Brennan would have invalidated it. Recalling the words of STANLEY V. GEORGIA (1969) [4], Brennan said that "if the First Amendment means anything, it means that the State has no business telling a man, sitting alone in his own house, what book he may read or what films he may watch."

Brennan's analysis was inapposite to the case at hand, however. No adult has the right to compel a child to appear in a pornographic film or photo; hence, it stretches the imagination to claim that someone else has the right to possess (and derive pleasure from) what the pornographer had no right to produce in the first place. Laws against the possession of child pornography not only help to stop the abuse of children through the production of the pornography; they also protect the child victims' right to privacy after the unlawful photographs or films have been produced.

JOHN G. WEST, JR.

Bibliography

ATTORNEY GENERAL'S COMMISSION ON PORNOGRAPHY 1981 *Attorney General's Commission on Pornography, Final Report*, part II, chapter 7. Washington, D.C.: U.S. Government Printing Office.

CHILD WITNESSES

See: *Coy v. Iowa* [I]; *Maryland v. Craig* [I]

CHILDREN AND THE FIRST AMENDMENT

Because many conceptions of the FIRST AMENDMENT's [2,I] protection of speech and press are premised on a model of human rationality and human choice and because traditional views about children take them to be incapable of having the rationality and exercising the capacity of choice assumed for adults, issues about the free speech rights of children have always been problematic. Indeed, the need to protect children from harmful ideas they may be incapable of evaluating has been explicitly a part of the free speech tradition since John Stuart Mill's *On Liberty*.

Treating minors as different for free speech purposes has been a recurring feature of OBSCENITY [3] law. Although the Supreme Court reaffirmed in *Pinkus v. United States* (1978) that it is impermissible to judge the obscenity of material directed primarily to adults on the basis of its possible effect on children, the Court has also held in *Ginsberg v. New York* (1968) that where sexually explicit material is directed at juvenile readers or viewers it is permissible to apply the test for obscenity in light of a juvenile rather than an adult audience. In addition, the Court in NEW YORK V. FERBER (1982) [3] relied on the importance of protecting juvenile performers in allowing CHILD PORNOGRAPHY [I] prosecution for the distribution of material not legally obscene, although it is clear that analogous justifications for restrictions on publications remain impermissible with respect to adult participants. Still, the Court has been sensitive to the likely overuse of children-protecting rationales for restricting speech, and although in FEDERAL COMMUNICATIONS COMMISSION V. PACIFICA FOUNDATION (1978) [2] it relied on a protection of children rationale in upholding restrictions on the times during which sexually explicit or offensive radio programs might be broadcast, in *Sable Communications of California, Inc. v. FCC* (1989) it unanimously struck down a federal law restricting "indecent" telephone communications because of an insufficient showing that a restriction of this magnitude was necessary to protect children. *Sable* thus continued a tradition going back at least to BUTLER V. MICHIGAN (1957) [1], in which Justice FELIX FRANKFURTER [2] made clear that a law reducing the adult population to reading only what was fit for children would be an impermissible encroachment on First Amendment freedoms.

More commonly, the issue has arisen in the context of restrictions on speech in the public schools. Although it is so obvious as never to have generated a Supreme Court case that children as speakers in the PUBLIC FORUM [3,I] or other open environment have the same free speech rights as adults, the question is more complicated with reference to speech within the confines of the public schools. In upholding a student's right to wear a protest armband even in class, the Supreme Court in TINKER V. DES MOINES INDEPENDENT COMMUNITY SCHOOL DISTRICT (1969) [4] observed that "[n]either students [n]or teachers shed their constitutional rights to freedom of speech or expression at the schoolhouse gate" and proceeded to hold content-based restrictions on student speech in the schools invalid unless supported by evidence of actual or potential "disturbance," "disruption," or "disorder."

Both the language in *Tinker* and its "disturbance" standard proved difficult to square, however, with the fact that much of the mission of the schools involves controls on communication, of which the most obvious is the hardly unconstitutional practice of rewarding certain answers and penalizing others. As a result, subsequent cases, themselves frequently criticized as too much of a departure from *Tinker* and too easy an acquiescence to teacher or administrator authority, have tempered the *Tinker* approach. In BETHEL SCHOOL DISTRICT V. FRASER (1986) [I] the Court upheld disciplinary action against a high-school student who had made a sexually suggestive, but plainly not legally obscene, speech in a school assembly, and in HAZELWOOD SCHOOL DISTRICT V. KUHLMEIER (1988) [2], the Court allowed the school to exercise content-based control over a school-sponsored student newspaper produced on school property with school resources, the writing and editing of which was part of a journalism course offered by the school. More significantly, *Hazelwood* explicitly substituted a seemingly more lenient "reasonableness" standard for the *Tinker* "disturbance" standard, although it remains too early to assess the actual import of the new approach. It does seem clear that the recent cases represent a willingness to defer to decisions of school authorities more than has been the case in the past and a consequent willingness to allow school authorities at the primary and secondary level to choose to have an "indoctrination" rather than a "market place of ideas" model as the major purpose of primary and secondary education. Thus, the recent trend will likely result in little judicial review of content-based restrictions on student speech within the primary and secondary schools. But the Court's unwillingness to overrule *Tinker*, combined with decisions like BOARD OF EDUCATION V. PICO (1982) [1], dealing (unclearly) with political censorship of school libraries, indicates that judicial intervention remains appropriate where the content-based restrictions are excessively viewpoint based or where they stem not from the decisions of primary professionals such as teachers and principals, but rather from the selective involvement of more political and less professional elected officials.

FREDERICK SCHAUER

Bibliography

GARVEY, JOHN 1979 Children and the First Amendment. *Texas Law Review* 57:321–366.

—— 1981 Freedom and Choice in Constitutional Law. *Harvard Law Review* 94:1756–1794.

YUDOF, MARK G. 1984 Library Book Selection and the Public Schools: The Quest for the Archimedean Point. *Indiana Law Journal* 59:527–564.

CHRISTIAN RIGHT

See: Religious Fundamentalism [I]

CITIZENSHIP
(Update)

American citizenship can be obtained in three ways. The most common way, citizenship by birth in the United States (jus soli), is secured by the FOURTEENTH AMENDMENT [2,I] citizenship clause. Although customary exceptions to this principle exist (e.g., children born on foreign vessels or of diplomatic personnel), this birthright citizenship has been understood (wrongly, I have argued) to extend even to native-born children of ALIENS [1] in the country illegally or on a temporary visa.

A second route to citizenship is through NATURALIZATION [3]. To naturalize, one must be a resident alien who has resided in the United States continuously for five years (a longer period than in Canada and the Scandinavian countries); be of good moral character; and demonstrate an ability to speak, read, and write English and a basic knowledge of United States government and history. These requirements are relaxed for certain individuals, such as spouses of U.S. citizens.

The third route to citizenship is through parentage (jus sanguinis). Statutory law enumerates a number of parentage categories, sometimes augmented by RESIDENCY REQUIREMENTS [3], that confer eligibility for citizenship on the child. The Supreme Court held in *Rogers v. Bellei* (1971) that in regulating this form of citizenship, Congress is not limited by the citizenship clause of the Fourteenth Amendment. In recent years Congress has liberalized eligibility.

Dual and triple citizenships, which arise as a result of the combination of the American jus soli rule with the jus sanguinis rules of other nations, are tolerated and legally protected. Still, the government discourages multiple citizenship; aliens who wish to naturalize must renounce any prior allegiance, which may or may not effectively terminate their foreign citizenships.

U.S. citizenship, once acquired, is almost impossible to lose without the citizen's expressed consent. The Supreme Court has severely restricted the government's power to denationalize a citizen for disloyalty, divided allegiance, or other reasons. Birthright citizens cannot be deprived of their citizenship unless the government proves that they specifically intended to renounce it. Naturalized citizens who procured their citizenship through fraud or misrepresentation are subject to DENATURALIZATION [2], but to prevail the government must satisfy demanding standards, most recently defined in *Kungys v. United States* (1988). This tiny risk of denaturalization is the only permissible difference between naturalized and other citizens.

As a result of a steady expansion of the equal protection and due process principles, legal resident aliens today enjoy almost all the significant rights and obligations that citizens enjoy, including access to most public benefits. Only five differences are worth noting. Three of them are political: citizens, but not aliens, may vote, serve on juries, and serve in certain high elective offices and certain high (and not so high) appointive ones. Modern practice (many states in the nineteenth century permitted aliens to vote) and political inertia, more than sound policy, probably account for the durability of these differences. A fourth difference, which Congress has considered eliminating, is that citizens can bring their noncitizen family members to the United States more easily than aliens can. Finally, aliens are subject to DEPORTATION [2], although the actual risk of deportation for a long-term resident alien who does not engage in serious criminal behavior is very low.

This progressive convergence of the citizen and resident-alien statuses suggests some devaluation of American citizenship. As public philosophy, this devaluation carries with it certain dangers for the polity. But it also represents an immense gain for the liberal values of inclusiveness and equal treatment. By maximizing individual opportunity and preventing the formation of a legally disabled underclass, the equality and due process principles have fostered the social mobility and optimism that seem essential to the success of American democracy. Moreover, the constitutional JURISPRUDENCE [I] through which this has been achieved is probably irreversible, reflecting fundamental dynamics in domestic law and international relations that enjoy widespread support.

The conception of political membership has grown steadily more fluid, functional, and context-dependent. Before the rise of the modern nation-state, political membership was based upon kinship and ethnic ties. Today, membership is a far more complex, variegated, multipurpose idea. For purposes such as voting, citizenship is the crucial status, whereas mere territorial presence suffices for attributing most constitutional rights. For purposes of participation in an economic common market, membership is constituted by supranational groupings, exemplified by the recently established United States–Canada free-trade zone and the still-evolving European Community.

We live in an increasingly integrated world. Transnational economic relationships are ubiquitous, international travel has become inexpensive, migratory pressures are enormous, environmental problems are often global, scientific and cultural exchanges are highly valued, and political cooperation among nations is more essential than ever before. Even within America's borders, citizenship represents an increasingly hollow ideal. It neither confers a distinctively advantageous status nor demands much of the individuals who possess it.

National citizenship, however, is not anachronistic. It provides a focus of political allegiance and emotional energy on a scale capable of satisfying deep human longings for solidarity, symbolic identification, and community. This is especially important in a liberal polity whose cosmopolitan aspirations for universal principles of human rights must somehow be balanced against the more parochial social commitments to family, ethnicity, locality, region, and nation. Although these political and emotional aspects of citizenship remain significant, American society seems resolved that little else of consequence shall be allowed to turn on citizenship. But within that general understanding and social consensus, the precise role of citizenship and the special rights and obligations that should attach to it are open questions. Here, only one proposition seems certain: Today's conceptions of citizenship may not be adequate to meet tomorrow's needs.

PETER H. SCHUCK

Bibliography

BRUBAKER, W. R., ED. 1989 *Immigration and the Politics of Citizenship in Europe and North America.* New York: University Press of America.

SCHUCK, PETER and SMITH, ROGERS 1986 *Citizenship Without Consent: Illegal Aliens in the American Polity.* New Haven, Conn.: Yale University Press.

CITY OF RENTON v. PLAYTIME THEATRES
475 U.S. 41 (1986)

Renton, Washington, passed a ZONING [4,I] ordinance that prohibited adult theaters from locating within 1,000 feet of any residence, church, park, or school. The owners of two adult theaters filed suit, claiming the ordinance violated the FIRST AMENDMENT [2,I]. The Supreme Court disagreed, holding 7–2 that the ordinance was a constitutional response to the serious social problems created by adult theaters.

Writing for six members of the majority, Justice WILLIAM H. REHNQUIST [3,I] argued that, even though the ordinance was clearly directed at theaters showing a certain kind of film, the law was properly analyzed as a "content neutral" regulation because it was "aimed not at the *content* of the films shown at 'adult motion picture theatres,' but rather at the *secondary effects* of such theatres on the surrounding community." According to Rehnquist, because the ordinance left 520 acres of land on which adult theaters could still locate, it represented a valid time, place, and manner regulation of the type upheld by the Court in many other "content neutral" cases. Rehnquist did not dispute that the zoning restriction might impose financial hardship on adult theaters, but said the First Amendment does not compel the state "to ensure that adult theaters, or any other kinds of speech-related businesses . . . will be able to obtain sites at bargain prices."

In dissent, Justice WILLIAM J. BRENNAN [1,I] objected to the majority's classification of the ordinance as "content neutral." But even under that standard, the ordinance was still unconstitutional according to Brennan because it was not narrowly tailored to fit a significant governmental interest.

JOHN G. WEST, JR.

(SEE ALSO: *Young v. American Mini Theatres* [I].)

CIVIL LIBERTIES
(Update)

The significant increase in the constitutional protection of CIVIL RIGHTS [1,I] and civil liberties that has occurred since the late 1950s has brought dramatically renewed focus to the question of the appropriate scope of JUDICIAL POWER [3,I]. Some argue that the federal judiciary, especially the Supreme Court, should play an active role in helping to shape public values—pushing a sometimes reluctant populace to make more meaningful the broad constitutional guarantees of liberty and equality. Others warn of the antidemocratic nature of JUDICIAL REVIEW [3]. Constitutional decision making often invalidates the policy choices of popularly elected officials in favor of the rulings of life-tenured unelected judges. Schools are desegregated, prisons are ordered restructured, ABORTION [1,I] regulations are voided, and SCHOOL PRAYERS [I] are prohibited—regardless of how the majority of Americans feel about these decisions.

This countermajoritarian "difficulty" has led to consistent demands for a more passive judiciary. Only if violations of the Constitution are unambiguous, involving significant deprivations of clearly understood civil liberties, the argument goes, should the independent federal judiciary intervene. Otherwise, American democracy should be allowed a loose rein. The choices of the majority, even in most areas that implicate liberty and equality interests, should be considered determinative. And most fundamentally, they should be respected by courts.

How one comes out on this perennial debate, of course, has a major impact upon how one regards the performance of the judiciary in the post–World War II era. The VINSON

COURT (1946–1953) [4] exercised its authority to invalidate governmental practices relatively rarely. As a result, for example, the criminal prosecution of communists under the Smith Act was upheld and the continued implementation of the SEPARATE-BUT-EQUAL DOCTRINE [4] by the states went largely undisturbed by the Court.

The WARREN COURT (1954–1969) [4], however, took a much different tack. Following BROWN V. BOARD OF EDUCATION (1954, 1955) [1], the Court launched a virtual constitutional revolution. In fairly rapid succession the Court handed down decisions not only combating RACIAL DISCRIMINATION [3,I] on a number of fronts but also requiring the REAPPORTIONMENT [3] of legislatures, the application of the bulk of the provisions of the BILL OF RIGHTS [1] against the states through the INCORPORATION DOCTRINE [2,I], giving more content to the FIRST AMENDMENT's [2,I] speech and press guarantees, protecting VOTING RIGHTS [4], prohibiting orchestrated public school prayer, assuring the poor some measure of ACCESS TO THE COURTS [1], and bolstering the demands of PROCEDURAL DUE PROCESS [3,I]. Other institutions of government, both state and federal, were forced to comply with the Justices' aggressive, and often inspiring, vision of the equal dignity of black and white, rich and poor, high and low.

The almost breathless pace of change wrought by the Warren Court led to significant calls for a judicial counterrevolution. President RICHARD M. NIXON [3] named jurists to the Court whom he believed would strictly construe the Constitution. In his view, this meant that the Court would interfere far less frequently with the political branches of government. In many ways, however, the BURGER COURT (1970–1986) [1] failed to fit the bill of STRICT CONSTRUCTION [4]. Some Warren-era doctrines—CRIMINAL PROCEDURE [1] guarantees and legal protections for the poor, for example—were pared back. But the Supreme Court, if anything, became even more accustomed to enforcing its vision of constitutional mandate against other government actors. Important women's rights, including a right to choose to have an abortion, were recognized for the first time. Protections for FREEDOM OF SPEECH [2,I] were expanded. More surprisingly, perhaps, the Burger Court aggressively patrolled what it considered the appropriate division and SEPARATION OF POWERS [4] among the branches of the federal government. By striking down the LEGISLATIVE VETO [3] procedure in IMMIGRATION AND NATURALIZATION SERVICE V. CHADHA (1983) [2], for example, the Court voided, in one stroke, more federal legislative enactments than it had previously in its entire history. The Burger Court may not have been an inspiring Court; it was, however, a powerful one.

The REHNQUIST COURT [I], of course, has yet to sketch fully its vision of judicial authority. WILLIAM H. REHN-

QUIST [3,I] was confirmed as CHIEF JUSTICE [1] in 1986. ANTONIN SCALIA [I] joined the Court in the same year. ANTHONY M. KENNEDY [I] replaced Justice LEWIS F. POWELL [3,I] in early 1988. Although it is true that a few terms do not a Court make, significant signs are beginning to appear which suggest that the Rehnquist Court may reject much of the activism of its two immediate predecessors. It is possible that the Court will, in the coming decade, intentionally reduce its role in protecting civil liberties through the interpretation of what Justice WILLIAM J. BRENNAN [1,I] has termed the "majestic generalities" of the Constitution and the Bill of Rights. There is increasing reason to believe that after thirty years of political turmoil over the role of the judiciary in American government, a passive Court may be in the making.

Consider a few prominent examples. In 1986 the Supreme Court dramatically announced a halt to the growth of a favorite Burger Court product, the RIGHT OF PRIVACY [3,I]. The decision in BOWERS V. HARDWICK (1986) [I] refused to afford constitutional protection to the private, consensual homosexual acts of an adult male. Michael Hardwick had been arrested—though the prosecution was subsequently dropped—for violating Georgia's sodomy statute by having sexual relations with another adult man in his own bedroom. Hardwick claimed that the Georgia law violated the right to privacy. Earlier decisions like GRISWOLD V. CONNECTICUT (1965) [2], which protected the right to use contraceptives, and ROE V. WADE (1973) [3], recognizing the right to terminate a pregnancy, had characterized the right to privacy as "fundamental" and "deeply rooted in this Nation's history and tradition."

The Court in *Bowers* declared that it was not "incline[d] to take a more expansive view of [its] authority to discover new fundamental rights. . . . The Court is most vulnerable and comes nearest to illegitimacy when it deals with judge-made constitutional law having little or no cognizable roots in the language or design of the Constitution." The majority of the Court claimed that if it were to give credence to claims such as that made by Hardwick, it would be "tak[ing] to itself further authority to govern the country without express constitutional authority." The adjective "further" assumes that the Supreme Court has already moved beyond any supportable role in the constitutional structure. It may also suggest that if *Bowers* is the reversal of a significant trend of decision making in the privacy arena, others will not be far behind.

In the same year, the Supreme Court upheld a municipal ZONING [4,I] ordinance making it illegal to locate an "adult" theater within a thousand feet of a residential area, single-family dwelling, church, park, or school. The opinion in CITY OF RENTION V. PLAYTIME THEATRES, INC. (1986) [I] carried many of the suggestions of the diminished JUDICIAL ROLE that appeared in *Bowers*. As a result, the decision allowed the regulation of constitutionally protected (nonobscene) speech in order to "maintain property values . . . and preserve the . . . quality of the city's neighborhoods."

Perhaps even more telling, though, was the crux of the Court's rationale. The fact that the statute "may" have been motivated, at least in part, by the city's desire to restrict "the exercise of First Amendment rights" was ruled beyond the scope of the Court's review; "[T]his Court will not strike down an otherwise constitutional statute on the basis of an alleged illicit legislative motive." Furthermore, the Court declared that it is beyond the judicial function to "appraise the wisdom of the city's decision. . . . The city must be allowed a reasonable opportunity to experiment with solutions to admittedly serious problems." This language is at least somewhat surprising in a case involving the regulation of speech that is, as even the Court admits, protected by the First Amendment. In an earlier time, one can almost imagine Justice HUGO L. BLACK [1] reminding in dissent that legislatures retain a great deal of leeway for experimentation without violating the Bill of Rights.

In the context of public education, the Supreme Court has taken these declarations of deference to local decision makers considerably farther. In BETHEL SCHOOL DISTRICT V. FRASER (1986) [I] the Court sustained a school's suspension of a student for making a sexually suggestive nominating speech at a voluntary assembly, concluding flatly that the "determination of what manner of speech in . . . school assembly is inappropriate properly rests with the school board." And in HAZELWOOD SCHOOL DISTRICT V. KUHLMEIER (1988) [I], in which the Court upheld the censorship of a high school newspaper, it determined that judicial oversight must be reduced in order to give local school administrators the opportunity to "disassociate" themselves from the messages contained in school-sponsored student publications. Accordingly, principals may constitutionally exercise editorial control over high school newspapers "so long as their actions are reasonably related to legitimate pedagogical concerns."

The Supreme Court's controversial abortion ruling in WEBSTER V. REPRODUCTIVE HEALTH SERVICES (1989) [I] reflects a major change in emphasis as well. Although a majority refused to overrule *Roe v. Wade*, the Court recognized considerably greater authority in state governments to regulate the abortion process. Chief Justice Rehnquist's PLURALITY OPINION [3] characterized the Court's prior abortion decisions as "unsound in principle, and unworkable in practice." *Roe's* privacy protections are, in his view, "not found in the text of the Constitution or in any place else one would expect to find a constitutional principle." Moreover, they result in the Justices of the Supreme Court acting as the country's "ex officio medical board," accepting or rejecting medical practices and standards throughout the United States. Surely, the Chief Justice wrote, the goal of constitutional adjudication is not "to remove inexorably politically divisive issues from the ambit of the legislative process."

Justice Scalia was even clearer in his declarations that the Supreme Court has no business deciding sensitive policy issues like abortion. He described *Roe* as asserting a "self-awarded sovereignty over a field where [the Court] has little proper business since the cruel questions posed are political . . . not juridical." As a result, he would overrule the 1973 abortion decision outright, returning the difficult human rights issue to the legislatures for determination.

Other examples—such as the Supreme Court's rulings that minors and mentally retarded defendants can be subjected to CAPITAL PUNISHMENT [1,I]—could be mentioned. No doubt, though, these few instances constitute far less than a major cross-sampling of the Court's work. In the past several terms the Court has occasionally ventured into new arenas of judicial purview. These areas have primarily involved separation of powers claims rather than classic civil liberties issues. But the Justices have also bolstered the protection afforded to some economic rights and, even more surprising, tentatively entered the difficult thicket of the GERRYMANDER [2].

Still, the likelihood is strong that a significant trend is afoot. The present Supreme Court seems determined to reduce its role as a policymaker in American government. If new and difficult civil liberties claims are pressed, the judiciary may be less inclined to impose its will on the more democratically accountable branches of government. Even the Court's higher-profile constitutional decisions reflect something of this tendency. In the controversial and widely noted FLAG DESECRATION [2,I] case, *Texas v. Johnson* (1989), a majority of the Court voted to reverse a state conviction based upon the burning of a flag. Justice Kennedy's influential concurring opinion, however, emphasized that the Court "cannot here ask another branch to share responsibility . . . for we are presented with a clear and simple statute to be judged against a pure command of the Constitution." This desire to defer to other government actors—if possible—may be the hallmark of the judiciary in the years to come. As a matter of democratic theory, that choice may be a wise one. For this constitutional democracy, however, the verdict may be significantly more complex.

GENE R. NICHOL

(SEE ALSO: *Desegregation* [2]; *Freedom of the Press* [2,I]; *Prisoners' Rights* [3,I]; *Religious Liberty* [3,I]; *Separation of Church and State* [4,I]; *Sexual Orientation* [I]; *Sexual Preference and the Constitution* [4].)

Bibliography

DWORKIN, RONALD 1986 *Law's Empire*. Cambridge, Mass.: Harvard University Press.

FISHER, LOUIS 1988 *Constitutional Dialogues*. Princeton, N.J.: Princeton University Press.

GARVEY, J. and ALEINIKOFF, ALEXANDER 1989 *Modern Constitutional Theory: A Reader*. St. Paul, Minn.: West Publishing Co.

GREENWALT, KENT 1988 *Religious Convictions and Political Choice*. New York: Oxford University Press.

LEVINSON, SANFORD 1988 *Constitutional Faith*. Princeton, N.J.: Princeton University Press.

MACKINNON, CATHERINE 1987 *Feminism Unmodified*. Cambridge, Mass.: Harvard University Press.

NAGEL, ROBERT 1989 *Constitutional Cultures*. Berkeley: University of California Press.

PERRY, MICHAEL 1988 *Morality, Politics and Law*. New York: Oxford University Press.

SYMPOSIUM 1987 The Bork Nomination. *Cardozo Law Review* 9:1–530.

TRIBE, LAURENCE 1988 *American Constitutional Law*, 2nd ed. New York: Foundation Press.

CIVIL RIGHTS
(Update)

In contemporary legal discourse, civil rights refer principally to legislative and judicial proscriptions against racial SEGREGATION [4] and RACIAL DISCRIMINATION [3,I]—although some branches of civil rights law concern SEX DISCRIMINATION [4,I] and discrimination based on religion, ethnicity, national origin, physical or mental handicap, and SEXUAL ORIENTATION [I]. The primary sources of civil rights are the Civil War amendments to the Constitution and congressional legislation enacted pursuant to these amendments. In common usage, however, the term civil rights includes antidiscrimination legislation enacted under Congress's other constitutional powers, federal regulations, executive orders, and state laws, as well as judicial decisions interpreting all of these sources.

There have been two major periods of civil rights activity. The first, commonly referred to as Reconstruction, began at the end of the Civil War and lasted little more than a decade. The beginning of the second period, sometimes called the Second Reconstruction, is often placed at 1954, with the Supreme Court's decision in BROWN V. BOARD OF EDUCATION OF TOPEKA (1954) [I].

Although all three branches of the national government have participated in establishing the scope of civil rights, in recent years the Supreme Court has been the focus of continuing interest and often heated debate. The Court has played a highly visible role in determining the applicability of formal civil rights guarantees to social activity, and since *Brown*, the Court has been widely seen as the institution primarily responsible for articulating the morality of racial equality. This perception is ironic, considering the Court's role in eviscerating civil rights legislation during the first RECONSTRUCTION [I]—a history that seems especially vivid in light of some of the Court's recent decisions narrowing the substantive content of civil rights.

Civil rights jurisprudence generally involves two broad issues: defining the right that has allegedly been violated and determining the scope of the remedy once a violation has been found. In theory, the latter follows the former because the Supreme Court often says that the nature of the violation determines the scope of the remedy. However, in practice, the relation between the two is not so neatly defined. First, civil rights remedies do not ineluctably follow the finding of a violation. For example, although the Court in *Brown v. Board of Education* determined that segregation violated the constitutional rights of black school children, the aggrieved children were forced to await *Brown II v. Board of Education* (1955) before the Court issued a remedy. Even this remedy was partial; school boards were not required to eliminate the violation immediately, but "with all deliberate speed." It is also not clear that determining the scope of civil rights remedies actually follows the determination that a violation has occurred. The reverse may occasionally be true: commentators often speculate that the Court's decision to reject a claim of constitutional injury has been influenced by concerns over its ability to administer a manageable and effective remedy. Whatever the exact sequence may be, the narrowed conception of civil rights that evolved during the midstages of the Second Reconstruction has been accompanied by a correspondingly limited scope for remedial policies.

Recent conflicts over civil rights issues reflect the ongoing effort to derive specific resolutions from general principles set forth in the Constitution—an effort that historically has produced shifting and sometimes contradictory interpretations. The THIRTEENTH AMENDMENT [4], for example, renders SLAVERY [4] and its badges and incidents unconstitutional, whereas the FOURTEENTH AMENDMENT [2,I] guarantees equal CITIZENSHIP [1,I] and equality before the law. The late-nineteenth-century Court determined that neither PRIVATE DISCRIMINATION [3] nor state-mandated segregation implicated these civil guarantees. Yet these principles are currently interpreted to permit statutory regulation of private discrimination and to prohibit state-sponsored racial segregation.

Thus, although it seems clear that equality before the law is a basic civil right guaranteed by the Fourteenth Amendment, this ideal has historically offered no clear basis for determining the scope of civil rights because

equality is subject to multiple interpretations. In the modern civil rights era, equality has been interpreted to forbid racial discrimination, but even this formula offers no clear basis for determining the scope of civil rights. For example, it is not clear whether the proscription against racial discrimination applies only to explicit racial categories or whether it applies more broadly to policies, practices, and customs that appear, on their face, neutral, but exact similar exclusionary effects. It is also not clear whether race-conscious efforts to remedy the effects of racial discrimination are consistent with or a violation of the prohibition. It is also not clear which background circumstances and conditions are relevant and which are not in determining whether an act or policy is discriminatory. Anatole France's oft-quoted saw that "Law in its majestic equality forbids the rich and poor alike from sleeping under bridges" illustrates the transparency of purely formal conceptions of equality that do not acknowledge the importance of social and economic inequality.

Post-1986 developments manifest a ripening of conflict over the question of whether civil rights law contemplates only formal equality or whether it contemplates something more. Judges, scholars, legislators, and laymen have debated whether racial equality requires only the cessation of practices that explicitly discriminate on the basis of race or whether it also demands a full dismantling of practices, policies, and structures that continue to produce racial inequality. The opposing approaches to these questions derive from competing conceptualizations of civil rights: the antidiscrimination approach and the antidomination approach.

The antidiscrimination approach focuses on achieving formal equality through the eradication of racial classifications and purposeful discrimination. It emphasizes individual-centered harms and colorblind remedies. In contrast, the antidomination view tends to look beyond formally manifested or intentional discrimination to the circumstances and conditions of inequality. Ultimately, this wider perspective envisions the creation of legal remedies and social practices that will foster greater RACIAL BALANCE [3] throughout society.

Many, if not most, civil rights decisions are consistent with either approach. However, rough distinctions between the two are apparent in current debates over the extent to which pervasive conditions of racial inequality implicate civil rights and bear on the scope of civil rights remedies. The doctrinal arenas in which this conflict is most apparent have involved discriminatory intent and AFFIRMATIVE ACTION [1,I].

Although the scope of the intent doctrine was largely determined in the 1970s, its full impact has become increasingly apparent in subsequent years. Discriminatory intent was first articulated as the *sine qua non* of an EQUAL

PROTECTION [2] claim in WASHINGTON V. DAVIS (1976) [4]. In this case, plaintiffs challenged the use of a reading and writing test to screen applicants for employment in Washington, D.C., as police officers. Not shown to measure skills necessary for effective performance as a police officer, the test served as an effective barrier to black recruitment. The Court nevertheless determined that an equal-protection claim could be sustained only if the test had been adopted with the intent to discriminate against minority applicants. This intent standard, as further clarified in later cases, could not be satisfied even where the employer adopting the challenged policy or practice did so with full knowledge of its disproportionate impact. In recent years, the discriminatory-intent doctrine has, in effect, provided a presumption of constitutionality to most racially unequal conditions because it is the unusual case in which some discriminatory intent is manifest in a governmental decision. Thus, racial inequalities that have historically burdened nonwhite communities and that continue to exist today in employment, education, housing, and criminal justice generally do not implicate civil rights. Although the Supreme Court has acknowledged that such disparities often result from societal discrimination, unless a particular discriminatory decision can be identified and isolated, such inequalities are not seen to raise any civil rights issues and thus require no remedy.

Many commentators and some members of the Court have criticized the Court's use of the discriminatory-intent test to distinguish inequalities that violate the Constitution from those that do not. They assert that the presence of explicit intent should not exhaust the definition of constitutional injury. Some point out that the model of discrimination contemplated by the intent requirement is simply anachronistic. In the aftermath of *Brown*'s rejection of formal white supremacy, few decision makers currently adopt policies that explicitly discriminate against blacks.

Even on its own terms, the intent standard is inadequate, for racial animus may play a role in decision making, yet be difficult to prove. Indeed, racial motivation may remain hidden even to the actor. Yet another problem is that the intent standard tends to focus inquiry on a single allegedly discriminatory actor when there are often multiple actors, many of whom have acted without animus, but who, in the aggregate, perpetuate the discriminatory effects of past discrimination.

The principle of purposeful discrimination also fails to address inequality that is reproduced by social practices that have now become ingrained in American society. Critics have argued that the intent standard embodies a superficial conceptualization of formal equality in that its critical scope focuses only on the most external aspects of racial discrimination. This framework virtually excludes consideration of racial categories that are effectively created through apparently neutral practices. Sometimes referred to as "procedural discrimination," practices and policies that do not discriminate on their face, but predictably produce racial disparities throughout society are more common sources of inequity than are formal racial categories. Unvalidated standardized tests, subjective evaluation procedures, nepotism, word-of-mouth hiring practices, and even the high-school diploma requirements can unfairly limit the opportunities of minorities. Whether intentional or unthinking, these practices disadvantage and burden minorities in ways that are closely related to the formal discriminations of the past.

Such criticisms are informed by a view that the moral and political objective of the Fourteenth Amendment is to empower the national government to eliminate the effects of white supremacy. Eliminating intentional discrimination does not fully satisfy this mandate, as purposeful harm is simply one of many means of perpetuating white supremacy.

Despite the effective limits that the intent standard places on the scope of civil rights litigation, defenders marshal several arguments to justify its currency. One is that intentional discrimination prevailed during the period preceding *Brown*, and it is this form of discrimination that is now understood as incompatible with the nation's ideals. Institutionally, the intent standard is justified because intentional racial discrimination is precisely the kind of perversion of democracy that the Court is empowered to correct. Remedying these harms and eliminating these tendencies justify and exhaust the moral and ideological commitment of civil rights. Any other rule, it is argued, would involve judicial overreaching and undue interference with myriad governmental and private practices that sometimes produce racially disproportionate results. Moreover, it would stretch the Court's institutional and symbolic resources to fashion appropriate remedies if a broader standard were used. In sum, there is no ideological, political, or moral justification to move beyond intentional discrimination. Racially disparate results do not themselves speak to civil rights; it is racially unequal treatment that constitutes the crux of the injury. Under this view, the intent standard thus effectively mediates between legitimate and illegitimate conceptions of civil rights.

The intent standard, along with other doctrines in current vogue with the Supreme Court's majority, represents a refusal to extend constitutional protections to preclude institutional and systemic discrimination. Although aggregate views of racial disparities suggest that racial separation and stratification are still common in employment, housing, voting, and the criminal justice system, this view is rendered irrelevant by the Court's current framework that seeks one actor when there are often several and current and demonstrably direct causes when many are historical and cumulative.

Those who support an antidomination view of racial equality note that aggregate views of race paint a picture of society that resembles conditions prevailing during periods in which white supremacy was more openly advocated and racial discrimination more explicitly practiced. They regard these disparities as raising legitimate civil rights issues not only because of their probable connection to the more explicit policies of the not-too-distant past, but also because of the devastating effect on the life chances of minorities and the likelihood that such conditions will reproduce themselves for generations to come.

Earlier decisions suggested that the Court might be receptive to this view. For example, in GRIGGS V. DUKE POWER CO. (1971) [2], the Court ruled that an employment practice that disproportionately harmed minorities constituted EMPLOYMENT DISCRIMINATION [2] under the CIVIL RIGHTS ACT OF 1964 [1], whether or not the practice was adopted with the intent to discriminate. The fact that the practice disparately burdened minorities was enough to require the employer to produce evidence that the practice was a business necessity.

In subsequent years, however, the Court increasingly disfavored such systemic views of discrimination. An ominous indication of the full implications of this trend was suggested by MCCLESKEY V. KEMP (1987) [I] and was reinforced in *Wards Cove Packing Co. v. Antonio* (1989).

In *McCleskey v. Kemp,* Justice LEWIS F. POWELL [3,I] accepted the validity of a study indicating that African-Americans in Georgia who killed whites were significantly more likely to receive the death penalty than were blacks who killed blacks or whites who killed either whites or blacks. Nonetheless, the Court determined that these statistics did not substantiate an equal-protection challenge to the Georgia death penalty. Aggregate statistics could not be used because they could not support an inference that intentional racial discrimination had influenced the disposition of the defendant's particular case. Moreover, other factors, such as the state's interests in imposing the death penalty, in maintaining prosecutorial discretion, and in protecting the integrity of jury deliberations, precluded the defendant from gaining access to information needed to prove that racial discrimination affected the disposition of his case.

Although *McCleskey v. Kemp* might have been reconciled as consistent with the distinction that the Court drew between constitutional claims (in which systemic claims were generally disfavored) and statutory claims (in which the Court had adopted a more flexible approach toward such claims), *Wards Cove* demonstrates that the Court's rejection of systemic claims is not limited to constitutional claims. In *Wards Cove,* the Court significantly narrowed *Griggs* to require, in part, that employees challenging employment practices that create racial disparities must specify and isolate each practice and its effects.

McCleskey and *Wards Cove* are two of several cases that illustrate how the Court in the 1980s has employed various analytical and normative preferences to reject the appeal for systemic relief. Its techniques include viewing causation as isolated rather than interrelated, demanding showings of contemporary rather than historical explanations for racial disparities, and embracing merely formal rather than substantive equality as the objective of civil rights law.

The predominance of the intent standard has significantly affected the development of affirmative action, another area in which the conflict between competing visions of civil rights has been most apparent over the past decade. Affirmative action, while largely referring to race-conscious remedial measures, also encompasses more general efforts to dismantle segregation and to cease the reproduction of racial inequality. GREEN V. COUNTY SCHOOL BOARD OF NEW KENT (1968) [2] best represents this broader conceptualization of affirmative action. In this case, the Supreme Court determined that a "free choice" policy was insufficient to remedy the dual school system created by the defendant school board's previous *de jure* segregation. Equality required not only a cessation of discriminatory practices, but in addition, an affirmative effort to dismantle the racial segregation that had been created through express governmental policy and that would likely be maintained by the practices that were institutionally and societally ingrained.

The current controversy over affirmative action centers on the extent to which this task of dismantling a dual society should be undertaken by governmental and private entities in various contexts. Affirmative efforts have been made to integrate public and private industries, higher education, and professional trades. Affirmative-action plans have been developed as remedies following findings of discrimination; some were included in consent decrees and still others were developed voluntarily, sometimes under the threat of suit, but other times out of genuine commitments to increase the numbers of underrepresented groups in various walks of life.

Critics of affirmative action vigorously assailed the use of race-conscious strategies to benefit minority individuals who had not themselves been shown to be victims of discrimination. Their principal argument is that affirmative action is simply "disease as cure," in that it makes use of race classification to distribute opportunities on the basis of race rather than on individual merits. This is precisely the harm that was imposed on racial minorities and that cannot be justified on nondiscrimination grounds. They argue, moreover, that whites harmed by such efforts are in fact victims of racial discrimination and that the use of race-conscious efforts to correct racial imbalances violates the Fourteenth Amendment.

Affirmative action has been most often justified by supporters as necessary to remedy the effects of past discrimination. Most of the arguments boil down to a view that a full remedy for racial discrimination requires affirmative efforts to restructure racial hierarchy by redistributing educational, economic, and employment opportunities across racial groups. Affirmative action has also been characterized as essential to the nondiscrimination principle. In this view, it is a bottom-line effort to minimize the effects of racial bias that works its way into evaluation systems that have historically favored dominant values and interests. Some argue that affirmative action serves as reparation for past discrimination, whereas others justify affirmative action as essential to creating a future society that is not racially stratified. In the words of one Justice, "to get beyond race, we must first take race into account."

Despite the polarized nature of the ongoing affirmative-action debate, affirmative action is a doctrinal area in which the fluctuating majorities on the Court and its shifting sensibilities since 1986 are best illustrated. Indeed, the Court has only recently reached an apparent consensus on the constitutionality of affirmative action.

The much awaited decision in REGENTS OF UNIVERSITY OF CALIFORNIA V. BAKKE (1978) [3] produced something of a stalemate: state universities were permitted to use race as one factor in admission decisions; but, absent some evidence of past discrimination on their part, they could not set aside seats for which only minorities could compete. After Bakke, the constitutional status of affirmative action remained murky. In subsequent cases, a shifting majority upheld affirmative-action plans adopted by the federal government in construction contracts (in FULLILOVE V. KLUTZNICK [1980] [2]) and in private industry (in UNITED STEELWORKERS OF AMERICA V. WEBER [1979] [4]). However, growing concerns over the rights of whites disadvantaged by these efforts finally came to the fore in FIREFIGHTERS' LOCAL #1784 V. STOTTS (1984) [2], in which the Court precluded federal courts from ordering a city employer subject to an affirmative-action CONSENT DECREE [1] to protect the jobs of less-senior minorities by laying off more-senior whites.

Foes of affirmative action subsequently interpreted Stotts to ban all affirmative-action remedies that benefited persons other than actual victims of discrimination. The U.S. Justice Department, after urging the Court to make such a ruling, used Stotts as a basis for challenging affirmative-action programs operated by hundreds of cities and states pursuant to consent decrees. Yet Stotts failed to produce a clear consensus regarding the constitutionality of affirmative action. Subsequent Court decisions upholding other affirmative-action plans benefitting "non-victims" indicated that Stotts was not read as encompassing a broad rejection of race-conscious remedies.

Despite these decisions, however, there remained on the Court a vocal opposition to such race-conscious measures. That slim majorities upheld these measures suggested that the constitutionality of affirmative action remained highly contested and subject to limitation. In 1989, a majority finally coalesced in CITY OF RICHMOND V. J. A. CROSON CO. (1989) [I] to hold that race-conscious affirmative-action programs were subject to STRICT SCRUTINY [4]. The city of Richmond adopted a thirty percent set-aside program for minority contractors. Although Richmond was fifty percent black, only one sixty-seventh of one percent of all city contracts had gone to minority contractors. The Court held that the city could not undertake an affirmative-action program to correct such gross disparities without some evidence that black contractors had been discriminated against in the past and that this discrimination had caused the disparities. Particularly striking is the Court's refusal to recognize the relevance of Congress's previous findings of industry-wide discrimination, and its willingness to reduce centuries of white supremacy to the same plane as two decades of affirmative action. Such findings could not be "shared," but had to be proven anew in Richmond.

Croson demonstrates how the combination of the intent requirement and the application of strict scrutiny to affirmative action combine to create the tragic irony that institutional and systemic perpetuation of racial inequality escapes constitutional scrutiny, while efforts to break these patterns and practices are constitutionally prohibited.

Moreover, Croson represents a decisive victory of the more formal antidiscrimination approach over the more contextual antisubordination approach, at least where Congress has not adopted the latter approach. (See METRO BROADCASTING V. F.C.C. [1990] [I].)

Critics argue that traditional protections for nonwhites are being eroded while the civil rights laws are being interpreted vigorously to preclude some of the more effective remedies. This claim is not implausible when one compares, for example, the language in Croson (explaining how the Court's deep commitment to eliminate all forms of racial discrimination mandates a rejection of even remedial race classifications) with the Court's willingness in PATTERSON V. MCLEAN CREDIT UNION (1989) [I] to interpret the CIVIL RIGHTS ACT OF 1866 [I] to leave a private employer's racial harassment unremedied under this statute. Although the contrasting protections in each of these cases might be reconciled by focusing on the distinctions between the separate doctrinal categories under which these cases arise, it is hard to ignore the apparent trend in which minorities are receiving less protection against traditional forms of race discrimination while the racially privileged are receiving more.

The Court's recent race jurisprudence also suggests that civil rights litigation no longer occupies the status of "high priority litigation." The Court seems to have rejected the view that civil rights plaintiffs play a special role as private attorneys general seeking to effectuate society's highest interest in eradicating discrimination, root and branch. In technical interpretations, the Court has narrowed the availability of remedies and simultaneously shifted advantages to employers and often to white males. Most troubling are rule 11 cases, in which courts have levied severe penalties against civil rights litigants for bringing suits that were judged to be "frivolous." Although rule 11 of the FEDERAL RULES OF CIVIL PROCEDURE [2] lay dormant until it was raised in 1983, nearly half of all rule 11 sanctions have involved civil rights and public-interest cases. Other research also suggests civil rights cases are also disproportionately likely to be dismissed given the heightened pleading threshold placed on such claims. The overall effect of these "technical" opinions has been to raise the risk and cost of litigating civil rights claims at precisely the same time that shifts in substantive rules make it unlikely that a plaintiff will prevail. The probable consequence of such decisions is the chilling of the civil rights bar. The long-term consequence may be that law may cease to serve as a meaningful deterrent to discriminatory behavior.

These recent developments have led many to conclude that the Second Reconstruction is largely a dead letter and that the period is now more aptly described as a post–civil rights era. Indeed, the parallels with the Second Reconstruction seem to confirm the cyclical nature of civil rights protection and, more troubling, the cyclical nature of its decline.

KIMBERLÉ CRENSHAW

(SEE ALSO: *Race-Consciousness* [I]; *Racial Preference* [I].)

Bibliography

FREEMAN, ALAN 1990 Antidiscrimination Law: The View from 1989. *Tulane Law Review* 64:1407–1441.

LAWRENCE, CHARLES 1987 The Id, the Ego, and Equal Protection: Reckoning with Unconscious Racism. *Stanford Law Review* 39:317–387.

ORTIZ, DANIEL 1989 The Myth of Intent in Equal Protection. *Stanford Law Review* 41:1105–1150.

SCHNAPPER, ERIC 1983 Perpetuation of Past Discrimination. *Harvard Law Review* 96:828–864.

STRAUSS, DAVID A. 1986 The Myth of Colorblindness. *Supreme Court Review* 1986:99–134.

TRIBE, LAURENCE H. 1988 *American Constitutional Law*, 2nd ed. New York: Foundation Press.

WILLIAMS, PATRICIA 1989 The Obliging Shell: An Informal Essay on Formal Equal Opportunity. *Michigan Law Review* 87:2128–2151.

CIVIL RIGHTS MOVEMENT

Because the basic rights of CITIZENSHIP [1,I] were not equally available to all Americans at the nation's inception, civil rights movements involving groups excluded from full political participation have been a continuing feature of U.S. history. Males without property, African Americans, and women are among the groups that have engaged in sustained struggles to establish, protect, or expand their rights as American citizens. These struggles have resulted in fundamental departures from the limited conceptions of citizenship and the role of government that prevailed during the early national era.

The term "civil rights movement" more narrowly refers to the collective efforts of African Americans to advance in American society. These efforts are aspects of a broader, long-term black freedom struggle seeking goals beyond CIVIL RIGHTS [1,I], but they have had particularly important impact on dominant conceptions of the rights of American citizens and the role of government in protecting these rights. Although the Supreme Court in the DRED SCOTT [2] decision of 1857 negated the citizenship status of African Americans, the subsequent extensions of egalitarian principles to African Americans resulted in generalized expansions of the scope of constitutionally protected rights. In particular, both the FOURTEENTH AMENDMENT [2,I] and the FIFTEENTH AMENDMENT [2] to the Constitution, despite retrogressive Court decisions such as PLESSY V. FERGUSON (1896) [3], ultimately served as foundations for major civil rights reforms benefiting black Americans and other groups. During the twentieth century, African Americans have participated in many racial advancement efforts that have enlarged the opportunities and protections available to individuals in other groups. More recently, as a result of sustained protest movements of the period after WORLD WAR II [I], the term "civil rights" has come to refer not only to governmental policies relating to the equal treatment of individuals but also to policies equalizing the allocation of resources among groups. In short, the modern civil rights movement in the United States has redefined as well as pursued rights.

The National Association for the Advancement of Colored People (NAACP), an interracial group founded in 1909, has been the most enduring institution directing the course of twentieth-century American civil rights movements. Although many organizations later challenged the NAACP's priorities and its reliance on the tactics of litigation and governmental lobbying, the group's large membership and its increasingly effective affiliate, the NAACP LEGAL DEFENSE & EDUCATIONAL FUND [3], made civil rights reforms into principal black political objectives. Among the outgrowths of NAACP-sponsored legal suits were the Supreme Court's SMITH V. ALLWRIGHT (1944) [4] decision outlawing white primary elections and the BROWN V. BOARD OF EDUCATION (1954, 1955) [1] decision against segregated public schools. These landmark cases helped to reverse earlier Court decisions—such as *Plessy*—that limited the scope of civil rights protections.

In the years after the *Brown* decision, other civil rights organizations departed from the NAACP's reform strategy and placed more emphasis on protest and mass mobilization. Starting with the Montgomery bus boycott of 1955–1956, southern blacks, aided by northern allies, successfully used boycotts, mass meetings, marches, rallies, sit-ins, and other insurgent tactics to speed the pace of civil rights reform. The Southern Christian Leadership Council (SCLC), founded in 1957 and led for many years by MARTIN LUTHER KING, JR. [3], and the Student Nonviolent Coordinating Committee (SNCC), founded in 1960, spearheaded a series of mass struggles against white racial domination in the South. The NAACP also supplied many of the participants and much of the legal support for these struggles, while the predominantly white Congress of Racial Equality (CORE) contributed activists and expertise in the use of Gandhian nonviolent tactics. Although DESEGREGATION [2] was initially the main focus of southern mass movements, economic and political concerns were evident from their inception.

King and the SCLC played especially important roles in mobilizing mass protest campaigns in the Alabama cities of Birmingham and Selma in 1963 and 1965. SCLC leaders orchestrated clashes between nonviolent demonstrators and often brutal law enforcement personnel. Such highly publicized confrontations made northern whites more aware of southern racial inequities, particularly the pervasive and antiquated Jim Crow system of public SEGREGATION [4]. As the southern struggle's best-known spokesperson, King sought to link black civil rights aspirations with widely accepted, long-established political principles. During 1961 he identified the democratic ideals of the Founding Fathers as an unrealized "noble dream." "On the one hand, we have proudly professed the principles of democracy, and on the other hand, we have sadly practiced the very antithesis of those principles," he told an audience at Lincoln University. Speaking at the 1963 March on Washington, he insisted that the DECLARATION OF INDEPENDENCE [2] and the Constitution were "a promissory note" guaranteeing all Americans "the unalienable

rights of life, liberty, and the pursuit of happiness." By exposing the contradictions between American ideals and southern racial realities, the SCLC's southern campaigns strengthened northern white support for civil rights reforms.

Although the SNCC was an outgrowth of the student sit-in movement of 1960, its most significant activities were concentrated in the rural areas of Mississippi and Alabama. In these areas, SNCC staff members worked with indigenous black leaders seeking to overcome economic and political oppression. During the first half of the 1960s, SNCC concentrated its efforts on the achievement of voting rights for southern blacks and federal protection for civil rights workers. SNCC organizers also helped to create new institutions, such as the Mississippi Freedom Democratic party and the Lowndes County (Alabama) Freedom Organization, under local black leadership. By 1966, the "black power" slogan, popularized by SNCC's chair Stokely Carmichael, summarized the group's emerging ideas of a struggle seeking political, economic, and cultural objectives beyond narrowly defined civil rights reforms.

By the late 1960s, organizations such as the NAACP, SCLC, and SNCC faced increasingly strong challenges from "black nationalist" leaders and new militant organizations, such as the Black Panther party. Often influenced by Malcolm X and by Pan-African ideologies, proponents of "black liberation" saw civil rights reforms as insufficient because they did not address the problems of poor blacks. Black nationalists also pointed out that African American citizenship had resulted from the involuntary circumstances of enslavement. In addition, racial-liberation proponents often saw the African American freedom struggle in international terms, as a movement for "human rights" and national "self-determination" rather than for civil rights.

The most significant legislation to result from the mass struggles of the 1960s were the CIVIL RIGHTS ACT OF 1964 [1] and the VOTING RIGHTS ACT OF 1965 [4]. (Congress also passed notable civil rights bills in 1968, 1972, and 1990.) Taken together, these laws greatly enhanced the civic status of blacks, women, and other minority groups and placed greater responsibility on the federal government to protect such groups from discriminatory treatment. Although the 1964 and 1965 acts were in some respects simply restatements of protections specified in the constitutional amendments enacted during RECONSTRUCTION [I], the impact of the new legislation was greater because of the expanded scope of federal regulatory powers and the continued militancy by victims of discrimination.

Since the mid-1960s, national civil rights policies have evinced awareness that antidiscrimination legislation was not sufficient to achieve tangible improvements in the living conditions of many blacks or to bring about equalization of the distribution of resources and services among racial groups in the United States. In 1968 the National Advisory Commission on Civil Disorders (the Kerner Commission) concluded that despite civil right reforms, the nation was "moving toward two societies, one black, one white—separate and unequal." By the time of this report, the liberal coalition that had supported passage of the major civil rights legislation was divided over the role, if any, government should play in eliminating these persistent racial inequities. A "white backlash" against black militancy and claims that black gains had resulted in "reverse discrimination" against whites undermined support for major new civil rights initiatives during the 1970s and 1980s.

Although militant protest activity declined after the 1960s, civil rights movements have remained a significant feature of American political life. The increased black participation in the American political system that resulted from previous struggles lessened black reliance on extralegal tactics, but civil rights issues continued to stimulate protest, particularly when previous gains appeared to be threatened. Furthermore, women, homosexuals, disabled people, and other groups suffering discriminatory treatment have mobilized civil rights movements and created organizations of their own, thereby contributing to the continuing national dialogue regarding the scope of civil rights and the role of government.

During the 1970s and 1980s, debate continued over the appropriateness of employment AFFIRMATIVE ACTION [1,I] programs and court-ordered compensatory remedies for historically rooted patterns of discrimination. Nevertheless, despite contention regarding these issues and notwithstanding the conservative political climate of the period, most national civil rights policies established during the 1960s have survived. Moreover, civil rights advocates have continued to press, with limited success, toward implementation of policies for group advancement rather than individual rights, tangible gains rather than civil status, and equality of social outcomes rather than equality of opportunity. The modern African American freedom and liberation struggles of the 1960s therefore produced a major but still controversial shift in prevailing norms regarding the nature of civil rights in the United States.

CLAYBORNE CARSON

(SEE ALSO: Race-Consciousness [I]; Racial Discrimination [3, I]; Racial Preference [I].)

Bibliography

BRANCH, TAYLOR 1988 Parting the Waters: America in the King Years, 1954–63. New York: Simon and Schuster.
CARSON, CLAYBORNE 1981 In Struggle: SNCC and the Black Awakening of the 1960s. Cambridge, Mass.: Harvard University Press.
GRAHAM, HUGH DAVIS 1990 The Civil Rights Record. New York: Oxford University Press.
KLUGER, RICHARD 1975 Simple Justice: The History of Brown v. Board of Education and Black America's Struggle for Equality. New York: Knopf.
LAWSON, STEVEN F. 1985 In Pursuit of Power: Southern Blacks and Electoral Politics. New York: Columbia University Press.

CIVIL WAR

The Civil War was the greatest constitutional crisis in the nation's history. It tested the nation–state relationship and the powers of Congress, the President, and the courts. By ultimately destroying SLAVERY [4], the conflict removed the most destructive element in the constitutional system and produced promises of equality under law throughout the United States. The addition of the THIRTEENTH AMENDMENT [4], FOURTEENTH AMENDMENT [2,I], and FIFTEENTH AMENDMENT [2] dramatically changed the structure of the federal system in important respects. In the short run these amendments ended slavery and gave state and national CITIZENSHIP [1] to over four million black men, women, and children. They also opened the door for black participation in politics. By the mid-twentieth century the amendments would place a great many individual rights under federal protection.

The war also finally settled the long-debated question of SOVEREIGNTY [4]. When a state and the national government clashed over ultimate authority, the national government would prevail. This primacy did not mean, however, that the states were stripped of power or influence. Both state and national governments involved themselves energetically and successfully in war-making and hence increased both their influence and their stature before the people. State and federal taxation increased along with state and federal expenditures for public projects. The war thus produced an ironic dual legacy: freedom for black Americans and a vital federal system in which states would retain significant, though no longer unique, influence over the amount of freedom these freedmen would exercise.

Because Congress was in recess when the conflict began, the President had to cope with the crisis alone. ABRAHAM LINCOLN [3] answered secessionist rhetoric with a powerful argument that sustained national authority by noting the danger of anarchy in SECESSION [4] and by emphasizing the sovereignty of people, not states. "A majority, held in restraint by constitutional checks, and limitations, and always changing easily, with deliberate changes of popular opinions and sentiments, is the only true sovereign of a free people," Lincoln said. To preserve the constitutional system that embodied this process, Lincoln was willing to lead the Union into war.

Lincoln marshaled northern resources to fight secession. He called for troops, paid $2 million from the treasury, pledged federal credit for $250 million more, and proclaimed a blockade of southern ports. These initiatives raised the constitutional problem of whether the conflict was legitimate at all, for Lincoln had acted without statutory authority and only Congress had power to declare war. In the March 1863 PRIZE CASES [3], the Supreme Court gave its answer on the disposition of several ships seized by the Union navy after Lincoln's 1861 blockade. The constitutional question was whether the President could blockade the South without a DECLARATION OF WAR [2] by Congress. Emphasizing the distinction between an international war, which Congress had to declare, and a civil war thrust upon the President and demanding immediate response, the Court defined the war as an insurrection, thus recognizing the President's power to subdue the rebellion without recognizing the Confederacy as an independent nation. The Court also justified Lincoln's action on the basis of the Militia Act of 1795, which allowed the President to call up the federal militia to stop insurrections. Presidents JOHN QUINCY ADAMS [1], JAMES K. POLK [3], MILLARD FILLMORE [2], and FRANKLIN PIERCE [3] had established precedents in exercising this power, and the 1827 case of MARTIN V. MOTT [3] had sustained it.

Executive authority over CIVIL LIBERTIES [1,I], the rights of civilian justice, FREEDOM OF SPEECH [2,I], and FREEDOM OF THE PRESS [2,I] provoked the most criticism. Fearing prorebel judges and juries in border states, Lincoln in 1861 suspended the privilege of the writ of HABEAS CORPUS [2,I] in the area between New York and Washington. This action gave the military control over civil liberty. Union soldiers arrested men near Baltimore for recruiting rebels and burning bridges linking Washington to the North. Chief Justice ROGER BROOKE TANEY [4] went to Baltimore especially to challenge Lincoln's suspension of the writ. Congress, not the President, retained constitutional suspension authority, Taney claimed. But over fifty pamphlets quickly surfaced to debate the issue, and authoritative voices supported Lincoln. Lincoln ignored Taney, and habeas corpus remained suspended. In fact, in 1862 suspension of the writ was expanded to cover the entire North.

The Union army arrested about 15,000 people; however, the vast majority were taken as rebel territory was occupied. The number of northern civilians subject to military law owing to the suspension of habeas corpus was limited, perhaps to a few hundred, and press, plat-

form, and pulpit continued to sound with criticism of the "Lincoln dictatorship." On the other hand some newspapers, including the *National Zeitung*, the Philadelphia *Evening Journal*, the Chicago *Times*, and the New York *World*, were temporarily shut down, and the editors of others were arrested, held for short periods of time, and then released—a practice that often restrained their criticism. Furthermore, Lincoln defended the suspension policy with sweeping rhetoric that may have had its own chilling effect on criticism: "The man who stands by and says nothing when the peril of his government is discussed cannot be misunderstood. If not hindered he is sure to help the enemy."

In the most famous civil liberties case of the time, a leading Ohio Democratic congressman, Clement Vallandigham, was arrested in Ohio in 1863 for protesting General Burnside's prohibition of "declaring sympathy for the enemy." Tried and convicted by a military tribunal, Vallandigham was banished to the Confederacy after the Supreme Court denied itself jurisdiction of the case in EX PARTE VALLANDIGHAM (1864) [4]. Vallandigham and his arrest were popular causes, however, and the Democratic party sought votes with some success as the party of civil liberties throughout the conflict. Still, when northern voters had to choose between Lincoln's suspensions and Vallandigham's defiance, they usually sided with Lincoln and his explanation that preserving the constitutional system as a whole in wartime required limiting speech that threatened the war effort. The Confederate government also suspended the writ of habeas corpus, provoking protest from state-sovereignty radicals, but such protest did little to weaken the Confederacy.

The abiding health of the constitutional system in the North during the war was demonstrated by the ongoing electoral process, within which civil liberty restrictions could be discussed and debated and through which the voters might throw out of office the very government that was restricting civil liberties. In Dixie, too, elections continued for the Confederate Congress, although not for the presidency, which had a six-year term, beginning in 1861. One advantage the North had over the South was an established political system that generated alternatives, focused political discussion, used patronage to keep intraparty rivalries in line, and kept opposition to the administration within reasonable bounds. Confederate political quarrels, lacking party apparatus, became personal and hence more intense.

LEGISLATIVE POWER [3] also expanded during the war, as Congress and executive cooperated to preserve and strengthen national authority. Legislators enacted a series of military drafts that brought national authority directly into the life of every American. Congress endorsed Lincoln's habeas corpus suspension in March 1863, although the tardiness of the Indemnity Act suggests the sensitivity of voters to the issue. Congress established the Joint Committee on the Conduct of the War to investigate generals perceived as not vigorous enough or not in accord with REPUBLICAN PARTY [I] policies. Lincoln used committee pressure to prod generals toward advanced measures. The one major division between executive and legislative branches, over RECONSTRUCTION [I], began with the anti-Lincoln diatribe of the Wade-Davis Manifesto, but soon found Lincoln and Congress working out their differences, agreeing on the need to protect freedmen and provide them with economic support through the FREEDMEN'S BUREAU [2] Act. Wade and Davis both supported Lincoln for reelection in 1864, and just before his death Lincoln was apparently contemplating a change in his Reconstruction policies that would have moved him closer to Congress. The two branches still debated which southern governments should be restored to the Union—those following Lincoln's plan or Congress's alternative—but both agreed that once war ended Congress would effectively control the Reconstruction process.

There was no disagreement about the wartime economic program. The first federal income tax law, the creation of the first national currency in the Greenback Act of 1862, the development of a national banking system, the taxing out of existence of state-based currency, the huge subsidy to build railroads to the Pacific Ocean, the opening up of millions of acres to homesteading with the HOMESTEAD ACT [2], the establishment of the Department of Agriculture, and the MORRILL ACT [3], which helped found and sustain major universities throughout the nation, all received Lincoln's unequivocal approval.

None of this national government activity was accompanied by federal regulation. The first national regulative agency, the Interstate Commerce Commission of 1887, lay twenty-two years into the postwar era. But people now accepted Congress's constitutional authority to shape the economy. Despite the Jeffersonian rhetoric of the Democratic party, it was the old Hamiltonian program and Hamiltonian views of national power, now infusing Whig and Republican political economy, that shaped national government policymaking. State governments, too, became more active. Some states set up public health boards and railroad oversight commissions. In the South, Reconstruction state governments established the region's first public schools. Cities also expanded their activities, having seen what government energy might accomplish.

The death of slavery was the largest constitutional change of the war. The conflict helped to resolve a growing contradiction within the constitutional system itself. On the one hand, the Constitution of 1787 recognized and protected slavery in several of its provisions. FEDERALISM [2,I] left states free to determine whether they would be free or slave. The Supreme Court had declared the territories open to slavery. Democratic presidents had endorsed proslavery demands. On the other hand, by 1860 slavery had become, in many northern eyes, a major threat to constitutional liberties and the operation of the political/constitutional system.

The prewar era saw proslavery attempts to stifle antislavery voices—in Congress through gag rules, in the free states through anti-abolitionist mobs, and in politics generally through the prohibition of antislavery arguments in the slave states and the territories. All these efforts helped generate sectional parties. In addition, the South used threats of secession to protect slavery, thus hardening northern hostility to the peculiar institution and to what it termed "the Slave Power Conspiracy." People did not have to be racial egalitarians to be enemies of slavery. The threat to individual rights and the political process made slavery a target of northern hostility. The Constitution thus was at war with itself—promising open elections, free debate, the right to petition, the whole process of government by consent, on the one hand, and protecting slavery, on the other. The war ended the conflict.

Freed from obstruction by southern congressmen, the wartime northern Congress not only enacted much nationalizing legislation but also attacked slavery whenever the Constitution put it within congressional reach. Congress ended slavery in the DISTRICT OF COLUMBIA [2] and in the territories. Then, acting on the theory that slaves might be contraband of war, Congress turned on the South and passed laws first confiscating property used directly to attack the Union (First Confiscation Act, August 1861) and then taking all slaves of rebels (Second Confiscation Act, July 1862). But these two laws freed no slaves, for the judicial procedures to prove disloyalty were too cumbersome. The laws did, however, demonstrate growing support for executive action against slavery.

Lincoln had two arenas in which he might act. In civilian areas his emancipation goals were restrained by the Constitution, which let states choose freedom or slavery. He asked border slave states to free their slaves. When that effort failed, he turned his attention to places still in rebellion, places where his constitutional war powers could operate. The EMANCIPATION PROCLAMATION [2] of January 1, 1863, freed slaves wherever the Union advanced after that day, and it permitted freedmen to acquire claims on citizenship by serving as soldiers.

Emancipation ended the national government's protection for slavery, which had existed since 1787. With the adoption of the Thirteenth Amendment in 1865, the national government promised to eradicate, not defend, slavery. The death of slavery ended the reason for secession and for obstructing open debate in Congress and in the polity at large. It also meant that the institution that had most conspicuously challenged the ideal of equal justice under law was gone. As the Civil War ended, a robust constitutional system of active states and a proven nation awaited new challenges to that ideal.

PHILLIP S. PALUDAN

(SEE ALSO: *Confederate Constitution* [1]; *Confiscation Acts* [1]; *Constitutional History, 1861–1865* [1]; *Jeffersonianism* [I]; *War Powers* [4,I]; *Whig Party* [I]; *Executive Power* [I]; *Executive Prerogative* [I].)

Bibliography

BELZ, HERMAN 1978 *Emancipation and Equal Rights: Politics and Constitutionalism in the Civil War Era.* New York: Norton.

———— 1984 *Lincoln and the Constitution: The Dictatorship Question Reconsidered.* Fort Wayne, Ind.: Louis Warren Lincoln Library.

FEHRENBACHER, DON E. 1979 Lincoln and the Constitution. In Cullom Davis, ed., *The Public and Private Lincoln.* Carbondale: University of Southern Illinois Press.

HYMAN, HAROLD 1973 *A More Perfect Union: The Impact of the Civil War and Reconstruction on the Constitution.* New York: Knopf.

————, and WIECEK, WILLIAM 1982 *Equal Justice Under Law: Constitutional Development, 1835–1875.* New York: Harper and Row.

MCKITRICK, ERIC 1967 Party Politics and the Union and Confederate War Efforts. In Walter Dean Burnham and William Chambers, eds., *The American Party System.* New York: Free Press.

NEELY, MARK E., JR. 1991 *The Fate of Liberty: Abraham Lincoln and Civil Liberties,* New York: Oxford.

PALUDAN, PHILLIP S. 1988 *"A People's Contest": The Union and Civil War, 1861–1865.* New York: Harper and Row.

RANDALL, JAMES G. (1926) 1951 *Constitutional Problems Under Lincoln,* rev. ed. Urbana: University of Illinois Press.

COLORADO v. CONNELLY
479 U.S. 157 (1986)

Narrowly seen, this case deals with true confessions by mentally deranged people, but it resulted in the major holding that the Fifth Amendment's right against compulsory self-incrimination operates only when the coercion is linked to government. A confession that is involuntary in the sense that it is not the product of a rational intellect or free will may, nevertheless, be introduced in EVIDENCE [2] because no government agent misbehaved or was responsible for the involuntary character of the confession.

In this case, the murderer confessed in obedience to God's voice. He received his MIRANDA [3,I] rights, waived them, and insisted on confessing. The court, in a 7–2 decision, found no violation of DUE PROCESS OF LAW [2] and no involuntary self-incrimination. The dissenters believed that the Court was wrong to think that the only involuntary confessions are those obtained by government misconduct. Justice JOHN PAUL STEVENS [4,I], concurring with the decision, sensibly acknowledged that the confession in this case was involuntary but not of such a character that it had to be excluded from evidence.

LEONARD W. LEVY

(SEE ALSO: *Police Interrogation and Confessions* [3,I]; *Right Against Self-Incrimination* [3,I].)

COMMERCIAL SPEECH

For most of this century commercial speech was regarded as outside the scope of the FIRST AMENDMENT [2,I]. Indeed, the Supreme Court so held in 1942. But in 1976 the Supreme Court reversed course in the case of VIRGINIA STATE BOARD OF PHARMACY V. VIRGINIA CITIZENS' CONSUMER COUNCIL [4]. There the Court held that Virginia had violated the First Amendment by prohibiting pharmacists from advertising prices of prescription drugs. The Court was unpersuaded that the state's fear that product advertising would lower the "professional" character of the practice of pharmacy outweighed the First Amendment interest in open competition of information and ideas, even about products of commerce.

In 1980 in CENTRAL HUDSON GAS & ELECTRIC CORPORATION V. PUBLIC SERVICE COMMISSION [1], the Court announced a four-part test for deciding when commercial speech is entitled to First Amendment protection. To determine whether commercial speech is protected, the Court held, it must be found that the speech concerns a lawful activity and is not misleading, that "the regulation directly advances the governmental interest asserted," and that the regulation "is not more extensive than is necessary to serve that interest." Applying that standard to the case before it, the Court invalidated a Public Service Commission regulation that prohibited electrical utilities from engaging in promotional advertising. While the Court acknowledged that the commission's purpose was legitimate (namely, to conserve energy), the commission's case failed in the Court's view because there was no showing that this legitimate purpose could not be achieved by regulation less intrusive on First Amendment interests.

In recent years the Supreme Court has seemed to retreat from the *Central Hudson* trend of extending broader First Amendment rights when it comes to protection of commercial speech. In a major decision in 1986 in POSADAS DE PUERTO RICO ASSOCIATES V. TOURISM COMPANY [I], the Court upheld a Puerto Rican government regulation that forbade casino advertising directed at Puerto Rican residents; advertising aimed at tourists, on the other hand, was permitted. Though casino gambling was legal in Puerto Rico, and though the advertising prohibited was neither misleading nor fraudulent, the Court held that the government's interest in avoiding the debilitating effects of gambling on the internal culture of Puerto Rico was "substantial," that the restriction "directly advanced" that goal, and that the legislature could reasonably conclude that residents would "be induced by widespread advertising to engage in such potentially harmful conduct." The Court refused to require Puerto Rico to use means other than an advertising prohibition to achieve its goal of discouraging gambling by residents. The Court reasoned that, because casino gambling could be prohibited entirely, that power "includes the lesser power to ban advertising of casino gambling."

The *Posadas* case seems a step backward from the direction taken in *Virginia Pharmacy* and *Central Hudson* for two reasons. First, it appears to signal that the Court will not demand that governments demonstrate the inadequacy of nonspeech restrictive measures in controlling supposedly harmful effects of commercial speech. While *Central Hudson* required the state to "demonstrat[e] that its interest in conservation cannot be protected adequately by more limited regulation," *Posadas* was satisfied by the assumption that the legislature "could" conclude, as it "apparently did," that alternative remedies were insufficient. The Court explicitly articulated this limitation in the *Central Hudson* formula in BOARD OF TRUSTEES OF STATE UNIVERSITY OF NEW YORK V. FOX (1989) [I].

Second, the Court's reasoning in *Posadas* that the state's potential power to forbid gambling includes the power to regulate the speech itself even when gambling is not prohibited raises serious questions about the continuing strength of earlier decisions protective of commercial speech. In *Virginia Pharmacy*, for example, although prescription drugs presumably could have been banned by Virginia, that fact did not stop the Court from holding that a ban on advertising for such drugs was unconstitutional.

The most that can be said at the present time about the commercial speech doctrine is that it is not yet on a consistent track, although some level of First Amendment protection for commercial speech is now firmly established.

LEE C. BOLLINGER

(SEE ALSO: *Freedom of Speech* [2,I].)

COMMUNISTS

See: Extremist Speech and the First Amendment [I]

COMPARABLE WORTH

The term "comparable worth" refers to the claim that workers in predominantly female occupations should be compensated at rates similar to those paid to workers in predominantly male occupations, when the labor involved in both is comparable in value to the employer. The claim assumes (1) that significant sex segregation exists in American employment; (2) that, as a result, women are disadvantaged economically; and (3) that job classifications that are different can nonetheless be compared by analyzing their component skill, effort, responsibility, working conditions, and training requirements.

The first assumption is not controversial. More than half of the jobs that fall under the most commonly used occupational designations are over eighty percent male- or female-dominated. At least part of the second claim is likewise firmly established. On average, women earn only sixty percent of what men do, and the higher the percentage of women in a particular job category, the lower the average wage tends to be.

One of the controversies over comparable worth centers on how much of the male-female wage disparity can be explained by "nondiscriminatory" factors, such as length of time in continuous employment, trade-offs between work and family responsibility, and personal choice. Although these factors may themselves be products of prior SEX DISCRIMINATION [4,I], they can nevertheless be distinguished from the employer's own current intentional discrimination, reliance on sex stereotypes, or use of wage-setting devices that do not measure job requirements or performance. Proponents of comparable-worth claims argue that the latter factors produce a significant part of the general wage disparity, so that the disparity is properly challenged as discriminatory under laws guaranteeing equal employment opportunity. Opponents who agree that there is a relationship between employers' undervaluation of certain kinds of work and the fact that such work is predominantly done by women, nonetheless reject comparable-worth claims as a useful strategy for improving the economic condition of women. They prefer strategies that would move large numbers of women into fields in which men are currently overrepresented.

Controversy also surrounds the questions of which jobs are comparable and how to measure comparability. Courts generally accept statistical analysis in claims of EMPLOYMENT DISCRIMINATION [2], but do not always agree on the validity, appropriateness, or evidentiary weight of particular statistical analyses. Neither do they agree on whether and how comparable-worth claims should fit within the framework of employment discrimination claims created by Title VII of the CIVIL RIGHTS ACT OF 1964 [1], the Equal Pay Act of 1964, or the EQUAL PROTECTION [2,I] clause of the FOURTEENTH AMENDMENT [2,I] to the Constitution. *County of Washington v. Gunther* (1981), the only Supreme Court opinion to mention comparable worth, expressly declined to address the issue, although it did hold that intentional sex discrimination in wages could be challenged under Title VII, despite differences in male and female job classifications.

Most comparable worth litigation is brought against public employers, who generally employ large numbers of people in a wide variety of job classifications. Although public employers are subject to both Title VII and constitutional prohibitions on discrimination, equal protection claims are generally not raised by plaintiffs seeking comparable-worth decrees. As PERSONNEL ADMINISTRATOR OF MASSACHUSETTS V. FEENEY (1979) [3] illustrates, an employment practice does not violate the Constitution unless its discriminatory impact has been intentionally created. Employers are more likely to set wages on the basis of prevailing market rates for certain job classifications or even on unconscious stereotypes about the relative worth of female-dominated occupations than on an intentional desire to undercompensate women simply because they are women.

Even in the statutory arena, much uncertainty remains. For example, it is unclear whether the availability of statutory "disparate impact" claims against other types of alleged employment discrimination extends to sex-based wage discrimination. Some courts have asserted that wage-setting practices are too subjective, too multifaceted, or both, to be effectively tested by the disparate impact model of discrimination. Others have simply stated that an employer's reliance on the market in setting wages is not the kind of practice to which the model should apply. The Supreme Court has spoken only obliquely on these issues.

Given uncertainty whether equal pay for work of comparable worth is required by existing federal law, advocates of comparable worth have not confined their efforts to the courtroom. Pay equity, including comparable worth, has to date been more successfully achieved through collective bargaining, state legislation, and local ordinances than through litigation.

CHRISTINE A. LITTLETON

(SEE ALSO: *Feminist Theory* [I].)

Bibliography

BLUMROSEN, RUTH G. 1980 Wage Discrimination, Job Segregation and Women Workers. *Women's Rights Law Reporter* 6:19–57.

DOWD, NANCY E. 1986 The Metamorphosis of Comparable Worth. *Suffolk University Law Review* 20:833–865.
FELDSTEIN, HYDEE R. 1981 Sex-based Wage Discrimination Claims. *Columbia Law Review* 81:1333–1347.
NOTE [LITTLETON, CHRISTINE] 1981 Toward a Redefinition of Sexual Equality. *Harvard Law Review* 95:487–508.

COMPUTERS

The rapid advance of computer technology has drastically expanded our ability to store, analyze, and disseminate information. This development has implications for three areas of constitutional doctrine: the RIGHT OF PRIVACY [3,I], PROCEDURAL DUE PROCESS OF LAW [3,I], and the FREEDOM OF SPEECH [2,I] and FREEDOM OF THE PRESS [2,I].

Because the field is so new, the Supreme Court has not yet had many opportunities to confront these issues. An account of the Court's JURISPRUDENCE [I] so far reveals that it is only slowly beginning to recognize in computer technology a danger different in kind from that presented by information technologies supplanted. Thus, in LAIRD V. TATUM (1972) [3], the earliest of the Court's computer cases, the question presented was whether the Constitution limits the government's right to store publicly available information in computerized form. One of the complaints in *Laird* was that the storage of such information in army-intelligence data banks for undefined subsequent use had a CHILLING EFFECT [1] on the expression of those targeted for observation. In finding that the effect was so speculative that the controversy was not ripe for adjudication, the Court in effect held that government storage of personal information in a computer does not in itself give rise to a constitutionally based complaint.

WHALEN V. ROE (1977) [4] was the first opinion expressly addressing the right of privacy in a computer context. A New York law required centralized computer storage of the names and addresses of persons prescribed certain drugs. The Court acknowledged "the threat to privacy implicit in the accumulation of vast amounts of personal information in computerized data banks." In a CONCURRING OPINION [1], Justice WILLIAM J. BRENNAN [1,I] noted that the potential for abuse of computerized information might necessitate "some curb on such technology." Nonetheless, the Court analyzed the law under the same BALANCING TEST used in other cases involving government invasions of privacy, balancing the state's interest in collecting drug-use information against the interest in privacy, and upheld the statute. Although the Court emphasized the stringent security measures taken to prevent unnecessary or unauthorized access to New York's computer files, lower courts have given *Whalen* a narrow reading and placed few constitutional restrictions on government use of computerized data banks. These lower courts have given greater weight to the earlier decision in PAUL V. DAVIS (1976) [3], where the Court had held that alleged LIBEL [3] and public disclosure of arrest records by government officials did not amount to a deprivation of "liberty."

Although the Court seems headed toward a narrow conception of privacy of computerized records as protected by the Constitution, it has embraced a broader view in statutory contexts. In *Department of Justice v. Reporters' Committee for Freedom of the Press* (1989), for example, the Court upheld a privacy interest against a request by CBS News under the FREEDOM OF INFORMATION ACT [2] for disclosure of "rap sheets." Here, the Court noted that "there is a vast difference between public records that might be found after a diligent search of courthouse files, county archives, and local police stations throughout the country and a computerized summary located in a single clearinghouse of information."

A second important set of privacy questions raised by governmental use of computers is the extent to which computers may be used as an aid or substitute for other decision-making processes. This is a question not merely of the use of stored information but also the use of sophisticated programs that make possible new modes of analysis. One example is computerized matching, now a widespread practice at both the federal and state levels. These powerful programs can, for instance, help determine the eligibility of recipients of governmental benefits by matching lists of the individuals receiving such benefits with other governmental records (such as tax returns, employment files, and automobile licenses), with publicly available information, or with privately supplied information. Although some statutes and regulations limit these computerized matching programs, most courts have failed to perceive the practices as raising constitutional concerns. Some, however, have suggested that computerized matching is the kind of search that should require a SEARCH WARRANT [4].

The more important issue posed by computerized matching is what action is to be taken on a "hit" (that is, a match between records). What, for example, happens when an individual on a list of recipients of unemployment benefits also turns up on a file of federal employees? This is a question of procedural due process, and once again, the analysis applied so far has not differed from situations in which computers are not used. Similar questions arise in the criminal context, where computerized records may be used to determine whether a person has outstanding arrest warrants or is driving a stolen vehicle.

A closely related question is whether sophisticated computerized analysis techniques may be utilized to develop profiles of certain kinds of individuals that are then used to identify specific people as the focus of governmental law enforcement and investigation. Thus, the government has, in part through computerized analysis of cases, developed certain statistically based profiles of typical drug smugglers. Those who meet the profile are targeted for intense examination, sometimes involving other computerized techniques. In *United States v. Sokolow* (1989) the Court analogized drug-courier profiles to the "hunches" on which police officers typically operate. It then required the same showing of reasonable suspicion required in other instances in which persons are stopped for questioning. Although the Court did not see in the "empirical documentation" of the profile any greater basis for suspecting persons meeting the profile, it also did not find in the profiling technique any cause for heightened constitutional scrutiny.

A final area in which computers figure directly in constitutional analysis is the freedom of speech and freedom of the press. In this area, the question is the extent to which computerized forms of communication are protected by the FIRST AMENDMENT [2,I]. Is, for example, a computerized bulletin board protected against libel judgments to the same extent as a newspaper under the standard of NEW YORK TIMES V. SULLIVAN (1964) [3]? Can the government subject computers to greater restrictions than other forms of communication? In *Marshfield Family Skateland, Inc. v. Town of Marshfield* (1983), the Supreme Court dismissed a challenge to an ordinance banning video games on the ground it failed to present a substantial federal question, but has not otherwise addressed the issue. Lower court cases have thus far largely involved criminal prosecution, for example, for using computers in gambling. Although these decisions held that the computer programs were unprotected speech, the computers were so integral to the commission of the crime that these cases are not necessarily indicative of the extent to which courts will find that computers raise unique constitutional questions.

ROCHELLE C. DREYFUSS
DAVID W. LEEBRON

(SEE ALSO: *Science, Technology, and the Constitution* [I].)

Bibliography

FREEDMAN, WARREN 1987 *The Right of Privacy in the Computer Age.* New York: Quorum Books.
PRIVACY PROTECTION STUDY COMMISSION 1977 *Personal Privacy in an Information Society.* Washington, D.C.: U.S. Government Printing Office.
SHATTUCK, JOHN 1984 In the Shadow of 1984: National Identification Systems, Computer Matching, and Privacy in the United States. *Hastings Law Journal* 35:991–1005.
U.S. DEPARTMENT OF HEALTH, EDUCATION AND WELFARE

1973 *Records, Computers and the Rights of Citizens* (Report of the Secretary's Advisory Committee on Automated Personal Data Systems). Washington, D.C.: U.S. Government Printing Office.

WESTIN, ALAN F. 1972 *Databanks in a Free Society: Computers, Record-Keeping and Privacy*. New York: Quadrangle Books.

CONDITIONAL SPENDING

The United States Constitution allocates legislative authority between a federal Congress and state governments. Congress may legislate or regulate only pursuant to specific powers expressly delegated in the Constitution; excepting IMPLIED POWERS [2], all powers not delegated to the national government are retained by the state governments. The power to spend money for the common defense or the GENERAL WELFARE [2], however, is a power separate from, and in addition to, all of Congress's other ENUMERATED POWERS [2]. Thus, Congress may spend federal funds for any purpose that can be thought to contribute to the general welfare, even though none of Congress's enumerated powers encompasses the subject of the expenditure. Congress may not impose regulatory requirements, however, even though admittedly in the interest of the common defense and general welfare, unless the area regulated is one over which regulatory control is delegated to Congress.

The power to spend carries with it the power to attach certain conditions to the expenditure. Those conditions in effect specify how federal grants will be used. For example, if Congress grants the states funds to build highways, Congress has the concomitant power to specify where the highways should run or how they should be built. This power to impose conditions permits Congress to ensure that its money is actually spent as Congress intends.

The conditional spending problem is presented when Congress seeks to purchase, not the usual goods and services, but compliance with a legislative objective that normally would be pursued by a simple regulation backed by a regulatory penalty such as a fine. When Congress uses its spending power to offer a financial inducement— a reward—for conduct that it could not directly require or regulate under any of its other enumerated powers, the core constitutional conception of specifically delegated powers is threatened. The problem posed by conditional spending is the extent to which federally induced state reliance on federal moneys gives Congress effective regulatory authority over the states beyond the powers delegated to Congress in the Constitution.

The question is of central importance to the basic constitutional scheme of FEDERALISM [2,I]. Over the course of the last several decades, the federal tax burden on individuals has increased substantially, making it increasingly difficult as a political matter for state legislatures to raise state taxes. At the same time that the federal tax burden has deterred states from raising their own revenue, national grant programs for general welfare purposes, such as highways, education, and health, have induced states to rely increasingly on national funds to finance state services. Substantial state reliance on the distribution of money raised by national taxation is now a fact of political life in the federal system. This financial dependence of the states on Congress's beneficence invites Congress to extract concessions from the states, to require the states to accept "conditions" in return for the revenues now under Congress's control. If there are no constitutional limitations on the conditions Congress can attach to federal grants, Congress may extract tax revenue from the citizens of the several states, pursuant to the taxing power, and then return that revenue to the states, under the spending power, on the condition that the states impose on themselves or their citizens some regulation that Congress constitutionally could not have imposed under its other enumerated powers.

There are two competing views on the constitutionality of conditions attached by Congress to federal grants. The first view holds that offering a government benefit as a reward for compliance with some congressional objective is in effect identical to regulatory coercion by imposition of a fine to obtain the same end. Under this view, if achievement of an end is beyond Congress's delegated regulatory powers, it also should be constitutionally invalid when pursued through a conditional spending scheme. The second view is that the use of the spending power to offer a reward for compliance with some congressional objective is distinguishable from regulatory coercion in the form of a fine for noncompliance because the latter removes the freedom of choice while the former does not. According to this view, a state or individual confronted with the offer of a conditional grant may refuse the reward and persist in noncompliance, while one confronting a regulatory fine has no freedom of choice. Moreover, a fine takes money but a spending scheme awards it; refusing takes no money. Under this view, then, direct congressional regulation is confined to the enumerated powers, but Congress's purchase of compliance through a scheme of conditional spending is not similarly restrained.

Early spending power cases asserted that there is no conceptual difference between withholding a benefit and imposing a fine to achieve a regulatory end, and applied this principle to protect STATES' RIGHTS [4]. UNITED STATES V. BUTLER (1936) [1] involved a challenge to the AGRICULTURAL ADJUSTMENT ACT OF 1933 (AAA) [1]. Under the act, processors of agricultural goods were taxed and the proceeds from the tax were used to pay farmers to allow their land to lie fallow. The purpose of the scheme was to stabilize farm prices by reducing the supply of farm goods in the market. Respondents challenged the scheme as beyond the scope of Congress's delegated powers, primarily the INTERSTATE COMMERCE [2] power, because the act sought to regulate the purely local activity of agricultural production. The United States did not attempt to defend the scheme as a valid commerce regulation, but argued it could be sustained as a valid exercise of Congress's authority to spend "for the general welfare."

The Court disagreed in *Butler*, holding that the scheme was invalid precisely because Congress used its spending power to achieve a regulatory effect on agriculture, otherwise outside the scope of its delegated powers and subject only to state control. The Court expressly endorsed the Hamiltonian view that although Congress has limited powers, the spending power is not limited to the subjects of the enumerated powers; but the Court said the scheme was not a simple exercise of Congress's power to spend. It was "at best . . . a scheme for purchasing with federal funds submission to federal regulation of a subject reserved to the states." The Court distinguished between a conditional appropriation where the condition specifies how the money is to be spent, which is valid, and a conditional appropriation where the goal of the condition is regulation: "There is an obvious difference between a statute stating the conditions upon which moneys shall be expended and one effective only upon assumption of a contractual obligation to submit to a regulation which otherwise could not be enforced. . . . If in lieu of compulsory regulation of subjects within the states' reserved JURISDICTION [3], which is prohibited, the Congress could invoke the taxing and spending power as a means to accomplish the same end, clause 1 of Section 8 of article I would become the instrument for total subversion of the governmental powers reserved to the individual states."

By modern standards *Butler* was decided wrongly. *Butler's* real error, however, was not in holding that spending legislation could not be used to accomplish regulatory ends outside Congress's delegated powers; rather, it was in adopting a narrow interpretation of Congress's power under the COMMERCE CLAUSE [1,I] that disallowed price-support legislation. Such a result would not hold up today. But in *Butler* the Court's perception that the AAA was regulation, not spending, seems unassailable.

The conceptual foundation of *Butler*—that a reward for compliance is regulation, not spending—has been carried forward and expanded by the modern Court in some CIVIL LIBERTIES [1,I] cases, FIRST AMENDMENT [2,I] cases in particular. In those cases, the Court has recognized that offering a governmental benefit on the condition that the individual refrain from engaging in protected activities

is the economic and constitutional equivalent of imposing a fine for the violation of a regulation prohibiting the activity. For example, the Court has held that if government offers a financial reward in return for the recipient's agreement to forgo a practice commanded by her religion, the conditional grant presents the same RELIGIOUS LIBERTY [3,I] problem that would be presented by a fine for engaging in the religious practice. Either presents the same governmental interference with the individual's constitutionally protected liberty. In either case, the individual may choose to continue the protected activity and suffer the economic loss or forgo the protected activity and avoid the economic loss. In individual liberties cases this proposition is known as the doctrine of UNCONSTITUTIONAL CONDITIONS [4] and is often identified with the Court's decision in SHERBERT V. VERNER (1963) [4].

In its most recent encounter with conditional spending, the Supreme Court appears to have abandoned the conceptual foundation of *Butler* and ignored its currency in the individual liberties area. In *South Dakota v. Dole* (1987) the Court confronted a challenge to the national minimum drinking age (NMDA) amendment to the National Surface Transportation Act. The act authorizes federal grants to the states for the construction of national highways. The NMDA instructed the secretary of transportation to withhold up to ten percent of a state's federal highway funds if that state fails to enact a minimum drinking age of twenty-one within the next year. Thus, by attaching a condition to a grant, Congress sought to impose a uniform national minimum drinking age. In *Dole* the Court assumed for purposes of the case that Congress, after the TWENTY-FIRST AMENDMENT [4], could not have enacted a regulation requiring each state to adopt such a minimum drinking age for the state. Nor, the Court assumed arguendo, could Congress constitutionally have enacted a simple regulation directly prohibiting the purchase or consumption of alcohol by persons under twenty-one years of age. Thus, the only issue left for the *Dole* Court to resolve was whether the MNDA was constitutional as a condition accompanying a grant of federal funds to the states, even assuming that Congress could not regulate drinking ages directly under any of its delegated legislative powers.

The *Dole* Court observed that "Congress has acted indirectly under its spending power to encourage uniformity in the States' drinking ages." Thus, the legislation was held to be "within constitutional bounds even if Congress may not regulate drinking ages directly." In essence, the Court held that although Congress lacks regulatory authority to achieve a legislative end directly, Congress may "purchase" state compliance through the use of conditions attached to spending grants. The basis of the Court's holding is that there is a difference between coercing compliance (an exercise of regulatory power) and buying compliance (an exercise of the spending power). The *Dole* holding is in tension with other Supreme Court PRECEDENTS [3], notably *Butler* and the individual liberties cases, which recognize that conditional spending can be the conceptual and economic equivalent of direct regulation. In effect, the Court in *Dole*, voting 7–2, reverted to the notion that compliance with a condition attached to a benefit is "voluntary" as long as the potential recipient can choose to forgo the benefit in order to avoid compliance with the condition.

The Supreme Court's decision in *Dole* appears to invite the complete abrogation of all limits on delegated federal LEGISLATIVE POWER [3] through the simple device of burdensome taxes accompanied by "financial incentives" to comply with any federal legislative objective that is outside the range of concerns constitutionally delegated to Congress. Chief Justice WILLIAM H. REHNQUIST's [3,I] opinion in *Dole*, however, suggested some limitations on the breadth of the Court's holding.

First, said the Chief Justice, Congress may "induce" or "tempt" voluntary compliance, but may not "coerce" compliance. The difficulty with the coercion/inducement test as a limit on congressional action is that it simply restates the distinction—discredited in some modern individual liberties cases—between achieving an end by regulation and achieving an end by withholding a benefit. The question of "how much benefit" simply is beside the point, for as *Sherbert v. Verner* concluded, any benefit withheld is tantamount to a fine in that amount. One who is subject to the threat of a regulatory fine may choose to violate the regulation and pay the fine because the amount of the fine is modest. But that "freedom" of choice does not eliminate constitutional objections to the substance of the regulation.

The facts of the *Dole* case suggest that Chief Justice Rehnquist was relying upon a distinction Congress would not even credit. Congress's very purpose in enacting the NMDA would have been undercut seriously if not every state had complied; it is clear that Congress had no intention of offering a choice, but threatened to withhold a benefit to obtain regulatory compliance.

Second, in a footnote Rehnquist suggested a constitutional requirement that any condition attached to a federal grant bear some relationship to that grant. In applying this suggestion to the facts of *Dole*, however, the Chief Justice simply noted that the condition related to the national problem of teenage drunk driving. Teenage drunk driving may well be a problem national in scope, but the condition did not in any way specify the characteristics of the highways that the conditioned funds were intended to purchase. Requiring only that the condition relate to a national problem rather than specify characteristics of

the particular goods and services to be purchased by the grant seems tantamount to a statement that Congress can regulate perceived national problems through the spending power. Of course, Congress may with greater legitimacy reach many of the same subjects by the exercise of its wide-ranging commerce powers.

THOMAS R. MCCOY
BARRY FRIEDMAN

(SEE ALSO: *Federal Grants-in-Aid* [2]; *Taxing and Spending Powers* [4].)

Bibliography

MCCOY, THOMAS R. and FRIEDMAN, BARRY 1988 Conditional Spending: Federalism's Trojan Horse. *Supreme Court Review* 1988:85–127.

MIZERK, DONALD J. 1987 The Coercion Test and Conditional Federal Grants to the States. *Vanderbilt Law Review* 40:1159–1195.

ROSENTHAL, ALBERT J. 1987 Conditional Federal Spending and the Constitution. *Stanford Law Review* 39:1103–1164.

SULLIVAN, KATHLEEN 1989 Unconstitutional Conditions. *Harvard Law Review* 102:1413–1506.

CONFESSIONS

See: Police Interrogation and Confessions [3, I]

CONFRONTATION, RIGHT OF
(Update)

The Supreme Court has explained that the accused's Sixth Amendment right "to be confronted with the witnesses against him" has the primary function of furthering the trial's truth-determining process. But recent cases reveal conflicts over the best way to ascertain truth and competing visions of a trial's shape. Cases involving children especially have posed the question whether a dramatic and adversarial trial, with the accusing witness and accused as protagonist and antagonist, tends to produce the most accurate results. They have also posed the question of the extent to which values other than truth-seeking—such as protecting a witness from the trauma of trial—can supervene the confrontation right.

Taking its cue from Shakespeare's *Richard II*—"Then call them to our presence; face to face and frowning brow to brow, ourselves will hear the accuser and the accused freely speak" (1.1.15–17)—the Court in COY V. IOWA (1988) [I] held that the core of the right, manifest in the Sixth Amendment's text, involves physical face-to-face confrontation between witness and accused. Keeping the dramatis personae together on the trial's stage contributes not only to honest testimony but to maintaining our dramatic sense of what a trial is: "There is something deep in human nature that regards face-to-face confrontation between accused and accuser as 'essential to a fair trial.' " Accordingly, *Coy* held unconstitutional a statute allowing in all such cases a screen to obstruct a sexually abused minor witness's view of the accused.

MARYLAND V. CRAIG (1990) [I] answered affirmatively the question *Coy* reserved: whether a court may employ such a device if it first makes an individualized finding that an important state interest justifies its use in a particular case. But *Craig* did not clarify whether protecting a witness from serious distress or trauma can justify a device that does not also aid truth-seeking by enabling a child, whom distress would otherwise render substantially unavailable, to testify. The device, upheld in *Craig*, altered the nature of the trial by mixing the media of stage and television: in the courtroom, the defendant, judge, and jury watched, via closed-circuit television, real-time pictures of the child testifying in another room in the presence of the prosecutor and defense counsel. In contrast to *Coy*, the *Craig* decision described face-to-face confrontation only as a preference and emphasized that the confrontation clause's interest in reliability can be furthered sufficiently by a witness's testifying under oath and being cross-examined while observed by the trier of fact. In addition, *Kentucky v. Stincer* (1987) determined that the accused may be excluded from a routine witness-competency hearing of a sexually abused minor, because his right to confrontation regarding the witness's substantive testimony remains intact.

Other opinions focus entirely on cross-examination as the core of the confrontation right. While emphasizing that a judge has wide latitude to impose reasonable limits on cross-examination to avoid harassment, prejudice, confusion, trauma, repetition, and the like, recent cases, such as *Delaware v. Van Arsdall* (1986) and *Olden v. Kentucky* (1988), hold that, save for HARMLESS ERROR [2], a trial judge cannot exclude all inquiry into traditionally relevant subject areas, such as bias and other credibility matters. For example, *Davis v. Alaska* (1974) holds that a court cannot restrict cross-examination about a witness's juvenile court record, despite a statute protecting the record's confidentiality. With respect to the adversarial manner of cross-examination, lower courts do not readily restrict the cross-examination of children to a gentle inquiry using age-appropriate language and concepts, despite claims that traditional cross-examination on counsel's terms is not conducive to a child's truth-telling.

The Court is divided on whether the cross-examination right is exclusively a procedural trial right that guarantees only an opportunity to cross-examine or whether it is also a right that can enhance effective cross-examination

by affording PRETRIAL DISCLOSURE [3], and DISCOVERY [2]. The EYEWITNESS IDENTIFICATION [I] rules established by UNITED STATES V. WADE (1967) [4] exemplify this latter approach. The former is found in *Pennsylvania v. Ritchie* (1987), in which a trial court refused to give defense counsel access to a child welfare office's investigatory file of a sexual abuse case, pursuant to a statute establishing its confidentiality. Because defense counsel had the opportunity to examine the accusing daughter at trial, a plurality found no confrontation clause violation. The Court did require the trial judge to conduct a review of the file in camera to determine whether the accused's due process rights required disclosure. The view that the confrontation clause assures an opportunity to cross-examine but not effective cross-examination led the Court, in *United States v. Owens* (1988) and *Delaware v. Fensterer* (1985), to uphold the admission of a testifying witness's out-of-court statements, even though he had lost all memory concerning the statements other than the fact that he had previously made them.

Finally, the Supreme Court continues to address the admission of HEARSAY [2] and of codefendant statements. *Ohio v. Roberts* (1980), involving the admission of the prior testimony of an unavailable witness, indicated that the confrontation clause imposes a strong preference for in-court statements, which requires the state to make a good-faith effort to produce the declarant in court, and a requirement that the admission of an out-of-court statement be based on indicia of reliability, established either by its coming "within a firmly rooted hearsay exception" or by a showing of "particularized guarantees of trustworthiness." But in *Bourjaily v. United States* (1987) and *United States v. Inadi* (1986), the Court interpreted the two *Roberts* requirements as applying primarily to the admission of prior testimony. *Bourjaily* limited the *Roberts* indicia of reliability requirement by admitting coconspirator statements under an agency theory without regard to their reliability. *Inadi* permitted the prosecutor to introduce out-of-court statements of a coconspirator without making much effort to produce him. It distinguished prior testimony in *Roberts* from these coconspirator statements, in that the latter, precisely because they were made during the conspiracy, may be more probative than a declarant's subsequent postconspiracy in-court statements. This view—that a trial can best achieve truth through the consideration of statements made in a natural setting rather than through the artifice of a dramatic and adversarial replaying at trial—finds support in some lower court decisions admitting children's out-of-court statements made near the time of their abuse or in the context of a trusted relationship. However, by reemphasizing the *Roberts* requirements, the Supreme Court, in *Idaho v. Wright* (1990), rejected the admission, under a residual hearsay exception, of a sexual abuse accusation made by an unavailable three-year-old in response to the allegedly suggestive questions of an examining pediatrician. With little consideration of the growing psychological evidence on the subject, the Court emphasized that to be admissible the out-of-court statement must have been made under circumstances evidencing such trustworthiness that, subsequently at trial, "adversarial testing would add little to its reliability."

With respect to codefendant confessions, in *Cruz v. New York* (1987), *Richardson v. Marsh* (1987), *Lee v. Illinois* (1986), and *Tennessee v. Street* (1985), the Court reaffirmed (if only narrowly) and refined *Bruton v. United States* (1968) by prohibiting the limited admission against a nontestifying codefendant of that portion of his confession that directly implicates the defendant but is not admissible against him.

In noncriminal cases, the DUE PROCESS [2] clause can afford some sort of confrontation right to enhance the truth-determining process. IN RE GAULT (1967) [2] held that a minor who risks loss of liberty in a state juvenile institution enjoys a right of confrontation, including sworn testimony subject to cross-examination. Lower courts have similarly guaranteed such a right in civil commitment proceedings for those suffering from MENTAL ILLNESS [3,I], even though these proceedings in practice are not particularly adversarial and rely heavily on out-of-court statements not strictly within traditional hearsay exceptions. The scope of confrontation rights in proceedings involving the custody of children, as in civil child abuse cases, is currently disputed in doctrine and in practice. The Supreme Court recognized the right to confront and cross-examine adverse witnesses in administrative hearings prior to the termination of WELFARE BENEFITS [4] in GOLDBERG v. KELLY (1970) [2] and prior to a prisoner's transfer to a mental hospital in *Vitek v. Jones* (1980). But the Court has permitted decision making without confrontation, based on a written record or on hearing the affected individual's side of the story, in other cases, such as a prison disciplinary proceeding in *Wolff v. McDonnell* (1974) and a PUBLIC EMPLOYEE [3] pre-discharge review that precedes a fuller post-deprivation hearing in *Cleveland Board of Education v. Loudermill* (1985).

ROBERT D. GOLDSTEIN

Bibliography

GRAHAM, MICHAEL H. 1988 The Confrontation Clause, the Hearsay Rule, and Child Sexual Abuse Prosecutions: The State of the Relationship. *Minnesota Law Review* 72:523–601.

HADDAD, JAMES B. 1990 The Future of Confrontation Clause Developments: What Will Emerge When the Supreme Court Synthesizes the Diverse Lines of Confrontation Decisions. *Journal of Criminal Law and Criminology* 81:77–98.

JONAKAIT, RANDOLPH N. 1988 Restoring the Confrontation Clause to the Sixth Amendment. *UCLA Law Review* 35:557–622.

CONGRESS AND FOREIGN POLICY

Congress has three principal functions. As a forum for debate, it is a vital instrument for creating and crystallizing public opinion, the source of all legitimate governmental power and policy in a democratic society. Through the investigatory power of its committees, it is the grand inquest of the nation, watching society and government with an eye for new and emerging problems. And it has the sole power of legislation on certain subjects, qualified only by the President's veto. All three aspects of Congress's work are important to its activities in the field of FOREIGN AFFAIRS [2]. This article, however, will concentrate on Congress's role in legislation and its attempt to become a major participant in administration, the only area of its foreign policy agenda currently generating serious constitutional problems.

The Constitution divides the task of making and carrying out foreign policy in accordance with the rule that except where the Constitution provides otherwise, Congress is vested with the legislative part of American foreign policy and the President with the executive portion. Articles I and II mention certain subjects that illustrate the distinction between "legislative" and "executive" functions, and Article I, section 6, paragraph 2, provides that "no person holding any office under the United States shall be member of either House during his continuance in office." In a sentence focused on safeguards against corruption of the governmental process by either Congress or the President, paragraph 2 reveals the clear expectation that the new American constitutional order was not to be a cabinet government, but that Congress and the executive were to be separated institutionally as well as by function. During the period of drafting the Constitution, the presidency was deliberately made unitary rather than plural. And much was said and written about an executive capable of "energy, secrecy, and dispatch," as contrasted with a deliberative legislature not directly involved in the execution of the laws.

Drawing a line between the legislative and executive spheres has been conspicuously difficult in the area of foreign policy, however. One reason why this should be so is that foreign policy includes much more than the passage of statutes and the negotiation of international agreements and their subsequent execution. Much foreign policy is necessarily made in the ordinary course of diplomacy. And from the beginnings under the Constitution of 1787, the President has been recognized as the sole agent of the nation in its dealings with other states. He alone receives ambassadors and, from time to time, declares them unacceptable and sends them away. The power to recognize nations and to withhold recognition was accepted early as entirely presidential. The President is the chief diplomat of the nation; he smiles and frowns, speaks or remains silent, warns, praises, protests, and negotiates.

Even when diplomacy results in treaties that require approval by the Senate before ratification or in EXECUTIVE AGREEMENTS [2], which the President may or may not submit for a congressional vote, the process of making foreign policy is more heavily influenced by the President than is the passage of most statutes, which make policy in advance of action. The President can shape the circumstances in which issues of foreign policy come before Congress more often and more effectively than he can in dealing with issues of domestic policy. On the other hand, the negotiating process has its own constitutional pitfalls. If the Senate has to consent to the ratification of a major treaty or if Congress must pass enabling legislation in support of a treaty or executive agreement, members of Congress may be surly and uncooperative if they have not somehow participated in the negotiations themselves within or even beyond the limits of Article I, section 6, of the Constitution. Since the failure of the Versailles Treaty in 1919, every President has sought to anticipate the problem through briefings, consultations, or even membership or observer status for senators on negotiating delegations. If, on the other hand, members of Congress are suitably consulted about the instructions given to the negotiators and the ultimate bargain falls short of the goals specified in the instructions, pitfalls of another kind appear. The relation of Congress and the President in the making and ratification of treaties and executive agreements has therefore been a major political and constitutional irritant at least since 1795, when JAY'S TREATY was barely ratified.

ALEXANDER HAMILTON [2] took the view that the executive, legislative, and judicial powers were to be distinguished by their "nature." The EXECUTIVE POWER [I], he said, is all governmental power that is neither judicial nor legislative in character. From this somewhat circular eighteenth-century axiom, Hamilton, THOMAS JEFFERSON [3], and JOHN MARSHALL [3] drew a conclusion that has been of critical importance to CONSTITUTIONAL INTERPRETATION [1] ever since. Where a power is executive in character, Hamilton wrote, it is deemed to be presidential unless that conclusion is excluded by the constitutional text. In such cases, presidential supremacy is the rule and congressional authority the exception, and exceptions are to be strictly construed. The same rule of construction applies when powers are characterized as legislative or judicial. Here, too, the granted power is to be construed broadly, and the exceptions narrowly.

This rule is not without its modern critics. A few recent writers have urged that Congress be considered the supreme institution of government in all realms, and not only in the legislative sphere. They forget that the Constitution of 1787 was composed and adopted by men who found congressional supremacy under the ARTICLES OF CONFEDERATION [1] an unsatisfactory mode of government. The only reason such critics offer for their conclusion is that the United States is "a republic which has become a democracy" and that the imperious rise of modern democracy makes presidential and perhaps even judicial independence an anachronism.

In making and carrying out foreign policy, Congress and the President are forced to work together: neither Congress nor the President can conduct foreign policy alone for long. Sooner or later, a President will need money, new statutes, or both. And, as presently constituted, Congress is incapable of conducting diplomacy or commanding the armed forces, save by sporadic intervention in highly charged episodes. The history of American foreign policy is therefore necessarily the history of a rivalrous and uneasy partnership between Congress and the President, with occasional intervals of harmony and a few of utter frustration, such as WOODROW WILSON's [4] tragic final days.

The normal congressional impulse to nibble at the President's executive authority has gained momentum in recent years from four major sources. The first and perhaps the most important has been the growth in congressional staff, which goes back to the Legislative Reorganization Act of 1946. Before that fateful reform was adopted, Congress and its committees relied largely on the administration of the day for assistance in research and drafting. The Congressional Research Service of the Library of Congress provided some supplemental help, but until the recent past, that service was extremely small. Today, congressional staffs include 35,000 people, and the Congressional Research Service, several hundred more.

The influence of an able young congressional staff on the relations between Congress and the President has been reinforced by a second source of congressional ascendency: the modern habit of electing a Democratic Congress and a Republican President. The habit has been rather popular with the voters, but has decidedly negative features. For example, it encourages partisan irresponsibility on the part of Congress even on major national issues, especially in the field of foreign affairs.

These two tendencies together produce a third: the practice of writing long and elaborate statutes intended to control the President and the courts in detail as they apply statutes and treaties to new situations. As an astute observer recently noted, one of the most influential statutes ever enacted by Congress, the SHERMAN ANTITRUST ACT [4], consists of six brief paragraphs occupying less than half a page, whereas statutes now tend to be hundreds, if not thousands, of pages long.

Fourth and finally, congressional attacks on the President's prerogatives in the field of foreign affairs draw strength from widespread protest against the foreign policy the United States has pursued since 1945. That protest is based on a nostalgic yearning for the neutrality and comparative isolation of the United States during the century between 1815 and 1914.

These flows of change were suddenly accelerated in the late 1960s and early 1970s by the growing unpopularity of the VIETNAM WAR [4,I] and the WATERGATE [4] scandal. Protest movements against the war in Vietnam became ominous. In turn, this phenomenon led Congress to move decisively both to stop "Johnson's War" and to alter the traditional constitutional balance between Congress and the President so that such "presidential" wars could never happen again. Thomas M. Franck and Edward Weisbard call this vague and many-sided movement a congressional revolution that has radically redistributed the foreign affairs powers in favor of Congress at the expense of the presidency. Foreign policy, they proclaim, will now be made by "co-determination," without regard to the distinction between legislative and executive functions. The Bastille Day of the congressional revolution, they say, was June 29, 1973, the day when President RICHARD M. NIXON [3] surrendered to a congressional effort to end the American military involvement in Indochina and promised to stop bombing in Cambodia. "With that sullen concession, power over foreign policy shifted: from the imperial President and his discreet and decorous professional relations managers to the undisciplined, rambunctious rabble of the House and Senate."

The power to end wars by armistice and cease-fire agreements had always been regarded as part of the President's authority as COMMANDER-IN-CHIEF [I]. In the case of the Vietnam War, however, the explosion of opinion against the war and the coincidence of the Watergate scandal and the revulsion it produced against President Nixon led to the success of Congress's attempt to end the war independently by using its power over appropriations and forcing a gravely wounded President to acquiesce in its action. This extraordinary conjuncture of political forces also permitted Congress to override President Nixon's veto of the WAR POWERS ACT [4].

Actually, the revolt of Congress against the Hamiltonian conception of the presidency began long before the explosion of opinion against the Vietnam War and President Nixon. A key weapon of Congress in that battle was, and remains, the LEGISLATIVE VETO [3] in all its forms. The

legislative veto was invented in 1932. It allows Congress to overrule presidential constructions and applications of existing law by CONCURRENT RESOLUTION [1], that is, to reverse purely executive actions without having to confront the President's VETO POWER [4]. Since that time, the practice had spread throughout the statute books, but particularly in the realm of foreign policy. The Lend-Lease Act of 1941, for example, contained a legislative veto provision, stipulating that Congress could terminate the act by concurrent resolution. President FRANKLIN D. ROOSEVELT [3] thought the provision unconstitutional, but acquiesced in it silently because the act was of transcendent importance, and it was by no means clear that it would have passed without the legislative veto.

During the prolonged struggle between Congress and the President over foreign policy during the 1960s and 1970s, legislation of this kind became a flood. That legislation attempted to control presidential discretion in interpreting and applying statutes and treaties not only by concurrent resolutions passed by both houses but also by veto-free delegations of executive power to one house and even to particular committees of either house.

The Supreme Court held the legislative veto unconstitutional in IMMIGRATION AND NATURALIZATION SERVICE V. CHADHA (1983) [2], but Congress has not yet seriously undertaken to comply with the decision by removing from the books more than 200 statutes directly affected by it. Indeed, Congress is still defying the Court by passing or seriously considering bills that would openly violate the rule of the decision.

How far can Congress go in using its power of the purse as a sword in its struggle to seize executive power? In the past, both political usage and Supreme Court opinions made clear that the appropriations power had constitutional limits. Several congressional conditions on the spending of appropriated funds have been ruled or declared to be unconstitutional in cases that include UNITED STATES V. LOVETT (1946) [3], MYERS V. UNITED STATES (1926) [3], *United States v. Klein* (1872), and FLAST V. COHEN (1968) [2]. Congress's recent experiments with expanded uses of its appropriations power have stimulated original and provocative law review articles suggesting that the President now has the power to use a line item veto and a limited power to spend in emergencies without prior appropriations and that Congress cannot use its appropriations power to prevent the President from carrying out his constitutional duties. Future constitutional development along some of these lines would be a normal response to perceptions of a congressional thrust for excessive power.

Twelve years after Franck proclaimed the success of what he regarded as Congress's wholesome and cleansing revolution, it is clear that while much has changed, his optimism was premature. Whether the congressional attempt to transform the constitutional relationship between Congress and the President in the field of foreign affairs will prevail in the end remains to be seen. Institutions 200 years old normally reflect the necessities of function. As Franck remarks, if Congress demonstrates that it cannot in fact use its new powers or if its key members are unwilling or unable to devote the necessary time and attention to their new foreign policy responsibilities, "power will run off Capitol Hill."

What is clear, however, is that the historical conflict between Congress and the President about the making and implementation of foreign policy has changed fundamentally. It is no longer the push and pull of a natural tug of war between the legislative and executive branches, operating within the framework of well-understood rules and habits. Congress has been pressing with new determination to take over executive functions in many areas of government, and particularly in foreign affairs. The constitutional balance between Congress and the President has shifted so radically that "the inevitable friction" about which Justice LOUIS D. BRANDEIS [1] wrote in *Myers v. United States* has become war, marked both by episodes of bitter hostility and by a slow presidential retreat that is transforming the President into a prime minister or constitutional monarch, ceremoniously presiding over an increasingly strong Congress. Whether we describe this transformation as a glorious revolution or as a constitutional crisis is immaterial. What is at stake in the battle is far more than constitutional piety or even the effectiveness of government, important as it is. What is at stake is the future of liberty. The accumulation of the legislative and executive powers in the same hands, as Jefferson, JAMES MADISON [3], and others have said over the years, is "the very definition of tyranny."

The powers of the presidency have not been formally annulled. They are still latent in the bloodstream of the government. But they encounter more and more resistance each time a President tries to use them. As a result, the presidency is being stripped of some of its more important prerogatives.

If the present trends are not reversed by the courts, the President will soon be wrapped like Gulliver in a web of regulatory statutes and hopelessly weakened. Although the President has the sole constitutional authority to conduct foreign relations, congressional leaders sometimes negotiate independently with foreign governments, as they have done recently with Nicaragua, for example. Substantive riders on appropriations bills and other devices to evade the President's veto power are more popular than ever. Congress has already put the President under the control of a congressional cabinet in the exercise of his responsibilities for intelligence and is actively considering applying that model to the process of making "presidential" decisions about the use of force and foreign policy more generally. If that possibility should materialize, the presidency the nation has known since 1789, the presidency of ABRAHAM LINCOLN [3] and Franklin D. Roosevelt, would be no more.

The Persian Gulf crisis of 1990–1991, however, demonstrated once again the functional necessity for the historic powers of the President. The abject failure of Congress to manage that episode should do much to restore the constitutional balance.

EUGENE V. ROSTOW

(SEE ALSO: *Advice and Consent* [1]; *Congressional War Powers* [I]; *Senate and Foreign Policy* [I]; *Treaty Power* [4].)

Bibliography

CRABB, CECIL V., JR. and HOLT, PAT 1989 *Invitation to Struggle: Congress, the President, and Foreign Policy*, 3rd ed. Washington, D.C.: Congressional Quarterly Press.

FISHER, LOUIS 1985 *Constitutional Conflicts Between Congress and the President*. Princeton, N.J.: Princeton University Press.

———1988 *Constitutional Dialogues*. Princeton, N.J.: Princeton University Press.

FRANCK, THOMAS M. and WEISBAND, EDWARD 1979 *Foreign Policy by Congress*. New York: Oxford University Press.

ROSTOW, EUGENE V. 1989 *President, Prime Minister, or Constitutional Monarch?* Washington, D.C.: National Defense University Press.

WILSON, WOODROW (1885)1967 *Congressional Government*. Cleveland, Ohio: Meridan Books.

CONGRESSIONAL WAR POWERS

The Constitution assigns the power to declare war solely to the Congress, one of the wisest of the many CHECKS AND BALANCES [1] built into the American political system. Throughout American history, however, Presidents have committed acts of war without congressional authorization. The question of where to assign the power to initiate and conduct war was thoroughly debated during the framing of the Constitution. The outcome of that debate was a document that clearly did not give the President unlimited WAR POWERS [4,I] but in fact separated the power to conduct war from the power to initiate war.

The Constitution grants Congress the power to issue a DECLARATION OF WAR [2] and to "grant letters of Marque and reprisal." There is no question that the ORIGINAL INTENT [I] of the Framers of the Constitution was to vest in the Congress the complete power to decide on war or peace, with the sole exception that the President could respond to sudden attack on the United States without congressional authorization. During the CONSTITUTIONAL CONVENTION OF 1787 [1], the debates centered on an original draft of the war power providing that "the legislature of the United States shall have the power . . . to make war." One member of the convention, CHARLES PINCKNEY [3], opposed giving this power to Congress, claiming that its proceedings would be too slow; PIERCE BUTLER [1] said that he was "voting for vesting the power in the President, who will have all the requisite qualities, and will not make war but when the Nation will support it." Butler's motion received no second, however.

JAMES MADISON [3] and ELBRIDGE GERRY [2], meanwhile, were not satisfied with the original wording, that the legislature be given the power to make war. They moved to substitute "declare" for "make," "leaving to the Executive the power to repel sudden attacks." The meaning of this motion, which eventually was carried by a vote of seven states to two, was clear. The power to initiate war was left to Congress, with the reservation from Congress to the President to repel a sudden attack on the United States. As THOMAS JEFFERSON [3] explained in 1789, "We have already given . . . one effectual check to the dog of war by transferring the power of letting him loose, from the executive to the legislative body, from those who are to spend to those who are to pay."

Acts of war, acts of reprisal, and acts of self-defense—all have been taken by past Presidents, but seldom without a rationalization of the legal implications of their actions that reflected recognition of the necessity of congressional authorization of all presidential acts of war except self-defense. At a time of national crisis, notably during the CIVIL WAR [I], the President has acted illegally and depended on Congress to ratify his action after the fact. In the latter half of the twentieth century, however, a major change in the concept of the war power began to be propounded. Beginning with the KOREAN WAR [3] and the VIETNAM WAR [4,I], some presidents, congressmen, and publicists claimed for the executive the power to initiate war without the consent of Congress.

Covert war, as we have come to know it, grew out of the United States' experiences in WORLD WAR II [I]. Two factors have combined to encourage covert action and covert war. First, nuclear weapons—forces of utter destruction—have deterred more overt and massive forms of violence. Second, the intensity of the ideological and geopolitical struggle between the United States and the Soviet Union nevertheless assured that violence, albeit covert, would continue. Shortly after World War II, in January 1946, President HARRY S. TRUMAN [4] issued a directive establishing the Central Intelligence Group, the precursor of the Central Intelligence Agency. Previously, no nonmilitary covert operations group had existed in the United States during peacetime. Later intelligence groups would build on this meager institutional foundation, often without questioning either the appropriateness of its methods or the basic assumptions behind its organization.

The Constitution commits the entire power to decide for war or peace to Congress, not the President, with the exception noted above—in the event of sudden attack. No action of covert war is likely to fit within that narrow exception. The COMMANDER-IN-CHIEF [1] clause gives the President no additional power to commit forces of the United States to war or acts of war when the nation is at peace. Only Congress is empowered to change this condition.

The Constitution's grant to Congress of the power to grant "letters of Marque and reprisal" covers most of what we think of as covert war. Originally a letter of marque merely authorized crossing into a foreign state to obtain redress for wrongs inflicted by a foreigner, and a letter of reprisal permitted the use of force to secure compensation for an unlawful taking of property or goods within the territorial jurisdiction of the sovereign. When combined, a letter of marque and reprisal permitted a particular person to seize property or even foreign citizens who refused to redress injuries they caused. By the eighteenth century, letters of marque had evolved into means of legitimating acts of war against other sovereign states by private parties. Likewise, reprisals developed into public acts of war against another state or citizens of another state in retaliation for an injury for which the state is held responsible. Under international law a reprisal is legal only if the acts are responsive and proportional to previous hostile acts of another state and the reprisal is first preceded by unsuccessful attempts at a peaceful resolution.

The war clause in its completeness, then, grants to Congress all power to decide on war, including both public and private or covert war, declared or undeclared. The Constitution grants no power to the President to wage private war against states with whom the nation is at peace by hiring modern mercenaries, pirates, or privateers without the express authorization of Congress. Nor does the President or the National Security Council have the authority to privatize the conduct of American foreign policy in the sale of arms or transfer of money. Absent a direct attack on the United States, a decision to go to war is constitutional only when it is publicly arrived at by congressional debate.

EDWIN B. FIRMAGE

(SEE ALSO: *Congress and Foreign Policy* [I]; *Executive Power* [I]; *Executive Prerogative* [I]; *Foreign Affairs* [2]; *Senate and Foreign Policy* [I]; *War, Foreign Affairs, and the Constitution* [4].)

Bibliography

LOBEL, JULES 1986 Covert War and Congressional Authority: Hidden War and Forgotten Power. *University of Pennsylvania Law Review* 134:1035–1110.

PRADOS, JOHN 1986 *Presidents' Secret Wars: CIA and Pentagon Covert Operations Since World War II.* New York: William Morrow.

WORMUTH, FRANCIS D. and FIRMAGE, EDWIN B. 1989 *To Chain the Dog of War: The Power of Congress in History and Law*, 2nd ed. Urbana: University of Illinois Press.

CONSERVATISM

Conservatives would agree with Robert Bork's understanding of the role of the Supreme Court under the Constitution and with its implicit understanding of the Constitution itself. Bork concluded a 1984 lecture at the American Enterprise Institute in Washington with the following words:

In a constitutional democracy the moral content of the law must be given by the morality of the framer or the legislator, never by the morality of the judge. The sole task of the latter—and it is a task quite large enough for anyone's wisdom, skill, and virtue—is to translate the framer's or the legislator's morality into a rule to govern unforeseen circumstances. That abstinence from giving his own desires free play, that continuing and self-conscious renunciation of power, that is the morality of the jurist.

Bork's is not, of course, the popular view of the judge's role, a fact made manifest by the reaction to his nomination for a seat on the Supreme Court. Some 1,925 law professors—surely a good proportion of the total—publicly opposed his appointment and took the trouble of communicating their opposition to the Senate Judiciary Committee. Bork, they said in one way or another, was out of the "mainstream," as surely he was and is. Whereas Bork would appeal to the Framers' morality, mainstream lawyers, arguing that the Framers represented "a world that is dead and gone," tend to prefer their own; some of them go so far so to accuse the Framers of being morally indifferent, a view popularized by Ronald Dworkin, one of Bork's principal opponents. Dworkin sees the Constitution as in need of moral principles and would supply that need. What is required, he says, is a "fusion of constitutional law and moral theory, a connection that, incredibly, has yet to take place."

Conservatives would protest that a Constitution that secures the rights of man—the *equal* rights of man—to the end of "securing the blessings of liberty" is not lacking in moral principle. Still, had he chosen to do so, Dworkin could have found in the mill of the founding documents an abundance of the grist he wants to grind. There is,

for example, JAMES MADISON's [3] famous statement in *The Federalist* #10 to the effect that the first object of government is the protection of different and unequal faculties of acquiring property. Protecting the equal rights of unequally endowed men can only lead to what Madison said it would lead to, and has in fact led to, namely, different degrees and kinds of property. In short, liberty leads to inequality, not of Madisonian rights but of wealth, position, and rank.

Unlike mainstream (or liberal) lawyers, conservatives are willing to live with this dispensation, and not only because they object to the means used by the mainstream lawyers to change it. The history of Title VII of the CIVIL RIGHTS ACT OF 1964 [1] provides an example of those means. That piece of legislation was enacted by Congress to put an end to EMPLOYMENT DISCRIMINATION [2] against blacks and women. But the Supreme Court, over the objections of conservative Justices, including Chief Justice WILLIAM REHNQUIST [3,I] and Justice ANTONIN SCALIA [I], has converted it into a statute permitting, and in effect compelling, discrimination favoring blacks and women. Concurring in a case dealing with gender discrimination, a somewhat shamefaced Justice SANDRA DAY O'CONNOR [3,I] indicated how this was accomplished: "As Justice Scalia illuminates with excruciating clarity, [Title VII] has been interpreted . . . to permit what its language read literally would prohibit." When necessary to further their political agendas, mainstream lawyers, on and off the bench, favor appeals to the "spirit," instead of the written text, of statutes and to what they contend is the "unwritten," instead of the written, Constitution.

No case better illustrates this practice than the 1965 BIRTH CONTROL [1] case GRISWOLD V. CONNECTICUT [2], and none has given rise to so much criticism from conservatives (and even from a few liberals) as the most prominent of the cases it spawned, ROE V. WADE [3], the 1973 ABORTION [1,I] decision. To strike down the Connecticut statute forbidding the use of contraceptives—a statute that for practical reasons could not be enforced and for political reasons could not be repealed—the Court found a right to privacy not in a specific constitutional provision but in "penumbras, formed by emanations" from the FIRST AMENDMENT [2,I], THIRD AMENDMENT [4], FOURTH AMENDMENT [2,I], FIFTH AMENDMENT, NINTH AMENDMENT [3], and ultimately the FOURTEENTH AMENDMENT [2,I]. To strike down the abortion laws of all fifty states, the Court again invoked this right to privacy, now locating it in the "liberty" protected by the Fourteenth Amendment.

The principal proponent of this kind of constitutional construction, and the chief target of conservative criticism, was Justice WILLIAM J. BRENNAN [1,I], and nothing better illustrates his understanding of JUDICIAL POWER [3] than a draft opinion he wrote during the Court's consideration of FRONTIERO V. RICHARDSON (1973) [2], a case decided when the so-called EQUAL RIGHTS AMENDMENT [2] was awaiting ratification by the states. Frontiero was a female air force officer who was denied certain dependents' benefits—benefits that would automatically have been granted with respect to the wife of a male officer—because she failed to prove that her husband was dependent on her for more than one half of his support. The issue on which the Court was divided was whether sex, like race, should be treated as a suspect, and therefore less readily justified, classification. Brennan, we are told, circulated an opinion declaring classification by sex virtually impermissible. "He knew that [this] would have the effect of enacting the equal rights amendment [but he] was accustomed to having the Court out front, leading any civil rights movement" (Bob Woodward and Scott Armstrong, *The Brethren*, p. 254). The authors of this account conclude by quoting Brennan as being of the opinion that there "was no reason to wait several years for the states to ratify the amendment"—no reason other than the fact, which Brennan knew to be a fact, that the Constitution *as then written* would not support the decision he wanted the Court to render.

Conservatives call this JUDICIAL ACTIVISM [3], or government by the judiciary. It is not for the judiciary—the least responsible and, conservatives could charge, frequently the most irresponsible branch of government—to make the laws or amend the Constitution (or "bring it up to date"). Those powers belong, in the one case, to the Congress and, in the other, to the people in their sovereign capacity. Judges, they say, quoting *The Federalist* #78, are supposed to be "faithful guardians of the Constitution," not evangels of new modes and orders: "Until the people have, by some solemn and authoritative act, annulled or changed the established form, it is binding upon themselves collectively, as well as individually." As conservatives see it, one issue dividing them from mainstream (or liberal) lawyers is that of legitimacy: The legitimacy of judge-made law and, ultimately, the legitimacy of the Constitution itself. If, as James Madison put it, the judges are not guided by the sense of the people who ratified the Constitution, "there can be no security for a consistent and stable, more than for a *faithful* exercise of its powers." The legitimacy of government depends on adherence to the written text, the text the people ratified.

The classic statement of these (conservative) propositions can be found in JOHN MARSHALL's [3] opinion for the Court in MARBURY V. MADISON (1803) [3]: The "whole American fabric has been erected" on the principle that government derives from, and is dependent on, the will of the people. "The original and supreme will organizes

the government, and assigns to different departments their respective powers."

Statements of this sort abound in the literature of the founding period. "In a government which is emphatically stiled [*sic*] a government of laws, the least possible range ought to be left for the discretion of the judges." "If the constitution is to be expounded, not by its written text, but by the opinions of the rulers for the time being, whose opinions are to prevail, the first or the last? [And if the last] what certainty can there be in those powers [which it assigns and limits]?" Both certainty and legitimacy would be put in jeopardy by rules of constitutional construction that, in effect, permit the judges to do as they will. "Would [the Constitution] not become, instead of a supreme law for ourselves and our posterity, a mere oracle of the powers of the rulers of the day, to which implicit homage is to be paid, and speaking at different times the most opposite commands, and in the most ambiguous voices?"

Connected to this issue of legitimacy is the cause of constitutional government itself. As conservatives see it, inequality of wealth, rank, and position is the price we pay for liberty, and it was to secure the blessings of liberty that the Constitution was ordained and established. In Madison's words in *The Federalist* #10, the Constitution serves to secure liberty by providing "a republican remedy for the diseases most incident to republican government," egalitarian diseases manifested in "a rage for paper money, for an abolition of debts, for an equal division of property, or for any other improper or wicked project." The remedy was to be found in the limits embodied "in the extent and proper structure of the Union"—in a word, in the Constitution. And as Marshall said in *Marbury*, The Constitution is written in order that "those limits not be mistaken or forgotten." THOMAS JEFFERSON [3] made the same point when he said that "the possession of a written constitution [was America's] peculiar security."

What conservatives want to conserve is this *liberal* Constitution, which, as they see it, is endangered by persons styling themselves liberals today. First, there are academic lawyers who treat the Constitution not as *law*—in Marshall's words, "a superior paramount law, unchangeable by ordinary means"—but as a mere "epiphenomenon," which is to say, as merely one of the factors (and, typically, not a controlling factor) entering into judicial decisions. As one of them puts it, rather than carry any precise meaning that judges are bound by oath to recognize and obey, the most important constitutional provisions "do *not* rule out any answer a majority of the Court is likely to want to give." The social, historical, and economic conditions take precedence over the Constitution's written text, and they may dictate any outcome. "There is nothing that is unsayable in the language of the Constitution," writes another.

Second, there is Justice Brennan, who writes that "the genius of the Constitution rests not in any static meaning it might have had in a world that is dead and gone, but in the adaptability of its great principles to cope with current problems and current needs."

Third are historians who, in the course of ridiculing the conservatives' appeal for a jurisprudence of ORIGINAL INTENT [I], insist that "our Constitution is no more important to the longevity and workability of our government than MAGNA CARTA [3] is to the longevity and workability of the British government. Our Constitution is as unwritten as theirs."

Finally, there are journalists who say that "the mere idea of original intent is an absurdity . . . [that] those men in Philadelphia could not have possibly had an 'original intent.' "

As these statements indicate, the conservative effort to preserve that liberal Constitution will gain little support in the liberal community. Unlike the Framers, today's liberals prefer equality to liberty, an equality of status to an equality of rights, a development foreseen by ALEXIS DE TOCQUEVILLE [4]. Democratic peoples have a natural taste for liberty, he wrote, but their passion for equality is "invincible" and "irresistible," and anyone who tries to stand up against it "will be overthrown and destroyed by it."

In addition, conservatives have to contend with developments in the realm of political thought that, it is said, deprive the Constitution of its philosophical foundations. The Constitution put constraints on the popular will, but, according to Professor Sanford Levinson, those constraints have been deprived of whatever moral authority they might once have had. Constitutional arguments have been rendered meaningless. Indeed, the very idea of CONSTITUTIONALISM [2] is dead: "The death of 'constitutionalism' may be the central event of our time," Levinson writes, "just as the death of God was that of the past century (and for much the same reason)." If, as he claims, this view of our situation is "shared by most major law schools," conservatives are engaged in an almost hopeless enterprise. Care of the Constitution was put in the hands of the judges, but the judges are trained in those "major law schools."

Admittedly, and quite apart from the influence of this legal and political thought, governing within the limit imposed by a STRICT CONSTRUCTION [4] of the Constitution has never been an easy matter. FEDERALISM [2,I] is one of its prominent features, and conservatives, today if not in the past, would preserve it in its integrity. They would do so for political, as well as for constitutional, reasons. Like Tocqueville, they appreciate the political importance of what he called "mores," those "habits of the heart" that characterize a people and, in our case, he argued, made free goverment possible. Conservatives would attribute the Constitution's "longevity and workability" not to its flexibility but, at least in part, to the laws of the states where these mores, or morals and manners, are fostered and protected. Directly or indirectly (by supporting the private institutions whose business it is to provide it), these laws are intended to promote the sort of civic or moral education required of citizens in a democracy. Many of them—such as laws dealing with FLAG DESECRATION [2], OBSCENITY [3], indecency, illegitimacy, school prayer, and religious instruction and institutions, the list of which is not endless but is long—have been declared unconstitutional under the Fourteenth Amendment INCORPORATION DOCTRINE [2,I]. These laws have been declared unconstitutional, conservatives insist, in the absence of any evidence that the framers of the Fourteenth Amendment intended it—originally intended it—to be used for that purpose.

There is, however, an abundance of evidence that the Fourteenth and other post–Civil War amendments were intended to affect the federal structure of the Constitution in material respects. The same freedom that allowed the states to be concerned about the moral character of their citizens also allowed them to decide who among their residents were to be citizens and, therefore, who among them were to enjoy the CIVIL RIGHTS [1,I] and the PRIVILEGES AND IMMUNITIES [3] of citizens. Thus, and without any question, those amendments were intended to deprive states of this power; they would do so by providing what Madison in 1787 criticized the original Constitution for its failure to provide, namely, "a constitutional negative on the laws of the States [in order to] secure individuals agst. encroachments on their rights."

The consequence—if only in our own time—has been a tremendous growth of national power at the expense of the states, and especially national judicial power. Conservatives cannot (and, in most cases, do not) complain when this power has been used to put an end to RACIAL DISCRIMINATION [3,I]; as amended, the Constitution not only authorized this but required it. Given what proved to be almost a century of congressional inaction, they would also agree with the Supreme Court's decision in BROWN V. BOARD OF EDUCATION (1954,1955) [1], the public school desegregation case. Read literally (or construed strictly), the words of the equal protection clause do not lend themselves to the use to which they were put in that case, but—to paraphrase what was said by conservative Chief Justice CHARLES EVANS HUGHES [2] on an earlier occasion—while emergencies may not create power, they do furnish the occasions when it may properly be exercised. On such occasions, the conservative rule of "strict construction" must give way to necessity.

Conservatives concede, as they must, that necessity

is the mother of invention; where they differ from mainstream liberals, to cite still another aphorism, is in their refusal to make a virtue of necessity. They cannot say, because it would be foolish to say, that the times must be kept in tune with the Constitution; but because our freedom and prosperity depend upon it, they do say, and say emphatically, that the times, *to the extent possible*, should be kept in tune with the Constitution.

WALTER BERNS

(SEE ALSO: *Bork Nomination* [I]; *Critical Legal Studies* [I]; *Liberalism* [I]; *Political Philosophy of the Constitu 'on* [3, I]; *Suspect Classifications* [4]; *Unwritten Constitution* [4].)

Bibliography

BORK, ROBERT H. 1990 *The Tempting of America: The Political Seduction of the Law.* New York: Free Press.

GOLDWIN, ROBERT A. and ART KAUFMAN, EDS. 1987 *How Does the Constitution Protect Religious Freedom?* Washington: American Enterprise Institute.

LERNER, RALPH 1987 *The Thinking Revolutionary: Principle and Practice in the New Republic.* Ithaca, N.Y.: Cornell University Press.

MCDOWELL, GARY L. 1988 *Curbing the Courts: The Constitution and the Limits of Judicial Power.* Baton Rouge: Louisiana State University Press.

PANGLE, THOMAS L. 1988 *The Spirit of Modern Republicanism: The Moral Vision of the American Founding and the Philosophy of Locke.* Chicago: University of Chicago Press.

RABKIN, JEREMY 1989 *Judicial Compulsions: How Public Law Distorts Public Policy.* New York: Basic Books.

CONSPIRACY LAW

The crime of conspiracy is charged regularly in state and federal courts throughout the United States. This crime consists in an agreement by two or more individuals to commit an additional crime. The conspiracy charge is widely used in a number of different areas, particularly with respect to white-collar crimes and narcotics offenses. The prosecution views the crime of conspiracy as advantageous because it allows, in a single trial, for the prosecution of all conspirators wherever they are located, and it allows the government to prosecute the case in any city in which any act in furtherance of the agreement took place. In addition, statements made by any conspirator are allowed to be used against all other conspirators, and each conspirator can be found criminally responsible for other conspirators' crimes found to be in furtherance of the agreement.

Three major constitutional questions have arisen in conspiracy trials in the United States. The first deals with the DOUBLE JEOPARDY [2,I] clause of the Fifth Amendment, which provides in part, "nor shall any person be subject for the same offense to be twice put in jeopardy

of life or limb." Most judges have concluded that the purpose of the double jeopardy clause was to ensure that a person could not be charged more than once for the same offense in the same jurisdiction. Individuals who are prosecuted for the conspiracy offense contend that if they are also charged with the crime that was the subject of the agreement (for example, bank robbery), their double jeopardy rights have been violated. The courts have consistently rejected this claim, however, holding that conspiracy (the agreement to commit bank robbery) and the crime (the actual bank robbery) are separate offenses. Hence, the defendant can receive separate punishment for each without the double jeopardy clause being violated.

Defendants also contend that being charged with conspiracies in two different courts violates their double jeopardy rights. For instance, conspiracy to rob a bank may be a violation of both state and federal law. It is a violation of state law because robbing any institution within the state is a crime. It is a violation of federal law because the bank may be a federally insured institution. Under the principle of "dual sovereignties" the Supreme Court has concluded that separate prosecutions and separate penalties for a federal conspiracy and a state conspiracy do not violate the double jeopardy clause, because such prosecutions are not multiple trials for the same offense by the same jurisdiction.

An additional constitutional issue is raised when defendants are charged with conspiring not to commit a crime but to commit acts that are "injurious to the public health or morals." These cases usually involve situations in which a particular form of behavior, such as charging usurious interest rates, is not itself criminal, but the defendant is charged with *conspiring* to commit that act. The Supreme Court in *Musser v. Utah* (1948) cast considerable doubt on the constitutionality of these prosecutions. The chief argument here is that such conspiracy prosecutions violate the DUE PROCESS [2] clause of both the Fifth Amendment and FOURTEENTH AMENDMENT [2,I] because the phrase "acts injurious to the public health or morals" is so vague as to give insufficient guidance to citizens. As a consequence of the *Musser* decision, few prosecutions have been based upon this rather open-ended charge; instead, the government typically contends that the defendants have conspired to commit a particular crime and that crime is then set forth in some detail.

The third constitutional issue is perhaps the most famous and controversial, involving free speech implications under the FIRST AMENDMENT [2,I]. The problem surfaces when the defendants are charged with agreeing to advocate activities challenging the government. In such situations, the question is whether the agreement can be viewed as purely criminal behavior or whether, under the First Amendment, the behavior is protected speech. The most important Supreme Court case in the area is YATES V. UNITED STATES (1956) [4]. There the defendants were mid-level officials of the Communist party charged with conspiring to advocate the overthrow of the government of the United States by force and violence. In construing the Smith Act, the Court concluded that the prosecution, to succeed, must show an agreement to engage in unlawful action and a specific intent by each conspirator to engage in that action. If, however, the charge against the defendants were based upon their agreement to advocate the abstract principle of forcible overthrow of the government, that agreement would not violate the statute, even if such advocacy promoted violent activity.

PAUL MARCUS

Bibliography

COOK, JOSEPH and MARCUS, PAUL   1991   *Criminal Procedure,*
     3rd ed. New York: Matthew Bender.
MARCUS, PAUL   1991   *The Prosecution and Defense of Criminal Conspiracy Cases.* New York: Matthew Bender.

CONSTITUTION AND CIVIC IDEALS, THE

The renowned constitutional scholar ALEXANDER M. BICKEL [1] believed that "the concept of citizenship plays only the most minimal role in the American constitutional scheme." The Constitution "bestowed rights on people and persons, not . . . some legal construct called citizen"—a state of affairs Bickel thought "idyllic."

Indeed, the unamended Constitution mentioned citizenship remarkably infrequently. Three times it made citizenship "of the United States" required for the elective federal offices (Article I, sections 1–2; Article II, section 1). It mentioned citizenship of a "State" four times in describing the JURISDICTION [3] of the federal courts (Article III, section 2), and once in protecting citizens' PRIVILEGES AND IMMUNITIES [3] by a principle of interstate equality (Article IV, section 2). Article I, section 8, also gave Congress the power to establish "an uniform Rule of naturalization." That was all. The Constitution did not define United States or state citizenship, explain their relationship, or specify their "Privileges and Immunities." Strikingly, it did not demand citizenship of voters, Supreme Court Justices, or even traitors (Article III, section 3).

Yet, despite its silences on citizenship, the Constitution embodied not one but several civic ideals, all of which presented a conception of the nature and meaning of membership in the Union that its Framers aimed to perfect. With deference to Bickel, the Constitution's reticence about these ideals traces only partly to an exaltation of

universal personal rights over all particular political identities. In important ways the different civic ideals visible in the Constitution were in sharp tension with each other. The Constitution's silences also reflected the Framers' decisions not to confront, much less resolve, those difficulties. Subsequently, these initially postponed conflicts over rival civic ideals have shaped the nation's evolution profoundly. Over time, Americans have modified their original civic conceptions, and in the twentieth century many have supported a new ideal of American civic identity.

In framing the Constitution, American leaders drew on the classical republican tradition espoused by James Harrington and analyzed by Baron de MONTESQUIEU [3] and from colonial and revolutionary struggles men like LUTHER MARTIN [3] derived their beliefs that legitimate governments must be popularly controlled and that popular governance must be conducted preeminently in small republics. Hence, they favored FEDERALISM [2,I], opposed lodging any extensive power in the national government, and continued to believe in the primacy of state citizenship over national citizenship. From the Enlightenment LIBERALISM [I] of JOHN LOCKE [3] and, in most American readings, WILLIAM BLACKSTONE [1], others such as JAMES WILSON [4] and JAMES MADISON [3] derived their esteem for sacred personal rights, including rights of property and conscience (expressed in the CONTRACT CLAUSE [2] limits on the states and the Article IV ban on RELIGIOUS TESTS [3] for national office). Such men tended to favor national power and the primacy of Americans' more extended membership in their nation.

But beyond their liberalism and REPUBLICANISM [I], American leaders from GOUVERNEUR MORRIS [3] to CHARLES PINCKNEY [3] also expected that to be a full member of the American community, one would share in a special ethnocultural heritage clustered around Protestant Christianity, the white race, European or (preferably) American birth, and male predominance in most spheres. This version of "Americanism" led them to require all Presidents after the revolutionary generation to be "natural born" citizens (Article II, section 1); to countenance black chattel SLAVERY [4] implicitly but recurrently (e.g., Article I, sections 2 and 9; Article IV, section 2; Article V); to distinguish tribal Indians from both Americans and foreigners twice (Article I, sections 2 and 8); and to accept tacitly the subordinate status of women. Such an Americanism was often bound up with Protestant visions of the new Union as a "redeemer nation," providentially selected to serve divine purposes. Christianity also pervaded the other early American civic conceptions, intertwining with republican espousals of public virtue as well as liberal precepts of human dignity that transcended temporal politics and nationalities.

None of these civic conceptions could gain exclusive

sway in the Constitution; none could be wholly ignored. In some respects, the Framers invented a novel kind of national liberal republic that was a significant contribution to the development of modern regimes. But some fundamental conflicts were compromised or evaded precisely by leaving citizenship and the touchy relation between state and national political membership undefined: by avoiding, explicitly accepting, or opposing the illiberal institution of black chattel slavery; by not specifying civic privileges and immunities; and by refusing to establish a national religion while permitting state establishments to continue. Even the relationship of state authority to Congress's new power to naturalize citizens was left for later resolution.

Almost immediately, state-oriented republican anxieties about the Constitution's expansions of national power compelled Congress to propose the BILL OF RIGHTS [1], explicitly reserving powers to the states and protecting local institutions like MILITIA [I] and juries, although several amendments, the FIRST AMENDMENT [2,I] especially, also specified liberal protections of basic personal freedoms. Clashes between Jeffersonianism and Jacksonian STATES' RIGHTS [4] republicanism and the FEDERALISTS' [I] and Whigs' nationalist economic liberalism continued through the antebellum years, accompanied by growing conflicts pitting liberal and Christian advocates of expanded rights for blacks and other ethnic and religious minorities against Americanist defenses of Protestant white male supremacy. Finally, of course, issues of the primacy of state versus national citizenship and the status of blacks fueled the Union's great crisis in the 1860s. The CIVIL WAR [I] amendments appeared to decide those disputes in favor of liberal nationalistic civic conceptions, but in the late nineteenth century both traditional republican views of federalism ·and Americanist views of racial and gender hierarchies were in many respects successfully reasserted.

Most Progressive Era reformers remained narrow Protestant Americanists, but Progressive intellectuals on the left, including John Dewey, Randolph Bourne, and Horace Kallen, began formulating a broader conception of American civic identity. They drew on republicanism's calls for democratic participation, liberalism's emphasis on equal human dignity, and Americanism's stress on the importance of constitutive social identities. But, relying on pragmatist philosophic foundations, these thinkers reformulated those conceptions into one that may be termed "democratic cultural pluralism." It represented American nationality as a democratically organized confederation of disparate ethnic, religious, and cultural groups, all entitled to equal respect in public institutions and policies; these groups would serve as the primary loci of most persons' social identities. Democratic pluralists saw na-

tional membership essentially as a means to advance the welfare of all such groups on a fair, neutral basis. The democratic cultural pluralist conception of American civic identity increasingly came to prevail in judicial constitutional doctrines and in American citizenship statutes after the NEW DEAL [I] and especially during the Great Society years. The federal government repudiated racial SEGREGATION [4], ended ethnically exclusionary IMMIGRATION [2] and naturalization policies, reduced legal discriminations against women, and promoted broader opportunities via bilingual and AFFIRMATIVE ACTION [1] programs. In the 1970s and 1980s, criticisms of these measures mounted, with many contending that they promoted fragmentation and group selfishness instead of national unity. Thus, the great questions about American civic ideals that the Constitution did not answer still remain far from settled.

ROGERS M. SMITH

(SEE ALSO: *Gender Rights* [I]; *Jacksonianism* [I]; *Jeffersonianism* [I]; *Political Philosophy of the Constitution* [3,I]; *Pragmatism* [I]; *Progressive Constitutional Thought* [3]; *Progressivism* [I]; *Sex Discrimination* [4]; *Whig Party* [I].)

Bibliography

KARST, KENNETH L. 1989 *Belonging to America: Equal Citizenship and the Constitution.* New Haven, Conn.: Yale University Press.

KETTNER, JAMES H. 1978 *The Development of American Citizenship, 1608–1870.* Chapel Hill: University of North Carolina Press.

CONSTITUTION AS CIVIL RELIGION

That there exist similarities between religious devotion and esteem for the Constitution of the United States is scarcely a new notion. JAMES MADISON [3] wrote in 1792 that our fundamental charter should be the object of "more than common reverence for authority," treated indeed as "political scriptures" protected against "every attempt to add to or diminish them." Conversely, but in the same terms, Madison's great friend and colleague THOMAS JEFFERSON [3] complained in 1816 about the propensity of Americans to "look at constitutions with sanctimonious reverence and deem them like the ark of covenant, too sacred to be touched." By 1885 the young scholar WOODROW WILSON [4] could write in his classic *Congressional Government* of the "almost blind worship" directed at the Constitution's principles.

Perhaps the most important scholarly formulation of the role played by the Constitution within what later scholars would come to call the American civil religion was Max Lerner's 1937 article "Constitution and Court as Symbols." Influenced by Justice OLIVER WENDELL HOLMES, JR.'s [2] famous assertion that "we live by symbols" and by the contemporary political-anthropological analysis of THURMAN ARNOLD [1], Lerner emphasized the "totem-[ic]" aspect of the Constitution "as an instrument for controlling unknown forces in a hostile universe." It was no coincidence with Lerner that an American culture so influenced by Protestant Christianity would fix on the Constitution: "The very habits of mind begotten by an authoritarian Bible and a religion of submission to a higher power have been carried over to an authoritarian Constitution and a philosophy of submission to a higher law." The United States, whatever the prohibition of the FIRST AMENDMENT [2,I] on an ESTABLISHMENT OF RELIGION [2], "ends by getting a state church after all, although in a secular form."

The very title of Lerner's article points to the dual aspect of this purported state church: there is not only an authoritative text but also an equally authoritative institution that can give privileged interpretations of that text. That institution, of course, is the Supreme Court. No less a skeptic than HENRY ADAMS [1] confessed that "he still clung to the Supreme Court, much as a churchman clings to his bishops, because they are his only symbol of unity; his last rage of Right." Even the more scholarly Alpheus Mason suggested that the marble palace of the Supreme Court constituted our "Holy of Holies."

It is, then, easy enough to show that religious language and metaphors come readily to analysts of the Constitution. And it is also easy enough to agree with contemporary scholars like Robert Bellah that all societies, very much including our own, amass a variety of myths, symbols, narratives, and rituals that can be brought together under the rubric of "civil religion." But one may still wonder about such concepts, especially when applied quite specifically to suggest that an understanding of American CONSTITUTIONALISM [2] is enhanced by placing it within the analogical context of religion. What, then, is genuinely learned by reference to Constitution "worship" or comparing the Supreme Court to the Vatican?

For almost all the persons mentioned and many others besides, the lesson has to do with the central role of the Constitution, as declared by the Court, in providing the basis of national unity. A striving for sources of unity is especially important in what Justice THURGOOD MARSHALL [3,I] aptly described in *Gillette v. United States* (1971) as "a Nation of enormous heterogeneity in respect of political views, moral codes, and religious persuasions." The Constitution overcomes such heterogeneity by offering the individual membership in what one nineteenth-century analyst termed a "covenanting community." From this perspective, it is the Constitution that provides the political basis of the "unum" that overcomes the "pluribus" of American civil society.

One way of achieving this ostensible unity is by explicitly asking (or demanding) that the citizenry pledge commitment to it. The Constitution itself, in Article VI, even as it prohibits religious tests for public office, formally requires all public officials to take an oath recognizing the supremacy of the Constitution over alternate sources of political authority. Such oaths are scarcely meaningless. Thus, Justice WILLIAM J. BRENNAN [1,I], when asked if he had "ever had difficulty dealing with [his] own religious beliefs in terms of cases," responded by pointing to the oath he had taken upon appointment to the Court in 1956 as having "settled in my mind that I had an obligation under the Constitution which could not be influenced by any of my religious principles. . . . To the extent that [any duty of a Roman Catholic] conflicts with what I think the Constitution means or requires, then my religious beliefs have to give way."

Not only public officials must take oaths of allegiance to the Constitution: nationalized citizens since 1790 have been required to take an oath of allegiance not simply to the United States but to the Constitution. The United States has been rent by recurrent controversy over the propriety of loyalty oaths as a means both of achieving unity and of identifying those who, by their unwillingness to subscribe to such oaths, are insufficiently integrated into the civil faith.

Although analyzing the Constitution in terms of American civil religion is suggested here, the emphasis on the Constitution as the basis of unity has limits. No doubt there is some validity to this notion, but its adherents often overlook the extent to which shared belief in the abstract idea of the Constitution may often generate significant political conflict, including civil war. Just as the history of traditional religion is replete with actual, often extremely bitter, conflict even among persons purporting to share a common faith, so does the history of constitutional faith present a far more complex picture than the conventional focus on unity would suggest. The notion of the Constitution as the focus of attention in an American civil religion may have more ominous implications than are suggested by an analysis that sees only unity as the outcome of such attention.

Indeed, there are direct analogies between the cleavages observed within traditional religious communities and those seen within the American constitutional community. Two questions common to law and religion seem especially important. First, what constitutes the body of materials that counts as authoritative teachings for the community organized as a faith community? Within traditional religion, this question can take the form of debates about "canonical" texts, for example. But a recurrent struggle, seen vividly, in the history of Western Christianity, concerns the propriety of viewing as authoritative only the materials within a closed body of canonical texts. Counter to such a textual, or scriptural, understanding would be one emphasizing as well the authority of traditions derived from sources other than these canonical texts. From an early time the Catholic church invoked the propriety of its own teachings as a supplement to the teachings of the Bible. That propriety, of course, was specifically challenged by those Protestant reformers who took "Only the Scriptures" as their cry and rejected all nonscriptural teachings as totally without authority.

The second question common to law and religion centers on the need for an institutional structure that can authoritatively resolve disputes. Against the claims of the particular institutional authority of the Vatican, Protestants asserted a "priesthood of all believers" that could come to its own conclusions about the meaning of scripture. The more radical Protestant sects were often accused, not unfairly, of being anarchic in their implications. These are obviously oversimplified "ideal typical" evocations of Catholicism and Protestantism (which have their analogues within Judaism and Islam as well). Nonetheless, how might they help to illuminate the role played by the Constitution within the overall structure of American political culture?

What constitutes the Constitution? Is it composed only of the particular words of the canonical text associated with the outcome of the CONSTITUTIONAL CONVENTION OF 1787, as amended thereafter, or does it also include "unwritten" materials that are equally authoritative? Second, does there exist a particular institution whose interpretations of the Constitution (however defined) are treated as authoritative? Both of these questions allow divergent responses, each of them with their Protestant and Catholic analogues.

As to the first dimension, it is almost certainly true that an important strain of American constitutionalism is Protestant inasmuch as it emphasizes, like Chief Justice JOHN MARSHALL [3] in MARBURY V. MADISON (1803) [3], a "reverence" for written constitutions, with the linked suggestion that the Constitution consists *only* of what is written down. Perhaps the most important twentieth-century judicial explicator of this strain was Justice HUGO L. BLACK [1], who began his book *A Constitutional Faith* (1968) by stating, "It is of paramount importance to me that our country has a written constitution." More recent adherents include former Attorney General Edwin Meese and ROBERT H. BORK [I], whose defeat for a seat on the Supreme Court can be explained in part by his antagonism to the legitimacy of any notion of an UNWRITTEN CONSTITUTION [4] on which judges could draw equally with the written one.

The competing view, emphasizing a more Catholic, unwritten dimension to the Constitution, goes back at least as far as *Marbury*. Indeed, Justice SAMUEL CHASE [1] made free reference to "certain vital principles in our free Republican government" that would "overrule an apparent and flagrant abuse of legislative power" even if not explicitly expressed. Many other Justices, including Chief Justice Marshall himself in FLETCHER V. PECK (1810) [2], have expressed similar sentiments.

The most important modern Justice in this tradition is almost certainly JOHN MARSHALL HARLAN [2], who joined in an epic debate with Justice Black in the 1965 decision GRISWOLD V. CONNECTICUT [2], in which the Court invalidated a Connecticut birth control law on the grounds that it violated the RIGHT OF PRIVACY [3,I]. Justice Black dissented. He could "find in the Constitution no language which either specifically or implicitly grants to all individuals a constitutional 'right to privacy.' " Though he "like[d] my privacy as well as the next person," he refused to find it protected against state interference. For Black, evocation of an unwritten aspect of the Constitution threatened a return to the discredited jurisprudence of LOCHNER V. NEW YORK (1905) [3] and its endorsement of a nontextual FREEDOM OF CONTRACT [2]. Harlan, however, joined in striking down the Connecticut law and endorsed the necessity when interpreting DUE PROCESS OF LAW [2] to look at "what history teaches are the traditions from [this country] developed as well as the traditions from which it broke. That tradition is a living thing." A central fault line of debate within the Supreme Court can thus be understood as pitting "Protestants," who emphasize a solely textual Constitution, against "Catholics," who look to unwritten tradition as well.

The second dimension of the Protestant-Catholic distinction—that concerning institutional authority—does not so much explain debate within the Supreme Court as it does the fundamental debate about the primacy of the Court as an expositor of the meaning of the Constitution. The Court has several times in the modern era, most notably in the 1958 Little Rock school case COOPER V. AARON [2], interpreted *Marbury* to stand for the proposition that it is the "ultimate interpreter" of the Constitution. Justice Black, however Protestant his theory of the Constitution, was thoroughly Catholic in his embrace of the ultimate authority of the Supreme Court as constitutional interpreter.

Not surprisingly, it has usually been nonjudges who have proclaimed the merits of a more Protestant understanding of judicial authority. A classic account was given by President ANDREW JACKSON [3] in his 1832 message (written by ROGER BROOKE TANEY [4]) vetoing on constitutional grounds the renewal of the charter of the BANK OF THE UNITED STATES [1]. He dismissed Marshall's opinion in MCULLOCH V. MARYLAND (1819) [3], which upheld the constitutionality of the bank, stating that the "authority" of the Supreme Court opinions was restricted only to "such influence as the force of their reasoning may deserve." ABRAHAM LINCOLN [3], when running against

STEPHEN A. DOUGLAS [2] for the Senate in 1858, took a similar stance in regard to the infamous DRED SCOTT V. SANDFORD [2] decision of the previous year. More recently, former Attorney General Meese provoked significant controversy when he criticized JUDICIAL SUPREMACY [3] and called for recognizing the primacy of the Constitution as against the decisions of the Supreme Court. Meese was castigated by many who not only defended the role of the Court as "ultimate interpreter" but also pronounced Meese's views as having dangerously anarchic tendencies.

To the extent that one accepts a reading of traditional religion as providing a base for disruption and fragmentation as well as unity, one should be prepared to accept the suggestion that the Constitution-oriented civil religion will have similar aspects and tendencies. In particular, the debates about the sources underlying legitimate decision making and about institutional authority to give privileged interpretations are likely to last at least as long as the schism between the Roman Catholic church and Protestant sects, however much the proponents of any given view would like to bring the debate to an end through surrender by the other side.

Finally, one should note that some critics have condemned the notion of civil religion not so much on empirical grounds—they often concede the existence of the phenomenon analyzed by Bellah, Lerner, and others—but rather on normative grounds. Embrace of the tenets of constitutional faith has been described by some of these critics as the equivalent of idolatry. They argue instead that constitutional faith, however important, must always be judged by the distinctly different claims of more traditional faith communities.

SANFORD LEVINSON

(SEE ALSO: *Constitution and Civic Ideals* [I]; *Political Philosophy of the Constitution* [3,I].)

Bibliography

BELLAH, ROBERT   1970   Civil Religion in America. Pages 168–189 in Bellah, ed., *Beyond Belief*. New York: Harper and Row.

GREY, THOMAS C.   1984   The Constitution as Scripture. *Stanford Law Review* 37:1–25.

KAMMER, MICHAEL   1986   *A Machine That Would Go of Itself: The Constitution in American Culture*. New York: Knopf.

LERNER, MAX   1937   Constitution and Court as Symbol. *Yale Law Journal* 42:1290–1319.

LEVINSON, SANFORD   1988   *Constitutional Faith*. Princeton, N.J.: Princeton University Press.

CONSTITUTION AS LITERATURE

Although presumably no one would say that the Constitution offers its readers an experience that cannot be distinguished from reading a poem or a novel, there is nonetheless a sense in which it is a kind of highly imaginative literature in its own right (indeed its nature as law requires that this be so), the reading of which may be informed by our experience of other literary forms. But to say this may be controversial, and the first step toward understanding how such a claim can be made may be to ask what it is we think characterizes imaginative literature in the first place.

It is common in our culture to marginalize "high literature," even while admiring it, and this mainly by thinking of it as offering nothing more than a refined pleasure, merely aesthetic in kind, and by assuming that it can therefore have nothing to do with practical affairs, with money or power. Those who think of themselves as literary people sometimes reciprocate with a marginalization of their own, speaking as if the merely practical offered nothing of interest to one who is devoted to what Wallace Stevens once called "the finer things of life." But this mutual marginalization impoverishes both sides, and the rest of us too, for it rests on a false dichotomy, between the aesthetic and the practical, which is like—and related to—those between fact and fiction, form and content, science and art.

For there is an important sense in which all literature is constitutive, great literature greatly so, of the resources of culture, which are simultaneously employed and remade in the creation of the text, and of what might be called the textual community as well. (By this I mean the relations that each text establishes between its author and its reader, and between those two and the others that it talks about.)

Beginning with the second point, we can say that every text, whether self-consciously literary or not, establishes what Aristotle called an ethos (or character) for its speaker and its reader and for those it speaks about as well; in addition, it establishes, or tries to establish, a relation among these various actors. In this sense every text is socially and ethically constitutive, a species of ethical and political action, and can be understood and judged as such. In fact, we make judgments of this sort all the time—although perhaps crudely so—for example whenever we find a politician's speech patronizing or a commercial advertisement manipulative or when we welcome frank correction at the hand of a friend.

The first point, that the text reconstitutes its culture, is perhaps more familiar, for we have long seen works of art as remaking the culture out of which they are made. This observation establishes a significant connection between the Constitution (and other legal texts) on the one hand and literary texts on the other; for in both, the material of the past is reworked in the present, and part of the art of each of these kinds of literature is the transformation, or reconstitution, of its resources.

To say this is to leave open, of course, the question how, and by what standards, such judgments of art and ethics are to be made. To pursue this question would be the work of a volume at least; let it suffice here to say these are judgments that expression of all sorts permits and that expression of a self-conscious kind—in the law and in fiction, as well as poetry and history—invites. Perhaps we can say in addition that through the reading of texts that address this question in interesting and important ways we may hope to develop our own capacities of analysis and judgment. For present purposes, the point is simply to suggest that once literature is seen as socially and culturally constitutive, the connection with the Constitution, and with the judicial literature elaborating it, may seem less strange than it otherwise might.

This line of thought began by rethinking what we mean by literature. We might wish to start from the other side, by thinking again about our ways of imagining law. In our culture the law is all too often seen simply as a set of rules or directives issuing from a sovereign to be obeyed or disobeyed by those subject to it. This is the understanding—crudely positivistic—that for many years dominated much of our theoretical thinking and much of our teaching as well; it still holds sway deeper in our minds than we may like to admit. In fact, as the history of the Constitution itself demonstrates with exemplary clarity, the meaning of legal directives is not self-evident or self-established, but requires the participation of readers who offer a variety of interpretations, often in competition with each other. In this sense the readers, as well as the writers, of our central legal texts are makers of the law, and any view of the law and the Constitution should reflect this fact.

Law is perhaps best thought of, then, not as a structure of rules, but as a set of activities and practices through which people engage both with their language (and with the rest of their cultural inheritance) and with each other. One of its aims, deeply literary in character, is to give meaning to experience in language; this is the backward-looking role of law. When it looks forward, as it does above all in the Constitution (but also in contracts, statutes, loan agreements, and trust indentures), it seeks to establish through language a set of relations among various actors, each of whom is given by the legal text certain tasks, obligations, or opportunities that otherwise would not exist, but none of which can be perfectly defined in language. By its nature, then, the legal text gives rise to a set of rhetorical and literary activities through which alone it can work.

The point of such a line of thought is not to assert there is no difference between a judicial opinion, or a constitutional amendment, and a lyric poem—that would be silly—but that, by looking to the deeper structures of the activities in which we engage, we may see them as sharing certain concerns and do this in ways that improve our capacity to understand, to judge, and to perform them. We may perhaps free literature from the veil drawn over it by the claim that it is merely aesthetic and, at the same time, free law from its veil, made of the claims that it is purely practical, only about power, or simply a branch of one of the policy sciences.

The Constitution is constitutive in the two ways in which every text is: it recasts the material of its tradition into new forms, for good or ill; and it establishes a set of relations among the actors it addresses and defines. The first point is historical and quite familiar and usually takes the form of observing that the U.S. Constitution is not a wholly radical innovation, but built upon certain models—British and colonial—out of which it grew. To this fact indeed it owes much of its durability and, perhaps as well, much of its capacity to make what really was new (that is, dual sovereignty) both intelligible and real. The second point is really a suggested way of reading the Constitution: not as a document allocating something called "power" but as a rhetorical creation defining new places and occasions for talk, creating new speakers, and establishing conditions of guidance and restraint. All of these activities are imperfectly determinate and therefore call for the literary and rhetorical practices of reading and writing, intepretation and argument, that lie at the center of the law. Before the Constitution was adopted, none of its official actors existed; there was no President, no Senate, no Supreme Court. One of the effects of the text, as ratified, was to bring these actors into existence. But that is not the end of it; every act of these new actors depends for its validity upon a claim, implied or expressed, about the meaning of the Constitution itself, and every such claim is in principle open to argument. This is not to say that the Constitution is incoherent, but that as a work of language it has much uncertainty built into it. In fact, it has the only kind of coherence that is open for human institutions to have.

This brings us to the most obvious, and best rehearsed, connection between literature and the law, especially constitutional law, namely, both of these fields work by the reading of texts, or by what it is now the fashion to call "interpretation." That word, however, is not without its dangers, for it may be taken to imply that an interpreter of a text reproduces in her own prose, in her "interpretation," a statement of what the original text means that is in some sense complete and exhaustive, which can indeed serve as an adequate substitute for it. But in neither literature nor the law can this be done; any "interpretation" is of necessity partial, in the sense that it is both incomplete and motivated by a set of understandings and desires that belong to the present reader (formed though these are in part from the materials of the past). The "interpretation" of an earlier text does not so much restate its meaning as elaborate possibilities of meaning that it has left open; the new text is the product of a new time, as well as the old.

Not solely the product of the present and of its partialities, both law and literature are grounded on the premise that the past speaks to us in texts that illumine and constrain though always incompletely so. Accordingly, there are similar interpretive vices in both fields; for example, the attempt to collapse the text, with all its difficulties and uncertainties, into some simplified statement of its "plain meaning," all too often in denial of the uncertainties that both kinds of texts necessarily have and with them the responsibilities for judgment that they generate. Or we may seek simplicity in another direction, defining the meaning of the text by reference to something outside it (for example, the biography of the writer or the "original intention" of the framer or legislator), usually without recognizing that what we think of ourselves as simply referring to is also, in part at least, our own creation—a text which itself requires interpretation. The result of both of these methods is the hidden arrogation of power to the so-called interpreters, who pretend to yield to an external authority, but actually exercise the power in question themselves. Or the vice may be of an opposite kind: to see so much complexity and indeterminacy in a text as to make its responsible reading hopeless and to say, therefore, that nothing can be clear but our own desires (if those) and that no respect needs to be paid (because none can) to the putatively authoritative texts of others. At its extreme, the tendency of this method is to destroy both law and culture.

In both kinds of work the process of reading requires a toleration of ambiguity and uncertainty: a recognition of complexity, an acknowledgment that our own habits of mind condition both what we see in a text and what we feel about it, and a relinquishment of the hope of universal and absolute clarity. Yet it requires a recognition as well that the past can speak to the present, that culture can be transmitted and transformed, that it is possible, and worth doing, to look beyond ourselves to that which we have inherited from others. Here, in this uncertain struggle to discover and state meaning, to establish a connection with the texts of another, is the life of law and literature alike.

One feature of legal interpretation that is distinctive, or distinctively clear, and of special relevance to the Constitution is its idealizing character. The reading of legal texts inherently involves us in the expression of our ideals, and this in two ways. First, whenever we interpret the Constitution, or any other legal text, we necessarily imagine for it an author, with a certain imagined character and set of values, situated in a certain set of circumstances,

and actuated by a certain set of motives or aims. For whatever our theory may pretend, the text cannot be read simply as an abstract order or as the decontextualized statement of an idea; it must be read as the work of a mind speaking to minds. Thus, in our every act of interpretation we define—indeed, we create—a mind behind the text. This is necessarily the expression of an ideal; although, of course, our sense of the past helps to shape it, and to call it an ideal is not to say that it is one that all people share. But we idealize the speakers of the law, or it is not law.

Second, the literature of the law is inherently idealizing in the way in which lawyers idealize their official audiences. We speak to a judge not as to the small-minded angry person we actually think him to be, but as his own version of the wisest and best judge in the world, as we imagine it. And the judge too speaks not to a world of greedy, selfish, and lazy people, as he may see us, but to an ideal audience, the best version of the public he can imagine. In both cases our acts of imagining are acts of idealization for which we are responsible; it is in this way the nature of law to make the ideal real.

JAMES BOYD WHITE

(SEE ALSO: *Constitutional Interpretation* [I.])

Bibliography

LEUBSDORF, JOHN 1987 Deconstructing the Constitution. *Stanford Law Review* 40:181–201.

VINING, JOSEPH 1986 *The Authoritative and The Authoritarian*. Chicago: University of Chicago Press.

WHITE, JAMES BOYD 1984 *When Words Lose Their Meaning: Constitutions and Reconstitutions of Language, Character, and Community*. Chapter 9. Chicago: University of Chicago Press.

CONSTITUTIONAL CONVENTION, RECORDS OF

The records of the CONSTITUTIONAL CONVENTION OF 1787 [1] are not so full as scholars and jurists would like them to be. A verbatim account of the proceedings does not exist and, absent modern technology, could not have been produced. Stenographers in Philadelphia covered the state ratifying convention, which met in the fall of 1787; but the Federal Convention met in secrecy and, even if the local stenographers had been admitted, the rudimentary state of their craft and assorted personal shortcomings would have made a satisfactory result unlikely.

We must rely for information about the Convention on a journal kept by its secretary, William Jackson, and on notes kept by various delegates. Some of the notes, especially those made by JAMES MADISON [3], are extensive; others are fragmentary. Taken together, the existing records give us a satisfactory narrative of events at the Convention—although details of the drafting of many key provisions are sparse, leaving the ORIGINAL INTENT [I] of the Framers enigmatic. It is also true that the documentation becomes poorer toward the end of the Convention. The delegates, tired and eager to go home, recorded less than they did earlier, and what they recorded was sketchier. This is unfortunate, because the last weeks of the Convention saw many important compromises and changes about which, in the absence of adequate records, we know far too little.

The story of how Madison created his notes is familiar: "I chose a seat in front of the presiding member, with the other members, on my right and left hand. In this favorable position for hearing all that passed I noted in terms legible and in abbreviations and marks intelligible to myself what was read from the Chair or spoken by the members; and losing not a moment unnecessarily between the adjournment and reassembling of the Convention I was enabled to write out my daily notes during the session or within a few finishing days after its close." Conscientiously completed at considerable physical cost—Madison later confessed that the task "almost killed" him—these notes are the principal source of information about the convention. That Madison kept his notes in his possession until his death caused one suspicious scholar, WILLIAM W. CROSSKEY [2], to charge that during his life he had tampered with them—"forged" them, in fact—to make them consistent with political actions he had taken after 1787, an accusation since proven to be without foundation. The one considerable problem with Madison's notes is that they contain only a small proportion of each day's debates. They should not be used with the assumption that they are comprehensive.

The source next in importance to Madison's notes is the Convention records kept by New York delegate ROBERT YATES [4]. They were published in 1821 under the title *Secret Proceedings and Debates of the Convention Assembled at Philadelphia in the Year 1787* by an anonymous editor, who turned out to be Citizen Edmond Genêt, the incendiary ambassador of revolutionary France to the United States in 1793. When Madison first saw the published version of Yates's notes, he warned against their "extreme incorrectness"—and with good reason, for it has been discovered that Genêt was guilty of the sin Crosskey laid at Madison's door: tampering with the manuscript version of Yates's notes, deleting some parts and changing others. The *Secret Proceedings* must therefore be used with extreme caution.

Several other delegates left notes, records, and scraps of paper that shed varying amounts of light on what occurred at Philadelphia, among which the notes of RUFUS KING [3] and JOHN DICKINSON [2] are the fullest. ALEXANDER HAMILTON [2], JAMES MCHENRY [3], WILLIAM PIERCE [3], PIERCE BUTLER [1], WILLIAM PATERSON [3], CHARLES PINCKNEY [3], and JAMES WILSON [4] left more fragmentary materials. OLIVER ELLSWORTH [2] and LUTHER MARTIN [3] said a good deal about the workings of the Convention in polemics generated by the campaign for the RATIFICATION OF THE CONSTITUTION [3] during 1787–1788. Their accounts should be consulted, but their partisanship obviously dictates that their statements be used with caution.

The remaining source of information about the Convention is the official journal published in 1819 at the direction of Congress and edited by then Secretary of State JOHN QUINCY ADAMS [1]. Although Adams complained that the manuscript record left by Convention Secretary William Jackson was "very loosely and imperfectly kept," he was able to make perfect sense of it, with the result that the journal that issued from his editorship is a reliable, if bare-bones, narrative of the daily business of the Convention.

Scholars are aware that several delegates kept manuscript notes of Convention proccedings that have not been found. It is possible that in the future our understanding of Convention proceedings will be enriched, if not fundamentally changed, by the discovery of yet another set of Convention notes.

JAMES HUTSON

Bibliography

FARRAND, MAX, ED.   1987   *The Records of the Federal Convention of 1787*, rev. ed., 4 vols. New Haven, Conn.: Yale University Press.

HUTSON, JAMES H.   1986   The Creation of the Constitution: The Integrity of the Documentary Record. *Texas Law Review* 65:1–39.

CONSTITUTIONAL FICTIONS

The leading modern American discussion of legal fictions remains Lon Fuller's articles first published in 1930–1931. Fuller argued that legal fictions promote function, form, and sometimes fairness. It has become increasingly clear, however, that legal fictions no longer serve merely as an "awkward patch" on the fabric of law, as Fuller put it. Fuller considered legal fictions a necessary evil for systematic thinking about law. He viewed legal fictions as akin to working assumptions in physics: they provide a kind of scaffolding, but are not intended to give essential support nor to deceive. After their useful function ends, legal fictions should and could be readily removed.

Fuller defined a legal fiction as "either (1) a statement

propounded with a complete or partial consciousness of its falsity, or (2) a false statement recognized as having utility." In today's postrealist world, however, there is a widespread sense that legal fictions are not some small awkward patch, but rather virtually all of law's seamless cloth. This transforms the problem of defining and explaining legal fictions. The very pervasiveness of legal fictions helps to camouflage them. We may generally ignore a phenomenon that permeates our LEGAL CULTURE [I].

Fuller's taxonomy of legal fictions illuminated Henry Maine's earlier assertion that legal fictions "satisfy the desire for improvement, which is not quite wanting, at the same time that they do not offend the superstitious disrelish for change which is always present." To Maine, legal fictions were "invaluable expedients for overcoming the rigidity of law," but they were also "the greatest of obstacles to symmetrical classification." Fuller advanced beyond Maine's complacent legal anthropology, but he still somewhat desperately sought symmetry. Today we tend to regard all law as a gyrating classification system full of overlaps, gaps, and incommensurate variations. In Grant Gilmore's words, "The process by which a society accommodates to change without abandoning its fundamental structure is what we mean by law."

Precisely because legal fictions are not static, they may grow to influence or even control how we think or refuse to think about basic matters. The fiction that a corporation is a person warranting certain constitutional protections, for example, obviously has spread like kudzu since the Supreme Court first propounded this notion in dicta in *Santa Clara County v. Southern Pacific Railroad* (1886). We employ legal fictions to preserve a notion of continuity with the past, yet legal fictions help short-circuit attempts to comprehend the complexity behind the assumptions a legal fiction conveys. Like sunlight, legal fictions affect the directions of growth.

There is a basic irony in our commitment to preserving the RULE OF LAW [3] alongside our reverence for pragmatic immediate solutions to pluralistic problems. Nevertheless, few Americans have ever gone as far in condemning legal fictions as did Jeremy Bentham. Bentham claimed that "[i]n English law, fiction is a syphilis, which runs in every vein, and carries into every part of the system the principle of rottenness." If fictions are to justice "[e]xactly as swindling is to trade," as Bentham put it, Americans tend to exalt trade so much that we tolerate and even celebrate the trader, the flimflam man, and the innovative judge.

In constitutional law, legal fictions are at least as pervasive as in what is still nostalgically called private law. Obviously, a great judge in a constitutional case has to do more than look up the answer in the constitutional text. But what it is we want a good or great postrealist judge to do remains intensely controversial.

The paradoxical way in which Americans revere but fail to heed closely constitutional law suggests that it may be impossible to separate basic constitutional fictions from constitutional governance. Yet political history in the United States has been dominated by an ongoing, multi-faceted debate about proper interpretation of the Constitution. Controversies about specific instances of JUDICIAL REVIEW [3] and proposals for constitutional change ebb and flow, but debate about what is true to the Constitution never disappears.

Americans generally display remarkable respect for an old ambiguous text despite—perhaps because of—widespread uncertainty about what it contains. Yet the Constitution and its most important amendments surely were not ratified by a majority of Americans. Moreover, whoever "we the people" may have excluded or included, it is clear that the American people have not actually endorsed the centuries of judicial gloss on the Constitution that provides much basic constitutional law. Nevertheless, sacerdotalizing of the Constitution amounts to a civic religion. General acquiescence in the interpretations of the text by unelected judges thus provides a central constitutional fiction that ironically also has proved to be a notably sturdy foundation. It is important to distinguish this crucial, general trapeze act involving the assumption of societal consent from the more specific uses of fictions in constitutional law.

As early as the 1830s ALEXIS DE TOCQUEVILLE [4] declared: "The government of the Union rests almost entirely on legal fictions. The union is an ideal nation which exists, so to say, only in men's minds and whose extent and limits can only be discerned by understanding." Tocqueville made his point about the central role of legal fictions in American governance, ironically, just as constitutional debate about the abolition of SLAVERY [4] began to spiral toward the CIVIL WAR [I]. That example of the terrible cost of fundamental disagreements about the meaning of the Constitution helps explain why most Americans most of the time are willing to accept the central constitutional fiction that judicial interpretations of the Constitution somehow can settle even the most controversial questions.

An important initial question is whether the American model of judicial review, promulgated most famously by Chief Justice JOHN MARSHALL [3] in *Marbury v. Madison* (1803) [3], may not itself be a fiction of elemental proportions. Marshall insisted that to deserve the "high appellation" of "a government of laws and not of men," the American system required the power of federal judges to declare legislative acts unconstitutional, but this was hardly necessary to decide the case before the Court and lacked explicit support in the constitutional text. Additional fictions that have played particularly important roles in our constitutional history range from markedly inconsistent judicial declarations enforcing FEDERALISM [2,I] to decisions granting FOURTEENTH AMENDMENT [2,I] protection to CORPORATIONS [2]. Among the most important recent examples are decisions applying most but not all of the BILL OF RIGHTS [1] to the states, on the theory that their protections were incorporated through the DUE PROCESS [2] clause of the Fourteenth Amendment, and decisions making EQUAL PROTECTION [2] doctrine applicable to the federal government through a theory of "reverse incorporation" premised on the Fifth Amendment.

Less obvious but equally important constitutional fictions limit or ignore the constitutional text. For example, the SLAUGHTERHOUSE CASES (1873) [4] rendered the privileges or immunities [3] clause of the Fourteenth Amendment essentially redundant. Also, there has been longstanding reluctance to give the NINTH AMENDMENT [3] any content at all. Constitutional fictions thus may restrain as well as enlarge judicial authority.

Particularly flagrant constitutional fictions have produced a smattering of serious scholarly and political criticism, but most Americans apparently continue to revere the Supreme Court and to accept its interpretations even when not pleased by the results in specific cases. For example, there were withering attacks on the Court's aggressive use of what many saw as fictional limitations on progressive legislation in the 1920s and 1930s, but the failure of President FRANKLIN D. ROOSEVELT's [3] COURT-PACKING PLAN [I] suggested that Americans, even when outraged at specific results and dubious about their bases, nevertheless were more willing to accept judicially created fictions than to tinker with the institution of judicial review.

As James Russell Lowell stated in 1888, "After our Constitution got fairly into working order it really seemed as if we had invented a machine that would go of itself, and this begot a faith in our luck which even the civil war itself but momentarily disturbed." But Lowell sardonically continued, "I admire the splendid complacency of my countrymen, and find something exhilarating and inspiring in it. . . . And this confidence in our luck with the absorption in material interests, generated by unparalleled opportunity, has in some respects made us neglectful of our political duties."

It might be thought that legal fictions ought to play a diminished role in constitutional law, in contrast to their prevalence in COMMON LAW [I]. For instance, constitutional law does not lack a text, whereas the common law, in Frederick Pollock's words, "professes . . . to develop and apply principles that have never been committed to any authentic form of words." Despite the best efforts of interpretivists, originalists, and self-proclaimed strict constructionists, however, constitutional law as we know it— and as it has been from the start—demonstrates clearly that even our written "authentic form of words" requires

additional criteria for everyday construction and interpretation. In fact, we seem to grow ever more doubtful about what sources we should consult, to say nothing of what might be thought authoritative.

We lack any rule of recognition to distinguish constitutional truth from constitutional fiction. Moreover, our constitutional history clearly reveals that some sections of the authentic text have been relegated to limbo through nonoriginalist hierarchical principles, whereas other sections have acquired so many levels of added meaning that it is now hard to discern any original shape beneath the layers of barnacles added over the years.

The constitutional text is manipulable, but that need not mean it is infinitely manipulable. Federal judges have declared themselves less bound by STARE DECISIS [4] in the constitutional realm than they are in other domains, but they tend to remain concerned with the past and with their won places in history. Yet these same judges use legal fictions to purge the past of its blemishes and discontinuities.

There seems to be a kind of ideological frontier thesis in constitutional law. Justices who start anew and never actually look back are applauded. Because they usually can find PRECEDENTS [3] readily and tend not to consider contexts, these judges reinforce a tendency to turn our backs on past unpleasantness. Fundamental assumptions in constitutional doctrine posit an America full of openings: we may all escape the sins of the past; we all enjoy a fair and equal start in the race of life.

Equality among citizens, for example, is virtually always assumed, whether actual or not. This formal ideal of equality generally provides a complete defense against those who seek remedies for past discrimination unless they can demonstrate that the defendants actually violated the plaintiffs' equality; thus, the victim must place the defendant at the scene of past crimes. This fiction was essential a century ago in the CIVIL RIGHTS CASES (1883) [1] and PLESSY V. FERGUSON (1896) [3]; a similar fiction was crucial when the Court vigorously enforced its version of FREEDOM OF CONTRACT [2] before the NEW DEAL [I]; and its formal fictional counterpart seems prevalent in RACIAL DISCRIMINATION [3,I] cases today.

In constitutional law we are devoted to the artificial doctrinal categories and analytic tests that judges create. This remains so even if we are subliminally aware, as Justice OLIVER WENDELL HOLMES [2] noted, that a particular doctrine may be "little more than a fiction intended to beautify what is disagreeable to the sufferers." Judicial reliance on binary tests to foster pseudocertainty is not new, of course, as anyone who recalls the twilight zone of DUAL FEDERALISM [2] must acknowledge. In constitutional cases today, however, judges seem to rely even more frequently on multipart formulas to convey that "delusive exactness" Holmes decried—and sometimes practiced.

Legal fictions are quite different from literary fictions. As ROBERT COVER [I] pointed out, potential violence lurks beneath the fictions created by judges, whereas the nexus between real force and even the most powerful literary fiction is attenuated. Additionally, the author of literary fiction enjoys more freedom than the creator of legal fiction. The poet, even the novelist, usually tries to operate on multiple levels and even dreams of reaching a broad and varied audience. Writers of literary fiction also tend to acknowledge and even to use the possibility of complicity between the teller of the tale and the recipient of it, so that shared understanding is a core concern. By contrast, legal fiction employs a specialized shorthand; many creators and users of legal fiction intend their work product to be confined to, or even ignored by, only a narrow audience of professionals.

Americans find it easy to read prepossessions into the Constitution. We resemble religious sects who are able to find diverse creeds in the same Bible. A century ago, CHRISTOPHER G. TIEDEMAN [4], a leading conservative treatise writer, admiringly noted that "when public opinion . . . requires the written words to be ignored the court justly obeys the will of the popular mandate, at the same time keeping up a show of obedience to the written word by a skillful use of legal fictions." Today heated political and social controversies often revolve around whether the Constitution resolves, or is even relevant to, the debate over ABORTION [1,I] or AFFIRMATIVE ACTION [1,I], for example. Many people will consider whatever answers the Supreme Court hands down to be constitutional fictions at best. Yet, as the historian CHARLES BEARD [1] put it in 1930, "Humanity and ideas, as well as things, are facts." Constitutional fictions tend to grow into fundamental facts of life in a culture that reveres law.

AVIAM SOIFER

(SEE ALSO: *Constitution as Civil Religion* [I]; *Constitutional Interpretation* [1]; *Incorporation Doctrine* [2]; *Legal Realism* [3].)

Bibliography

FULLER, LON 1967 *Legal Fictions*. Palo Alto, Calif.: Stanford.
KAMMEN, MICHAEL 1986 *A Machine That Would Go of Itself*. New York: Knopf.
SOIFER, AVIAM 1986 Reviewing Legal Fictions. *Georgia Law Review* 20:871.

CONSTITUTIONAL HISTORY, 1980–1989

The major constitutional development of the 1980s was the confirmation of divided government as a legitimate alternative to presidential party government as a model for constitutional administration. In the elections of 1980 and 1984 the people chose a Republican President while returning a Democratic majority to the HOUSE OF REPRESENTATIVES [I]. In 1986 the Democratic party regained control of the Senate, which it retained in 1988 as the REPUBLICAN PARTY [I] again won the presidency. This type of split-ticket voting was a relatively new phenomenon in modern American politics. From 1889 to 1953, no President on his inauguration faced a Congress one house of which was controlled by the opposition party. The contemporary period of divided government began in 1969 when the Republican RICHARD M. NIXON [3] was elected President and the Democrats controlled Congress. After the resignation of Nixon in 1974, the Democrats briefly revived presidential party government with the election of JIMMY CARTER [1] in 1976. Their inability to govern effectively despite having power over both political branches prepared the way for the Republican capture of the White House in 1980.

Throughout the 1980s, assessments of divided government tended to be uncertain because such government contradicted what had come to be accepted since the NEW DEAL [1] as the constitutional norm, namely, presidential government under a dominant party after a critical or realigning election. In fact, there were indications in Nixon's two election victories of a disintegration of the New Deal liberal coalition and an expectation of a political realignment that would enable the presidential party system to continue. The problem with this analysis was that while twentieth-century presidential government was historically liberal, many students of politics believed it was also inherently or in its nature liberal. Many observers were therefore reluctant to conclude that divided government could represent the deliberate choice of the electorate or that it could be a satisfactory approach to running the Constitution, despite the fact that it brought the constitutional principle of the SEPARATION OF POWERS [4] more directly to bear on the conduct of government.

Part of the difficulty observers had in recognizing the legitimacy of divided government was attributable to the political popularity of RONALD REAGAN [3,I]. Despite having twice been elected governor of California, Reagan was an improbable candidate for President. This improbability owed less to his being a former Hollywood actor than to his advocacy of NATURAL RIGHTS [3] individualism, LIMITED GOVERNMENT [2], and middle class social values that had come to be identified in the dominant political culture as the essence of right-wing reactionism. Labeled an "ideological" candidate by the national media, he ran on a platform that proposed to reverse the tide of centralized BUREAUCRACY [1,I], restore equal opportunity for individuals, stimulate economic growth through deregulation and market incentives, and rebuild national defense. Reagan's assertion of these policies made the election of 1980 the most significant since 1932. In effect, it was a REFERENDUM [3] on the regulatory WELFARE STATE [I], broadly conceived in the light of the liberal reforms of the 1960s and 1970s. When President Reagan won reelection in 1984, and Vice-President GEORGE BUSH [I] won election as President in 1988, in a significant sense the era of welfare state liberalism was over, a fact difficult to deny. Divided government was the constitutional expression of this political change.

In one sense, the source or cause of divided government was the Constitution. The FUNDAMENTAL LAW [2] organizes government into three coordinate branches and, in the words of *The Federalist* #51, guards against a concentration of the several powers in the same department by "giving to those who administer each department the necessary constitutional means and personal motives to resist the encroachments of the others." Moreover, the Constitution permits voters to make a free political choice, including that of ticket splitting (which some critics of divided government have proposed to restrict by a constitutional amendment). Furthermore, the Constitution does not establish POLITICAL PARTIES [3,I] in the structure of government, but allows them to exist as voluntary associations regulated by state and federal law. A contributing factor to divided government was the decline of partisan loyalty in the electorate, caused in part by antiparty reform measures, such as CAMPAIGN FINANCE [1,I] laws. With the decline of party, political choice was based in part on the political values, principles, and governmental duties and functions associated with the executive and legislative branches or their leading officials. The separation of powers, one of the basic concepts of limited government, was thus the organizing principle of divided government.

A second apparent cause of divided government was uncertainty or ambivalence in the electorate about the basic direction of public policy. In electing Republican chief executives, the people approved of policies aimed at economic expansion, control of inflation, tax reform, limitations on government spending, and strengthened national defense. In voting Democratic control of Congress, the people expressed a desire to maintain the social welfare and regulatory programs that constituted the achievement of modern liberalism. These included ENTITLEMENT [I] programs and legally conferred benefits for individuals and groups in every social class. Although politically contradictory, these policy alternatives might be seen as reflecting complementary dimensions of the public philosophy underlying American CONSTITUTIONALISM [2]: individualism, based on natural rights principles that limit government power, and the public interest, based on community consensus that requires government regulation.

Nevertheless, in a relative historical sense, by contrast with the period of presidential party government which it succeeded, the public philosophy of divided government represented a partial attempt to restore an older conception of limited government. This was the idea that federal power was limited to specific ends or objects in accordance with the federal principle of divided SOVEREIGNTY [4]. Reagan administration proposals for a new FEDERALISM [2,I] that would return certain policy matters to the states expressed this outlook. Underlying these proposals was the more basic idea of restoring a sense of discipline and limitation in the conduct of government, seen in attempts to limit government spending, reduce the federal deficit, and revive the concept of a balanced BUDGET [1].

The political expression of this conservative idea was a state-based movement for a CONSTITUTIONAL CONVENTION [1] to limit federal spending and achieve a balanced budget. By the mid-1980s this movement had begun to produce political effects in Washington. The Republican-controlled Senate and executive branch supported a BALANCED-BUDGET CONSTITUTIONAL AMENDMENT [I]. The Democratic party switched from supporting deficit spending to arguing for deficit reduction as a reaction against Reagan administration defense spending in a year (1985) when the deficit reached $200 billion. With the executive and legislature each blaming the other for the deficits, the situation was ripe for a bipartisan solution. The result was the Balanced Budget and Emergency Deficit Control Act of 1985.

Known as the GRAMM-RUDMAN-HOLLINGS ACT [2], the law required the federal budget to be reduced by stages until it was eliminated in 1991. It contained a triggering mechanism by which automatic across-the-board spending cuts were mandated if deficits exceeded specified levels at certain target dates. Finding it difficult to meet the reduction requirements, Congress put some spending items "off budget" so that they would not be counted in the reckoning of the deficit problem. In 1987 it revised the law to postpone the balanced budget date to 1993. Although the Washington political establishment generally disliked the law, it had the effect of reducing the deficit and slowing the rate of increase in government spending. Despite sharp differences over spending priorities, limitation of spending had become a bipartisan objective or requirement, replacing the presumption of indefinite government expansion based on taxing and spending that marked the 1960s and 1970s. In this sense, divided government signaled the kind of change in the policy agenda associated with a political realignment.

Although compromise could be said to be the logic of government under the separation of powers, as seen in the disposition of such major issues as the budget deficit, tax reform, and control of immigration, ideological conflict was the predominant political effect of divided government. The struggle between the executive and legislature for control of the administrative state, a continuing theme in twentieth-century CONSTITUTIONAL HISTORY [1], was exacerbated by the ideological polarization of the 1980s.

Powerful governing instruments were available for carrying on the struggle for policymaking and administrative control. Having forced President Nixon to resign through application of the IMPEACHMENT [2] power, Congress curbed EXECUTIVE POWER [I] by passing laws respecting presidential actions in regard to WAR POWERS [4,I], intelligence activities, and budgetary matters. In 1978, Congress took the major step of creating the office of special prosecutor outside the executive branch to investigate wrongdoing in high-level executive offices. By vigorous use of the LEGISLATIVE VETO [3] and the appropriations and oversight powers, Congress in the 1980s challenged the president not only in domestic policy but also in FOREIGN AFFAIRS [2].

Although the executive was weaker than in the era of presidential party government, this branch also experienced a restoration of authority under divided government. Despite legislative measures aimed at limiting the executive, the principal elements of presidential power from the pre-WATERGATE [4] period remained intact. The White House staff of 600 and the Executive Office of the President staff of 5,000 employees were powerful institutions that functioned as a policymaking structure parallel to the regular executive departments. Perhaps the main element in the power of the chief executive was the fact that political responsibility for government continued to fall primarily upon the president. On the whole, despite severe second-term problems in the IRAN-CONTRA AFFAIR [I], President Reagan was reasonably successful in meeting that responsibility. Possessing aptitude suitable for a plebiscitary type of presidency, he used the media effectively to communicate directly with the electorate and shape public opinion in support of administration policies.

Although President Reagan's political appeal rested in part on his opposition to big government, he responded to the constitutional imperative of the modern administrative state by expanding executive authority to achieve the policy ends of his administration. In 1981 he issued Executive Order 12291, giving the OFFICE OF MANAGEMENT AND BUDGET (OMB) [3] authority to require executive agencies to submit cost-benefit analyses. Focused on budgetary impact, the order was intended as a check on the regulatory process, aimed at eliminating waste and inefficiency. In 1985, President Reagan issued a more far-reaching directive, Executive Order 12498, intended to coordinate and establish White House control over bureaucratic policymaking. This order required executive agencies to submit proposed regulations to OMB for sub-

stantive approval to ensure that they were consistent with overall White House policy.

The Reagan EXECUTIVE ORDERS [2] resisted an inherent tendency in Congress toward micromanagement of the executive branch, a tendency encouraged by the politics of divided government. Reaction to the directives revealed the ambiguous constitutional status of ADMINISTRATIVE AGENCIES [I] subject to the control of both the President and Congress. Functionally the executive departments and independent REGULATORY AGENCIES [3] are in the executive branch, for they are concerned with enforcing and administering laws. The President can order administrative officers to carry out policies within their statutory discretion, and if they fail to follow his direction, he should be able to remove them, on the theory that the Constitution intends law enforcement to be managed by the chief executive. Adminstrative departments and agencies owe their existence, however, to Congress. By its lawmaking power, it creates the units of the administrative state, defining the purpose and powers of each department or agency and the terms and conditions of holding office. From this point of view, the executive departments and regulatory agencies are accountable to Congress and may exercise rulemaking discretion only within their statutory mandates.

Claiming discretionary rulemaking authority exercised by previous administrations, Reagan officials frequently acted to withdraw, revoke, or alter agency rules. When they did so, they were sometimes charged, by congressional committees and by private INTEREST GROUPS [I] that opposed the changes, with violating their statutory authority. In the period of divided government, rulemaking under the delegation of LEGISLATIVE POWER [3] to the executive, usually considered a basic feature of the modern administrative state, was thus subject to attack as lawless executive conduct.

Despite serious deregulatory efforts, the structure of the regulatory welfare state changed very little in the 1980s. Few agencies were eliminated, and given the balance of political forces and congressional defense of the status quo, it was difficult to effect major policy changes. On the government-expansion side, the Veterans Adminstration was elevated to cabinet rank. The main difference between this period and the 1970s was that the regulatory state functioned in a more accommodating and less antagonistic spirit in relation to regulated groups and associations. Corporations opposed the wholesale dismantling of regulatory structures that the "Reagan revolution" at first seemed to threaten, because it would reopen costly political and legal battles. What corporations wanted was greater flexibility in government—business relations and greater reliance on economic analysis in regulatory policy. After initially strong deregulatory efforts met stiff resistance in the subgovernments of the administrative constitution, the Reagan administration moderated its regulatory policy accordingly.

In seeking to preserve the regulatory welfare state, the Democratic congressional establishment evinced tendencies toward legislative supremacy inherent in the doctrine of the separation of powers and the theory of POPULAR SOVEREIGNTY [3]. As in the past, the appropriations power, regarded as the quintessential legislative power, was the most effective instrument for asserting the congressional will.

The CONGRESSIONAL BUDGET AND IMPOUNDMENT CONTROL ACT [1] of 1974 made Congress an equal participant in budget planning. The act created the Congressional Budget Office to compete with the OMB, and it solved the problem of presidential IMPOUNDMENT OF FUNDS [2] by placing tight restrictions on presidential nonspending (called deferrals and rescissions). At the same time, the act succeeded in one of its implicit purposes, to facilitate congressional spending, which increased significantly in the 1970s and 1980s. Under divided government, the cooperation envisioned in the budget act between the executive and legislature was elusive, and by 1985 it was widely believed that the BUDGET PROCESS [I] was not working satisfactorily, for reasons that implicated both branches. The Gramm-Rudman-Hollings Act did not improve the process.

Failing to reach agreement on the series of executive department appropriations bills required by the law, Congress from 1986 to 1988 enacted each year a single measure, the omnibus continuing resolution, to fund the entire federal government. The continuing resolution previously had been a technical expedient used to keep an agency in operation when action on an appropriations bill was not complete by the end of the congressional session. It now was transformed into a comprehensive budget act. Concealed within the continuing resolutions were many substantive policy decisions, unknown to anyone but their subcommittee sponsors, that were enacted into law without public scrutiny and debate. The continuing resolution for 1988, for example, appropriated $605 billion, was 1,057 pages long, and was accompanied by a 1,194-page conference report. President Reagan, with only one day to consider the bill, was virtually forced to sign it if he did not want to shut down the government for lack of funds. In effect, Congress deprived the President of his VETO POWER [4].

Another constitutional innovation of Congress was the creation of commissions outside the government to decide public policy matters. For example, Congress established the National Economic Commission; the Commission on Executive, Legislative, and Judicial Salaries; and the Commission on Sentencing Guidelines to deal with politically controversial subjects. These were but a few of 596 federal commissions created in 1988 by Congress, 117 of which were determined by the General Accounting Office to be concerned with substantive policy questions. A contemporary manifestation of the progressive belief that government could be purified by separating politics from administration, government by commission added a new wrinkle by proposing to separate politics from legislation. It was an acknowledgment that the legislative process itself, where interests are properly expressed, was so immobilized by faction and ideology that Congress was prepared to abdicate its constitutional responsibility for lawmaking.

If the policy environment was not conducive to legislation, Congress could influence administrative policymaking through the legislative veto. In the era of presidential party government the legislative veto was used mainly to effect executive reorganization plans and strengthen presidential policymaking. In the aftermath of Watergate, Congress used the veto extensively to supervise regulatory policymaking, including it in more than 200 statutes. The Supreme Court declared the legislative veto unconstitutional in the case of IMMIGRATION AND NATURALIZATION SERVICE V. CHADHA [2]. Nevertheless, Congress continued to employ devices that were the functional equivalent of the legislative veto. For example, it required agencies to get the approval of appropriations committees before taking an action and used committee reports and notification requirement to supervise bureaucratic policymaking.

The most significant congressional constitutional innovation in the period of divided government was the creation of a major executive office, the INDEPENDENT COUNSEL [I], outside the executive branch. The independent counsel is a SPECIAL PROSECUTOR [I] whose duty is to investigate allegations of criminality by high-level officials in the executive branch. After the Watergate affair, bills were introduced into Congress to provide for the prosecution of executive branch wrongdoing by an officer not subject to the political influence or legal control of the President. The premise on which these proposals rested was that an inherent conflict of interest prevented the President and the Justice Department from conducting an unbiased investigation of malfeasance in the executive branch. Publicly the proponents of the special prosecutor defended it as an "auxiliary precaution" under the theory of separation of powers and CHECKS AND BALANCES [1] for controlling the government, especially the executive power. The Carter administration supported this legislation, and the office of special prosecutor—renamed independent counsel in 1983—was included in the Ethics in Government Act of 1978.

The independent counsel act assumes that the executive

branch is peculiarly prone to illegal activity and conflict of interest. Its provisions apply to the President, vice-president, cabinet officers, senior White House staff, and sundry directors of agencies constituting a class of about seventy officials. The law provides that upon receiving information about a possible criminal violation by a covered official, the ATTORNEY GENERAL [1] shall conduct an inquiry to decide whether an investigation by an independent counsel is needed. Restrictions on the attorney general make further investigation almost necessary for dealing with allegations of wrongdoing. The judiciary committee of either house is also authorized to request the appointment of a special prosecutor. At the request of the attorney general, a panel of judges from the District of Columbia Circuit Court (called the Special Division) appoints an independent counsel, whose jurisdiction is defined by the Special Division and who can be removed by the attorney general only for cause.

Although the act purports to separate the independent counsel from the legislative branch, the effect of the law is to create a major executive office outside the executive branch. It provides a means by which Congress can do things that for political reasons it might not wish to do through the use of constitutional powers otherwise available to it, such as impeachment. Investigation and INDICTMENT [2] through the independent counsel process can be seen as a substitute for impeachment. Despite the appointment of the counsel by the attorney general and the appearance of administrative independence, the independent counsel is in effect an agent of Congress, for congressional committee investigations are the primary source of information on which the appointment process is based. Furthermore, when an executive official is targeted for investigation, the independent counsel is under political pressure to find a violation. The counsel searches for a crime to pin on the executive official, rather than looking for the person to fit the crime, as traditional law enforcement does.

In *Morrison v. Olson* (1988) the Supreme Court upheld the constitutionality of the independent counsel act. In earlier decisions, such as *Chadha*, NORTHERN PIPELINE CO. V. MARATHON PIPE LINE CO. (1981) [3], and BOWSHER V. SYNAR (1986) [I], the Court had struck down acts of Congress as violations of the separation of powers. Its acceptance of the independent counsel was therefore a major victory for Congress. The independent counsel's functions appeared to be a "purely executive power" that under the Court's previous separation of powers decisions required placing the officer under the full removal power of the President. The Court dropped this line of analysis, however, concluding simply that the removal provisions of the act and other limits on the President's ability to control the discretion of the independent counsel did not interfere with the President's exercise of his constitutional duty to execute the laws. *Morrison v. Olson* in effect invited Congress to create additional special prosecutors to enforce laws that are judged to be too important to leave to the discretionary litigation policy of politically appointed officers in the executive branch.

Although the office of independent counsel was created ostensibly to assure impartial investigation of executive branch improprieties, it encouraged lawmakers to pursue policy disagreements with the executive branch in a partisan manner, to the point of criminalizing them. The Iran-Contra affair illustrated this tendency. It also epitomized the conflicts of divided government carried into the sphere of foreign policy. In this pivotal event, the President relied on executive discretion in foreign affairs, congressional committees investigated executive officials in the accusatorial manner established in the McCarthy era, and independent counsel obtained indictments leading to criminal trials that obviated impeachment proceedings.

The Iran-Contra affair initially involved the secret sale of arms to Iran, with which the United States had been in a state of undeclared war since 1979. The sale was a foreign policy maneuver intended to secure the release of American hostages held by Arab terrorists. This covert action arguably violated the requirement of the NATIONAL SECURITY ACT [3] that the President, in conducting such an operation, make a factual "finding" and notify Congress. The Reagan administration used the profits from the Iranian arms sale to aid the Contras in Nicaragua seeking to overthrow the left-wing Sandinista government. The foreign policy question here was whether the United States should support the rebels. Congress cast the dispute in legal terms, which was made easier by a series of riders it had attached to defense appropriations acts from 1982 to 1986. These riders, known as the BOLAND AMENDMENTS [I], prohibited any funds from being spent by any agency of the United States involved in "intelligence activities," for the purpose of supporting the military overthrow of the Nicaraguan government.

Fundamental constitutional issues concerning the powers of President and Congress in foreign policy were hung on the peg of narrow statutory questions concerning the meaning of the Boland amendments. Yet as products of legislative compromise and executive-legislative accommodation in the (unacknowledged) spirit of divided government, the riders were deliberately vague and ambiguous. A key question was whether the National Security Council (NSC) was an "intelligence activity" in the sense intended by the legislation. The riders did not expressly identify it as such, although they did so identify other agencies. A further question, assuming that NSC was covered, was whether its activities conformed to the permissible scope of intelligence activities assisting the Contras that the Boland amendments approved. Neither the Iran-Contra hearings nor subsequent judicial trials of NSC officials satisfactorily resolved these questions.

If basic constitutional questions could not be reached, answers to narrow legal questions were also elusive because of the basic ambiguity in congressional foreign policy. Sometimes Congress voted for military and humanitarian aid to the Contras; at other times it barred using military equipment to overthrow the Nicaraguan government. Congress desired to challenge the President's control of foreign policy, but was afraid of critical public reaction if it did so too clearly or extremely. Therefore, it resorted to imprecise statutory language that did not unequivocally block the executive branch from carrying out its pro-Contra policy. For his part, President Reagan did not veto the Boland amendments, either because he viewed them as a compromise that permitted the administration to pursue its policy or because he feared impeachment.

The latter was a reasonable fear, for when information about the Iranian arms sale was revealed in 1986 a Watergate-type impeachment mood gripped many lawmakers and critics of the executive branch. The office of independent counsel, however, in conjunction with the traditional legislative power of investigation, was available as a less politically risky alternative. In November 1986, President Reagan promptly agreed to a congressional request to seek the appointment of an independent counsel to investigate the Iran-Contra affair. NSC officers Lt. Col. Oliver North, Admiral John Poindexter, and Robert McFarlane were the most prominent targets of the investigation, which resulted in at least six criminal convictions.

The trial of Oliver North illustrated the process by which constitutional controversy over the conduct of foreign policy was reduced to minor criminal convictions. North was a principal figure in the administration's policy who was called to testify in 1987 before the House and Senate select committees investigating the Iran-Contra matter. He was given a grant of criminal-use IMMUNITY [2], which meant that his testimony—televised to the nation in dramatically staged hearings—could not be used against him in any criminal prosecution that might result from the independent counsel's investigation. North's testimony was subsequently used against him, however, in a supposedly nonevidentiary way that arguably violated North's Fifth Amendment RIGHT AGAINST SELF-INCRIMINATION [3, I] as interpreted by the Supreme Court in KASTIGAR V. UNITED STATES (1972) [3]. North was indicted on a dozen counts. He was not charged with violating the Boland amendments, and he was acquitted on the most serious charges, such as defrauding the government by diverting funds to the Contras. North was convicted on three charges: accepting an illegal gratuity, falsifying

and destroying government documents, and obstructing Congress.

The precise purpose of Congress in the Iran-Contra affair was a matter of some dispute. In policy terms, the Democratic leadership opposed aiding the rebels, yet it pursued this policy ambiguously and inconsistently. More clear was the constitutional purpose of Congress—to assert the power of the legislative branch in foreign affairs. Historical practice and constitutional law recognized a broad sphere of executive power and discretion in this area. Congress therefore required cogent arguments against the administration's policy to overcome the presumption that tended to favor executive authority in the making of foreign policy, especially in the twentieth century. To bring foreign policy in a detailed operational sense under the RULE OF LAW [3], as the Boland amendments purported to do, asserted a congressional claim of authority to rival that of the President. Criminalizing the foreign policy disagreement through the use of independent counsel prosecutions was a suitable means of discrediting executive authority. An administration that conducted foreign policy by illegal or lawless means could not be considered constitutionally legitimate. This was the point that criminal convictions in the Iran-Contra affair were intended to make.

Criminal conviction was an effective policymaking tool because it could be justified by the traditional republican goal of imposing the rule of law on executive power, which is always the potential source of tyranny, according to the antiexecutive strain in American political thought. Although the Iran-Contra defendants were not tried for violating the Boland amendments, members of Congress did not hesitate to make accusations and to conclude that officials of the executive branch broke the laws enacted by Congress to prevent the United States from getting involved in a war in Latin America. Senators and representatives could make these accusations, confident that under the separation of powers doctrine their possession of the lawmaking power makes them superior to the executive branch and establishes a presumption that the will of Congress is tantamount to the rule of law.

Even if the Boland amendments are considered constitutional, it is questionable whether the lawmaking power can be effectively employed in making foreign policy. The reason is that in foreign affairs U.S. officials are required to deal with the representatives of other countries, who are not subject to the authority and rules of action that constitute U.S. law. The rule of law as propounded by legislative enactments under the separation of powers is further questionable because the purpose of foreign policy is to protect the public safety and national security. Prudence, wisdom, and discretion in the exercise of power are required to achieve this end, rather than the general and prospective rules of action that characterize the rule of law. The statesmanship on which the successful conduct of foreign policy depends has usually been thought more likely to result from the actions of the chief executive, who can be held politically accountable, than from the deliberations of hundreds of lawmakers in Congress.

In the 1980s, tendencies toward legislative assertiveness clashed with an executive authority that had significantly recovered from the power deflation and loss of respect suffered during the eras of the VIETNAM WAR [4,I] and Watergate. President Reagan was in many respects a nonpolitical chief executive, uninterested in the details of partisan maneuvering and administrative management, who in spite of himself refurbished the presidential office. That he successfully served two terms and employed military force in foreign affairs without interference from Congress under the War Powers Resolution was evidence of executive branch revitalization.

Divided government contradicted the theory of presidential party government. Yet it was not, as some observers argued, a historical and procedural accident. On the contrary, divided government resulted from a reconsideration of the public philosophy of interest-group liberalism and the constitutional theory of the regulatory welfare state. It was a partial repudiation of the twentieth-century tendency toward governmental activism and centralized sovereignty. Divided government was a confirmation of the relevance and utility of the separation of powers principle, one of the basic concepts of limited government.

HERMAN BELZ

(SEE ALSO: *Bork Nomination* [I]; *Civil Liberties* [I]; *Civil Rights* [I]; *Congress and Foreign Policy* [I]; *Congressional War Powers* [I]; *Conservatism* [I]; *Constitutional Reform* [I]; *Criminal Justice System* [I]; *Economy* [I]; *Establishment Clause* [I]; *First Amendment* [I]; *Freedom of Speech* [I]; *Freedom of the Press* [I]; *Line Item Veto* [I]; *Procedural Due Process of Law, Civil* [I]; *Procedural Due Process of Law, Criminal* [I]; *Racketeer Influenced and Corrupt Organizations Act* [I]; *Religious Fundamentalism* [I]; *Religious Liberty* [I].)

Bibliography

CARTER, STEPHEN L. 1988 The Independent Counsel Mess. *Harvard Law Review* 102:105–141.
EASTLAND, TERRY 1989 *Ethics, Politics, and the Independent Counsel: Executive Power, Executive Vice, 1789–1989.* Washington, D.C.: National Legal Center for Public Interest.
HARRIS, RICHARD A. and MILKIS, SIDNEY M., EDS. 1989 *Remaking American Politics.* Boulder, Colo.: Westview Press.
HELCO, HUGH 1986 General Welfare and Two American Political Traditions. *Political Science Quarterly* 101:179–196.
JONES, GORDON S. and MARINI, JOHN A., EDS. 1988 *The Imperial Congress: Congress in the Separation of Powers.* New York: Pharos Books.
LOWI, THEODORE J. 1985 *The Personal President: Power In-*
vested, Promise Unfulfilled. Ithaca, N.Y.: Cornell University Press.
MANSFIELD, HARVEY C., JR. 1985 Pride Versus Interest in American Conservatism Today. *Government and Opposition* 20:194–205.
SHAPIRO, MARTIN 1985 The Constitution and the Bureaucracy. *This Constitution* 9:11–16.
SUNDQUIST, JAMES L. 1989 Needed: A Political Theory for the New Era of Coalition Government in the United States. *Political Science Quarterly* 103:613–636.
WILDAVSKY, AARON 1980 *How to Limit Government Spending.* Berkeley: University of California Press.

CONSTITUTIONAL REFORM

Although any change in the Constitution can be labeled a reform, the broad term "constitutional reform" is usually reserved for proposed amendments that would alter in some fundamental way the structure of the government established by the nation's charter—that is, the organization of the legislative, executive, and judicial branches, the distribution of power among them, and their interrelationships.

Rarely have structural amendments to the Constitution been adopted. Of the twenty-six amendments ratified since 1787, only two have affected the form or character of the institutions as they were designed by the Framers. The SEVENTEENTH AMENDMENT [4], ratified in 1913, required United States senators to be chosen by popular election rather than by state legislatures. The TWENTY-SECOND AMENDMENT [4], approved in 1951, limits presidential tenure to two full terms. The other twenty-four amendments either have added substantive provisions (guaranteeing FREEDOM OF SPEECH [2,I] and RELIGIOUS LIBERTY [3,I], abolishing SLAVERY [4], providing for WOMAN SUFFRAGE [I], and so on) or, while dealing with the governmental structure, have corrected flaws or made minor adaptations in the constitutional design without altering the nature or relationships of the institutions that compose the government.

The stability of the American constitutional structure contrasts sharply with the impermanence of governmental systems in many other countries, some of which have written, discarded, and rewritten entire constitutions during the period that the United States constitutional structure has remained virtually unchanged. The American experience undoubtedly reflects a general satisfaction with the governmental system, particularly with that system's original and distinctive feature—its SEPARATION OF POWERS [4] and CHECKS AND BALANCES [1]. It may also reflect the fact that the Constitution embodies probably the most difficult AMENDING PROCESS [1] of any constitution in the world. In the normal process, an amendment must be approved by two-thirds of each house of Congress and then be ratified by the legislatures (or constitutional conventions) of three-fourths of the states. The requirement for such extraordinary majorities confers an effective VETO POWER [4] on any sizable political bloc; an amendment must be favored by Republicans and Democrats alike, by both conservatives and liberals, by advocates of a strong presidency as well as defenders of Congress. Yet structural amendments redistribute power and hence create winners and losers among the political blocs. The potential losers can usually muster enough support, either in the Congress or in the state legislatures, to block action. (As an alternative to initiation by the Congress, amendments may be proposed by a CONSTITUTIONAL CONVENTION [1] organized at the request of two-thirds of the state legislatures; but no such convention has ever been called. RATIFICATION [3] by three-fourths of the states would still be required.)

During the 1980s, the objective of constitutional reform attracted authoritative and well-organized support, expressed through two organizations made up of persons with long experience in high office. One, which included former officials of every administration from DWIGHT D. EISENHOWER [2] to RONALD REAGAN [3,I], was created in 1982 to advocate a single six-year term for the President—a proposal with a history of support going back to ANDREW JACKSON [3]. Ineligibility for reelection, the group argued, would enable the President to rise above politics and put the national interest ahead of personal reelection concerns. But the proposal encountered the objections, among others, that if the President is ineligible for reelection, he becomes a "lame duck" and hence loses authority, and that six years would be too long for a President who turned out to be ineffective. The proposal failed to win widespread support, and the movement faded.

The second organization, established in 1981, was the Committee on the Constitutional System, consisting of former members of Congress, former high executive officials, academics, and other political observers. Identifying the principal structural problem as one of conflict and deadlock between the executive and legislative branches, the committee undertook a broad consideration of remedies. Rejecting the six-year term for the President, the group recommended instead that the term of members of the HOUSE OF REPRESENTATIVES [I] be extended from two years to four (a proposal advanced in 1966 by President LYNDON B. JOHNSON [3]) and the term of senators from six years to eight. All House members and half the senators would be chosen in each presidential election, thus eliminating the present midterm congressional contests. Proponents contend that a four-year time horizon for the whole government would enable it to make difficult decisions

that it does not now make because the next election is always imminent; opponents respond that the midterm election is a necessary check to enable the voters to register approval or disapproval of their government.

The committee also endorsed an amendment to permit members of Congress to serve in the presidential CABINET [1] and other executive branch positions (a variation of proposals that won considerable support in earlier decades to give cabinet members nonvoting seats in the Congress and to require cabinet members, or even the President, to appear before Congress to answer questions). And it proposed to ease the process for approving treaties, by reducing the present requirement for a two-thirds vote of the SENATE [I] to either 60 percent of the Senate or a constitutional majority of both houses.

Finally, the committee recommended consideration of two more radical reforms. One would reduce the likelihood of divided government (that is, one party controlling the executive branch and the opposing party ruling one or both houses of Congress), which the committee identified as conducive to deadlock and inaction, by requiring voters to choose between party slates for President, vice-president, Senate, and House. The second would provide a means for reconstituting a government that had proved incapable of governing—because of deadlock between the branches, presidential incapacity, corruption, or any other reason—by means of a special election in which the presidency, vice-presidency, and congressional seats would be at stake. Such a procedure would correspond to those by which legislatures in parliamentary democracies are dissolved and new elections held. These proposals, too, attracted little popular support, and constitutional reform remained a subject only for academic debate.

JAMES L. SUNDQUIST

Bibliography

ROBINSON, DONALD L. 1989 *A Government for the Third American Century.* Boulder, Colo.: Westview Press.
SUNDQUIST, JAMES L. 1986 *Constitutional Reform and Effective Government.* Washington, D.C.: Brookings Institution.

CONSTITUTIONAL REMEDIES

Constitutional remedies take different forms, including defenses to criminal prosecutions, postconviction HABEAS CORPUS [2,I] actions, civil actions for DAMAGES [2], and declaratory and injunctive relief. Remedies for violations of constitutional rights, at first indistinguishable from more general legal remedies, became the focus of special congressional concern after the CIVIL WAR [I] and are now a highly developed set of modern rules shaped by both Congress and the Supreme Court.

Until well into the twentieth century, misbehavior by state or federal officials was more likely to be viewed as tortious or otherwise merely unlawful rather than as unconstitutional. As in MARBURY V. MADISON (1803) [3] and DRED SCOTT V. SANDFORD (1857) [2], federal courts would refuse to enforce unconstitutional legislation, but the question of additional remedies for constitutional violations rarely arose. CRIMINAL PROCEDURE [2] had not yet been federalized, and there were few constitutional rights that could give rise to distinctive remedies. Thus, early remedies against official misbehavior, such as the effort to vest jurisdiction in the Supreme Court to issue writs of MANDAMUS [3], invalidated in *Marbury*, were not thought of as distinct constitutional remedies. Even today, the liability for damages of the United States (but not United States officials) is governed largely by the FEDERAL TORT CLAIMS ACT [2], which does not by its terms distinguish between constitutional violations and other tortious conduct. It authorizes an action against the United States only if the challenged behavior also happens to violate state law. The conflating of constitutional violations and other legal wrongs limited and obscured constitutional remedies.

The Civil War led to the creation of new constitutional rights, and Reconstruction era CIVIL RIGHTS [1,I] statutes demonstrated a new congressional belief in the need to give such rights special protection. Section 4 of the CIVIL RIGHTS ACT OF 1866 [1], "with a view to affording reasonable protection to all persons in their constitutional rights of equality before the law," increased the number of federal judicial officers authorized to enforce the statutory protections of the act. The HABEAS CORPUS ACT OF 1867 [1] established federal habeas corpus relief as a remedy in all cases "where any person may be restrained of his or her liberty in violation of the constitution," a provision that survives with little substantive change today. The Enforcement Act (the Civil Rights Act of 1870) imposed criminal penalties for the violation of constitutionally protected voting rights and for conspiracies to violate constitutional rights. The Ku Klux Klan Act (the Civil Rights Act of 1871)—part of which is now SECTION 1983, TITLE 42, U.S. CODE [4]—created a civil action for every person deprived, under color of state law, of constitutional rights. Similar criminal prohibitions, largely ineffective, against violating constitutional rights continue in force in Sections 241 and 242, Title 18, U.S. Code.

These Reconstruction statutes, combined with increasing substantive constitutional protections, led to important judicially generated growth of constitutional remedies in both the criminal and civil areas. In the 1920s the Supreme Court began to treat the DUE PROCESS [2] clause of the FOURTEENTH AMENDMENT [2,I] as a limitation on state criminal procedure. The resulting constitutionalization of criminal procedure led to expanded direct review by the Supreme Court of the constitutionality of state court convictions and to greater use of federal habeas corpus to vindicate constitutional rights. The EXCLUSIONARY RULE [2] for FOURTH AMENDMENT [2,I] violations has been a particularly controversial remedy in the criminal sphere.

In the civil arena, the term "constitutional remedies" usually refers to damages actions and injunctive relief, each of which has had a distinct historical development. Injunctive relief for constitutional violations developed first. EX PARTE YOUNG (1908) [2] established the availability, despite the ELEVENTH AMENDMENT [2,I] and the doctrine of SOVEREIGN IMMUNITY [4], of injunctive relief against unconstitutional behavior by state officers. The remedial power to enjoin unconstitutional behavior figured prominently in the fight against SEGREGATION [4] statutes.

As the use of the INJUNCTION [2] to protect constitutional rights grew, different forms of injunctive relief emerged. Injunctions protecting constitutional rights may be subdivided into simple injunctions and structural, or institutional, injunctions. The simple injunction, ordering, for example, that the unconstitutional statute not be enforced, has remained relatively uncontroversial. The proper scope of broader injunctive relief has been debated since the 1960s, when federal courts found that recalcitrant state officials and legislatures did not comply with court orders to desegregate school systems and to improve conditions in prisons or mental institutions. Remedial orders in such INSTITUTIONAL LITIGATION [2] involved courts in the details of running institutions. DESEGREGATION [2] orders not promptly obeyed led to hard choices about obedience to the RULE OF LAW [3] in the face of resistance to one particular remedy, court-ordered SCHOOL BUSING [4]. Some observers raised questions about the legitimacy of judicial intervention in the operations of other public institutions and the capacity of courts as institutional managers. In a few cases, courts faced with years of noncompliance ordered local governments to finance constitutionally prescribed remedies, even going so far as to order increases in local taxes. In MISSOURI V. JENKINS (1990) [I] the Court held that a federal district court may direct a local government to levy taxes to comply with desegregation requirements.

Damages were awarded against public officials in a few early twentieth-century decisions in cases brought under section 1983, and damages are one traditional remedy under the Fifth Amendment's TAKING OF PROPERTY [4,I] clause. However, the modern right to recover damages against officials for constitutional violations is mainly traceable to MONROE V. PAPE (1961) [3] and BIVENS V. SIX UNKNOWN NAMED AGENTS (1971) [1]. In *Monroe* the Court held that section 1983 authorized a damages action against police officers who violated the Fourth Amendment in an illegal arrest and search. Actions based on section 1983 have since grown to encompass most constitutional harms, and litigation under the section constitutes one of the largest segments of federal court civil dockets. The remedies available under section 1983 include compensatory damages, punitive damages (against individuals, but not governments), injunctive relief, and the award of attorneys' fees. The Eleventh Amendment severely limits monetary remedies for constitutional violations, but the Supreme Court made clear that a state may be required to pay the cost of prospective compliance with the Constitution, such as the cost of desegregating a school system.

Section 1983 authorizes actions only against state officials. In *Bivens* the Court allowed a damages action against federal officials for violating the Fourth Amendment. After *Bivens* the Court recognized IMPLIED CONSTITUTIONAL RIGHTS OF ACTION [2] under the FIRST AMENDMENT [2,I], Fifth Amendment, and Eighth Amendment. In the 1980s, however, the Court began to rein in the *Bivens* remedy. In *Chappell v. Wallace* (1983) and *United States v. Stanley* (1987) the Court refused to recognize *Bivens* actions for enlisted military personnel who alleged that they had been injured by unconstitutional actions of their superiors and who had no cause of action against the United States. In *Bush v. Lucas* (1983) the Court refused to create a *Bivens* remedy for a violation of a civil service employee's First Amendment rights, because the violation arose "out of an employment relationship that is governed by comprehensive procedural and substantive provisions giving meaningful remedies against the United States." And in *Schweiker v. Chilicky* (1988) the Court held that the denial of SOCIAL SECURITY [4] benefits in violation of due process did not give rise to a *Bivens* action against the wrongdoing officials.

Congress greatly influences constitutional remedies by expanding, contracting, and shaping them. The Fourteenth Amendment and other constitutional provisions authorize Congress to enact legislation, both remedial and substantive, to enforce constitutional rights. The Reconstruction statutes were enacted largely under this authority. Section 1983 and federal habeas corpus, both federal statutory remedies, are the two most frequently used constitutional remedies, aside from defenses to criminal prosecutions.

The limits of congressional power over constitutional remedies have not been fully tested. Congress has left in place the two most-used statutory protections and regularly rejects proposals to restrict federal court jurisdiction to hear particular classes of cases or to issue specific remedies. Congress did limit section 1983 by requiring, in the Civil Rights of Institutionalized Persons Act, that certain prisoners first exhaust state administrative remedies before bringing section 1983 actions. And, in refusing to extend *Bivens* actions, the Supreme Court, in *Bush v. Lucas* and *Schweiker v. Chilicky*, emphasized that comprehensive alternative congressional remedial schemes were already in place for protecting the constitutional rights asserted. Congress's refusal to enact jurisdictional limitations, together with the implausibility of repealing section 1983 or federal habeas corpus, suggests a deep national commitment to the ideal of remedying constitutional wrongs.

The modern growth of constitutional remedies may have modified that commitment in one important way. The increased availability of injunctive and damages relief taught that fully remedying each constitutional wrong comes at a cost, either in challenging the authority of governing officials or in increasing confrontations between the judicial and political branches of government or between federal courts and state officials. A full panoply of remedies to fix each constitutional wrong may have increased the Supreme Court's reluctance to acknowledge new constitutional rights. In PAUL V. DAVIS (1976) [3], *Parratt v. Taylor* (1981), and subsequent cases involving both the due process clause and section 1983, the Court may have curtailed substantive constitutional protections in order to avoid triggering extensive remedial relief.

THEODORE EISENBERG

(SEE ALSO: *Damage Claims* [I]; *Prisoners' Rights* [3,I].)

Bibliography

EISENBERG, THEODORE 1982 Section 1983: Doctrinal Foundations and an Empirical Study. *Cornell Law Review* 67:482–556.

——— 1991 *Civil Rights Legislation*, 3rd ed. Charlottesville, Va.: Michie.

NAHMOD, SHELDON H. 1986 *Civil Rights and Civil Liberties Litigation*, 2nd ed. Colorado Springs, Colo.: Shepard's.

SCHWAB, STEWART J. and EISENBERG, THEODORE 1988 Explaining Constitutional Tort Litigation: The Influence of the Attorney Fees Statute and the Government as Defendant. *Cornell Law Review* 73:719–784.

CONSTITUTIONAL THEORY

The term "constitutional theory" refers to two aspects of constitutional law. First, it refers to general theories of the Constitution, which deal with the overall structure of the government, the relations among the branches, and the relation between the national and state governments. Second, it refers to theories of JUDICIAL REVIEW [3,I], which provide justifications for the occasions on which the courts, ruling on constitutional issues, will and will not displace the judgments of elected officials.

General theories of the Constitution consider the structure of the government as defined in the Constitution and, more important, as the institutions of the government have developed historically. The primary subjects of this sort of constitutional theory are the SEPARATION OF POWERS [4] of the three branches of the national government, and FEDERALISM [2,I], or the division of authority between the national government and state governments. Constitutional theories of this sort attempt to explain how the institutional arrangements of the United States government promote the public interest by allowing the adoption of socially beneficial legislation that does not threaten FUNDAMENTAL RIGHTS [2].

Theories of the separation of powers fall into two basic groups. In one, the primary concern is the separateness of the branches of the national government. Within this version of constitutional theory, problems arise when one branch begins to assume duties historically performed by another branch. The LEGISLATIVE VETO [3], invalidated in IMMIGRATION AND NATURALIZATION SERVICE V. CHADHA (1983) [2], offers an example. In the other version, the emphasis is on CHECKS AND BALANCES [1], and so the legislative veto is treated as a useful innovation to deal with problems of legislative control of executive actions in a government much larger than it was when created in 1789.

In general, checks and balances theories are more receptive to institutional innovations than separation of powers theories. Innovations tend to be seen as democratically chosen devices by which the executive and legislative branches respond to the demands for expansive substantive action generated by the political process; the public asks that the government expand its activity in the provision of social welfare or in international affairs, and the government responds first by acting to satisfy those demands and then, finding that either Congress or the President has grown too powerful, by developing new institutions like the legislative veto to check the branch that seems more threatening.

Yet, if checks and balances theories allow for institutional innovation and therefore for the adoption of policies that the public believes to be in its interest, they are less sensitive than separation of powers theories to the threats to fundamental freedoms that institutional innovations pose. If the original design of the Constitution carefully balanced the branches, as separation of powers theories suggest, then it is unlikely that current majorities will improve on that design.

Similar tensions pervade theories of federalism. At the outset, federalism appeared to be an important protection of democracy and social experimentation: state and local government, being closer to the people, could more readily be controlled by them than the more remote government in the national capital; and the variety of problems faced on the local level might elicit various responses, some of which would prove valuable enough to be adopted elsewhere while those that failed would do so only on a small scale. As the nation expanded, however, economic conditions appeared to require more coordinated responses than local governments could provide. As a result, federalism lost some of its value, to the point where on most issues the national government is free to act as national majorities wish, no matter how much some local governments and local majorities might object. The impairment of local democracy is apparent, yet alternative theories of federalism rely on notions of a sharp division of authority between state and nation that tend to seem quite artificial under modern circumstances.

These examples show how changes in both the scope of the national economy and the reach of the national government pose questions for general theories of the Constitution. Most dramatically, neither POLITICAL PARTIES [3] nor ADMINISTRATIVE AGENCIES [I] were contemplated by the designers of the Constitution, and yet any overall theory of the operation of the national government—a constitutional theory of the first sort—must somehow accommodate the importance of parties and BUREAUCRACIES [1,I].

General constitutional theory also deals with the role of the courts, though on a relatively high level of abstraction. Such theories agree that the courts exist to protect fundamental rights, but disagree primarily on the sources of those rights. One approach finds fundamental rights rooted in transcendental conceptions of rights, of the sort identified in classical theories of natural law. This approach often meets with skepticism about the existence of natural law. Another approach finds the fundamental rights enumerated in the text of the Constitution, but has difficulty dealing with what have been called the "open-ended" provisions of the Constitution, such as the NINTH AMENDMENT [3] and the PRIVILEGES AND IMMUNITIES [3] clauses, which appear to refer to UNENUMERATED RIGHTS [I].

When general theories of the Constitution deal with the role of judicial review, they sometimes adopt varieties of the other basic type of constitutional theory, the concern of which is the justification of judicial review. Constitutional theories of this type must divide the universe of constitutional claims into those that the courts should uphold and those that they should reject. A powerful argument against a court's decision to exercise its power to invalidate legislation is that such a decision necessarily overturns the outcome of processes of majority rule that are themselves an important value in the American constitutional system. It should be noted, however, that the strength of the "countermajoritarian difficulty," as ALEXANDER M. BICKEL [1] called it, can vary, depending on which government actor actually promulgated the rule in question—a city council, a state government, an administrative agency, Congress, or the President? Majoritarianism alone cannot answer the questions about judicial review. The constitutional system, though it values majority rule, does not take majority rule to be the sole value, as the Constitution's inclusion of limitations on the power of government demonstrates. If there is to be any judicial review, which seems required by the structure of the Constitution, on some occasions courts will displace the decisions of the majoritarian legislatures.

Most constitutional theories of the second type agree, however, that the courts should not simply substitute their determination of what is wise public policy for the legislature's. Not only do courts often lack the competence that legislatures have in developing information about social problems and possible methods of responding to those problems, but, more to the point, the countermajoritarian implications of such freewheeling exercises of the power of judicial review are, for most, unacceptable in the American constitutional system. Theories of this type therefore set themselves two tasks: they must specify when and why courts can invalidate legislation, and when and why they cannot.

Modern constitutional theories of this type fall into several basic groups, though many variants have been offered:

1. ORIGINALISM [I] insists that the courts should invalidate legislation only when the legislation is inconsistent with provisions of the Constitution as those provisions were intended to be applied by their authors. This theory might significantly limit the power of courts if, as most of its proponents believe, the Framers of the Constitution did not intend to place substantial limits on government's powers. The theory is vulnerable on a number of grounds. For some provisions, the evidence is at least mixed, sometimes suggesting that the Framers did indeed intend to limit government power a great deal. Originalist theories, because they seem to be primarily concerned about imposing limits on judicial discretion, have difficulty dealing with the kinds of ambiguities about intentions that historical inquiry almost invariably generates. The framers of the FOURTEENTH AMENDMENT [2,I], for example, were a coalition of Radical Republicans, who desired substantial changes in the overall operation of government with respect to individual rights, and more conservative Republicans, who wanted to preserve a substantial amount of state autonomy in that area. Whose intentions are to control in interpreting the amendment? In addition, technological change presents society with innovations that could not have been within the contemplation of the Framers, and social change sometimes means not only that contemporary values are different from those of the Framers of

the Constitution but also that the meaning of practices with which they were familiar has changed so much that it is unclear why contemporary society ought to respond to those practices as the authors intended. WIRETAPPING [4], a practice that clearly has something to do with the values protected by the FOURTH AMENDMENT [2,I] but which is significantly different from the practices the Framers actually contemplated, is an example of the first problem. The second problem is illustrated by the changed role of public schools between 1868, when the Framers of the Fourteenth Amendment foresaw little impact on SEGREGATION [4] of public schools, and 1954, when the Supreme Court held that segregated public education is unconstitutional.

2. Natural law theories rely on substantive moral principles determined by philosophical reflection on the proper scope of government in relation to individual liberty, to specify the choices that are within the range of legislative discretion and those that violate individual rights. Contemporary versions of these theories are offered by conservative libertarians, who stress the importance of private property as a domain of liberty, and by liberal supporters of the WELFARE STATE [I], who stress the importance of nondiscrimination and the provision of the basic necessities of life for people to be able to lead morally acceptable lives. Natural law theories often face general skepticism about the existence of the kinds of rights on which they rely, and a more specific skepticism about the ability of judges as compared to legislators to identify whatever rights there might in fact be.

3. Precedent-oriented constitutional theories rely on past decisions by the courts to guide contemporary decisions. PRECEDENTS [3] are taken to identify with sufficient clarity the kinds of choices that are to be left to legislatures. Using the ordinary techniques of legal reasoning, the courts can use precedents to determine constitutional questions that they have not faced before. Proponents of these theories argue that the techniques of legal reasoning are sufficiently constraining that courts will not be able to do whatever their policy inclinations would suggest, but are also sufficiently loose that courts will be able to respond appropriately to innovations and social change. Precedent-oriented theories face a number of problems. Many critics find it difficult to give normative value to the decisions of prior courts simply because those decisions happen to have been made; for them, just because the courts at one time "got off the track" is no reason to continue on an erroneous course. Other critics are skeptical about these theories' claims regarding the degree to which precedent actually constrains judges. Influenced by the American legal realists, they argue that the accepted techniques of legal reasoning are so flexible that judges can choose policies they prefer and disguise those choices

as dictated by, or at least consistent with, prior decisions.

4. Process-oriented theories attempt to minimize the countermajoritarian difficulty by pressing judicial review into the service of majority rule. They do so by identifying obstacles that make the government less than truly majoritarian. For theories of this sort, the democratic process is bound to malfunction when some people are excluded from the franchise, so that majoritarian legislatures can freely disregard their views. Similar problems arise when rights of expression are limited, so that supporters of certain positions are punished for advocating their adoption; majoritarian legislatures would not learn what these people actually prefer, and the outcome of the political process would therefore be distorted. Process-oriented theories have also dealt with questions of discrimination, which they typically treat as arising from situations in which, though there is no formal disfranchisement, prejudice leads legislators systematically to undervalue the true wishes of their constituencies taken as a whole, that is, including the victims of prejudice.

Critics of process-oriented theories point to limitations that the Constitution places on government that, though perhaps explicable in terms of preserving a majoritarian process, somehow seem devalued when treated solely in process terms; the THIRTEENTH AMENDMENT [4] ban on SLAVERY [4] is a notable example, as is the body of constitutional privacy law that the Supreme Court has developed. Other critics suggest that process-oriented theories, while purporting to serve majoritarian goals, actually subvert them, because the theories are loose enough to allow judges to identify so many obstacles in the processes of majority rule that they can use process-oriented theories to serve their own political goals. A libertarian process theory, for example, might rely on the economic theory of public choice to argue that the courts should be much more active in invalidating social and economic legislation because the beneficiaries of such laws tend to be concentrated INTEREST GROUPS [I] that can readily organize and lobby for their interests, while the costs of the laws are borne by consumers and taxpayers who, because no individual has much at stake, are systematically underorganized in the political process. A social welfare process theory, in contrast, would argue that poor people are at a systematic disadvantage in the political process because they have insufficient income, compared to wealthier people, to devote to political activity; such a theory would suggest that the courts should invalidate restrictions on the provision of public assistance, and should uphold— and perhaps even require—limitations on contributions to political campaigns.

5. The final group of theories of judicial review focuses less on the limits that courts should face in deciding individual cases and more on the practical political limits the courts actually do face in exercising the power of judicial review. These theories stress that the courts are part of the general political process and can be constrained by the actions of the other branches. Some of these theories emphasize the formal limitations on judicial power built into the Constitution, such as Congress's ability to restrict the jurisdiction of the courts, its power to impeach judges, and the public's power to amend the Constitution. These formal limitations have rarely been invoked successfully where Congress or the public has simply disagreed with the results the judges have reached. Another mechanism built into the Constitution, the power to replace judges who resign or die in office with judges sympathetic to the political program of current political majorities, has been more effective in the long run. Replacement of judges in the ordinary way has often shifted the general tenor of the courts, though no one can guarantee that this mechanism will succeed in overturning any particular decision, such as the Supreme Court's ABORTION [1,I] decision in 1973.

Other versions of this type of theory note that the courts have only infrequently succeeded in imposing their agenda on the public without having some substantial support in the political branches. In short, these theorists argue that the courts cannot get away with very much; the countermajoritarian difficulty, though real, has been exaggerated. Further, in this view, the courts have a limited amount of "political capital": they can invest their capital in decisions designed to enhance their reputation, either by invalidating unpopular laws that somehow have survived in the political process or by upholding popular laws, and thereby generate returns that they can use to preserve their public support when they invalidate genuinely popular statutes. These types of constitutional theory seem to pay attention to the realities of the operation of politics, but they are often too informal in their understanding of politics to be fully persuasive, and in any event, they fail to capture the important normative dimensions of most discussions of constitutional law.

MARK TUSHNET

(SEE ALSO: *Conservatism* [I]; *Constitutional Interpretation* [1]; *Critical Legal Studies* [I]; *Deconstructionism* [I]; *Interpretivism* [I]; *Jurisprudence and Constitutional Law* [I]; *Law and Economics Theory* [I]; *Legal Fictions* [I]; *Liberal Constitutional Construction* [I]; *Liberalism* [I]; *Noninterpretivism* [I]; *Political Philosophy of the Constitution* [3,I].)

Bibliography

BICKEL, ALEXANDER 1962 *The Least Dangerous Branch: The Supreme Court at the Bar of Politics.* Indianapolis, Ind.: Bobbs-Merrill.

ELY, JOHN HART 1980 *Democracy and Distrust.* Cambridge, Mass.: Harvard University Press.

TUSHNET, MARK 1988 *Red, White, and Blue: A Critical Analysis of Constitutional Law.* Cambridge, Mass.: Harvard University Press.

CONTROLLED-SUBSTANCE ABUSE

Throughout the quarter-century from 1965 to 1990 the federal government waged a frustrating "war" against the growing problem of trafficking in, and abuse of, marijuana, heroin, cocaine, and other drugs. The government's war on drugs raises a number of issues of constitutional dimension: To what extent does the EQUAL PROTECTION [2,I] clause permit differences in the regulation of various controlled substances? How specific must regulations be to conform to the requirements of the DUE PROCESS [2] clause? To what extent is the use of controlled substances protected by a constitutional RIGHT OF PRIVACY [3,I] or by RELIGIOUS LIBERTY [3,I]? Does the FOURTH AMENDMENT [2,I] prohibition of unreasonable SEARCH AND SEIZURE [4,I] contain an exception for seizure of illicit drugs? Does the prohibition of CRUEL AND UNUSUAL PUNISHMENT [2,I] impose any limitations on the sanctions imposed on drug offenders?

The FOURTEENTH AMENDMENT [2,I] guarantee of equal protection of the laws has been interpreted to require a RATIONAL BASIS [3] for governmental classifications. A classification is "underinclusive" if it does not include all who are similarly situated and "overinclusive" if it includes those who do not rationally belong with the other members of a prohibited class. The earliest efforts to regulate the abuse of controlled substances raised substantial issues under the equal protection clause, because they failed to include many drugs and tended to apply the same punitive sanctions to all drugs, despite substantial differences in their dangerousness. In 1937, for example, the Marijuana Tax Act classified marijuana with narcotic drugs, imposing the same harsh penalties for possession of marijuana as for heroin or cocaine. For more than thirty years, the drug policy of the United States recognized no distinctions among drugs. The same strategy was used to control all drugs, and that strategy was simply to keep escalating the penalties. Only one exception was recognized, and that was ALCOHOL [I]. Alcohol was treated as though it were not a drug at all. Drug treatment programs racked it up as a success if they converted a drug addict into an alcoholic. Separate federal bureaucracies were created to deal with alcohol abuse and drug abuse so that no one would get the idea that America's ten million alcoholics were addicted to a drug.

In 1970 the federal Controlled Substances Act codified a comprehensive scheme for the classification of drugs on five different schedules, depending on their potential for abuse, risk of addiction, and legitimate medical use. Penalties for trafficking vary substantially, depending on the schedule on which a drug is placed. Since 1970, continuous legal challenges have been mounted against the classification of marijuana on Schedule I, along with heroin, LSD, and other drugs having no recognized medical use. Other drugs, such as PCP, have been moved from a lower schedule to a higher one as awareness of the potential for their abuse has increased.

The guarantee of due process of law contained in both the Fifth and Fourteenth Amendments has been interpreted to require adequate notice of a criminal prohibition, to ensure both that potential violators can comply with the law and that law enforcement officers are not given broad authority to discriminate in the enforcement of the laws. Laws not meeting this standard are struck down as unconstitutionally vague.

In two spheres drug laws have raised substantial problems of VAGUENESS [4]. The first problem lies in the description of the prohibited drug itself. The development of "designer drugs" in clandestine laboratories has enabled new drugs to appear in the illicit market faster than laws can be amended to prohibit them. Congress reponded in 1986 by prohibiting controlled-substances "analogues," which are defined as substances whose chemical structure is "substantially similar" to previously controlled substances. Legal challenges asserting that this language is unconstitutionally vague are currently pending.

Second, attempts to regulate the marketing of drug paraphernalia have run into vagueness challenges, because drug "paraphernalia" include common household objects, such as spoons and scales. In 1982 the Supreme Court upheld an ordinance regulating the sale of items "designed or marketed for use with illegal cannabis or drugs." The Court concluded that any problem of vagueness was cured by a requirement of proof of actual intent that the items be used for illegal purposes.

The constitutional guarantee of privacy has been interposed against many governmental efforts to regulate drug use, but the most significant battleground has been urine testing of employees to detect drug use. In 1989 the Supreme Court gave the green light to programs requiring DRUG TESTING [I] of railway employees involved in train accidents and U.S. Customs Service employees applying for positions involving interdiction of drugs. The Court declared that the expectations of privacy are diminished for employees who participate in industries that are pervasively regulated or who are employed in drug enforcement efforts.

Whether drug use can ever be constitutionally protected as part of a religious exercise came before the Court in a 1990 case presenting a constitutional challenge to the discharge of Oregon employees who participated in a Native American Church ceremony that included the chewing of peyote buttons. In EMPLOYMENT DIVISION, DEPT. OF HUMAN RES. V. SMITH [I], the Court declared that a general criminal prohibition of the use of peyote could be enforced even when peyote was used as part of a legitimate, bona fide religious ceremony. The dissenting Justices argued that preference was being shown to some religions over others, noting that the alcohol used for sacramental wine in Catholic services was exempted from the PROHIBITION [3] laws enacted in the 1920s.

The prohibition of UNREASONABLE SEARCHES [4,I] and seizures in the Fourth Amendment has frequently been viewed as an obstacle by police charged with the enforcement of drug laws. The EXCLUSIONARY RULE [2], which requires the suppression of illegally seized evidence, may result in the dismissal of drug trafficking charges if the illicit drugs were seized without a valid SEARCH WARRANT [4]. A study of New York City police revealed that immediately after the exclusionary rule was first announced in 1961, arrest reports in half of all cases related that the defendant "dropped the drugs on the ground upon seeing the police officer." Any inquiry into the grounds for a search was thus avoided. During the prior year only fourteen percent of the reports claimed the defendant dropped the drugs. Obviously, the new rule did not cause an outbreak of "dropsy" in New York; it caused an outbreak of police perjury. Police were willing to lie to avoid application of the exclusionary rule to their searches.

Congress has frequently responded to the complaints of narcotics officers that the exclusionary rules make their jobs too tough. As part of President RICHARD M. NIXON's [3] war on drugs, Congress enacted a NO-KNOCK ENTRY [3] provision for drug cases in 1970, providing that search warrants for drugs could dispense with the normal requirement that police knock and announce themselves before entering the premises to be searched. Police argued that the exemption was necessary for drug cases because drugs are quickly destroyed if violators are warned of the police presence. What was forgotten was that police occasionally make mistakes. A series of "wrong-door" raids led to shootouts that left four innocent people dead, including one police officer. In 1974, Congress repealed the no-knock provision, restoring the requirement of a knock on the door even in drug cases.

During the 1980s the argument that search and seizure requirements should be relaxed in drug cases gained a receptive ear in the Supreme Court. In case after case, the Court carved out exceptions to the requirements of PROBABLE CAUSE [3] and search warrants, citing the need for more pervasive police surveillance to prevent the smuggling of illicit drugs.

A common legislative response to the frustration of escalating drug use is simply to escalate the penalties for illegal possession or trafficking of drugs. Does the cruel and unusual punishment clause of the Eighth Amendment impose any limitation? In 1962 the Supreme Court struck down a California law that made it a criminal offense "to be addicted to the use of narcotics." The Court characterized addiction as an illness over which the victim had no control, and concluded it would be "cruel and unusual punishment" to imprison someone for simply being sick. Subsequent cases, however, have held that addiction offers no defense to someone arrested for such activities as possession of drugs or being intoxicated in public. The imposition of life prison sentences has been challenged as disproportionate to the seriousness of drug offenses, but the Supreme Court currently gives states a wide berth in setting the level of punishment for drug offenses.

In the early 1970s, New York's Governor Nelson Rockefeller successfully sponsored a law imposing mandatory life imprisonment for drug pushers. The law was hailed as the ultimate solution, one that would make drug selling such a serious offense that no one would want to take the risk. The total failure of that policy quickly became an embarrassment. Motorists began complaining that they could not drive down some streets in Harlem in broad daylight without being accosted at every corner by drug hustlers. The hustlers, of course, were addicts on the lowest rung of the distribution ladder. The threat of a mandatory prison sentence had little impact on them.

Today legislators are stymied. Although they have imposed a mandatory sentence of ten years to life and a fine of $100,000 for engaging in a drug enterprise, these penalties have no perceptible impact on the number of drug enterprises flourishing in America. A serious suggestion has been made that CAPITAL PUNISHMENT [1,I] is the answer.

A potent weapon against drug traffickers has been found in the enactment of forfeiture laws. Under the Comprehensive Forfeiture Act of 1984, federal authorities can seize any property derived from the proceeds of a drug transaction or any property used to facilitate a drug offense. Houses, businesses, automobiles, airplanes, and boats have been forfeited to the government. In 1990 the Supreme Court ruled that money paid to criminal defense lawyers for representation in drug prosecutions could also be seized, without violating the Sixth Amendment RIGHT TO COUNSEL [3]. Courts have split on the question of whether the Eighth Amendment prohibition of cruel and unusual punishment requires that a forfeiture be proportionate to the seriousness of the offense. In one case, forfeiture of a house worth $100,000 was upheld even though the property was used to grow less than $1,000 worth of marijuana plants.

As the war on drugs escalates, the tension between law enforcement techniques and traditional constitutional liberties will increase. In applying a BALANCING TEST [1], courts can be expected to give greater and greater weight to the need to suppress drug trafficking. One may hope that the casualties in the war on drugs will not include the Constitution itself.

GERALD F. UELMEN

(SEE ALSO: *Drug Regulation* [2,I].)

Bibliography

KAPLAN, JOHN   1970   *Marijuana: The New Prohibition.* New York: Simon and Schuster.
NATIONAL COMMISSION ON MARIJUANA AND DRUG ABUSE   1973   *Drug Use in America: Problem in Perspective*, Second Report (March).
TREBACH, ARNOLD   1982   *The Heroin Solution.* New Haven, Conn.: Yale University Press.
UELMEN, GERALD F. and HADDOX, VICTOR G.   1990   *Drug Abuse and the Law.* New York: Clark Boardman.
WISOTSKY, STEVEN   1986   *Breaking the Impasse in the War on Drugs.* Westport, Conn.: Greenwood Press.

COUNTY OF ALLEGHENY v. AMERICAN CIVIL LIBERTIES UNION
109 S.Ct. 3086 (1989)

Each year the County of Allegheny set up a variety of exhibits to commemorate the holiday season. Inside the county courthouse, a crèche was displayed on the grand staircase. Outside the courthouse stood a Christmas tree and a menorah, the latter a symbol of Hanukkah. The outside display was accompanied by a sign describing it as part of the city's salute to liberty. A splintered Supreme Court ruled that the crèche violated the ESTABLISHMENT CLAUSE [I], but the menorah did not.

Justice HARRY A. BLACKMUN [1,I] delivered the opinion of the Court with respect to the crèche. He argued that the crèche violated the second prong of the LEMON TEST [I] because it expressed a patently religious message, as indicated by an accompanying banner with the words "Gloria in Excelsis Deo!" ("Glory to God in the Highest!"). However, Blackmun argued that the menorah did not endorse religion because in context it was devoid of religious significance. The menorah and Christmas tree together merely symbolized the different facets of the "same winter-holiday season, which has attained a secular status in our society."

Justice SANDRA DAY O'CONNOR [3,I] rejected Blackmun's reasoning with respect to the menorah, although she concurred in the Court's judgment. Unlike Blackmun, O'Connor readily acknowledged the religious meaning of the menorah, but argued that its display was permissible because in context it "conveyed a message of pluralism

and freedom of belief" rather than endorsement. Justices WILLIAM J. BRENNAN [1,I], JOHN PAUL STEVENS [4,I], and THURGOOD MARSHALL [3,I] disagreed. They contended that both the Christmas tree and the menorah were religious symbols and that their display effected a dual endorsement of Christianity and Judaism.

Four Justices on the Court—WILLIAM H. REHNQUIST [3,I], ANTONIN SCALIA [I], BYRON R. WHITE [4,I], and ANTHONY M. KENNEDY [I]—took issue with the Court's ruling on the crèche. Writing for this group, Justice Kennedy argued that the guiding principle in establishment-clause cases should be government neutrality toward religion—but neutrality properly understood. Given the pervasive influence of the "modern administrative state," said Kennedy, complete government nonrecognition of religion would send "a clear message of disapproval." Hence, some government recognition of religion may actually further the goal of neutrality. As applied to this case, for the government to recognize only the secular aspects of a holiday with both secular and religious components would signal not neutrality but "callous indifference" toward the religious beliefs of a great many celebrants. Such hostility is not required by the Constitution according to Kennedy. As long as holiday displays do not directly or indirectly coerce people in the area of religion and the displays do not tend toward the establishment of a state religion, they should be constitutional. Under this standard, the crèche, the Christmas tree, and the menorah were all permissible.

JOHN G. WEST, JR.

(SEE ALSO: *Establishment of Religion* [2]; *Lynch v. Donnelly* [3]; *Religious Liberty* [3,I]; *Separation of Church and State* [4,I].)

COURT-PACKING PLANS

"Court packing" is an ambiguous phrase. It arises more frequently as an epithet in political disputation than as an analytical term in scholarly discourse. "Packing" connotes a deliberate effort by an executive, especially a President, to appoint one or more (usually more) judges to assure that decisions will accord with the ideological predisposition of that executive. *Webster's New International Dictionary* defines "pack" as "to . . . make up unfairly or fraudulently, to secure a certain result." Yet not everyone agrees on what is unfair, and it is not at all extraordinary for Presidents to take pains to ascertain that a prospective nominee is likely to behave in ways that will not be out of harmony with the ends of their administrations.

Furthermore, the word "packing" has been employed with respect to two different situations—when a President is filling vacancies that have arisen in the natural course of events, and when a President seeks legislation to increase the membership of courts to create additional opportunities for appointments that may shape the outcome of pending and future litigation.

Although political antagonists have taken advantage of the elasticity of the word to raise the charge of Court packing through much of our history, scholars have largely concentrated their attention on three particular episodes. The first of these events took place on the night of March 3, 1801, when in his final hours in office, President JOHN ADAMS [1] sat up very late signing commissions of sixteen appointees to circuit judgeships and forty-two justices of the peace for the District of Columbia, including one William Marbury. All these offices had been created in the last three weeks of his term by an obliging Federalist Congress, and Adams, outraged by the victory of the Democratic Republicans in 1800 and fearful of its consequences for the nation, busied himself filling the posts with faithful partisans to serve as a restraint on his successor, THOMAS JEFFERSON [3]. This melodrama of the "midnight judges" would subsequently lead to the landmark case of MARBURY V. MADISON (1803) [3].

Historians long thought they had detected another instance of Court packing during RECONSTRUCTION [I]. In 1870, at a time when the membership of the Court had been reduced, the Supreme Court, in *Hepburn v. Griswold*, struck down the Legal Tender Act of 1862 as applied to debts incurred before its enactment. The 4–3 vote strictly followed party lines. A year later, in *Knox v. Lee* and *Parker v. Davis*, the decision was reversed when the three dissenters in the earlier ruling were joined by two new appointees, both Republicans, of President ULYSSES S. GRANT [2]. Their appointments followed the action of Congress restoring the Court to nine Justices. This sequence gave credibility to the allegation that the Court had been packed in order to save the Republican administration's monetary policy. In fact, however, scholars now agree that neither the augmentation of the size of the bench nor these appointments resulted from partisan or ideological motivations.

By far the most important Court-packing plan in American history emerged out of a conflict between the Supreme Court and the administration of FRANKLIN D. ROOSEVELT [3] in the Great Depression. In 1935 and 1936, the Court again and again struck down NEW DEAL [I] laws, including those creating the two foundation stones of Roosevelt's recovery program, the NATIONAL INDUSTRIAL RECOVERY ACT [3] and the AGRICULTURAL ADJUSTMENT ACT OF 1933 (AAA) [1]. Most of these rulings came on split decisions, with OWEN J. ROBERTS [3] joining the conservative "Four Horsemen"—PIERCE BUTLER [1], JAMES C. MCREYNOLDS [3], GEORGE SUTHERLAND [4], and WILLIS VAN

DEVANTER [4]—to form a five-man majority, sometimes augmented by the Chief Justice, CHARLES EVANS HUGHES [2].

The Roosevelt administration responded by exploring a number of possibilities for curbing the powers of the Supreme Court. As early as May 1935, Attorney General HOMER S. CUMMINGS [2] directed one of his aides to look into how the Court's authority to pass on constitutional questions could be limited. Rumors had circulated from the beginning of the New Deal era that Court packing might someday be attempted, and at a cabinet meeting at the end of 1935, the President mentioned packing the Court as the first of a series of options. A cabinet official noted in his diary, however, that Roosevelt characterized it as "a distasteful idea." Still, Roosevelt more than once alluded to the episode in Great Britain earlier in the century when the threat of creating several hundred new peers had compelled the House of Lords to approve reform legislation.

Initially, critics of the judiciary assumed that redress could be achieved only by amending the Constitution, but the behavior of the Court in 1936 turned the thinking of the administration in new directions. When Justice HARLAN F. STONE [4], in a biting dissent in BUTLER V. UNITED STATES (1936) [1], accused the majority in the 6–3 ruling invalidating the AAA processing tax of a "tortured construction of the Constitution," he fostered the idea that Congress need not alter the Constitution because properly interpreted it could accommodate most of the New Deal. Instead, Congress should concern itself with the composition of the Court.

The replacement of even one Justice could shift 5–4 decisions toward approval of FDR's policies without any modification of the Constitution. Yet, although this Court was the oldest ever, not a single vacancy developed in all of Roosevelt's first term. Increasingly, the administration looked for a solution that would eschew the tortuous process of constitutional amendment and instead, by the much simpler procedure of an act of Congress, overcome obstruction by elderly judges.

Shortly after winning reelection in November 1936, Roosevelt told Cummings that the time to act had come. Not only had the Court struck down fundamental New Deal laws in his first term, but in addition, it was expected to invalidate innovative legislation such as the National Labor Relations Act and the SOCIAL SECURITY ACT [4] when it ruled on these statutes early in his second term. Moreover, although he had won an overwhelming endorsement from the people in a contest in which he had carried all but two of the states, he was constrained from taking advantage of this mandate because if he tried to put through measures such as a wages and hours law the Court was likely to wipe out those laws too. He saw little prospect that the Court might change its attitude; in the very last decision of the term, MOREHEAD V. NEW YORK EX REL. TIPALDO (1936) [3], it had shocked the nation by striking down a New York State minimum wage law for women, thereby indicating that it did not merely oppose concentrated power in Washington, but was in the President's words, creating a "'no-man's land' where no Government—State or Federal—can function." Under these circumstances, FDR was determined not to be like President JAMES BUCHANAN [1], who sat passively while his world collapsed about him.

During the month of December, Cummings put together the specific proposal that Roosevelt embraced. Cummings was influenced by the political scientist EDWARD S. CORWIN [2], who suggested linking an age limit of seventy years for Justices to the appointment of additional members of the bench, but he did not find the precise formula until he came upon a 1913 memorandum by James C. McReynolds, then attorney general, recommending that when a judge of the lower federal courts did not retire at seventy the President be required to appoint an additional judge. Cummings seized McReynolds's idea and applied it to the Supreme Court as well. He also worked out a rationale for the scheme by incorporating it in a package of proposals for relieving congestion in the federal judicial system. Roosevelt, for his part, savored the irony that the original notion had come from McReynolds, now the most hostile Justice on the Court.

Through all these months, the President had given little indication of what he was considering. After the adverse decision in SCHECHTER POULTRY CORPORATION V. UNITED STATES (1935) [4], he had said, "We have been relegated to the horse-and-buggy definition of interstate commerce," but so loud were objections to this remark that he made almost no public utterance about the Court for the next year and a half and did not raise the issue in the 1936 campaign. No cabinet officer save Cummings knew of the surprise he was about to spring, and he confided nothing to his congressional leaders until the very end.

On February 5, 1937, Roosevelt stunned the nation by sending to Congress a plan to reorganize the federal judiciary. He prefaced the proposal by claiming that aged and infirm judges and insufficient personnel had created overcrowded federal court dockets and by asserting that "a constant and systematic addition of younger blood will vitalize the courts." To achieve this goal, he recommended that when a federal judge who had served at least ten years waited more than six months after his seventieth birthday to resign or retire, a President might add a new judge to the bench. He could appoint as many as six new Justices to the Supreme Court and forty-four new judges to the lower federal tribunals.

The President's message elicited boisterous opposition. From the very first day, opponents characterized his scheme as "court packing" and accused Roosevelt of tampering with the judiciary. Within weeks, they had forced him to back away from his crowded dockets–old age rationale by demonstrating that the Supreme Court was abreast of his work. Especially effective was a letter from Chief Justice Hughes read by Senator BURTON K. WHEELER [4] at the opening of hearings before the SENATE JUDICIARY COMMITTEE [I]. An increase in the size of the Court, Hughes objected, would not promote efficiency, but would mean that "there would be more judges to hear, more judges to confer, more judges to discuss, more judges to be convinced and to decide."

Despite fervent and well-organized protests, commentators concluded that the legislation was likely to be approved because Roosevelt had such huge Democratic majorities in both houses of Congress. After the 1936 elections, the Republicans were reduced to only sixteen members in the Senate. In the House, the Democrats had a 4–1 advantage. Although there were some conspicuous defectors, such as Wheeler, it seemed unlikely that enough Democrats would break with a President who had just won such an emphatic popular verdict of approval to deny him the legislation he sought.

A series of unanticipated decisions by the Court, however, drastically altered this situation. On March 29, the Court, in a 5–4 ruling in WEST COAST HOTEL CO. V. PARRISH (1937) [4], validated a minimum wage act of the state of Washington essentially the same as the New York law it had struck down the previous year. Two weeks later, in a cluster of 5–4 decisions, it upheld the constitutionality of the WAGNER (NATIONAL LABOR RELATIONS) ACT [4]. In May, by 5–4 and 7–2, it validated the Social Security Act. The critical development in these votes was the switch of Justice Roberts, who for the first time since the spring of 1935, broke away from the Four Horsemen to uphold social legislation. Roberts's turnabout gave Roosevelt a 5–4 advantage, which swelled to a prospective 6–3 when, also in May, one of the Four Horsemen, Willis Van Devanter, announced that he was retiring. On that same day, the Senate Judiciary Committee voted, 10–8, to recommend against passage of the bill, and administration polls of the Senate found that as a consequence of these developments Roosevelt no longer had the votes. "A switch in time," it was said, "saved nine."

Roosevelt, however, persisted in trying to put through a modified Court-packing measure, and he almost succeeded. In June, he advanced a compromise raising the suggested retirement age from seventy to seventy-five years and permitting him only one appointment per calendar year. Although watered down, this new version preserved the principle of the original bill and would give him two new Justices by January 1, 1938 (one for the calendar year 1937 and one for 1938), as well as a third Justice for the Van Devanter vacancy. In July, when Court-packing legislation finally reached the Senate floor, the opposition found that Roosevelt had a majority for this new proposal if it could be brought to the floor. The President's advantage, however, rested on the influence of the domineering Senate Majority Leader, Joseph T. Robinson, but when shortly after the debate began, Robinson died, Roosevelt's expectation went down with him. On July 22, the Senate voted to inter the bill in committee.

Roosevelt had suffered a severe defeat, but he insisted that, although he had lost the battle, he had won the war. To the Van Devanter vacancy, he soon named HUGO L. BLACK [1], an ardent New Dealer and supporter of Court packing, and within two and a half years of his defeat, he was able to appoint a majority of the nine Justices. This "Roosevelt Court," as it was called, never again struck down a New Deal law. Indeed, it took so expansive a view of the commerce power and the spending power and so circumscribed the due process clause that scholars speak of the "Constitutional Revolution of 1937." Not once since then has the Court stuck down any significant law—federal or state—regulating business. The struggle over Court packing, however, cost Roosevelt dearly, for it solidified a bipartisan conservative coalition arrayed against further New Deal reforms.

Although no President since Roosevelt has advocated a Court packing statute, the charge of packing has been raised against three of his successors. When, in his final year in office, LYNDON B. JOHNSON [3] sought to elevate Associate Justice ABE FORTAS [2] to the Chief Justiceship, conservative Republicans charged him with a "midnight judge" kind of maneuver to deny his probable successor, RICHARD M. NIXON [3], the opportunity to make the selection, and after revelations about Fortas's comportment, the endeavor failed. So frank was Nixon in turn about stating his desire to reverse the doctrines of the WARREN COURT [4] that he was accused of trying to pack the Supreme Court with conservative jurists when he made nominations such as those of Clement Haynsworth and G. Harrold Carswell. Both of these nominations were rejected, but Nixon won confirmation of four other choices, including WARREN E. BURGER [1] as Chief Justice, although they were sometimes to disappoint him by their subsequent behavior. An even louder outcry arose over RONALD REAGAN's [3,I] selections. His attempt to place Robert Bork on the Supreme Court was turned aside, but he secured approval of four other nominees, all regarded as sharing his conservative outlook. He had even greater success in the lower federal courts. His efforts

were decried as, in the title of one book, *Packing the Courts: The Conservative Campaign to Rewrite the Constitution*, but neither Reagan nor Nixon had acted markedly differently from such twentieth-century predecessors as WILLIAM HOWARD TAFT [4], WARREN G. HARDING [2], and Franklin D. Roosevelt, although none of the others may have exhibited such sedulous ideological zeal.

WILLIAM E. LEUCHTENBURG

(SEE ALSO: *Bork Nomination* [I].)

Bibliography
ALSOP, JOSEPH and CATLEDGE, TURNER 1938 *The 168 Days.* Garden City, N.Y.: Doubleday, Doran.
LEUCHTENBURG, WILLIAM E. 1966 The Origins of Franklin D. Roosevelt's "Court Packing" Plan. In Philip B. Kurland, ed. *The Supreme Court Review: 1966.* Pages 347–400. Chicago: University of Chicago Press.
_____ 1969 Franklin D. Roosevelt's Supreme Court "Packing" Plan. In Harold M. Hollingsworth and William F. Holmes, eds., *Essays on the New Deal.* Pages 69–115. Austin: University of Texas.

COVER, ROBERT M.
(1943–1986)

Born in Boston in 1943, Robert M. Cover earned his B.A. from Princeton University in 1965. In 1963 Cover had left Princeton to work for the Student Nonviolent Coordinating Committee (SNCC) in Georgia, where he was jailed and beaten. Although he became a superb scholar and an inspirational teacher and friend, Cover remained an engaged activist. He believed that "legal meaning is a challenging enrichment of social life, a potential restraint on arbitrary power and violence." He never separated himself or his work from that pursuit.

Cover received his LL.B. from Columbia Law School in 1968, at which time he immediately joined the Columbia faculty. He moved to Yale Law School in 1972 and was named the Chancellor Kent Professor of Law and Legal History in 1982.

Cover won the Ames Prize for *Justice Accused: Antislavery and the Judicial Process* (1975). This book probed the moral dilemma confronting northern judges opposed to slavery [4] on moral grounds who nonetheless believed that the law of antebellum America required them to order fugitive slaves returned to their masters. In addition, Cover coauthored books on procedure and wrote numerous articles about how narrative, myth, and history "invite new worlds" by illuminating the tension between law and the normative worlds we construct.

Cover's pathbreaking work stressed that judicial language is unlike literary language because it involves actual violence, pain, and death. He explored new facets of jurisdiction [3], law and religion, civil rights [1,I], and civil liberties [1,I]. If a dominant theme emerged in the radically interdisciplinary work of this "anarchist who love[d] law," it was exploration of how law might be a bridge toward the creation of new narratives and better actualities. To Cover, law should involve a conscious quest for a juster justice.

Cover died of a heart attack in 1986.

AVIAM SOIFER

Bibliography

MEMORIAL ISSUE 1987 *Yale Law Journal* 96:1699–1984.

COY v. IOWA
487 U.S. 1012 (1988)

Coy was convicted of sexually assaulting two thirteen-year-old girls. During his trial, the girls gave testimony in front of a screen that blocked Coy from their sight. Coy claimed that use of the screen violated his right to CONFRONTATION [1,I] guaranteed by the Fifth Amendment. The Supreme Court agreed, holding that face-to-face examination of witnesses testifying at trial is a fundamental guarantee of the confrontation clause.

Writing for the majority, Justice ANTONIN SCALIA [I] argued that open accusations seem integral to the very idea of fairness; moreover, face-to-face confrontation serves the end of truth because it is more difficult for witnesses to lie (or lie convincingly) when they must do so to the face of the person their testimony will harm. Scalia argued that the Court's previously carved out exceptions to the confrontation clause were inapposite because they dealt with out-of-court statements and not testimony given during trial. Whether there may be exceptions to the confrontation clause even at trial, Scalia was unwilling to say. All he would acknowledge is that if such exceptions exist they must be "necessary to further an important public policy."

Justice SANDRA DAY O'CONNOR [3,I], in one of her characteristically narrow concurrences, claimed that nothing in the ruling should be construed as forbidding state efforts to protect child witnesses, and she listed several types of state action that she thought would not raise a "substantial Confrontation Clause problem." O'Connor also seized on the majority's concession that exceptions to the confrontation clause may exist when "necessary to further an important public policy." The key word, O'Connor pointed out, was "necessary," and this would likely be the focus of future litigation. It was; and in 1990, the Court took up the issue again in MARYLAND V. CRAIG [I].

JOHN G. WEST, JR.

CREATIONISM

Creationism is the belief that plants and animals were originally created by a supernatural being substantially as they now exist. Proponents of creationism today are primarily evangelical Christians who adopt a literal reading of the book of Genesis in the Bible. Several hundred creationists also hold advanced science degrees and claim that the best scientific evidence supports creationism; these creationists advocate what they call "scientific creationism."

Scientific creationism is far afield from prevailing scientific orthodoxy, and although most of its proponents are evangelicals, many evangelicals do not subscribe to it. Scientific creationism teaches that the earth is several thousand years old, rather than several billion, and that much of the fossil record was created in a worldwide deluge, rather than by the gradual accumulations of the ages. It harkens back to catastrophism of the type dominant in the scientific community before the theories of Charles Lyell and Charles Darwin gained acceptance. Scientific creationists claim that the fossil record supports the idea that when life first appeared it was already complicated and multifaceted; at the very least, they argue, the fossil record shows no support for the gradual progression of life forms taught by classical Darwinian theory. Much of the evidence cited by creation scientists comes from evolutionists, who continue to have marked disagreements with one another about the mechanism by which evolution occurs.

Creationism originally became a constitutional issue because creationists tried to keep evolution from being taught in the public schools, a policy the Supreme Court struck down as violative of the ESTABLISHMENT CLAUSE [I] in EPPERSON V. ARKANSAS (1968) [2]. Creationism remains a constitutional issue, however, because creationists now seek to have scientific creationism taught in public schools. In fact, they have sought state laws that require the teaching of creationism side-by-side with evolution.

Opponents of these laws maintain that teaching creationism is tantamount to teaching religion and hence abridges the establishment clause; as evidence for their position, they point to the religious underpinnings of creationism and claim that few if any scientists hold creationist beliefs. Creationists respond that how they derived their theory is irrelevant; the sole question is whether or not it can be validated by scientific research. As for the dearth of scientists who are creationists, creation scientists point to their own doctorates in science from secular universities. Nevertheless, creationists readily admit that few scientists have adopted creationism, but claim that this is the result of prejudice on the part of evolutionists, marshaling evidence that graduate students and professors believing in creationism have been systematically discriminated against because of these beliefs. Creationists argue that laws requiring the teaching of scientific creationism alongside evolution are required to break the stranglehold of such prejudice.

In response to creationist concerns, Louisiana enacted a law requiring the balanced treatment of the theories of "evolution science" and "creation science" in the public schools. The act defined the respective theories as "the scientific evidences for [creation or evolution] and inferences from those scientific evidences." The act did not mandate that either theory be taught in the schools; but it did demand that if one was taught the other must be taught. The act also required that neither evolution nor creation science be taught "as proven scientific fact."

The Supreme Court held 7–2 that the act failed the first part of the LEMON TEST [I] because it did not have a valid secular purpose; hence, the statute was unconstitutional on its face under the establishment clause.

Writing for the majority, Justice WILLIAM J. BRENNAN [1,I] rejected the act's explicitly stated secular purpose of "protecting ACADEMIC FREEDOM [1]" because the statute did not in any way enhance the freedom of teachers to teach science. Brennan also rejected the contention that Louisiana wanted to ensure "fairness" by requiring that all the evidence regarding origins be taught, noting that the law unequally provided for the development of curriculum guides for creation science, but not evolution.

The core of Brennan's argument, however, was his determination that creation science embodies "religious doctrine" and that the "preeminent purpose of the Louisiana legislature was . . . to advance the religious viewpoint that a supernatural being created humankind." Brennan sought to show from the legislative record that legislators in fact supported the act because evolution contradicted their own religious beliefs. Hence, the motivations of the legislators, rather than the clear language of the act, was the decisive factor in invalidating the law.

Justice ANTONIN SCALIA [I], joined by Chief Justice WILLIAM H. REHNQUIST [3,I], filed a lengthy dissent attacking many of the central premises of the majority's opinion. Scalia maintained that the majority was able to dismiss the act's stated secular purpose only by misconstruing it. According to Scalia, the "academic freedom" the act sought to guarantee related not to the teachers, but

to the students, whom the legislature wanted to be able to study various views of the origin and development of life. Furthermore, the act on its face treated evolution and creation science equally, and the few differences that did exist could be readily explained. For example, the state provided for the development of study guides for creation science, but not evolution because "of the unavailability of works on creation science suitable for classroom use . . . and the existence of ample materials on evolution."

Scalia saved his most cutting remarks, for the majority's inquiry into the subjective motives of Louisiana's legislators. Scalia showed through copious citations that the majority had distorted legislators' intentions. But in Scalia's view, even had the majority correctly read the motives in this case, motives alone should not have invalidated the law. The act should have been struck down only if its objective language clearly violated the Constitution or if the primary effect of the law in practice was to advance religion impermissibly (a question not before the Court).

Edwards v. Aguillard raises questions both difficult and deep; it is not really analogous to cases dealing with school prayer or Bible reading because these practices are devotional exercises clearly designed to inculcate religious truth. In this case, however, the state officially disclaimed any intention to present creationism as "true." So even if creationism is inherently religious—as the Court determined—it is not necessarily the case that teaching about it promotes religion in violation of the establishment clause. As Justice LEWIS F. POWELL [3,I] pointed out in his concurring opinion, the Court has often maintained that public schools have the right to teach objectively about religion. So to strike down the Louisiana law, the Court not only had to find creationism religious, but it had to maintain that the purpose of the law was to teach creationism as true. As a factual matter, however, this was by far the weakest link in the Court's logic.

Why then did the Court rule as it did? One can only speculate; but it would not be inappropriate to point out the obvious: creationism conjures up images of the Scopes trial and intolerant fundamentalists who are none too bright. In the battle between science and superstition, creationism has been accounted superstition, and one can readily understand why the Court would be reluctant to uphold a law that might appear to sanction creationism. Unfortunately, there are problems with excluding beliefs like creationism from the classroom entirely.

Evolution remains so controversial primarily because it is part of a much larger debate over the nature and meaning of life. The study of how life began almost inevitably raises questions of why: Why did life begin? Why are humans rational? Why is there order in the universe?

Men and women have debated these questions for thousands of years, considering them to be some of the most important inquiries human beings can undertake. Yet these are the very sorts of questions that modern science cannot answer. All modern science can legitimately offer are tentative explanations about the physical process by which life developed after it first appeared; of its own accord, it can tell us nothing of the purpose or meaning of the development of life. Nor, in all probability, will it ever unravel the mystery of how life first arose from nonlife. The result is that if one relegates the discussion of the origin and development of life to science textbooks that discussion will be, at best, incredibly impoverished because modern science cannot legitimately provide answers to questions of meaning and purpose. At worst, the discussion will be disingenuous because attempts will be made to answer the questions of meaning in the guise of science. One does not need to know much of recent history to realize that science has been used quite often to justify a variety of philosophically laden schemes, from social darwinism to eugenics. The encroachment of science into the domains of philosophy and theology may be more subtle in the public schoolroom, but it occurs nevertheless. It can be seen in the 1959 biology text that declared that "nothing supernatural happened" when life first arose or in more recent texts that emphasize "chance" and "randomness" as the sole determinants of how life developed. Such statements advance philosophical and theological claims just as surely as creationism; yet these claims are allowed because they are made in the name of science. In such a situation, one can readily understand why some creationists have tried to distance their theory from its religious underpinnings; they know this is the only way their ideas will get a fair hearing.

It might be better if public schools—and the Court—recognized more forthrightly that both philosophy and theology have a place in the discussion of origins and that their inclusion in school curricula need not be equated with their advancement by the state. One can teach about various theories, after all, without advocating any of them.

JOHN G. WEST, JR.

(SEE ALSO: *Religious Fundamentalism* [I]; *Separation of Church and State* [4,I].

Bibliography

BERGMAN, JERRY   1984   *The Criterion: Religious Discrimination in America.* Richfield, Minn.: Onesimus.

BIRD, WENDELL R.   1978   Freedom of Religion and Science Instruction in Public Schools. *Yale Law Journal* 87:515–570.

CURTIS, V. KAY   1988   Religion: Church and State Relations: Balanced Treatment of Theories of Origins—Edwards v. Aguillard. *Oklahoma Law Review* 41:740–758.

CRIMINAL JUSTICE SYSTEM

The BILL OF RIGHTS [I] has sometimes been likened to a national code of CRIMINAL PROCEDURE [2]. However, the Constitution regulates many important aspects of criminal justice that are not "procedural" in any sense; at the same time, it fails to regulate many other important aspects, both procedural and nonprocedural. Moreover, features of the criminal justice system that are subject to extensive constitutional limitations are not, in practice, so strictly regulated as is commonly believed. It is therefore appropriate to reflect on which important aspects of criminal justice are and are not governed by the Constitution, what factors explain these patterns, and what the future role of the Constitution should be in defining fundamental norms of criminal justice.

To evaluate the role of constitutional norms in criminal matters, it is necessary to analyze the entire criminal justice system. Each political entity in the United States (local, state, or federal) has such a system; it consists not only of the rules of EVIDENCE [2] and procedure applicable in criminal matters, but also the major institutions of criminal justice (for example, the police, lawyers, judges, court and correctional officials), as well as the provisions of the criminal law (crimes, defenses, and penalties). This system can be envisioned as a process that begins with the definition of the criminal law and the institutions of justice; proceeds "chronologically" through increasingly selective stages of investigation, charging, adjudication, appellate review, and punishment; and ends with the continuing careers of convicted offenders, who all too often, begin the process all over again. Each of these stages of the process raises fundamental issues of justice and of individual-state relations that might be, but often are not, regulated by constitutional norms. At the same time, the enforcement of any such norm is limited by that norm's systemic context; specific rules are dependent on other rules, many of which are not subject to federal constitutional regulation. Thus, changes in specific constitutional norms are often canceled by compensating changes in other rules or practices in the same or different parts of the system.

The following is a list of the major issues at each stage of the above chronological flow model that are and are not subject to significant constitutional regulation:

1. The definition of crimes and penalties is largely unregulated by the Constitution, except for certain limitations imposed by the EX POST FACTO [2], BILL OF ATTAINDER [1], and EQUAL PROTECTION [2] clauses, the FIRST AMENDMENT [2] and Eighth Amendment, the RIGHT OF PRIVACY [3,I], and the VAGUENESS [4] and fair notice doctrines. Almost all issues relating to the definition of

defenses (e.g., self defense, intoxication, and insanity) are unregulated.

2. Except for the appointment and tenure of federal judges, the requirements of judicial neutrality in the issuance of warrants and at trial, and certain First Amendment limitations on the hiring and firing of public employees, the institutions of criminal justice are not regulated at all by the federal Constitution; many are also not closely governed by STATE CONSTITUTIONS [I]. Important unregulated issues include selection and internal supervision of police, prosecutors, and correctional officials; selection and tenure of state judges; and training of police, prosecutors, judges, and defense attorneys.

3. The investigation of criminal charges is covered by highly detailed constitutional limitations as to SEARCH AND SEIZURE [4,I], POLICE INTERROGATION AND CONFESSIONS [3,I], the RIGHT TO COUNSEL [3], and BAIL [1,I]. Important unregulated issues include police decisions to investigate or not investigate, to use informants and undercover police officers, and to charge some offenders and offenses, but not others; magistrate shopping; nighttime arrests and searches; searches when no one but police are present; use of arrest and pretrial detention in minor cases; prompt appearance in court; appellate review of pretrial detention; and nonbail release conditions.

4. Prosecutorial decisions to select offenders and charges, to later drop charges, and to engage in PLEA BARGAINING [3] as to charges and the sentence, or both, have an enormous impact on case outcomes. However, except for very limited equal-protection and "vindictive prosecution" standards, these critical decisions are not regulated by the Constitution.

5. Other pretrial procedures covered by the Constitution include the GRAND JURY [3,I] (in federal cases only), certain aspects of DISCOVERY [2], motions to exclude evidence, and SPEEDY TRIAL [4,I]. However, the powers of the prosecution and the defense to obtain statements from potential witnesses (other than the defendant) before a trial are not regulated by the Constitution.

6. Extensive FAIR TRIAL [2] rights are provided by the Constitution; examples are TRIAL BY JURY [3], right to counsel, CONFRONTATION [1] with state witnesses, BURDEN OF PROOF [1], RIGHT AGAINST SELF-INCRIMINATION [3,I], and DOUBLE JEOPARDY [2,I]. Important unregulated issues include the admissibility of the defendant's prior convictions or other misconduct, separation of guilt and sentencing evidence and findings, the necessity of written findings of guilt, multiple trials for the same offense in different states or in both state and federal systems, and most issues involving joinder of offenses and offenders in a single trial.

7. Many of the fair trial standards also apply to SENTENCING [I] proceedings, but they apply more flexibly.

The Constitution does not require formal findings or reasons for a particular sentence, nor does it limit guilty plea concessions. Except for the imposition of CAPITAL PUNISHMENT [1,I], sentencing decisions need not be structured by guidelines. The Eighth Amendment sets some limits on disproportionately severe prison terms and fines, and sentences are also limited by certain First Amendment, equal protection, and right of privacy rules, but most sentences are not constitutionally regulated either as to their form or severity.

8. The FREEDOM OF THE PRESS [2] and fair trial principles govern media publicity and access to trials and certain pretrial proceedings.

9. Although HABEAS CORPUS [2,I] rights are guaranteed, it is not clear whether the Constitution guarantees defendants any right to direct appeal in state cases. If an appellate system is provided, it must meet minimal equal protection and DUE PROCESS [2] requirements, but the number of appellate levels, composition of courts, and nature of appealable issues are not regulated.

10. Victims have no rights under the Constitution—to be heard or to appeal, to be protected, or to receive compensation.

11. Compensation of citizens for unconstitutional search, arrest, pretrial detention, or imprisonment is available under federal CIVIL RIGHTS [1] statutes, but is subject to important limitations (for example, judicial immunity and police officer's defense of reasonable belief that arrest or search was lawful).

12. The Constitution guarantees very few PRISONERS' RIGHTS [3,I]. Most fair trial rights do not apply to decisions such as prison discipline, transfers, parole, and revocation of probation.

To understand why the Constitution regulates criminal matters so selectively, it is necessary to consider not only the implications of FEDERALISM [2,I], but also the textual sources and historical development of federal constitutional norms. The constitutional texts applicable to criminal cases are mostly found in the Bill of Rights (1791) and the FOURTEENTH AMENDMENT [2,I] (1868). Of these, only the latter applies directly to the states, and it did not provide much concrete guidance until the 1960s, when the WARREN COURT [4], with use of the INCORPORATION DOCTRINE [2], began to hold that certain Bill of Rights guarantees were implicit in the Fourteenth Amendment's due process clause. Because there were very few federal criminal cases until the twentieth century, there was little early case law interpreting Bill of Rights guarantees. Indeed, before the adoption of the EXCLUSIONARY RULE [2] in federal cases in 1914, there was virtually no case law, because there was no criminal court remedy encouraging defendants to litigate constitutional claims.

The Supreme Court's application of the exclusionary

rule to state criminal cases in 1961, along with its expansion of the availability of habeas corpus and right to counsel in 1963, set the stage for a veritable explosion of constitutional case law during the final years of the Warren Court. Nevertheless, this expansion was constrained by the texts of the Bill of Rights. These texts were written in response to specific perceived abuses of the late eighteenth century. Moreover, they were written at a time when crime tended to be local and relatively disorganized, and before the development of organized police forces and the emergence of the public prosecutor's monopoly over the bringing of cases to trial. Considering these dramatic changes in the nature of crime and criminal justice, the Bill of Rights remains remarkably relevant today, but it fails to address many fundamental issues of modern criminal justice. In the absence of specific provisions, the courts have had to create new rights either by broad analogy to specific rights, or by applying the more open-ended provisions of the due-process clauses of the Fifth and Fourteenth Amendments. However, both approaches weaken the legitimacy of such newly recognized rights and make them vulnerable to attack.

This inherent vulnerability of the Warren Court's jurisprudence, combined with the appointment of more conservative Justices by Presidents RICHARD M. NIXON [3] and RONALD REAGAN [3, I], substantially slowed the expansion of criminal-process safeguards during the 1970s; indeed, the Supreme Court began to cut back on the scope of substantive rights and the availability of exclusionary and habeas corpus remedies. Notions of federalism also provided justification for this conservative shift; many believed that the Warren Court had gone too far in imposing strict federal standards on state criminal justice systems faced with rapidly rising crime rates and inadequate resources. Also, the relatively late development of these standards in federal cases and their very recent application to state cases lent some support to the view that they were not truly fundamental, at least in state cases.

But the Supreme Court did not simply relax the standards in state cases. Because the majority of Justices still accepted the premise of the selective incorporation doctrine—that a uniform definition of each right should apply in state and federal criminal cases—the conservative decisions of the 1970s and 1980s resulted in the lowering of constitutional standards in federal cases as well. Congress responded with a few statutory safeguards, and the Supreme Court's own FEDERAL RULES OF CRIMINAL PROCEDURE [2] continued to provide certain standards more restrictive than the Constitution requires. At the same time, many state courts responded by relying more and more on STATE CONSTITUTIONAL LAW [4] to provide greater protections. In addition, state statutes, rules of procedure, and evidence codes continued to provide important safeguards in areas where constitutional law had retreated or had never been applied.

The degree of the Supreme Court's conservative shift since 1970 should not be overstated. Indeed, a closer analysis of the jurisprudence of the Warren Court reveals that it too had doubts about the wisdom of expanding and strictly enforcing constitutional standards in state and federal criminal cases. Six themes that cut across the spectrum of specific rights illustrate this ambivalence. Although these themes became much clearer in the 1970s and 1980s, they were already evident in the Warren Court era.

First, even the Warren Court recognized that some procedural rights are less important than others. The most important rights were those directly related to the integrity of the adversary system, particularly the right to counsel. Such rights, when violated, were more likely to receive retroactive application and to lead to automatic reversal of a conviction. At the other end of the spectrum, receiving the least protection, were FOURTH AMENDMENT [2, I] rights. In theory, such rights involve fundamental issues of individual freedom from governmental oppression. In practice, however, they tend only to be asserted by defendants who, in light of illegally seized physical evidence, appear to be clearly guilty of criminal conduct. Thus, the Warren Court recognized several important limitations on these rights and related exclusionary remedies; for example, these rights received little if any retroactive application. Post–Warren Court decisions reflect this "hierarchy of rights" theme even more strongly.

Second, even the adversary-system rights given highest priority by the Warren Court were not applied with equal strictness at all stages of the criminal process. Except for police interrogations covered by MIRANDA V. ARIZONA (1966) [3], the right to counsel was not applied before the filing of formal charges. Similarly, the Court did not show much interest in extending fair trial standards to critical decisions made by correctional authorities, such as disciplinary isolation and revocation of parole. Indeed, the Supreme Court (along with most lower courts) adopted a "hands off" approach toward the entire correctional process. Decisions after 1970 did recognize some rights for prisoners and extended counsel rights to some preindictment proceedings. It remains true, however, that constitutional fair trial guarantees apply primarily *at* trial; the criminal justice system is not, on the whole, really an "adversary" system.

Third, even some trial rights were not deemed applicable to all criminal cases: the Warren Court held that there is no right to a jury trial for "petty offenses" (maximum sentence not exceeding six months' imprisonment). The petty-offense limitation was later applied in different form to the right to counsel at trial. The rationale for this limitation, also widely followed in nonconstitutional procedural rules, is that more severe penalties require more exacting procedures of adjudication. During the pretrial investigative stage, however, the opposite rule applies: more serious offenses give the citizen fewer rights and the police greater power, for example, to make warrantless entries to arrest.

Fourth, the Warren Court's failure to condemn certain problematic features of American criminal justice implied that fundamental concepts, such as due process and equal protection, may mean different things in criminal cases than they do in other contexts. This view was later explicitly adopted by the Court in *Gerstein v. Pugh* (1975), holding that the Fourth Amendment defines (sometimes less strictly) "the 'process that due' for seizures of person or property in criminal cases." The Warren Court never questioned the traditional use of money bail to condition pretrial release, even though such use often constitutes blatant WEALTH DISCRIMINATION [4]. The Court held that the right to vote could not be lost by inability to pay a POLL TAX [3], yet it allowed the right of physical liberty before conviction to be lost by inability to post bail. Similarly, the Warren Court never seriously questioned the dominant form of adjudication of criminal cases, that is, plea bargaining, which would seem to be either an UNCONSTITUTIONAL CONDITION [4] on the exercise of rights or a case of coerced waiver of rights. It scarcely seems imaginable that the Warren Court would have tolerated in any other context an institutionalized practice whose main purpose is to discourage the exercise of constitutional rights.

Fifth, the Warren Court recognized that police and courts have a practical need for easily administered "bright-line" rules that disregard the specific circumstances of each case. Although most of the Warren Court's bright lines tended to be overly broad with respect to individual rights, some tilted more in the other direction, for example, the automatic right to conduct a limited SEARCH INCIDENT TO ARREST [4]. Later Supreme Court decisions have struck the opposite balance: most, but not all, bright-line rules favor the police.

Finally, the Warren Court undercut many of its liberal, prodefendant rights by recognizing significant limitations on the scope of exclusionary remedies. Thus, defendants lack STANDING [4] to object to even the most outrageous violations of another person's rights; they cannot object to the use of illegally seized evidence to contradict their own testimony on the witness stand; remote products ("fruits") of illegality remain admissible in the prosecution's case, and there is no criminal court remedy for an illegal arrest that does not produce any such evidentiary fruits; and the admission of clearly excludable evidence generally does not require reversal if the reviewing court

concludes, in light of the untainted evidence, that admission was HARMLESS ERROR [2]. These exceptions were greatly expanded (and became more numerous) in later Supreme Court decisions; meanwhile, field studies of the exclusionary rule confirmed what perhaps was true even under the Warren Court: exclusion of evidence is rare, occurring in less than one percent of cases, many of which still result in conviction.

Why are fundamental constitutional rights so weakly enforced, even by liberal judges? In addition to the important reasons of history and federalism, noted earlier, there are a number of factors peculiar to the criminal process. First, enforcement of rights usually costs money, and the criminal justice system is inherently underfunded: crime often increases much faster than prisons can be built; legislatures enact moralistic and "get tough" laws, but not the tax increases necessary to pay for their enforcement; and criminal laws are rarely repealed or reduced in severity because there are no votes for the elected official who is, or even appears to be, "soft" on crime or immorality. Second, in part as a result of the first problem, almost all cases are resolved by a guilty plea rather than by trial; defendants who plead guilty waive not only their trial rights, but frequently also their rights to contest the introduction of illegally obtained evidence.

Third, the remedies for constitutional violations create problems of their own. The exclusionary rule often requires courts to throw out reliable evidence; retrial after appellate reversal of conviction may be impossible because of lost evidence, witnesses, and testimony. Fourth, the actors purportedly regulated by constitutional norms retain substantial unregulated discretion—not only because of the need to limit caseloads to stay within resource limits, but also because the correctness of the actors' decisions often turns on case-specific factual determinations, such as voluntariness of consent or waiver, which does not permit close regulation by legal norms. In any case, such norms govern relatively few issues; officials deal with cases and defendants under many rules and at many stages of system processing, and each stage provides opportunities to undercut or evade the occasionally strict rule.

Finally, it must be admitted that Americans are deeply ambivalent about some of their most fundamental ideals of justice. Such ideals often make it more difficult to arrest and convict criminals; particularly in times of rapidly increasing crime rates, most citizens prefer to protect themselves and their property rather than criminals. Even where constitutional norms are designed to protect the innocent, they are necessarily most likely to be asserted by a guilty defendant. As noted earlier, this is almost always true in the Fourth Amendment area, but it is generally true throughout the system. The presumption of innocence itself is somewhat counterintuitive: most arrested persons and certainly most defendants brought to trial are guilty, or ought to be; if they were not, our criminal justice system would be grossly defective. Similarly, the right against compelled self-incrimination is contrary to the general duty to testify and the view that wrongdoers have a duty to admit their mistakes; the right to a vigorous defense is contrary to the view that wrongdoers should not be assisted in their efforts to conceal the truth and avoid punishment; and limits on deceptive police practices are contrary to the view that sometimes it is necessary to fight fire with fire. In light of these value conflicts, citizens—and sometimes even lawyers and judges—may lose sight of the importance of our most fundamental criminal-procedure safeguards.

What, then, can we conclude about the proper role of the Constitution in criminal matters? Despite the problems described, Americans certainly must not stop trying to improve the quality of criminal justice. Moreover, constitutional norms play a central role in these efforts—defining, as the Supreme Court said of the CRUEL AND UNUSUAL PUNISHMENT [2,1] clause, "the evolving standards of decency which mark the progress of a maturing society." At the same time, constitutional norm setting has its limits. Only the most fundamental and lasting norms can be expressed in the constitutional text. Moreover, the case law articulating such norms must not get too far ahead of our ability and willingness to enforce these rules; otherwise, idealism and hope turn to hypocrisy and cynicism.

The Constitution is only one source of norms in criminal cases; other major sources are state constitutions, statutes, codes of criminal procedure and evidence, model law and procedural codes, administrative regulations, and the COMMON LAW [1]. Increasingly, Americans have begun to look to statements of international human rights; although the INFLUENCE OF THE AMERICAN CONSTITUTION ABROAD [2] once made the United States a leader in this field, international norms have now progressed to the point where they sometimes set standards more strict than, or in areas not covered by, the American Constitution.

RICHARD S. FRASE

Bibliography

AMERICAN BAR ASSOCIATION   1980   ABA Standards for Criminal Justice, 4 vols., 2nd ed. Boston: Little, Brown.
AMERICAN LAW INSTITUTE   1975   A Model Code of Prearraignment Procedure. Philadelphia: American Law Institute.
FRASE, RICHARD S.   1986   Criminal Procedure in a Conservative Age: A Time to Rediscover the Critical Nonconstitutional Issues. Journal of Legal Education 36:79–82.
FRIENDLY, HENRY J.   1965   The Bill of Rights as a Code of Criminal Procedure. California Law Review 53:929–956.
KAMISAR, YALE; LAFAVE, WAYNE; and ISRAEL, JEROLD H.   1990   Modern Criminal Procedure: Cases, Comments, Questions, 7th ed. St. Paul, Minn.: West Publishing Co.
LAFAVE, WAYNE R. and SCOTT, AUSTIN W., JR.   1986   Criminal Law, 2nd ed. St. Paul, Minn.: West Publishing Co.
ZIMRING, FRANKLIN E. and FRASE, RICHARD S.   1980   The Criminal Justice System: Materials on the Administration and Reform of the Criminal Law. Boston: Little, Brown.

CRIMINAL JUSTICE AND TECHNOLOGY

In 1928 Justice LOUIS D. BRANDEIS [1] warned that "discovery and invention have made it possible for the government, by means far more effective than the rack, to obtain disclosure in court of what is whispered in the closet." And, he went on to ask, "can it be that the Constitution affords no protection against such invasion of individual security?" In OLMSTEAD V. UNITED STATES (1928) [3] the Supreme Court responded yes to Brandeis's question: the Constitution "affords no protection."

Today the Court continues to give virtually the same answer. Thus, in *United States v. Knotts* (1983), Justice WILLIAM H. REHNQUIST [3,I] wrote that "nothing in the FOURTH AMENDMENT [2,I] prohibit[s] the police from augmenting the sensory facilities bestowed upon them at birth with such enhancement as science and technology afforded them in this case." That case involved a mobile tracking device, but the same attitude is reflected in many other cases and contexts. The Court has virtually abdicated any role in shaping a response to the threats to liberty and individual rights posed by the new technology, leaving the problem to the occasional efforts of the Congress and to the state legislatures and courts.

The *Olmstead* WIRETAPPING [4] controversy set the pattern. There the Court construed the Fourth Amendment to deny any constitutional protection against devices that do not involve a physical trespass and the seizure of tangible documents. Nine years later, in NARDONE V. UNITED STATES (1937) [3], the Court construed a federal statute codifying federal radio and telecommunications law to prohibit wiretapping, much to everyone's surprise. The limitations of this approach were reflected in the virtual failure of the statute to reduce wiretapping significantly and in the Court's understandable refusal in *Goldman v. United States* (1942) to apply the statute to the next significant technological development, a detectaphone placed against a wall that could overhear conversations in another room without physically trespassing.

Now, a half century later, Brandeis's warning is more timely than ever, for we have developed technologies that make these early devices seem primitive. These new technologies include tiny, almost invisible video and audio surveillance devices that can function at short or long distances and by night as well as day, such as a "mini-awac," which can spot a car or a person from 30,000 feet in the air; electronic bracelets and anklets that signal a probation or parole officer if his or her charge goes more than a short distance from home; and chemical dust that can be used with ultraviolet detectors for tracking. Computer matching of records in different places can also provide vast amounts of information about a person. Many other techniques involving new biological and medical technology are also being developed.

The Court's resistance to imposing constitutional controls on the use of technological advances in the CRIMINAL JUSTICE SYSTEM [I] stems in part from the law enforcement and constitutional contexts in which these issues arise. Almost always the question before the Court has been whether a convicted criminal is to go free because the enforcement authorities have used some technological device without meeting constitutional requirements. Only for a brief period in its history (1961–1967) has the Court not been reluctant to tolerate such an outcome.

The constitutional provision at issue in these cases is usually the Fourth Amendment, which imposes restrictions only on SEARCH AND SEIZURE [4,I]. The Court's analytic approach has been to dichotomize surveillances into "searches" and "nonsearches," with the latter denied any Fourth Amendment protection at all; other constitutional provisions, such as the Fifth Amendment's ban on compelled self-incrimination, have been construed as inapplicable to the use of most technological devices. SCHMERBER V. CALIFORNIA (1966) [4] illustrates that point.

This dichotomous approach, together with the Court's general reluctance to recognize the special impact of modern technology on individual liberty, was illustrated just a few years after it overruled *Olmstead* in KATZ V. UNITED STATES (1967) [3]. A sharply divided Court in UNITED STATES V. WHITE (1971) [4] refused to recognize a constitutionally protected right not to have one's conversation with another person secretly transmitted electronically by the latter to police listening some distance away. "Inescapably, one contemplating illegal activity must realize and risk that his companions may be reporting to the police," wrote Justice BYRON R. WHITE [4,I], and to him there was no significant difference "between probable informers on the one hand and probable informers with transmitters on the other." But as the dissenting Justice JOHN MARSHALL HARLAN [2] wrote, "third-party bugging

. . . undermine[s] that confidence and sense of security that is characteristic of . . . a free society. It goes beyond the . . . ordinary type of 'informer situation.'" The "assumption of risk" analysis used by the Court is circular, insisted Justice Harlan, for "the risks we assume are in large part reflections of laws that translate into rules [our] customs and values. . . . The critical question, therefore, is whether . . . we *should* impose on our citizens [such] risks . . . without at least the protection of a warrant." Moreover, the Fourth Amendment is designed to protect all of us, not just people "contemplating illegal activities," and the Court's approach precluded constitutional protections when a confidential conversation turns out to be wholly innocent.

The *White* unconcern for differences in degree that become differences in kind has been reflected in virtually every constitutional case involving modern technology that the Court has faced. For example, seeking anonymity in a crowd and moving to out-of-the-way places are ways to preserve some privacy in a surveillance-pervaded crowded society. In *United States v. Knotts* the Court ruled that an electronic device, a "beeper," surreptitiously attached to a container that emitted electronic signals, enabling the police to trace the container wherever it went, did not call for constitutional protection; the Court reasoned that "visual surveillance from public places along [the] route" of the person with the container would have provided the same information. Only if the beeper enters a house with the container and continues to operate is there a privacy encroachment requiring a SEARCH WARRANT [4]. The same reasoning can obviously apply to beepers secretly attached to people.

The Court has been equally indifferent to the threats to privacy and liberty posed by modern expansions of visual surveillance. Walls and distance—which we ordinarily use to protect privacy—are not very effective safeguards in today's world. Video surveillance can now be conducted from great distances and often with the capability of listening as well. So far, the Court has tended to ignore distance as a factor. In a series of three decisions in the late 1980s the Court consistently upheld surveillance from above enclosed areas, even when the surveillance was made possible only by the use of highly sophisticated equipment. In *Dow Chemical Co. v. United States* (1986), Dow had a 2,000-acre chemical factory, around which it maintained elaborate security that barred ground-level views; it also investigated any low-level flights. Any further protection against intrusion, such as a roof over the entire facility, would have been prohibitively expensive. An Environmental Protection Agency airplane took approximately seventy-five pictures of the plant from altitudes as high as 12,000 feet. The camera's precision was so great that the pictures could be enlarged over 240 times without significant loss of detail or resolution; it was possible to see pipes and wires as small as one-half inch in diameter. Finding the plant similar to an OPEN FIELD [I], a 5–4 majority of the Court denied constitutional protection against the surveillance.

In *Dow*, the Court suggested that more protection might be available to a private residence than to a large industrial complex. But in *California v. Ciraolo* (1986) the same 5–4 majority decided the same way when police flew a private plane 1,000 feet above Ciraolo's yard, which he tried to protect with a six-foot outer fence and a ten-foot inner fence; the police saw a marijuana plant in the yard on a small plot, which they photographed. Despite Ciraolo's precautions, Chief Justice WARREN E. BURGER [1] concluded that even though Ciraolo had a REASONABLE EXPECTATION OF PRIVACY [I] in his backyard, it was "unreasonable for [him] to expect that his marijuana plants were constitutionally protected from being observed with the naked eye from an altitude of 1,000 feet," because the observation occurred in public "navigable air space" and the members of the public could look down as they flew overhead. As Justice LEWIS F. POWELL [3,I] observed in dissent, however, the likelihood of such an observation by a private person on a public or private plane is "virtually nonexistent."

The Court confirmed its indifference to the privacy of areas under surveillance a few years later in *Florida v. Riley* (1989), when it concluded that observations from a helicopter hovering 400 feet above a partially covered greenhouse in the defendant's backyard did not implicate the Fourth Amendment. The Court stressed that the helicopter was not violating the law, "did not interfere with respondent's normal use of the greenhouse," observed no "intimate details," and caused "no undue noise, no wind, dust or threat of injury." The Court did not explain why any of these should be determinative in deciding whether the greenhouse was entitled to be free from unrestricted surveillance.

An especially serious threat to individual liberty arises from the computer revolution. Seeking medical care, participating in public welfare programs, engaging in regulated activities, or even acting as consumers requires us to provide third parties vast amounts of personal information that previously we could have kept confidential. Data that were once either nonexistent or kept in a shoebox or file cabinet are now on someone else's computer disks. Moreover, those records that did exist were stored in public or private files usually scattered in a great many places, making it difficult to develop a full dossier on anyone. That difficulty is now a thing of the past. Computer matching pulls together masses of information in different files, information that can dog one throughout one's exis-

tence. As sociologist Gary Marx points out, "this can create a class of permanently stigmatized persons," making it impossible for people to overcome past mistakes and failures and to start a new life. Rehabilitation may be rendered impossible.

The Supreme Court has not dealt directly with computer matching, but has effectively denied constitutional protection to the privacy of a key element in that process: the records themselves. In *United States v. Miller* (1976) the Court refused to require police to meet Fourth Amendment requirements when they subpoenaed a bank's microfilm records of a suspect's checks, bank statements, deposit slips, and other bank transaction records. The Court found no "legitimate expectation of privacy in these records and documents because all contain only information voluntarily conveyed to the banks and exposed to their employees in the ordinary course of business. . . . The depositor takes the risk, in revealing his affairs to another, that the information will be conveyed by that person to the government." The result is that the enormous mass of information that we must "voluntarily convey" in order to live in a modern world is now without constitutional protection. This includes not only bank and medical records but even the telephone numbers we call, which are not conveyed to any one at all but simply recorded for billing purposes by usually inanimate equipment. In *Smith v. Maryland* (1979) the Court refused to require constitutional prerequisites for installation of a pen register that recorded the numbers of outgoing telephone calls. Justice HARRY A. BLACKMUN [1,I] wrote that "the switching equipment that processed those numbers is merely the modern counterpart of the operator who, in an earlier day, personally completed calls for the subscriber." Wayne LaFave noted the "ominous proposition that modern technology cannot add to one's justified expectation of privacy, but can only detract from it."

Finally, the Court has extracted a principle from one of the oldest forms of "technology" that would render newer technology one of the greatest threats to privacy and other individual rights. In concluding in *United States v. Place* (1983) that use of a dog's sense of smell to detect drugs in a suitcase did not raise Fourth Amendment concerns, the Court said, "A 'canine sniff' by a well-trained narcotics detection dog . . . does not expose non-contraband items that otherwise would remain hidden from public view . . . [and is] limited both in the manner in which the information is obtained and in the content of the information revealed." This approach would seem to be counter to the proposition that an intrusion cannot be validated by what it turns up. Moreover, if accuracy and unobtrusiveness are criteria, then what lies in store if, as Justice Brandeis feared, we do indeed develop ways that can unobtrusively detect the presence of incriminating materials by foolproof methods?

And why should techniques be limited to searching out tangible items; what of incriminating expressions or even thought revealed by new medical or chemical technology? At this point the Court might balk, but so far its CONSTITUTIONAL THEORY [I] would impose few if any controls.

HERMAN SCHWARTZ

(SEE ALSO: *Electronic Eavesdropping* [2].)

Bibliography

FISHMAN, CLIFFORD S. 1985 Electronic Tracking Devices and the Fourth Amendment: *Knots, Karo* the Questions Still Unanswered. *Catholic University Law Review* 34:277–395.
LAFAVE, WAYNE 1987 *Search and Seizure*. St. Paul, Minn.: West Publishing Co.
MARX, GARY T. 1988 *Undercover Police Surveillance in America*. Berkeley: University of California Press.
OFFICE OF TECHNOLOGY ASSESSMENT 1985 *Federal Government Information Technology: Electronic Surveillance and Civil Liberties*. Washington, D.C.: U.S. Government Printing Office.

CRITICAL LEGAL STUDIES

"Critical legal studies" refers to a development in American jurisprudence in the late 1970s and 1980s. Its originators were self-consciously affiliated with leftist political movements. Their understanding of the law, including constitutional law, was influenced by the experience of the movements for CIVIL RIGHTS [1,I] and against the VIETNAM WAR [I], in which, as they saw it, appeals to legality—in the form of saying that RACIAL DISCRIMINATION [3,I] was unconstitutional and that the war was being conducted illegally—played an important but complex role. Their intellectual position was shaped in large measure by an understanding of American LEGAL REALISM [3] that took realism's implications to be more radical than many of its first proponents may have believed. The radical reading of legal realism was supported, in critical legal studies, by an understanding of what were perceived as the intellectual difficulties of the liberal tradition, which produced the tensions that the realists attempted unsuccessfully to resolve.

The most direct legacy of legal realism to critical legal studies was the idea of indeterminacy. Critical legal studies understood the realist message to be that law, again including constitutional law, was shot through with "contradictions," in the sense that, at least in any socially significant case, legal arguments that were professionally defensible were available for a rather wide range of outcomes and rules, some of which might differ radically from others.

According to critical legal studies, this indeterminacy resulted from the fact that the liberal tradition attempted to, but could not, suppress what Duncan Kennedy, an early proponent of critical legal studies, called "the fundamental contradiction" of social life—that people are both fearful of, and dependent upon, other people. In the critical legal studies analysis, the central themes of the liberal tradition, expressing suspicion of government efforts to promote "the good" in societies where there were fundamental differences over what constitutes the good, drew primarily on the fear of other people. Yet, according to critical legal studies, because social life necessarily places people in relations of dependence on each other, law cannot, and does not, simply express the fear of others. Rather, law attempts to express both aspects of the fundamental contradiction, which is what generates the possibility of acceptable legal arguments leading to radically different results.

To deal with the point that the indeterminacy thesis is in tension with the fact that lawyers can predict with some assurance how judges will resolve many contentious legal issues, even if the issues could in some sense be regarded as open to decision either way, critical legal studies relies on claims about law as ideology. In one version, influenced by Marxist social thought, indeterminacy is resolved in fact by the political predispositions of the judges, and predictability occurs because the judges, and lawyers too, are drawn from a relatively narrow range of social classes, whose interests they promote. The conspiratorial overtones of this account are reduced in another version of the argument that law is a form of ideology. This version, influenced by the work of Michel Foucault, argues that indeterminacy is resolved because on a higher level of abstraction some general ideology about reason and the state is embedded in modern culture, so that many of the more radical possibilities are ruled out of contention from the start.

Critical legal studies is a form of general jurisprudence, and the indeterminacy thesis was developed primarily in connection with private law. The critical legal studies analysis of constitutional law has two important strands. The first, drawing on the private law studies, is a critique of the distinction between public and private that pervades law and appears in constitutional law in the form of the STATE ACTION [4,I] doctrine. According to that doctrine, the Constitution regulates only actions by government, leaving private parties free to shape their relations and to control their property without regard to constitutional norms. One key element in the legal realist analysis of private law, however, was that the private law of property and contract could fairly be characterized as a form of delegating public authority to private individuals, subject always to public control through, for example, doctrines restricting the enforcement of contracts on the ground that they violate public policy. Given that analysis of private law, the state action doctrine appears incoherent, and for critical legal studies SHELLEY V. KRAEMER (1948) [4], holding unconstitutional judicial enforcement of racially restrictive property covenants, is not an anomaly, as it is in many mainstream accounts of constitutional law, but is instead a necessary implication of the analysis of the public/private distinction.

The second important strand in the critical legal studies analysis of constitutional law has been the "critique of rights." The critique of rights applies the indeterminacy thesis to the individual rights provisions of the Constitution. Vacillation by the Supreme Court over the importance of intent versus effect in antidiscrimination law, for example, is taken to reflect not just the political shift from the WARREN COURT [4] to the BURGER COURT [1] and now the REHNQUIST COURT [I] but also the indeterminacy of the idea of nondiscrimination itself. The critique of rights accepts the proposition that there is general agreement on the importance of certain FUNDAMENTAL RIGHTS [2], so long as the claims are either that there are such rights (without specifying what they are) or that the rights are acknowledged and enforced in abstract terms. But, the critique of rights contends that, as is always the case when socially significant claims are made, when it comes to enforcing these abstract rights in particular contexts, neither the Constitution nor the Court's precedents even weakly determine what the Court does. Rather, what matters are the current political predispositions of the members of the Supreme Court, a fact that is reflected in the general understanding that we can talk about "conservatives" and "liberals" on the Court.

The critique of rights is augmented and given a political twist by an analysis of the Supreme Court as one of the branches of a unitary government. In this analysis, influenced by mainstream political science, the Court is treated as a political body whose central role, symbolized by the political processes by which Justices are appointed, is to act on behalf of those interests who control the political system over the medium to long run. With this political understanding as a background, the critique of rights argues that, as a general matter with some exceptions, the Supreme Court will interpret—and historically has interpreted—the individual rights provisions of the Constitution primarily to protect the interests of established groups, particularly the owners of large aggregations of property. LOCHNER V. NEW YORK (1905) [3], for an earlier period, and the Court's recent CAMPAIGN FINANCE [1,I] decisions, for the modern period, exemplify the Court's commitment to an interpretation of the Constitution in the service of established power groups.

Apart from general challenges to the indeterminacy

thesis across the board, the main criticism of the critique of rights has been offered by minority scholars and liberal defenders of the legacy of the Warren Court. For them, the Warren Court's decisions show that, at least on occasion, the Supreme Court's articulation of individual rights can both advance the interests of minority groups and express a vision of a way of organizing society in which existing holders of power might be displaced.

Most proponents of the critique of rights accept both of these points. As to the first, though, they make several points. First, if we examine the entire history of the Supreme Court, the Warren era appears almost as an aberration. Second, many of the Warren Court's decisions might be understood in political terms as advancing the political agenda of the NEW DEAL [I] political coalition, which may have retained control of the courts after it shattered in the political branches. BROWN V. BOARD OF EDUCATION (1954, 1955) [1], a key example used against the critique of rights, would be seen as the Court's enforcement of a national view against SEGREGATION [4]—which was, among other things, embarrassing the United States during the period of Cold War ideological competition with the Soviet Union—against the wishes of a recalcitrant region. If the Warren Court was the judicial expression of the New Deal coalition, it is not surprising, according to the critique of rights, that when the New Deal coalition lost power in the political branches, the Supreme Court eventually abandoned the Warren Court's ideology.

The critique of rights also argues, in response to both of the minority challenges, that the appeal to rights may indeed be a way of expressing opposition to the existing social order, but that those appeals may also be politically damaging. The appeal to rights can be politically damaging because it may divert resources into litigation and a focus on the courts. According to this view, successful legal appeals to rights may sometimes be more harmful than unsuccessful ones. Having secured one victory in the courts, a minority movement may rest on its laurels, relying on the courts to continue to protect its interests and overlooking the fact that permanent victories occur, given the role of the courts in the political system, only if the winners in the courts eventually secure the backing of the political branches. In addition, once a movement achieves a major victory in the courts, such as ROE V. WADE (1973) [3] was for the women's movement, it may make the reasonable short-term judgment that it should devote resources to further judicial action—for example, relying on the courts to strike down laws aimed at undermining or whittling away at *Roe*. This would allow its opponents to adopt the strategy (which may be more successful in the long run) of influencing state and local legislatures, Congress, and the President.

In this view, however, the appeal to rights can also

be an expression of opposition to the established order, precisely because the indeterminacy of law rests on the fundamental contradiction of social life. That contradiction means that any system of law contains competing views of the good social order. Thus, adherents of utopian visions of an alternative social order can argue that their preferred social order would realize values already acknowledged in the law but imperfectly implemented in the present order. In addition, the general public respect for fundamental human rights—at least when they are stated in the abstract—gives the advocate of some novel right or of the extension of an acknowledged right an initial rhetorical advantage in public discussions of those claims.

According to the critique of rights, then, the utility of appeals to rights will depend on a careful analysis of the particular circumstances and settings in which the appeals are made. If a social movement can rely on the language of rights without diverting its resources into litigation, for example, many of the disadvantages of the appeals to rights disappear. Yet, although the idea of making appeals to rights without relying on the courts is sensible, in the political culture of the United States, people who invoke rights but do not seek to have the courts implement them are likely to be seen as using a form of language that their behavior belies. Similarly, political circumstances sometimes are favorable for the use of the utopian appeals to rights in litigation as a method of securing legal victories or as a method of mobilizing a constituency. Such favorable circumstances appear to have been present for the civil rights movement during the Warren era. Proponents of the critique of rights would caution, however, that careful analysis of the particulars is necessary in order to make a judgment about whether the advantages of an appeal to rights outweigh the disadvantages.

With the apparent dissolution of much of the Warren Court legacy on the Supreme Court in the late 1980s, the critical legal studies perspective on constitutional law may gain some added force, for the Warren era may become understood as the kind of aberration that critical legal studies has always contended it was. On the other hand, to the extent that critical legal studies is a self-consciously leftist political movement, leftists and liberals may find recourse to the language of rights even more essential in a conservative era.

MARK TUSHNET

(SEE ALSO: *Civil Rights Movement* [I]; *Conservatism* [I]; *Constitutional Interpretation* [1]; *Contract Clause* [2]; *Liberalism* [I]; *Property Rights* [I].)

Bibliography

KELMAN, MARK 1987 *A Guide to Critical Legal Studies.* Cambridge, Mass.: Harvard University Press.
TUSHNET, MARK 1988 *Red, White, and Blue: A Critical Analysis of Constitutional Law.* Cambridge, Mass.: Harvard University Press.
UNGER, ROBERTO 1986 *The Critical Legal Studies Movement* Cambridge, Mass.: Harvard University Press.

CRUEL AND UNUSUAL PUNISHMENT
(Update)

The Eighth Amendment's cruel and unusual punishment clause, derived from COMMON LAW [1] and held to restrain the states as well as the federal government, applies to noncapital as well as capital criminal punishments. The concept of cruel and unusual punishments, while undoubtedly meant to address extremely harsh or painful methods and kinds of PUNISHMENT [I], also incorporates ideas of excessiveness, proportionality, and appropriateness. It is therefore relative, and whether a particular punishment is cruel and unusual depends on prevailing societal standards, objectively determined, regarding punishments. The Supreme Court has held that the clause outlaws not only punishments that are barbarous, involving torture or the intentional and unjustifiable infliction of unnecessary pain, but also forbids confinements whose length or conditions are disproportionate to the severity of crimes, serious deprivations of prisoners' basic human needs, loss of CITIZENSHIP [1,I] as a punishment, and punishments for status.

In WEEMS V. UNITED STATES (1910) [4] the Court held the Philippine punishment of *cadena temporal* unconstitutional as applied. The imposed punishment for the crime of making a false entry in a public record—not shown to have injured anyone—was fifteen years' imprisonment at hard and painful labor with chains, loss of CIVIL LIBERTIES [1,I], and governmental surveillance for life. The Court, in *Estelle v. Gamble* (1976), also held that deliberate indifference to a prisoner's serious medical needs constitutes cruel and unusual punishment. In *Hutto v. Finney* (1978) it upheld a lower court's conclusion that routine conditions in the Arkansas prison system were so inhumane as to be cruel and unusual. Earlier, the Court had determined in TROP V. DULLES (1968) [4] that imposing loss of citizenship on a native-born citizen for desertion in wartime was cruel and unusual because it destroyed the person's political existence and made him stateless. In implicit recognition that states may define as crimes only acts, conduct, or behavior, the Court, in *Robinson v. California* (1962), held criminal imprisonment for the status of being a drug addict, unaccompanied by any acts, cruel and unusual.

The question to what degree the Eighth Amendment's cruel and unusual punishment clause may limit the power of a state to define the length of a prison sentence has been troublesome. The issue arises most often in challenges to recidivist statutes mandating life sentences on persons having three or more consecutive felony convictions or to sentencing statutes requiring extremely long sentences for those convicted of small drug offenses. Originally, in a number of cases raising disproportionate-length challenges to such statutes, the Court took the view that legislatures had extremely wide latitude in setting felony sentence lengths and that it would rarely, if ever, find such statutes unconstitutional. Thus, in RUMMEL V. ESTELLE (1980) [3] the Court upheld a life sentence imposed on a person who was separately convicted and imprisoned for three nonviolent felonies, involving illegally acquiring money in the amounts of $80, $28.36, and $120.75. The only mitigation in the sentence was a possibility of parole after twelve years. In *Hutto v. Davis* (1982) the defendant received a sentence of forty years in prison and a fine of $20,000 for possession and distribution of nine ounces of marijuana, and the Court upheld this statute as well, although the average sentence for similar offenders was approximately three years.

Although these two cases suggested that the Court, in practice, did not accept any constitutional standard of length proportionality in felony cases, in a subsequent case a different Court majority strongly endorsed and articulated just such a standard. In SOLEM V. HELM (1983) [4] the Court struck down, as uconstitutionally disproportionate in length, a sentence of life imprisonment without possibility of parole for a defendant convicted for a seventh felony, which involved uttering a "no-account" check for $100. The Court held that although no sentence is per se unconstitutional, the cruel and unusual punishment clause requires that criminal sentences must be proportionate to the crime for which the defendant has been convicted. The judgment whether a sentence is proportionate turns on an analysis guided by consideration of the gravity of the offense and harshness of the penalty; sentences imposed on other criminals in the same JURISDICTION [3]; and sentences imposed on commission of the same crime in other jurisdictions. *Solem*, however, overturned no prior case law, and the current Court is strongly disposed to accept legislative judgments. The only reasonable conclusion to draw is that the principle of length proportionality is weak and, except in rare cases, unlikely to stand as a check on disparate and extremely long sentences.

GARY GOODPASTER

(SEE ALSO: *Prisoners' Rights* [3,I].)

Bibliography

GRANUCCI, ANTHONY F.   1969   "Nor Cruel and Unusual Punishments Inflicted": The Original Meaning. *California Law Review* 57:839–865.

CRUZAN v. DIRECTOR, MISSOURI DEPARTMENT OF HEALTH (1990)

See: Right to Die [I]

CURTILAGE

See: Open Fields Doctrine [I]

DAMAGES CLAIMS
(Update to Damages)

At least since MARBURY V. MADISON [3] was decided in 1803, it has been understood that the United States Constitution is law, enforceable by courts and superior in status to LEGISLATION [3]. In some surprising particulars, however, exactly what that means is far from clear. Since the early 1970s a good deal of both judicial and academic attention has been focused on the propriety of recognizing what are called constitutional damages claims. Compensatory and punitive actions based directly on the Constitution raise significant questions concerning the role of the judiciary in the American system of government. The Supreme Court's response to the tensions presented by the creation of constitutional damages actions has been a complex and confusing one.

The Constitution has traditionally been enforced through a variety of remedial mechanisms. *Marbury's* embrace of JUDICIAL REVIEW [3,I] itself adopts a constitutional enforcement measure—a "negative" judicial authority to ignore statutes that conflict with the terms of the Constitution. Since OSBORN V. BANK OF THE UNITED STATES [3] was decided in 1824, INJUNCTIONS [2] have been used to prevent government officials from engaging in future constitutional violations. In this century, the judiciary's equitable enforcement powers have been stretched to include certain nontraditional remedies, such as the exclusion of relevant evidence in criminal trials and the busing of school children in DESEGREGATION [2] cases.

On one level, lawsuits seeking monetary compensation for the violation of constitutional rights are commonplace.

SECTION 1983, TITLE 42, U.S. CODE [4], creates an action at law for constitutional injuries sustained at the hands of persons acting "under color" of state or local authority. Public employees terminated unconstitutionally by state agencies, the victims of unlawful arrests, persons subjected to discrimination prohibited by the FOURTEENTH AMENDMENT [2,I], and myriad other plaintiffs have successfully recovered money damages from state and local officials in constitutional causes of action based on section 1983.

There is, however, no counterpart to section 1983 for federal officials. If, for example, an FBI agent or a treasury officer exceeds the strictures of the FOURTH AMENDMENT [2,I], any damage claim instigated by the victim must be rooted directly in the Constitution. The general federal-question jurisdictional statute (28 U.S.C. § 1331) empowers the UNITED STATES DISTRICT COURTS [4] to entertain cases arising under the Constitution. But no statutory directive explicitly creates a cause of action for money damages. And the power of federal judges to infer such claims from the sparse language of the constitutional charter has proven a matter of considerable complexity.

In BIVENS V. SIX UNKNOWN NAMED AGENTS [1], decided in 1971, the Supreme Court held for the first time that federal officials can be sued for damages under the Fourth Amendment. Bivens, allegedly without PROBABLE CAUSE [3], had been "manacled . . . in front of his wife and children" while federal officials threatened to "arrest the entire family." The Court concluded that the "injuries consequent" to an illegal search provide the basis for an "independent claim both necessary and sufficient to make out . . . [a] cause of action." The *Bivens* case thus seemed to open the door to the recognition of a full complement of constitutional damage claims.

To a significant degree, however, *Bivens*'s promise has remained unfulfilled. The decision determined that the Fourth Amendment is directly enforceable against federal officials through damage decrees. It was silent, however, about other provisions of the BILL OF RIGHTS [1]. In the decade following the ruling, the Supreme Court held that the implied antidiscrimination component of the Fifth Amendment (DAVIS V. PASSMAN (1979) [2]) and the CRUEL AND UNUSUAL PUNISHMENTS [2,I] prohibition of the Eighth Amendment (*Carlson v. Green*, 1980) would sustain damages actions. But in *Stanley v. Lucas* (1987), the Justices determined that a former serviceman could not assert a constitutional damage claim against the ARMED FORCES [I] for being involuntarily subjected to LSD testing—in apparent violation of the DUE PROCESS [2] clause of the Fifth Amendment. And other decisions have disapproved free speech (*Bush v. Lucas*, 1983) and PROCEDURAL DUE PROCESS [3,I] (*Schweiker v. Chilicky*, 1988) claims lodged against federal officials.

The set of principles that guide the Supreme Court's constitutional damages claims cases is, in several aspects, surprising. According to *Carlson v. Green*, victims of individualized constitutional violations by federal officials are said to "have a right to recover damages . . . in federal court despite the absence of any statute conferring such a right." The action may be defeated, however, in two instances. First, relief will be denied if the government official demonstrates the existence of "special factors counselling hesitation in the absence of affirmative action by Congress." Second, the constitutional claim will fail if Congress, by providing an alternative remedy or by clear legislative directive, has indicated that JUDICIAL POWER [3] should not be exercised. "Special factors" have been found to exist in the military and civil service contexts, and more recently, intricate statutory schemes like the SOCIAL SECURITY [4] system have been deemed adequate substitutes for constitutional review.

It is unusual, of course, for exercises in CONSTITUTIONAL INTERPRETATION [1]—like *Bivens* itself—to be effectively overturned or displaced by congressional enactment. *Marbury v. Madison* would seem to argue otherwise. Nor is it commonplace for the Court openly to admit that constitutional violations will be remedied unless "special factors" counsel against enforcement. Chief Justice JOHN MARSHALL [3] argued in COHENS V. VIRGINIA (1821) [1], for example, that "we have no more right to decline the exercise of jurisdiction which is given, than to usurp that which is not given."

Damages actions are typically either created by statute or, if fashioned through the COMMON LAW [1] process, subject to legislative revision or rejection. *Bivens*-type cases occupy a hazy middle ground between traditional constitutional interpretations and common law adjudica-

tion. It is perhaps not surprising, therefore, that the decisions are riddled with compromise as well.

GENE R. NICHOL

Bibliography

DELLINGER, WALTER E.   1972   Of Rights and Remedies: The Constitution as a Sword. *Harvard Law Review* 85:1532–1564.

HILL, ALFRED   1969   Constitutional Remedies. *Columbia Law Review* 69:1009–1161.

MERRILL, THOMAS W.   1985   The Common Law Powers of Federal Courts. *University of Chicago Law Review* 52:1–72.

MONAGHAN, HENRY P.   1975   Foreword: Constitutional Common Law. *Harvard Law Review* 89:1–45.

NICHOL, GENE R.   1989   *Bivens, Chilicky* and Constitutional Damages Claims. *Virginia Law Review* 75:1117–1154.

DEATH PENALTY

See: Capital Punishment [1,I]; Capital Punishment Cases of 1972 [1]; Capital Punishment Cases of 1976 [1]; Capital Punishment and Race [I]

DECONSTRUCTION

The topic of deconstruction and the Constitution arises chiefly because of work done since 1978 by the left-oriented scholars of the Conference on CRITICAL LEGAL STUDIES [I], who have applied modern continental critical theory, including literary theory, to Anglo-American law. The issues involved also descend from the rise of PRAGMATISM [I] in American philosophy in the late nineteenth century and its influence on American JURISPRUDENCE [I] via the skepticism of OLIVER WENDELL HOLMES, JR. [2], and the later adherents of LEGAL REALISM [3]. This dual ancestry is not coincidental. Deconstruction was popularized by the French critical philosopher Jacques Derrida, especially in his 1974 book *Of Grammatology*. Though most influenced by Friedrich Nietzsche, Derrida also drew on a forebear of American pragmatism, Charles Peirce.

Like many pragmatists, deconstructionists take a radical stance toward the epistemological doubts that have occupied modern philosophy since Descartes. In their view, although the various ways in which human minds represent their experiences to themselves (from organic sensations to oral languages, to conventional writing) may bear some complex relationship to an external physical reality, they never provide a direct, unmediated grasp of it. The visual sensation of seeing the color "red," the sounds of the English adjective "red," and the written word "red" may somehow signify to us something that is really out there, but we cannot claim that our physical sensation or our oral or written terms are full or necessary representations of it. The something might cause different physical sensations in different individuals or sensory apparatuses, and certainly it can be signified by different sounds or written marks. All this is uncontroversial in most modern epistemologies.

What deconstructionists distinctively stress is that our sense of the meaning of our particular representations, our regard of those representations as signs for external somethings, is heavily dependent on the relationship of the representations or signs to some existing system of representations or signs. Obviously, the meaning readers of written English assign to the written marks "red" requires familiarity with the system of signs that is written English. The meaning speakers of English assign to the spoken sounds of "red" requires knowledge of English as a system of sound signs. Even the visual sensation we call "red" has its meaning for us only by reference to other sensations and to a system of terms that classifies and labels those sensations for us, a system that partly constitutes our knowledge of colors. The sensation, too, is for us a sign that gains much of its sense from a system of signs.

Deconstructionists therefore see all human experience as heavily defined and constructed by vast webs of signs that get their meaning more clearly from their relationship to other signs than from reality. We still presume that some such reality exists, that human minds have formed systems of signs to give reality a measure of order and meaning, and that reality can somehow prompt sensations in us that may persuade us to revise the signs we use to depict it. But deconstructionists stress that our choice of particular signs to represent reality is always in some measure arbitrary, influenced more by the preexisting set of signs available to us than any self-evident demands of external reality. Hence, we cannot have much confidence that any set of signs is an accurate representation of reality. All such systems are but partial interpretations, discernibly built out of other partial interpretations that at best show aspects of the world, and those through a glass darkly.

Yet we persist in taking our interpretations, our systems of signs, to be something more. We present them to ourselves (or they present themselves to us) as reliable windows or maps revealing an external reality of matter and/or reason that can be rendered present to our minds and senses. Like Nietzsche and the pragmatists, deconstructionists urge us to abandon this old dualistic "metaphysics of presence," in which we try to pierce through our mental limitations to grasp fully an external truth beyond. Instead, we should admit that our world of experience is *always* composed largely of questionable interpretations, partial perspectives, and contingent systems of signs. We should

therefore turn inquiry away from the "reality" for which signs allegedly stand, toward a greater understanding of the components, possibilities, and limitations of systems of signs. The world will then be seen as sets of signs or texts, melding philosophy and other modes of inquiry into literary theory.

Deconstruction is one means toward a better understanding of these texts. One deconstructs something—a novel, a treatise, a law, a political institution—by viewing it as a system of signs and unraveling it to reveal its reliance on preexisting systems of signs to make it meaningful; its consequent vulnerability to multiple meanings, depending on which of the systems of signs it incorporates, is stressed, along with its embodiment of those systems' biases and of the contradictions within them and among them, and thus its inevitable incompleteness and incoherencies. To be sure, one may also find insights that seem worth preserving. But ultimately one can always show any text to be another partial, ambiguous system of signs constructed out of other such systems.

Unlike the early scientific resolutive-compositive method of inquiry, moreover, the point of deconstruction is not to give us a fuller understanding of how the object of analysis functions while otherwise leaving it intact after we mentally reconstruct it. Deconstruction always invalidates much of what a text initially appeared to do or say, altering our sense of it. We may then strive to construct new accounts of the text's themes that are more comprehensive because they encompass what we have learned; but those accounts will ultimately remain partial interpretations.

The appeal of all this for critical scholars in Anglo-American law should be clear. National legal systems can plausibly be viewed as systems of signs for which people make strong claims. They are said to have considerable internal coherence and to be largely accurate representations of external social and political worlds and of appropriate moral principles. Those claims seem integral to a legal system's very legitimacy. But, via deconstruction, one can often show that many legal terms derive from preexisting discourses identified with particular ruling groups and that they express those groups' interests more clearly than they express any objective moral principles. Legal language can also be shown to be subject to multiple inconsistent interpretations, depending on which elements are stressed. Thus, the law may seem indeterminate or incoherent, gaining definition only from those who wield enough power to make their interpretations stick.

Critical legal scholars have deconstructed the doctrines of judicial and ADMINISTRATIVE LAW [1] in numerous areas of American law, such as contracts, property, and criminal law, in just these ways. At times, however, they have moved too quickly to two types of conclusions that represent shallow readings of the implications of deconstruction. Some align deconstruction with Marxism, attempting to show that legal doctrines at bottom express capitalist class interests rooted in material relations of production. Such readings have some force, but in deconstructionist terms they do not go far enough unless they concede that the various Marxisms are but further systems of signs and that Marxist claims to have grasped the truth of external material reality are highly vulnerable to deconstructionist debunking. Other critical legal scholars write as if the American legal system is peculiarly guilty of insuperable internal contradictions and ambiguities, implying that a system ordered on different principles would overcome these problems. But again deconstruction suggests that although there are more or less encompassing interpretations, all systems of signs will always be vulnerable to demonstrations of their inadequacy.

These points can be exemplified by showing how we might begin deconstructing the Constitution. Its PRE-AMBLE [3] says that "We the People of the United States" are ordaining and establishing the document. Those words seem to assume a traditional understanding of flesh-and-blood persons consciously using words as authoritative signs, accurately representing themselves and their thoughts and giving new order to their lives.

But deconstructing interpreters can challenge that picture in all the ways just suggested. "We the People" is, after all, plainly a kind of metaphor: no reader really thinks all the people of the United States directly established the Constitution. Interpreters can easily show, moreover, that the text's terms, derived largely from the discourse of American elites, treat many as virtually invisible non-people (e.g., indentured servants, women, African Americans, Native Americans, all of whom the document relegates to lesser categories, explicitly or implicitly). Thus, deconstruction might first suggest that the Constitution is a misleading, biased creation of elites alone, as leftist critics assert.

Next, one can deconstruct the Constitution to display internal dissonances. For instance, in contrast to the Preamble, the last article of the original Constitution (Article VII) indicates that the Constitution must be ratified by nine state conventions. Here the Constitution seems established more by a supermajority of the states, or of these state conventions, than by "We the People." Wrestling with whether the text finally describes itself as a product of the national populace or the states has long led analysts to conclude that it is opaque or inconsistent, incapable of constituting a government without added meaning supplied by its interpreters. If so, it is less a constitution than it purports to be.

Deconstruction of "We the People" can be taken still deeper yet. We might question how much of its meaning derives from reference to *any* flesh-and-blood inhabitants of the United States, then or now, be they a national populace, ruling elites, or state citizens. For some readers, the opening words actually summon up thoughts of Founding Fathers who are plainly not all "the People," but a few, and whose identities are provided much more by enduring national myths than any perceptions of the Founders' physical reality. Insofar as readers do think of "the People," moreover, they are likely to imagine the type of entity portrayed in certain traditions of political writing and novels—a heroic demos of anti-aristocratic republicans, unified by a general will and acting as a collective moral agent capable of political transformations. That may be a stirring image, but it is one expressing knowledge of certain systems of signs, not of the particular persons living in the United States in 1787–1789.

The power of those political traditions in shaping our reading of the Constitution suggests in turn that these systems of signs are actually providing much of the Constitution's meaning that the text purports to derive from "the People." If so, the most fundamental political claim of the Constitution, the claim that it is the creation of responsible human agents who are guiding their own collective destiny, may appear to be a myth. The Constitution now seems much more a set of signs drawn from other systems of signs that constituted the consciousness of "We the People" than a law created by "We the People." In short, deconstruction of "We the People" can lead us to think of political agency in a different way, a subjectless way that is sharply opposed to what the text initially seemed to suggest.

There is something to be learned from each of these three deconstructionist readings of the Constitution, culminating in this challenge to meaningful human agency itself. Yet we should also recall that the partiality of every existing interpretation does not by itself show that they are all simply false. The existence of contradictions in a text or a body of laws does not alone prove that its essential themes are indefensible. And the dependence of our minds on the many systems of signs that order our worlds of experience does not prove that we cannot play a significant role in coming to understand those worlds somewhat better and in reordering them beneficially.

Like the "cynical acid" concerning the determinacy of legal rules and factual judgments that the legal realists earlier provided, deconstruction simply renders certain particular claims of these sorts less credible. It does not prevent us, after encompassing the insights it provides us, from going on to construct systems of ideas and institutions that seem more satisfactory than their predecessors, albeit still imperfect. Nor does it tell us much about how such constructive efforts should proceed. Thus, deconstruction itself represents but a partial contribution to understanding the Constitution and judging what it can and should mean, how and whether it can and should work, today and in the future.

ROGERS M. SMITH

(SEE ALSO: *Political Philosophy of the Constitution* [3,I].)

Bibliography

DERRIDA, JACQUES 1974 *Of Grammatology*, trans. Gayatri Spivak. Baltimore: Johns Hopkins University Press.

KELMAN, MARK 1987 *A Guide to Critical Legal Studies*. Cambridge, Mass.: Harvard University Press.

NIETZSCHE, FRIEDRICH 1966 *Beyond Good and Evil: Prelude to a Philosophy of the Future*, ed. Walter Kaufmann. New York: Random House.

DELEGATION OF POWER
(Update)

The delegation doctrine concerns Congress's power to give or delegate the rulemaking authority it has to the executive or judicial branches. In most of the cases involving the doctrine, litigants have challenged congressional delegation of rulemaking authority to ADMINISTRATIVE AGENCIES [I].

By the early 1980s the Supreme Court seemed to have a well-established position on the scope of Congress's power to delegate its rulemaking power. The Court held, as a matter of formal doctrine, that Congress could not delegate its power "to legislate," for such a delegation would violate the Constitution's command that "all legislative Powers . . . shall be vested in a Congress." But the Court also held that Congress could seek "assistance" from the other branches in exercising its LEGISLATIVE POWER [3] and therefore could give the other branches authority to enact rules to "fill in" the details of congressional policy. Yet, although the formal doctrine purported to set some judicially enforceable limits on congressional delegations, the Court's application of the doctrine imposed virtually no limits on Congress's power to delegate rulemaking authority.

The Court's decisions held that to be constitutional a delegation must contain a congressionally adopted policy or set of "intelligible principles" to guide and confine the other branch in its rulemaking activity. The Court stated that such intelligible principles were necessary to ensure that the other branch merely implemented or filled in the details of policy that Congress had adopted. It also held that the standards were necessary to give the courts a means of measuring whether the other branch

had complied with the scope of Congress's delegation and thus to measure whether the other branch had acted in conformity with the "will of Congress."

This delegation doctrine was virtually without force. With two exceptions in the 1930s, the Court found that all of Congress's delegations contained sufficient intelligible principles. Many of the approved principles—such as "consistent with public convenience, interest and necessity" and "just and reasonable"—were so broad and vague that they gave the other branch seemingly unconfined discretion in exercising its rulemaking authority.

The Court's lenient, accommodating approach in applying the "intelligible principles test" led many commentators to charge that the Court paid mere lip service to the test and, as a result, failed to enforce a meaningful judicial limitation on Congress's delegations. Indeed, the Court's approach seemed to reflect a judicial judgment that congressional delegation of rulemaking authority is inevitable and desirable and that the difficulties of creating more restrictive constitutional rules or principles were greater than the benefits of doing so.

Then, in 1983, the Supreme Court did invalidate a congressional delegation of its decision-making power, and some thought that the Court might be signaling a stricter approach to delegation challenges. In IMMIGRATION AND NATURALIZATION SERVICE V. CHADHA (1983) [2] the Court held that the one-house LEGISLATIVE VETO [3] was unconstitutional. For over fifty years, some legislation delegating congressional authority to the executive branch had provided that specified executive action could be annulled by one house of Congress. In *Chadha*, for example, Congress delegated power to the ATTORNEY GENERAL [1] to allow ALIENS [1] to remain in the country, even though their visas had expired. The legislation delegating this power provided that either house of Congress could, nonetheless, overturn the attorney general's determination in a particular case by adopting a resolution. The attorney general allowed Chadha to stay after his visa expired, but the HOUSE OF REPRESENTATIVES [I] passed a resolution ordering him to leave. Accepting that Congress has the power to set the terms for aliens to remain in the country, the Court ruled that setting or revising those terms was a legislative act and that Congress could exercise its legislative power only through legislation, which requires action by both houses and presentation to the President. Congress could not vest its legislative power in one of its own houses.

The *Chadha* majority did not consider the one-house veto as a delegation issue. But as Justice BYRON R. WHITE [4,I] pointed out in dissent, *Chadha* in effect imposed a significantly more stringent limitation on Congress's power to delegate its authority than the Court had imposed in the preceding fifty years. Some thought that the Court's more stringent approach would be limited to congressional delegations to parts of Congress. Others speculated that *Chadha* might signal the Court's willingness to scrutinize all the delegations more closely, as some members of the Court, most notably Chief Justice WILLIAM H. REHNQUIST [3,I], have sometimes urged.

The Court has recently indicated that speculation about the broader implications of *Chadha* probably is not warranted. In two significant cases during the 1988 term, the Court reaffirmed its use of the intelligible principles test and emphasized its long tradition of upholding delegations in light of the need for flexibility in formulating and enforcing federal policy. In MISTRETTA V. UNITED STATES (1989) [I], the Court upheld Congress's delegation of power to the Sentencing Commission to promulgate a new system of determinate sentences for federal crimes. And in *Skinner v. Mid-America Pipeline* (1989), the Court sustained Congress's delegation of power to the secretary of transportation to establish and collect pipeline-safety user fees. The pipeline case seems particularly significant because in an earlier decision the Court had seemed to suggest that it might employ greater scrutiny in testing the constitutionality of Congress's delegation of its power to tax. *Skinner* belies that suggestion.

The Court's approach in delegation cases can be contrasted with its approach in cases charging that Congress has appropriated the powers of another branch. In those cases, the Court is far less deferential. For example, in BOWSHER V. SYNAR (1986) [I] the Court held that Congress acted beyond its authority in attempting to give "executive" power to the comptroller general, who is responsible to Congress, not the executive branch. The difference in judicial scrutiny may reflect a conclusion that JUDICIAL POWER [3,I] need not be exercised to prevent one branch from giving away some of its powers but should be exercised to prevent one branch from usurping the powers of another. A branch can protect against relinquishing its own power simply by refusing to delegate; it must rely on the courts to prevent another branch from invading its domain.

Moreover, although the Court rarely invalidates congressional delegation of its rulemaking authority on constitutional grounds, the Court does require that such delegations be clearly made. Such a requirement protects against congressionally unauthorized rulemaking by the other branches. For example, in *National Cable Television Association v. United States* (1974), the Court held that the Federal Communications Commission overstepped its delegated authority in seeking to cover its administrative costs through user fees, noting that such fees could be viewed as taxes and that congressional delegations of its revenue-raising power should be "narrowly construed."

As the *Skinner* case shows, Congress can delegate the power to collect revenue when it chooses to do so, but the Court will require a clear statement that such delegation is intended, lest the other branches intrude without permission into the congressional domain.

SCOTT H. BICE

Bibliography

ARANSON, PETER H.; GELLHORN, ERNEST; and ROBINSON, GLEN O. 1982 A Theory of Legislative Delegation. *Cornell Law Review* 68:1–67.
SYMPOSIUM 1987 The Uneasy Constitutional Status of the Administrative Agencies: Part 1, Delegation of Powers to Administrative Agencies. *American University Law Review* 36:295–442.

DESHANEY v. WINNEBAGO COUNTY DEPARTMENT OF SOCIAL SERVICES
488 U.S. 189 (1989)

When Joshua DeShaney was one year old, his parents were divorced; the court awarded custody of Joshua to his father, who moved to Wisconsin and remarried. When Joshua was three, his father's second wife complained to the county department of social services (DSS) that the father was abusing the child, hitting him and leaving marks on him. DSS officials interviewed the father, who denied the charges; DSS did not pursue the matter. A year later Joshua was admitted to a hospital with multiple bruises and abrasions; the examining doctor notified DSS; DSS immediately obtained a court order taking custody over Joshua, but the DSS investigating team decided there was insufficient evidence of child abuse to retain Joshua in the court's custody. The father promised DSS that he would enroll Joshua in a preschool program and undertake counseling for himself. A month later the hospital emergency room notified DSS that Joshua had been treated again for suspicious injuries; the caseworker concluded there was no basis for action. Over the next six months the caseworker visited the home, repeatedly saw injuries on Joshua's head, and noted that he had not been enrolled in the preschool program. She recorded all this in her files and did nothing more. About a month later, the emergency room notified DSS that Joshua had been admitted with injuries they believed caused by child abuse. On the caseworker's next two home visits, she was told Joshua was too ill to see her. DSS took no action. Four months later, the father beat four-year-old Joshua, who lapsed into a coma; Joshua suffered severe brain damage, but lived. He is expected to spend the rest of his life in an institution for the profoundly retarded.

The father was tried and convicted of child abuse, but

the case that reached the Supreme Court was a civil action, brought by Joshua's mother against DSS and some DSS employees, seeking damages on the ground that DSS had deprived Joshua of SUBSTANTIVE DUE PROCESS OF LAW [4,I] in violation of the FOURTEENTH AMENDMENT [2]. The lower courts denied relief and the Supreme Court affirmed, 6–3. For the majority, Chief Justice WILLIAM H. REHNQUIST [3,I] concluded that the due process clause imposed no affirmative duty on the state or its officers to protect a citizen's life or liberty against private persons' invasions. Furthermore, no such constitutional duty arose merely because DSS had known of Joshua's situation and indicated its intention to protect him. The case differed from those in which the Court had recognized a state duty to assure minimal safety and medical treatment for prisoners and institutionalized mental patients, for here the state had done nothing to restrain Joshua or otherwise prevent him from protecting himself or receiving protection from other persons. The harm, in other words, "was inflicted not by the State of Wisconsin, but by Joshua's father."

For the dissenters, Justice WILLIAM J. BRENNAN [2,I] castigated the majority for so limited a view of the prison- and mental-hospital cases. Here the state had set up DSS to protect children in precisely Joshua's situation, thus encouraging citizens generally to rely on DSS to prevent child abuse. One had to ignore this context to conclude, as the majority did, that the state had simply failed to act. Justice HARRY A. BLACKMUN [1,I], in a separate dissent, objected to the majority's formalistic distinction between STATE ACTION [4,I] and state inaction; the state had assumed responsibility for protecting Joshua from the very abuse that deprived him of much of what it means to have a life.

In a great many ways the Supreme Court has imposed affirmative duties on the states to compensate for inequalities or other harms not directly of the states' making. (See ACCESS TO THE COURTS [1]; RIGHT TO COUNSEL [3]; MENTAL RETARDATION AND THE CONSTITUTION [3]; PROCEDURAL DUE PROCESS OF LAW, CIVIL [3,I].) Its decisions in these areas recognize, if only partially, the artificiality of insisting that constitutional guarantees be rigidly confined to action that is formally governmental, ignoring the interlacing of public and private action that characterizes much behavior in America's complex society. As *DeShaney* sadly illustrates, a mechanical application of the judge-made state-action limitation on the Fourteenth Amendment can permit the systematic evasion of public responsibility.

KENNETH L. KARST

Bibliography

TRIBE, LAURENCE H. 1989 The Curvature of Constitutional Space: What Lawyers Can Learn from Modern Physics. *Harvard Law Review* 103:1–39.

DIAL-A-PORN

With the development of new telephone technologies, the transmission of sexually explicit messages over the phone lines has become a multimillion dollar business. Telephone pornography raises special difficulties because many children call telephone sex lines unbeknown to parents. Some companies engaged in telephone pornography actually solicit business from minors, distributing advertisements for their services on school playgrounds. In one highly publicized case in California, a twelve-year-old boy who had been exposed to a pornographic phone message sexually assaulted a four-year-old girl.

In response to concerns about the effects of telephone pornography on children, Congress in 1983 banned all "obscene or indecent" commercial phone messages transmitted to persons under the age of eighteen. Pursuant to provisions of the law, the Federal Communications Commission developed procedures by which telephone pornography companies could restrict their services to adults, including message scrambling, mandatory payment by credit card, and special access codes for users. Use of these procedures provided a defense against prosecution under the law. In 1988, however, an appellate court held the FCC regulations unconstitutional; and a few months later, Congress decided that its previous law was not sufficient to remedy the problem and subsequently banned "obscene or indecent" telephone messages directed to all persons, regardless of age.

In *Sable Communications of California, Inc. v. F.C.C.* (1989), the Supreme Court upheld Congress's ban on "obscene" phone messages by a vote of 6–3, but it unanimously struck down the prohibition against "indecent" messages. Writing for the majority, Justice BYRON R. WHITE [4,I] noted that the Court had already decided that OBSCENITY [3] is not protected by the FIRST AMENDMENT [2,I]; hence the ban on obscene phone messages was clearly constitutional under the Court's previous decisions. The indecency restriction was a different matter. Applying the COMPELLING STATE INTEREST [1] test the Court regularly uses in free speech cases, White argued that the government undoubtedly has a compelling interest in eliminating indecent messages directed at children. However, the wholesale ban on indecent phone messages was not narrowly tailored to further that interest. According to White, nothing indicated that the regulations promulgated under the previous law would not have protected children sufficiently. White hinted, but did not decide, that those previous regulations were constitutional.

Concurring, Justice ANTONIN SCALIA [I] pointed out that while the Court forbade the government from prohibiting all indecent phone messages, it did not hold that public utilities have an obligation to carry such messages. In other words, regardless of the provisions of federal law, a utility could make a business decision not to carry sexually explicit message services.

Justice WILLIAM J. BRENNAN [1,I] agreed with the Court's invalidation of the ban on indecent phone messages, but he objected to its approval of the obscenity provisions, noting: "I have long been convinced that the exaction of criminal penalties for the distribution of obscene materials to consenting adults is constitutionally intolerable."

JOHN G. WEST, JR.

(SEE ALSO: *Child Pornography* [I]; *Meese Commission* [I]; *Pornography* [3]; *Pornography and Feminism* [I].)

DIRECT DEMOCRACY

Those who framed the Constitution opted for a system of representative government rather than direct democracy. The true distinction between the "pure democracies of Greece" and the American government, explained JAMES MADISON [3] in *The Federalist* #63, lay "in the total exclusion of the people in their collective capacity from any share in the latter." It was this distinction that the Federalists believed might permit American government to succeed where other democracies had failed. Placing the exclusive power of ordinary lawmaking in governors distinct from the governed, said Madison, would refine and enlarge public views "by passing them through the medium of a chosen body of citizens" whose wisdom, patriotism, and love of justice would make them unlikely to sacrifice the interest of the country "to temporal or partial considerations." Representative bodies afforded greater opportunities for deliberation and debate. Popular masses were perceived as too quick to form preferences, frequently failing to consider adequately the interests of others, and overly susceptible to contagious passions.

Part of the Framers' distrust of popular rule was the threat it posed to creditor rights and individual property interests. And the well-heeled delegates had plenty to fear from the masses of have-nots. Indeed, some historians contend that the central problem that prompted the convening of the delegates at Philadelphia was not the weaknesses of the ARTICLES OF CONFEDERATION [1] but concern over an excess of POPULISM [I] in the states. In any case, Madison and his fellow Federalists labored mightily—and successfully—to block an attempt to include in the FIRST AMENDMENT [2,I] a right of the people to "instruct their representatives."

In the early part of the twentieth century the Progressives successfully introduced two forms of direct democracy at the state level—the INITIATIVE [2] and the REFERENDUM [3]. These innovative reforms, now a part of the lawmaking process in more than half the states, were a response to the widely perceived corruption and control of legislators by wealthy interest groups. The Progressives sought to curb legislatures by placing corrective power in the citizenry. The initiative allows the voters to propose and enact legislation by simple majority vote. Initiatives are thus designed to rectify corruption that impedes legislation by circumventing the legislative framework. Conversely, referenda are directed against corruption that produces legislation by adding an additional layer to the lawmaking process. The referendum allows the voters to reject laws previously enacted by the legislature. Thus, the two Progressive reforms simultaneously make it both less difficult and more difficult to enact laws.

Not long after many of the western states began to use the initiative device, its constitutionality came under attack. In *Pacific States Telephone & Telegraph Co. v. Oregon* (1912), the Supreme Court was asked to rule whether a state's use of a voter initiative to enact a tax measure was consistent with the REPUBLICAN FORM OF GOVERNMENT [3] guaranteed to the states by Article IV, section 4, of the Constitution. The taxpayer argued that the representative nature of republican government precluded the people from taking legislative functions into their own hands. The Court never reached the merits of this claim, holding instead that whether a state government is "republican" was a POLITICAL QUESTION [3,I] that courts were not competent to answer. The Court, treating the challenge as an attack on the legitimacy of the Oregon government, relied on LUTHER V. BORDEN (1849) [3] for the proposition that such a matter was properly to be resolved by the political branches of the national government (Congress and the President).

The JUSTICIABILITY [3] bar to the resolution of the constitutional challenge to citizen lawmaking remains securely in place. But although the Supreme Court has never passed on the constitutionality of direct democracy devices in general, the Court has condemned its use in particular applications. In HUNTER V. ERICKSON (1969) [2] the Supreme Court struck down a voter initiative altering a city charter to require that any OPEN HOUSING LAWS [3] passed by the city council be approved by voter referendum before taking effect. The Court's majority held that by making open housing laws more difficult to enact, the charter amendment erected special barriers to legislation favoring ethnic and religious minorities and therefore violated the EQUAL PROTECTION [2,I] clause of the FOURTEENTH AMENDMENT [2,I].

Similar concerns led the Court to invalidate an anti-SCHOOL BUSING [4] initiative passed by the voters of the state of Washington. In *Washington v. Seattle School District No. 1* (1982), a 5–4 majority thwarted the voter reversal of an attempt by Seattle school authorities to achieve racial balance through involuntary busing. The majority's route to its conclusion that the initiative offended the equal protection clause cannot easily be mapped. At times, Justice HARRY A. BLACKMUN [1,I], the opinion's author, appears to find impermissible racial motivation. He notes that "there is little doubt that the initiative was effectively drawn for racial purposes," a fact of which he believed the Washington electorate was "surely aware." Elsewhere in the opinion, he seems to rest the decision on the customized alteration of the normal decision-making process for issues of unique interest to minority groups. In such instances, Blackmun suggests, inquiry into motivation is not necessary. This latter reading is reinforced by the 8–1 decision in CRAWFORD V. BOARD OF EDUCATION (1982) [2], handed down the same day.

Over Justice THURGOOD MARSHALL's [3,I] lone dissenting observation that the case was indistinguishable from *Seattle*, the Court in *Crawford* sustained an amendment to the California Constitution (approved overwhelmingly by both houses of the California legislature and ratified by the voters) stripping state courts of the power to order busing, except in cases of Fourteenth Amendment violations. It is not uncommon for commentators to express amazement that the two cases were decided by the same Court, much less on the same day. The Court's conclusion in *Crawford* that the California amendment was not adopted with a racially discriminatory purpose is difficult to square with its opposite assessment on a similar record in *Seattle*.

What differentiates *Seattle* from *Crawford*, however, is the role of direct democracy. The sponsors of the Washington initiative sought to circumvent the representative process that produced Seattle's pupil reassignment plan. The school board had historically made considerable efforts to alleviate the isolation of the district's sizable minority population. Local attempts to recall the board members responsible for some of these efforts had failed. The initiative process afforded an opportunity for the populace to reverse the minority's gains. In marked contrast to the Washington process, the California amendment in *Crawford* was a joint effort of the legislature and the voters. Here was not a case of the people bypassing a representative body. The Madisonian nightmare, so stark in *Seattle*, was largely absent from the California reaction against a zealous judiciary. None of this is explicit in the two opinions. Indeed, neither opinion makes any serious effort to distinguish its companion case. The Justices were understandably hesitant to announce explicitly a distinction

grounded on a distrust of electoral majorities. But it is hard to reconcile the two results on any other ground.

Nowhere is the tension between the Madisonian fears of popular masses and the American democratic ideal more in evidence than in an interchange between Justice HUGO L. BLACK [1] and Thurgood Marshall, then solicitor general, that occurred during the oral argument in REITMAN V. MULKEY (1967) [3]. By an overwhelming majority, California voters had adopted an initiative measure amending the state constitution to repeal existing open housing laws and forbid the enactment of new ones. During ORAL ARGUMENT [3], Marshall stressed that this authorization of RACIAL DISCRIMINATION [3,I] in the private housing market had been the result of voters bypassing the representative process. "Wouldn't you have exactly the same argument," he was asked, if the provision challenged "had been enacted by the California legislature?" "It's the same argument," Marshall replied, "I just have more force with this." "No," interjected Justice Black, "it seems to me you have less. Because here, it's moving in the direction of letting the people of the States . . . establish their policy, which is as near to a democracy as you can get."

Hugo Black was undoubtedly right in observing that direct voter legislation is quite a bit closer to "democracy" than legislative products. What his vision obscures, however, is the intentional nature of the gap between true democracy and the republican form of government carved out by those who drafted the Constitution. Representative government was designed to capture the virtues of POPULAR SOVEREIGNTY [3] without being tainted by its vices. Accountability to the electorate was to be the touchstone of legitimacy. But the Framers opted for the virtues of agency, favoring a removed deliberation over the impassioned decision making of participatory democracy.

Two-thirds of those questioned in a 1987 nationwide Gallup survey said that citizens ought to be able to vote directly on some state and local laws, and a poll conducted in 1977 found more than half in favor of a constitutional amendment for a national initiative. In the late 1970s, the Senate held extensive hearings on just such a proposed amendment. Despite the sponsorship of more than fifty members of Congress and supportive testimony by a wide range of both conservatives and liberals, the proposal died in committee. Americans are not, it seems, quite ready to abandon their commitment to the Framers' preferences.

JULIAN N. EULE

Bibliography

BELL, DERRICK 1978 The Referendum: Democracy's Barrier to Racial Equality. *Washington Law Review* 54:1–29.
CRONIN, THOMAS E. 1989 *Direct Democracy.* Cambridge, Mass.: Harvard University Press.
EULE, JULIAN N. 1990 Judicial Review of Direct Democracy. *Yale Law Journal* 99:1503–1590.

DISABILITIES, RIGHTS OF PERSONS WITH

When Justice OLIVER WENDELL HOLMES, JR. [2] declared in BUCK V. BELL (1927) [1] that the state's POLICE POWER [3] authorized involuntary sterilization of individuals thought to be mentally impaired, he asserted, "It is better for all the world, if instead of waiting to execute degenerate offspring for crime, or to let them starve for their imbecility, society can prevent those who are manifestly unfit from continuing their kind. . . . Three generations of imbeciles is enough." His statement embodied three assumptions about people with disabilities that have since provoked repeated and partially successful constitutional challenges. The first assumption was that people with disabilities do not enjoy the same basic rights as anyone else, such as the rights to procreate or to be free from involuntary medical treatment. The second assumption was that people with disabilities have no special rights should their conditions leave them vulnerable to legal, social, or physical jeopardy. The third assumption was that society's interests always outweigh the interests of people who have or who are perceived to have disabilities.

Inspired by the CIVIL RIGHTS MOVEMENTS for blacks and for women, in the 1950s and 1960s, advocates for people with disabilities drew on changing medical knowledge about mental and physical disabilities. During the same years, increased federal funds for research and services reached those with mental disabilities and helped to support a movement for their rights. Advocates attacked the segregation produced by institutional settings. They also challenged the deprivation of VOTING RIGHTS [4]; rights to have sexual relations; rights to marry; rights to have children; rights of access to jobs, housing, and transportation; and rights to treatment and services. The disability rights movement attained periodic success in constitutional adjudication in the lower federal courts, which in turn supported federal legislation backed by congressional findings of constitutional rights and also provided the backdrop for landmark Supreme Court DUE PROCESS [2], and EQUAL PROTECTION [2,I] decisions.

Initial lawsuits maintained that people with disabilities retained the same rights held by others. On this theory, confinement of persons on grounds of MENTAL ILLNESS [3,I] or MENTAL RETARDATION [3] should not deprive them of other liberties, and the confinement itself should be justified by provision of services or treatment. The court of appeals so reasoned in *Donaldson v. O'Connor* (1974) and then built on this judgment with *Wyatt v. Aderholt* (1974), which declared on PROCEDURAL DUE PROCESS [3,I] grounds a right to treatment for persons civilly committed to state mental institutions. It was this right to treatment

that Congress incorporated in the DEVELOPMENTALLY DISABLED ASSISTANCE AND BILL OF RIGHTS ACT (1975) [2].

Although the Supreme Court refrained from endorsing the right to treatment at that time, it reinforced the disability rights movement by unanimously announcing in O'CONNOR V. DONALDSON (1975) [3] that "a State cannot constitutionally confine without more [justification] a nondangerous individual who is capable of surviving safely in freedom by himself or with the help of willing and responsible family members or friends." The Court also reasoned that mere public intolerance could not justify the deprivation of physical liberty.

Elaborating the FOURTEENTH AMENDMENT [2,I] due process theory of liberty, advocates argued that the right to treatment included a right to be treated in the least restrictive setting possible, which meant the setting least confined and removed from the rest of the community. A series of lawsuits challenging the conditions and absence of treatment at a large institution in Pennsylvania produced the disappointing decision in PENNHURST STATE SCHOOL V. HALDERMAN (1981) [3] that the Developmental Disability Act did not confer any substantive right to appropriate treatment in the least restrictive environment. This Supreme Court conclusion occurred after years of litigation had already propelled the states to move people from institutions to community-based facilities.

Then the Supreme Court took the occasion of one more lawsuit arising from the same Pennsylvania institution to announce a constitutional right to treatment for people with disabilities confined in state institutions. In *Youngberg v. Romeo* (1982) the Court declared that the due-process clause of the Fourteenth Amendment assures (1) safe conditions of confinement; (2) freedom from bodily restraints; and (3) training or "habilitation," meaning a duty to provide at least "such training as an appropriate professional would consider reasonable to ensure the individual's safety and to facilitate his ability to function free from bodily restraints."

The emerging right to treatment also spawned arguments for a right to refuse treatment. Lower federal courts in cases such as *Rennie v. Klein* (1978) recognized a constitutional privacy right of involuntary mental patients to refuse medication. In WASHINGTON V. HARPER (1990) [I] the Supreme Court announced that forced administration of antipsychotic drugs violates a constitutional liberty interest, but that due process can be satisfied by administrative processes less formal than a court hearing. During the same term, the Court acknowledged in *Cruzan v. Missouri Department of Health* (1990) that a constitutionally protected liberty interest in refusing unwanted medical treatment may be inferred from its prior decisions. In *Cruzan*, the first Supreme Court decision addressing the RIGHT TO DIE [I], the Court acknowledged that incompetent as well as competent persons have a constitutionally protected liberty interest in consenting to or refusing treatment. Yet this interest did not forbid a state from requiring clear and convincing evidence that the patient herself would want to terminate life-sustaining treatment. Having spoken on this issue, the Court, like many state courts, may start to hear right-to-die and treatment cases affecting severely disabled adults, infants, and children.

Implicit in the due process liberty cases is the theme of equal protection, which has also inspired an independent line of opinions articulating rights of persons with disabilities. Advocates achieved early constitutional successes by linking claims about disabilities to arguments against racial SEGREGATION [4]. Thus, in *Hobson v. Hansen* (1967), affirmed in *Smuck v. Hobson* (1969), the district court ruled a public-school ability-tracking system unconstitutional in light of its racially segregative impact. In *Larry P. v. Riles* (1979) the district court found unconstitutional the use of I.Q. tests for placing students in classes for the "educable mentally retarded" because of a foreseeable racial impact.

Charges of RACIAL DISCRIMINATION [3,I] trigger STRICT SCRUTINY [4] under the equal-protection clause. Yet the Supreme Court has resisted claims that strict scrutiny should also apply to charges of discrimination on the basis of disability. In *Cleburne v. Cleburne Living Center, Inc.* (1985) the Court expressly rejected the assertion that persons with disabilities are members of a suspect or semisuspect classification.

Nonetheless, the Court in *Cleburne* did give unusually sharp teeth to its low-level rational-relationship scrutiny. It found that a city requirement of a special-use permit for a proposed group home for persons with mental retardation violated the equal-protection clause. Locating group homes in residential neighborhoods would be essential to the goal of moving disabled people out of remote institutions and into the mainstream community. The city of Cleburne had created a special ZONING permit requirement for the operation of a group home for mentally retarded persons. The majority of the Court found no RATIONAL BASIS [3] for believing that the proposed group home would pose a special threat to the city's interests and rejected fear and negative attitudes by community members as inadequate bases for treating mentally retarded individuals differently from others. Justice THURGOOD MARSHALL [3,I], joined by Justices WILLIAM J. BRENNAN [1,I] and HARRY A. BLACKMUN [1,I], maintained that the Court's majority had in effect applied heightened scrutiny and should explicitly accord such scrutiny given the history and continuing legacy of segregation of and discrimination against people with mental retardation.

A combination of equal protection and due process arguments produced the landmark decisions in *Mills v. Board of Education* (1973) and *Pennsylvania Ass'n for Retarded Children v. Pennsylvania* (1971), which decreed that children with disabilities have constitutional rights to equal educational opportunity, and exclusion from public schooling violates these rights. Congress expressly relied on the constitutional dimensions of these district court decisions in promulgating the EDUCATION FOR ALL HANDICAPPED CHILDREN ACT [2] of 1975. Sometimes known as the "special education" statute, this act provides federal moneys to assist states in extending free appropriate public education to children with disabilities.

Drawing from procedural due-process doctrines, the act calls for individualized evaluations of each child's educational and health needs and an administrative process providing opportunities for parents to participate and raise objections to proposed placements. The act also echoes the right to treatment, but locates it within the context of compulsory schooling. The act introduces the desegregation concept of mainstreaming children with disabilities in regular classrooms to the extent possible. For students who still require instruction in separate classrooms or separate facilities, the act calls for selecting the placement that is the least restrictive—the one most approximating the mainsteam classroom. Finally, the statute calls for related medical services to ensure that students with special physical needs are not excluded from instruction due to medical needs.

Disability rights advocates have struggled to combine arguments for extending to people with disabilities the same liberty interests enjoyed by others with the use of arguments for special claims for treatment and even rights to refuse treatment that might not arise for others. The REHABILITATION ACT [3] of 1973 included section 504, a nondiscrimination provision modeled after the CIVIL RIGHTS [1,I] statutes drafted to guard against both racial discrimination and SEX DISCRIMINATION [4,I]. A central idea developed in this context is that people entitled to protection against discrimination include those who are perceived to be disabled, whether or not they actually are disabled. On this basis, people who have had a disease or an illness or people who may be perceived to have an illness or a deformity have been extended statutory protections, as in *School Board of Nassau County v. Arline* (1987).

Antidiscrimination principles also animate the Fair Housing Act Amendments of 1988 that protect persons with disability and the AMERICANS WITH DISABILITY ACT (1990) [I], heralded by many as the most important and extensive legislation ever adopted on behalf of persons with disability. Yet enduring questions about the meaning of equality and the degree of requisite accommodation will arise both as statutory questions and as constitutional questions concerning the scope of JUDICIAL POWER [3,I] to order expenditures to accommodate previously excluded groups. Ending the exclusion of physically handicapped persons requires architectural renovation, new communication technologies, and other potentially costly changes. Ending the exclusion of persons with mental disabilities may require the creation of new kinds of institutions, like group homes, which involve money and trained personnel as well as changed community attitudes. Devising programs for persons with AIDS or at risk of AIDS would also involve large expenditures.

Federal courts implementing statutory and constitutional rights for persons with disabilities may confront claims of ELEVENTH AMENDMENT [2,I] immunity asserted by states against court-ordered expenditures. In analogous cases involving court-ordered remedies for school segregation and prison conditions, courts have ruled that inadequate resources can never be an adequate justification for a state to deprive persons of their constitutional rights.

Much has changed since Justice Holmes's 1927 opinion in *Buck v. Bell;* the law recognizes many of the same rights for persons with disabilities as for others. Courts and legislatures have articulated special rights to help disabled persons overcome legal, social, and physical jeopardy. Will the Constitution direct an answer to the question when societal interests outweigh the interests of persons with disabilities? Perhaps the future constitutional challenge is to locate within societal interests the interests of persons with disabilities so the very terms of the questions will change.

MARTHA MINOW

Bibliography

BURGDORF, ROBERT L. and BURGDORF, MARCIA PEARCE 1977 The Wicked Witch Is Almost Dead: *Buck v. Bell* and the Sterilization of Handicapped Persons. *Temple Law Quarterly* 50:955–1034.
MINOW, MARTHA 1990 *Making All the Difference: Inclusion, Exclusion, and American Law.* Ithaca, N.Y.: Cornell University Press.
NOTE 1973 Right to Treatment. *Harvard Law Review* 86: 1282–1306.
STUDENT AUTHORS 1974 Developments in the Law: Civil Commitment of the Mentally Ill. *Harvard Law Review* 87:1190–1406.
TRIBE, LAURENCE 1988 *American Constitutional Law*, 2nd ed. Mineola, N.Y.: Foundation Press.

DORMANT COMMERCE CLAUSE

The Constitution does not explicitly restrict STATE REGULATION OF COMMERCE [4,I]. While the COMMERCE CLAUSE [1,I] of Article I authorizes congressional displacement of state commercial regulation, the constitutional text is silent regarding the residuum of power left to the states where Congress has not acted. It has long been accepted, however, that the mere grant of authority to Congress—even if unexercised—implies some restrictions on the states. A panoply of terms is applied to this constitutional implication. Among the most popular are the "negative commerce clause" or the "dormant commerce clause."

Surprisingly, there was little discussion at the CONSTITIONAL CONVENTION OF 1787 on the subject of free trade. Consequently, the Supreme Court felt obligated to justify the implied limitation on the state by reference to the events that precipitated the call for a convention rather than to what transpired at that gathering. The ARTICLES OF CONFEDERATION [1] era was marked by commercial warfare between the states. The resulting barriers to national trade, which threatened the vitality and peace of the Union, are often viewed as a primary catalyst for the Convention of 1787.

Judging from the constitutional language alone, one might conclude that the Framers left protection of national trade to congressional supervision rather than judicial enforcement. This expectation, however, does not appear to have been the vision of the principal Framer. JAMES MADISON [3] anticipated that competing economic interests would neutralize each other in Congress and prevent the enactment of national regulation of interstate trade. The commerce clause, explained Madison in a letter written a half-century after the Constitution's drafting, would act "as a negative and preventive provision against injustice among the States themselves, rather than as a power to be used for the positive purposes of the General Government." Under Madison's impasse theory, Congress would be unable to act because of political impediments, and the state would be powerless to act because of limited authority.

Madison's theory did not address the question of who was to bring the states back in line when they transcended their authority. Logic pointed to the courts. If Congress were paralyzed in the face of potent and conflicting local interests, only the courts could protect the national interest in free trade. Few expressed this sentiment better than OLIVER WENDELL HOLMES, JR. [2]. Too often, observed Holmes, state action is taken "that embodies what the Commerce Clause is meant to end." The Union "would be imperiled," he warned, if the Court lacked power to void such laws. The Court's active role in scrutinizing state commercial regulation suggests that most of Holmes's successors have shared his concern.

The Court's dormant commerce clause jurisprudence has two distinctive branches. Under the "discrimination" branch, the Court invalidates state legislation discriminating against INTERSTATE COMMERCE [2]. Under the "undue burdens" branch, the Court will strike down even neutral state regulation if the burden imposed on interstate commerce is clearly excessive in relation to the local benefits.

The discrimination branch has been relatively noncontroversial. Even those who question the propriety of judicial balancing of trade burdens and local benefits generally concede the need for discrimination review. The dormant commerce clause, however, seems an odd vehicle for attacking interstate discrimination. The antidiscrimination provision of Article IV's PRIVILEGE AND IMMUNITIES [3] clause seems far more appropriate.

In its original form, as contained in the Articles of Confederation, the privileges and immunities clause specifically addressed the problem of commercial isolationism, providing that the inhabitants of each state "shall be entitled to all privileges and immunities of free citizens in the several states; and . . . shall have free ingress and regress to and from any other States, and shall enjoy therein all the privileges of trade and commerce, subject to the same duties, impositions and restrictions as the inhabitants thereof." Little evidence exists on why the clause was pared down when carried over to the Constitution. CHARLES PINCKNEY [3], generally believed to have drafted the shorter version, assured the convention that no change in substance was intended. The term "privileges and immunities" probably was seen as sufficiently comprehensive to obviate the need for explicit references to ingress, regress, trade, and commerce.

If the positive command of the privileges and immunities clause were given the broad scope that was likely intended, resort to the commerce clause's negative inferences would be unnecessary for resolution of the discrimination cases. That the Court has not followed this route is attributable largely to PAUL V. VIRGINIA (1869) [3]. *Paul* held that CORPORATIONS [2] were not "citizens" within the privileges and immunities clause. Notwithstanding subsequent construction of the DUE PROCESS [2] and EQUAL PROTECTION [2,I] clauses to encompass corporations as "persons" and the recognition of corporate CITIZENSHIP [1,I] for purposes of Article III's diversity provisions, the holding in *Paul* remains a bar to corporate invocation of the antidiscrimination shield of Article IV.

Although some Justices and commentators believe that the Court may be proceeding under the wrong constitutional provision, almost no one questions the validity of the judicial role in voiding state discrimination against interstate commerce. However, the Court's continued willingness to strike down evenhanded state regulation because of "undue" burdens on the nation's free trade is a matter of substantial controversy. The present scope of congressional power dwarfs whatever James Madison may have anticipated. Moreover, the judicial expansion of the national commercial power is punctuated by the frequency with which Congress exercises its authority. Madison's image of a Congress deadlocked by competing geographic economic interests is seldom visible. Naturally, differences of perspective within Congress sometimes prevent consensus. But Congress has mechanisms to circumvent such stalemates. When impasses occur, Congress can shift decision-making responsibility onto the shoulders of REGULATORY AGENCIES [3] by broad and often standardless delegations of power.

The rationale for the Court's zealous oversight of state commercial regulation has thus been substantially undermined. This led Justice ANTONIN SCALIA [I], in a CONCURRING OPINION [1] in *CTS Corp. v. Dynamics Corp.* (1985) and a dissent in *Tyler Pipe Industries, Inc. v. Washington State Department of Revenue* (1987), to observe that absent rank discrimination—which he suggested is better dealt with under the privileges and immunities clause— the role of invalidating state legislation that unduly burdens free trade properly belongs with Congress. This view parallels another FEDERALISM [2,I] development.

In GARCIA V. SAN ANTONIO METROPOLITAN TRANSIT AUTHORITY (1985) [2], the Supreme Court abdicated any role in preserving the balance of power between the states and the federal government, deciding that the struggle over the scope of Congress's commercial power was best suited for the political arena. The states that petitioned for judicial assistance were told to fight their battle in Congress. This, said the Court, is how the Framers wished the scales of power to be balanced. Yet when a state regulates commerce in a congressional vacuum, the Court is there to ensure that the national economic interest will be adequately protected. The scales are not, after all, allowed to tip according to the political wind. The Court is keeping its thumb on the congressional side.

JULIAN N. EULE

(SEE ALSO: *Dormant Powers* [2].)

Bibliography

EULE, JULIAN N. 1982 Laying the Dormant Commerce Clause to Rest. *Yale Law Journal* 99:425–485.

REGAN, DONALD H. 1986 The Supreme Court and State Protectionism: Making Sense of the Dormant Commerce Clause. *Michigan Law Review* 84:1091–1287.

DOUBLE JEOPARDY
(Update)

Over the past few years, the Supreme Court has decided a substantial number of cases involving double jeopardy issues. For the most part, these decisions continued a trend noted in the *Encyclopedia* of giving additional flexibility to the doctrine, although several notable exceptions expanded the protection provided by the clause. The most significant developments concerned two topics: multiple crimes arising from the same conduct and sentencing. The most disturbing development occurred under the dual-sovereignty doctrine.

In the area of multiple offenses, the Supreme Court continued to adhere to the position that the legislative branch has virtually unlimited power to define as separate crimes and to punish cumulatively individual steps within a criminal transaction and the completed transaction as well. The well-worn test set out in *Blockberger v. United States* (1932) determined whether the offenses are separate by asking if each "requires proof of a fact which the other does not." This has been construed as a rule of statutory construction, which is not controlling within a single prosecution if the LEGISLATIVE INTENT [3] is clear that multiple punishments are intended.

However, where individual crimes arising from the same events are adjudicated separately, a sharply divided Court expanded the protection of the double jeopardy clause beyond the confines of the *Blockberger* test. In *Grady v. Corbin* (1990), the Court concluded that a prosecution for vehicular manslaughter was barred where the defendant had been convicted previously of driving while intoxicated based on the same automobile accident. The Court reasoned that successive prosecutions present dangers that require protection under the double jeopardy doctrine even in circumstances where the two crimes do not constitute the "same offense" under the *Blockberger* test. It formulated a new and certainly more complicated test: The guarantee against double jeopardy is violated by subsequent criminal prosecution when the government establishes an essential element of that crime by proving conduct that constituted an offense for which the defendant has been previously prosecuted.

The decision in *Grady v. Corbin* unsettled the law with regard to the important concept of what constitutes the "same offense." Its immediate practical effect will be to encourage, if not require, the government to prosecute in a single case all charges arising from the same transaction because some of those that share a common element will be barred by the double jeopardy clause if they are prosecuted later. How this decision will be reconciled with the body of related doctrine—and even whether it will stand the test of time given the Court's history of dramatically changing course on double jeopardy issues—remains to be seen. Indeed, the conflicting nature of the Court's double jeopardy jurisprudence was apparent from cases decided during the same term. In *Dowling v. United States* (1990), the Supreme Court determined that EVI-DENCE [2] of criminal conduct was not barred by the collateral estoppel concept of double jeopardy, even though the defendant had been found not guilty in an earlier trial of that criminal conduct. *Dowling* and *Grady v. Corbin* can be reconciled because the crimes in *Dowling* were not part of the same transaction, but the two cases demonstrate that there is no broad consensus within the Court on basic principles, particularly the application of this "same transaction" concept.

In the area of SENTENCING [I], the Court decided a number of significant cases. Although the clause does not apply to civil penalties, the Court concluded that in a very rare case a penalty traditionally considered remedial can be so overwhelmingly disproportionate to the damage caused that it must be considered punishment with a purpose of deterrence or retribution. In this circumstance, presented by a series of penalties in *United States v. Halper* (1989), the double jeopardy clause bars imposition of civil penalties subsequent to criminal conviction and punishment.

The Court has determined that the double jeopardy clause does not in general prohibit the government, pursuant to statutory authorization, from appealing a sentence or prohibit a court from increasing that sentence after review. In contrast, the double jeopardy clause does impose some limits on resentencing in CAPITAL PUNISHMENT [1,I] litigation. In *Bullington v. Missouri* (1981), the Court concluded that the clause prohibits imposing a death sentence on resentencing where a jury initially imposed a life sentence. The trial-type proceedings involved in such a determination render a decision not to impose a death penalty the equivalent of an acquittal at trial. The double jeopardy clause does not, however, bar the trial judge, under statutory authorization, from overriding a jury recommendation of life imprisonment and imposing a death sentence.

The Court concluded that the double jeopardy doctrine permits either resentencing or judicial modification of a sentence in two other areas. First, it held in *Morris v. Mathews* (1986) that where the defendant is convicted of both a jeopardy-barred greater offense and a lesser offense that is not so barred the error may be corrected without resentencing by simply substituting the lesser-included conviction, unless the defendant can demonstrate a reasonable probability that he or she would not have been convicted of the lesser offense absent the joint trial with the jeopardy-barred offense. Second, the decision in *Jones v. Thomas* (1989) held that as long as the resentencing remains within legislatively intended limits an appellate court could modify an initially invalid consecutive sentence by vacating the shorter sentence and crediting the defendant for the time served even after the defendant had fully satisfied the shorter sentence. In reaching this conclusion, the Court dismissed longstanding PRECE-DENT [3] apparently prohibiting resentencing after the defendant had satisfied one of two alternative sentences.

In a disturbing, although not doctrinally surprising, opinion, the Court extended to prosecutions by separate states its very broad HOLDING [2] that double jeopardy is inapplicable where the same conduct is prosecuted by state and federal governments. Reasoning that this dual-sovereignty doctrine rests on the critical determination that two entities draw authority to punish from separate sources of power, the Court concluded in HEATH V. ALA-BAMA (1985) [I] that the doctrine operates between states as it does between state and federal governments.

On first examination, applying the doctrine to two states appears to present no major issues. However, an examination of the facts of the case and the underlying policies presents a different picture. *Heath* involved a kidnapping that began in Alabama and ended in a murder across the nearby state line in Georgia. Pursuant to a plea bargain in Georgia, the defendant avoided the death penalty in exchange for a life sentence. He was then prosecuted in Alabama for the same murder and sentenced to death. The Supreme Court's decision resulted in affirming that death sentence.

At a practical level, the operation of the dual-sovereignty doctrine permitted two states to enjoy all the advantages of multiple prosecutions that the double jeopardy clause was intended to prevent. Admittedly, however, these advantages can accrue to the prosecution whenever the dual-sovereignty doctrine is applied. The major difference in this case is that the two sovereigns were protecting the same policy interest—punishing the taking of human life. When the state and federal government are involved, there has historically been not only a separate source of political power, but also a separate interest protected.

Heath demonstrates that the Supreme Court is steadfast in its commitment to a monolithic and absolute dual-sovereignty doctrine in the context of double jeopardy. Given the expansion of federal JURISDICTION [3] to almost every area of state criminal law, this position is understandable, if not defensible. Currently, the different policy interest protected by the federal prosecution is often imaginary, and the decision in *Heath* makes recognition of this fact unnecessary.

ROBERT P. MOSTELLER

(SEE ALSO: *Criminal Justice System* [I]; *Criminal Procedure* [2].)

Bibliography

LaFave, Wayne R. and Israel, Jerold H.   1985   *Criminal Procedure*. St. Paul, Minn.: West Publishing Co.

Thomas, George C.   1988   An Elegant Theory of Double Jeopardy. *University of Illinois Law Review* 1988:827–885.

DRUG ABUSE

See: Controlled Substance Abuse [I]; Drug Regulation [2,I]

DRUG REGULATION
(Update)

The breadth of congressional power under the COMMERCE CLAUSE [1] to regulate the manufacture, distribution, and possession of psychoactive drugs remains unquestioned. In recent years, however, strong measures taken by the federal and state governments to prevent and punish drug offenses have raised constitutional objections grounded in the BILL OF RIGHTS [1]. The most controversial of these measures has been the use of chemical testing to detect the presence of illicit drugs in a person's urine or other body fluids.

Beginning in the mid-1980s, many public and private employers began to require urine testing as a condition of employment. The FOURTH AMENDMENT [2,I] ban against UNREASONABLE SEARCHES [4,I] is implicated when a governmental agency requires its employees or applicants for employment to submit to urine testing or when the government requires private employers (such as railroads) to test their employees. The collection and subsequent analysis of a person's urine is clearly a "search" for Fourth Amendment purposes, so the constitutional controversy has focused on when such testing is "reasonable" in light of the government's objectives and the employees' interests in personal privacy. It is generally agreed that urine testing is "reasonable," even in the absence of a SEARCH WARRANT [4], if it is based on PROBABLE CAUSE [3], or "individualized suspicion," that a particular employee has used illicit drugs. The controversial question is whether, and under what circumstances, employees can be required to submit to urine testing as part of a random or universal screening program.

In 1989 the Supreme Court upheld two screening programs, rejecting the argument that urine testing is per se unreasonable in the absence of individualized suspicion. However, in upholding testing programs for U.S. Customs agents and for railroad employees, the Court closely scrutinized the governmental objectives and the testing protocols. For example, in NATIONAL TREASURY EMPLOYEES UNION V. VON RAAB (1989) [I], the Court held that the Customs Service's interests in the integrity and safety of its work force and in the protection of sensitive information justified the urine testing of all employees applying for or holding positions involving interdiction of illicit drugs or requiring the carrying of firearms. Taking its cue from

Von Raab, the District of Columbia Court of Appeals subsequently held in *Harmon v. Thornburgh* (1989) that these same interests did not justify the random testing of attorneys in the Justice Department's antitrust division.

Measures taken to suppress drug use have also been challenged under the Eighth Amendment's prohibition against CRUEL AND UNUSUAL PUNISHMENT [2,I]. Trafficking in illicit drugs is typically punishable by lengthy periods of imprisonment, and under many statutes, severe sentences are mandatory. However, in *Hutto v. Davis* (1982), the Supreme Court rejected a proportionality challenge to two consecutive twenty-year sentences for possessing and distributing nine ounces of marijuana, and the Sixth Circuit Court in *Young v. Miller* (1989) refused to set aside a mandatory nonparolable life sentence imposed by Michigan on a female first offender who had been convicted of possessing at least 650 grams of heroin. Acknowledging that the sentence "borders on overkill," that Michigan permits parolable life sentences for armed robbery or second-degree murder, and that only one other state authorized a sentence of such severity for drug offenses, the Sixth Circuit Court nonetheless found no constitutional impediment to "Michigan's efforts to punish major drug traffickers to the fullest extent of the law, even those who are first offenders."

In 1990 the Supreme Court resolved a question discussed at length in the main volumes of the *Encyclopedia*—whether bona fide sacramental use of peyote is protected by the FIRST AMENDMENT [2,I] guarantee of RELIGIOUS LIBERTY [3,I]. In EMPLOYMENT DIVISION, DEPARTMENT OF HUMAN RESOURCES OF OREGON V. SMITH (1990) [I] the Court held that Oregon's criminal prohibition against possession of peyote could constitutionally be applied to sacramental use of the drug and that a state employee could therefore be fired and denied unemployment compensation for having used peyote at a religious ceremony of the Native American Church. The Court's opinion is less noteworthy for the result it reached than for its reformulation of the governing constitutional rule. As noted in the *Encyclopedia*, under the BALANCING TEST [1] articulated in SHERBERT V. VERNER (1963) [4], the issue is whether the state's interest in suppressing use of illicit drugs is sufficiently compelling to override the individual's interest in religious liberty. However, in the peyote case, the Court held that the government is not required to exempt religiously motivated actors from generally applicable and otherwise valid criminal prohibitions.

RICHARD J. BONNIE

Bibliography

ROTHSTEIN, MARK   1987   Drug Testing in the Workplace: The Challenge to Employment Relations and Employment Law. *Chicago-Kent Law Review* 63:683–743.

DRUG TESTING

Increasingly through the 1980s, federal and state governments required testing of a person's blood, urine, breath, and hair to try to determine recent drug or alcohol use. President Ronald Reagan's Executive Order No. 12564 hastened this trend by ordering federal executive agencies to develop and implement such programs for their employees. Other tested groups have included military personnel, defendants subject to pretrial release, probationers, PRISONERS [3,I] and parolees, state employees (especially those involved in law enforcement and transportation), high school and college athletes and other students, women seeking obstetrical care and their neonates, and parents in child abuse and neglect cases.

When required or encouraged by the government, drug-testing programs raise fundamental issues for FOURTH AMENDMENT [2] jurisprudence. Judicial legitimation of such programs may over time lead to substantial alteration of the predominant paradigms of privacy. Such programs present very different issues from the blood test in SCHMERBER V. CALIFORNIA (1966) [4], which the Supreme Court permitted on the grounds that medical personnel administered it based on PROBABLE CAUSE [3] of intoxication and that EXIGENT CIRCUMSTANCES [2] excused the lack of a SEARCH WARRANT [4].

In its 1988 term the Supreme Court upheld in large part two federal testing programs. In SKINNER V. RAILWAY LABOR EXECUTIVES' ASS'N. (1989) [I], the Court upheld regulations of the Federal Railroad Administration that required railroads to test the urine and blood of employees in major train accidents. NATIONAL TREASURY EMPLOYEES UNION V. VON RAAB (1989) [I] upheld urine testing of Customs Service employees as a condition of promotion to positions that involve direct drug interdiction or the carrying of guns. The Court remanded for further consideration the issue of employee testing for promotion to positions allowing access to "sensitive" information.

All Justices agreed that a compelled production and subsequent chemical analysis of urine, blood, and breath are invasions of a person's REASONABLE EXPECTATION OF PRIVACY [I] and therefore a search and possibly a seizure. For the first time outside of a prison context, the Court's majority concluded that a search of a person's body may be analyzed as an ADMINISTRATIVE SEARCH [1,I] and thus may be upheld without individualized suspicion. Applying a test derived from a 1985 school search case, NEW JERSEY V. T.L.O. [3], and developed in the 1986 term in cases involving searches of a junkyard, a probationer's home, and an employee's desk, the Court concluded that a government's "special needs," apart from those of normal law enforcement, can justify dispensing with the presumption that compliance with the warrant clause determines the reasonableness of the search. Such justification occurs at least when a warrant or probable clause requirement (or some lesser standard of individualized suspicion) would interfere with the state's satisfying its special needs.

Finding that such requirements were not practical because they would frustrate the government's achievement of its goals, the Court concluded that the drug-testing programs were reasonable in view of the importance of the state's interest, as weighed against individual privacy interests. It treated the latter as limited because of the reduced privacy expectation of employees, especially those in such highly regulated and scrutinized jobs as railroaders and Customs Service officers. The Court also noted the programs' efforts to employ accurate tests and to obtain employee medical data that could improve test interpretation, recognizing that the accuracy of a test affects a search's reasonableness (as well as the due process validity of any decision, such as dismissal, predicated on the test). To the extent the testing procedure is not particularly reliable, as can easily be the case, the government's interest is reduced.

Although these decisions approve widespread testing without individualized suspicion, they involve only testing that is triggered by a special event such as an accident or an application for promotion. Some lower court decisions have more deferentially reviewed the facts of challenged programs and upheld testing that lacked some of the restrictions crafted into the Customs Service program. Such programs involve more sustained and less predictable invasions of privacy and increase the discretionary power of superiors over subordinates that Fourth Amendment jurisprudence can limit. For example, courts have upheld repeated random or systematic drug tests of employees, such as flight controllers, police officers, and prison guards, without a triggering event. With respect to large classes of employees among whom the interest in deterring drug use is less substantial, lower courts have also approved testing based on an individualized suspicion that is less than probable cause.

As the Court gives more scope to administrative search doctrine, officials may rely increasingly on such searches rather than on a police officer's discretionary decision to search based on an individual suspicion of crime. Any such development will increasingly pose the question of the appropriate standard of JUDICIAL REVIEW [3] in assessing the reasonableness not of an individual officer's acts but of a general legislative or executive program. The evidence justifying the program and the rules limiting discretion will be relevant to such an assessment. While in *Von Raab* the government plausibly hypothesized risks that might arise from a Customs officer's drug use, no evidence of drug abuse within the Customs Service was available. In accepting such hypothetical justifications,

the Court's scrutiny was far from searching. This deference is consistent with the Court's explicit refusal to consider the availability of less intrusive means in determining reasonableness. Yet, in remanding some of the regulations for further consideration, the Court showed that its scrutiny was not of the lowest order.

The Court could confine the reach of these two cases largely to governmental employment by attributing them to the special scrutiny to which public employees may be subjected in hiring, retention, and promotion and thus treat these cases as variants of an UNCONSTITUTIONAL CONDITIONS [4] problem. Yet, the numbers of persons covered by such testing and the intensity of these searches raise the question whether these decisions may signal a basic paradigm shift in Fourth Amendment law away from the presumption that reasonableness is defined by the warrant clause. The BURGER COURT [1] and the REHNQUIST COURT [I] have for years been edging in this direction rhetorically and in a series of ad hoc judgments; whether in retrospect *Von Raab* will be a watershed case cannot yet be determined.

The "special needs" rule risks a doctrinal unraveling of the warrant clause presumption in two ways. If the range and number of administrative searches increase, distinguishing administrative searches with a civil enforcement rationale from criminal enforcement searches will become ever more difficult. Second, a burgeoning of administrative searches will have the doctrinally unjustified and politically unattractive result of affording the criminal suspect more privacy protection than the populace at large.

These decisions are also noteworthy for the extent to which they permit intrusions on the body as a routine matter. They legitimate the role that intruding on bodily privacy can play in disciplining the civilian adult population. No appreciation is found in the Court's opinions that the body is the home of the self. The only noticeable concern is with the shame of scrutinized urination, a matter that testing programs sometimes address by providing only for aural supervision.

Also of note is their impact on the Fourth Amendment values of particularity and informational privacy. Depending on the kind of chemical analyses permitted, drug tests can provide a recent history—whether accurate or not, extending back many weeks—of legal and illegal drug use, which may have occurred solely in the home's privacy. They can also provide information about bodily and psychosomatic conditions such as pregnancy, HIV antibodies, diabetes, epilepsy, and depression.

In other, often more public situations that do not involve the employment relationship, the need to identify and seize a person may present a preliminary practical impediment to drug testing. In MICHIGAN DEPARTMENT OF STATE POLICE v. SITZ (1990) [I], the Supreme Court upheld the constitutionality of temporary seizures at sobriety checkpoints. Officers briefly stopped all cars, examined the driver for signs of intoxication, and presumably observed what was in plain view. Upon finding signs of intoxication, the officer would direct the driver to a side location to examine his license and registration and to test sobriety. The state police established these checkpoints for short periods of time without prior notice to the public and without providing reasons for their location and timing.

The Court reviewed these seizures by applying a reasonableness BALANCING TEST [1] derived from *Brown v. Texas* (1979), but without first making a finding of "special needs" as in *Von Raab*. Presumably the distinction between these two tests is that the Court treats brief seizures of persons in cars upon the highway, even for routine law enforcement purposes, as less intrusive than searches. Subjecting the program's justifications to a more lenient scrutiny than was used in *Von Raab*, the Court easily concluded that the state's interest in a program that is rationally related to deterring drunk driving outweighs the individual's liberty interest in avoiding brief detention.

As in *Von Raab*, the Court refused to base its reasonableness judgment on the availability of other effective means of achieving state objectives that less seriously burden Fourth Amendment values. Accordingly, it refused to consider substantial evidence that checkpoints are far less effective in identifying and apprehending drunk drivers than are seizures based on articulable suspicion. It is too early to tell whether and how the power to seize without individualized suspicion will be combined with a *Von Raab* drug search.

ROBERT D. GOLDSTEIN

(SEE ALSO: *Search and Seizure* [4,I].)

Bibliography

LaFAVE, WAYNE 1987 *Search and Seizure: A Treatise on the Fourth Amendment*. St. Paul, Minn.: West Publishing Co.

SCHULHOFER, STEPHEN 1989 On the Fourth Amendment Right of the Law-Abiding Public. *Supreme Court Review* 1989:87–163.

ZEESE, KEVIN 1989 *Drug Testing: Legal Manual*. New York: Clark Boardman.

ECONOMIC DUE PROCESS

"Economic due process" is the name given to the doctrine that the Supreme Court used to strike down a variety of economic regulations in the first third of the twentieth century. The core of the doctrine is the conception that the central interest protected by the DUE PROCESS [2] clauses is "liberty of contract." Given that assumption, the Court could not justify ECONOMIC REGULATION [2] as a means to redress inequality of bargaining power between contracting parties, such as workers and employers. Moreover, economic legislation that purported to be based on other objectives—such as protecting public health, morals, or safety—was examined by the Court to ensure that the challenged legislation reasonably advanced those objectives.

The doctrine reached its full form in LOCHNER V. NEW YORK (1905) [3], where a bare majority of the Court struck down a state law limiting bakery workers' maximum hours to sixty per week. Because the Constitution protected liberty of contract, economic regulation for its own sake was invalid, and thus, a state legislature could not regulate the hours of bakery workers to protect them from exploitation. A "labor law, pure and simple" would be unconstitutional. The hours of workers could be regulated only to protect the interests within the POLICE POWER [3]—health, safety, welfare, or morality. Even if the legislature passed the law with the stated purpose of protecting workers' health, the Court would still ask whether the law was necessary for that purpose. This inquiry was designed to ensure that the law was not in fact a pretext for forbidden economic regulation.

There were two distinct criticisms of the *Lochner* deci-

sion. One was that the Court did not give sufficient weight to the judgment of the New York legislature that excessive hours of work jeopardized the health of bakery workers. Three of the four dissenting Justices in *Lochner* conceded that New York could not limit bakers' hours to prevent their economic exploitation. They would, however, have accepted New York's judgment that the measure was necessary to protect health. A more fundamental objection was that the Constitution permitted economic regulation for economic motives. A prophetic solo dissent by Justice OLIVER WENDELL HOLMES, JR. [2] disagreed with the Court's major premise that the Constitution protected liberty of contract. He said, "A Constitution is not intended to embody a particular economic theory. . . . It is made for people of fundamentally differing views."

In the three decades that followed, the Court upheld most challenged economic regulations on the ground that they protected public health, safety, or morals. Indeed, in BUNTING V. OREGON (1971) [1] it upheld a law fixing maximum hours for factory workers. However, the Court struck down a significant number of laws that it considered to be interferences with a free market. In ADAIR V. UNITED STATES (1908) [1] and COPPAGE V. KANSAS (1915) [2], the Court invalidated laws that outlawed labor contracts forbidding employees to join labor unions. The Court overturned a minimum wage law in ADKINS V. CHILDREN'S HOSPITAL (1923) [1] and a law that fixed prices in TYSON & BROTHER V. BANTON (1927) [4]. And in NEW STATE ICE COMPANY V. LIEBMANN (1932) [3], the Court invalidated a law that limited business entry for businesses that were not public utilities.

The Court abandoned its free-market approach to the due process clause in NEBBIA V. NEW YORK (1934) [3], where it sustained a Depression-era law fixing minimum prices for milk. A bare majority of the Court concluded that a "state may regulate a business in any of its aspects, including the prices to be charged for the products or commodities it sells." Two years later, in MOREHEAD V. NEW YORK EX REL. TIPALDO (1936) [3], the Court unexpectedly invalidated a law setting minimum wages for women workers. That decision was, however, overruled the following year in WEST COAST HOTEL CO. V. PARRISH (1937) [4]. Since 1937, no decision of the Supreme Court has held an economic regulatory measure invalid under the due process clause.

The decision in *Nebbia* abandoned the idea that business regulation for economic motives was forbidden. During the *Lochner* era, the Court had decided whether laws were reasonably necessary to promote police-power objectives only because it sought to ensure that the police power was not a subterfuge for economic regulation. Once the Court decided that economic regulation need not be justified by the police power, it might have been concluded that economic regulations are valid whether or not they are reasonable, and occasionally, the Supreme Court has said this. In FERGUSON V. SKRUPA (1963) [2], Justice HUGO L. BLACK [1], writing for the Court, said that in rejecting *Lochner* the Court had abandoned the doctrine "that due process authorizes courts to hold laws unconstitutional when they believe the legislature has acted unwisely."

Conventional due process doctrine seems to say, however, that economic regulatory legislation might be invalid if sufficiently unreasonable. In *Nebbia* the Court stated that laws violated due process if they did not have "a reasonable relation to a proper legislative purpose" or if they were "arbitrary." In UNITED STATES V. CAROLENE PRODUCTS CO. (1938) [1], the Court upheld the Filled Milk Act of 1923, which prohibited the shipment of skimmed milk compounded with vegetable oil in interstate commerce. A lower federal court decided that the law lacked RATIONAL BASIS [3] because filled milk was not deleterious to health. The opinion of Justice HARLAN F. STONE [4] said that in the application of the rational basis test, "the existence of facts supporting the legislative judgment is to be presumed, for regulatory legislation affecting ordinary commercial transactions is not to be pronounced unconstitutional unless in the light of the facts made known or generally assumed it is of such a character as to preclude the assumption that it rests upon some rational basis within the knowledge and experience of legislators."

Although the Court, in the *Carolene Products* case, concluded that the Filled Milk Act did rest on a permissible congressional finding that filled milk was injurious to health, its OBITER DICTA [3] suggested that the law could be challenged if the facts presented to the lower court proved that the law's lack of wisdom was not debatable:

"Where the existence of a rational basis for legislation whose constitutionality is attacked depends upon facts . . . such facts may properly be made the subject of judicial inquiry, . . . and the constitutionality of a statute predicated upon the existence of a particular state of facts may be challenged by showing to the court that those facts have ceased to exist."

In one sense, there is no difference between the dictum in *Ferguson v. Skrupa*—that the due process clause does not permit an inquiry into legislative reasonableness—and the dictum of *Carolene Products* that suggests the possibility of a trial to show that a law lacks a rational basis. For more than fifty years, Supreme Court decisions, without exception, have upheld all economic regulations challenged under the due process clause.

In another sense, however, the *Carolene Products* approach has produced a different outcome than would have occurred if the Court had adhered consistently to the *Ferguson* dictum. Lower courts frequently conduct trials to determine whether laws challenged as a violation of due process are reasonable. Occasionally, lower federal courts decide that state or federal laws lack a rational basis. Although the Supreme Court has uniformly reversed those decisions when appealed, the laws may be effectively invalidated when there is no appeal. For example, in *Milnot Co. v. Richardson* a lower federal court decided that the Filled Milk Act—the same law sustained in *Carolene Products*—was unconstitutional because it lacked a rational basis. The federal government, not sympathetic to the objectives of the statute, did not appeal.

A few academic commentators have argued that the Court's withdrawal from judgment in the economic due process area has gone too far. Some have argued that the Court should use the rational basis formula to invalidate laws that have no real purpose except to favor one economic interest at the expense of a competing interest or the public. Indeed, some state courts use the due process clause, or some other provision, in state constitutions in exactly this manner. The Supreme Court, however, has neither acknowledged nor followed that advice. In WILLIAMSON V. LEE OPTICAL COMPANY (1955) [4], for example, the Court sustained a state law forbidding a dispensing optician to duplicate eyeglasses without a prescription from an optometrist or ophthalmologist. Opticians argued, with some merit, that the law was unnecessary to protect public health and that the legislature's real purpose was to give optometrists and ophthalmologists a monopoly on the sale of eyeglasses. The Court answered that the law might encourage people to have their eyes examined more often, although a more candid answer might have been that it did not matter whether the law was unabashed economic favoritism.

All the Justices appointed in the last fifty years have

agreed that the *Lochner* line of decisions represented an abuse of JUDICIAL POWER [3]. The consensus about economic due process is the starting point of current debate about constitutional law. The point of Justice Holmes's *Lochner* dissent was that it was irresponsible for Justices to read their own subjective economic preferences into the due process clause. Is it equally an abuse of power to read the due process clause to overturn state legislation that restricts noneconomic liberties? Justice WILLIAM O. DOUGLAS [2], writing for the Court when it struck down a state ban on BIRTH CONTROL [1] devices in GRISWOLD V. CONNECTICUT (1965) [2], insisted that there was a difference between judging the propriety of laws that "touch economic problems, business affairs or social conditions" and those that involve such personal liberties as "an intimate relation of husband and wife." Justice HARRY A. BLACKMUN [1], writing for the Court in ROE V. WADE (1973) [3], which struck down laws restricting ABORTION [1,I], acknowledged and quoted Holmes's admonition in his *Lochner* dissent that the Constitution "is made for people of fundamentally differing views, and the accident of our finding certain opinions natural and even familiar, or novel, and even shocking, ought not to conclude our judgment upon the question whether statutes embodying them conflict with the Constitution of the United States." The opinion went on, however, to conclude that the due process clause protects "personal rights that can be deemed 'fundamental.'"

Lochner is a discredited and overruled decision, but its ghost continues to haunt contemporary constitutional law debate.

WILLIAM COHEN

(SEE ALSO: *Labor Movement* [I]; *State Police Power* [4].)

Bibliography

COX, ARCHIBALD 1987 *The Court and the Constitution.* Boston: Houghton Mifflin.

HETHERINGTON, JOHN A. C. 1958 State Economic Regulation and Substantive Due Process of Law. *Northwestern University Law Review* 53:13–32.

LINDE, HANS A. 1970 Without "Due Process": Unconstitutional Law in Oregon. *Oregon Law Review* 49:125–187.

MCCLOSKY, ROBERT G. 1962 Economic Due Process and the Supreme Court: An Exhumation and Reburial. *Supreme Court Review* 1962: 34–62.

WONNELL, CHRISTOPHER T. 1983 Economic Due Process and the Preservation of Competition. *Hastings Constitutional Law Quarterly* 11:91–134.

ECONOMIC EQUAL PROTECTION

During the heyday of the doctrine of ECONOMIC DUE PROCESS [I], the EQUAL PROTECTION [2,I] clause took a backseat to the DUE PROCESS [2] clause. In BUCK V. BELL (1927) [1], Justice OLIVER WENDELL HOLMES, JR. [2], called an argument that a law was invalid because its application was confined to an unreasonably small number of people "the usual last resort of constitutional arguments." Still, the "last resort" succeeded, and laws were invalidated under the equal protection clause when burdensome business regulations unreasonably (in the Court's view) exempted some businesses from the burden. In *Smith v. Cahoon* (1931), for example, the Supreme Court invalidated a law requiring compulsory insurance for trucks because it exempted those carrying agricultural products. The next-to-last decision of this kind was *Hartford Steam Boiler Inspection & Insurance Co. v. Harrison* (1937). The Court held that a law forbidding stock insurance companies from acting through salaried agents violated equal protection because the restriction did not apply to mutual insurance companies.

Since 1937, the Court has invalidated an economic regulatory law on the basis of similar reasoning only once: *Morey v. Doud* (1957) struck down an Illinois law regulating the sale of money orders because American Express money orders were exempted by name. In NEW ORLEANS V. DUKES (1976) [3] the Court characterized *Morey* as "the only case in the last half century to invalidate a wholly economic regulation solely on equal protection grounds" and overruled it.

Since 1976, two cases have applied the equal protection clause to "wholly economic regulations," but each case was unique. In METROPOLITAN LIFE INSURANCE COMPANY V. WARD (1985) [3], a bare majority of the Court invalidated a tax on insurance companies because local companies were exempted. This discriminatory tax statute would have been invalid under the COMMERCE CLAUSE [1,I], except that Congress had authorized states to impose taxes that burdened out-of-state insurance companies. The Court concluded that discrimination against out-of-state business was nonetheless prohibited by the equal protection clause. *Allegheny Pittsburgh Coal Co. v. County Commission of Webster County* (1989) invalidated a tax assessor's practice of valuing recently sold property at its sale price for property tax purposes, while valuing property that had not changed hands at a level far below its present market value. In a footnote, the Court commented that its decision was only applicable to an "aberrational" administrative practice that was illegal under state law. The Court did not decide whether the assessor could justify an identical but legally authorized practice on the ground that it was unfair to tax "unrealized paper gains in the value of property."

In a much-cited CONCURRING OPINION [1] in an earlier case, Justice ROBERT H. JACKSON [3] argued that there was a substantial difference between economic due process, which the Court had appropriately rejected, and economic equal protection. In RAILWAY EXPRESS AGENCY V. NEW YORK (1949) [3], the Court upheld a law that prohibited advertising signs on vehicles, but exempted a sign advertising the business of the vehicle owner. The Court lamely concluded that the distinction between signs advertising the vehicle owner's own business and those advertising some other business was reasonable, because New York could reasonably conclude that the latter signs were more distracting. Concurring, Justice Jackson concluded that signs of both classes were equally distracting, but argued that a better reason to uphold the distinction was that New York could decide that it was fair to exempt those who advertised their own businesses. In a much-quoted OBITER DICTUM [3] he argued that a requirement of equality should be given more than lip service in cases of ECONOMIC REGULATION [2]: "There is no more effective practical guaranty against arbitrary and unreasonable government than to require that the principle of law which officials would impose upon a minority must be imposed generally. . . . Courts can take no better measure to assure that laws will be just than to require that laws be equal in operation."

Justice Jackson's dictum has had only a minor influence on Supreme Court decisions. Government lawyers rarely respond to equal protection challenges with the bald reply that the difference in treatment between groups is simply the outcome of INTEREST GROUP [I] politics. Most often, there is an attempt to justify a particular group's exemption from a burden with the argument that exemption promotes a praiseworthy public purpose. The Court has uniformly credited those arguments, no matter how farfetched, in economic regulation cases. In WILLIAMSON V. LEE OPTICAL COMPANY (1955) [4], for example, the Court sustained a law prohibiting opticians from duplicating eyeglasses without a prescription from an ophthalmologist or optometrist. The Court said that a legislature might conclude that although the optician had the ability to duplicate the lenses without a prescription, the prohibition would encourage people to have their eyes examined more often. It is easy enough to show that the public health justification in *Williamson* was an afterthought to uphold a law that the legislature passed to protect the business of two groups of eye-care professionals from competition of a third.

Much contemporary legislation is, in fact, based on interest-group politics. But because the Court has rejected the free-market constitutional command of economic due process, it is doubtful that the Court would accept the argument of a few legal commentators that it should seriously ask whether the outcomes of interest-group pressures further the public good. Questions about whether it is fair to promote the interests of one economic group at the expense of another will likely be left to the political processes for the foreseeable future.

One prominent argument in this area begins by conceding the point that laws can be justified as the outcomes of interest-group politics. So long as government lawyers seek to uphold a law's exemptions and classifications on good-government grounds, however, courts should limit themselves to those arguments and insist that there be a "real and substantial" relationship to those good-government grounds. Critics of this approach argue, among other things, that its adoption would only promote more elaborate legislative "boilerplate," to supply stronger less-than-candid good-government justifications to explain the outcomes of interest-group politics.

Be that as it may, in cases involving economic regulation, economic equal protection has met the same fate as economic due process.

WILLIAM COHEN

(SEE ALSO: *Economic Freedom* [I]; *Economy* [I].)

Bibliography

GUNTHER, GERALD 1972 Forward: In Search of Evolving Doctrine on a Changing Court: A Model for a Newer Equal Protection. *Harvard Law Review* 86:1–48.
LINDE, HANS A. 1975 Due Process of Lawmaking. *Nebraska Law Review* 55:197–255.
SUSTEIN, CASS R. 1985 Interest Groups in American Public Law. *Stanford Law Review* 38:29–87.

ECONOMY

The United States Constitution is much more than the formal document ratified in 1789. It is the preeminent symbol of the American preference for continuity over radical change, a collection of myths that provides a common faith, and a complicated dialogue between written and unwritten rules of law. As such it reflects and embodies many of the conflicting values at the core of American culture. The law itself, as an extended commentary on the Constitution, has perpetuated many of those conflicts by seeking to balance essentially irreconcilable objectives. It has always attempted, with mixed success, to reconcile elitism and democracy, individual opportunity and community, enterprise and equity, growth and stability, competition and cooperation, and freedom and responsibility. Moreover, it has both liberated and encouraged economic growth even as it has tried to make economic institutions responsible and accountable.

The Constitution's Framers could not anticipate the dramatic changes that occurred in the United States during the first half of the nineteenth century. After all, they drafted the document to serve an economy in which most farmers practiced subsistence agriculture and in which factories were rare, transportation limited, banking and credit primitive, and business transactions simple and direct. Nevertheless, the Constitution provided a congenial legal environment during the first phase of industrialization. The rapid expansion of the nation in size and population was an inherently decentralizing force, as the Supreme Court recognized when it began to interpret the COMMERCE CLAUSE [1,I] and the CONTRACT CLAUSE [2]. The Court might have defined constitutional power over the economy in several ways. For example, in explaining the meaning of the commerce clause, it might have prohibited the states from enacting any statutes regarding interstate trade. It might also have ruled that state laws could coexist with federal laws in the absence of direct conflict between the two or that the states could legislate only until Congress decided to address the same subject. But in an age when the fear of centralized power was all-pervasive, particularly in the South, the Court's decisions were inevitably compromises. Although the Court prohibited states from taxing the federal government, blocked them from limiting or excusing debts, denied their right to violate corporate charters, banned them from directly interfering with INTERSTATE COMMERCE [2], confirmed the sanctity of contracts between individuals in two or more states, and granted CORPORATIONS [2] perpetual existence—all important prerequisites to the establishment of national markets—it left the states plenty of responsibilities. They could charter, license, and regulate businesses, and they could regulate working conditions. And because the Constitution provided for a government of ENUMERATED POWERS [2], leaving a broad economic arena to the states under the TENTH AMENDMENT [4], the relationship between federal and state law hinged on the assumption that state statutes were constitutional unless prohibited by the Constitution or preempted by Congress.

In short, even JOHN MARSHALL's [3] most nationalistic decisions reinforced the idea of separate realms of power with separate responsibilities. The Supreme Court's commentary on economic powers did not end with its early decisions regarding the commerce and the contract clauses. Following the depression of 1837, the Court formally recognized a general federal commercial law and a national credit system protected by "impartial" federal courts. That business law provided national rules for the marketplace, but did not entirely displace state rules. Hence, corporations could "forum shop" for the laws, state or federal, best suited to their needs. Then, at the end of the century, the I. M. Singer Company and the Big Four meat-packing firms persuaded the Court to strike down state licensing and tax laws designed to exclude the products of out-of-state corporations. By doing so, the Court may have played an even more important part in creating a continental market than did the railroads.

During the nineteenth century the Constitution was defined as much by the inaction of Congress as by the actions of the Supreme Court. Preoccupied as it was with a host of thorny sectional issues, Congress refused to intervene in new questions concerning the relative powers of the states and the federal government. For example, although the Constitution granted the power to coin money to the national government, Congress did not authorize the issuance of national bank notes until the CIVIL WAR [I]. In the meantime, state-chartered commercial banks issued debt instruments that doubled as the nation's currency. Equally significant, Congress used the central government's power to issue corporate charters, which Marshall had read into the Constitution in 1819, only to create national banks and to encourage a few land-grant railroads. Congress might have used the commerce power to license bridges and highways—a logical extension of the power over interstate trade—but transportation decisions were left almost entirely to the states and to private enterprise. Moreover, although the Constitution permitted Congress to enact uniform BANKRUPTCY [1] laws, Congress used that power seldom and reluctantly, leaving the states to pass extensive debtor legislation.

By failing to limit the states' powers in most economic spheres, the Constitution indirectly encouraged legal experimentation and innovation. So did the structure of government mandated by the Constitution. The tendency of FEDERALISM [2,I] to disperse power to the local level reinforced the dependence of Americans on quasi-governmental associations, such as commercial federations, civic organizations, and booster clubs—organizations that often served as better forums for collective action than did formal institutions of government. Given the decentralized nature of the pre–Civil War political system and the lack of major ideological differences between the POLITICAL PARTIES [3], the controversies over tariffs, banks, and internal improvements reflected localism and particularism more than STATES' RIGHTS [4]. Not only did federalism institutionalize the nation's centrifugal, localistic impulses; it also reinforced the American tendency to view economic conflicts in constitutional and legal terms, and it reduced tension among competing economic groups by providing a variety of jurisdictions in which to fight for their objectives.

By barring certain acts, the Constitution encouraged the states to expand powers indisputably their own, especially their POLICE POWERS [3] over private property. For example, had the EMINENT DOMAIN [2,I] power not been granted to private companies, the construction of bridges, turnpikes, canals, and railroads—and industrial development in general—would have been impeded. Individual property owners could be recalcitrant. Railroads needed to acquire broad ribbons of land; without the state's power of condemnation, the property had to be purchased at great expense on the open market. In 1807 the Schuylkill and Susquehanna Navigation Company failed to complete its canal because of the high prices it had to pay for land and water rights.

But under the new eminent domain statutes, which spread throughout the nation after the 1830s, indirect damages were not subject to compensation, and benefits to property not taken—such as any appreciation in property values—could be deducted from required compensation. Those were important subsidies to public works. The courts also limited the liability of transportation companies for injuries to workers, and the legislatures enacted new laws relaxing penalties for usury and debt.

The transformation of law was linked to the emergence of the business corporation, which tapped a vast pool of small investors, permitted them to transfer and withdraw their funds quickly, spread the risk of investment, and limited their liability. But the railroads grew so fast and became so powerful that by the 1870s and 1880s the promotion of capital investment had given way to demands for regulation in many parts of the nation.

Regulation has served many purposes, including the disclosure of illicit activities, the restraint of monopolies and oligopolies, fact gathering, the protection of industries from harmful competition, publicizing the problems of various businesses, and coordinating business activities. It has also served more ritualistic, almost mythic, purposes consistent with the dictates of CONSTITUTIONALISM [2]. For example, it has maintained the illusion of accountability, the notion that the economy works in rational ways subject to public control. It has also perpetuated the idea that there is a "public interest," not just a multitude of special interests competing for preference in an open market. And it has formally acknowledged free competition, one of the most cherished American values. The classical model of free competition was valued not only because it promoted economic efficiency or even provided maximum individual opportunity but also because it built character and mollified some of the antisocial elements in unrestrained individualism.

The promotion of businesses by the state—such as providing exclusive charters, tax exemptions, land, or capital—had always implied a right to regulate those businesses. That right had been freely admitted, at least by businesses that served the public, such as canals and railroads. But by the end of the nineteenth century, corporations tried to free themselves from restrictions—except when restrictions served their interests. State and federal courts aided them in many ways, such as by limiting the state police powers, exalting freedom of the courts, and devising SUBSTANTIVE DUE PROCESS [4,I] to limit the power of Congress and the state legislatures. Because

many congressional leaders shared the assumptions of the Supreme Court's conservative majority, Congress failed to provide the basic ground rules needed for effective antitrust actions. It did not, and probably could not, define what size business should be. Those who supported antitrust actions were not well armed with evidence concerning the potential impact of that policy on income distribution, on the concentration of wealth, on the efficiency of production, and on a host of related matters.

The American respect for private property and the RULE OF LAW [3], as well as the inability of Congress and the legislatures to decide how big was too big and what constituted "unfair" business practices, made regulation all the more difficult. The SHERMAN ANTITRUST ACT (1890) [4] failed more for this reason than because of opposition from the courts or the power of special interests. Not surprisingly, the regulatory commission became the favored alternative not just to antitrust prosecutions but also to using taxation, federal incorporation, or NATIONAL POLICE POWER [3] to discipline the economy. The Interstate Commerce Commission, created in 1887, set the legalistic precedent of case-by-case regulation, and that approach blended well with the faith of many Progressive politicians in panels of experts working through a process relatively immune from political influence. Many reformers favored regulatory commissions because they considered the political process clumsy and easily corrupted. They also assumed that men of good will could compromise or reconcile their differences if they could find reliable facts and that fact-finding was a job for experts.

At the federal level, the regulatory commission was a child of the Progressive Era, but the number of commissions proliferated during the 1930s with the establishment of the Civil Aeronautics Board, the Tennessee Valley Authority, the Bonneville Power Authority, the Securities and Exchange Commission (SEC), and the multitude of National Recovery Administration code boards. The SEC brought credibility and order to the securities industry largely because the agency's first chairman, James M. Landis, recognized the value of close relations with the stock industry. For example, the SEC provided "advance opinions" in response to specific regulatory questions, a dramatic departure from the formal adjudicatory procedures followed by both the ICC and the Federal Trade Commission (FTC). Yet, despite the number and influence of the NEW DEAL [I] commissions, they did little to change the shape of industrial America. Instead, they showed the limits of commission-style regulation. The reform movement of the 1930s included many competing visions: a cartelized industrial order regulated by business leaders through trade associations; a sink-or-swim free market economy; a corporate state in which government provided both centralized planning and a forum where different interest groups could resolve their differences; and the older Progressive ideal of government as a referee, intervening only to insure that participants followed the rules. The regulatory commission had become a cheap alternative to structural reform.

After WORLD WAR II [I], regulatory commissions faced increasing criticism. Some critics charged that the commissions were elitist and undemocratic: by combining executive, legislative, and judicial functions in appointive bodies, the agencies constituted a "fourth branch of government" that was clandestine, remote, and capricious. Other critics insisted that over time regulatory boards became narcissistic and bureaucratized as the reform impulse suffocated under crushing caseloads and the staggering range of trivial detail encountered in day-to-day deliberations. Others complained that commissions were not independent enough, that they were too subject to political interference, such as being staffed by political hacks and cronies unsympathetic to regulation. Still another criticism was that commissions were easily "captured" by those they regulated, either through direct means or through the subtle process by which the regulator gradually came to speak the same language and to hold the same economic philosophy as the regulated. Finally, many politicians and academics charged that commissions were grossly inefficient, a judgment hard to dispute when cases brought before the Civil Aeronautics Board and the FTC often took years to settle.

Two things happened in the postwar period. First, the old constitutional goal of balancing public and private, individual acquisitiveness and the common welfare, and stability and growth seemed anachronistic—perhaps even faintly absurd—to many Americans who had come of age in the RONALD REAGAN [3,I] era. And second, to most Americans the size of a business became far less important than its sense of social responsibility. During the 1960s and 1970s, Americans discovered the dangers of DDT, phosphates in laundry detergents, propellants in aerosol cans, lead-based paints, nuclear power, radioactive wastes, chemical dumps, oil spills, saccharin, Pintos, Corvairs, Volkswagens, and dozens of other staples of modern industrial society. Economic regulation gave way to social and environmental regulation as the Environmental Protection Agency (1970), the Occupational Safety and Health Review Commission (1970), the Consumer Product Safety Commission (1972), the Mining Enforcement and Safety Administration (1973), the Office of Strip Mining Regulation and Enforcement (1977), and a host of other agencies demonstrated their popularity. In 1981 the EPA alone had more employees than the ICC, FTC, SEC, and Federal Power Commission, even though the youngest of those four had been around for nearly fifty years and the oldest for almost a hundred. Moreover, while "con-

sumers" had little affect on New Deal regulatory policies, the Sierra Club, the National Audubon Society, Common Cause, and many other citizen groups gave the public far greater influence over the new regulation.

Over time, the law has been far more successful in its quest to encourage economic growth than in its representation of interests outside the marketplace. The Framers faced many difficult problems, none more vexing than how to elevate basic principles of law above the push and pull of day-to-day politics without rendering those principles blind to new economic needs. Of necessity, the Constitution transcended time and place. To ensure that the law would be responsive yet responsible, two choices were made: vast economic power was granted to state and local governments to decide their economic futures, and the courts and stand-in regulatory commissions were left to resolve most conflicts. Promotion and regulation were clearly complementary, and they often pulled in the same direction, but the balance inherent in the nineteenth-century law was impossible to maintain.

DONALD J. PISANI

(SEE ALSO: *Environmental Regulation* [2,I]; *Federal Trade Commission Act* [2]; *Interstate Commerce Act* [2]; *Preemption* [3]; *Progressive Constitutional Thought* [3]; *Progressivism* [I]; *Property Rights* [I]; *Regulatory Agencies* [3]; *Securities Law* [4].)

Bibliography

FRIEDMAN, LAWRENCE M. 1985 *A History of American Law.* New York: Simon and Schuster.

——— and SCHEIBER, HARRY N., EDS. 1988 *American Law and the Constitutional Order: Historical Perspectives.* Cambridge, Mass.: Harvard University Press.

HALL, KERMIT L. 1989 *The Magic Mirror: Law in American History.* New York: Oxford University Press.

PISANI, DONALD J. 1987 Promotion and Regulation: Constitutionalism and the American Economy. *Journal of American History* 74:740–768.

EDUCATION
(Update)

Although the first compulsory attendance law was enacted in Massachusetts in 1852, public and private education were almost exclusively governed by state constitutional provisions and statutes until the 1920s. In three landmark constitutional decisions from 1923 to 1927—MEYER V. NEBRASKA (1923) [3], PIERCE V. SOCIETY OF SISTERS (1925) [3], and *Farrington v. Tokushige* (1927)—the Supreme Court affirmed the authority of the states to compel attendance at public or private schools. In so doing, however, it declared that the states may neither abolish private education nor regulate it so severely that private schools are effectively turned into public schools.

The "Pierce compromise," which recognized the role of the state in compelling school attendance, but preserved private alternatives, was premised on the economic rights of private schools, the recognition that there are constitutional limits on the states' legitimate authority to inculcate particular values and attitudes in children, and on natural law theories of the rights of parents to direct the upbringing of their children. Put somewhat differently, parents may choose to supplement the basic education provided by the state by relying on private schools, but governments have no constitutional obligation to pay for private education. Parents may choose a private school that reflects their religious, educational, and other values, but the state has the authority to regulate those schools reasonably to accomplish its legitimate socialization and citizenship objectives.

Meyer and its progeny have never been overruled by the Supreme Court, despite their reliance on now repudiated notions of SUBSTANTIVE DUE PROCESS [4,I] in the economic sphere, and they provide the foundation for all subsequent constitutional decisions in the education field. Only one narrow constitutional exception to compulsory attendance has been fashioned, in WISCONSIN V. YODER (1972) [4], and this exception was for Amish students claiming that modern public high schools undermined their religious faith and practices. Furthermore, state courts, under federal and state constitutional provisions, have restrained state authorities from too closely constraining the operation of private religious schools.

Some modern commentators, however, believe that the "Pierce compromise" would rest more comfortably on FIRST AMENDMENT [2,I] grounds. The idea is that a state monopoly over elementary and secondary education would imperil democratic values as government agencies sought to establish an ideological conformity that would jeopardize the rights of adult citizens to formulate and express their own points of view, particularly with respect to matters of public policy. The underlying assumption is that indoctrination by the state may be as dangerous to freedom of expression as direct government censorship of what speakers may say.

The theme of *Meyer* and *Pierce* was carried forward in *West Virginia Board of Education v. Barnette*, decided by the Court in 1943. A majority of the Justices held that West Virginia could not constitutionally require its students to salute the American flag in violation of their personal beliefs. Justice ROBERT H. JACKSON [3] did not challenge the notion that public schools may seek to inculcate patriotic values, but he held that the compelled expression of belief was an unconstitutional means of achieving that end. Although the case involved Jehovah's Witnesses, the decision rested on the students' freedom of expression, not their right of free exercise of religion.

AMBACH V. NORWICK (1979) [1] reinforces the view that the key factual element in *Barnette* was the coerced declaration of belief. In *Ambach*, the Court held that a state may prefer American citizens to resident aliens in selecting teachers on the theory that citizens are more knowledgeable and effective in communicating American cultural and political values.

Two decades after *Barnette*, the Court, acting under the ESTABLISHMENT CLAUSE [I] of the First Amendment, declared in ENGEL V. VITALE (1962) [2] and ABINGTON TOWNSHIP SCHOOL DISTRICT V. SCHEMPP (1963) [1] that the states and school districts may not require or sponsor SCHOOL PRAYER [I]. The Court, evidencing some skepticism as to whether such prayers ever might be genuinely voluntary, completely abolished sponsored prayer in public schools, even for students wishing to engage in such prayer. In effect, the Court treated the ban on establishing religion as a substantive limit on governmental expression in public schools. In reaching this result, the Court was at pains to distinguish between ritual indoctrination of religion and the study of religion as an academic subject.

But in the years after World War II, the major concern of the federal courts was less the need to cabin state indoctrination than it was to vindicate the rights of African-Americans and other groups to an equal educational opportunity. The landmark decision, of course, was BROWN V. BOARD OF EDUCATION OF TOPEKA, a 1954 decision in which a unanimous Supreme Court declared that segregation of students by race in public schools violated the EQUAL PROTECTION [2,I] clause of the FOURTEENTH AMENDMENT [2,I]. *Brown* was elaborated on in a series of decisions—including GREEN V. COUNTY SCHOOL BOARD OF NEW KENT (1969) [2], SWANN V. CHARLOTTE-MECKLENBURG BOARD OF EDUCATION (1971) [4], KEYES V. SCHOOL DISTRICT NO. 1 OF DENVER (1973) [3], MILLIKEN V. BRADLEY (1974) [3], and *Board of Education of Oklahoma City Public Schools v. Dowell* (1991)—seeking to define unlawful SEGREGATION [4], to establish the legal framework for remedying past RACIAL DISCRIMINATION [3,I] (including the constitutionality of continuing to rely on neighborhood assignment of pupils), to pass on the appropriateness of interdistrict remedies, and to define when a "unitary" or nondiscriminatory school system had been established. Much of the debate centered on what affirmative steps a school district must take, including the busing of children to more remote schools to achieve a racial balance, once a constitutional violation has been proven.

In the 1960s and early 1970s, a number of groups sought to be included under the umbrella of *Brown*, urging that they had been victims of discrimination in the public schools. For example, handicapped students argued that they could not constitutionally be excluded from public schooling, students from poor families urged that the District of Columbia allocated less money to schools in the poorer neighborhoods, and Asian-American students, in LAU V. NICHOLS (1974) [3], alleged that the absence of special instruction in English for students with limited proficiency in English functionally excluded them from a public education in violation of the equal protection clause. These lawsuits met with varying degrees of success.

The era of equal educational opportunity in constitutional litigation largely came to an end in 1973 with the Supreme Court's ruling in SAN ANTONIO INDEPENDENT SCHOOL DISTRICT V. RODRIGUEZ (1973) [4]. Texas relied extensively on local property taxes to support public education, and students from poor districts, with low property values, alleged that the resultant distribution of funds discriminated against them in violation of the equal protection clause. In this context, the Court held that education is not a fundamental interest under the Fourteenth Amendment. Unless a particular group was the object of a SUSPECT CLASSIFICATION [4] (that is, historically disadvantaged groups such as African-Americans), the Court would not apply a rigorous standard of review to relative denials of educational opportunity, but would uphold educational policies that "bear some rational relationship to legitimate state purposes." The Court concluded that the state's interest in local control of education constituted such a legitimate purpose and that local financing was a rational means of achieving it. After *Rodriquez*, and with few exceptions outside the realms of race and alienage (e.g., PLYLER V. DOE, 1982 [3]), equal educational opportunity claims were litigated under federal statutes enacted to protect particular classes of students (for example, the handicapped, students with limited English proficiency, and women) and under state constitutional provisions.

The modern era in constitutional litigation in the education field is dominated by the struggle for the hearts and minds of coming generations of citizens. The public schools have become the battlegrounds for essentially ideological wars. Under a variety of constitutional provisions, most notably the speech and religion clauses of the First Amendment, the Supreme Court has been asked to intervene to resolve disputes over Darwinism and creationism, fundamentalist Christianity and secularism, CONSERVATIVISM [I] and LIBERALISM [I], and feminism and advocacy of traditional roles for women. In addressing these divisive and controversial issues, the Court has tended to focus on the motivation of school authorities. If they make curricular and other choices in good faith and if they seek to advance educational objectives, then the decision is virtually insulated from JUDICIAL REVIEW [3,I]. If, in contrast,

they act to suppress a political ideology or to indoctrinate religious values in children, then their actions may violate the First Amendment.

By way of example, under WALLACE V. JAFFREE (1985) [4], moments of silence are permissible only if their purpose, in context, is not to advance religion. Similarly, according to *Edwards v. Aguillard* (1987), a state may not require that theories of the origin of Homo sapiens contrary to Darwinism be taught if the decision is motivated by religious concerns. And federal appellate courts have held in *Smith v. Board of School Commissioners* (1987) and *Mozert v. Hawkins County Board of Education* (1987) that an emphasis on secular values in textbooks and courses is permissible so long as the impetus is not hostility toward religion.

The socialization perspective also yields insights into constitutional decisions involving students and teachers. In TINKER V. DES MOINES INDEPENDENT COMMUNITY SCHOOL DISTRICT (1969) [4] the Supreme Court held that students may engage in expressive activity in public schools (wearing black armbands to protest the VIETNAM WAR [4,I]) as long as their speech does not threaten a substantial disruption of or material interference with the schools' educational activities. In other words, students may not thwart the schools' ability to communicate, but subject to that caveat, they may express their personal points of view—even if they are inconsistent with those taken by school authorities, thereby reducing the schools' ability to indoctrinate students.

Under BETHEL SCHOOL DISTRICT V. FRASER (1986) [I], *Tinker* is inapplicable to vulgar student expression because limits on such expression are appropriate to schools' educational mission. Furthermore, according to the Court's decision in HAZELWOOD SCHOOL DISTRICT V. KUHLMEIER (1988) [I], *Tinker* protects only the personal speech of students. When they participate in curricular activities—for example, as staff members for a school newspaper organized as part of a journalism course—they must conform to reasonable school policies on the content of the publication. Finally, a majority of the Justices have stated in BOARD OF EDUCATION V. PICO (1982) [1] that library books may be removed from a school library if the books are pedagogically unsuitable or vulgar; they may not be removed because the school board wishes to suppress an ideology with which it disagrees.

A similar analysis may be applied to the academic freedom of elementary and secondary school teachers. If a school district insists on educational grounds that teachers assign particular books, then their academic freedom in the classroom has not been violated, according to a Tenth Circuit decision in *Carey v. Board of Education* (598 F.2nd 535, 1979). If, however, there is a systematic effort to suppress a type of book in order to exclude particular ideas or ideologies, then the school authorities have invaded the academic freedom of the teachers. Thus, for example, it is one thing to exclude books on Russian history because no courses on Russian history are offered or resources are limited; it is quite another thing to do so because the books discuss Marxist ideas.

The current constitutional standard seeks to distinguish between indoctrination and education. It is questionable whether such a distinction can be applied by federal courts in a principled and predictable manner. Schools stress many values: students are told that racial discrimination, drug abuse, and murder are wrong; they are told that democratic participation, civility, and honesty are right. Thus, the source of the distinction between indoctrination and education may lie more in the nature of the values being promulgated than in the process of communication.

MARK G. YUDOF

Bibliography

VAN GEEL, TYLL 1987 The Court and American Education Law. Buffalo, N.Y.: Prometheus Books.
YUDOF, MARK G. 1983 When Government Speaks. Berkeley: University of California Press.
———— 1984 The Quest for the Archimedean Point. Indiana Law Journal 59:527–564.
YUDOF, MARK G.; KIRP, DAVID L.; and LEVIN, BETSY 1991 Educational Policy and the Law, 3rd ed. St. Paul, Minn.: West Publishing Co.

EDWARDS v. AGUILLARD
(1987)

See: Creationism [I]

EICHMAN, UNITED STATES v.
(1990)

See: Flag Desecration [I]

EIGHTH AMENDMENT

See: Cruel and Unusual Punishment [2,I]; Punitive Damages [I]

ELECTED JUDICIARY

Federal judges are appointed by the President, with the advice and consent of the Senate. Appointment is for life. Although there was substantial disagreement among the delegates to the CONSTITUTIONAL CONVENTION OF 1787 [1] about how to select judges, ALEXANDER HAMILTON's [2] proposal for lifetime presidential appointments ultimately prevailed and has remained intact for two centuries.

This system was not without its critics, however. Chief among them was THOMAS JEFFERSON [3], who argued that the independence of the judiciary should be subject to the people's will. While President, Jefferson urged that federal judges should be removed from office upon the recommendation of Congress to the President. In his old age, Jefferson expressed regret that the Constitution did not provide for the removal of judges on a simple majority vote of the legislature, the branch most responsive to the public will. Many historians have attributed Jefferson's antipathy toward the judiciary to his personal animosity toward his distant cousin, Chief Justice JOHN MARSHALL [3].

Initially, the states also established appointive systems for the selection of judges. Five states entrusted the appointive power to the governor, and eight vested the appointive power in one or both houses of the legislature. To this day, the legislature selects most judges in Connecticut, South Carolina, and Virginia, and state supreme court justices are elected by the legislature in Rhode Island.

Gradually, however, states began adopting systems by which judges were popularly elected. Public perception that property owners controlled the judiciary led to reform, initially at the lower trial court levels. In 1832, Mississippi became the first state in which all judges were popularly elected. An electoral system was adopted in New York at the New York Constitutional Convention of 1846. By the time the CIVIL WAR [I] began, twenty-four of the thirty-four states had established elected judiciaries. Newly admitted states all adopted popular election for most judges.

Disenchantment with the popular election of judges grew during the latter half of the nineteenth century. Judicial candidates were invariably selected by political machines, which typically controlled them after their election. Judicial corruption and incompetence became commonplace. In 1906, in his classic address on the "Causes of Popular Dissatisfaction with the Administration of Justice," ROSCOE POUND [3] claimed that "putting courts into politics, and compelling judges to become politicians in many JURISDICTIONS [3] . . . has almost destroyed the traditional respect for the bench." By the turn of the century, several states converted their judicial elections into nonpartisan races. Today, nonpartisan elections are used to select most or all judges in seventeen states. Only thirteen states still utilize partisan elections to select most or all judges.

A return to the appointive system, utilizing a commission to make nominations, was endorsed by the American Bar Association in 1937. Three years later, Missouri became the first state to adopt this scheme, since known as the Missouri Plan. Thirty-one states now use some variation of the plan for selection of at least some of their judges. In many of these states, the appointment is not for life, however. The judge serves a limited term and must face the voters in a retention election. Normally, retention elections are uncontested. In 1986, however, a well-financed campaign against the retention of three justices of the state supreme court in California succeeded in removing them from the court.

The rising cost of election campaigns for judicial offices has led to increasing concerns about the propriety of campaign fund-raising by judges. In many states, million-dollar campaigns for state supreme court seats represent the largest share of judicial campaign expenditures and large corporations are major contributors to the campaigns. In 1986, for example, five justices of the Texas Supreme Court received $387,700 in campaign contributions from Texaco and Pennzoil while a lawsuit between them was pending before the court.

Unfortunately, the debate between proponents of judicial independence and those who exalt judicial accountability frequently masks a hidden agenda. Thus, in one era, those with a liberal agenda decry the entrenched power of a conservative judiciary; in another era, liberal judges are defended with fervent loyalty to the concept of judicial independence.

At a time when political campaigns have been reduced to raising large campaign chests to finance blizzards of fifteen-second television commercials, however, the wisdom of subjecting judges to election contests must be seriously questioned. In political campaigns the complex issues being decided by judges tend to be oversimplified. Frequently, an emotional issue such as CAPITAL PUNISHMENT [1,I] or ABORTION [1,I] becomes the campaign's focal point. The risk becomes substantial that judicial outcomes will become simple reflections of the prevailing political winds. The death penalty offers a startling example. The three justices removed from the California Supreme Court in 1986 were subjected to a bitter campaign that characterized voting for their removal as "three votes for the death penalty." After they were replaced, the affirmance rate in review of death penalty judgments jumped from 7.8 percent to 71.8 percent, with very few precedents being overtly overruled. Nationally, there is a close correlation between the method of selection of justices of a state supreme court and that court's affirmance rate in death penalty appeals. For the period 1977–1987, death penalty affirmance rates varied among state supreme courts according to manner of judicial selection as follows:

Executive appointment:	26.3%
Uncontested retention elections:	55.3%
Nonpartisan contested elections:	62.9%
Partisan contested elections:	62.5%
Legislative appointments:	63.7%

The dependence of judges upon traditional sources of campaign funds also raises serious questions about their ability to remain impartial when their campaign supporters appear as litigants or lawyers in cases before them. The Code of Judicial Conduct, adopted by the American Bar Association in 1972, does not require a judge to disqualify himself or herself if a campaign contributor is a party to a case.

Often when lawyers have a choice of filing a case in state or federal court, they opt for federal court because they have greater confidence the case will be decided by an impartial tribunal, unaffected by the vagaries of local politics. Even the most conscientious state judges have expressed discomfort with the prospect of campaigning for reelection and with that prospect's subliminal impact upon their decision-making process. As California Supreme Court Justice Otto Kaus put it, "It's hard to ignore a crocodile in your bathtub."

Although many of those appointed to the state and federal benches are politicians before they get there, the goal should be to permit them to cease political activity once they put on their robes. At the federal level, that goal has been largely achieved. At the state level, however, it does not appear that an elected judiciary can be insulated from the corrupting influence of campaign fund-raising. A 1971 report of the American Bar Association concluded, "There is no harm in turning a politician into a judge. He may become a good judge. The curse of the elective system is that it turns every elected judge into a politician."

GERALD F. UELMEN

Bibliography
BERKSON, LARRY; BELLER, SCOTT; and GRIMALDI, MICHELLE 1981 *Judicial Selection in the United States: A Compendium of Provisions.* Chicago: American Judicature Society.
DUBOIS, PHILLIP L. 1980 *From Ballot to Bench: Judicial Elections and the Quest for Accountability.* Austin: University of Texas Press.

ELECTION FINANCE

See: Campaign Finance [1,I]

ELEVENTH AMENDMENT
(Update)

The Eleventh Amendment is at the center of an important debate about state accountability under federal law. Part of the debate is historical: What was the amendment originally intended to do? Part of the debate concerns modern doctrine: What should the amendment mean today?

Everyone agrees that the Eleventh Amendment was adopted to overturn the result reached by the Supreme Court in CHISHOLM V. GEORGIA (1793) [1]. In *Chisholm*, the Court heard a case brought by a citizen of South Carolina against the state of Georgia on a contract. The suit involved no question of federal law. It was brought under a provision of Article III conferring jurisdiction over "Controversies between a State and Citizens of another State." Despite Georgia's claim of SOVEREIGN IMMUNITY [4] from suit, the Court held that Georgia could be compelled to appear.

The amendment provides: "The Judicial power of the United States shall not be construed to extend to any suit in law or equity, commenced or prosecuted against one of the United States by Citizens of another State, or by Citizens or Subjects of any foreign state." The historical debate concerns not whether but how the amendment was intended to overrule *Chisholm*. There are two ways to understand what the adopters of the amendment intended.

The first is to read the amendment as *forbidding* suits brought against states by out-of-state citizens or by foreign citizens or subjects. Under this reading, federal courts cannot take jurisdiction over such suits, even if a federal question is involved. The second is to read the amendment as *repealing* a jurisdiction that had previously been authorized. Under this reading, suits cannot be brought against states by out-of-state citizens or by foreign citizens or subjects merely because of the character of the parties. But if there is any other basis for jurisdiction, such as the existence of a federal question, suits are permitted. Under either reading of the amendment, ADMIRALTY AND MARITIME JURISDICTION [1] is not affected, for the amendment refers only to suits "in law or equity."

The Supreme Court was not forced to choose between the two readings of the amendment until after the CIVIL WAR [I]. Eventually, the Court chose to read the amendment as *forbidding* jurisdiction whenever an out-of-stater or a foreigner sued a state, as a way of protecting southern states from suit under the federal CONTRACT CLAUSE [2] after they defaulted on state-issued revenue bonds. The Court then filled in the "missing" term of the amendment by holding in *Hans v. Louisiana* (1890) that the underlying principle of the amendment required that suits by instaters be forbidden as well. In this century, the Court has further expanded the prohibition of the amendment by reading it to prohibit suits by foreign countries (*Principality of Monaco v. Mississippi*, 1934) and in admiralty (*Ex parte New York, No. 1*, 1921).

In recent years, a number of legal scholars have argued that reading the amendment as only *repealing* the party-based jurisdiction of Article III is historically more accurate. Four Justices of the Supreme Court, led by Justice WILLIAM J. BRENNAN [1,I], have shared this view and have argued that modern doctrine should be brought into line with this understanding. In *Pennsylvania v. Union Gas Co.* (1989), however, a majority of the Court refused to incorporate this historical view into modern doctrine.

Although the Court reads the Eleventh Amendment to forbid federal court jurisdiction even when federal law provides the basis for private parties' suits against the states, the prohibition may be avoided or overcome in a number of ways. First, a state may waive its sovereign immunity by a voluntary appearance. As *Edelman v. Jordan* (1974) illustrates, however, a state may raise a sovereign immunity defense for the first time on appeal after having made a voluntary appearance at trial and having lost on the merits of the dispute. Second, the Supreme Court held in *Cohens v. Virginia* (1821) that the Eleventh Amendment does not apply to appeals to the Supreme Court from the state courts. Third, a state's subdivisions are not protected by the amendment. Under the principle enunciated in *Lincoln County v. Luning* (1890) a municipality, county, or school board may be sued in federal court under federal law without regard to the Eleventh Amendment.

Fourth, suit may be brought against a state officer for prospective relief. The foundation case is *Ex parte Young* (1908), in which the Court permitted an INJUNCTION [2] prohibiting a state officer from acting unconstitutionally. The principle was expanded to permit injunctions ordering affirmative actions by state officials in *Edelman v. Jordan* (1974). But the same decision held that a federal court is forbidden to award monetary relief that will necessarily come out of the state treasury.

Finally, Congress may abrogate the states' sovereign immunity by statutes explicitly so providing. Under an abrogating statute, a state may be sued directly for the retroactive monetary relief otherwise unavailable under *Edelman*. The first case to allow congressional abrogation was *Fitzpatrick v. Bitzer* (1976), which sustained a statute enacted under the FOURTEENTH AMENDMENT [2,I]. The Court suggested in *City of Rome v. United States* (1980) that statutes passed under the FIFTEENTH AMENDMENT [2] could also abrogate state sovereign immunity. Most recently, the Court sustained an abrogating statute passed under the COMMERCE CLAUSE [1,I] in *Pennsylvania v. Union Gas* (1989). The combined reach of the Fourteenth Amendment and the commerce clause is such that Congress has considerable freedom to abrogate state sovereign immunity so long as it employs language making its intention clear.

After the Court's decision in *Union Gas*, the debate

among the Justices over the original meaning of the amendment may have lost most of its practical significance. Under current doctrine there appears to be no significant constraint on the power of Congress to authorize suit against the states, beyond the limitations inherent in the ENUMERATED POWERS [2] under which Congress has acted. This position is not greatly different from that which would be achieved if the Eleventh Amendment were read as merely repealing party-based jurisdiction, leaving intact FEDERAL QUESTION JURISDICTION [2] for private suits brought under valid federal law. The most important difference is that the present doctrine requires Congress to speak clearly in lifting the states' Eleventh Amendment immunity from suit in federal court.

WILLIAM A. FLETCHER

Bibliography

FLETCHER, WILLIAM A. 1983 A Historical Interpretation of the Eleventh Amendment: A Narrow Construction of an Affirmative Grant of Jurisdiction Rather than a Prohibition Against Jurisdiction. *Stanford Law Review* 35:1033–1131.

GIBBONS, JOHN J. 1983 The Eleventh Amendment and State Sovereign Immunity: A Reinterpretation. *Columbia Law Review* 83:1889–2005.

ORTH, JOHN V. 1987 *The Judicial Power of the United States: The Eleventh Amendment in American History.* New York: Oxford University Press.

EMINENT DOMAIN
(Update)

One of the most challenging and enduring puzzles in American constitutional law is how one distinguishes a compensable TAKING OF PROPERTY [4,I] from a legitimate and noncompensable exercise of the POLICE POWER [3]. To suggest the Supreme Court's approach to the question, Harry N. Scheiber, author of the *Encyclopedia*'s principal article on eminent domain, looked back and away from the Court to Chief Justice LEMUEL SHAW [4] of Massachusetts. Shaw had observed in 1839 that much depends "upon the nature of the exigencies as they arise, and the circumstances of individual cases." As of 1985, Scheiber concluded, Shaw's view "lacked prescriptive potential, but it has proved remarkably accurate in predicting the direction that the law would take—and the perplexities that would beset the best efforts of lawmakers and judges to produce definitive formulae."

Even in 1985, however, there were at least some "definitive formulae" by which to identify regulatory takings. First, it had long been thought that government regulatory action resulting in physical invasion of private property should always be regarded as a taking, no matter how trivial the intrusion, and this per se rule was firmly endorsed by the Court in LORETTO V. TELEPROMPTER, INC. (1982) [3], at least if the government invasion was "permanent." A second per se rule—that government regulation of nuisance-like activity was never to be regarded as a taking, no matter how substantial the burden of the regulation—was also clear enough.

Neither of these per se rules could be of much importance in the modern regulatory state, for modern regulation seldom results in physical invasions and commonly reaches beyond the mere control of nuisances. Yet, in this broad and important middle ground, the Court in 1985 was self-consciously drawing the line between takings and the police power in just the ad hoc fashion that Shaw had long ago foreseen. The two per se rules aside, the Court's approach was one of balancing a number of considerations, including the mix and breadth of benefits and burdens worked by a regulation, its economic impact, and the extent of its interference with concrete investment-backed expectations. The ad hoc approach played into the two per se rules as well, because temporary physical invasions were to be examined in terms of balancing and because the characterization of something as a nuisance is itself a matter of more or less.

Have matters changed since 1985? The answer depends in large part on three cases decided by the Court in 1987: *Nollan v. California Coastal Commission, Keystone Bituminous Coal Association v. DeBenedictis,* and *First English Evangelical Lutheran Church v. County of Los Angeles.* Unfortunately, the meaning of these cases is hardly clear. Some analysts see in them an unwelcome move away from ad hoc balancing. In their view, the Court has now confirmed the two per se rules mentioned above and added more, such that the law of regulatory takings is being resolved into a series of categorical "either–ors." *Either* a regulation (controlling other than nuisances) is categorically a taking because it results in a permanent physical invasion, specifically undermines a distinct investment-backed expectation, or totally eliminates the property's economic value, *or* it is categorically not a taking at all. But other commentators see in the 1987 decisions yet more evidence that the Court remains unable to develop what Scheiber called "definitive formulae."

The foregoing disagreement aside, there are other puzzles in the takings cases of 1987. *Nollan* found a taking where the regulatory authority had conditioned a development permit on the property owners' dedication of a lateral easement of public passage across their land. This decision suggests that some regulatory programs will be subjected to heightened judicial scrutiny in the course of determining takings questions, but it is far from clear how broadly this suggestion should be read. *Keystone Bituminous,* in the course of upholding Pennsylvania's Subsidence Act against a takings claim, seems to overrule the opinion of Justice OLIVER WENDELL HOLMES, JR. [2] in *Pennsylvania Coal Company v. Mahon* (1922), the centerpiece of regulatory takings law; yet the Court never says as much. And Justice JOHN PAUL STEVENS [4,I], in his dissent in *First English Evangelical Lutheran Church*, poses a nice problem for the Court's endorsement in that case of INVERSE CONDEMNATION [2] as a remedy for regulatory takings.

First English finally announced what had been anticipated ever since the dissenting opinion of Justice WILLIAM J. BRENNAN [1,I] in *San Diego Gas and Electric Company v. City of San Diego* (1981). *First English* holds that in the event of regulatory takings, property owners are entitled to the JUST COMPENSATION [3] required by the Fifth Amendment, including interim DAMAGES [2] for the period the offending regulation remains in effect. "Once a court determines that a taking has occurred, the government retains the whole range of options already available—amendment of the regulation, withdrawal of the invalidated regulation, or exercise of eminent domain." But amendment or withdrawal no longer permits the government to escape liability, as it did before. Once the taking has occurred, "no subsequent action by the government can relieve it of the duty to provide compensation for the period during which the taking was effective."

Of all that the Court has decided about takings since 1985, only the remedy of inverse condemnation appears to be clear, yet even it is cloudy. The cloud looms because of the Court's admonition that it is not dealing "with the quite different questions that would arise in the case of normal delays in obtaining building permits, changes in zoning ordinances, and the like which are not before us." Here a temporary loss of use might not be a taking at all. But how, Justice Stevens wonders, is one to draw the line between such "everyday regulatory inconveniences" and compensable temporary takings? In any event, if a regulation can affect a significant percentage of some property's *value* without being held a taking—and this is clearly the law—then why should a regulation not be allowed to affect as well a significant percentage of the property's useful *life*?

The law of takings seems little clearer today than it did in 1985, inverse condemnation *in principle* aside.

JAMES E. KRIER

(SEE ALSO: *Environmental Regulation* [2,I]; *Property Rights* [I]; *Regulatory Agencies* [3].)

Bibliography

SYMPOSIUM 1988 The Jurisprudence of Takings. *Columbia Law Review* 88:1581–1794.

EMPLOYMENT DIVISION, DEPARTMENT OF HUMAN RESOURCES OF OREGON v. SMITH
110 S.Ct. 1595 (1990)

Two drug and alcohol abuse counselors were fired from their jobs after ingesting the hallucinogenic drug peyote during a religious ceremony of the Native American Church. They were subsequently denied unemployment compensation by the state of Oregon because the state determined they had been discharged for work-related "misconduct." The workers filed suit, alleging that the denial of compensation violated the free exercise clause of the FIRST AMENDMENT [2,I]. The Supreme Court disagreed by a vote of 6–3.

If the Court had handled *Smith* as it had handled most of its previous cases in the field of RELIGIOUS LIBERTY [3,I], it would have first asked whether Oregon had a COMPELLING STATE INTEREST [1] to deny unemployment compensation to the fired workers. If Oregon could demonstrate such an interest, and the denial of compensation was narrowly tailored to further that end, the denial would have been upheld. But the Court did not treat *Smith* as it had previous cases. Instead, it used *Smith* to abolish the compelling-interest standard for challenges brought under the free exercise clause.

Writing for five members of the Court, Justice ANTONIN SCALIA [I] made the astonishing claim that the Court had never really applied the compelling-interest standard to free exercise claims. According to Scalia, the Court had "never held that an individual's religious beliefs excuse him from compliance with an otherwise valid law prohibiting conduct that the State is free to regulate." Of course, the Court had held precisely that in several cases, most notably CANTWELL V. CONNECTICUT (1943) [1] and WISCONSIN V. YODER (1972) [4]. But Scalia noted that these cases implicated other constitutional rights besides free exercise, and he suggested that those other rights were the decisive factor in the Court's decisions to hold unconstitutional particular applications of certain general laws. In *Cantwell*, the invalidated licensing law impinged on the FREEDOM OF SPEECH [2,I]; in *Yoder*, the compulsory education law infringed on the "right of parents . . . to direct the education of their children." Scalia concluded from this that only when the free-exercise clause is joined with other constitutional protections may it invalidate particular applications of general laws. As a practical matter, this means that the free exercise clause alone means very little. Generally applicable laws that do not implicate other constitutional rights are constitutional, no matter how difficult they make it for certain persons to practice their religion; indeed, it is conceivable that a generally applicable law could destroy certain religious groups entirely and yet survive a free exercise challenge under Scalia's approach. Only laws that expressly seek to regulate religious beliefs or to proscribe certain actions only when they are engaged in for religious reasons violate the free exercise clause according to the Court's new standard.

Concurring in the judgment, but disavowing the Court's reasoning, Justice SANDRA DAY O'CONNOR [3,I] attacked the majority opinion as "incompatible with our Nation's fundamental commitment to individual religious liberty." Carefully recalling prior precedents, O'Connor showed that the compelling-interest test had been applied much more consistently by the Court in free exercise cases than Scalia had suggested. O'Connor further defended the test as an appropriate method by which to enforce "the First Amendment's command that religious liberty is an independent liberty. . . ." Applied to the case at hand, O'Connor believed that the free exercise claim could not prevail, however, because exempting the two workers from drug laws would significantly impair the government's "overriding interest in preventing the physical harm caused by the use of a Schedule I controlled substance."

Justices THURGOOD MARSHALL [3,I], WILLIAM J. BRENNAN [1,I], and HARRY A. BLACKMUN [1,I] joined most of Justice O'Connor's concurring opinion, but they disagreed with her ultimate conclusion, arguing that enforcement of drug laws against the religious ingestion of peyote was in no way necessary to fulfill the state's legitimate interest in circumscribing drug use. The state had argued that an exemption of the claimants in *Smith* would invite a flood of other claims for exemption to drug laws based on religious beliefs; but Blackmun pointed out that many states already have statutory exemptions for religious peyote use and have suffered no such difficulty.

The debate on the Court that erupted in *Smith* over what standard to apply to free exercise claims was dramatic; and yet it was not entirely unexpected, having been foreshadowed in several previous cases, including GOLDMAN V. WEINBERGER (1986) [I] and O'LONE V. ESTATE OF SHABAZZ (1987) [I]. It also had been preceded for some years by a vigorous debate among scholars such as Walter Berns and Michael McConnell. Berns had long characterized the Court's decision in *Yoder* as contrary to American republicanism. His view clearly triumphed in *Smith*. Whether or not the Court's new approach is any better than its old one, however, is open to question.

One can certainly understand why the Court might want to restrict challenges under the free exercise clause. When only the members of a particular religious group may use an illegal drug or ignore compulsory education laws, the free exercise clause appears to undermine the equality before the law established by the rest of the

Constitution. Scalia's approach seeks to avoid this contradiction by defining free exercise in terms of other constitutional rights, such as freedom of speech, FREEDOM OF ASSOCIATION [I], and EQUAL PROTECTION [3,I]. Scalia has a keen theoretical mind, and one can readily see the analytical power of his approach. Under his scheme, religious liberty will be protected by general rights applicable to all, rather than by specific exemptions granted only to those who hold peculiar religious beliefs. The principle of equality before the law will be maintained. That this approach may indeed afford protection to religious liberty is demonstrated by the recent development of the doctrine of EQUAL ACCESS [I], which is premised on free-speech and free-association protections rather than the free-exercise clause.

Yet one can legitimately wonder—as Justice O'Connor did in *Smith*—whether Scalia's approach will actually protect the free exercise of religion to its fullest extent. One suspects that it could only do so if the Court were willing to give an expansive reading to other constitutional rights in order to make up for its restricted interpretation of free exercise. Indeed, Scalia himself had to resort to an UNENUMERATED RIGHT [I] of parental control over a child's education to explain the Court's previous ruling in *Wisconsin v. Yoder* within his framework. But the REHNQUIST COURT [I] appears to be in no mood to give a broad reading to any rights just now, which makes its evisceration of the free exercise clause all the more troubling.

Government today wields a wide array of regulatory powers that the Court no longer even presumes to question; the "compelling state interest" test may be the only practical way to insulate religious groups from the destructive effects of such regulatory powers. The Court's failure to appreciate this fact raises troubling questions about its commitment to religious freedom for all.

JOHN G. WEST, JR.

Bibliography

BERNS, WALTER   1976   *The First Amendment and the Future of American Democracy*, Chapter 2. New York: Basic Books.
McCONNELL, MICHAEL W.   1990   The Origins and Historical Understanding of Free Exercise of Religion. *Harvard Law Review* 103:1409–1517.

ENTITLEMENT

Both the Fifth Amendment and the FOURTEENTH AMENDMENT [2,I] protect "life, liberty or property" against deprivation "without due process of law." At least according to the constitutional text, when citizens seek to challenge a government's action as a violation of the due process clause, they must adduce some interest in "life, liberty or property" of which they have been deprived.

In the field of PROCEDURAL DUE PROCESS OF LAW [3,I], the Supreme Court traditionally read the phrase "life, liberty or property" as an undifferentiated whole, giving individuals the right to appropriate NOTICE [3] and hearing whenever the government subjected them to "grievous loss." This broad interpretation, however, was often limited by the RIGHT/PRIVILEGE DISTINCTION [3], according to which benefits that the government was not legally obligated to grant could be denied or terminated without constitutional constraint. Thus, a "grievous loss" occasioned by a denial of "largess" would not trigger constitutional requirements of fair procedure under the due process clause.

In the years following WORLD WAR II [I], as the involvement of government in social welfare programs and the domestic economy continued to increase, it became clear that government allocation of largess constituted a powerful mechanism for government oppression if left unconstrained. In GOLDBERG V. KELLY (1970) [2], in the course of an opinion imposing constitutionally mandated procedural requirements on the termination of WELFARE BENEFITS [4], the Court announced in obiter dictum the elimination of the largess or privilege exception to the demands of due process. The claim that "public assistance benefits are a privilege and not a right" was unavailing, according to Justice WILLIAM J. BRENNAN [1,I], because "welfare benefits are a matter of statutory entitlement for persons qualified to receive them," functioning more like "property" than "gratuity." The loss of benefits imposed a "grievous loss" and thus called forth the demands of due process.

Two years later, in BOARD OF REGENTS V. ROTH (1972) [1] and *Perry v. Sinderman* (1972), the Court moved the concept of "entitlement" from the margins of due process doctrine to its core. In passing on the claims of untenured professors employed by state colleges to hearings before being dismissed from their posts, the majority opinions of Justice POTTER STEWART [4] took the position that it was not the "weight" of interests affected by public action that invoked the protection of due process but their "nature." Rather than evaluating the "grievousness" of injuries inflicted by discharge, the Court required the instructors to demonstrate that their discharge amounted to a deprivation of technically defined "liberty" or "property."

The liberty protected by due process was delineated in *Roth* as a matter of federal constitutional law. The Court referred to historically rooted concepts of liberty: beyond freedom from bodily restraint and assault, it included the "privileges long recognized as essential to the orderly pursuit of happiness by free men." Property interests, on the other hand, were said to find their source outside the Constitution in "rules or understandings that secure certain benefits and that support claims of entitlement to those benefits." Beyond the areas protected as

liberty, therefore, an entitlement grounded in "some independent source such as state law" was a necessary condition for a claim to procedural due process protection. Because under state law Roth's employment was terminable at will, he had no property entitlement upon which to base his demands for due process. The Court left it open for Perry to show some "binding understanding" not embodied in the written terms of his contract that could support a "legitimate claim of entitlement."

In subsequent cases, the Court clarified the proposition that legislative alteration of the terms of the entitlement does not trigger a requirement of notice and hearing, but only administrative action predicated upon alleged failures to meet the terms of the entitlement. Decisions involving prison release and good-time credit programs, like *Wolff v. McDonnell* (1974) and *Greenholtz v. Inmates of Nebraska Penal and Correctional Complex* (1979) have extended the entitlement concept to conditions of liberty conferred by state laws or regulations. A hearing before deprivation of credit toward release or other prison perquisites granted to a duly sentenced prisoner is required only when the law granting the liberty is sufficient to vest an entitlement.

The reliance on positive law entitlements outside of the Constitution to define the applicability of constitutional protection forces the Supreme Court to spend considerable effort defining what constitutes a sufficiently clear and binding entitlement to invoke the protection of procedural due process. In *Roth* the Court differentiated between an unprotected "unilateral expectation" and a "legitimate claim of entitlement" that could support a property interest. Subsequent opinions have looked primarily to statutes, regulations, and contractual provisions to draw the line of demarcation, but have not required great specificity of entitlement to generate protection. Positive law that leaves official decision makers entirely unconstrained in dispensing benefits or employment has been held to create no protected interests; when criteria in positive law provide substantive limitations on official discretion binding on the decision-makers, even standards as vague as "good cause" or "probable ability to fulfill the obligations of a law abiding life" have enabled citizens to claim the protection of due process.

A great deal has been held to turn on the particular official choice of language, as well as state court glosses on it. The difference between benefits that "shall be granted if" and that "shall not be granted unless" particular criteria are met can lead to outcomes that vary considerably among cases that seem otherwise quite similar. Under current doctrine, policymakers who seek to control the decisions of street-level bureaucrats with written criteria for actions must pay the price of providing due process to the citizens whom those decisions affect. Given the rule-governed nature of most modern bureaucracies, this doctrine means hearings are widely available. It also means, however, that policymakers who seek to escape federal due process constraints have an incentive to leave their subordinates entirely without formal guidance.

The reliance on positive law in defining entitlements has led to a doctrinal conundrum. It is not uncommon for the very statute or regulation that defines the property or liberty entitlement to provide procedures to terminate that interest. In these cases, it has been argued that the entitlement protected is simply the entitlement to retain the benefit until it has been terminated in accordance with statutory procedures. If those procedures have been followed, the argument goes, termination deprives the citizen of no property and federal due process can require nothing more.

Whatever its logical appeal, this argument, originally articulated by Justice WILLIAM H. REHNQUIST [3,I] in his plurality opinion in ARNETT V. KENNEDY (1974) [1], is an invitation for government to eliminate the constraints of due process in the administration of statutorily created interests by attaching nugatory procedural protections to their statutory definition of interests. The Court, in *Cleveland Board of Education v. Loudermill* (1985), acknowledged this danger in forcefully rejecting the Rehnquist argument. Justice BYRON R. WHITE [4,I] wrote for eight members of the Court that once the positive law of a state lays the groundwork for an entitlement, the constitutionally mandated procedures for terminating that interest were unaffected by the procedures that a state might attach. Although state law determines whether an individual is entitled to the protections of due process by defining their entitlements, the Constitution defines what due process requires. "The categories of substance and procedure are distinct," the Court held. "Were the rule otherwise, the due process clause would be reduced to a mere tautology."

SETH F. KREIMER

Bibliography

MONAGHAN, HENRY P. 1977 Of Liberty and Property. *Cornell Law Review* 62:401–444.
SMOLLA, RODNEY 1982 The Reemergence of the Right-Privilege Distinction in Constitutional Law: The Price of Protesting Too Much. *Stanford Law Review* 35:69–120.
TRIBE, LAURENCE H. 1987 *American Constitutional Law*, 2nd. ed. pp. 663–714. Westbury, N.Y.: Foundation Press.

ENVIRONMENTAL REGULATION
(Update)

In recent years, three issues have dominated the constitutional side of environmental law. The first issue involves the ability of administrative agencies to obtain access to private property and business records for purposes of inspection. These FOURTH AMENDMENT [2,I] problems are not, however, distinctive to the environmental area, but are typical of those involving ADMINISTRATIVE SEARCH [1,I] in general.

The second issue involves FEDERALISM [2,I]. Since the doctrine of NATIONAL LEAGUE OF CITIES V. USERY (1976) [3] met its demise in GARCIA V. SAN ANTONIO METROPOLITAN TRANSIT AUTHORITY (1985) [2], Congress has faced no constitutional obstacles to environmental regulation. Where state regulation is concerned, however, COMMERCE CLAUSE [1,I] and PREEMPTION [3] problems remain recurring sources of litigation. State environmental regulations often burden interstate businesses and may sometimes be a pretext for protectionism. Although some state regulatory measures have fallen afoul of the dormant commerce clause, courts on the whole have been sympathetic to environmental measures and willing to give them the benefit of the doubt in commerce clause cases. The results in preemption cases are much less predictable. As the federal regulatory presence has grown, the difficulties of coordinating local regulations with federal rules have become more widespread. As a result, state regulations are not infrequently held to be preempted by federal law.

The third major constitutional issue involves government regulation of private lands. Under some circumstances, a regulation that "goes too far" can be an unconstitutional TAKING OF PROPERTY [4,I]. Efforts at environmental preservation can severely restrict the use of property, thereby raising taking problems.

One of the best-known cases is a Wisconsin Supreme Court decision, *Just v. Marinette County* (1972). *Just* involved a Wisconsin statute that allowed only limited uses of wetlands, such as harvesting of wild crops, forestry, hunting, and fishing. Other uses required a special permit. Essentially, this law required special permission before any commercial or residential use could be made of the property. The Wisconsin Supreme Court upheld the statute, despite the severe restriction on land use, because of the strong public interest in preserving wetlands. Other state courts have split on the constitutionality of similar statutes.

The Supreme Court has considered several environmental takings cases. In *Keystone Bituminous Coal Association v. DeBenedictus* (1987) the Court upheld a Pennsylvania statute that required underground coal miners to provide support for surface structures. A similar Pennsylvania statute had been held unconstitutional in a well-known opinion by Justice OLIVER WENDELL HOLMES, JR., [2], but the current statute was found to be unobjectionable because it required only a small fraction of the total coal deposits to be left in the ground. On the other hand, in *Nollan v. California Coastal Commission* (1987) the

Court took a much different approach. *Nollan* involved a couple who wanted to build a larger beach house. As a condition for receiving a permit, the California Coastal Commission required them to allow the public to walk along the beach. Justice ANTONIN SCALIA [I] found a taking because there was an insufficient nexus between the state's goal of preserving the public's right to view the ocean and the requirement that the public be allowed to walk along the beach.

As these two decisions indicate, the outcomes in taking cases are often unpredictable. This uncertainty is a particular problem for environmental regulators and land-use planners, for a mistake can result in an award of damages as well as an injunction against the taking.

With these exceptions, constitutional issues have not loomed large in federal environmental law. By and large, like most regulations of economic activities, environmental statutes have received only minimal judicial scrutiny. As a result, the major issues in environmental law have involved statutory interpretation rather than constitutional disputes.

DANIEL A. FARBER

(SEE ALSO: *Eminent Domain* [2,I]; *Land Use* [I]; *Property Rights* [I]; *State Regulation of Commerce* [4].)

Bibliography

MICHELMAN, FRANK   1988   Takings, 1987. *Columbia Law Review* 88:1600–1629.

ROSE, CAROL   1984   *Mahon* Reconsidered: Why the Takings Issue Is Still a Muddle. *Southern California Law Review* 57:561–599.

EQUAL ACCESS

For over two decades litigation involving religion and the public schools focused on state-sponsored religious exercises. This pattern changed during the 1980s, as student-led religious groups sought access to school facilities on the same basis as other student groups. These groups claimed that once a public school opened its premises to extracurricular student groups, it created a limited PUBLIC FORUM [3,I] and could not discriminate against some groups on the basis of the content of their speech; hence, the school was obliged to grant "equal access" to religious student groups that wanted to use school facilities. Equal access found a legal footing in WIDMAR V. VINCENT (1981) [4], where the Supreme Court held that a public university could not close its facilities to religious student groups once it had opened them for use by other groups because to do so would violate the religious students' FREEDOM OF SPEECH [2,I] guaranteed by the FIRST AMENDMENT [2,I].

Despite *Widmar*, most secondary schools continued to reject requests by religious students to meet on school premises, as did most federal courts; indeed, until 1989 every federal appellate court to rule on the issue held that it would violate the ESTABLISHMENT CLAUSE [I] for secondary schools to allow religious student groups to meet on the same basis as other student groups. The basic rationale for these lower-court holdings came from a federal appellate opinion by Judge Irving Kaufman in *Brandon v. Guilderland* (1980). In *Brandon*, a group of high school students sought permission to meet before school in an empty classroom to pray and read the Bible. The school district denied the request. Judge Kaufman argued that the district could not accede to the students' petition because to do so would impermissibly advance religion and excessively entangle church and state in violation of the second and third prongs of the LEMON TEST [I].

Kaufman's main argument was psychological: "To an impressionable student even the mere appearance of secular involvement in religious activities might indicate that the state has placed its imprimatur on a particular creed. This symbolic inference is too dangerous to permit." Critics of the decision disagreed. Chief Justice WARREN BURGER [1], dissenting in BENDER V. WILLIAMSPORT (1986) [I], argued that one must objectively distinguish between state advancement of religion and individual advocacy of religion; whereas the former activity is prohibited by the First Amendment, the latter is "affirmatively protected." The fact that "some hypothetical students" might mistake individual religious expression for state religion was irrelevant according to Burger, who added: "No one would contend that the State would be authorized to dismantle a church erected by private persons on private property because overwhelming evidence showed that other members of the community thought the church was owned and operated by the state."

When the Supreme Court declined to resolve the constitutionality of equal access, Congress intervened by passing the Equal Access Act in 1984. The act applies to all public secondary schools receiving federal money that also maintain a "limited open forum," which exists whenever a school allows "one or more noncurriculum related student groups to meet on school premises during noninstructional time." The act forbids schools with a limited open forum from discriminating against student groups because of the content of their speech.

In WESTSIDE COMMUNITY SCHOOLS V. MERGENS (1990) [I] the Supreme Court held that the act does not violate the establishment clause as applied to religious student groups, but declined to rule whether the equal-access rights guaranteed by statute are also required by the First Amendment. The Court will likely have another opportunity to deal with this First Amendment issue. As equal-access theory is based primarily on the freedom of speech, it lends itself to a broader range of activities than just the student meetings protected by the Equal Access Act. More recent cases have focused, for example, on the right of students to distribute religious publications to classmates on school premises. These cases have yet to reach the Supreme Court.

JOHN G. WEST, JR.

(SEE ALSO: *Religious Fundamentalism* [I]; *Religion in Public Schools* [3,I]; *Religious Liberty* [3,I]; *Separation of Church and State* [4,I].)

Bibliography

WEST, JOHN G., JR. 1991 The Changing Battle over Religion in the Public Schools. *Wake Forest Law Review* 26:361–401.
WHITEHEAD, JOHN W. 1989 Avoiding Religious Apartheid: Affording Equal Treatment for Student-Initiated Religious Expression in Public Schools. *Pepperdine Law Review* 16:229–258.

EQUAL PROTECTION OF THE LAWS
(Update)

Two questions have dominated the Supreme Court's EQUAL PROTECTION [2] opinions since 1985. The first, largely a matter of rhetoric, is the question of the appropriate STANDARD OF REVIEW [4]. The second and more important question is the relevance of racial groups in determining the existence of discrimination and in providing legislative or judicial remedies for the harms of discrimination.

The uninitiated reader of the Court's opinions surely would think the process of decision in an equal protection case begins with a selection of the appropriate standard of judicial review from among three well-worn formulas: (1) STRICT SCRUTINY [4], which requires the government to offer compelling justification for an inequality it has imposed, and so generally results in the invalidation of governmental action; (2) RATIONAL BASIS [3], in which the Court pays strong deference to the government's assertions of justification and generally upholds the governmental action; or (3) the "intermediate," "heightened" scrutiny that falls between these two polar extremes, requiring "important" justification. Then, the same reader might imagine, the Court measures the government's asserted justifications against the proper standard of review, and on that basis reaches judgment.

More skeptical readers know that the order of the decisional process is often quite the reverse, with a judgment on the merits of the case preceding—even dictating— the selection of a standard of review as an opinion's rhetorical structure. The skeptics know, too, how misleading it is to speak of "the" standard of review, given the Court's occasional willingness to require significant justification in the name of "rational basis" review. Justice THURGOOD MARSHALL [3,I] has long (and accurately) insisted that the Court's decisions add up to a sliding scale in which the standard of review varies according to the importance of the interests at stake. Justice JOHN PAUL STEVENS [4,I] made a similar point when he said, "There is only one equal protection clause." In equal protection cases, as in other cases, the Court decides by weighing interests.

The Court's post-1985 equal protection decisions are illustrative. A 6–3 majority of the Justices used the traditional, highly deferential, "rational basis" standard to uphold two acts of Congress governing eligibility for welfare benefits and food stamps in *Lyng v. Castillo* (1986) and *Lyng v. Automobile, Aerospace and Agricultural Implement Workers* (1988). Similarly, in *Kadrmas v. Dickinson Public Schools* (1988), the Court upheld, 5–4, a state law authorizing some school districts to impose on unwilling parents user fees for school-bus transportation. The majority specifically rejected the argument of two dissenting Justices that PLYLER V. DOE (1982) [3] demanded heightened judicial scrutiny for wealth classifications governing access to public education. *Plyler*'s opinion had been written in the language of "rational basis" review, but no one among the Justices or the Court's commentators had been deceived into believing that the Court was being deferential to the legislature's judgment. In fact, the Court in *Kadrmas* explicitly called *Plyler* a case of heightened scrutiny. The post-1985 decisions may be less than satisfying, but they are conventional applications of existing doctrine.

The dissenters' invocation of *Plyler v. Doe* reminds one, however, that Justices can make "rational basis" into the equivalent of heightened scrutiny when they are so inclined. Two recent cases evoked such responses. ATTORNEY GENERAL OF NEW YORK V. SOTO-LOPEZ (1986) [I] was a challenge to a state law that gave veterans of the armed forces a preference in civil-service hiring, but only if the veterans were New York residents when they entered the forces. A four-Justice plurality concluded that the law failed to pass the heightened scrutiny demanded by the RIGHT TO TRAVEL [3]. Two other Justices rejected both the "right to travel" argument and the conclusion that heightened scrutiny was appropriate; nonetheless, they concluded that the law lacked a rational basis and so violated the equal protection clause. Plainly, this is not a classical "rational basis" decision, any more than was *Plyler v. Doe*.

In *Cleburne v. Cleburne Living Center* (1985) the Justices were unanimous in holding unconstitutional a Texas town's refusal to grant a ZONING [4,I] variance to allow the operation of a group home for mentally retarded persons. The court of appeals had concluded that an official classification based on MENTAL RETARDATION [3] required justification at the level of "intermediate" scrutiny, but a majority of the Supreme Court disagreed. Vigorously arguing that the proper standard was "rational basis," the majority proceeded to a meticulous examination of the justifications offered by the town, rejecting each one as insufficient. As Justice Marshall, concurring, pointed out, *Cleburne* has taken its place alongside *Plyler* as a leading modern example of the sliding scale of standards of review in action.

In at least two kinds of cases, the "rational basis" standard, initially given "bite" in the fashion of *Plyler* and *Cleburne*, has been transformed into candid recognition of a more rigorous judicial scrutiny of governmental justifications. The law of SEX DISCRIMINATION [3,I] moved from the "rational basis" explanation of *Reed v. Reed* (1971) to the explicit "intermediate" scrutiny of CRAIG V. BOREN (1976) [2]. A similar rhetorical change is visible in the law governing classifications based on the legal status of ILLEGITIMACY [2]. First came the "rational basis" language of LEVY V. LOUISIANA (1968) [3]; eventually, the open adoption of "intermediate" scrutiny in *Clark v. Jeter* (1988). These progressions exemplify the normative power of the factual: the practice of heightened scrutiny eventually leads to its formal recognition as doctrine. It is not extravagant to expect a similar treatment of the claims of the mentally retarded in some future opinion. In the end, the standard of JUDICIAL REVIEW [3,I] seems not so much to govern decisions as to provide a rhetorical framework on which lawyers and judges can fasten the substantive considerations that are the heart of argument and decision: the harms of governmental actions to constitutionally protected interests and the government's justifications for those actions.

In contrast, arguments about the relevance of group harms and the validity of group remedies are of major importance in deciding cases—and, indeed, in deciding whether the nation will seriously address the continuing harms of RACIAL DISCRIMINATION [3,I]. Certainly racial discrimination happens to people one by one, but it happens because they are members of a racial group. The harms of group subordination have multiple causes; actions are harmful because of their contexts. Yet our current constitutional law pays little attention to context and, instead, centers on a principle demanding no more of government than formal racial neutrality. To establish a claim of racial discrimination that violates the equal protection clause, normally one must show that identifiable officers of the government have purposefully acted on a racial

ground to produce the harm in question—a proposition typically hard to prove.

A rare case in which the requisite purpose was found was *Hunter v. Underwood* (1985). The Supreme Court concluded that a clause in Alabama's 1901 state constitution disenfranchising persons convicted of crimes of "moral turpitude" had been adopted for the purpose of preventing black citizens from voting and continued in the present to have racially disparate effects. Accordingly, the Court held that it was unconstitutional for the state to deny the vote on the basis of a conviction for the MISDEMEANOR [3] of passing a worthless check. The Court based its conclusion about the law's continuing racially disparate effects on statistics showing that blacks in two Alabama counties had been disenfranchised under the law at a rate at least 1.7 times the rate for whites.

Two years later, however, in rejecting an equal protection attack on the constitutionality of the death penalty, a majority of the Justices refused to give similar weight to a statistical demonstration of racial discrimination. A study of some 2,000 Georgia murder cases in the 1970s showed dramatic racial disparities in the likelihood that CAPITAL PUNISHMENT [1,I] would be imposed. In MCCLESKEY V. KEMP (1987) [I] the Court decided, 5–4, that those statistics were irrelevant; to prevail on a claim of racial discrimination, a defendant must show some specific acts of purposeful discrimination by the prosecutor, jury, or judge in his or her own case. Surely the majority Justices understood that a contrary decision would have threatened wholesale reversals of death sentences—a course they were unwilling to take.

Both the *Hunter* and *McCleskey* cases raised questions concerning the relevance of group subordination in equal protection analysis. *McCleskey* illustrates the present majority's devotion to the principle of formal racial neutrality and its reluctance to accept a showing of disparity among racial groups as proof of the discrimination that violates the equal protection clause. In interpreting a number of federal CIVIL RIGHTS [1,I] statutes, however, the Court has accepted this sort of statistical proof of discrimination.

The issue of the constitutionality of AFFIRMATIVE ACTION [1,I] brings together the rhetorical question of the standard of judicial review and the more substantive question of group remedies. Although, since 1985, the Supreme Court has remained fragmented on both these aspects of affirmative action, the practical effects of the decisions show a remarkable stability.

Given the acceptability of statistical proof of violation of a number of major antidiscrimination laws, many an affirmative-action program amounts to the substitution of one group remedy for another. Accordingly, there is broad agreement among the Justices on the validity of affirmative-action programs that are seen to be genuinely remedial. Yet the dominant principle for the Court's current majority is one of formal racial neutrality, and there is some awkwardness in squaring affirmative action with this principle. In two recent affirmative-action cases—WYGANT V. JACKSON BOARD OF EDUCATION (1986) [I], on public hiring, and RICHMOND (CITY OF) V. J. A. CROSON CO. (1989) [I], on public contracting—the key opinions were written by Justices LEWIS F. POWELL [3] and SANDRA DAY O'CONNOR [3]. On the surface, these opinions minimize group concerns, but together they make clear how a public institution can constitutionally adopt an affirmative action program. The approved method, explained as a form of remedy for past discrimination, makes judicious use of statistics showing racial disparities. In short, Justices Powell and O'Connor have found a way to use the language of individual justice in the cause of ending group subordination.

The prevailing opinions in *Wygant* and *Croson* emphasize the "strict scrutiny" standard of review, employing this standard both in evaluating the justifications for affirmative action as a remedy for past discrimination and in requiring "narrow tailoring" of a racially based remedy. In METRO BROADCASTING, INC. V. F.C.C. (1990) [I], however, a different 5–4 majority announced that the less demanding "intermediate" scrutiny was appropriate in evaluating an affirmative-action program approved by Congress. In an opinion by Justice WILLIAM J. BRENNAN [1,I], the majority upheld a congressionally approved program of the Federal Communications Commission (FCC) for a limited number of racial preferences in the distribution of broadcast licenses. Here the majority said that Congress was not limited to providing remedies for past discrimination; rather, the affirmative-action program was aimed at achieving a greater diversity in broadcast programming. The four dissenters, in opinions by Justice O'Connor and Justice ANTHONY M. KENNEDY [I], insisted on "strict scrutiny" for congressional affirmative action as well as for state or local governmental programs and argued that the nonremedial purpose of broadcasting diversity was not a sufficiently compelling governmental purpose to pass the test.

Even after the retirement of Justice Brennan, there remains a majority of Justices who agree that Congress has the power, in enforcing the FOURTEENTH AMENDMENT [2], to remedy societal discrimination, both private and governmental, through affirmative-action programs. Presumably, in future cases, that result will be described, as it was in *Croson*, as consistent with "strict scrutiny." Indeed, in *Metro Broadcasting* itself one might have imagined an opinion upholding the FCC's diversity program as broadly "remedial." In the affirmative-action context,

as elsewhere in equal protection doctrine, discussions of the standard of review serve purposes that are mainly rhetorical.

KENNETH L. KARST

(SEE ALSO: *Capital Punishment and Race* [I]; *Discrete and Insular Minorities* [2]; *Race and Criminal Justice* [I]; *Race-Consciousness* [I]; *Racial Preference* [I].)

Bibliography

BELL, DERRICK A.   1987   *And We Are Not Saved: The Elusive Quest for Racial Justice.* New York: Basic Books.
KARST, KENNETH L.   1989   *Belonging to America: Equal Citizenship and the Constitution.* New Haven, Conn.: Yale University Press.
KENNEDY, RANDALL L.   1988   McCleskey v. Kamp: Race, Capital Punishment, and the Supreme Court. *Harvard Law Review* 101:1388–1433.
LAWRENCE, CHARLES R., III   1987   The Id, the Ego, and Equal Protection: Reckoning with Unconscious Racism. *Stanford Law Review* 39:317–388.
MINOW, MARTHA   1987   The Supreme Court, 1986 Term—Foreword: Justice Engendered. *Harvard Law Review* 101:10–95.

ESTABLISHMENT CLAUSE

Three themes dominate recent Supreme Court decision making under the First Amendment's ESTABLISHMENT OF RELIGION [2] clause. First, the Court has continued to follow the doctrinal framework of EVERSON V. BOARD OF EDUCATION (1947) [2] and LEMON V. KURTZMAN (1971) [3], but with increasing emphasis on the "endorsement or disapproval" inquiry advocated by Justice SANDRA DAY O'CONNOR [3,I]. Second, the Court has steered a selective course in applying this framework, upholding certain governmental practices but invalidating others. Third, and potentially most significant, the Justices stand at the brink of a radical change in doctrine. Although a majority of the Court continues to follow *Everson* and *Lemon*, there is growing support for an alternative interpretation that would dramatically weaken the principle of SEPARATION OF CHURCH AND STATE [4,I].

In *Everson*, the Supreme Court adopted a broad interpretation of the establishment clause, one that forbids governmental favoritism for religion over irreligion as well as for one religion over another. Since 1971, this broad interpretation has been implemented through the three-part LEMON TEST [I]. Under *Lemon*, a statute (or other governmental action) can be upheld only if it satisfies three requirements: "First, the statute must have a secular legislative purpose; second, its principal or primary effect must be one that neither advances nor inhibits religion . . . ; finally, the statute must not foster 'an excessive governmental entanglement with religion.' "

Despite persistent criticism, the Court continues to embrace the *Everson* interpretation and the *Lemon* test. The Court has reformulated the first two parts of *Lemon*, however, by emphasizing the "endorsement or disapproval" inquiry that Justice O'Connor initially proposed in her concurring opinion in LYNCH V. DONNELLY (1984) [3]. In WALLACE V. JAFFREE (1985) [4] and *Edwards v. Aguillard* (1987), the Court adopted O'Connor's formulation of the "purpose" inquiry: "The purpose prong of the *Lemon* test asks whether government's actual purpose is to endorse or disapprove of religion." In COUNTY OF ALLE-GHENY V. ACLU (1989) [I] the Justices likewise relied on O'Connor's formulation to modify *Lemon*'s "primary effect" requirement. Thus, the Court held that regardless of purpose, governmental action has a constitutionally impermissible effect if it *appears* to endorse or disapprove religion. "The Establishment Clause, at the very least," wrote the Court, "prohibits government from appearing to take a position on questions of religious belief."

Justice O'Connor's approach does not eliminate difficult questions of application. As suggested by *Corporation of Presiding Bishop v. Amos* (1987), for example, there is no "endorsement" when government merely "accommodates" religion by removing burdens that government itself has created. More generally, the line between partisan "endorsement" and neutral "acknowledgment" may be exceedingly difficult to draw.

With or without the O'Connor reformulation, the *Lemon* test provides no more than a framework for analysis. Its application requires an exercise of judgment, an exercise of judgment that depends on the context of specific cases and on the individual philosophies of the Justices. In its recent cases, the Court's applications of *Lemon* have suggested a relaxation of establishment clause restraints on GOVERNMENT AID TO RELIGIOUS INSTITUTIONS [2,I] and activities. At the same time, the Court has applied the clause forcefully to prohibit government from advancing religion through the public school curriculum, and it has adopted a fact-specific approach for cases involving religious symbols.

If government singles out religion for special economic benefits, the Supreme Court continues to find an establishment clause violation. Thus, in TEXAS MONTHLY, INC. V. BULLOCK (1989) [I] the Court invalidated a Texas sales tax exemption that was limited to religious periodicals. For governmental programs that include secular as well as religious beneficiaries, however, the Court's decisions in WITTERS V. WASHINGTON DEPARTMENT OF SERVICES FOR THE BLIND (1986) [I] and BOWEN V. KENDRICK (1988) [I] suggest a relaxation of the Court's prior doctrine. In *Witters*, the question was whether the establishment

clause required the state of Washington to deny vocational rehabilitation funds to an individual attending a Christian college in preparation for a religious career. The Washington State Supreme Court had held that the denial was mandated by *Lemon*'s second prong, but the United States Supreme Court unanimously disagreed. Although the opinion of the Court was narrowly drawn, separate concurring opinions, joined by a majority of the Justices, gave a broad reading to MUELLER V. ALLEN (1983) [3], one that apparently would support the constitutionality of any neutrally drawn educational assistance program, even if most of the individual beneficiaries used the funds for religious training.

In *Bowen* the Court rejected a facial challenge to a federal statute designed to combat teenage sexual relations and pregnancy. In addressing these religiously sensitive topics, the statute not only permitted but expressly encouraged the involvement of religious organizations. Nonetheless, the Court refused to invalidate the statute either in its entirety or with respect to religiously affiliated grantees. Although the Court remanded for a determination of whether particular grants might render the statute unconstitutional as applied, it refused to presume that religiously affiliated grantees would use their grants "in a way that would have the primary effect of advancing religion."

The Court's permissive treatment of governmental funding programs has not been duplicated in the public school context. In *Edwards v. Aguillard* the Court considered a challenge to Louisiana's Balanced Treatment Act, which provided that evolution could not be taught in the public schools unless accompanied by the teaching of CREATIONISM [I]. With only two Justices dissenting, the Court concluded that the act violated the first prong of *Lemon* and therefore was unconstitutional. Citing mandatory attendance policies and the impressionability of young students, the Court noted that it was "particularly vigilant in monitoring compliance with the Establishment Clause in elementary and secondary schools." Unpersuaded by the legislature's articulation of a secular purpose, the Court concluded that the act was designed "to alter the science curriculum to reflect endorsement of a religious view that is antagonistic to the theory of evolution." The Court found that this "preeminent religious purpose" was at least the "primary purpose" of the act and that the act therefore "endorses religion in violation of the First Amendment."

The Supreme Court's treatment of governmental displays of religious symbols shows neither the permissiveness of the funding cases nor the "particular vigilance" the Court has exercised in policing the public school curriculum. Instead, the Court has adopted a fact-specific approach that requires case-by-case determinations of whether particular religious displays have the purpose or effect of endorsing religion. In *County of Allegheny v. ACLU* the Court considered challenges to two separate holiday displays in downtown Pittsburgh, one of a crèche, the other of a menorah. A sharply divided Court found that the crèche violated the establishment clause but that the menorah did not. The Court emphasized that the crèche stood essentially alone in the Allegheny County Courthouse and included a banner that read "Gloria in Excelsis Deo." By contrast, the menorah was placed beside a large Christmas tree and was accompanied by a sign proclaiming the City of Pittsburgh's "salute to liberty." Focusing on the second prong of *Lemon*, as modified by Justice O'Connor, the Court concluded that the crèche sent an impermissible message of religious endorsement, whereas the menorah, in context, sent a permissible message of cultural diversity and freedom of belief.

The Court's recent applications of its establishment clause doctrine are significant and controversial in their own right. A far more important development, however, may be just around the corner. For years, critics have attacked *Everson* and *Lemon* for their alleged hostility to religion. To date, the Court has resisted these attacks, affirming the basic wisdom of its doctrinal framework and continuing to enforce a meaningful separation of church and state. The Court is changing, however, and it may be within one vote of a dramatic shift in doctrine. Speaking for four Justices in *County of Allegheny*, Justice ANTHONY M. KENNEDY [I] wrote that "substantial revision of our Establishment Clause doctrine may be in order." Suggesting the direction such revision might take, he argued that governmental "support" for religion should be permitted unless it involves coercion, "proselytizing" for a particular religion, or "direct benefits" so substantial as to in fact establish or tend to establish a state religion. It seems clear that the four Justices joining this opinion would support a fundamental retreat from the Court's existing doctrine.

Justice Kennedy's suggested course would seriously threaten the political-moral principles and policies that are furthered by the Court's prevailing approach. Governmental "support" for religion causes harm to the religious and irreligious individuals who are not within the government's favor. This harm creates feelings of resentment and alienation, which in turn cause injury to the political community itself. At the same time, the purported support for religion is often illusory; it may demean religion and work to its long-term detriment. The Supreme Court's establishment clause doctrine works to ensure a proper respect for the religious and irreligious beliefs of individuals, supports the maintenance of a religiously inclusive political community, and does no disservice to the important role of religion in our society. Whatever

its weaknesses, this doctrine should not be abandoned.
DANIEL O. CONKLE

Bibliography

CONKLE, DANIEL O. 1988 Toward a General Theory of the Establishment Clause. *Northwestern University Law Review* 82:1113–1194.
NOTE 1987 Developments in the Law: Religion and the State. *Harvard Law Review* 100:1606–1781.
SMITH, STEVEN D. 1987 Symbols, Perceptions, and Doctrinal Illusions: Establishment Neutrality and the "No Endorsement" Test. *Michigan Law Review* 86:266–332.

EUTHANASIA

See: Right to Die [I]; Euthanasia [2]

EVANGELICALS AND THE CONSTITUTION

See: Religious Fundamentalism [I]

EXCESSIVE FINES

See: Punitive Damages [I]

EXECUTIVE POWER

Article II of the Constitution vests "the executive power" of the United States in the President, whereas Article I vests in Congress those legislative powers "herein granted," and Article III says that the JURISDICTION [3] of the federal courts extends only to the subjects enumerated in the article. The common reader would normally construe these provisions to confer the entire executive power on the President, while granting Congress and the courts only parts of the legislative and judicial authority of the United States. As so often happens, however, the common reader has had a difficult time. From the first term of President GEORGE WASHINGTON [4], there has been a considerable debate over the scope of the President's executive power.

One party, labeled "Super-Whigs" by EDWARD S. CORWIN [2], views all the powers of the national government with grudging suspicion as necessary but distasteful restraints on the powers of the states or the people. For members of this party, the first principle of constitutional exegesis is that the Constitution provides limited and ENUMERATED POWERS [2] that should be narrowly construed. They read the first sentence of Article II as a "mere designation" of the President's office and would confine the President's authority strictly to those examples of the executive power mentioned in the constitutional text: the VETO POWER [4], the power to receive ambassadors, the duty to execute faithfully the laws, and the others.

The other participant in the debate, the party of those who interpret law in the manner of JOHN MARSHALL [3], read the vesting clause of Article II as a grant to the President of a broad and independent range of authority to be defined historically and by the necessities of circumstance, and not limited to the powers and duties mentioned in the text. For this party, "the executive power" includes not only IMPLIED POWERS [2], but also the prerogative and emergency powers of the British Crown unless limited or denied to the President by the Constitution.

The issue has long since been settled by usage and by decisions of the Supreme Court in cases such as EX PARTE MILLIGAN [3], *In re Neagle* (1890), and IN RE DEBS (1895) [2], but it continues to enjoy a half-life in the literature of the Constitution.

In his perceptive study, *The Creation of the Presidency, 1775–1789*, C. C. Thach, Jr. concludes that Article II admits "an interpretation of executive power which would give to the President a field of action much wider than that outlined by the enumerated powers." Thach has no doubt that this consequence of the text was contemplated and intended because the dominant force governing the CONSTITUTIONAL CONVENTION OF 1787 [1] was not the theories of MONTESQUIEU [3] and WILLIAM BLACKSTONE [1], popular as they were, but the experience of the state and the national governments between 1776 and 1787. To the majority of the founding fathers, led by JAMES WILSON [4], JOHN JAY [3], JAMES MADISON [3], and GOUVERNEUR MORRIS [3], the lesson of this experience was the danger of unbridled legislative power and the necessity for a strong and accountable national executive "to counterbalance legislative predominance. Neither theorist nor foreign model was needed to demonstrate that fact. The state legislatures' excesses and the incompetency of Congress as an administrative body produced the presidency." This is why Article I, section 6, forbids any member of Congress from holding an executive office during his or her term and why the Convention rejected several proposals that would have diluted the unity of the presidency or subordinated the office to a congressional committee.

Thach's judgment has been vindicated by the ebb and flow of history, despite the survival of a minority view favoring congressional supremacy. Upheavals of public opinion like those of the later stages of the VIETNAM WAR [4,I] and the WATERGATE [4] scandal caused the pendulum to swing more violently than usual in the direction of congressional power, but—thus far, at any rate—James Wilson's conception of the presidency has recovered from the vehemence of periodic congressional attacks and pre-

vails in public opinion, governmental practice, and constitutional law.

The reasons for this pattern are simple, but fundamental: they correspond to functional necessity. Congress cannot conduct the day-to-day business of a vast government, the central task of the executive power. The size, history, and habits of Congress make it an admirable legislative body, but for these reasons also make it impossible for Congress, even through committees and committee staff, to constitute the operational arm of a government capable of "energy, secrecy, and dispatch."

It is equally apparent that no American President can preempt the legislative power and rule by decree, at least not for long. It is not always easy to discover at what point in the process of government a statute is constitutionally necessary. But as a matter of principle, there is a boundary between the legislative and executive functions, no matter how difficult it sometimes is to draw. As a matter not only of legal obligation, but of institutional resistance, every President is forced sooner or later to respect the limits of the tripartite system of government, sanctioned as it is by the conviction that "there can be no liberty" in a society where the executive and legislative functions are combined and where the judiciary is not separated from both the other branches.

Congress had to consider the indispensable elasticity of these concepts when it met for the first time in 1789. In considering a statute to establish the first three departments of the government, Congress faced the question as to whether it was constitutionally required to give the President the power to remove heads of the departments or whether the President had that power under Article II, with or without a statute. The Constitution made it clear that only the President could nominate these officers, but could not appoint them without the ADVICE AND CONSENT [1] of the SENATE [I]. Congress could provide other procedures for "inferior" officers or officers to be appointed by the courts. Were the new cabinet ministers to serve at the President's pleasure or was IMPEACHMENT [2] required to remove them? Could the President remove them only with the advice and consent of the Senate? Could the Senate or Congress as a whole remove them on its own motion, whatever the President thought?

Madison led the extended debate on the bill in the HOUSE OF REPRESENTATIVES [I], and in the end, Congress decided to say nothing on the subject, but to leave the outcome to practice and to the courts. Madison contended that the officers should be deemed to serve at the President's pleasure. The principal reason he offered for discovering an "implied" power of removal in Article II was that the President could not be expected faithfully to execute the laws if he were not given a free hand to dismiss his chief subordinates; neither the Senate nor Congress as a whole should have a binding vote in the conduct of the administrative business of the government, save through legislation. It followed, Madison concluded, that the President alone was responsible and accountable for the removal of officials.

Madison's position on the constitutional basis of the President's removal power was tested in a famous episode. During the passionate battles between President ANDREW JOHNSON [3] and Congress over policy in the military occupation of the South, Congress passed the TENURE OF OFFICE ACT [4], providing that certain heads of departments could serve until their successors were qualified. The provision was designed by Congress to prevent Johnson from dismissing Secretary of War EDWIN M. STANTON [4], who was in charge of the military occupation of the South. Stanton was removed by Johnson, however, and the House of Representatives proceeded to impeach the President, largely for violating the statute. The President, of course, was acquitted by the Senate. Some sixty years later, the Supreme Court declared the Tenure of Office Act unconstitutional in MYERS V. UNITED STATES (1926) [3].

To confirm that the authority of a President to remove a member of his CABINET [1] is an integral part of "the" executive power was hardly the end of the story. The *Myers* case did not concern the removal of a cabinet member, but of a postmaster. At the present stage in the evolution of the law on the subject, it can be said that the President's "absolute" power to remove federal officials is clear only for those of senior political responsibility whose appointments have been confirmed by the Senate. In contrast, military officers and foreign-service officers receive their commissions from the President after a senatorial vote of consent, but can only be discharged after compliance with statutory procedures for assuring them justice. For officials below the political level, Congress can qualify or abolish the President's removal power by passing civil-service legislation or by other means and direct the appointment of members of boards, commissions, and independent agencies for fixed terms. However, the Supreme Court has held in RUTAN V. REPUBLICAN PARTY OF ILLINOIS (1990) [I] that the FIRST AMENDMENT [2,I] prevents state governors from discriminating among lower-level state officials on political grounds with regard to promotions, dismissals, and other aspects of employment. This line of cases surely applies also to the national government.

The same pattern of adjustment and accommodation between President and Congress is manifest in other lines of decisions that distinguish between the executive and the legislative functions—those on pardons, for example.

This *Encyclopedia* considers the relations of Congress and the President in the field of FOREIGN AFFAIRS [2] in a number of articles, so this phase of the problem will not be addressed here. This article will, however, recall the ways in which the President and Congress share powers with respect to the important subject of appropriations.

It is often said that Congress has exclusive authority over the national purse because of the provisions in Article I, section 9, that "no money shall be drawn from the Treasury but in Consequence of appropriations made by law," and in Article I, section 7, that all money bills must originate in the House of Representatives. From the beginning, however, questions have arisen about the import of these words. The questions were raised with new intensity by the controversy over President RONALD REAGAN's [3,I] handling of the IRAN-CONTRA AFFAIR [I].

Does the word "law" in the phrase "appropriations made by law" mean only statutory law, or does it include the President's actions pursuant to his prerogative and EMERGENCY POWERS [2] under the Constitution as well? President Washington spent unappropriated funds to put down the WHISKEY REBELLION [4], and ABRAHAM LINCOLN [3] spent two million dollars in unappropriated funds for war material during the early months of the CIVIL WAR [I], while Congress was not in session. President WOODROW WILSON [4] and a number of other Presidents have taken comparable actions.

Article I, section 9, prohibits the spending of unappropriated funds. Does it therefore by implication allow the President not to spend funds, even when they have been appropriated? When the Armistice in Europe was signed in 1945, could President HARRY S. TRUMAN [4] cancel military procurement contracts? The practice of presidential IMPOUNDMENT OF FUNDS [2] already appropriated goes back at least to President THOMAS JEFFERSON [3]. On rare occasion, Presidents have relied on their inherent constitutional powers both to spend funds without benefit of statutory authority and not to make expenditures that had been authorized by statute.

Such acts have been treated as presenting a special constitutional problem fraught with overtones of tyranny. In situations of this kind, it has been normal practice for Presidents to report such expenditures or decisions not to spend to Congress, often with a request that Congress join its authority to that of the President by approving the action already taken. While some conclude that President Lincoln acted unconstitutionally in spending two million dollars of unappropriated funds in 1861 for the purpose of resisting the Confederacy, this author is of the opinion that Lincoln was legally correct in characterizing his action as constitutional.

The existence of an emergency does not suspend the

Constitution; it merely changes the state of facts to which the law must be applied. As a matter of international law and constitutional law alike, the government of the United States possesses all the powers it requires to function in the society of nations. Like every other constitution, the Constitution of the United States contemplates the possibility of emergencies and makes provision for dealing with them. When Presidents invoke their emergency powers, they are acting under the Constitution, not beyond its limits, regardless of whether they are right or wrong in judging the scope of their powers. There is no other way for them to act. The general constitutional norms of reasonableness apply to the field of emergency actions as they do to other exercises of executive (and legislative) authority. In scrutinizing actions taken by the executive in the name of emergency, however, Congress, the courts, and the people may conclude that what the President did was justifiable as going no further than was reasonably necessary to carry out the President's constitutional responsibility under the circumstances.

Even if Lincoln could have assembled Congress in emergency session in the spring of 1861, his political judgment that such a session would have been impolitic, to say the least, was an important part of this constitutional responsibility. In defending Washington's unorthodox method of financing the suppression of the Whiskey Rebellion, ALEXANDER HAMILTON [2] spoke of a presidential prerogative to make temporary "advances" against future congressional appropriations. This is a possible approach to the constitutional problem; it is analytically more precise, however, to treat such presidential actions as exercises of an autonomous presidential power. Congress may approve after the event, as frequently happens when Presidents use the national force on their own authority. The PRIZE CASES (1863) [3]. But the President's action meets the standard of Article I, section 9, whether Congress approves or not.

Involving the claim of emergency, however, by no means justifies every decision the President (or Congress) takes to resolve it, as shown in *Ex Parte Milligan* (1866). In the context of the Constitution as a whole and considering the possibilities of abuse, the President's power to spend unappropriated funds should be confined to the minimum necessary for the purpose.

During the administration of RICHARD M. NIXON [3], a major controversy between Congress and the presidency developed about the existence and the extent of the President's power not to spend appropriated funds. The controversy resulted in the CONGRESSIONAL BUDGET AND IMPOUNDMENT ACT [1] of 1974. This statute distinguishes between appropriations that authorize expenditures and those that mandate them. In the first category, the Act acknowledges a power in the President to sequester appropriated funds for a limited period, giving Congress time to reconsider its prior decision. Where an appropriation is mandatory, however, the President is required to carry it out.

These problems in determining the respective role of the legislature and the executive in spending public funds, important as they are, do not address the principal constitutional issues raised by the growing tendency of Congress to use riders on appropriation bills, LEGISLATIVE VETOES [3], standing congressional oversight committees, and other legislative methods as devices for taking executive powers unto itself. The pracitce of "tacking foreign matter to money bills" was familiar to the Constitutional Convention and has been familiar ever since, both in money bills and more generally. No constitutional way to protect the President's veto by requiring Congress to enforce a rule of "germaneness"—that is, a rule that would confine each act to one subject—has yet been developed. Two approaches to the problem are currently being discussed: the LINE ITEM VETO [I] and a more vigorous judicial development of the Supreme Court's analysis and conclusions in cases like *Springer v. Government of the Philippine Islands* (1928), IMMIGRATION AND NATURALIZATION SERVICE V. CHADHA (1983) [2], BOWSHER V. SYNAR (1986) [I], and *Commodity Future Trading Commission v. Schor* (1986), all of which recognize the importance of enforcing the constitutional distinction between legislative and executive power, whatever form the encroachment may take. There has been some support for the novel argument that a constitutional basis for the item veto already exists and should be declared by the Supreme Court rather than by constitutional amendment. Whether or not so radical a step is taken, however, it is to be expected that the Court will pursue the initiative it took in *Chadha* and *Bowsher*.

EUGENE V. ROSTOW

(SEE ALSO: *Congress and Foreign Policy* [I]; *Congressional War Powers* [I]; *Executive Prerogative* [I]; *Pardoning Power* [3]; *Senate and Foreign Policy* [I].)

Bibliography

CORWIN, EDWIN S. 1940 and 1957 *The President: Office and Powers.* New York: New York University Press.

FISHER, LOUIS 1975 *Presidential Spending Power.* Princeton, N.J.: Princeton University Press.

THACH, CHARLES C., JR. 1922 *The Creation of the Presidency, 1775–1789.* Baltimore Md.: The Johns Hopkins Press.

EXECUTIVE PREROGATIVE

Executive prerogative refers to the President's constitutionally based authority to declare policy, take action, and make law without congressional support or in the face of inconsistent congressional LEGISLATION [3]. This authority may be seen as a corollary of the SEPARATION OF POWERS [4] under which the President has exclusive EXECUTIVE POWER that Congress may not invade because Congress's authority is limited to LEGISLATIVE POWERS [3]. Executive prerogative may also refer to certain EMERGENCY POWERS under which the President may act contrary to the Constitution, such as spending funds without an appropriation or contrary to an act of Congress that would properly be classified as a legislative act. In the view of some eighteenth-century political theorists, the President could act extraconstitutionally or illegally if circumstances required, but he would have to seek subsequent ratification of the act. More recently, the President has justified such action on the basis of an inherent or implied authority conferred by the Constitution.

Executive prerogative mostly relates to FOREIGN AFFAIRS [2] but may also include domestic acts, such as actions during war or national emergency, dismissal of CABINET [1] officers appointed with Senate participation, and assertion of EXECUTIVE PRIVILEGE [2] to protect communications of executive branch officials from congressional or judicial inquiry.

The Constitution does not expressly delegate a "foreign affairs" power to the President or to any single branch of the government. Indeed, the Constitution delegates most specific foreign relations powers to the Congress. These powers include the powers to declare war, to regulate FOREIGN COMMERCE [2], and to define and punish offenses against the law of nations, piracy, and FELONIES [2] committed on the high seas, as well as the powers to authorize an army, navy, and MILITIA [I] and to make rules for the regulation of land and naval forces. Congress therefore has concurrent authority and substantial practical influence over all aspects of foreign affairs. Notwithstanding this authority, the President dominates foreign affairs. Yet the Constitution delegates relatively few foreign relations powers to the President, and several of these powers are shared with the Senate or Congress. The President has the power to make treaties and appoint ambassadors, but only with the participation of the Senate. His power as COMMANDER-IN-CHIEF [1] is subject to limitation by the congressional war, legislative, and appropriations powers. The President has the power to receive ambassadors, the duty (and implicitly the power) to take care that laws (including treaties and customary international law) be faithfully executed, and a general executive power. But executive prerogative rests more on historical practice and functional necessity than on constitutional text.

Much of the President's dominance of foreign affairs is based on extralegal factors, such as access to the media and political party status. Most presidential foreign affairs authority derives from congressional support. For example, Congress has delegated to the President plenary authority over foreign commerce. It has also authorized and funded a standing armed force, a vast intelligence bureaucracy, and dozens of agencies with thousands of officials participating in all facets of international organization and activities. Having created the bureaucracies, Congress has generally been content to let the executive run them. Executive prerogative has historically sanctioned the President's right to recognize foreign states and governments, establish diplomatic relations, initiate negotiations, determine the content of communications with foreign governments, conduct intelligence operations, conclude presidential EXECUTIVE AGREEMENTS [2], and initiate military action.

Executive prerogative has been controversial since the first administration of GEORGE WASHINGTON [4]. After Washington declared neutrality in 1793 in the war between France and Great Britain, ALEXANDER HAMILTON [2] and JAMES MADISON [3] debated his authority under the pseudonyms Pacificus and Helvidius. The structure of the debate, and even the arguments advanced, have been used repeatedly in foreign policy clashes between the President and Congress, most recently in the IRAN-CONTRA AFFAIR [I]. The Washington declaration amounted to a decision not to declare war and implicitly interpreted a treaty with France not to require U.S. entry into the war.

Madison rejected Washington's authority to issue the declaration because in his view neutrality pertained to declaration of war, a congressional power, and to the application of a treaty, a power shared with the Senate. Madison viewed constitutional powers as strictly separated so that any activity within the scope of a legislative power was precluded to the President. He also advocated a narrow construction of the executive power and other presidential authorities specified in the constitutional text. In Madison's view, the President could only execute laws and policies established by Congress.

Hamilton took a broad view of the executive power, arguing that its scope was limited only by explicit exceptions such as Senate participation in treaty making and congressional power to declare war. Thus, the President could preserve peace until Congress declared war. As the "organ of intercourse" between the United States and foreign nations, the President could make, interpret, suspend, and terminate treaties; recognize foreign governments; and execute the laws of nations (including the law of neutrality). In Hamilton's view, the President shared power with the legislature in war and treaty making.

Washington established other important precedents supporting presidential foreign affairs power. He authorized military actions against AMERICAN INDIANS [1] without congressional authorization and dispatched an envoy without Senate approval. He also asserted executive privilege against both the Senate and Congress to protect treaty-negotiating instructions, and he effectively eliminated the Senate's "advice" function in treaty making. Other early Presidents also established major precedents justifying presidential foreign affairs power. JOHN ADAMS [1] initiated presidential executive agreements. THOMAS JEFFERSON [3] committed funds to purchase military supplies without an appropriation and dispatched the navy to protect U.S. vessels against pirates off Africa.

Since then, presidential authority has fluctuated with the strength of particular Presidents and the exigencies of the moment, depending on what the President has claimed and what the Congress has tolerated. The courts generally have declined to adjudicate these controversies. On the few occasions when the Supreme Court has addressed questions of presidential power, it has almost always sided with the President.

In a much-quoted passage, Justice GEORGE SUTHERLAND [4], in UNITED STATES V. CURTISS-WRIGHT EXPORT CORP. (1936) [2], referred to "the very delicate, plenary and exclusive power of the President as the sole organ of the federal government in the field of international relations." Sutherland explained that "[t]he President alone has the power to speak or listen as a representative of the nation. He *makes* treaties with the advice and consent of the Senate; but he alone negotiates. Into the field of negotiation the Senate cannot intrude; and Congress itself is powerless to invade it." Sutherland offered a functional explanation: "if, in the maintenance of our international relations, embarrassment . . . is to be avoided and success for our aims achieved, congressional legislation . . . must often accord to the President a degree of discretion and freedom. . . . [H]e, not Congress, has the better opportunity of knowing the conditions which prevail in foreign countries. . . . He has his confidential sources of information. He has his agents in the form of diplomatic, consular and other officials. Secrecy in respect of information gathered by them may be highly necessary, and the premature disclosure of it productive of harmful results. . . ."

In *Chicago and Southern Air Lines v. Waterman S. S. Corp.* (1948) Justice ROBERT H. JACKSON [3], after noting the importance of secret intelligence in executive decision making, added: "[T]he very nature of executive decisions as to foreign policy is political, not judicial. Such decisions are wholly confided by our Constitution to the political department of the government. . . . They are delicate, complex and involve large elements of prophecy. They are and should be undertaken only by those directly responsible to the people whose welfare they advance or imperil. They are decisions of a kind for which the Judiciary has neither aptitude, facilities nor responsibility and have long been held to belong in the domain of political power not subject to judicial intrusion or inquiry."

In YOUNGSTOWN SHEET & TUBE CO. V. SAWYER (1952) [4], however, the Court denied an executive emergency power to seize steel mills during the KOREAN WAR [3]. The determinative factor was that Congress had earlier declined to give the President such authority. Jackson's concurring opinion [1], which is now the standard framework for analysis, held that the President's authority is maximum when exercised pursuant to express or implied congressional authorization, but is "at its lowest ebb" when exercised contrary to the express or implied will of Congress. Jackson recognized a "zone of twilight" where there is neither a grant nor a denial of presidential authority. The branches then have concurrent authority, and "Congressional inertia, indifference or quiescence may sometimes, at least as a practical matter, enable if not invite, measure on independent presidential responsibility." In DAMES & MOORE V. REGAN (1981) [2] the Court upheld a presidential executive agreement eliminating causes of action in federal courts for claims against foreign governments, contrary to a statute conferring jurisdiction over such cases, on the basis of congressional acquiescence to earlier executive agreements dealing with such claims. Presidents have also negotiated export restraint measures covering steel and automobiles at odds with the antitrust laws, and Congress has acquiesced.

In the absence of much judicial guidance, presidential foreign affairs power has been shaped by political compromises between Congress and the President. Almost all exercises of presidential power, including politically controversial ones, have the sanction of congressional acquiescence.

Executive prerogative builds on the negotiation function. Everyone agrees that the President has exclusive authority to recognize foreign states and governments, establish diplomatic relations, and control official communications with foreign governments. The President declares foreign policy, although important declarations like the MONROE DOCTRINE [3] or support for the African National Congress typically require congressional action to be effective. Executive branch officials, with congressional acquiescence, have also construed executive prerogative to include the right to preserve confidentiality of diplomatic communications and related executive deliberations.

The President may negotiate an international agreement on any subject matter. He decides whether to conclude it on the basis of Article II or the constitutionally equivalent procedure of authorization by Congress. He may conclude some international agreements without any congressional participation. These agreements have sometimes been controversial, but the Supreme Court has approved. In UNITED STATES V. BELMONT (1937) [1] and UNITED STATES V. PINK (1942) [3], the Court upheld an executive agreement that superseded state law. In *Dames & Moore v. Regan* (1981) the Court upheld an executive agreement inconsistent with a federal statute. After the VIETNAM WAR [4,I] and WATERGATE [4], the President fended off congressional attempts to regulate executive agreements. The President may also interpret, suspend, and terminate Article II treaties without Senate participation.

The most controversial aspect of executive prerogative concerns the presidential war power. This authority rests in part on the commander-in-chief clause and in part on congressional authorization of military forces and acquiescence in their use. Since WORLD WAR II [I], the President has frequently initiated military activities without a congressional DECLARATION OF WAR [2]. Examples include military actions in Korea, the Dominican Republic, Lebanon, Grenada, the Persian Gulf, and Panama. During the Vietnam War, Congress challenged the President, passing the War Powers Resolution over the President's veto. Subsequent presidents disregarded its major limitation, sending troops to the Middle East, Asia, Africa, and Latin America. Some members of Congress complained, but Congress acquiesced to presidential military action, at least for limited purposes. Executive branch officials have also claimed constitutionally based authority to initiate covert intelligence operations.

Only rarely has a President acted contrary to congressional prohibition. In some contexts, however, functional theory and historical practice constitutionally justify such action, whether as an emergency power or, under contemporary theory, as a synergistic product of the textual powers of the President. One cannot anticipate the contexts in which such action may be required, and it is therefore difficult to define rules in principled terms. The prospect for congressional acquiescence seems crucial. The President does not have a general power to override acts of Congress for foreign-policy purposes. Nevertheless, the foreign relations power may justify action inconsistent with acts of Congress when foreign policy urgency requires and Congress seems likely to acquiesce. Presidential exercise of power is subject to congressional review to weigh the genuineness of the urgency and wisdom of the action. If Congress disagrees, it can repudiate the President formally. Congressional action in response to assertions of presidential prerogative should in turn prevail and constitutional lawmaking continue.

PHILLIP R. TRIMBLE

(SEE ALSO: *Congress and Foreign Policy* [I]; *Congressional War Powers* [I]; *Senate and Foreign Policy* [I]; *War, Foreign Affairs, and the Constitution* [4]; *War Powers* [4,I].)

Bibliography

BALDWIN, GORDON 1976 The Foreign Affairs Advice Privilege. *Wisconsin Law Review* 1976:16–46.
CORWIN, EDWARD 1917 *The President's Control of Foreign Relations*. Princeton, N.J.: Princeton University Press.
FISHER, LOUIS 1985 *Constitutional Conflicts Between Congress and the President*. Princeton, N.J.: Princeton University Press.
GLENNON, MICHAEL J. 1990 *Constitutional Diplomacy*. Princeton, N.J.: Princeton University Press.
HENKIN, LOUIS 1972 *Foreign Affairs and the Constitution*. Mineola, N.Y.: Foundation Press.
KOH, HAROLD HONJU 1990 *The National Security Constitution*. New Haven, Conn.: Yale University Press.
LOBEL, JULES 1989 Emergency Power and the Decline of Liberalism. *Yale Law Journal* 98:1385–1433.
NOTE 1968 Congress, the President, and the Power to Commit Forces to Combat. *Harvard Law Review* 81:1771–1805.
NOTE 1984 The Extent of Independent Presidential Authority to Conduct Foreign Intelligence Activities. *Georgetown Law Journal* 72:1855–1883.
WRIGHT, QUINCY 1922 *The Control of American Foreign Relations*. New York: Macmillan.

EXTREMIST SPEECH

Extremist speech is generously protected under the FIRST AMENDMENT [2,I] to the Constitution as interpreted by the Supreme Court in this century. What speech should be classified as "extremist" is, of course, a difficult matter, one that will vary from culture to culture. In some countries advocating FREEDOM OF SPEECH [2,I] may itself be "extremist." But in the United States the label of extremist speech is reserved for speech that advocates violent overthrow of the government, the commission of serious crimes (such as assassination), racism, and anti-Semitism or discrimination against other minorities or groups. And, in this country, it has been decided that this speech will receive constitutional protection.

Probably the most widely known contemporary instance of the protection of extremist speech arose in the late 1970s when a small group of neo-Nazis from Chicago announced their intention of conducting a march in the Chicago suburb of Skokie, home to some 40,000 Jews and several thousand survivors of World War II German concentration camps. The city resisted, enacting a number of ordinances prohibiting, among other things, speech known as group libel, that is, speech that would "portray criminality, depravity or lack of virtue in, or incite violence, hatred, abuse or hostility toward a person or a group of persons by reason of reference to religious, racial, ethnic, national or regional affiliation." The AMERICAN CIVIL LIBERTIES UNION [1], on behalf of the neo-Nazi group, challenged the city's interference with the proposed march as unconstitutional under the First Amendment. The Courts sustained the challenge. Both the Illinois Supreme Court and the U.S. Court of Appeals for the Seventh Circuit, in two separate cases, held that under modern Supreme Court precedents it was beyond doubt that even this most offensive speech was constitutionally protected, absent a showing that the speech was about to turn into illegal conduct.

In fact, cases involving extremist speech constitute the backbone of the First Amendment jurisprudence. This is true, in part, because the very first cases involving free speech issues to come before the Supreme Court (which did not occur until 1919) involved extremist speech. The Supreme Court, therefore, began the process of developing modern First Amendment jurisprudence in contexts where the issue at hand was to define the outer boundaries of the principle of free speech. Many cases followed over the next seventy years, of which the Skokie case was one.

As a result of these cases, much judicial and academic ink has been spent on deciding what should be the test for establishing the limits of the First Amendment. Various formulations have been devised. It has been said that First Amendment protection ends when there is a CLEAR AND PRESENT DANGER [1] to the society (the test OLIVER WENDELL HOLMES [2] initially proposed in 1919); when speech explicitly advocates illegal action (the test proposed by Judge LEARNED HAND [2] in 1918); when speech will in the due course of events threaten the overthrow of government (which was approximately the test the Court followed during the nadir of First Amendment protection in the era of MCCARTHYISM [3]); or when speech threatens imminent serious illegal behavior and is directly intended to incite such action (the prevailing test today).

Cases involving extremist speech have been so important to the development of First Amendment jurisprudence because they have raised independent, or separate, theoretical issues about the role and meaning of the modern idea of freedom of speech. Two major issues should be noted.

First, drawing the boundaries of freedom of speech involves more than just knowing what the basic purposes of the First Amendment are. Because we live in an imperfect world, rules of law, including constitutional law, must prepare for tears and snags of a practical world. Language is rarely precise enough to foreclose mistaken applications of the rules we devise. Institutions must be relied upon to apply the rules, and the quality of institutional decisions will be dependent on the quality of the people who compose them. Thus, the extremist speech cases have posed a second issue: To what extent must *unworthy* speech be protected in order to insure that truly *worthy* speech—

speech that advances the purposes of the First Amendment—will in fact be preserved? The difficulties of drawing that line, to achieve in a practical world the right level of free speech, are immense. One must consider to what extent legislative institutions will themselves be sensitive to freedom of speech, the degree to which citizens will be deterred from speaking by the perceived possibility of hostile government action, and the courage of judges to stand up to improper legislative attempts to interfere with valuable speech. Therefore, drawing the outer line at which constitutional protection stops generates its own important and fascinating issues, beyond the issue of deciding what purposes or values underlie the First Amendment. As a general proposition it may be said that modern First Amendment protection uses extremist speech to give "breathing space" to the right of freedom of speech.

But there is an even more important reason why extremist speech cases have commanded such attention over the past seventy years. It may well be the case that extremist speech protection furthers a *distinctive* First Amendment value, separate from its function of affording ample leeway to valuable speech. The classic rationales for free speech see the relationship between free speech and the discovery of truth and a democratic system of government. These have been forcefully articulated in cases involving extremist speech. But there is another potential First Amendment meaning, or value, at stake in these cases involving speech deeply threatening to basic values of American society. Extremist speech is often bad, as socially harmful as other bad acts that are regularly subject to social regulation. That means that free speech may be a special context in which the society chooses to let bad acts go unregulated as a symbolic act of self-recognition of the difficulties of dealing appropriately with bad acts— as, for example, by being too intolerant in the ordinary political process or by reacting with excessive harshness when bad acts are punished. This rationale of free speech focuses on the relationship between that principle and the general virtue of tolerance. It may well be, in other words, that the centrality of the extremist speech cases in the First Amendment jurisprudence arises out of the fact that they have added a new and significant, and distinctively American, role to the idea of freedom of speech.

LEE C. BOLLINGER

Bibliography

BAKER, C. EDWIN 1989 *Human Liberty and Freedom of Speech.* New York: Oxford University Press.

BOLLINGER, LEE C. 1986 *The Tolerant Society: Freedom of Speech and Extremist Speech in America.* New York: Oxford University Press.

EYEWITNESS IDENTIFICATION

Eyewitness identification can be powerful EVIDENCE [2] in a criminal prosecution. Yet an identification can easily be wrong, whether made soon after the crime or in court. Because identifications can have a potentially devastating impact and are of questionable reliability, courts are especially concerned with them. Triers of fact typically assume that an eyewitness to a crime can accurately discern and remember the physical characteristics of the perpetrator. However, extensive research proves that powers of observation and recall are quite deficient.

The legal system cannot fully rectify problems with identification; it cannot affect a witness's perceptual and recall capabilities. However, the law can try to control any conscious or unconscious attempt by the police or prosecution to supply what perception and memory cannot.

Although the courts have never directly supervised the use of identification techniques, the Supreme Court has tried to minimize mistaken identification by requiring that procedures most likely to produce inaccurate results comport with certain constitutional requirements. Both the Sixth Amendment RIGHT TO COUNSEL [3] and the DUE PROCESS [2] clauses of the Fifth Amendment and FOURTEENTH AMENDMENT [2,I] provide defendants with substantive bases for questioning identifications.

In UNITED STATES V. WADE (1967) [4] the defendant participated in a postindictment LINEUP [3] conducted without notice and in the absence of his counsel. The Supreme Court held that the Sixth Amendment required invalidation of the defendant's subsequent conviction because a postindictment lineup was a "critical stage," when substantial prejudice to defendant's rights could result and counsel could help to avoid the prejudice.

However, the Supreme Court held in KIRBY V. ILLINOIS (1972) [3] that the right to counsel does not extend to pretrial identification procedures employed before adversarial judicial proceedings are initiated. In *Kirby* the defendant was arrested and later identified in a police station confrontation at which the defendant was not advised of his right to counsel and his attorney was not present. The Court clarified the "initiation of adversarial proceedings" in *Moore v. Illinois* (1977), where the defendant was identified by a victim during a preliminary hearing where his counsel was not present. In *Moore* the Court held that adversarial proceedings had begun at the preliminary hearing, rather than only after the indictment.

In UNITED STATES V. ASH (1973) [1] a witness observed a photographic array prior to trial, and defendant's counsel was not present. The Court held that there is no right to counsel at such displays and that right to counsel is limited to "trial-like confrontations." In a photographic display, the defendant is not present and does not confront the prosecutor or the adversarial system.

The Supreme Court held in *Stovall v. Denno* (1967) that the guarantee of due process of law protects an accused from identification procedures that are "so unnecessarily suggestive and conducive to irreparable mistaken identification" as to deny a defendant due process of law. In *Stovall* the Court held that a one-to-one emergency confrontation between the accused and an injured witness in a hospital room did not violate due process because it was not unnecessarily suggestive and was not substantially likely to lead to misidentification.

The due process questions of suggestibility returned to the Court in the following years. In *Simmons v. United States* (1968) the felons who had robbed a bank were still at large. The police showed six snapshots to witnesses, who identified the defendants from the photos. Guidelines of the International Association of Chiefs of Police require a photographic array to include eight photographs. However, in this case, the Court found that the compelling need for identification of the robbers justified the suggestive procedure as long as there was little danger of misidentification and rejected the defendants' due process claim. Then in *Neil v. Biggers* (1972) the Court emphasized reliability over suggestibility in analyzing a due process claim. In *Neil* the Court accepted the reliability of a stationhouse show-up at which the defendant was identified in an accidental encounter at a water fountain seven months after the crime. The Court denied the defendant's due process claim.

In *Manson v. Brathwaite* (1977) the Court reaffirmed that the reliability of an identification is the "linchpin" of due process analysis. In *Manson* an undercover police officer purchased heroin from a seller while standing near him in a well-lit hallway for two or three minutes. A few minutes later the undercover officer described the seller to another officer, who gave the undercover officer a picture of the defendant. Two days later, the undercover officer identified the picture as a photograph of the person from whom he had bought heroin. The *Manson* Court held that a single photographic display of an accused did not create a substantial likelihood of irreparable misidentification, for it was done by a trained police officer. To prevail on a due process claim, then, a defendant must prove both unnecessary suggestiveness and substantial likelihood of misidentification.

The remedy for violation of either the Sixth Amendment right to counsel or the due process standards is exclusion of the pretrial evidence and of any in-court identification derived from the tainted pretrial identification. To limit the application of this severe remedy, the Supreme Court has developed the "independent source" test, by which an in-court identification is admissible if it derives from a source independent of the tainted identification. A source is independent if there has been prior opportunity to observe the criminal act, an easy identification, and no past misidentification. However, in *Moore* the Court held that criminal prosecution may begin as early as the initial appearance, at least for the purpose of determining the right to counsel.

At a suppression hearing, usually held prior to trial, the court determines admissibility of pretrial identification evidence. Generally, the prosecution bears the burden of establishing the presence of counsel or intelligent waiver by the accused or of showing that an in-court identification derives from a source independent of tainted pretrial identification. The burden of proving a violation of due process, however, is on the defendant. In some jurisdictions, if the defendant can show that an identification process was unnecessarily suggestive, then the burden shifts to the government to show the justification of exigent circumstances.

Admissibility and credibility are separate questions. Identification evidence found admissible, usually by the judge, is not necessarily credible. The jury decides whether it believes that the witness has made an accurate identification.

Properly conducted lineups are least likely to result in misidentification. A court has the authority to order an accused to participate in a lineup. A court may, in its discretion, order a lineup at the request of the defendant, but the defendant has no constitutional right to a lineup either before trial or in the courtroom during trial. A court may also allow the defendant to sit in the audience. Sound litigation tactics require counsel for the defendant to observe the lineup procedure for reliability but not participate or use the lineup for DISCOVERY [2].

CHARLES H. WHITEBREAD

(SEE ALSO: *Procedural Due Process of Law, Criminal* [3,I].)

Bibliography

BUCKOUT, ROBERT 1980 Nearly 2,000 Witnesses Can Be Wrong. *Bulletin of the Psychonomic Society* 16:307–310.

WHITEBREAD, CHARLES H. 1986 *Criminal Procedure*. Mineola, N.Y.: Foundation Press.

FBI

The Federal Bureau of Investigation (FBI) is a division of the Department of Justice supervised by the attorney general. Although a CABINET [1] officer since the 1790s, the ATTORNEY GENERAL [1] did not oversee federal law enforcement and did not even head a federal department until congressional legislation of 1870 created the Department of Justice. The attorney general's responsibilities originally involved arguing major cases before the Supreme Court and advising the President on constitutional questions. The combination of the Reconstruction experience with the enactment of legislation regulating INTERSTATE COMMERCE [2] in 1887 and preventing corporate mergers in 1890, however, led attorneys general to recognize the need for experienced investigators to secure evidence to prosecute violators of the anti-trust and interstate commerce laws. Accordingly, in July 1908 Attorney General Charles Bonaparte, by EXECUTIVE ORDER [2], created a special investigation division within the Department of Justice, the Bureau of Investigation, formally renamed the Federal Bureau of Investigation in 1935.

Thereafter, the FBI's investigative reponsibilities increased as new laws expanded the definition of interstate commerce crime (the MANN ACT [3] of 1910 and the Dyer Act of 1919) and law enforcement responsibilities (laws criminalizing kidnapping and bank robbing) and barred specified political activities that threatened the nation's internal security (the ESPIONAGE ACT [2] of 1917 and the Smith Act of 1940). Yet this expansion raised no unique constitutional question both because it was legislatively mandated and because the Supreme Court upheld the constitutionality of the Espionage and Smith Acts, which impinged on speech and association.

The FBI's activities have raised constitutional issues because of the Bureau's monitoring of "subversive" activities, particularly since 1936. In striking contrast even to the abusive PALMER RAIDS [3] of 1920, which had been based on the 1918 Immigration Act's alien deportation provisions, after 1936 the FBI did not seek evidence to effect prosecution; and its "intelligence" investigations were authorized solely under secret executive directives (President FRANKLIN D. ROOSEVELT's [3] oral directive of August 1936) or public executive orders (President HARRY S. TRUMAN's [4] March 1947 order establishing the Federal Employee Loyalty Program). In acquiring intelligence about dissident activities, the FBI's purposes became either to service White House interests and those of the increasingly powerful FBI director or, in the case of federal loyalty/security programs, to anticipate espionage by identifying "potentially disloyal" federal employees. In time, the FBI's dissemination activities extended beyond the executive branch—at first, during the 1940s, informally and then after the 1950s formally, to governors and to carefully selected reporters, columnists, prominent national leaders, and members of Congress. Rather than prosecuting individuals for violating federal laws, the FBI instead brought about the dismissal of "subversive" employees by disseminating information on state employees to state governors under a code-named Responsibilities Program and by exposing publicly other "subversives," often through covert assistance to the HOUSE COMMITTEE ON UN-AMERICAN ACTIVITIES [2], Senator Joseph McCarthy, and the Senate Internal Security Subcommittee. Adopting a more aggressive tack after 1956, FBI officials instituted two other formal programs, COINTELPRO and

Mass Media, both having as their purpose the discrediting of targeted organizations and their adherents.

These programs were not subject to JUDICIAL REVIEW [3,I] both because they had no law enforcement purpose and because they were conducted secretly. Furthermore, these covert efforts to "harass, disrupt and discredit" targeted organizations or to disseminate derogatory information about political activists to favored journalists, members of Congress, Presidents, governors, and prominent citizens were based on a commitment to contain political change.

The FBI's activities raised other constitutional questions in view of some of the Bureau's investigative techniques. Despite the legislative ban against WIRETAPPING [4] of the COMMUNICATIONS ACT [1] of 1934 and the FOURTH AMENDMENT [2,I] prohibition of UNREASONABLE SEARCHES and seizures, from 1940 forward the FBI installed wiretaps and bugs and conducted break-ins when investigating "subversive" activities and at times during sensitive criminal investigations. These techniques were authorized under secret directives issued either by Presidents (Franklin Roosevelt's May 1940 authorization of wiretapping), the attorney general (Herbert Brownell's May 1954 authorization of bugging), or solely by the FBI director (J. EDGAR HOOVER's [2] 1942 authorization of break-ins). Theoretically, information so obtained could not be used for prosecution. However, two individuals inadvertently uncovered the FBI's ELECTRONIC EAVESDROPPING [2] at a time when they were the subjects of criminal inquiries. Intercepted messages included attorney–client conversations, and in both cases, the disclosures led the courts to overturn the defendants' convictions.

Contrary to the rationale that gained currency during the 1960s of inherent presidential powers, when FBI officials first employed these electronic surveillance techniques in the 1940s they privately conceded their illegality and accordingly sought to preclude public discovery of potentially controversial practices. For example, when outlining how requests for his approval to conduct break-ins were to be submitted, FBI Director Hoover characterized this technique as "clearly illegal." Because break-ins offered the opportunity to acquire otherwise unobtainable information about "subversive" activities (membership and subscription lists, financial records, correspondence and memoranda), Hoover was willing to risk use of this technique. To avert discovery, however, the FBI director devised a special records procedure, "Do Not File," to ensure the undiscoverable destruction of such records and further to allow FBI officials to affirm, in response to congressional SUBPOENAS [4] or court-ordered DISCOVERY [2] motions, that a search of the FBI's "central records system" uncovered no evidence of illegal conduct.

This FBI practice raised additional constitutional question insofar as, beginning in the late 1950s, break-ins were employed during some criminal investigations.

The Founding Fathers had not anticipated the constitutional questions posed by FBI "intelligence" investigations, some of which employed intrusive investigative techniques. In view of both their scope and purpose, FBI intelligence investigations raise two difficult policy questions, the first concerning investigation and the second concerning controls. First, should FBI investigations be confined to law enforcement based on a PROBABLE CAUSE [3] standard, or should the attorney general issue guidelines authorizing and defining the scope of such investigations, or instead, should Congress, through a legislative charter, define the scope of FBI investigative authority? Second, should the Bureau be subject primarily to the oversight of the attorney general and only indirectly to selected review during court proceedings and congressional hearings? Or should Congress assume this ongoing oversight role? The attorney general has been unwilling, historically, to assume this responsibility by creating written records of his review and has authorized FBI "intelligence" investigations (excepting during the brief period of 1976–1981).

(SEE ALSO: *McCarthyism* [3].)

ATHAN THEOHARIS

Bibliography

THEOHARIS, ATHAN and COX, JOHN STUART 1988 *The Boss: J. Edgar Hoover and the Great American Inquisition*. Philadelphia: Temple University Press.
UNGAR, SANFORD 1975 *FBI*. Boston: Atlantic/Little, Brown.

FEDERAL CRIMINAL LAW

In the past two decades, Congress has enacted many new types of criminal statutes, such as the RACKETEER INFLUENCED AND CORRUPT ORGANIZATIONS ACT (RICO) [I] and the continuing criminal enterprise and money-laundering offenses. New approaches to criminal penalties and sentencing have also been adopted, including criminal forfeiture, high mandatory sentences, and the sentencing guidelines. Although the government has been prosecuting these new crimes and penalties, often in combination, for many years, with few exceptions their constitutionality has not been tested in the Supreme Court.

The Constitution as applied to the substantive federal criminal law is largely dormant. The Supreme Court infrequently agrees to review cases raising issues of interpretation of federal criminal statutes. Even rarer is the case in which the Court agrees to consider the constitutionality of a substantive criminal statute. And cases in which the Court holds either substantive criminal legislation or prosecutorial action to be unconstitutional are rarer still. This is not for want of a large number of federal criminal cases in which such issues are raised, nor for a lack of applicable constitutional provisions or doctrines against which federal criminal statues and prosecutions can be tested—for example, DOUBLE JEOPARDY [2,I], VAGUENESS [4], and CRUEL AND UNUSUAL PUNISHMENT [2,I].

There have been a few recent exceptions to the prevailing pattern. In *Grady v. Corbin*, a 1990 decision arising out of a state drunk driving–criminal homicide prosecution, the Supreme Court adopted a revised double-jeopardy test that, among its most important effects, may have an impact on federal RICO and continuing criminal enterprise prosecutions.

Before *Grady*, the principal test for determining whether the Constitution was violated by successive prosecutions under two different criminal statutes for the same criminal act or transaction was the doctrine described in *Blockburger v. United States* (1932): that the double-jeopardy prohibition is not violated if each of the statutes involved in the two prosecutions requires proof of a fact that the other statute does not.

The effect of *Blockburger* has been generally to permit separate prosecutions growing out of the same conduct (even if the essence of the charges are similar) as long as they were based on different federal criminal statutes. In the federal criminal context, the *Blockburger* standard is easily met; there is little coherence or consistency in the way federal crimes are drafted, and the nature of most of these statutory offenses is such that they have elements quite different from all others.

In *Grady*, the Court ruled that the *Blockburger* test should still be applied in the first instance. If this standard is satisfied by a comparison of the elements of the two offenses, it is to be followed by a further inquiry under which the subsequent prosecution is barred if "the government, to establish an essential element of an offense charged in that prosecution, . . . prove[s] conduct that constitutes an offense for which the defendant has already been prosecuted."

Rather than focusing, as does *Blockburger*, on the statutory elements alone, this latter test requires a comparison of what the prosecutor attempts to prove at both of the trials. Justice WILLIAM J. BRENNAN [1,I], writing for the majority in *Grady*, took pains, however, to note that "[t]his is not . . . [a] same evidence test. The critical inquiry is what conduct the . . . [government] will prove, not the evidence . . . [it] will use to prove that conduct."

Depending on its subsequent interpretation, application of the *Grady* test could impose an important restriction on the government's ability to prosecute RICO and continuing criminal-enterprise cases. The RICO offense is committed when a person conducts the affairs of an enterprise (a continuing conspiratorial group or legal entity, such as a corporation or a governmental agency) through a pattern of racketeering activity that involves the commission of two or more related predicate offenses.

Before *Grady*, the government could, and often did, prosecute RICO cases relying on predicate offenses for which the accused had previously been tried and convicted (and even offenses of which the accused had been acquitted). *Grady*'s abandonment of *Blockburger* as the exclusive test of double jeopardy in successive-prosecution cases can be argued to bar the use as predicate offenses in RICO (and, for similar reasons, in continuing criminal enterprise cases) of crimes for which the accused has previously been tried. If the *Grady* test is applied as Justice ANTONIN SCALIA [I], in dissent, suggested it would be —that is, "where the charges arise from a single criminal act, occurrence, episode, or transaction, they must be tried in a single proceeding"—the decision will have the effect of barring separate trials of a RICO charge and the predicate offenses on which the RICO count is based.

An early post-*Grady* decision, *United States v. Esposito* (1990), handed down by a federal court of appeals, has taken a contrary view, however, holding that *Grady* does not bar a prosecution of the predicate crimes where there has been a prior acquittal on the related RICO charge. *Esposito* relied mainly on the earlier Supreme Court decision in *Garrett v. United States* (1985), a case only briefly cited in *Grady*.

Garrett involved the double-jeopardy implications of a continuing criminal-enterprise prosecution where the facts underlying a prior conviction of marijuana importation were used to prove one of the three predicate offenses on which the continuing criminal-enterprise charge was based. The Supreme Court ruled that the double-jeopardy prohibition was not violated where the prior conviction was only one incident of conduct that occurred on two single days during the five-year course of conduct that was the basis for the continuing criminal-enterprise charge.

Although *Garrett* seems to be a relevant precedent in deciding on the effect of *Grady* on RICO and continuing criminal-enterprise prosecutions, the question remains whether, after *Grady*, *Garrett* is still good law and, if so, whether in a RICO or continuing criminal-enterprise prosecution, the government in proving conduct underlying a prior conviction as a predicate offense is trying to "establish *an essential element* of . . . [the] offense charged in that prosecution" (emphasis added).

Grady does not affect another application of the same *Blockburger* test—its use as the constitutional standard for determining whether separate punishments can be imposed for offenses tried together. Accordingly, even after *Grady*, there is no constitutional bar to the practice of prosecuting, along with a RICO count, separate predicate offenses (even those based in essentially the same harmful conduct) whose statutory elements differ from each other and those in the RICO statute and, following conviction on all of the charges, imposing separate punishments for each of the several crimes.

Grady is a modern rarity, a constitutional decision that may impose a substantive restriction on the enforcement of the federal criminal law, but there is a chance that it will not remain very long on the books. It was a 5–4 decision, with Justice Scalia, joined by Justices SANDRA DAY O'CONNOR [3,I], ANTHONY M. KENNEDY [I], and Chief Justice WILLIAM H. REHNQUIST [3,I] dissenting. Given the close division in the case, the subsequent retirement of the author of the majority opinion, Justice Brennan, and the fact that the Court's articulation of double-jeopardy doctrine seems to be continually evolving, the case is a possible candidate for early overruling.

Apart from *Grady*, no other recent significant constitutional decision has served to restrict the use of the many innovative federal crime statutes and punishments enacted during the past two decades. The closest that the Court has come recently to such a decision is Justice Scalia's concurring opinion in *H.J., Inc. v. Northwestern Bell Telephone Co.* (1989) (joined by the same three Justices who joined him in dissent in *Grady*), in which he raised doubts about whether a key element of the RICO statute—the "pattern" requirement in the "pattern of racketeering activity" phrase—meets the constitutional proscription against vagueness in criminal statutes.

The *H.J.* decision itself involved a civil action under the provision of the RICO statute that authorizes a private treble-damage suit to be brought by a person injured by a criminal RICO violation. Justice Scalia noted that because RICO has criminal applications "as well," it "must, even in its civil applications, possess the degree of certainty required for criminal laws." A corollary follows from this proposition. A decision in a civil RICO suit that the "pattern of racketeering" phrase used in defining the criminal violation is constitutionally infirm would apply equally in the criminal context. Thus, a constitutional decision that might in its immediate impact serve to insulate business people from treble-damage actions could also serve to protect organized-crime figures from federal criminal prosecution. Of course, it remains to be seen whether the concurring opinion in *H.J.* will gain another adherent and ripen into a constitutional restriction on the breadth of the RICO statute.

An innovative aspect of the RICO and drug statutes, the punishment of criminal forfeiture, was recently considered in *Caplin and Drysdale, Chartered v. United States* (1989), where the Court held that neither the Fifth nor the Sixth Amendment exempts from forfeiture assets that a criminal defendant proposes to use to pay defense counsel. In a related case, *United States v. Monsanto* (1989), the Court upheld the constitutionality of a pretrial order freezing such assets in a defendant's possession.

A more central constitutional challenge to criminal forfeiture, litigated in some of the courts of appeals, but yet to be considered by the Supreme Court, is the question as to whether, given the nature and circumstances of the offense, a forfeiture might be grossly disproportionate under the Eighth Amendment's cruel and unusual punishment clause.

Under the RICO statute, the prosecutor may seek forfeiture of the convicted person's entire interest in an enterprise the affairs of which were carried on in violation of the statute; the statutory forfeiture provision contains no limitation. Moreover, once the accused is convicted, forfeiture is mandatory; the judge has no discretion to reduce the amount. Thus, a person who owns all or most of a corporation and violates the federal criminal law, for example, by accepting or paying some kickbacks may, as a result of a RICO conviction, forfeit his or her entire interest in the corporation to the government.

In *United States v. Busher* (1987), taking to heart the Supreme Court's ruling in SOLEM V. HELM (1983) [4] (the Eighth Amendment "prohibits not only barbaric punishments, but also sentences that are disproportionate to the crime committed"), the Ninth Circuit Court of Appeals ruled that the Eighth Amendment limits extreme criminal forfeitures under RICO (and under the drug laws) to insure that the punishment imposed is not "disproportionate to the crime committed." Some of the other circuits have ruled similarly.

None of these decisions has been reviewed by the Supreme Court. However, the Court has agreed to consider an appeal on an Eighth Amendment ground in a drug case that might shed some light on the forfeiture punishment issue. In *Harmelin v. Michigan*, the Court will decide whether a mandatory term of life imprisonment without parole imposed on a person with no prior criminal record, who has been convicted of possession of slightly more than a pound of cocaine, violates the eighth amendment proscription against cruel and unusual punishment. The case will be considered in the 1990–1991 term.

There has been one recent important constitutional decision affecting a key element in the federal criminal enforcement system, MISTRETTA V. UNITED STATES (1989) [I], where the Court sustained the United States Sentencing Commission against a constitutional challenge claiming that the legislation setting up the Commission delegated excessive legislative power to the Commission and violated separation of powers doctrine.

In 1984, with a view to eliminating excessive disparity in federal sentences, the Congress enacted the Sentencing Reform Act setting up the Sentencing Commission as an independent body in the Judicial Branch, with authority to establish binding Sentencing Guidelines that, based upon detailed factors relating to the offense and the offender, provide for a range of determinate sentences for all federal offenses.

In *Mistretta*, the Court ruled that the Sentencing Reform Act sets forth "more than . . . [the] 'intelligible principle' or minimal standards" that are required under traditional nondelegation doctrine prohibiting excessive delegations of legislative authority: "Developing proportionate penalties for hundreds of different crimes by a virtually limitless array of offenders is precisely the sort of intricate, labor-intensive task for which delegation to an expert body is especially appropriate."

While recognizing that the Sentencing Commission "unquestionably is a peculiar institution within the framework of our Government", the Court rejected the argument that the structure of the Commission violated separation of powers doctrine insofar as it required Article III judges, who sit on the Commission with other nonjudicial appointees selected by the President, to exercise legislative authority; and also required those judges to share their judicial rulemaking authority with nonjudges; and threatened judicial independence insofar as the President is given authority to remove the judges from the Commission.

Mistretta is a significant decision since it sustains against constitutional attack the basic structural change relating to federal sentencing that Congress had effected by enacting the Sentencing Reform Act. Although there are further constitutional issues that may be raised in cases applying the guidelines—for example, whether the guidelines violate due process insofar as they restrict judicial discretion to weigh individual factors in sentencing—the message of *Mistretta* is that the Sentencing Commission and its guidelines are here to stay.

Although *Mistretta* is significant, it is also *sui generis*. It is a unique decision relating to a new institutional structure and does not detract at all from the observation made earlier that the Constitution is largely dormant as applied to the substantive federal criminal law.

Of course, given the current makeup of the Court, public attitudes toward crime, and the historical reluctance of the Court to adjudge substantive federal criminal legislation unconstitutional, even were the Court to agree to review the constitutionality of these new measures, it would be unlikely that any of them would be found invalid.

Still, even if declarations of unconstitutionality are unlikely, it would be helpful to the bench and bar if the Court were to review these issues with greater frequency.

The import of the Court's general reluctance to review many issues of statutory interpretation and the constitutionality of substantive federal criminal laws and related issues (while inexplicably continuing frequently to delve deeply into the minutiae of Fourth Amendment search and seizure issues) goes far beyond the direct effect of the Court's failure to consider the relevant issues; it influences the lower federal courts, which see many more federal criminal cases than the high court, and it may also be having an impact on the Congress.

Not surprisingly, federal district courts and courts of appeals generally do not give extended consideration to claims challenging the constitutionality of the new federal criminal statutes such as RICO. Correspondingly and perhaps more importantly, they also appear generally not even to be influenced very much by constitutional values in their interpretation of federal criminal statutes. This may not be unexpected in a climate created by a high court that itself is paying little attention to such issues. Yet in a system of judicial review, one expects constitutional values to be applied not only as a basis for determining the validity of criminal statutes, but as an element influencing, in appropriate cases and to a limited extent, issues of statutory interpretation.

In recent years, Congress has legislated an explosion in federal criminal statutes. At the same time, the legislature seems to be paying less and less attention to statutory details and has even become careless in the drafting process. In 1984, 1986, and 1988, Congress enacted comprehensive legislative packages encompassing a large number of federal criminal subjects; in the 1988 legislation, for example, a significant number of the provisions were directed to correcting drafting errors in the earlier legislation. Although it is not possible to demonstrate any direct linkage between the Supreme Court's inattention to the federal criminal law and the increase in legislative action in this area and the corresponding increase in drafting sloppiness, one might expect the Congress to be affected in its actions if the Court were to enter this arena more frequently.

Were the Court more actively to review and perhaps occasionally invalidate federal legislative or executive action in the criminal sphere affecting substantive interests, the effect might go far beyond the specific issues being decided. It might influence federal judges' approach to issues of interpretation of federal criminal statutes and also affect the kinds of cases prosecutors bring and the kind of positions they take in cases being brought. Most important, it could influence the Congress and have a significant impact on the form and content of future federal criminal legislation.

NORMAN ABRAMS

Bibliography

ABRAMS, NORMAN 1986 *Federal Criminal Law and Its Enforcement.* St. Paul, Minn.: West Publishing Co.

———— 1989 The New Ancillary Offenses. *Criminal Law Forum* 1:1–39.

KURLAND, ADAM H. 1989 The Guarantee Clause as a Basis for Federal Prosecution of State and Local Officers. *Southern California Law Review* 62:367–491.

LYNCH, GERARD E. 1987 RICO: The Crime of Being a Criminal, Parts I & II, Parts II & III. *Columbia Law Review* 87:661–764, 920–984.

FEDERAL JUDICIAL APPOINTMENTS, TENURE, AND INDEPENDENCE

In the federal judicial system the appointment and tenure of judges are governed by the Constitution and by statutes enacted by Congress. Neither the Constitution nor Congress controls the structure of state judicial systems or the appointment and tenure of judges of those courts; under state laws, judges are variously popularly elected or appointed by the governor or another state officer, with or without the consent of the legislature, a commission, or a confirming election. State judges do not have life tenure.

Federal courts are classified as "Article III courts," also known as CONSTITUTIONAL COURTS [1], and "Article I courts," also known as LEGISLATIVE COURTS [3]. The constitutional courts are those courts specified in Article III, section 1, vesting the JUDICIAL POWER OF THE UNITED STATES [4] "in one supreme Court, and such inferior Courts as the Congress may from time to time ordain and establish." These judges have lifetime tenure and compensation that cannot be reduced during their judicial service. Legislative courts encompass the remaining adjudicative tribunals that are congressionally established but do not have all of the characteristics required by Article III. Judges of legislative courts are appointed for terms of years; the jurisdiction of those courts is not coextensive with Article III courts' jurisdiction.

Except for recess appointments by the President to fill vacancies when the Senate is not in session (Article II, section 1), constitutional Justices and judges hold their offices "during good behavior," as Article III provides. In UNITED STATES EX REL. TOTH V. QUARLES (1955) [4], the Court held that the GOOD BEHAVIOR clause guarantees such judges lifetime tenure, subject to removal only by IMPEACHMENT [2].

Article II, section 2, requires nomination of Article III Justices and judges by the President "with the advice and consent of the Senate." The role of the Senate under the ADVICE AND CONSENT [1,I] clause has been debated since the CONSTITUTIONAL CONVENTION OF 1787 [1]. The clause was adopted as a compromise in the closing days of the Convention as an alternative to proposals to grant appointing power to the President alone or to the Senate alone; the delegates did not discuss the meaning of the clause.

Senators have variously interpreted their constitutional obligations in proceedings to confirm presidential nominations to the judiciary. Some senators have treated their task as little more than a procedural formality unless the nominee is egregiously unfit for the judicial post to which he or she has been named or a serious flaw in the candidate's background is revealed during the deliberations. Other senators have expansively interpreted their responsibility to "advise" the President, including the advice that the President's choice is wrong. The history of confirmation battles strongly suggests that the fate of a particular nominee more often depends on the political views of the senators than on intellectual differences over CONSTITUTIONAL INTERPRETATION [2]. Apart from the individual characteristics of the nominee and the personal and political philosophies of the senators who act on a nomination, the outcome of the process is heavily influenced by the sensitivity of the judicial post to which the candidate has been named, the existing composition of that particular court, the relative power of the President and the Senate at the time of the nomination, and the prevailing national political climate. The closest senatorial scrutiny is usually given to nominees for the Supreme Court. The obvious reason is the tremendous importance of the Court. Less obvious is that senatorial courtesies do not have the same significance in confirmation of Supreme Court nominees as they do in nominations to district courts and courts of appeals. In the latter instances, the opposition of one senator from the nominee's home state is usually enough to doom confirmation, especially if the senator is a member of the President's political party.

Scant attention was given to the public interest in judicial confirmations before 1929 because, until then, the Senate acted upon all nominations in closed executive session unless the hearing was ordered open by a two-thirds vote of the Senate. Except in rare instances, such as the nomination of Justice LOUIS D. BRANDEIS [1] in 1916 and of Justice HARLAN FISKE STONE [4] in 1925, the necessary votes could not be mustered. The Senate rules were amended in 1929 to open all confirmation hearings.

Even after hearings were open, they were usually quiet events. Nominees were not called to appear before the

SENATE JUDICIARY COMMITTEE [I] until 1939, when the nomination of FELIX FRANKFURTER [2] was under consideration. Although he initially declined to appear, he later testified and was unanimously approved by the Senate. Since then, with few exceptions, nominees to Article III courts are routinely called to, and do testify before, the Judiciary Committee. The addition of televised hearings probably has not changed confirmation results, but at a minimum it has heightened the drama of controversial appointments and encouraged oratory.

Although the confirmation process is now generally available in living color, the roles of the actors in the prenomination process are neither public nor well known. The large cast includes the President, the inner circle of the White House, senators who are not members of the Judiciary Committee, congressional delegations, the ATTORNEY GENERAL [1], the Department of Justice, the Federal Bureau of Investigation, the American Bar Association, and sometimes others.

Presidential means and motives for selecting nominees to the Supreme Court defy facile description. Supreme Court vacancies occur unpredictably and sporadically. For example, no vacancies on the Court appeared during President JIMMY CARTER's [1] term, but Justice POTTER J. STEWART's [4] retirement gave President RONALD REAGAN [3,I] his first appointment to the Court within a few months of his assuming office.

History gives substance to Justice Felix Frankfurter's description of Supreme Court nominations as "that odd lottery." Sometimes the presidential motivation for a particular appointment is evident, even if the means by which the person came to presidential attention are not. Thus, President HERBERT HOOVER's [2] reason for nominating CHARLES EVANS HUGHES [2] as CHIEF JUSTICE [1] in 1930 was the economic plight of the country and his belief that Hughes would forward views that would help the President's economic policies. On the other hand, the source of President ULYSSES S. GRANT's choice of Caleb Cushing is known, but his motives in selecting him are not. The nominee was seventy-four years old, and his political philosophy was unknown. President Grant withdrew the nomination after he discovered Cushing's ties to the Confederacy. Both the source and motive are occasionally clear, as is true of President LYNDON B. JOHNSON's [3] nomination of Solicitor General THURGOOD MARSHALL [3,I].

History permits only a few generalizations about presidential choices for the Supreme Court. For example, the nominee will almost always be a member of the political party of the President, and in making selections the President will rely on the advice of trusted friends within and outside his administration and of those persons whose support, or nonopposition, will be needed to confirm the nominee or to assist the President in achieving other objectives on his political agenda.

Presidents have sometimes selected candidates for lower courts without initial outside consultation. Usually, however, the President makes his choice from a list of potential nominees submitted to him. For district courts, typically a nomination is initiated by a senator of the candidate's home state if the senator is of the President's political party. When no senator of the candidate's home state is of the President's party, the names may be suggested by the state governor, leaders of the President's party, members of the congressional delegation, or members of his administration. President Carter encouraged all senators to use regional or local panels to gather and submit potential nominees for district courts before making recommendations to him. Some senators still use such panels, although the White House has not recently urged them to do so.

Proposals for appointments to courts of appeals are initiated by an analogous process. Because courts of appeals' geographical jurisdiction is not confined within state lines, as the jurisdiction of a district court is, more senators have a say in these appointments than in appointments of district judges. Senators of the President's party continue to play an important initiating role, but some degree of senatorial courtesy is also extended to other senators in the affected states. President Carter departed from prior practice by issuing an EXECUTIVE ORDER [2] establishing a nationwide commission, with panelists chosen from all states within each circuit to propose nominations. Senators could propose nominees in addition to those proposed by panels. The Reagan administration abolished the commission, relying instead on members of his administration and selected senators to perform the task, a process that more nearly resembled the practices before President Carter.

When potential nominees have been reduced to a short list, the candidates are screened by the Department of Justice and discussed with key senators and with leaders of the congressional delegation of the President's party. The Federal Bureau of Investigation is directed to search the background of potential nominees to discover evidence that might disqualify the candidate or embarrass the administration. Further screening is usually done by White House personnel to whom the President has delegated that task.

If all these preliminary tests look positive, the names on the short list will be submitted to the American Bar Association's Standing Committee on Federal Judiciary to test their professional qualifications. Committee rankings of district and circuit judge nominees are self-explanatory: "exceptionally well qualified," "well qualified," "qualified," and "not qualified." The rating system for

Supreme Court nominees describes the candidates as "well qualified," "not opposed," and "not qualified." In committee parlance, "not opposed" means that the nominee is considered barely qualified. Presidents do not have to accept these ratings, but it is rare that a nomination has been forwarded to the Senate when the candidate has received poor grades from the Bar Association.

Appointments and tenure of judges to Article I courts do not follow the same scenario. Article I courts display almost as many variations as Charles Darwin's "singular group of finches," and Congress has adapted the system to each of the jurisdictional environments in which these courts sit. Even a partial taxonomy of Article I courts reveals their jurisdictional diversity: the district courts of the Canal Zone, Virgin Islands, Guam, and Northern Mariana Islands; the High Court of American Samoa; certain ADMINISTRATIVE AGENCIES [I] with adjudicative powers; the United States COURT OF MILITARY APPEALS [2]; the TAX COURT [4]; the bankruptcy courts; and the local judiciary of the DISTRICT OF COLUMBIA [2]. Appointment to these courts is made variously by the President, with or without senatorial confirmation, and, in the instance of the bankruptcy courts, by federal district judges. Judges of these courts serve designated terms in office, rather than having life tenure.

The constitutional legitimacy of Congress's establishing courts other than Article III courts has been repeatedly questioned from the early days of our Republic. The issue first came before the Supreme Court in AMERICAN INSURANCE COMPANY V. CANTER (1828) [1], testing the constitutionality of Congress's creating TERRITORIAL COURTS [4] staffed by judges without life tenure. Chief Justice JOHN MARSHALL [3], writing for the Court, held that Congress had the power to create "legislative courts," having judges of limited tenure with jurisdiction that was not coextensive with that of Article III courts. Since then, the Court has had second thoughts about the vexing constitutional restrictions on congressional delegation of jurisdiction to adjudicative tribunals that do not have all of the characteristics of Article III courts. Although the former Court of Claims survived constitutional attack when the Supreme Court held that it was a peculiar Article III court in *Glidden Co. v. Zdanok* (1962), the reorganized bankruptcy courts did not fare so well in NORTHERN PIPELINE CO. V. MARATHON PIPE LINE CO. (1982) [3], in which a sharply divided Court struck down part of the legislative grant of jurisdiction to bankruptcy courts as an unconstitutional delegation of Article III jurisdiction.

Although appointments to the federal judiciary are heavily politicized, federal judges are thereafter completely independent of the politics that brought them to the bench, as some Presidents have unhappily learned when their appointees have not followed the philosophies they anticipated. Despite the divorce of the judges from politics, judges and Justices have not always been removed from the political realm. For example, in 1790, Chief Justice JOHN JAY [3] and Associate Justice OLIVER ELLSWORTH [2] temporarily shed their robes to represent the government in treaty negotiations with France and England. Chief Justice WILLIAM HOWARD TAFT [4] actively participated in helping President WARREN G. HARDING [2] select federal judges, and Chief Justice EARL WARREN [4] in 1962 chaired the commission investigating the assassination of President JOHN F. KENNEDY [3]. A number of Justices have been continuing confidants of Presidents and assisted them in formulating national policies.

Inevitable tensions are generated between independence and politics because the judiciary depends on Congress to authorize needed judgeships, to pay judicial salaries and authorize and pay for nonjudicial personnel assisting courts, and to provide for courtrooms and courthouses. Justices and judges commonly testify before Congress and write and speak on such issues affecting the judiciary and the administration of justice. Statutes and canons of judicial ethics announce rules designed to avoid collisions between independence and political influences.

Particularly sensitive conflicts are also generated when the need for judicial independence must be balanced against the need to sideline judges who are physically or mentally unable to perform their duties and to discipline errant federal judges short of impeachment. Little controversy has arisen from involuntarily retiring judges for disability. A storm of criticism followed the enactment of the 1980 Judicial Councils Reform and Judicial Conduct and Disability Act, which empowered a panel of judges to investigate complaints against a federal judge accused of "conduct prejudicial to the effective expeditious administration of the business of the courts" and authorized the panel to impose discipline, short of removal from office, if the panel should find wrongdoing. The act was attacked on two grounds: for infringing the constitutional freedom of judges from removal by procedures other than impeachment, and for posing a threat that such disciplinary proceedings could be used to subject judges to reprisals for unpopular decisions. Nonetheless, the statute has been sustained, and the opponents' fears of retaliation have not been realized.

The independence of the judiciary implies more than political neutrality. Numerous statutes, rules, and ethical principles seek to preserve judicial independence by foreclosing parties to litigation and other persons from improperly influencing judicial decisions. With a few carefully guarded exceptions, litigants, their lawyers, and others are forbidden to contact a judge about a pending case without prior permission and without contemporaneously informing all parties and their lawyers about the existence and substance of any such communications. Both civil and criminal penalties are used to punish persons who violate those rules.

SHIRLEY HUFSTEDLER

(SEE ALSO: *Appointing and Removal Power (Presidential)* [1]; *Appointments Clause* [I].)

Bibliography

EDWARDS, DREW E. 1987 Judicial Misconduct and Politics in the Federal System: A Proposal for Revising the Judicial Councils Act. *California Law Review* 75:1071–1092.

FOWLER, W. GARY 1984 Judicial Selection Under Reagan and Carter: A Comparison of Their Initial Recommendation Procedures. *Judicature* 67:265–283.

FREUND, PAUL A. 1988 Appointment of Justices: Some Historical Perspectives. *Harvard Law Review* 101:1146–1163.

SLOTNICK, ELLIOT E. 1988 Federal Judicial Recruitment and Selection Research: A Review Essay. *Judicature* 71:317–324.

FEDERALISM
(Contemporary Practice)

The Supreme Court does not enforce constitutional FEDERALISM [2]. Rather, it enforces sufferance federalism, that is, federalism as determined by Congress, a weak form of federalism in which state laws govern particular subjects only so far as Congress decides and in which Congresss controls such subjects as it sees fit. The Court also does not now recognize any significant distinction between taxing a state and taxing a private business; the former may be subjected to national taxes imposed by Congress in any circumstance applicable to the latter. And the Court interprets the SPENDING POWER [I] not as a limited power enabling the government to defray the expenses of its own operations and programs but as a power available to Congress to use to eliminate diversity among state laws according to its own choice. At the same time, the Supreme Court also deems Congress to possess power to restrict the means by which state or LOCAL GOVERNMENTS [I] might attempt to raise their own revenue for their own programs, without depending on appropriations from Congress. This renders each state dependent on such funds as Congress may see fit to budget, with such strings attached as Congress decides as a way to force changes in laws otherwise not subject to its control. In brief, in the aggregate of its federalism decisions the Court acts overall as an agency of the national government on federalism questions. "Judicially constrained dual federalism" does not accurately describe federalism in the United States. Rather, "sufferance federalism"—federalism to such extent as the national government decides to be appropriate—is the system virtually de jure in the United States.

Several examples of mere sufferance federalism have been provided in four recent decisions of the Supreme Court. Instructive on the point is *South Dakota v. Dole* (1987), which sustained an act of Congress that disapproved state statutes permitting any person over eighteen years of age to purchase beer. Congress desired that the minimum state drinking age should be raised to twenty-one. The means selected by Congress were efficient to this end. It reduced federally appropriated matching highway funds to any state in which the lawful minimum drinking age was lower than Congress desired the state legislature to enact and reduced these funds by such a fraction as Congress could be confident would be sufficiently harsh that no state could hold out against the penalty thus imposed.

The Court, over two dissents, rejected the view that the spending power is a power merely to meet the government's own operating BUDGET [1] as a national government (the view JAMES MADISON [3] had held). It also rejected the view that Congress's power was at most a power to set the conditions of a general or a specific program it would be willing to help fund (e.g., the construction of such highways as would be built to congressional specifications of design, quality, and materials). Rather in *Dole* the Court accepted the additional view that the spending power is available to Congress to use as an oblique power for the "indirect achievement of objects which Congress is not empowered to achieve directly." It is a power, in short, to require states to adopt the same substantive law on a given subject as their neighbors have, insofar as Congress sees fit, or be penalized under federal programs of assistance at such level of disadvantage Congress is confident will be sufficient to bring about the change it desires in their laws. As illustrated by the *Dole* case, the Court thus acts as an *active* department in federalism matters, that is, an enforcing department of the national government, validating Congress's preferences not merely in respect to its own laws but in respect to the content of state law as well. The three other major federalism decisions by the Court in the most recent five years (1985–1990) are of the same general hue.

In *South Carolina v. Baker* (1988), for example, the Court sustained an act of Congress eliminating the federal tax deductibility of interest income received on bearer bonds issued by state or local governments, bonds commonly used as a means of financing state or local operations. In sustaining this act, the Court overruled its own unanimous holding in POLLOCK V. FARMERS' LOAN & TRUST (1895) [3]. Then, going beyond the facts of the case and the immediate legal question, Justice WILLIAM J. BRENNAN [1,I] volunteered that Congress might also forbid states from attempting to raise revenue by issuing such bonds *at all*. In Justice Brennan's view, if Congress felt that such bonds would be a hindrance to its own collection of national taxes, it might outlaw their use by the states. To the objection that this would leave the states effectively subject to Congress ("sufferance federalism"), Justice Brennan was unfazed: "[S]tates must find their protection from congressional regulation through the national political process, not through judicially defined spheres of [respective national and state powers]."

In a related federalism development involving the ELEVENTH AMENDMENT [2,I] and state immunity from suits brought by private parties in federal court, a majority of the Court overruled still another unanimous and equally long-standing contrary decision. It held that Congress could subject states to money DAMAGE CLAIMS [I] in federal courts without their consent or waiver of SOVEREIGN IMMUNITY [4] despite the Eleventh Amendment, which as applied by the Court a full century earlier in *Hans v. Louisiana* (1890), was deemed by the Court to preclude such FEDERAL JURISDICTION [I]. In this third new case, *Pennsylvania v. Union Gas Co.* (1989) the Court thus reinterpreted the Constitution to favor congressional power once again.

The fourth case in the Court's recent quartet is of the same character. In GARCIA V. SAN ANTONIO METROPOLITAN TRANSIT AUTHORITY (1985) [2], the Court overruled its own decision that was then less than a decade old, holding that Congress may directly command the terms of state employment to the same extent it had presumed to regulate wages and hours in private employment. The case overruled was NATIONAL LEAGUE OF CITIES V. USERY (1976) [3].

In large measure, however, these developments are not thematically new, despite the fact that three of the four constituitonal federalism cases involved such complete inconsistencies with the Supreme Court's own prior decisions as to require its previous interpretations of the Constitution to be set aside. Rather, the passing terms of the Supreme Court have but hardened what has been, overall, a one-way twentieth-century trend. Writing in 1950 in the *Virginia Law Review*, the distinguished constitutional historian EDWARD S. CORWIN [2] summarized the developments in "The Passing of Dual Federalism." His conclusions were accurate even for the time:

[T]he Federal System has shifted base in the direction of a consolidated national power. . . . [The] entire system of constitutional interpretation touching the Federal System is today in ruins. Today neither the State Police Power nor the concept of Federal Equilibrium is any "ingredient of national legislative power," whether as respects subject-matter to be governed, or the choice of objectives or of means for its exercise. [Today] "Cooperative Federalism" spells further aggrandizement of national power. . . . Resting as it does primarily on the superior fiscal resources of the National Government, Cooperative Federalism has been, to date, a short expression for a constantly increasing concentration of power at Washington in the instigation and supervision of local policies.

To be sure, even as implied in Corwin's article a half-century ago, the system of dual federalism was not originally expected to be administered by the Supreme Court in this one-sided fashion. Rather, in theory, it spoke to the Constitution's original differential apportionment of legislative powers (between the national and state governments) and a certain equilibrium in different spheres of respective national and constrained state powers that was meant to be held in place under the superintendence of the Supreme Court. The powers constitutionally apportioned were separated between limited—albeit important—powers under congressional control and the larger number left to the separate determination by legislature within each state. Subjects not believed to require a common regime of uniform national regulation—and thus not identified in Article I or elsewhere as subject to congressional disposition—were reserved from the national government to such differential treatment as the domestic law of each state might reflect. Madison characterized this basic arrangement in THE FEDERALIST [2] #45: "The powers delegated by the proposed Constitution to the federal government are few and defined. Those which are to remain in the State governments are numerous and indefinite."

The Supreme Court, while fully expected to grant full enforcement to acts of Congress within its ENUMERATED POWERS [2] ("few and defined"), was equally expected to withhold enforcement from any not within them. Indeed, it was the latter obligation of the courts that was particularly emphasized in the course of the RATIFICATION [3] debates. In Pennsylvania, JAMES WILSON [4] put the point reassuringly in the following terms: "If a law should be made inconsistent with those powers vested by this instrument in Congress, the judges, as a consequence of their independence, and the particular powers of government being defined, will declare such law to be null and void." In *The Federalist* #78, ALEXANDER HAMILTON specifically adverted to the federalism-checking function of the courts: "If it be said that the legislative body [Congress] are themselves the constitutional judges of their own powers, . . . it may be answered that this cannot be the natural presumption, where it is not to be collected from any particular provision in the constitution. . . . It is far more rational to suppose that the courts were designed to be an intermediate body between the people and the legislature, in order, among other things, to keep the latter within the limits assigned to their authority." In the Virginia convention, JOHN MARSHALL [3] took the same view: "If they [Congress] were to make a law not warranted by any of the powers enumerated, it would be considered by the judges as an infringement of the Constitution which they are to guard. They would not consider such a law as coming under their jurisdiction. *They would declare it void.*"

Moreover, according to Marshall, a law that might nominally come within the limits of some enumerated power vested in Congress should—and would—be held void by the courts if it were discoverable that it was but a means to effectuate a control over a matter not entrusted to Congress, a matter reserved to the internal disposition of each state. On the very point of policing the equilibrium of federalism against abuse by congressional indirection in the exertion of its powers (as in *South Dakota v. Dole*), Marshall insisted in McCULLOCH V. MARYLAND [3] on the obligation of the judges to disallow the attempt: "[S]hould congress, under pretext of executing its powers, pass laws for the accomplishment of objects not trusted to the [national] government it would become the painful duty of this tribunal, should a case requiring such a decision come before it, to say, that such an act was not the law of the land." This is the same position Justice FELIX FRANKFURTER [2] repeated concretely, dissenting in *United States v. Kahriger* (1953): "[W]hen oblique use is made of the taxing power as to matters which substantively are not within the powers delegated to Congress [in this instance, whether gambling within a state ought or ought not be suppressed—a commonplace criminal law subject of state and local law and nowhere entrusted to Congress to decide], the Court cannot shut its eyes to what is obviously, because designedly, an attempt to control conduct which the Constitution left to the responsibility of the States, merely because Congress wrapped the legislation in the verbal cellophane of a revenue measure."

The constitutional checks felt to be desirable in respect to state laws not subject to congressional pleasure were in turn expressly (albeit quite narrowly) provided for principally in the special provisions of Article I, section 10 (forbidding state EX POST FACTO LAWS [2] or impairing the OBLIGATION OF CONTRACT [3]). Later, to be sure, between 1865 and 1870, these limitations were significantly enlarged in the Civil War amendments—in respect to which Congress is given strong powers of enforcement. However, subject to these limitations and such others as might be variously reflected internally in each state in keeping with its own constitution as interpreted by the states' own courts (rather than as the federal courts might want), it was the varietals of state law—not national law—that were meant to occupy the fields not given to Congress to command.

The main check against persistent immoderation of state law (for example, criminal law, family law, TORTS [1], local business regulation, trusts and estates) lay not in any possible PREEMPTION [3] by Congress—it being understood that there was no such general power of preemption provided or vested in Congress by the Constitution. Instead, the main check that might keep the character of state laws from reaching extremes not forbidden by the constitution itself inhered in the porousness of state boundaries and the freedom of state citizens to move away from a state to a different state, taking their skills and personal property with them. Any persistent tendency toward immoderation in state legislation was thus constrained to the extent it was deemed constitutionally desirable to have it constrained—not by a supererogatory general authority in Congress, but by the consciousness of each state that it could not prevent its citizens from considering the comparative advantage of a different state or veto the free movement of persons and of personal property within the United States.

In contrast, modern federalism, or sufferance federalism, eliminates this alternative check on state laws, as it tends also to eliminate differences among the states themselves. Insofar as processes of democratic centralism (Congress) can impose uniform preemptive national legislation regardless of subject matter (as the Constitution is now construed by the Supreme Court to permit—largely via the COMMERCE CLAUSE [1]), such difference as any particular state law might provide as a contrast with that of some other state can be made of no consequence even within that state. Whatever the state law may permit to those within that state, it remains true that even all those moving to or residing in that state must reckon with the separate and enforceable prohibition Congress has already enacted and made applicable to them as a matter of federal law, a law fully enforceable via the federal courts. They must therefore conform to that law, rather than merely to the law of the state, regardless of where they reside. And insofar as Congress has been persuaded to regulate them in keeping with how others (though not including the state of their residence) may want them to be regulated by federal law, it will make no difference where they attempt to go. However, even more obtains under sufferance federalism than this. Because powers vested in Congress are interpreted to permit it to effectively determine the very content of state laws (as they are now so interpreted in general), then to the extent that INTEREST GROUPS [2] and states with influence in Congress find themselves embarrassed or vexed by some distinction the internal laws of some few other states provide by way of contrast with themselves, they may act through Congress to compel the legislatures in every state to revise those states' own laws to conform to the preference already adopted in their states. Either way, then, such differences as may tend to exhibit themselves in certain laws of different states even today remain subject to congressional sufferance and elimination, if, as, and when Congress so decides.

It is the interpretive stance of the Supreme Court (e.g., on the scope of the power to "regulate commerce among the several states," equating it with a power to regulate or prohibit whatever may affect commerce, whether or not it is commerce that Congress cares about in the particular case) and not the literal abrogation of JUDICIAL REVIEW [2,I] on the federalism question that is solely responsible for the change to sufferance federalism in the United States. The Court continues to be nominally willing to review substantive federalism, but it invariably sustains such preemptions of directions or commands that Congress presumes to enact as long as Congress goes through certain formal motions in the course of enacting its bills; however, it is not a refusal to hear or to entertain the case as such. This distinction might appear to be merely scholastic insofar as the practical results would appear to be the same as though the Court had abrogated judicial review of federalism cases. But it is more than scholastic precisely because the Court's current position does not leave the merits of the federalism objection unaddressed; rather, it denies the merits of those objections—that is, it decides the cases in which they arise. Accordingly, an amendment currently being pressed in thirty-three state legislatures (approved by fifteen legislatures, by one house in six others, and pending in twelve more) that, if proposed and ratified, would require the Court to address and decide the merits of federalism objections in cases otherwise appropriately raising such questions, would change nothing at all. Proposals of this sort proceed on a misunderstanding of judicial behavior on the Supreme Court. Sufferance federalism in the United States is not the result of the nonreviewability of federalism cases arising under the Constitution; rather, it is the result of the Supreme Court's own disposition to find that it is merely this form of federalism the Constitution of the United States provides.

WILLIAM VAN ALSTYNE

Bibliography

CORWIN, EDWARD 1950 The Passing of Dual Federalism. *University of Virginia Law Review* 36:1–23.
EPSTEIN, RICHARD 1989 The Proper Scope of the Commerce Clause. In Ellen Frankel Paul, ed., *Liberty, Property, and Government*. Albany: State University of New York Press.
PATTERSON, JAMES 1969 *The New Deal and the States: Federalism in Transition*. Princeton, N.J.: Princeton University Press.
STERN, ROBERT 1973 The Commerce Clause Revisited—The Federalization of Intrastate Crime. *Arizona Law Review* 15:271–285.

VAN ALSTYNE, WILLIAM 1985 The Second Death of Federalism. *Michigan Law Review* 83:1709–1733.
——— 1987 Federalism, Congress, the States and the Tenth Amendment: Adrift in the Cellophane Sea. *Duke Law Journal* 87:769–799.
——— 1989 Dual Sovereignty, Federalism and National Criminal Law: Modernist Constitutional Doctrine and the Nonrole of the Supreme Court. *American Criminal Law Review* 26:1740–1759.

FEDERALISM AND CIVIL RIGHTS

In the scheme of the United States Constitution, the concept of FEDERALISM [2,I] requires respect for the distinct legal authorities and diverse cultures of the separate states, but the concept of CIVIL RIGHTS [1,I] requires adherence to uniform rules emanating either directly from the national Constitution or indirectly from various congressional enactments. The two concepts are thus bound in a structural tension.

This tension has persisted since the RECONSTRUCTION [I] amendments, when the national government first seriously began to create federal civil rights that could be asserted against the states. These rights, together with the expansion of federal JUDICIAL POWER [3] necessary to enforce them, were self-conscious efforts to eradicate aspects of the indigenous culture of the southern states traceable to the institution of SLAVERY [4]. Federal civil rights were thus born in a burst of national centralization.

Ironically, these rights were interpreted by courts in such a way as to permit racial subordination to endure even in the absence of slavery. The FOURTEENTH AMENDMENT [2,I] in particular was understood to establish civil rights that were primarily economic in nature, most notably the right of FREEDOM OF CONTRACT [2]. In the era after LOCHNER V. NEW YORK (1905) [3], federal courts were so persistent in using this right to strike down social reform legislation in the states that Thomas Reed Powell was moved to "question whether judicial centralization is not pushed to an extreme under our federal system."

In this context, the values of federalism acquired a distinctively progressive cast. In 1932, for example, Justice LOUIS D. BRANDEIS [2], in his dissent in NEW STATE ICE COMPANY V. LIEBMANN [3], gave his influential and ringing defense of federalism as a "laboratory" for "novel social and economic experiments." When, after the constitutional crisis of the NEW DEAL [I], the Supreme Court backed off from its enforcement of laissez-faire economic rights, these same federalist values led some to challenge the Court's creation of a vigorous regime of noneconomic civil rights. In ADAMSON V. CALIFORNIA (1947) [1], for example, Justice FELIX FRANKFURTER [2] opposed Justice HUGO L. BLACK's [1] proposal to "incorporate" the guarantees of the BILL OF RIGHTS [1] into the Fourteenth Amendment for application against the states. Frankfurter argued that the INCORPORATION DOCTRINE [2,I] would "tear up by the roots much of the fabric of law in the several States, and would deprive the States of opportunity for reforms in legal process designed for extending the area of freedom."

In this way the values of federalism became associated with conservative opposition to the establishment of federal noneconomic civil rights. This association reached its apex when the concept of STATES' RIGHTS [4] was used to challenge the legitimacy of BROWN V. BOARD OF EDUCATION (1954, 1955) [1] and the CIVIL RIGHTS MOVEMENT [I], a conjunction that came close to discrediting the values of federalism as effective limitations on the establishment of civil rights.

Certainly by the mid-1960s, as the nation committed itself to the recognition and implementation of civil rights, the values of federalism were in eclipse. The Supreme Court incorporated virtually all of the Bill of Rights into the Fourteenth Amendment for application against the states, and it aggressively enlarged its interpretation of the scope and application of those rights. The incorporation of most of the FOURTH AMENDMENT [2,I], Fifth Amendment, and Sixth Amendment forced the states to comply with uniform national standards in the area of CRIMINAL PROCEDURE [2]. The Court's expansion of FIRST AMENDMENT [2,I] guarantees of FREEDOM OF SPEECH [2,I] and RELIGIOUS LIBERTY [3,I] resulted in the invalidation of numerous state regulations that had heretofore been deemed perfectly acceptable reflections of local culture. And the Court's firm commitment to rights of racial and ethnic equality effectively outlawed the Jim Crow culture of the southern states. Congress significantly participated in this process of establishing national civil rights through its enactment of the CIVIL RIGHTS ACT OF 1964 [1], the CIVIL RIGHTS ACT OF 1968 [1], and the VOTING RIGHTS ACT OF 1965 [4].

By the end of the WARREN COURT [4] era, the rhetoric of federalism had virtually disappeared from the ongoing debate about the substance of civil rights. For example, when the BURGER COURT [1] deliberated whether the EQUAL PROTECTION [2,I] clause should require STRICT SCRUTINY [4] of gender classifications, it argued the question almost entirely in terms of the independent merits of the position, rather than in terms of the effect that such scrutiny would have on the ability of diverse states to enact laws that reflected distinct cultural attitudes toward controversial issues of gender equality. Similarly, when the Burger Court in ROE V. WADE [3] endowed women with the constitutional right to have an ABORTION [1,I], it barely discussed the implications of the decision for the values of federalism.

The end of the 1960s witnessed a political renaissance of the values of federalism, a renaissance that later intensified during the presidency of RONALD REAGAN [3,I]. This renaissance found judicial expression in debates over the reach of federal judicial power, rather than in debates over the nature of the substantive civil rights protected by that power. Thus, both the Burger Court and the REHNQUIST COURT [I] invoked values of federalism in order to curb the authority and accessibility of federal courts, which the Warren Court had greatly expanded in an attempt to enforce fully the civil rights that it had recognized.

For example, in an important line of cases that originated with YOUNGER V. HARRIS [4], the Burger Court invoked the principles of "our Federalism" in order to limit the availability of federal EQUITY [2] relief. The Court explained these principles as a "notion of 'comity,' that is, a proper respect for state functions," and the belief that the nation "will fare best if the States and their institutions are left free to perform their separate functions in their separate ways." The Court invoked similar notions of COMITY [1] to justify restrictions on ACCESS TO THE COURTS [1] for federal writs of HABEAS CORPUS [2,I], expansive interpretations of state immunity from federal judicial power under the ELEVENTH AMENDMENT [2,I], strict presumptions against waivers of that immunity, and limitations on the authority of federal courts to issue injunctions broadly restructuring state and local government institutions. The tension between civil rights and federalism thus continued, although in a somewhat modulated key.

That tension may profitably be analyzed by inquiring into the values served by the concepts of civil rights and federalism. Civil rights, at least those that emanate from the Constitution, serve mainly to protect persons from the exercise of governmental authority. The persistent image is that of individuals safeguarded by courts from the domination of an overpowering government. From this perspective, it makes no difference whether government power is exercised at the state or federal level.

Yet federalism is committed to the proposition that it is usually preferable to exercise power at the local rather than national level. There are many different rationales for this preference, ranging from efficiency to experimentation. But there are two justifications that are most directly responsive to the values underlying the claim for civil rights.

The first accepts the premise that it is vitally important to protect individual liberty from the excesses of state power, but it views courts as, in the long run, unreliable institutions for securing that protection. Individual freedom is better served, so the argument runs, by establishing the states as centers of power that are competitive with the federal government, in the expectation that the resulting diffusion of power will effectively check the potential for abusive government. To establish the states as independent centers of power, however, requires ceding to them autonomy from a uniform regime of civil rights emanating from the federal government. On this account, then, the resolution of the tension between civil rights and federalism ought to depend upon how the long-term benefits to civil rights anticipated from the structural arrangements of federalism compare against the short-term benefits that would result from judicial enforcement of federal civil rights.

The second justification for federalism strikes deeper, for it denies that the image underlying the rationale for civil rights is adequate as a description of local state governments. State governments, according to this argument, are closer to the people and hence more fully realize the values of political participation. Thus, they should not be pictured as overreaching and impersonal governments estranged from their citizens, but rather as more nearly authentic communities, in which political processes both form and express genuine social commitments. The national imposition of uniform civil rights would therefore be both unnecessary and deeply disruptive of these positive local processes. On this account, then, the resolution of the tension between civil rights and federalism ought to depend upon whether states can more accurately be described as representing authentic and inclusive communities or as impersonal and potentially oppressive governments.

Given the difficult and perplexing nature of these inquiries, it is clear why the tension between federalism and civil rights has endured, and in all likelihood will continue to do so.

ROBERT C. POST

Bibliography

POST, ROBERT C. 1988 Justice Brennan and Federalism. In Harry N. Scheiber, ed., *Federalism: Studies in History, Law and Policy*, pp. 37–45. Berkeley, Calif.: Berkeley Press.
POWELL, THOMAS REED 1931 The Supreme Court and State Police Powers, 1922–1930. *Virginia Law Review* 17:529–556.
RAPACZYNSKI, ANDRZEJ 1985 From Sovereignty to Process: The Jurisprudence of Federalism After *Garcia. Supreme Court Review* 43:29–38.
SANDALOW, TERRANCE 1980 Federalism and Social Change. *Law and Contemporary Problems* 43:29–38.

FEDERALISM AND SHARED POWERS

Federalism and SEPARATION OF POWERS [4] are the two principal techniques in America for dividing political power. Federalism allocates power between the national government and the states; separation of powers distributes power among three branches of the national government and within each of the state governments. Although these divisions of power characterize national and state government, many essential functions of government are shared. Justice ROBERT H. JACKSON [3] deftly noted in YOUNGSTOWN SHEET & TUBE CO. V. SAWYER (1952) [4], "While the Constitution diffuses power the better to secure liberty, it also contemplates that practice will integrate the dispersed powers into a workable government. It enjoins upon its branches separateness but interdependence, autonomy but reciprocity." Jackson directed his observation to the doctrine of separation of powers, but it applies equally well to federalism.

Independence from England in 1776 left the thirteen American states without a central government. Under the ARTICLES OF CONFEDERATION [1], drafted in 1777 but not ratified until 1781, each state retained "its sovereignty, freedom and independence," with the exception of a few powers expressly delegated to the national government. Various attempts were made over the years to bring a measure of effectiveness to the Confederation, but it was finally agreed after the ANNAPOLIS CONVENTION [I] in 1786 to meet in Philadelphia the following year "to devise such further provisions as shall appear to them necessary to render the constitution of the Federal Government adequate to the exigencies of the Union."

The delegates at Philadelphia rejected MONTESQUIEU's [3] theory that republican government could function only in small countries. He had argued that as a country increased in size, popular control must be surrendered, requiring aristocracies for moderate-sized countries and monarchies for large countries. JAMES MADISON [3], in THE FEDERALIST [2] #10, made precisely the opposite argument: that republican government was more likely the larger the territory. In a small territory, a dominant faction could gain control. "Extend the sphere," Madison reasoned, "and you take in a greater variety of parties and interests; you make it less probable that a majority of the whole will have a common motive to invade the rights of other citizens."

Critics of the 1787 Constitution claimed that it promoted a national or consolidated form of government instead of preserving the independence of the states. An exceptionally blunt challenge came from the Virginia ratification convention, where PATRICK HENRY [2] attacked the opening words of the Constitution: "What right had they to say, *We, the people?* . . . Who authorized them to speak the language of, *We, the people,* instead of, *We, the states?*" Madison answered these critiques in *Federalist* #39, pointing out that the Constitution contained features of a national character but also vested some power directly in the states. The proposed Constitution, he said, "is, in strictness, neither a national nor a federal Constitution, but a composition of both." By "federal" Madison meant *confederal*: a confederation of sovereign states, such as existed under the Articles of Confederation.

The Philadelphia Convention wrestled with two rival proposals. The VIRGINIA PLAN [4] called for a strong central government, while the NEW JERSEY PLAN [3] advocated a confederation with few national powers. The latter attracted little support. The GREAT COMPROMISE [2], promoted by OLIVER ELLSWORTH [2] of Connecticut, combined two antagonistic ideas: representation by population in the HOUSE OF REPRESENTATIVES [I] and equal voting power for each state in the SENATE [I]. He explained to the Convention on June 29, "We were partly national; partly federal. The proportional representation in the first branch [the House] was conformable to the national principle & would secure the large States agst. the small. An equality of voices [in the Senate] was conformable to the federal principle and was necessary to secure the Small States agst. the large. He trusted that on this middle ground a compromise would take place."

The compromise gave the central government the power to collect taxes, regulate commerce, and declare war, along with other express functions, including the NECESSARY AND PROPER CLAUSE [3] to carry into effect the ENUMERATED POWERS [2]. National powers are reinforced by the SUPREMACY CLAUSE [4] in Article VI, section 2: "This Constitution, and the laws of the United States which shall be made in pursuance thereof; and all treaties made, or which shall be made, under the authority of the United States, shall be the supreme law of the land; and the judges in every State shall be bound thereby, anything in the constitution or laws of any State to the contrary notwithstanding." Article I, section 9, prohibits the national government from taxing articles exported from any state or preferring the ports of one state over another, while Article I, section 10, prohibits a number of state actions, including entering into any treaty, alliance, or confederation; coining money; passing any BILL OF ATTAINDER [1] or EX POST FACTO LAW [2]; impairing the OBLIGATION OF CONTRACTS [3]; or laying any IMPOSTS [2] or duties on imports or exports without the consent of Congress, except what is "absolutely necessary" to execute its inspection laws.

The TENTH AMENDMENT [4] provides that the powers "not delegated to the United States by the Constitution, nor prohibited by it to the States, are reserved to the States respectively, or to the people." The Articles of Confederation gave greater protection to the states, which retained all powers, except those "expressly delegated" to the national government. When it was proposed in 1789 that the same phrase be inserted in the Tenth Amendment, Madison objected to the word "expressly" because it was impossible to delineate every function and responsibility of the federal government. There had to be, he said, room for IMPLIED POWERS [2] "unless the Constitu-

tion descended to recount every minutiae." On the force of his argument, the word "expressly" was eliminated from the Tenth Amendment. In MCCULLOCH V. MARYLAND (1819) [3], Chief Justice JOHN MARSHALL [3] relied on Madison's argument in upholding the power of Congress to establish a national bank, even though that power is not expressly included in the Constitution.

The suggestion that the Tenth Amendment contains substantive powers for states, even to the point of reinserting the word "expressly," has been made in such cases as *Lane County v. Oregon* (1868) and HAMMER V. DAGENHART (1918) [2]. In MISSOURI V. HOLLAND (1920) [3], however, the Supreme Court denied that the TREATY POWER [4] was restricted in any way "by some invisible radiation from the general terms of the Tenth Amendment," and Justice HARLAN F. STONE [4], in UNITED STATES V. DARBY LUMBER COMPANY (1941) [2], dismissed the Tenth Amendment as a "truism," meaning only "that all is retained which has not been surrendered." Nevertheless, the decisions in *Fry v. United States* (1975) and NATIONAL LEAGUE OF CITIES V. USERY (1976) [3] demonstrate that the Tenth Amendment retains vitality.

Many of the turf battles between the national government and the states have been fought over the scope of the COMMERCE CLAUSE [1,I]. Commercial friction among the states after 1776 was a principal reason for discarding the Articles of Confederation and adopting a government with greater national powers. The enumerated powers given to Congress in Article I include the power to "regulate commerce with foreign nations, and among the several States, and with the Indian tribes." In GIBBONS V. OGDEN (1824) [2], Chief Justice Marshall advanced a broad interpretation of the power of Congress to regulate commerce, but over the years, the Court employed other doctrines to distinguish between national and state powers. At times the two levels of government could exercise CONCURRENT POWERS [1]. States were able to regulate commerce within their borders unless preempted by Congress. The Court also created the doctrine of exclusive JURISDICTIONS [3], promoting the theory of DUAL FEDERALISM [2], under which the states and the national government exercised mutually exclusive powers.

These doctrines appeared to be increasingly artificial with the rapid nationalization of the American economy. Traditional boundaries between INTRASTATE COMMERCE [2] and INTERSTATE COMMERCE [2] were swept aside when the operations of railroads, agriculture, and livestock acquired national structures. The Court even held that Congress could regulate actions inside a state that were simply related to interstate commerce. During World War I and World War II commercial and economic activities that normally fell within the jurisdiction of the states were controlled by the federal government.

During the period of SUBSTANTIVE DUE PROCESS [4,I],

which lasted from the 1890s to 1937, the Supreme Court struck down a number of regulatory efforts by Congress and state legislatures on the theory that the statutes interfered with the "liberty of contract," a fiction created by the judiciary to limit governmental power. Statutes enacted to establish minimum wages and maximum hours, to protect children from harsh labor practices, or to create better working conditions were regularly invalidated by state and federal courts.

Those judicial doctrines were eventually cast aside during the NEW DEAL [I] revolution, especially after the COURT-PACKING PLAN [I] in 1937. Although at one period the Court struck down congressional statutes because they invaded "local" activities within the control of state governments or because "manufacturing" was considered by the judiciary as local and thus beyond congressional control, these barriers to national action were eventually removed. A series of rulings, such as *NLRB v. Jones & Laughlin Steel Corp.* (1937) and *United States v. Darby Lumber Company* (1941), gave solid support to Congress's interpretations of its powers under the commerce clause. In PRUDENTIAL INSURANCE COMPANY V. BENJAMIN (1946) [3], a chastened Court offered this revealing assessment: "The history of judicial limitation of congressional power over commerce, when exercised affirmatively, has been more largely one of retreat than of ultimate victory."

In *National League of Cities v. Usery* (1976), the Supreme Court appeared to resuscitate state SOVEREIGNTY [4] and the Tenth Amendment. The case involved the decision of Congress to extend federal hours-and-wages standards to state employees. In *Maryland v. Wirtz* (1968), the Court had upheld the extension of federal minimum wages and overtime pay to state-operated hospitals and schools. It even upheld, in *Fry v. United States* (1975), the short-term power of the President to stabilize wages and salaries for state employees. Nevertheless, *National League* refused to permit federal minimum-wage and maximum-hour provisions to displace state powers in such "traditional governmental functions" as fire prevention, police protection, sanitation, public health, and parks and recreation. This 5–4 decision overruled *Wirtz* on the ground that the congressional statute threatened the independent existence of states. In his dissent, Justice WILLIAM J. BRENNAN [1,I] objected that the Court had delivered "a catastrophic judicial body blow at Congress' power under the Commerce Clause."

The Court's bifurcation between "traditional" and "nontraditional" governmental functions spawned confusion in the lower courts. Many of the efforts of federal district courts to apply the standard in *National League* were rejected by the Supreme Court. Finally, in *Garcia v. San Antonio Metropolitan Transit Authority* (1985), Justice HARRY A. BLACKMUN [1,I], whose concurrence had

provided the fifth vote in *National League*, swung in the other direction to join with the four dissenters in overruling *National League*. He called attention to the frustrating struggle in federal and state courts to distinguish between traditional and nontraditional functions. He called the criteria in *National League* "unworkable," "inconsistent with established principles of federalism," and "both impracticable and doctrinally barren." Because of this decision, the protection of federalism has been left largely to the political process of Congress. The tone of the four dissents, however, suggests that *Garcia* might be living on borrowed time, reflecting the position of older members of the Court: Blackmun, Brennan, THURGOOD MARSHALL [3,I], BYRON R. WHITE [4,I], and JOHN PAUL STEVENS [4,I]. WILLIAM H. REHNQUIST [3,I], the author of *National League*, offered this advice in his *Garcia* dissent: "I do not think it incumbent on those of us in dissent to spell out further the fine points of a principle that will, I am confident, in time again command the support of a majority of this Court."

Although the position of the Court on *National League* and *Garcia* might be in a state of flux and easily reversible, the judgment of ANTONIN SCALIA [I] during his nomination hearings in 1986 to be Associate Justice seems well grounded in history: "The primary defender of the constitutional balance, the Federal Government versus the states, . . . the primary institution to strike the right balance is the Congress. . . . The court's struggles to prescribe what is the proper role of the Federal Government vis-à-vis the State have essentially been abandoned for quite a while."

LOUIS FISHER

(SEE ALSO: *Preemption* [3].)

Bibliography

ADVISORY COMMISSION ON INTERGOVERNMENTAL RELATIONS 1988 *State Constitutional Law: Cases and Materials.* Washington, D.C.: U.S. Government Printing Office.

ANTON, THOMAS J. 1989 *American Federalism and Public Policy.* Philadelphia: Temple University Press.

CONLAN, TIMOTHY 1988 *New Federalism: Intergovernmental Reform from Nixon to Reagan.* Washington, D.C.: Brookings Institution.

O'BRIEN, DAVID M. 1989 Federalism as a Metaphor in the Constitutional Politics of Public Administration. *Public Administration Review* 49, no. 5:411–419.

FEDERALISTS

Arguments about the meaning of the Constitution can be dated to the controversy over its adoption or to the congressional debates of 1789 about the power to remove subordinate executive officials. But not until the conflict over ALEXANDER HAMILTON's [2] proposal to create a BANK OF THE UNITED STATES [1] did these disputes assume a partisan configuration and begin to take the form of two conflicting modes of CONSTITUTIONAL INTERPRETATION [1]. When Hamilton's proposal came before the HOUSE OF REPRESENTATIVES [I] in February 1791, Congressman JAMES MADISON [3] remembered that the CONSTITUTIONAL CONVENTION OF 1787 [1] had specifically declined to add the right to charter CORPORATIONS [1] to the list of Congress's powers. Madison contended that incorporation of a bank was not an exercise of any of the delegated powers and could not be justified on other grounds without confiding an "unlimited discretion" to a limited regime and threatening its gradual transmutation into a unitary national system. Disturbed by Madison's objections, President GEORGE WASHINGTON [4] requested the opinions of his principal advisers before he signed the bill. EDMUND RANDOLPH [3] and Secretary of State THOMAS JEFFERSON [3] agreed with their Virginia friend. Elaborating Madison's insistence that to step beyond the constitutional enumeration was "to take possession of a boundless field of power, no longer susceptible of any definition," Jefferson maintained that the incorporation of a bank was not a regulation of the nation's commerce, not a tax, and not a borrowing of money. To derive the power from the "general phrases," he continued, would render the enumeration useless, reduce the Constitution "to a single phrase," and, in practice, authorize the federal government to do anything it pleased.

Hamilton's rebuttal of his colleagues, which persuaded Washington to sign the bill, erected the essential framework for the BROAD CONSTRUCTION [1] of the document that would prevail throughout the 1790s. In fact, the reasoning and phrasing of this great opinion would be closely followed by JOHN MARSHALL [3] in MCCULLOCH V. MARYLAND [3] in 1819. "If the *end* be clearly comprehended within any of the specified powers, and if the measure have an obvious relation to that *end*, and is not forbidden by any particular provision of the Constitution," Hamilton maintained, "it may safely be deemed to come within the compass of the national authority." Insisting that the Constitution's grant of sovereign powers necessarily implied a power to decide which means were most appropriate to federal ends, the secretary of the treasury rejected Jefferson's contention that the boundaries of federal power would be washed away if "NECESSARY AND PROPER" [3] was construed to mean "convenient," "useful," "requisite," and "needful." A liberal interpretation of this phrase was vital, he observed, to an effective federal system: "The means by which national exigencies are to be provided for . . . are of such infinite variety, extent, and complexity that there must, of necessity, be great latitude

of discretion in the selection and application of those means."

Hamilton's opinion on the national bank began with the assumption "that every power vested in a government is in its nature *sovereign,* and includes . . . a right to employ all the means requisite and fairly applicable to the attainment of the ends." It was not to be denied, the secretary argued, "that there are *implied* as well as *express powers.*" Similar assumptions underpinned his "Letters of Pacificus" in 1793, with their defense of the inherent power of the chief executive to issue the Neutrality Proclamation. And yet, a "liberal" or "broad" construction of the reach of federal powers only partially describes the general tendency of Federalist interpretations of the Constitution. While the party was in power, Hamilton and other leaders generally assumed that the enduring dangers to the new regime would issue for the most part from the states' continual encroachments on the federal government's preserve and from a democratic people's tendency to favor an increasing concentration of the powers of the central government itself in the popularly elected lower house. Thus, the Federalists did seek as broad and flexible a definition of the general government's authority as reason would admit. They also usually attempted to defend the independence and prerogatives of the executive and the courts against encroachments by the Congress, which the Framers had intended to be more immediately responsive to the people. The most important constitutional collisions of the decade can all be helpfully illuminated in these terms. So could Federalist resistance to the Jeffersonians' repeal of the JUDICIARY ACT OF 1801 [3], when many argued that the tenure of judges during GOOD BEHAVIOR [2] should not be subverted by an abolition of their posts.

After 1793, foreign policy and its domestic repercussions dominated the intensifying party conflict, and Hamilton's defense of presidential leadership initiated an extended public argument about the meaning of the clause that vested "the executive power . . . in a President of the United States." "Pacificus" interpreted this phrase as granting an inherent body of executive prerogatives to the head of the executive department, "subject only to the *exceptions* and *qualifications*" defined by the Constitution. Writing as "Helvidius" at Jefferson's request, Madison condemned this doctrine as derived from the theory and practice of monarchical Britain and as striking "at the vitals" of a republican Constitution. Hamilton's interpretation, he insisted, would enable an ambitious President to take the country into war without congressional consent.

In practice, the conduct of the first two administrations did establish lasting precedents for firm executive direction of the country's international relations. In 1796 the

House of Representatives asked Washington for documents relating to JOHN JAY's [3] negotiation of a commercial treaty with Great Britain. Some members hoped to defeat the unpopular treaty by declining to appropriate the money necessary to carry it into effect. Washington's refusal to submit the papers to the House, which had no constitutional role in making treaties, was consistent with his general practice of an active leadership in foreign-policy concerns. JOHN ADAMS's [1] decision to initiate a diplomatic resolution to hostilities with France, undertaken in the face of active opposition from his CABINET [1] and from Federalists in Congress, was yet another potent contribution to the chief executive's command of his department and to presidential guidance in this field.

The diplomatic impasse that resulted in the naval war with France—undeclared but authorized by acts of Congress—also ended in the most ferocious constitutional collision of the decade. Fearing French collusion with their Jeffersonian opponents, as well as with a host of recent immigrants to the United States, Federalists in Congress took advantage of the patriotic fury sparked by revelation of the XYZ Affair to pass a range of crisis legislation. Their opponents sharply criticized the Alien Acts of 1798, which authorized the President—without judicial process and merely on suspicion—to deport any ALIEN [1] whose presence he considered dangerous to the United States. But the Republicans reserved their most ferocious condemnations for a controversial companion law, aimed at the repression of domestic opposition.

The Sedition Act of 1798 made it a criminal offense to "write, print, utter, or publish . . . any false, scandalous, and malicious writing or writings against the government of the United States, or either House of Congress of the United States, or the President of the United States, with the intent to defame [them] or to bring them . . . into contempt or disrepute." To the Republicans, whose opposition culminated in the VIRGINIA AND KENTUCKY RESOLUTIONS [4], this legislation was a flagrant violation of the limits of Congress's delegated powers and of the FIRST AMENDMENT [2,I]. Little less objectionable, they thought, were prosecutions grounded on the supposition that there was, in any case, a federal COMMON LAW [1] of SEDITIOUS LIBEL [4].

The crisis laws of 1798 were major threats to private rights and public liberties as these would later be defined. Together with the argument for the existence of a FEDERAL COMMON LAW OF CRIMES [2], they were supreme examples of the readiness of many Federalists to broaden federal authority by means of constitutional constructions that advanced a sweeping doctrine of inherent sovereign powers along with a constricted reading of the BILL OF RIGHTS [1]. In defense of the Sedition Law, the Federalists contended that the First Amendment's guarantee of FREEDOM OF THE PRESS [2,I] extended only to a prohibition of true censorship (or PRIOR RESTRAINT [3]), not to prosecutions in the aftermath of publication. Because the act provided that the truth of a seditious utterance would be an adequate defense—and because it allowed juries, rather than judges, to decide whether such an utterance was libelous or not—the Sedition Act, its advocates maintained, was actually a liberalization of existing common law. These arguments did not disguise the Federalists' desire to break an opposition that was intensifying as danger of a French invasion disappeared. Neither did they hide the party's underlying fear of the results of open political competition; that fear was amply justified by the defeat of 1800.

From the LOUISIANA PURCHASE TREATY [3] through the War of 1812, growing numbers of beleaguered Federalists retreated from the party's early, broad construction of the Constitution. In 1803 a few objected to the treaty, not because they shared the President's concern that there was no explicit constitutional foundation for the acquisition, but because the treaty promised that a territory not within the boundaries of the original United States (and likely to support their Jeffersonian opponents) would in time be granted statehood. If such a promise were constitutional at all, they argued, it lay within the prerogative of Congress. After 1808, with slighter strain, a larger number of Federalists bitterly denounced Jefferson's embargo, the Enforcement Acts, and other efforts to compel the warring European powers to respect the country's rights as a neutral. Congress's constitutional authority to regulate the nation's commerce, they maintained, did not include the power to prohibit it entirely. Moreover, the EMBARGO ACTS [2] produced a vast extension of executive authority and nearly dictatorial intrusions by the military and the revenue collectors into the nation's economic life, violating both the spirit of the Constitution and the FOURTH AMENDMENT [2,I] guarantees against UNREASONABLE SEARCHES [4,I] and seizures. To New Englanders especially, the long experiment with economic warfare, which was pressed in a variety of ways through the next three years, seemed evidence of Jeffersonian hostility to commerce in general and to New England as a region. For them, accordingly, a narrow definition of the commerce power proved a milepost on a general withdrawal into constitutional interpretations that the Federalists had once condemned.

The quick retreat into a narrow, sometimes tortured understanding of the Constitution was primarily, though not exclusively, a sectional response to the Republican ascendancy in national affairs. Although this doctrinal switch ended by discrediting the party as a whole, it won approval neither from the Federalist judiciary nor from many of the greatest architects of Federalist ideas. After the commencement of the War of 1812, the Massachusetts legislature, governor, and courts, building on the compact theory of the Constitution, insisted that the state executive, not Congress, should determine whether an "invasion" authorized the federal government to call forth the militia. All the New England states impeded federal employment of these forces, practicing state interposition in a way that even the Virginia and Kentucky legislatures had never actually attempted. Regional resistance to the war extended to flirtations with SECESSION [4] or a separate peace and culminated in the HARTFORD CONVENTION [2] of December 1814. This effort to extort concessions in the midst of war discredited the Federalists beyond redemption and nationalized a constitutional interpretation that all New England states had once condemned. The constitutional amendments the convention urged would have gravely weakened the effective federal regime, which was the most impressive legacy of Federalist administrations. Yet, even as the party died, the nationalistic constitutional construction of its greatest years were winning the endorsement of the MARSHALL COURT [3].

LANCE BANNING

(SEE ALSO: *Alien and Sedition Acts* [1]; *Commerce Clause* [1,I]; *Foreign Affairs* [2]; *Implied Powers* [2]; *Jeffersonianism* [3]; *Militia Clause* [3]; *Republicanism* [3]; *Treaty Power* [4].)

Bibliography

MILLER, JOHN C. 1960 *The Federalist Era, 1789–1801.* New York: Harper and Row.
SMELSER, MARSHALL 1968 *The Democratic Republic, 1801–1815.* New York: Harper and Row.
SMITH, JAMES MORTON 1956 *Freedom's Fetters: The Alien and Sedition Laws and American Civil Liberties.* Ithaca, N.Y.: Cornell University Press.

FEMINIST THEORY

Feminist theory encompasses such a large and diverse body of work that it can no longer be described succinctly. A partial definition might stress the relationships among and between, on the one hand, women, women's experience, perceptions and treatment of women, gender as a social category, masculinity and femininity, and sexuality, and, on the other, social and personal identity, language, religion, economic and social structures, law, philosophy, and knowledge. The multifaceted nature of current feminist theory has even led many feminists to use the term "feminist theories." This diversity also marks the use of feminist theory with respect to law.

Feminists trained in law tend to describe their theoretical work as "feminist legal theory" or "feminist jurisprudence." The early development of the field, in the late 1970s and early 1980s, was closely tied to traditional legal

categories and analysis, even while it posed a significant challenge to the traditional use of such categories and methods. Its existence was made possible by the movement of significant numbers of women into the legal profession, and especially onto law school faculties, and by changes in interpretation of constitutional doctrine wrought by the CIVIL RIGHTS MOVEMENT [I]. The extent of these changes began to manifest itself in *Reed v. Reed* (1971), in which the Supreme Court first interpreted the EQUAL PROTECTION [2,I] clause as demanding significant justification for laws that formally discriminated against women. At first, then, feminist jurisprudence concerned itself primarily with elaboration of what equality might mean for women; a large proportion of the scholarship in the field remains focused on this question. However, in the 1990s the directions of feminist legal theory are likely to respond more to developments in feminist theory than to developments in legal theory or doctrine.

In some way all feminist theory concerns itself with describing, explaining, criticizing, and changing the social condition of women as a class from the perspective of, and on behalf of, all women. This project is pursued, however, in radically different ways, posing several kinds of challenges to traditional constitutional JURISPRUDENCE [I] and practice: doctrinal, culture, textural, and structural.

Feminist theory criticizes constitutional doctrine primarily for its failure to center, or often even to consider, women's experience in fashioning, elaborating, and applying rules presented as "neutral." Decisions such as *Geduldig v. Aiello* (1974)—in which a majority of the Supreme Court rejected an equal protection challenge to the exclusion of pregnant women from a state disability insurance plan, finding the exclusion based on medical condition rather than on sex—are used to demonstrate the extent to which nonfeminist interpretations of equal protection treat as irrelevant or unimportant experiences that many women consider quite important to them as women. While agreeing on this criticism, however, feminist theorists tend to disagree among themselves on whether constitutional law should attempt to develop more "truly neutral" doctrines, what such doctrines might be like, and whether neutrality itself is possible or desirable.

Cultural challenges to constitutional law are of two primary types. Some theorists suggest that the replacement of a predominantly white male judiciary, legislature, and practicing bar with a profession that more closely represents the sex and race composition of the general population would tend to change law and legal practice in a variety of ways. Attempts to test these propositions range from examination of the opinions of women jurists, such as Supreme Court Justice SANDRA DAY O'CONNOR [3,I], to documentation of shifts in political language, to interviews with, and observations of, female lawyers. Other theorists abstract certain characteristics thought to be associated with women and attempt to elaborate the potential effects of a closer integration of such characteristics into constitutional law. Both of these types of cultural critique often draw on Carol Gilligan's suggestion that an "ethic of care," with its attendant focus on responsibility, connection, and relationship, could validly be added to the "ethic of justice" that biases both moral and legal theory toward an exclusive focus on rights, autonomy, and individualism.

Textual criticism focuses on the language of law, especially law's written texts. Judicial opinions, legislation, and even the Constitution itself may be read as examples of literary production not fundamentally dissimilar from novels, plays, or newspaper articles. Some feminist textual criticism examines language as it communicates certain assumptions about the appropriateness or relevance of women's presence or experience, and shares with doctrinal criticism the project of identifying the sex bias concealed under seemingly neutral practices. This type of criticism has led to some minor changes in legal language (e.g., the replacement of "reasonable man" with "reasonable person"), as well as to textual revisions with more substantive force, such as recrafting jury instructions on self-defense so that their language does not presume the situation of one man resisting another. More literary-oriented theory focuses on the use and deployment of words, images, and metaphors that may be understood as gendered, either in their conscious association with traditional notions of masculinity and femininity or in their historical or psychosocial association with sexuality, sexual courtship, or heterosexual intercourse. Such theorists find within legal texts a process of dichotomization between male and female and a hierarchical ordering of male over female that mirror the insights of structural theories.

Finally, feminist theory also examines both conceptual and rhetorical structures within law and the structure of law itself. Probably the most widely disseminated insight to arise from feminist theory with respect to law is the critique of the process by which law divides human life into a "public" realm, in which law, justice, equality, and politics are thought to be appropriate, and a "private" realm, in which ideals of harmony, sacrifice, and intimacy are to be protected from public scrutiny. The feminist critique of this public-private distinction makes several key points: (1) Legal actors, such as courts, which are themselves "public," decide where the line will be drawn between public and private, and thus shape "the private" through public actions. (2) The association of men with the public sphere and women with the private sphere is used to legitimize women's exclusion from the political life of the nation. (3) When women's experience with intimacy is one of violence—marital rape, wife battering, incest, or sexual coercion—the public-private distinction

operates not to protect women's privacy from public scrutiny but to block women's ability to hold male intimates publicly accountable for their violence. (4) The very process of dichotomization that makes it possible to think of public and private life as two separate spheres reflects and strengthens the notion that women and men are fundamentally, necessarily, and naturally different, separate, and unequal. This critique has obvious implications for STATE ACTION [4,I] doctrine, the choice to place women's reproductive rights under the rubric of the RIGHT OF PRIVACY [3,I], and interpretations of what PROCEDURAL DUE PROCESS [3,I] requires in a variety of situations.

Other structural critiques question traditionally presumed relationships between the state and the individual, law and society, normality and deviance, identity and politics, freedom and coercion, and the subjective and objective. The results of these inquiries have led some feminists to characterize the state, the law, or both as "male" in the social, rather than biological, sense of that term.

The Constitution plays a major role in creating or maintaining the structures critiqued by feminist theory. Feminist theory suggests that the Framers' constitution of a polity that excluded women of all races and classes, as well as men of certain races and classes, did not simply result in a partial realization of a vision that could, over time, be extended to those who had been left out. Instead, that decision created gaps and contradictions within the very definitions of what it means to be a polity, to create and limit a government, to "promote the general welfare," and even what it means to subscribe to a rule of "laws, not men [sic]."

CHRISTINE A. LITTLETON

(SEE ALSO: *Constitution as Literature* [I]; *Gender Rights* [I]; *Women in Constitutional History* [I]; *Woman Suffrage* [I].)

Bibliography

DUBOIS, ELLEN; DUNLAP, MARY; GILLIGAN, CAROL; MACKINNON, CATHERINE; and MENKEL-MEADOW, CARRIE 1985 Feminist Discourse, Moral Values and the Laws—A Conversation. *Buffalo Law Review* 34:11–87.
KAY, HERMA HILL and LITTLETON, CHRISTINE A. 1988 Feminist Jurisprudence: What Is It? When Did It Start? Who Does It? Pages 844–887 in Herma Hill Kay, ed., *Sex-Based Discrimination*, 3rd ed. St. Paul, Minn.: West Publishing Co.
LITTLETON, CHRISTINE A. 1987 Reconstructing Sexual Equality. *California Law Review* 75:1279–1337.
MACKINNON, CATHARINE A. 1989 *Toward a Feminist Theory of the State*. Cambridge, Mass.: Harvard University Press.
SHERRY, SUZANNA 1986 Civic Virtue and the Feminine Voice in Constitutional Adjudication. *Virginia Law Review* 72:543–616.

WEST, ROBIN L. 1988 Jurisprudence and Gender. *Chicago Law Review* 55:1–72.

WILLIAMS, PATRICIA 1988 On Being the Object of Property. *Signs* 14:5–24.

WILLIAMS, WENDY 1985 Equality's Riddle: Pregnancy and the Equal Treatment/Special Treatment Debate. *New York University Review of Law and Social Change* 13:325–380.

FIFTH AMENDMENT

See: Double Jeopardy [2,I]; Due Process of Law [2]; Grand Jury [2,I]; Right Against Self-Incrimination [3,I]; Taking of Property [3,I]

FIRST AMENDMENT
(Update)

Within the legal culture, the First Amendment is typically understood to protect from government abridgment a broad realm of what might be called "symbolic activity," including speech, religion, press, association, and assembly. Because these symbolic activities are intertwined with many other activities that the government is clearly empowered to regulate—for instance, education and economic relations—the courts have experienced considerable difficulty in distinguishing impermissible infringement on First Amendment freedoms from legitimate exercises of government authority. Much of Supreme Court doctrine in the First Amendment area is an attempt to develop and refine precisely this sort of distinction.

One dominant principle that has informed the Supreme Court's doctrinal development of this distinction is the principle of content neutrality. The principle of content neutrality suggests that government must be neutral as to the conceptual content of speech, religion, press, and symbolic activity in general. Hence, according to First Amendment doctrine, it is only in extreme circumstances and for the most important reasons that the Court will allow government to regulate symbolic activity because of its conceptual content. The converse of this judicial principle is that the Court will recognize a relatively broad governmental power to regulate symbolic activity because of its effects or its form. Putting these two principles side by side, the result is that content-based regulation is often found unconstitutional, whereas content-neutral regulation is often found to be constitutional. These two broad imperatives with their sharply divergent implications for case outcomes place great conceptual pressure on distinguishing the content-based from the content-neutral, or more specifically on distinguishing the conceptual or substantive content of symbolic activity from its form and effects.

Although there has been no shortage of attempts, both scholarly and judicial, to specify and refine the gist of this distinction, First Amendment doctrine remains relatively undeveloped and unstable in dealing with this recurrent tension. Indeed, the Supreme Court seems continually to shift the terrain for making the predicate determination of whether the government action is content-based or content-neutral. Often the Justices are divided on the question whether the critical content-neutrality determination should be made with respect to the express or apparent state interest, the underlying governmental intent or motivation, the statutory or regulatory description of the symbolic activity, the judicial description of the symbolic activities actually affected, or the judicial description of symbolic activities conceivably affected. Although the Supreme Court has fashioned numerous diverse and detailed doctrines to specify the appropriate grounds on which to make the content-neutrality determination, there is so much of this doctrine and it is so obviously overlapping that ample room remains for disagreement among the Justices, the advocates, and the commentators about how to characterize and hence decide particular First Amendment cases. The result is that in the 1980s the First Amendment—especially in the area of religion—has followed the FOURTH AMENDMENT [2,I] in an entropic proliferation of fragmentary, ephemeral, and highly bureaucratized doctrine.

In consequence, it has become easy for Justices to find ample legal resources to disagree about whether some particular government action is content-neutral. The result is that a government action that is described as content-based by one group of Justices will often be characterized as effect-based or form-based by another group of Justices. Often the Justices will disagree about whether—and if so, to what extent—the conceptual content of a symbolic activity is divisible from its form or effects. In making determinations about whether some government action is content-neutral and in deciding to what extent the conceptual content of symbolic activity is distinguishable from its form, there is virtually no guiding Supreme Court doctrine. The result is that the importance of political ideology in the production of the legal conclusions of the Justices has become relatively transparent in the First Amendment area.

In *Texas v. Johnson* (1989), for instance, the Court overturned the conviction of a flag burner on the ground that the FLAG DESECRATION [2,I] statute was aimed at suppressing speech on the basis of its content. Counsel for Texas had argued that the statute was aimed at preserving the flag as a symbol of nationhood and national unity. The majority concluded that this state interest was an instance of content-based suppression because it singled out for punishment those messages at odds with what

Texas claimed to be the flag's meaning. For the majority, the state interest was intricately related to the content-based suppression of certain ideas. The dissent by Chief Justice WILLIAM H. REHNQUIST [3,I] (joined by Justice BYRON R. WHITE [4,I] and Justice SANDRA DAY O'CON-NOR [3,I]), by contrast, viewed flag burning in less conceptual, less content-oriented terms. The dissent characterized flag burning as "a grunt and a roar"—not an essential part of the expression of ideas. Unlike the majority, these dissenters characterized the form and the content of the flag burner's protest as easily divisible. Indeed, the dissenters argued that the defendant could easily have chosen any number of vehicles other than flag burning to express his views. Accordingly, for the dissenters the Texas flag desecration statute merely removed one of these vehicles from the defendant's arsenal of available forms of expression.

This pattern of conflicting characterizations of state interests aimed at content, on the one hand, or form or effect, on the other, recurs frequently throughout the law of FREEDOM OF SPEECH [2,I] and FREEDOM OF THE PRESS [2,I]. For instance, in *American Booksellers Assn., Inc. v. Hudnut* (1986), Judge Frank Easterbrook of the Seventh Circuit Court of Appeals, struck down the Indianapolis version of an antipornography civil rights ordinance originally drafted by Catharine MacKinnon and Andrea Dworkin. The ordinance defined PORNOGRAPHY [3,I] as the graphic sexually explicit subordination of women and provided various civil rights remedies for injured parties. The proponents of the ordinance emphasized the subliminal socializing effects of pornography. They described pornography as harmful in its institutionalization of a subordinate role and identity for women. The proponents of the ordinance thus emphasized the material, constitutive, and hence instantaneous manner in which pornography visits its injurious effects on women. Judge Easterbrook, however, characterized the ordinance as based on content viewpoint, for the ordinance had the explicit aim and effect of condemning the view that women enjoy pain, humiliation, rape, or other forms of degradation. Judge Easterbrook noted that the harmful effects of pornonoraphy, like the effects of political views, depend upon—and are indeed indivisible from—the conceptual content of pornography.

In the related context of zoning restrictions on adult theaters, the Court, in CITY OF RENTON V. PLAYTIME THEATERS, INC. (1986) [I], upheld a zoning ordinance that prohibited adult motion picture theaters from locating within 1,000 feet of a residential zone, church, park, or school—the effect being to exclude such theaters from approximately ninety-four percent of the land in the city. Writing for the Court, Chief Justice Rehnquist rejected the view that this ordinance was content-based and instead found that the "predominate intent" was to prevent undesirable secondary effects such as crime or decrease in property value. On the basis of this conception of predominant intent, the Chief Justice classified the zoning ordinance as one that did not offend the fundamental principle against content-based regulation. By contrast, Justice WILLIAM J. BRENNAN [1,I], dissenting with Justice THURGOOD MARSHALL [3,I], argued that the ordinance's exclusive targeting of adult motion picture theaters—theaters that exhibit certain kinds of motion pictures—demonstrated the absence of content neutrality. For the dissent, the content-based character of the regulation was further evidenced by indications of the city council's hostility to adult motion pictures and by the failure of the ordinance to target other activities that could conceivably give rise to the undesirable secondary effects.

These divergences among the judges and commentators are readily understandable, given that as yet no coherent basis has been provided to distinguish content-neutral from content-based regulation or to specify the extent to which content is divisible from form or effect in the various kinds of symbolic activities. The absence of a coherent basis for such a distinction permits political preferences concerning the speech at issue and the importance of governmental interests at stake to play a role, though not necessarily a determinative role, in the decisions of the courts.

The same kind of politicization, the same problem of distinguishing content-neutral from content-based regulation, and the same tendency to produce more complex context-specific doctrine has been evident in the Supreme Court's treatment of religion cases. In COUNTY OF ALLEGHENY V. ACLU (1989) [I], for instance, the Court fragmented over the constitutionality of two religious displays on public property during the Christmas-Hanukkah season. One display was of a crèche; the other display exhibited a Christmas tree and a menorah. On the basis of some exceedingly fine distinctions, the various opinions established that the menorah exhibition was constitutional while the crèche was not.

The importance of the distinction between content, on the one hand, and form and effect, on the other, was especially evident in the judicial disagreement over the constitutionality of the crèche display. Writing at times for the Court, for a plurality, and for himself, Justice HARRY A. BLACKMUN [1,I] concluded that the display of a crèche on public property during the Christmas season violated the ESTABLISHMENT CLAUSE [I] because it endorsed a patently Christian message. Focusing on the message conveyed by the display, Justice Blackmun noted that the crèche was accompanied by the words "Glory to God in the Highest" and that unlike the crèche in the case of LYNCH V. DONNELLY (1984) [3], there was nothing in the context of the display to detract from the crèche's religious message. Accordingly, Justice Blackmun concluded that the government was endorsing a religious message in violation of the establishment clause. One group of dissenting and concurring justices, Justice ANTHONY M. KENNEDY [I], Justice White, and Justice ANTONIN SCALIA [I], rejected Justice Blackmun's establishment clause requirement of no government endorsement of religion. Turning away from an inquiry into the meaning of the government display of a crèche, this group of Justices focused attention on the effects of the crèche: they noted that there was no evidence of coerced participation in religion or religious ceremonies or of significant expenditures of tax money. On the whole then, the judicial disagreement here also organized itself around the determination of whether it is the conceptual meaning of the government action that matters or its forms and effect.

In the area of freedom of the press, the distinction between content-based and content-neutral regulation also plays an important role. In *Arkansas Writers' Project, Inc. v. Ragland* (1987) the Court found unconstitutional a state law that imposed taxes on general-interest magazines but exempted newspapers and religious, professional, trade, and sports journals. The Court found this selective taxation scheme particularly disturbing because the different treatment accorded to the various magazines depended upon their content. The dissent of Justice Scalia and Chief Justice Rehnquist, by contrast, focused on the form and the effects of the tax scheme. Noting that the tax scheme merely withheld an exemption from the disfavored magazines, the dissent refused to equate the denial of an exemption to regulation or penalty on the disfavored magazines. The dissent noted that unlike direct regulation or prohibition, the denial of a subsidy was unlikely to be coercive. Focusing next on the effects of the tax scheme, the dissent noted that the tax was so small that it would be unlikely to inhibit the disfavored magazines. The dissent closed by hinting that given the indivisibility of form from subject matter in written material, it would not be possible to insist on a principled—that is, neutral—basis to distinguish permissible from impermissible subsidization.

It would be an overstatement to say that all of First Amendment doctrine turns upon the distinction between content-based regulation, on the one hand, and form-based or effect-based regulation, on the other. But the distinction does play an important role in the jurisprudence of the First Amendment. And yet, despite the important role played by this distinction, the Court has failed thus far to provide any coherent interpretation of the distinction. Indeed, at times, individual Justices deny the very possibility of making such a distinction—as in the selective yet oft-repeated claim that in a given sym-

bolic context, form and effect are indeed inseparable from content.

PIERRE SCHLAG

(SEE ALSO: *Extremist Speech and the First Amendment* [I], *Freedom of Assembly and Association* [2]; *Freedom of Petition* [2]; *Religious Liberty* [3,I]; *Religious Symbolism and the First Amendment* [I]; *Separation of Church and State* [4,I].)

Bibliography

BOLLINGER, LEE 1986 *The Tolerant Society*. New York: Oxford University Press.
GREENAWALT, KENT 1988 *Religious Convictions and Political Choice*. New York: Oxford University Press.
LEVY, LEONARD W. 1985 *Emergence of a Free Press*. New York: Oxford University Press.
———— 1986 *The Establishment Clause: Religion and the First Amendment*. New York: Macmillan.
SHRIFFRIN, STEVEN 1990 *The First Amendment, Democracy, and Romance*. Cambridge: Harvard University Press.
TRIBE, LAURENCE H. 1988 *American Constitutional Law*, 2nd ed. Pages 785–1061, 1154–1301. Mineola, N.Y.: Foundation Press.

FIRST CONGRESS

One year after the CONSTITUTIONAL CONVENTION OF 1787 [1] adjourned, the Confederation Congress called the first federal elections. An overwhelming majority of Federalists were elected to this First Congress, which was expected to function as a quasi-constitutional convention. The tasks facing the new Congress were formidable because, according to Congressman JAMES MADISON [3], the legislators would be traveling "in a wilderness without a single footstep to guide" them. If Congress acted wisely, however, Madison felt that its "successors [would] have an easier task."

Not surprisingly, experienced men were selected to serve in the new Congress. Eleven of the first senators and nine congressmen had been delegates to the federal convention, and fourteen senators and twice as many congressmen had served in state ratifying conventions. GEORGE WASHINGTON [4] told Lafayette that the new Congress "will not be inferior to any Assembly in the world."

The whole country anxiously anticipated the meeting of Congress at Federal Hall in New York City on March 4, 1789. However, much to the chagrin of Federalists, neither house had a quorum on the appointed day. Almost a month elapsed before the HOUSE OF REPRESENTATIVES [I] attained a quorum on April 1, followed five days later by the SENATE [I]; at this time, a joint session of Congress performed its constitutionally assigned function of counting the presidential electoral votes. George Washington was declared President by a unanimous vote, while JOHN ADAMS [1], a distant second, was proclaimed vice president. Messengers were sent to Washington and Adams as Congress made plans for their reception and inauguration.

Early in April the House elected Frederick A. Muhlenberg of Pennsylvania speaker and John Beckley of Virginia clerk. The Senate elected JOHN LANGDON [3] of New Hampshire president pro tempore and Samuel A. Otis of Massachusetts secretary. The House voted to hold open sessions except on sensitive matters such as Indian or military policy, whereas the Senate chose to keep its sessions closed. Two delegations came to the House under a cloud; opponents formally contested the elections of William Loughton Smith of South Carolina and the entire New Jersey delegation. Acting under Article I, section 5, of the Constitution, the House investigated the elections and declared that Smith and the New Jersey congressmen had been duly elected. The Senate, acting under Article I, section 3, drew lots to determine which senators would have initial terms of two, four, or six years that would give the Senate its distinctive staggered election every second year.

A week before Washington's inauguration, the Senate debated the titles to be given the President and vice president. Advocates of grandiose titles, such as "His Highness the President of the United States of America, and Protector of their Liberties," felt that the new republic needed such titles to command the respect of European nations. The House, however, disagreed, and the first conference committee settled the matter when the Senate agreed to the simple title of "Mr. President." The debate set the tone for the new government and symbolically marked a clear break with monarchy.

As expected, the House of Representatives initiated most legislation and the Senate became primarily a revisory body. The House proposed 143 bills to the Senate's 24. Except for the JUDICIARY ACT OF 1789 [3], the Residency bill, and the act establishing the postmaster general, all major legislation originated in the House. Because neither house established a system of standing committees, each bill was submitted to an ad hoc committee that drafted legislation which was then considered by the committee of the whole.

The first bill enacted by Congress required all federal and state officials to take an oath to support the new Constitution. Within two years, Congress created the executive departments, provided for the federal judiciary, set the country's finances in order, proposed a federal BILL OF RIGHTS [1], approved a federal tariff, reenacted the NORTHWEST ORDINANCE [3], took over the states' lighthouses, and passed legislation for NATURALIZATION [3] and COPYRIGHTS [2] and PATENTS [3,I].

Early in Congress's first of three sessions, James Madison notified the House that he intended to introduce amendments to the Constitution. With little support from other congressmen who thought that the consideration of amendments was premature, Madison persevered; and on August 24, the House sent seventeen amendments in the form of a bill of rights to the Senate. The Senate combined some of Madison's amendments, tightened the language of others, and eliminated the amendments prohibiting the states from infringing on the freedoms of conscience, speech, and press and the right to jury trial. On September 25, 1789, Congress approved twelve of Madison's amendments, which were sent to the states for their legislatures to adopt.

Unquestionably, the most controversial issues during the First Congress centered on the secretary of the treasury's *Report on Public Credit*. In his report ALEXANDER HAMILTON [2] proposed the funding of the federal debt, the federal assumption of the states' debts, the levying of an excise on distilled spirits, and the incorporation of a federal bank. No one denied the responsibility of the federal government to pay its own debt; however, some congressmen, led by Madison, opposed paying the debt at face value to speculators who had over the years accumulated a large percentage of the outstanding federal securities at greatly depreciated prices. Madison advocated paying speculators only a fraction of the face value of their holdings while providing partial compensation to the original holders. Madison also led the fight against other aspects of Hamilton's plan, arguing that the Constitution gave Congress no authority to take over the states' debts or to create a bank. To a great extent, the debate over these issues centered over a strict or broad interpretation of the Constitution. Did Congress only have delegated powers or, as Hamilton argued, did the NECESSARY AND PROPER CLAUSE [3] allow Congress to exercise implied powers? President Washington agreed with Hamilton's broader interpretation and refused to veto the bank bill. Madison, in fact, had earlier compromised his strict interpretation of the Constitution by supporting the federal assumption of state debts in exchange for northern support for the movement of the federal capital from New York City, first to Philadelphia for ten years, and then permanently to a site on the banks of the Potomac River.

Precedents were also set by the First Congress in establishing the relationship between the Senate and the President. With some hesitation, the Senate welcomed President Washington to its chamber as he presented the Treaty of New York with the Creek Nation for ratification. The Senate felt uncomfortable with the executive waiting in its chamber for an immediate adoption of the treaty, and the President disliked the Senate's insistence on examining the treaty in greater detail. Washington vowed never again to present a treaty in person. Except in one case, the Senate confirmed Washington's appointments. A protracted debate occurred over the President's power to dismiss department heads without the Senate's approval. The controversy ended when John Adams broke a tie vote on a motion to strike wording from a foreign-relations bill giving the President the right of removal. By not specifying this right in terms of a congressional grant, Congress strengthened the presidency while restricting the Senate's executive power.

In two short years the new Congress had assuaged the fears of Anti-Federalists and stifled their attempts to call a second constitutional convention. Congress had breathed life into the new Constitution, set legislative precedents, created a structure of government, enacted the first phases of Hamilton's financial plan, and established working relationships between its two houses, between itself and the other two branches of the federal government, and between the federal government and the states. The actions of the First Congress, particularly its handling of the financial morass left by the Revolution, divided the new nation economically and ideologically and set the groundwork for the first nationwide political parties. John Trumbull wrote to Vice President Adams that "In no nation, by no Legislature, was ever so much done in so short a period for the establishing of Government, order public Credit & general tranquility." It was an auspicious beginning.

JOHN P. KAMINSKI

Bibliography

BAKER, RICHARD ALLAN 1989 The Senate of the United States: "Supreme Executive Council of the Nation," 1787–1800. *Prologue* 21:299–313.

BICKFORD, CHARLENE BANGS and BOWLING, KENNETH R. 1989 *Birth of the Nation: The First Federal Congress 1789–1791.* Madison, Wis.: Madison House.

SILBEY, JOEL H. 1987 "Our Successors Will Have an Easier Task": The First Congress under the Constitution, 1789–1791. *This Constitution* 17:4–10.

SMOCK, RAYMOND W. 1989 The House of Representatives: First Branch of the New Government. *Prologue* 21:287–297.

FIRST WORLD WAR

See World War I [I]

FLAG BURNING

See: Flag Desecration [I]

FLAG DESECRATION
(Update)

The word "desecration" has religious overtones. It means defiling the sacred. Flag burning is the secular equivalent of the offense of BLASPHEMY [1], a verbal crime signifying an attack, by ridicule or rejection, against God, the Bible, Jesus Christ, Christianity, or religion itself. Flag burning is comparable to a verbal attack on the United States. Burning the nation's symbol signifies contempt and hatred by the flag burner of the things he or she believes the flag stands for, such as colonialism, imperialism, capitalism, exploitation, racism, or militarism. To the overwhelming majority of Americans, however, the flag embodies in a mystical and emotional way the loyalty and love they feel for the United States. With few exceptions we venerate the flag because it symbolizes both our unity and diversity; our commitment to freedom, equality, and justice; and perhaps above all, our constitutional system and its protection of individual rights.

Like blasphemy, therefore, flag burning tests the outermost limits of tolerance even in a free society. Burning the flag is a most offensive outrage that stretches to the breaking point the capacity of a nation to indulge dissidents. But that same form of desecration is not only an act of vandalism; it is symbolic expression that claims the protection of the free speech clause of the FIRST AMENDMENT [2,I]. Therein lies the problem and the paradox: should the flag represent a nation whose people have a right to burn its revered symbol?

Imprisoning flag burners would not mean that book burning and thought control are next. We know how to distinguish vandalism from radical advocacy; we would not regard urinating on the Jefferson Memorial or spray painting graffiti on the Washington Monument as a form of constitutionally protected free speech. Special reasons exist for protecting the flag from the splenetic conduct of extremists. A society should be entitled to safeguard its most fundamental values, but dissenters have a right to express verbal opposition to everything we hold dear. Yet, nothing is solved by saying that it is better to live in a country where people are free to burn the flag if they wish, rather than in a country where they want to burn it but cannot. We know the difference between suppressing a particularly offensive mode of conduct and a particularly offensive message. The problem is, however, that the particular mode of conduct may be the vehicle for communicating that offensive message. To suppress the message by suppressing the conduct involves governmental abridgment of a First Amendment freedom. So the Supreme Court held in *Texas v. Johnson* in 1989.

In 1984 in Dallas, Gregory Johnson, a member of the Revolutionary Communist Youth Brigade, a Maoist society, publicly burned a stolen American flag to protest the renomination of RONALD REAGAN [3,I] as the Republican candidate. While the flag burned, the protesters, including Maoists, chanted, "America, the red, white, and blue, we spit on you." That the flag burning communicated an unmistakable political message was contested by no one. The police arrested Johnson not for his message but for his manner of delivering it; he had violated a Texas statute that prohibited the desecration of a venerated object by acts that seriously offended onlookers.

State appellate courts reversed Johnson's conviction on ground that his conduct constituted constitutionally protected SYMBOLIC SPEECH [4]. Given its context—the Republican convention; Reagan's foreign policy; the protestors' demonstrations, marches, speeches, and slogans—Johnson's burning the flag was clearly speech of the sort contemplated by the First Amendment. The Texas courts also rejected the state's contention that the conviction could be justified as a means of preventing breach of the public peace. In fact, the state admitted that no BREACH OF THE PEACE [1] occurred as a result of the flag desecration. The Supreme Court, 5–4, affirmed the judgment of the Texas Court of Criminal Appeals.

Justice WILLIAM J. BRENNAN [1,I], spokesman for the majority, showed his political savvy by emphasizing that the courts of the Lone Star State, where red-blooded John Wayne patriotism flourishes, recognized "that the right to differ is the centerpiece of our First Amendment freedoms." Government cannot mandate a feeling of unity or "carve out a symbol of unity and prescribe a set of approved messages to be associated with that symbol." Brennan added that although the First Amendment literally forbids the abridgment of only "speech," the Court had labeled as speech a variety of conduct that communicated opinions, including the wearing of black arm bands to protest war, a sit-in by blacks to protest racial segregation, picketing, and the display of a red flag. Indeed the state conceded that Johnson's conduct was politically expressive. The question was whether that expression could be constitutionally proscribed, like the use of FIGHTING WORDS [2] calculated to provoke a breach of peace. Apart from the fact that no breach occurred here, Brennan reminded, a prime function of free speech is to invite dispute. The "fighting words" doctrine had no relevance in this case because the message communicated by flag burning did not personally insult anyone in particular.

Whether the state could justify the conviction as a means of preserving the flag as a symbol of nationhood and national unity depended on the communicative impact of the mode of expression. Brennan insisted that the restriction on flag desecration was "content-based." Johnson's political expression, he declared, was restricted because of the content of the message that he conveyed. This point is important and unpersuasive. As Chief Justice WILLIAM H. REHNQUIST [3,I] for the dissenters said, burning the flag was no essential part of the exposition of ideas, for Johnson was free to make any verbal denunciation of the flag that he wished. He led a march through the streets of Dallas, conducted a rally on the front steps of the city hall, shouted his slogans, and was not arrested

for any of this. Only when he burned the flag was he arrested. Texas did not punish him because it or his hearers opposed his message, only because he conveyed it by burning the flag.

Brennan replied that by punishing flag burning the state prohibited expressive conduct. "If there is a bedrock principle underlying the First Amendment," he wrote, "it is that the Government may not prohibit the expression of an idea simply because society finds the idea itself offensive or disagreeable." By making an exception for the flag, Texas sought to immunize the ideas for which it stands. Whatever it stands for should not be insulated against protest. In the context of this case, the act of flag burning constituted a means of political protest. Compulsion is not a constitutionally accepted method of achieving national unity.

Brennan believed that the flag's deservedly cherished place as a symbol would be "strengthened, not weakened, by our holding today. Our decision is a reaffirmation of the principles of freedom and inclusiveness that the flag best reflects, and of the conviction that our toleration of criticism such as Johnson's is a sign and source of our strength." This was the Court's strongest point.

Texas v. Johnson provided Court watchers with the pleasure of seeing judicial objectivity at work, for the Court did not divide in a predictable way. The majority included Justices ANTONIN SCALIA [I] and ANTHONY M. KENNEDY [I], Reagan-appointed conservatives, whereas the dissenters included Justice JOHN PAUL STEVENS [4,I], a liberal moderate. Stevens wrote his own dissent. He believed, oddly, that public desecration of the flag "will tarnish its value." He also thought that the Texas statute that the Court struck down did not compel any conduct or profession of respect for any idea or symbol. The case had nothing to do with disagreeable ideas, he said; it involved offensive conduct that diminishes the value of the national symbol. Texas prosecuted Johnson because of the method he used to express dissatisfaction with national policies. Prosecuting him no more violated the First Amendment than prosecuting someone for spray painting a message of protest on the Lincoln Memorial.

Rehnquist's dissent was suffused with emotional theatrics about the flag and patriotism. His point was that the flag was special, as two hundred years of history showed. Even if flag burning is expressive conduct, he reasoned, it is not an absolute. But he thought it not to be expressive conduct. Flag burning was no essential part of any exposition of ideas, he claimed, but rather was "the equivalent of an inarticulate grunt" meant to antagonize others. By the same reasoning, however, one might say that flag flying is also a grunt of patriotism. That does not alter the point that flag burning is malicious conduct—vandalism rather than speech.

Zealous politicians, eager to capitalize on their love for the flag and opposition to those who burned it, sought to gain political advantage from the Court's opinion. President GEORGE BUSH [I], a war hero, had helped spur a paroxysm of patriotism in 1988 by assaulting his opponent for having vetoed a bill that would have compelled teachers to lead their students in a Pledge of Allegiance every day. Bush, having made a photo opportunity of visiting a flag factory in 1988, made another after the decision in *Texas v. Johnson*, by holding a ceremony in the White House rose garden. Accepting a replica of the Iwo Jima Memorial, depicting the marines hoisting the flag on a bloody wartime site, Bush condemned flag burning as a danger to "the fabric of our country" and demanded a constitutional amendment outlawing desecration of the flag.

Cynical observers shouted "cheap politics" and criticized the President and his supporters for trying to cover up problems concerning the savings and loan scandals, the deterioration of the nation's schools, the ballooning national debt, the urban underclass, and the army of homeless beggars in American cities. Bush's opponents declared that he sought to desecrate the Constitution by indulging in escapist politics and seeking the first revision of the BILL OF RIGHTS [1] in two centuries. Many conservatives in Congress agreed that tampering with the Bill of Rights was not the way to treat the problem of flag burning. Democrats, who felt obligated to "do something" at the risk of being branded unpatriotic, offered the Flag Protection Act of 1989, and so headed off the amendment movement. The new act of Congress provided that whoever knowingly mutilates, defaces, physically defiles, or burns the flag shall be fined or imprisoned for a year, or both.

Members of the "lunatic left" promptly defied the act of Congress by burning the flag on the Capitol steps for the benefit of the TV cameras. Shawn Eichman and company got the publicity they wanted and were arrested. They quickly filed motions to dismiss, on grounds that the act of Congress was unconstitutional; that is, the flag they burned symbolized their freedom to burn it. The government asked the Supreme Court to reconsider its holding in *Texas v. Johnson* by holding that flag burning is a mode of expression, like fighting words, that does not enjoy complete protection of the First Amendment.

The Court, by the same 5–4 split, refused to alter its opinion. Brennan, again the majority spokesman, acknowledged that the government may create national symbols and encourage their respectful treatment, but concluded that it went too far with the Flag Protection Act "by criminally proscribing expressive conduct because of its likely communicative impact." Desecrating the flag was deeply offensive to many people, like virulent racial and religious epithets, vulgar repudiations of conscription, and scurri-

lous caricatures, all of which came within the First Amendment's protection, notwithstanding their offensiveness.

The government sought to distinguish the Flag Protection Act from the state statute involved in *Johnson*, on the theory that the act of Congress did not target expressive conduct on the basis of the content of its message. The government merely claimed its authority to protect the physical integrity of the flag as the symbol of our nation and its ideals. Brennan replied that destruction of the flag could in no way affect those ideals or the symbol itself. The invalidity of the statute derived from the fact that its criminal penalties applied to those whose treatment of the flag communicated a message. Thus, *United States v. Eichman*, resulting in the voiding of the act of Congress, was a replay of *Johnson*.

Stevens, for the dissenters, recapitulated his previous contentions. He believed that the majority opinion concluded at the point where analysis of the issue ought to begin. No one, he declared, disagreed with the proposition that the government cannot constitutionally punish offensive ideas. But, he argued, certain methods of expression, such as flag burning, might be proscribed if the purpose of the proscription did not relate to the suppression of ideas individuals sought to express, if that proscription did not interfere with the individual's freedom to express those ideas by other means, and if on balance the government's interest in the proscription outweighed the individual's choice of the means of expressing themselves. Stevens expatiated on the flag as a symbol and insisted that the government should protect its symbolic value without regard to the specific content of the flag burner's speech. Moreover, Eichman and the other dissidents were completely free to express their ideas by means other than flag burning. Stevens apparently missed the point that Eichman had a right to choose his own means of communicating his political protest. What disturbed Stevens most was the belief that flag burners actually have damaged the symbolic value of the flag. And he added the following in a veiled allusion to the shenanigans of would-be amenders of the Constitution: "Moreover, the integrity of the symbol has been compromised by those leaders who seem to advocate compulsory worship of the flag even by individuals whom it offends, or who seem to manipulate the symbol of national purpose into a pretext for partisan disputes about meaner ends."

Every nation in the world has a flag, and many of them, including some democracies, have laws against desecrating their flag. No other nation has our Bill of Rights. The year 1991 marked the 200th anniversary of its ratification. It requires no limiting amendment. The American people understand that they are not threatened by flag burners, and the American people prefer the First Amendment undiluted. They understand that imprisoning a few extremists is not what patriotism is about. Forced patriotism is not American. Flag burning is all wrong, but a lot of wrongheaded speech is protected by the Constitution. When the nation celebrated the bicentennial of the Bill of Rights, it celebrated a wonderfully terse, eloquent, and effective summation of individual freedoms. Time has not shown a need to add "except for flag burners." That exception, as the Court majority realized, might show that the nation is so lacking in faith in itself that it permits the Johnsons and Eichmans to diminish the flag's meaning. They are best treated, as Brennan urged, by saluting the flag that they burn or by ignoring them contemptuously.

LEONARD W. LEVY

Bibliography

GREENAWALT, KENT 1990 O'er the Land of the Free: Flag Burning as Speech. *UCLA Law Review* 37:925–947.

KMIEC, DOUGLAS W. 1990 In the Aftermath of *Johnson* and *Eichman. Brigham Young University Law Review* 1990:577–638.

FORD v. WAINWRIGHT
477 U.S. 399 (1986)

The Supreme Court held, 5–4, that the infliction of CAPTAIL PUNISHMENT [1,I] on an insane prisoner violates the ban on CRUEL AND UNUSUAL PUNISHMENTS [2,I] imposed by the Eight Amendment and the FOURTEENTH AMENDMENT [2,I]. Justice THURGOOD MARSHALL [3,I] for the majority applied the principle that the Eighth Amendment recognizes the evolving standards of decency of a maturing society. No state today permits the execution of the insane. Even at the time of the adoption of the BILL OF RIGHTS [1], the COMMON LAW [1] disapproved execution of the insane because it lacked retributive value and had no deterrence value. Marshall ruled that Florida's procedure for determining a condemned prisoner's sanity failed to rely on the judiciary to ensure neutrality in fact-finding.

The dissenting Justices contended that the Eighth Amendment did not mandate a right not to be executed while insane. Justice WILLIAM H. REHNQUIST [3,I] observed that at common law the executive controlled the procedure by which the sanity of the condemned prisoner was judged. The dissenters refused to endorse a constitutional right to a judicial determination of sanity before the death penalty could be imposed. Justice LEWIS F. POWELL [3,I] was the swing vote in this case. He agreed that the Eighth Amendment prohibited the execution of the insane, but declined to endorse Justice Marshall's virtual requirement of a judicial proceeding to determine sanity.

LEONARD W. LEVY

(SEE ALSO: *Mental Illness and the Constitution* [3,I].)

FOREIGN POLICY

See: Congress and Foreign Policy [I]; Congressional War Powers [I]; Foreign Affairs and the Constitution [2]; Senate and Foreign Policy [I]

FOURTEENTH AMENDMENT AND SECTION 5
(Framing)

The FOURTEENTH AMENDMENT [2,I] was proposed by Congress in 1866 and ratified in 1868. Section 1 made persons born in the nation citizens and prohibited states from abridging the PRIVILEGES AND IMMUNITIES [3] of citizens of the United States and from denying DUE PROCESS [2] or EQUAL PROTECTION [2,I] to any person. Section 5 gave Congress the power to enforce the amendment by appropriate legislation. However, in 1866, the exact scope of the enforcement power was not clear. Particularly, it was unclear whether the amendment was designed to reach purely private action and conspiracies or only those in which state officials were involved. Controversy on this question has continued from 1866 to the present.

Although the debates on the Fourteenth Amendment did not emphasize the mechanics of the enforcement authorized by section 5, broad themes in the debate were clearly relevant to enforcement. Most members of the REPUBLICAN PARTY [1,I] insisted on protection for FUNDAMENTAL RIGHTS [2] of American citizens, were committed to a federal system that required states to respect basic rights, and were unwilling for the federal goverment to supplant the basic jurisdiction of the states over crimes and civil matters. At the same time, Republicans were determined to protect blacks and loyalists in the South.

A prototype of the Fourteenth Amendment written by Republican JOHN A. BINGHAM [1] provided congressional power to pass all laws necessary to secure all persons equal protection in their rights to life, liberty, and property. Several Republicans objected to the prototype because they thought it would allow federal statutes broadly to supplant state civil criminal law. Bingham denied that was his purpose and said he intended to authorize Congress to punish state officers for violations of the BILL OF RIGHTS [1]. Bingham's prototype was recast with limitations on the states in section 1 and the enforcement power in section 5. Bingham explained that the final version of the amendment would allow Congress to protect the privileges and immunities of citizens and the inborn rights of every person when these rights were abridged or denied by unconstitutional acts of any state.

Although Republicans generally believed that state laws denying privileges or immunities, due process, or equal protection could be struck down by the courts, they expected Congress to take a direct and substantial role in enforcing the guarantees of section 1. Many believed that the equal protection clause required the states to supply the protection of the laws to blacks, Unionists, Republicans, and others who faced private violence.

Republicans thought enforcement could reach state officials who violated the rights secured by the amendment. One object of the Fourteenth Amendment was to ensure that Congress had the power to pass the CIVIL RIGHTS ACT OF 1866 [1]. That act had punished persons who, under color of state law or custom, had deprived citizens of the rights it guaranteed. Senator LYMAN TRUMBULL [4], chairman of the SENATE JUDICIARY COMMITTEE [1] and manager of the civil rights bill in the Senate, thought that state judges who maliciously violated rights secured in the act were subject to prosecution.

In 1871, Congress considered an act to deal with terrorism by the Ku Klux Klan. The most difficult issue confronting the Congress was whether the power to enforce the Fourteenth Amendment under section 5 allowed Congress to make private action a crime. Republicans generally supported provisions that would punish those, like state officers, who deprived persons of rights, privileges, and immunities of citizens of the United States under COLOR OF LAW [1]. However, Democrats and several leading Republicans objected to provisions designed to reach private acts and private conspiracies to deny constitutional rights. They insisted that the power to enforce the Fourteenth Amendment was limited to STATE ACTION [4,I] or, some Republican dissenters thought, to cases where the state failed to supply equal protection. Congressional critics pointed to the change from the prototype of the Fourteenth Amendment, which granted Congress power to secure equal protection in life, liberty, or property, to the amendment's final version, which provided restriction on the states in section 1 together with congressional power to enforce the amendment in section 5.

According to the state-action argument, Congress had less power to reach private terrorism intended to deny constitutional rights than the Supreme Court in 1842 had found it had to punish private individuals who interfered with the return of FUGITIVE SLAVES [2].

In 1871, most Republicans thought the states had the duty to protect their citizens against politically or racially motivated violence and that private individuals who interfered with this duty could be punished. As finally passed, the 1871 act punished private individuals who conspired to deprive persons of equal protection or equal privileges or immunities or who conspired to interfere with state officials supplying equal protection. In this form, the act secured the support of Republicans who had expressed constitutional doubts. Still, in UNITED STATES V. HARRIS (1883) [2], the United States Supreme Court held a section of the 1871 act unconstitutional because it reached con-

spiracies by private persons to deny constitutional rights and did so regardless of how well the state had performed its duty of equal protection. In 1966, in the midst of a second RECONSTRUCTION [I], six Justices suggested that Congress could reach some private conspiracies designed to interfere with constitutional rights. In JONES V. ALFRED H. MAYER CO. (1968) [3] the Supreme Court recognized power in Congress to enforce the THIRTEENTH AMENDMENT [4] by prohibiting private racial discrimination in housing contracts. Still, the power of Congress to reach private conduct under the Fourteenth Amendment remains controversial.

MICHAEL KENT CURTIS

Bibliography

AVINS, ALFRED 1967 The Ku Klux Act of 1871: Some Reflected Light on State Action and the Fourteenth Amendment. *Saint Louis University Law Journal* 11:331–381.

CARR, ROBERT K. 1947 *Federal Protection of Civil Rights.* Ithaca, N.Y.: Cornell University Press.

FRANTZ, LAURENT B. 1964 Congressional Power to Enforce the Fourteenth Amendment Against Private Acts. *Yale Law Journal* 73:1352–1384.

HYMAN, HAROLD and WIECEK, WILLIAM 1982 *Equal Justice Under Law.* New York: Harper and Row.

KACZOROWSKI, ROBERT J. 1985 *The Politics of Judicial Interpretation: The Federal Courts, Department of Justice and Civil Rights 1866–76.* New York: Chelsea House.

ZUCKERT, MICHAEL 1986 Congressional Power Under the Fourteenth Amendment—The Original Understanding of Section Five. *Constitutional Commentary* 3:123–155.

FOURTEENTH AMENDMENT, SECTION 5
(Judicial Construction)

Section 5 of the FOURTEENTH AMENDMENT [2,I] empowers Congress to "enforce, by appropriate legislation" the other provisions of the amendment, including the guarantees of the DUE PROCESS [2] and EQUAL PROTECTION [2,I] clauses of section 1. Congress can, of course, enact criminal penalities or provide civil remedies to redress violations of the due process and equal protection clauses. The more difficult issue is whether the Fourteenth Amendment enforcement power is large enough to allow Congress to forbid conduct that does not violate due process or equal protection.

In the CIVIL RIGHTS ACT OF 1875 [1], Congress made RACIAL DISCRIMINATION [3,I] in "inns, public conveyances . . . , theatres and other places of public amusement" a crime. The CIVIL RIGHTS CASES (1883) [1] held that the Fourteenth Amendment enforcement power did not provide sufficient support for the law. Congress only had the power under section 5 to "enforce" the amendment, which forbade only discrimination by the state. Therefore, legislation outlawing a "private wrong" was beyond the enforcement power. The same limit applies to the enforcement power in section 2 of the FIFTEENTH AMENDMENT [2], for section 1 of that amendment is similarly interpreted to forbid only state abridgment of the right to vote.

Despite the holding of *Civil Rights Cases*, it has been settled that the Fourteenth Amendment gives Congress power to prohibit some behavior by private individuals. In UNITED STATES V. GUEST (1966) [2] six Justices agreed to an OBITER DICTUM [3] that Congress can "punish private conspiracies that interfere with fourteenth amendment rights, such as the right to utilize public facilities." That concept supports provisions of 1968 legislation that make it a federal crime for private individuals to deny others, "because of . . . race, color, religion or national origin," their rights to attend public schools or participate in programs provided or administered by the state.

It is less clear whether the holding of the *Civil Rights Cases* is still valid in denying Congress the power, under section 5 of the Fourteenth Amendment, to control private conduct that is not connected to any relationship between the victim and the states. No Supreme Court decision since *Guest* has spoken to that question. Because Congress has a wide range of other legislative powers available to it, this abstract question probably will not be answered in the foreseeable future. The CIVIL RIGHTS ACT OF 1964 [1], for example, went further than the law invalidated in the *Civil Rights Cases*, outlawing discrimination by hotels, restaurants, and private employers. The 1964 Act was upheld, in *Katzenbach v. McClung* (1964), under Congress's broad power to regulate INTERSTATE COMMERCE [2]. The commerce power also supports 1968 federal legislation regulating private housing discrimination.

One question concerning the scope of the Fourteenth Amendment enforcement power may be more than academic. In cases like NATIONAL LEAGUE OF CITIES V. USERY (1976) [3] and GARCIA V. SAN ANTONIO METROPOLITAN TRANSIT AUTHORITY (1985) [2], questions have been raised about the constitutionality of federal laws that impose obligations directly on state governments—for example, that the state pay its workers a minimum wage. It may be necessary to decide whether legislation imposing some obligations on state or LOCAL GOVERNMENTS [I] can be sustained under the Fourteenth Amendment enforcement power. The Court has concluded in *City of Rome v. United States* (1980) that the three constitutional amendments enacted following the CIVIL WAR [I]—the THIRTEENTH AMENDMENT [4], the Fourteenth Amendment, and the Fifteenth Amendment—"were specifically designed as an expansion of federal power and an intrusion on state sovereignty." Thus, constitutional limits on na-

tional power imposed to protect state sovereignty are inapplicable to legislation authorized by these amendments. In *City of Rome* the Court upheld federal VOTING RIGHTS [4] legislation requiring the city to obtain approval of the United States ATTORNEY GENERAL [1] before it could reduce the size of its city council.

The power to provide "remedies" to prevent violations of the Fourteenth and Fifteenth Amendments allows Congress to invalidate some state laws that courts otherwise would have sustained. State LITERACY TESTS [3] for voters are a clear example. The Supreme Court upheld literacy tests as a requirement for voters in *Lassiter v. Northampton County Board of Elections* (1959). Federal voting rights laws, however, have since suspended all state literacy tests. The Court sustained that legislation in OREGON V. MITCHELL (1970) [3]. Congress could reasonably find that the states had used literacy tests to engage in racial discrimination. Even if literacy tests for voting did not themselves violate the Constitution, Congress decided that they were being used to violate the Fifteenth Amendment. Congress could then invalidate all literacy tests as a remedy to prevent racial discrimination in voting.

Modern cases have uniformly sustained federal laws enacted to provide broad remedies for possible violations of the Fourteenth and Fifteenth Amendments. There has been more controversy concerning the question of whether Congress has power to interpret the guarantees of section 1 of the Fourteenth Amendment. In KATZENBACH V. MORGAN (1965) [3] the Court sustained a provision of the VOTING RIGHTS ACT OF 1965 [4] that suspended literacy tests for voting in New York by persons who had completed six grades of school in Puerto Rico. The Court sustained that legislation, in part on the ground that Congress could decide that New York's literacy test law, which waived the test only for citizens who had completed six grades of school in the English language, violated the equal protection clause of section 1 of the Fourteenth Amendment. Two dissenters argued that only courts could interpret the Constitution and warned that the power to interpret the Constitution's guarantees of liberty could authorize Congress to dilute those guarantees as well as amplify them.

The continuing authority of the interpretive theory of *Katzenbach v. Morgan* is now in some doubt. Amendments to the Voting Rights Act in 1970 extended the right to vote to eighteen-year-olds in both state and federal elections, interpreting the equal protection clause to declare that it was unconstitutional to deny them the right to vote because of their age. Different 5–4 majorities of the Court in *Oregon v. Mitchell* upheld the statute as applied to federal elections and invalidated it as applied to state elections. Four of the Justices would have upheld the statute in its entirety, while four would have held that Congress lacked the power to change the voting age in either state or federal elections. The specific issue of voting age has, of course, been mooted by enactment of the TWENTY-SIXTH AMENDMENT [4] the following year. Since 1970 Congress has not relied on the interpretive theory in enactments enforcing the Fourteenth and Fifteenth Amendments.

WILLIAM COHEN

(SEE ALSO: *Conspiracy Law* [I]; *Private Discrimination* [I]; *Racial Preference* [I].)

Bibliography

BICKEL, ALEXANDER M. 1966 The Voting Rights Cases. *Supreme Court Review* 1966:79–102.

COHEN, WILLIAM 1975 Congressional Power to Interpret Due Process and Equal Protection. *Stanford Law Review* 27:603–620.

COX, ARCHIBALD 1971 The Role of Congress in Constitutional Determination. *University of Cincinnati Law Review* 40:199–261.

FOURTH AMENDMENT

The Fourth Amendment gives citizens the "right . . . to be secure" in their "persons, homes, papers, and effects" by prohibiting the government from engaging in unreasonable SEARCHES AND SEIZURES [4,I]. The nature and scope of this "right" depends on how the Supreme Court resolves three central questions of Fourth Amendment jurisprudence: which government information-gathering techniques merit Fourth Amendment regulation, what type of regulation applies to these "searches" and "seizures" to ensure their "reasonableness," and what remedies follow Fourth Amendment violations.

The amendment's text yields no answers to the questions of coverage and remedy. It does not specify the criteria for determining whether a particular governmental practice qualifies as a Fourth Amendment "search" or "seizure." Nor does the amendment say whether the evidentiary products of "unreasonable" Fourth Amendment activity should be excluded from a defendant's criminal trial to deter future governmental violations of the amendment. The Supreme Court resolved this latter problem when it "read" an exclusionary remedy into the Fourth Amendment in WEEKS V. UNITED STATES (1914) [4] and applied it to the states in MAPP V. OHIO (1961) [3].

The amendment does provide some clues as to what constitutes "reasonable" Fourth Amendment activity because its "warrant" clause identifies the conditions that must be satisfied for the issuance of a valid SEARCH WARRANT [4] or ARREST WARRANT [1]. The government must show a neutral magistrate that it has PROBABLE CAUSE [3] for believing that it will find what (or whom) it is looking for and that the seizure of such EVIDENCE [2] serves a legitimate governmental purpose. The warrant must contain a particular description of the place to be searched or person or items to be seized. The violation of these guidelines could provide the exclusive or primary criteria for assessing what constitutes an unreasonable search or seizure prohibited by the first clause of the amendment. But the text certainly does not dictate this interpretation, and the Court has not consistently embraced this "warrant" model of Fourth Amendment regulation.

To aid its interpretation of the text, the Supreme Court has sought to ascertain the goals and concerns of those who drafted and ratified it. Translating the "Framers' intent"—when it can be discovered—to a radically different social, cultural, and institutional context is, however, an exercise of dubious value. We know that the Framers wanted to eliminate GENERAL WARRANTS [2] because such warrants placed few limits on the scope of the search or on what could be seized. More generally, the Framers wanted to confine the nascent federal government's powers. However, their vision of what those powers entailed bears little resemblance to the vast regulatory capacities of the modern welfare state. Drawing comparisons between their concerns and ours works only at the highest level of generality. The vague principles generated by such analogies cannot resolve the difficult interpretive questions the Court faces when it applies the amendment to governmental functions and uses of modern technology the Framers could not have imagined.

These intractable uncertainties in the text and historical record help explain why the Supreme Court has rarely relied on a "Framers' intent" methodology to resolve the three central questions of Fourth Amendment jurisprudence. Instead, the Court's fundamental interpretive strategy is to identify and balance the competing values implicated by this restraint on governmental power.

To resolve the threshold question of whether a particular governmental information-gathering practice constitutes Fourth Amendment activity, the Court has identified the individual "interests" protected by the Fourth Amendment and then determined whether that practice significantly implicates these Fourth Amendment values. A Fourth Amendment "seizure" of a person's tangible "effects" takes place when the government interferes with an individual's legitimate property interests. A fourth amendment "seizure" of a person occurs when the governmental agent takes some action that restrains a REASONABLE PERSON's [I] liberty of movement. A Fourth Amendment "search" occurs when the government intrudes on the individual's REASONABLE EXPECTATION OF PRIVACY [I] as to the place searched (including the individual's body) or information examined.

The Court's test for evaluating what constitutes a reasonable expectation of privacy comes from Justice JOHN MARSHALL HARLAN's [2] CONCURRING OPINION [1] in KATZ V. UNITED STATES (1967) [3]. Harlan articulated "a twofold requirement, first that a person have exhibited an actual (subjective) expectation of privacy and, second, that the expectation be one that society is prepared to recognize as 'reasonable.'" Harlan subsequently rejected the subjective component of his test, and the Court endorsed his rejection of it in *Hudson v. Palmer* (1984). Focusing on the individual's subjective expectations is unsatisfactory because the government can destroy our actual privacy expectations by engaging in the very type of intrusive surveillance practices that the amendment was designed to regulate. Harlan insisted that the question of reasonable privacy expectations demanded a normative inquiry into the types of privacy expectations a free society *should* protect. Or, as Anthony Amsterdam put it, the Court should determine "whether if the particular form of surveillance practiced by the police is permitted to go unregulated by constitutional restraints, the amount of privacy and freedom remaining to citizens would be diminished to a compass inconsistent with the aims of a free and open society."

Amsterdam's inquiry reminds us of the risks generated by the Court's decision *not* to subject some governmental information-gathering activity to constitutional constraints. When the courts hold that a surveillance practice does not qualify as Fourth Amendment activity, the government may employ the practice against any citizen without any basis for believing either that the citizen merits governmental scrutiny or that such attention will promote any legitimate public interest. Amsterdam's query brilliantly characterizes the ultimate issue implicated by this threshold question of Fourth Amendment coverage; it does not, however, provide any guidelines for resolving the coverage question.

First, application of Amsterdam's formulation requires an empirical prediction about how the police will use (or abuse) the information-gathering technique if it is not subject to any constitutional regulation. But whose prediction of future police behavior should govern? A majority of the Justices on the WARREN COURT [4] feared potential abuse of unregulated police power against racial and ethnic minorities. In contrast, a majority of the Justices on both the BURGER COURT [1] and the REHNQUIST COURT [I] appear more sanguine about the police's good-faith use of unregulated surveillance tactics.

Second, Amsterdam's characterization of the ultimate normative judgment does not tell us *whose* norms should define what counts as a loss of privacy that is "inconsistent" with the aims of a free society. Do these norms come from some independent political theory about the minimal

amount of privacy and liberty necessary for a free society; from a moral theory about the minimal privacy due to any human being; or from current majoritarian preferences as expressed by customs, laws, and moral conventions?

The Rehnquist Court does not appear to be relying on any independent normative account of the minimal privacy expectations necessary for a free society in its Fourth Amendment coverage decisions. According to the Court, individuals cannot legitimately demand privacy protection for information that they "knowingly" expose to the public. Thus, in *California v. Ciraolo* (1986) and *Florida v. Riley* (1989) the Court concluded that citizens cannot reasonably demand some privacy protection from governmental aerial surveillance of the private property adjoining their homes so long as these flights operate at altitudes where private flights frequently occur. By "exposing" their activity in this area to view from private aircraft, citizens have assumed the risk that this information will be disclosed to the public and therefore have no legitimate privacy expectation against unregulated govermental snooping. Similarly, in CALIFORNIA V. GREENWOOD (1988) [I], the Court concluded that no Fourth Amendment search occurs when governmental agents rummage through people's discarded trash, because they have exposed that trash (and all the information about their lives that can be gleaned from its inspection) to any private citizen who wishes to examine it.

The question-begging nature of the Court's "assumption of risk" analysis hardly suggests that the Justices are relying on any coherent theoretical account of privacy. The Court fails to ask whether individuals have any meaningful choice to avoid exposure of some information to private third parties in these cases. How, for example, are homeowners supposed to protect their backyards from those curious airline passengers armed with high-powered binoculars? More importantly, the empirical risks of disclosure that citizens assume as to some private third party (for example, the scavenger going through their trash) cannot resolve the normative question of what risks of disclosure they should bear when the government is the information-gatherer. Must we incinerate our own trash to keep the government from rummaging through it to learn the most intimate details about our lives? Must we remain indoors behind shrouded windows to prevent the government from learning what we might otherwise do in our backyards? Why, in short, must information remain secret before we can demand that the government have some good reason for gaining access to it?

All of these objections have considerable force if the Fourth Amendment's privacy norms derive from some coherent theoretical account. But why does the constitution endorse any particular theoretical account about how to determine what constitutes a reasonable expectation of privacy? What if a majority of American citizens approved of these decisions because they accurately reflected their own judgments about what types of privacy expectations should be considered legitimate? Admittedly, the majority's normative judgments might reflect the public's acquiescence to a range of intrusive governmental information-gathering practices that have gradually lowered its normative expectations. But there are other possible explanations for such majoritarian views.

Majoritarian preferences about the degree of desirable protection from unregulated government surveillance may reflect an assessment of how much privacy and liberty is lost from the high incidence of crime in our communities. People who live in a drug-infested high-crime area might be happy to have the police engage in suspicionless searches of their trash in hope that these unregulated practices will generate more drug arrests, more convictions, and a lower level of criminal activity in their neighborhoods. In short, the majority might be willing to forgo some protection from unregulated governmental intrusions into their lives to increase their protection from violent criminal intrusions.

Linking a "reasonable expectation of privacy" test to majoritarian preferences is, of course, very problematic. Courts will have difficulty determining whether majoritarian preferences reflect acquiescence to intrusive governmental practices or considered judgments about the best trade-off between different types of privacy losses. Moreover, "majoritarian" calculations of this trade-off are suspect because the losses of privacy and liberty from governmental intrusion probably will not be equally distributed among all citizens. Finally, basing Fourth Amendment privacy norms on majoritarian preferences offers no constitutionally mandated minimal floor of privacy protection against the government. If crime sufficiently threatened the basic fabric of society, the majority might prefer a trade-off that gave governmental authorities the powers of a police state. If the majority expressed these preferences in a political process that gave equal weight to all citizens' choices, the Court could not invalidate any resulting crime-control legislation without appealing to some independent normative privacy theory.

The conclusory nature of the Court's analysis in cases like *Ciraolo* and *Greenwood* precludes any confident conclusion about the sources from which the Court is deriving its privacy-expectation norms. Indeed, the incoherence of these opinions might be the inevitable product of the Court's refusal to rely exclusively on either majoritarian preferences or some normative privacy theory to justify its coverage decisions.

However, an examination of the Rehnquist Court's answers to the second central question of Fourth Amendment jurisprudence—the type of regulation applicable to governmental practices that are covered by the amendment—strongly suggests that the Court's "reasonableness" analysis reflects current societal assessments of when these practices are cost-justified.

What constitutes a "reasonable" search or seizure depends in part on the nature of the Fourth Amendment "interest" or "right" at stake. Consider the RIGHT OF PRIVACY [3,I] implicated by governmental intrusions into our bodies. The Supreme Court faced this issue in *Winston v. Lee* (1985) when it decided that a court-approved surgery to remove a bullet that could link the individual to a crime constituted an unreasonable search and seizure.

The Court could have justified this decision by viewing bodily privacy as a right of personhood that merits respect and protection regardless of the beneficial social consequences that might be generated by its impairment. A court-ordered surgical procedure performed for nonmedical reasons against the individual's will would constitute an "unreasonable" search because it violated this norm.

Instead, the Court said that a search's reasonableness "depends on a case by case approach, in which the individual's interests in privacy and security are weighed against society's interests in conducting the procedure." In this case, the balance tipped in the individual's favor. The state did not need the incriminating bullet because it already possessed sufficient independent evidence of Lee's guilt to secure his conviction. While acknowledging that an intrusion into bodily privacy might be so egregious and life-threatening that it would be deemed unreasonable on that basis alone, the Court endorsed a utilitarian cost-benefit–balancing analysis to determine the reasonableness of intrusive BODY SEARCHES [I] in future cases.

Winston offers an extreme example of a general judicial trend to view Fourth Amendment values in liberty, property, and privacy as "individual interests" that will be protected from state interference only when doing so will promote our general welfare. In theory, a comprehensive utilitarian calculation of whether a particular search was "reasonable" might consider several factors, including: the strength of the Fourth Amendment interest that is being impaired, the degree of its impairment, the strength of the societal interest at stake, the extent to which the Fourth Amendment activity under review actually furthers that societal interest, and whether the government could further that societal interest by means that intruded less on the individual's Fourth Amendment interests.

But who should balance these competing interests? From what sources should the balancer derive the standard for determining how much social cost the protection of the individual's Fourth Amendment interests is worth? And what kinds of regulatory guidelines should follow from this balancing methodology?

Courts could defer to majoritarian resolutions of such

questions in those cases where majoritarian preferences are expressed through political processes that treat all individual choices with equal weight. Under such a "fair process" model, the Court might limit its constitutional inquiry to determining whether the manner by which these trade-off judgments were reached provided a fair opportunity for all interests, values, and alternatives to be considered by politically accountable decision makers. Searches and seizures would be unreasonable if the political process for making the cost-benefit judgment was flawed by some form of discrimination or if the trade-off judgment was delegated to the "arbitrary" discretion of officers in the field who do not qualify as "democratically accountable" officials.

Deriving Fourth Amendment norms exclusively from majoritarian preferences (even those expressed by a well-functioning democratic process) remains problematic for those who view the Constitution as a source of rights and principles that are designed in part to check majoritarian will. But what is the alternative if an assessment of reasonableness requires a cost-benefit analysis? Some commentators have suggested that the Framers of the Fourth Amendment have already done all the necessary balancing of competing interests and that their judgments are reflected in the amendment's warrant-clause requirements.

According to this "warrant" model of Fourth Amendment regulation, the probable cause requirement embodies the Framers' balancing judgment of what constitutes a reasonable search or seizure. Prior judicial authorization ensures that a neutral magistrate, and not the officer in the field, will decide whether the probable cause standard is satisfied. The warrant also controls the discretion of governmental field agents because its particular description of what can be searched and seized limits the scope of their justifiable intrusion.

The Warren Court appeared to embrace this warrant model; it treated searches and seizures without probable cause and most warrantless Fourth Amendment activity as presumptively unreasonable. That Court identified only two narrowly defined exceptions (STOP AND FRISK [4] and ADMINISTRATIVE SEARCHES [1,I]) where it was willing to engage in its own balancing analysis to assess the reasonableness of Fourth Amendment activity that did not satisfy the warrant clause's requirements.

In TERRY V. OHIO (1968) the Court applied a watered-down version of probable cause (individualized reasonable suspicion) to justify warrantless investigative seizures (stops) and protective searches (frisks) that were less intrusive than ARRESTS [1] and full evidentiary searches. But these stop-and-frisk cases retained a core Fourth Amendment criterion for assessing reasonableness: the government had to demonstrate an individualized factual basis for engaging in Fourth Amendment activity.

The Warren Court's second deviation from the warrant model of regulation came in CAMARA V. MUNICIPAL COURT (1967) [1], where it recognized that governmental civil regulatory interests may render some administrative searches reasonable even in the absence of any individualized factual bases for conducting them. *Camara* upheld the reasonableness of housing-code inspection searches even though there were no individualized ground for believing that the homes searched contained code violations. Having concluded that an individualized suspicion requirement would destroy the state's ability to promote its valid civil regulatory interest, the Court sustained the constitutionality of housing-code inspections conducted in conformity with "reasonable administrative or legislative standards" that limited the discretion of inspectors in the field.

The Burger and Rehnquist Courts have shown a far greater willingness to engage in their own context-specific balancing of competing interests to decide what constitutes reasonable Fourth Amendment activity. At a rhetorical level, they have not explicitly repudiated the warrant model of regulation for criminal cases. However, they have greatly expanded the range and scope of Fourth Amendment intrusions governed by the *Terry* exception to probable cause. On the basis of individualized reasonable suspicion, the police may now "frisk" the passenger compartment of cars to look for dangerous weapons and conduct protective "sweep" searches of homes to look for dangerous accomplices of the person they have arrested. Moreover, the Court has watered down the quality of the evidence needed to establish reasonable suspicion by holding in ALABAMA V. WHITE (1990) that police corroboration of nonincriminating details from an anonymous tip may satisfy the standard of founded suspicion.

More importantly, the Court has greatly expanded both the rationale and scope of the administrative search doctrine. In several decisions, the Court has used a balancing approach to justify intrusive searches and seizures without a warrant, probable cause, or even individualized suspicion where the governmental interest furthered by the search is viewed as particularly compelling. Two significant themes emerge from these cases.

First, the Court has dispensed with individualized suspicion as a minimal Fourth Amendment requirement even in contexts in which such a requirement would not preclude the government from promoting the societal interests at stake. Thus, in NATIONAL TREASURY EMPLOYEES UNION V. VON RAAB (1988) [I], the Court upheld the constitutionality of suspicionless DRUG TESTING [I] of employees who were in or were seeking certain sensitive positions within the Customs Service. The Court found mandatory urine testing reasonable despite the absence of any showing that the Service had a drug problem or that a founded suspicion standard would prevent the Service from adequately dealing with any problem it did have.

Second, the Court has not confined its interest-balancing approach to civil regulatory searches and seizures. Despite language in *Von Raab* that some special "governmental need" beyond the normal imperatives of law enforcement must be shown for interest balancing to be appropriate, the Court used interest balancing in MICHIGAN DEPARTMENT OF STATE POLICE V. SITZ (1990) [I] to uphold the reasonableness of seizures of all drivers at sobriety checkpoints. The Court did not concern itself with whether these suspicionless seizures better promoted the detection and deterrence of drunk driving than did police patrols that stopped drivers on the basis of individualized reasonable suspicion. Nor did the availability of less intrusive police practices that served the same societal interests render these checkpoint stops unreasonable. In essence, this law enforcement seizure was "reasonable" because the state's compelling interest in fighting drunk driving outweighed the individual's interest in liberty that was only "minimally" intruded on by a momentary detention and examination for signs of intoxication.

When the Court uses this interest-balancing approach, it never identifies the source of its standard for assessing why the state interest outweighs the individual's Fourth Amendment interests. But opinions like *Sitz* strongly suggest that the Court is relying on its interpretation of majoritarian assessments of when searches and seizures are cost-justified. The Court certainly is not making its own probing cost-benefit analysis. Instead, it defers to the judgments of upper-level law enforcement officials concerning the most appropriate use of their scarce law enforcement resources because the Fourth Amendment "was not meant to transfer [such decisions] from politically accountable officials to the courts." Left unstated is the assumption that the tenure of "politically accountable" officials depends on their ability to gauge accurately majoritarian preferences about the appropriate trade-off between individual and societal interests. Left unexamined is whether the political process generating these trade-off decisions has fairly considered the competing interests at stake or adequately examined alternative ways to accommodate them. The Court appears to be using a "fair process" model in name only to legitimate majoritarian preferences concerning what constitutes cost-justified Fourth Amendment activity.

The Court's Fourth Amendment jurisprudence reflects a fundamental tension within constitutional law concerning two different functions that can be served by constitutional principles in a democratic system. The Court sometimes treats the Constitution as a source of norms whose justification is not linked either to the satisfaction of majoritarian preferences or to the promotion of general social welfare. When the Court views the Fourth Amendment from this perspective, its determination of what constitutes "reasonable" Fourth Amendment activity will sometimes frustrate majoritarian preferences. Recently, the Court has viewed the Constitution's requirements as embodied in the expression of the preferences that emerge from a democratic process. The Rehnquist Court, however, does not engage in any searching inquiry about the nature of the process that generated these preferences; it simply assumes that a well-functioning democratic process was in place. When the Court views the Fourth Amendment from this more positivistic perspective, it shows far greater deference to the judgments and actions of the governmental actors subject to the amendment's constraints.

PETER ARENELLA

(SEE ALSO: *Fourth Amendment (Historical Origins)* [2]; *Search and Seizure* [4]; *Unreasonable Search* [4].)

Bibliography

AMSTERDAM, ANTHONY G. 1974 Perspectives on the Fourth Amendment. *Minnesota Law Review* 58:349–477.
LAFAVE, WAYNE 1987 *Search and Seizure: A Treatise on the Fourth Amendment*, 2nd ed. Vols. 1–3. St. Paul, Minn.: West Publishing Co.
SCHULHOFER, STEPHEN J. 1989 On the Fourth Amendment Rights of the Law-Abiding Public. *Supreme Court Review* 1989:87–163.
WASSERSTROM, SILAS J. and SEIDMAN, LOUIS M. 1988 The Fourth Amendment as Constitutional Theory. *Georgetown Law Journal* 77:19–112.

FRAZEE v. ILLINOIS DEPARTMENT OF EMPLOYMENT SECURITY
489 U.S. 829 (1989)

This case expanded the protection of the free-exercise clause of the FIRST AMENDMENT [2,I] by allowing a Christian to refuse work on the Sabbath without being denied unemployment benefits. Earlier, the Court had held that such benefits may not be denied to persons whose religious beliefs obligated them to refuse work on the Sabbath, but in all the PRECEDENTS [3], such as SHERBERT V. VERNER (1963) [4], the claimant had belonged to a religious sect or particular church. Frazee was not a member of either and did not rely on a specific religious tenet. The Illinois courts therefore upheld the denial to him of unemployment compensation.

Unanimously, the Supreme Court sustained Frazee's free-exercise right. He had asserted that he was a Christian, and no authority had challenged his sincerity. As a Christian, he felt that working on Sunday was wrong. The Court held that a professing Christian, even if not a church-goer or member of a sect, was protected by the free-exercise clause from having to choose between his or her religious belief and unemployment compensation. Denial of compensation violated the clause.

LEONARD W. LEVY

FREEDOM OF ASSOCIATION
(Update to *Freedom of Assembly and Association*)

The freedom of association derives from the free speech and free assembly provisions of the FIRST AMENDMENT [2,I], and it protects the right of persons to enter into relationships with one another unhampered by intrusive governmental regulation. More precisely, the freedom of association encompasses two distinct guarantees: the FREEDOM OF INTIMATE ASSOCIATION [2] and the freedom of expressive association. The freedom of intimate association protects "certain kinds of highly personal relationships," such as marriage. The freedom of expressive association, on the other hand, protects "the right to associate with others in pursuit of a wide variety of political, social, economic, educational, religious, and cultural ends."

In recent cases the Court has made clear the limits of these two guarantees with respect to ANTIDISCRIMINATION LAWS [I]. In *Roberts v. United States Jaycees* (1984) and *Board of Directors of Rotary International v. Rotary Club* (1987), the Court rejected arguments by both the Jaycees and Rotary International that laws prohibiting SEX DISCRIMINATION [4,I] could not be applied to them without violating their members' freedom of association. Both organizations limited their regular membership to men. The Court held that neither the freedom of intimate association nor the freedom of expressive association protected this type of discrimination by the organizations in question. The freedom of intimate association did not apply at all because both organizations tended to have unlimited memberships and open meetings. The freedom of expressive association may have been implicated, but not sufficiently to override the government's COMPELLING STATE INTEREST [1] to eradicate discrimination. As the Court said in *Rotary,* "The evidence fails to demonstrate that admitting women . . . will affect in any significant way the existing members' ability to carry out their various purposes."

In *New York State Club Association v. New York City* (1988), the Court turned back yet another free association challenge to an antidiscrimination law. New York City prohibits discrimination on the basis of race, gender, and other grounds by any "place of public accommodation, resort or amusement," but exempts from this restriction any group "which is in its nature distinctly private." In 1984 the city passed a new law providing that no groups shall be considered private if it "has more than four hundred members, provides regular meal service and regularly receives payment . . . from or on behalf of nonmembers. . . ." The new law exempted religious and benevolent associations from this provision. A consortium of private clubs and associations challenged the ordinance, claiming that it abridged on its face both the First Amendment and the EQUAL PROTECTION [2,I] clause. The Supreme Court unanimously disagreed.

Writing for the Court, Justice BYRON R. WHITE [4,I] argued that the First Amendment facial challenge failed both because the law was not invalid in all its applications and because its provisions were not overbroad. Under the previous rulings in *Roberts* and *Rotary,* the law clearly could be applied constitutionally to some of the groups that challenged it, and no evidence was presented showing that the law applied impermissibly to a substantial number of other groups. White acknowledged that the law still might be unconstitutional as applied to certain associations, but noted that these groups maintained the right to sue in order to invalidate particular applications of the ordinance. White also rejected the consortium's equal protection challenge, arguing that the city council could have reasonably believed that exempted religious and benevolent groups differ from those covered by the ordinance because of the level of business activity conducted by the groups.

No member of the Court has dissented in these cases, but Justice SANDRA DAY O'CONNOR [3,I] has tried to clarify when discriminatory activities might be protected by the freedom of expressive association. In *Roberts* and again in *New York,* O'Connor filed concurring opinions that sought to distinguish expressive associations from commercial ones. An expressive association exists to promote a particular message; thus, according to O'Connor, it should be protected by the full force of the First Amendment against state control of its membership. A commercial association, however, exists primarily to engage in certain commercial activities, and the protection afforded it by the Constitution subsequently should be much more limited. In O'Connor's view, groups like the Jaycees are predominantly engaged in commercial activities; hence, the freedom of expressive association should not exempt them from rational state regulations such as antidiscrimination laws. In contrast, gender-exclusive groups such as Boy Scouts or Girl Scouts probably should be protected as expressive associations because "even the training of outdoor survival skills or participation in community service might become expressive when the activity is intended to develop good morals, reverence, patriotism, and a desire for self-improvement."

JOHN G. WEST, JR.

FREEDOM OF RELIGION

See: Religious Liberty [3,I]

FREEDOM OF SPEECH
(Update)

Although the Supreme Court decided almost thirty cases addressing freedom of speech issues between 1985 and 1989, most of these decisions merely reaffirmed or only modestly refined existing doctrine. Perhaps most important, the Court in this period continued to invoke its content-based/content-neutral distinction as a central precept of FIRST AMENDMENT [2,I] jurisprudence. For purposes of this distinction, a content-based restriction may be defined as a law that limits speech because of the message it conveys. Laws that prohibit SEDITIOUS LIBEL [4], ban the publication of confidential information, or outlaw the display of the swastika in certain neighborhoods are examples of content-based restrictions. To test the constitutionality of such laws, the Court first determines whether the speech restricted occupies only "a subordinate position on the scale of First Amendment values." If so, the Court engages in a form of categorical balancing, through which it defines the precise circumstances in which each category of LOW-VALUE SPEECH [I] may be restricted. In this manner, the Court deals with such speech as false statements of fact, commercial advertising, FIGHTING WORDS [2], and OBSCENITY [3]. If the Court finds that the restricted speech does not occupy "a subordinate position on the scale of First Amendment values," it accords the speech virtually absolute protection. Indeed, outside the realm of low-value speech, the Court has invalidated almost every content-based restriction it has considered in the past thirty years.

Content-neutral restrictions, the other half of the content-based/content-neutral distinction, limit expression without regard to the content of the message conveyed. Laws that restrict noisy speeches near a hospital, ban billboards in residential communities, or limit campaign contributions are examples of content-neutral restrictions. In dealing with such restrictions, the Court engages in a relatively open-ended form of balancing: the greater the restriction's interference with the opportunities for free expression, the greater the government's burden of justification.

It may seem odd that the Court uses a stricter standard of review for content-based restrictions (other than those involving low-value speech) than for content-neutral restrictions, since both types of restrictions reduce the sum total of information or opinion disseminated. The explanation is that the First Amendment is concerned not only with the extent to which a law reduces the total quantity of communication but also—and perhaps even more fundamentally—with at least two additional factors: the extent to which a law distorts the content of public debate, and the likelihood that a law was enacted for the constitutionally impermissible motivation of suppressing or disadvantaging unpopular or "offensive" ideas. These two factors, which are more clearly associated with content-based than with content-neutral restrictions, explain both why the Court strictly scrutinizes content-based restrictions of high-value speech and why it does not apply that same level of scrutiny to all content-neutral restrictions. As indicated, most of the Court's decisions about freedom of speech from 1985 to 1989 reaffirmed this basic analytical structure.

Perhaps the two most important Supreme Court decisions in the realm of freedom of speech in this era were HUSTLER MAGAZINE V. FALWELL (1988) [I] and *Texas v. Johnson* (1989). In *Hustler Magazine* the Court held that the First Amendment barred an action by the nationally known minister Jerry Falwell against *Hustler* magazine for a "parody" advertisement. The ad contained a fictitious interview with Falwell in which he allegedly said that he had first engaged in sex during a drunken rendezvous with his mother in an outhouse. The Court held that a public figure may not recover DAMAGES [2] for the intentional infliction of emotional harm caused by the publication of even gross, outrageous, and repugnant material. In *Johnson* the Court held that an individual may not constitutionally be prosecuted for burning the American flag as a peaceful political protest. The Court explained that "if there is a bedrock principle underlying the First Amendment, it is that the Government may not prohibit the expression of any idea simply because society finds the idea itself offensive or disagreeable." Justice ANTHONY M. KENNEDY [I] observed in a concurring opinion, "It is poignant but fundamental that the flag protects those who hold it in contempt." In each of these decisions, the Court emphatically reaffirmed the central structure of free speech analysis and declined the invitation significantly to expand the concept of low-value speech.

Although *Hustler Magazine* and *Johnson* involved expansive interpretations of freedom of speech, in at least three other areas in this era the Court appreciably narrowed the scope of First Amendment protection. First, there is the issue of COMMERCIAL SPEECH [1,I]. Although the Court once had held that commercial advertising is of such low value that it is entirely outside the protection of the First Amendment, the Court overturned that doctrine in 1974 and held that commercial advertising is entitled to substantial—though not full—First Amendment protection. Specifically, the Court held that government may not constitutionally ban the truthful advertising of lawfully sold goods and services on the "highly paternalistic" ground that potential consumers would be "better off" without such information. More recently, however, the Court has retreated from this position. Indeed, in POSADAS DE PUERTO RICO ASSOCS. v. TOURISM COMPANY OF PUERTO RICO (1986) [I], which involved restrictions on advertising for lawful gambling activities, the Court held that even truthful advertising of lawful goods and services can be extensively regulated or banned in order to discourage "undesirable" patterns of consumption.

Second, the Court in recent years has increasingly granted broad authority to local governments to regulate expression that is sexually explicit, but not legally obscene. Although failing to classify sexually explicit expression as low-value speech, the Court has repeatedly sustained restrictions that curtail such expression in a discriminatory manner. In CITY OF RENTON v. PLAYTIME THEATRES (1986) [I], for example, the Court upheld a city ordinance prohibiting adult-film theaters from locating within 1,000 feet of any residential zone, church, park, or school, even though this effectively excluded such theaters from more than 95 percent of the entire area of the city.

Third, in dealing with speech in "restricted environments," such as the military, prisons, and schools, which are not structured according to traditional democratic principles, the Court has increasingly deferred to the judgment of administrators in the face of claimed infringements of First Amendment rights. In BETHEL SCHOOL DISTRICT v. FRASER (1986) [I], for example, the Court upheld the authority of a public high school to discipline a student for making a campaign speech that contained sexual innuendo; in HAZELWOOD SCHOOL DISTRICT v. KUHLMEIER (1988) [I] the Court upheld the authority of a public high school principal to exclude from a student-edited school newspaper stories dealing with pregnancy and with the impact of divorce on students; in *Turner v. Safley* (1987) the Court upheld a prison regulation generally prohibiting correspondence between inmates at different institutions; and in *Thornburgh v. Abbott* (1989) the Court upheld a Federal Bureau of Prisons regulation authorizing wardens to prevent prisoners from receiving any publication found to be detrimental "to the security, good order or discipline of the institution." These decisions are in sharp contrast to earlier decisions that granted considerable protection to the freedom of speech even in such restricted environments. It should be noted that the Court's recent inclination to grant broad deference to administrative authority is evident not only in its restricted environment decisions but also in decisions dealing with PUBLIC FORUMS [3,I] and with the speech of PUBLIC EMPLOYEES [3].

Although not involving the Supreme Court, there was extensive debate and activity with respect to several other free speech issues between 1985 and 1989. First, there has been considerable controversy concerning the law of LIBEL AND THE FIRST AMENDMENT [3]. In NEW YORK TIMES V. SULLIVAN [3] (1964) the Court held that in order to prevent the chilling of "uninhibited, robust and wide-open" debate, public officials could not recover for libel without proof that the libelous statements were false and that they were published with a knowing or reckless disregard of the truth. In recent years, critics have maintained that *New York Times* not only has prevented injured plaintiffs from obtaining judicial correction of published falsehoods but also has produced excessive damage awards against publishers. These critics argue that *New York Times* has thus effectively sacrificed legitimate dignitary interests of the victims of libel without protecting the "uninhibited, robust, and wide-open" debate the rule was designed to promote. Such criticism has provoked a wide range of proposals at both the state and national levels for either judicial or legislative reform. The most common and most intriguing of these proposals calls for the recognition of a civil action for a declaration of falsity, which would require no showing of fault on the part of the publisher but would authorize no award of damages to the plaintiff.

A second area that has generated increased attention in recent years concerns the advent and expansion of cable television. REGULATORY AGENCIES [3] and state and federal courts have confronted a broad range of issues arising out of the cable revolution, including the regulation of sexually explicit programming, the applicability of political "fairness" principles, the constitutionality of mandatory access and "must carry" rules, the regulation of subscription rates and franchise fees, and the constitutionality of government restrictions on the number of cable systems. Most fundamentally, the expansion of cable television may ultimately undermine the "scarcity" rationale for government regulation of radio and television BROADCASTING [1,I].

Perhaps the most interesting and most controversial development in recent years relating to freedom of speech concerns the issues of obscenity and PORNOGRAPHY [3]. Sixteen years after the 1970 Report of the Commission on Obscenity and Pornography, which found "no evidence that exposure to explicit sexual materials plays a significant role in the causation of delinquent or criminal behavior," a new government commission, the Attorney General's Commission on Pornography, concluded that there is indeed a causal relationship between exposure to sexually violent material and aggressive behavior toward women. This conclusion, which stirred immediate controversy among social scientists, led the 1986 commission to recommend additional legislation at both the state and federal levels and more aggressive enforcement of existing antiobscenity laws.

In a related development, many feminists in recent years have actively supported a more extensive regulation of pornography. Distinguishing "obscenity," which offends conventional standards of morality, from "pornography," which subordinates women, such feminists as Catharine MacKinnon and Andrea Dworkin have proposed legislation that would restrict the sale, exhibition, and distribution of pornography, which they define as "the sexually explicit subordination of women, graphically depicted, in which women are presented dehumanized as sexual objects, as sexual objects who enjoy pain, humiliation or rape, as sexual objects tied up, or cut up or mutilated or physically hurt, or as whores by nature."

This type of legislation poses a profound challenge to free speech. Opponents maintain that these laws constitute censorship in its worst form and that they are nothing less than blatant attempts to suppress specific points of view because they offend some citizens. Supporters of such legislation maintain that pornography is of only low First Amendment value, that it causes serious harm by shaping attitudes and behaviors of violence and discrimination toward women, and that it is futile to expect "counter-speech" to be an appropriate and sufficient response to such material. Although the courts that have considered the constitutionality of this kind of legislation have thus far held it incompatible with freedom of speech, the pornography issue will no doubt continue to generate constructive debate about the occasionally competing values of equality, dignity, and freedom of speech for some time to come.

GEOFFREY R. STONE

(SEE ALSO: *Balancing Test* [I]; *Child Pornography* [I]; *Dial-A-Porn* [I]; *Feminist Theory* [I]; *Flag Desecration* [2,I]; *Pornography and Feminism* [I].)

Bibliography

BOLLINGER, LEE C. 1986 *The Tolerant Society: Freedom of Speech and Extremist Speech in America.* Oxford: Clarendon Press.

KALVEN, HARRY, JR. 1988 *A Worthy Tradition: Freedom of Speech in America.* New York: Harper and Row.

STONE, GEOFFREY R.; SEIDMAN, LOUIS M.; SUNSTEIN, CASS R.; and TUSHNET, MARK V. 1986 *Constitutional Law*, Chap. 7. Boston: Little, Brown.

FREEDOM OF THE PRESS
(Update)

The FIRST AMENDMENT's [2,I] guarantee of freedom of the press is vitalized, as is FREEDOM OF SPEECH [2,I], by the synergy among the justifications for the protection of freedom of expression: (1) the marketplace of ideas is the best way of ascertaining truth; (2) full discussion of options is necessary to maintain a self-governing polity; (3) choice of both the means and the content of conveying one's messages is inherent to the notion of individual self-expression; and (4) free discussion is necessary as a check on governmental power by providing information for a resisting citizenry. The justifications have been translated into a set of DOCTRINES [2] that preclude the following in declining order of absoluteness: government licensing the printed press; prepublication censorship; demands that certain information be published; and with tightly circumscribed exceptions, civil or criminal liability for what is published. The right to publish is thus highly protected, but the right to gather news, although essential to the operation of freedom of the press, has proved difficult to implement by judicial decision.

Licensing the printed media, as Great Britain required before its Glorious Revolution, has never been seriously suggested. Occasionally, Congress has debated a specific wartime or national security preclearance censorship provision, but none has been adopted; and if adopted, it would almost certainly have been successfully challenged. When Minnesota did appear to have enacted a limited preclearance scheme with its so-called gag law, the Supreme Court held it UNCONSTITUTIONAL [4] in NEAR V. MINNESOTA EX REL. OLSON (1931) [3].

MIAMI HERALD PUBLISHING COMPANY V. TORNILLO (1974) [3], invalidating a right-to-reply law, suggests that a newspaper may never be required to publish or be punished for not publishing an item it wishes to exclude. Tornillo, a candidate for the Florida legislature, had been savaged by a pair of editorials in the *Miami Herald* just before the election. He demanded that the *Herald* print his responses as required by a state law regulating electoral debates. The Court, however, unanimously held the law unconstitutional, reasoning that it would "chill" the newspaper's willingness to enunciate its views and that it intruded into editorial choice. The latter rationale sweeps broadly enough to assure autonomy in deciding what to exclude.

The contested areas of freedom of the press involve attempts by the press to acquire information and attempts by the state to punish publication of certain sensitive information. Under very limited circumstances, government may successfully block publication by an INJUNCTION [2] remedy. Under broader, but still limited circumstances both civil and criminal remedies may be allowable.

Near analogized the Minnesota gag law, which placed a newspaper under a permanent injunction banning future "malicious, scandalous and defamatory" publication, to the traditional common law PRIOR RESTRAINT [3] created by preclearance licensing. Because a barebones guarantee of freedom of the press was a ban on prior restraints, the Minnesota gag law was unconstitutional—the first statute ever found to violate the First Amendment. *Near* did not go all the way and ban all prior restraints. Thus, in *Near*'s most famous passage, the Court implied that national security might well be a ground for a prior restraint: "No one would question but that a government [during actual war] might prevent actual obstruction to its recruiting service or the publication of the sailing dates of troops and transports or the number and location of troops." Subsequently, it has been assumed that if a prior restraint were ever appropriate, national security would be the justification. Nevertheless, in NEW YORK TIMES V. UNITED STATES (1971) [3], its most publicized national security case, the Supreme Court concluded that the government had not met its BURDEN OF PROOF [1] to prevent publication of the *Pentagon Papers*, which described top secret decision making involving the VIETNAM WAR [4,I]. The modern reality of copying machines and computer disks has made injunctive prior restraints obsolete because the materials will always show up somewhere else and any injunction will be futile to prevent disclosure—facts not yet reflected in the doctrine.

Despite upholding the press in every single case involving PRIVACY AND THE FIRST AMENDMENT [3] and in other noncopyright contexts where the press has published truthful information noncoercively obtained from governmental sources, the Court has avoided sweeping rules and always assumed that somewhere lies a situation where the press ought not publish. Again, national security heads the list, and the Court has recognized the enforceability of contracts that forbid publication without approval of the Central Intelligence Agency; it would undoubtedly sustain the federal prohibition on disclosing the identities of intelligence agents as part of a pattern of activities intended to expose covert action. Beyond national security, the protection of sensitive private information of nonpublic figures is the next most likely candidate for a limitation on publication, although any such limitation will have to be carefully circumscribed. Thus, in *Florida Star v. B.J.F.* (1989), a civil privacy case, the Court set aside an award of DAMAGES [2] for negligent publication of a rape victim's name because the paper had lawfully obtained the information through governmental disclosure. The Court recognized, as it had previously, that the state is in the best position to protect against disclosure through careful internal procedures.

Florida Star may usefully be contrasted with *Seattle*

Times v. Rhinehart (1984), where the Court held that a trial court can forbid publication of information acquired by the press in state-mandated DISCOVERY [2], unless the information actually comes out in the litigation. *Rhinehart's* balance demonstrates that there are some circumstances where it is too unfair to allow the press to publish (without sanction) information that it has. One may extrapolate from *Rhinehart* that, if the press were to break into property and pillage files (or plant bugs) and later to publish, then the publication could also be penalized.

But these examples of coercive acquisition of information are a far cry from the issue ducked ever since the *Pentagon Papers Cases* (1971): what if the press should publish information unlawfully taken by a third party (as federal law forbids)? Here, outcomes of the Court's decisions, rather than the reasons offered, appear to preclude sanctions in cases where the press does not coercively acquire the information, while leaving the potential deterrent of criminal penalties hanging as a last resort.

A similar outcome prevails in cases of efforts of the press to obtain information. Constitutional rhetoric surrounding the importance of information to a self-governing citizenry supports a right of the press to obtain the information necessary for self-governance, but this rhetoric also leaves no principled stopping places. As a result, the Court has stated that news gathering is part of freedom of the press, but has also found implementation of such a right to be largely beyond its skills. When BRANZBURG V. HAYES (1972) [1] raised the claim of a reporter's privilege not to disclose sources, the Court rejected it, although in OBITER DICTA [3] it stated that orders designed to "disrupt a reporter's relationship with news sources would have no justification." Despite fears of the press, government generally has not abused its limited right to require disclosure.

The Court initially rejected claims of the press of access to prisons and pretrial hearings, but in RICHMOND NEWSPAPERS V. VIRGINIA (1980) [3], it held that the press and public have a right to watch criminal trials. Although the press acted as if *Richmond Newspapers* might convert the First Amendment into a freedom of information sunshine law, it is not. This decision opens courtroom doors, but not those of GRAND JURIES [2] or the other branches of government.

The least satisfying area of the Court's JURISPRUDENCE [I] on freedom of the press is the one where the Court has been the most active: the constitutionalization of the law of LIBEL [3] in the wake of NEW YORK TIMES V. SULLIVAN (1964) [3]. Despite this decision's promise to balance successfully the interests of reputation against the CHILLING EFFECT [1] that civil liability imposes on the press, over the years the constitutional law of defamation has become an ever more intricate maze of rules that in operation protect neither reputation, the press, nor the public's interest in knowing accurate information.

Although the best-known feature of current libel law may be its division of defamed plaintiffs into two classes— PUBLIC FIGURES [3] and private figures, with the former having to meet the *New York Times* actual-malice standard—this distinction has had little impact on litigation. The reason is that private figures also need to show actual malice if they are to recover punitive damages—the financial key to their attorneys' taking their cases on contingent fees. At trial, the current constitutional rules attempt to minimize jury discretion. According to *Milkovich v. Lorain Journal* (1990), the plaintiff bears the burden of proving falsity, and those statements that "cannot reasonably be interpreted as stating actual facts" are fully protected. There is also strict appellate supervision of the evidence, something unmatched in any other area of law.

The intricate structure of First Amendment libel law has been widely criticized. In operation, the overwhelming number of libel suits are disposed of before trial; in such a case, the plaintiff is never granted an opportunity to show that the defamatory statements were false. If the case goes to a jury, the odds shift heavily to the plaintiff, although the damage awards are likely to be set aside either by the trial judge or the appellate court. It is the rarest of plaintiffs who successfully hurdles all the rules designed to protect the press. As a result, the rules do not provide the public with an opportunity to know the truth about injured plaintiffs; the law underprotects reputation; and in all likelihood, individuals are deterred from entering the public arena where, rightly or wrongly, they are often perceived as fair game.

Nevertheless, current law also fails to serve the interests of the press. A wholly unanticipated aspect of *New York Times* was the way it turned the libel trial away from what the defendant said about the plaintiff to scrutiny of how the press put the story together. When the trial focuses on the practices, care, motives, and views of the press—especially when, as is likely for a case reaching trial, the story is false—the dynamics of the case invite punishment of the press. A good trial lawyer will be able to paint the dispute as a contest between good and evil, and the evidence necessary to prove reckless disregard of the truth leaves no doubt as to which side is evil. In the 1980s, the average jury award in cases where reckless disregard was found exceeded $2 million.

It does not reduce the chill on newspapers to learn that few plaintiffs get to keep their awards and that the average successful plaintiff receives a mere $20,000. There seems to be a damages explosion in tort verdicts generally, and newspapers know catastrophe can arrive with just one huge verdict. An example was the $9 million judgment against the *Alton (Illinois) Evening Telegraph*, which sent the paper to bankruptcy court (although a subsequent settlement allowed the 38,000-circulation paper to stay

in business). What makes defamation a special tort is that the injury that plaintiffs suffer seems far less severe than that suffered by a physically injured tort plaintiff. Large jury verdicts, both for punitive damages and those for emotional pain and suffering, thus seem designed more to punish than to compensate.

The operation of *New York Times* has thus produced a strange landscape. Issues of truth and falsity rarely surface, and reputations are not cleared for the vast majority of plaintiffs. For those few that get to a jury, however, trying the press can lead to a large, albeit momentary, windfall. The possibility of that windfall, coupled with the necessary legal fees to avoid it, maintains a chilling effect, even though appellate supervision typically cuts the verdicts to size. Libel law, having been wholly remade in the wake of *New York Times*, needs to be rethought again. It is not that the Court has misunderstood what to balance; rather, its balance systematically undermines all the values it attempts to protect.

A free press is essential in a democracy, and the Court's doctrines have never lost sight of this. Typically, press cases parallel speech cases, but one area where the Court has split the two is taxation. To protect the press, the Court has struck down press taxes that are unique to the press or treat different parts of the press differently. Whatever the imperfections of the law of freedom of the press, few areas of constitutional law have achieved a more coherent whole than freedom of the press. Even an "outrageous" parody of the Reverend Jerry Falwell in HUSTLER MAGAZINE V. FALWELL (1988) (I), found by a jury to have inflicted extreme emotional distress, received the unanimous protection of a Court certain that freewheeling caustic discussion must be a central object of constitutional protection if we are to have a free and therefore secure press.

L. A. POWE, JR.

Bibliography

ANDERSON, DAVID A. 1975 The Issue Is Control of Press Power. *Texas Law Review* 54:271–282.
POWE, LUCAS A., JR. 1991 *The Fourth Estate and the Constitution: Freedom of Press in America*. Berkeley: University of California Press.
SMOLLA, RODNEY A. 1986 *Suing the Press*. New York: Oxford University Press.
SYMPOSIUM 1977 Nebraska Press Association v. Stuart. *Stanford Law Review* 29:383–624.

FRIENDLY, HENRY J.
(1903–1986)

Henry J. Friendly was among the greatest federal judges of the twentieth century. After graduating from Harvard Law School (where he was president of the *Harvard Law*

Review) and clerking for Justice LOUIS D. BRANDEIS [1], Friendly entered private practice in New York City, where he had a distinguished career. Appointed to the UNITED STATES COURT OF APPEALS [4] for the Second Circuit in 1959 by President DWIGHT D. EISENHOWER [2], Judge Friendly served on the court for twenty-seven years until his death.

Judge Friendly's unquestioned brilliance, his towering intellect, and his unrelenting concern with the facts are reflected in his judicial opinions in almost every area of the law. His contributions to ADMINISTRATIVE LAW [1] and federal jurisdiction, two areas in which he took a special interest, are unsurpassed in their analytical power and insight. In addition, Judge Friendly's opinions on SECURITIES LAW [4] and CRIMINAL PROCEDURE [2] are widely regarded as unequaled in their thoughtfulness, craft, and scholarship. Perhaps Judge Friendly's extraordinary ability for deft analysis of legally and factually complex issues was most impressively displayed in the series of comprehensive opinions he wrote during the 1970s for the Special Railroad Court. This court was established to handle the litigation arising over the congressionally directed reorganization of the eastern railroads, many of which were in bankruptcy reorganization.

In addition to his prolific output of judicial opinions, Judge Friendly wrote a number of influential law review articles as well as a short book on federal jurisdiction. He was also active in the American Law Institute. Perhaps the unique combination of talents that Judge Friendly possessed are most succinctly captured by the thought that he was considered to be a lawyer's lawyer, a scholar's scholar, and a judge's judge.

WALTER HELLERSTEIN

Bibliography

SYMPOSIUM 1984 In Honor of Henry J. Friendly. *University of Pennsylvania Law Review* 133:1–77.

FRISBY v. SCHULTZ
487 U.S. 474 (1988)

In response to anti-abortion protesters picketing the home of a local abortionist, a Wisconsin town passed an ordinance forbidding picketing "before or about the residence . . . of any individual." The Court held in a 6–3 vote that the ordinance did not on its face violate the FIRST AMENDMENT [2,I]. Writing for five members of the majority, Justice SANDRA DAY O'CONNOR [3,I] narrowly construed the law as applying only to picketing directed at a particular home. The law served a significant government interest, according to O'Connor, because it sought to protect the sanctity of the home from unwanted—and inescapable—intrusions. O'Connor noted that "[t]he First Amendment permits the government to prohibit offensive speech as intrusive when the 'captive' audience cannot avoid the objectionable speech. . . . [Here] [t]he resident is figuratively, and perhaps literally, trapped within the home, and because of the unique and subtle impact of such picketing is left with no ready means of avoiding the unwanted speech."

The dissenters sympathized with the intent of the law, but found that its language suffered from OVERBREADTH [3].

JOHN G. WEST, JR.

FUNDAMENTALISTS AND THE CONSTITUTION

See: Religious Fundamentalism [I]

GENDER DISCRIMINATION

See: Sex Discrimination [4,I]

GENDER RIGHTS

Strictly speaking, there can be no distinct class of gender rights under the Constitution, but only the same rights for all persons, or all citizens, regardless of sex. The Constitution secures rights only of individuals, not of groups, and makes no distinction between men and women.

No nouns or adjectives denote sex in the Constitution except for the use of the word "male" in the FOURTEENTH AMENDMENT [2,I], in a provision no longer operative, which never provided any positive authority for SEX DISCRIMINATION [4,I].

There are, to be sure, many masculine pronouns in the text, but they have always been understood to be genderless; to hold that these pronouns refer only to men would mean, unless the Constitution is amended, that women are ineligible to serve in the Congress or the presidency, that a female FUGITIVE FROM JUSTICE [2] fleeing to another state need not "be delivered up" (Article IV, section 2), and that accused women do not have the RIGHT TO COUNSEL [3]—absurdities that have not been indulged in by courts or responsible scholars.

The only mention of sex is in the NINETEENTH AMENDMENT [3], forbidding denial of the right of citizens to vote "on account of sex," but its ratification did not require any change in the text of the Constitution. If the EQUAL RIGHTS AMENDMENT [2], forbidding denial of "equality of rights . . . on account of sex," had been ratified, the

same would have been true: nothing already in the text of the Constitution would have been altered, because there is in it no positive authorization for denial of the right to vote, or of any other right, "on account of sex."

There is another indication that no distinction between men and women is intended in the Constitution. For purposes of determining representation, "the whole number of persons" is to be counted (Article I, section 2, as amended by the Fourteenth Amendment, section 2)—that is, females and males equally. This contrasts strikingly with similar provisions in other documents of the time; for example, the NORTHWEST ORDINANCE [3] of 1787 provides that only "male inhabitants" be counted for purposes of representation.

The fact that there has never been any constitutional justification for denying rights or privileges to any person or citizen on account of sex has not prevented legislatures and courts from discriminating against women. Judicial discrimination often relied on sources and doctrines extraneous to the Constitution and, ironically, was frequently expressed in terms of protective concern for the well-being of women. In BRADWELL V. ILLINOIS (1873) [1], Justice JOSEPH P. BRADLEY [1] gave classic form to the pronouncement that the denial of a woman's right was for her own good: "The civil law as well as nature herself has always recognized a wide difference in the respective spheres and destinies of man and woman. Man is, or should be, women's protector and defender. The natural and proper timidity and delicacy which belongs to the female sex evidently unfits it for many of the occupations of civil life."

To justify his denial that women have the same constitutional right as men "to engage in any and every profession, occupation, or employment," Justice Bradley cited "the civil law," "nature herself," "the divine ordinance," "the nature of things," "the law of the Creator," and, finally, "the general constitution of things"—but not the Constitution of the United States.

Well past the middle of the twentieth century, this combination of protective concern, extraneous doctrines, and silence about the text of the Constitution served as the foundation of sex discrimination in many areas, including employment, PROPERTY RIGHTS [I], jury duty, voting, pensions, EDUCATION [2,I], and WELFARE BENEFITS [4]. The decisive turn around finally began in the courts in *Reed v. Reed* (1971) and FRONTIERO V. RICHARDSON (1973) [2]. But the correction of centuries of denying women their rights does not establish gender rights, which, like all other group rights, lacks constitutional justification.

In the series of cases since Reed, the Supreme Court sought for the appropriately strict "level of judicial scrutiny of legislation" under the Fourteenth Amendment's equal protection clause. The effort to afford EQUAL PROTECTION OF THE LAWS [2,I] is a belated acknowledgment that there is no affirmative basis in the Constitution, and never was, for treating the rights of one person differently from the rights of others on account of sex.

ROBERT A. GOLDWIN

(SEE ALSO: *Women in Constitutional History* [I]; *Woman Suffrage* [I].)

Bibliography

GOLDWIN, ROBERT A.   1990   *Why Blacks, Women, and Jews Are Not Mentioned in the Constitution.* Washington, D.C.: AEI Press.
WORTMAN, MARLENE STEIN   1985   *Women in American Law.* Vol. 1. New York: Holmes and Meier.

GERRYMANDER
(Update)

By the mid-1980s the focus of attention in racial gerrymandering controversies had shifted from the FOURTEENTH AMENDMENT [2,I] to the VOTING RIGHTS ACT of 1965 [4], which Congress had amended in 1982 to assist minority-group plaintiffs. In *Thornburgh v. Gingles* (1986) the Supreme Court laid down guidelines for application of the revised Section 2 of the act.

While constitutional controversy over racial gerrymandering was subsiding, the issue of partisan gerrymandering was nearing its climax. In *Davis v. Bandemer* (1986) a 6–3 majority held that attacks on partisan gerrymanders under the EQUAL PROTECTION [2,I] clause were justiciable, but only two Justices voted to strike down the districting plan that was being challenged by Indiana Democrats.

Justice BYRON R. WHITE's [4,I] plurality opinion for the four Justices who believed the question was justiciable but that the Indiana plan was constitutional has received divergent interpretations. In one common view, the opinion is simply confused or self-contradictory. Others have read it to mean that plans yielding a legislative seat distribution sharply disproportionate to the statewide partisan vote will be struck down.

In *Davis*, the Republican National Committee supported the Indiana Democrats in an AMICUS CURIAE [1] brief, while the Democratic congressional delegation from California supported the Indiana Republicans. This apparent display of political disinterestedness might have been influenced by the pending Republican challenge to the California congressional districting plan on similar grounds. After *Davis*, a lower court dismissed the California case, interpreting White's opinion in *Davis* to require pervasive discrimination against the plaintiff group beyond the gerrymander that is being challenged. Under this interpretation, major-party gerrymandering claims would rarely if ever be successful. The Supreme Court refused to review the California dismissal in *Badham v. Eu* (1988).

After much sound and fury, the prospects for judicial invalidation of partisan gerrymanders may have been no greater at the end of the 1980s than at the beginning.

DANIEL HAYS LOWENSTEIN

Bibliography

GROFMAN, BERNARD, ED.   1990   *Political Gerrymandering and the Courts.* New York: Agathon Press.
SYMPOSIUM 1985 Gerrymandering and the Courts. *UCLA Law Review* 33:1–281.

GOLDMAN v. WEINBERGER
475 U.S. 503 (1986)

Goldman, an orthodox Jew and ordained rabbi, was forbidden from wearing a yarmulke while on duty as an Air Force officer. The prohibition was pursuant to an Air Force regulation enjoining the wearing of headgear indoors "except by armed security police." Goldman sued, claiming that the prohibition violated his FIRST AMENDMENT [2,I] right to the free exercise of religion. The Supreme Court disagreed, 5–4.

Writing for the majority, Justice WILLIAM H. REHNQUIST [3,I] declined to require a government showing of either a COMPELLING STATE INTEREST [1] or a RATIONAL BASIS [3] to justify the yarmulke prohibition. Rehnquist argued that the military must be accorded wide-ranging deference by the courts in order to carry out its mission; hence he refused to second-guess the Air Force's "professional judgment" about how to maintain a uniform dress code. Rehnquist used similar reasoning a year later to uphold the power of prison authorities to restrict the free-exercise rights of prisoners in O'LONE V. ESTATE OF SHABAZZ (1987) [I].

Justices WILLIAM J. BRENNAN [1,I], HARRY A. BLACKMUN [1,I], and SANDRA DAY O'CONNOR [3,I] each filed separate dissents. All three believed that the Court should have attempted to weigh Goldman's free-exercise rights against the government interest at stake; they further agreed that the government interest should give way in this case because the military had made no attempt to show a reasonable basis for the regulation as applied to Goldman. They noted, in particular, that Goldman had been allowed to wear his yarmulke by the Air Force for almost four years before the practice was challenged.

JOHN G. WEST, JR.

(SEE ALSO: *Armed Forces* [I]; *Employment Division v. Smith* [I].)

GOVERNMENT AID TO RELIGIOUS INSTITUTIONS
(Update)

A theme of equality has dominated recent Supreme Court [4,I] decisions in the area of church–state relations. This may be seen most dramatically in the shrunken protection for RELIGIOUS LIBERTY [3,I] under the Court's peyote ruling in EMPLOYMENT DIV., DEPT. OF HUMAN RES. V. SMITH (1990) [I], which held that the free-exercise clause of the FIRST AMENDMENT [2,I] affords no religious exemption from a neutral law that regulates conduct even though that law imposes a substantial burden on religious practice. Similarly, on the subject of RELIGION IN PUBLIC SCHOOLS [3,I], the Court held in BOARD OF EDUCATION OF WESTSIDE COMMUNITY SCHOOLS V. MERGENS (1990) [I] that the First Amendment's ban on laws respecting an ESTABLISHMENT OF RELIGION [2] permits student religious groups in secondary schools to meet for religious purposes (including prayer) on school premises during noninstructional time as long as other non–curriculum-related student groups are allowed to do so. This theme of neutral treatment of religious and secular groups has been prominent in regard to the subject of governmental aid as well.

It has long been the rule that a government subsidy to religious institutions violates the ESTABLISHMENT CLAUSE [I] when the subsidy's purpose or primary effect is to finance religious (rather than secular) activities. The decision in BOWEN V. KENDRICK (1988) [I] affirmed this proposition and also revealed the present Court's inclination to give a generous interpretation to the term "secular" activities. The case upheld the constitutionality of Congress's granting funds to a variety of public and private agencies (including religious organizations) to provide counseling for prevention of adolescent sexual relations and to promote adoption as an alternative to ABORTION [1,I]. Whereas this program may be fairly characterized as having a "secular" purpose (even though it coincides with the approach of certain prominent religious groups), there appears to be a substantial danger that the program's primary effect will be to further religious precepts when religiously employed counselors deal with a subject so closely and inextricably tied to religious doctrine.

Substantial constitutional controversy continues to revolve around government financing of church-related schools that combine the inculcation of religious doctrines with the teaching of secular subjects substantially, although not necessarily entirely, as they are taught in public schools. Most forms of public aid for parochial schools, even to support secular courses, have been held to violate the establishment clause, particularly when the aid has been provided directly to the schools themselves rather than to the parents. The Court has usually reasoned that although the aid had a secular (in contrast to a religious) purpose, it was still invalid. The Court's analysis of the problem began with a critical premise: The mission of church-related elementary and secondary schools is to teach religion, and all subjects either are, or carry the potential of being, permeated with religion. Therefore, if the government funds any subjects in these schools, the primary effect will be to aid religion unless public officials monitor the situation to see to it that those courses are not infused with religious doctrine. However, if public officials engage in adequate surveillance, there will be excessive entanglement between government and religion—the image being government spies regularly in parochial school classrooms.

Although no holding of the Supreme Court has overturned this approach, the separate opinion of Justices ANTHONY M. KENNEDY [I] and ANTONIN SCALIA [I] in *Bowen v. Kendrick* reasons that the fact that the assistance goes directly to the schools is not important. Rather, these Justices believe that the use to which the aid is put is crucial. This opinion strongly suggests that a majority of the Court would no longer invalidate most forms of aid to the schools themselves as long as there were adequate controls to assure that the funds were not spent for religious purposes. This is a sound precept. If governmental assistance to parochial schools does not exceed the value of the secular educational service the schools render, then there is no use of tax-raised funds to aid religion and thus no threat of this historic danger to religious liberty.

Tax relief—either exemptions for property used exclusively for worship or other religious purposes, or income tax deductions for parents who send their children to parochial schools—had been held not to violate the establishment clause as long as the benefits extended beyond religion-related recipients. For example, the Court had upheld property-tax exemptions for educational and charitable institutions and tax deductions for school expenses to all parents of school children. By the same token, in TEXAS MONTHLY, INC. V. BULLOCK (1989) [I] the Court invalidated a state sales-tax exemption for books and magazines that "teach" or are "sacred" to religious faith. Because the exemption was for religious purposes only and not the broad-based type of tax relief provided in the earlier cases, the Court held that this governmental aid violated the establishment clause.

In the mid-1980s, probably the most important uncertainty regarding governmental assistance to parochial schools concerned VOUCHERS [I]. Although the decision in WITTERS V. WASHINGTON DEPARTMENT OF SERVICES FOR THE BLIND (1986) [I] involved only a special type of voucher and did not speak to the constitutionality of school vouchers generally, its rationale goes a long way to sustaining their validity. The case upheld a state program giving visually handicapped persons a voucher (although it was not called that) for use in vocational schools for the blind. Witters was studying religion at a Christian college "in order to equip himself for a career as a pastor, missionary or youth director." A majority of the Court, even before Justices Kennedy and Scalia had been appointed, agreed that "state programs that are wholly neutral in offering educational assistance to a class defined without reference to religion do not violate the [establishment clause], because any aid to religion results from the private choices of individual beneficiaries." The state's money, however, was plainly being spent for religious purposes. If the government, whether through a voucher or a direct grant to parochial schools, is financing not only the value of secular education in those schools, but also all or part of the cost of religious education, the support is an expenditure of compulsorily raised tax funds for religious purposes and should be held to violate the establishment clause.

JESSE H. CHOPER

Bibliography

CHOPER, JESSE H. 1987 The Establishment Clause and Aid to Parochial Schools—An Update. *California Law Review* 75:5–14.

CORD, ROBERT L. 1982 *Separation of Church and State: Historical Fact and Current Fiction.* New York: Lambeth Press.

GOVERNMENT AS PROPRIETOR

Constitutional litigants in disparate contexts have sought to characterize particular government acts as proprietary, rather than sovereign, in order to substitute for the constitutional standards otherwise applicable to government something like those applicable to private proprietors. Government at any level—local, state, or federal—not only may regulate and tax (the most coercive and quintessentially sovereign exercises of power), but may borrow, spend, buy or sell goods and services, build and operate offices or mass transit, manage property of many kinds, and employ workers. Our constitutional regime sharply differentiates between government and private spheres. When government acts in capacities that resemble the proprietary activities of private owners, managers, and employers, suggestions of modified constitutional analysis may be inevitable. Sometimes the litigant who suggests such a modification seeks to enlarge government power by skirting the constitutional limitations that normally bind federal or state sovereigns, but not private proprietors, in their treatment of individuals; the courts have grappled with this problem through the STATE ACTION [4,I] doctrine. Sometimes the objective is to dislodge SOVEREIGN IMMUNITY [4] in its various forms and render government accountable to individuals or to subject it to regulation and taxation by superior sovereigns, just as other individuals are. As a double-edged sword that can cut down either constitutional obligation or constitutional immunity, the proprietary analogy is potentially a formidable and versatile tool.

This analogy's checkered past includes adoption, and later rejection, in some constitutional contexts and continuing influence in various forms in others. Courts that reject the government–proprietor distinction make two main arguments: first, it is impossible to draw a sensible line between government's proprietary and sovereign activities, and second, there is questionable legitimacy in drawing such a line in order to discount the value of using proprietary means to accomplish democratically chosen ends. The government–proprietor distinction's frequent recurrence and continued influence rests, in the strongest version, on the superficial appeal of the private analogy or, in a weaker version, on factors sometimes associated with the difference between proprietary and regulatory conduct. Proprietary activity sometimes may implicate other constitutional values to a lesser degree than does more "sovereign" activity: it may interfere less with individual freedom or other values such as interstate harmony; it may provide additional legitimate justifications for governmental policy; or, by analogy to the lesser constitutional protection afforded private COMMERCIAL SPEECH [1,I] and activity than is afforded political speech and activity, sovereign immunity may be deemed less important for government's proprietary than for its "sovereign" behavior. But the proprietary designation is often too inexact a shorthand for these relevant elements of constitutional analysis. Furthermore, as a determinative or even very strong factor, the proprietary designation too readily slights other important considerations that sometimes should temper or overwhelm it. The designation's mixed success is partially attributable to the fact that it is far too broad and insensitive a constitutional measure and partially to the fact that stronger principles often obviate any value it might otherwise have.

Other drawbacks further limit the utility of treating government as if it were a private business. The government as proprietor may be analogous to a private proprietor, but it differs in its motivations and responsibilities. It is still government, subject to political as well as commercial or proprietary influences and to constitutional restraints inapplicable to private actors.

Imprecise and multiple meanings also limit the usefulness of the proprietary designation. Acting as an owner may differ from one kind of property to another and may differ from acting as a business, a consumer, or an employer. Not only are there varying kinds and gradations of proprietary activity, but the line between regulatory or other sovereign activity and proprietary activity is often blurred. The difference between management policy with respect to government property, business, or employees and regulation of the citizenry at large is a matter of degree, not kind.

Perhaps most fundamentally, in each kind of constitutional controversy, claims of proprietary prerogative or liability encounter varying responses depending on the perceived nature and strength of the countervailing constitutional values. According to PUBLIC FORUM [3,I] analysis, people free to speak at home may be prevented from speaking at will in government offices—an example of a proprietary justification for limiting the locations of FREEDOM OF SPEECH [2,I]—yet may not be prevented from speaking in parks or on street corners. Proprietary prerogatives of government thus may affect FIRST AMENDMENT [2,I] free speech analysis with respect to some but not all publicly owned property. Nor may a government business discriminate on an invidious basis, such as by race or political viewpoint, any more than it may so discriminate in a tax or regulatory capacity. These antidiscrimination restrictions on government behavior are so strong that they may apply fully whether government behaves in a sovereign or proprietary capacity.

The idea of government as proprietor thus has not worked as a categorical concept of overarching importance. It must be understood by reference to the particular kind of proprietary activity involved, the reasons why that activity is thought relevant to solving the specific constitutional controversy, the nature and strength of the constitutional values with which the activity competes, and the practical consequences of the concept. A survey of relevant constitutional controversies reveals this complexity. The contro-

versies include intergovernmental claims by municipalities that their proprietary acts, just like those of private parties, are constitutionally protected from state interference; claims by states of constitutional immunity from control by Congress or the federal courts; state claims of freedom to prefer their own citizens over residents of other states with respect to proprietary policies; and claims by government at all levels that the constitutional rights of individuals may be more circumscribed on government property than on private property. Each set of controversies has its own story.

The simplest story is the unsuccessful attempt of LOCAL GOVERNMENT [I] to carve out a proprietary-rights exception from the principle that each state's power over its political subdivisions generally is unrestricted by the federal Constitution. The Supreme Court easily rejected municipal claims that constitutional provisions like those prohibiting impairment of the OBLIGATIONS OF CONTRACTS [3] or the TAKING OF PROPERTY [4,I] without JUST COMPENSATION [3] should limit state interference, not only with private contracts and property, but with city contracts and property used in the city's proprietary activities. Even with respect to contract and PROPERTY RIGHTS [I] that the state had originally granted to a private business, that the business then assigned to a city, the Court refused in *City of Trenton v. New Jersey* (1923) to adopt a proprietor–sovereign distinction that would impose on the states constitutional obligations toward the "proprietary" acts of their constituent governments. Originally a judge-made distinction designed to circumvent the sovereign immunity doctrine of COMMON LAW [1] and hold municipalities liable for tortious injuries caused by their proprietary conduct, the proprietor–sovereign distinction lacked a principled basis or definable content and would not be transferred to this area of constitutional law.

The proprietary notion had already been adopted in disputes about the extent of Congress's power to tax state activities, however, though it was ultimately rejected for some of the same reasons in this very different context. Congress expanded its tax programs at the turn of the century just as state trading activity increased. The Supreme Court, in cases like *South Carolina v. United States* (1905), sustained federal taxes on state-sold liquor and other commodities by holding that the constitutional DOCTRINE [2] of INTERGOVERNMENTAL TAX IMMUNITY [1], which otherwise prohibited federal taxation of state operations, did not extend to state proprietary operations. This proprietary exception was designed to preserve common federal-revenue sources and, possibly, in this area of strong constitutional protection for private enterprise (LOCHNER V. NEW YORK [3] also was decided in 1905), to equalize the competitive positions of state and private business. But by 1947, in *New York v. United States*, the Court, in sustaining a federal tax on state-bottled water, adopted new standards that were more generous to congressional authority and expressly rejected "limitations upon the taxing power of Congress derived from such untenable criteria as 'proprietary' against 'governmental' activities of the States."

Congress's power to regulate, rather than tax, state operations has followed a different story line. Even if some form of state tax immunity might be important to preserve, *United States v. California* (1936) established for forty years that, when Congress exercised a plenary regulatory power like the power to regulate INTERSTATE COMMERCE [2], there was no need to distinguish between sovereign and proprietary operations because both were subject to federal regulation. Federal safety, price control, and labor regulations could be applied to state operations because, as the Court said in *Maryland v. Wirtz* (1968), "the Federal Government, when acting within a delegated power, may override countervailing state interests whether these be described as 'governmental' or 'proprietary.'"

The overruling of the *Wirtz* decision, by a 5–4 vote, in NATIONAL LEAGUE OF CITIES V. USERY (1976) [3] did backtrack and protect certain state operations from federal regulatory as well as taxing power. Ostensibly, the boundary was not drawn according to whether a state operation was governmental or proprietary, but by whether it was an "integral" or "traditional" government function. However, this formulation led to distinguishing between impermissible federal labor regulation of state police and fire-department employees and permissible labor regulation of the employees of state-owned railroads. The state as employer would sometimes be immune, but not with respect to employees providing services like those the private sector traditionally provided.

The *Usery* case was soon itself overruled, however, by the 5–4 decision in GARCIA V. SAN ANTONIO METROPOLITAN TRANSIT AUTHORITY (1985) [2], which held that, at least with respect to congressional regulation—if not possibly taxation—the states must rely on their political influence in Congress, not on judicial enforcement of the Constitution, for protection against burdensome congressional interference with state operations. By withdrawing from the task of defining any core of state SOVEREIGNTY [4], the *Garcia* decision again obviated the need to draw a government–proprietor or similar distinction. The Court had now concluded that such distinctions were not only "unworkable in practice," but "unsound in principle" because they wrongly devalued an important principle of federalism—each state's lawful and democratically selected means of carrying out its legitimate policy objectives should be equally respected, however unconventional the choice of means might be.

The complete rejection of the proprietor–sovereign distinction in virtually all hierarchical intergovernmental disputes—whether invoked by municipalities claiming more constitutional protection from state control for proprietary than for governmental activities or by states conversely claiming more constitutional immunity from Congress for governmental than for proprietary activities—so far has not been replicated outside the constitutional clashes between superior and subordinate levels of government. Yet, doctrinal turbulence and perennial dissatisfaction with reliance on proprietary notions remain.

The tale of changing Supreme Court responses to state policies that give preference to their residents in the distribution of "proprietary" commercial benefits is a major example. To further political and economic union, the PRIVILEGES AND IMMUNITIES [3] clause of Article IV, Section 2, generally prohibits each state from discriminating against citizens of other states, and the DORMANT COMMERCE CLAUSE [I] prohibits state discrimination against interstate business. However, each state's primary obligation to serve its own residents necessitates some resident preference. Various proprietary concepts have been employed to mediate the Constitution's interstate equality demands and its conflicting recognition of state sovereignty.

Under the privileges and immunities clause, no state, absent substantial justification, may limit nonresident access to private-sector commercial opportunities more severely than it limits resident access. Beginning in the nineteenth century, however, the Court permitted resident preference regarding commercial exploitation of state-owned natural resources. The Court concluded that government property owners, like private owners, generally may be selective in sharing what they own with whom they wish. This proprietary escape hatch from the regulatory nondiscrimination rule was criticized as "a fiction," but not fully abandoned, in TOOMER V. WITSELL (1948) [4], just a year after the decision in *New York v. United States* had discarded the proprietor–sovereign distinction as a standard for demarcating the line between federal taxing authority and state tax immunity. *Toomer* rejected South Carolina's attempt to justify charging nonresidents 100 times more than it charged its own residents for a license to shrimp in state coastal waters; the Court called the state's claim to "own" the shrimp and the sea extravagant. Since then, even true state resource ownership does not render the privileges and immunities clause wholly inapplicable. Although ownership is "often the crucial factor" in evaluating the constitutionality of discriminatory resource distribution, the Court in HICKLIN V. ORBECK (1978) [2] limited resident preference to the state's direct proprietary dealings and disallowed conditional policies requiring those in the immediate proprietary relationship to prefer residents in "downstream" relationships.

The proprietary idea followed a similar but not identical course in dormant-commerce-clause jurisprudence. At the end of the nineteenth century, the Court carved a generous proprietary exception from the usual rule that a state may not prevent the shipment of local goods to other states. In *Geer v. Connecticut* (1896), for example, it allowed a complete ban of shipping game birds out of state; the Court applied the fictitious theory that the state owned the wildlife within its borders and thus could control its disposition, even after the birds lawfully had been reduced to private possession. *Geer* was eventually overruled a year after *Hicklin* in *Hughes v. Oklahoma* (1979), which applied the same dormant-commerce-clause standards applicable to regulation of private goods to the regulation of wildlife. At a minimum, *Hughes* limited the proprietary justification to instances of actual, not pretended, state ownership.

Moving in the other direction, several decisions in the last two decades have allowed states to discriminate against interstate commerce on the basis of a different kind of proprietary prerogative—that of the state acting as a commercial buyer or seller, rather than just as owner of property. Whether favoring in-state suppliers for government purchases, as in *Hughes v. Alexandria Scrap Corp.* (1976), or preferring in-state customers when demand for state-manufactured goods exceeds supply, as in *Reeves v. Stake* (1980), states have been exempted from the normal dormant-commerce-clause antidiscrimination limits when acting as "market participants" rather than as regulators of private buyers or sellers in the interstate market. The Court's position articulated in *United Building and Construction Trades Council v. Mayor and Council of the City of Camden* (1984) is that the grant to Congress of the power to regulate interstate commerce serves only as an "implied restraint upon state regulatory powers." Thus, the nonregulatory activities of the states are not subject to dormant-commerce-clause scrutiny—a rationale that assumes a ready distinction between state regulatory and proprietary activity. Even so, the Court sought to limit the state-as-trader exception in two ways. First, as with proprietary prerogatives under the privileges and immunities clause, the market-participant doctrine allows local favoritism only in the state's dealings with its direct trading partners and disallows requiring those partners to favor residents in their independent economic relationships with others. Second, the Court in the *Camden* case held that discriminatory state market participation, which is free from dormant-commerce-clause restraints, is not wholly exempt from privileges-and-immunities-clause analysis. The latter provision directly restrains state action in the interests of interstate harmony, whether regulatory or not. Both these attempts to confine the damage that might be done by a wholesale lifting of interstate equality

obligations for state proprietary activity are familiar symptoms of the beguiling but dubious use of proprietary justifications.

Several elements in the history of proprietary adjustments to interstate equality doctrine also appear in the history of proprietary adjustments to free-speech doctrine. The general question is whether government has power to deny the right to communicate on public property what freely may be communicated on private property. In the late nineteenth century era, when the Supreme Court forcefully protected private property from government intrusion and state property from nonresident demands of equal access, the excessive attribution of plenary control to property ownership prevailed. In *Davis v. Massachusetts* (1897) the Court affirmed a ruling by OLIVER WENDELL HOLMES, JR. [2], then a state judge, that "[f]or the legislature absolutely or conditionally to forbid public speaking in a highway or public park is no more an infringement of rights of a member of the public than for the owner of a private house to forbid it in the house." By the late 1930s, however, as the Court found constitutional room for extensive government regulation of private property, it also found government's proprietary claims insufficient to justify complete denial of public communication in streets and parks. The power associated with property, governmental or private, would not categorically overwhelm other important considerations.

Neither was ownership always irrelevant. What ensued, with frequent division within the Court, was the development of public-forum doctrine, which sometimes distinguishes among different kinds of public property to determine what rights of access private speakers may enjoy. The core First Amendment principle that government may not discriminate against viewpoints it dislikes is so strong that it applies to all public property. Moreover, quintessential public forums like streets and parks cannot be completely closed to speech, even though banning all access would be viewpoint neutral. Yet, the Court remains excessively influenced by proprietary prerogatives. Rather than directly weighing the particular property-management interests of government against the First Amendment importance of speaker access to the particular public location, the Court has permitted government to deny access altogether—at least when the denial is not viewpoint selective—to other forms of public property, ranging from prison grounds to schools to offices to military bases, even where the speech would not interfere with the property's intended purpose. In the leading case of PERRY EDUCATION ASSOCIATION V. PERRY LOCAL EDUCATORS ASSOCIATION (1983) [3] the Court said, "The existence of a right of access to public property and the standard by which limitations upon such a right must be evaluated differ depending on the character of the property at issue." In that and other cases where access claims have been denied, the Court has hearkened back to Justice HUGO L. BLACK's [1] statement for the majority in the jail-grounds case of ADDERLEY V. FLORIDA (1966) [1]: "The State, no less than a private owner of property, has power to preserve the property under its control for the use to which it is lawfully dedicated." The Court's deference to government's proprietary prerogatives thus depends not on property ownership alone, but at least formally, on distinctions among different kinds of public property.

If the fact of ownership is sometimes still weighed too heavily in public-forum doctrine generally, that weight may be even more excessive when, as with the market-participant exception to dormant-commerce-clause doctrine, government property is used in a commercial setting. Normally, if the government, with respect to public property that could be closed to all, voluntarily makes it available for speech on some subjects, it cannot deny access to speakers on other subjects. In *Lehman v. Shaker Heights* (1974), however, the Court allowed a city that sold space on its buses for commercial and public-service advertising to refuse to sell space for political and public-issue advertising. Putting aside First Amendment norms of equal treatment of subject matter in the "voluntary" public forum, four Justices emphasized that the city was "engaged in commerce" and acting "in a proprietary capacity."

Some deference to government's proprietary powers in managing its property, its business dealings, or its PUBLIC EMPLOYEES [3] is undoubtedly appropriate, at least so long as those powers are not exercised for invidiously selective reasons. The Court's opinion in RUTAN V. REPUBLICAN PARTY OF ILLINOIS (1990) [I] is a recent example of the limits of such deference; *Rutan* invalidated government personnel decisions based on political patronage over the dissent of three Justices, who complained that government should be less restricted as employer than as lawmaker. The extent to which proprietary interests permit regulation that otherwise would violate the individual rights of the general populace should, and sometimes (if not often enough) does, depend on additional considerations, such as the importance of the competing constitutional right and its claim to affirmative public support, including the availability of alternative opportunities to exercise that right and the degree to which government monopolizes those opportunities. These considerations surely support the Court's willingness to override proprietary prerogatives in favor of free speech in the streets, parks, and other traditional areas of popular assembly. (Although the recent 5–4 decision in *United States v. Kokinda* [1990] upheld a postal regulation barring solicitation on postal property as applied to soliciting political contributions on a sidewalk separating a post office from

its parking lot, only four Justices relied on proprietary justifications for the exclusion; even they agreed that the "Government, even when acting in its proprietary capacity, does not enjoy absolute freedom from First Amendment constraints, as does a private business.") Having safeguarded these public locales, perhaps the Court is more comfortable in approving limits on access rights in others.

In determining whether government has left too little room for individual liberty, however, the proprietary idea is too indirect and blunt an instrument, just as it is too imprecise a measure in determining whether state autonomy should be protected against congressional regulation and in determining whether a state's preferences for its own residents will threaten interstate harmony. The government–proprietor distinction's complete rejection in some spheres and its resilience and mutations in others counsel us to acknowledge its intuitive appeal, but to beware excessive reliance on its seductive power.

JONATHAN D. VARAT

Bibliography

GILLEN, TERESA 1985 A Proposed Model of the Sovereign/Proprietary Distinction. *University of Pennsylvania Law Review* 133:661–684.
KREIMER, SETH F. 1984 Allocational Sanctions: The Problem of Negative Rights in a Positive State. *University of Pennsylvania Law Review* 132:1293, 1314–1324.
LINDE, HANS 1964 Justice Douglas on Freedom in the Welfare State: Constitutional Rights in the Public Sector. *Washington Law Review* 39:4–46.
———— 1965 Constitutional Rights in the Public Sector: Justice Douglas on Liberty in the Welfare State. *Washington Law Review* 40:10–77.
POST, ROBERT C. 1987 Between Governance and Management: The History and Theory of the Public Forum. *UCLA Law Review* 34:1713–1835.
VARAT, JONATHAN D. 1981 State "Citizenship" and Interstate Equality. *University of Chicago Law Review* 48:487–572.
WELLS, MICHAEL AND HELLERSTEIN, WALTER 1980 The Governmental-Proprietary Distinction in Constitutional Law. *Virginia Law Review* 66:1073–1141.

GOVERNMENT SECRECY

The FIRST AMENDMENT [2,I] guarantees of FREEDOM OF SPEECH [2,I] and FREEDOM OF THE PRESS [2,I] are essential to democratic rule because they protect the right to communicate and receive information needed for self-government. Self-government might seem to require that "the public and the press" also enjoy "rights of access to information about the operation of their government," as Justice JOHN PAUL STEVENS [4,I] stated in RICHMOND

NEWSPAPERS V. VIRGINIA (1980) [3]. Yet, despite its broad protection of speech and the press, the Constitution imposes meager limits on government secrecy. Judicial recognition of a RIGHT TO KNOW [3] generally has been limited to the right to learn what others may choose to disclose and not a right to know what the government elects to conceal.

The most prominent right of access to an official event recognized by the Supreme Court is the right to attend criminal trials and proceedings. Even here, however, early signs were inauspicious. In GANNETT CO., INC. V. DEPASQUALE (1979) [2] a newspaper relied on the Sixth Amendment to require a judge to open pretrial hearings over objections from the accused and prosecutor. The Sixth Amendment guarantees "the accused . . . the right to [a] public trial." The Court rejected the newspaper's argument on the ground that the amendment gave *the public* no "right . . . to insist upon a public trial."

A year later, after much criticism, a fragmented Court found such a right in the First Amendment. In *Richmond Newspapers* the trial judge had closed a murder trial at the defendant's request. Chief Justice WARREN E. BURGER [1], writing for himself and Justices BYRON R. WHITE [4,I] and John Paul Stevens, acknowledged that the First Amendment did not explicitly mention a right of access to governmental functions. But he found a right to attend criminal trials "implicit in the guarantees of the First Amendment." He emphasized that other "unarticulated rights" had been found implicit in the Constitution, including the right of association, the RIGHT OF PRIVACY [3,I], and the RIGHT TO TRAVEL [3]. The CHIEF JUSTICE [1] also cited the NINTH AMENDMENT [3], which he said was adopted "to allay . . . fears . . . that expressing certain guarantees could be read as excluding others."

Justice WILLIAM J. BRENNAN [1,I] (joined by Justice THURGOOD MARSHALL [3,I]) took a broader view of the right to government information, as did Justice Stevens in a separate opinion. For Justice Brennan, the First Amendment had "a *structural* role to play in securing and fostering our republican system of self-government. Implicit in this structural role is [the] assumption that valuable public debate . . . must be informed." His structural analysis extended to "governmental information" generally, not only criminal trials, with the "privilege of access . . . subject to a degree of restraint dictated by the nature of the information and countervailing interests in security or confidentiality." Justice WILLIAM H. REHNQUIST [3,I] alone dissented.

The Court has since relied on the First Amendment to invalidate a law that excluded the press and public during the trial testimony of a minor alleged to be the victim of a sexual offense in GLOBE NEWSPAPER COMPANY

v. SUPERIOR COURT (1982) [2]; to overturn a trial court's secret examination of prospective jurors in *Press-Enterprise Co. v. Superior Court* (1984); and to uphold public access to a pretrial hearing at which the prosecution must prove the existence of PROBABLE CAUSE [3] to bring a defendant to trial in *Press-Enterprise Co. v. Superior Court* (1986). In each case, the Court said that the interest in public access could be outweighed in particular cases by demonstrated need for exclusion.

Beyond criminal proceedings, the argument for public access to government information has fared poorly. After suggesting in BRANZBURG V. HAYES (1972) [1] that "news gathering is not without its First Amendment protections," the Court has recognized almost none. In *Houchins v. KQED, Inc.* (1978) the Court said that the Constitution accords the press no greater rights than it gives the public generally. But some members of the Court, notably Justice Stevens, have argued that the press should nonetheless receive greater access "to insure that the citizens are fully informed regarding matters of public interest and importance." The seven Justices participating in *Houchins* could not agree on a majority opinion, but a combination of views granted the press more frequent visits to a local jail than the public enjoyed and the right to bring recording equipment, which the public could not. But journalists had no right to enter a problem area of the jail or to interview randomly encountered inmates.

The Supreme Court has not recognized a First Amendment right of access to civil trials, although individual Justices have supported one, as have lower courts. A right of access in criminal matters is easier to uphold for two reasons. First, the Sixth Amendment, although not the source of an access right, already contemplates constitutional limits on societal efforts to close criminal proceedings. No equivalent limit exists for civil matters. Second, when the Constitution was adopted, "criminal trials both here and in England had long been presumptively open," as Chief Justice Burger pointed out in *Richmond Newspapers*.

A right of access to fiscal information would seem to reside in the accounts clause of the Constitution, which provides that "a regular Statement and Account of the Receipts and Expenditures of all public Money shall be published from time to time." Even if this provision does guarantee fiscal information, it is not clear who might be able to enforce it. In *United States v. Richardson* (1974) a taxpayer challenged the government's failure to disclose the CIA budget. The Court refused to address the merits of the challenge because the taxpayer lacked STANDING [4] to assert it. Taxpayer status did not confer a right to sue.

Judicial and congressional SUBPOENAS [4] would seem one way to require the executive branch of government to produce information. But a constitutional EXECUTIVE PRIVILEGE [2] of uncertain dimension will sometimes entitle the President and other executive officers to maintain the secrecy of their communications by resisting such subpoenas. UNITED STATES V. NIXON (1974) [3] recognized a qualified executive privilege, but declined to apply it to protect the President's Watergate tapes.

FREEDOM OF INFORMATION ACTS [2] afford the single best route around official secrecy. These acts, which exist at the federal level and in many states, guarantee access to a great deal of information. However, the guarantee is legislatively, not constitutionally, created.

STEPHEN GILLERS

Bibliography
BRENNAN, WILLIAM J. 1979 Address. *Rutgers Law Review* 32:173–183.
LEWIS, ANTHONY 1980 A Public Right to Know About Public Institutions: The First Amendment as a Sword. *Supreme Court Review* 1980:1–25.

GOVERNMENT WRONGS

In his *Commentaries on the Law of England* (1765), WILLIAM BLACKSTONE [1] articulated what he took to be the fundamental principle governing legal redress against the Crown: "The King can do no wrong." This maxim, which Bracton had reported in the thirteenth century, was for Blackstone and for the legal historians who followed him an implication of the royal prerogative signifying that the Crown could not be brought to account judicially without its consent. Even in Bracton's time, however, the Crown had established remedies for many wrongs committed by royal officers. The maxim, then, probably meant not that the king was above the law but that he would not ordinarily suffer wrong to be done to his subjects by his officers without remedy.

Prior to the AMERICAN REVOLUTION [I] the law in England, as summarized in *Lane v. Cotton* (1701), recognized the personal liability of individual officers for negligent wrongs committed in the course of their duties, but denied governmental liability for negligence. The American Constitution, however, established political and legal principles that were radically different from those that prevailed in English public law. State-law principles also reflected certain departures from the English model. This discussion focuses on tort claims, not contractual disputes. The discussion will distinguish between state and federal government wrongs, between immunity doctrine in the state courts and in the federal courts, and between actions asserting DAMAGE CLAIMS [I] and suits for injunctive relief.

In CHISHOLM V. GEORGIA (1793) [1] the Supreme Court upheld state government liability, ruling that Article III conferred federal court jurisdiction over COMMON LAW [1] actions against states initiated by citizens of other states. In an OBITER DICTUM [3], however, the Court stated that Article III immunized the United States from suit, a position affirmed in later cases. The *Chisholm* ruling on state liability aroused a firestorm of political protest, culminating in the adoption of the ELEVENTH AMENDMENT [2,I], which was understood to bar any federal court action against a state, even one claiming a constitutional violation.

The JURISPRUDENCE [I] relating to the states' Eleventh Amendment immunity soon became quite complex and remains so. For example, in *Hans v. Louisiana* (1890) the immunity was extended to suits brought against states by their own citizens, contrary to Article III's text, and to suits that were effectively, though not nominally, against states. In EX PARTE YOUNG (1908) [4], however, the Court created what proved to be a transformative exception to the immunity. There, the Court permitted the federal courts to grant injunctive relief against state officials in their individual capacities if their actions, although valid under state law, violated the Constitution. From this seed, the CIVIL RIGHTS [1,I] revolution in the courts would grow.

The most far-reaching federal-law limitation on state and local government wrongs, SECTION 1983, TITLE 42, U.S. CODE [4], authorizes courts to grant monetary or injunctive relief against "any person who, under color of [state or local] law," deprives the plaintiff of rights secured by federal law. Enacted in 1871 to implement the newly ratified FOURTEENTH AMENDMENT [2,I], it was of little significance until the Court, in *Monroe v. Pape* (1961), interpreted the statute to cover official wrongs that were authorized by state law. Only two years after the decision, Section 1983 litigation had increased by more than sixty percent. Subsequent decisions expanded this remedy even further. In 1976 Congress authorized the award of attorneys' fees to successful plaintiffs in Section 1983 cases.

Today, the main limitations on Section 1983 liability are the following: A LOCAL GOVERNMENT [I] is not liable for its officials' wrongs unless the illegal actions reflect an "official policy or custom"; punitive damages may be awarded against individual officials but ordinarily not against governments; comprehensive regulatory schemes may override Section 1983's remedy; simple negligence is not actionable; and, most important, certain immunities may protect governments and officials from actions for damages and other retrospective relief. These immunities are absolute as to judicial, legislative, and prosecutorial actions, and are qualified (protecting an official who acts in good faith) as to administrative actions.

Each state has established its own regime of liability and immunity law for its officials' wrongs. These regimes usually center on statutory waivers of SOVEREIGN IMMU-

NITY [4]. In interpreting these statutes, state courts often distinguish between "discretionary" and "governmental" decisions, which are absolutely immune, and "ministerial" and "proprietary" decisions, which are not. These state-law regimes are largely unaffected by the Constitution, although they may provide remedies under state law for federal-law violations.

Wrongs committed by federal officials are subject to three different remedies under federal law: (1) the Federal Tort Claims Act of 1946 (FTCA); (2) the "Bivens action" and (3) direct JUDICIAL REVIEW OF ADMINISTRATIVE ACTION [I] under the Administrative Procedure Act of 1946 or particular review provisions in statutes.

The FTCA is a limited waiver of the United States's sovereign immunity derived, as noted above, from judicial interpretations of Article III. It creates a damage remedy for federal officials' negligence and for certain intentional torts of "investigative or law enforcement officers" so long as the conduct is tortious under the applicable state law. The FTCA substitutes governmental for official liability; although it confers no immunities, it creates some broad exceptions. The two most important ones deny liability for most intentional torts, and for "any claim . . . based upon the exercise or performance or the failure to exercise a discretionary function or duty . . . whether or not the discretion involved be abused." Neither a jury trial nor punitive damages is available under the FTCA.

The eponymous *Bivens* action, from BIVENS V. SIX UNKNOWN NAMED AGENTS (1971) [I], is a judicially created remedy against individual federal officials (not the government) for violations of certain constitutional rights; the Court has specifically extended it to FOURTH AMENDMENT [2,I], Fifth Amendment EQUAL PROTECTION [2,I], and Eighth Amendment rights. In *Bivens* actions, the FTCA exceptions do not apply, but the official may claim an absolute or qualified immunity (depending on the nature of the act). Punitive damages and jury trials are permitted.

The Administrative Procedure Act authorizes JUDICIAL REVIEW [3] of the decisions of almost all federal agencies at the instance of one who is aggrieved by an agency action and seeks injunctive, mandatory, or declaratory relief. The only important exceptions are cases in which a statute precludes judicial review, as in *Block v. Community Nutrition Institute* (1984), or in which the agency action "is committed to agency discretion by law," as in *Heckler v. Chaney* (1985).

The legal structure for remedying governmental wrongs, especially at the federal level, is formidable. That structure, however, displays some problematic features. First, certain doctrines limit victims' redress. These include the Eleventh Amendment immunity; the Court's rejection, in MONELL V. DEPARTMENT OF SOCIAL SERVICES OF NEW YORK CITY (1978) [3], of local governments' vicarious liability for their employees' Section 1983 violations; and the limitations on liability, damages, and fee-shifting under the FTCA. Such doctrines, by effectively confining many victims to a remedy against an individual official, may defeat both the compensation and deterrence goals of the law. Individual officials are unlikely to be able to pay substantial damages. They are also likely to be poorly situated to alter the bureaucratic policies or practices that may have caused their wrongdoing and may cause more of it in the future. In addition, doctrines about STANDING [4], RIPENESS [3], and irreparable harm have sometimes been used to restrict access to injunctive relief against governmental wrongdoing of a more or less systematic nature. An example is *City of Los Angeles v. Lyons* (1983).

Second, this focus on the liability of individual officials, some of whom will be neither legally represented nor indemnified by the governments that employ them, creates incentives for the officials to adopt self-protective strategies of inaction, delay, formalism, and change in the character of their decisions. The circumstances in which many low-level officials work also provide ample opportunity to pursue such incentives. Although these strategies may succeed in minimizing the officials' personal exposure to liability, they tend to undermine the officials' functions and impose wasteful costs on the public.

A remedial structure that limited the liability of individual officials for damages, transferring remedial responsibility to the governmental entities that employed them, would strike a better balance among the competing social interests. Those interests are to deter official wrongdoing, maintain vigorous decision making, compensate victims of illegality, respect the distinctive institutional competences of different decision makers, and accomplish these ends at a tolerable public cost.

PETER H. SCHUCK

(SEE ALSO: *Executive Immunity* [2]; *Judicial Immunity* [3]; *Legislative Immunity* [3]; *Torts* [I].)

Bibliography

NAHMOD, SHELDON 1986 *Civil Rights and Civil Liberties Litigation: The Law of Section 1983.* Colorado Springs, Colo.: Shepard's/McGraw-Hill.

SCHUCK, PETER 1983 *Suing Government: Citizen Remedies for Official Wrongs.* New Haven, Conn.: Yale University Press.

GRAND JURY
(Update)

The grand jury clause of the Fifth Amendment is an anomaly. It gives constitutional stature to a secret inquisitorial process that is quite at odds with the open adversarial character of the remainder of the federal judicial system. The clause preserves the institution of the grand jury without placing it clearly within any of the three branches of the federal government. The federal grand jury, like its English progenitor, has two conflicting functions. The guarantee of review by a grand jury was included in the Fifth Amendment because the grand jury serves as a shield or buffer protecting individuals against baseless or malicious charges. But the grand jury also has another side: it serves as an investigatory agency that ferrets out crime.

Since the original publication of this encyclopedia in 1986 the Supreme Court has decided six grand jury cases. Four involved prosecutorial errors or abuses that could impair the grand jury's ability to shield individuals from unfounded charges. In each case, the question was the availability of a judicial remedy. The other two cases considered the ramifications of grand jury secrecy.

The issue of remedies for abuse of the grand jury reached the Supreme Court because of the lower courts' increasing willingness to invalidate federal INDICTMENTS [2] if the government committed errors at the grand jury phase. Until the mid-1970s, federal courts showed little inclination to police the grand jury process to ensure that it fulfilled its constitutional function of protecting the accused against unfounded criminal charges. In *Costello v. United States* (1956) the Supreme Court held that the federal grand jury was to operate, like its English progenitor, free of technical rules of evidence and procedure. Under the influence of *Costello*, the lower federal courts typically refused to consider claims of error or abuse in the grand jury process. Beginning in the mid-1970s, some lower courts became increasingly willing to review grand jury proceedings and consider claims of abuse, with the understanding that the indictment might be dismissed if the claims were well founded. Grand jury litigation was attractive to the defense because, even if the indictment was not dismissed, the review process offered an opportunity for discovery otherwise precluded by jury secrecy.

Three of the Supreme Court's recent decisions rebuffed the lower courts' efforts to ensure that the grand jury fulfilled its protective function. In the first of the three decisions, *United States v. Mechanik* (1986), the Court held that any error that had occurred at the grand jury stage was harmless in light of the jury's guilty verdict. The Court stated that the federal rule limiting the persons who could be present during grand jury sessions was designed to protect against the danger of charges not supported by PROBABLE CAUSE [3]. The trial jury's guilty verdict established that there was proof beyond a REASONABLE DOUBT [3] of the defendant's guilt and thus any violation of the procedural rule at the grand jury phase was harmless. Reversal of a conviction entails significant social costs. A retrial burdens witnesses, victims, the prosecution, and the courts. If the prosecution is unable to retry the defendant after the first conviction is reversed, the social cost is even greater. These costs are not justified, the Court concluded, where an error at the grand jury stage had no effect on the outcome of the trial.

Although *Mechanik* was criticized as an open invitation to prosecutors to disregard grand jury procedures, it left open two possible avenues of JUDICIAL REVIEW [3,I] and relief. First, some lower courts held that *Mechanik* did not limit the federal courts' supervisory powers. This interpretation left the courts free to grant relief from grand jury abuse, even in the absence of demonstrable prejudice in the exercise of supervisory power. Second, several circuits permitted defendants to bring interlocutory appeals seeking review of unfavorable pretrial rulings on grand jury issues under the collateral order doctrine, on the theory that the issues would be mooted by the verdict.

The Supreme Court eventually resolved both of these issues, again rebuffing the lower courts' efforts to police the grand jury process. In *Bank of Nova Scotia v. United States* (1988), the Court applied the HARMLESS ERROR [2] rule announced in *Mechanik* to supervisory power rulings. *Mechanik* and *Bank of Nova Scotia* increased the pressure on the appellate courts to grant interlocutory review on claims of grand jury abuse, and the Supreme Court was forced to turn next to the issue of interlocutory appeals. In *Midland Asphalt Corp. v. United States* (1989), the Court concluded that interlocutory review would be available on claims of grand jury abuse only when the defendant alleged a defect so fundamental that it caused the grand jury not to be a grand jury or the indictment not to be an indictment.

Taken together, *Mechanik*, *Bank of Nova Scotia*, and *Midland Asphalt* demonstrate the Supreme Court's unwillingness to subject the grand jury's internal proceedings to judicial review. *Midland Asphalt* holds that interlocutory appeal ordinarily is not permitted if the trial judge denies relief on a grand jury claim before trial. *Mechanik* and *Bank of Nova Scotia* hold that if the defendant is convicted and appeals, the jury's guity verdict moots any error in the grand jury process. Relief is theoretically available in the district court before trial, but given grand jury secrecy, the defendant will seldom have sufficient information about the grand jury process at this point to make the necessary showing of government error and resulting prejudice. These decisions reflect a firm consensus on the Court. Eight members of the Court joined the opinion in *Bank of Nova Scotia*, and the opinion in *Midland Asphalt* was unanimous. Give the limited resources available to the CRIMINAL JUSTICE SYSTEM [I], the Court is simply unwilling to divert judicial resources to a preliminary trial of the grand jury process, particularly when there is no indication that the outcome of a case will change. The Court's decisions avoid not only the cost of reversals in cases where there has been a serious abuse of the grand jury but also the cost of extensive judicial review (with the resultant breach in grand jury secrecy) in all cases.

The Supreme Court did reverse one conviction because of an error at the grand jury stage in a case involving what the Court called the "special problem of racial discrimination." In *Vasquez v. Hillery* (1986) the Court held that racial discrimination in the selection of the grand jury required the reversal of a twenty-year-old murder conviction, even if the state could not reprosecute so long after the original conviction. In a striking contrast to *Mechanik*, which was decided during the same term, the Court rejected the argument that the discrimination at the grand jury phase was harmless error in light of the jury's guilty verdict after a fair trial. Emphasizing that racial discrimination strikes at the fundamental values of the criminal justice system, the Court concluded that the remedy of dismissing the indictment and reversing the resulting conviction was not disproportionate. Although the constitutional prohibition against racial discrimination was the driving force behind this decision, it is worth noting that claims of racial discrimination at the selection stage (unlike the claims in *Mechanik, Bank of Nova Scotia,* and *Midland Asphalt*) can be adjudicated without any breach of grand jury secrecy. Traditionally secrecy is required only after the grand jury has been impaneled.

The Court also decided two cases involving facets of grand jury secrecy. *United States v. John Doe, Inc. I* (1987) dealt with the question of when the government can use materials collected in a grand jury investigation. *Doe* effectively cut back on an earlier decision that held grand jury secrecy prohibits prosecutors from disclosing grand jury evidence to other government lawyers for use in civil proceedings unless the prosecutors obtain a court order based upon a showing of particularized need. This rule ensured that prosecutors had no incentive to misuse the grand jury for civil discovery and decreased the likelihood that grand jury secrecy will be breached. *Doe* gave the grand jury secrecy rule a narrow interpretation, allowing prosecutors conducting grand jury proceedings freely to disclose grand jury materials to civil division attorneys with whom they were consulting about the desirability of filing a civil suit. Permitting informal disclosure without judicial supervision facilitated the government's determination whether to proceed civilly or criminally without duplicative investigations by civil attorneys.

The Court also recognized that the FIRST AMENDMENT [2,I] places limits on the principle of grand jury secrecy. *Butterworth v. Smith* (1990) held that the Florida rule prohibiting a witness from ever diclosing his own testimony violates the First Amendment. The Court found that the state's interests were not sufficient to justify a permanent ban on a reporter's right to make a truthful statement of information that he gathered on his own before he was called to testify. Although neither the federal rules nor those in the majority of states would have prohibited disclosure under those circumstances, fourteen other states have secrecy rules like Florida's. The Court did not question the validity of the more narrowly drawn federal and state secrecy rules.

SARA SUN BEALE

Bibliography

ARNELLA, PETER 1980 Reforming the Federal Grand Jury and the State Preliminary Hearing to Prevent Conviction Without Adjudication. *Michigan Law Review* 78:463–585.

BEALE, SARA SUN and BRYSON, WILLIAM C. 1986 and Supp. 1990 *Grand Jury Law and Practice.* Wilmette, Ill.: Callaghan.

NOTE [ARFAA, CHRISTOPHER M.] 1988 *Mechanikal* Applications of the Harmless Error Rule in Cases of Prosecutorial Grand Jury Misconduct. *Duke Law Journal* 1988:1242–1271.

HABEAS CORPUS
(Update)

A federal court is empowered to grant a writ of habeas corpus to any individual who is held in custody by federal or state government in violation of the Constitution of the United States. Although state courts also can provide habeas corpus relief to those in state custody, the most important contemporary use of habeas corpus is as a vehicle for federal court review of state court criminal convictions. After almost 200 years of habeas corpus litigation in the United States, including more than a century under the RECONSTRUCTION [I] statutes that made federal court relief available to state prisoners, the scope of habeas corpus remains controversial.

Conservatives view habeas corpus as a means for guilty people to escape punishment. They seek to limit the availability of the writ, arguing that habeas corpus undermines the finality of criminal convictions and creates friction between federal and state courts. Liberals, in contrast, see federal habeas corpus review as an essential protection to assure that no person whose constitutional rights have been violated—whether factually innocent or guilty—is imprisoned.

The debate over the scope of habeas corpus review implicates major underlying disputes in constitutional law. For example, federal district court review of state court criminal convictions raises questions of FEDERALISM [2,I], along with the question of whether state judiciaries can be trusted to protect federal constitutional rights. Moreover, disagreements about the availability of habeas corpus reflect different views about the value of the constitutional rules governing CRIMINAL PROCEDURE [2]. Those who oppose Supreme Court protections for criminal defendants (such as the EXCLUSIONARY RULE [2] and MIRANDA RULE [3,I] warnings) seek to limit their enforcement by narrowing the scope of habeas corpus review.

Not surprisingly, the Supreme Court frequently splits along ideological lines in ruling on habeas corpus issues. The WARREN COURT's [4] expansion of habeas corpus relief was halted by the BURGER COURT [1], which adopted substantial new restrictions on federal court habeas review. Most recently, the REHNQUIST COURT [I] has announced important additional limits on the matters that can be raised in federal habeas corpus proceedings. Three restrictions are particularly significant.

First, a petitioner is allowed to present in federal habeas corpus only those matters that were argued in the proceedings that led to his or her conviction, unless the individual can demonstrate cause for the failure to raise the objection and prejudice from the asserted constitutional violation. Under the Warren Court decision in FAY V. NOIA (1963) [2], an individual could present a constitutional issue on habeas corpus, even if not argued earlier, unless it could be demonstrated that the person "deliberately by-passed" the earlier opportunity to litigate the matter. But the Burger Court expressly overruled this standard, which presumptively allowed issues to be presented in federal court, and instead held that new matters could be raised only if there was "cause" for the earlier default and "prejudice" arising from it.

In recent years, the Court has made it clear that the "cause and prejudice" standard is a difficult one to meet. In *Murray v. Carrier* (1986) the Supreme Court summarized the circumstances under which an individual has sufficient cause to raise a new matter on habeas corpus. The Court explained that there was sufficient cause to permit a federal habeas petition to raise a new matter only if defense counsel could not reasonably have known of a legal or factual issue, if the government's attorney interfered with the presentation of the issue, or if there was ineffective assistance of counsel. Each of these proofs of cause is hard to accomplish, and the difficulty reflects the Court's expressly stated view that federal habeas corpus relief has significant costs and should be limited. The Court, however, has said, in *Smith v. Murray* (1986), that individuals who can demonstrate that they are probably innocent of the crime for which they were convicted should be able to secure relief, regardless of the reason for the earlier procedural default.

Although several Supreme Court opinions define "cause," the Court has found fewer occasions to clarify the meaning of "prejudice." The Court indicated in *United States v. Frady* (1982) that a petitioner can meet this requirement only by demonstrating that the constitutional violations caused "actual and substantial disadvantage" that infected the "entire trial with errors of constitutional dimension."

Second, the Supreme Court has restricted the ability of individuals to relitigate on habeas corpus issues that were raised and decided in state court. In BROWN V. ALLEN (1953) [1] the Court ruled that individuals claiming to be held in custody in violation of the United States Constitution could present their claims in federal court even if those claims had been fully and fairly litigated in the state court. But in STONE V. POWELL (1976) [4] the Burger Court limited this PRECEDENT [3], holding that a petitioner could not relitigate the claim that a state court improperly had admitted evidence that was the product of an illegal search or seizure, provided that the state court had offered a full and fair opportunity for a hearing on the issue. The Court emphasized that exclusionary rule claims do not relate to the accuracy of the fact-finding process. Furthermore, the Court said, state judges could be trusted to protect the FOURTH AMENDMENT [2,I].

The Court refused to extend *Stone v. Powell* to challenges to racial discrimination in GRAND JURY [2] selection (*Rose v. Mitchell*, 1979), to BURDEN OF PROOF [1] issues (*Jackson v. Virginia*, 1979), or to claims of ineffective assistance of counsel based on the failure to object to admission of evidence (*Kimmelman v. Morrison*, 1986). But in the 1989 case of *Duckworth v. Eagan*, two Justices, SANDRA DAY O'CONNOR [3,I] and ANTONIN SCALIA [I], stated that they would apply *Stone* to bar habeas corpus review of claims of Fifth Amendment violations because of improper administration of *Miranda* warnings. In light of the evident desire of the conservative majority on the Court to con-

strict the availability of habeas corpus, the O'Connor-Scalia position may come to command a majority of the Court.

Finally, in *Teague v. Lane* (1989) the Supreme Court restricted the power of a federal court in habeas corpus to recognize new constitutional rights. Until *Teague*, federal courts considered habeas corpus petitions alleging constitutional violations, regardless of whether the court would be recognizing a new right that would not be applied retroactively in other cases. But in *Teague*, the Court held that habeas petitions may raise only claims to rights that are "dictated" by precedent, except where the recognition of a new right would have retroactive effect. Because few newly recognized criminal procedure rights are given retroactive application, *Teague* will effectively prevent federal habeas petitioners from presenting claims, except as to rights that have been established previously.

These three sets of restrictions on federal habeas corpus reflect the Supreme Court's desire to limit the procedural protections available to criminal defendants. But these decisions are disturbing for those who believe that a federal forum should be available to those convicted through violations of federal constitutional rights. Moreover, given a conservative Court that sees the costs of habeas corpus as generally outweighing its benefits given legislative pressures for federal statutes limiting habeas corpus review, further restrictions seem likely.

ERWIN CHEMERINSKY

(SEE ALSO: *Procedural Due Process of Law, Criminal* [3,I].)

Bibliography

FRIEDMAN, BARRY   1988   A Tale of Two Habeas. *Minnesota Law Review* 73:247–347.

YACKLE, LARRY   1985   Explaining Habeas Corpus. *New York University Law Review* 60:991–1060.

HAZELWOOD SCHOOL DISTRICT *v.* KUHLMEIER
484 U.S. 260 (1988)

In TINKER V. DES MOINES INDEPENDENT SCHOOL DISTRICT (1969) [4] the Supreme Court held that school officials could not interfere with students' speech unless that speech threatened substantial disorder, a material disruption of the educational program, or invasion of the rights of others. The *Kuhlmeier* decision continues the erosion of *Tinker* that had begun in the BETHEL SCHOOL DISTRICT V. FRASER (1986) [I].

A journalism class in a Missouri public high school wrote and edited the school newspaper. The school's principal, after reviewing proofs, ordered the deletion of two of the paper's projected six pages to avoid publication of two articles: one detailing the experiences of three pregnant students and another on students' feelings about their parents' divorces. The first story, the principal said, was inappropriate for the school's younger students; the second contained derogatory comments by a named student about her father. With no notice to the student writers or editors, the paper was printed with the offending pages deleted. Three of the students brought suit against school officials, seeking a DECLARATORY JUDGMENT [2] that the censorship violated their FIRST AMENDMENT [2,I] rights. They lost in the federal district court, but prevailed in the court of appeals on the theory of the *Tinker* decision. The Supreme Court reversed, 5–3.

Justice BYRON R. WHITE [4,I], for the Court, first concluded that the paper was not a PUBLIC FORUM [3,I] because its pages had not been opened up to students generally or to any other segment of the general public. He distinguished *Tinker* in two main ways. First, the school could legitimately seek to inculcate the community's values, and thus could act to avoid the inference that it endorsed the conduct that led to student pregnancy. Second, the principal's control over the school paper was a series of decisions about the educational content of the journalism curriculum, and courts must pay deference to educators in such matters. Thus, the proper STANDARD OF REVIEW [4] was not STRICT SCRUTINY [4] but one of "reasonableness"—a standard satisfied by the principal's decision.

For the three dissenters, Justice WILLIAM J. BRENNAN, [1,I] argued that the majority's "reasonableness" test effectively abandoned the much more demanding standards of *Tinker*. Surely some members of the *Kuhlmeier* majority would be satisfied to paint *Tinker* into a corner where its value as a PRECEDENT [3] would be severely limited. Whether the Court will complete this process of doctrinal retrenchment remains to be seen.

KENNETH L. KARST

HEATH v. ALABAMA
474 U.S. 82 (1985)

By the same act, Heath committed crimes in two states. Men whom he hired kidnapped his wife in one state and killed her in another. He pleaded guilty in one state to avoid CAPITAL PUNISHMENT [2,I], and he received a life sentence. However, the other state tried him for essentially the same offense, convicted him, and sentenced him to death. Heath claimed that the second trial exposed him to DOUBLE JEOPARDY [2,I] in violation of the clause

of the Fifth Amendment, applicable to the states via the INCORPORATION DOCTRINE [2,I].

In many cases, the Court had held that a state and the federal government may prosecute the same act if it was a crime under the laws of each. Never had the Court previously decided whether two states could prosecute the same act.

Justice SANDRA DAY O'CONNOR [3,I], for a 7–2 Court, declared that although the Fifth Amendment's double-jeopardy clause protects against successive prosecutions for the same act, if that act breached the laws of two states, it constituted distinct offenses for double-jeopardy purposes. The "dual sovereignty" rule in such cases meant that each affronted sovereign had criminal JURISDICTION [3]. The states are as sovereign toward each other as each is toward the United States. In a sense, the case created no new law because the double-jeopardy clause had never previously barred different jurisdictions from trying the same person for the same act. Nevertheless, Justices WILLIAM J. BRENNAN [1,I] and THURGOOD MARSHALL [3,I] sharply dissented.

LEONARD W. LEVY

HODGSON v. MINNESOTA
110 S.Ct. 2841 (1990)

OHIO v. AKRON CENTER FOR REPRODUCTIVE HEALTH
110 S.Ct. 2841 (1990)

Minnesota and Ohio adopted laws requiring that parents be notified before abortions were performed on minors. By shifting 5–4 votes, the Supreme Court struck down one version of Minnesota's law and upheld another. The Court upheld the Ohio law, 6–3. Four Justices thought all the laws were valid, and three thought they were all invalid; the swing votes were Justices SANDRA DAY O'CONNOR [3,I] and JOHN PAUL STEVENS [4,I].

Minnesota required notification to both of a minor's biological parents before she could have an abortion. A majority concluded that this law "[did] not reasonably further any legitimate state interest." This formulation avoided the question whether a restriction on the right to have an ABORTION [1,I] must pass the test of STRICT SCRUTINY [4], as ROE V. WADE (1973) [3] had held. Whatever the rhetoric, the effective STANDARD OF REVIEW [4] was a demanding one. Justice Stevens, for the majority, acknowledged the state's interest in supporting parents' authority and counseling, but said that any such interest could be served by a one-parent notification rule. He also conceded that the state might wish to protect parents' interests in shaping their children's values, but said this interest could not "overcome the liberty interests of a minor acting with the consent of a single parent or court." Justice O'Connor, too, found this version of the Minnesota law "unreasonable," especially considering that only half the minors in the state lived with both biological parents.

The Minnesota legislature, anticipating that the Court might hold the statute invalid, had adopted a fall-back procedure: If a minor could convince a judge that she was mature enough to give her informed consent to an abortion or that an abortion without two-parent notification was in her best interests, the judge might dispense with that notification. This "judicial bypass" was enough to secure the approval of Justice O'Connor, and so was upheld, 5–4.

The Ohio law required notification of only one parent. Here Justices O'Connor and Stevens joined the four Justices who had considered both Minnesota laws valid. Justice ANTHONY M. KENNEDY [I] wrote the principal opinion, most of which was joined by a majority of the Court. The dissenters in this case, who also dissented as to the Court's disposition of Minnesota's fall-back law, emphasized the severe costs of any parental notification requirement to a minor who dared not tell her parents she was pregnant and who was likely to find a judicial proceeding intimidating. As Justice THURGOOD MARSHALL [3,I] said, those costs are not merely psychological; the fear of confronting parents may cause a young woman to delay an abortion, with attendant increases in risks to her health.

Justice ANTONIN SCALIA [I], who voted to uphold all three laws, took note of the way in which different majorities were pieced together in these cases and concluded that the reason lay in the lack of a principled way to distinguish the results when the Court persists in "this enterprise of devising an Abortion Code." Given the retirement from the Court of Justice WILLIAM J. BRENNAN [1,I], who formed part of the five-Justice majority that invalidated the first Minnesota law, the issue of parental notification seems sure to return to the Court. When it does so, some Justices seem prepared to avoid the complications identified by Justice Scalia in a single doctrinal stroke, sweeping abortion rights—and thus, in some states, abortions—into the back alley.

KENNETH L. KARST

HOLLAND v. ILLINOIS

See: *Batson v. Kentucky* [I]

HOMOSEXUALITY

See: *Bowers v. Hardwick* [I]; Sexual Orientation [I]; Sexual Preference and the Constitution [4]

HOUSE OF REPRESENTATIVES

The House of Representatives was born of compromise at the CONSTITUTIONAL CONVENTION OF 1787 [1]. Early during the Convention, the VIRGINIA PLAN [4], favored by the larger states, proposed a bicameral legislature in which states would be represented on the basis of wealth or population. New Jersey and other small states balked at this plan and proposed maintaining a unicameral legislature in which each state would have equal representation. The present structure of Congress was accepted as the heart of the GREAT COMPROMISE [2]. In the SENATE [I] each state was guaranteed equal representation, while in the House, representation was to be determined by each state's population, excluding Indians but including three-fifths of the slave population.

The compromise served dual purposes: it resolved a major conflict between the delegates, and it created one of the CHECKS AND BALANCES [1] within the Congress to guard against the flawed legislation that might come from a unicameral legislature. The House of Representatives was planned to reflect populist attitudes in society.

Article I, section 2, of the Constitution establishes the structure of the House. Members are chosen every second year. By law, this occurs the Tuesday after the first Monday in November in even-numbered calendar years. The frequency of elections was expected to make House members particularly responsive to shifting political climates. The Framers believed this influence would be balanced by requiring legislation to be passed by the Senate and House together. Senators are elected for six-year terms, with a third of the seats contested in each biennial election. The two-year term in the House was a compromise between those favoring annual elections and others, including JAMES MADISON [3], who favored elections once every third year. Subsequent attempts to set House terms at four years have failed. Opponents of such plans believe that having all congressional elections coincide with presidential elections would make House candidates unduly vulnerable to the effects of coattail politics. There is no limit to the number of terms a representative or senator may serve.

The Constitution requires that representatives be chosen by "the People of the several States," as opposed to the indirect election of the President and Vice-President by the ELECTORAL COLLEGE [2], and the original plan called for election of senators by the state legislatures.

The SEVENTEENTH AMENDMENT [4] now requires direct election of senators. The precise method of direct election is not constitutionally determined. Until 1842, some states allowed voters to select a slate of at-large representatives, making it possible for voters to select every representative from a given state. Congress forbade this practice, mandating the use of congressional districts—that is, equally apportioned subdivisions within the states. Each district sends one representative to the House.

Congressional districts have been the subject of continuous controversy. Districts are drawn by the state legislatures, and the political parties in control of the individual legislatures often GERRYMANDER [2,I] boundary lines, creating oddly shaped districts that benefit the fortunes of the majority party. The federal courts have been loath to intervene in these disputes, although the issue does not fall squarely into the category of the unreviewable POLITICAL QUESTION [3,I], and the Supreme Court has hinted that an extreme partisan gerrymander might be unconstitutional.

The Court has been far more strict in requiring that state legislatures draw district lines to achieve population equality among the several districts within a given state. This principle, first set forth in WESBERRY V. SANDERS (1964) [4], has been consistently reaffirmed.

Anyone who can vote in an election for "the most numerous Branch of the State Legislature" can vote for members of the House of Representatives. Early in the country's history, VOTING RIGHTS [4] were limited to white males and were often linked to property holdings. As a result, voter eligibility varied from state to state. The scope of suffrage has broadened over time, through the adoption of the FIFTEENTH AMENDMENT [2] (vote for former slaves), the NINETEENTH AMENDMENT [3] (vote for women), the TWENTY-FOURTH AMENDMENT [4] (abolition of poll taxes), the VOTING RIGHTS ACT of 1965 [4], and the TWENTY-SIXTH AMENDMENT [4] (vote for all citizens eighteen or older). Indians are also now eligible to vote and are counted for purposes of apportionment.

Article I, section 2, requires that representatives be at least twenty-five years old, U.S. citizens for at least seven years, and citizens of the states they represent. Although not constitutionally required, political practice in the United States requires House members to reside in the districts they represent. This practice is not common to all national legislatures, most notably the British House of Commons.

Under Article I, section 5, the House and the Senate are the judges of the qualifications of their members, as well as the final arbiters of contested elections. On ten occasions, elected candidates have failed to meet constitutional requirements for House membership. Prior to 1969, both chambers occasionally refused to seat victorious candidates who were thought unacceptable for moral or political reasons. The Supreme Court limited Congress's ability to make such judgments in POWELL V. MCCORMACK (1969) [3]. The Court ruled that the House could not refuse to seat Adam Clayton Powell, Jr., on the basis of his being held in contempt of court. So long as an elected candidate meets the constitutional requirements of age, CITIZENSHIP [1], and residence, the member's chamber must seat him or her, although members may be censured or expelled for violating internal chamber rules. Article I grants each chamber of Congress the power to establish and enforce internal rules.

The number of House seats allotted to each state is determined by the decennial census. Article I, section 2, paragraph 3, sets forth the original apportionment scheme. The apportioning mechanism remains, but the size of the House has increased with the growth of the country. The House was initially designed to seat 65 members, each representing not less than 30,000 countable constituents. During the twentieth century, allowing the maximum membership under the Constitution would have produced an unwieldly body of several thousand members, Congress has permanently capped the size of the House at 435 voting members. In the 1980s, members from all but the smallest states represented an average of approximately 520,000 constituents.

When a vacancy occurs in the House of Representatives because of death or other circumstances, the governor of the state with the vacant seat calls a special election. Vacant Senate seats are filled by gubernatorial appointment. The special-election requirement reaffirms the constitutional principle that representatives are the elected national officals most directly tied to their constituents. In practice, when vacancies occur in the second year of a congressional term, seats often remain vacant until the next general election.

Article I, section 2, paragraph 5, provides for the election of the Speaker of the House and other officers. The Speaker is actually chosen by the majority-party caucus and then formally elected by the House. House rules dictate the specific functions of the Speaker and other officers, and by Act of Congress the Speaker is second in the line of PRESIDENTIAL SUCCESSION [3], behind the vice–president. The Speaker is not constitutionally required to be a member of the House, although political practice has limited the Speaker's office to senior House members from the majority party.

Few specific powers are granted exclusively to the House of Representatives. In the event that no presidential candidate receives a majority of Electoral College votes, representatives, voting in state delegations with one vote per state, choose the President from among the three candidates with the greatest number of electoral votes.

This process, set forth in Article II, section 1, and modified by the TWELFTH AMENDMENT [4], has been used only following the elections of 1800 and 1824.

The House has the sole constitutional power to impeach officers of the United States. When impeaching a federal officer, the House brings formal charges of high crimes or misdemeanors against the accused. Following a vote to impeach by the House, the Senate may vote to convict the officer by a two-thirds majority. The House has impeached only one President, ANDREW JOHNSON [3], in 1868. The Senate failed to convict him by a single vote. A dozen federal judges have been formally impeached, and four convicted. In July 1974 the House Committee on the Judiciary initiated IMPEACHMENT [2] hearings against President RICHARD M. NIXON [3] and recommended his impeachment on three counts. Nixon resigned following his court-ordered release of the Watergate tapes, and the House dropped its proceedings.

The final power held exclusively by the House is the "power of the purse." The Constitution requires that all bills to raise federal revenues originate in the House. The larger states at the Constitutional Convention insisted on linking taxation and representation, believing that the direct and frequent election of the representatives would cause them to proceed with caution in proposing tax measures. In fact, the Senate can propose revenue measures through the process of amending bills from the House. The adoption of the Seventeenth Amendment has diluted much of the original concern regarding taxation and direct representation.

ROBERT F. DRINAN, S.J.

Bibliography

CONGRESSIONAL QUARTERLY 1982 *Powers of Congress*, 2nd ed. Washington, D.C.: Congressional Quarterly.

CORWIN, EDWARD SAMUEL 1985 *Corwin and Peltason's Understanding the Constitution*, 10th ed. New York: Holt, Rinehart & Winston.

GALLOWAY, GEORGE B. 1976 *History of the House of Representatives*, 2nd ed. New York: Thomas Y. Crowell.

HINCKLEY, BARBARA 1987 *Stability and Change in Congress*, 4th ed. San Francisco: Harper & Row.

HUSTLER MAGAZINE AND LARRY FLYNT v. JERRY FALWELL
485 U.S. 46 (1988)

On first glance, this appears to be a case in which the FIRST AMENDMENT [2,I] ran amok because the Supreme Court extended its constitutional protection to a malevolent and disgusting LIBEL [3] that in no way expressed an opinion or an idea. *Hustler Magazine*, which caters to prurient interests, published a parody of an advertisement in which Jerry Falwell, a nationally syndicated television preacher and head of a political organization called The Moral Majority, was purportedly interviewed. By innuendo, the parody suggested that his first experience with sexual intercourse was with his mother in an outhouse when he was drunk. At the bottom of the page in small print was a disclaimer, "ad parody—not to be taken seriously."

Falwell sued for DAMAGES [2], claiming libel and the intentional infliction of emotional distress. A jury found for him on the issue of emotional distress but against him on the libel claim because the parody could not reasonably be understood to describe actual facts. *Hustler* appealed the verdict on the emotional distress issue, arguing that the "actual malice" standard of NEW YORK TIMES V. SULLIVAN (1964) [3] must be met before one could recover for emotional distress. The Fourth Circuit sustained the verdict on ground that the *Sullivan* standard had been met because *Hustler* acted recklessly. Unanimously, the Supreme Court sustained *Hustler* in an opinion by Chief Justice WILLIAM H. REHNQUIST [3,I].

His opinion makes little sense unless one understands that the dispositive fact was the trial jury's refusal to find that *Hustler* had libeled Falwell. One might think that if the parody was not believable, it was false, and if it was false and recklessly published with malice, the *Sullivan* standard had been met; but the Court took as decisive the jury's finding that *Hustler* had not published a libel because no one would reasonably believe the parody described a fact. Accordingly, the question before the Court was not whether Falwell's reputation had been maliciously and recklessly libeled. Rather, the question was whether his emotional distress overcame a First Amendment protection for offensive speech calculated to inflict psychological injury, "even when that speech could not reasonably have been interpreted as stating actual facts about the public figure involved."

In response to this question, Rehnquist discoursed on the importance of the First Amendment to the free flow of "ideas and opinions" and the need for "robust debate" concerning PUBLIC FIGURES [3] involved in important public issues. One might read this section of the opinion as a parody of the Court's great free-speech opinions, for nothing in *Hustler*'s alleged interview with Falwell related to any public issues or reflected the expression of ideas or opinions. The interview reflected slime and sleaze.

More persuasive was Rehnquist's argument that to hold that public figures or public officials might recover damages for the infliction of emotional distress might mean that "political cartoonists and satirists would be subjected to damages awards without any showing that their work falsely defamed its subject." Nevertheless, Thomas Nast's depictions of the Tweed Ring or Herblock's of Richard Nixon seem wholly different from *Hustler*'s of Falwell; *Hustler* carried no ring of truth and addressed no issues other than, broadly speaking, Falwell's moral character. The outrageousness of the allegation against him places it apart from traditional political cartooning and satire, but the Court was unable to make distinctions. It relied on the *Sullivan* standard by concluding that a public figure victimized by a publication inflicting emotional injury could not recover damages without showing false facts published with actual malice.

Justice BYRON R. WHITE [4,I] in an inch of space, separately concurring, noted that as he saw the case, the *Sullivan* precedent was irrelevant because the jury found that the *Hustler* parody contained no assertion of fact. That being so, one may conclude that the Court correctly decided that the First Amendment barred Falwell from recovering damages on the sole ground that he had suffered emotional distress.

LEONARD W. LEVY

ILLEGAL ALIENS

See: Alien [1]; Immigration Law [2,I]

ILLINOIS v. PERKINS
110 S.Ct. 2394 (1990)

An eight-member majority of the Supreme Court held that the RIGHT AGAINST SELF-INCRIMINATION [3,I] is not abridged when prisoners incriminate themselves in statements voluntarily made to a cellmate who is an undercover officer. Justice ANTHONY M. KENNEDY [I] for the Court reasoned that the officer posing as a prisoner did not have to give *Miranda* warnings before asking questions that sought incriminating responses because Perkins, although in custody, was not in a coercive situation when he boasted to his cellmate about a murder. He spoke freely to a fellow inmate. He was tricked, but the MIRANDA RULES [3,I] prohibit coercion, not deception. Any statement freely made without compelling influences is admissible in evidence. The Court also held that because the prisoner had not yet been charged for the crime that was the subject of the interrogation, the RIGHT TO COUNSEL [3] had not yet come into play. Therefore, the prisoner suffered no violation of his Sixth Amendment right. Justice WILLIAM J. BRENNAN [3,I] who concurred separately, agreed completely on the Fifth Amendment issue, but believed that the police deception raised a question of DUE PROCESS OF LAW [2].

Justice THURGOOD MARSHALL [3,I], the lone dissenter, contended that because the prisoner was in custody, the interrogation should not have occurred without Miranda warnings. He believed that the Court had carved out of *Miranda* an undercover-agent exception.

LEONARD W. LEVY

(SEE ALSO: *Miranda v. Arizona* [3]; *Police Interrogation and Confessions* [3,I].)

ILLINOIS v. RODRIGUEZ
110 S.Ct. 2793 (1990)

This is another in a growing list of recent decisions that circumscribe the protections of the FOURTH AMENDMENT [2,I]. In this case, a woman who made a criminal complaint against Rodriguez accompanied police to his apartment where they might arrest him. She had a key, claimed to be a cotenant, and consented to their entrance. In PLAIN VIEW [3,I], they found EVIDENCE [2] of his possession of illegal drugs, and a state court convicted him for the narcotics violation. The facts showed that the woman was no longer a cotenant and possessed the key without Rodriguez's knowledge. The Court held that even if the police receive permission to search a home from one who does not have authority to grant consent, the SEARCH AND SEIZURE [4,I] is reasonable if the police act in the good-faith belief that they have received consent from one entitled to give it.

The liberal trio of Justices, led by THURGOOD MARSHALL [3,I], dissented from Justice ANTONIN SCALIA's [I] opinion for a six-member majority. Marshall asserted that THIRD-PARTY CONSENT [I] must be more than "reasonable"; it must be based on actual authority to give consent

257

because one possesses a legitimate expectation of privacy in the home. Absent a voluntary limitation on one's expectation of privacy, the police should not be able to dispense with the Fourth Amendment's requirement of a SEARCH WARRANT [4]. The majority had extended the exceptions to the warrant requirement by broadening the concept of a CONSENT SEARCH [I].

LEONARD W. LEVY

IMMIGRATION AND ALIENAGE
(Update to Immigration)

Federal regulation of immigration did not begin until late in the nineteenth century, and the current code of complex admissions categories and limitations is wholly a product of the twentieth century. The first significant tests of congressional authority to exclude and deport noncitizens came in CHAE CHAN PING v. UNITED STATES (1889) [1] and *Fong Yue Ting v. United States* (1893), cases challenging federal immigration law that barred the entry of Chinese laborers, notably the CHINESE EXCLUSION ACT of 1882. Although the Constitution includes no express provision authorizing the enactment of immigration laws, the Supreme Court held that such a power inhered in the notion of SOVEREIGNTY [4] and was closely associated with exercise of the FOREIGN AFFAIRS [2] power of the United States. It also ruled that congressional decisions as to which classes of aliens should be entitled to enter and remain in the United States are largely beyond judicial scrutiny.

Modern cases reaffirm that the Constitution provides virtually no limit on Congress's power to define the substantive grounds of exclusion and DEPORTATION [2]. It is also well established that removal of aliens from the United States is not "punishment" in a constitutional sense, and therefore, prohibitions against CRUEL AND UNUSUAL PUNISHMENT [2,I], EX POST FACTO LAWS [2], and BILLS OF ATTAINDER [1] are not deemed to apply to regulations of immigration. Nor does the due process clause of the Constitution offer protection to ALIENS [1] applying for initial admission to the United States. Such an alien, the Court stated most recently in *Landon v. Plasencia* (1982), requests a "privilege" and has "no constitutional rights regarding his application" for admission.

It is a dramatic overstatement, however, to conclude that noncitizens in the United States have no constitutional rights. Aliens are generally afforded the constitutional rights extended to citizens (although they are not eligible for federal elective office and do not come within the protection of constitutional provisions prohibiting discrimination in voting). An alien arrested for a crime is entitled to the various protections of the FOURTH AMENDMENT

[2,I], Fifth Amendment, Sixth Amendment, and Eighth Amendment; an alien may assert FIRST AMENDMENT [2,I] rights in a situation in which such claims may be made by citizens. In the important case of *Wong Wing v. United States* (1896), the Court invalidated a provision of the 1892 immigration statute providing for the imprisonment at hard labor of any Chinese laborer determined by executive branch officials to be in the United States illegally. Distinguishing this provision from immigration regulations that bar entry or mandate removal of aliens—which are virtually immune from judicial scrutiny—the Court held that such "infamous punishment" could not be imposed without a judicial trial.

Even within the immigration context, the Court has ruled that DUE PROCESS [2] applies to proceedings aimed at removing an alien who has entered the United States. Similar protections must be afforded permanent resident aliens seeking to reenter the United States after a trip outside the country.

Furthermore, the Supreme Court has adopted interpretations of the immigration code that temper the harsher aspects of its constitutional doctrine. "Because deportation is a drastic measure and at times the equivalent of banishment or exile," the Court stated in *Fong Haw Tan v. Phelan* (1948), ambiguities in deportation grounds should be resolved in an alien's favor. In *Jean v. Nelson* (1985), the Court held that federal statutes do not authorize immigration officials to discriminate on the basis of race or national origin in deciding whether to release aliens from detention prior to a determination of their right to enter the United States.

While the current constitutional doctrine may be described in fairly short order, it is harder to provide a coherent theoretical justification for the case law. The cases may reflect the existence of two conflicting norms. One, based on a theory of membership in a national community, views immigration as a privilege extended to guests whose invitation may be revoked at any time for any reason; the other, grounded in a notion of fundamental human rights, protects all individuals within the United States, irrespective of their status.

Those two norms seem to underlie the Court's bifurcated approach to federal and state laws that discriminate on the basis of alienage. In YICK WO v. HOPKINS (1886) [4], the Supreme Court held that a local ordinance invidiously applied against Chinese aliens violated the FOURTEENTH AMENDMENT [2,I]. While *Yick Wo* may be read as a case primarily condemning racial prejudice, later cases make clear that state classifications drawn on the basis of alienage will be subjected to searching judicial scrutiny. Discriminatory state legislation is deemed suspect for two reasons. First, because immigration regulation is characterized as an exclusive federal power, state laws that burden aliens conflict with federal policy. Second, as announced by the Supreme Court in GRAHAM v. RICHARDSON (1971) [2], aliens constitute a "discrete and insular minority for whom heightened judicial solicitude is appropriate." Since *Graham*, which struck down laws disqualifying aliens from state WELFARE BENEFITS [4], scores of state laws excluding aliens from public benefit programs and economic opportunities in the private sphere have been invalidated. Supreme Court opinions have sustained Fourteenth Amendment challenges to law prohibiting aliens from receiving state scholarships and from serving as lawyers, civil engineers, state civil servants, and notaries public.

In PLYLER v. DOE (1982) [3], the Court held that the EQUAL PROTECTION [2,I] clause protects undocumented aliens in the United States against some forms of state discrimination. The Court invalidated a Texas statute that authorized local school districts to exclude undocumented alien children from school. Although the Court eschewed STRICT SCRUTINY [4]—concluding that EDUCATION [2,I] was not a FUNDAMENTAL RIGHT [2] protected by the Constitution and that laws discriminating against undocumented aliens were not based on a SUSPECT CLASSIFICATION [4]—it nonetheless appeared to apply a standard more strict than the traditional RATIONAL BASIS [3] test. Important to the Court were the nature of the interest burdened and the consequences of denying an education to children, many of whom were likely to remain resident in the United States. The Court also noted that no federal policy authorized the exclusion of children from local schools.

Not all state classifications that discriminate against aliens have fallen. CITIZENSHIP [1,I] is viewed as a legitimate qualification for those jobs or functions deemed to be closely linked with the exercise of a state's sovereign power. According to Justice BYRON R. WHITE [4,I], writing for the Court in *Cabell v. Chavez-Salido* (1982), "exclusion of aliens from basic governmental processes is not a deficiency in the democratic system but a necessary consequence of the community's process of self-definition." Aliens may therefore be excluded from voting, eligibility for elective office, and jury service. The "political function" exception has also been applied where the linkage to usual conceptions of citizenship seems more attenuated. The Court has upheld state laws prohibiting aliens from serving as police officers, public school teachers, and probation officers. In these cases, the Court does not apply the strict scrutiny test. Rather, it deems the presence of the governmental function as warranting application of a rational basis test.

Federal statutes that draw distinctions based on alienage have been judged by a very lenient constitutional standard. In *Fiallo v. Bell* (1977), the Court refused to invalidate a section of the Immigration and Nationality Act that permitted children born out of wedlock to enter the United States based on their relationship with their natural mother but did not accord a similar entitlement to nonmarital children seeking to enter based on their relationship with their natural father. Noting that "Congress regularly makes rules that would be unacceptable if applied to citizens," the Court refused to apply heightened scrutiny to the statutory provision, despite its alleged "double-barreled" discrimination based on sex and illegitimacy.

Outside the immigration context, the Court has likewise demonstrated great restraint in its review of federal legislation regulating aliens. *Mathews v. Diaz* (1976) upheld a provision of the federal Medicare program that denied eligibility to permanent resident aliens unless they had resided in the United States for five years. The Court rejected the claim that the strict scrutiny applied to discriminatory state laws should control, reasoning that given congressional power to regulate immigration, federal laws may classify on the basis of alienage for noninvidious reasons. In *Diaz* the five-year RESIDENCE REQUIREMENT [3] was not irrational, for "Congress may decide that as the alien's tie grows stronger, so does the strength of his claim to an equal share" in "the bounty that a conscientious sovereign makes available to its own citizens and some of its guests." And although the Court held in HAMPTON v. MOW SUN WONG (1976) [2] that a regulation excluding aliens from the federal civil service was beyond the authority of the Civil Service Commission, lower courts subsequently sustained a presidential order reimposing the exclusion.

Despite its constitutional authority to limit federal programs to citizens, Congress has generally made available to permanent resident aliens those benefits and opportunities provided to citizens. Such practice may indicate a political norm that membership in the American community arises from entry as a permanent resident alien rather than through NATURALIZATION [3] several years later.

T. ALEXANDER ALEINIKOFF

Bibliography

ALEINIKOFF, T. ALEXANDER 1989 Federal Regulation of Aliens and the Constitution. *American Journal of International Law* 83:862–871.
LEGOMSKY, STEPHEN H. 1984 Immigration Law and the Principle of Plenary Congressional Power. *Supreme Court Review* 1984:255–307.
MARTIN, DAVID A. 1983 Due Process and Membership in the National Community: Political Asylum and Beyond. *University of Pittsburgh Law Review* 44:165–235.
ROSENBERG, GERALD M. 1977 The Protection of Aliens from Discriminatory Treatment by the National Government. *Supreme Court Review* 1977:275–339.

SCHUCK, PETER H. 1984 The Transformation of Immigration Law. *Columbia Law Review* 84:1–90.

INCORPORATION DOCTRINE AND ORIGINAL INTENT

Scholars have variously concluded that the FOURTEENTH AMENDMENT [2,I] was intended to require the states to obey all, some, or none of the guarantees of the federal BILL OF RIGHTS [2]. To understand the relationship of the Fourteenth Amendment to the Bill of Rights requires examining history leading up to the 1866 framing of the Fourteenth Amendment.

In 1833 the Supreme Court ruled in BARRON v. CITY OF BALTIMORE [1] that the guarantees of the Bill of Rights did not limit state and local governments. Confronted with abolitionist literature and fearing slave revolts, in the 1830s southern states made it a crime to criticize SLAVERY [4].

On the eve of the CIVIL WAR [I], two southern states prosecuted their citizens for disseminating an antislavery book. Republicans had used an abridged version of the same book as a campaign document. In the LINCOLN–DOUGLAS DEBATES [3] both ABRAHAM LINCOLN [3] and STEPHEN DOUGLAS [2] recognized that Republicans could not campaign in the South. To protect slavery, federal, territorial, and state governments violated other basic liberties as well.

In the 1857 case of DRED SCOTT v. SANDFORD [2], Chief Justice ROGER BROOKE TANEY [4] said blacks (even free blacks) belonged to a degraded class when the Constitution was written, could not be citizens of the United States, and were entitled to none of the rights, privileges, and immunities secured by the Constitution to citizens, including rights in the Bill of Rights.

Concern for CIVIL LIBERTIES [1,I] became part of the ideology of the REPUBLICAN PARTY [I]. The Republican campaign slogan in 1856 was "Free Speech, Free Labor, Free Soil, and Fremont."

Leading Republicans adhered to an unorthodox, antislavery legal philosophy. Although the Supreme Court had suggested that blacks could not be citizens of the United States, Republicans insisted that free blacks were citizens. Leading Republicans also thought, contrary to Supreme Court decisions, that the Bill of Rights protected American citizens against state violation of their liberties. From 1864 to 1866 these views were expressed by Republican conservatives, moderates, and radicals.

When Congress met in 1866, the defeated southern states sought readmission to the Union and to Congress. Southern states and localities had passed BLACK CODES [1] restricting for blacks many FUNDAMENTAL RIGHTS [2]

accorded to whites, including freedom to move, to own property, to contract, to bear arms, to preach, and to assemble. Congress appointed the Joint Committee on RECONSTRUCTION [I] to consider the condition of the southern states and to consider whether further conditions should be required before their readmission.

To deal with the Black Codes, Congress passed the CIVIL RIGHTS ACT OF 1866 [1]. It provided that persons born in the United States were citizens and gave such citizens the same rights to contract, to own property, to give evidence, and "to full and equal benefit of laws and proceedings for the security of person and property as enjoyed by white citizens." Because leading Republicans accepted the idea that the Bill of Rights liberties limited the states even before the passage of the Fourteenth Amendment, they could read "the full and equal benefit of laws . . . for the security of person and property" to include Bill of Rights liberties.

Democrats, along with President ANDREW JOHNSON [3], denied the power of the federal government to pass the Civil Rights Act. Republicans insisted that the power to pass the act could be found in the THIRTEENTH AMENDMENT [4], which abolished slavery; in the original PRIVILEGES AND IMMUNITIES [3] clause of Article IV, section 2; and, in the view of several leading Republicans, in the DUE PROCESS [2] clause of the Fifth Amendment.

Although most Republicans thought Congress had the power to pass the Civil Rights Act, Congressman JOHN A. BINGHAM [1], later principal drafter of the Fourteenth Amendment's first section, argued that a constitutional amendment was required. Bingham and James Wilson, chairman of the House Judiciary Committee, understood the Civil Rights Act as an attempt to enforce the guarantees of the Bill of Rights.

The final version of Section 1 of the Fourteenth Amendment provided that all persons born in the United States and subject to its jurisdiction were citizens and that no state should make or enforce any law abridging the privileges and immunities of citizens of the United States or deny due process or EQUAL PROTECTION [2,I] to any person. Bingham explained that the amendment provided the power "to protect by national law the privileges and immunities of all citizens of the Republic and the inborn rights of every person within its jurisdiction whenever the same shall be abridged or denied by the unconstitutional acts of any State."

Senator JACOB M. HOWARD [2] presented the amendment to the Senate on behalf of the joint committee. He explained that court decisions had held that the rights in the Bill of Rights did not limit the states. The privileges and immunities of citizens of the United States, Howard said, included the rights in the Bill of Rights. "The great object of the first section of this amendment is, therefore, to restrain the power of the States and compel them at all times to respect these great fundamental guaranties."

Both in Congress and in the election campaign of 1866, discussion of Section 1 was brief. Republicans said variously that the amendment would ensure that the rights of citizens of the United States would not be abridged by any state; that it would protect the rights of American citizens; that it would protect constitutional rights, including free speech and the right to bear arms; or that it embodied the Civil Rights Act or its principles. Suggestions that the amendment was identical to the Civil Rights Act imply that the act incorporated the due process guarantee and that guarantees of the Bill of Rights limited the states prior to the ratification of the Fourteenth Amendment.

Many state ratification debates were not recorded. Often Republicans said nothing at all, being content to wait and vote. In Pennsylvania, Republicans said the amendment was necessary to secure freedom, including FREEDOM OF SPEECH [2,I]; was needed to protect citizens in all their constitutional rights; and embodied both the principles of the Civil Rights Act and the inalienable rights to life and liberty referred to in the DECLARATION OF INDEPENDENCE [2]. Radicals in Massachusetts insisted that the amendment was useless because it provided for things already secured by the Constitution, including black CITIZENSHIP [1,I] and protection of Bill of Rights guarantees against state action.

In Congress and in the campaign of 1866, except for statements by Bingham and Howard, there were few extended discussions, and often none at all, of the legal meaning of Section 1. Discussions of application of one or more Bill of Rights liberties to the states under Section 1 of the Fourteenth Amendment were similarly brief. Republicans concentrated their attention on different questions—on the merits of the contest between President Andrew Johnson and Congress, on the readmission of southern states, and on broad statements of political principle. Still, in 1866 many Republicans indicated that Section 1 would protect particular Bill of Rights liberties, and none explicitly said that it would leave the states free to deny their citizens privileges set out in the Bill of Rights.

MICHAEL KENT CURTIS

(SEE ALSO: *Freedom of Assembly and Association* [2]; *Freedom of Contract* [2]; *Freedom of the Press* [2,I]; *Incorporation Doctrine* [2]; *Property Rights* [I]; *Second Amendment* [4].)

Bibliography

BERGER, RAOUL 1989 *The Fourteenth Amendment and the Bill of Rights.* Norman: University of Oklahoma Press.

CURTIS, MICHAEL KENT 1986 *No State Shall Abridge: The Fourteenth Amendment and the Bill of Rights.* Durham, N.C.: Duke University Press.

GRAHAM, HOWARD 1968 *Everyman's Constitution.* Madison: State Historical Society of Wisconsin.

HYMAN, HAROLD and WIECEK, WILLIAM 1982 *Equal Justice Under Law.* New York: Harper and Row.

TEN BROEK, JACOBUS 1965 *Equal Under Law.* New York: Macmillan.

WIECEK, WILLIAM 1977 *The Sources of Anti-Slavery Constitutionalism in America, 1760–1848.* Ithaca, N.Y.: Cornell University Press.

INDEPENDENT COUNSEL

In 1978, Congress established a permanent framework for dealing with allegations that a senior official of the federal government had committed federal crimes. The fundamental element of the new process is the selection of a special officer with the sole responsibility of investigating the allegations. The special selection of a person from outside the government frees the person from the institutional and personal restraints that might affect the judgment and objectivity of a regular Justice Department prosecutor called upon to investigate his governmental superiors or colleagues.

As originally enacted as part of the Ethics in Government Act of 1978, this officer was called a SPECIAL PROSECUTOR [I]. Congress later changed the officer's title to "independent counsel" in order to diffuse criticism that appointment of an official called a "special prosecutor" prejudged the outcome of the investigation. The original title seemed to suggest that the offense being investigated was special and that prosecution was probable or necessary. The title "independent counsel" signifies that the official's responsibility is to be more neutral and dispassionate.

Before Congress acted in 1978 to provide a permanent mechanism for appointing an independent counsel, the decision whether to take any unusual steps to respond to reports of high-level corruption was left to an unpredictable combination of public notoriety and political integrity. For example, in order to deal with reports of massive corruption in the WARREN HARDING [2] administration concerning the sale of the Teapot Dome petroleum reserves, Congress enacted a special statute authorizing the President, with Senate confirmation, to appoint "special counsel" to investigate and prosecute criminal violations relating to the leases on oil lands in former naval reserves. The incumbent ATTORNEY GENERAL [1], Harry Daugherty, lacked public trust, since he himself faced separate criminal allegations. President CALVIN COOLIDGE [2] appointed a former Ohio senator and a private lawyer from Pennsylvania (later a Supreme Court Justice) to serve as special counsel. Among those prosecuted was the former secretary of the interior, Albert B. Fall, who was convicted of bribery and sentenced to prison.

During the administration of HARRY S. TRUMAN [4], public pressure forced Attorney General J. Howard McGrath to appoint a highly respected former New York City official to serve as his "special assistant" to investigate widespread corruption in federal tax cases. The special assistant, however, had no statutory mandate. When he tried to press his investigation by seeking information from high-level Justice Department officials, including the attorney general himself, Attorney General McGrath fired him. President Truman immediately fired the attorney general, but did not see to the appointment of any replacement special prosecutor. Not until a new administration took over did the allegations yield prosecutions and convictions, including the convictions of the former assistant attorney general in charge of the Tax Division and of President Truman's own appointments secretary.

Then came WATERGATE [4]. Shortly after the beginning of President RICHARD M. NIXON's [3] second term, allegations surfaced that his senior aides in his reelection committee, the White House, and the Justice Department had been personally involved in planning a burglary at the offices of the Democratic National Committee during the 1972 presidential campaign or had helped to cover up the guilt of the conspirators. Public skepticism about a Justice Department investigation led the new attorney general, Elliot Richardson, to appoint a Harvard Law School professor, Archibald Cox, as the "Watergate special prosecutor." When Cox insisted on subpoenaing tape recordings that President Nixon had made in his White House office and refused to yield voluntarily, the President fired him.

The public firestorm that followed Cox's firing and Richardson's resignation forced the President to agree to the appointment of a new special prosecutor, Leon Jaworski, whose authority was derived from newly issued Justice Department regulations that the President pledged to respect. Those regulations guaranteed that the special prosecutor would not be removed except for "gross impropriety" or other special cause. In UNITED STATES v. NIXON (1974) [3], the Supreme Court upheld the constitutional authority of the Special Prosecutor to press another subpoena directed to the President, despite the President's objection that it invaded his constitutional right to invoke executive privilege. The Court concluded that the Justice Department regulations to which the President had agreed and which remained in effect provided the special prosecutor with autonomy to pursue the investigation, regardless of the President's wishes.

During the JIMMY CARTER [1] administration, Attorney General Griffin Bell appointed an official outside the Justice Department to serve as his "special counsel" to investigate allegations concerning the financial interests of the President and his brother.

The 1978 legislation goes well beyond any of the prior approaches. It requires the attorney general to apply to a special court to appoint a special prosecutor (or independent counsel) whenever preliminary inquiry into allegations against the President or other senior government officials specified in the statute leads the attorney general to conclude that there are "reasonable grounds" for further investigation. The court then must appoint an independent counsel from outside the government. That counsel becomes vested with all of the investigative and prosecutorial authority that the attorney general and his subordinates would otherwise have. In exercising his judgment, the independent counsel is not subject to supervision or direction by the attorney general or even the President. The statute protects the independent counsel's autonomy by specifying that he may be removed only by the attorney general personally and only for "good cause." The statute also makes the removal decision subject to JUDICIAL REVIEW [3].

In the first ten years of experience under the statute, there were more than thirty instances in which the statute came into play and at least eight special prosecutors or independent counsels were formally appointed. In *Morrison v. Olson* (1988) the Supreme Court upheld the constitutionality of the independent-counsel provisions. Their constitutionality had been challenged by the target of an investigation, a former assistant attorney general. The Justice Department itself joined in urging the Court to strike down the statute as an invasion of the President's constitutional prerogatives. The constitutional attack rested on two basic arguments: first, that the provisions for court appointment and protected tenure violated the President's right to appoint and remove all senior "officers" of the government and, second, that the independent counsel's autonomy invaded the prerogatives assigned to the President under the SEPARATION OF POWERS [4], particularly the responsiblity for enforcing federal law.

The Court ruled, however, that an independent counsel is only an "inferior officer" within the meaning of the APPOINTMENTS CLAUSE [1] of Article II of the Constitution, so that Congress may vest the appointment power in a court. The Court reasoned that the narrowness of the investigative charter and other statutory constraints put an independent counsel into the "inferior officer" status.

The Court also rejected the more fundamental objection that the independent-counsel mechanism violates the Constitution's separation of powers. The Court agreed that investigation and prosecution of federal crimes is essentially an executive-branch function, but concluded that the attorney general's role in the initial decision to apply for appointment of an independent counsel and his power to remove the counsel "for good cause" provide adequate executive-branch control over the assertion of these powers. The Court also concluded that Congress' solution to a difficult problem of assuring public confidence in the integrity of the criminal process satisfies the constitutional separation of powers because neither the legislature nor the judiciary had "aggrandized" its powers at the expense of the executive branch.

Although the Court's decision settles the constitutional question, doubts about the wisdom of the statute remain. An independent counsel lacks either an electoral base or public accountability. The appointment to investigate a particular set of allegations, with virtually no limit on the resources that can be devoted to the investigation, may tend to distort, rather than protect, the fair and objective judgment that the statutory mechanism is supposed to promote. This special charter may also lead to relentlessly intensive and sweeping investigations that subject government officials to substantially more onerous treatment than an "ordinary" criminal suspect would receive at the hands of a full-time, professional prosecutor.

PHILIP A. LACOVARA

Bibliography

BAKER, HOWARD H. 1975 The Proposed Judicially Appointed Independent Office of Public Attorney: Some Constitutional Objections and an Alternative. *Southwestern Law Journal* 29:671–683.

CUMMINGS, HOMER S. and MCFARLAND, CARL 1937 *Federal Justice: Chapters in the History of Justice and the Federal Executive.* New York: Macmillan.

HUSTON, LUTHER A. 1967 *The Department of Justice.* New York: Praeger.

———— 1968 *Roles of the Attorney General of the United States.* Washington, D.C.: American Enterprise Institute.

JACOBY, JOAN E. 1980 *The American Prosecutor: A Search for Identity.* Indianapolis: Lexington Books.

TIEFER, CHARLES 1983 The Constitutionality of Independent Officers as Checks on Abuses of Executive Power. *Boston University Law Review* 63:59–103.

INTEREST GROUPS

Interest groups, or groups of people who try to use the power of government to advance their own interests, have played an important part in the development of both constitutional law and CONSTITUTIONAL THEORY [I].

CHARLES A. BEARD [1] argued that a particular array of interest groups lay behind the support for and opposition to the Constitution in 1787–1789. Examining the property holdings of supporters and opponents, Beard argued that debtors and owners of real property opposed the Constitution, while personalty interests, especially creditors whose property consisted largely of promises to repay loans, supported it. Beard's specific conclusions have been rejected by later scholars, who have found more complex patterns of property holding than Beard's argument required. Even if the specific argument is rejected, however, consistent patterns of support and opposition based on interests can be found. Constitutional provisions like the ban on state impairments of the OBLIGATION OF CONTRACTS [3] and the prohibition of state issuance of money are best explained by the fact that the supporters of the Constitution feared that they would be outvoted in state legislatures on important issues related to debt and might be able to defend their interests better in the national Congress. Similarly, the likelihood that the new government would be able to resolve controversies over ownership of the undeveloped lands to the west meant that speculators who had purchased western lands were inclined to support the Constitution. Many of the Constitution's compromises over SLAVERY [4] resulted from the sort of interest-group bargaining that characterizes politics. At the same time, the action of interest groups alone seems insufficient to account for the RATIFICATION OF THE CONSTITUTION [3]. Because too many people with too many conflicting interests supported ratification, interest alone cannot explain the adoption of the document. In the end, the Constitution was ratified because of the interaction between interest-group support and conviction that the new government promised to be better as a matter of principle than the Confederation.

Supporters of the new Constitution were alert to the problems that interest groups posed for good government. The central theme in THE FEDERALIST [2] is probably the necessity of designing a government to "curb the influence of faction." *The Federalist*'s notion of "faction" is not precisely the same as modern ideas about interest groups, for "factions" included groups brought together by a common "passion" as well as those acting to advance a common "interest." Nonetheless, the arguments in *The Federalist* about the evils of faction capture many modern concerns about the problems interest groups pose for government. For *The Federalist*, factions must be checked because they are motivated by passions or interests "adverse to the rights of other citizens or to the permanent and aggregate interests of the community"—what we would today call the public interest. This remains true, even if the faction amounts to a majority; even a majority can invade the interests of others, and more controversially, even a majority can act in ways that fail to advance the public interest, conceived of as something different from the interests of a majority.

According to *The Federalist* the new government was well suited to check the influence of faction. Its federal structure allowed the government to extend over a rather large territory. By extending the geographic scope of government, the Constitution made it more difficult for individual factions to gain control of the government. Because the nation would be large, it was unlikely that any single faction or interest group would be represented in sufficient numbers throughout the country to gain control of the machinery of the national government. Even if different factions attempted to put together a coalition, the size of the nation would make coordination of their plans difficult. In addition, the SEPARATION OF POWERS [4] in the national government meant that interest groups would have to mobilize their political forces for a long time and in a number of forums before they could control the government. DIRECT ELECTIONS [2] for the HOUSE OF REPRESENTATIVES [1] might register factional concerns every two years, but gaining control of the SENATE [1], elected by the people indirectly acting through their state legislatures, would be more difficult. In the initial conception, the ELECTORAL COLLEGE [2], which was to select the President, was another constraint on the ability of interest groups to control the government. The life-tenured judiciary, too, could stand in the way of factional control, invalidating legislation that contravened constitutional provisions designed to limit faction, such as the CONTRACT CLAUSE [2].

As a theoretical matter *The Federalist*'s defense of the new government as a means of checking the influence of interest groups is quite powerful. Yet it has some limitations. The structures of the government of a territorially extended republic might be sufficient to protect against the influence of interest groups, but on *The Federalist*'s theory as here summarized, it is difficult to understand why the national government would be able to adopt programs that were truly in the national interest. Moreover, modern developments have undermined the cogency of *The Federalist*'s arguments. The rise of national political parties makes it somewhat easier for interest groups scattered throughout the nation to coordinate their programs. The direct election of members of the Senate and the elimination of the electoral college as a body that seriously deliberates about who the President should be have limited the power of those institutions to stand up to factional influence.

Modern constitutional law deals with interest groups in two ways. Where the interest groups are organized around economic concerns, in recent years the Supreme Court has never found their ability to secure government aid conclusively unconstitutional. WILLIAMSON V. LEE OPTICAL COMPANY (1955) [4] is typical. The Court upheld a statute requiring that consumers purchase duplicate lenses for their glasses only with a prescription from an eye doctor. The statute obviously was the result of lobbying pressure from eye doctors facing competition from

opticians who lacked medical training. According to the Court, the statute was constitutional because the state legislature might have believed that requiring a new prescription was helpful in assuring that consumers would get glasses whose prescriptions suited their needs. As most commentators have recognized, this explanation is extremely weak. In general, the Court's approach to constitutional claims by or against economic interest groups, framed as violations of the DUE PROCESS [2] or EQUAL PROTECTION [2,I] clauses, leaves the matter entirely to the legislature. In that sense, factions are now allowed to control the government.

Some areas of JUDICIAL REVIEW [3,I] dealing with economic matters remain of interest. In enforcing the restrictions that the COMMERCE CLAUSE [1,I] places on STATE REGULATION OF COMMERCE [4,I], the Court has sometimes been sensitive to the role that local interest groups play in securing restrictionist legislation. In *Washington State Apple Advertising Commission v. Hunt* (1977), the Supreme Court invalidated a statute requiring that apples be repackaged in ways that concealed from purchasers the fact—which they might be interested in learning—that some of the apples came from Washington, where particularly good apples are grown. The Court noted in passing that the statute had been adopted at the behest of North Carolina's apple growers, whose apples were less attractive to consumers. In other cases, however, the Court has not been so concerned about the interest-group politics that lies behind legislation. *Exxon Corp. v. Governor of Maryland* (1978) upheld a statute, designed to aid corner gas station owners, prohibiting national gasoline producers from owning retail gas stations in the state.

In addition, the Constitution bars governments from TAKINGS OF PROPERTY [4,I] without JUST COMPENSATION [3] and from impairing the obligation of contracts. In extreme cases, the Supreme Court has been willing to invalidate laws that seem to it to be the product of pure interest-group motivation rather than of sincere consideration of the public interest. In UNITED STATES TRUST CO. OF NEW YORK V. NEW JERSEY (1977) [4], the Court invoked the contract clause to invalidate a New Jersey statute that diverted revenue from tolls on automobiles, which were by contract supposed to be used to pay off road-building bonds, instead using them to support mass transit. In *Nollan v. California Coastal Commission* (1987), the Court invalidated a California statute that had been interpreted to allow an owner of a beachfront residence to expand his house only if he allowed the public to walk across the beach in front of the house. The New Jersey statute might be seen as the result of interest-group lobbying by mass transit commuters, who might be easier to organize than the holders of the road-building bonds, while the California law might be seen as imposing costs on isolated individual owners in the service of the interests of a majority faction.

The significance of these decisions, though, should not be exaggerated; they are controversial, in part because in both there does seem to be a genuine public interest promoted by each of the statutes the Court invalidated. In general, where economic interests are involved, the Court tolerates a great deal of interest-group legislation, even if there seems to be little "public interest" justification for the legislation, although the Court most often does require that the state offer a public interest justification, no matter how weak, for what it does.

Interest groups play another role in modern constitutional law. In UNITED STATES v. CAROLENE PRODUCTS CO. (1938) [1], Justice HARLAN FISKE STONE [4] suggested that laws adversely affecting DISCRETE AND INSULAR MINORITIES [2] would have to be strongly justified to be constitutional. Such minorities might be thought of as a type of interest group, which because of its position in the society is unable to attain political power commensurate with its numbers. Their political opportunities might be blocked by a history of discrimination against them, which might lead members of the groups to believe that attempting to secure government assistance is futile or might demonstrate that a majority consistently undervalues the interests of the minority.

The idea that the courts should be alert to protect these minorities gains much of its force from the experience of blacks in the period before BROWN V. BOARD OF EDUCATION (1954, 1955) [1] and the VOTING RIGHTS ACT OF 1965 [4]. Other candidates for inclusion in the group of DISCRETE AND INSULAR MINORITIES are women, nonmarital children, and the poor. But the Supreme Court has been reluctant to expand the group of protected minorities. In *City of Cleburne v. Cleburne Living Center* (1985), the Court refused to give the mentally retarded formal inclusion in the group, noting that many legislatures had acted to promote the interests of the mentally retarded and that, were they to be treated as a special group, many other groups with "perhaps immutable disabilities" and unable to "mandate the desired legislative responses" (e.g., the aging, the disabled, and the mentally ill) might "claim some degree of prejudice."

The Court has not expanded the list of discrete and insular minorities because it believes that with respect to most groups, the ordinary operation of politics allows any interest group to participate in the process of bargaining and trading votes that leads coalitions to achieve their goals. In many ways, that is the image of politics offered in *The Federalist*, and if the political process works in that way, the Court's reluctance is well founded. Yet Stone's insight regarding the imperfections of the political process suggests that on occasion interest groups might

be unable to secure legislative action no matter how hard they try. Recent theories of the political process offered by students of "public choice" indicate, however, that the difficulty may not be that minority interest groups cannot get their way, but rather that majority groups, those that wish to advance the public interest, might find themselves defeated by well-organized interest groups: the members of the smaller interest groups are likely to have more at stake, and are therefore more likely to organize effectively, than the members of the majority, each of whom has so little at stake that none will make any effort to oppose legislation that imposes substantial costs on the group as a whole.

Public choice theories of the Constitution reinvigorate *The Federalist*'s concern that factions or interest groups might control the government and lead to the adoption of legislation that impairs the public interest. If those theories accurately describe the contemporary scene, however, they show that neither judicial review nor the structures of government on which *The Federalist* relied have been sufficient to curb the influence of faction.

MARK TUSHNET

(SEE ALSO: *Economic Analysis* [2]; *Mental Illness* [3,I]; *Mental Retardation* [3]; *Political Philosophy of the Constitution* [3,I].)

Bibliography

BEARD, CHARLES 1913 *An Economic Interpretation of the Constitution.* New York: Macmillan.

OLSEN, MANCUR 1965 *The Logic of Collective Action.* Cambridge, Mass.: Harvard University Press.

SUSTEIN, CASS 1985 Interest Groups in American Public Law. *Stanford Law Review* 38:29–87.

INTERGOVERNMENTAL TAX IMMUNITIES

To what extent should the federal government be able to collect taxes from the states? To what extent should the states be able to collect taxes from the federal government? The Supreme Court has struggled with these questions for over 170 years.

In 1819, in MCCULLOCH V. MARYLAND [3], the Court held that a state tax on the operations of a bank created by the United States was in violation of the SUPREMACY CLAUSE [4] of the Constitution. Speaking for the Court, Chief Justice JOHN MARSHALL [3] asserted that "the power to tax is the power to destroy" and stated "that the states have no power, by taxation or otherwise, to retard, impede, burden, or in any manner control the operations of the constitutional laws enacted by Congress to carry into the execution the powers vested in the general government." This same logic was used in WESTON V. CITY COUN-

CIL OF CHARLESTON (1829) [4,I] to hold that a city tax imposed on stocks and bonds generally could not be applied to bonds issued by the federal government and in *Dobbins v. Commissioners of Erie County* (1842) to hold that states could not tax the salaries of federal employees.

In COLLECTOR V. DAY (1871) [1] the Court took a major step and held the federal income tax could not be applied to the salaries of state officials. It said the immunity was reciprocal and that the exemption from taxation of the federal government by the states and the states by the federal government "rests upon necessary implication, and is upheld by the great law of self-preservation."

For over half a century the Court applied the intergovernmental immunity doctrine to permit large numbers of private taxpayers to escape federal and state taxes on the ground that the tax burden would be passed on to the federal or state governments. For example, in *Indian Motorcycle Co. v. United States* (1931) the Court held invalid a tax imposed by the United States on the sale of a motorcycle to a city for use in its police force. The Court said that the state and federal governments were equally exempt from taxes by the other. "This principle is implied from the independence of the national and state governments within their respective spheres and from the provisions of the Constitution which look to the maintenance of the dual system." The only exception to this broad doctrine recognized by the Court was that the federal government could impose taxes on state enterprises which departed from usual government functions and engaged in businesses of a private nature, such as running a railroad or selling mineral water.

In the late 1930s, the Court began a process of dismantling the tax immunity doctrine. In GRAVES V. NEW YORK EX REL. O'KEEFE (1939) [2], the Court upheld the imposition of a state income tax on the salary of a federal official, saying, "So much of the burden of a non-discriminatory general tax upon the incomes of employees of a government, state or national, as may be passed on economically to that government through the effect of the tax on the price level of labor or materials, is but the normal incident of the organization within the same territory of two governments, each possessing the taxing power." And, in *Alabama v. King & Boozer* (1941) the Court upheld a state sales tax imposed on a government contractor, even though the financial burden of the tax was entirely passed on to the federal government through a cost-plus contract.

Over the past half-century the Court has reduced the tax immunity doctrine to a very narrow scope. Private parties doing business with the federal government or leasing government property, even for completing a government contract, may be subjected to state taxation. In *United States v. New Mexico* (1982) the Court upheld the right of a state to tax fixed fees paid by the United States to private contractors in return for managing government installations, saying that "tax immunity is appropriate in only one circumstance: when the levy falls on the United States itself, or on an agency or instrumentality so closely connected to the Government that the two cannot realistically be viewed as separate entities." The only limit on the states is that they cannot impose taxes that discriminate against the United States. Thus, in *Davis v. Michigan Department of Treasury* (1989), a state was not permitted to tax the pensions received by federal retirees when it exempted state employees from the same tax.

The immunity of the states is even narrower. The Court assumes that the states themselves or their property cannot be directly subjected to federal taxation, but even here there is an exception permitting the application of nondiscriminatory federal taxes directly to some kinds of state enterprises. Recently, in *South Carolina v. Baker* (1988), the Court said the intergovernmental tax immunity doctrine had been "thoroughly repudiated" and held that the federal government could impose its income tax on the income received from state and local bonds. The federal tax was limited in this case to income from bonds issued in bearer form, but the Court said it could apply to all such bonds if Congress so provided.

Under the supremacy clause the federal government has one additional power: it can expand or retract its immunity from state taxation, permitting states to tax what the Court otherwise would forbid or denying the states the right to tax what the Court would otherwise permit.

The intergovernmental tax immunity doctrine now has so little vitality that it should not interfere with any reasonable, nondiscriminatory taxation by either state or federal governments. Yet attempts to use it persist. In 1989 the Supreme Court had cases in which it held that a state could tax an oil company on profits from producing oil on an Indian reservation; that a state could tax BANKRUPTCY [1] liquidation sales by a bankruptcy trustee; and that a tax on pensions of federal retirees was invalid when it exempted state employees from the same tax.

EDWARD L. BARRETT

(SEE ALSO: *Federalism (History)* [2]; *Federalism (Theory)* [2]; *Federalism (Contemporary Practice)* [I]; *Federalism and Shared Powers* [I].)

Bibliography

ROTUNDA, RONALD D. 1986 Intergovernmental Tax Immunity and Tax-Free Municipals After *Garcia. University of Colorado Law Review* 57:849–869.

INTERPRETIVISM

The rationale that JOHN MARSHALL [3] provided for constitutional review in MARBURY V. MADISON (1803) [3] declared that the Constitution is law and that the courts as courts of law are obliged to apply its dictates, even when the consequence is invalidation of a duly enacted statute. JUDICIAL REVIEW [3] has, of course, evolved into a major pillar of the American governmental system, but exercise of the power has never ceased to arouse controversy. Marshall used several examples of clear violations of explicit constitutional language to bolster the case for judicial review, but such easy cases seldom get to court. In cases that typically do get to court, the constitutional language leaves room for doubt and debate, and the consequent clash between democratic decision making and judicial choice has been a focal point of an ongoing national concern about judicial review.

The contemporary phase of the national soul-searching about judicial review can be traced to a period of JUDICIAL ACTIVISM [3] that began with the Supreme Court's 1954 decision in BROWN V. BOARD OF EDUCATION [1], holding that racial SEGREGATION [4] in public schools is a violation of the EQUAL PROTECTION [2,I] clause of the FOURTEENTH AMENDMENT [2,I]. Starting with *Brown*, the Supreme Court, under the leadership of EARL WARREN [4], tackled a broad range of controversial social issues in the name of the Constitution. Much legislation was struck down, and Warren himself and the WARREN COURT [4] became familiar targets in political debate in 1950s and 1960s. Despite the controversy, the Court did not really approach center stage of the nation's politics until 1973, when, under the leadership of WARREN E. BURGER [1], it held in ROE V. WADE [3] that a woman's interest in decisions about ABORTION [1,I] was constitutionally protected from most state criminal laws and many forms of state regulation. *Brown* had led the way to a rough social consensus in opposition to racial segregation, but *Roe*'s resolution of the abortion issue proved much less prescient. Abortion became the most divisive public issue in the United States in the late twentieth century, and the Supreme Court found itself the object of a great deal of attention in the ensuing political controversy.

Before *Roe*, opponents of the Court's activism had not found much common theoretical ground for their concern. *Roe*, like *Brown*, was decided under the Fourteenth Amendment, but the abortion issue, unlike the racial segregation issue in *Brown*, was rather remote from the problems that had originally inspired the amendment. This fact helped stimulate an academic literature questioning the Court's activism on the ground of its disregard of the ORIGINAL INTENT [I] behind constitutional provisions. These critics urged that constitutional language and original intentions were the preeminent sources on which courts were permitted to draw for guidance in CONSTITUTIONAL INTERPRETATION [1]. This general approach was dubbed "interpretivism," and the neologism stuck, as did the even uglier NONINTERPRETIVISM [I] to mean an insis-

tence that the courts could legitimately be guided in constitutional decisions by values of the culture not fairly traceable to constitutional language or to original intentions.

The dispute between interpretivists and noninterpretivists found its way into political discourse, especially during the presidency of RONALD REAGAN [3,I], when Attorney General Edwin Meese railed against judicial activism and called for a return to a "jurisprudence of original intention." The dispute achieved an unusual degree of public visibility in 1987 when President Reagan nominated Robert Bork to succeed LEWIS F. POWELL [3,I] for a seat on the Supreme Court. Powell had been a swing vote on a Court closely divided on a variety of issues, and the identity of his successor drew unusual attention from various interested groups. Bork had aligned himself with the interpretivist position, first in academic writings and later in speeches he gave while serving as a judge on the United States Court of Appeals for the District of Columbia Circuit. He viewed noninterpretivism as rampant among judges and scholars and as an illegitimate intrusion by the courts into both LEGISLATIVE POWER [3] and EXECUTIVE PREROGATIVE [I]. On that ground, Bork had expressed doubt about such decisions as GRISWOLD V. CONNECTICUT (1965) [2], protecting access to BIRTH CONTROL [1] devices against state prohibition. This and other positions on constitutional law that Bork viewed as matters of interpretivist principle became points of contention in the televised hearings on his nomination and surely contributed to his defeat in the Senate.

In addition to being ugly, the terms "interpretivism" and "noninterpretivism" were never terribly apt, for both sides purported to "interpret" the constitution. Gradually the synonymous and more descriptive (though perhaps not much less ugly) terms ORIGINALISM [I] and "nonoriginalism" gained currency in the 1980s. Terminology aside, the distinction between interpretivism and noninterpretivism proved elusive under close examination. The most extreme form of interpretivism insisted that constitutional questions must be referred to an almost mechanical process of application of constitutional language and original intentions. In this strong form, interpretivism would surely defang the activist tiger, but commentators quickly exposed weaknesses in any pretense of interpretivism to answer constitutional questions by resorting to constitutional language and intention alone. Many of the criticisms suggested difficulties in softer versions of interpretivism as well.

Perhaps the most obvious problem is with the inadequacy of the historical record for so many key constitutional provisions. Lawyers and judges are not trained in historical research, and even if they were, they would find that history itself requires interpretation that necessarily draws on the cultural framework, and hence the values, of the inquirer. But those interpretive difficulties are substantially compounded by the sparseness of the historical record in the case of the original Constitution and many of the amendments. Reports of the debates in the state conventions called to ratify the original Constitution are particularly sketchy. In some cases, the official reports are virtually nonexistent, and newspaper or other informal reports that have survived are suspect or even demonstrably inaccurate.

This historical problem plays on another—the conceptual difficulty of combining intentions of the individual actors in enactment of constitutional provisions into an authoritative corporate intention. The Confederation Congress, the CONSTITUTIONAL CONVENTION OF 1787 [1], and the several state ratifying conventions all played important roles in the original Constitution. But there is no consensus about the right way to sum the individual states of mind of the participants for any one body, let alone for all the relevant bodies combined. In the case of the original Constitution, for instance, we usually recur to the intentions of the Framers at the Constitutional Convention, who did not have a formal role in the adoption of the document, and ignore the intentions of the delegates to the state ratifying conventions, who did. This is done without any particular theoretical justification. Just suggestive of the many questions that any thoroughgoing response to the summing problem would have to address are whether the mental frameworks of persons who voted against the Constitution or some provision of it are to be counted, whether views of sponsors of language count more than views of others with equal votes, and whether ratifying conventions after the required nine initial ratifications matter.

In practice, of course, we do rely comfortably on explanations by participants expressed contemporaneously with the enactment process. The dominant source in the case of the original Constitution is THE FEDERALIST [2]. The essays of *The Federalist* are attractive for a variety of reasons, but most especially because of JAMES MADISON's [3] authorship of so many of them and because they represent an intellectual tour de force that provides a compelling rationale for the Constitution. But those are hardly answers to the historical difficulty or to the summing problem. Indeed, *The Federalist* was produced after the Convention and as advocacy, rather than as a faithful reflection of the contemporaneous intentions of the Constitution's draftsmen. As such, *The Federalist* may well have been influential for members of the ratifying conventions in ways it could not have been for members of the Constitutional Convention. Ironically, *The Federalist* may thus provide evidence of intention—albeit strictly circumstantial evidence—for a group that is largely ignored in the literature about original intentions, while not providing much evidence at all for the group with which, because of Madison's central role at the Convention, they are more commonly associated.

It is interesting that the summing and historical problems have caused so little anguish. We have not seemed disabled by the lack of a summing algorithm or by the lack of historical evidence. This is probably so because we appreciate intuitively that all those states of mind were important as inputs to the real product of the constitutional process, the language of the document itself, about which there is no doubt at all. Intentions, in contrast, are suggestive guides to interpretation, helpful because language does not apply itself, because the views of those involved in the process are likely to provide useful perspectives, and because we have come to learn that the views of some—Madison and ALEXANDER HAMILTON [2] in particular—contain special insight and special wisdom about the American constitutional system. The usefulness of what can be learned about original intentions is surely not unrelated to their historic association with the enactment of the Constitution, but their usefulness is not logically bound up with that association. And we need neither summing formulas nor definitive evidence to make use of the ideas those intentions provide.

Other critics of interpretivism have emphasized the ambiguity of what in an individual's mental framework is meant by his "intentions." Ronald Dworkin, for example, has pointed out that there may be a distinction between the hopes and the expectations of a constitutional draftsman. And these two may be different from what the draftsman fears his language may come to mean. A further difficulty of this sort is in specifying the level of generality at which the authoritative intentions are taken to be held. Lawmakers, for instance, will typically have had exemplary instances in mind of things that would be fostered or forbidden by the law. The language they enact, however, will usually be expressed generally rather than as a list of specific goals or specific evils. The framers of the Fourteenth Amendment, for instance, clearly assumed that specific discriminatory statutes of the southern states, known collectively as the BLACK CODES [2], would be forbidden by the amendment, while the constitutional language they chose is exceedingly general. When the language is that general, it would be strange indeed to confine the reach of the amendment to the exemplary instances, or even to matters closely analogous to those exemplary instances. Nor would it likely be faithful to any probable reconstruction of original intentions. The generality of the language suggests that many of those involved must have had more general norms in mind in addition to the exemplary instances. Thus, even if the historical evidence is plentiful and the summing problem somehow overcome, the interpreter must at a minimum mediate between levels of generality at which intentions almost surely were simultaneously held.

A further difficulty lies in the role of PRECEDENT [3] in an interpretivist scheme. The animating force behind the interpretivist approach is a desire for stability and certainty in constitutional law that requires the taming of judicial activism. Original intentions are assumed to be an unchanging lodestar providing both stability and certainty. But what then happens if there has been an earlier decision that now appears mistaken by original-intention lights? The earlier decision will have induced reliance and will for a time at least have defined the "law" on the question. If that decision must be overruled on the basis of persuasive new historical data—to say nothing of a new judgment about the import of old data—the goals of stability and certainty are not served, but undermined. In addition, it is not clear how one would approach the role of precedent in original-intention terms. This is really part of a larger problem that Paul Brest has referred to as the problem of "interpretive intention." It is perfectly possible for someone involved in constitution making to believe that a given problem will be resolved one way under language he votes to enact but that precedential developments, a change in external circumstances, or even a change of heart by judges might appropriately lead to a different result. It is perfectly possible, that is, for constitution makers to appreciate that they are setting in motion a decisional process, grounded in a desire to eradicate certain bad things or foster certain good ones, but not inextricably tied to any list of what is forbidden or desired. In that case, the intender's substantive and interpretive intentions can well suggest opposed results. If we somehow had access to the full complexity of original intention, we might resolve the conflict, but not necessarily in any way that would provide stability and certainty in the law. This problem of interpretive intention is particularly acute in a system like the American one, where long tradition antedating the Constitution requires courts to defer significantly to prior decisions. In such a context, it seems quite likely that constitution makers took for granted that STARE DECISIS [4] would have its due in constitutional law.

Interpretivist responses to these criticisms were complex and varied. While some interpretivists clung to a vision of original intentions that virtually applied themselves, most acknowledged that generally stated constitutional language had to leave room for judgment and hence choice by the courts. Some interpretivists, for instance, acknowledged that the intentions the judges were to apply were appropriately conceived at a level of substantial generality. Others embraced a role for precedent in constitu-

tional law. Still others saw room for arguments from changed circumstances or from aspects of the constitutional system that did not come neatly packaged in a clause or an amendment. But the more these extratextual and extraintentional considerations are allowed to intrude, the more blurred becomes the line between the opposed interpretivist and noninterpretivist camps.

This is not to say that either side relented or that there was no difference between the two. Noninterpretivism had no unified approach to interpretation to offer. Some noninterpretivists advanced moral and POLITICAL PHILOSOPHY [3,I] as the appropriate source for constitutional values when constitutional language ran out. Others urged judges to search for answers in conventional morality. Some saw judges as striving for a sort of global coherence in the law, while others urged adherence to precedent in more restricted domains. They were united only in their disdain for the oversimplified view of interpretation advanced by interpretivists, but the lack of any coherent noninterpretivist program reinforced the interpretivist view that noninterpretivism invited judicial tyranny.

As the debate proceeded, it became increasingly apparent that what was really at issue was the appropriate degree of judicial activism in a constitutional democracy, that interpretivism represented an appealing if ultimately unpersuasive theoretical grounding for the position that judges are constitutionally bound to exercise the judicial veto in only the clearest of cases. Despite protestations to the contrary, the two sides differed more in how clear the case had to be than in the type of evidence that could be considered. Differences over the role of original intentions were thus really ones of attitude and degree rather than anything more fundamental. It was interesting that, aside from Robert Bork, few judges joined the fray, and when they did, they seldom did so in the language of interpretivism and noninterpretivism. As the 1980s drew to a close, it appeared that political conservatives had largely prevailed in their campaign for a constrained judiciary. After ANTHONY M. KENNEDY [I] succeeded to Lewis Powell's seat on the Court, Chief Justice WILLIAM H. REHNQUIST [3,I] presided over a Supreme Court majority that articulated a philosophy of "judicial restraint" in constitutional review, but it was not a majority that did so under the banner of interpretivism.

ROBERT W. BENNETT

(SEE ALSO: *Bork Nomination* [I]; *Judicial Activism and Judicial Restraint* [3]; *Ratifier Intent* [I].)

Bibliography

BENNETT, ROBERT W. 1984 Objectivity in Constitutional Law. *University of Pennsylvania Law Review* 132:445–496.

BREST, PAUL 1980 The Misconceived Quest for Original Understanding. *Boston University Law Review* 60:204–238.

DWORKIN, RONALD   1981   The Forum of Principle. *New York University Law Review* 56:469–518.

MONOGHAN, HENRY P.   1981   Our Perfect Constitution. *New York University Law Review* 56:353–396.

IRAN-CONTRA AFFAIR

The Iran-Contra hearings by a joint committee of both houses of Congress (the Senate Committee on Secret Military Assistance to Iran and the Nicaraguan Opposition and the House of Representatives Select Committee to Investigate Covert Arms Transactions with Iran) were but one more episode in the almost constant twentieth-century battle between the presidency—not necessarily the President, but the executive branch and particularly the officials of the White House—and Congress for power over FOREIGN AFFAIRS [2] assigned by the Constitution to the national government. Iran-Contra, like WATERGATE [4] and the Steel Seizure Controversy, stands out among the few instances in which Congress mounted a successful, albeit short-lived, challenge to a thrust for power by the White House.

Following the debacle of the VIETNAM WAR [4,I], initiated by President JOHN F. KENNEDY [3] and carried on disastrously by Presidents LYNDON B. JOHNSON [3] and RICHARD M. NIXON [3] without a specific congressional declaration of war, the United States found itself chastened, but not necessarily enlightened, by the experience. A large but by no means unanimous portion of the population wished to continue the fight against communism wherever it could be found, but preferably on foreign soil and, if necessary, without the endorsement of Congress. If American lives were wasted by unsuccessful military adventures in Korea and Vietnam, eventually bringing peace without honor, perhaps clandestine support of anticommunist guerrillas, in Central America with the approval of Congress could bring us honor without peace. After many years of unrestrained but unsuccessful activity in which American matériel and largess were profligately expended, along with the lives of the residents, Congress decided to call a halt to at least some of its clandestine support for insurgent forces below America's southern border, absent congressional approval. And when Congress discovered—it was an all but open secret—that secret operations in the foreign affairs apparatus of the White House were providing the wherewithal for much of the military resistance in Central America, in defiance of congressional law, a hearing was called to establish who, what, why, and when. As in Watergate, the hearings were politically dangerous because they came so close to involving the President himself in illegality. Unlike the case of Watergate, however, the President—in this instance,

RONALD REAGAN [3,I]—seemed more guilty of nonfeasance than malfeasance, as an investigation by a committee that the President had appointed, with former Senator John Tower as chairman, seemed to indicate in its report.

Fundamentally, the obligation of the President and his aides to abide by the terms of the laws enacted by Congress are not to be gainsaid. According to Article II, section 3, of the Constitution, the President "shall take care that the Laws be faithfully executed." Occasionally, the question may legitimately arise whether in fact that language rightfully cabins the chief executive in the circumstances and there is a conflict between the two branches, which becomes a question of constitutional dimensions. Usually, the contesting sides reach a peaceful understanding. Sometimes the issue has to be resolved by the courts, as was the case when President HARRY S. TRUMAN [4] seized the steel mills or when the executive branch froze the assets of the Iranian government without congressional authorization. Sometimes the controversy reaches the forum of a congressional hearing, as was the case with Watergate and again with the Iran-Contra controversy.

Prior to WORLD WAR I [I], the United States was governed by what Woodrow Wilson could label "congressional government" in his 1913 book of that title, which did not mean that Congress did not succumb to strong presidential leadership, such as ABRAHAM LINCOLN's [3], in times of crisis. During and after WORLD WAR II [I], government in the United States became the eponymous "presidential dictatorship" of CLINTON ROSSITER's [3] 1985 volume, with Congress usually subordinated to the will expressed by the President. Since the KOREAN WAR [3], there has been a further realignment of power, again described by an astute critic's title, Arthur Schlesinger's *The Imperial Presidency* (1973), this time marking not a shift between Congress and the President but a development within the presidency of an unelected, politically irresponsible BUREAUCRACY [1,I].

It may well be that a congressional investigation of alleged wrongdoing at the level of the White House serves its function when it is called to the public's attention, when the wrongdoing that has taken place is brought to an end, and when some of the principal responsible presidential subordinates are subjected to criminal processes in the United States courts or otherwise chastised. Clearly the intent of the Framers was to fix the responsibility on the President for the conduct of his office. But we live now in more perilous times. If the continued threat of serious malefaction is to be eliminated, the price of the IMPEACHMENT [2] process to determine whether the chief executive has erred is nevertheless too destabilizing in times of crisis for the nation to pay for such hearings. The national government was paralyzed for months in the Watergate crisis. Thus, the Iran-Contra affair may not have afforded as satisfying a resolution of the questions first raised by Senator Howard Baker: "What did the President know? And when did he know it?" But the Constitution's interests were served, and the nation's interests were protected.

The Iran-Contra hearings, however consequential in theory, were a contest for constitutional power between President and Congress, and were generally regarded by the American public as entertainment rather than enlightenment. It was as if some of Hollywood's second-rate script writers had concocted a "B" version of the Watergate hearings. Everyone was covering up for a generally beloved and pathetically inept President, who could not remember what had occurred in his meetings with his national security staff. There was a handsome Marine veteran wrapped in the flag and dedicated to the extermination of communists and communism by means in or out of the Constitution's limits. There was his beauteous secretary devoted to her boss, who helped destroy and remove secret documents. There were professional spies, cabinet officers locked out of the deliberations, national security chiefs, past and present. There were strange and sinister-looking Middle Eastern arms merchants. And there was a Rasputin figure, who, fortunately for the goals of the hearings, had died before his evidence could be secured. If the purpose of the Iran-Contra hearings were to prove that congressional hearings about the conduct of the presidential office can be a futile and useless CHECK AND BALANCE [1] of one branch of the government on the other, the hearings succeeded beyond a peradventure of doubt. They also proved what "every schoolboy knew," that the American government had been secretly negotiating with Iran for the release of American prisoners and that it was supplying weapons to the Contra forces in Nicaragua—the first, in contradiction of the Reagan administration's own frequently announced policy; the second, at least without and likely in contradiction of congressional mandate. This is not the way American government is supposed to work.

After the hearings, many of the witnesses were indicted and some pleaded guilty to various offenses while others were found guilty. None of the major figures received heavy sentences. Lt. Col. Oliver North, the popular hero of the tale, was sentenced to 1200 hours of community service and fined $150,000 on three felony counts of willfully obstructing the congressional investigation, but his conviction was reversed—ironically, on civil liberties grounds. Robert McFarlane, former national security adviser to the President, pleaded guilty to four misdemeanor counts of assisting in secret efforts illegally to aid the Contras. He received two years probation, a $20,000 fine and 200 hours of community service. Admiral John M. Poindexter, Reagan's national security adviser and North's superior, did get six months on five counts of conspiracy.

PHILIP B. KURLAND

(SEE ALSO: *Constitutional History 1980–1989* [I].)

Bibliography

COHEN, WILLIAN and MITCHELL, GEORGE 1988 *Men of Zeal.* New York: Viking.
JOINT HEARINGS ON THE IRAN-CONTRA INVESTIGATION. 1987–1988 Washington D.C.: U.S. Government Printing Office.
REPORT OF THE JOINT CONGRESSIONAL COMMITTEE INVESTIGATING THE IRAN-CONTRA AFFAIR 1988 Washington, D.C.: U.S. Government Printing Office.

ITEM VETO

SEE: Line Item Veto

J

JACKSONIANISM

The election of ANDREW JACKSON [3] to the presidency in 1828 was only the second time since the adoption of the Constitution that the "out" party came to power. The first occurred in 1800 with the election of THOMAS JEFFERSON [3], who at that time opted for a course of action that stressed moderation and reconciliation. Jefferson revised several of the government's policies and changed many of its personnel, but he refused to go along with any assault on the Constitution itself or on major FEDERALIST [I] enactments. If anything, through the LOUISIANA PURCHASE TREATY [3] and the EMBARGO ACTS [2] of 1807–1809, he increased the powers of the national government. Jackson took a very different approach. He favored amendment of the Constitution and other policies to make the central government more amenable to popular control. Jackson also championed a strict interpretation of the Constitution and the decentralization of authority, stressing the close links between the will of the people, majority rule, and STATES' RIGHTS [4]. He also was critical of the broad powers of interpretation that the Supreme Court had arrogated to itself over the preceding quarter-century.

Although the campaign of 1828 was particularly scurrilous, with much of it centered on the candidates' personalities, it also involved fundamental constitutional and even ideological considerations. Jackson's opponent, JOHN QUINCY ADAMS [1], had organized his whole administration and run for reelection on a platform of the AMERICAN SYSTEM [I]—a federal program of INTERNAL IMPROVEMENTS [2], a high protective tariff, and the second BANK OF THE UNITED STATES [1]—which was predicated upon a loose interpretation of the Constitution and the need

for a strong and active national government. These views were a major issue in the election of 1828, and opposition to them explains much of the support Jackson received in the South, the Old West, and the Middle Atlantic states, from people who had strong emotional and ideological ties to ANTIFEDERALISM [1] and Old Republicanism. This group—which included THOMAS HART BENTON [1], Amos Kendall, Silas Wright, Francis Preston Blair, NATHANIEL MACON [3], and Thomas Ritchie—was strongly committed to the view of the origin and nature of the Union that had been articulated in the VIRGINIA AND KENTUCKY RESOLUTIONS [4] of 1798–1799. These resolutions viewed the Constitution as the product of a compact between the different states and asserted that the federal government was one of clearly defined and specifically delegated and limited powers. The resolutions denied that the Supreme Court was either the exclusive or final arbiter of constitutional questions and argued instead that the states should act as sentinels to watch over the activities of the federal government. They believed that these principles had been validated by Jefferson's election in 1800, but that they had been abandoned as the country pursued wealth and power between 1801 and 1828. Jackson's most avid supporters wanted him to reverse this development and to return the country to plain republican principles, and they justified this by invoking the "Spirit of '98."

Jackson did not disappoint them. He began by advocating the principle of rotation of office for federal officeholders. This had been a popular constitutional concept in the 1780s and had found expression in the ARTICLES OF CONFEDERATION [1], the PENNSYLVANIA CONSTITUTION OF 1776 [3], and a number of other STATE CONSTITUTIONS [4]. The failure to include it in the United States Constitution had been a major concern of the Antifederalists, and Jackson's espousal of it in regard to presidential appointments was considered by his opponents to be a direct assault on the Constitution. Throughout his first administration Jackson also urged that the Constitution be amended to eliminate the ELECTORAL COLLEGE [2], limit the tenure of the President and vice-president to a single term of four or six years, provide for the popular election of senators and members of the federal judiciary, and give self-government to the DISTRICT OF COLUMBIA [2]. He and most of his closest advisers also favored a repeal of section 25 of the JUDICIARY ACT OF 1789 [3].

But these proposals were never endorsed by Congress, which was at odds with Jackson throughout most of his two terms in office. As a consequence, Jackson was forced to enunciate his views of the Constitution through his various annual addresses, veto messages, proclamations, policy decisions, and appointments. In these ways, Jackson made clear his opposition to a federal program of internal improvements on both constitutional and policy grounds. He also vetoed the bill to recharter the second Bank of the United States, in large part because its activities impinged on the rights of the states. Moreover, in exercising this veto and in implementing his policy toward AMERICAN INDIANS [I], he took direct issue with the nationalist claim that the Supreme Court was the exclusive or final arbiter in disputes between the federal and state governments. Jackson also appointed five Justices to the Supreme Court—JOHN MCLEAN [3], HENRY BALDWIN [1], JAMES M. WAYNE [4], PHILIP P. BARBOUR [1], and ROGER BROOKE TANEY [4] as CHIEF JUSTICE [1]—who were unsympathetic to the BROAD CONSTRUCTION [1] and the nationalist decisions of the MARSHALL COURT [3].

Although deeply committed to the concept of states' rights, the Jacksonians had no sympathy for the doctrine of NULLIFICATION [3], promulgated by JOHN C. CALHOUN [1] and South Carolina, who believed that the protective tariffs of 1828 and 1832 were unconstitutional and who were concerned with protecting the institution of SLAVERY [4] from outside interference. The Jacksonians, for their part, advocated states' rights as a way of achieving majority rule, while the proslavery interests espoused the doctrine of states' rights as a way of protecting the interests of a minority. The difference can be seen most clearly in the two groups' positions on the issues of when and by whom the Constitution should be amended. The Jacksonians, consistent with their faith in majority rule, took upon themselves the burden of obtaining amendments to the Constitution in order to make the federal government more directly responsive to the will of the people and to limit and clarify the powers of the Supreme Court. Such a course would require the approval of two-thirds of both houses of Congress and three-quarters of the states.

Historically, these have been difficult majorities to obtain, and the Jacksonians were never successful. Proslavery interests, on the other hand, argued during the nullification crisis that a single state had a right to nullify federal law and that, in the event of nullification, the law's proponents would have the responsibility of gaining the requisite majorities to alter the Constitution. This argument shifted in a decisive way the burden of obtaining the amendment.

Jacksonians also opposed Calhoun's version of the states' rights doctrine because they believed it threatened the existence of the Union. The right of states to secede from the Union had not traditionally been part of the concept of states' rights. The Jacksonian commitment to the rights of the states in no way precluded a belief that the Union was perpetual or that within its properly limited sphere of power (like the making of tariff laws) the federal government was supreme. The Jacksonians rejected the nullifiers' claim that SECESSION [4] was a legal or constitutional right that could be peacefully exercised. Instead, they insisted it was only a natural or revolutionary right that had to be fought for and could be suppressed.

After Jackson left office, the Jacksonian interpretation of the Constitution dominated the administrations of three other Presidents. MARTIN VAN BUREN [4] was a product of the Virginia–New York alliance that played such a dominant role in the politics of the early Republic and that had its roots in the strong Antifederalist tradition in both these states. As President, Van Buren was a strong advocate of states' rights, opposed a federal program of internal improvements, and implemented the independent treasury system, which divorced banking from the federal government. JAMES K. POLK [3] was also a doctrinaire Jacksonian. He prevented the creation of a third Bank of the United States, reinstated the independent treasury system, and further circumscribed federal spending on internal improvements. FRANKLIN PIERCE [3] also viewed the world from a Jacksonian perspective. He had a great respect for states' rights and opposed the federal government's involvement in the ECONOMY [I].

The Jacksonians were never proslavery in the sense that Calhoun and other southerners were, but they shared an antipathy to abolitionists, who wanted the federal government to move against the "peculiar institution." In fact, the Jacksonians never developed an effective position on the slavery question—a failure that, as much as anything else, explains the lack of success of two other Presidents who had roots in Jacksonianism, JAMES BUCHANAN [1] and ANDREW JOHNSON [3].

Nonetheless, while the Jacksonian constitutional position did not lead to any basic changes in the Constitution itself and its orientation toward states' rights and strict interpretation was overturned by the extreme nationalist thrust of the CIVIL WAR [I], it did dominate much of

American politics in the second third of the nineteenth century.

RICHARD E. ELLIS

(SEE ALSO: *Amending Process* [1]; *Cherokee Indian Cases* [1]; *Tariff Act of 1828* [4]; *Whig Party* [I].)

Bibliography

ELLIS, RICHARD E. 1987 *The Union at Risk: Jacksonian Democracy, States' Rights, and the Nullification Crisis.* New York: Oxford University Press.

REMINI, ROBERT V. 1988 *The Legacy of Andrew Jackson: Essays on Democracy, Indian Removal, and Slavery.* Baton Rouge: Louisiana State University Press.

VAN DEUSEN, GLYNDON G. 1959 *The Jacksonian Era, 1828–1848.* New York: Harper and Row.

JEFFERSONIANISM

THOMAS JEFFERSON [3] wished to be remembered as the author of the DECLARATION OF INDEPENDENCE [2] and as the founder of the University of Virginia, but history has credited him with much more. In the world of practical politics, Jefferson's achievements were legion—legal reformer, wartime governor of Virginia, author of the VIRGINIA STATUTE OF RELIGIOUS LIBERTY [4], draftsman of the great Ordinance of 1784, first secretary of state, leader of the "loyal opposition" in the administration of JOHN ADAMS [1], third President of the United States, purchaser of Louisiana, father of the Democratic party, and founder of the first political party system. In the world of ideas, Jefferson was the nation's premier advocate of political democracy, POPULAR SOVEREIGNTY [3], and a republican system of government. He was also a staunch advocate of public education, progressivism, and the RULE OF LAW [3] both at home and abroad.

Somewhat less appreciated than these enduring contributions to the nation's history was Jefferson's role in the development of a theory of CONSTITUTIONALISM [2] that, after two centuries, continues to inform the American commitment to constitutional government. Jefferson's first inaugural address (March 4, 1801), one of the nation's great state papers, provides a glimpse into part, though not all, of Jefferson's constitutional vision. Directing his remarks to the Washington community in the newly established seat of government in the DISTRICT OF COLUMBIA [2], Jefferson reflected upon those axioms of the American system that he prized above all. Referring to majoritarian rule as a "sacred principle," Jefferson reminded his listeners "that though the will of the majority is in all cases to prevail, that will to be rightful must be reasonable; that the minority possess their equal rights, which equal law must protect, and to violate would be oppression." In

one of the most remarkable statements on the value of FREEDOM OF SPEECH [2,I] in a free society, Jefferson declared, "If there be any among us who would wish to dissolve this Union or to change its republican form, let them stand undisturbed as monuments of the safety with which error of opinion may be tolerated where reason is left free to combat it." And with a single phrase, Jefferson identified the constitutional value whose full implementation has been the cornerstone of modern American constitutional JURISPRUDENCE [I]: "Equal and exact justice to all . . . of whatever state or persuasion, religious or political."

The elements of Jeffersonian constitutionalism were these: the preservation of FUNDAMENTAL RIGHTS [2]; the preeminence of the legislative branch in a government of separated powers; the integrity of the sovereign states in a federal union of shared and divided powers; strict adherence by Congress to those powers delegated to it in the written Constitution; RELIGIOUS LIBERTY [3,I] as guaranteed by a regime in which church and state remained apart; and a recognition of the need for frequent constitutional change through the process of constitutional amendment. The fact that Jefferson himself, out of political necessity, may have trespassed upon some of these principles when he became President does not undercut their value, importance, and durability to the development of American constitutionalism.

Jeffersonian constitutionalism emerged in sharp relief to the constitutionalism of the Federalists in the political crisis brought on by the passage of the ALIEN AND SEDITION ACTS [1] in 1798. These Federalist enactments had two chief purposes—to undermine the support the Jeffersonian opposition was receiving from French refugees, recent immigrants, and resident aliens (the Alien Act) and to stifle the Jeffersonian press (the Sedition Act). Although never tested definitively in the Supreme Court, the Sedition Act was recognized and implemented by the lower federal courts. The Jeffersonian response took cogent form as resolutions of principle adopted by the legislatures of Kentucky and Virginia. Jefferson, who was then vice-president of the United States in the administration of the Federalist John Adams, secretly prepared the Kentucky Resolutions, while JAMES MADISON [3], Jefferson's closest political ally, wrote the Virginia Resolutions.

The VIRGINIA AND KENTUCKY RESOLUTIONS [4] vigorously defended the cause of CIVIL LIBERTIES [1,I] against encroachment by the federal government. At a time when the Supreme Court had yet to assert its power of JUDICIAL REVIEW [3,I] over Congress and when FIRST AMENDMENT [2,I] and Fifth Amendment guarantees were nothing more than "parchment barriers" against governmental tyranny, the resolutions represented the only formal defense then available against the exercise of excessive federal power.

The resolutions are replete with Jeffersonian principles of constitutionalism—defense of civil liberties, support for the integrity of the states, LIMITED GOVERNMENT [3], DUE PROCESS OF LAW [2], faithfulness to the language of the written constitutional text, fear of federal "consolidation," and the importance of having an authority located somewhere (in this case, the states) with jurisdiction to declare federal laws unconstitutional.

Although the Virginia and Kentucky resolutions were primarily designed as a "solemn protest" against the abuse of power, the resolutions also advanced a theory of federal union. Both Jefferson and Madison characterized the union as a "compact" among the several states. Under this theory of FEDERALISM [2,I], each state reserved to itself, as a contracting party to the compact, the "equal right to judge for itself, as well of infractions [by the general government] as of the mode and measure of redress." In subsequent resolutions, the Virginia and Kentucky legislatures even proposed the doctrine of state NULLIFICATION [3] as a proper remedy against unlawful federal usurpations. However, the states north of Virginia repudiated this notion as well as the compact theory itself and called upon the federal judiciary rather than the states to decide upon matters of constitutionality. As the Rhode Island legislature would put it, Article III of the Constitution "vests in the Federal Courts, exclusively, and in the Supreme Court, ultimately, the authority of deciding on the constitutionality of any act or law of the Congress of the United States." Thus, the Virginia and Kentucky Resolutions, in an indirect way, helped to pave the way for MARBURY V. MADISON (1803) [3], the Supreme Court's first clear assertion of its power of judicial review.

The compact theory proposed by the Jeffersonians in the Virginia and Kentucky Resolutions did not die with the demise of the Alien and Sedition Acts. Rather, it was resurrected and then distorted by the state of South Carolina in an ordinance nullifying the tariff of 1832. Even James Madison repudiated South Carolina's version of the compact theory. So did the then President ANDREW JACKSON [3]. Subsequently, the theory became closely identified with the cause of the slaveholding states, who used it to defend SECESSION [4] in the winter of 1860–1861. The Union victory in the CIVIL WAR [I] thoroughly discredited the theory once and for all, and the Supreme Court finally repudiated it as a doctrine of constitutional law in the case of TEXAS V. WHITE (1869) [4]. Nevertheless, compact theory continued to show signs of life in the twentieth century in the fight for STATES' RIGHTS [4] against centralization in Washington during the NEW DEAL [I], in the conservative response to the CIVIL RIGHTS MOVEMENT in the 1950s and 1960s, and even more recently when states with unique problems, such as Alaska, have protested against perceived unfairness in treatment by the national government.

Jeffersonian constitutionalism had many notable adherents. The well-known Virginia senator John Taylor of Caroline County attacked Federalist constitutional theories and defended local democracy and states' rights in numerous books and pamphlets. St. George Tucker, the Virginia jurist, annotated the most influential edition of *Blackstone's Commentaries* (five volumes, 1803). But Jeffersonian constitutionalism achieved its most forceful and articulate expression in the jurisprudence of Judge SPENCER ROANE [3] of the Virginia Supreme Court of Appeals. From the time of his election to that court in 1794 until his death in 1822, Roane became one of the staunchest advocates of Jeffersonianism, speaking from one of the nation's most important state courts. He became Chief Justice John Marshall's chief antagonist in the debate over federal power, a debate that surfaced in a series of great constitutional cases. In numerous pamphlets and newspaper articles, as well as in his judicial opinions, Roane applied Jeffersonian constitutional principles with unparalleled consistency. He believed in the coequal power of the states, he challenged the JUDICIAL SUPREMACY [3] of the Supreme Court in deciding matters of federal constitutionality, and he believed that the preservation of the Union depended upon a narrow construction of the powers delegated to Congress.

But the Jeffersonians were not single-minded in their views on the federal Constitution. Justice WILLIAM JOHNSON [3], a Jefferson appointee to the Supreme Court who sat from 1804 to 1834, shared the Jeffersonian belief in the primacy of the legislative branch in any government of separated powers and the Jeffersonian fear of the federal judiciary. Thus, in the case of *United States v. Hudson and Goodwin* (1812), Johnson wrote that the federal courts did not have jurisdiction to try COMMON LAW [1] crimes without expressed legislative authorization from Congress. But where powers were given to the legislature, as in Article I, section 8, of the Constitution, Johnson believed that they should be amply interpreted. Although he was noted for his many dissents to the strongly nationalist jurisprudence of the Marshall Court, Johnson went along with Marshall's great decision in McCULLOCH V. MARYLAND (1819) [3], which broadly defined congressional power under the NECESSARY AND PROPER CLAUSE [3]. And in a CONCURRING OPINION [1] in the famous COMMERCE CLAUSE case [3] of GIBBONS V. OGDEN (1824) [2], Johnson declared that "the [commerce] power must be exclusive; it can reside but in one potentate; and hence, the grant of this power carries with it the whole subject, leaving nothing for the State to act upon." Johnson thus invited the wrath of Jeffersonian purists, who rejected the doctrines of IMPLIED POWERS [2] and exclusive federal control over commerce. They believed that Johnson had become something of a crypto-Federalist.

JOHN C. CALHOUN [1], secretary of war in the administration of JAMES MONROE [3], vice-president under both JOHN QUINCY ADAMS [1] and Andrew Jackson, United States senator from South Carolina from 1832 to 1844, and secretary of state under John Tyler, was one of Jefferson's principal political heirs. While history has rightly tagged Calhoun as the architect of southern nationalism and as a principal defender of southern SLAVERY [4], Calhoun also composed one of America's most original political treatises, the *Disquisition on Government* (1853), which advanced novel theories of the Constitution. Although Calhoun's specific interest was the antebellum South's sectional concern for its "peculiar institution" (slavery), his articulation of the special problems of minorities in a majoritarian culture and his efforts to devise mechanisms to protect minority interests—such as the notion of the "concurrent majority"—contributed much to the totality of the American political experience. This, too, was part of the tradition of Jeffersonian constitutionalism.

Despite the checkered history of the compact theory, Jeffersonian views on the importance of the states in the structure of the Union have become the basis of modern neofederalism. Neofederalism rests upon an efficiency-utility theory that posits that the central government cannot take repsonsibility for all domestic issues and that, as Justice LOUIS D. BRANDEIS [1] said in dissent in the case of NEW STATE ICE COMPANY V. LIEBMANN (1932) [3], states can serve as "laboratories" for social experimentation, particularly in times of economic distress. Because the states have often been ahead of the federal government in devising innovative solutions to novel social problems, state power and authority need to be promoted. A second rationale for modern neofederalism is that some states have unique problems that only they can properly address. A national solution may be inappropriate. Therefore, the integrity of state power deserves respect because state governments are, as Jefferson himself said in his first inaugural, "the most competent administrations of domestic concerns."

Jeffersonian constitutionalism has had its most dramatic manifestation in the twentieth century in the Supreme Court's development of civil liberties as the cornerstone of constitutional law. In their protest against the Alien and Sedition Acts, the Jeffersonians anticipated this development when they articulated a very liberal theory of speech and press freedom. And it was Jefferson who spoke of "a wall of separation between church and state," a concept that the modern Supreme Court has repeatedly affirmed. American religious pluralism, nurtured by the Supreme Court's sensitivity to the requirements of the ESTABLISHMENT CLAUSE [I] of the First Amendment, owes much to the works and thought of Jefferson and Madison, the foremost champions of religious freedom in the early Republic.

The revival of state constitutional law as an alternative forum and mechanism for constitutional adjudication is another legacy of the Jeffersonian tradition. As the Supreme Court continues to consolidate and, in some instances, to cut back on its past advances in the field of individual rights, state supreme courts, under their own separate STATE CONSTITUTIONS [I], have broadened the scope of constitutional law and have broken new ground in rights jurisprudence. This is a development that the original Jeffersonians would have understood and approved.

GEORGE DARGO

Bibliography

HORSNELL, MARGARET E. 1986 *Spencer Roane: Judicial Advocate of Jeffersonian Principles*. New York: Garland.

KOCH, ADRIENNE and PEDEN, WILLIAM, EDS. 1944 *The Life and Selected Writings of Thomas Jefferson*. New York: Modern Library.

MORGAN, DONALD G. 1954 *Justice William Johnson, The First Dissenter: The Career and Constitutional Philosophy of a Jeffersonian Judge*. Columbia: University of South Carolina Press.

PATTERSON, CALEB P. 1953 *The Constitutional Principles of Thomas Jefferson*. New York: Books for Libraries.

PETERSON, MERRILL D. 1962 *The Jeffersonian Image in the American Mind*. New York: Oxford University Press.

JIMMY SWAGGART MINISTRIES v. BOARD OF EQUALIZATION OF CALIFORNIA
110 S.Ct. 688 (1990)

In conjunction with its evangelistic activities in the state of California, Jimmy Swaggart Ministries sold religious books, tapes, records, and other merchandise. The group agreed to pay state sales tax on the nonreligious merchandise sold, but maintained that merchandise with specific religious content—such as Bibles, sermons, and Bible study manuals—were exempt from taxation on the basis of the FIRST AMENDMENT [2,I]. The Supreme Court unanimously disagreed, holding that application of a sales tax to the religious merchandise did not violate either the free exercise clause or the excessive entanglement provision read into the ESTABLISHMENT CLAUSE [I] by the LEMON TEST [I].

The Court distinguished the case from prior precedents that had invalidated the application of general licensing fees to those who sold and distributed religious materials door-to-door. In both MURDOCK V. PENNYSLVANIA (1943) [3] and *Follett v. McCormick* (1944), the Court had objected to such licensing fees because they acted as a prior retraint on the free exercise of religion. In the same cases, however, the Court made clear that the First Amendment did not exempt religious groups from generally applicable taxes on income and property. The Court reaffirmed that principle here, noting that the tax under attack was a general levy on revenues raised from the sale of certain products. The Court acknowledged that in some cases a generally applicable tax of this sort might "effectively choke off an adherent's religious practices," but reserved for the future a determination on whether such a tax would violate the free exercise clause.

JOHN G. WEST, JR.

(SEE ALSO: *Employment Division Dept. of Hum. Res. of Oregon v. Smith* [I]; *Texas Monthly, Inc. v. Bullock* [I].)

JOHNSON v. TRANSPORTATION AGENCY
480 U.S. 616 (1987)

Paul Johnson sought promotion to the position of road dispatcher with the Transportation Agency of Santa Clara County, California; he was deemed the best-qualified applicant for the job by a board of interviewers and by the Road Operations Division Director, who normally would have made the promotion decision. But the agency's affirmative-action officer intervened, recommending to the agency director that a woman seeking the position be appointed instead. The agency director agreed, and the woman was selected over Johnson. Johnson subsequently filed a suit alleging SEX DISCRIMINATION [4,I], and a federal district court found gender to be "the determining factor" in the promotion. The Supreme Court nevertheless sustained the agency's action, 6–3.

Writing for the majority, Justice WILLIAM J. BRENNAN [1,I] invoked the language of UNITED STEELWORKERS V. WEBER (1979) [4] and argued that the agency's AFFIRMATIVE ACTION [1,I] program was justified because it sought to correct a "manifest imbalance" that existed in job categories that had been "traditionally segregated" on the basis of gender. According to Brennan, the determination of whether a "manifest imbalance" exists usually rests on the disparity between the percentage of a protected group employed in specific job categories and the percentage of the protected group in the local labor force who are qualified to work in those categories. Precisely how high the disparity has to be before a "manifest imbalance" arises, Brennan did not say; but he did indicate that the requisite disparity was something less than that required in cases like WYGANT V. JACKSON BOARD OF EDUCATION (1986) [I], where employees had to establish a prima facie case of discrimination against their employer.

Concurring, Justice JOHN PAUL STEVENS [4,I] sought to push open the door to affirmative action still further. He implied that private employers should be able to discriminate in favor of "disadvantaged" racial and gender groups for a wide variety of reasons, including improving education, "averting racial tension over the allocation of jobs in a community," and "improving . . . services to black constituencies."

Justice SANDRA DAY O'CONNOR [3,I] concurred in the Court's judgment, but on narrower grounds than the majority. She maintained that affirmative-action programs can be invoked only to remedy past discrimination. But her standard of proof for past discrimination was nearly the same as the majority's standard for "manifest imbalance": a statistical disparity between the percentage of an organization's employees who are members of a protected group and the percentage of the relevant labor pool that is made up of members of the group. Unlike Brennan, however, O'Connor did claim that the disparity must be enough to establish a prima facie case that past discrimination in fact occurred. In the present case this was a distinction without a difference, because O'Connor found that her standard had been met.

Writing for the dissenters, Justice ANTONIN SCALIA [I] attacked the Court for converting "a statute designed to establish a color-blind and gender-blind workplace . . . into a powerful engine of racism and sexism . . . ." Scalia noted that although Brennan cited *Weber* as controlling, he had in fact dramatically extended *Weber* by redefining the meaning of the phrase "traditionally segregated job categories." In *Weber*, the phrase had "described skilled jobs from which employers and unions had systematically and intentionally excluded black workers. . . ." But in the present case, few women were employed in categories such as road maintenance workers because women themselves did not want the jobs. "There are, of course, those who believe that the social attitudes which cause women themselves to avoid certain jobs and to favor others are as nefarious as conscious, exclusionary discrimination. Whether or not that is so . . . the two phenomena are certainly distinct. And it is the alteration of social attitudes, rather than the elimination of discrimination, which today's decision approves as justification for state-enforced discrimination. This is an enormous expansion. . . ."

JOHN G. WEST, JR.

(SEE ALSO: *Race-Consciousness* [I]; *Racial Discrimination* [3,I].)

Bibliography

UROFSKY, MELVIN I. 1991 *A Conflict of Rights: The Supreme Court and Affirmative Action*. New York: Scribners.

U.S. COMMISSION ON CIVIL RIGHTS 1987 *Toward an Understanding of Johnson*. Clearinghouse Publication 94. Washington, D.C.: U.S. Government Printing Office.

JUDICIAL CONFERENCE OF THE UNITED STATES

The Judicial Conference of the United States is a legacy of WILLIAM HOWARD TAFT's [4] chief justiceship. Its establishment in 1922 constituted a part of the former President's broad campaign against progressives' demands for changes in the substance of then-prevailing federal law. Taft responded with a structural reform proposal: unprecedented administrative integration of a geographically dispersed court system manned by virtually autonomous judges. Thus, the third branch as a whole would achieve enhanced independence coincident with, and protective of, the uniqueness of the essential judicial function.

The Judicial Conference remains the linchpin of national judicial administration. From its beginnings as an annual meeting of the presiding judges of the UNITED STATES COURTS OF APPEALS [4] chaired by the CHIEF JUSTICE [1], the organization's membership has grown to include a representative from one of the UNITED STATES DISTRICT COURTS [4] in each of the eleven numbered circuits and the District of Columbia and the chief judges of those circuits, the UNITED STATES COURT OF APPEALS FOR THE FEDERAL CIRCUIT [4], and the COURT OF INTERNATIONAL TRADE [2]. Biennial meetings at Washington, held in executive session, are largely repositories for reports from an extensive committee system involving the participation of approximately two hundred federal judges. This system provides status differentiation among the more than 700-member federal judiciary, but more significantly responds to a work load spawned both by the brevity of conference sessions and by a voluminous and complex agenda associated with the growth of judicial business and personnel.

Further structural changes in the conference-related administrative organization originated in causes both within and without the third branch. Congress in 1939 established the Administrative Office of the United States Courts and provided for regional administrative units: circuit judicial councils and circuit judicial conferences. Chief Justice CHARLES EVANS HUGHES [2] promoted the Administrative Office Act as a response to FRANKLIN D. ROOSEVELT's [3] 1937 "Court-packing" bill, perceived by conference members as threatening executive-branch domination of the judiciary.

The new act vastly increased the functions performed by the Judicial Conference and its committees. Although the director and deputy director are appointed by the Supreme Court, the Office acts under "the supervision and direction" of the conference. Consequently, housekeeping, personnel, aud budgetary duties once performed by the ATTORNEY GENERAL AND DEPARTMENT OF JUSTICE [1] now fall within the oversight of the conference. These and subsequent congressionally mandated duties, some of which affected the district judges, ignited trial judge demands for conference representation, achieved in 1957, and led to establishment in 1967 of the Federal Judicial Center. This research, development, education, and training arm of the courts is directed by a governing board whose members are appointed by the conference.

The Judicial Conference has from its inception promoted administrative centralization, a functional tendency enhanced by the information-gathering and supportive services available from the Administrative Office. Consonant with the 1922 act's charge "to promote uniformity of management procedures and expeditious conduct of court business," the conference formulates policies for allocating budgetary, personnel, and space resources. It similarly addresses administrative questions raised in areas such as legal defenders, bankruptcy, probation, magistrates, and rules of practice and procedure.

The Judicial Conference promulgates standards of judicial ethics. Its role in disciplining wayward judges received explicit congressional authorization in 1980. The Judicial Councils Reform and Judicial Conduct Act empowered the circuit judicial councils to certify intractable misbehavior problems to the conference for "appropriate action." Remedies include referral of such cases to the House Judiciary Committee upon finding "that consideration of IMPEACHMENT [2] may be warranted," a procedure followed in three instances from 1986 through 1988.

The SEPARATION OF POWERS [4] makes the federal judiciary dependent on Congress for support. Since Taft's chairmanship and later with congressional authorization, the Judicial Conference has developed and promoted legislative programs. Additional judgeships, appropriations, judicial salaries, court organization, jurisdiction, procedural rules, and impeachment recommendations have been among the proposals brought to Capitol Hill, usually by conference committee chairmen. Thus, judges do and must lobby Congress to obtain necessary resources. Yet, legislative liaison may embroil the judiciary in visible political conflict, as occurred when Chief Justice WARREN E. BURGER [1] lobbied against portions of the 1978 BANKRUPTCY ACT [1].

The strategic position of the Judicial Conference, its policymaking functions, and its implementation responsibilities pose dilemmas. A quest by the conference for efficiency, uniformity, and equity has induced intrabranch policies favorable to development of "managerial" judges and has produced unavoidable tensions between centralized policymaking and individual court administration. Conference recommendations to Congress permit submission of proposals freighted with substantive public policy implications packaged in the wrappings of judicial administration, a characteristic that marked the struggle to divide the Fifth Circuit.

PETER GRAHAM FISH

(SEE ALSO: *Progressive Constitutional Thought* [3]; *Progressivism and the Constitution* [I].)

Bibliography

BARROW, DEBORAH J. and WALKER, G. THOMAS 1988 *A Court Divided: The Fifth Circuit Court of Appeals and the Politics of Judicial Reform.* New Haven, Conn.: Yale University Press.

FISH, PETER GRAHAM 1973 *The Politics of Federal Judicial Administration.* Princeton, N.J.: Princeton University Press.

JUDICIAL POWER AND LEGISLATIVE REMEDIES
(Update to Judicial Power)

Article III of the Constitution states that "[t]he judicial Power of the United States, shall be vested in one Supreme Court, and in such inferior Courts as the Congress may from time to time ordain and establish." The Article itself fails to detail the nature and extent of the phrase "judicial Power." However, the Constitution, taken as a whole, is not so silent as to its meaning.

The Framers, borrowing from MONTESQUIEU [3] the idea of SEPARATION OF POWERS [4], believed that each of the branches had to have a discrete role if the overall government was to avoid tyranny. Each branch was to have specific functions and tasks that would prevent the acquisition of too much power by any one branch. Montesquieu, writing in *The Spirit of the Laws*, stated that "there is no liberty, if the judiciary power be not separated from the legislative and executive. Were it joined with the legislative, the life and liberty of the subject would be exposed to arbitrary control; for the judge would be then the legislator. Were it joined to the executive power, the judge might behave with violence and oppression."

The Constitution is more explicit in its explanation of legislative and executive powers. Article I, section 8, lists many of the specific powers to be exercised by Congress in carrying out its constitutional duties. Section 8 contains, among many duties, the power "to lay and collect Taxes, Duties, Imposts, and Excises . . . [t]o coin Money . . . [t]o establish Post Offices . . . [t]o raise and support Armies." Likewise, the executive powers described in Article II include the power to fill vacancies and to act as COMMANDER-IN-CHIEF [1] of the ARMED FORCES [I].

Nevertheless, when one reviews the Constitution as a complete document and notes the placement of powers under specific articles, the power of the judiciary becomes something clear and distinct as well. That power is by nature a limited one. Publius wrote in THE FEDERALIST #78, "Whoever attentively considers the different departments of power must perceive, that in a government in which they are separated from each other, the judiciary, from the nature of its functions, will always be the least dangerous . . . [It] has no influence over either the sword or the purse, no direction either of the strength or of the wealth of society, and can take no active resolution whatever. It may truly be said to have neither Force nor Will, but merely judgment."

The debate concerning judicial power should not focus on JUDICIAL REVIEW [3,I]. In fact, the question as to whether the Court should exercise judicial review is a moot one, at best. The writings of both *The Federalist* [2] and the ANTI-FEDERALISTS [1] assumed that the Court would rule on matters of law to determine whether statutory law complied with the standards of constitutionality.

The nature of judicial power, however, remains a subject of debate in the political arena because the Supreme Court continues to expand its role by directly implementing specific public-policy choices. In doing so, it has employed such constitutional provisions as EQUAL PROTECTION [2,I] and DUE PROCESS [2,I] in order to secure remedies in cases such as BROWN V. BOARD OF EDUCATION (1954) [1], which effectively overturned the SEPARATE-BUT-EQUAL DOCTRINE [4] of PLESSY V. FERGUSON (1896) [3]. More recently, courts have begun to propose remedies that encroach on the powers specifically delegated to the legislative branch. In some cases, courts have formulated the exact legislative programs by which wrongs will be righted. Two cases from the 1989 term illustrate the difference between legitimate exercise of judicial power and encroachment on legislative prerogatives.

In *Spallone v. United States* (1990) the Supreme Court reversed, by a 5–4 vote, the civil CONTEMPT [2] charges and fines imposed by a UNITED STATES DISTRICT COURT [4] on the city council members of Yonkers, New York. The city had been found in violation of Title VIII of the CIVIL RIGHT ACT OF 1968 [1] and the equal protection clause of the FOURTEENTH AMENDMENT [2,I] by "intentionally engag[ing] in a pattern and practice of housing discrimination." Chief Justice WILLIAM H. REHNQUIST [3,I], writing the majority opinion, framed the question narrowly, asking "whether it was a proper exercise of judicial power for the District Court to hold petitioners, four Yonkers city councilmembers, in contempt for refusing to vote in favor of legislation implementing a consent decree earlier approved by the city."

The Supreme Court, concluding that the district court lacked authority to impose the contempt fines against the individual members of the city council, upheld the contempt fines levied against the city. With the question framed so narrowly, the five-Justice majority explained that "[t]he imposition of sanctions on individual legislators is designed to cause them to vote, not with a view to the interest of their constituents or of the city, but with a view solely to their own personal interest." In so doing, the district court jeopardizes the legitimate exercise of deliberation by representative institutions accountable to a legitimate constituency and removes the legislative immunity that is essential to enable elected representatives to consider the common good of the community.

Although the mounting fines against the city (nearly one million dollars a day) had forced the council to vote in favor of the housing plan, the members of the council still could have decided that it was in the best interest of the city to go bankrupt, thereby defying the court. However, when the individual members of the council were forced to vote under threat of personal financial catastrophe, they were no longer able to represent the interest of the community. This point is of great consequence. A legislative body must have a will of its own while working collectively (and even if at time in conflict) with the courts toward the implementation of the Constitution and laws passed pursuant to it.

The second recent Supreme Court case concerning the limits of judicial power is MISSOURI V. JENKINS (1990) [I]. In this case, a unanimous Court agreed that a federal district court had exceeded its authority when, in fashioning a remedy for school desegregation, it ordered an increase in a school district's property tax levy, even though the increase exceeded the limits imposed by state law. The majority opinion by Justice BYRON R. WHITE [4,I], however, raises a serious question as to the limits of judicial authority. Justice White "agree[d] with the State that the tax increase contravened the principles of comity." But he went on to suggest that the district court, under the SUPREMACY CLAUSE [4] of the Constitution, could order the school district to levy taxes at the rate needed to pay for the desegregation remedy.

In a CONCURRING OPINION [1] by Justice ANTHONY M. KENNEDY [I], a four-Justice minority argued that the majority opinion's OBITER DICTUM [3] had endorsed "an expansion of power in the federal judiciary beyond all precedent." The minority argued that "while courts have

undoubted power to order that schools operate in compliance with the Constitution, the manner and methods of school financing are beyond federal judicial authority." It was apparent from the majority's decision that there was a "fear that failure to endorse judicial taxation power might in some extreme circumstance leave a court unable to remedy a constitutional violation." But, as the minority noted, "this possibility is nothing more or less than the necessary consequence of *any* limit on judicial power."

Spallone and *Jenkins* are merely the most recent examples in a long history of judicial attempts to impose remedies on legislative bodies. With the growing reluctance of representatives to raise taxes and to fashion rules and laws to meet the costs of constitutional obligations determined by the courts, the conflict between the branches is sure to continue.

Thus, the basic question concerning the nature and extent of judicial power returns to the focus. Judicial power obviously is not the same as the power of the legislative or executive branches. The courts have the power to order officials to comply with the Constitution's demands; however, the extent of this judicial power is limited in scope. An extraordinary situation may arise in which a court is unable to enforce a judicial remedy—in effect lowering the status of the court, but granting courts unlimited remedial power derogates from the principle of representative government.

JEFFREY D. SCHULTZ

Bibliography

BICKEL, ALEXANDER M. 1978 *The Supreme Court and the Idea of Progress.* New Haven, Conn.: Yale University Press.
CAREY, GEORGE W. 1989 *The Federalist: Design for a Constitutional Republic.* Urbana: University of Illinois Press.
COX, ARCHIBALD 1987 *The Court and the Constitution.* Boston: Houghton Mifflin.
WOLFE, CHRISTOPHER 1985 Three Contemporary Theories of Judicial Review. *The Political Science Reviewer* 15:215–260.

JUDICIAL REVIEW OF ADMINISTRATIVE ACTS

To conform to basic SEPARATION OF POWERS [4] precepts, JUDICIAL REVIEW [3] of administrative actions must be limited yet effective. It must be limited to avoid entangling courts in policy decisions that belong to other branches; it must be effective to bind ADMINISTRATIVE AGENCIES [I] to the RULE OF LAW [3]. Many ADMINISTRATIVE LAW [1] doctrines attempt to accommodate these two purposes. Often they do so by adapting COMMON LAW [1] remedies against government to the American scheme of separated powers. This process began with MARBURY V. MADISON (1803) [3], which announced that a court having jurisdiction could issue common law MANDAMUS [3] against a cabinet officer. The Supreme Court emphasized the need to avoid judicial intrusion in the political discretion of executive officers, while conforming their decisions to the dictates of law.

Modern administrative agencies perform functions that are characteristic of all three constitutional branches: adjudication, rule-making, and execution. The legitimacy of these activities depends on the relationships between the agencies and the branches that the courts have defined. For example, *Crowell v. Benson* (1932) allowed agencies to exercise adjudicative authority only because judicial review could assure that agency decisions had adequate factual and legal support.

The delegation doctrine states that when Congress grants LEGISLATIVE POWER [3] to agencies it must provide intelligible standards to guide and confine agency discretion. Yet this doctrine is aspirational today: no congressional delegation to an agency has been invalidated for over fifty years. The delegation doctrine has been supplanted by a series of inquiries into the legality of particular agency actions.

First, courts review the substantive conformity of agency actions with constitutional requisites, such as those in the BILL OF RIGHTS [1]. Substantive constitutional criteria apply to statutes.

Second, courts review the fairness of agency procedures under DUE PROCESS [2] and statutory guarantees. PROCEDURAL DUE PROCESS [3] involves a two-stage inquiry that identifies the presence of an interest that constitutes "liberty" or "property," and then considers the individual and government interests at stake and the value of a more elaborate process. Statutory guarantees often flow from the generally applicable Administrative Procedure Act (1946), which defines the basic procedures of federal agencies for adjudication and rulemaking, and further defines the scope of judicial review of administrative acts. Such statutory procedures often are more elaborate than the minimal constitutional requisites.

Third, courts review the statutory interpretations that underlie administrative acts. Courts usually defer to agency interpretations of law that are consistent with ascertainable LEGISLATIVE INTENT [3] and that are otherwise reasonable. The purpose of this doctrine is to give maximum scope to agency discretion within statutory bounds.

Fourth, courts review the factual basis for agency actions. Here they compare administrative explanations for decisions with materials in the administrative record and accept conclusions of fact and policy that are reasonable. The courts try to ensure that agencies have carefully con-

sidered the policy options before them and have inquired fully into the facts. Thus, ordinary rationality review is much more demanding in administrative law than it is under constitutional EQUAL PROTECTION [2,I] or SUBSTANTIVE DUE PROCESS [4,I] guarantees.

Any of several threshold considerations can prevent courts from reviewing the merits of administrative actions. STANDING [4] to seek review is partly a constitutional doctrine. To present a "case" or "controversy" within the federal JUDICIAL POWER [3,I], parties must show that they are injured in fact by the government and that judicial relief will remedy the injury. In administrative cases, courts also require the parties challenging agency actions to be within the zone of interests affected by the governing statute. There are constitutional overtones in this latter test, because it denies review to persons so tangentially interested in a statute's administration that they are unlikely to present a concrete, sharply adversarial claim.

Parties must ordinarily exhaust their administrative remedies before seeking judicial review. Separation of powers considerations partly explain this doctrine, which enforces delegations of decision-making power to agencies. The courts make exceptions to this exhaustion requirement when the issues are ready for judicial review, delay would cause hardship to private parties, or agency autonomy would be unduly threatened by immediate judicial review.

Finally, not all administrative acts are reviewable. Statutes sometimes entirely preclude judicial review, subject to uncertain due process limitations. As in *Johnson v. Robinson* (1974), courts usually interpret statutes that preclude review to allow at least inquiries into the constitutionality of agency actions. In this way, the courts avoid deciding whether Congress can forbid all review of an administrative act for which review is otherwise appropriate. Courts do hold that certain agency functions are intrinsically unsuited for review, such as agency decisions not to undertake enforcement action. Here as elsewhere, courts attempt to control agencies only to an extent that is consistent with traditional notions of the limits of the JUDICIAL ROLE [I].

HAROLD H. BRUFF

(SEE ALSO: *Cases and Controversies* [1]; *Procedural Due Process, Civil* [3,I].)

Bibliography

DAVIS, KENNETH CULP 1978–1984 *Administrative Law Treatise*, 2nd ed., vols. 1–5. San Diego, Calif.: K. C. Davis.
PIERCE, RICHARD J., JR.; SHAPIRO, SIDNEY A.; and VERKUIL, PAUL R. 1985 *Administrative Law and Process.* Mineola, N.Y.: Foundation Press.

JUDICIAL ROLE

Theories about the proper role of the Supreme Court have proliferated in recent decades. These theories have been too political in one sense and not political enough in another. They are too political in that they tend to be thinly veiled rationalizations of political preferences, valued less for their own sakes than for the results they entail in specific controversies. Today, knowing someone's attitude about the role of the Court, one can usually deduce his or her political positions, not so much on ECONOMIC REGULATION [2] as on some divisive social questions.

To arrive at a consensus about JUDICIAL ACTIVISM [3], we need a political situation in which most groups feel that they have at least as much to gain as to lose by subscribing to an agreed conception of the Court's role. No such consensus exists. Today the country is divided over several major social issues: crime, PORNOGRAPHY [3], race, women's roles, homosexuality, and religion. Ever since the 1950s, social liberals have believed that on most of those issues they have everything to gain and little to lose by judicial intervention; conversely, social conservatives have usually had a stake in confining the Court's role. Each camp has fashioned jurisprudential theories that reflect its perceived stake in judicial activism or restraint. In this sense, the debate about the Court's role is basically political.

Yet the debate is usually couched in legal terms, and in this sense, it is excessively legalistic. Commentators usually do not directly discuss the appropriate role of the Court; instead, they argue about how to interpret the Constitution. Thus, proponents of judicial activism espouse loose-constructionist theories of interpretation, and advocates of judicial restraint usually defend a more literal adherence to the text and its original meaning.

This familiar argument has long since become repetitive and unenlightening. Worse still, it treats fundamental political questions as if they were analogous to disputes over the meanings of contracts. To analyze judicial governance solely in legal terms implies that objections to a broad judicial role can be fully met by a cogent legal response, such as an interpretation of a PRECEDENT [3], the NINTH AMENDMENT [3], or the EQUAL PROTECTION [2,I] clause. Admittedly, such analyses are essential, and they may indeed solve the purely legal aspect of a constitutional problem. But fidelity to law is not the only constitutional virtue, for the Constitution is a political charter as well as a legal text. If judicial lawlessness were the sole issue, we could solve every problem with a constitutional amendment saying, "It shall be unconstitutional to treat any social problem unwisely; the Supreme Court may enforce this provision on its own motion." That would eliminate every legal ground for objecting to a large judicial role,

and yet the political objections obviously would remain.

Legalism is popularly identified with a restrictive view of the Court's role, but as this hypothetical amendment illustrates, that assumption is only a half-truth. After the Justices sweep past the Maginot Line of ORIGINAL INTENT [I], legalism is as likely to justify judicial activism as restraint, offering no solid resistance to continual enlargement of JUDICIAL POWER [3]. Legal training breeds indifference to trends; in most fields of law, lawyers ordinarily evaluate decisions as correct or incorrect, not as contributing to a tendency that should be evaluated as such. The law is expected to evolve and grow toward the limits of its logic; indeed, the very word "trend" connotes gradualism, a legal virtue. In COMMON LAW [1] fields, that attitude is generally harmless. The doctrine of promissory estoppel, idling in a backwater of the law of contracts, does not affect our system of government, and even if it did, the legislature could change it. In constitutional law, by contrast, the Court's role has enormous political implications; as in all politics, constitutional trends may be ominous well before the day of reckoning arrives.

In an effort to supplement narrow legal standards, some scholars have offered political objections to judicial activism. The most common of these objections may be called "the argument from democracy": America is a democracy, but the Court is not electorally accountable; therefore, excessive judicial activism is illegitimate, undermines public respect for the institution, and thus impairs its ability to perform its proper functions.

The argument from democracy, and the usual responses to it, are not narrowly legalistic, and their emphasis on democratic theory is explicitly political. Still, the search for criteria of democratic legitimacy has important similarities to conventional legal analysis: it focuses on individual decisions and doctrines, it asks whether each of them is correct (legitimate) or incorrect, and it seeks to answer that question by applying broad, consistent principles.

Without denying the value of such neolegalistic inquiries, it is important to emphasize that there is another way of looking at the Court's role, focusing less on individual decisions and more on trends and aggregates and recognizing that a decision may be justifiable from one point of view yet harmful from another. Conventional discussions of constitutional JURISPRUDENCE [I], with their legalistic tendency to label decisions as correct or incorrect, tend to obscure the fact that judicial governance, even when it is lawful and legitimate, exacts a price—not always an excessive or even a high price, but a price. For constitutional rights tend to diminish the role of self-government. This is not simply a question of lawfulness or legitimacy. When the Court enforces a constitutional right—even one fairly discoverable in text, traditions, and precedents—it reduces, however slightly, the responsibilities of politicians and reformers. Within the scope of legal expectations aroused by a specific right, they have less incentive to participate in politics. Within the scope of hopes aroused by the Court's general willingness to create rights, they may choose to forgo the onerous burden of self-government, waiting instead for an edict from Washington. Even if reformers lose in the Court, three or four dissents may nourish the hope that new Justices will solve the problem. To that extent, rights tend to relieve reformers of the tasks of CITIZENSHIP [1]: studying public policy, creating reform commissions, drafting statutes, talking to bureaucrats and politicians, bargaining with opponents, persuading the uncommitted, and compromising. Likewise, judicially created rights sometimes enable politicians to avoid accountability to sharply divided constituencies.

Even as a legal issue, one open to creative solutions, a constitutional right is a problem that has been removed from the fifty states, with all their judges, to one Supreme Court. All other judges, though still free to interpret and suggest, cease to be ultimately responsible.

Admittedly, these hidden prices are nebulous and incalculable. No doubt the price of judicial governance is often low in individual cases, and even when it seems to be high, it may be worth paying. It may be offset by the beneficial effects of judicial intervention, for example, in opening up opportunities for an oppressed class (as in BROWN V. BOARD OF EDUCATION OF TOPEKA (1954) [1]), in protecting FREEDOM OF SPEECH [2,I], or in purifying the electoral process. The essential point is that the citizenry should try to appraise the enlarged judicial role cumulatively—as it appraises the federal budget—and as a problem in government, not merely in law. In constitutional jurisprudence one should consider the destination, not just the next step of the journey. Do we want the Supreme Court to decide, case-by-case over the decades, just when and how the government may regulate sex, marriage, and privacy? To establish national standards for criminal punishment, fashioned case-by-case in litigation? To oversee regulation of the economy? Or provision of housing, under the aegis of a "constitutional right to shelter?" We generally discuss such questions as if they were discrete and legal. Yet they are more than that. They are political choices, most of which can be resolved either way in the long run by the accumulation of precedent, without violating the conventions of legal reasoning and the RULE OF LAW [3]. It may sometimes take a more or less lawless decision to get the process started, but every kingdom begins as a usurpation. Given the leading role of precedent in legal analysis, judicial activism is ultimately self-legitimating.

Powell v. Texas (1967) exemplifies the difference between legal and political grounds for judicial restraint. In *Powell* the issue was whether it was CRUEL AND UN-USUAL PUNISHMENT [2,I] for Texas to punish a chronic alcoholic for public drunkenness. The trial judge had found that chronic alcoholism is a disease whose symptoms include loss of will power and "a compulsion" to appear drunk in public. This being so, argued Powell's attorney, it would be unconstitutional to treat Powell as a criminal. By a 5–4 vote, the Court rejected this argument and upheld the conviction.

A proponent of STRICT CONSTRUCTION [4] would presumably applaud this decision on the ground that it conformed to the original meaning of "cruel and unusual." But as precedents accumulate, such arguments often lose much or all of whatever cogency they originally possessed. The leading precedent in *Powell* was *Robinson v. California* (1962), in which the Court had reversed a conviction for the crime of being "addicted to the use of narcotics." The opinion in *Robinson* distinguished between punishing someone for an act and punishing him for a "status," the latter being unconstitutional. Some of the language of the opinion implied that the basic defect of a status crime is that a status (insanity or a disease, for example) is, or may be, involuntary. Arguably, therefore, the rationale of *Robinson* extended beyond status crimes to involuntary acts, including drunken behavior by an alcoholic. To so hold might have been scientifically unsound or unwise, and it might not have been the most persuasive interpretation of *Robinson*, but given *Robinson* it could hardly have been described as a blatantly lawless decision. It would have been the sort of expansive but plausible interpretation of a precedent that courts have been handing down for centuries.

A decision in Powell's favor would also have been consistent with some of the neolegalistic criteria fashioned by jurisprudents to identify fields in which the Supreme Court's activism is legitimate. Criminal law is an area in which the courts have traditionally played a major role, and properly so because of their expertise and the tendency of popular majorities to be insensitive to the need for fairness toward criminals. Criminal defendants can be thought of as the functional equivalent of racial and religious minorities. In displacing a state court's rules of criminal responsibility, the Supreme Court is not overriding democracy but merely correcting other judges.

Although not violative of the rule of law, a broad reading of *Robinson* would have vastly expanded the Court's role, for it would have made a potential constitutional case out of every issue of free will—for example, defenses based on drunkenness and insanity. Legalistic arguments for judicial restraint do not adequately describe the implications of this sort of decision. On one side of the scale are the virtues, real or imagined, of uniformity and rationality. On the other side is the impact not only on the Court's caseload but on the values of FEDERALISM [2,I]:

freedom, diversity, and relatively widespread citizen participation in government. Federalism's values are embedded in our constitutional order, but in a case like *Powell* they are not "the law" in the usual sense of an authoritative rule of decision on whose binding force well-trained lawyers would agree; they are, rather, the political virtues without which constitutional jurisprudence becomes sophistry.

DAVID P. BRYDEN

Bibliography

BRYDEN, DAVID P. 1986 Politics, the Constitution, and the New Formalism. *Constitutional Commentary* 3:415–437.

HARLAN, JOHN M. 1964 The Bill of Rights and the Constitution. *American Bar Association Journal* 50:918.

NAGEL, ROBERT F. 1989 *Constitutional Cultures: The Mentality and Consequences of Judicial Review.* Berkeley: University of California Press.

THAYER, JAMES BRADLEY 1893 The Origin and Scope of the American Doctrine of Constitutional Law. *Harvard Law Review* 7:129–156.

JURISDICTION, FEDERAL

As ALEXANDER HAMILTON [2] stressed in THE FEDERALIST [2] #78, the power and obligation of federal judges to measure the conduct of public officials and bodies against the precepts of the Constitution mean that federal courts must sometimes act to thwart these officials and bodies. On occasion this is, at least in some quarters, a very unpopular enterprise. From time to time, Congress has entertained the possibility of responding to controversial decisions by the Supreme Court or the lower federal courts by strategically removing the JURISDICTION [3] of part or all of the federal judiciary over the controverted matters.

Proposals of this sort raise the important and sensitive question of whether the lower federal courts and, possibly, even the Supreme Court, ultimately act at the sufferance of Congress or whether the Constitution secures the existence of an independent federal judicial voice. Article III of the Constitution, which provides for the establishment of the federal judiciary, invites rather than stills speculation on this fundamental question of institutional structure. The first sentence of Article III provides: "The judicial power of the United States, shall be vested in one supreme Court, and in such inferior Courts as the Congress may from time to time ordain and establish." Following this is the provision without which Hamilton felt the Constitution would have been "inexcusably defective": "The Judges, both of the supreme and inferior Courts, shall hold their Offices during GOOD BEHAVIOR [2], and shall, at stated Times, receive for their Services

a Compensation, which shall not be diminished during their Continuance in Office."

Section 2 of Article III begins with a menu of matters over which the judicial power "shall extend." Nine categories are delineated. The first three are styled as classes of "cases," the most important being cases "arising under this Constitution, the Laws of the United States, and treaties." The remaining six are styled as classes of "controversies," the most prominent being controversies "between Citizens of different States." Section 2 then specifies two narrow classes of cases over which the Supreme Court has ORIGINAL JURISDICTION [3] and concludes with the following stipulation: "In all the other Cases before mentioned, the supreme Court shall have APPELLATE JURISDICTION [1], both as to Law and Fact, with such Exceptions, and under such Regulations as the Congress shall make."

Remarkably, there is no well-settled understanding of the scope of Congress's authority under these provisions to restrict federal jurisdiction. Cooler and more responsible heads have usually prevailed in Congress when "court-stripping" proposals have been floated, and the Supreme Court has been carefully diplomatic in sounding deference to Congress when it can afford to do so; as a result, there is little authority on the question. Most of the Court's pertinent statements have been by way of broad OBITER DICTUM [3] and have been Janus-faced. Broad statements welcoming Congress's plenary license to sculpt federal jurisdiction have been balanced by the Court's insistence that the very fabric of national union depends on the existence of final federal judicial authority over legal affairs.

The two most prominent cases in this area both grew out of the CIVIL WAR [I]. In EX PARTE MCCARDLE (1869) [3] the Court faced jurisdiction-limiting legislation plainly intended to protect Reconstruction LEGISLATION [3] from constitutional invalidation. Although the legislation gestured at pushing the Court aside, it only touched one statutory basis of the Court's appellate jurisdiction, leaving—as the Court itself pointedly observed—another statutory route to the same end. With an angry and somewhat dangerous Congress in the wings and with little at stake for the moment, the Court gave broad deference to Congress's power to reduce its appellate jurisdiction. Three years later, in an attempt to prevent the presidential pardon of supporters of the Confederacy from entitling them to compensation for property lost during the hostilities, Congress denied the federal courts jurisdiction over property claims that depended on presidential pardon. In *United States v. Klein* (1872) the Court promptly struck down this law as a means to the unconstitutional end of interfering with the President's authority to grant pardons and as an unconstitutional attempt to dictate how federal courts otherwise seized with jurisdiction should decide cases. Most commentators are skeptical about the applicability of either the generous tone of *McCardle* or the special circumstances of *Klein* to modern court-stripping issues.

A few propositions are reasonably clear. In one sense, the lower federal courts do indeed exist at the sufferance of Congress. Although there is some scholarly dissent, most commentators agree that Congress was not obliged to create the lower federal courts at all and could disband them today. Most also agree that when Congress does establish lower courts it need not give them all or any particular part of the jurisdiction enumerated in Article III. Events at the CONSTITUTIONAL CONVENTION OF 1787 [1] support the conclusion that the Framers intended to resolve their sharp division over what form, if any, the lower federal judiciary should assume by leaving the matter for congressional resolution, and the first sentence of Article III plainly executes this compromise. Although it is logically possible to hold that Congress must give all of the federal judicial power to any lower federal court it creates, such an inflexible view seems arbitrary and at odds with the idea of remanding the shape of the lower federal courts to the judgment of Congress in the first place. Congress has never given all of Article III jurisdiction to the lower federal courts, and the Supreme Court, from *Sheldon v. Sill* (1850) forward, has firmly assumed that Congress can order à la carte from the Article III menu.

Sheldon v. Sill can be read to say that Congress can choose any package of lower-court jurisdiction it likes, as long as the bounds of Article III jurisdiction are not exceeded. But this is surely not the case. Were Congress to parse access to civil plaintiffs on the ground of their religion or political affiliation, for example, the FIRST AMENDMENT [2,I] would surely be violated. A diversity case with no pertinent wrinkles, *Sheldon* reliably stands only as a negation of the binary view of congressional authority over the lower federal courts.

With respect to the Supreme Court, once it is observed that the first sentence of Article III clearly contemplates the existence of a Supreme Court with some modicum of jurisdiction, the textual focus shifts to the last sentence of Article III: "In all the other Cases before mentioned, the supreme Court shall have appellate Jurisdiction, both as to Law and Fact, with such Exceptions, and under such Regulations as the Congress shall make." Most commentators agree that Congress's authority under this provision includes the power to remove some Article III CASES or CONTROVERSIES [1] from the appellate jurisdiction of the Supreme Court. Congress has always kept some classes of cases from the Supreme Court, and the Court consistently has endorsed this reading of the exceptions language. Substantial housekeeping concerns support this institutional consensus. Some Article III matters have seemed unnecessary or even inappropriate candidates for the Court's appellate jurisdiction, such as controversies between citizens of different states that have been fully adjudicated in the courts of one of the states.

But beyond the propositions that the Supreme Court must have some jurisdiction and that Congress can take some cases out of the Court's appellate jurisdiction, little is clear, and much remains open to scholarly reflection. The orthodox view among legal scholars has been very generous to Congress. As long as Congress leaves the jurisdiction of state courts intact, avoids patent constitutional problems such as selecting plaintiffs on the basis of their religious or political beliefs, and avoids untoward interference with the federal courts that do have jurisdiction, the orthodox view licenses Congress to tailor federal jurisdiction, including that of the Supreme Court, as it pleases. On this view, for example, Congress could respond to decisions by the Supreme Court that extended the protections of the First Amendment to the burning of the American flag by depriving the entire federal judiciary of jurisdiction over FLAG DESECRATION [2,I] cases. Most, if not all, of the scholars who hold this view—their ranks have included Paul Bator, Charles Black, Gerald Gunther, Michael Perry, and Herbert Wechsler—would deplore such an event, and they would urge Congress not to trifle with the federal judiciary in this fashion. But the orthodox view rests on the unshakable conviction that the first section of Article III gives Congress unlimited plenary authority over the lower federal courts and that the last sentence of Article III gives Congress the same authority over the Supreme Court. For some, this reading of the Constitution has been a cause for regret; but others have seen an important institutional virtue in the federal judiciary's vulnerability to such treatment. Charles Black and Michael Perry, for example, have argued that Congress's power to silence the federal courts, when not exercised, supports the claim that Congress has acquiesced in the general run of the courts' decisions and, hence, lends democratic legitimacy to these nonmajoritarian tribunals.

A revisionist strand of Article III scholarship has developed, arguing for substantial constitutional restraints on Congress's power to shape federal jurisdiction. The claims for such restraints group around two propositions: first, that the Constitution secures a core function for the federal judiciary against congressional interference; and second, that Congress cannot act to reduce federal jurisdiction selectively out of manifest hostility to federal judicial doctrine.

Henry Hart, in a famous written dialogue on Congress's

jurisdiction-limiting authority, first argued that there was an essential role of the Supreme Court that Congress could not constitutionally impair. Leonard Ratner has given more concrete content and support to what is called the "essential functions" thesis, arguing that the demands of supremacy and uniformity require that the Supreme Court be available to review all matters of federal legal substance. Although lacking in explicit textual support in its Hart-Ratner form, the essential-functions thesis can draw support from the commitment of the Constitutional Convention and its product, the Constitution, to subordinate the states to federal authority and to do so through the federal judicial process. In some of its variations, the thesis can also draw support from congressional precedent: in the course of two centuries of meandering Supreme Court appellate jurisdiction, the Court has always been permitted jurisdiction to review unrequited claims of constitutional right against state and local conduct.

A structurally distinct form of the essential-functions thesis has also emerged, attached not to the Supreme Court alone but to the Article III federal judiciary as a whole. The claim is that there are certain matters for which *some* Article III court must be provided. Only in default of Congress's having provided a lower federal court with jurisdiction over these matters does the Constitution require that the Supreme Court be available to them. Although given modern voice in the past decade, this appears to have been Alexander Hamilton's view, as reflected in *The Federalist* #82, and is familially related to Justice JOSEPH STORY's [4] views in MARTIN V. HUNTER'S LESSEE (1816) [3]. The scholars who have been attracted to this version of the essential-functions thesis have regarded it as better supported by legally relevant materials. This author, in the first modern statement of this form of the essential-functions thesis, has argued that Article III's textually explicit commitment to an independent judiciary can be honored only if politically sensitive cases—those involving claims of constitutional right being the strongest possible candidates—are assured review in an Article III forum. Robert Clinton has argued from a close analysis of events at the Constitutional Convention that the Framers intended to oblige Congress to distribute all Article III jurisdiction among the federal courts and used the "exceptions and regulations" language only to permit Congress to distribute Article III matters among Article III courts. Akhil Amar, observing, in effect, that every instance of the word "cases" in Article III is modified by a preceding "all," has argued that the first three items on the Article III menu—those styled as categories of "cases"—are textually required to be assigned to some Article III court.

The alternative revisionist claim, that Congress cannot act to reduce federal jurisdiction selectively out of manifest hostility to federal judicial doctrine, has been advanced on a number of connected grounds. Laurence Tribe has borrowed equal-protection analysis from the HUNTER V. ERICKSON (1969) [2] tradition to argue that it is unconstitutional for Congress to burden the exercise of particular constitutional rights by depriving those who claim such rights the benefits of a federal forum. John Hart Ely has argued that the motive of Congress in such cases—hostility to federal judicial doctrine—is impermissible and can serve to invalidate selective removals of jurisdiction. This author has argued that some selective deprivations of jurisdiction carry the appearance of congressional hostility to controversial constitutional claims, invite the disregard of those claims, and are for that reason unconstitutional.

Although the best possible protection against untoward congressional manipulation of federal jurisdiction is the sound judgment of Congress, there is a growing, but still much disputed, view among academic commentators that the Constitution protects against a lapse of congressional responsibility here as elsewhere.

LAWRENCE G. SAGER

Bibliography

AMAR, AKHIL 1985 A Neo-Federalist View of Article III: Separating the Two Tiers of Federal Jurisdiction. *Boston University Law Review* 65:205–272.

BATOR, PAUL M. 1982 Congressional Power over the Jurisdiction of Federal Courts. *Villanova Law Review* 27:1030–1041.

CLINTON, ROBERT L. 1984 A Mandatory View of Federal Court Jurisdiction: A Guided Quest for the Original Understanding. *University of Pennsylvania Law Review* 132:741–866.

EISENBERG, THEODORE 1974 Congressional Authority to Restrict Lower Federal Court Jurisdiction. *Yale Law Journal* 83:498–533.

GUNTHER, GERALD 1984 Congressional Power to Curtail Federal Court Jurisdiction: An Opinionated Guide to the Ongoing Debate. *Stanford Law Review* 36:895–922.

HART, HENRY M., JR. 1953 The Power of Congress to Limit the Jurisdiction of Federal Courts: An Exercise in Dialectic. *Harvard Law Review* 66:1362–1402.

REDISH, MARTIN H. and WOODS, CURTIS E. 1975 Congressional Power to Control the Jurisdiction of Lower Federal Courts: A Critical Review and a New Synthesis. *University of Pennsylvania Law Review* 124:45–109.

SAGER, LAWRENCE GENE 1981 Foreword: Constitutional Limitations on Congress' Authority to Regulate the Jurisdiction of the Federal Courts. *Harvard Law Review* 16:129–156.

TRIBE, LAURENCE H. 1981 Jurisdictional Gerrymandering: Zoning Disfavored Rights Out of the Federal Courts. *Harvard Civil Rights–Civil Liberties Law Review* 16:129–156.

WECHSLER, HERBERT 1965 The Courts and the Constitution. *Columbia Law Review* 65:1001–1014.

JURISPRUDENCE AND CONSTITUTIONAL LAW

Constitutional jurisprudence is the most abstract and philosophical part of CONSTITUTIONAL THEORY [I]. We may divide the subject into general areas or departments, although these areas will be densely interconnected. The most general division is between "foundational" and "interpretive" constitutional jurisprudence.

Foundational constitutional jurisprudence considers abstract normative questions about ideal constitutional structure. Is a written political CONSTITUTION [1] better than a conventional or informal one? Does the best constitutional structure vest EXECUTIVE POWER [I] in a president independent of the legislature, as the American Constitution does? Would it have been better to adopt the British practice that vests executive power in the head of the party that controls the legislature? Should a constitution protect the interests of individual citizens against the wishes or interests of the majority? If so, which interests should it protect? Should it protect economic interests, for example? Should it deny either the national or state government power to raise taxes for purposes of redistributing the wealth? Should the constitution guarantee moral liberty or independence? Should it ensure homosexuals their own SEXUAL ORIENTATION [I]? Should it ensure women freedom of ABORTION [1,I]?

Most of these questions raise issues of philosophical depth. What reasons could justify granting individuals legal rights of immunity from a decision a majority of citizens want, for example? Two answers are common among philosophers, and these answers lead to different conclusions about which individual rights a constitution should protect. The first is instrumental: It holds that constitutional rights are legitimate if, but only if, recognizing and enforcing the right produces an aggregate benefit for the community as a whole. Some philosophers have argued in favor of a constitutionally protected right to FREEDOM OF SPEECH [2,I] on this instrumental ground, for example. They argue that protecting free speech for individuals benefits the community as a whole by providing it with valuable information, challenge, and debate.

The second answer insists that constitutional rights are justified not because they produce aggregate benefits, but because they protect rights that individuals have on intrinsic moral grounds. Under this latter view, people have rights as "trumps" over collective-interests goals. Obviously, these different views about the ground of constitutional rights produce different views about their scope. An instrumental approach to free speech, for example, will not support extending this right to speech that has little or no chance of producing collective benefit, even indirectly or in the long term—to racist or obscene speech, for example, or to speech that calls for revolutionary or illiberal change. But someone who thinks that people have an inherent right to express their opinions, even in circumstances in which it is against the interests of their community for them to do so, would not use this test for limiting freedom of speech.

Another independent distinction is of great importance in foundational jurisprudence: the distinction between procedural issues of fairness and substantive issues of justice. The question as to whether an ideal constitution would grant individuals a right of choice in sexual orientation, for example, raises both sorts of issues. Some might deny that individuals should have a right even in principle; they might believe that every society should force its members to follow the traditional moral code with which most citizens identify because this is the best way to preserve the proper sense of communal integrity and unity. But even if they do *not* believe this—even if they think that a society of this sort would be deeply unjust—they still might resist a constitutional right to sexual independence on grounds of procedural fairness. They might say that democracy is the only acceptable form of government, and that it is undemocratic to use a constitution to prevent the majority from having the law it thinks best, even when the majority is profoundly wrong. This last claim—that individual constitutional rights are undemocratic—is one of the two most widely discussed issues of foundational constitutional jurisprudence in America and will be discussed further.

The second, interpretive part of constitutional jurisprudence considers issues closer to those of traditional jurisprudence and also closer to constitutional legal practice. It asks not what constitution would be ideal but what constitution we actually have, both in general and in detail. The central question of interpretive jurisprudence is a methodological one. It is only indirectly concerned with the right answer to the substantive questions the Supreme Court must eventually decide, like the question as to how far the Constitution as it stands, properly interpreted, now grants individuals constitutional rights to free speech, abortion, or economic protection. Interpretive jurisprudence is concerned, rather, with the strategies of investigation and argument that should be used to answer these questions.

The clauses of the Constitution that grant individual rights are drafted in very abstract language. The FOURTEENTH AMENDMENT [2,I], for example, says that no state may deny DUE PROCESS OF LAW [2] or EQUAL PROTECTION OF THE LAW [2,I]. How should lawyers and judges decide whether the legal effect of that language is to create a constitutional right for blacks to attend integrated rather than segregated schools, for whites to resist AFFIRMATIVE ACTION [1,I], or for a woman to have an abortion when she and her doctor believe it necessary or desirable? One answer, which is particularly popular among conservative politicians, insists that CONSTITUTIONAL INTERPRETATION [1] can only be a matter of discovering and respecting the wishes of those who made the Constitution, who are often called, compendiously, the "Framers." Did the framers of the Fourteenth Amendment intend blacks (or whites or women) to have such a constitutional right? If so, then the correct interpretation of the amendment's legal force includes that right; but if not, then it does not.

The question as to whether this ORIGINAL INTENT [I] method of constitutional interpretation is appropriate is the second of the two most debated issues of constitutional jurisprudence and will be further discussed. Two other answers to the methological question as to how the abstract language of the Constitution should be interpreted each have support among constitutional lawyers and teachers. "Passivism" holds that when the language of the Constitution is abstract or its legal effect is for another reason unclear or debatable, then it should be interpreted to interfere least with the power of state or national legislators or other political officials to do what they think best for the community. Passivism presupposes the foundational thesis that individual constitutional rights are in principle antidemocratic. It therefore acts to shrink the scope of such rights whenever possible.

The method of "integrity" presupposes a very different interpretive attitude: the Constitution is not just a set of discrete political decisions allocating power in different ways but a system of principle. It therefore insists that each of the abstract clauses and provisions should be interpreted and applied in a way that makes it coherent in principle with accepted interpretations of other parts of the Constitution and with principles of political morality that provide the best available foundational justification for the constitutional structure as a whole.

This brief and schematic discussion illustrates the inevitable interconnections between foundational and interpretive issues. Although the original-understanding method denies that foundational morality should figure prominently in constitutional interpretation, it cannot be applied without relying on controversial foundational positions, as will be discussed. The passivist method presupposes a controversial foundational position about the conflict between CONSTITUTIONALISM [2] and democracy, and the method of integrity insists that foundational morality must play an overt, although limited, role in detailed constitutional interpretation.

The Constitution contains both structural and disabling provisions. The structural provisions describe the various branches of the national government, provide methods for electing or selecting their members, and define the powers of these institutions and officials vis-à-vis the institutions and officials of the various states. These structural provisions constitute the American form of democracy; they create government by the people. In contrast, the disabling provisions of the BILL OF RIGHTS [1] and the Civil War amendments, like the FIRST AMENDMENT [2,I] and the due process clause and the equal protection clause, set limits to the overall authority of elected officials. Many lawyers and politicans believe these provisions impede government by the people and are undemocratic for that reason.

Some who take this view regard this friction as a cardinal defect of our constitutional system. They argue that the antidemocratic provisions should be narrowly interpreted to give individuals as few trumps over majority decision as possible. Other lawyers who agree that the disabling provisions are antidemocratic do not agree this is a cause for regret; they believe that a limited democracy is superior to a pure one simply because the former respects individual rights. Is the assumption both these views share— that the Constitution impedes as well as creates democracy—correct? This depends on what we take democracy to be.

Democracy is collective government by the people. But which sense of collective is meant? There are two kinds of collective actions—statistical and communal—and our conception of democracy will turn on which kind we take democratic government to require. Collective action is statistical when what the group does is only a matter of some function—rough or specific—of what the individual members of the group do on their own, that is, with no sense of doing something as a group. In contrast, collective action is communal, when it cannot be reduced to some statistical function of individual action because it is collective in the deeper sense that requires individuals to assume the existence of the group as a separate entity or phenomenon. An orchestra can play a symphony, although a single musician cannot. This is a case of communal rather than statistical action because it is essential to an orchestral performance, not just that a specified function of musicians each plays some appropriate score, but that the musicians play *as* an orchestra, each intending to make a contribution to the performance of the group and not just as isolated individual recitations.

On the statistical understanding, democracy is government according to the wishes of a majority or at least a plurality of the eligible voters. Under communal understanding, democracy is government by distinct entity— the people as such—rather than any set of individuals one by one. These two conceptions of democracy take different views of the distinction previously drawn between the structural and disabling provisions of the Constitution. By the statistical reading, structural provisions are mainly limited to those that are procedurally structural—those that define how members of Congress are elected, what proportion of them it takes to enact legislation, and so forth. By the communal conception, the structural provisions include not only those that are procedurally structural in these ways but also provisions needed to create a genuine political community that can be understood to be acting as a collective unit of political responsibility. A genuine community is one in which government is not only of and for the majority, but of and for all the people, and a genuine community will therefore need to insure not only that each citizen have an opportunity to participate in political decisions through a vote, but that each decision allows each citizen equal concern and respect.

Several of the apparently disabling constitutional provisions can be understood as necessary to guarantee equal respect and concern and, therefore, to be functionally structural rather than disabling of democracy understood by the communal conception. The First Amendment guarantee of free speech, for example, might be thought necessary not only to full and equal participation, but to equal respect as well, and the equal protection clause can be interpreted as requiring equality of concern for all citizens in the deliberations that produce political decisions. Thus, the foundational question of constitutional jurisprudence—whether and how far the Constitution is undemocratic—is actually a deep question that draws on the most fundamental parts of moral and POLITICAL PHILOSOPHY [3,I].

But how should lawyers and judges decide whether some state or statute violates the requirement that states follow "due" process, deny no one the "equal" protection of the laws, or avoid punishments that are cruel and unusual? The original-understanding thesis insists that abstract constitutional provisions should be interpreted to have only the force that the Framers intended or expected them to have. Although this thesis has generally been rejected in Supreme Court practice, lawyers and politicians have offered various arguments in its support. Some say, for example, that because the Framers were the people whose decision made the Constitution our FUNDAMENTAL LAW [2], their convictions about its correct application should be respected.

We must recognize three points about this kind of argument, however. First, any such argument for the original-understanding thesis necessarily draws on normative assumptions about the proper allocation of authority in a democracy among remote constitutional architects, contemporary legislators, and past and contemporary judges.

Second, these normative assumptions cannot be justified, without the most blatant and absurd circularity, by appealing to the intentions, wishes, or decisions of the people whose authority they propose to describe. It would absurd to argue that judges should respect the expectations of the Framers because the Framers expected that they would or believed or decided that they should.

The third point is particularly important: Such arguments, even if supported by independent normative assumptions, are radically incomplete if they purport to establish only the general proposition that lawyers and judges should respect the Framers' wishes or intentions. In most pertinent cases, the question at issue is not whether judges should respect the convictions of the Framers but which of their convictions judges should respect, and how. Suppose the following historical information is discovered: All the framers of the equal-protection clause believed, as a matter of political conviction, that people should all be equal in the eye of the law and the state. They were convinced that certain forms of official RACIAL DISCRIMINATION [3,I] against blacks were morally wrong for that reason, and they adopted the amendment mainly to prevent states from discrimination against blacks in those ways. They agreed, for example, that it would be morally wrong for a state to create certain special remedies for breach of contract and make these remedies available to white plaintiffs, but not black ones. The framers assumed that the clause they were adopting would prohibit that form of discrimination.

They also shared certain opinions about which forms of official discrimination were not wrong and would not be prohibited by the clause. They shared the views, for example, that racial SEGREGATION [4] of public schools did not violate the clause. (Many of them, in fact, voted to segregate schools.) None of them even considered the possibility that state institutions would one day adopt affirmative-action RACIAL QUOTAS [3] designed to repair the damages of past segregation; therefore, none of them had any opinion about whether such quotas would violate the clause. Some of them thought that laws that discriminate in favor of men treat women unjustly. Most framers of the equal protection clause were not of this opinion and assumed that the clause did not outlaw the gender-based distinctions then common. Most of them thought that homosexual acts were grossly immoral and would have been mystified by the suggestion that laws prohibiting such acts constituted an unjustified form of discrimination.

Many contemporary lawyers and judges think that some or all these concrete convictions are inconsistent with the framers' more abstract intention to establish a society of equal CITIZENSHIP [1,I]. Almost everyone now agrees, for example, that racially segregated schools are inconsistant with this ideal. Many people think that affirmative action is inconsistent with the ideal as well, and many people, although not necessarily the same people, think that laws that subordinate women or homosexuals violate the ideal. If a contemporary judge believes that the framers' concrete convictions were inconsistent with their abstract ones on one or more of these matters because the framers of the clause did not reach the correct conclusions about the moral consequences of their own principles, then that judge has a choice to make. It is unhelpful to tell him or her to follow the framers' intentions. The judge needs to know which intentions—at how general a level of abstraction—he or she should follow and why.

In other words, a judge can compose sharply different versions of the original understanding of the equal protection clause, each of which has support in the collection of framers' convictions and expectations. The judge might adopt a reductive version that emphasizes the framers' concrete opinions and hold that the clause condemns only the cases of discrimination that the framers of the clause collectively expected it to condemn. So understood, the clause forbids discrimination against blacks in legal remedy for breach of contract, but it does not forbid racially segregated schools, affirmative-action quotas that disadvantage whites, or discrimination against women or homosexuals. Or, the judge might adopt an abstract version of the original understanding that emphasizes the framers' general conviction to provide equal citizenship, properly understood, for all Americans. Under this version, if we assume that equality is in fact denied by school segregation, quota systems, or laws that subordinate people on the basis of gender or sexual orientation, the clause condemns these discriminations, despite what the framers themselves thought or would have approved.

The important choice judges and other interpreters of the Constitution must make, therefore, is not between the original understanding and some other method of interpretation but between reductive and abstract versions of the original understanding. Many proponents of the original-understanding method have not made this choice coherently; they believe the equal protection clause outlaws racial segregation and affirmative action quotas, but does not outlaw laws discriminating against women or homosexuals, for example. Lawyers and judges must not only choose between the reductive and abstract versions coherently but also on principle, that is, with adequate support in foundational jurisprudence. The passivist interpretive method, which supports the choice of reductive understanding of the framers' intention, is based on the statistical conception of democracy and, accordingly, fails if this conception is rejected. The method of integrity, which presupposes an abstract understanding, is based on a communal conception in which individual rights are not subversive, but constitutive of genuine democracy. Even at the practical level of adjudication, constitutional law is deeply embedded in political philosophy.

RONALD DWORKIN

(SEE ALSO: *Conservatism* [I]; *Judicial Review and Democracy* [3]; *Liberalism* [I].)

Bibliography

DWORKIN, RONALD 1985 *A Matter of Principle.* Cambridge, Mass.: Harvard University Press.

———— 1986 *Law's Empire.* Cambridge, Mass.: Belknap Press of Harvard University Press.

PERRY, MICHAEL J. 1988 *Morality, Politics, and Law.* New York: Oxford University Press.

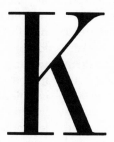

K

KENNEDY, ANTHONY M.
(1936–   )

Anthony M. Kennedy has fulfilled the objectives of President RONALD REAGAN [3,I] in choosing him to fill the vacancy on the Supreme Court created by the retirement of Justice LEWIS F. POWELL [3,I].

First, President Reagan expected that Kennedy's noncontroversial background would ensure him swift confirmation by the Senate. After graduating from Harvard Law School in 1961, Kennedy had worked as a lawyer and lobbyist in California until President GERALD R. FORD [2] appointed him to the Ninth Circuit Court of Appeals in 1975. While on the bench, Kennedy, who also taught constitutional law at McGeorge School of Law, evolved as a relatively colorless, nonideological conservative, but gained notoriety for writing the lower court opinion striking down the LEGISLATIVE VETO [3]—a result subsequently affirmed by the Supreme Court in IMMIGRATION AND NATURALIZATION SERVICE V. CHADHA (1983) [2]. In February 1988 the Senate unanimously confirmed Kennedy.

President Reagan also hoped that Kennedy would join Chief Justice WILLIAM H. REHNQUIST [3,I] and Justices BYRON R. WHITE [4,I], SANDRA DAY O'CONNOR [3,I], and ANTONIN SCALIA [I] to form a conservative majority that would curtail the initiatives of both the WARREN COURT [4] and the BURGER COURT [1]. During his first two terms on the Court, Kennedy did in fact cast the crucial fifth vote with these Justices in several 5–4 decisions expanding state control in the fields of ABORTION [1,I],

CAPITAL PUNISHMENT [1,I], CRIMINAL PROCEDURE [2], and CIVIL RIGHTS [1,I].

However, Kennedy has demonstrated little potential as a leader of the current conservative Justices, others of whom have striven to apply complex interpretative theories to constitutional issues. Instead, Kennedy has emerged as a classically conservative Justice: he has thus far avoided articulating any overarching philosophy of CONSTITUTIONAL INTERPRETATION [1] and has been reluctant to challenge PRECEDENT [3].

Kennedy's votes support a view of FEDERALISM [2,I] under which the states check federal power and are responsible for matters on which the Constitution provides no clear prohibitions. For example, Kennedy joined Justice Scalia's separate opinion in *Pennsylvania v. Union Gas Co.* (1989), which would have denied Congress the power to lift the states' ELEVENTH AMENDMENT [2,I] immunity in exercising its legislative powers under Article I. Kennedy also joined *Will v. Michigan* (1989) and DESHANEY V. WINNEBAGO COUNTY DEPARTMENT OF SOCIAL SERVICES (1989) [I], which effectively held that neither the FOURTEENTH AMENDMENT [2,I] nor SECTION 1983, TITLE 42, U.S. CODE [4] significantly altered state sovereignty. Similarly, Kennedy maintained in dissent in MISSOURI V. JENKINS (1990) [I] that by upholding a federal court order commanding a school district to impose a tax, the majority impermissibly expanded federal court power at the expense of "fundamental precepts for the democratic control of public institutions."

Kennedy's opinions reflect his belief in a living constitution that recognizes, even against claims of individual liberties, the need for government to adapt to changes in technology and its responsibilities. For example, in SKINNER V. RAILWAY LABOR EXECUTIVES ASSOCIATION (1989) [I] and TREASURY EMPLOYEES UNION V. VON RAAB (1989) [I] Kennedy explained that the FOURTH AMENDMENT [2,I] did not preclude DRUG TESTING [I] of railway workers after railroad accidents and of customs workers when there was no individualized suspicion and no evidence of drug abuse in the customs service. Similarly, Kennedy rejected FIRST AMENDMENT [2,I] challenges to a municipal regulation in *Ward v. Rock Against Racism* (1989) that required performers at an outdoor theater to use the city's sound system and technician, even though the requirement restricted certain speakers and messages.

Kennedy's hesitancy to reverse or to expand precedent reflects his preference for deciding cases on the narrowest available grounds and to affect settled doctrine as little as possible. Accordingly, in *Saffle v. Parks* (1990) Kennedy read precedents narrowly in order to deny federal HABEAS CORPUS [2,I] relief because the respondent had raised a new legal claim that could not be applied retroactively on collateral review. Kennedy also hewed closely to precedent in *Barnard v. Thorstenn* (1989) in holding that residency requirements for admission to the Virgin Islands bar violated the PRIVILEGES AND IMMUNITIES [3] clause of Article IV.

In WEBSTER V. REPRODUCTIVE HEALTH SERVICES (1989) [I], Kennedy refused to join Justice Scalia's concurrence urging overruling of ROE V. WADE (1973) [3], but joined Chief Justice Rehnquist's PLURALITY OPINION [3] that rejected the trimester analysis used by the *Roe* Court for measuring the importance of the state's interest. Similarly, in CITY OF RICHMOND V. J. A. CROSON CO. (1989) [I] Kennedy refused to join Justice Scalia's concurrence challenging a city's set-aside of public funds for minority contractors, as well as the congressional program on which it was modeled, which had been upheld in FULLILOVE V. KLUTZNICK (1980) [2]. Kennedy's concurrence emphasized that *Fullilove* posed a difficult but separate issue concerning the scope of congressional power under section 5 of the FOURTEENTH AMENDMENT [2,I].

In PATTERSON V. MCLEAN CREDIT UNION (1989) [I], Kennedy narrowly reaffirmed RUNYON V. MCCRARY (1976) [3]. Although the *Runyon* Court had applied 42 U.S.C. section 1981 to restrict racial discrimination in private school admissions, Kennedy refused to apply the statute's prohibitions of discrimination in the "formation" or "making" of contracts to racial harassment in the conditions of employment.

Dissenting in *James v. Illinois* (1990), Kennedy reluctantly accepted precedents imposing the EXCLUSIONARY RULE [2] on the states, but suggested the rule should not have been applied to prevent the prosecution from using illegally obtained evidence to impeach the defendant

and other defense witnesses in a criminal trial. Similarly, in *Jones v. Thomas* (1989), Kennedy acknowledged, but refused to extend, the traditional DOUBLE JEOPARDY [2,I] prohibition (against multiple sentences for the same offense) to preclude the petitioner's continued confinement under a longer sentence after he had completed a commuted sentence imposed for the same offense. He also explained in WASHINGTON V. HARPER (1990) [I] that the involuntary administration of antipsychotic drugs to a violent prisoner comported with both SUBSTANTIVE DUE PROCESS [4,I] and PROCEDURAL DUE PROCESS [3,I].

However, in his dissent in COUNTY OF ALLEGHENY V. ACLU (1989) [I], Kennedy urged abandoning the Court's traditional test in ESTABLISHMENT CLAUSE [I] cases. He argued that the Court's test separated church and state more than the Framers intended.

The major exception to Kennedy's narrow construction of individual rights is his concurrence in TEXAS V. JOHNSON (1989) [I], in which the Court held 5–4 that the First Amendment protected flag burning as political speech. Kennedy explained that "the flag protects even those who would hold it in contempt."

Kennedy's steadfast refusal to offer a sophisticated alternative to the grander constitutional visions of his fellow conservatives may foretell a modest role for him. Ironically, such a role would reflect Kennedy's vision of the Court's modest role in a system governed by traditional notions of federalism.

MICHAEL J. GERHARDT

(SEE ALSO: *Flag Desecration* [2,I]; *Fourteenth Amendment and Section 5, Framing* [I]; *Fourteenth Amendment and Section 5, Judicial Construction* [I].)

Bibliography

CHEMERINSKY, ERWIN 1989 Foreword: The Vanishing Constitution. *Harvard Law Review* 103:43–104.
MALTZ, EARL M. 1990 The Prospects for a Revival of Conservative Activism in Constitutional Jurisprudence. *Georgia Law Review* 24:629–668.

KENNEDY, ROBERT F.
(Update)

Robert Kennedy was named ATTORNEY GENERAL [1] of the United States in 1961 by his brother President JOHN F. KENNEDY [3]. A graduate of Harvard College and the University of Virginia Law School, he had served as counsel for Senate committees in the 1950s and acquired a reputation as an able and relentless prosecutor. His appointment was ascribed to nepotism and provoked widespread criticism.

Kennedy surrounded himself with an exceptionally able group of lawyers, headed by Archibald Cox of the Harvard Law School as SOLICITOR GENERAL [4,I] and by BYRON R. WHITE [4,I], later of the Supreme Court, as deputy attorney general. In time, he won general respect for capable, humane, and nonpolitical administration of the Department of Justice.

The major challenge was the enforcement of CIVIL RIGHTS [1,I] statutes and decisions. Robert Kennedy brought about the end of SEGREGATION [4] in interstate transportation and used government intervention, including federal marshals, to support black students seeking entry to the University of Mississippi (1962) and the University of Alabama (1963).

Civil rights activists criticized the Justice Department for segregationist appointments to the southern bench and for unwillingness to assume local POLICE POWER [3] in protection of civil rights workers. The problem of FEDERALISM [2,I] and civil rights caused Kennedy anguish, but he believed that LOCAL GOVERNMENTS [I] had primary responsibility for law enforcement and feared the implications of a national police force.

The key to racial justice in his view was voting: "From participation in the elections," he said, "flow all other rights." Department of Justice lawyers fanned out across the South to fight VOTING RIGHTS [4] cases. In 1963, after outrages in Birmingham and elsewhere in the South, the Kennedys submitted a comprehensive civil rights bill to Congress. The CIVIL RIGHTS ACT OF 1964 [1], passed after President Kennedy's assassination, was the most far-reaching civil rights statute since RECONSTRUCTION [I].

Like all attorneys general from 1920 to 1970, Kennedy had the problem of J. EDGAR HOOVER [2], the autocratic and increasingly tendentious chief of the Federal Bureau of Investigation (FBI). Kennedy required the FBI to hire black agents, to reduce its obsession with communism, and to move into such neglected fields as civil rights and organized crime.

Kennedy personally argued the case of GRAY V. SANDERS (1963) [2], in which the Supreme Court struck down the Georgia county-unit system and affirmed the principle of ONE PERSON, ONE VOTE [3]. He secured provision of counsel and reform of the BAIL [1] system in the interests of INDIGENT [2] defendants, and his Committee on Juvenile Delinquency laid the foundation for the War on Poverty in the later 1960s.

He also played a role in foreign affairs but as the President's troubleshooter, not as his legal adviser. The Central Intelligence Agency covert action that the younger Kennedy promoted against Fidel Castro's Cuba, like all covert action, violated international law. During the Cuban missile crisis, however, he opposed a surprise air strike on Cuba, observing that "a sneak attack was not in our traditions." After serving nine prickly months as LYNDON B. JOHNSON's [3] attorney general, Kennedy resigned and ran successfully for the Senate from New York. He was assassinated in 1968.

As attorney general, Robert Kennedy, though not a legal technician himself, had a high appreciation of technical legal ability in others, sought impartial enforcement of domestic law, gave new impetus to the movement for racial justice, and organized one of the strongest Departments of Justice in recent times.

ARTHUR M. SCHLESINGER, JR.

Bibliography

NAVASKY, VICTOR 1971 Kennedy Justice. New York: Atheneum.

SCHLESINGER, ARTHUR M., JR. 1978 Robert F. Kennedy and His Times. Boston: Houghton Mifflin.

LABOR

Labor relations present three principal kinds of constitutional issues. First, to what extent does the FIRST AMENDMENT [2,I] protect employees' efforts to organize labor unions and solicit support, and to what extent does it limit the power of unions over their members? Second, how does the doctrine of federal preemption restrict the states in regulating union and management activities? Third, what DUE PROCESS [2] guarantees may employers and employees invoke in response to federal and state laws establishing new substantive rules and remedies in employment?

Although the Supreme Court has never squarely determined whether there is a constitutional right to form a labor organization, the existence of such a right has generally been assumed since the decision of the Seventh Circuit in *McLaughlin v. Tilendis* (1968), dealing with public school teachers. Many Supreme Court cases have considered the validity of restrictions on unions' collective action, including attempts to enlist the aid of fellow employees or the public. In *Dorchy v. Kansas* (1926) the Court declared that there is no "absolute right to strike" under the Constitution and held that a state could prohibit a strike or group work stoppage for an illegal purpose, such as extortion. The Court also sustained, in *Steelworkers v. United States* (1959), the constitutionality of the provisions in the TAFT-HARTLEY LABOR MANAGEMENT RELATIONS ACT [4] authorizing an eighty-day INJUNCTION [2] against a strike that "imperil[s] the national health or safety." Finally, summary affirmance in *Postal Clerks v. Blount* (1971) of a three-judge federal district court decision seems to confirm that government employees have

no constitutional right to strike. But the Court has never ruled whether there are any circumstances that would give rise to such a right on the part of private employees.

Separate articles in the main volumes of this encyclopedia cover the constitutionality of restraints on BOYCOTTS [1] and PICKETING [3] by labor unions. In *DeBartolo Corp. v. Florida Gulf Coast Building Trades* (1988), the Supreme Court engaged in some rather strained statutory interpretation to avoid "serious constitutional concerns" and held that a union's handbilling, as distinguished from picketing, did not "coerce" a shopping mall's tenants within the meaning of the National Labor Relations Act. (The handbills asked customers not to deal with any of the neutral or "secondary" retailers in the mall.) The Court pinpointed the critical distinction between handbilling and picketing: "The loss of customers because they read a handbill urging them not to patronize a business, and not because they are intimidated by a line of picketers, is the result of mere persuasion." This emphasis on the means of communication does not fully explain why the same message, if delivered by a solitary picket wearing a large placard, should necessarily be intimidating and not persuasive.

Federal laws governing private employment and many state laws governing public employment authorize "union security" agreements. Such an agreement requires financial support of the union that acts as COLLECTIVE BARGAINING [1] agent by all employees benefiting from its representation. The Supreme Court sustained these provisions against First Amendment claims of freedom of association in *Railway Employees' Department v. Hanson* (1956) and ABOOD v. DETROIT BOARD OF EDUCATION (1977) [1]. But to counter constitutional free speech issues, the Court also held in *Machinists v. Street* (1961) and *Abood* that a union could use compulsory financial contributions only for collective bargaining activities and not for political or ideological purposes opposed by an employee. The Court recognized there would be "difficult problems in drawing lines" in this area.

The WAGNER (NATIONAL LABOR RELATIONS) ACT [4] enacted in 1935 and substantially revised in 1947 and 1959, forbids both employers and unions in INTERSTATE COMMERCE [2] from coercing employees in their right to join, or not join, a labor organization. In addition, the 1947 Taft-Hartley Act amendments made the contracts of such employers and unions enforceable in the courts under federal law. Previously, state law generally applied to all these matters. In *San Diego Building Trades v. Garmon* (1959), the Supreme Court held that if activity in the labor field is "arguably subject" to federal protection or prohibition, the states must ordinarily yield jurisdiction. The Court added in *Machinists Lodge 76 v. Wisconsin Employment Relations Commission* (1976) that the states also cannot regulate conduct that Congress intended to leave unregulated.

There are several exceptions to this doctrine of federal PREEMPTION [3]. Compelling local interests in the maintenance of domestic peace or minimum labor standards enable the states to deal with violence, malicious LIBEL [3], or TRESPASS [4] to private property, and to prescribe requirements for job safety and insured health care plans. Even if conduct is arguably protected by federal law such as union access to employer premises during an organizing campaign—thus implicating federal supremacy most acutely—preemption does not follow invariably. In *Sears, Roebuck and Co. v. San Diego Carpenters* (1978), the Court concluded that a state court could determine whether a union's trespassory picketing was actually protected by federal law when the union had declined to seek a federal ruling on the issue, the employer had no way of obtaining one, and the trespass was "far more likely to be unprotected than protected." Finally, although federal substantive law is now applicable to union–employer contracts, the Supreme Court held in *Dowd Box Co. v. Courtney* (1962) that state courts retain concurrent jurisdiction over suits for their violation.

Federal and state labor legislation enacted during the twentieth century has often abrogated COMMON LAW [1] claims, created new statutory rights and obligations, and substituted administrative proceedings for TRIAL BY JURY [4]. These laws have posed due process and other constitutional questions. After some initial opposition, the courts have tended to sustain these innovations. The Supreme Court upheld the constitutionality of a state WORKERS' COMPENSATION [4] law in NEW YORK CENTRAL RAILROAD COMPANY V. WHITE (1917) [3], of the federal unemploy-

ment tax in STEWARD MACHINE COMPANY V. DAVIS (1937) [4], and of the National Labor Relations Act in *NLRB v. Jones and Laughlin Steel Corp.* (1937). But to avoid constitutional problems, the Court declared in *Steele v. Louisville & Nashville Railroad Co.* (1944) that the federal labor laws, in granting majority unions the power of exclusive representation, also implied a duty to represent all the members of a bargaining unit fairly and nondiscriminatorily. A new round of battles over due process may have opened when the Montana Supreme Court ruled 4–3 in *Meech v. Hillhaven West, Inc.* (1989) that the state's pioneering "wrongful discharge" statute, which displaced common law claims for dismissal, did not violate the Montana Constitution's guarantee of "full legal redress."

THEODORE J. ST. ANTOINE

(SEE ALSO: *Freedom of Assembly and Association* [2]; *Freedom of Speech* [2,I].)

Bibliography

GORMAN, ROBERT A. 1976 *Basic Text on Labor Law: Unionization and Collective Bargaining.* Pages 209–215, 257–262, 655–661, 695–728. St. Paul, Minn.: West Publishing Co.
WELLINGTON, HARRY H. 1968 *Labor and the Legal Process.* Pages 145–184, 223–266. New Haven, Conn.: Yale University Press.

LABOR MOVEMENT

The American labor movement has had a passionate, paradoxical, and often bitter relationship with the Constitution. During the era of LOCHNER V. NEW YORK (1905) [3], from the 1880s to the 1920s, most judges agreed that labor was a commodity like any other; the Constitution guaranteed workers the right freely to sell their labor "just as the employer may sell his iron or coal." During these decades, state and federal courts protected employers' and individual workers' rights to contract and compete in the marketplace free from what judges deemed unwarranted governmental interferences. Courts voided many hours and safety laws as unconstitutional interferences with liberty of contract. Courts enjoined strikes and BOYCOTTS [1] as tortious interferences with employers' freedom of enterprise. Even in "legal" strikes, many state and federal courts held that there was no such thing as peaceful PICKETING [3].

The burdens of repression and semi-outlawry drove trade unionists to develop an alternative constitutional outlook. They assailed the COMMON LAW [1] view that labor was a mere commodity and that employers could acquire a property right in their workers' labor or "human capacities." The INJUNCTIONS [2] that forbade strikers' "interference" with this right were, in labor's view, "judicial re-enactments of slavery." The THIRTEENTH AMENDMENT [4]—even some of the Supreme Court's own Thirteenth Amendment decisions—seemed to support these claims. According to the unions, the Thirteenth Amendment, which abolished slavery, was a "glorious labor amendment" that stood not only for self-owernship but also for labor's dignity and independence. These ideas drew upon the Lincolnian "Free Labor" philosophy of the Thirteenth Amendment's framers who vowed that the amendment would always stand as a shield against the oppression of "free labor both black and white."

Labor's constitutional critique of the injunction also invoked the FIRST AMENDMENT [2,I]. However slight a feature of official constitutional doctrine, the First Amendment, in the eyes of nineteenth-century trade unionists, always stood for the sanctity of association by citizens and "uniting peaceably to redress wrongs." Injunctions against peaceful persuasion, meetings, publications, parades, and picketing "trampled on" this vision of the First Amendment.

During the *Lochner* era, only a few dissenting jurists embraced aspects of labor's constitutional vision. But labor's constitutional views were seconded by many NEW DEAL [I] congressmen who championed the NORRIS-LaGUARDIA ACT [3] and WAGNER ACT [4]. These statutes supplanted the old common law regime and ushered in the modern labor-law era. Then, with the demise of *Lochner*-era SUBSTANTIVE DUE PROCESS [4,I] and the emergence of a New Deal majority on the Supreme Court, the Court began to extend First Amendment protection to labor protest.

In THORNHILL V. ALABAMA (1940) [4] the Court struck down a state antipicketing statute, declaring that "the dissemination of information concerning the facts of a labor dispute must be regarded as within that area of free discussion that is guaranteed by the Constitution." Picketing was a means of communicating with the public about matters of public concern. Although decided on the narrow ground of OVERBREADTH [3], *Thornhill* established that restrictions on picketing were subject to the constraints of the First Amendment.

In *Thornhill*, the Court did not adopt organized labor's—and New Deal reformers'—view that liberty of labor protest was bound up with an alternative conception of labor and of industrial democracy. Instead, the *Thornhill* Court classified picketing as political speech, perhaps because it had just abandoned the economic due-process doctrines of the *Lochner* era and did not want to appear to be meddling anew in economic affairs. But the marketplace dimension of picketing was inescapable. Picketing is inextricable from strikes and boycotts: a form of moral and political expression at the same time it aims to produce marketplace pressure and advantage. The Court could not recognize and define a constitutional right to picket without confronting the question of constitutional protection for strikes and boycotts. After *Thornhill*, several lower federal courts began to forge substantial First and Thirteenth Amendment limits on the states' power to bar peaceful strikes and boycotts.

But the Supreme Court soon disappointed those who expected it to recognize these nascent rights. Instead, the Court returned the issue to the common-law terrain, reaffirming the law's traditional role of restricting the scope of allowable protest and mutual aid. In *Carpenters & Joiners Union, Local No. 213 v. Ritter's Cafe* (1942) the Court upheld a state court injunction against peaceful picketing. "[R]ecognition of peaceful picketing as an exercise of free speech," the Court reasoned, "does not imply that the states must be without power" to confine the bounds of industrial disputes—in this case, to forbid any pickets urging the public to boycott a cafe whose owner "had awarded a building contract to a man who was unfair to organized labor." The state court had found that the boycott violated the state's ANTITRUST LAWS [1]; the Supreme Court held that state courts and legislatures remained free to "draw the line" in this fashion, balancing "the effort of the employer to carry on his business free from the interference of others against the effort of labor to further its economic self-interest."

In the new regime of judicial deference toward state regulation of business and commerce, this characterization of labor conflicts—as clashes of private economic interests—was a gloomy sign from labor's perspective. Beginning with *Ritter's Cafe*, the Court ceased characterizing industrial disputes and labor picketing as involving matters of public concern. By the 1950s, labor protest was held to involve "purely commercial activities which may be regulated by the state upon any reasonable basis." Organized workers once again were sellers of a commodity like any other, and judicial restraint was therefore the appropriate posture. Since the New Deal, primary strikes over wages and working conditions have enjoyed considerable statutory protection; but strikes or boycotts that fall outside the narrow circle of statutory or state court approval have found almost no shelter in the Constitution. Today, even peaceful picketing urging consumers not to buy the products of "unfair" employers continues to be routinely enjoined, and First Amendment challenges are routinely rebuffed.

Meanwhile, First Amendment doctrine has undergone transformations that render its treatment of labor protest anomalous. Nonlabor picketing now enjoys full First Amendment protection from content-based restrictions.

Moreover, in *NAACP v. Claiborne Hardware Co.* (1982), the Court held that peaceful picketing by CIVIL RIGHTS [1,I] groups in support of a boycott of white merchants was fully shielded by the First Amendment. The Court rejected the argument that the picketing was unprotected because the pickets frequently had no direct dispute with the merchants. The pickets' main goal was DESEGREGATION [2] of local public facilities; thus, the boycott was largely a "secondary" one, in labor-law jargon. The *Claiborne* Court noted that no similar First Amendment protection shields picketing in support of labor boycotts, but the Court found the difference in constitutional status justified by the difference it perceived between the two kinds of boycotts. The black citizens' boycott involved "expression on public issues, which has always rested on the highest rung of the hierarchy of first amendment values." Labor boycotts, by contrast, involve mere clashes of economic interests. Forgetting what it once had recognized—that labor protest also involves "public issues"—the Court relegated labor picketing to a second-class status.

Many commentators have assailed the Court's "public issue" versus "labor" picketing distinction, particularly in light of the elevation of commercial advertising to the status of constitutionally protected speech. At the time of *Thornhill*, the Court regarded government regulation of COMMERCIAL SPEECH [1,I] as falling within that domain of social and economic policy that it behooved the Court to leave alone. More recently, however, the Court in CENTRAL HUDSON GAS AND ELECTRIC CORP. V. PUBLIC SERVICE COMMISSION (1980) [1] extended substantial First Amendment protection to commercial advertising so that it now enjoys more constitutional protection than peaceful labor picketing.

It may be that the Court continues to relegate labor protest to a second-class constitutional status because it does not view industrial conflict as a matter of much public concern. Other factors may also figure. Many current decisions rest on the hoary nineteenth-century assumption that picketing is inherently coercive. Today's courts still frequently seem unable to distinguish physical coercion on the part of pickets from the economic force exerted on an employer if uncoerced listeners are simply persuaded by the pickets' message.

Courts may also tolerate severe governmental restraints on labor protest in part because they see unions as powerful political and economic players, more or less evenly matched with their employer-adversaries. In fact, this parity has rarely existed; today, the labor movement is extremely weak—as weak, in some respects, as it was before the New Deal reforms. But it is unlikely that the courts will change the Constitution's treatment of labor protest unless workers and unions themselves again create

on a massive scale a protest movement that appeals beyond existing law to an alternative constitutional tradition and the moral imagination of the public.

WILLIAM E. FORBATH

Bibliography

FORBATH, WILLIAM 1989 The Shaping of the American Labor Movement. *Harvard Law Review* 102:1109–1256.

NOTE (Cynthia Estlund) 1982 Labor Picketing and Commercial Speech: Free Enterprise Values in the Doctrine of Free Speech. *Yale Law Journal* 91:938–960.

POPE, JAMES 1987 Labor and the Constitution: From Abolition to Deindustrialization. *Texas Law Review* 65:1071–1136.

LAND USE

See: Eminent Domain [2, I]; Zoning [4, I]

LAW AND ECONOMICS THEORY

The "positive" economic theory of law argues that one can discern an economic logic implicit in law, constitutional as well as any other. Economic analysis can also play a normative role, providing a benchmark for assessing the soundness of any particular constitutional clause or interpretation. (As economics itself does not establish indisputable criteria of judgment, the benchmark itself may be blurry.) For some constitutional provisions or doctrines, the relevance of economics is obvious; the Fifth Amendment's takings clause is an example.

A market economy requires private property. One can imagine an economy of government firms relating to each other, to workers, and to consumers primarily through market operations. But if capital were allocated by government, this would be an odd parody of a market economy, and if capital were allocated by markets in the sense that individuals were free to place their capital where they chose, the firms would not be government firms. The Fifth Amendment's requirement of JUST COMPENSATION [3] for the TAKING OF PROPERTY [4,I] thus supplies a qualified protection for the market economy. The economist naturally asks how alternative constructions of the clause will affect incentives—the feature of a market economy that accounts in large measure for its productivity.

One might view the clause as aimed at assuring owners correct incentives to invest and improve property. The Supreme Court's focus on "investment-backed expectations" in PENN CENTRAL TRANSPORTATION CO. V. NEW YORK CITY (1978) [3] suggests such a concern. But insurance against such risks could be provided by private insurers, and so the question arises why the duty to pay should fall on government. At least one answer—again looking at incentives—is that such a duty will improve incentives for government decision makers, deterring the pursuit of programs that sacrifice a greater value than they produce.

Does such a view lead to a rule that compensation is required for government acts that fail some sort of cost-benefit test, and not for ones that pass? Clearly not. To resolve claims on such a basis would require the courts to assess the wisdom of virtually every government decision, a costly repetition of other branches' work. Because many of the benefits and costs of a program are political, this inquiry would take courts into areas where other institutions might have a comparative advantage. Finally, the Constitution establishes rights. Whether created for instrumental or for ethical reasons (e.g., a sense of the moral fitness of people's owning themselves and what they receive in free exchanges with others), a right would hardly be worthy of the name if it succumbed whenever a cost-benefit test ran against it. Thus, the economist, along with everyone else, would not define the protections of the taking clause by reference to "case utilitarianism" (assessing particular acts in terms of their direct effect on aggregate utility).

But the criterion of maximizing utility may help define the rules that embody constitutional rights—"rule utilitarianism." Reading the takings clause to require compensation for all government acts, for instance, would provide a strong incentive against wasteful government acts. But such a rule would entail enormous administrative and information costs—though never the costs of evaluating the program's benefits, as the rejected case-utilitarian view would. The concern for administrative costs suggests a reading of the takings clause that requires compensation for any act (or class of acts), except where its costs are relatively widespread—in the extreme case, for example, those of a change in monetary policy—so that the administrative costs of awarding compensation are high. (The compensation itself is not a social cost, but a transfer from taxpayers or users to whoever's property is taken. Effecting the transfer through raising taxes will usually impose secondary costs, however, by reducing economic incentives to engage in the taxed activity.)

In fact, many features of taking law seem to fit such a notion comfortably: the refusal to view all regulatory losses as automatically compensable, coupled with compensability for at least some extreme cases; consideration of "average reciprocity of advantage," offsetting benefits that a property owner may gain from a scheme as a whole, such as a historic district, and that would complicate any effort to compute compensation; and award of compen-

sation for even a very small loss where it takes the form of a complete taking of all rights in a diminutive piece of property.

On the other hand, the courts' relative indifference to regulations sweeping away much of the value of undeveloped land raises a question about the judicial vision of the clause. Focus on incentives for property owners might support such relative indifference; the existence of land, as opposed to buildings, typically requires no investor effort. (In *Kaiser Aetna v. United States*, 1979, where human effort had created a waterway, the Supreme Court extended protections to private interests beyond what it would have afforded similar interests in a natural waterway.) Focus on incentives for government and recognition of the opportunity costs of undeveloped resources preempted by government might tilt the balance toward protection in some of these cases.

The takings clause may seem easy territory for demonstrating a constitutional concern for economic incentives, but broadly defined, such a concern pervades the document. The Framers' fear of excessive governmental power led them to rely on institutional incentives as a check. The SEPARATION OF POWERS [4] rests on an assumption about human behavior familiar to economists: even in government, people will pursue personal advantage to a large degree. Thus, as in the private marketplace, the Constitution used private incentives to achieve a public end, ambition being made to counteract ambition, as JAMES MADISON [3] put it in THE FEDERALIST [2] #51.

The system of checks exposes a complex relation between efficiency at different levels. While Judge Richard Posner has argued that separation of powers is at least in part an effort to increase government efficiency by tailoring the institutional structure to particular government tasks, the structure also impedes government action, making it less efficient as an institution. But if some sort of overall efficiency is the constitutional goal (e.g., getting the maximum human benefit out of scarce resources), the Framers must have found certain activities per se inefficient. If government action itself is typically inefficient, hobbling it may increase overall efficiency by forestalling inefficient ECONOMIC REGULATION [2]. On the other hand, once inefficient regulations exist, separation of powers may decrease efficiency by delaying deregulation long after a consensus has developed that government intervention is unwise.

Another example of a per se inefficient activity may be the FIRST AMENDMENT [2,I] ban on an ESTABLISHMENT OF RELIGION [2], which would seem to negate even government subsidies to religion that offset market failure and would thus presumably be efficient. But reading the clause as a requirement of government neutrality in religion, one can readily find a justification in economics, broadly conceived. The Framers could easily have thought that the costs of any government nonneutrality, in social and political divisiveness, would generally outweigh benefits.

If the Constitution does prefer a set of social "goods," such as minimal government and government neutrality toward religion and speech, there remains the problem of defining the degree of preference. Few good things come without costs, and one would naturally expect courts to be wary of constitutional interpretations that extend constitutional goods to a point of extravagant cost. The Constitution is not a "suicide pact," as Justice ROBERT H. JACKSON [3] cautioned in TERMINIELLO V. CHICAGO (1949) [4]. Similarly, if "cost-benefit" sounds like an economist's approach, "balancing" the costs of alternative rules is surely no more than recognition that at some point one set of rights must yield to another. Justice OLIVER WENDELL HOLMES, JR. [2] wrote in *Hudson County Water Co. v. McCarter* (1908), "All rights tend to declare themselves absolute to their logical extreme. Yet all in fact are limited by the neighborhood of principles of policy which are other than those on which the particular right is founded, and which become strong enough to hold their own when a certain point is reached."

Still, the economist's concern for cost may be special. The subject of economics is the problem of maximizing something (e.g., utility, wealth), subject to the constraint of scarcity. Whether the relevant scarcity is of conventional commodities or of constitutional goods, such as opportunities to communicate, the economist should have something useful to say. Indeed, an important insight of economics is that costs are simply benefits (goods) given up in pursuit of other goods. An economist should be quicker than most to spot opportunity costs and to dispel the fallacy that costs could ever be purely pecuniary. The costs of a policy, including a constitutional rule, are the goods, services, and benefits that it destroys or sacrifices. To the extent economic analysis of law flourishes, one may expect to find cost arguments more common, explicit, and sophisticated. Thus, although in CLEVELAND BOARD OF EDUCATION V. LAFLEUR (1974) [1] the Court declared that "administrative convenience alone is insufficient to make valid what is otherwise a violation of due process of law," MATHEWS V. ELDRIDGE (1976) [3] made such costs integral to its analysis of procedural due process.

What, then, is distinctive about the economic approach? Neither the interest in costs nor the balancing of the costs of various approaches seems unique to analysts of economic bent, even if economists typically press them furthest. There are, however, analytic tools employed by economists as a matter of course, but by others rarely, if at all.

One specialty of economics is the search for the true incidence of the costs of taxes, subsidies, and regulations. Inelastic suppliers and demanders bear these costs. A supply is inelastic if suppliers have few alternative uses of the relevant resources. A tax on coal production is likely to fall largely on the owners of coal in place, as there are few activities to which they can divert their coal-mining property. This is still more true if users of coal have many alternatives—that is, if demand is quite elastic. This is clearest where the coal tax of a single state is at issue, and demanders' substitutes include the supply of all coal producers outside the taxing state.

Use of the analysis is obvious for issues of the constitutionality of state taxes or regulations that are challenged as offending the DORMANT COMMERCE CLAUSE [I], that is, the courts' implied authority to strike down state rules that unduly intrude on INTERSTATE COMMERCE [2], even where Congress has been silent. Indeed, in assessing a coal severance tax against a COMMERCE CLAUSE [1,I] attack, the Court alluded in *Commonwealth Edison Co. v. Montana* (1981) to the elasticity of demand as an important consideration, but declined to pursue the matter. The decision not to pursue it appears correct, for the "export" of the tax seems unlikely unless the taxing state has market power in the good. This will not be true unless the state accounts for a high proportion of supply or colludes with other supplying states. In either case, the state is likely to be so drastically outnumbered by importing states as to make a congressional remedy easy.

The search for incidence is useful in other, less obvious areas. The Supreme Court's PUBLIC FORUM [3,I] jurisprudence, for example, rests on the notion that for a special class of speakers the burden of restrictions on the communicative use of public property is relatively severe because of their lack of alternative means of reaching an audience. Thus, Justice HUGO L. BLACK [1] argued in *Martin v. City of Struthers* (1943) that "door to door distribution of circulars is essential to the poorly financed causes of little people." The question raised is a good one, but the asserted answer may be an oversimplification. Though doubtless the poor buy a lower per capita share of the food supply than the nonpoor, the nonpoor obviously do not "buy up" all the food. Similarly, it is far from clear that messages relating to causes involving the poor are underrepresented in market channels of communication. (To the extent that the poor are a demoralized underclass, they likely would not initiate many communications of any kind, including circulars and street demonstrations.)

The economist's training generally leads to a search for effects on ultimate consumers and providers. Where would-be speakers challenge a private property owner's speech restrictions, as at the shopping center in *Lloyd Corp. v. Tanner* (1972), or where a shopping center owner challenges a state's limits on his ability to restrain speech, as in PRUNEYARD SHOPPING CENTER V. ROBINS (1980) [3], the Court has framed the dispute as one between the property rights of the owner and the free speech rights of speakers. But to the economist a more relevant formulation is the conflict between one set of property users' interest in communication and another set's interest in being free from the communications. A profit-seeking owner of a shopping center is a middleman, presumably seeking an economically optimal tradeoff: to allow speech up to the point where the benefit (captured by him in rents) exceeds the costs (suffered by him as diminished rentals as result of user resistance). The point suggests yet another perspective on the idea that the cost of communication on sidewalks, streets, or other government property is low. The speaker's out-of-pocket cost is low, to be sure, but in part because some of the burden is borne by those whose convenience or tranquillity is reduced. Of course, if government officials cannot charge fees to capture some of the benefits of free communication, yet do bear some of its costs (in the form of less personal tranquillity themselves), the public forum doctrine may be a justifiable subsidy to offset their skewed incentives in other branches.

If there is an economic logic implicit in constitutional law, is the reason that the Framers and the courts have used the tools of economic analysis intuitively rather than explicitly or that some process (e.g., the selection of cases for litigation as opposed to settlement) tends to screen out economically unsound precedents? To the extent that the first explanation is sound, there may appear some tension between the positive economic theory and any special claim for the tools of economic analysis; highly refined economic thinking might lead to results at odds with those of an intuitive economic sense. But the essential concerns of economic theory—with incentives, with maximizing values subject to constraints, with tradeoffs at the margin, with identifying the true nature and incidence of costs—seem basic to any coherent approach to social structure, of which constitution making is a variety. Economic analysis thus seems inextricably linked to CONSTITUTIONAL INTERPRETATION [1], with perhaps no more at stake than degrees of sophistication.

STEPHEN F. WILLIAMS

(SEE ALSO: *Economic Analysis* [2]; *Economic Development* [I]; *Economic Equal Protection* [I]; *Economic Liberties* [2].)

Bibliography

COASE, R. H. 1977 Advertising and Free Speech. *Journal of Legal Studies* 6:1–34.
CONFERENCE 1975 Economic Analysis of Political Behavior. *Journal of Law and Economics* 18:587–918.
EASTERBROOK, FRANK H. 1984 Foreword: The Court and the Economic System. *Harvard Law Review* 98:1–60.
EPSTEIN, RICHARD A. 1985 *Takings*. Cambridge, Mass.: Harvard University Press.
McCONNELL, MICHAEL W. and POSNER, RICHARD A. 1989 An Economic Approach to Issues of Religious Freedom. *University of Chicago Law Review* 56:1–60.
POSNER, RICHARD A. 1986 *Economic Analysis of Law*, 3rd ed. Boston: Little, Brown.
SOWELL, THOMAS 1980 *Knowledge and Decisions*. New York: Basic Books.
SYMPOSIUM 1987 The Constitution as an Economic Document. *George Washington Law Review* 56:1–186.

LEGAL CULTURE

The expression "legal culture" refers to opinions, attitudes, values, and expectations with regard to law and legal institutions. Every man and woman in society has at least some opinions on this subject—about judges, courts, the Supreme Court, or lawyers—but the expression, as the word "culture" implies, refers not so much to individuals as to generalizations about the opinions and values of members of some distinct group, class, category, or jurisdiction. One can speak about the legal culture of men as opposed to women, blacks as opposed to whites, or of salespeople, teachers, drug addicts, or people who live on farms. It may also be possible to make statistical generalizations about particular countries, so that it may make sense to talk about American legal culture as opposed to Portuguese or Korean legal culture.

One can distinguish between an "external" and an "internal" legal culture. The internal legal culture is the legal culture of those members of society "inside" the legal system, so to speak—that is, those who perform specialized legal tasks, for example, lawyers and judges. The legal culture of everybody else is external legal culture.

Concepts of legal culture are, or ought to be, significant for the understanding of constitutional history and in explaining how constitutional doctrine gets made. Political and social movements always provide the motor force for constitution making and for constitutional change; the decisions of high courts, which create the fabric of constitutional law, are always the product of concrete lawsuits, in which real parties with real social and economic interests are contending. In both cases, purposes, goals, and ideals of litigators and other actors (and of lawyers and judges) are the immediate cause of both stasis or change. Hence, legal culture, it can be argued, is what creates constitutional law and gives meaning and life to the constitutional system.

It is obvious that the texture of constitutional law has changed radically in the course of American history; yet the text of the Constitution itself has been extremely durable, not to say sluggish. The leading cases of modern constitutional law are or pretend to be "interpretations" or glosses on the post–Civil War amendments, which have not been altered in over a century; the BILL OF RIGHTS [1]; or the text of the original Constitution, which is now some two centuries old. A scholar of 1870 or 1880 who woke from a century's sleep would simply not recognize today's body of constitutional doctrine; current EQUAL PROTECTION [2,I] doctrine, for example, would be totally beyond his or her comprehension. Yet much of the standard work on both CONSTITUTIONAL THEORY [I] and constitutional history has a strongly normative flavor, and it fails to come to grips with the powerful forces that have turned old doctrines topsy-turvy and pulled new doctrines into existence like rabbits from a magician's hat.

The radical changes in constitutional doctrine imply radical changes in internal legal culture; but these in turn are reflexes of radical changes in external legal culture, the culture of the educated community, of business and political leaders, and indeed, of the public at large. The Constitution, in fact, is always interpreted (and necessarily so) in the light of ruling ideas of the times. The Justices may make use of general social norms either consciously or unconsciously; because of the standardized and formalistic style in which Supreme Court decisions are written, it is not easy to know the level of awareness of the Justices or the way in which they conceive of their judicial role.

In the broadest sense, studies of constitutional doctrine and constitutional history that are sensitive to social context are studies of legal culture, although they do not necessarily use this term. Other studies deal with American culture and the Constitution more explicitly: Michael Kammen, for example, has written a history of the meaning and imagery of the Constitution in American culture— an exploration, among other things, of the symbolic importance of the Constitution in American politics and the cult of the Constitution as a "sacred" document.

Constitutional doctrine itself is a reflection of legal culture, but it would be naive to assume that the general public or any particular segment of it share the same views as the justices who enunciate legal doctrine. There has been some research on public attitudes toward CIVIL LIBERTIES [1,I] and the Bill of Rights; such studies are necessarily studies of the congruence (or lack of congruence) of external and internal legal culture. The most important recent study (by Herbert McClosky and Alida Brill, in 1983) found that the general public tends to agree strongly with the general ideas behind the Bill of Rights, but on many specific issues, public opinion differs from the current state of doctrine—and from the views of legal and political elites. These differences tilt in a particular direction. The general public is less "liberal" than the

Court and less "liberal" than legal and political elites on such issues as whether PORNOGRAPHY [3] can be banned, whether atheists should be allowed to teach or hold public office, or how far to carry the SEPARATION OF CHURCH AND STATE [4,I].

So-called impact studies are also relevant to the study of legal culture. These are studies of the ways in which decisions of the Supreme Court, or other courts, are received, used, followed, evaded, or flouted by the public, or some particular part of the public. Legal culture is not only the source of doctrine; it monitors the reaction to doctrine and to specific decisions of the courts. There is a sizeable literature, for example, on reactions to the Supreme Court's decisions barring prayers from public schools. In the broadest sense, much of the vast literature on the controversy over ABORTION [1,I] or on school DESEGREGATION [2] is impact literature and, hence, relevant to the role of legal culture in the constitutional system. But there has not been much success as yet in framing general theories about impact or about the role of legal culture in producing compliant or noncompliant behavior.

The neglect of legal culture by constitutional scholars has undoubtedly impoverished the understanding of constitutional law. Normative arguments are tossed back and forth on many crucial issues: for example, what ways of "interpreting" the Constitution are legitimate and what ways are illegitimate. "Originalists" claim that the duty of judges is to seek out the ORIGINAL INTENT [I] of the Framers; judges have no legitimate right to read their own values into the Constitution. Such arguments, rhetorically speaking, put the issue very starkly as a kind of either-or position. Apparently, the only alternative to STRICT CONSTRUCTION [4] is a situation in which judges act arbitrarily, according to whim, and simply spin constitutional doctrines out of their heads. In a system of CHECKS AND BALANCES [1], where are the checks and balances on the power of the Supreme Court Justices to create law out of thin air?

One answer (there are many others) is that the Justices are constrained by internal and external legal cultures. The internal legal culture is inescapably inside the heads of the Justices. The Justices are lawyers, trained in a particular tradition. The internal legal culture has its own powerful symbols, its own language and etiquette; and the Justices operate in this context. Of course, each Justice is an individual man or woman; each has his or her own take on the internal legal culture. But this culture sets boundaries and limits within which the Court, of necessity, does its work.

The external legal culture is an even more powerful curb, in fact, if not in theory. The concept of legal culture assumes that judges never "invent" doctrine; that in any given period, the general legal culture sets limits, defines boundaries, and establishes a range of opinions no less than does the internal legal culture (the legal tradition). It is out of the question for a Supreme Court Justice today, no matter how "conservative," to be as retrograde on racial issues as the most "liberal" judge of the 1880s. The whole spectrum of opinion has shifted in the direction of racial equality, and the corresponding interpretation of the meaning of equal protection has shifted accordingly. The social context is the source of the norms that mold general opinion on matters of race. The norms change over time as context changes. The Justices today live in a world of computers, gene-splicing, and communication satellites, and their views are profoundly affected by the world all about them. They also live in a society dedicated more deeply to individual rights and to race and gender equality than the world of their predecessors. The study of legal culture is a study of this world, and those who stress this factor believe it is one of the best ways to understand where the Court has been, where it is, and where it is going.

                                    LAWRENCE M. FRIEDMAN

Bibliography

FRIEDMAN, LAWRENCE M. 1975 *The Legal System: A Social Science Perspective.* New York: Russell Sage Foundation.
——— 1990 *The Republic of Choice: Law, Authority, and Culture.* Cambridge, Mass.: Harvard University Press.
KAMMEN, MICHAEL 1986 *A Machine that Would Go of Itself: The Constitution in American Culture.* New York: Alfred A. Knopf.
MCCLOSKY, HERBERT and BRILL, ALIDA 1983 *Dimensions of Tolerance: What Americans Believe About Civil Liberties.* New York: Russell Sage Foundation.
MUIR, WILLIAM K., JR. 1967 *Prayer in the Public Schools: Law and Attitude Change.* Chicago: University of Chicago Press.
UROFSKY, MELVIN I. 1988 *A March of Liberty: A Constitutional History of the United States.* New York: Alfred A. Knopf.

LEGISLATIVE PURPOSES AND MOTIVES

Article I of the Constitution vests all legislative powers in the Congress of the United States. Congress is thus ordained to be the policymaking arm of the government. Since Congress exercises this authority through the separate flexing of 435 members of the HOUSE OF REPRESENTATIVES [I] and the 100 members of the Senate, the statutes passed by Congress are always collective works—written, amended, and propounded by many. As a result, discerning a single purpose or motive for most statutes is not easy.

An individual member of Congress proposes legislation to solve a problem. As that proposal winds its way through the legislative process, many forces affect the proposal and its meaning. Witnesses favoring and opposing the proposal testify before committees, and their testimony may present an interpretation altogether different from that intended by the proposal's sponsor. While the bill remains in committee, amendments may be offered and voted upon, further changing the purposes or effects of the proposal. Constituents, hearing about the proposal, will express their views to their representatives, voicing still other potentially competing concerns and perceptions about the proposal. After the proposal comes out of the committee, frequently in amended form, it is further refined and amended in floor debate. Again, the purposes and perceptions of the legislators are vast and varied. Once the proposal is approved in one chamber, the whole process is replicated in the other chamber. If further amendments are adopted in the second chamber, the differences between the two chambers' versions are ironed out in a "conference committee," consisting of legislators from both chambers. Only when the House and Senate approve an identical bill does the proposal go to the President for his approval.

With such a tortuous journey to complete, a piece of legislation rarely survives its odyssey with a clear purpose intact. As a result, judges and lawyers must devote much of their time and attention to the process of interpreting statutes. Although the judges, lawyers, and lawmakers have developed many rules and strictures for performing this task, there is much disagreement on what rules or strictures apply in a particular case.

Sometimes a legislative body will seek to ease the task of interpretation by putting a "preamble" or "statement of purposes" into the statute. Unfortunately, such efforts frequently end up as broad platitudes that do not help readers to discern more subtle nuances, such as the LEGISLATIVE INTENT [3] or purpose of a statute. On occasion, the preamble is used to reassure dubious legislators that the statute does not have the effect that its plain words imply. Because these preambles are usually included as window dressing, most courts have rejected efforts to use the preamble to "trump" the plain meaning of the words of the statute. The title of a statute can also be misleading as to the law's real purposes. An infamous example from one of the state legislatures involved a statute entitled An Act Relative to Sheep and Swine that also imposed a residence requirement for candidates for public office.

The rules that the courts use in interpreting statutes are usually called the "canons of construction." There are perhaps a dozen well-known canons that are most frequently employed. The most commonly accepted canon is the "plain-meaning rule," which requires that a court first look at the words of the statute without regard to the floor debate or committee reports. On this view, if the plain meaning of the statute can be discerned from such a review of the wording, the court should look no further; the statute should be construed in accord with such plain meaning. Few statutes lend themselves easily to the plain-meaning approach. When the meaning is not clear, both judges and lawyers differ as to where to look next. Some look to the floor debate, and others look to the committee reports that accompany such a legislative proposal when it goes to the floor for debate. Some judges and scholars apply other canons of construction, on the theory that the legislators knew and used such canons in deciding what words to use. Still others delve into the testimony of committee witnesses for clues about congressional intent. All of the congressional activities that took place before the statute was passed are called collectively the "legislative history" of the statute. Because the activities are so multifarious, use of legislative history by the courts is sometimes disparaged as being comparable to a performer looking out at an audience and waving to his friends.

There is not much to indicate that the legislators in fact do their work with the canons of construction in mind. One of the canons states that expression of one thing excludes another, similar thing. Legislators frequently will insert specific amendments to emphasize a particular concern without considering this canon. Another canon (ejusdem generis) states that when an enumeration of examples is followed by a general catchall phrase, the catchall phrase can apply only to persons or things of the same general kind or class that were specifically mentioned. Notwithstanding this canon, the statutes and court decisions are full of examples where the catchall phrase was not so limited. In any event, the canons frequently contradict each other, and even when they are consistent, they are not always consistently applied.

All agree that the individual expressions of purposes by individual members of Congress ought not be controlling—not even when such an expression comes from the sponsor of the legislation. Statements of purpose voiced after the statute is passed are almost never given any weight; the theory of legislative interpretation turns on deciphering the purposes of the legislative body *before* the statute was voted upon.

Even the record of congressional debate may be suspect. Members of Congress frequently engage in artificial floor debate in an effort to influence the way in which a statute will be interpreted in the future. A dialogue will be written out between two or more members in which questions of interpretation of particular parts of the statute will be asked and answered. Because these dialogues usu-

ally involve only a few members and are not voted upon by the entire membership, the weight to be accorded such "debate" should be light. However, many judges are beguiled by such artificial legislative maneuvers.

Congress sometimes avoids elaborating the minute details of its intent by delegating the effectuation and elaboration of its purpose to an ADMINISTRATIVE AGENCY [I]. A large number of statutes establish agencies to administer programs created by Congress. Two examples are the Environmental Protection Agency, which is mandated to administer and enforce the environmental laws passed by Congress, and the Securities and Exchange Commission, which is mandated to administer and enforce the securities laws passed by Congress. The laws usually provide that an appeal may be taken from the final decision of the administrative agency to the federal courts. In such an appeal, the interpretation placed on the statute by the agency charged with its administration is to be given great weight by the reviewing courts. Unless the agency has violated the plain meaning of the statute, the courts are supposed to defer to whatever interpretation the agency places upon the statute. The theory behind this doctrine, derived from *Chevron USA, Inc. v. Natural Resources Defense Council* (1984), is that the agency has been charged by Congress to be the main actor in that particular field, and the courts should not interfere with the discretion exercised by the agency.

Many STATE CONSTITUTIONS [I] require the state legislatures to enact statutes limited to a single subject. This limitation makes it easier for the legislators and the citizenry to know what is in a statute and assists courts in interpreting the meaning of a statute. The United States Constitution has never contained such a limitation, and Congress routinely includes a variety of provisions and subjects in a single bill. A single continuing appropriation bill passed by the Congress can contain substantive law provisions covering a wide range of topics. Because some of these provisions are inserted during floor debate and do not have much legislative history, it is frequently difficult to decipher a provision intention or purpose except from the brief explanation that may be made by the sponsor.

Finding the legislative purpose or motive of a particular statute is one of the difficult tasks given over to administrative agencies and the courts.

ABNER J. MIKVA

(SEE ALSO: *Environmental Regulation and the Constitution* [2,1]; *Securities Law and the Constitution* [4].)

Bibliography

FRANKFURTER, FELIX 1947 Some Reflections on the Reading of Statutes. *Columbia Law Review* 47:527–546.

LLEWELLYN, KARL N. 1950 Remarks on the Theory of Appellate Decision and the Rules or Canons About How Statutes Are to Be Construed. *Vanderbilt Law Review* 3:395–406.

MIKVA, ABNER J. 1987 Reading and Writing Statutes. *University of Pittsburgh Law Review* 48:627–637.

LEMON TEST

The *Lemon* test is the three-part formula used by the Supreme Court to decide whether or not a government action violates the ESTABLISHMENT CLAUSE [I]. The first part requires that the government action have a secular purpose; the second part demands that the action neither advance nor inhibit religion as its primary effect; and the final part dictates that the act not cause an excessive entanglement between church and state. The test was first announced in LEMON V. KURTZMAN (1971) [3], though its major components date back, at least, to the majority opinion in ABINGTON TOWNSHIP SCHOOL DISTRICT V. SCHEMPP (1963) [1].

The test's first prong remained noncontroversial throughout most of the 1970s, with the Court invariably finding a secular purpose for statutes under review. Then came the Court's decision in *Stone v. Graham* (1979), which struck down a Kentucky law requiring the posting of the Ten Commandments in public classrooms. Kentucky claimed that the purpose of the posting was to inform students of the influence of the Ten Commandments on secular history—and, in fact, the Commandments were to be accompanied by a message pointing out their influence on the development of Western law. But the Court found this "avowed" secular purpose insufficient and claimed that the state's actual purpose was to promote religion. This distinction between "actual" and "avowed" secular purposes was adopted by Justice SANDRA DAY O'CONNOR [3,I] in her restatement of the *Lemon* test in LYNCH V. DONNELLY (1984) [3], and the distinction became increasingly important thereafter. In WALLACE V. JAFFREE (1984) [4] the Court struck down a law providing for a schoolroom moment of silence because the legislators' actual motive was to promote religion; and in *Edwards v. Aguillard* (1987) the Court invalidated for the same reason Louisiana's Balanced Treatment Act, which claimed to promote ACADEMIC FREEDOM [1] in the discussion of CREATIONISM [I].

The actual-purpose approach has drawn serious criticism; the most sustained critique of the approach was delivered by Justice ANTONIN SCALIA [I] in his dissent in *Aguillard*. If religious motivation by itself invalidates a piece of legislation, wrote Scalia, then a great deal of legislation indeed may have to be invalidated: "Today's religious activism may give us the Balanced Treatment Act, but yesterday's resulted in the abolition of slavery, and tomorrow's may bring relief for famine victims." Moreover, if the Court really wants to strike down legislation on the basis of motivations, it had better go about it in a more thorough manner. Scalia suggested that to ascertain the dominant motivation behind a bill reliably, one would need to tally the views of every legislator. Scalia's criticism may have had an effect, for Justice O'Connor took a step back from the actual-purpose standard in her majority opinion in WESTSIDE COMMUNITY SCHOOLS V. MERGENS (1990) [I].

But the first prong of *Lemon* is not the only part of the test to spark debate in recent years; controversy has also erupted over its second prong—spurred in part by the Court's maze of contradictory decisions involving GOVERNMENT AID TO RELIGIOUS INSTITUTIONS [2,I]. Seeking greater clarity in the application of the second prong, Justice O'Connor has convinced a majority of her colleagues to reformulate it. The inquiry under the second prong has shifted from determining the primary effect of a government act to ascertaining whether the government action has "in fact conveyed a message of endorsement or disapproval" of religion. Under this new inquiry, an act may (or may not) violate the establishment clause, regardless of whether it advances or inhibits religion as a primary effect; the crucial factor is the public message conveyed by the act.

Justice ANTHONY M. KENNEDY [I] has been the Court's most vocal critic of O'Connor's endorsement inquiry, and in COUNTY OF ALLEGHENY V. AMERICAN CIVIL LIBERTIES UNION (1989) [I] he offered his own reformulation of *Lemon*'s second prong in response. Kennedy's reformulation prohibits two types of government action: direct government benefits that tend to establish a state religion, and government coercion to engage in religious activity. Kennedy's opinion was joined by Chief Justice WILLIAM H. REHNQUIST [3,I] and Justices Antonin Scalia and BYRON R. WHITE [4,I]. All four Justices have indicated a dislike for the *Lemon* test, and Kennedy may be laying the groundwork to replace it altogether.

JOHN G. WEST, JR.

(SEE ALSO: *Religious Fundamentalism* [I]; *Separation of Church and State* [4,I].)

Bibliography

LEVY, LEONARD W. 1986 *The Establishment Clause: Religion and the First Amendment.* Chapter 6. New York: Macmillan.

THEUER, JEFFREY S. 1988 The Lemon Test and Subjective Intent in Establisment Clause Analysis: The Case for Abandoning the Purpose Prong. *Kentucky Law Journal* 76:1061–1075.

LESBIANISM

See: *Bowers v. Hardwick* [I];
Sexual Orientation [I];
Sexual Preference and the
Constitution [4]

LIBERAL CONSTITUTIONAL CONSTRUCTION

The liberal attitude toward the Constitution—admitting a range of internal differences—centers on the proposition that the Framers, as talented a group of democratic politicians as ever lived, expected their descendants to be at least as experimental as they were. When the Framers gathered in Philadelphia, they were improvising a *novus ordo seclorum* without a blueprint. JOHN ADAMS [1], working feverishly in London compiling the history of attempts at republican government, tried to summarize the lessons of history. JAMES MADISON [3] had prepared himself by reading every relevant work that he and his mentor THOMAS JEFFERSON [3], then in Paris, could lay their hands on. ALEXANDER HAMILTON [2] was satisfied that Thomas Hobbes had provided the essentials.

But delegates to the CONSTITUTIONAL CONVENTION OF 1787 [1] mainly brought with them their experience in running provincial, state, and Confederation government. Collectively they had well over a thousand years of experience in office, from governor and Chief Justice down to mayor and justice of the peace. Of the fifty-five chosen, forty-four were, or had been, members of the CONTINENTAL CONGRESS [2]; at a time when being a lawyer was very different from emerging from a law school assembly line and vanishing into a vacuum-packed corporate environment, thirty-four had done their apprenticeships, and JAMES WILSON [4] and GEORGE WYTHE [4] were eminent professors and legists. The only outstanding absentees from the political class were JOHN JAY [3], secretary of foreign affairs under the Confederation; John Adams in London; Thomas Jefferson in Paris; and PATRICK HENRY [2], who was elected but refused to attend as he "smelt a rat," that is, he thought Jefferson was masterminding the convention through Madison, as had been the case in the Virginia legislature with the VIRGINIA STATUTE OF RELIGIOUS LIBERTY [4].

Although with the exception of Madison and perhaps Hamilton they had not arrived with specific plans, they clearly shared a sense of mission: The United States government under the ARTICLES OF CONFEDERATION [1] had to be strengthened to prevent the infant nation from being eaten by the sharks that infested the international environ-

ment. Here the presence of GEORGE WASHINGTON [4] was of immense symbolic value because of his known dedication to the principles of a free republic and the respect he had from the people. Washington was unanimously elected president of the Convention.

The Framers were well aware that they were not free-floating Platonic "guardians" who could impose their concept of a "republic" upon an unresisting populace. Hence, when the final document was signed on September 17, its principal architects considered it the best they could get rather than the fulfillment of an ideal. George Washington put it well in a letter: "You will readily conceive . . . the difficulties which the Convention had to struggle against. The various and opposit [*sic*] interests which were to be subdued, the diversity of opinions and sentiments which were to be reconciled; and in fine, the sacrifices which were necessary to be made on all sides for the General Welfare, combined to make it work of so intricate and difficult a nature that I think it is much to be wondered at that any thing could have been produced with such unanimity."

Hamilton and Madison, disappointed by the convention's rebuff to their centralizing initiative, agreed that the Constitution was an improvement over the Articles and set to work to get it ratified. South Carolina's PIERCE BUTLER [1] probably spoke for most of his fellow Framers when he wrote, "View the system then as resulting from a spirit of Accommodation to different Interests, and not the most perfect one that the Deputies cou'd devise for a Country better adapted for the reception of it than America is at this day, or perhaps ever will be."

In the course of RATIFICATION OF THE CONSTITUTION [3] by the state conventions, questions inevitably arose on the meaning of various articles. When one reads the replies that were given—in a universe wholly lacking in modern communications techniques—it rapidly becomes clear that a number of the delegates often were not quite sure what they had approved. They knew that in general terms they had established a republic with strong legislative and executive branches—the judicial article received little attention either in the Convention or in ratification debates—and hoped that the new government would provide the United States with the authority and the funds that were so sorely lacking under the Articles.

To head off a potentially dangerous demagogic anti-constitutionalist attack—claiming in essence that Hobbes's Leviathan was being covertly imposed on unsuspecting citizens—the Framers promised a BILL OF RIGHTS [1]. The Constitution was ratified, the states organized presidential and congressional elections for that fall, and the Founding Fathers set to work finding appropriate positions for themselves and their friends in the new administration.

Now they had to make this experiment in republican government work.

To summarize, the Framers had not descended from Mount Sinai with the Law carved in stone; they had contrived a mechanism designed to establish law and, if necessary, change it. The FIRST CONGRESS [I], for example, set up the Treasury Department as a dependency of Congress with the secretary reporting in person or in writing to the House and Senate. Alexander Hamilton's masterful recommendations on the public credit, the BANK OF THE UNITED STATES [1], and the encouragement of manufactures were in the form of reports to Congress. In practice, however, the secretary was responsible to the President, and the law was later changed to reflect this. The Constitution requires the President to get the ADVICE AND CONSENT [1,I] of the Senate to treaties; the advice provision vanished after Washington's one attempt to discuss pending Indian treaties with the Senate ended on such a chilly note that no President since has made the pilgrimage.

Indeed, there is a substantial body of evidence to suggest that the widely discussed "intent of the Framers" is a will-o'-the-wisp. We know their intention on structural matters—the division of powers between the executive, legislative, and judicial branches—but beyond that, things get murky. Once again the First Congress gives us a sense of the extent to which the Framers were not sure of their own objectives, for an intense debate arose over the question of the Senate's role in the President's dismissal power. In other words, if Senate approval is necessary for the appointment of, say, an ambassador, is Senate approval required to fire him? The consensus seemed to be that it was not, but the matter was not settled until MYERS V. UNITED STATES [3] in 1926, and even today there is some ambiguity on the status of members of so-called independent regulatory commissions.

Without going into further detail, it is obvious that early generations of politicians and jurists were more concerned with how a problem could be solved than with how the Framers would have dealt with it. ABRAHAM BALDWIN [1], one of the most intelligent men who was both a politician and jurist, put it thus to his House colleagues in March 1796:

It was not to disparage [the Constitution] to say that it had not definitely, and with precision, absolutely settled everything on which it had spoke. He had sufficient evidence to satisfy his own mind that it was not supposed by the makers of it at the time but that some subjects were left a little ambiguous and uncertain. It was a great thing to get so many difficult subjects definitely settled at once. . . . The few that were left a little unsettled might without any great risk be settled by practice or by amendments. . . . When he reflected on the immense difficulties and dangers of that trying occasion—the old Government prostrated and a chance whether a new one

could be agreed on—the recollection recalled to him nothing but the most joyful sensations that so many things had been so well settled, and that experience had shown there was very little difficulty or danger in settling the rest.

This liberal spirit of experimentation was brilliantly exemplified by the Supreme Court under the leadership of Chief Justice JOHN MARSHALL [3]. Marshall's enmity toward his cousin Thomas Jefferson was surely fortified by the latter's penchant (at least before and after he served as President) for STRICT CONSTRUCTION [4] of the Constitution. In the famous 1819 case MCCULLOCH V. MARYLAND [3], the Chief Justice, in the course of echoing Hamilton's 1791 defense of the constitutionality of the Bank of the United States, took some time out to condemn this unimaginative perception of the nature of the Constitution. Wrote Marshall:

A constitution to contain an accurate detail of all the subdivisions of which its great powers will admit, and of all the means by which they may be carried into execution, would partake of the prolixity of a legal code, and could scarcely be embraced by the human mind. It would probably never be understood by the public. Its nature therefore requires that only its great outlines should be marked, its important objects designated, and the minor ingredients which compose these objects be deducted from the nature of the objects themselves. . . . To have prescribed the means by which government should in all future time execute its powers . . . would have been an unwise attempt to provide by immutable rules for exigencies which, if foreseen at all, must have been seen dimly, and which can best be provided for as they occur.

Five years later in the steamboat case of GIBBONS V. OGDEN (1824) [2] the Chief Justice really dispatched the narrow-minded critics of federal power: "Powerful and ingenious minds taking as postulates that the powers expressly granted to the government of the Union are to be contracted by construction into the narrowest possible compass, and that the original powers of the states be retained if any possible construction will retain them, may by a course of well-digested but refined and metaphysical reasoning, founded on these premises, explain away the constitution of our country and leave it a magnificent structure indeed to look at, but totally unfit for use." So much for metaphysicians and political philosophers.

In concrete terms Marshall's talent for improvisation to cope with pressing problems was spectacular. He invented the doctrine of POLITICAL QUESTIONS [3,I] to provide the Court with a safe exit from risky enfilades in *Foster v. Nielson* (1829); in AMERICAN INSURANCE COMPANY V. CANTER (1828) [1] he belatedly provided the constitutional rationale for acquiring new territories and, while he was at it, invented LEGISLATIVE COURTS [3], created under Article I and distinct from the CONSTITUTIONAL COURTS [1] of Article III; and, to mention only two more, he developed the ORIGINAL PACKAGE DOCTRINE [3] in BROWN V. MARYLAND (1827) [1] and the status of Indian tribes as "dependent domestic nations" in *Worcester v. Georgia* (1831). One could argue that John Marshall, following in the footsteps of the Framers (and he had been a delegate to the Virginia ratifying convention), set the pattern of creative experimentation for liberal CONSTITUTIONALISM [2].

Rather than compiling a catalog of constitutional improvisations, many of which have been initiated by the executive (ABRAHAM LINCOLN [3] moved the power to suspend the writ of HABEAS CORPUS [2,I] into Article II, where it has since remained) and the legislature (Congress in 1871 conferred citizenship on corporations for federal jurisdictional purposes), it would be wise to narrow the inquiry to a few specific areas. For example, what do steamships and television waves have in common? The answer is that they are subject to regulation by the federal government under the COMMERCE CLAUSE [1,I]. The first stages in this triumph of fungibility were easy, for interstate water shipping, interstate railways, interstate trucking, and interstate telegraphs were tangible. The big jump took place in 1933 when the Supreme Court, in *Federal Radio Commission v. Nelson Bros.*, held radio waves to be analogous to telegraph signals and subsequently widened this to include television. The principle applied was Marshall's, namely, that it did not make any difference whether a boat was propelled by sail or engine; the vital aspect was that something was going from one state to another.

The liberal approach to constitutionalism has infuriated a lot of individuals and groups of all political persuasions. The focus here is not on whether the experiments were successful but on the modus operandi. At some points the improvisations were considered politically "reactionary" (for example, when the Court in the YELLOW DOG CONTRACT [9] Case assumed that individual workers and industrial giants were bargaining-table equals and when it negated state minimum-wage laws). In other cases a howl went up that the Justices were "radical" (for example, when the Court protected criminal rights and when it legitimized ABORTION [1,I]). Whatever the outcome, the result was founded on the experimental attitude. To put it differently, it would be extremely difficult to find a decision in which the majority view was buttressed by better probative evidence of the intention of the Framers than was the view of the dissenting minority.

To say that experimentation has been the only game in town since 1787 is a statement of historical fact, a fundament of the liberal tradition. Indeed, one could argue that the one area where stasis set in and experimentation became increasingly difficult and finally impossible was the mesh of SLAVERY [4] and STATES' RIGHTS [4], leading

to a ferocious Civil War in which roughly a million males out of a population of sixteen million ages fifteen to thirty-nine were killed or wounded. The Constitution of 1787 was a sanguinary failure.

If this is the liberal attitude toward the Constitution, what are the critical differences between it and the conservative view? In candor, it is hard to find substantial differences at the level of principle, for America's so-called conservatives have always found themselves carrying the intellectual baggage of that magnificent cadre of improvisers who founded the Republic. In Ireland in the 1690s many a big house had a portrait of the king over the mantelpiece mounted on pivots top and bottom. When the Jacobites came to town one pushed the picture around to display King James II; when the forces of William and Mary appeared, a similar push put their visages front and center. The problem with such a portrait in the context of the founding era is that the same portraits would appear on both sides: conservative constitutionalists have always endorsed experimentation *sub silentio*, but then denied that this in fact was their methodology. Presumably they have learned the technique at the feet of John Marshall.

For example, JOHN C. CALHOUN [1] has been described as a man of rigid conservative principles, the hero of the states' rights cause. Yet in 1817 Calhoun casually observed that the Constitution "was not intended as a thesis for the logician to exercise his ingenuity on it. It ought to be construed with plain good sense."

Similarly, Robert H. Bork has become an icon of contemporary conservative jurisprudence, but in his book *The Tempting of America: The Political Seduction of the Law* (1990) he provides us with an example of the liberal, experimental mode worthy of John Marshall himself. In discussing BAKER V. CARR (1962) [1]—which required states to establish election districts based on the formula ONE PERSON, ONE VOTE [3]—Bork excoriated the WARREN COURT [4] not for the result ("There is no doubt in my mind . . . that plaintiffs [demanding the end of rigged districting] deserved to win") but because the Court based its decision on the EQUAL PROTECTION [2,I] clause of the FOURTEENTH AMENDMENT [2,I].

As it happens, the authors of the Fourteenth Amendment, like the Framers, had a talent for ambiguity, so it is an exercise in soothsaying to attempt a reconstruction of the precise meaning of equal protection. Let us simply say that the jury is still out, and will doubtless remain out indefinitely, on the legal consequences the drafting Committee of Fifteen had in mind in 1866. What is interesting is Bork's solution to the inequities created by malapportionment and how he explicates the constitutional rationale that would enable those who "deserved to win" to win. Let no one deny his imaginative creativity: he indicates that the Court could have avoided the equal protection quagmire quite simply by using the provision in Article IV, section 4, that "the United States shall guarantee to every State in this Union a REPUBLICAN FORM OF GOVERNMENT [3]."

This provision, launched by Madison in the VIRGINIA PLAN [4], was discussed on two occasions during the Convention. The weight of the evidence suggests it was designed to prevent any state from setting up, or having imposed upon it from without, a monarchical form of government. When it was invoked by the Dorrite rebels against the obsolete Rhode Island Charter in 1849, the Court said in LUTHER V. BORDEN [3] that the legitimacy of Rhode Island's government was a "political question"; and when the clause was subsequently invoked in a desultory fashion in several other cases, the Justices echoed Chief Justice ROGER BROOKE TANEY's [4] decision in *Luther* and held that the determination of republican governance was nonjusticiable.

Bork states that "for no very good reason" the Court held the proviso to be judicially unenforceable and suggests it should be overruled after 113 years as STARE DECISIS [4]. Actually, some supporters of the liberal, experimental approach who thought of this at the time of COLEGROVE V. GREEN (1946) [I] (the first major assault on malapportionment) and hit a brick wall would cheer Bork on. However, the historical evidence for the use of the "guarantee clause" is tenuous, at least as flimsy as that underpinning the equal protection clause of the Fourteenth Amendment, for at the time of the ratification of the Constitution malapportionment was a major concern in a number of states. ELBRIDGE GERRY [2], a Framer, refused to sign the document, but not because it forbade the GERRYMANDER [2,I]. It would seem that even Bork cannot resist temptation. As David Hume pointed out, creating a useful past is a delightful form of political entertainment. It is also a persistent highlight of American judicial behavior.

JOHN P. ROCHE

(SEE ALSO: *Bork Nomination* [I]; *Cherokee Indian Cases* [1]; *Conservatism* [I]; *Justiciability* [3]; *Original Intent* [I]; *Political Philosophy of the Constitution* [3,I]; *Positivism* [I]; *Pragmatism* [I]; *Progressive Constitutional Thought* [3]; *Progressivism* [I].)

Bibliography

BORK, ROBERT H. 1990 *The Tempting of America: The Political Seduction of the Law.* New York: Free Press.

JACKSON, ROBERT H. 1941 *The Struggle for Judicial Supremacy.* New York: Knopf.

LEVY, LEONARD W. 1988 *Original Intent and the Framers' Constitution.* New York: Macmillan.

MCDONALD, FORREST 1985 *Novus Ordo Seclorum.* Lawrence: University Press of Kansas.

PETERSON, MERRILL 1987 *The Great Triumvirate.* New York: Oxford University Press.

ROCHE JOHN P. 1961 *Courts and Rights.* New York: Random House.

——— 1974 *Shadow and Substance.* New York: Macmillan.

WARREN, CHARLES 1922 *The Supreme Court in United States History*, 2 vols. Boston: Little, Brown.

LIBERALISM

In today's America the term "liberalism" is circulated mainly by those who pronounce it with scorn—by the political right and by academic theorists who have little else in common with the right. Yet the American nation was conceived in liberalism. The DECLARATION OF INDEPENDENCE [2] proclaimed the liberal ideals of individual liberty, legal equality, and the rule of law. It also embraced the liberal doctrine that located the legitimacy of governmental power not in divine right but in the consent of the governed.

The Constitution, too, was mainly seen by its Framers through liberal lenses. What they saw was a SOCIAL COMPACT [4] deriving its authority from "the people of the United States" and designed in major part to serve liberal purposes: "to establish justice," "to secure the blessings of liberty," and by dampening the causes of civil strife, "to insure domestic tranquility." What they did not see—or would not see—was the fundamental inconsistency of SLAVERY [4] with all these purposes. Putting this enormity out of their minds, the Framers of the Constitution and the BILL OF RIGHTS [1] saw the chief source of oppression in the power of the state and placed much of their hope for achieving liberal ends in a system of LIMITED GOVERNMENT [3].

The limits were both structural and substantive. Liberty was to be achieved both by the dispersal of the powers of government (see FEDERALISM [2,I]; SEPARATION OF POWERS [4]) and by broadly worded prohibitions on various kinds of governmental interference with the rights of individuals. Although the liberalism of the Framers was strongly influenced by the Enlightenment's notions of rationality, these substantive limitations were not the product of abstract reason. Rather, they were designed to serve intensely practical purposes for the new nation. The liberal doctrines of FREEDOM OF SPEECH [2] and FREEDOM OF THE PRESS [2], for example, seemed essential to the citizen participation on which the continued legitimacy of government would depend. Similarly, the liberal doctrine rejecting divine authority as the basis for governmental legitimacy served the cause of domestic peace. The Framers, well versed in recent British history, need not stretch their imaginations to see how the interactions of religion and government might plunge a nation into civil strife. A major purpose of both the SEPARATION OF CHURCH

AND STATE [4] and the guarantee of RELIGIOUS LIBERTY [3] was to promote tolerance and thereby to moderate religion's capacity for political divisiveness.

Today's Constitution, the product of two centuries' worth of interpretation, differs dramatically from the Constitution of the Framers. Yet, what Louis Hartz called "the liberal tradition" has remained central in American constitutional law, surviving political and social upheavals and even a civil war of our own. Like all paradoxes, this contradiction of continuity and change is more apparent than real. Over the years liberalism, like the Constitution, has taken on a series of new meanings in response to changes in America's economic, social, and political conditions. Jacksonian democracy, the Civil War and RECONSTRUCTION [3], the late-nineteenth-century industrial expansion, the NEW DEAL [I], and the CIVIL RIGHTS MOVEMENT [I] each brought a new version of liberalism that made its mark on the Constitution. The constitutional law of our time—like the term liberalism itself—evidences overlays of all these eras of social change, from the days of Adam Smith to the days of MARTIN LUTHER KING, JR. [2]. The decisions of the Supreme Court, the nation's leading expositor of the Constitution, have both reflected the transformations of liberalism and contributed to them.

In the nation's early years the individualist liberalism of JOHN LOCKE [2] was tempered by a vision of REPUBLICANISM [I] that imposed on the people's governors a moral responsibility to attune their public decisions to the general good, not merely their own self-interest or the interests of their constituents. This republican ideal was not wholly unrealistic so long as government was largely in the hands of the gentry. By around 1820, however, gentry rule had crumbled under the dual pressures of democratization and geographical expansion. In the era of ANDREW JACKSON [3] the consent of the governed implied an electorate that was expanded to include most adult white men, and the body of citizens who could make effective use of individual freedom—especially economic freedom—was similarly expanded by a doctrine of equal liberties. The widening of the franchise was almost entirely the work of legislatures. The protection of economic freedom, however, became the business of the courts, acting in the name of the Constitution. The JUDICIAL ACTIVISM [3] of the MARSHALL COURT [3] (1803–1835) led the way in promoting a nationwide free-trade unit by striking down a number of state regulatory laws (see STATE REGULATION OF COMMERCE [4]; CONTRACT CLAUSE [2]).

During the period before the Civil War, another doctrine of liberalism came to the fore, with major assists from the adherents of ABOLITIONIST CONSTITUTIONAL THEORY [1] and from those who opposed SLAVERY IN THE TERRITORIES [4]. "Free labor" became a slogan of the new REPUBLICAN PARTY [I] and of ABRAHAM LINCOLN

[3] in particular (see LABOR MOVEMENT AND CONSTITUTIONAL DOCTRINE [I]). The doctrine of free labor, infused with the liberal goals of democracy and individualism, received a strong impetus when the EMANCIPATION PROCLAMATION [2] converted a war to save the Union into a war to free the slaves—a process that culminated in the THIRTEENTH AMENDMENT [4], ratified in 1865.

Generously interpreted, the Thirteenth Amendment might have served as a foundation for a sweeping constitutional guarantee of racial equality and for congressional legislation serving this end. The politics of Reconstruction impeded such an expansive interpretation, but did produce the FOURTEENTH AMENDMENT [2], with its broad guarantees of EQUAL PROTECTION [2,I] and DUE PROCESS [2,I], and the FIFTEENTH AMENDMENT [2], prohibiting racial discrimination in VOTING RIGHTS [4]. The three Civil War amendments, along with a series of civil rights acts, were seen by their proponents as establishing a principle of equal citizenship that would carry out some of the unfulfilled liberal promises of the Declaration of Independence.

These hopes were soon dashed. By the end of the century, politics—North and South—had turned away from a concern for racial equality. The Supreme Court had followed suit in a series of decisions that converted the Civil War amendments and the Reconstruction CIVIL RIGHTS [1,I] laws into guarantees of formal equality that offered little real protection for the substantive values of equal citizenship: respect, responsibility, and participation (see CIVIL RIGHTS CASES [1883] [1]; PLESSY V. FERGUSON [1896] [3]).

As politics increasingly turned to the business of industrial expansion, the dominant version of liberal individualism now focused on the freedom of industry and enterprise from ECONOMIC REGULATION [2]. Beginning in the 1880s, for half a century the Supreme Court policed the boundaries of economic liberty, striking down a great many regulatory laws in the name of ECONOMIC DUE PROCESS [2] and holding a number of federal statutes invalid as exceeding the power of Congress under the COMMERCE CLAUSE [1]. During this period, and especially during WORLD WAR I [I] and the Red Scare of 1919–1920, the Court gave little comfort to those who were urging a similarly expansive reading of other constitutional legacies of the Framers' liberal individualism—such as FIRST AMENDMENT [2] freedoms.

It took the Great Depression and World War II to effect a realignment that would give the center of the political stage to the liberalism of the New Deal. This rendering of liberalism, like the liberalism of Reconstruction, emphasized the necessity of substantive underpinnings for individual liberty. The New Deal's legislative program centered on economic democracy and social welfare, and to achieve these ends its leaders sought to guide the national economy with governmental regulation on an unprecedented scale. During the first term of President FRANKLIN D. ROOSEVELT [3], an activist majority of the Supreme Court fought a rear-guard action against the new liberalism in the name of the old. In 1937, however, before Roosevelt had made a single appointment to the Court, the majority shifted. From that day to the present, the Court has routinely upheld economic regulation both by Congress and by the states and has also upheld the legislative framework of the modern welfare state (see TAXING AND SPENDING POWERS [4]; SPENDING POWER [I]). During the 1930s and 1940s, the Court also took its first steps toward reinvigorating the First Amendment.

All these developments in constitutional doctrine supported a liberalism in which equality meant not just formally equal laws but the substance of equal citizenship. The Court cooperated with the political branches in an effort to bring freedom and security to people who had been seen as outsiders and so to achieve a more inclusive definition of the national community. For a time, the Cold War, like the Red Scare before it, laid a restraining hand on political freedom and also marked a group of dissidents as outsiders. But just as the Cold War reached the peak of its influence on domestic politics, the new liberalism, with its impulse to extend the blessings of liberty to all Americans, took a giant step forward. The WARREN COURT [4] opened the modern civil rights era with the decision in BROWN V. BOARD OF EDUCATION OF TOPEKA (1954) [1].

The *Brown* decision began a "second Reconstruction," not only by expanding the meaning of constitutional doctrines of racial equality, but also by providing a catalyst for a vigorous political movement. Congress responded with two momentous laws aimed at extending the substance of equal citizenship to the members of racial and ethnic minorities: the CIVIL RIGHTS ACT OF 1964 [1] and the VOTING RIGHTS ACT OF 1965 [4]. In its active liberal reshaping of constitutional doctrine, the Warren Court began in the civil rights field, but did not end there. Particularly during the last six years of the tenure of EARL WARREN [4] as Chief Justice, the Court not only extended judicial remedies for racial DESEGREGATION [2] but also promoted political equality by ordering the REAPPORTIONMENT [3] of legislatures on the principle of "one person, one vote." The Court also greatly expanded the substantive protections of the First Amendment and recognized a constitutional RIGHT OF PRIVACY [3,I]. In the field of criminal justice the Court accomplished the INCORPORATION [2] of nearly all the guarantees of the Bill of Rights into the Fourteenth Amendment, thus applying them to the states as well as the national government. Furthermore, the Court tightened the requirements of many of those

guarantees, making the Constitution a significant limitation on police practices and the procedures of state criminal courts.

Even after Chief Justice Warren retired in 1969, the constitutional momentum of the Warren Court carried the Court to further liberal activism. Most notably, the BURGER COURT [1] in the 1970s expanded the reach of the equal protection clause to the field of SEX DISCRIMINATION [4] and held in ROE V. WADE (1973) [3] that the right of privacy largely forbade a state to criminalize a woman's choice to have an ABORTION [1,I]. These two developments were closely related; women's right to control their own sexuality and maternity is critical to their ability to participate in society as equal citizens.

Political liberals generally have applauded all these constitutional developments. Yet each of them has produced its own "backlash" in the political arena. When President LYNDON B. JOHNSON [3] signed the 1964 act into law, he predicted that the South would thus be handed to the Republican party. In Presidential politics, this prediction has been validated, starting with the successful "southern strategy" of RICHARD M. NIXON [3] in 1968. Nixon explicitly criticized the Warren Court's decisions in the criminal justice area, and the four Justices that he appointed to the Court began the process that would eventually dismantle a considerable part of that doctrinal structure. As for civil rights, critics of the REHNQUIST COURT [I] have said that the second Reconstruction lasted only a little longer than the first one did. In the 1980s a firm majority of the Court has embraced a doctrinal model centered on formal racial equality, sharply limiting the uses of AFFIRMATIVE ACTION [1,I] and other group-based remedies for the group harm of racial discrimination. The right of privacy has not yet fulfilled its promise as a generalized protection of individual freedom in matters of intimate personal relations, but rather has been narrowed even in the area of abortion rights. Recent First Amendment developments are typified by the PUBLIC FORUM [3] doctrine, which began as a means to expand expressive freedom and now serves mainly as a threshold barrier to turn away would-be speakers' claims. In the world of constitutional doctrine, as in the larger political world, modern liberalism has been obliged to assume a posture of defense.

The constitutional liberalism that animates political liberals today—and serves as the political right's *bête noire*—is a far cry from the liberalism of nineteenth-century economics that dominated constitutional doctrine for five decades. Its primary modern sources are the New Deal's social welfare concerns and the Warren Court's concerns for CIVIL LIBERTIES [1,I] and for the inclusion of subordinated groups in the promise of America. Even so, today's liberalism continues to draw on the liberalism that infused the framing of the Constitution and the Fourteenth Amendment: the rule of law, tolerance as a means to civil peace, individual rights to freedom from excessive governmental intrusion, and equal citizenship.

Although the political resistance to the New Deal had its main base in the business sector, today business has largely made its peace with the newer liberalism—not exactly embracing regulation, but accepting it. The most vehement opposition to affirmative action programs, for example, comes not from business groups, but from "social issues" conservatives who equally oppose the recognition of abortion rights or claims to sexual freedom. These citizens, who are presently the dominant voices on the political right, do not reject the liberal constitutional ideals of equality, individual rights, or tolerance, but argue that in recent decades liberals on the bench have abused their power to write a perverted version of those ideals into constitutional law.

For the "social issues" conservatives, these constitutional ideals are unchangeable; they took permanent shape when they were written into the Constitution. In this view constitutional equality means formally equal laws and no more; individual constitutional rights are limited to the specific rights of life, liberty, and property that the Framers had in mind; and the reach of constitutionally required tolerance is permanently confined by the morality of the Framers (see CONSERVATISM AND THE CONSTITUTION [I]). They emphatically reject, for example, any claim to equality or rights of tolerance in the context of governmental discrimination on the basis of SEXUAL ORIENTATION [I], insisting that such matters be left to majoritarian community morality.

Constitutional liberalism is also under attack from quite another political direction, notably by theorists in the CRITICAL LEGAL STUDIES [I] movement. These writers seek to "deconstruct" the very idea of rights by showing that all legal doctrine is indeterminate and therefore subject to manipulation in the interest of the powerful. Here, a countercurrent has developed among racial and ethnic minority writers who argue the practical utility of claims of rights in overcoming group subordination and point to the civil rights movement as an example of the liberating possibilities of rights—an argument the Framers of the Constitution surely would understand.

Another attack on liberalism by critical theorists, now joined by a number of feminist writers, centers on the potential of liberal-individualist attitudes for impoverishing the sense of self and submerging the sense of community responsibility—especially responsibility toward the down-and-out. Related to these concerns is the criticism that classical liberalism, locating the threat to individual freedom in the power of the state, neglects the oppressive capacity of nongovernmental actors, compounding the wrong by insisting on a strong public/private distinction. (See STATE ACTION—BEYOND RACE [4].)

From both sides, then, liberalism is challenged for undercutting the claims of community. A liberal tolerance may result in constitutional protections not only for consensual homosexual behavior but for racist speech or PORNOGRAPHY [3,I]. (The antipornography cause in particular has produced an alliance between the political right and one branch of feminists.) Similarly, liberalism's long-standing devotion to Enlightenment-style rationality is under attack from both sides. The dominance of secular rationality is attacked by those who would promote SCHOOL PRAYERS [I] or the teaching of CREATIONISM [I] in public schools; and feminists and others argue that the instrumental rationality of the liberal welfare state's BUREAUCRACY [I] is alienating and dehumanizing.

The critical theorists' critique of liberalism has yet to make a significant impact on constitutional law. The critique from the right, however, has been warmly received by the federal judiciary, which in large measure was reconstituted during the 1980s. Now it is liberal judges who are fighting a rear-guard action. Yet some important elements of the liberal constitutional inheritance from the New Deal and the Warren Court seem secure. Citizens at all points on the political spectrum continue to hold the federal government responsible for maintaining the health of the national economy, including high levels of employment. Although social welfare programs perceived as aiding the minority poor are anything but robust, SOCIAL SECURITY [4] is the nearest thing we have to a political sacred cow, and some form of national health insurance seems likely to emerge soon. Explicit governmental discrimination against the members of subordinated racial or ethnic groups, we can assume, will be unconstitutional as long as we have the Constitution.

These examples are modest when they are measured against the modern liberal agenda; saying that the constitutional clock will not be turned back to 1950 or 1930 is not saying very much. For the moment, surely, liberals must seek their goals primarily in political arenas. In these arenas, however, we have already seen some important effects of racial equality in voting rights—for example, in the process of confirmation of Supreme Court Justices.

Undoubtedly, "the liberal tradition" will remain central in American constitutional jurisprudence because our constitutional culture is indelibly imprinted with the rhetoric of liberalism: equality, tolerance, individual rights. Another certainty, however, is that the meanings of these large abstractions will change in response to changes in American society. Today's political liberals will applaud some of those changes and regret others. But the process is one that no true liberal can lament.

KENNETH L. KARST

Bibliography

ALTMAN, ANDREW 1990 *Critical Legal Studies: A Liberal Critique.* Princeton, N.J.: Princeton University Press.

CRENSHAW, KIMBERLÉ 1988 Race, Reform and Retrenchment: Transformation and Legitimation in Antidiscrimination Law. *Harvard Law Review* 101:1331–1387.

DIGGINS, JOHN P. 1984 *The Lost Soul of American Politics: Virtue, Self-Interest, and the Foundations of Liberalism.* New York: Basic Books.

FERGUSON, KATHY E. 1984 *The Feminist Case Against Bureaucracy.* Philadelphia: Temple University Press.

HARTZ, LOUIS 1955 *The Liberal Tradition in America: An Interpretation of American Political Thought Since the Revolution.* New York: Harcourt Brace Jovanovich.

KARST, KENNETH L. 1989 *Belonging to America: Equal Citizenship and the Constitution.* New Haven, Conn.: Yale University Press.

SHIFFRIN, STEVEN 1983 Liberalism, Radicalism, and Legal Scholarship. *UCLA Law Review* 30:1103–1217.

SMITH, ROGERS M. 1985 *Liberalism and American Constitutional Law.* Cambridge, Mass.: Harvard University Press.

UNGER, ROBERTO MANGABEIRA 1975 *Knowledge and Politics.* New York: Free Press.

WOLFF, ROBERT PAUL 1968 *The Poverty of Liberalism.* Boston: Beacon Press.

LINE-ITEM VETO

The Constitution permits the President to sign or veto a bill as a whole. He may not pick and choose among the parts of a bill, signing some portions while vetoing others. Although most governors have VETO POWER [4] over individual items, constitutional amendments to grant similar authority to the President have thus far been unsuccessful.

The Framers were familiar with the powers exerted by the British Board of Trade, which routinely reviewed thousands of acts submitted by the mainland of American colonies and disallowed some "in whole or in part." These disapprovals were more similar to JUDICIAL REVIEW [3] than to an item veto, in the sense that vetoes prevent proposals from taking effect, while the board's actions came after the colonial measures were law. In any event, the Framers did not find the British precedent appealing for the Constitution being drafted.

The item veto did not materialize until the CONFEDERATE CONSTITUTION [1] of 1861. Since that time, forty-three states have adopted some variation of the item veto for their governors. In 1873 President ULYSSES S. GRANT [2] requested an item veto for the national executive, and at least a dozen Presidents have made similar appeals.

The fact that so many governors have the item veto is not a sufficient justification for giving the same power to the President. The federal–state analogy suffers from a number of deficiencies. The item veto exercised by governors is inseparable from a constitutional design that differs dramatically from the design of the federal Constitution, especially in the distribution of executive and legislative powers. A much greater bias against LEGISLATIVE POWER [3] operates at the state level. State budget procedures also differ substantially from federal procedures. Appropriation bills in the state are structured to facilitate item vetoes by governors, but appropriation bills passed by Congress contain few items. Money is provided in large, lump-sum accounts.

Presidents regularly claim that with item-veto power they could carve out the "boondoggles and pork" that Congress supposedly includes in bills. However, Congress does not specify "pork barrel" projects in the bills presented to the President. Particular projects are identified in the conference report that accompanies a bill. These reports, which are not submitted to the President for his signature or veto, explain to executive departments and agencies how lump-sum funds are to be spent. The President cannot veto items, because there are no items to veto.

Congress could pattern itself after the states, taking the details from conference reports and inserting them into public laws. The results would not be attractive for agency officials, who like the latitude and flexibility of lump-sum funding. They do not want details, or items, locked into public law.

During the administration of RONALD REAGAN [3,I], the editorial page of the *Wall Street Journal* argued that the President already had item-veto authority. The theory is that the Framers anticipated that each discrete subject would be placed in a separate bill and presented to the President, giving him maximum discretion in using the veto power. Because Congress currently passes omnibus bills—including continuing funding and authorization for various programs—it is argued that an effective veto requires a power in the President to exercise item veto within these massive bills.

The historical record does not support this theory's view of the Framers' expectations. The first appropriations bill passed in 1789 was an omnibus measure, containing all funds for civilian and military programs. The same kinds of bills were enacted in 1790 and 1791. Evidently the members of the First Congress, which included many of the Framers who had participated in the CONSTITUTIONAL CONVENTION OF 1787 [1], did not believe that Congress should pass separate appropriations bills for every discrete program or activity.

A presidential item veto would have little effect on reducing federal deficits. Most of the federal budget is "uncontrollable" because of fixed costs to pay interest on the federal deficit, provide ENTITLEMENTS [I] (such as SOCIAL SECURITY [4]) for individuals, and reimburse contractors for work already done. Those appropriations could not be vetoed. However, an item veto could greatly increase EXECUTIVE POWER [2]. Presidents and their assistants could use the threat of an item veto to coerce legislators into supporting presidential nominees, treaties, legislative goals, and spending priorities.

LOUIS FISHER

(SEE ALSO: *Budget Process* [I].)

Bibliography

FEIN, BRUCE and REYNOLDS, WILLIAM BRADFORD 1989 Wishful Thinking on a Line-Item Veto. *Legal Times*, November 13, pp. 20, 24.

FISHER, LOUIS and DEVINS, NEAL 1986 How Successfully Can the States' Item Veto Be Transferred to the President? *Georgetown Law Journal* 75:159–197.

LOCAL GOVERNMENT

The Constitution does not mention local governments, but because of their ubiquity and importance questions have inevitably arisen about how they are to be fitted into the conceptual world it creates. Differences in the structures and functions of local governments might have led the Supreme Court to develop a complex set of responses to those questions. Both history and state law, for example, furnish materials that would have permitted the Court to conclude that some activities of some local governments should be characterized as "private," thereby freeing those local governments from the limitations the Constitution imposes on the exercise of governmental power and permitting them to claim the protections it confers upon private interests.

Instead, the Court has, with minor exceptions, treated all local governments alike. In all their activities, all are "political subdivisions of the State created as convenient agencies for exercising such of the powers of the State as may be entrusted to them," as the Court wrote of municipal corporations in *Hunter v. City of Pittsburgh* (1907). Several important conclusions flow from this conception of local government.

First, in exercising whatever authority the state may have conferred on them, local governments are subject to the same limitations the Constitution imposes on the exercise of state power. Second, local governments have no constitutional rights against the state that created them. A state may, for example, dispose of a local government's property as though it were the state's own, with no obligation to compensate the local government from which the property is "taken." Third, states have plenary control over the distribution of governmental authority within their borders. Individuals do not have a constitutional right to be governed by local institutions rather than by

the state directly, nor do they have a right to be governed by one rather than another local government.

The states' plenary authority over governmental organization is, of course, subject to the limitations the Constitution imposes on the exercise of all state authority. Thus, in GOMILLION V. LIGHTFOOT (1961) [2], a state statute redrawing the boundaries of a municipality so as to exclude virtually all its black, and none of its white, residents was invalidated as racially discriminatory. And in *Washington v. Seattle School District No. 1* (1982), the Court sustained a challenge to a statewide initiative that denied local school boards authority to bus students for the purpose of eliminating DE FACTO [2] school SEGREGATION [4]. Relying on HUNTER V. ERICKSON (1969) [2], the Court held that a state could not structure its decision-making process "in such a way as to place special burdens on the ability of minority groups to achieve beneficial legislation." But in so holding, the Court was careful to reaffirm the state's power to assume control of the schools or, presumably, of all decisions concerning student placement. The invalidated initiative differed from such measures, in the Court's view, because it did not operate "in a race-neutral manner."

The states' plenary authority over their local governments may also be circumscribed by federal legislation. Thus, in *Lawrence County v. Lead-Deadwood School District* (1985) a federal statute authorizing local governments that receive federal payments in lieu of property taxes to spend funds "for any governmental purpose" was held to preempt a state statute which required that the funds be spent in the same way as general tax revenues. Just how far Congress may intrude on the states' power to control their local governments is uncertain, but in principle the question appears to be no different from that which arises whenever Congress regulates internal affairs of the states. In *FERC v. Mississippi* (1982) the Court sustained Congress's power to impose certain duties on state utility commissions, and in GARCIA V. SAN ANTONIO METROPOLITAN TRANSIT AUTHORITY (1985) [2] the Court sustained Congress's power to subject states to the wage and hour provisions of the FAIR LABOR STANDARDS ACT [2]. These decisions establish that the power of Congress is very broad, perhaps extending to the limits of Congress's authority under its ENUMERATED POWERS [2]. Neither decision, however, quite forecloses the possibility that the Court may yet find in the TENTH AMENDMENT [4] a principle of state autonomy that imposes some limits on Congress's power to interfere with state control of the agencies of state government.

The doctrine that local governments are merely state agencies, if taken to a logical extreme, might be understood to undermine the devolution of state authority to them. To the extent that a state relies on local governments for the performance of various governmental functions, differences in the circumstances and policies of the local governments inevitably lead to disparate treatment of the state's citizens. If local governments are merely state agencies, it can be argued, the state should be held responsible for the disparities to the same extent it would if it had directly ordered them. Although territorial discrimination by the state of ͺ ͺ can be justified and has in particular circumstances been upheld by the Court, it seems plain that the acceptance of that argument would seriously threaten the institution of local self-government. Thus far, however, the Supreme Court has refused to apply the *Hunter* doctrine in so drily logical a fashion.

In SAN ANTONIO INDEPENDENT SCHOOL DISTRICT V. RODRIGUEZ (1973) [4], the Court held that a state policy of relying on local school districts to finance a substantial percentage of the cost of operating local schools did not violate the EQUAL PROTECTION [2,I] clause of the FOURTEENTH AMENDMENT [2,I], even though there were marked differences among the school districts in both taxable resources and expenditures per pupil. Among the considerations that influenced the Court were the deeply embedded national tradition of local financing and control of schools and the more general threat that a contrary decision would have posed to traditional reliance on local governments to support and provide a broad range of other services.

MILLIKEN V. BRADLEY (1974) [3] reflects similar deference to the tradition of local self-government. In that case, the Court reversed a decree ordering interdistrict SCHOOL BUSING [4] as a remedy for unlawful segregation of the Detroit schools. In doing so, it rejected the district court's argument that "school district lines are no more than arbitrary lines on a map drawn 'for political convenience'" that may be ignored whenever interdistrict relief is necessary to achieve an effective remedy. Said the Court, "No single tradition in public education is more deeply rooted than local control over the operation of schools." Due respect for that tradition, the Court held, precluded an interdistrict remedy unless other districts participated in bringing about the unlawful segregation or the state drew district lines to foster segregation.

A number of commentators have argued that *Rodriguez*, *Milliken*, and several other recent Supreme Court decisions that accord weight to the nation's traditions of local self-government are, if not inconsistent with the *Hunter* doctrine, at least in tension with it. But the Court has gone no further than to recognize those traditions when they are expressed in state law. For that reason, its recent decisions seem more an affirmation of the state's plenary authority over governmental organization than a retreat from it.

For reasons that have never been adequately explained, however, the Court has not followed the logic of *Hunter* in determining the reach of federal JUDICIAL POWER [3].

A local government is treated as a "citizen of a state" for purposes of DIVERSITY JURISDICTION [2], though the same is not true of either the state or those of its political subdivisions of statewide authority that are regarded as merely its alter ego. Nor do local governments share the state's ELEVENTH AMENDMENT [2,I] immunity from federal court suit.

TERRANCE SANDALOW

(SEE ALSO: *Racial Discrimination* [3,I]; *State Action* [4,I].)

Bibliography

BRIFFAULT, RICHARD   1989   Our Localism. *Columbia Law Review* 89:85–111.
LEE, CAROL F.   1982   The Federal Courts and the Status of Municipalities: A Conceptual Challenge. *Boston University Law Review* 62:1–73.

LOW-VALUE SPEECH

The role that assessments of the value of particular speech or categories of speech should play in FIRST AMENDMENT [2,I] theory is much contested. Everyone agrees, however, that at some point judges should be barred from making assessments about the value of particular speech in deciding whether it may be regulated or prohibited. Moreover, the image of a content-neutral government, at least as a regulative ideal, is a powerful force in First Amendment law.

Commentators ordinarily describe judicial judgments about the value of speech as "exceptions." The norm is said to be that speech is protected and that judgments about the value of speech are foreign to the judiciary. Exceptions are often explained in terms of "low value" theory. Speech does not get protection or it gets less protection than other speech because it has low value.

Geoffrey R. Stone, the theory's principal exponent, argues that low-value theory justifiably plays a major role in the JURISPRUDENCE [I] of the First Amendment. It is necessary, he argues, because otherwise we should have to apply the same standards to private blackmail as to public debate. If we do not treat harmful but relatively unimportant speech differently, we will dilute the expression "at the very heart of the guarantee." As Stone characterizes the law, "the Court, applying [the low-value] approach, has held that several classes of speech have only low first amendment value, including express incitement, false statements of fact, obscenity, commercial speech, fighting words, and child pornography." Once the Court has decided that speech has low value, according to Stone, it engages in "categorical balancing, through which it defines the precise circumstances in which the speech may be restricted." By contrast, in assessing high-value speech, "the Court employs, not a balancing approach akin to its content-neutral balancing, but a far more speech-protective analysis." Thus, low-value theory functions to preserve the autonomy of high-value speech from government regulation.

No doubt, many categories of unprotected speech are explainable in part because they are thought to be of low value. Moreover, some forms of otherwise protected speech are afforded less generous protection than is given to other forms of protected speech almost exclusively because they are seen to have less value. But no sharp line divides low-value from high-value speech, and low-value theory cannot account for all of its important exceptions.

Consider the First Amendment's standard testing ground: advocacy of illegal action. Such advocacy is protected unless it is directed to inciting imminent lawless action and is likely to incite or produce imminent lawless action. Is unprotected advocacy really a form of low-value speech? One approach might be to say that any speech that can be prohibited is low-value by definition. This approach, however, substitutes tautology for analysis, and it does nothing to provide an *ex ante* divide between high-value and low-value speech.

In what sense, then, is INCITEMENT [2] or unprotected advocacy a form of low-value speech? Notice that advocacy of illegal action is not in itself a form of low-value speech. Indeed, noninciting advocacy of illegal action in itself is fully protected by the First Amendment. This conclusion has been reached in light of powerful opinions by Justices OLIVER WENDELL HOLMES JR. [2], and LOUIS D. BRANDEIS [1] about the value of such speech. Thus, advocacy of illegal action appears to be high-value speech. The reason why some types of advocacy of illegal action can be prohibited seems to have less to do with their value as speech than with their potential for harm.

Alternatively, even if the Court had silently repudiated Holmes and Brandeis, the label "low-value speech" would obscure the decision-making process. The Court did not start, and need not have started, its analysis of illegal action by asking whether the category of speech was valuable or not. Indeed, in dealing with the issues, the Court has ordinarily begun with an assessment of state interests. What ultimately is at stake in this context is an accommodation of the values of order and FREEDOM OF SPEECH [2,I]. If the rules in the context of advocacy of illegal action are good ones, the reason is that those rules have protected order without unnecessary sacrifice of First Amendment values. But First Amendment values have surely been sacrificed. If the rules governing advocacy of illegal action have the effect of muffling the voices of those who are most agitated against the system, we have suffered a substantial First Amendment loss. It demeans the speech

and underestimates that loss to think about this as a part of low-value theory.

The same can be said for the rules attempting to regulate false statements of fact in LIBEL [3] law. Certainly, from one perspective, high-value speech is at risk. Many think criticism of public officials and other PUBLIC FIGURES [3] is "at the very heart of the guarantee." To fashion a set of rules in which plaintiffs succeed in allowing juries to scrutinize that criticism risks a major chilling effect. Moreover, the fact-finding process may simply mask the unleashing of juror prejudices about what speech should be free.

Presumably the protection of reputation requires findings of truth and falsity by juries, but that protection must be accompanied by a sense of First Amendment loss. To characterize any such process as a part of low-value theory would deemphasize the major risk to high-value speech, however the latter might be defined. The conflict between reputation and free speech necessitates a difficult choice. Something important must be abandoned, and that choice deserves emphasis.

Low-value theory avoids that emphasis. It offers the soothing prospect of characterizing free-speech doctrine as generally unthreatening to speech of general importance, but low-value theory cannot deliver. Like it or not, so-called high-value speech is subject to government regulation if a strong enough showing can be made.

STEVEN H. SHIFFRIN

(SEE ALSO: *Balancing Test* [1]; *Child Pornography* [I]; *Commercial Speech* [1,I]; *Fighting Words* [2]; *Obscenity* [3]; *Pornography* [3]; *Pornography and Feminism* [I].)

Bibliography

SHIFFRIN, STEVEN H. 1990 *The First Amendment, Democracy, and Romance.* Cambridge, Mass.: Harvard University Press.

STONE, GEOFFREY R. 1983 Content Regulation and the First Amendment. *William and Mary Law Review* 25:189–252.

LYNG v. NORTHWEST INDIAN CEMETERY
485 U.S. 439 (1988)

The U.S. Forest Service planned to build a paved road and allow timber harvesting in an area held sacred by certain AMERICAN INDIANS [1]. The Indians used the area, now part of a national forest, to perform religious rituals. The Supreme Court held 5–3 that the Forest Service action would not violate the free exercise clause of the FIRST AMENDMENT [2,I].

Writing for the majority, Justice SANDRA DAY O'CONNOR [3,I] maintained that the free exercise clause was not implicated here because the Indians would not be coerced by the government's action into violating their religious beliefs. Hence, the government did not have to supply a COMPELLING STATE INTEREST [1] to justify its action. The fact that the government activity would interfere with the Indians' religion was irrelevant because "the Free Exercise Clause is written in terms of what the government cannot do to the individual, not in terms of what the individual can extract from the government." Moreover, even if the Forest Service actions should " 'virtually destroy the Indians' ability to practice their religion,' . . . the Constitution simply does not provide a principle that could justify upholding" their claims.

Writing for the dissenters, Justice WILLIAM J. BRENNAN [1,I] rejected the majority's narrow reading of the free exercise clause and argued that because the beliefs and activities implicated by the government action were "central" to the religion of the American Indians, the government must supply a compelling state interest to justify its action.

JOHN G. WEST, JR.

(SEE ALSO: *Religious Liberty* [3,I].)

MARSHALL, THURGOOD
(1908–)
(Update)

Thurgood Marshall has earned a unique place in American history on the basis of a long, varied, and influential career as a private attorney, government lawyer, and appellate jurist. Two achievements in particular stand out. First, as counsel for the National Association for the Advancement of Colored People (NAACP), he shaped the litigation that destroyed the constitutional legitimacy of state-enforced racial SEGREGATION [4]. Second, as an Associate Justice of the Supreme Court—the nation's first black Justice—he has boldly articulated a liberal jurisprudence on a Court dominated by conservatives. No person in the history of the Supreme Court better illustrates the limits and possibilities of the jurist as dissenter.

Marshall was born July 2, 1908, in Baltimore, Maryland, attended that city's racially segregated public schools, and was graduated from Lincoln University. Excluded from the University of Maryland Law School by that state's racial policies, he received his law degree from Howard Law School. He excelled at Howard and came to the attention of the school's dean, CHARLES H. HOUSTON [2], a pioneer in the use of litigation as a vehicle of social reform. Although Marshall embarked on a conventional commercial practice upon graduation, he also participated, under Houston's guidance, in important, albeit unremunerative, CIVIL RIGHTS [1,I] cases. Appropriately enough, his first consisted of a successful suit against the same state university system that had earlier excluded him. In MURRAY V. MARYLAND (1937) Marshall convinced the Court of Appeals of Maryland that the Constitution required the state to do more for black residents seeking legal education than merely offer them scholarships to attend out-of-state law schools.

In 1939 Marshall succeeded Houston as special counsel of the NAACP. Over the next two decades he traveled ceaselessly, addressing problems of racial inequality in a wide array of settings: from obscure local courts in which he sought to extract from hostile juries and judges a measure of justice for black defendants, to Korea where he investigated the treatment of black soldiers by United States military authorities, to black churches and lodges where he encouraged people in aggrieved communities to seek to vindicate their rights. He also argued thirty-two cases before the Supreme Court, prevailing in twenty-nine of them. His brilliant advocacy helped to convince the Supreme Court to invalidate practices that excluded blacks from primary elections (SMITH V. ALLWRIGHT [1944] [4]), to prohibit segregation in interstate transportation (MORGAN V. VIRGINIA [1946] [3]), to overturn convictions obtained from juries from which blacks had been illicitly barred (PATTON V. MISSISSIPPI [1947]), and to prohibit state courts from enforcing racially restrictive real estate covenants (SHELLEY V. KRAEMER [1948] [4]). Marshall's greatest triumph arose from the skillfully orchestrated litigation that culminated in BROWN V. BOARD OF EDUCATION OF TOPEKA (1954) [1], which invalidated state-enforced racial segregation in public schooling. By the close of the 1950s, Marshall had attained widespread recognition as a leading public figure and was known affectionately in much of black America as "Mr. Civil Rights."

The next stage in Marshall's career was marked by a series of high-level appointments. In 1961, President JOHN

F. KENNEDY [3] appointed him to the United States Court of Appeals for the Second Circuit over the strong objections of segregationist senators who delayed his confirmation for nearly a year. In 1965, President LYNDON B. JOHNSON [3] appointed Marshall SOLICITOR GENERAL [4] of the United States. The first black American to hold this post, Marshall argued several important cases before the Court, including MIRANDA V. ARIZONA (1966) [3], in which he successfully urged the Court to impose greater limitations on the power of police to interrogate criminal suspects; HARPER V. VIRGINIA STATE BOARD OF ELECTIONS (1966) [2], in which he successfully argued that state POLL TAXES violated the federal Constitution; and UNITED STATES V. GUEST (1966) [2], in which he successfully defended the federal prosecution of white supremacists in Georgia who committed a racially motivated murder during the era of the CIVIL RIGHTS MOVEMENT [I].

In 1967, President Johnson set the stage for Marshall to cross the color line in another area of governmental service when he named him to a seat on the Supreme Court. Marshall's elevation vividly symbolized the ascendancy of values and interests he had long sought to advance. At the outset of Marshall's career on the Court, it was presided over by Chief Justice EARL WARREN [4] and animated by a decidedly reformist ethos. Ironically, however, the liberal wing whose ranks Marshall fortified began to disintegrate soon after he took his seat. By the mid-1970s, the appointments of Chief Justice WARREN E. BURGER [1] and associate Justices LEWIS F. POWELL [3,I] and WILLIAM H. REHNQUIST [3,I] had brought to the fore a conservative ethos that has long confined Justice Marshall to the periphery of judicial power.

During his years on the Court, Justice Marshall has seldom held sway in the middle as a "swing" vote. Rather, he has made his mark as a judicial maverick—always independent, consistently bold, frequently dissenting. Keenly attentive to allegations of INVIDIOUS DISCRIMINATION [2], Justice Marshall has been strongly favorable to the claims of members of historically oppressed groups. However, he has repeatedly found himself at odds with the Court. MEMPHIS V. GREENE (1981) [3] involved a city's decision to close a street, mainly used by blacks, which traversed a predominantly white neighborhood. The Court upheld the legality of the city's action. Justice Marshall perceived a violation of the THIRTEENTH AMENDMENT [4], concluding that the city's action constituted a racially prejudiced "badge or incident of slavery." PERSONNEL ADMINISTRATOR OF MASSACHUSETTS V. FEENEY (1979) [3] called into question a state law that provided an absolute preference for veterans of the ARMED FORCES [I] in civil service positions, a system of selection that tended overwhelmingly to disadvantage women in relation to men. The Court upheld the statute. Justice Marshall condemned it as a

violation of the EQUAL PROTECTION [2,I] clause of the FOURTEENTH AMENDMENT [2,I]. MOBILE V. BOLDEN (1980) [3] concerned an at-large voting scheme under which, for almost seventy years, no black had ever been elected to a seat on the ruling city commission in Mobile, Alabama, even though blacks constituted nearly a third of the city's population. The Court held that this electoral arrangement could be invalidated only if it were used as a vehicle of purposeful discrimination. Justice Marshall concluded that the system's racially disparate impact violated the FIFTEENTH AMENDMENT [2]. ROSTKER V. GOLDBERG (1981) [3] brought into question the constitutionality of a federal statute that requires men but not women to register for the military draft. Differing with the majority of his colleagues, Justice Marshall declared that the Court erred in placing its "imprimatur on one of the most potent remaining public expressions of 'ancient canards about the proper role of women.'"

Critical of the Court for showing too little solicitude for those who have been historically victimized on the basis of race and gender, Justice Marshall has also rebuked the Court for displaying undue aggressiveness in defending the asserted rights of those who challenge affirmative action policies that provide preferences to women and racial minorities. Sharply distinguishing between benign and invidious discrimination, he has voted to uphold every AFFIRMATIVE ACTION [1,I] plan the Court has reviewed. Here, too, he has been forced into dissent, objecting bitterly to decisions that have increasingly limited the permissible scope of affirmative action measures. In REGENTS OF UNIVERSITY OF CALIFORNIA V. BAKKE (1978) [3], the first affirmative action case that the Court resolved, Justice Marshall declared that "It must be remembered that during most of the past 200 years, the Constitution as interpreted by the [Supreme] Court did not prohibit the most ingenious and pervasive forms of discrimination against the Negro. Now, when a State acts to remedy the effects of that legacy of discrimination, I cannot believe that this same Constitution stands as a barrier."

A decade later, Justice Marshall continued to rail against an interpretation of the Fourteenth Amendment that he considers perverse. In RICHMOND V. J. A. CROSON CO. (1989) [I], for instance, he dissented against a ruling that invalidated Richmond, Virginia's policy of reserving that for enterprises owned by racial minorities a designated percentage of business generated by the city. Observing that "It is a welcome symbol of racial progress when the former capital of the Confederacy acts forthrightly to confront the effects of RACIAL DISCRIMINATION [3,I] in its midst," he angrily chided his colleagues for taking "a deliberate and giant step backward." The Court's decision, he predicted, "will inevitably discourage or prevent governmental entities, particularly States and localities, from acting to rectify the scourge of past discrimination. This is the harsh reality of the majority's decision, but it is not the Constitution's command."

Other areas in which Justice Marshall's strongly held views have frequently been at odds with the Court's conclusions involve CAPITAL PUNISHMENT [1,I], ABORTION [1,I] and the legal status of the poor—areas in which Marshall's jurisprudential commitments frequently overlap. Insisting that death penalties under all circumstances violate the Eighth Amendment's prohibition against CRUEL AND UNUSUAL PUNISHMENT [2], Justice Marshall has filed dissents against all executions that the Court has sanctioned. In AKE V. OKLAHOMA (1985) [1], his advocacy on behalf of those charged with capital crimes succeeded in wringing from his colleagues a rare broadening of rights to which criminal defendants are entitled. Writing for the Court, Justice Marshall held that, at least in cases possibly involving the death penalty, DUE PROCESS [2] requires states to afford indigent defendants the means to obtain needed psychiatric experts.

With respect to abortion, Justice Marshall has been among the most stalwart defenders of ROE V. WADE (1973) [3], dissenting in every case in which the Court has upheld legislative inroads on what he views as a woman's broad right to decide whether or not to terminate a pregnancy. An example of his allegiance to *Roe v. Wade* (1973) [3] is his dissenting opinion in MAHER V. ROE (1977) [3], where he maintained that a state violated the Constitution by denying poor women funding for abortions while making funds available to them for expenses of childbirth. "Since efforts to overturn [*Roe v. Wade*] have been unsuccessful," he charged, "the opponents of abortion have attempted every imaginable means to circumvent the commands of the Constitution and impose their moral choices upon the rest of society." Articulating his anger with characteristic sharpness, Justice Marshall asserted that this case involved "the most vicious attacks yet devised" in that they fell on poor women—"those among us least able to help or defend themselves."

Throughout Justice Marshall's career on the Court he has vigorously attempted to improve the legal status of the poor. He has argued, for instance, that the federal courts should subject to heightened scrutiny state laws that explicitly discriminate on the basis of poverty. For the most part, however, his efforts have been stymied. One particularly memorable expression of Justice Marshall's empathy for the indigent is his dissent in *United States v. Kras* (1973), a case in which the Court held that federal law did not violate the Constitution by requiring a $50 fee of persons seeking the protections of bankruptcy. Objecting to the Court's assumption that the petitioner could readily accumulate this amount, Justice Marshall wrote that he could not agree with the majority

that it is so easy for the desperately poor to save $1.92 *each week* over the course of six months. . . . The 1970 Census found that over 800,000 families in the Nation had annual incomes of less than $1,000 or $19.23 a week. . . . I see no reason to require that families in such straits sacrifice over 5% of their annual income as a prerequisite to getting a discharge in bankruptcy. . . . It may be easy for some people to think that weekly savings of less than $2 are no burden. But no one who has had close contact with poor people can fail to understand how close to the margin of survival many of them are. . . . It is perfectly proper for judges to disagree about what the Constitution requires. But it is disgraceful for an interpretation of the Constitution to be premised upon unfounded assumptions about how people live.

On occasion Justice Marshall's dissents have succeeded in changing the mind of the Court. An example is the Court's response to claims of racially invidious discrimination in peremptory challenges. In SWAIN V. ALABAMA (1965) [4] the Court had ruled that prosecutors could properly use race as a basis for peremptorily excluding potential jurors so long as they did so as a matter of strategy relating to a particular trial and not for the purpose of barring blacks routinely from participation in the administration of justice. By repeatedly dissenting from orders in which the Court refused to reconsider *Swain* and by showing in detail this decision's dismal practical consequences, Marshall finally convinced the Court to reverse itself—though even when it did in BATSON V. KENTUCKY (1986) [I], Marshall still maintained that his colleagues had neglected to go far enough in ridding the criminal justice system of invidious practices.

For much of Justice Marshall's career on the bench, he seems to have deliberately avoided any extrajudicial controversies. Beginning in the 1980s, however, he appears to have altered his habits. He publicly criticized RONALD REAGAN [3,I], declaring that his civil rights record as President of the United States was among the worst in the twentieth century. He also chided President GEORGE BUSH [I] for selecting DAVID H. SOUTER [I] to occupy the seat on the Court vacated by Justice Marshall's long-time ally, Justice WILLIAM J. BRENNAN [1,I]. In an unprecedented action, Justice Marshall declared on a televised broadcast that, in his view, the President's choice was inappropriate.

Although Justice Marshall received considerable criticism for his comments on Presidents Reagan and Bush, extrajudicial remarks that generated an even greater amount of controversy stemmed from a speech that he gave in 1987 in the midst of the bicentennial celebration of the United States Constitution. Boldly challenging the iconography of American CONSTITUTIONALISM [1], he asserted that he did not find "the wisdom, foresight, and sense of justice exhibited by the framers [to be] particularly profound. To the contrary," he declared, "the government they devised was defective from the start," omitting, for example, blacks and women as protected members of the polity. Eschewing "flag waving fervor," Justice Marshall noted his intention to commemorate the bicentennial by recalling "the suffering, struggle, and sacrifice that has triumphed over much of what was wrong with the original document" and by also acknowledging the Constitution's unfulfilled promise.

Some detractors fault Justice Marshall on the grounds that his penchant for dissent has robbed him of influence that he might otherwise have wielded. Judging influence, however, is a dangerous endeavor. Justices JOHN MARSHALL HARLAN [2,I], OLIVER WENDELL HOLMES, JR [2], and LOUIS D. BRANDEIS [1] are as well respected on the basis of their dissenting opinions as they are respected for any other aspect of their illustrious careers. History may well bequeath the same fate to Justice Thurgood Marshall. Justice Marshall resigned from the Court in 1991.

RANDALL KENNEDY

(SEE ALSO: *Badges of Servitude* [1]; *NAACP Legal Defense Fund* [3]; *Race and Criminal Justice* [I]; *Race-Consciousness* [I].)

MARYLAND v. CRAIG
110 S.Ct. 3157 (1990)

This is another Sixth Amendment case in which the Supreme Court [4,I] declined to follow the express words of the text. Although the Court engaged in what is usually described as JUDICIAL ACTIVISM [3,I], it acted in a good cause and had PRECEDENT [3] for its exception to the CONFRONTATION [1,I] clause of the amendment. In every case in which HEARSAY [2] evidence of any sort is admitted, the right of the accused to confront the witnesses against him or her becomes empty. In this case the Court held, 5–4, that the victim of child abuse may testify on closed circuit television to avoid the trauma of face-to-face confrontation with the accused.

Justice SANDRA DAY O'CONNOR [3,I], for the Court, reasoned that the state had a legitimate interest in protecting the child witness from psychological trauma. Face-to-face confrontation, assured by the text of the Sixth Amendment, turned out not to be an indispensable element of the confrontation guarantee.

Justice ANTONIN SCALIA [I], an unlikely spokesman for the liberal Justices who joined him, rested his dissent on the clear language of the text. He accused the majority of a line of reasoning that "eliminates the right." But his view on the admission of hearsay ("not expressly excluded by the Confrontation Clause") would also justify admission

of television testimony in the presence of defense counsel—because the amendment does not expressly exclude such a procedure. Scalia further questioned whether the evidence of a frightened child was reliable. But the state, not the Court, should decide whether the child required protection. Scalia's final proposition, that the Court is not at liberty to ignore the confrontation clause, was at war with his several illustrations to the contrary.

LEONARD W. LEVY

MCCLESKEY v. KEMP
481 U.S. 279 (1987)

McCleskey, a black Georgian, on being sentenced to death for the murder of a white person, sought a writ of HABEAS CORPUS [2,I] on the claim that Georgia's capital-sentencing procedures violated the EQUAL PROTECTION [2,I] clause of the FOURTEENTH AMENDMENT [2,I] and the CRUEL AND UNUSUAL PUNISHMENT [2,I] clause of the Eighth Amendment. He based his claim on "the Baldus study," a statistical examination of Georgia's more than 2,000 murder cases during the 1970s. The study showed a significant correlation between race and prosecutors' decisions to seek the death penalty and jurors' recommendations of the death penalty. For example, death was the sentence in twenty-two percent of the cases involving black defendants and white victims, in eight percent of the cases involving white defendants and white victims, and in three percent of the cases involving white defendants and black victims. The Supreme Court [4,I], held 5–4, that McCleskey did not show that Georgia had acted unconstitutionally in sentencing him to CAPITAL PUNISHMENT [1,I].

The infirmity of McCleskey's argument, according to Justice LEWIS F. POWELL [3,I], for the Court, consisted in his failure to prove that he personally had been the target of RACIAL DISCRIMINATION [3,I] or that the race of his victim had anything to do with his sentence. Anyone invoking the equal-protection clause in a capital-sentencing case has the burden of showing that deliberate discrimination had a discriminatory effect "in *his* case." McCleskey's reliance on the Baldus study proved nothing with respect to him; moreover, every jury is unique, so that statistics concerning many juries do not establish anything regarding a particular one.

McCleskey also argued that the state violated the equal protection clause by enacting the death penalty statute and retaining it despite its supposedly discriminatory application. Powell dismissed this argument because it had no support from proof that the legislature passed and kept a capital punishment act because of its racially discriminatory effect. The Court had previously held in *Gregg v. Georgia* (1976) that Georgia's capital-sentencing system could operate fairly.

The Court found McCleskey's Eighth Amendment argument no more persuasive. In *Gregg* it had ruled that the jury's discretion was controlled by clear and objective standards. The statute even required the trial court to review every sentence to determine whether it was imposed under the influence of prejudice, whether the evidence supported it, and whether the sentence was disproportionate to sentences in similar cases. Moreover, the judge had to consider the question whether race had any role in the trials. Absent proof that the Georgia system operated arbitrarily, McCleskey could not prove a violation of the Eighth Amendment by showing that other defendants had not received the death penalty.

McCleskey also argued that Georgia's system was arbitrarily applied "because racial considerations may influence capital sentencing decisions." Statistics, Powell replied, show only a "likelihood," which was insufficient to establish an "unacceptable risk" of racial prejudice.

Justice WILLIAM J. BRENNAN [1,I], for the dissenters, argued the Eighth Amendment issue. He believed that a death sentence should be voided if there was a risk that it might have been imposed arbitrarily. Brennan believed that McCleskey should not have to prove discrimination in his own case; it was enough that the risk of prejudice, which Brennan believed was established by the statistical study, "might have infected the sentencing decision." McCleskey's claim warranted the Court's support because his was the first case challenging the system, not on how it might operate but "on empirical documentation of how it does operate." Black Georgians who killed whites were sentenced to death at nearly twenty-two times the rate of blacks who killed blacks and at more than seven times the rate of whites who kill blacks. This proved the point about disproportionate sentencing for the dissenters.

Justice HARRY A. BLACKMUN [1,I], who also spoke for them, used similar evidence to maintain that Georgia's capital-sentencing procedures conflicted with the equal-protection clause. Racial factors impermissibly affected the system from indictment to sentencing: "The Baldus study demonstrates that black persons are a distinct group that are singled out for a different treatment in the Georgia capital sentencing system." The BURDEN OF PROOF [1], Blackmun contended, should be on the state to demonstrate that racially neutral procedures yielded the racially skewed results shown by the study.

The Court's opinion is not easy to explain, unless one accepts the belief of dissenters that the Court did not wish to open a can of worms. McCleskey's claims taken to their logical conclusion undermined principles that buttressed the entire CRIMINAL JUSTICE SYSTEM [I]. His equal-protection and "cruel and unusual punishment" arguments, if accepted, could have applied to punishments in noncapital cases and to procedures before SENTENCING [4,I] and might have resulted in abolition of the death penalty as well.

LEONARD W. LEVY

(SEE ALSO: *Capital Punishment and Race* [I]; *Capital Punishment Cases of 1972* [1]; *Capital Punishment Cases of 1976* [1]; *Race and Criminal Justice* [I].)

MCCREE, WADE HAMPTON, JR.
(1920–1987)

Wade McCree was a member of the generation of black lawyers Governor G. Mennen Williams of Michigan once described as "revolutionaries," individuals who by talent and determination succeeded in opening doors that previously had been closed to members of their race. A graduate of Fisk University and Harvard Law School, McCree spent several years in private practice, but then entered upon a career of public service that continued through four decades and earned for him a reputation as one of the most distinguished lawyers of his time.

After serving as a member of the Michigan Workmen's Compensation Commission and as an elected Wayne County circuit judge, he was appointed by President JOHN F. KENNEDY [3] to the UNITED STATES DISTRICT COURT [4] for the Eastern District of Michigan. Five years later, in 1966, President LYNDON B. JOHNSON [3] elevated him to the UNITED STATES COURT OF APPEALS [4] for the Sixth Circuit, on which he served until 1977, when President JIMMY CARTER [1] appointed him SOLICITOR GENERAL [4,I]. In 1981, he joined the faculty of the University of Michigan Law School, where he served as the Lewis M. Simes Professor until his death. McCree was the first black or among the first blacks to hold each of these positions.

Widely admired for his judicious manner and temperament, his careful craftsmanship, and the breadth and depth of his knowledge, McCree quickly gained a reputation as a judge's judge. As a judge, and more particularly as a judge on an "inferior court," he was constrained within limits set by others, but within the limits of his office he sought to advance what he regarded as the deepest purposes of law, the fair treatment of individuals and the protection of their liberty and security. McCree's career, both on the bench and off, demonstrates the contribution to those goals that can be made in a life spent in the law.

TERRANCE SANDALOW

Bibliography

TRIBUTES 1987 Wade Hampton McCree, Jr. *Michigan Law Review* 86:217–265.

MCGOWAN, CARL
(1911–1987)

Carl McGowan served on the UNITED STATES COURT OF APPEALS [4] for the District of Columbia Circuit from 1963 until his death. Before his appointment, he had a private practice and served on the law faculty of Northwestern University. He was a judge whose intelligence and humanity made him suited to the craft. His opinions were lucid in style and expression, sound in analysis, and combined intellectual acuity, practical understanding, and good sense.

McGowan could not be pigeonholed as a "liberal" or a "conservative." He was the sort of judge a lawyer might wish for before knowing which side of the case he had to argue. McGowan won the respect and affection of his colleagues on the bench as well as of the bar of the DISTRICT OF COLUMBIA [2]. He counseled not by preaching but by example. He was learned in the law, evenhanded in approach, honest, and wise. His ability to conciliate between opposing views allowed his court to resolve cases on common ground. McGowan's dissents barely match the number of terms he served on the court—some twenty-five dissents in a quarter century's service. From the mid-1960s to the mid-1980s, the overall dissent rate in the D.C. Circuit in cases with published opinions hovered around 13 percent; indicative of McGowan's moderating influence, in cases in which he was a panel member, that rate was five percent.

Judge McGowan's patient genius worked through many perplexing constitutional issues. In *Rothstein v. Wyman* (2d Cir. 1972), for example, his opinion delineated the critical line drawn by the ELEVENTH AMENDMENT [2] between what federal courts can and cannot order states to do. In *Nixon v. Administrator of General Services* (D.D.C. 1976) he persuasively analyzed a panoply of constitutional objections pressed on behalf of a former president. In high tribute to Judge McGowan, the Supreme Court's majority essentially adopted his reasoning on the hard questions of SEPARATION OF POWERS [4], EXECUTIVE PRIVILEGE [2], invasion of privacy, freedom of expression, and BILL OF ATTAINDER [1].

RUTH BADER GINSBURG

Bibliography

POWELL, LEWIS F., JR., ET AL. 1988 In Memoriam Judge Carl McGowan. *George Washington Law Review* 56:681–702.

MEESE COMMISSION

The Attorney General's Commission on Pornography, better known as "The Meese Commission" after Attorney General Edwin Meese, was charged to "determine the nature, extent, and impact on society of pornography in the United States, and to make specific recommendations to the Attorney General concerning more effective ways in which the spread of pornography could be contained, consistent with constitutional guarantees." The committee included three attorneys, two psychologists, a city council member, a federal judge, a social worker, a magazine editor, and a priest. It had a balanced religious and political composition as well.

After a year of extensive hearings, field trips, and study, the commission produced a 1,960-page report. If the size of the report were not daunting enough, the findings of the commission were relatively inconclusive. Although the commission did take a stand on the issue of PORNOGRAPHY [3]—something a similar presidential commission established during the Nixon administration failed to do—it did not wholly condemn pornography as the right, especially the religious right, and feminists had hoped. Instead, it unanimously condemned sexually explicit material that is violent in nature; sexually explicit materials that show situations where women are humiliated, demeaned, and subjugated; and CHILD PORNOGRAPHY [I] in any form.

A major problem the commission faced was its inability to define key terms. The commission found it difficult to define "pornography," "obscenity," and "hardcore." In the end, it could do no better than Justice POTTER J. STEWART [4] had in JACOBELLIS V. OHIO (1964) [3]. Stewart, although not defining pornography, qualified it by stating, "I know it when I see it." Hampered by the inability to define key terms, the commission called for further research.

JEFFREY D. SCHULTZ

(SEE ALSO: *Pornography and Feminism* [I].)

Bibliography

ATTORNEY GENERAL'S COMMISSION ON PORNOGRAPHY 1986 *Final Report.* Washington, D.C.: U.S. Government Printing Office.
KEATING, CHARLES H. JR. 1970 *Report of Charles H. Keating, Jr., Commissioner: Commission of Obscenity and Pornography.* Cincinnati, Ohio: Charles H. Keating, Jr.
STANMEYER, WILLIAM 1986 The Pornography Commission Report: A Plea for Decency. *Benchmark* II:227–236.

MENTAL ILLNESS
(Update)

Beginning in the 1960s, lower federal courts scrutinized with increasing intensity state claims that special statutory treatment of mental illness, either as a basis for civil commitment to psychiatric institutions or for apparent exemptions from ordinary criminal liability, were in fact beneficial to the affected individual. For almost two decades the Supreme Court was cautiously supportive of this effort, though only equivocally addressing the lower courts' most expansive findings of constitutional protections. In 1983, however, the Court definitively rejected one protective path that some lower courts had pursued; in *Jones v. United States*, the Court ruled that a criminal defendant found not guilty by reason of insanity could be confined to a mental institution without regard to the maximum term for which he might have been sentenced for the offense charged and, moreover, that the defendant could be confined without regard to the standards for mental illness civil commitment.

Two significant decisions since 1983 suggest that the Court more generally has resolved to abandon its prior tolerance, if not wholehearted support, for judicial scrutiny of state authority regarding mental illness. In *Allen v. Illinois* (1986), the Court ruled that the Fifth Amendment RIGHT AGAINST SELF-INCRIMINATION [3,I] does not apply to commitment proceedings based on mental illness, thus upholding the use of derogatory evidence obtained from a court-ordered psychiatric interview. The Court accepted at face value both the state's characterization of the proceedings as "civil" (even though the statute under review applied only to mentally ill people who were "sexually dangerous" and had already been charged with a criminal offense) and the state's claim that the purpose of the commitment was "treatment, not punishment" (even though the person would be confined for an indeterminate term in a maximum-security facility adjoining, though administratively distinct from, a state prison). Similarly, in WASHINGTON V. HARPER (1990) [I] the Court ruled that a criminally convicted prisoner could be compelled to take psychotropic medication without any recourse to judicial proceedings to examine either the prisoner's mental competency or need for the medication. The Court thus effectively disapproved the extensive prior efforts of lower federal courts to establish constitutional protections against forced medication for civilly committed people, as in *Rennie v. Klein* (1983) and *Rogers v. Okin* (1984).

The Supreme Court's disavowal of this kind of judicial scrutiny comes at a time of popular arousal about homeless people in urban areas, many of whom appear to be mentally ill. Their visibly disturbing presence has been widely blamed on past judicial inquiries into conditions in mental institutions and the "deinstitutionalization" movement given impetus by these court decisions. Many states have responded to this popular concern by enacting more liberal standards for civil commitment, not only to avert "dangerous" conduct but also to forestall "substantial mental deterioration." Though some lower courts have constitutionally

invalidated such liberalized criteria, it is unlikely that the Supreme Court today would agree.

In one limited context the Supreme Court has recently enlarged the state's obligation to give special advantage to mentally ill people; in FORD V. WAINWRIGHT (1986) [I] the Court ruled that states are constitutionally prohibited from executing a mentally incompetent person. But this apparent beneficence has a twist that ironically corresponds to the overall direction of the Court's recent jurisprudence regarding mental illness: the state will now provide psychiatric treatment to incompetent people so that, when cured, they can be killed.

ROBERT A. BURT

Bibliography

KIESLER, CHARLES A. and SIBULKIN, AMY E. 1987 *Mental Hospitalization: Myths and Facts About a National Crisis.* Newbury Park, Calif.: Sage.

MERCY-KILLING

See: Euthanasia [2];
Right to Die [I]

MERITOR SAVINGS BANK, FSB
v. VINSON
477 U.S. 57 (1986)

In *Meritor* the Supreme Court unanimously held that sexual harassment that created a "hostile environment" in the workplace constituted EMPLOYMENT DISCRIMINATION [2,I] in violation of Title VII of the CIVIL RIGHTS ACT OF 1964 [1]. The Court thus gave its blessing to an interpretation that was already well established in the guidelines of the Equal Employment Opportunity Commission (EEOC) and in the lower federal courts.

A woman who had been employed by a bank for four years sued her branch manager and the bank for injunctive relief and for both compensatory and punitive damages, alleging that the manager had demanded and obtained sexual favors from her, including some incidents of forcible rape. She stated that she had not reported these facts to the manager's superiors because she was afraid of her manager. The manager disputed these allegations, and the bank contended that it neither knew nor approved of any sexual harassment by the manager. The bank further argued that the prohibitions of Title VII were limited to discrimination causing economic or tangible loss, not psychological harm.

Justice WILLIAM H. REHNQUIST [3,I], writing for the

Court, rejected the latter argument. Title VII was intended to strike at all disparate treatment of men and women. The EEOC guidelines were also persuasive authority that Title VII is concerned with noneconomic injury. The guidelines had explicitly recognized sexual harassment that creates "an intimidating, hostile, or offensive working environment" to be a form of SEX DISCRIMINATION [4,I] that violates the act, and lower courts had arrived at a similar interpretation in cases involving both racial harassment and sexual harassment.

Even if the plaintiff's sexual relationship with the manager were "voluntary," the Court said, that is not a defense to a Title VII action; rather, the question is whether the manager's sexual advances were "unwelcome," a determination to be made on the totality of the circumstances shown in the record. The Court declined to rule in the abstract on the question of the bank's liability for the actions of its manager. It followed the EEOC's brief, agreeing that an employer is absolutely liable when a supervisory employee offers economic benefits for sexual favors, but refusing to extend the rule of absolute liability to a "hostile environment" case. The Court also rejected the bank's argument that the mere existence of a grievance procedure insulated it from liability. The issue of the employer's liability, the Court suggested, should first be addressed by the lower courts in the context of specific findings of fact.

Justice THURGOOD MARSHALL [3,I], writing for four Justices, concurred separately to address the question of employer liability. He would follow the EEOC guidelines on this point. These guidelines went beyond the EEOC's own brief to the Court, making an employer generally responsible for supervisory employees' sexual harassment whether or not that conduct was authorized or forbidden and whether or not the employer knew or should have known of the conduct.

KENNETH L. KARST

Bibliography
ABRAMS, KATHRYN 1989 Gender Discrimination and the Transformation of Workplace Norms. *Vanderbilt Law Review* 42:1183–1248.
MACKINNON, CATHARINE A. 1979 *Sexual Harassment of Working Women.* New Haven, Conn.: Yale University Press.

METRO BROADCASTING, INC. v. F.C.C.
110 S.Ct. 2997 (1990)

In this decision the Supreme Court, 5–4, upheld two aspects of an AFFIRMATIVE ACTION [1,I] program approved by Congress in the area of BROADCASTING [1,I]. In 1986

members of racial and ethnic minorities, who constitute about one-fifth of the nation's population, owned just over two percent of the radio and television broadcasting stations licensed by the Federal Communications Commission (FCC). Two FCC policies aim to bring a greater racial and ethnic diversity to broadcast ownership. First, the FCC considers minority ownership as one factor among many in making comparative judgments among applicants for new licenses. Second, the FCC seeks to increase minority ownership through a "distress sale" policy. Normally, a licensee cannot transfer its license during the time when the FCC is considering whether the license should be revoked. As an exception to this policy, such a broadcaster may sell its license before the revocation hearing to a minority-controlled broadcaster that meets the FCC's qualifications, provided that the price does not exceed seventy-five percent of the station's value. Congress, in appropriating money for the FCC, ordered that these programs be continued.

In *Metro Broadcasting* both of these policies were challenged as denials of the guarantee of EQUAL PROTECTION [2,I] that the Court has recognized in the Fifth Amendment's DUE PROCESS [2] clause. Writing for the majority, Justice WILLIAM J. BRENNAN [1,I] strongly emphasized Congress's adoption of the two minority ownership policies. The proper STANDARD OF REVIEW [4] for congressional affirmative action was not STRICT SCRUTINY [4] but the intermediate standard that the Court has previously used, for example, in cases of SEX DISCRIMINATION [4]. This standard requires that Congress have an "important" purpose for its legislation and that the racial classification be "substantially related" to achieving that purpose.

For the majority of the Court, the FCC's policies easily satisfied this test. The interest in diversifying broadcast programming accorded with the long-recognized policy of the Federal Communications Act to ensure the presentation of a wide variety of views. The Supreme Court had recognized this need in the context of the scarcity of electronic frequencies in RED LION BROADCASTING CO. V. F.C.C. (1969)[3], sustaining the FCC's "fairness doctrine." The FCC had quite reasonably determined that racial and ethnic diversity in broadcast ownership would promote diversity in programming, and Congress had repeatedly endorsed this view by rejecting proposals that would arguably reduce opportunities for minority ownership, such as a proposal to deregulate broadcasting. The Court, said Justice Brennan, must give great weight to the joint administrative-congressional determination of a connection between minority ownership and programming diversity. The minority ownership policies did not rest on impermissible stereotyping, but on the need to diversify programming. The FCC had considered other means of achieving this diversification and had reasonably concluded that these means were relatively ineffective. The burden imposed by these two policies on nonminority applicants for broadcast licenses was not impermissibly great.

Justice SANDRA DAY O'CONNOR wrote for the four dissenters. Arguing that any race-conscious program must pass the test of strict scrutiny, she rejected the claim that broadcasting diversity was a COMPELLING STATE INTEREST [1] or even an important one. Furthermore, the policies were not narrowly tailored; they assumed a connection between minority ownership and program content, and they ignored other race-neutral means of assuring programming to serve a diversity of audiences, such as direct regulation of programming.

The importance of *Metro Broadcasting* as a precedent remains to be seen. Justice Brennan's retirement from the Court may lead to a resurgence of the rhetoric of strict scrutiny, even for congressional programs of affirmative action. However, as Justice O'Connor noted in her concurrence in WYGANT V. JACKSON BOARD OF EDUCATION (1986) [I], the practical difference between compelling and important purposes, or between necessary and substantially related means, may be less than a surface reading of opinions suggests.

KENNETH L. KARST

(SEE ALSO: *Race-Consciousness* [I]; *Racial Preference* [I].)

Bibliography

EULE, JULIAN N. 1990 Promoting Speaker Diversity: Austin and Metro Broadcasting. *Supreme Court Review* 1990: 105–132.

MICHIGAN DEPARTMENT OF STATE POLICE v. SITZ
110 S.Ct. 2481 (1990)

Recent FOURTH AMENDMENT [2,I] cases reflect a pattern of rejection by the Supreme Court of claims based on the right against unreasonable SEARCH AND SEIZURE [4,I]. This case fits that pattern, yet the decision of the Court seems right.

Because of the slaughter on public highways caused by drunk drivers, the Michigan State Police instituted a program of sobriety checkpoints. All drivers passing through a checkpoint, usually after midnight, were stopped and examined briefly for signs of intoxication. Suspected drunk drivers were directed out of the flow of traffic for further investigation; all others were permitted to continue. The average stop took twenty-five seconds. A 6–3 Supreme Court held that although the stop was

a seizure in the sense of the Fourth Amendment, it was a reasonable one because the intrusion was slight and served a substantial public interest. The dissenters, led by Justice JOHN PAUL STEVENS [4,I], believed that the intrusion violated the Fourth Amendment. Much of Steven's opinion challenged the wisdom of the legislative policy authorizing the sobriety-checkpoint program. His challenge to its constitutionality was founded on the absurd proposition that "unannounced investigatory seizures are, particularly when they take place at night, the hallmarks of regimes far different from ours," and he referred to Nazi Germany. Moreover, Stevens weakened his argument based on the Fourth Amendment by offering the opinion that a permanent, nondiscretionary checkpoint program would not violate the amendment. He supposed that a state could condition the use of its roads on the uniform administration of a breathalyzer test to all drivers, thereby keeping drunks off the roads.

The intrusiveness of the means upheld by the Court's majority, led by Chief Justice WILLIAM H. REHNQUIST [3,I], was considerably less than that of the means favored by Stevens. In addition, the majority did not debate the wisdom of the policy before it. Its deference to the legislature seemed submissive, however, and its constitutional analysis stopped when it took notice of the twenty-five-second intrusion.

LEONARD W. LEVY

(SEE ALSO: *Unreasonable Search* [4,I].)

MILITARY AND THE CONSTITUTION

See: Armed Services and the Constitution [I]; Military Justice and the Constitution [3]

MILKOVICH v. LORAIN JOURNAL CO.
110 S.Ct. 2695 (1990)

This is a major free press case that has been widely misunderstood, especially by the news media. The *Los Angeles Times*, for example, called it a "huge setback" for freedom of the press. Under the heading, "Supreme Court Strips Away 'Opinion' as Libel Defense," the *Times* announced that the Court had unanimously demolished "a widely used media defense against libel suits, ruling that a writer or speaker may be sued for statements that express opinion." The *Times* censured the Court for having acted "with astonishing recklessness . . . when it overturned nearly two decades of precedent and ruled that the First Amendment does not automatically protect expressions of opinion from being found libelous." A dramatic increase in LIBEL [3] litigation was foreseen as a result of the Court's chilling just the sort of "serious speech the First Amendment was intended to protect." Every critic, editorialist, cartoonist, and commentator faced trial, the *Times* predicted.

In fact, the Court did not diminish the First Amendment's [2,I] protection of opinion and overruled no precedents, let alone two decades of them. It did hold, however, that opinion requires no new constitutional protection because the conventional safeguards of freedom of expression adequately protect opinion in libel cases. It held, too, that if an expression of opinion implied an assertion of objective fact on a matter of public concern, no liability for defamation would exist unless the party bringing suit proved that the publication was false and published with malice in the case of a public official or a PUBLIC FIGURE [3], or false and published with "some level of fault" in the case of a private individual involved in a matter of public concern.

In this case, the publication accused a private individual of perjuring himself in a judicial proceeding on a matter of public concern, but the accusation was couched in terms of opinion, for example, "anyone who attended the [wrestling] meet . . . knows in his heart that [Coach] Milkovich . . . lied at the hearing." Chief Justice WILLIAM H. REHNQUIST [3], for the Court, observed that the writer should not escape liability merely because he used words such as "I think," because he might do as much damage to an individual's reputation as he would by saying flatly that he had lied.

The publishing company sought a special rule distinguishing "fact" from "opinion" and exempting opinion from the law of libel. This is what the Court refused to do because some opinions connoted facts for which their authors ought to be responsible. The Court made clear, however, that "a statement of opinion relating to a matter of public concern which does not contain a provably false factual connotation will receive full constitutional protection."

Justices WILLIAM J. BRENNAN [1,I] and THURGOOD MARSHALL [3,I] dissented, but only on the question as to whether the publisher in this case should be held accountable for libel. Significantly, Brennan, who was the Court's foremost exponent of FREEDOM OF THE PRESS [2,I] in libel cases, declared that Rehnquist addressed the issue of First Amendment protection of opinion "cogently and almost entirely correctly. I agree with the Court that . . . only defamatory statements that are capable of being proved false are subject to liability under state libel law." Thus, the Court did not diminish constitutional protections of opinion and held, properly, that existing First Amendment doctrines adequately served to insulate from libel prosecutions the expression of sheer opinion in matters of public interest.

LEONARD W. LEVY

MIRANDA RULES
(Update)

MIRANDA V. ARIZONA (1966) [3] held that a statement obtained from a criminal defendant through custodial interrogation is inadmissible against that defendant unless the police obtained a waiver of the RIGHT AGAINST SELF-INCRIMINATION [3,I] after warning the suspect of both the right to remain silent and the RIGHT TO COUNSEL [3]. Recently, the Supreme Court has issued decisions favorable to the government concerning several *Miranda* issues: the definition of custodial interrogation, in *Arizona v. Mauro* (1989); the adequacy of warnings provided to persons in custody, in *Duckworth v. Eagan* (1989); and the standard that governs the validity of waiver, in *Colorado v. Spring* (1987) and *Colorado v. Connelly* (1986). Although in *Arizona v. Robertson* (1988) the Court reaffirmed the proscription of questioning until counsel appears, once the suspect requests counsel, the police need not advise the suspect of a lawyer's efforts to consult with him or her, as the Court held in *Moran v. Burbine* (1986).

The most significant of these developments is the holding in *Connelly* and *Spring* that a *Miranda* waiver is valid so long as the police did not obtain the waiver through conduct that would render a confession "involuntary" as a matter of PROCEDURAL DUE PROCESS [3,I]. The *Miranda* opinion stated that "a heavy burden rests on the Government to demonstrate that the defendant knowingly and intelligently waived his privilege against self-incrimination and his right to . . . counsel." Connelly, a lunatic, confessed at the behest of "the voice of God." Spring waived *Miranda* rights after government agents led him to believe that the questioning would concern an illegal firearms transaction, but the interrogation eventually included questions about a homicide. Spring's waiver was not knowing, and Connelly's was not intelligent. The Court nonetheless approved admission of both CONFESSIONS [I], stating in *Connelly* that "there is obviously no reason to require more in the way of a 'voluntariness' inquiry in the *Miranda* waiver context than in the FOURTEENTH AMENDMENT [2,I] confession context."

The Justices would not likely approve waiver of the right to counsel *at trial* by a person in Connelly's condition or by a person like Spring, who misunderstood the seriousness of the charge. Yet in *Patterson v. Illinois* (1988), the Court held that in the interrogation context the claimed waiver of the Sixth Amendment right to counsel, a right initiated by a formal charge with the prospect of a trial, is tested under the *Connelly* standard. Ironically, the standard governing the waiver of rights is strictest in the courtroom, where coercion and deception are least likely, and most lenient in the stationhouse or the police cruiser, where these dangers are greatest.

Not many police departments are likely to depart from the verbal formulation of the warnings given by the *Miranda* opinion, and in few cases does a lawyer attempt to advise an arrested person who did not invoke the *Miranda* right to counsel. Commonly, however, the government claims that the accused waived his or her *Miranda* rights. The ability of police interrogators to induce suspects to waive their rights explains the consistent empirical finding that the *Miranda* doctrine has had a negligible effect on police effectiveness. Because *Miranda* was inspired by dissatisfaction with the vacuous and unpredictable due process approach, stating the test for waiver in the same terms as the voluntariness test comes close to full circle from the law that preceded *Miranda*.

But the Court's retrenchment of the *Miranda* doctrine is not the whole story. In one sense, the most important development in confessions law is *Miranda*'s continued survival, emphasized by cases such as *Roberson*, in which the Court approved the exclusion of valuable evidence obtained without police brutality. At least since HARRIS v. NEW YORK (1971) [2], a majority of the Justices have believed that *Miranda* was wrongly decided. A majority continues to describe the *Miranda* rules as prophylactic safeguards rather than constitutional entitlements, a distinction that is not compatible with *Miranda*'s presumption that statements obtained without a valid waiver are compelled within the meaning of the Fifth Amendment. Despite the erosion of their Fifth Amendment foundation, the Court refuses to abandon the *Miranda* rules.

The failure of recent efforts to have *Miranda* overruled confirms that STARE DECISIS [4], even without more, will sustain the decision. During the presidency of RONALD REAGAN [3,I], the Justice Department's Office of Legal Policy issued a lengthy report calling for *Miranda*'s demise. The report effectively pointed out the inconsistency of *Harris* and its progeny with *Miranda* itself; but on several points, including the key issue of law enforcement effectiveness, the report made an embarassingly weak case for obliterating a landmark. Not only did the Court as a whole reject the department's effort; the report was not approved by a single Justice in any concurring or dissenting opinion.

So *Miranda* lives, a symbol of commitment to civil liberty that conveniently does little to obstruct the suppression of crime. But at the borders of the *Miranda* rules, a skeptical Supreme Court majority has taken frequent opportunities to limit their scope. The most likely future development along these lines is approval of the suggestion advanced by two Justices, concurring in *Duckworth v. Eagan*, to the effect that claims by state prisoners that their convictions violated *Miranda* should not be cognizable in federal HABEAS CORPUS [2,I] proceedings.

DONALD A. DRIPPS

(SEE ALSO: *Police Interrogation and Confessions* [3,I]; *Procedural Due Process of Law, Criminal* [3,I].)

Bibliography

KAMISAR, YALE; LAFAVE, WAYNE; and ISRAEL, JEROLD 1989   *Modern Criminal Procedure*, 6th ed. St. Paul, Minn.: West Publishing Co.

UNITED STATES DEPARTMENT OF JUSTICE, OFFICE OF LEGAL POLICY 1986   *Report to the Attorney General on the Law of Pre-trial Interrogation*. Washington, D.C.: U.S. Government Printing Office.

MISSOURI v. JENKINS
110 S.Ct. 1651 (1990)

Jenkins produced a unanimous result but with two sharply differing opinions on an important question concerning the power of federal courts to remedy school DESEGREGATION [2]. A federal district court, after ordering the desegregation of the Kansas City school district, ordered the state of Missouri and the district to share the costs of the remedy, which included substantial capital improvements to make the integrated schools more attractive and thus to reduce "white flight." The district had exhausted its capacity to tax as defined by state law, and so the court ordered the district's property-tax levy increased through the next several fiscal years. The court of appeals affirmed the tax increase order, but the Supreme Court unanimously reversed. The majority, in an opinion by Justice BYRON R. WHITE [4,I], held that the district court had abused its discretion in imposing the tax itself when an alternative to such an intrusive order was available. That alternative, said Justice White, would be for the district court to order the school district to levy property taxes at a rate adequate to fund the desegregation remedy.

Justice ANTHONY M. KENNEDY [I], joined by three other Justices, concurred in the result but disagreed strongly with the majority's conclusion that the district court had power to order the district to levy such a tax. That order, he said, would exceed the JUDICIAL POWER OF THE UNITED STATES [3] established in Article III of the Constitution. Taxation would be a legislative function, and the hiring and supervision of a staff to administer the funds so levied would be a political function. Justice Kennedy distinguished GRIFFIN V. COUNTY SCHOOL BOARD OF PRINCE EDWARD COUNTY (1964) [2], in which the Court had upheld the power of a district court to order a school district to levy taxes to reopen schools that had been closed in evasion of a desegregation order. *Griffin*, he said, involved an order to exercise an existing power to tax; in *Jenkins*, the school district would have to exceed its powers under state law. He suggested that the district court might have accomplished the desegregation of Kansas City's schools—although not with the particular remedies chosen—by means that did not require funding beyond the district's current means. Desegregating schools was an important objective, he said, but the limits on judicial power must be strictly observed.

KENNETH L. KARST

(SEE ALSO: *Judicial Power and Legislative Remedies* [I].)

MISTRETTA v. UNITED STATES
488 U.S. 361 (1989)

In *Mistretta* the Supreme Court, 8–1, upheld the Sentencing Reform Act of 1984 against the constitutional challenges that it was an unconstitutional DELEGATION OF POWER [2,I] and that it violated the principle of SEPARATION OF POWERS [4] by intruding the federal judiciary into functions that are legislative.

Congress has the power to fix the sentence for a federal crime. Historically Congress has, in practical effect, delegated a considerable part of this power to the judicial branch through the mechanism of setting a range of possible sentences for the same offense—for example, one to five years of imprisonment. This scheme gives the judge authority to select the sentence appropriate in a particular case—typically including the possibility of probation—in light of the circumstances of the offense, the defendant's history and sense of responsibility, and the like. The possibility of a presidential pardon remained. In recent years, too, Congress allowed the judge to sentence the defendant to an indeterminate term, leaving the actual release date to the U.S. Parole Commission, an agency located in the executive branch. The system not only divided power among the three branches of the federal government, but also produced wide-ranging variation in the severity of sentences.

These disparities persisted despite the best efforts of sentencing institutes, judicial councils, and the Parole Commission. Concern for sentencing inequities, combined with a desire to express a tough attitude toward crime, led Congress to adopt the 1984 act. This act authorized the creation of the United States Sentencing Commission, "an independent commission in the judicial branch" composed of seven members appointed by the President with the ADVICE AND CONSENT [1,I] of the Senate. Three of the members must be federal judges chosen by the President from a list of six submitted by the JUDICIAL CONFERENCE OF THE UNITED STATES [I]. The commission was authorized to prepare guidelines for essentially determinate SENTENCING [I], specifying sentences for various types of crimes and categories of defendants. A judge must adhere to the guidelines except when a case presents aggravating or mitigating circumstances of a kind not specified in the guidelines. The commission is to review and revise the guidelines periodically.

John Mistretta, sentenced on the basis of the guidelines by a federal district court for the sale of cocaine, appealed to the UNITED STATES COURT OF APPEALS [4] and petitioned the Supreme Court for CERTIORARI [1] before judgment in the court of appeals. The Supreme Court granted the petition and affirmed the sentence. Justice HARRY A. BLACKMUN [1,I], writing for the Court, quickly rejected *Mistretta*'s delegation of power challenge. Congress can constitutionally delegate its legislative power to an agency if it specifies clear standards for the agency to follow in carrying out its rule-making power. Congress gave the Sentencing Commission a clear set of specific goals, including lists of the factors to be considered in establishing grades of offense and categories of defendants. These lists leave considerable discretion to the commission, but the statute's standards are sufficiently clear to allow a reviewing court to determine whether the commission had followed the will of Congress.

Justice Blackmun wrote at greater length in rejecting the broader separation of powers challenge that the Sentencing Commission was a judicial body exercising legislative powers. The commission's work undoubtedly involved political judgment, but the practical consequences of locating the commission within the judicial branch did not threaten to undermine either the integrity of the judiciary or the power of Congress. On the question of locating the commission within the judicial branch, Justice Blackmun emphasized that the commission is not a court and does not exercise judicial power; that Congress can override the commission's determinations at any time; and that the questions assigned to the commission had long been exercised by the judiciary in the aggregate, deciding case by case.

Justice Blackmun found "somewhat troublesome" the participation in the commission of judges appointed under Article III of the Constitution. Nonetheless, he concluded that the Constitution does not prohibit Article III judges from taking on extrajudicial functions in their individual capacities, that Congress and the President had historically acquiesced in federal judges' assumption of such duties, and that the Court's own precedents supported the constitutionality of the practice. Some kinds of extrajudicial service might have adverse effects on the public's sense of the judiciary's independence, but the commission's work was "essentially neutral" in the political sense and designed primarily to govern tasks done entirely within the judicial branch. Although the President could remove commission members for neglect of duty or malfeasance, this power did not extend to the dismissal of federal judges as judges. Justice Blackmun made clear that there were limits to such extrajudicial service by judges of CONSTITUTIONAL COURTS [1], but he could find no constitutionally significant practical effect on the work of the judicial branch from these judges' service on this commission. The emphasis on "practical" and "functional" considerations is the central theme throughout Justice Blackmun's opinion.

Justice ANTONIN SCALIA [I] dissented, arguing that Congress could not constitutionally delegate its legislative power to an agency whose sole power was to make laws, even laws going under the name of "guidelines." This opinion represents the strongest effort in the modern era to revive the delegation doctrine as a serious limit on congressional authority to enlist other agencies in lawmaking. Justice Scalia lamented the Court's tendency to tolerate blurring of the lines separating the powers of the three branches of the federal government. Scolding the majority in a manner now familiar, he offered a restatement of today's operative rule: "the functions of the Branches should not be commingled too much—how much is too much to be determined, case-by-case, by this Court." If we disregard the tone, this restatement seems exactly on the mark. Even so, it is not clear how the national government can be run on a formalistic model of separation of powers that already seemed too confining in 1794 when JOHN JAY [3], while he was Chief Justice of the United States, went to London to negotiate the agreement we now call JAY'S TREATY [3.]

KENNETH L. KARST

MORRISON v. OLSON
[1988]

See: Constitutional History, 1980–1989 [I]; Independent Counsel [I]; Special Prosecutor [I]

NATIONAL TREASURY EMPLOYEES UNION v. VON RAAB
489 U.S. 656

In this companion case to SKINNER V. RAILWAY LABOR EXECUTIVES ASSOCIATION [I], the Supreme Court upheld 5–4, the constitutionality of federal regulations requiring urine testing of all Customs employees involved in drug interdiction, carrying weapons, or handling classified materials. Justices ANTONIN SCALIA [I] and JOHN PAUL STEVENS [4,I], who had supported the majority in *Skinner*, joined the *Skinner* dissenters in this case.

Scalia believed that considerations of public safety and the relation between drugs and accidents had justified the departure from individualized suspicion in *Skinner*. These considerations did not prevail in this case. No EVIDENCE [2] existed to show that Customs employees used drugs, let alone that such use jeopardized the public. Accordingly, the public safety could not be furthered by the urinalysis required of these employees. The search itself, Scalia believed, was "particularly destructive of privacy and offensive to personal dignity." The Court majority, however, remained convinced that the government had a compelling interest in ensuring the physical fitness of the employees required to submit to urine testing.

LEONARD W. LEVY

NAZIS

See: Extremist Speech and the First Amendment [I]

NEW CHRISTIAN RIGHT

See: Religious Fundamentalism [I]

NEW DEAL

During the New Deal years, from 1933 to the end of WORLD WAR II [I], the nation experienced an era of protracted economic crisis and social dislocation, a dramatic change in national political alignments, and then mobilization for total war. A society contending with changes and emergencies of this order, especially with an enormously popular reformist President in office, cannot easily avoid profound challenges to its constitutional order; and so it was for America in this era. Every major aspect of political controversy in this period found expression of varying kinds in constitutional discourse and conflict, and these constitutional battles both reflected and actively intensified the bitter ideological polarization that bedeviled the nation's politics.

When the New Deal era came to a close just after the war, the constitutional as well as political landscape of the country had been transformed. With respect both to governmental institutions and policies and to formal constitutional doctrine, things as they had stood in 1933 had been largely swept away. The transformations of governance and politics in the New Deal era brought far-reaching reform of constitutional law, accomplished without benefit of formal constitutional amendment on any question except the repeal of PROHIBITION [3]. The new constitutional order that emerged, moreover, would stand firmly for half a century as the basic framework of the modern welfare, regulatory, and national-security state. In most particulars, the new order proved durable enough to survive determined efforts by neoconservatives in the 1980s to overturn some of the most important New Deal doctrines and reforms.

President FRANKLIN D. ROOSEVELT [3] at the outset of his presidency characteristically struck a pose that seemed to dismiss offhandedly the need for worries about constitutional difficulties. "Our Constitution is so simple and practical," he declared in his first inaugural address in 1933, "that it is possible always to meet extraordinary needs by changes in emphasis and arrangement without loss of essential form." But what changes in "emphasis" and "arrangement" he had in mind! Even the legislative programs and executive actions of the "First Hundred Days" posed a broad challenge to prevailing doctrines in constitutional law, especially regarding the protection of vested economic rights against government's hand and the proper limits of the national government's authority in the federal system. Nor did the challenge recede or soften significantly in the years immediately following, as Roosevelt and his party generated a prolix legislative and administrative record that would repeatedly inspire bitter constitutional controversies.

Virtually every element of the New Deal administration's policies, especially their ideological nuances and implications, bore the imprint of Roosevelt's own thinking. The direction and extraordinary scope of the New Deal's challenge to the traditional role and prerogatives of the states, for example, were signaled early by Roosevelt when he was governor of New York: "In our business life and in our social contracts," he declared in 1929, "we are little controlled by the methods and practices employed by our forefathers." Why, then, he asked, be "content . . . to accept and continue to use the local machinery of government which was first devised generations or even centuries ago?" This kind of iconoclasm and willingness to experiment with governmental structures was soon to be directed against the states. Impatience with antiquated institutional legacies was linked with Roosevelt's robust "Old Progressive" faith in bringing expertise to bear on social and economic problems. Hence, the President readily endorsed the regional approach (exemplified by the TENNESSEE VALLEY AUTHORITY ACT OF 1933 [4]) to problems that transcended state lines. Similarly, he was sympathetic to a national planning approach (as was espoused by his National Resources Planning Board and the agricultural price-support and production-control efforts); and he also fostered the system of direct federal grant-in-aid support to city governments for public housing, airports, and other projects in ways that dramatically enhanced municipal autonomy within the states.

Perhaps of greatest long-run importance to governmental practice was Roosevelt's own proclivity to devolve on appointive agencies and their expert staffs the responsibility for defining the "public interest" in the course of setting regulatory policies—a preference shared by the New Deal majorities in Congress as they crafted the design of new regulatory agencies. Roosevelt regularly pressed on Congress and the public the urgency of the social and economic programs he was proposing—both the programs of the "Hundred Days," designed to break the terrible spiral of despair, and those of the ensuing years, designed to effect enduring reforms, including a systematic (and, to many, a radical) redistribution of income and wealth. The argument for urgent action, for room to experiment, and for administration with maximal flexibility and discretion was cast from the start in terms of the necessities associated with a "national emergency." As New Deal programs expanded, however, this view was translated into the more general argument for wide-ranging agency discretion and a reliance on experts for policy making. In the context of the war emergency after 1938, this tendency became even more pervasive.

The question remained: what constitutional principles, if any, restrained such claims by the chief executive? The New Deal answer in light of the Depression crisis tended increasingly to be couched as a majoritarian rationale: "Does anybody believe," asked Senator Lewis Schwellenbach of Washington, one of Roosevelt's closest allies in Congress, "that the founding fathers intended to set up a form of government which would prevent that government from solving the current problems of the people?" Roosevelt phrased the issue similarly in his first radio speech of his second term, the address in which he fired the first shot in the COURT-PACKING [I] battle. It was the entire "modern movement for social and economic progress through legislation" that was at stake, the President declared, referring dramatically to "one-third of a nation ill-nourished, ill-clad, ill-housed." He rejected as outrageous the notion that the judiciary might deny Congress the authority "to protect us against catastrophe by meeting squarely our modern social and economic conditions."

In private correspondence with Schwellenbach, the President referred to their common view of the constitutional issues as the cause of "liberal democracy." New Deal victories by "overwhelming" popular majorities in 1932 and 1936, the President repeatedly contended in his public messages on the constitutional question, had provided an "overwhelming mandate" for immediate action to put the programs of "liberal democracy" in place.

Roosevelt and the constitutional imperatives embodied in his programs for this "liberal democracy" successfully prevailed beginning in 1937, as a new majority in support of the New Deal emerged virtually overnight on the HUGHES COURT [2] and later became a dependable reliance for Roosevelt as he made new appointments. Similarly, the President would prevail in virtually all particulars when he assumed vastly expanded executive emergency authority in the military and foreign-policy realms during the prewar neutrality period and the years of combat in a global arena that followed the Pearl Harbor disaster.

The President thus placed his personal stamp on the most dramatic political initiatives of the era; however, there were also more enduring legacies of the New Deal in the nation's constitutional development. An inventory of this heritage from the 1930s and World War II must embrace not only the dramatic changes that were ardently debated in their own day, but also the various effects of conflict and innovation only dimly discerned by either friends or critics of Roosevelt's social and economic programs and the wartime initiatives.

Prominent in the inventory of change was the movement of national authority and active intervention into many vital areas of social and economic life that before 1933 had been left by Congress largely to the states and had been only marginally affected by national law. A vast array of legislation from 1933 to 1937 bespoke this dramatic occupation by Congress of policy areas that traditionally had been extremely decentralized in practice; some of them, moreover, had been specifically designated by the Supreme Court's conservative majority as being within the exclusive purview of the states as a matter of TENTH AMENDMENT [4] guarantees, or as a matter of judicially defined categories that differentiated "national" from "local" activities under terms of the COMMERCE CLAUSE [1] or in light of the doctrine of a limited number of enumerated powers.

Thus, by 1941 the working constitutional system had become a system in which formal constitutional issues of FEDERALISM had been recast completely in light of new realities generated by New Deal innovations. A definitive redistribution of both policy responsibilities and power had occurred. There was comprehensive restructuring of agriculture as a managed sector, a formal preemption of labor law through the Wagner Act and its guarantees of the right to organize, adoption of minimal federal standards for wages and hours, and the establishment of a vast regional energy and economic development program through the Tennessee Valley Authority. Federal regulatory authority was extended over the securities markets, and there was a dramatic expansion of national regulation in the transportation, antitrust, and banking fields. The New Deal also instituted the first massive ENTITLEMENT programs with the passage of the SOCIAL SECURITY ACT [4] in 1935; this measure became the foundation stone of the modern national WELFARE STATE [1].

One concomitant of this powerful move toward centralization of governmental responsibilities was a transformation in the distribution of funds and expenditures. In 1929, with expenditures of $2.6 billion, the budget of the national government was only one-third the amount of state and local expenditures; but a decade later, federal expenditures were $9 billion, exceeding the combined amounts spent by state and local government. Linked with this aspect of new "giant government"—emergence of the national government as a modern Leviathan—was the New Deal's explicit adoption in 1938 of Keynesian principles for fiscal policy. Although growth of the national government establishment was not in itself a development that implicated constitutional questions directly, as a reality of governance and power, "big government" transformed the entire context of the debate over constitutional principles.

More explicitly cast in constitutional terms was the matter of federal grants in aid to state and local government, which rose from $193 million in 1933 to a floodtide level of $2.9 billion in 1939. Although welfare and relief comprised some eighty percent of these sums in each year, the vast aggregate amount in 1939 embraced a range of new programs for natural-resources management, public housing, and health services as well as the more traditional highway aid and agricultural research funds. In this arena of initiative, the Supreme Court posed no serious obstacles; in the 1923 case of FROTHINGHAM V. MELLON [2], it already had upheld the practice of attaching conditions to federal grants. Decisions in the late 1930s reaffirmed this view. Taken as a whole, the grant-in-aid programs became an important element of what has been termed the modern system of COOPERATIVE FEDERALISM [2], displacing the older principles and practices of DUAL FEDERALISM [2].

In its devastating response to the early New Deal measures for industrial reorganization and agricultural market controls, the Supreme Court in SCHECHTER POULTRY CORPORATION V. UNITED STATES (1935) [4] did strike down key legislation in part because of what it found to be a promiscuous violation of the principles of SEPARATION OF POWERS [4]. After the new liberal majority had established the credo of Roosevelt's "liberal democracy" in a dominant position in the Court's decisions after 1936, however, the delegation of rule-making authority to the new administrative and regulatory agencies won virtually routine approval with the Justices. Indeed, judicial deference to agency discretion became one of the most durable—and also most problematic—features of the longer-term New Deal legacy in American law.

For the most part, it was regulation of economic interests that was at stake when challenges were raised against administrative prerogatives; and as the Court abandoned its commitment to defend economic or entrepreneurial liberty on the same basis as it would the political elements of liberty (see PREFERRED FREEDOMS [3]), such challenges lost their doctrinal authoritativeness. Not until the 1960s did political leaders and legal scholars entirely sympathetic with the goals of New Deal–style benefit programs and regulatory regimes begin to worry much about excessive paternalism and discretion. They became concerned particularly with the degree to which the New Deal legacy had produced a system of social benefits, franchises, subsidies, and services that were dispensed by elaborate bureaucracies. In this system, some groups and individuals were favored, while others might be held virtually in thrall because of Byzantine or Kafkaesque procedural standards or simply because of high-handedness and capriciousness. Only then, thirty years after the system had begun to emerge from New Deal legislation and twenty years after the Administrative Procedure Act became law, were the Constitution's procedural guarantees reappraised with a view toward real equality of treatment and fairness in the agencies' administration of social programs and regulations.

When war broke out in Asia and Europe, the Roosevelt administration's policies carried the "emergency" doctrine and delegation of powers to an entirely new level. In September 1939, the President declared a "limited emergency" by EXECUTIVE ORDER [2], thereby assuming the authority to expand the military forces and to take other measures under war statutes. After the Pearl Harbor attack, the two WAR POWERS ACTS [4] (December 1941 and March 1942) gave the President unprecedented delegated powers under which he erected a massive bureaucracy with coercive powers to direct mobilization. The March 1941 Lend-Lease Act also delegated the spending power, providing the legal basis for over $50 billion in grants of supplies and credits to the Allies.

In one of the most extraordinary documents in the entire history of American constitutional law, Roosevelt in September 1942 threatened that if Congress failed to meet his wishes with respect to repealing a section of the price-control laws in light of the war emergency, he would assume the power to nullify the law on his own authority. Congressional deference averted a constitutional confrontation on the issue.

The war period was of special importance with respect to civil liberties. In one of the most grievous violations of any groups' rights in the modern era, the Roosevelt administration authorized by EXECUTIVE ORDER 9066 [2] (later validated by Congress) the removal in 1942 of the entire Japanese-ancestry population from the West Coast and their prolonged internment in concentration camps until nearly the end of the war. Meanwhile, the army took advantage of a declaration of martial law in Hawaii by the territorial governor in the hours after Pearl Harbor, maintaining a comprehensive military regime with suspension of civilian justice in criminal matters until late 1944, long after any credible threat of invasion of the Hawaiian Islands had passed. In the notorious JAPANESE AMERICAN CASES (1943–1944) [3], the Supreme Court upheld the removal and internment decisions; but when the Hawaiian policy was finally challenged (DUNCAN V. KAHANAMOKU [1946] [2]), the Court ruled that the army had acted illegally in suspending civilian government and justice beyond the time justified by military necessity.

Although the wartime record on CIVIL LIBERTIES [1,I] was thus marred by excesses of the military authorities—and although the army in each instance had full support of the White House—the more enduring heritage of the New Deal in race relations and constitutional equal protection has a different face. Although failing to support federal antilynching bills or any positive CIVIL RIGHTS [1,I] legislation that would have attacked SEGREGATION [4], Roosevelt and the agency administrators generally pressed hard to see that blacks received an equitable share of the benefits of federal welfare and relief programs. The President supported the Justice Department's creation in 1939 of what became the Civil Rights Division; and within a few years, this unit's lawyers had undertaken a variety of prosecutions—the most significant being the case of UNITED STATES V. CLASSIC (1941) [1]—challenging RACIAL DISCRIMINATION [3,I] in the electoral process in the southern states. The Justice Department's new concern for equal rights and civil liberties also served to enhance the significance of Supreme Court decisions (including especially HAGUE V. C.I.O. [2] in 1939) (that were then strengthening FIRST AMENDMENT [2,I] guarantees and laying the essential doctrinal groundwork for the much farther-reaching civil liberties and civil rights jurisprudence of the WARREN COURT [4] era. In sum, racial equality and civil liberties had been brought within the ambit of the New Deal agenda—the essential counterweight to unrestrained majoritarianism that many feared was embodied in Roosevelt's attack on the Court in 1936 and even, albeit in a more reflective mode, in the constitutional theories calling for "judicial self-restraint" championed in the wake of the Court fight (see JUDICIAL REVIEW AND DEMOCRACY [3]).

The American constitutional order in 1945, at President Roosevelt's death, had thus witnessed far-reaching changes in the allocation of state versus federal powers, in the extent and style of intervention by government in social and economic affairs, and in the role of the national authorities in regard to individual rights and liberties. In the realm of doctrine, the Supreme Court had reinterpreted the commerce clause so completely that the Justices would soon declare it to be simply "as broad as the economic needs of the nation" (*American Power & Light v. SEC* [1947]). After the decision of WICKARD V. FILBURN (1942) [4], the economic regulatory powers of the Congress seemed to be plenary, with no economic activity protected from congressional determination of what was of national significance. As early as 1934, in NEBBIA V. NEW YORK [3], the Court had discarded traditional economic due process and AFFECTED WITH A PUBLIC INTEREST [1] doctrine—two of the main props of traditional VESTED RIGHTS [4] analysis that had been used to restrain severely the state's regulatory powers. In UNITED STATES V. DARBY LUMBER COMPANY (1941) [2] the Court cast into the dustbin of history, it seemed, the old view of the Tenth Amendment, declaring now that the amendment "states but a truism" and was merely "declaratory." Meanwhile, the New Deal administration posed a new challenge to state sovereignty over valuable natural resources by asserting a federal property claim based on "paramount rights" over the offshore oil and any other resources of the continental shelf, long considered to be under state ownership out to a distance of three miles. With the emergence of the new civil rights and civil liberties jurisprudence exemplified by *Classic*, the university-segregation decision of MISSOURI EX REL. GAINES V. CANADA (1938) [3], and other decisions, the potentialities of the emerging changes in law became clear. Whether one interprets these changes, as friends of the Roosevelt Administration sought to do, as a "return to the Constitution" (a reversal of conservative doctrines that had become dominant in violation of correct principles), or instead, as a positive advancement of law to meet the urgent requirements of a modern industrial society in crisis, the New Deal era did indeed bequeath to postwar America a constitutional order dramatically transformed.

HARRY N. SCHEIBER

Bibliography

BIXBY, DAVID M. 1981 The Roosevelt Court, Democratic Ideology, and Minority Rights: Another Look at United States v. Classic. *Yale Law Journal* 90:741–814.

HURST, JAMES WILLARD 1977 *Law and the Social Order in the United States.* Ithaca, N.Y.: Cornell University Press.

MURPHY, PAUL L. 1972 *The Constitution in Crisis Times, 1919-1969.* New York: Harper & Row.

PARRISH, MICHAEL E. The Great Depression, the New Deal, and the American Legal Order. *Washington Law Review* 59:723–750.

SCHEIBER, HARRY N. 1989 Economic Liberty and the Constitution. In *Essays in the History of Liberty.* San Marino, Calif.: The Huntington Library.

——— AND SCHEIBER, JANE L. 1990 Constitutional Liberty in World War II: Army Rule and Martial Law in Hawaii. *Western Legal History* 3:341–378.

NEW RIGHT

As a political phenomenon New Right jurisprudence is a reaction against the broad protection of individual rights advanced by the WARREN COURT [4]. Intellectually the New Right proposes a style of CONSTITUTIONAL INTERPRETATION [1] that emphasizes fidelity to received historical materials and legal forms in order to foreclose judicial reliance on moral philosophy. Among the most prominent proponents of New Right jurisprudence are former Attorney General Edwin Meese, Chief Justice WILLIAM H. REHNQUIST [3,I], and scholar-jurist Robert H. Bork.

The great aim in fashioning an approach to constitutional interpretation must, for the New Right, be to find public, politically neutral standards that curb judicial willfulness. "The framers' intentions with respect to freedoms," as Bork put it, "are the sole legitimate premise from which constitutional analysis may proceed." The great temptation for judges armed with the power to review legislative acts (and for losers in the political process who retain the capacity to influence judges) is to strike down laws that they do not like on the grounds furnished by some broad, vague, and easily manipulated constitutional phrase. The only antidote for judicial tyranny is history—the authority of the original, public sense of what a particular phrase or clause was meant to accomplish.

This reliance on ORIGINAL INTENT [I], however, cannot be a mechanical process. Principles must be discerned and applied to particular circumstances and problems (such as WIRETAPPING [4]) that the Framers could not have foreseen. Most originalists seek to discern and apply the primary purpose of a clause rather than the Framers' specific intentions. And so even a practice specifically accepted by the Framers of the EQUAL PROTECTION [2,I] clause of the FOURTEENTH AMENDMENT [2,I], such as segregated schooling, might be unconstitutional.

The second element in New Right jurisprudence is an emphasis on democracy or majority rule as the touchstone of constitutional authority. Against the background of POPULAR SOVEREIGNTY [3], the power of unelected judges to strike down laws made by the people's representatives appears anomalous and in need of close containment. The emphasis on popular rule also supports the resort to historical intentions: When judges rely on the Framers' intentions, they can claim simply to be upholding a superior expression of popular will (the Constitution as originally understood) to an inferior one (the will of this legislature).

The New Right's third basic commitment is its four-square opposition to the role of moral theory in constitutional interpretation. Whatever one might think of natural law or moral objectivity, in political practice moral arguments must always be regarded as nothing more than expressions of personal preferences and desires. Thus, according to Bork, "every clash between a minority claiming freedom from regulation and a majority asserting its freedom to regulate requires a choice between the gratifications (or moral positions) of the two groups." The New Right believes that to allow moral judgment any substantial role in constitutional interpretation licenses judges to overturn duly made laws on personal, ideological grounds.

The fourth and final plank in the New Right program is the identification of the extension of individual rights with an assault on community in the name of moral relativism. Both Bork and Meese approvingly quote the conservative British jurist Lord Patrick Devlin: "What makes a society is a community of ideas, not political ideas alone but also ideas about the way its members should behave and govern lives." More judicially mandated individual freedom, it seems, equals more relativism and less community.

Each of the components of New Right jurisprudence has been subjected to criticism. Original intentions, it has been said, are often extremely difficult to discern. What is to count as evidence? How do we distinguish intentions from hopes and aspirations? Did the Framers intend us to be guided by their intentions? Perhaps most tellingly, what do we make of the broad moralistic language that was often chosen and written into the Constitution? Bork wants to regard the NINTH AMENDMENT [3] and the Fourteenth Amendment's PRIVILEGES AND IMMUNITIES [3] clause as unintelligible "ink blots" on the document because to treat them as the broad delegations that they appear to be would give too much power to judges. The New Right's sense of how much JUDICIAL POWER [3] is too much seems, in spite of professions of political neutrality, rooted less in a careful reading of history than in a reaction against the JUDICIAL ACTIVISM [3] spawned by the Warren Court.

The New Right's emphasis on the Constitution's basically democratic character misses, some have charged, the equally basic role of individual liberty in the founding design. A basic commitment to broad individual rights helps legitimate the powers of a Court remote from popular passions and prejudices. The practical moral skepticism of the New Right is also subjected to debate: Do we not have widely shared working standards of morality? Does not the New Right itself implicitly invoke and depend upon a democratic political morality and an ethic of judicial self-restraint?

The New Right's claim that individual rights will replace community morality with relativism seems highly dubious, not to mention odd, in light of the New Right's own professed skepticism. In becoming more tolerant, open, and respectful of individual freedom a community would seem to be changing, perhaps even improving, its morality rather than dropping it. With its capacity to insist that majorities treat minorities reasonably, the Supreme Court appears well situated to improve community morality.

New Right jurisprudence appeals to political skeptics who identify judicial activism, new and old, with elite tyranny. The sharpest opponents of the New Right are those who believe that the Constitution itself raises moral questions for interpreters and that an active, morally reflective Court advances the causes of individual liberty and reasonable self-government.

STEPHEN MACEDO

(SEE ALSO: *Bork Nomination* [I]; *Conservatism* [I]; *Constitution and Civic Ideals* [I]; *Critical Legal Studies* [I]; *Deconstructionism* [I]; *Liberalism* [I]; *Originalism* [I]; *Political Philosophy of the Constitution* [3,I]; *Segregation* [4].)

Bibliography

BERGER, RAOUL   1977   *Government by Judiciary.* Cambridge, Mass.: Harvard University Press.

BORK, ROBERT H.   1990   *The Tempting of America: The Political Seduction of the Law.* New York: Free Press.

MACEDO, STEPHEN   1987   *The New Right v. the Constitution.* Washington, D.C.: Cato Institute.

REHNQUIST, WILLIAM H.   1976   The Notion of a Living Constitution. *Texas Law Review* 54:693–704.

NEW YORK STATE CLUB ASSOCIATION v. NEW YORK CITY (1988)

See: Freedom of Association [I]

NIMMER, MELVILLE B.
(1923–1985)

After his graduation from Harvard Law School Melville Nimmer practiced law in Los Angeles for more than a decade. During that time he wrote the foundational article elaborating the "right of publicity," a right to control the commercial use of one's own identity. He also produced *Nimmer on Copyright* (1st ed., 1963), a four-volume treatise rightly called "magisterial," which soon became the nation's leading authority on copyright law. In 1962 he joined the law faculty of the University of California, Los Angeles, where he was a much-loved teacher of copyright law (later expanded into entertainment law), contracts, and constitutional law.

Although Nimmer's constitutional law scholarship ranged over such diverse topics as American CIVIL RIGHTS [1,I] legislation and judicial review in Israel, the main focus of his attention was the FIRST AMENDMENT [2]. He practiced what he preached, serving the AMERICAN CIVIL LIBERTIES UNION [1] as counsel in a number of cases, including COHEN V. CALIFORNIA (1971) [1]. In *Cohen* the Supreme Court adopted Nimmer's argument severely restricting the assumption, casually made in CHAPLINSKY V. NEW HAMPSHIRE (1942) [1], that profanity lay outside the First Amendment's protection. The case produced one of Justice JOHN MARSHALL HARLAN's [2] most noteworthy opinions, and today it is widely taught in law school courses dealing with the FREEDOM OF SPEECH [2,I].

Nimmer's First Amendment articles dealt with movie censorship, LIBEL [3] and invasion of privacy (see PRIVACY AND THE FIRST AMENDMENT [3]), SYMBOLIC SPEECH [4], national security secrets, the special role of the press clause, and—inevitably—the relation of COPYRIGHT [2] to the First Amendment. (He wrote on three of these topics for this *Encyclopedia*.) In these writings he developed a theory of "definitional balancing" that became one of the theoretical centerpieces of his last major work on constitutional law, *Nimmer on Freedom of Speech: A Treatise on the Theory of the First Amendment* (1984). Nimmer planned to supplement this treatise regularly, and specifically to apply his theories to "national security, breach of the peace, commercial speech and obscenity." When he died the next year, his colleagues and the larger community lost much more than those products of a gifted legal mind.

KENNETH L. KARST

Bibliography

MELVILLE B. NIMMER SYMPOSIUM 1987 *UCLA Law Review* 34:1331–1903 (includes a complete list of Nimmer's published works).

NINTH AMENDMENT

See: Ninth Amendment [3]; Unenumerated Rights [I]

NONINTERPRETIVISM

This ungainly name was invented as a counterpart of INTERPRETIVISM [I], the view that courts, in deciding on the meaning of the Constitution, should find their authoritative sources only in the constitutional text and the clearly established intentions of those who adopted the text. A noninterpretivist, then, was one who believed that courts might properly go beyond these sources, enforcing constitutional norms not readily discernible in the text or the Framers' intentions, narrowly conceived. These terms lost their vogue fairly quickly because few commentators (and no judges) wanted to admit that their views were anything other than interpretations of the Constitution.

Today's commentary uses other terms that are more descriptive of their referents. "Textualism," for example, refers to a view that focuses closely on the Constitution's words. Almost no commentators now profess to be strict textualists. Justice HUGO L. BLACK [1] is the modern Supreme Court's strongest claimant to being a textualist, and even he had his moments of backsliding. ORIGINALISM [I], which limits the authoritative sources to the text and the ORIGINAL INTENT [I] of the Framers, has a number of adherents among today's commentators and a smaller number among the federal judiciary, but none among the Justices. By the end of the 1980s, however, sightings of noninterpretivists had become rarer than sightings of Bigfoot.

KENNETH L. KARST

Bibliography

BREST, PAUL 1980 The Misconceived Quest for the Original Understanding. *Boston University Law Review* 60:204–238.
ELY, JOHN HART 1980 *Democracy and Distrust: A Theory of Judicial Review*, chaps. 1 and 2. Cambridge, Mass.: Harvard University Press.
LEVY, LEONARD W. 1988 *Original Intent and the Framers' Constitution*. New York: Macmillan.
PERRY, MICHAEL J. 1982 *The Constitution, the Courts, and Human Rights*. New Haven, Conn.: Yale University Press.
TUSHNET, MARK V. 1983 Following the Rules Laid Down: A Critique of Interpretivism and Neutral Principles. *Harvard Law Review* 96:781–827.

NONJUDICIAL INTERPRETATION OF THE CONSTITUTION

The requirement in Article VI, section 3, that public officers "support the Constitution" applies to all three branches of government, not merely the judiciary. In compliance with this constitutional mandate, legislators and executive officials have made major contributions over the years in interpreting and shaping the Constitution. Because judicial doctrines often exclude the courts from deciding certain questions, the meaning of the Constitution may depend exclusively on determinations reached by the legislative and executive branches.

In the early decades of the American republic, before the Supreme Court began to establish PRECEDENTS [3] for constitutional law, the Constitution had to be interpreted solely by members of Congress and executive officials. Such critical issues as FEDERALISM [2,I], INTERSTATE COMMERCE [2], the President's APPOINTING AND REMOVAL POWER [1], the investigative power of Congress, the TREATY POWER [4] and FOREIGN AFFAIRS [2], SLAVERY [4], and INTERNAL IMPROVEMENTS [4] were debated and resolved by the political branches without any assistance from the judiciary. Many of these constitutional judgments were later accepted by the federal courts as binding interpretations.

The idea of JUDICIAL SUPREMACY [3] begins with Chief Justice JOHN MARSHALL's [3] declaration in MARBURY V. MADISON (1803) [3] that it is "emphatically the province and duty of the judicial department to say what the law is." Bold words, but the political situation required Marshall to finesse the legal issue to avoid a confrontation with President THOMAS JEFFERSON [3] he knew he could not win. Significantly, Marshall never again, throughout his long tenure on the bench, invalidated another act of Congress.

It is doubtful whether Marshall actually believed that the Supreme Court possessed the exclusive authority to decide the meaning of the Constitution. After Congress impeached and removed Judge JOHN PICKERING [3] in 1804 and began proceedings to impeach Supreme Court Justice SAMUEL J. CHASE [1] (with Marshall probably next in line), Marshall wrote to Chase on January 23, 1804, suggesting that members of Congress did not have to impeach judges because they objected to their legal opinions. Congress could simply reverse the decisions. Marshall advised Chase, "I think the modern doctrine of impeachment should yield to an appellate jurisdiction in the legislature. A reversal of those legal opinions deemed unsound by the legislatures would certainly better comport with the mildness of our character that [would] a removal of the Judge who has rendered them unknowing of his fault."

Marshall's letter to Chase is somewhat ambiguous. Could Congress reverse only statutory interpretations or constitutional decisions as well? Did reversal require a constitutional amendment or merely a statute? The context of Marshall's statement implies that he was quite willing to share with the other two branches the task of CONSTITUTIONAL INTERPRETATION [1].

Obviously, neither Congress nor the Presidents accepted the Court as the final arbiter of constitutional law. Jefferson believed that constitutional decisions by one branch, including the judiciary, were to be given "no control to another branch." Each branch "has an equal right to decide for itself what is the meaning of the Constitution in the cases submitted to its action; and especially, where it is to act ultimately and without APPEAL." An example is the President's PARDONING POWER [3]. Although the ALIEN AND SEDITION ACTS [1] of 1798 had never been declared unconstitutional in the federal courts, Jefferson considered it a nullity when he became President and, accordingly, pardoned those who had been convicted under it. Congress later appropriated funds to reimburse individuals who had been fined under the Sedition Act, declaring in committee reports that the statute was "unconstitutional, null, and void." The Court later admitted in NEW YORK TIMES V. SULLIVAN (1964) [3] that the Sedition Act had been repudiated not by a court of law, but by the "court of history."

President ANDREW JACKSON [3] also believed that each branch of government had an independent duty to interpret the Constitution. The Court upheld the constitutionality of the BANK OF THE UNITED STATES [1] in McCULLOCH V. MARYLAND (1819) [3], and Congress passed legislation to recharter it, but Jackson nevertheless vetoed the bill on the ground that Congress, the President, and the Court "must each for itself be guided by its own opinion of the Constitution. Each public officer who takes an oath to support the Constitution swears that he will support it as he understands it, and not as it is understood by others." This broad concept of the VETO POWER [4] has been adopted by all subsequent Presidents.

In a series of speeches in 1858, ABRAHAM LINCOLN [3] denied that the Court's decision in DRED SCOTT V. SANDFORD (1857) [2] represented the "last word" on the slavery issue, particularly with regard to the power of Congress to prohibit SLAVERY IN THE TERRITORIES [4] and the rights of blacks. Lincoln considered the Court a co-equal, not a superior, branch of government. In his inaugural address in 1861, he warned that if government policy on "vital questions affecting the whole people is to be irrevocably fixed" by the Court, "the people will have ceased to be their own rulers."

The Supreme Court may be the ultimate interpreter of the Constitution in a particular case, but once it releases an opinion, it is helpless to control the political forces and pressures that shape constitutional meaning. In 1918 and again in 1922, the Court struck down congressional efforts to regulate child labor. The first statute, according to the Court, exceeded Congress's power under the COMMERCE CLAUSE [1,I] because manufacturing was not "interstate commerce." The second statute, the Court held, exceeded the taxing power because the tax was really a "regulation." Despite these precedents, the New Deal Congress passed legislation in 1938 to regulate wages and hours in manufacturing, relying again on the commerce clause, and a unanimous Court overrode the 1918 child labor decision and upheld the statute in UNITED STATES V. DARBY LUMBER COMPANY (1941) [2].

For a period of several decades in the twentieth century, the Supreme Court invoked its power of JUDICIAL REVIEW [3,I] to restrict the power of Congress to regulate the national economy. These decisions did little more than delay the momentum for national control. In time, the constitutional meaning of interstate commerce and federalism fell almost exclusively to Congress and the President. In PRUDENTIAL INSURANCE COMPANY V. BENJAMIN (1946) [3] the Court conceded: "the history of judicial limitation of congressional power over commerce, when exercised affirmatively, has been more largely one of retreat than of ultimate victory." In GARCIA V. SAN ANTONIO METROPOLITAN TRANSIT AUTHORITY (1985) [2] the Court essentially delegated to Congress the responsibility for defining federalism.

Relying on the commerce clause and its powers to enforce the Civil War amendments, Congress has taken the initiative to establish the constitutional rights of black citizens in such areas as education, housing, VOTING RIGHTS [4], employment, and equal access to PUBLIC ACCOMMODATIONS [3]. Virtually all these legislative actions in recent decades have been sustained by the courts.

Dissenting in GERTZ V. ROBERT WELCH, INC. (1974) [2], Justice WILLIAM J. BRENNAN [1,I] claimed that the courts are "the ultimate arbiters of all disputes concerning clashes of constitutional values." Two hundred years of history present quite a different picture. Clashes of constitutional values are fought out in every arena—national and state—and within all of the branches of government. No single branch can claim ultimate control. Constitutional judgments of the courts are frequently overturned by the political branches.

In ZURCHER V. STANFORD DAILY (1978) [4] the Court balanced the right of a free press against the needs of law enforcement officials and sided with the latter. In 1980, Congress passed legislation giving much greater protection to FIRST AMENDMENT [2,I] interests. In *United States v. Miller* (1976) the Court supported the right of law enforcement agents to subpoena banks for information in a depositor's account. Two years later, Congress passed legislation that placed limits on warrantless searches of bank and credit records.

Another example of a Court–Congress dialogue, with Congress again defending constitutional rights left unprotected by the judiciary, is GOLDMAN V. WEINBERGER (1986) [I]. The Court upheld an Air Force regulation that prohibited an Orthodox Jew from wearing his yarmulke indoors while on duty. The Court reasoned that the Air Force's values of obedience, discipline, and unity outweighed any interference with the religious beliefs of Captain Goldman. Congress disagreed, passing legislation the next year that told the Air Force to change its regulation to permit officers and airmen to wear religious apparel while in uniform.

On special occasion, an authoritative and binding decision by the Supreme Court may be helpful in resolving a political impasse. The unanimous decision in COOPER V. AARON (1958) [2] defused the smoldering Little Rock crisis, but the CIVIL RIGHTS [1,I] stalemate persisted until the two political branches confronted the issue squarely and passed the CIVIL RIGHTS ACT OF 1964 [1]. This statute provided more of a "last word" on the constitutional rights of black citizens than any court decision, including such landmark rulings as BROWN V. BOARD OF EDUCATION OF TOPEKA (1954) [1]. Similarly, the unanimous decision in UNITED STATES V. NIXON (1974) [3] signaled a dramatic turn in the WATERGATE [4] affair, leading to the resignation of President RICHARD M. NIXON [3], but the decision added little clarity to the constitutional meaning of EXECUTIVE PRIVILEGE [2] and even introduced new areas of confusion and uncertainty.

Sometimes an effort by the Court to announce the last word on a divisive constitutional issue simply backfires, attempting to do through the judiciary what must be accomplished through the political process. A notable example is the inaugural address by one President who explained that a difficult constitutional issue was before the Supreme Court, where it belonged, and that it would be "speedily and finally settled." The address was by JAMES BUCHANAN [1], two days before the Court announced the *Dred Scott* case.

The belief that the judiciary is the ultimate arbiter of constitutional issues finds no support in our history. The Court itself often shows a keen awareness that constitutional interpretation is an exceedingly delicate and complex task that must be shared with Congress, the President, the states, and society at large.

LOUIS FISHER

Bibliography

ANDREWS, WILLIAM G., ED. 1969 *Coordinate Magistrates: Constitutional Law by Congress and the President.* New York: Van Nostrand Reinhold.

FISHER, LOUIS 1988 *Constitutional Dialogues: Interpretation as Political Process.* Princeton, N.J.: Princeton University Press.

MURPHY, WALTER F. 1986 Who Shall Interpret? The Quest for Ultimate Constitutional Interpreter. *Review of Politics* 48:401–423.

O'BRIEN FORMULA

The Supreme Court has occasionally stated that the test set out in UNITED STATES V. O'BRIEN (1968) [3] should be employed in cases involving the content-neutral regulation of speech. Under that test such a regulation is "sufficiently justified if it furthers an important or substantial government interest . . . and if the incidental restriction on alleged FIRST AMENDMENT [I] freedoms is no greater than is essential to the furtherance of that interest."

Current doctrine is more complicated than such statements imply. First, the *O'Brien* test often is not employed in important cases involving content-neutral regulations. For example, when speakers seek access to government property, the Court turns to a body of tests and rules that fall under the heading of PUBLIC FORUM [3,I] doctrine. The *O'Brien* test has been largely absent from the opinions in those cases.

Second, even when the *O'Brien* test is applied, the Court often deviates from the test's original language in ways that seem to make the test more speech-protective. For example, the *O'Brien* test implies that the furtherance of a substantial state interest by the appropriate means *always* outweighs the interest in FREEDOM OF SPEECH [2,I]. But the Court will sometimes ask whether the government interest is *sufficiently* substantial to justify the effect of the ordinance on expression. In addition, the Court may consider factors not mentioned in the test—principally, the adequacy of alternative channels of communication.

Nonetheless, the Court's application of the test has been less rigorous than its wording might connote. Indeed, some commentators have been led to suggest that the

O'Brien test really means that the government always wins. This is a plausible reading of the test's treatment in the Supreme Court, but not of its treatment in the lower courts. In fact, the *O'Brien* test is simply a mangled attempt to state that courts should consider competing interests and arrive at appropriate decisions.

STEVEN H. SHIFFRIN

Bibliography

SHIFFRIN, STEVEN H. 1990 *The First Amendment, Democracy, and Romance.* Cambridge, Mass.: Harvard University Press.

O'CONNOR, SANDRA DAY
(1930–)

Sandra Day O'Connor was born in Arizona in 1930. After leaving high school at the age of sixteen, she completed both her undergraduate and law degrees at Stanford University in five years. She spent the next decade as a county attorney and in private practice in Arizona and elsewhere, and she became an Arizona assistant attorney general in 1965. She served in the Arizona state senate from 1969 until 1974, when she moved into the state judiciary—first as a trial judge and later on the state's intermediate court of appeals. President RONALD REAGAN [3,I] nominated her as the first female Justice of the Supreme Court of the United States in 1981.

O'Connor took the oath of office on September 25, 1981, as the first Supreme Court appointee of the most conservative President since CALVIN COOLIDGE [2]. Not surprisingly, she immediately became part of the conservative wing of the Court, voting with Justice WILLIAM H. REHNQUIST [3,I] more than ninety percent of the time by 1984. She has continued to be a reliable conservative vote in CRIMINAL PROCEDURE [2] and FEDERALISM [2,I] cases. After 1984, however, she began striking out on her own in several areas. She became considerably less predictable in cases involving SUBSTANTIVE DUE PROCESS [4,I], discrimination, and complex jurisdictional or procedural questions.

By 1989 O'Connor had become a pivotal center vote on the Court. Although this change resulted in part from the appointment of two more conservative Justices, it was also the result of the changes in O'Connor's own views: by 1987 she was voting with Rehnquist only seventy-eight percent of the time. Moreover, during this period O'Connor often wrote separate concurrences and dissents, approaching cases from independent points of view; and by the end of the 1988 Term, her originally solo viewpoints commanded majorities in several doctrinal areas. Three topics illustrate both her influence and her central position on the Court: the ESTABLISHMENT CLAUSE [I] of the FIRST AMENDMENT [2,I], AFFIRMATIVE ACTION [1,I], and CAPITAL PUNISHMENT [1,I].

At the time O'Connor joined the Court, establishment clause challenges were virtually always governed by the test of LEMON V. KURTZMAN (1971) [3]: a statute violates the establishment clause if it has a primary purpose or a primary effect of advancing or inhibiting religion, or if it causes excessive government entanglement with religion. Beginning with LYNCH V. DONNELLY (1984) [3], O'Connor proposed a "refinement" of the LEMON TEST [I] emphasizing the questions "whether the government's purpose is to endorse religion and whether the statute actually conveys a message of endorsement." Unlike the standard view of the *Lemon* test, which centers on the practical effect of governmental action, O'Connor's test focuses on the communicative or symbolic aspects of that action. Thus, O'Connor would find a constitutional violation when "[e]ndorsement sends a message to non-adherents that they are outsiders, not full members of the political community, and an accompanying message to adherents that they are insiders, favored members of the political community."

Between 1984 and 1989, O'Connor's application of this principle made her the swing vote in many establishment-clause cases. She provided the fifth vote to uphold a public Christmas display including a crèche in *Lynch v. Donnelly* and to uphold federal funding of religious family-planning organizations in BOWEN V. KENDRICK (1988) [I]. She also provided the fifth vote to invalidate a state-mandated moment of silence for meditation or prayer at the beginning of the public school day in WALLACE V. JAFFREE (1985)

[4] and to invalidate a public Christmas display of a crèche alone in COUNTY OF ALLEGHENY V. ACLU (1989) [I]. In *County of Allegheny*, moreover, she appeared to have converted a majority of the Court to her test, at least where the display of religious symbols is at issue.

O'Connor also fashioned what has become the majority test for constitutional challenges to affirmative action programs. For over a decade, the Court was unable to produce a majority opinion in any constitutional case involving affirmative action. Badly fragmented, the Court could not agree on either the level of scrutiny to be applied to such challenges or the factual prerequisites that might make an affirmative action program valid. Beginning with WYGANT V. JACKSON BOARD OF EDUCATION (1986) [I], O'Connor wrote several separate opinions answering both questions with great specificity: affirmative action programs should be tested by STRICT SCRUTINY [4], and such scrutiny typically requires that there be a remedial need for the program, shown by some evidence—not necessarily contemporaneous—of prior government discrimination (remedying past societal discrimination is an insufficient governmental interest). In 1989, in RICHMOND (CITY OF) V. J. A. CROSON CO. (1989) [I], O'Connor obtained majority support for her position.

O'Connor has also had a significant influence in cases dealing with the death penalty for juveniles. Although she has not generally been the swing vote in ordinary capital cases, her vote has been crucial in deciding whether the state may execute persons who committed crimes when they were under the age of majority. In THOMPSON V. OKLAHOMA (1988) [I], she voted with the four liberal Justices to overturn a death sentence imposed on a girl who had committed murder at the age of fifteen. O'Connor did not join Justice JOHN PAUL STEVENS's [4,I] plurality opinion, however, because it categorically denied the constitutionality of executing anyone who was under sixteen when the crime was committed. Instead, O'Connor concluded that the legislature, in failing to set any minimum age limit, did not give proper consideration to a question on which no national consensus existed and, thus, that the penalty was CRUEL AND UNUSUAL PUNISHMENT [2].

This distinctive approach allowed her to vote the very next year in STANFORD V. KENTUCKY (1989) [I] to uphold death sentences imposed on two juveniles who had committed crimes at the ages of sixteen and seventeen. Again she was the fifth vote, this time combining with the conservative wing of the Court, and again she wrote a separate concurrence basing her decision on a "sufficiently clear . . . national consensus." In a case decided the same day as *Stanford*, PENRY V. LYNAUGH (1989) [I], O'Connor provided the pivotal vote (and wrote the majority opinion) for two separate majorities: one concluding that the Eighth Amendment generally permits the execution of mentally retarded adults and the other reversing the death sentence of the particularly mentally retarded defendant on the ground that the jury instructions deprived the jury of any meaningful opportunity to take the defendant's handicap into account as a mitigating factor.

Finally, O'Connor may prove to be the crucial vote on ABORTION [1,I]. From 1981 to 1989, O'Connor consistently voted to uphold all antiabortion laws; and in *Akron v. Akron Center for Reproductive Health* (1983), she even wrote that ROE V. WADE (1973) [3] was "on a collision course with itself." In WEBSTER V. REPRODUCTIVE HEALTH SERVICES (1989) [I], however, O'Connor declined to join with the four other Justices wishing to modify *Roe*. Instead, she wrote a separate concurrence upholding the challenged statute under *Roe* itself and explicitly refusing to reach the question of *Roe's* continued validity. Indeed, her earlier opinions had suggested that the Court abandon the trimester approach to abortion and instead ask whether a challenged statute "unduly burdens" a woman's right to an abortion. In *Webster*, Rehnquist's plurality opinion adopted this approach almost verbatim, but O'Connor nevertheless declined to join his opinion.

Two additional trends are evident in O'Connor's opinions. First, she frequently writes separately in order to "clarify" the majority's opinion. Her clarifying concurrences are often attempts to point out the limits of the Court's decision or to minimize the distance between the majority and dissent. In *Wygant*, for example, her concurrence stressed that there was little difference in application between a "compelling" governmental interest and an "important" one and that both majority and dissenting opinions agreed that remedying past discrimination constitutes such an interest. In other cases she has made a great effort to specify what issues the Court has not decided.

The second common thread during O'Connor's tenure on the Court to date is her tendency to demand fact-specific decision making in a wide variety of contexts. For example, in *Lanier v. South Carolina* (1985), she wrote a separate concurrence to a per curiam opinion on the voluntariness of a confession, stressing that on remand the Court should look at the particular circumstances of the confession. In two cases involving the appropriate state statute of limitations to be borrowed in SECTION 1983 [4] actions, she dissented from nearly unanimous Court decisions imposing a single standard, preferring instead to examine the circumstances of each Section 1983 suit (*Wilson v. Garcia* [1985] and *Goodman v. Lukens Steel Co.* [1987]). In a series of HABEAS CORPUS [2,I] cases, she wrote majority opinions fashioning a test whereby defendants who could produce evidence of "actual innocence" might avoid the newly strengthened strictures of the "cause and prejudice" test (*Smith v. Murray* [1986] and *Murray v. Carrier* [1986]). In COY V. IOWA (1988) [I], she concurred in a decision invalidating on CONFRONTATION [1] clause grounds a state statute permitting courts to place a screen between the accused and the accuser in child sexual abuse cases, but refused to join the majority's conclusion that such screens *always* violate the right to confrontation. In ALLEN V. WRIGHT (1984) [1], she demanded greater specificity by parents seeking STANDING [4] to challenge Internal Revenue Service regulations that they alleged were inadequate to prevent discriminatory private schools from obtaining and keeping charitable exemption status. Finally, her position on affirmative action, noted above, makes clear the need for some factual predicate for the adoption of any affirmative-action plan.

When O'Connor joined the Court in 1981, it was expected that her votes would reflect three influences: her CONSERVATISM [I] would align her with the right wing of the Court, her state legislative background would give her a strong STATES' RIGHTS [4] tilt, and her gender would make her more receptive to claims of SEX DISCRIMINATION [4,I]. Only the last of these expectations has proved both accurate and significant. Although as already indicated, she has voted conservatively on some issues, in other cases she has followed an independent path. Her deference to state legislatures is reasonably consistent, but she has virtually always been outvoted, as in GARCIA V. SAN ANTONIO METROPOLITAN TRANSIT AUTHORITY (1985) [2] and *South Dakota v. Dole* (1987).

O'Connor has, however, been a consistent supporter of gender equality. During her tenure on the Court, she has joined the majority—and sometimes provided a crucial vote—in making partnership decisions subject to Title VII (*Hishon v. King & Spalding* [1984]), declaring sexual harassment as actionable under the same statute (MERITOR SAVINGS BANK V. VINSON [1986] [I]), rejecting a PREEMPTION [3] challenge to a state law requiring employers to give pregnancy leave to employees who want one (*California Federal Savings & Loan v. Guerra* [1987]), upholding discrimination claims based on sexual stereotyping (*Price Waterhouse v. Hopkins* [1989]), invalidating an all-female state nursing school (MISSISSIPPI UNIVERSITY FOR WOMEN V. HOGAN [1982] [3]), and upholding an affirmative action program for women (JOHNSON V. TRANSPORTATION AGENCY [1987] [I]). Only in the area of abortion has her support of women's rights been less consistent.

Thus, after eight years on the Court, O'Connor has proved herself an independent and sometimes unpredictable thinker. It is clear, however, that the first female Supreme Court Justice has already left her mark on the Court and will continue to do so.

SUZANNA SHERRY

(SEE ALSO: *Gender Rights* [I]; *Race-Consciousness* [I]; *Racial Discrimination* [3,I]; *Racial Preference* [I]; *Rehnquist Court* [I].)

Bibliography

CORDRAY, RICHARD M. and VRADELIS, JAMES I. 1985 The Emerging Jurisprudence of Justice O'Connor. *University of Chicago Law Review* 52:389–459.

O'CONNOR, SANDRA DAY 1981 Trends in the Relationship Between the Federal and State Courts from the Perspective of a State Court Judge. *William and Mary Law Review* 22:801–815.

SHEA, BARBARA C. S. 1986 Sandra Day O'Connor—Woman, Lawyer, Justice: Her First Four Terms on the Supreme Court. *University of Missouri, Kansas City Law Review* 55:1–32.

SHERRY, SUZANNA 1986 Civic Virtue and the Feminine Voice in Constitutional Adjudication. *Virginia Law Review* 72:543–616.

OHIO v. AKRON CENTER FOR REPRODUCTIVE HEALTH (1990)

See: *Hodgson v. Minnesota* [I]

O'LONE v. ESTATE OF SHABAZZ
482 U.S. 342 (1987)

Regulations at a New Jersey prison forbade minimum-security inmates who worked outside the main prison building from reentering the building during the day, thus preventing certain Muslim PRISONERS [3,I] from attending their weekly worship service held on Fridays. Required by the Koran to attend the service, the prisoners filed suit, claiming violation of their rights under the free exercise clause. Adopting what was essentially a COMPELLING STATE INTEREST [1] test, the court of appeals held that the prison had to prove "that no reasonable method exists by which [the prisoners'] religious rights can be accommodated without creating bona fide security problems." In a 5–4 decision the Supreme Court reversed, ruling that the court of appeals paid insufficient deference to prison officials, who have authority to enact any prison regulations "reasonably related to legitimate penological interests."

Justice WILLIAM J. BRENNAN [1,I], writing for the dissenters, accused the majority of uncritically accepting the assertions of prison administrators. Brennan did not claim

that the courts should never defer to the judgment of prison authorities; but when the prison completely deprives prisoners of a right and where the activity in question is not presumptively dangerous, Brennan maintained that prison officials should be required to show that the denial of the right is no greater than necessary to achieve the government's objective.

Shabazz foreshadowed the Court's eventual abolition of the compelling-state-interest test for all free-exercise cases in EMPLOYMENT DIVISION, DEPARTMENT OF HUMAN RESOURCES OF OREGON V. SMITH (1990) [I].

JOHN G. WEST, JR.

(SEE ALSO: *Religious Liberty* [3,I].)

OPEN FIELDS DOCTRINE

The FOURTH AMENDMENT [2,I] protects "persons, houses, papers, and effects against unreasonable searches and seizures." The amendment, held to embody a RIGHT OF PRIVACY [3,I], shelters certain enclaves from arbitrary government examination and interference. Within these enclaves, roughly defined as places where persons have a subjective expectation of privacy that society recognizes as reasonable—the paradigmatic case is the home—governmental SEARCHES AND SEIZURES [4,I] are unreasonable unless authorized by a SEARCH WARRANT [4] issued on PROBABLE CAUSE [3]. There are some exceptions to this rule against WARRANTLESS SEARCHES [4], however, and the open fields doctrine presents one of them.

In applying the Fourth Amendment to detached dwellings the Supreme Court has held that persons have a REASONABLE EXPECTATION OF PRIVACY [I] in the home and its "curtilage." Curtilage is the area immediately surrounding the home that harbors the intimate activities associated with domestic life and home privacies. Proximity to the home, containment within an enclosure surrounding the home, use for domestic and private purposes, and steps taken to protect the area from observation all help to define its ambit.

The open fields doctrine permits warrantless searches of private land outside the curtilage. The right of privacy that the Fourth Amendment protects is therefore not congruent with the right of property ownership, and exercise of the COMMON LAW [1] right to exclude persons from land cannot make governmental searches of it unlawful. Further, under the doctrine open fields need be neither open nor fields, but only areas of land outside the curtilage. Fenced dense woods could therefore qualify as open fields. Consequently, neither the natural seclusion of property, which might be thought to make it private, nor efforts to keep trespassers out, such as posting with signs or surrounding with fences, secures it from governmental search.

GARY GOODPASTER

(SEE ALSO: *Plain View Doctrine* [3,I].)

Bibliography

LaFAVE, WAYNE 1987 *Search and Seizure: A Treatise on the Fourth Amendment.* St. Paul, Minn.: West Publishing Co.

OPERATION RESCUE

See: Antiabortion Movement [I]

ORIGINAL INTENT

"Original intent" is a shorthand term for both a familiar topic of CONSTITUTIONAL HISTORY [1,I] and a problematic theory of CONSTITUTIONAL INTERPRETATION [1]. As a historical problem, the quest for original intent seeks to discover what particular provisions of the Constitution meant at the moment of their adoption, whether to the Framers in the CONSTITUTIONAL CONVENTION OF 1787 [1] (or Congress, in the case of subsequent amendments), the ratifiers in the state conventions and legislatures, or the citizenry in general. As a mode of constitutional interpretation, however, original intent suggests that the true meaning of these provisions was in some sense fixed at the point of their adoption and that later interpreters of the Constitution should adhere to that original meaning.

The earliest version of original intent can be traced as far back as the 1790s, when JAMES MADISON [3] sought to develop a mode of interpretation that could counter the loose canon of Hamiltonian construction. More recently, the call for a return to a "jurisprudence of original intent" held a central place in the campaign by the administration of RONALD REAGAN [3,I] to challenge controversial decisions taken by the Supreme Court under Chief Justices EARL WARREN [4] and WARREN E. BURGER [4]. In many areas of constitutional law, conservatives argued, the Court had freely ignored the original meaning of particular provisions of the Constitution in order to impose its own values on society. In so doing, conservatives further alleged, the Court had also usurped powers the Constitution vested in the political branches of government, thereby violating its original meaning in a second and more fundamental sense.

Yet the appeal of the theory of original intent has never been confined to conservatives alone. On many issues, liberals can invoke the authority of the Framers and ratifiers of the Constitution just as easily. In recent controversies over the conduct of FOREIGN AFFAIRS [2], for example, liberals have effectively argued that the Framers and ratifiers of the Constitution did not expect the executive to have unilateral initiative in making foreign policy or the power to commit American forces to combat without the active approval of Congress. Judged pragmatically, the theory of original intent is neither inherently conservative nor inherently liberal. It is, instead, a style of constitutional argument that particular parties can invoke whenever the available historical evidence promises to support their immediate cause.

Modern proponents of a jurisprudence of original intent rest their case on democratic norms. The Constitution is the supreme law of the land not merely because Article VI says so but because its authority can be traced to extraordinary acts of POPULAR SOVEREIGNTY [3], whether in the state ratification conventions of 1787–1790 or through the congressional and state legislative supermajorities required to secure amendments. By contrast, the Supreme Court Justices who ultimately interpret the Constitution are the least politically accountable officers in the entire system of governance. When judges abuse the power of JUDICIAL REVIEW [3] to impose values not securely rooted in the constitutional text, originalists argue, they effectively nullify the sovereign will of the people as that will is expressed in the great acts of constitution-making or in the ordinary legislative decisions the Court chooses to overturn. If fundamental constitutional change is called for, originalists suggest, it should be achieved through the amendment procedures of Article V, not by judicial fiat.

Critics of this modern version of ORIGINALISM [I] challenge this position on several grounds. They argue, first, that the unwieldy requirements of Article V render the Constitution so difficult to amend that it is far better to rely on constitutional evolution through judicial interpretation and political innovation than to insist that its original meaning be preserved inviolate until the necessary supermajoritarian consensus can be mobilized. Nor is it clear why decisions made by judges who are appointed by politically accountable Presidents and senators should be regarded as more arbitrary or less democratic than those earlier decisions imposed by generations dead and gone. Finally, the criticism that judges act undemocratically by extending the definition and protection of constitutional rights misses the obvious point that it has always been the duty of the judiciary to protect individual and minority rights against majority abuse.

These objections are, in a sense, normative: they ask whether a jurisprudence of original intent is desirable, not whether it is practicable. But other reservations about the merits of this theory of interpretation rest on narrower grounds of practicality. Some of these reservations concern the adequacy of the historical evidence on which all appeals to the original meaning rest; others reflect doubts about the capacity of judges or other officials to use this evidence intelligently and objectively. The idea that adherence to original intent would always work to constrain judges is itself questionable. A historical record that is ambiguous or murky may actually broaden the interpretive latitude within which a willful judge might choose to roam.

Perhaps the single most telling problem of evidence involves the difficult task of recovering what the ratifiers of the Constitution understood they were adopting when they expressed the sovereign will of the people. Under the strict theory of original intent, the understandings of the ratifiers command the greatest weight in interpretive efforts, because it was their actions—as opposed to the proceedings in the Federal Convention or Congress—that alone gave legal force to the constitutional text. Unfortunately, the records of the debates in the state ratification conventions of 1787–1788 (or in the state legislatures for the BILL OF RIGHTS [1] and later amendments) seem less than adequate. Whole days of debate—and in some states, entire conventions—went unreported; numerous provisions of the Constitution went unexamined; and in the end, the delegates who passed judgment on the Constitution voted only on whether or not they wanted to accept the document as a whole. Thus, although the ratification records are rich enough to allow scholars to survey the general grounds on which the Constitution was supported or opposed, they cannot conclusively illuminate what its various provisions meant to the obscure state politicians who ratified it, much less the anonymous—though sovereign—people they represented.

James Madison was aware of this problem when, in the mid-1790s, he first argued that the understanding of the ratifiers could legitimately constrain the reach of interpretation. Although Madison never explained exactly how one could determine what the Constitution meant in a positive sense, he did believe that it was possible to challenge interpretations that either had not been offered at the time of adoption or would have been rejected out of hand if they had been candidly stated.

Regardless of the legal arguments that favor the authority of the ratifiers, in practice few interpreters of the Constitution are inclined to ignore evidence about the intentions of its actual Framers. Much of the debate about the original allocation of the WAR POWERS [4,I], for example, centers on the Federal Convention's decision to substitute the verb "declare" for "make" in the clause giving Congress the authority to declare war. Scholars have similarly canvassed the congressional debates about the FOURTEENTH AMENDMENT [2,I] for clues about the original meaning of its frequently controverted clauses.

The great advantage that inquiries into the Framers'

intentions enjoy over ratifiers' understandings is that the former may better help to explain how and why a particular provision acquired its precise textual form. Yet even then, there is no ready way to demonstrate how well any one comment or set of comments represented the range of intentions and expectations that typically inform any collective political decision. Many studies of legislative voting suggest that all exercises in collective decision making are inherently ambiguous.

Given all these difficulties, it is not surprising that most judicial forays into originalist interpretation receive low marks from knowledgeable scholars. Judges and their law clerks are not trained historians, and they repeatedly err in their treatment of the historical evidence on which they necessarily rely. On this basis alone it can be strongly argued that originalism can never offer much more than a rhetorical strategy to justify decisions taken on more complex grounds.

That argument does not imply, however, that originalism has no role to play in modern CONSTITUTIONALISM [2]. Even if it is impossible to ascertain fixed original meanings for the Constitution's most disputed and "open-textured" clauses, a sound historical approach can still reconstruct the general contours of the debates from which they emerged. Moreover, the fact that Americans repeatedly invoke the authority of Framers and ratifiers—especially "the founders" of 1787–1788—in their constitutional disputes may reveal something important about American political culture. Originalism can never be a dispositive theory of interpretation, but neither can it be entirely deposed from the place it has repeatedly claimed in American constitutional discourse.

JACK N. RAKOVE

(SEE ALSO: Conservatism [I]; Deconstructionism [I]; Incorporation Doctrine and Original Intent [I]; Interpretivism [I]; Liberalism [I]; Noninterpretivism [I]; Political Philosophy of the Constitution [3,I]; Strict Construction [4].)

Bibliography

LEVY, LEONARD W. 1988 Original Intent and the Framers' Constitution. New York: Macmillan.
LOFGREN, CHARLES 1986 "Government from Reflection and Choice": Constitutional Essays on War, Foreign Relations, and Federalism. New York: Oxford University Press.
RAKOVE, JACK N., ED. 1990 Interpreting the Constitution: The Debate over Original Intent. Boston: Northeastern University Press.

ORIGINALISM

"Originalism" is a term used to describe the view that judicial decisions regarding the Constitution must be based on the ORIGINAL INTENT [I] of those who participated in the framing and enactment of the original Constitution and later amendments. For example, originalists regard the issue of the constitutional validity of the death penalty as easily resolved by the explicit references in the Fifth and Fourteenth Amendments to the deliberate taking of life by government, indicating that the Constitution expressly contemplates the imposition of the death penalty. The Fifth Amendment states that "[n]o person shall be held to answer for a capital, or otherwise infamous crime, . . . put in jeopardy of life or limb; . . . be deprived of life, liberty, or property . . ." and the FOURTEENTH AMENDMENT [2,I] likewise guarantees that "[n]o state shall . . . deprive any person of life, liberty, or property. . . ."

Originalists justify their view on the grounds that focusing on original intent both limits the intrusion of the subjective political values of judges in constitutional decisions and gives due respect to democratic processes. Originalists argue that the intent of the Framers will sometimes accord with the personal views of judges and sometimes not. Application of this intent, therefore, will limit the ability of judges to impose their personal views on various issues upon the nation. Originalists also point out that the Constitution contains democratic amendment procedures and that the use of criteria other than original intent would enable judges to subvert both the democratic processes that led to the enactment of particular constitutional provisions and the democratic processes that provide for amendments. Finally, originalists argue that originalism is the only theory that can legitimate the institution of judicial review, which is a method of ensuring that the Constitution, as a superior law adopted by the people, constrains all organs of government, including the courts. *Marbury v. Madison*, 5 U.S. (1 Cranch) 137, 179–180 (1803).

Critics of originalism generally rely on two lines of attack. The first line is that the intent of the Framers is difficult and often impossible to determine. As Justice WILLIAM J. BRENNAN [1,I] said: "It is arrogant to pretend that from our vantage we can gauge accurately the intent of the Framers on application of principle to specific, contemporary questions." Doubt as to our present ability to learn the intent of the Framers fuels the suspicion among observers more cynical than Justice Brennan that lip service to supposed evidence of original intent is actually a façade behind which judges weave their subjective political values into the fabric of constitutional law. Second, critics argue that our concepts of civilized rule constantly evolve and that originalism affords too niggardly a protection for profoundly important rights. Again, Justice Brennan put the matter succinctly in describing his position on the constitutionality of the death penalty: "Because we are the last word on the meaning of the Constitution,

our views must be subject to revision over time, or the Constitution falls captive, again, to the anachronistic views of long-gone generations." He thus felt free to argue that the Eighth Amendment's prohibition on CRUEL AND UNUSUAL PUNISHMENT [2,I] (applicable to the states through the Fourteenth Amendment) prohibits the death penalty notwithstanding the specific references to the death penalty in the Fifth Amendment, which was part of the BILL OF RIGHTS [1] package that included the Eighth, and the more general reference to the death penalty in the Fourteenth Amendment itself.

In response to the first criticism—that the intent of the Framers regarding contemporary constitutional litigation is not ascertainable—originalists divide into what might be called an "intentionalist" school of thought and an "interpretivist" school of thought.

Members of the intentionalist school search for the actual state of mind of the Framers at the pertinent time, based on the language of the constitutional text, preconstitutional precedents, sometimes involving British law, or explicit legislative history. In their view, a judicial decision that is not based on explicit constitutional language or direct evidence of an actual intent held by the Framers is an illegitimate decision. The intentionalist school is best illustrated by the work of Raoul Berger. Berger has thus concluded that BROWN V. BOARD OF EDUCATION OF TOPEKA (1954) [1] was an illegitimate decision because of the lack of an explicit reference to DESEGREGATION [2] in the Fourteenth Amendment and because of evidence that some of the Framers stated during the framing and ratification period that public, segregated, educational institutions would pass constitutional muster under the Fourteenth Amendment. He has also denied the existence of an EXECUTIVE PRIVILEGE [2] because of the failure of the Constitution to mention such a privilege and the lack of precedent in colonial or preexisting law.

INTERPRETIVISM [I], on the other hand, insists only that constitutional decisions be, in Dean John Hart Ely's (not himself an originalist) words, "in accord with an inference whose starting point, whose underlying premise, is fairly discoverable in the Constitution. That the complete reference will not be found there—because the situation is not likely to have been foreseen—is generally common ground." For interpretivists, the name originalism is thus a bit of a misnomer, at least to the extent that it suggests that express language of the Constitution or evidence of the actual state of mind of the Framers are the sole legitimate criteria for constitutional adjudication.

Interpretivists take the view that CONSTITUTIONAL INTERPRETATION [1] must apply the conventional legal criteria used by lawyers in interpreting other legal texts. As Judge Robert H. Bork, certainly the most noted originalist, has stated, the search for original intent is "the everyday procedure of lawyers and judges when they must apply a statute, a contract, a will, or the opinion of a court." These criteria, of course, are designed to determine the purposes of the text. Democratic processes demand that statutory interpretation be governed by LEGISLATIVE IN-TENT [2]. Contract law stresses the purposes of the parties, estate law stresses the intent of the testator, and the doctrine of STARE DECISIS [4] stresses the meaning of prior decisions. Drawing on an analogy between these fields of law and constitutional law, interpretivists believe that constitutional law must stress the meaning of the document, which for them, as Professor Henry Monaghan has stated, is not so much the state of mind of the Framers as the "*public* understanding" of what particular constitutional provisions were intended to achieve.

Constitutional adjudication is thus for interpretivists much more than a search for express language, colonial or English precedent, or direct evidence of intent (or lack thereof) that produces a mechanical result in each case. Language or other direct evidence of intent is of course important in their view and dispositive when, as in the case of the death penalty, explicit consideration was given to the particular issue. Certainly, they would argue, the fact that the Fifth and Fourteenth Amendments prohibit imposition of the death penalty without DUE PRO-CESS OF LAW [2] is inconsistent with a judicial decision holding that the death penalty violates the Constitution in any and all circumstances.

Beyond such cases in which direct evidence of intent, such as language in the Constitution or legislative history, is dispositive, the interpretive view of originalism provides considerable scope for the exercise of judgment and for disagreement. This is not surprising because the conventional legal criteria applied by lawyers in interpreting statutes, contracts, or other legal documents extend well beyond language or express intent. Legal documents frequently provide evidence of only a very general purpose bb that courts must adapt to the circumstances of each case. Courts legitimately, therefore, read into statutes commands or exceptions to commands that have no basis in the express statutory language, but are believed necessary to effectuate the overall legislative purpose. For example, in *Reves v. Ernst & Young* (1990), the Supreme Court held that the phrase "any note" in the definitional section of the Securities Exchange Act of 1934 does not literally mean "any note," but must be understood in terms of what Congress sought to accomplish by enacting the statute; and in *Haggar Co. v. Helvering* (1940), the Court held in light of the statutory purpose that "[a] timely amended return is as much a 'first return' . . . as is a single return filed by the taxpayer. . . ." Courts must do this because of the inability of drafters to anticipate the myriad circumstances in which the meaning of the

statute must be divined, obvious drafting errors, or changes in the relevant industrial practice or technology. Similarly, courts may adapt contractual language to changed circumstances or impose duties, such as the duty to act in good faith where the contract accords considerable discretion to one party, notwithstanding the lack of express contractual language. Application of this mode of analysis to constitutional interpretation is essential because constitutional language is more general than most statutes and private contracts, and the interstices thus tend to be considerably wider.

Interpretivists believe that the Framers could not foresee all of the circumstances to which particular constitutional provisions might be applied and that judges must attempt to adapt what evidence of purpose there is to changed circumstances. Many interpretivists thus believe that contrary to Raoul Berger's conclusion *Brown* was fully legitimate. The interpretivists argue that the specific expectations of those Framers who stated that segregated education would survive the enactment of the Fourteenth Amendment were not faced with direct evidence that segregated educational systems were palpably inconsistent with the amendment's core purpose of relieving blacks of obstacles imposed by law. The interpretivist school thus takes into account the very limited experience these Framers had with both segregated schools and public education itself and feels free to override their particularized expectations in order to satisfy the basic philosophy of the EQUAL PROTECTION [2,I] clause.

Similarly, the interpretivist school is willing to adapt constitutional provisions to other changed circumstances. For example, in *Ollman v. Evans* (D.C. Circuit, 1984), Judge Bork wrote with regard to the interplay of the First Amendment and the law of LIBEL [3]:

We know very little of the precise intentions of the framers and ratifiers of the speech and press clauses of the first amendment. But we do know they gave into the judges' keeping the value of preserving free expression and, in particular, the preservation of political expression, which is commonly conceded to be the value at the core of these clauses. Perhaps the framers did not envision libel actions as a major threat to that freedom. . . . But if, over time, the libel action evolves so that it becomes a threat to the central meaning of the first amendment, why should not judges adapt their doctrines? . . . It is no different to refine and evolve doctrine here, so long as one is faithful to the basic meaning of the amendment, than it is to adapt the fourth amendment to take account of electronic means of surveillance, the commerce clause to adjust to interstate motor carriage, or the first amendment to encompass the electronic media. . . .

Moreover, interpretivists feel free to draw what Professor Charles L. Black has called inferences "from the structures and relationships created by the Constitution." Again, this interpretive method is commonly used by lawyers and judges to interpret legal texts. The Supreme Court's opinions regarding private actions under the securities laws brim with inferences as to the scope and content of one remedial provision drawn from the scope and content of other remedial provisions. Interpretation of contracts also often requires courts to infer obligations from the structure of the parties' relationship.

Because the Constitution established a nation to be governed by a designated governmental structure, this interpretive method is particularly suited to constitutional law. Black has thus argued that an inference from structure reconciles the Supreme Court's scrutiny of state regulation claimed to discriminate against INTERSTATE COMMERCE [2] with the absence in the constitutional texts of any explicit prohibition of such state conduct; the freedom of commerce from local discrimination is implicit in the economic structure of nationhood and the fact that "we are one people, commercially as otherwise. . . ." One can similarly infer some form of executive, legislative, or judicial privilege from the Constitution's SEPARATION OF POWERS [4]. Were one branch routinely to compel disclosure of the internal decisional consultations of another branch, the latter branch might find its decision making skewed and the exercise of its legitimate powers subject to substantial encroachment by the other branch. This result would be contrary to the Constitution's purpose of establishing separate and independent branches of government.

Drawing inferences from structure and relationships is thus a legitimate method of determining the intent of the Framers. This intent, of course, is not the Framers' conscious thoughts or expectations, but the adaptation of the general principle they sought to establish to particular factual situations. Indeed, unless a judge is willing to draw such inferences, the intent of the Framers may go unfulfilled. For example, as Black has argued, even if the First Amendment had not been adopted, a judge might legitimately conclude that the various provisions for free elections for federal office could not fulfill their purpose if either federal or state governments were free to prohibit speeches by candidates for federal office or their supporters. To effectuate the purposes of the electoral provisions—to effectuate original intent—some form of protection for political speech similar to First Amendment doctrine would have to be fashioned by courts.

Having concluded that neither the constitutional text, legislative history, nor inferences from structures and relationships address a claim of a right, originalists believe that courts should not recognize that right. Originalists thus typically argue that ROE V. WADE (1973) [3] was incorrectly decided because there is no evidence that either the generalized RIGHT TO PRIVACY [3,I] relied on in the decision's brief doctrinal discussion or the specific issue of ABORTION [1,I] has even been addressed by any constitutional provision. This view is fortified in the minds of originalists by the seeming disarray among *Wade*'s defenders as to the doctrinal basis for the decision, which ranges from an implied right of privacy protecting individual autonomy in sexual or procreative matters to the First Amendment's religion clause, to the equal protection clause, and to the THIRTEENTH AMENDMENT's [4] prohibition on involuntary servitude.

In some cases, evidence of purpose or inferences drawn from structures or relationships may yield no guidance for interpretation of a particular constitutional provision. In such a case, originalists believe that judges should accord no judicially enforceable meaning to that provision because the only available criteria for establishing that meaning are the judiciary's subjective views of what is good constitutional policy. Originalists thus typically view the NINTH AMENDMENT [3] ("The powers not delegated to the United States by the Constitution, nor prohibited by it to the States, are reserved to the states respectively, or to the people") or the PRIVILEGES AND IMMUNITIES [3] clause of the Fourteenth Amendment ("No state shall make or enforce any law which shall abridge the privileges or immunities of citizens of the United States") as such clauses. The language of these provisions does not make any cogent choice between alternative legal rules, and their history appears to lack any evidence of judicially enforceable purpose. This being the case, originalist theory holds that judges should not undertake to attribute meaning to these provisions. To the argument that the Framers may have intended that courts undertake the task of giving meaning to such clauses, originalists generally answer that there is nothing in the constitutional record to suggest that such substantial power was to be accorded to the judiciary.

On one issue—adherence to PRECEDENT [3]—originalist theory is unclear. As the preceding discussion has indicated, the interpretive school of originalism calls simply for the application of conventional legal criteria to constitutional interpretation. In nonconstitutional areas, such criteria certainly include judicial precedent. Thus, one does not infrequently encounter statutes whose interpretation over time seems to have departed rather far from their language or legislative purpose. The doctrine of stare decisis, however, generally precludes courts from undoing settled interpretations. Similarly, contractual clauses are used by lawyers to achieve particular purposes, even though the purposes and the particular language seem at best distantly related. Lawyers continue to use them, however, because courts have previously attributed to these clauses the purposes in question.

One would therefore expect interpretivists at least to put a heavy weight on precedent and to overrule precedent only infrequently. However, this expectation clashes with the argument that a reluctance to overrule precedent gives an advantage to those who would base constitutional decisions on criteria deemed by originalists to be invalid. Unless originalists are willing to overrule precedent, it can be argued, the Constitution will, over time, spawn a body of law considerably at odds with original intent. Indeed, Professor Monaghan has pointed out that much of present constitutional law "is at variance with what we know of the original understanding."

With regard to the criticism that originalism affords inadequate protection for profoundly important rights, originalists rarely answer with a denial. Originalism does not claim to offer a comprehensive formula for civilized rule or an optimal set of individual rights. Rather, it purports to offer the correct role for the judiciary in a democratic society. It posits that lodging the ultimate decision-making power of the state in a nonelected branch of government must ultimately subordinate the elected branches and subvert democratic rule itself. It denies the existence of a natural law that can be discovered and applied by judges in a manner consistent with democratic principles. Originalists see in the various attempts by scholars to fashion nonoriginalist criteria for constitutional decision making faintly disguised political movements seeking to achieve in court what they have been unable to secure in elections.

At bottom, then, originalism is based on the view that judges must confine their role to the application and enforcement of principles that have become constitutional law through the adoption of the Constitution or the amendment of the Constitution itself. Originalism is neutral with regard to particular rights in the sense that a persuasive argument that a right is necessary to civilized rule will not carry the day in court without an anchoring of that argument in the Constitution; nevertheless, originalism is not a nihilistic philosophy. Rather, it prizes democratic rule and demands that restrictions on this rule be the result of the adoption and amendment procedures set out in the Constitution. Originalists thus view the orderly democratic procedures of the Constitution as superior to claims of substantive rights that have not been adopted through such procedures. For originalists, rule by judiciary is not the road to civilized rule or optimal individual rights.

The future of originalism is unclear. The Senate's failure to confirm Judge Bork was based in part on the criticisms of originalism previously described. Many originalists are puzzled at the recent controversy over their view because many of their critics seem not to quarrel with the application of conventional legal criteria to other legal texts such as statutes or contracts. Moreover, originalists view their methodology as politically neutral. Nevertheless, the Bork controversy illustrated the difficulty of defending originalism in a political context. Because originalists do not believe that the Constitution enshrines every right necessary to avoid every wrong—including serious wrongs—originalists can be mistakenly perceived as favoring those wrongs. Judge Bork was thus depicted by some as favoring POLL TAXES [3] because he had written that such taxes did not violate the equal protection clause.

Originalists fear that the difficulty of defending their position politically will fundamentally alter the American system of government. In their view, judicial nominations and Senate confirmation proceedings may, in the worst-case scenario, become highly politicized in the sense that nominees may be required to make commitments about future decisions equivalent to political promises. These promises will be made to appease groups that seek to constitutionalize their claims and have sufficient political power to extract such promises. If so, originalists fear, constitutional law will become an incoherent body of rules having no connection with the document and resulting from random constellations of political forces and the idiosyncratic views of particular Supreme Court Justices.

RALPH K. WINTER

(SEE ALSO: *Conservatism* [I]; *Constitutional Theory* [I]; *Deconstructionism* [I]; *Liberalism* [I]; *Jurisprudence and Constitutional Law* [I]; *Noninterpretivism* [I]; *Pragmatism* [I]; *Textualism* [I].)

Bibliography

BLACK, CHARLES L. 1969 *Structure and Relationship in Constitutional Law.* Baton Rouge, La.: Louisiana State University Press.

BORK, ROBERT H. 1990 *The Tempting of America: The Political Seduction of the Law.* New York: Free Press.

FEDERALIST SOCIETY 1986 *Interpreting Our Written Constitution* (Occasional Paper No. 2). Washington, D.C.: The Federalist Society.

MCDOWELL, GARY 1985 *The Constitution and Contemporary Constitutional Theory.* Cumberland, Va.: Center for Judicial Studies.

MONAGHAN, HENRY 1981 Our Perfect Constitution. *New York University Law Review* 56:353–376.

OSBORNE v. OHIO (1990)

See: Child Pornography [I]

P

PARADISE, UNITED STATES v.
480 U.S. 149 (1987)

For several decades, the Alabama Department of Public Safety excluded blacks from employment as state troopers. Only after a federal district court imposed a hiring quota in the early 1970s did the department finally change its ways. Even then, however, the department failed to promote the black officers it hired. Thereafter, the district court again intervened, this time requiring the department to institute promotion procedures without an adverse impact on black officers. When the department failed to institute such procedures within a timely period, the court imposed a promotion quota until the department developed acceptable promotion procedures of its own. Under the court's scheme, one black officer had to be promoted for every white officer promoted. The United States challenged the court's order, claiming that it violated the EQUAL PROTECTION [2,I] clause of the FOURTEENTH AMENDMENT [2,I]. The Supreme Court disagreed and upheld the order 5–4.

Writing for a plurality, Justice WILLIAM J. BRENNAN [1,I] noted that members of the Court disagreed about what level of scrutiny to apply to discrimination remedy cases, but argued that this did not matter because the race-conscious remedy under review survived even the Court's highest standard of STRICT SCRUTINY [4] because it was "narrowly tailored" to serve a COMPELLING STATE INTEREST [1].

Rejecting the strict scrutiny approach in discrimination-remedy cases, Justice JOHN PAUL STEVENS [4,I] concurred in the judgment, but stressed that the federal judiciary has "broad and flexible authority" to fashion even race-conscious remedies once a violation of the Fourteenth Amendment has occurred.

Justice SANDRA DAY O'CONNOR [3,I] vigorously disagreed. Writing for three of the dissenters, O'Connor not only insisted that all remedies be subjected to strict scrutiny but she also took the plurality to task for adopting "a standardless view" of strict scrutiny's requirement that a remedy be narrowly tailored to accomplish its purpose. Maintaining that "there is simply no justification for the use of racial preferences if the purpose of the order could be achieved without their use," O'Connor argued there was no evidence that the district court considered any alternatives to the RACIAL QUOTA [3], even though several alternatives in fact existed, including an invocation of the court's CONTEMPT POWER [1].

JOHN G. WEST, JR.

(SEE ALSO: *Race-Consciousness* [I]; *Racial Discrimination* [3,I].)

PATENT
(Update)

A patent is a grant issued by the federal government that gives an inventor the right to exclude others from making, using, or selling his invention for a specific period of time. The historical purpose of granting these exclusive rights has not changed to this day: it is to encourage public disclosure of new scientific and technological developments that would have a favorable impact upon society and the economy.

The American patent system was largely based on early

European concepts. As far back as 1440, English "letters patent" were issued for a method of processing salt. Often, however, such royal grants of monopolies were offered not to encourage invention or business development but to reward court favorites. They generated a great deal of controversy and ultimately led to passage of the Statute of Monopolies (1623), which, by making a patent an exceptional case in which exclusive rights could be granted, restricted the crown's power to confer a monopoly.

The Framers of the Constitution, realizing the importance of stimulating science and technology, authorized Congress to establish and control a patent system. In September 1787 the CONSTITUTIONAL CONVENTION [1] adopted Article I, section 8: "The Congress shall have Power . . . To promote the Progress of Science and useful Arts, by securing for limited Times to Authors and Inventors the exclusive Right to their respective Writings and Discoveries."

Congress exercised this power by passing the Patent Act of 1790. The statute placed the burden of granting patents upon a committee made up of the secretary of state, the secretary of war, and the ATTORNEY GENERAL [1]. Secretary of State THOMAS JEFFERSON [3], an early champion of the idea that "ingenuity should receive liberal encouragement," became the first patent examiner.

For several decades there was no requirement that an inventor demonstrate his invention's patentability (its novelty and usefulness) in order to obtain exclusive rights. As a result, a patent was issued almost immediately upon receipt of an application. The process was modified in 1836, when the commissioner of patents was charged with examining every proposal to determine that an invention was both new and useful in concept (though not necessarily that it worked well in practice). These criteria are still applied, together with a requirement that the invention must be "unobvious to one skilled in the art."

Patents are to be distinguished from trademarks and COPYRIGHTS [2]; generally, the claiming of one does not preclude the claiming of any other, even though they may all apply to a single product. A copyright protects an author's original writing (the tangible expression of an idea). A trademark covers any words used to distinguish one product from another. For example, a computer's interior mechanism and software may be protected by a patent, its instruction manual by a copyright, and its market identification by a trademark. All three legal protections are now considered part of a larger jurisprudential framework called "intellectual property."

A patent may be obtained by anyone who invents or discovers a new, useful, and "unobvious" device or process. If a patent is granted, the inventor gains exclusive rights for a period of seventeen years (fourteen years for the developer of a new design). Any unauthorized manufacture, use, or sale of a patented device or design (or their equivalents) constitutes an infringement.

Patent cases begin at the district court level, may be appealed to the UNITED STATES COURT OF APPEALS FOR THE FEDERAL CIRCUIT [4], and can be reviewed by the Supreme Court. In *Graham v. John Deere Co. of Kansas City* (1968) the Court defined the three statutory conditions of patentability: novelty, usefulness, and nonobviousness. The classic modern doctrine of "equivalents" was described in *Graver Tank & Manufacturing Co. v. Linde Air Products Co.* (1950). One of the largest recent infringement cases was *Polaroid Corp. v. Eastman Kodak Co.* (1989).

KENNETH LASSON

Bibliography

CHISUM, DONALD S. 1978 *Patents: A Treatise on the Law of Patentability, Validity and Infringement.* New York: Matthew Bender.

DELLER, ANTHONY W. 1964 *Walker on Patents.* New York: Lawyers Co-operative.

LASSON, KENNETH 1986 *Mousetraps and Muffling Cups: One Hundred Brilliant and Bizarre United States Patents.* New York: Arbor House.

PATIENTS' RIGHTS

The constitutional status of patients' rights can be distilled into three general doctrinal propositions: First, there are constitutional constraints on state authority to force medical treatment on an unwilling person; second, when a person is in state custody (for whatever reason), the state is constitutionally obliged to provide at least minimally adequate health care; and third, the state is not otherwise constitutionally required to provide even a minimal level of health care to anyone. The Supreme Court has not been so solicitous, however, toward implementing the first and second propositions as it has been toward the third.

The Court long ago held, in JACOBSON V. MASSACHUSETTS (1905) [3] regarding smallpox vaccination, that an individual may be constitutionally subjected to involuntary medical treatment to protect community health. Beginning in the 1970s, in cases involving MENTAL ILLNESS [3,I], the Court found that forced treatment implicated FOURTEENTH AMENDMENT "liberty" interests and, accordingly, required the state to demonstrate, by "clear and convincing evidence," both the existence of mental illness and some measure of harm either to the affected individual or others that would follow without treatment. The principal decisions in this area were O'CONNOR V. DONALDSON (1975) [3] and *Addington v. Texas* (1979). The Court, however, has not been expansive in applying the "liberty" principle to require state respect for individuals' autonomous choice to refuse treatment even where the possibility of harm appears limited to themselves alone.

Two 1990 decisions exemplify this restrictive construction. In *Washington v. Harper* (1990) the Court ruled that a prisoner could be forced to take psychotropic medication without any judicial determination of his or her need for the medication or mental competency to refuse it. While the Court acknowledged the existence of a "significant liberty interest" and said that the state's purposes in forcibly administering the medication must be "therapeutic" rather than "punitive," the Court found that internal administrative determinations made by prison psychiatric professionals would be adequate to protect the PRISONER'S RIGHTS [3,1].

Cruzan v. Missouri Department of Health (1990) considered the rights of patients to refuse medical treatment in an apparently different context; and yet, the result, in the Court's restricted construction of the liberty interest at stake, seems strikingly similar. In *Cruzan*, the patient was in a state hospital, having been without cognitive function (in a "persistent vegetative state") since an automobile accident seven years earlier. Hospital staff refused to discontinue medical treatment without judicial authorization, notwithstanding the request of the patient's parents, and the state court found that there was no "clear and convincing evidence" that patient herself would have wanted termination of treatment. The Supreme Court ruled that a competent adult had a Fourteenth Amendment liberty interest against unconsented medical care, but that the state was free to erect stringent evidentiary standards in evaluating claims on behalf of incompetent patients.

There were special factors in these two cases that might have limited the Court's inclination to apply the liberty interest that it abstractly had endorsed. In *Harper*, the Court cited "legitimate needs of institutional confinement," including state "interests in prison safety and security," as a basis for withholding application of the prisoner's claimed right to refuse medication; there was, however, no specific factual finding that the prisoner's condition endangered prison safety or security. In *Cruzan*, the autonomy claim was advanced on behalf of an obviously incompetent patient; there was, however, evidence (which the state court refused to credit) that before her incapacitating accident, the patient had explicitly opposed such medical treatment. In accepting the restrictive evidentiary standard, the Supreme Court was apparently unconcerned with the practical likelihood that most people will not make clear prior indications of their wishes regarding medical treatment (notwithstanding the statutory recognition in many states of so-called "living wills"). The Court, moreover, referred favorably to the state's interest in prohibiting suicide, a reference that suggests that the state is free to impose stringent mental competency tests on individuals who, unlike Cruzan, have current capacity to articulate their resistance to treatment—tests so stringent as to undermine in practice the liberty interest to refuse medical treatment that the Court abstractly endorsed.

The Court may, however, be more hospitable to the practical implementation of patients' right to refuse treatment in future cases than it was in *Harper* or *Cruzan*. Indeed, there were strong dissents in both cases (three in *Harper* and four in *Cruzan*) urging respect for the refusal rights and although Justice SANDRA DAY O'CONNOR [3,1] concurred in the Court's opinion in *Cruzan*, she wrote separately to suggest that states may be constitutionally required to respect not only prior formal statements made by an individual, as in a "living will," but also the wishes of a surrogate decision maker who had been formally designated by the individual before incapacitating illness.

As in the current constitutional doctrine regarding a patient's right to refuse treatment, there is a disjunction in the Supreme Court's case law between the abstract formulation that the state must provide medical treatment to persons in its custody and the specific standards adopted to assure practical implementation of that right. The disjunction was visible on the face of the first opinion in which the Court announced that prisoners have a right to medical treatment: In *Estelle v. Gamble* (1976) the Court held that failure to provide necessary treatment could constitute CRUEL AND UNUSUAL PUNISHMENT [2,1] in violation of the Eighth Amendment, but only if such failure amounted to a "deliberate indifference to serious medical needs." Similarly, in *Youngberg v. Romeo* (1982), the Court found that a resident of a state mental retardation institution had a constitutional right to receive "minimally adequate or reasonable training" programs; at the same time, however, the Court held that in determining the minimal standards for adequacy of reasonableness, judges must defer to medical and behavioral professionals. (Indeed, in Chief Justice WILLIAM H. REHNQUIST'S [3,1] opinion for the Court in *Cruzan*, the force even of this minimally bestowed treatment right was subtly undermined with the observation that "the liberty interest" in *Youngberg* addressed only "safety and freedom from bodily restraint [and] did not deal with decisions to administer or withhold medical treatment.")

Whatever the uncertainties of its acknowledgment of the right to refuse medical treatment or the right to receive treatment while in state custody, the Court has been quite clear in rejecting the existence of any generally applicable constitutional right for the provision of medical services. The Court explicitly stated in *Youngberg* that there was no such right to "substantive services." In MAHER V. ROE

(1977) [3] and HARRIS V. MCRAE (1980) [2], moreover, the Court had held that neither state nor federal governments are constitutionally required to provide ABORTIONS [1,I] for women who are INDIGENT [2]; although these cases were colored by the surrounding public controversy about whether abortion should be considered an ordinary medical procedure, the decisions are nonetheless consistent with the Court's long-standing resistance to finding any constitutional ENTITLEMENTS [I] not only for medical care but for WELFARE BENEFITS [4] generally.

In *Cruzan* none of the other Court members joined with Justice ANTONIN SCALIA [I] in his separate statement that "the Constitution has nothing to say" about the right to refuse medical treatment. Notwithstanding the pervasive role of state and federal governments in the provision and regulation of health care, however, the Constitution—as currently construed by the Supreme Court—says very little about patients' rights generally.

ROBERT A. BURT

(SEE ALSO: *Right to Die* [I].)

Bibliography

ANNAS, GEORGE J.; LAW, SYLVIA; ROSENBLATTE, RAND; and WING, KENNETH 1990 *American Health Law.* Chapter VI, "Patients' Rights," pages 561–666. Boston: Little, Brown.
KATZ, JAY 1984 *The Silent World of Doctor and Patient.* New York: Free Press.

PATRONAGE AND THE CONSTITUTION

See: *Elrod v. Burns* [2]; *Rutan v. Republican Party of Illinois* [1]

PATTERSON v. McLEAN CREDIT UNION
109 S.Ct. 2363 (1989)

This decision's constitutional significance lies in what the Supreme Court did not do. The CIVIL RIGHTS ACT OF 1866 [1] guarantees "all persons . . . the same right . . . to make and enforce contracts . . . as is enjoyed by white persons." In RUNYON V. MCCRARY (1976) [3] the Court had held that this provision not only required a state to give blacks and whites the same legal rights in contracting but also forbade private racial discrimination in the making of contracts. Later decisions had applied the same section to employment contracts. *Patterson* raised the issue of whether this section gave a black employee a right to damages against her employer for acts of racial harassment. In 1988, after oral argument on this issue and without

any prompting from the parties, a 5–4 majority of the Court set the case down for reargument and asked the parties to consider whether *Runyon v. McCrary* should be overruled.

Four Justices bitterly dissented from this order, and outside the Court a clamor of protest rose. The majority that supported the order consisted of the two *Runyon* dissenters and the three Justices appointed by President RONALD REAGAN [3,I], and the order appeared to be the opening salvo in an assault on some of the major gains of the CIVIL RIGHTS MOVEMENT [I]. If *Runyon* were overruled, why should the Court not overrule JONES V. ALFRED H. MAYER CO. (1968) [3]? *Jones* was the landmark decision that (1) interpreted a parallel provision of the 1866 Act to forbid private racial discrimination in the disposition of property, and (2) upheld the law, as so interpreted, on the basis of Congress's power to enforce the THIRTEENTH AMENDMENT [4]. The latter possibility seems, in retrospect, to have been unlikely, but the depth of concern is understandable. Sixty-six United States senators and 118 representatives filed a brief urging the Court not to overrule *Runyon*, and so did the attorneys general of forty-seven states.

In the event, the Court unanimously reaffirmed the *Runyon* PRECEDENT [3]. The majority opinion (the same majority that had agreed on the reargument order) simply applied the doctrine of STARE DECISIS [4]. The Court went on to read the 1866 act extremely narrowly, rejecting the conclusion of most lower federal courts that the law allowed damages for a private employer's racial harassment of an employee.

Patterson's narrow interpretation of the 1866 act is vulnerable to criticism, as the opinion of the four dissenters and Congress's recent effort to overturn it both attest. But the Court's reaffirmation of *Runyon* stands as the doctrinal consolidation of a broad political consensus on CIVIL RIGHTS [1] that had seemed threatened in the 1980s.

KENNETH L. KARST

Bibliography

KARST, KENNETH L. 1989 Private Discrimination and Public Responsibility: Patterson in Context. *Supreme Court Review* 1989:1–51.

PENRY v. LYNAUGH
492 U.S. 302 (1989)

In this case on the prohition against CRUEL AND UNUSUAL PUNISHMENT [2,I] imposed by the Eighth Amendment and the FOURTEENTH AMENDMENT [2,I], the Court ruled that to inflict CAPITAL PUNISHMENT [1,I] on a mentally retarded prisoner was not necessarily unconstitutional. The Court, speaking through Justice SANDRA DAY O'CONNOR [3,I], also held that the ban on cruel and unusual punishments would be violated in a capital case if the sentencing jury were not instructed to consider all circumstances mitigating against the imposition of the death penalty. In this case, the jury had not properly considered whether Penry's MENTAL RETARDATION [3] and history of childhood abuse diminished his moral culpability and made capital punishment a disproportionate sentence. Because the Eighth Amendment mandates an individualized assessment of the appropriateness of the death penalty, no mitigating factor may be withheld from the jury. Punishment must be directly related to the personal culpability of the criminal. Accordingly, the Court vacated the death sentence and remanded the case for resentencing under proper jury instruction.

Nonetheless, Justice O'Connor, for the Court, rejected Penry's second claim, ruling that the Eighth Amendment does not categorically prohibit the execution of a criminal who is mentally retarded. One who is profoundly or severely retarded and wholly lacking in the capacity to understand the wrongfulness of his or her actions cannot, in the face of the amendment, be executed. But the degree of mental retardation must be considered. In Penry's case, that of an adult with the reasoning capacity of a child not more than seven years of age, there was some proof that his diminished abilities disabled him from controlling his impulses and learning from his mistakes; yet a jury could properly conclude that his disabilities did not substantially reduce his level of blameworthiness for a capital offense. The Court refused to accept mental age as a line-drawing principle in such cases.

Four dissenters argued that the execution of mentally retarded prisoners invariably violates the "cruel and unusual punishment" clause because such people lack the culpability that is prerequisite to the proportionate imposition of the death penalty.

The *Penry* decision also made law on the subject of HABEAS CORPUS [2,I] relief in federal courts, extending the nonretroactivity principle of *Teague v. Lane* (1989) to capital cases.

LEONARD W. LEVY

PEYOTE, RELIGIOUS USE OF

See: *Employment Division, Department of Human Resources v. Smith* [I]

PLAIN VIEW DOCTRINE
(Update)

Under the plain view doctrine of COOLIDGE V. NEW HAMPSHIRE (1971) [2], certain items found in a lawful search may be seized without a SEARCH WARRANT [4]

though they were not among the items that were legitimate objectives of the search. Though this issue also arises in other contexts, it most frequently comes into play when police, executing a search warrant naming certain things to be seized, find and immediately seize other items unnamed in the warrant.

The Supreme Court in *Coolidge* declined to hold that in such circumstances the police must always seek another warrant, reasoning that such a procedure "would often be a needless inconvenience, and sometimes dangerous—to the evidence or to the police themselves." At the same time, the Court was not prepared to uphold warrantless seizures made either without PROBABLE CAUSE [3] or as a consequence of an earlier circumvention of the warrant requirement, as where the police intended from the very beginning to seize the unnamed objects. Consequently, the *Coolidge* plurality concluded that a warrantless seizure was permissible only if three requirements were met: (1) there must have been a prior valid intrusion into the place where the seized evidence was found; (2) the discovery of the seized items must have been "inadvertent"; and (3) it must have been "immediately apparent" that the seized items were evidence of crime.

The *Coolidge* plurality did not explain what it meant by "inadvertent." It did not state explicitly what degree of expectation would make the subsequent discovery of an item other than inadvertent. Most lower courts took the inadvertent-discovery limitation to mean that a discovery is inadvertent, without regard to the hopes or expectations of the police, if there were not sufficient grounds to get a search warrant for that item. Moreover, for probable cause to nullify an inadvertent claim those grounds must have been in the hands of the police at a time when it would have been feasible to obtain a warrant, for otherwise the police cannot be faulted for failing to obtain a warrant also naming the seized item.

Even so interpreted, the inadvertent-discovery limitation is unsound. It is a limitation on seizure, not search, and thus protects possessory interests only, not privacy interests. Yet, one consequence of the inadvertence requirement is that lawfully discovered items seized on probable cause may be excluded merely because the officer, out of an abundance of caution, failed to seek a magistrate's approval for a more intrusive search through the premises for those items. If, as the Court declared in HOFFA V. UNITED STATES (1966) [2], "the police are not required to guess at their peril the precise moment at which they have probable cause," this result is not a desirable one. Such a result will no longer obtain, for in *Horton v. California* (1990) the Court rejected the inadvertent-discovery limitation on the plain view doctrine.

The "immediately apparent" limitation does not require the police to be certain of the incriminating character of the seized object; probable cause will suffice. But when must this probable cause become apparent? Assume a case in which police executing a search warrant for stolen stereo equipment see in the searched premises a television set. They turn the television set around to expose its serial number, and then determine that the number matches that of a set recently reported stolen. Many courts interpreted *Coolidge* to mean that such movement of the television set, though not authorized by the warrant, was nonetheless a lawful search if undertaken upon reasonable suspicion that the set was stolen. The appealing rationale of these cases was that the slight movement of the object to examine its exterior was such a minimal intrusion upon FOURTH AMENDMENT [2,I] interests as to not require full probable cause.

Though these decisions arguably found support in the Supreme Court's decision in *United States v. Place* (1983), holding that personal effects in transit such as luggage could be briefly detained for investigation upon mere reasonable suspicion, the Court in *Arizona v. Hicks* (1987) held that *Coolidge's* "immediately apparent" requirement means full probable cause must exist before the television set is even moved. The Court in *Hicks* reasoned that such movement was part of "a dwelling-place search," for which full probable cause had always been required, and distinguished such cases as *Place* on the ground that the "special operational necessities" existing there were not present. *Hicks* made the plain view doctrine of the *Coolidge* plurality a doctrine endorsed by a majority of the Justices, and *Hicks* held that the doctrine may not be invoked when the police have less than probable cause to believe that an item should be seized as evidence of crime.

WAYNE LaFAVE

(SEE ALSO: *Search and Seizure* [4,I]; *Unreasonable Search* [4,I]; *Warrantless Searches* [4].)

Bibliography

LaFAVE, WAYNE R.   1987   *Search and Seizure: A Treatise on the Fourth Amendment*, 2nd ed. St. Paul, Minn.: West Publishing Co.
MOYLAN, CHARLES E.   1975   The Plain View Doctrine: Unexpected Child of the Great Search Incident Geography Battle. *Mercer Law Review* 26:1047–1101.

POLICE INTERROGATION AND CONFESSIONS
(Update)

The government must comply with three constitutional requirements to use a confession against a defendant in a criminal case: a voluntariness requirement, a RIGHT TO

COUNSEL [3] requirement, and a warning requirement.

A court will refuse to admit into evidence a confession that was not voluntarily made by the defendant for two reasons. First, an involuntary confession may not be reliable. Second, the DUE PROCESS [1] clauses of the Fifth Amendment and FOURTEENTH AMENDMENT [2,I] and the Fifth Amendment's RIGHT AGAINST SELF-INCRIMINATION [3,I] prevent the government from using unconscionable methods to induce a person to confess to criminal activity.

A confession is not "involuntary" unless the police obtained the confession through means that were unfair and coercive. Thus, if the police use physical force, or the threat of physical force, against the defendant or against the defendant's family or friends in order to make a defendant confess to a crime, the defendant's confession is involuntary. The police may use a confession that they gained by lying to, or tricking, the defendant so long as the lies or tricks were not both unfair and coercive. A judicial finding of coercive police activity is a prerequisite to finding that a confession should be excluded from evidence under the voluntariness test. In *Colorado v. Connelly* (1986) the Supreme Court ruled that the government could use a confession from a man who, according to psychiatric testimony offered at trial, suffered from a psychosis that reduced his ability to invoke his right to remain silent when he was asked a question by police officers. The Supreme Court held that the defendant's statements were voluntary because the police had not used any unfair and coercive tactics to obtain his statement.

The Sixth Amendment guarantees each defendant a right to counsel. It does not restrict government questioning of a suspect prior to the time that criminal proceedings have been initiated against that suspect. However, the right to counsel is violated when the government actively elicits information from a defendant outside the presence of his attorney after the beginning of criminal proceedings.

The Sixth Amendment does not protect a defendant who voluntarily gives information to a government employee who did not actively elicit that information but only listened to the defendant's statement. Thus, after a defendant has been charged with a crime and placed in a jail cell, the police may place a government informant disguised as a prisoner in the cell with the defendant. If the informant asks the defendant questions, the defendant's answers cannot be used against the defendant at trial. If the informant does not actively elicit information from the defendant, and the defendant makes incriminating statements to the informant, the defendant's incriminating statements may be used against him at his trial.

In *Patterson v. Illinois* (1988) the Supreme Court ruled that a defendant who agreed to waive his Sixth Amendment right to counsel after he was given the *Miranda* warnings had made a knowing and intelligent waiver of his right to counsel and that his subsequent confession could be used against him. All questions whether a defendant waived his constitutional rights prior to confessing to a crime are to be determined by reference to the MIRANDA RULES [3,I], which comprise the third limitation on confessions.

In MIRANDA V. ARIZONA (1966) [3] the Supreme Court held that the police may not interrogate a person who is in police custody (or who has otherwise been deprived of his freedom by the police) unless the police clearly inform the person (1) that he has a right to remain silent; (2) that anything he says may be used against him in court; (3) that he has the right to an attorney and to have an attorney present during any questioning; and (4) that an attorney will be appointed for him if he is INDIGENT [2].

What happens after the suspect is given the *Miranda* warnings? If, following the *Miranda* warnings, the defendant "knowingly" and "intelligently" waives his right to remain silent and his right to an attorney, the police may interrogate him, and his subsequent confession may be used against him. If the person in custody indicates (either before or during the interrogation) that he does not want to talk to the police, the police must stop questioning the person. However, if the defendant has not requested an attorney, the police may at a later time give the defendant the *Miranda* warnings again and ask whether the defendant will waive his rights and talk with them. If the defendant says either before or during questioning that he wants to meet with an attorney, the police may not question the defendant at any later time, or ask the defendant at a later time to waive his rights, until the defendant has met with an attorney.

In the 1980s the Supreme Court ruled that a defendant's WAIVER OF CONSTITUTIONAL RIGHTS [4] after the *Miranda* warnings would be effective unless the police had used unfair and coercive methods to secure his waiver. In *Colorado v. Spring* (1987) the Court held that a defendant who had waived his rights after receiving the *Miranda* warnings did not have a right to be informed as to the nature of the charges that might be brought against him or the nature of the crime that was being investigated. In *Moran v. Burbine* (1986) the Court held that a defendant made a "knowing and intelligent" waiver of his rights following *Miranda* warnings, so that his statements could be used against him at trial, even though the police who gave him the warnings failed to tell him that an attorney had attempted to contact him.

The police are not required to use any specific set of words to inform the defendant of his rights so long as the statements made by the police to the defendant encompass the substance of the *Miranda* warnings. For example,

in *Duckworth v. Eagan* (1989) the police gave the defendant the *Miranda* warnings and then added, "We have no way of giving a lawyer, but one will be appointed for you, if you wish, if and when you go to court." The Supreme Court found that the statement did not undercut the substance of the *Miranda* warnings because it did not induce the defendant to waive his rights to forgo the presence of counsel at questioning. Therefore, the defendant's subsequent waiver of his rights was a valid waiver; his confession could be used against him.

In the 1980s confession cases, the Supreme Court was lenient in admitting into evidence incriminating statements made by defendants so long as the police did not engage in any coercive activity. However, the Court continues to protect the integrity of the adversary process by requiring police to honor a defendant's request for an attorney and to avoid any attempt at gaining information from a defendant outside of the presence of his counsel after judicial proceedings have been instituted against the defendant.

JOHN NOWAK

Bibliography

KAMIZAR, YALE; LAFAVE, WAYNE R.; and ISRAEL, JEROLD H. 1990 *Modern Criminal Procedure: Cases, Comments, and Questions*, 7th ed. St. Paul, Minn.: West Publishing Co.

LAFAVE, WAYNE R. and ISRAEL, JEROLD H. 1985 *Criminal Procedure*. St. Paul, Minn.: West Publishing Co.

POLITICAL ACTION COMMITTEES

For political action committees (PACs) and for all other contributors to campaigns for public office, the modern constitutional era began in 1976 with the Supreme Court's decision in BUCKLEY V. VALEO [1]. In sorting out the constitutionality of the many parts of the FEDERAL ELECTION CAMPAIGN ACT (FECA) [2] of 1971 and 1974, the Court reaffirmed the protections of the FIRST AMENDMENT'S [2,I] FREEDOM OF ASSEMBLY AND ASSOCIATION [2] for PACs, citing a long line of precedents that included NAACP V. ALABAMA (1958) [3]. The Court further held all campaign contributions and expenditures to be the expression of political views and thus protected by the First Amendment.

The protections of the First Amendment notwithstanding, the Court permitted much of the congressional regulation of PACs in the FECA to stand as a legitimate exercise of Congress's right to prevent "corruption or the appearance of corruption." All PAC contributions are limited to $5,000 per candidate per election. Moreover, in *California Medical Association v. FEC* (1981), Congress was within its constitutional powers in forbidding them to accept more than $5,000 per year from any group or individual. But because the Court in *Buckley* extended greater protections to campaign spending than to campaign contributions, PACs are free to pursue unregulated independent spending in campaigns—spending done, that is, without the cooperation or knowledge of the candidate being aided.

For a subset of PACs, those with sponsoring parent organizations, the burden of regulation is heavier. If a parent organization is a corporation or labor union, it is (and has long been) prohibited under federal law (and the laws of some states) from making direct political expenditures. The PAC, then, must be a "separate, segregated fund" that raises its own money for its political spending. The parent organization, however, is free under federal law to pay the overhead costs of the PAC and to direct its decisions. PACs with parent organizations are further restricted by law in their fund-raising: PACSs of membership organizations may solicit only their members; with a few rarely used exceptions, union PACs may solicit only their members; and corporate PACs may solicit only stockholders and nonunion employees. These limits were upheld in *FEC v. National Right to Work Committee* (1982).

Even though the major constitutional precedents in this area have arisen largely in cases under the FECA, they apply to state legislation as well—with one exception. In *Citizens Against Rent Control v. Berkeley* (1981) the Court ruled that those states with initiative and referendum elections are less free to limit PAC contributions in those elections. Because no potential officeholders receive campaign funds during such elections, there is no possibility of the campaign contributions eventually corrupting public officials.

By 1988 there were 4,268 PACs registered under federal law as against 608 in 1974; their contributions to congressional candidates had jumped from $12.5 million in 1974 to $148.1 million in 1988. That growth has given rise to proposals for new restrictions, proposals that have raised new constitutional questions. President GEORGE BUSH [I] in 1989 proposed that PACs with parent organizations be banned. No details were forthcoming, but certainly an outright ban would raise serious constitutional issues, more than, say, a change in the law to prohibit parent organizations from paying PAC overhead costs. Other common proposals would cut the limit on PAC contributions to candidates from $5,000 to $3,500 or even lower. One must determine, however, at what point restrictions on contributions become an invasion of First Amendment rights. Still other proposals would limit the total receipts a candidate might accept from PACs. As limits on receipts appear to stand logically between limits on contributions and limits on spending, these, too, would appear to be in a zone of constitutional uncertainty.

Clearly, the Supreme Court has not moved very far into the balancing of the legitimate regulatory interests of Congress and the First Amendment rights of PACs. It has in fact dealt only with one extended piece of legislation at one point in time; Congress has passed no major regulation of PACs since 1976, and the states began to do so only in the late 1980s. New issues will reach the courts (e.g., state limits on candidates' receipts from PACs), forcing new constitutional interpretations. Moreover, the changing status quo in campaign finance, and especially the growth of PACs, put old rules and precedents in a new legislative context.

FRANK J. SORAUF

(SEE ALSO: *Campaign Finance* [1,I].)

Bibliography

GOTTLIEB, STEPHEN E. 1985 Fleshing Out the Right of Association: The Problem of the Contribution Limits of the Federal Election Campaign Act. *Albany Law Review* 49:825–854.

SORAUF, FRANK J. 1986 Caught in a Political Thicket: The Supreme Court and Campaign Finance. *Constitutional Commentary* 3:97–121.

POLITICAL PARTIES, ELECTIONS, AND CONSTITUTIONAL LAW

Since the mid-1980s the Supreme Court has decided three significant FIRST AMENDMENT [2,I] cases affecting POLITICAL PARTIES [3] and one that will hamper states' efforts to reform the INITIATIVE [2] process.

In *Tashjian v. Republican Party of Connecticut* (1986), the REPUBLICAN PARTY [I] sought to "open" its PRIMARY ELECTION [3] for high-level offices by permitting independent voters to participate, but the Democratic legislature refused to modify statutes limiting participation to party registrants. The Supreme Court held that the First Amendment FREEDOM OF ASSOCIATION [2] guarantees a party the right to control its own nomination process; it therefore ruled that state law could not prohibit the Republicans from opening their primary.

Tashjian was a mixed blessing for adherents of the party-renewal movement, who were pleased by the extension of association rights to parties but who tend to favor a closed primary as more conducive to strong political parties with relatively sharp ideological focus. The party renewalists welcomed more uniformly the Court's unanimous decision in *Eu v. San Francisco County Democratic Central Committee* (1989), which relied on the parties' right of association to rule that state legislation can neither prevent party committees from endorsing candidates in primary elections nor require a particular governing structure for party organizations.

In *Tashjian* and *Eu*, the Court ignored a point that has been made by numerous commentators, that the extension of rights of association to parties is in tension with *Smith v. Allwright* (1944) and other cases, which treated parties, at least when they are conducting primary elections, as instrumentalities of the state for purposes of the doctrine of STATE ACTION [4,I]. Within the logic of the state action doctrine, it may be anomalous for the same entity to be treated as part of the state and yet to enjoy constitutional rights against the state. Nevertheless, the conclusion that parties should be protected by the First Amendment and at the same time barred from denying EQUAL PROTECTION [2,I] and other constitutional rights to citizens is not likely to offend many people.

A more serious deficiency in the Court's approach is its failure to recognize that party associational claims may reflect intraparty disputes rather than the typical CIVIL LIBERTIES [1,I] claim by a private person against the state. This was not the case in *Tashjian*, where, as Justice THURGOOD MARSHALL [3,I] noted in his majority opinion, a united Republican party was prevented from opening its primary by Democratic legislators. But in *Eu* the statutes governing each major party reflected the wishes of that party's delegation in the state legislature.

Eu establishes that over some range of decision making affecting parties, the wishes of state party committees or other extragovernmental party structures will prevail when they conflict with the wishes of the party's elected officials as reflected in state legislation. Mere invocation of the concept of freedom of association cannot establish that this result will strengthen parties in the long run or have other desirable consequences.

In RUTAN V. REPUBLICAN PARTY OF ILLINOIS (1990) [I], the Court significantly extended the range of its antipatronage doctrine. In *Elrod v. Burns* (1976) and BRANTI V. FINKEL (1980) [1], the Court had held that to fire nonpolicymaking PUBLIC EMPLOYEES [3] because of nonaffiliation with the party in power violated the employees' First Amendment rights of speech and association. In *Rutan* this principle was extended to transfers, promotions, and even hiring of public employees based on party affiliation.

Whereas *Tashjian* and *Eu* have been welcomed by many as empowering parties, *Rutan* has been criticized as weakening them. As Justice LEWIS F. POWELL [3,I] argued in dissent in *Elrod*, the prospect of reward often has been a stronger inducement to party activism than ideological conviction, and at many times and in many places, the main reward for party service has been public employment.

It may be doubted whether any of the recent party decisions actually will have the pro- or antiparty effects

that have been ascribed to them. The actual points at issue in *Tashjian* and *Eu*—open or closed primaries, party endorsements in primary elections, details of party governance—are not likely to have more than marginal consequences for the American party system. For example, some have hoped that the availability of party endorsements in primaries would permit party organizations to impose party discipline on public officials. But in the first primary held in California after the *Eu* decision, the Republican party opted not to make endorsements and the two statewide candidates in competitive races who were endorsed by the Democratic party were losers in the primary.

If *Tashjian* and *Eu* were extended to the point that parties could not be required by state law to use primaries at all to select their candidates, the effect on the American system could be considerable. Though Justice ANTONIN SCALIA [I] argued in dissent that just such a result was implied by *Tashjian*, there is no reason to expect the majority to press its reasoning that far. Even if it does, perhaps few, if any, party organizations would opt for nomination processes that could be perceived as less democratic than primaries.

The patronage cases, if enforced in a different era, might have had major effects. Even by the time of *Elrod*, patronage practices had declined sharply in most parts of the United States. *Rutan* may deliver a deathblow to patronage more surely than *Elrod* did, but even so, its effects on the political system should be limited to relatively few localities.

Meyer v. Grant (1988), though not affecting political parties, will be a significant restraint in those states whose STATE CONSTITUTIONS [4] provide for the initiative process. *Meyer* struck down a Colorado statute that prohibited the use of paid circulators to qualify initiative measures for the ballot.

Meyer came just as the "initiative industry" was exploding in California and beginning to spread to other initiative states. This industry assures a ballot position for proponents with deep pockets while rendering volunteer petition drives virtually obsolete.

As popular resistance grows to increased numbers of initiative measures proposed by well-funded but sometimes narrowly based groups, state legislatures are likely to look for ways of evading *Meyers v. Grant* or, if no such ways can be found, to increase the signature requirements as a means of cutting the number of proposals that qualify for the ballot.

DANIEL HAYS LOWENSTEIN

Bibliography

EPSTEIN, LEON D. 1986 *Political Parties in the American Mold*. Madison: University of Wisconsin Press.

LOWENSTEIN, DANIEL HAYS and STERN, ROBERT M.   1989
    The First Amendment and Paid Initiative Petition Circulators:
    A Dissenting View and a Proposal. *Hastings Constitutional
    Law Quarterly* 17:175–224.

POLITICAL PHILOSOPHY OF THE CONSTITUTION
(Update)

To speak of the political philosophy of the Constitution is to invite immediate controversy. Many allege that the Constitution has no coherent political philosophy; and those who maintain otherwise often regard its political philosophy as far from commendable.

Those who contend that the Constitution is theoretically incoherent point to its various inconsistences and the many provisions that were the products of compromise. The more charitable of such analysts try to make a virtue of the Constitution's supposed lack of an overarching political theory, arguing that this demonstrates the Framers' laudable ability to ignore their own prejudices. In the words of law professor Donald Horowitz: "What we ought to revere is the spirit of compromise the Framers brought to Philadelphia—compromise that accommodated large states and small, north and south, numbers and wealth, legislative supremacists and proponents of a strong executive."

Probably the most significant obstacle to this view is presented by THE FEDERALIST [2], the contemporaneous exposition of the Constitution by ALEXANDER HAMILTON [2], JAMES MADISON [3], and JOHN JAY [3]. Written during the turmoil of the battle for RATIFICATION [3], *The Federalist* presents a remarkably comprehensive and coherent exposition of the constitutional system, fleshing out its fundamental principles of NATURAL RIGHTS [3], CHECKS AND BALANCES [2], BICAMERALISM [1], SEPARATION OF POWERS [4], and FEDERALISM [2]. *The Federalist*, which was utilized extensively by ratification proponents, goes a long way toward explaining the shared principles that underlay the compromises of the CONSTITUTIONAL CONVENTION OF 1787 [1].

Perhaps a more challenging attack on the coherence of the Constitution comes from those who juxtapose its REPUBLICANISM [I] with its sanction of SLAVERY [4]. Article IV, section 2, effectively compelled northern states to return fugitive slaves to their southern masters; and Article I, section 9, protected the importation of slaves until 1808. Many of those who criticize the Constitution on this account accuse the Founders of having a contradictory understanding of inalienable rights, claiming that the Founders did not think such rights applied to black Americans.

These critics often cite as evidence for this proposition Justice ROGER BROOKE TANEY's [4] assertion in DRED SCOTT V. SANDFORD (1857) [2] that the Founders regarded black Americans "as beings . . . so inferior, that they had no rights the white man was bound to respect."

Yet Taney's claim in *Dred Scott* was a palpable fiction, one that Taney himself had rejected as defense counsel for an abolitionist preacher earlier in his career. In reality, the Founders were not inconsistent in understanding the principle of inalienable rights; but they were inconsistent in applying it, as they themselves recognized. Slaveholders such as GEORGE WASHINGTON [4] and THOMAS JEFFERSON [3] knew that slavery abrogated the natural rights on which the Constitution was premised and therefore had to be abolished. The question was how to abolish slavery. Although it is easy to condemn the Framers for their compromise on this issue, one may legitimately wonder how much longer the horrible oppression of slavery would have lasted if the bargain had not been struck and the South had stayed out of the Union.

Incoherency, however, is not the only charge leveled against the political philosophy of the Constitution. Other critics chide the Founders for creating a constitutional system that cannot sustain itself because it is based almost entirely on self-interest. They claim that the philosophy of the Constitution is best summarized by the statement in *The Federalist* #51 that one must supply "by opposite and rival interests, the defect of better motives." According to these observers, the two pillars of the constitutional system are the extended republic, which fosters such a multiplicity of factions that it will be difficult for any one of them to dominate the rest, and the separation of powers, which similarly aims at preventing any single faction from controlling the government by dividing and arranging "the several offices in such a manner as that each may be a check on the other—that the private interest of every individual may be a sentinel over the public rights."

According to this view, the Founders thought that if the Constitution was properly structured to rely on self-interest, good character on the part of citizens would become expendable. This thesis has been maintained, more or less vigorously, by a variety of scholars from across the political spectrum, including Richard Hofstadter, Benjamin Barber, and Martin Diamond. Yet there are grave difficulties with this interpretation, not the least of which is its negative formulation of the Constitution's principles. According to these critics, devices such as bicameralism, checks and balances, and separation of powers use self-interest to prevent a tyrannical concentration of authority. But this is only part of the story. The Framers also believed that these devices would promote good government by attracting virtuous leaders to federal office and by supplying those leaders with the tools needed to perform their governmental duties properly.

Nowhere can this be seen more clearly than in the separation of powers. The Framers believed that powers should be separated not only to prevent tyranny, but also because the executive, legislative, and judicial powers require by their very natures different talents in order to be exercised well. The executive power requires the capacity for energy, secrecy, and quick and decisive action; the legislative power demands deliberation, or the free and full consideration of diverging points of view; and the judicial power calls for a cool and dispassionate application of the laws. The Framers of the Constitution subsequently structured each of the three branches of government in such a way as to encourage these characteristics. The Framers provided for a unitary executive, believing that this would facilitate quick and decisive action. They created a bicameral legislature to promote the best kind of deliberation. Finally, they provided that federal judges would hold their posts during GOOD BEHAVIOR [2], thus insulating them from the partisan battles of the moment and promoting the impartial and dispassionate application of the laws.

In sum, the Framers sought to supply each branch of government with the tools necessary to carry out its assigned tasks in the best manner possible. Of course, this was not the same as assuring each branch *would* carry out its duties in the best manner possible. A despot elected President, for example, might use the power to pardon to shield the criminal activities of his or her subordinates; unscrupulous senators might hold presidential appointments hostage to extract special favors from the executive branch; and corrupt judges might use their lifetime tenure as a shield for their corruption. Thus, the structure of the various offices ensures that good people, if elected, can more easily fulfill the functions of their offices; but it does not guarantee that good and virtuous people will actually fill those offices.

The Framers of the Constitution were well aware of this, however, and they carefully crafted the selection procedures for the various offices to encourage the choice of persons eminent in both ability and virtue. For example, the Framers believed that the election process for the presidency would tend to elect outstanding individuals because it required a candidate to achieve a national consensus in order to win in the ELECTORAL COLLEGE [2]; no candidate who pandered to narrow or local interests would be likely to obtain such a national majority. Similarly, the selection of senators by their state legislatures would likely encourage the selection of distinguished statesmen because the legislatures would want to choose representatives that might bring luster and distinction to their respective states. More generally, higher age

requirements for the offices of senator and President made it more probable that candidates for these offices would have the wisdom and stature that comes from experience.

The Constitution also fosters virtuous leadership in yet another manner: it encourages persons of eminent ability to *seek* federal office by assuring them that they will have enough time to prosecute their projects for the public good. This is why the Constitution contains no provision for the rotation of offices; the Framers thought that renewability of terms would help attract the best people to federal office. In the case of the presidency, wrote Alexander Hamilton, a great man will be more likely to consider running for President if he knows that he will have the time to complete as well as to undertake "extensive and arduous enterprises for the public benefit. . . ."

In many different ways, then, the very structure of the Constitution aspires to cultivate virtue in government. One may readily question, of course, whether the Constitution's structural mechanisms are *sufficient* to bring about good government. To point to only one example: the Founders were certainly correct that the national consensus needed for the election of the President ensures that a candidate of merely local interests will likely fail in his or her bid for office, but this does not necessarily mean that the person chosen will be someone preeminent in ability and virtue. If the citizenry were consumed by self-interest, they might instead elect the most pliable candidate—the one they think can be bullied into supporting their interests by their representatives in Congress. In other words, even the electoral college cannot produce a good President in and of itself. The presidential electors—and ultimately, those who select those electors—must still be good enough to care about justice and virtue.

In the end then, the Constitution can only do so much. It is not a cure-all. But contrary to the claims of some critics, the Founders themselves recognized this. They did not believe that the Constitution was a machine that would run itself. They knew that its perpetuation ultimately depended on the character of the nation's citizens. Hence, even in *The Federalist*, "a dependence on the people" is acknowledged as the primary safeguard for republicanism, whereas the Constitution's various checks and balances are described as "auxilliary precautions."

Some may object that if the Founders truly considered the character of the citizenry important, they would have mentioned civic virtue in the Constitution explicitly. After all, certain early STATE CONSTITUTIONS [I] contained appeals to both God and virtue. The PREAMBLE [3] to the U.S. Constitution, in contrast, seems but a pale reflection of these earlier documents. It does speak of establishing justice, but instead of going on and listing the requisite civic virtues, it merely stresses the importance of "the blessings of Liberty." Some have interpreted the Founders' emphasis on liberty rather than virtue as proof that they envisioned a republic where self-interest, rather than self-sacrifice, was to be the guiding light. Yet those who interpret "liberty" in this manner are interpolating their own modern conceptions back into the founding.

It is not difficult to understand the reason for the confusion. Today, liberty is equated with the absence of all restraint. Indeed, people who call themselves "libertarians" argue against all government regulation of business and object to criminalizing PORNOGRAPHY [3], hallucinogenic drugs, and prostitution. Yet the Founders' conception of liberty was entirely different. Echoing the Aristotelian understanding of virtue, the Founding generation saw liberty as the golden mean between two extremes: it was the contrary of *both* slavery and anarchy. Liberty was freedom, but freedom within the confines of the laws of nature and of nature's God. It was the freedom to organize one's own affairs, live where one wanted, participate in politics, and buy and sell property, as long as a person did not violate the immutable moral law. In short, early Americans thoroughly agreed with John Milton's aphorism that "none can love freedom heartily, but good men; the rest love not freedom but license."

That this was the Founder's true conception of liberty should become self-evident to even the most cynical observers when they examine the public actions of the Founding Fathers. The same George Washington who presided over the Constitutional Convention of 1787 declared in his Farewell Address: "Of all the dispositions and habits which lead to political prosperity, Religion and Morality are indispensable supports." The same Congress that recommended the Constitution to the states enacted an ordinance for the Northwest Territories that announced: "Religion, morality and knowledge being necessary to good government . . . schools and the means of education shall forever be encouraged."

But perhaps it was Supreme Court Justice JAMES WILSON [4], arguably the most systematic political thinker during the founding, who best expressed the necessity of schooling Americans in their civil rights and civic responsibilities. In his inaugural law lecture at the College of Philadelphia, attended by such luminaries as Washington and Jefferson, Wilson declared:

On the public mind, one great truth can never be too deeply impressed—that the weight of the government of the United States, and of each state composing the union, rests on the shoulders of the people.

I express not this sentiment now, . . . with a view to flatter: I express it now, as I have always expressed it heretofore, with a far other and higher aim—with an aim to excite the people

to acquire, by vigorous and manly exercise, a degree of strength sufficient to support the weighty burthen, which is laid upon them—with an aim to convince them, that their duties rise in strict proportion to their rights; and that few are able to trace or to estimate the great danger, in a free government, when the rights of the people are unexercised, and the still greater danger, when the rights of the people are ill exercised.

JOHN G. WEST, JR.

(SEE ALSO: *Conservatism* [I]; *Constitution and Civic Ideals* [I]; *Constitutional History Before 1776* [I]; *Constitutional History, 1776–1789; Liberalism* [I].)

Bibliography

BARLOW, J. JACKSON; LEVY, LEONARD W.; and MASUGI, KEN, EDS. 1988 *The American Founding: Essays on the Formation of the Constitution.* New York: Greenwood Press.

HORWITZ, ROBERT H., ED. 1986 *The Moral Foundations of the Republic,* 3rd ed. Charlottesville: University Press of Virginia.

JAFFA, HARRY V. 1987 What Were the 'Original Intentions' of the Framers of the Constitution of the United States? *University of Puget Sound Law Review* 10:343–423.

KESLER, CHARLES R., ED. 1987 *Saving the Revolution: The Federalist Papers and the American Founding.* New York: Free Press.

POLITICAL QUESTION DOCTRINE
(Update)

Is the constitutionality of clandestine American involvement in Nicaragua an issue that the federal judiciary may decide? If the legislatures of two-thirds of the states apply to Congress to call a convention for proposing amendments and Congress ignores their application, should a federal court entertain an action by the states against Congress? Should the decision of the Republican National Committee not to seat a group of delegates at the party's national convention be subjected to federal court challenges?

All of these questions, in one way or another, implicate the political question doctrine. This doctrine counsels the judiciary to refrain from deciding constitutional questions involving subject matters or issues appropriate for resolution only by the national political branches—Congress and the executive. In effect, the doctrine aims to divide "politics" from the "law," which is the proper sphere of judicial interpretation.

The Supreme Court has long considered the identification of political questions necessary to national SEPARATION OF POWERS [4]. As early as MARBURY V. MADISON (1803) [3], the Court recognized that although federal courts are obliged to enforce the mandatory requirements of the Constitution, a life-tenured, unelected, and politically unaccountable judiciary must reserve discretionary policy-making for the elected representatives of the American people.

Not until BAKER V. CARR (1962) [1], however, did the Court articulate doctrinal standards for distinguishing a political question. Several of the *Baker* criteria call directly for judicial interpretation of the meaning and force of the Constitution's language; for example, does the text commit an issue to determination by the national political branches, and does the text lend itself to judicially manage-able standards for resolving the issue? Other criteria re-quire judges to assess realistically and pragmatically the political effects of a decision, such as asking if there is a significant potential for embarrassing or showing disre-spect for Congress or the executive or whether the finality of a prior political decision is more important than its legality. Applying these standards, the *Baker* Court held that the Tennessee state legislature's failure to reapportion electoral districts after substantial migration of rural popu-lations to urban centers raised a question of unconstitu-tional vote dilution and that the federal judiciary was com-petent to develop manageable standards for the vote dilution issue; it further held that the text of the FOUR-TEENTH AMENDMENT [2,I] did not commit an EQUAL PRO-TECTION [2,I] claim to the Congress or executive for deci-sion and that the federal political branches had taken no action that required finality and respect.

Judges and scholars have launched serious attacks on the *Baker* approach to the definition of political questions. As the Constitution does not even provide expressly for the federal judiciary's review powers, it is difficult to argue that the text discriminates between those provisions en-forceable by the judiciary and those consigned to Congress or the executive for construction. In addition, the indivi-dual-rights doctrines most fully developed by the judiciary are based on language in the BILL OF RIGHTS [1] and the Fourteenth Amendment that is cryptic and open-ended, embodying no apparent and manageable judicial standards. Moreover, the Court may undermine the legiti-macy of its own constitutional decisions by relying on pragmatic claims of institutional incompetence to super-vise the policy decision making of administrative experts.

Nevertheless, the Supreme Court has shown no inclina-tion to rethink the political question doctrine. In the most controversial political question ruling over the past five years, a solid majority of the Court expressly declined an invitation to modify or abandon the *Baker* standards. When several Indiana Democrats sued to invalidate a state legislative REAPPORTIONMENT [3] plan for gerryman-dering election district lines so as to disadvantage Demo-cratic candidates, the Court applied the *Baker* criteria point by point and concluded that a political group's claim to fair representation does not present a political question.

The opinion of Justice BYRON R. WHITE [4,I] in *Davis v. Bandemer* (1986) declared that the Constitution does not generally dedicate vote dilution issues to the Congress or President for resolution and that the courts are institu-tionally competent to formulate workable rules for decid-ing such claims, even though they had not yet devised a precise method for identifying an unconstitutional political GERRYMANDER [2,I].

Several reasons may explain the Court's reluctance to reexamine the functionality of the political question doc-trine. First, the judiciary has relied increasingly on other devices to limit its intervention in federal administrative policymaking, including the Supreme Court's rulings on STANDING [4], STATE ACTION [4,I], SOVEREIGN IMMUNITY [4], and constraints on equitable remedies. These alterna-tives have certain tactical and ideological advantages over the traditional political question doctrine: they apply to constitutional challenges against state and municipal, as well as federal, government violations, and without over-ruling the political question standards established during the WARREN COURT's [4] expansive enforcement of CIVIL RIGHTS [1,I], the BURGER COURT [1] and REHNQUIST COURT [I] have exploited these relatively fluid devices to impose more severe restrictions on judicial regulation of government operations.

A second reason the Court may be unwilling to reex-amine the doctrine is that scholarly criticism has chal-lenged the integrity of a conceptual division of politics and law. Surely there can be no definitive and principled distinction between a political decision and a legal one in terms of their real-world consequences. A legal decision will have political effects, just as any political decision might. For example, deciding whether federal minimum-wage standards for state employees unduly interfere with the sovereign authority of state government or whether federal restrictions on political campaign contributions vio-late a contributor's FREEDOM OF SPEECH [2,I] rights re-quires the judiciary either to approve the current balance of powers and rights struck by Congress or to disapprove it and redistribute the balance by imposing constitutional restraints on Congress. In another and less obvious sense, many constitutional decisions will turn on questions that are not essentially legal. Thus, some questions—for exam-ple, whether the state's interest in the preservation of fetal life during a woman's pregnancy is any less compelling before the point of viability than after it and whether a political party has been disadvantaged enough by a political gerrymander to claim unconstitutional vote dilution—may be legal because they are framed in intellectual ways famil-iar to lawyers and the federal judiciary assumes power to decide them. But the same questions are political in the sense that they cannot be answered except by refer-ence to some theory of value which is inherently political (in the examples, a theory underlying a right of reproductive choice or a right to an undiluted vote). The stronger the system of judicial supervision of governmental policy-making, the more likely it is that a legal question will implicate political considerations and consequences.

Reasonably, the Court may be loath to recognize a collapse of the formal distinction between politics and law, for the merger of political and legal questions muddles the role of the federal judiciary in the tripartite national governmental system. If the questions underlying most constitutional claims involve obvious political considerations, what justifies the federal judiciary in second-guessing the policy decisions of the political branches? Ultimately, the analytical flaws of the political question doctrine threaten to unseat the Court as the primary interpreter of the Constitution.

DAVID M. SKOVER

(SEE ALSO: *Campaign Finance* [1,I]; *Constitutional Interpretation* [1]; *Equity* [2]; *Judicial Policymaking* [3].)

Bibliography

BICKEL, ALEXANDER   1962   *The Least Dangerous Branch: The Supreme Court at the Bar of Politics.* Indianapolis, Ind.: Bobbs-Merrill.

KOMESAR, NEIL   1984   Taking Institutions Seriously: Introduction to a Strategy for Constitutional Analysis. *University of Chicago Law Review* 56:366–446.

NAGEL, ROBERT   1989   Political Law, Legalistic Politics: A Recent History of the Political Question Doctrine. *University of Chicago Law Review* 56:643–669.

REDISH, MARTIN   1985   Judicial Review and the "Political Question." *Northwestern University Law Review* 79:1031–1061.

SCHARPF, FRITZ   1966   Judicial Review and the Political Question: A Functional Analysis. *Yale Law Journal* 75:517–597.

POLITICAL TRIALS

Among Chief Justice JOHN MARSHALL's [3] better-known observations is his declaration in MARBURY V. MADISON (1803) [3] that the United States has "a government of laws and not of men." The assertion calls forth visions of a politically neutral legal system, dispensing evenhanded justice without regard to partisan concerns or to the identities of the parties. Yet, much in American legal history belies Marshall's aphorism. This country's past is replete with political trials, and they have done more than a little to shape its constitutional law.

In a sense, of course, all trials are political. Courts, judges, and the other institutions and individuals involved in the administration of justice are part of a system of government; even when they do no more than punish

an ordinary crime or resolve a private dispute, they help to demonstrate the utility of that system and to maintain its authority. To most people, though, the term "political trial" connotes something more; it designates a type of legal proceeding having peculiar properties that distinguish it from ordinary civil and criminal litigation. There is much disagreement about what those defining attributes are, but a political trial is probably best defined as any civil or criminal trial or IMPEACHMENT [2] proceeding that immediately affects, or is intended to affect, the structure, personnel, or policies of government; that is the product of political controversy; or that results when those in control of the machinery of government seek to use the courts to disadvantage their rivals or preserve their own economic or social position. Some commentators would dispute the inclusion of civil proceedings within this definition, but from the earliest days of the Republic, suits seeking damages, injunctions, and various special writs have been used to mobilize judicial machinery in support of political causes and to suppress critics of the government.

Most political trials are criminal, however. In some, the defendants are charged with offenses that are political in nature, involving direct challenges to governmental authority. TREASON [4] is the most serious crime of this type. Others include SEDITIOUS LIBEL [4], subversion, sabotage, and espionage. Prosecutions for bribery, corruption, abuse of official power, and vote fraud also belong in this category.

A trial can be political even if the defendant is not charged with one of these political offenses, for sometimes political issues pervade trials for ordinary crimes. As Otto Kirchheimer has pointed out, "political coloring [can] be imported to such a garden-variety criminal trial by the motives or objectives of the prosecution or by the political background, affiliation, or standing of the defendant." The 1886 Haymarket case, in which defendants were prosecuted and convicted on charges of CONSPIRACY [I] to commit murder and being accessories after the fact in a fatal bombing only because they were anarchists, is an example of the kind of proceeding to which he refers.

Like many political trials, the Haymarket case was a product of political persecution. Sometimes, though, the defendant imports the political coloring to a criminal case. A courtroom provides the accused with a public forum and an audience for his political message. Thus, during the 1920s, General Billy Mitchell deliberately provoked his superiors into court-martialing him for conduct prejudicial to the discipline and good order of the army so that he could gain a hearing for his views on air power and publicize what he regarded as the military's misuse of aviation.

Not all political trials involve such deliberate exploitation of judicial machinery for political purposes. Some earn this designation simply because political considerations determined their outcome. An example is the World War I trial of Joe Hill. Hill's affiliation with a radical labor organization, the Industrial Workers of the World (IWW), was unknown when he was arrested for a murder, but it was the reason for his ultimate unfair conviction on that charge.

A trial should also be considered political if the ordinary crime of which the defendant was accused was a product of political controversy or committed for political reasons. The Watergate burglary and coverup conspiracy trials exemplify this type of proceeding. The offenses with which the government charged the defendants were not inherently political, but the fact that the defendants were alleged to have committed them to advance RICHARD M. NIXON's [3] reelection campaign and to protect the reputation of his administration gave their trials a clearly political character.

Legal proceedings can sometimes take on that coloration simply because they happen to affect substantially the politics of their time. During the Vietnam War, Lieutenant William Calley was court-martialed for his role in the massacre of more than one hundred civilians at My Lai. Because it symbolized for hawks and doves alike all that they believed was wrong with the American military effort in Southeast Asia, the Calley case became one of the major political issues of the early 1970s.

Many of America's best-known political trials have arisen against the backdrop of military conflict. Both the Revolution and the Civil War generated prosecutions for treason and other explicitly political offenses. During and just after World War I the federal government and numerous states launched legal assaults on radicals and dissenters. World War II produced a circuslike sedition trial of some of the most vitriolic right-wing critics of President FRANKLIN D. ROOSEVELT [3], as well as postwar prosecutions of U.S. citizens alleged to have collaborated with the enemy and of leaders of the defeated Axis powers. Scores of American communists found themselves on trial during the KOREAN WAR [3]. The Vietnam War also unleashed a torrent of political trials, produced by the efforts of the administrations of LYNDON B. JOHNSON [3] and Richard Nixon to repress dissent and the determination of antiwar activists to obtain a judicial declaration of the war's illegality. International tensions falling short of shooting wars have also given rise to numerous political trials, such as those of Jeffersonian politicians and editors during the Quasi-War between the United States and France in the 1790s and, more recently, the trials of domestic communists during the early days of the Cold War.

Second only to military confrontations as a cause of political trials are conflicts between labor and capital. Indeed, during the period 1870–1930 they were more important. During that era big business exercised a growing influence over all levels and branches of government, and it could generally count on the assistance of prosecutors and judges in putting down challenges to its economic power. Prominent union leaders, such as EUGENE V. DEBS [2] of the American Railway Union and "Big Bill" Haywood of the IWW, found themselves cast as defendants in highly politicized legal proceedings, as did numerous other labor activists. During World War I federal criminal prosecutions devastated the IWW.

After the rise of organized labor to political power during the 1930s, labor–management conflict ceased to generate a significant number of political trials. Racial problems continued to do so, as they had since antebellum days when white southerners sometimes tried rebellious slaves, and numerous northern abolitionists suffered prosecution for interfering with enforcement of the FUGITIVE SLAVE [2] Law of 1850. The most spectacular political trial of the antebellum era was the 1859 state treason prosecution of abolitionist firebrand John Brown for his raid on Harpers Ferry, Virginia (now West Virginia). Although the Civil War destroyed SLAVERY [4], it did not put an end to political trials whose root cause was race. From West Point Cadet Johnson Whitaker in the 1880s to members of the Black Panther party in the late 1960s and early 1970s, African Americans who challenged white supremacy, whether violently or peacefully, found themselves defendants in political trials. The peak period for such prosecutions was the decade around 1970, which produced the highly publicized LeRoi Jones, Angela Davis, Bobby Seale, and Panther Twenty-one cases.

All of these black militants had positioned themselves well outside the political mainstream. Like the defendants in most American political trials, they were essentially scapegoats who lacked real power and posed threats to the system that were more symbolic than real. Seldom have those in authority hauled serious rivals into court. Early American history does offer some examples of legal attacks on potent challengers to incumbent regimes, such as the SEDITION ACT [4] prosecutions of the Republican opposition in the late 1790s. But most such trials occurred before the concept of a legitimate political opposition had fully established itself, and most triggered a popular reaction against those who had initiated them. There have been few prosecutions of mainstream opposition groups since the Civil War.

Nor has the United States produced many examples of that staple of political justice elsewhere, the "successor regime trial," a criminal prosecution brought by those who have recently captured control of the government to discredit their predecessors in power. The principal reason for this is no doubt the constitutional stability that has kept America under the same system of government for over two hundred years. But even after the North forcefully displaced the state and national governments of the South during the Civil War, it tried few leaders of the defeated Confederate regime. In the United States, political trials have usually occurred, not after wrenching transfers of power, but at times when the status quo was under challenge because of social and political ferment unleashed by war, economic conflict, or racial discord.

Although not associated with cataclysmic constitutional change, such legal proceedings have helped to shape the Constitution. In some doctrinal areas the precedents that supplement the language of the document itself are entirely the products of political trials. This is most obviously true of the procedures worked out by the House and Senate to supplement the purely political process of impeachment. The law of treason is also a product of political trials.

So are some FREEDOM OF SPEECH [2,I] doctrines. Justices OLIVER WENDELL HOLMES, JR. [2], and LOUIS D. BRANDEIS [1] worked out their CLEAR AND PRESENT DANGER [1] test in response to appeals by radicals prosecuted during World War I and the postwar Red Scare. That test gained the endorsement of a majority of the Supreme Court in HERNDON V. LOWRY (1937) [2], only to be restrictively reinterpreted in DENNIS V. UNITED STATES (1951) [2]. Both cases arose out of political trials of communists. In BRANDENBURG V. OHIO (1969) [1] the Court, in the process of overturning a conviction of a Ku Klux Klansman for the political offense of CRIMINAL SYNDICALISM [2], articulated a new principle even more protective of expression than the original clear and present danger test had been.

Political trials have affected other facets of constitutional law as well. For example, UNITED STATES V. NIXON (1973) [3], which recognized but limited the doctrine of EXECUTIVE PRIVILEGE [2], arose out of the efforts of SPECIAL PROSECUTOR [I] Leon Jaworski to obtain White House tapes for use in the Watergate conspiracy trial. The ringing declaration in EX PARTE MILLIGAN (1866) [3] that the Constitution "covers with the shield of its protection all classes of men, at all times, and under all circumstances" and cannot be "suspended during any of the great exigencies of government" represents a doctrinal response to the ABRAHAM LINCOLN [3] administration's efforts to use military commissions to punish civilian dissidents. Even *Marbury v. Madison*, the case in which the Supreme Court first applied the doctrine of JUDICIAL REVIEW [3], was a product of efforts to use judicial machinery to achieve political objectives.

The Court has, to be sure, exhibited some reluctance to decide issues thrust before it in this way. The POLITICAL QUESTION [3,I] doctrine is evidence of that attitude, as is the Court's refusal during the Vietnam conflict to hear appeals pressed upon it by litigants hoping to get the war declared unconstitutional. Nevertheless, political trials have led to rulings that have created precedents and shaped doctrine in important areas of the law. As ALEXIS DE TOCQUEVILLE [4] wrote in *Democracy in America*, "Scarcely any political question arises in the United States that is not resolved, sooner or later, into a judicial question." Often that resolution has begun in the context of a political trial. Although often condemned, such proceedings are an integral part of the American constitutional tradition.

MICHAEL R. BELKNAP

(SEE ALSO: *Iran-Contra Affair* [I]; *Military Justice and the Constitution* [3]; *Politics* [I]; [I]; *Special Prosecutor* [I].)

Bibliography

BECKER, THEODORE L., ED. 1971 *Political Trials*. Indianapolis, Ind.: Bobbs-Merrill.
BELKNAP, MICHAEL R., ED. 1981 *American Political Trials*. Westport, Conn.: Greenwood Press.
HACKMAN, NATHAN 1972 Political Trials in the Legal Order: A Political Scientist's Perspective. *Journal of Public Law* 21:73–126.
KIRCHHEIMER, OTTO 1961 *Political Justice: The Use of Legal Procedure for Political Ends*. Princeton, N.J.: Princeton University Press.

POLITICS

Constitutions are fundamentally linked to the character of politics. At the most obvious level constitutions structure the political process. The United States Constitution defines who may serve in various elected offices, the terms of office (the frequency of election), the number of representatives, and the manner of their election. But, as important if not as obvious, constitutions in general and the United States Constitution in particular are also shaped by basic concerns about the character of politics and its malfunctions or evils. These concerns are reflected in the structures of politics established in the Constitution, the debates about the Constitution, and the evolution of constitutional law over the last two hundred years.

Two basic visions of political malfunction—one that stresses fear of the many (majoritarian bias) and one that stresses fear of the few (minoritarian bias)—coexist in traditional American views of government and constitutional history. Minoritarian bias supposes an inordinate power in the few at the expense of the many. Political power and influence, whether gained by graft, propaganda, or campaign support, often require organization and resources. Here a majority, each of whose members suffers only small loss from a government action, can be at a significant disadvantage to a minority with large per capita gains. The total loss to the majority may far outweigh the gains to the minority, but if the per capita loss is small enough, members of the majority may not even recognize that loss. Even if a member of the majority knows of the proposed legislation and recognizes its dangers, each individual has small incentive to spend time or money in organizing others. These efforts are further frustrated by the likelihood that other members of the majority will be inclined to "free ride" (i.e., refuse to participate or assume that others will carry the load).

Majoritarian bias is a completely opposite response to the same skewed distribution of impacts that characterizes minoritarian bias. Here the numerical majority, with its small per capita interests, imposes disproportionate losses on an intense, concentrated minority. The difference between majoritarian and minoritarian bias lies in suppositions about the political process. If we suppose that everyone understands and votes his interests and if we assume a political process that counts votes for or against but does not consider the severity of impact or the intensity of feeling about the issue, a low-impact majority can prevail over a high-impact minority, even though the majority gains little and the minority is harmed greatly. The power of the many lies simply in numbers, and malfunctions arise because the few are disproportionately harmed.

Concerns about both majoritarian and minoritarian bias have been with Americans throughout their constitutional history, from the framing of the original Constitution to the modern era. The period of the framing and RATIFICATION OF THE CONSTITUTION [3] shows clear concern about these forms of bias. Indeed, the two opposing constitutional positions of the time—FEDERALISM [I] and ANTIFEDERALISM [1]—can be defined by differences in their concern about majoritarian and minoritarian bias.

The authors of THE FEDERALIST [2] recognized the existence of both forms of bias, expressed concern about both, but seemed to worry more about majorities. JAMES MADISON [3], in particular, placed great emphasis on the dangers of the majority in *Federalist #10*:

If a faction consists of less than a majority, relief is applied by the republican principle, which enables the majority to defeat its sinister views by regular vote: It may clog the administration, it may convulse the society; but it will be unable to execute or mask its violence under the forms of the Constitution. When a majority is included in a faction, the form of popular government on the other hand enables it to sacrifice to its ruling passion or interest, both the public good and the rights of other citizens. . . .

The majority . . . must be rendered, by their number and local situation, unable to concert and carry into effect schemes of oppression. . . .

A pure Democracy, by which I mean, a Society, consisting of a small number of citizens, who assemble and administer the Government in person, can admit of no cure for the mischiefs of faction.

Madison's comments reveal the major Federalist response to the perceived danger: the removal or insulation of federal government decision makers from local populations. They sought this insulation in several ways. First, the decision makers were physically distanced. The national capital was generally much farther from most citizens than was the seat of state or LOCAL GOVERNMENT [I]; physical distance was no small factor at a time when travel was so difficult. Second, each of the decision makers was to represent a large number of constituents, thereby making organization of a majority more difficult. Third, they served for relatively long terms, ranging from two to six years, so that their constituents had infrequent access through the ballot box and a complex record to decipher and judge. Fourth, the Senate and President were indirectly elected—the Senate by state legislatures and the President by the ELECTORAL COLLEGE [2].

The opponents of the Federalists, the more heterogeneous Antifederalists, appeared far more concerned about minoritarian bias. The Antifederalists feared that indirectly elected senators serving long terms would devolve into an aristocracy and combine with the indirectly elected President to allow an easy conduit for "the advantage of the few over the many." In response, they sought rotation in office, shorter terms, the possibility of recall, and easier IMPEACHMENT [2]. They also feared that the House of Representatives was insufficiently numerous to enable it "to resemble the people" and therefore would be subject to influence and corruption. They feared "the superior opportunities for organized voting which they felt to be inherent in the more thickly populated areas." They feared that a Supreme Court not subject to popular control would favor the rich. These fears were all signs of concern about minoritarian bias.

The tension between the Federalist and Antifederalist positions centered significantly on the controversy over the relative roles of large and small jurisdictions—in particular, the role of the states in relation to the national government. The Federalists, who feared the power of the majority more than that of the minority, believed in a strong national government and the indirect election of government officials. The Antifederalists believed in small jurisdictions and feared that as government grew larger and more remote, the concentrated few would subvert the process.

The Federalist and Antifederalist positions both possess inadequacies and inconsistencies. Antifederalists can be seen as heirs to the tradition of classical republicanism.

They envisioned a republic small in size, with a small and homogeneous population. The great problem for the Antifederalists was the extrapolation of republican ideals to a large, dispersed, and heterogeneous population. They did not have an alternative for a national government.

For the Federalists, whose vision of government was more directly embodied in the Constitution, the problems were both more subtle and more important. Madison and the Federalists stressed government on a relatively large scale, with political decision makers (legislators and executives) removed from the mass of the populace both by distance and by mode of selection. The analysis of political malfunction employed here suggests that to the extent that the Federalist structure achieved the insulation of officials from the general populace, it traded one bias for another.

Greater distance, more complex modes of selection, and larger, more diverse constituencies provide protection from the masses but not complete isolation. Other paths of influence—and therefore sources of bias—remain and in fact flourish. The more complex setting enhances the power of organization and the accumulation of funds and helps cover underhanded dealings. Isolation provides respite from the masses but far easier access to concentrated minorities. In other words, greater insulation of public officials may purchase protection from majoritarian bias by increasing the potential for minoritarian bias.

Madison and the Federalists were not necessarily wrong to emphasize majoritarian over minoritarian bias. The correct choice depends on a number of factors (such as size of the jurisdiction or complexity of the issues) that may make one or the other bias more likely. It is intriguing to wonder whether the correct choice might be different if one were writing a constitution on a clean slate for the larger, more complex United States of the late twentieth century than it was for the United States of Madison and the Federalists.

The tradeoffs and tensions between majoritarian and minoritarian bias have surfaced elsewhere in American constitutional history. The famous footnote four from UNITED STATES V. CAROLENE PRODUCTS CO. (1938) [1], where the Supreme Court set out the general outlines of modern constitutional law, is a microcosm of these tradeoffs and tensions. Footnote four reads:

There may be narrower scope for operation of the presumption of constitutionality when legislation appears on its face to be within a specific prohibition of the Constitution, such as those of the first ten amendments, which are deemed equally specific when held to be embraced within the Fourteenth.

It is unnecessary to consider now whether legislation which restricts those political processes which can ordinarily be expected to bring about repeal of undesirable legislation, is to be subjected to more exacting judicial scrutiny under the general prohibitions of the FOURTEENTH AMENDMENT [4,I] than are most other types of legislation. On restrictions upon the right to vote; on restraints upon the dissemination of information . . . ; on interferences with political organizations . . . ; as to prohibition of peaceable assembly. . . . .

Nor need we enquire whether similar considerations enter into the review of statutes directed at particular religious, or national, or racial minorities; or whether prejudice against discrete and insular minorities may be a special condition, which tends seriously to curtail the operation of those political processes ordinarily to be relied upon to protect minorities, and which may call for a correspondingly more searching judicial inquiry.

Examined form the perspective of the tension between majoritarian and minoritarian bias, the various components of *Carolene Products*—the holding of the case and the principle concerns expressed in the footnote—are very much interrelated.

In *Carolene Products* the Court applied minimal scrutiny to uphold the economic regulation before it. The legislation at issue in *Carolene Products* banned the interstate sale of "filled milk," skim milk supplemented with nonmilk fats such as coconut oil. It does not take much scrutiny to see the dairy lobby at work behind the passage and enforcement of the Filled Milk Act. Indeed, the dairy industry's efforts to employ legislation to keep "adulterated" products from grocery shelves and vending booths have a long history. It is perhaps not too uncharitable to suggest that concern for the dairies' pocketbooks rather than for the consumer's health best explains the dairy lobby's efforts: the dairy industry benefited from reduced competition and the resultant higher prices paid by consumers.

The holding of the case abandons serious judicial review of ECONOMIC REGULATION [2], thereby leaving dispersed majorities like consumers without direct judicial protection from the minoritarian bias that can characterize governmental decisions about economic regulation like that in *Carolene Products* itself. Seemingly in response to these concerns, paragraph two of the *Carolene Products* footnote promises indirect aid to dispersed majorities by strengthening their access to and participation in the political process. By protecting access to information, organization, and the vote, the Court focused on activities that would decrease the relative advantage of concentrated interests that trade upon their superiority in gathering information, organizing, and gaining access to power through nonvoting channels.

Yet, although these protections reduce minoritarian bias, they may do little for, and in fact aggravate, majoritarian bias. Government officials whose manipulations of programs reflect the will of a majority have little to fear from public exposure or an expanded franchise. Majoritarian bias is generated when simple democracy works too well. The majority knows its interest and votes it. Because that interest is unweighted, however, a minority suffers substantial losses for disproportionately small gains to the majority. From this vantage, judicial responses like the basic rule of American VOTING RIGHTS [4]—ONE PERSON, ONE VOTE [3]—are well suited to the dissipation of minoritarian bias, but can reinforce majoritarian bias. In the extreme, if it were possible to fully perfect the process by making every citizen totally aware of his or her own interest and able immediately to translate that interest into an effective vote, minoritarian bias would disappear, but majoritarian bias would be worse.

Paragraph three of the *Carolene Products* footnote responds to the need to protect against this danger of majoritarian bias by promising special judicial examination of those actions most likely infected by majoritarian bias. Subsequent equal protection law decisions made these concerns a central feature of modern constitutional law.

These important historical episodes indicate that the character of constitutions and the character of politics are tightly interwoven. Constitutions determine, and are determined by, the character of politics.

NEIL K. KOMESAR

(SEE ALSO: *Conservatism* [I]; *Federalists* [I]; *Jacksonianism* [I]; *Jeffersonianism* [I]; *Liberalism* [I]; *Populism* [I]; *Pragmatism* [I]; *Progressivism* [I]; *Republican Party* [I].)

Bibliography

KOMESAR, NEIL K. 1984 Taking Institutions Seriously. *University of Chicago Law Review* 51:366–446.

———— 1987 Back to the Future—An Institutional View of Making and Interpreting Constitutions. *Northwestern Law Review* 81:191–219.

———— 1987 Paths of Influence—Beard Revisited. *George Washington Law Review* 56:124–135.

———— 1988 A Job for the Judges: The Judiciary and the Constitution in a Massive and Complex Society. *Michigan Law Review* 86:657–721.

POPULISM

The industrialization of the United States in the late nineteenth century caused enormous social, economic, and political upheavals in nearly every sector of the nation. Perhaps no group suffered greater dislocations than the farmers, whose livelihood and prosperity were now subject to forces over which they had no direct control. In a series of movements, farmers joined together seeking remedies to their ills. Agrarian protest reached its peak in the Populist movement in the early 1890s, when farmers took to politics in an effort to implement specific economic and political programs.

One will find little evidence of a direct impact of populism on American constitutional development. Rather, the Populists, as part of their larger reform agenda, did make particular proposals that eventually found fruition in the Progressive era. The clearest statement of these demands can be found in the People's party platform of 1896.

The platform is notable for several reasons. First, it summed up two decades of resentment by the farmers against a system they believed ignored their needs and exploited them mercilessly. Several of the complaints directly addressed the structure and operation of government. To begin with, the Populists denounced the recent Supreme Court decision in POLLOCK V. FARMERS' LOAN & TRUST CO. (1895) [3] that had invalidated the 1894 income tax rider to the tariff. To the Populists, this decision represented another example of the government's siding with the rich, and the platform demanded "a graduated income tax, to the end that aggregated wealth shall bear its proportion of taxation." In *Pollock*, they argued, the Supreme Court had misinterpreted the Constitution and invaded "the rightful powers of Congress" over taxation.

The Populists were not the first to denounce the *Pollock* decision, but they did add a strong voice to the chorus demanding an income tax. The proposal for a constitutional amendment gradually gained support throughout the country, culminating in ratification of the SIXTEENTH AMENDMENT [4] in 1913.

The platform also called for the election of the President, vice-president, and the Senate by "a direct vote of the people." Under the Constitution, an ELECTORAL COLLEGE [2] selected the two executive officers, with each state's electors equal to the sum of its senators and representatives. Originally each state could chose its electors as it saw fit, but within a relatively short period of time all states adopted a system in which the popular vote determined which candidate received each state's electoral college ballots—typically in a winner-take-all system. This arrangement emphasized the importance of the larger states and created the possibility that a candidate with a majority of the popular vote could lose in the electoral college. The system has been criticized for decades, and constitutional amendments to abolish the electoral college are periodically introduced in Congress. So far, however, there has been no popular groundswell to carry through a change.

Initially, state legislatures also chose United States senators. In the Gilded Age, bribery and influence peddling often led to the selection of rich industrialists, so that by the 1890s the Senate had come to be known as a "millionaires' club." A few states had preferential primary elections to allow voters to indicate their choice for senator, but the Populists wanted direct election to eliminate what they saw as the corrupting influence of great wealth.

Any change in the election method would require a constitutional amendment, and the House of Representatives passed such an amendment in 1894, 1898, 1900, and 1902; in each session the Senate turned it down. By 1912, thirty states had preferential primaries, and the Senate finally bowed to the inevitable. It passed the SEVENTEENTH AMENDMENT [4], authorizing the direct election of senators, and the states ratified it the following year.

The 1896 Populist platform also called for other political reforms, some of which could be achieved without constitutional amendment. This list included the adoption of a secret ballot, limiting the use of the injunction in labor disputes, and public ownership of the railroad and telegraph. The Populists also proposed "a system of direct legislation through the initiative and referendum, under proper Constitutional safeguards."

The Populists saw many of their platform items enacted within a relative short period of time. They did not cause the adoption of the Sixteenth and Seventeenth Amendments, but certainly by adding their voices to the demand they helped to achieve these reforms. Except in wartime, we have never had government ownership or control of railroads and telegraph, but the regulatory powers finally given to the Interstate Commerce Commission in the first decade of the twentieth century provided an equivalent to the Populist demands—that public welfare take precedence over private interests.

The states did adopt secret ballots, and many of them also enacted initiative and referendum measures. Although the secret ballot proved effective in buttressing democratic elections, the other two proposals never proved as effective or easy to use as the Populists had anticipated. The elimination of the injunction as a judicial weapon against labor unions, however, had to wait until the New Deal era.

In sum, the Populist demand for political change itself had relatively little effect on American constitutional development. By adding their voices to the demand for change, however, they reinforced reform currents already underway.

MELVIN I. UROFSKY

Bibliography

POLLACK, NORMAN 1987 *The Just Polity: Populism, Law, and Human Welfare*. Urbana: University of Illinois Press.

PORNOGRAPHY AND CHILDREN

See: Child Pornograpy [I]; *New York v. Ferber* [I]

PORNOGRAPHY AND FEMINISM

In 1984 Indianapolis passed an "antipornography civil rights ordinance." Pornography was defined thus:

the graphic sexually explicit subordination of women, whether in pictures or in words, that also includes one or more of the following: (1) Women who are presented as sexual objects who enjoy pain or humiliation; or (2) Women [who] are presented as sexual objects who experience sexual pleasure in being raped; or (3) Women [who] are presented as sexual objects tied up or cut up or mutilated or bruised or physically hurt, or as dismembered or truncated or fragmented or severed into body parts; or (4) Women [who] are presented as being penetrated by objects or animals; or (5) Women [who] are presented in scenarios of degradation, injury, abasement, torture, shown as filthy or inferior, bleeding, bruised, or hurt in a context that makes these conditions sexual; or (6) Women [who] are presented as sexual objects for domination, conquest, violation, exploitation, possession, or use, or through postures or positions of servility or submission or display.

The ordinance afforded civil, but not criminal, remedies for trafficking in pornography (i.e., sales, exhibitions, or distribution with exceptions for libraries), forcing pornography on a person, coercing a person into pornography, attacking a person because of pornography, or causing such attacks. To some extent, the functional definition of pornography depends on the particular offense under the ordinance. For example, isolated parts of a book would not support a trafficking claim, but they could support a claim against an individual for forcing pornography on someone. Although the ordinance was crafted to protect women against SEX DISCRIMINATION [4,I], it provided that if men, children, or transsexuals were treated in the same manner, they, too, could be afforded protection.

Although there is substantial overlap, Indianapolis's "pornography" is not the Supreme Court's "obscenity." MILLER V. CALIFORNIA [1973] [3] defined OBSCENITY [3] to include material that the "average person, applying contemporary community standards," would find when "taken as a whole appeals to the prurient interest" and "depicts and describes in a patently offensive way, sexual conduct specifically defined by the applicable state law," and that "taken as a whole, lacks serious literary, artistic, political, or scientific value."

Some of the material falling under the sixth category of the Indianapolis ordinance (e.g., women presented as sexual objects through postures or display) might not be ruled offensive under contemporary community standards, though probably most graphic, sexually explicit material that subordinates women and that also falls within the six specified categories would meet the *Miller* standard for obscenity. Such material would in the general run of cases be thought to appeal to prurient interests and to be patently offensive under contemporary community standards. The only substantial question would be whether particular material had the serious value specified in the *Miller* test, and it is doubtful that much of it would.

The ordinance's proponents argue, however, that obscenity law is theoretically and functionally bankrupt. As Catharine MacKinnon writes, they doubt "whether the average person, gender neutral exists; [they have] more questions about the content and process of definition of community standards than deviations from them; [they wonder] why prurience counts but powerlessness does not; why sensibilities are better protected than are women from exploitation." They ask, "If a woman is subjected, why should it matter that the work has other value? Perhaps what redeems a work's value among men *enhances* its injury to women." They contend that the ordinance focuses on the real problem (harm to women rather than offense to the community), provides for more effective enforcement (by allowing women to bring civil actions), and is more precise in its definition of the material to be sanctioned than obscenity law has ever been.

Ironically, despite its efforts at precision, the ordinance has frequently been misread. For example, one respected commentator states that the "sweep of the Indianapolis ordinance is breathtaking. It would subject to governmental ban virtually all depictions of rape, verbal or pictorial. . . . The ban would extend from Greek mythology and Shakespeare to . . . much of the world's art, from ancient carvings to Picasso . . . and a large amount of commercial advertising."

It is not the case that virtually all depictions of rape are sexually explicit—let alone Shakespeare or commercial advertising in any large amount. Some ancient carvings and works of Picasso involve nudity, but how many of them are graphic? Do they involve the subordination of women? Where do they fall under the six categories? Do *any* of them fall under the first five categories? Could any breathtaking possibilities be cured by editing the sixth category? Is one person's breathtaking possibility another person's exercise of male domination? One suspects in any event that if an ordinance of this character were upheld, its opponents would find creative possibilities for limiting its scope and its proponents would be stressing the breadth of its reach.

Were the ordinance construed narrowly, what would be the case for its constitutionality? Many categories of speech are deemed beneath the protection of the FIRST AMENDMENT [2,1], including FIGHTING WORDS [2], some forms of advocacy of illegal action, some forms of defamation, and obscenity. The argument for the ordinance is not that it fits within such categories. Rather, proponents argue that a new category of nonprotection is justified. If defamation causes harm to specific individuals,

the proponents argue, pornography causes even more:

The harm of pornography includes dehumanization, sexual exploitation, forced sex, forced prostitution, physical injury, and social and sexual terrorism, and inferiority presented as entertainment. The bigotry and contempt pornography promotes, with the acts of aggression it fosters, diminish opportunity for equality of rights in employment, education, property, public accommodations and public services; create public and private harassment . . . ; promote injury and degradation such as rape, battery, child abuse, and prostitution and inhibit just enforcement of laws against these acts; contribute significantly to restricting women in particular from full exercise of citizenship and participation in public life, including in neighborhoods; damage relationships between the sexes; and undermine women's equal exercise of rights to speech.

Without questioning these harms, the UNITED STATES COURT OF APPEALS [4] for the Seventh Circuit declared the Indianapolis ordinance unconstitutional on its face in *American Booksellers Association v. Hudnut* (1985), and the Supreme Court affirmed without opinion. *Hudnut* is now the principal case in the pornography area.

Speaking for the Seventh Circuit, Judge Frank Easterbrook accepted the premise that "pornography is central in creating and maintaining sex as a basis of discrimination." Nonetheless, he maintained, the entire ordinance was premised on an unacceptable form of content discrimination: "The ordinance discriminates on the ground of the content of the speech. Speech treating women in the approved way . . . is lawful no matter how sexually explicit. Speech treating women in the disapproved way . . . is unlawful no matter how significant the literary, artistic, or political qualities of the work taken as a whole. The state may not ordain preferred viewpoints in this way. The Constitution forbids the state to declare one perspective right and silence opponents." Proceeding from this reading of the First Amendment, the court stated, "We do not try to balance the arguments for and against an ordinance such as this." The case was over.

From the court's perspective, the amount of harm to women caused by pornography was quite beside the First Amendment point and not to be weighed in the balance. But this reading of current doctrine is idiosyncratic. The categorical exceptions to First Amendment protection already involve discrimination on the basis of point of view.

The treatment of legislation involving advocacy of the overthrow of the government by force and violence is one obvious example. Obscenity is another. For example, appeals to prurient interests are defined as appeals to a "shameful or morbid interest in sex." The Court ruled in BROCKETT V. SPOKANE ARCADES (1985) [1] that appeals to prurient interests cannot be taken to include appeals to "normal" interests in sex, that is, appeals to an interest in "good, old fashioned, healthy" sex are constitutionally protected, even if they are patently offensive to contemporary standards and lack serious literary, artistic, political, or scientific value. Appeals to an "abnormal" interest in sex are treated differently. For them, when the other requirements are satisfied, it is permissible to bring down the full weight of the law. In short, appeal to one perspective is declared right and appeal to another is declared wrong.

The *Hudnut* court's unwillingness to balance the arguments was thus supported only by misreading the treatment of content discrimination in First Amendment law. Content discrimination in general and point-of-view discrimination are disfavored in First Amendment law, but they are not absolutely disfavored. The *Hudnut* court had no difficulty showing that pornography did not fall within any of the existing categorical exceptions to First Amendment protection. But the issue presented by pornography legislation is whether pornography's harm justifies the creation of a new categorical exception to First Amendment protection. That was the issue sidestepped by the court's decision of content discrimination.

One approach to the question is by analogy. The *Hudnut* court did consider that possibility. Obscenity, it observed, has been deemed by the Supreme Court to be LOW-VALUE SPEECH [I], and "pornography is not low value speech within the meaning of these cases" because pornography "is thought to influence social relations and politics on a grand scale, that it controls attitudes at home and in the legislature. This precludes a characterization of the speech as low value."

If analogy were the mode of argument, the issue would not be whether pornography falls into a category denominated as low value. The Supreme Court did not use the term "low value" in creating the obscenity exception. The Court maintained in ROTH V. UNITED STATES (1957) [3] that obscenity made such a slight contribution to truth that its possible benefits were categorically outweighed by the interests in order and morality. The proponents of pornography prohibitions insist that the same or something even stronger can be said of pornography. In addition, nothing in *Roth* speaks to the magnitude of the scale upon which obscenity was thought to influence order and morality (let alone in the home or the legislature). Certainly nothing in *Roth* or any subsequent decision supposes that if obscenity were demonstrated to have profound effects on order or morality, it would then emerge as protected speech.

The real animus of the *Hudnut* analysis is a deep hostility to the obscenity exception, a hostility that is tempered only by the view that obscenity does not matter much anyway. Thus, when Indianapolis says "pornography matters," the *Hudnut* court says, "all the more reason to protect it." But this response begs the question. First Amendment values are important; so are those of gender equality. As MacKinnon has observed, a victory for FREEDOM OF SPEECH [2,I] anywhere may be a victory for freedom of speech everywhere, but a victory for sexism anywhere may be a victory for sexism everywhere.

The case for or against pornography legislation cannot be decided in the abstract. Attention must be paid to the character and amount of the harm caused (e.g., whether pornography is cathartic, stimulates aggressive and discriminatory behavior, or both, and to what extent; the extent to which the ordinance would combat that harm (e.g., whether black markets would arise, to what extent the ordinance and its application would legitimize nonpornographic but equally harmful speech, and whether the absence of pornography would cause aggressive behavior); the possibility of less restrictive alternatives (e.g., what the impact of adding a serious-value test would be) and the impact on free speech (e.g., how serious the chilling effect on speech that ought to matter would be and whether the addition of a new category based on content discrimination and the raising of questions about the particular value of speech would require quite heavy justification).

Serious arguments can be made for and against the constitutionality of legislation like the Indianapolis antipornography ordinance. The scandal is that those arguments have yet to receive serious judicial consideration and expression.

STEVEN H. SHIFFRIN

(SEE ALSO: *Child Pornography* [I]; *Dial-A-Porn* [I]; *Feminist Theory* [I]; *Meese Commission* [I].

Bibliography

EMERSON, THOMAS I. 1985 Pornography and the First Amendment: A Reply to Professor MacKinnon. *Yale Law and Policy Review* 3:130–143.

MACKINNON, CATHARINE 1987 *Feminism Unmodified.* Cambridge, Mass.: Harvard University Press.

STONE, GEOFFREY R. 1986 Anti-Pornography Legislation as Viewpoint Discrimination. *Harvard Journal of Law and Public Policy* 9:461–480.

SUSTEIN, CASS R. 1986 Pornography and the First Amendment. *Duke Law Journal* 1986:589–627.

PORNOGRAPHY AND THE MEESE COMMISSION

See: Meese Commission [I]

PORNOGRAPHY OVER THE TELEPHONE

See: Dial-a-Porn [I]

POSADAS DE PUERTO RICO ASSOCIATES v. TOURISM COMPANY OF PUERTO RICO
478 U.S. 328 (1986)

In *Posadas* the Supreme Court upheld, 5–4, a Puerto Rico statute that authorized casino gambling but forbade advertising of casino gambling when the advertising was aimed at Puerto Rican residents. The majority, in an opinion by Justice WILLIAM H. REHNQUIST [3,I], followed the doctrinal formula in CENTRAL HUDSON GAS AND ELECTRIC CORP. V. PUBLIC SERVICE COMMISSION (1980) [1] for testing the constitutionality of regulations of COMMERCIAL SPEECH [1,I]. The advertising concerned a lawful activity and was not misleading or fraudulent. Thus, the Court proceeded to the interest-balancing part of the formula. The governmental interest was the reduction of demand for casino gambling; Puerto Rico's concerns for its residents' health, safety, and welfare was obvious, considering that a majority of the states prohibit such gambling altogether. The restrictions on advertising, said the Court, directly advanced that interest. Furthermore, the Commonwealth of Puerto Rico was not required to resort to advertising of its own as a LEAST RESTRICTIVE MEANS [3] for discouraging casino gambling. In support of the latter point Justice Rehnquist cited lower court decisions approving restrictions on advertising of cigarettes and alcohol. Puerto Rico could have banned casino gambling altogether; this greater power included the lesser power to regulate advertising.

Justice WILLIAM J. BRENNAN [1,I], writing for three Justices, dissented, arguing the the Commonwealth had not met its burden of substantial justification for regulating commercial speech. In particular, the Commonwealth had not shown that less restrictive means would suffice. Justice JOHN PAUL STEVENS [4,I] focused his dissent on the law's discrimination based on the advertising's intended audience.

There is little doubt that Congress or a state legislature could constitutionally ban the sale or use of cigarettes. Commentators have suggested that *Posadas* implies that, even if such a prohibition law were not adopted, a ban on cigarette advertising would be constitutional.

KENNETH L. KARST

POVERTY LAW

In a nineteenth-century COMMERCE CLAUSE [1,I] case, the Supreme Court characterized "paupers" and "vagabonds" as a "moral pestilence" against which the state could protect itself in the exercise of its POLICE POWERS [3]. Although we can still hear echoes of these sentiments in laws and practices segregating the poor and the institutions that serve them, the Supreme Court has now made clear that bare hostility to, or suspicion of, the poor is not a constitutionally permissible basis for STATE ACTION [4,I].

The decisive break came in the 1941 decision in EDWARDS V. CALIFORNIA [2], where the Court struck down as a violation of the DORMANT COMMERCE CLAUSE [I] a state law making it a crime knowingly to aid an indigent in coming into the state. The Court said in *Edwards* that "it will not now be seriously contended that because a person is without employment and without funds he constitutes a 'moral pestilence.' Poverty and immorality are not synonymous." In a much cited concurrence, Justice ROBERT JACKSON [3] went further, insisting that "'indigence' in itself is neither a source of rights nor a basis for denying them. The mere state of being without funds is a neutral fact—constitutionally an irrelevance, like race, creed, or color."

Since *Edwards*, indigence as such cannot be the basis for the imposition of governmental burdens. For indigence, as for race, however, the ideal of constitutional irrelevance has proved elusive. In dealing with issues of poverty since *Edwards*, the Court has found itself repeatedly confronting questions of what it might mean for the state to treat something as irrelevant that matters terribly in the society of which the state is a part. It is now settled that both state and federal legislatures can take action to alleviate poverty and its effects. The difficult problems that remain revolve around whether, and when, the Constitution may require relief for the poor from some of the burdens of indigence.

Constitutional solicitude for the poor emerged first in the context of CRIMINAL PROCEDURE [2], with the Supreme Court holding that indigent criminal defendants were entitled to state-appointed counsel, to trial transcripts on appeal, and, more recently, to limited forms of other important assistance in resisting prosecution. The first RIGHT TO COUNSEL [3] holding came in 1932, and the Court gradually developed a constitutional law of procedural rights for indigent criminal defendants in federal and then in state courts. These rights for the indigent accused developed without any overt prod from external influences. Expansion of the rights of the poor beyond the criminal procedure context had to await the development of larger social movements.

By the mid-1960s, problems of poverty were commanding political attention. Congress responded to President LYNDON B. JOHNSON's [3] call for a "war on poverty" with a variety of new programs designed to deal with the symptoms and the causes of poverty in America. One of the early poverty programs was federal subsidization of civil legal aid for the poor. Charitable legal aid programs had a long history in the United States, but the new federal subsidy helped channel the reformist zeal of large numbers of new lawyers acting on behalf of poor people. Their activities left a mark on many areas of the law, including much of constitutional law beyond the criminal procedure beginnings.

For a time it even appeared that litigation on behalf of welfare recipients might yield a constitutional right to subsistence support. In 1969 the Supreme Court held in SHAPIRO V. THOMPSON [4] that states could not impose durational RESIDENCE REQUIREMENTS [3] for the receipt of public assistance. The decision was based on the EQUAL PROTECTION [2,I] clause; the residence requirements impinged on the RIGHT TO TRAVEL [3] interstate, a right the Court characterized as "fundamental" and hence enjoying heightened constitutional protection. But the Court also suggested that the fact that WELFARE BENEFITS [4] were at issue was important to its decision. In the Court's words, the case involved "the very means to subsist—food, shelter, and other necessities of life." And the next year, the Court held in GOLDBERG V. KELLY (1970) [2] that a welfare recipient had a right to an administrative hearing before her welfare benefits could be withdrawn. Again the Court emphasized the nature of the benefits at stake—"the means to obtain essential food, clothing, housing, and medical care." This and other language helped stimulate a secondary literature advocating a constitutional right to what Frank Michelman called "minimum protection" of each individual's "just wants."

No such right ever gained much of a foothold in the courts, however, for reasons that came into focus early. In DANDRIDGE V. WILLIAMS (1970) [2], decided just one year after *Shapiro*, the Court rejected a claim that a family maximum on the size of the welfare grant deprived members of large welfare families of equal protection. The claim was plausible enough after *Shapiro*, but the prospect of continued expansion of the eligible population by virtue of equal protection decisions gave the Court pause, for it suggested that the legislative reaction might simply be to divide the same total public assistance resources among a larger eligible population. The Court's response to this tradeoff of equity and adequacy in welfare programs was to back off, saying in *Dandridge* that "conflicting claims

of morality and intelligence are raised by opponents and proponents of almost every measure, certainly including the one before us. But the intractable economic, social and even philosophical problems presented by public welfare programs are not the business of this Court. . . . The Constitution does not empower this Court to second-guess state officials charged with the difficult responsibility of allocating limited public welfare funds among the myriad of potential recipients." The Court did not abandon equal protection review of discrimination within welfare programs after *Dandridge*, but that review became much more subdued than the rhetoric of *Shapiro* had suggested.

The problem to which the Court referred in *Dandridge* is real enough in the equal protection context, where the claimant typically seeks to have a group to which he belongs made eligible for assistance according to standards of need the state has already defined. Indeed, each time the Court extends eligibility, it causes a realignment of political forces that might force legislative tradeoffs with nonwelfare programs such as defense, foreign aid, and the fight against pollution. In such a case, however, the legislature does retain the option to eliminate or scale back the amount of the welfare benefits. A claim for minimum subsistence, on the other hand, would require of the Court decisions not only about those entitled to the assistance but also about the appropriate level of assistance—what, in Michelman's terms, are "just wants" and how much is "minimum protection." The Court would be requiring the expenditure of funds absolutely rather than conditionally, thus necessitating, rather than just giving a nudge to, legislative tradeoffs between welfare programs and others competing for public support. The prospect would be daunting, and the Court never did more than flirt lightly with it.

The welfare cases did somewhat alleviate recurrent confusion in constitutional law with regard to the RIGHT/PRIVILEGE DISTINCTION [3]. Prior to those cases, when an interest characterized as a right was jeopardized by some legislative or executive action, constitutional protections were applicable; when privileges were at issue, it was sometimes said that no constitutional protections attached. This doctrine was never well developed, but it kept reappearing and posed a serious obstacle to constitutional succor for recipients under a growing array of government benefit programs, for those programs surely would fall on the privilege side of any such line. In both *Shapiro* and *Goldberg*, however, the Court rejected the distinction as constitutionally irrelevant. In subsequent cases, the notion behind the distinction has occasionally resurfaced (without the language of rights and privileges), but only as a consideration in defining the strength of constitutional protection, and not as a reason for denying protection altogether. Thus, the Supreme Court has repeatedly held that state and local governments need not subsidize ABORTION [1,I], even though a pregnant woman has a constitutionally protected interest in seeking out an abortion if she chooses. These decisions suggest that the state retains a higher degree of discretion over the dispensation of benefits than over the imposition of burdens, but they do not resurrect the sort of absolute discretion with which the right/privilege distinction was associated.

Lawyers for the indigent did have important constitutional triumphs, but usually by joining problems of the poor to some other theme with which the Court could feel more comfortable. Expansion of the franchise and perfection of the electoral system, for instance, have been important contemporary themes in constitutional law, and the Court has been responsive to the handicaps placed on the poor in participating in democratic institutions. In 1966 the Court struck down a state POLL TAX [3] as a condition on voting, and in subsequent cases, the Court limited property qualifications for voting in some specialized contexts. It has also restricted the filing fees that can be charged indigent candidates for public office.

The emphasis on fair process for indigents in the criminal cases and in *Goldberg* has been extended to certain civil proceedings. The movement, however, has been cautious as the Court undoubtedly keeps a wary eye on the costs involved. Thus, the state cannot require an indigent to pay court costs or filing fees as a condition to filing a divorce action. The state must pay for blood testing in a state-initiated paternity proceeding. And in compelling circumstances the state must provide counsel in an action to terminate parental rights. On the other hand, the state is not required to waive filing fees for a bankruptcy proceeding for an indigent or for an appeal of an adverse decision in a welfare hearing.

Some of the early opinions extending procedural protection to indigents in criminal cases used the language of equal protection, but the equal protection clause is not apt as a basis for procedural protections, because there is no obvious reference group with which the indigent defendant is to be compared. The more recent opinions have thus recurred to PROCEDURAL DUE PROCESS [3,I] notions of fundamental fairness as the standard against which arguments for subsidy are to be judged.

This attraction to themes that do not explicitly draw on the fact of poverty means that many of the advances in constitutional poverty law have resulted from litigation on behalf of groups whose members are mostly poor but not necessarily so. The Court has, for instance, established substantial constitutional protections for ALIENS [1] within the jurisdiction of the United States, for illegitimate children, for the mentally retarded, and for youngsters sub-

jected to JUVENILE PROCEEDINGS [3]. The opinions in these cases often draw on the impecuniousness of the protected group, but seldom in a way that makes the doctrines announced depend on that fact.

One important extension of constitutional rights of the poor has been snatched by state courts and state constitutional law out of the mouth of federal defeat. Primary and secondary education in the United States has been financed in large part through local property taxes, with the result that property-rich districts have been able to sustain much higher per-pupil expenditures for education than have property-poor districts. Drawing on the FUNDAMENTAL RIGHTS [2] branch of equal protection doctrine developed in *Shapiro* and other cases, students in property-poor districts challenged these financing schemes. The Supreme Court rejected the claim in its 1973 decision SAN ANTONIO INDEPENDENT SCHOOL DISTRICT V. RODRIGUEZ [4], holding that there was no fundamental right to a particular level of education and that the students in property-poor districts, who need not necessarily be poor, were entitled to no heightened constitutional protection. *Rodriguez*, like the welfare cases, suggests judicial disinclination to become involved in financing decisions for major public programs.

Faced with a reluctant federal court system, however, poverty lawyers and their clients increasingly have turned to state courts and state constitutional claims. In the case of educational financing, they could draw on equal protection provisions in state constitutions or on provisions assuming state responsibility for public education. The result has been court-ordered reform of educational financing in a substantial number of states.

Twenty-five years after the war on poverty began, there is no constitutional law of the poor in the way that there is a constitutional law of race relations or INTERSTATE COMMERCE [2]. But constitutional law has changed over that time in ways that have been important for the legal status of many people who are poor. It has changed mostly in small ways and in many different contexts, but those small and diverse changes add up to an altered landscape in which constitutional law is one tool among many in addressing the myriad legal problems that beset the poor.

ROBERT W. BENNETT

(SEE ALSO: *Illegitimacy* [2]; *Mental Retardation* [3]; *Rights of the Criminally Accused* [I]; *State Constitutions* [I].)

Bibliography

BENNETT, ROBERT W. 1983 The Burger Court and the Poor. Pages 46–61 in Vincent Blasi, ed., *The Burger Court*. New Haven, Conn.: Yale University Press.

LaFRANCE, ARTHUR B.; SCHROEDER, MILTON R.; BENNETT,

ROBERT W.; and BOYD, WILLIAM E. 1973 *Law of the Poor.* St. Paul, Minn.: West Publishing Co.

MICHELMAN, FRANK I. 1969 Foreword: On Protecting the Poor Through the Fourteenth Amendment. *Harvard Law Review* 83:7–59.

WINTER, RALPH K. 1972 Poverty, Economic Equality, and the Equal Protection Clause. *Supreme Court Review* 1972:41–102.

POWELL, LEWIS F., JR.
(Update)

From his appointment in 1971 until his resignation in 1987, Lewis F. Powell, Jr. was widely known as the "swing Justice" on a closely divided Supreme Court. As the term "swing Justice" implies, Powell's position on the Court was one of both loneliness and influence. The loneliness resulted because Powell lacked a stable set of allies on many of the most contentious issues that came before the Court. The influence stemmed largely from his capacity to make 5–4 majorities. In cases involving AFFIRMATIVE ACTION [1], ABORTION [1,I], CAPITAL PUNISHMENT [1,I], and the FIRST AMENDMENT [2,I], Powell's finely nuanced positions caused him to move back and forth between coalitions of Justices whose decisions depended less on the peculiar facts of individual controversies.

After a Justice has retired from the Court, his influence, if any, must depend on the power of his written opinions and his judicial philosophy to command respect. The question of Powell's long-term influence remains unsettled. With regard to the resolution of specific cases, Powell's successor, ANTHONY M. KENNEDY [I], has contributed to a perceptible conservative drift by the REHNQUIST COURT [I], including erosion of some of the doctrines to which Powell was committed. In addition, Powell's characteristic "balancing" philosophy, which emerged as perhaps the Court's predominant methodology during his tenure, has recently attracted sharp criticism.

Lewis F. Powell joined the Supreme Court at the age of sixty-four after thirty-five years of successful private practice in the state of Virginia. The son of well-to-do parents, Powell graduated from Washington and Lee College in 1929 and, just two years later, finished first in his class at Washington and Lee Law School. After a year of graduate study at Harvard Law School, Powell returned to Richmond and joined the prestigious firm of Hunton, Williams, Gay, Powell, and Gibson, where, with time out for military service during World War II, he remained until 1971.

Powell achieved unusual eminence as a private lawyer. Besides winning the trust and respect of clients and serving on the boards of directors of eleven major corporations,

Powell became active in a variety of lawyers' groups, including the American Bar Association, which he served as president in 1964–1965. Powell also took a leading role in a number of civic and cultural organizations. He was chairman of the Richmond school board from 1952 to 1961.

The Lewis Powell who took his seat on the Supreme Court in 1971 very much reflected his background and his experiences. In addition to possessing an acute analytical intelligence, he had a business lawyer's disposition to resolve disputes pragmatically, preferably in a way that would accommodate the reasonable interests of all parties. He also had a conservative respect for established institutions. Yet Powell was more than the archetype of the successful conservative lawyer. As chairman of the Richmond school board, he had resisted efforts by the Virginia political establishment to close public schools rather than accept racial DESEGREGATION [2]. And as vice-president of the National Legal Aid and Defender Society, he had worked to support publicly financed legal services for the poor.

Not surprisingly in light of his background, a respect for institutions of local government and especially for local school administration represented a consistent theme in Powell's Supreme Court opinions. Although cautious and nonideological in some areas, he consistently and even aggressively sought to protect state sovereignty interests under both the TENTH AMENDMENT [4] and the ELEVENTH AMENDMENT [2,I]. As a matter of "equitable restraint," he held that federal courts should virtually never interfere with proceedings before state courts and administrative agencies. And he favored the recognition of protective "immunities" for government officials whose official conduct entangled them in suits for money damages. Without such immunity, Powell reasoned in *Harlow v. Fitzgerald* (1982), able men and women would hesitate to accept positions of public responsibility. Powell also wrote germinal opinions in the field of STANDING [4] that had as their effect, if not their explicit purpose, the preclusion of lawsuits challenging the constitutionality of programs and policies—including those of LOCAL GOVERNMENTS [I]—whose effects were widely dispersed across large numbers of citizens. "Generalized grievances," he argued in an influential CONCURRING OPINION [1] in *Schlesinger v. Reservists* (1974) and later for a majority of the Court in *Warth v. Seldin* (1975), should generally be resolved in the legislature and at the ballot box, rather than by the nondemocratic federal courts.

The theme of deference to local political decision makers sounded particularly loudly in one of the earliest of Powell's major opinions, SAN ANTONIO INDEPENDENT SCHOOL DISTRICT V. RODRIGUEZ (1973) [4]. At issue in

Rodriguez was the constitutionality of Texas's system of school funding, which relied heavily on local property taxes to finance public EDUCATION [2,I] and, as administered, created a large disparity between the per-pupil expenditures in rich and poor school districts. The plaintiffs claimed that the disparate allocations offended the EQUAL PROTECTION [2,I] clause. Justice Powell, who wrote for a five-member majority, disagreed. Education was not a FUNDAMENTAL RIGHT [2] in the constitutional sense, he ruled, nor did a law disadvantaging students in impecunious school districts constitute a SUSPECT CLASSIFICATION [4] that would trigger close judicial scrutiny. Especially because the plaintiffs' argument called into question the educational financing system of "virtually every State," Powell found judicial restraint to be appropriate. "It would be difficult to imagine a case having a greater impact on our federal system than the one now before us," he wrote. "The ultimate solutions must come from the lawmakers and from the democratic pressures of those who elect them." Powell took a similarly deferential stand in cases challenging the infliction of various kinds of punishment in the public schools and the removal of books from a school library.

While Powell was a fairly traditional conservative on questions of federal jurisdiction and of federalism, his accommodationist impulses and penchant for balancing often asserted themselves in cases under the FIRST AMENDMENT [2,I], the EIGHTH AMENDMENT, and the FOURTEENTH AMENDMENT [2,I]. It was in these areas that he acquired his reputation as a swing Justice.

Powell's most famous opinion, in REGENTS OF UNIVERSITY OF CALIFORNIA V. BAKKE (1978) [3], epitomizes both Powell's judicial style and his role on an ideologically fractured Supreme Court. The case arose when Alan Bakke, a white male who was denied admission to the medical school of the University of California at Davis, challenged the school's practice of setting aside sixteen of one hundred places in its entering class for members of disadvantaged minorities. Four Justices of the Court would have upheld affirmative action programs under considerably looser constitutional standards than applied to INVIDIOUS DISCRIMINATION [2]. Four other Justices found all acts of RACIAL PREFERENCE [I], even those that favor discrete and insular minorities, to be absolutely prohibited by an applicable federal statute. That left Justice Powell, alone in the middle, to formulate the constitutional principles that would define the law of the case.

Upholding the ideal that race is irrelevant to moral worth, Powell argued that even discrimination in favor of minority persons must be subject to STRICT SCRUTINY [4] by the courts. But, carefully parsing the state's reasons for pursuing affirmative action, he also identified an interest in student diversity that was sufficiently "compelling" to justify attaching affirmative weight to prospective students' minority backgrounds as one of many factors relevant to admissions decisions. The end result was that RACIAL QUOTAS [3] were forbidden, but individualized "pluses" permitted. Steps could thus be taken to make amends for the legacy of past invidious racialism, but a narrow tailoring of program to rationale was required.

Although no other Justice joined Powell's opinion in *Bakke*, Powell generally succeeded in establishing both the framework and the tone for the Supreme Court's affirmative action JURISPRUDENCE [I] over the next ten years. The legal framework, subject to possible exception only in cases of congressional action, required compelling justifications, even for noninvidious or compensatory racial preferences. The tone reflected Powell's sense that the underlying issues were too hard, both morally and legally, to be settled other than on a case-by-case basis that would permit some accommodation, however crude, of the competing values at stake. In a series of cases involving employment and promotions, Powell's vote made the majority for the proposition that racial preferences would be allowed under the Constitution when reasonably necessary to correct for past discrimination by the institution implementing an affirmative action program or subject to a remedial judicial order. But he also insisted that racial classifications should be disfavored and, writing for a plurality of the Court in WYGANT V. JACKSON BOARD OF EDUCATION (1986) [I], held that dispreferred whites may not be required to carry too heavy a burden in order to compensate for wrongs of which they personally are likely innocent. The resulting balance was not always neat, but it reflected Powell's sense that some sort of accommodation was needed.

Careful balancing and accommodation of competing interests also marked Powell's approach to the First Amendment. Perhaps his most important opinion on this subject came in GERTZ V. ROBERT WELCH, INC. (1974) [2], which raised an issue about the scope of constitutional protection enjoyed by the press in suits for LIBEL [3]. The common law generally had presumed liability for all defamatory speech, with the burden resting on the defendant to prove truth as a defense. In the landmark case of NEW YORK TIMES V. SULLIVAN (1964) [3], however, the Supreme Court had recognized a constitutional privilege in cases involving speech about public officials in the performance of their official duties. Because of the public interest in promoting free and robust debate about governmental affairs, defamations of public officials were held to be constitutionally protected unless published "with actual malice," which the Court defined to mean with knowledge of their falsity or with reckless disregard for whether they were true or false. But the Court, following *New York Times*, had not reached a consensus on the scope of constitutional protection that should be accorded to other defamatory speech.

Carefully balancing the competing interests in FREEDOM OF SPEECH [2,I], FREEDOM OF THE PRESS [2,I], and the protection of individual reputation, Powell's *Gertz* opinion sought a middle ground. In order to avoid unwarranted "chilling" of the press as a result of threats of liability, Powell held that the states may not impose liability for libel in the absence of some showing of "fault." But neither, he concluded, did the First Amendment require that the state's interest in protecting its citizens' good names and reputations be sacrificed entirely. Where "private figures" are defamed, *Gertz* permits liability based on a showing that the press was negligent in publishing a false report. In actions brought by "public figures," whose stature or notoriety allows them greater opportunity to counter false allegations in the MARKETPLACE OF IDEAS [3], the balance shifts, and liability requires a demonstration of actual malice.

In addition to its balancing methodology, Powell's First Amendment jurisprudence was notable for its sensitivity to the role of a free press in making democracy work. In GANNETT CO., INC. V. DEPASQUALE (1979) [2] Powell argued in a concurring opinion that the First Amendment required at least a presumptive right of the press to attend and report on criminal trials. His views about rights of access to judicial proceedings were substantially adopted by the Court a year later in RICHMOND NEWSPAPERS V. VIRGINIA (1980) [3]. But Powell would have gone further. In provocative dissenting opinions in *Saxbe v. Washington Post Co.* (1974) and *Houchins v. KQED* (1978), he argued that the press, as a representative of the public, should have limited right of access to report on conditions inside prisons and presumably on the management of other governmental operations. From one perspective, Powell's views in these cases seem in tension with his generally respectful and deferential stance toward local government and political authority. From another, his position reflects a powerful inner logic. Local government deserves deference only insofar as it represents the informed judgments of its citizens. When government conducts its affairs in unnecessary secrecy, Powell believed, the moral foundations of democracy erode.

The need to strike a balance between deference to democratically accountable decision makers and the protection of competing constitutional values was also a main theme in Powell's opinions involving PROCEDURAL DUE PROCESS [3,I]. In this area, too, he emerged as one of the Court's intellectual leaders. Writing in MATHEWS V. ELDRIDGE (1976) [3], Powell developed a three-part BALANCING TEST [I] that has since become ubiquitous in the

Supreme Court's procedural due process cases. To determine whether the government has provided adequate procedural safeguards against the erroneous deprivation of a citizen's liberty or PROPERTY RIGHTS [I], Powell held, the Court must weigh and balance the magnitude of the individual interests at stake; the government's interests, including those in cheap and efficient administration; and the reduction in the risk of error that more-extensive procedures might yield.

Powell was also an important figure in cases involving SUBSTANTIVE DUE PROCESS [4,I] issues. He joined the initial 7–2 majority recognizing constitutional abortion rights in ROE V. WADE (1973) [3] and remained committed to *Roe*'s analytical framework throughout his tenure on the Court. As the Court later grew more polarized on abortion issues, Powell's centrist line-drawing often proved decisive in making 5–4 majorities. Powell also cast the swing vote in BOWERS V. HARDWICK (1986) [I], holding that the Constitution's protection of the right of PRIVACY [3,I] and the right of procreation does not extend to homosexual sodomy. In a characteristically accommodationist gesture, however, he suggested that a severe criminal penalty might offend the constitutional prohibition against CRUEL AND UNUSUAL PUNISHMENT [2,I].

Early in his career on the Supreme Court, Justice Powell won high praise from influential commentators for his skillful and judicious use of a balancing approach to constitutional questions. Although never defined with great precision, balancing—as practiced in *Mathews v. Eldridge*, for example—calls for the identification of all relevant and competing interests, and the striking of a balance for the case at hand; slight changes in the catalogue of affected interests, or the degree of their implication, could alter the result in the next case. Partly because of the looseness with which definitions of balancing are formulated, it is difficult to say how sharply balancing differs from other approaches to CONSTITUTIONAL INTERPRETATION [1]. Much depends on how the specification of relevant interests fits into, or competes with, judicial reliance on such factors as the constitutional text, constitutional history, precedent, constitutional structure, and traditional or consensus values.

Nevertheless, the view seems to be gaining currency that balancing is the currently predominant approach to constitutional interpretation and that Justice Powell was a leading figure in popularizing this methodology. Some commentators have offered the further argument that balancing is a deficient or even a bankrupt method of constitutional analysis. And at least one, Professor Paul Kahn, has argued that its deficiencies are damningly exhibited in Justice Powell's opinions. Powell's balancing, according to this criticism, was ad hoc, unpredictable, and subjective. Moreover, his approach to judging misconceived the JUDICIAL FUNCTION [I], which is to identify and hierarchically array constitutional principles of sufficient clarity and generality to offer clear guidance both to lower courts and to political decision makers.

These criticisms are at best overstated. Powell's case-by-case balancing approach located him in a time-honored tradition of practical thinking in which principles—whether legal or moral—represent the distilled wisdom of carefully individualized judgments. Adherents of this approach, which has found its way into the traditions of common law adjudication and of constitutional interpretation as well, argue forcefully that it is a practical and intellectual mistake to rest on rules that are too broad for their correctness to be rationally vindicated in advance. And Powell, when he thought rational vindication possible, did not hesitate to paint with a broad brush. He did so, for example, in establishing First Amendment lines and categories in *Gertz v. Robert Welch, Inc.*

It is a separate charge that Powell's mode of balancing—in the affirmative action cases, for example—represented JUDICIAL POLICYMAKING [3] that was insufficiently rooted in traditional sources of legal authority to qualify as anything more than judicial second-guessing of a political judgment. Powell, his critics argue, located himself too much "inside" the political community and wrongly tried to bring the community's values to bear on constitutional questions; instead, a Justice should locate himself outside the community in the lofty and frequently astringent principles of the Constitution. The fallacy in this criticism is that there is ultimately no helpful interpretive position "outside" the constitutional community. A Supreme Court Justice, like anyone, must read the Constitution from inside the society to which its lofty generalities must be applied. And it would be folly to think that a constitutional interpreter should try to ignore the society's needs and values. For Powell, traditional sources of legal authority retained their force. But Powell looked at them, and appropriately so, from a point of view that sought to reach sound, practical solutions to constitutional problems.

It is a somewhat more telling argument against the characteristic jurisprudence of Justice Powell that, in the search for a pragmatic balance—in the effort to keep competitive values in a position approaching equipoise or to achieve what he thought was a sensible result in a particular case—he sometimes drew lines that were too fine or too ad hoc to withstand critical scrutiny. Certainly Powell's humanitarian instincts sometimes caused him to distinguish relevant "conservative" precedents, including those that he had authored, by force of little more than ipse dixit. His concurring opinion in PLYLER V. DOE (1982) [3], distinguishing *San Antonio Independent School District v. Rodriguez* and holding that Texas could not withhold free public education from illegal-alien children, falls into this category. Some have argued that the *Bakke* line between forbidden racial quotas and permissible individual preferences is intellectually untenable.

Finally, Powell's sense of what was prudent or practically necessary sometimes overrode both the force of contending arguments and considerations of fairness. In McCLESKY V. KEMP (1987) [I], for example, the petitioner introduced statistical evidence establishing that blacks are more likely to be sentenced to death than are whites and that the killers of whites are more than four times more likely to be executed than are killers of blacks. This evidence, McClesky argued, required reversal of his death sentence under both the constitutional prohibition against cruel and unusual punishment and the equal protection clause. Justice Powell disagreed. In an opinion of unusual candor, he argued that the Court must reject the plaintiff's argument partly because of the far-reaching implications of its underlying premise. "McClesky's claim, taken to its logical conclusion, throws into serious question the principles that underlie our entire CRIMINAL JUSTICE SYSTEM [I]," Powell wrote. If statistical demonstrations of systemic disparities could establish individual unfairness, the Court "could soon be faced with similar claims [against] other types of penalty" from members of other disadvantaged groups. Powell plainly regarded this prospect as practically intolerable.

Although happily atypical in some respects, *McClesky* was, in fact, a characteristic Powell decision. Exemplifying the role of Justice as statesman, Powell repeatedly experienced conflicts of competing values about how a Supreme Court Justice, with his mission conceived to include a component of prudent statesmanship, ought to act. In cases in which competing values conflict, it is always easy to criticize any particular decision as striking the wrong balance. The harder and more interesting question is whether Powell, in embracing the obligations of prudent statesmanship, conceived his judicial role correctly. Although retirement encomiums are perhaps not the strongest evidence, Powell, upon stepping down from the Supreme Court, was widely hailed as a model Supreme Court Justice of the modern age.

RICHARD FALLON

Bibliography

ALEINIKOFF, T. ALEXANDER 1987 Constitutional Law in the Age of Balancing. *Yale Law Journal* 96:943–1005.

FREEMAN, GEORGE CLEMON 1988 Justice Powell's Constitutional Opinions. *Washington and Lee Law Review* 45:411–465.

GUNTHER, GERALD 1972 In Search of Judicial Quality on a Changing Court: The Case of Justice Powell. *Stanford Law Review* 24:1001–1035.

KAHN, PAUL W. 1987 The Court, the Community and the

Judicial Balance: The Jurisprudence of Justice Powell. *Yale Law Journal* 97:1–60.

MALTZ, EARL M.   1979   Portrait of a Man in the Middle—Mr. Justice Powell, Equal Protection, and the Pure Classification Problem. *Ohio State Law Journal* 40:941–964.

SYNPOSIUM   1982   In Honor of Justice Lewis F. Powell, Jr. *Virginia Law Review* 68:161–458.

TRIBUTE   1987   Tribute to Justice Lewis F. Powell, Jr. *Harvard Law Review* 101:395–420.

UROFSKY, MELVIN I.   1984   Mr. Justice Powell and Education: The Balancing of Competing Values. *Journal of Law and Education* 13:581–627.

PRAGMATISM

Pragmatism, generally considered to be our only indigenous school of philosophic thought, has profoundly influenced the development of American jurisprudence in the twentieth century. This influence is evident in a variety of legal settings, including the field of constitutional law, where debates over the proper interpretive role of the courts continue to focus upon issues first raised in a systematic way by the early philosophers of pragmatism, notably John Dewey.

The school of philosophical pragmatism emerged only in the late nineteenth century, but it is more deeply rooted in the American past than that date implies. Thus, we see in ALEXIS DE TOCQUEVILLE's [4] description of the American philosophical method a preview of what later became, in the works of Charles Peirce, William James, Dewey, and others, a schematically developed general theory: "To evade the bondage of system and habit, of family-maxims, class opinions, and, in some degree, of national prejudices; to accept tradition only as a means of information, and existing facts only as a lesson to be used in doing otherwise and doing better; to seek the reason of things for oneself, and in oneself alone; to tend to results without being bound to means, and to strike through the form to the substance—such are the principal characteristics of what I shall call the philosophical method of the Americans." In this account of philosophical temperament are the core elements of the reconstruction in philosophy that came to dominate constitutional discourse in the twentieth century: an instrumental approach to knowledge based upon a rigorous empiricism, a demystification of the past as a predicate for facilitating change, and an ethical orientation that finds in the application of a norm or concept the criterion of its value.

The emergence of the pragmatic movement in philosophy occurred at a critical juncture in American constitutional history. At a time when constitutional orthodoxy was embodied in the person of Justice STEPHEN J. FIELD [2], the appeal of pragmatic ideas to critics of the dominant view lay in the promise it held for achieving a congruence between law and the needs of a society undergoing rapid flux and transition. In place of a formalistic approach characterized by the derivation of absolute principles that are grounded in nature and from which constitutional conclusions can be deduced with certainty in support of social inequality, the pragmatists offered the prospect of deriving relative principles that are grounded in experience and from which constitutional conclusions of a tentative nature can be inductively assembled in support of a more egalitarian society. The application of pragmatism to constitutional reasoning supported the claim that law should not be an impediment to progress, that the Constitution was not a document embodying immutable principles but one whose meaning depended upon the circumstances of time and place.

In developing their legal theory, the pragmatists both drew on and rejected existing jurisprudential schools of thought. They were critical of the syllogistic process of legal reasoning that they found common to both the philosophical and analytical schools. In the application of ethical considerations by the NATURAL RIGHTS [3] theorists and in the abandonment of such considerations by the analytical positivists, they also found a similar detachment from the realities of the social situation. In the first case, ethics was not grounded in experience, and in the second, reality was distorted by the failure to understand the ethical imperatives implied in experience. The object of the pragmatists was thus to establish an empirical jurisprudence that included a consciousness of the moral basis of law. The attraction of pragmatic philosophy was its potential for steering a middle course between the positivistic separation of law and morality, on the one hand, and, on the other, the natural-rights fusion of law and morality according to standards derived outside of experience. Both extremes led to judicial protection of the status quo, the first by accepting the legitimacy of any existing legal arrangements and the second by freezing the law into a mold formed by metaphysical abstractions. Justice, for the pragmatists, was not to be defined a priori; nor was it identifiable with the will of the sovereign. Rather, it was to be defined "transactionally," emerging out of social experience as an end to be juridically achieved. Acceptance of this view by jurists would make it unnecessary to appeal to noncontextual sources, such as an absolute standard of right conduct embodied in the text of the Constitution.

The principal theorists of legal pragmatism, BENJAMIN N. CARDOZO [1] and ROSCOE POUND [3], wrote most often about private law, but both maintained that their prescriptions applied equally well to constitutional law. Cardozo's "method of sociology" and Pound's "theory of social interests" were intended in part to translate the precepts of Dewey and James into jurisprudential terms of potentially transformative significance for the Constitution. In the case of Dewey, who had addressed himself to legal questions, the translation was fairly straightforward. In his account of the law, legal rules and principles were viewed pragmatically as "working hypotheses" whose validity was to be ascertained by their application in concrete situations. Dewey also held the work of the Founding Fathers to be much less the object of reverence than had traditionally been the case: "The belief in political fixity, of the sanctity of some form of state consecrated by the efforts of our fathers and hallowed by tradition, is one of the stumbling-blocks in the way of orderly and directed change; it is an invitation to revolt and revolution." Just as the antifoundationalist emphasis in contemporary philosophy—the denial that knowledge must be based upon certain objective truths—owes much to the work of the early pragmatists, so too does the currently popular disparagement of the doctrine of ORIGINAL INTENT [I] in CONSTITUTIONAL INTERPRETATION [1]. Therefore, the contention that the Constitution embodies foundational principles of justice that reflect the original intentions of its Framers, is doubly problematic, and it carries minimal weight in the pragmatic account of constitutional interpretation.

The judge most often associated with philosophical pragmatism is OLIVER WENDELL HOMES, JR. [2]. Although he occasionally criticized some of the formulations of pragmatists, his work as a Supreme Court Justice (as well as his extrajudicial writings) often manifested a pragmatic approach to the Constitution. More important, his opinions inspired many others whose interest in pragmatism had less to do with the philosophical skepticism that appealed to Holmes than with the social reform possibilities implicit in its method. For example, Holmes's opinion in MISSOURI V. HOLLAND (1920) [3] suggested that the needs of the twentieth century need not be held hostage to the assumptions of the eighteenth or nineteenth centuries: "The case before us must be considered in the light of our whole experience and not merely in that of what was said a hundred years ago." His famous dissenting opinion in ABRAMS V. UNITED STATES (1919) [1] expressed in one short sentence the essence of the pragmatic conception of the Constitution. The theory of the Constitution, Holmes said, was that truth would emerge in the marketplace of ideas; the document "is an experiment, as all life is an experiment." This view often led Holmes to advocate judicial self-restraint; but in time it came to express a sentiment that provided jurisprudential support for a more activist, socially engaged judiciary. The work of the WARREN COURT [4] exemplified an important legacy of the pragmatists (especially Dewey): the increasing reliance by the judiciary upon social science evidence. Holmes's role in this development is suggested in an observation of his that Dewey, in the elaboration of his pragmatic philosophy, saw fit to quote: "I have had in mind an ultimate dependence of law [upon science] be-

cause it is ultimately for science to determine, as far as it can, the relative worth of our different social ends."

The pragmatic conception of the Constitution has generated considerable controversy. Criticism centers on two distinct but related problems. The first is that the importation of pragmatic ideas into the arena of constitutional interpretation inevitably leads to the abandonment of any meaningful distinction between judicial and legislative modes of decision making. This has the effect, it is claimed, of undermining the legitimacy of the Supreme Court, an unfortunate outcome rendered no less unfortunate by assertions about the enhanced quality of the Court's output. The second is that a pragmatic jurisprudence provides inadequate protection for constitutional rights. By effectively reducing self-evident and immutable truths to the level of tentative rules, pragmatic judges risk sacrificing FUNDAMENTAL RIGHTS [2] on the altar of social expedience. If the Constitution is a document lacking fixed points of reference and thus deprived of meanings that are not simply contextual (that is, situated in the experience of changing historical moments), can it serve as guarantor of rights that are in their ultimate sense expressive of an unchanging human nature?

GARY J. JACOBSOHN

(SEE ALSO: *Conservatism* [I]; *Judicial Activism and Judicial Restraint* [3]; *Liberalism* [I]; *Political Philosophy of the Constitution* [3,I] *Positivism* [I].)

Bibliography

GREY, THOMAS C. 1989 Holmes and Legal Pragmatism. *Stanford Law Review* 41:787–870.
JACOBSOHN, GARY J. 1977 *Pragmatism, Statesmanship, and the Supreme Court.* Ithaca, N.Y.: Cornell University Press.
SUMMERS, ROBERT SAMUEL 1982 *Instrumentalism and American Legal Theory.* Ithaca, N.Y.: Cornell University Press.

PRESIDENT AND THE TREATY POWER

Article II of the Constitution authorizes the President to "make" treaties with the ADVICE AND CONSENT [1] of the SENATE [I], provided two-thirds of the senators concur. An "Article II" treaty may be a bilateral or multilateral international agreement and is brought into force as an international obligation of the United States by the formal act of ratification or accession. This formal act (hereinafter called "ratification") is separate from the act of signing the treaty and is accomplished pursuant to an instrument executed by the President. Accordingly, the TREATY POWER [4] is a presidential power that requires Senate participation before its exercise.

The decision to open a treaty negotiation, like the process of negotiation itself, is an exclusive EXECUTIVE PRE-ROGATIVE [1]. The Senate or individual senators may influence the course of a negotiation, but the Senate has no constitutionally recognized role before the submission of a treaty for advice and consent to ratification. The original understanding of the treaty power envisioned Senate participation before the negotiation and conclusion of treaties. However, this understanding was quickly reinterpreted in an informal manner. In 1789, in connection with an upcoming negotiation, President GEORGE WASHINGTON [4] personally appeared before the Senate and asked its advice on a series of specific negotiating questions. The Senate postponed consideration of all but one such question to a second session. This procedure was unsatisfactory to both the President and the Senate and was abandoned. Even the practice initiated by Washington of seeking written advice on particular negotiating questions was abandoned by him before the end of his first administration. A congressional study reported that "[b]y 1816 the practice had become established that the Senate's formal participation in treaty-making was to approve, approve with conditions, or disapprove treaties after they had been negotiated by the President or his representative." An attempt in 1973 to affirm the "historic" role of the Senate in treaty making by constituting it as a council of advice for that purpose came to naught in the face of executive branch, constitutional objections. The Senate and individual senators may nevertheless informally influence the course of negotiations through expressions of views at hearings, participation as advisors to the U.S. delegation to a negotiation, and other informal methods.

If a negotiation produces an international agreement, the President must choose the most appropriate basis in domestic constitutional law for bringing the agreement into force. There are four distinct sources of authority for presidential conclusion of an international agreement on behalf of the United States. The President may submit the agreement as an Article II treaty to the Senate for its advice and consent to ratification. Alternatively, the President may seek congressional authorization of an international agreement by JOINT RESOLUTION [3] or act of Congress or may use existing legislation as a basis for ratification of the agreement. These agreements are called congressional–executive agreements. This alternative procedure has become accepted as constitutionally equivalent to the Article II procedure. Any international agreement so authorized is binding on the United States as a matter of international law, and both congressional–executive agreements and "self-executing" Article II treaties supersede earlier inconsistent federal statutes as a matter of domestic law. In general, a "self-executing" treaty is one that is intended by the United States to take effect as domestic law upon ratification.

Third, an international agreement may be contemplated by an earlier Article II treaty and may derive its authority from the earlier treaty. Such an agreement has the same legal force internationally and domestically as an Article II treaty. Fourth, an international agreement may be concluded on the basis of the President's power in FOREIGN AFFAIRS [2]. An international agreement concluded pursuant to the President's foreign-affairs power has the same effect internationally as an Article II treaty, but the President does not normally use a presidential EXECUTIVE AGREEMENT [2] if it would be inconsistent with domestic law (for an exception see DAMES & MOORE V. REGAN, 1981 [2]). Any international agreement, including an Article II treaty, supersedes inconsistent state law.

The President's choice as to whether to submit an international agreement to the Senate as an Article II treaty is guided by the State Department's Circular 175 Procedure. This State Department regulation requires that due consideration be given to such factors as the formality, importance and duration of the agreement, the preference of Congress, the need for implementing LEGISLATION [3] by Congress, the effect on state law, and past U.S. and international practice. Under Circular 175, officials of the executive branch may consult with the Senate Foreign Relations Committee as to the choice of constitutional procedure. Although the "Circular 175" factors are rather general and may sometimes suggest alternative inconsistent choices and although the choice of constitutional procedure is in part a political choice, historical factors are often decisive. Thus, international agreements dealing with boundaries, arms control, military alliances, extradition, and investment are normally submitted to the Senate as Article II treaties. In contrast, international agreements dealing with trade, finance, energy, fisheries, and aviation are normally concluded as congressional–executive agreements. Sometimes an agreement may be concluded as an Article II treaty that is non–self-executing and is therefore subject to the enactment of implementing legislation by Congress before its ratification. This procedure may be preferable if the treaty requires regular appropriation of funds.

If the President chooses to submit an international agreement to the Senate as an Article II treaty, the Senate may consent to its ratification subject to conditions that bind the President if the President chooses to ratify the treaty. These conditions may require the President to attach a reservation to United States adherence to the treaty or to amend the treaty by agreement with the other treaty party or parties. Senate-imposed conditions may also require the President to make a specified declaration to the other treaty party or parties in connection with ratification, or a Senate-imposed condition may state an understanding that the Senate seeks to impose on the President or the U.S. courts—for example, an understanding regarding a particular interpretation or the treaty's domestic effect. The President normally included Senate-imposed conditions requiring agreement by, or communication to, the other treaty party or parties in an instrument exchanged with the treaty partner or deposited specifically in connection with ratification. However, the President has claimed the constitutional power to comply with Senate-imposed conditions outside the formal ratification process. A Senate-imposed condition must relate to the subject matter of the treaty and may not infringe on other provisions of the Constitution, such as the BILL OF RIGHTS [1] or the President's foreign-affairs power. In MISSOURI V. HOLLAND (1920) [3], the Supreme Court upheld the validity of a treaty-related act of Congress that, absent the treaty, arguably contravened the TENTH AMENDMENT [4]. This decision caused considerable concern that a treaty might supersede other constitutional provisions, including the Bill of Rights. However, in REID V. COVERT (1957) [3], a plurality of Justices opined that a treaty may not contravene an individual liberty specifically protected by the Bill of Rights. Of course, the content of such a right may be altered by the existence of a treaty and the foreign location of the governmental activity.

Following the Senate's advice and consent, the President makes an independent decision as to whether to ratify the treaty, thereby bringing it into force as an international obligation of the United States subject to the conditions imposed by the Senate. Until 1950, ratified treaties were published in the *Statutes at Large*. Now they are published separately by the Department of State as part of the series entitled *United States Treaties and Other International Agreements*. The President has also exercised the power to accept or reject proposed reservations by other parties to a treaty without the participation of the Senate.

Once a treaty has been ratified, the President has the power to interpret it, unilaterally or in agreement with treaty partners, pursuant to the President's foreign-affairs power. However, the President normally does not commit the interpretation of treaties to third-party dispute resolution, such as arbitration or adjudication by the International Court of Justice, without Senate or congressional acquiescence or approval. Moreover, if the President changes an earlier, commonly held interpretation, Congress may use its legislative and appropriations powers to force the President to reconsider. The reinterpretation controversy involving the 1972 U.S.–U.S.S.R. Treaty on the Limitation of Anti-Ballistic Missile Systems (hereinafter called the "ABM Treaty") is a good example of this phenomenon. When the President sent the ABM Treaty to the Senate for its advice and consent to ratification, executive branch officials told the Senate that the treaty prohibited the development and testing of space-based ABM systems based on "other physical principles" than those existing in 1972, such as lasers. Thirteen years

later the administration of RONALD REAGAN [3,I] "reinterpreted" the treaty to permit the development and testing of those space-based ABM systems. However, several senators, former officials who negotiated the treaty, and academic commentators vigorously disputed the administration's case. Congress used its legislative and appropriations powers to force the executive branch to limit development and testing of ABM systems to activities permitted under the original interpretation.

In addition to the controversy over the substantive question of how the ABM Treaty should be interpreted, the reinterpretation attempt of the ABM Treaty sparked a dispute over the constitutional limits on presidential interpretation power. In 1987, the Senate considered, but declined to adopt, Senate Resolution 167, a general resolution stating that the meaning of a treaty cannot be unilaterally changed by the President from "what the Senate understands the treaty to mean when it gives its advice and consent to ratification." After another round of debate of the constitutional issue, the Senate attached a similar condition in its consent to ratification of the 1987 U.S.–U.S.S.R. Treaty on the Elimination of Intermediate-range and Shorter-range Missiles (hereinafter called the "INF Treaty") applicable only to that treaty. The President questioned the constitutionality of that condition, but only after he had ratified the INF Treaty.

After all the controversy, little is settled. Most commentators probably would agree that the President may not reinterpret fundamental treaty provisions in major respects, even with the agreement of a treaty partner, without seeking Senate or congressional approval. Such a change would probably be classified as a "major amendment" to the treaty and, as such, would require that consent. It would also seem that other reinterpretations could be made by the President with Senate or congressional acquiescence. If Congress disagrees with a presidential interpretation, it may reflect its nonacquiescence through its legislative or appropriations power. Finally, conditions formally adopted, like that to the INF Treaty, should bind the President if the President chooses to ratify the treaty.

Another area of recent controversy concerns the termination of treaties. President JIMMY CARTER [1] terminated an Article II defense treaty in accordance with its terms, despite a "sense of the Congress" expression that he should consult with Congress before any such change in policy. In GOLDWATER V. CARTER (1979) [2] the Supreme Court dismissed a complaint filed by some members of Congress to enjoin the presidential action. The PLURALITY OPINION [3] invoked the POLITICAL QUESTION [3,I] doctrine. Since that time, the President has claimed the right to terminate Article II treaties in accordance with their terms. Congress has acquiesced. The President has also successfully asserted the right to declare a treaty partner to be in "material breach" of its terms so the United States may withdraw from the treaty. Finally, the President has successfully asserted the right to violate the terms of a treaty or other norms of international law in the course of conducting the nation's foreign relations, at least in the absence of congressional action prohibiting such a violation. Those rights are based on the President's foreign-affairs power.

Because the judiciary rarely adjudicates SEPARATION OF POWERS [4] issues on the merits in foreign-affairs cases, the best guide to constitutional law defining presidential power in this area is recent historical practice; it constitutes a common law reflecting the pattern of accommodations reached by the President, the Senate, and the Congress in allocating responsibilities under the treaty power.

PHILLIP R. TRIMBLE

(SEE ALSO: *Congress and Foreign Policy* [I]; *Congressional War Powers* [I]; *Senate and Foreign Policy* [I].)

Bibliography

BESTOR, ARTHUR 1989 "Advice" from the Very Beginning, "Consent" When the End Is Achieved. *American Journal of International Law* 83:718–727.
CONGRESSIONAL RESEARCH SERVICE 1984 *Treaties and Other International Agreements: The Role of the United States Senate.* S-Print 98-205, 98th Congress, Second Session.
GLENNON, MICHAEL J. 1990 *Constitutional Diplomacy.* Princeton, N.J.: Princeton University Press.
HENKIN, LOUIS 1972 *Foreign Affairs and the Constitution.* Mineola, N.Y.: Foundation Press.
KOH, HAROLD HONGJU 1990 *The National Security Constitution.* New Haven, Conn.: Yale University Press.
SYMPOSIUM 1989 Arms Control Treaty Interpretation. *University of Pennsylvania Law Review* 137:1351–1557.

PRISONERS' RIGHTS
(Update)

Upon conviction and imprisonment, a profound change occurs in a person's legal status. Duly convicted prisoners lose entirely many freedoms enjoyed by free persons; however, they do not relinquish all rights. As the Supreme Court noted in *Wolff v. McDonnell* (1974), "though his rights may be diminished by the needs and exigencies of the institutional environment, a prisoner is not wholly stripped of constitutional protections when he is imprisoned for crime. There is no iron curtain drawn between the Constitution and the prisons of this country."

Prisoners always retain the right to the minimal conditions necessary for human survival (i.e., the right to food, clothing, shelter, and medical care). The right of prisoners to a non-life-threatening environment goes beyond the provision of life's necessities; it includes their right to be protected from each other and from themselves. On this last point, lower courts have been more responsive to prisoners' claims than the Supreme Court and have found that prison crowding is unconstitutional. As a federal district court in Florida asserted in *Costello v. Wainwright* (1975), prison crowding "endangers the very lives of the inmates" and therefore violates the Eighth Amendment's guarantee against CRUEL AND UNUSUAL PUNISHMENT [2,I]. The Supreme Court's reluctance to follow the lower courts is understandable, for empirical studies flatly contradict the assertion that crowding is life-threatening. Not only are the overall death rates, accidental death rates, and homicide and suicide rates of inmates two to three times lower than for comparable groups of parolees (controlling for age, race, and sex), but no statistically significant correlations exist between measures of crowding (density and occupancy) and inmate death rates.

Beyond agreement that inmates have the minimal right to a non-life-threatening environment, legal debate rages. Some courts and legal scholars have taken their cues from the Sixth Circuit Court of Appeals in *Coffin v. Reichard* (1944) and have declared that prisoners retain all the rights of ordinary citizens except those expressly or by necessary implication taken by law. The Supreme Court's decision in PROCUNIER V. MARTINEZ (1974) [3] followed this line of reasoning when it held that it would employ a STRICT SCRUTINY [4] standard of review to evaluate claims that the rights of prisoners were being denied. It declared that it would sustain limitations of prisoners' rights only if they furthered an important or substantial governmental interest and if they were no greater than necessary to protect that interest.

Fundamentally opposed to *Coffin* and *Procunier* is the view, now dominant on the Supreme Court, that inmates are without rights except for those conferred by law or necessarily implied and that, as a consequence, courts should employ the reasonableness test to assess the legitimacy of restrictions on what prisoners assert to be their rights. In *Turner v. Safley* (1987) the Supreme Court articulated this position and rejected the use of strict scrutiny in prisoners' rights cases. Writing for a five-member majority, Justice SANDRA DAY O'CONNOR [3,I] declared that "when a prison regulation impinges on inmates' constitutional rights, the regulation is valid if it is reasonably related to legitimate penological interests." O'Connor announced a four-prong test for measuring reasonableness: (1) Is there "a 'valid, rational connection' between the prison regulation and the legitimate government interest put forward to justify it?" (2) "Are alternative means of exercising the right . . . open to prison inmates?" (3) What is "the impact [that] accommodation of the asserted constitutional right will have on guards and other inmates, and on the allocation of prison resources generally"? (4) Is "the absence of ready alternatives . . . evidence of reasonableness of the prison regulation"? Employing this four-prong test, Justice O'Connor rejected a FIRST AMENDMENT [2,I] challenge to a Missouri ban on inmate-to-inmate correspondence because the prohibition on correspondence was "logically connected" to legitimate security concerns. In O'LONE V. ESTATE OF SHABAZZ (1987) [I], the Court applied the same reasonableness test to sustain New Jersey prison policies that resulted in Muslim inmates' inability to attend weekly congregational services.

Security concerns generally trump the claims of prisoners' rights; the Court is hesitant to recognize inmate claims that have the potential of putting at risk the prison itself, the guards, other inmates, or the petitioner. Justice WILLIAM H. REHNQUIST [4,I], in *Jones v. North Carolina Prisoners' Union* (1977), summarized well the Court's deferential approach to these issues: "It is enough to say that they [prison officials] have not been conclusively shown to be wrong in this view. The interest in preserving order and authority in prisons is self-evident."

Applying this reasoning, the Court has denied inmates' claims to a First Amendment right to organize as a prisoners' labor union, rejected the contention that an inmate's RIGHT OF PRIVACY [3,I] protects against routine strip and body-cavity searches, and refused to recognize any inmate legal rights in the ordinary classification process or inter-prison transfer. As the Court said in *Moody v. Daggett* (1976), no DUE PROCESS [2] issues are implicated by "the discretionary transfer of state prisoners to a substantially less agreeable prison, even where the transfer visit[s] a 'grievous loss' upon the inmate. The same is true of prisoner classification and eligibility for rehabilitative programs."

Beyond assuring life's necessities for inmates, the Court has consistently recognized inmates' claims in only two areas: their due process right of ACCESS TO THE COURTS [1] and PROCEDURAL DUE PROCESS [3] protection of their liberty interest in retaining "good time" and avoiding solitary confinement. Concerning the former, the Court has repeatedly insisted that inmates have the right to access to legal redress and that this right of access to the courts requires either an adequate law library or assistance from persons trained in law (although not necessarily lawyers). Concerning the latter, the Court held in *Wolff v. McDonnell* that inmates have a liberty interest in the good-time credit they have acquired and that they may not be stripped of these credits without a hearing before an impartial tribunal. The Court has not considered either of these rights to jeopardize prison security. Access to the courts poses no problems at all, and, as the Court made explicit in *Hewitt v. Helms* (1978) and *Superintendent v. Hill* (1985), prison disciplinary proceedings can follow (and

need not precede) solitary confinement and can impose sanctions based on the lax evidentiary standard of "some evidence."

RALPH A. ROSSUM

(SEE ALSO: *Body Search* [I].)

Bibliography
COHEN, FRED 1988 The Law of Prisoner's Rights: An Overview. *Criminal Law Bulletin* 24:321–349.
ROSSUM, RALPH A. 1984 The Problem of Prison Crowding: On the Limits of Prison Capacity and Judicial Capacity. *Benchmark* 1, no. 6:22–30.

PRIVATE DISCRIMINATION

The Constitution is a document filled with restraints upon the actions of government, but for the most part it has not been interpreted to extend its reach into the private sector. The FOURTEENTH AMENDMENT [2,I] to the Constitution, for example, guarantees the EQUAL PROTECTION OF THE LAWS [2,I], a command against discrimination that the Supreme Court has long read as applying only to the actions of states. The Supreme Court in BOLLING V. SHARPE (1954) [1] applied the antidiscrimination principle to the federal government, holding that the DUE PROCESS [2] clause of the Fifth Amendment contains within it an equal protection component. No provision of the Constitution, however, has ever been interpreted to apply rules of equal protection directly to private entities, prohibiting a private citizen or corporation from discriminating against others on the basis of race, sex, or religion.

Acts of private discrimination, nevertheless, do raise a number of significant constitutional issues. First, to what extent does the THIRTEENTH AMENDMENT's [4] abolition of SLAVERY [4] serve as a constitutional restraint on private acts of discrimination less severe than actual slavery? Second, when are the actions of private entities sufficiently intertwined with government to be brought within the coverage of the Fourteenth Amendment's equal protection clause under the rubric of the STATE ACTION [4,I] doctrine? Third, when the United States Congress forbids private discrimination, as in CIVIL RIGHTS [1,I] laws prohibiting racial bias in employment or housing, from where in the Constitution does Congress derive its affirmative authority to pass such legislation? Finally, when laws are passed at the federal, state, or local level banning discrimination by private individuals, businesses, or organizations, do such laws violate the FREEDOM OF ASSEMBLY AND ASSOCIATION [2] embodied in the FIRST AMENDMENT [2,I]?

The Thirteenth Amendment is one of the few constitutional provisions that directly implicates private conduct. That Amendment, the first of the three "Civil War Amendments," flatly bans slavery and involuntary servitude. It acts directly upon private entities; slaves were owned by private businesses and individuals. The Thirteenth Amendment, however, has not been interpreted to provide a significant source of constitutional proscription against acts of private discrimination. While the Amendment has been construed by the Supreme Court to protect individuals from the "badges and incidents" of slavery as well as actual slavery itself, the Supreme Court held in the CIVIL RIGHTS CASES [1] in 1883 that the Amendment does not restrict "mere discriminations on account of race or color." The Thirteenth is thus too narrow a prohibition to be of practical use as a restraint against the types of private discrimination prevalent in modern society. In 1968, however, the Supreme Court did hold that the Thirteenth Amendment serves as an important source of congressional power to pass legislation banning private acts of discrimination.

While the equal protection clause of the Fourteenth Amendment prohibits only governmental discrimination, under the so-called state action requirement many Supreme Court decisions have recognized that ostensibly private discrimination should be treated as state action because of some connection between the private actor and the government. When the private actor is performing a "public function," for example, its activities are treated as state action, and subject to the equal protection clause. The Supreme Court has thus held that segregated primary elections conducted by political parties in Texas involved public functions and violated the Fourteenth Amendment. In MARSH V. ALABAMA (1946) [3] the Court held that a "company town," a privately owned area encompassing both residential and business districts that looked exactly like any other town and in which the private company had assumed all the normal functions of running a city, was subject to the limitations of the First and Fourteenth Amendments. The Court has also held that apparently private activity will be treated as state action when the state and private entities have a "symbiotic relationship," as where a private restaurant leases space in a public parking garage, or when the state has commanded or encouraged acts of private discrimination.

When neither the Thirteenth Amendment nor the "state action" doctrine under the Fourteenth Amendment can be stretched to embrace a particular type of private discrimination, then the Constitution of its own force does not render the private discrimination illegal. Federal, state, and local governments may then choose to pass legislation filling this vacuum, banning discrimination through statutes and ordinances. Modern American law is pervaded with restrictions directed against private entities forbidding discrimination of all kinds, including discrimination on the basis of race, ethnic origin, sex, sexual

orientation, religion, age, and physical or mental disabilities. Many of these laws are acts of Congress. When Congress attempts to outlaw private discrimination, the first constitutional question to be addressed is whether Congress has affirmative constitutional power to enact the law.

Two principal constitutional sources have been advanced to support congressional legislation banning private discrimination: the COMMERCE CLAUSE [1,I], and Congress's powers under the enforcement clauses of the Thirteenth Amendment, Fourteenth Amendment, and FIFTEENTH AMENDMENT [2]. In the debates leading to the passage of the CIVIL RIGHTS ACT OF 1964 [1], one of the most important modern acts of legislation dealing with private discrimination, members of Congress debated whether the act should be grounded in Congress's power to regulate INTERSTATE COMMERCE [2] or in its power under Section 5 of the Fourteenth Amendment to enforce the Amendment by "appropriate legislation." Similar enforcement clauses exist under the Thirteenth Amendment, which abolished slavery; under the Fifteenth Amendment, which granted emancipated blacks the right to vote; and under several later amendments, including the NINETEENTH AMENDMENT [3] (WOMEN'S SUFFRAGE [I]), the TWENTY-THIRD AMENDMENT [4] (voting in the DISTRICT OF COLUMBIA [2]), the TWENTY-FOURTH AMENDMENT (abolition of POLL TAXES [3]), and the TWENTY-SIXTH AMENDMENT [4] (establishing eighteen as voting age).

The Civil Rights Act of 1964 banned most significant acts of discrimination in the private sector, including such areas as employment transportation, restaurants, and hotel accommodations. Some members of Congress argued that the act should be rooted in the enforcement clause of the Fourteenth Amendment, because it was in reality an exercise in social legislation aimed at attacking racial bias. Other members, doubtful that the Fourteenth Amendment could be used to reach private discrimination, argued for buttressing the act under the well-established powers of Congress to regulate interstate commerce. In two significant 1964 decisions shortly following passage of the act, HEART OF ATLANTA MOTEL V. UNITED STATES [2] and *Katzenbach v. McClung*, the Supreme Court upheld the Civil Rights Act on the basis of the commerce clause, and thus did not reach the question of congressional power under the Fourteenth Amendment.

As a practical matter, virtually any enactment of Congress aimed at private discrimination would be sustained under modern commerce clause analysis. Even localized acts of discrimination may, when considered cumulatively with other such acts around the nation, have a substantial impact on interstate commerce when aggregated. Under contemporary commerce clause theory, that potential aggregate impact would be enough to uphold the legislation.

Because Congress's power under the commerce clause is so sweeping, there has been little cause for the Court to determine precisely how far congressional enforcement powers under the post–Civil War amendments may be extended to reach private-sector discrimination.

The few decisions that have dealt with congressional enforcement power under the Civil War amendments, however, indicate that Congress's power does include an ability to proscribe private activity that would not be directly prohibited by the substantive reach of the amendment itself. In an important decision involving the Thirteenth Amendment, JONES V. ALFRED H. MAYER CO. (1968 [3]), the Court upheld an application of the Civil Rights Act of 1866 to forbid private discrimination in property dealings. The Court held that Congress's power to enforce the Thirteenth Amendment included the power to identify "badges or incidents of slavery" and to pass laws NECESSARY AND PROPER [3] to combat them.

In sum, there are ample sources of support in the Constitution for acts of Congress banning private discrimination. Congress has passed a considerable body of laws attacking such discrimination, often including in the legislation enforcement mechanisms or procedural advantages that actually make it easier to prove and obtain legal relief from acts of private discrimination than for claims based directly on the Constitution for discrimination by the government. Modern civil rights litigation frequently involves interpretation of such legislation, in which the courts are asked to determine just how far Congress has gone in a particular statute to ban discrimination in the private sector.

The final area of modern constitutional debate concerning discrimination in the private sector involves attempts by organizations engaged in discrimination to resist the application of laws banning such discrimination on the grounds that the laws infringe on the constitutional right of free association. The Civil Rights Act of 1964, and the many state and local civil rights laws passed in the 1960s and early 1970s modeled after that act, tended to reach only commercial private activity, such as employers, or stores, restaurants, and places of lodging generally "open for business to the public." A second generation of civil rights acts began to be passed by cities and states around the country, however, seeking to forbid discrimination by "private" clubs and organizations. Several of these groups claimed that these regulations violated their constitutional rights of free association.

These claims have, thus far, proved unsuccessful. In *Roberts v. United States Jaycees* (1984), the Supreme Court faced a Minnesota law that prohibited SEX DISCRIMINATION [4,I] in groups such as the Jaycees. The Supreme Court established two types of FREEDOM OF ASSOCIATION [I]: FREEDOM OF INTIMATE ASSOCIATION [2] and "freedom of expressive association." Groups with strong claims to freedom of intimate association tend to be relatively small, exercise a high degree of selectivity, and maintain seclusion from others as critical aspects of the relationship. The Jaycees, the Court held, were basically unselective, and lacked the attributes that would qualify for recognition of intimate associational claims. The second freedom of expressive association is an incident of the FREEDOM OF SPEECH [2,I] and assembly. The Court in *Roberts* held that application of state sex discrimination laws to the Jaycees would not impermissibly interfere with their freedom of expressive association, and it upheld the Minnesota law.

The Court next visited the freedom of association problem in *Board of Directors of Rotary International v. Rotary Club of Duarte* (1987). In characterizing the Rotary Club, the Court noted that although Rotary Clubs take no positions on "public questions," they do "engage in a variety of commendable service activities" protected by the First Amendment. These sorts of activities, however, posed no serious implications for infringement of the members' rights of expressive association. The lessons of these cases appear to be that attempts by private groups to resist imposition of antidiscrimination laws on free association grounds will probably fail, unless the groups possess genuinely impressive credentials as truly private organizations, with characteristics of exclusion or intimacy bordering on those of family or religious groups.

A related problem involves private religious schools that discriminate on the basis of race. The Supreme Court in *Norwood v. Harrison* (1973) held that a state could not lend textbooks to schools that practice racial SEGREGATION [4], even though such aid to a religious school would not be illegal under the ESTABLISHMENT CLAUSE [2,I]. Notwithstanding the lack of any violation of the principle of SEPARATION OF CHURCH AND STATE [4,I], the Court held that there is no constitutional protection for state aid to RACIAL DISCRIMINATION [3,I]. In BOB JONES UNIVERSITY V. UNITED STATES (1983) [1], the Court held that the Internal Revenue Service had been authorized by Congress to deny tax-exempt status to private schools that discriminate on a racial basis, and that this denial did not prohibit the free exercise of religion.

Modern constitutional law, in conclusion, generally does not impose restraints on private discrimination through direct application of the Constitution itself. On the other hand, by refusing to recognize any significant constitutional barriers to antidiscrimination legislation, modern constitutional law facilitates efforts on the part of federal, state, and local governments to eradicate such discrimination.

RODNEY A. SMOLLA

(SEE ALSO: *Affirmative Action* [1,I]; *Badges of Servitude* [1]; *Employment Discrimination* [2]; *Fourteenth Amendment and Section 5 (Framing)* [I]; *Fourteenth Amendment and Section 5 (Judicial Construction)* [I]; *Racial Quotas* [3]; *Racial Preference* [I].)

PRIVILEGE AGAINST SELF-INCRIMINATION

See: Right Against Self-Incrimination [3,I]

PROCEDURAL DUE PROCESS OF LAW, CIVIL

A claim for procedural due process is a claim that the government cannot undertake a particular act vis-à-vis an individual or set of individuals without according them an opportunity to be heard. Depending upon the situation, a constitutionally adequate opportunity to be heard may involve a "hearing" that is written or oral and may occur before or after the alleged "deprivation" has occurred. The contexts in which the issue of procedural due process arises vary; included among the litigants who have raised procedural due process challenges heard by the United States Supreme Court since the mid-1980s are PRISONERS [3,I], ALIENS [1], food-stamp recipients, veterans, and college athletes.

A procedural due process claim is not a challenge that the government is absolutely forbidden to act in a particular way. Rather, a procedural due process challenge is that as a predicate to action, the government must accord the person(s) subject to the action with a set of procedural safeguards, designed to make the government's decision more accurate and to recognize the dignitary and participatory interests in process that both the person(s) and society have.

Making the distinction in practice between SUBSTANTIVE DUE PROCESS [4,I] and procedural due process, however, is not always easy. For example, many due process opinions discuss whether or not a court in one jurisdiction can hale an outsider (a citizen of another state or country) before it and what jurisdiction's law may constitutionally be applied to that lawsuit. For more than a century, the Supreme Court has talked about these cases as raising due process problems, but has not always identified which kind of due process was at issue. Only relatively recently have commentators discussed such issues as substantive due process questions—despite the fact that the issue arises in the context of where and how to conduct a lawsuit. Another illustration is a group of due process cases that address access to EVIDENCE [2]. In *Arizona v. Youngblood*

(1988) the Supreme Court held that upon specific request of defendants, prosecutors have some obligation to disclose exculpatory information in their possession, but, absent bad faith on the part of police, "failure to preserve potentially useful evidence does not constitute denial of due process of law." Once again, although the rights involved related to litigation, the Court did not specify the kind of due process at issue but relied on a substantive due process analysis.

Supreme Court doctrine requires that for one to bring a procedural due process claim, two prefatory elements be established—STATE ACTION [4,I] and intent. Knowing when the state is acting is not always easy. For example, the Supreme Court concluded in *National Collegiate Athletic Association v. Tarkanian* (1987) that the National Collegiate Athletic Association was not engaged in state action, despite the fact that its 960 members include "virtually all public and private universities and four-year colleges conducting major athletic programs in the United States." Second, the governmental action must be intentional. In *Daniels v. Williams* (1986) the Supreme Court held that "the Due Process Clause is simply not implicated by a negligent act of an official causing unintended loss of or injury to life, liberty or property."

Once a claim has cleared the hurdles of intentional deprivations by government action, two more questions remain: (1) Does the governmental action threaten to deprive one of "life," "liberty," or "property"? (2) If so, how much process is due? The answers from the Supreme Court have limited both the instances when the clause applies and the quantum of process due.

"Property" continues to include both traditionally understood material possessions and state-created benefits, such as SOCIAL SECURITY [4], licenses, and other statutorily defined restrictions on governmental action. However, statutory ENTITLEMENTS [I] (whether characterized as "property" or "liberty") are now read more restrictively. To show such entitlement, the legislative or regulatory statement has to be positivistic (i.e., X "shall" occur) and the limits on official discretion must be express (i.e., X shall occur unless the official finds A, B, or C).

The question of what process is due might have many answers. For example, one might transfer the CRIMINAL PROCEDURE [2] requirements elaborated in the United States Constitution to the context of civil proceedings. (The line between "civil" and "criminal" is itself a complex one to draw; for example, the state may be a party, and seek penalties, in many civil contexts.) The Constitution is itself relatively silent about what procedures are to be provided in civil lawsuits. Article III sets forth the requirements for the federal judiciary, but its provisions are largely structural. The SEVENTH AMENDMENT [4] "preserves" the right to a TRIAL BY JURY [4] in federal court and places some limits on appellate review of jury verdicts. The FIRST AMENDMENT [2,I] speaks of the right to petition for redress, and the Fifth Amendment and FOURTEENTH AMENDMENT [2,I] include "due process" clauses but do not specify what process is due.

The doctrinal answer to the question of the amount of process due—supplied by Supreme Court interpretations of the due process clauses—continues to rely upon the adversarial, judicial model as its touchstone, but increasingly the Court has accepted departures from that model as constitutionally sufficient. The Court's formula in MATHEWS V. ELDRIDGE (1976) [3] remains a vital part of the analysis of how much process is due. A court asks about the private interest at stake, the government interest at stake (often assumed to be the conservation of resources by having inexpensive process), and the risk of error in the current procedure as compared to the risk of error if additional procedural safeguards were in place. Commentators have observed that this utilitarian approach assumes that accuracy is the only goal of the process accorded. Moreover, none of the three prongs of the test can be measured; the Court's utilitarian cost-benefit analysis may mask the subjectivity of the measurements of the costs and benefits. To the extent courts attempt to ascertain both, it is difficult, if not impossible, to measure the harms of false positives (giving benefits when the state should withhold them) and false negatives (withholding benefits when the state should grant them).

As a result of this approach, the Court frequently approves of minimal procedural safeguards. One example comes from the context of prison litigation, in which the Court, in *Superintendent, Massachusetts Correctional Institution v. Hill* (1985), permitted a relatively low standard of evidentiary proof ("some evidence") when prisoners' good-time credits are revoked and they must remain incarcerated. Another illustration comes from *Brock v. Roadway Express, Inc.* (1987), in which a trucking company challenged the secretary of transportation's order to reinstate a trucker who allegedly had been a whistle-blower and complained about the company's safety regulations. The Court concluded that although the company had the right to be informed of relevant evidence supporting the grievant, the company had no right to a "live" evidentiary hearing prior to being required to reinstate the trucker temporarily. Further, the Court, in *Walters v. National Association of Radiation Survivors* (1985), refused to hold that civil litigants have a procedural due process RIGHT TO COUNSEL [3] whenever they contest government decisions.

One aspect of the entitlement- or process-due approach of the Supreme Court reveals the analytic limits of current doctrine. In ARNETT V. KENNEDY (1974) [1] the Supreme Court faced a statute that both created (in the Court's

terms) an entitlement to a job and also provided a specific and limited set of procedures to determine whether termination of employment was appropriate. A plurality of the Court upheld the package as having provided all the process due; Justice WILLIAM H. REHNQUIST [3,I] remarked that the employee had to accept the "bitter with the sweet." When the Supreme Court faced the issue again in *Cleveland Board of Education v. Loudermill* (1985), a majority held that while the question of whether an entitlement (a "property" interest) existed was to be decided by reference to statutory statements, the question of what process is due was one reserved for the Court. The current state of the law as expressed in *Loudermill* has a conceptual flaw: why conclude that the question of interpreting "property" in the due process clauses is to be decided by deferring to the legislature but that the "process due" is to be determined solely by the Court?

Another aspect of the CONSTITUTIONAL INTERPRETATION [1] problem remains unclear: How great a role should the legislature play in defining "liberty"? Some opinions suggest that deference to the legislature is appropriate to decide whether liberty rights or PROPERTY RIGHTS [I] are at stake, while other opinions suggest that liberty is not, and can never be, dependent upon positive legislative enactment. The issue arose in *Kentucky Department of Corrections v. Thompson* (1989), in which a majority of the Court concluded that prisoners' interests in "unfettered visitation" by nonprisoners is not "guaranteed directly by the Due Process Clause," while Justices THURGOOD MARSHALL [3,I], WILLIAM J. BRENNAN [1,I], and JOHN PAUL STEVENS [4,I] concluded that "the exercise of such unbridled governmental power over the basic human need to see family members and friends strikes at the heart of the liberty protected by the Due Process Clause." In contrast, the Supreme Court, in *Lassiter v. Department of Social Services* (1981), assumed without discussion the existence of a liberty interest in being provided a lawyer when a parent faced state termination of her right to parent.

Writing in this encyclopedia in 1986, Frank Michelman noted that the critique of the due process model frequently arose from challenges to decision making by agencies, in the "pressure of the 'mass justice' conditions imposed by modern governmental benefit programs involving very large numbers of eligibility decisions." Since then, the same issue—pressures of "mass justice"—have moved from the context of agencies to the context of courts. Contemporary commentary focuses on the question of what process is due when considering the adequacy of procedure in the federal and state courts. Of late, judicial decision making has been much criticized as too slow, too expensive, too cumbersome, and too unresponsive to litigants' needs. Suggested alternatives, often labeled "alternative dispute resolution" (ADR), range from simplified trials and court-annexed arbitration to judicially conducted settlement programs and diversion to non-court-based decision making assistance. Some of these programs are then challenged on various grounds, such as that they fail to accord procedural due process, they unduly burden state or federally based rights to a jury trial, and they exceed the powers authorized to courts or to judges.

The creation and growing popularity of ADR mechanisms and the criticism of court-based adjudicatory mechanisms lend further strength to the weakening of the procedural due process model, at least as exemplified by GOLDBERG V. KELLY (1970) [2], in which the Court required an evidentiary hearing prior to the termination of WELFARE BENEFITS [4]. Proponents of ADR argue that the formal, trial-like model embodied in *Goldberg* has proven inadequate and that other modes are to be preferred. These modes are generally less formal, lawyer-free, and conducted in private; they may use arbitrators or mediators in lieu of judges. The claims (debated in the literature and by empirical studies) are that such modes are speedier and more economic and that they produce better outcomes than does trial.

The increased reliance on procedural requirements, the "due process model," has been criticized not only by those who seek to conserve the expenditure of private and government resources but also by those who challenge government action but question the utility of the means. Some argue that procedural requirements wrongly place the risk of error on the state; others, who are proponents of state aid, argue the procedural due process model implicit in *Goldberg* wrongly equates procedural regularity and adversarial modes with good outcomes. Commentators have wondered about the utility of providing procedural opportunities to individuals with few, if any, resources to exercise them. For example, of what value is the right of cross-examination if no provision is made for a state-paid attorney? Given the resource disparities between government and individuals, procedural due process may create a facade of legitimacy for decisions that are intrinsically unfair. At a more fundamental level, this critique questions the assumptions of procedural due process opinions that a conflict between the state and the individual is inevitable. The hope is that communitarian approaches may well hold more promise for giving indigent individuals access to the riches of society. Those who endorse the *Goldberg* paradigm have been criticized for their limited vision—premised upon a classic liberal assumption of autonomous individuals confronting the state and relying on legalistic solutions.

In response, proponents of the *Goldberg* paradigm,

while sympathetic to communitarian goals, note that the state "as friend" almost never materializes. Further, the formality of the *Goldberg* procedures embodies hopes of empowering actors otherwise less powerful. Although not a comprehensive solution, the requirement of formal procedure may be better than its absence. Moreover, many within the legal services community who participated in the *Goldberg* litigation did not, at the time, see its goal as procedural reform. Claims around procedural rights were used as organizing tools; the hopes were that procedural reform, along with changes in other court-based rules, such as greater use of CLASS ACTIONS [1], the provision of free attorneys, and easier ACCESS TO THE COURTS [1], would all result in diminished social inequities. Yet another possibility is that the classic due process conception of the state versus an individual can be reenvisioned as an interaction of the state, an individual, and the community in which both litigants are situated. The debate about the utility of the procedural due process model is still alive in this decade, as conferences and law-review articles address the problems of what kinds of dispute resolution governments should be offering, funding, and encouraging.

One's view of procedure, of the aspirations of *Goldberg*, of the limits imposed under the *Mathews* approach, and of the critique from both the Right and the Left depends in large measure upon one's understanding of the proper role of the state and of the relationship between government and individuals. Procedure (procedural due process included) is a vehicle for the expression of political and social values—a vision of a state in need of restraint or not, a vision of human dignity as enhanced or not enhanced by formalized interaction between decision maker and individual.

JUDITH RESNIK

(SEE ALSO: *Welfare Rights* [I]; *Welfare State* [I].)

Bibliography

COVER, ROBERT M.; FISS, OWEN M.; and RESNIK, JUDITH 1988 *Procedure*. New York: Foundation Press.

DELGADO, RICHARD; DUNN, CHRIS; BROWN, PAMELA; LEE, HELENA; and HUBBERT, DAVID 1985 Fairness and Formality: Minimizing the Risk of Prejudice in Alternative Dispute Resolution. *Wisconsin Law Review* 1985:1359–1404.

HANDLER, JOEL 1986 *The Conditions of Discretion: Autonomy, Community, Bureaucracy.* New York: Russell Sage Foundation.

LIND, E. ALLEN, ET AL. 1989 *The Perception of Justice: Tort Litigants' Views of the Civil Justice System.* Santa Monica, Calif.: Rand Corporation, Institute for Civil Justice.

RESNIK, JUDITH 1986 Failing Faith: Adjudicatory Procedure in Decline. *University of Chicago Law Review* 53:494–560.

SPARER, EDWARD 1984 Fundamental Human Rights, Legal Entitlements, and the Social Struggle: A Friendly Critique of the Critical Legal Studies Movement. *Stanford Law Review* 36:509–574.

PROCEDURAL DUE PROCESS OF LAW, CRIMINAL

Integral to the law's aspirations is the set of variables differentiating law and politics: reason and passion, rationality and bias, free inquiry and ideology, fairness and self-interest. The law's ardent hope is that these variables permit distinctions between what will endure and what will pass, for it is the relative mix of the enduring and the ephemeral that determines whether a nation is one of disinterested laws or of self-interested individuals. Thus it is that the Supreme Court strives to justify its decisions through well-reasoned opinions. The task of the Court is to resist the allure of politics and rest judgment on principle.

But is this task possible? The difficulties are legion. Disagreements abound concerning the correct interpretative methodology, the data relevant to the various interpretive approaches, and the proper role of the judiciary in a democratic scheme. These disagreements are compounded because the Supreme Court often does not speak with one voice but instead is spoken for by each of the Justices in a setting that seriously complicates a consistent ordering of preferences in enduring legal doctrine. Superimposed over all these difficulties is the fact that the Supreme Court is essentially a reactive institution, responding to problems generated for it by social factors beyond its control. No matter how fervently the Justices may wish to promulgate a consistent and principled JURISPRUDENCE [I], the diversity and unpredictability of the grist for the Court's mill make the task formidable.

The more open-ended the interpretive problem, the more formidable the task, and among the most open-ended of the Supreme Court's tasks is the interpretation of the twin DUE PROCESS OF LAW [2] clauses in the Fifth Amendment and FOURTEENTH AMENDMENT [2,I]. The language of these clauses is not confining, their historical purposes are unclear, and to the extent there is agreement concerning those purposes, their implications for contemporary issues are not obvious. The due process clause of the Fifth Amendment, for example, was adopted as part of a set of guarantees that the newly created central government would respect its proper sphere, and the similar clause of the Fourteenth Amendment was adopted to recognize and reflect the changes wrought in the country by the Civil War. Neither was adopted with the contemporary set of issues in mind to which these clauses have been asserted to be relevant by litigants and judges.

For all these reasons, the Supreme Court's interpretation of the due process clauses is consistently as much a reflection of the times as the product of timeless interpretive methodologies. The nation's first century was a time of territorial expansion and of the creation and consolidation of governmental institutions in which criminal due process adjudication played virtually no role, and there were virtually no criminal due process cases. The second century brought an increasing emphasis on the role of individual rights, which culminated in the remarkable creativity of the Supreme Court's procedural revolution in the mid-1960s. The question now is what the third century will bring.

Certain trends are already apparent. The procedural revolution is over and the resulting legal landscape is stable. Whatever its theoretical attraction, the theory of total INCORPORATION [2] has substantially won, even though a majority of the Court has never adopted the theory. Most of the criminal provisions of the BILL OF RIGHTS [1] have been found to be binding on the states through the due process clause of the Fourteenth Amendment. Furthermore, notwithstanding the dramatic reorientation of the Supreme Court owing to recent appointments, the Court has not overruled a single majority CRIMINAL PROCEDURE [2] decision holding a Bill of Rights provision incorporated into the Fourteenth Amendment. The incorporationist controversy is so definitively over that the opinions of the Court addressing questions of state criminal procedure discuss directly the applicable Bill of Rights provision with at most a cursory reference to the due process clause of the Fourteenth Amendment. The casualness with which the distinction is drawn between Fourteenth Amendment due process and the specific provisions of the Bill of Rights is exemplified by the opinion for a unanimous court in *Crane v. Kentucky* (1986). In holding that due process was violated by the exclusion of testimony concerning the circumstances of a defendant's confession, the Court said that "whether rooted directly in the Due Process Clause of the Fourteenth Amendment or in the compulsory PROCESS OR CONFRONTATION [1,I] clauses of the Sixth Amendment, the Constitution guarantees criminal defendants 'a meaningful opportunity to present a complete defense.'"

Justices also appear to have little interest in giving either due process clause much independent significance. In those few instances in recent years in which the Court has discussed either clause directly rather than as a surrogate for some other constitutional provision, it typically has done so to deny that due process has any meaning independent of the specific provisions of the Bill of Rights.

In *Moran v. Burbine* (1986) the Court held that there was no violation of due process when the police failed to inform a criminal suspect subjected to custodial interrogation of the efforts of an attorney to reach him. Due process also does not require appointed counsel for collateral review of a conviction (*Pennsylvania v. Finley*, 1987), not even for collateral review of capital convictions (*Murray v. Giarratano*, 1989). Similarly, in *Strickland v. Washington* (1984) the Court commented that although "the Constitution guarantees a fair trial through the Due Process Clauses, it defines the basic elements of a fair trial largely through the several provisions of the Sixth Amendment." The Court applied this approach in *Caplin & Drysdale, Chartered v. United States* (1989) to find that the Fifth Amendment due process clause adds little or nothing to the Sixth Amendment RIGHT TO COUNSEL [3] clause and in UNITED STATES V. SALERNO (1987) [I] to reach a similar conclusion concerning the relationship between Fifth Amendment due process and the requirement of BAIL [1] in the Eighth Amendment.

The failure of the Court to overrule prior criminal decisions and to give independent force to the due process clauses does not mean that the creative energies of the Court are quiescent. Rather, they are finding outlets in different directions. Through the mid-1960s the Court's agenda was to tame the unruly manner in which the criminal justice process operated, particularly in the states. Employing the due process clause of the Fourteenth Amendment as its primary weapon, the Court succeeded in subjecting the state criminal justice process to the formal limits on governmental power in the Bill of Rights and in breaking down resistance to its innovations in the lower state and federal courts. One measure of this success is the increasingly common phenomenon of state supreme courts using state law to impose greater constraints on state officials than the federal constitution requires.

Because its previous messages have been largely absorbed by the lower courts and perhaps in response to increasingly conservative politics in the country, the Court has refocused the target of criminal procedural due process analysis from the specific provisions of the Bill of Rights to the question of the appropriate remedy. There are three interrelated variables driving the refocusing: first, a concern that exclusion of evidence premised upon the policy of deterring undesirable state action has a reasonable chance of advancing that goal; second, an increasingly intense belief that finality is an important value in adjudication; and third, an emphasis on accuracy in outcome.

The primary remedies that the Court has employed to effect its revisions of criminal procedure were the exclusionary rule and the threat of reversing convictions. Cases such as GIDEON V. WAINWRIGHT (1963) [2], MAPP V. OHIO (1961) [3], and MIRANDA V. ARIZONA (1966) [3] fit a general pattern of announcements of new rules to be enforced by the threat of excluding EVIDENCE [2] seized in violation of those rules or the reversals of convictions if the rules are not followed. The theory was that law enforcement officials would not jeopardize convictions by ignoring the new rules and that the threats of exclusion and reversal would thus deter unwanted behavior.

The present Court perceives two difficulties with this theory. First, as the new rules became accepted, and thus became the norm, the power of exclusion or the threat of reversal to affect law enforcement behavior diminished. It is one thing to exclude evidence or reverse a conviction because the police broke into a person's house, in the process apparently lying about whether they possessed a SEARCH WARRANT [3], as occurred in *Mapp*, but it is another to exclude evidence where the police made every effort to comply with the Court's pronouncements, as the Court refused to do in *United States v. Leon* (1984). Second, the nature of Supreme Court innovation is that it begins with the core problem an area poses and then expands into peripheral areas. As the cases press the logic of the original innovations further, the relationship between the cases and the policies underlying the original innovations becomes increasingly attenuated. It is one thing to sanction state officials for extensively interrogating an individual without warning him of his rights or allowing him to consult counsel, as occurred in *Miranda*, but it is another to do so because the state official gave a set of *Miranda* warnings differing somewhat from the language specifically approved in *Miranda*, as the Court refused to do in *California v. Prysock* (1981).

The Supreme Court has fashioned a number of principles to limit the EXCLUSIONARY RULE [2] to situations in which there are reasonable prospects that deterrence will operate. Chief among these limiting principles is the GOOD FAITH EXCEPTION [2] to the exclusionary rule fashioned in *Leon*. Exclusion of evidence is not likely to deter behavior if the law enforcement personnel had a good-faith belief in the correctness of their conduct. Similarly, the Court has refused to extend the exclusionary rule into peripheral areas where deterrence is unlikely to result, such as the GRAND JURY [2,I] setting (UNITED STATES V. CALANDRA, 1974 [1]) and civil matters such as forfeiture proceedings (*United States v. Janis*, 1976) and DEPORTATION [2] proceedings (*Immigration and Naturalization Service v. Lopez-Mendoza*, 1984).

The Court has also limited those who may litigate the legality of state action to restrict exclusion of evidence to cases where a deterrent effect is likely. Because law enforcement officials will not typically know in advance who the culprit is or who will be permitted to litigate the legality of their behavior, they will not jeopardize an investigation through illegal action so long as someone affected by their behavior may be in a position to complain. Thus, in *Rakas v. Illinois* (1987), the Court held that the passengers of a car could not contest the legality of a search of the car that included a search of the glove compartment, which had been used with the owner's apparent knowledge. In *Rawlings v. Kentucky* (1980) the Court held that the defendant could not contest the validity of the search of an acquaintance's purse where, again, the defendant had placed items with the knowledge of the purse's owner.

Intimately related to the Court's concern about the deterrent efficacy of its remedies is its growing emphasis on finality of decision. As the time increases between alleged state misbehavior and judicial intervention, the likelihood that reversals will affect behavior decreases. In addition, permitting federal relitigation of issues is an intelligent tactic if the work product of the state courts is not trusted, as was the case three decades ago; but as greater confidence in that work product is achieved, departures from finality are less desirable. A system that allows multiple attacks on the legitimacy of its work product undermines itself in various ways. Allowing repetitive relitigation of issues increases the probability of aberrational results simply because a litigant will eventually come before a court that for whatever reason—randomness, bias, or simple lack of attention—will act aberrationally. Reversals in such cases are not likely to advance deterrence of undesirable behavior or any other significant value. Allowing relitigation may also detract from the primary values of the penal system by encouraging individuals to deny responsibility for their acts. Regardless of whether confession is good for the soul, it is less likely to occur while avenues of appeal remain open.

Finality has been advanced in various ways. In particular, the scope of HABEAS CORPUS [2,I] has been reduced. In STONE V. POWELL (1976) [4] the Court held that FOURTH AMENDMENT [2,I] issues could not be relitigated on habeas corpus if the defendant had been provided an adequate opportunity to litigate the issue at trial. In *Teague v. Lane* (1989) the Court held that the retroactivity of new constitutional rulings is limited to cases still pending on direct appeal at the time the new decision is handed down. In a series of cases, the Court has also developed a strict "waiver" rule to the effect that failure to raise an issue in a timely manner in state court precludes litigating it in federal habeas corpus unless failure to raise it amounted to ineffective assistance of counsel or unless a miscarriage of justice would result.

The third variable informing the Court's recent due process jurispurdence is a heightened focus on accuracy in adjudication. As the Court has become convinced that little remains of the disrespect for individual rights that it believed previously characterized the criminal justice process, it has become increasingly concerned with encouraging accurate outcomes. On the one hand, this has resulted in a further tightening of the avenues on appeal for a convicted defendant. In a series of cases beginning with *Chapman v. California* (1967), the Court has held that HARMLESS ERROR [2]—error that does not cast doubt on the outcome of the trial—does not justify reversing a conviction. In NIX V. WILLIAMS (1984) [3] the Court held that a conviction would not be reversed as a result of the admission of evidence illegally seized that would have been inevitably discovered by legitimate means. On the other hand, the Court has extended rights integral to the accuracy of convictions. For example, the Court has continued in its broad reading of the right to counsel, holding in EVITTS V. LUCEY (1985) [2] that a defendant convicted of a crime is guaranteed effective assistance of counsel on a first appeal as a matter of right, even though a state is not required to provide for an appeal, and in AKE V. OKLAHOMA (1985) [1] that a state must guarantee a criminal defendant access to a competent psychiatrist to assist in evaluation, preparation, and presentation of the defense.

The present state of due process adjudication is accurately captured by the holding in *James v. Illinois* (1990). In *James* the Court held that the principle that illegally obtained evidence can be used to impeach defendants' testimony so that exclusionary rules do not encourage perjury—first fashioned in *Walder v. United States* (1954)—did not extend to defense witnesses other than the defendant. Allowing the state to impeach witnesses other than the defendant would increase significantly the value of illegally obtained evidence, thus substantially impairing the efficacy of the exclusionary rule. Increasing the incentive of law enforcement officials to obtain evidence illegally would in turn put core constitutional values at risk. As significant as finality and accuracy are, they remain less significant than the core values of the various provisions of the Bill of Rights.

The implication of decisions like *James* is that criminal due process has evolved from a club to beat recalcitrant officials into line with the Court's innovations into a more subtle tool for adjusting the margins of the various doctrines. This use of procedural due process will surely continue for the foreseeable future. The next stage in the development of due process is presently unknowable, but its origins are predictable. The nation is in the midst of a subtle devolution of political authority from the central government to the states. Due process jurisprudence has mirrored this trend, as the Court has shown an increasing reluctance to intervene in the criminal justice process. As state officials become aware of their increasing autonomy, they will take advantage of it to rework state criminal processes. As innovations are implemented over the next decades, they will be subjected to constitutional challenges, and out of that process will come the next stage in the continuing evolution of the meaning of the due process clauses for criminal procedure.

RONALD J. ALLEN

(SEE ALSO: *Automobile Search* [1,I]; *Criminal Justice System and the Constitution* [I]; *Inevitable Discovery* [I].)

Bibliography

AMSTERDAM, ANTHONY G.   1970   The Supreme Court and the Rights of Suspects in Criminal Cases. *New York University Law Review* 45:785–815.

BLASI, VINCENT A., ED.   1983   *The Burger Court: The Counter-Revolution That Wasn't.* New Haven, Conn.: Yale University Press.

NOWAK, JOHN E.   1979   Due Process Methodology in the Post-incorporation World. *Journal of Criminal Law and Criminology* 70:397–493.

WILKES, DONALD E., JR.   1985   The New Federalism in Criminal Procedure: Death of the Phoenix? Pages 166–200 in Bradley D. McGraw, ed., *Developments in State Constitutional Law.* St. Paul, Minn.: West Publishing Co.

PROCHOICE MOVEMENT

See: Abortion, I [I]; Reproductive Autonomy [3]

PROGRESSIVISM

In the decades after the Civil War, American law was forced to accommodate to the increasing pace of economic change as the United States was transformed from an agrarian, rural nation of small operatives into an urban, industrial nation characterized by huge transportation, manufacturing, extractive, and financial corporations that served national rather than local or regional markets. The Standard Oil trust, formed in 1882, consisted of thirty-nine different companies that pumped oil in eight states, refined it in six, and sold it everywhere. Railroad mileage increased from 36,801 miles in 1866 to 193,346 in 1900, and the gross national product increased by a factor of twelve. By 1900, the United States was producing more steel than Great Britain and Germany combined. Nevertheless, the devastating depression of 1893–1897 underscored the pain, human suffering, and dislocation caused by industrialization—ranging from child labor to burgeoning farm tenancy, strikes, and massive unemployment (which ran as high as twenty percent during the darkest months of the depression). It also underscored the lack of rationality and order in the marketplace. The century ended with a flurry of mergers as 2,274 firms disappeared during the years 1898–1910.

Historians have questioned whether there was a "Pro-gressive movement," disagreed about who were its leaders and followers, and argued about its dates. Around the beginning of the twentieth century, institutional reform occurred at many levels of government, but Progressives were not unified by party, class, or objectives. For example, those who favored economic efficiency, such as the conservationists, seldom showed much sympathy for those who championed social issues. Not surprisingly, the Progressives never decided how the business corporation could be made more accountable to public opinion or what role it should play in American society. Since the colonial period, American law has attempted to blend pormotional and regulatory elements, though the former prevailed for most of the nineteenth century. It has proved far easier to promote economic growth—through such legal mechanisms as EMINENT DOMAIN [2], the power of incorporation, tax policy, and limits on liability for personal injury—than to regulate it.

For constitutional and legal scholars, it is appropriate to define the Progressive Era as the years from about 1886 to 1917. Some recent historians look more charitably on the Supreme Court during this era than did scholars who wrote before the 1970s. They argue that many Justices were by training and inclination classical liberals who saw the Constitution as the embodiment of natural law. These judges wanted to preserve higher law rights and individual liberty, limit monopoly and government "paternalism," and protect the central government from expanding STATE POLICE POWER [4]. They rejected "special privilege" in all forms. Earlier historians had charged that most members of the Court regarded the Constitution as primarily designed to protect property, that they knew little about American history and institutions, that they stubbornly clung to an organic, almost feudal view of society, and that they contributed to the growth of vast economic oligarchies. The critics insisted that state courts—particularly in their reliance on liberty of contract and in their use of injunctions to break strikes—were no less activistic, regressive, or anachronistic than the High Court.

It is not clear that the Supreme Court was out of step with public opinion or that its members held substantially more "conservative" values than did the mass of Americans. (Even in the midst of the depression, the Republicans won in a landslide in 1894 and WILLIAM MCKINLEY [3] beat William Jennings Bryan easily in 1896.) Nevertheless, no charge was more popular during the Progressive Era than that the courts had systematically violated the basic structural principle of the Constitution—the independence of the three branches of government. In 1895 the High Court rendered two decisions that struck at the heart of national LEGISLATIVE POWER [3]. In UNITED STATES V. KNIGHT CO. [3] the Court, which traditionally had defined the COMMERCE CLAUSE [1] very broadly, emasculated the SHERMAN ANTITRUST ACT (1890) [4] by ruling that the American Sugar Company, which refined more than 90 percent of the nation's supply, monopolized manufacturing but only indirectly commerce. (The Court drew the same kind of fine distinction when it refused to accept use of the commerce clause as a limit on child labor because only the products of labor, not the labor itself, was involved in INTERSTATE COMMERCE [2].) In the same year, the second POLLOCK V. FARMERS' LOAN AND TRUST CO. [3] decision ignored well-settled precedent by invalidating the national income tax of 1894. And in 1896 INTERSTATE COMMERCE COMMISSION V. CINCINNATI, NEW ORLEANS, & TEXAS PACIFIC RAILWAY [2] denied that Congress had granted the Interstate Commerce Commission power to set rates.

Simultaneously, the Court, led by Justice STEPHEN J. FIELD [2], reinterpreted the DUE PROCESS [2] clause of the FOURTEENTH AMENDMENT [2,I], making it a substantive protection of property against "arbitrary" and "confiscatory" state and federal regulations, not just the constitutional guarantee of a fair trial. *Munn v. Illinois* (1877) had clearly upheld the power of individual states to regulate the use of private property in the public interest; it had rejected SUBSTANTIVE DUE PROCESS [4] as the Court had done earlier in the SLAUGHTERHOUSE CASES (1873) [4]. But substantive due process—which won its first great victory in STONE V. FARMERS' LOAN AND TRUST COMPANY (1886) [4]—added new power to JUDICIAL REVIEW [3]. A similar spirit permeated the Court's statutory interpretations, as in the RULE OF REASON [3] articulated in STANDARD OIL COMPANY V. UNITED STATES (1911) [4], which suggested that monopoly in and of itself was not illegal and that only the courts could define what charges, rates, or business practices were "reasonable." In LOCHNER V. NEW YORK (1905) [3] it relied on the liberty and contract doctrine, which was based on substantive due process of law, to argue that the state could not use its police powers to regulate maximum work hours, except in dangerous jobs or jobs that immediately affected the public health; the Court held that bakers, unlike miners, did not do dangerous work. The right of workers to sell their labor at the highest price and of employers to buy it at the cheapest price took precedence. And in HAMMER V. DAGENHART (1918) [2] the Court went against well-established precedent in declaring that the first federal child labor law went beyond Congress' commerce power, threatening the police power of the states and the balance between federal and state authority.

Many jurists and politicians fought against the conservative drift of the courts during the Progressive Era, proposing reforms that included the recall of judges, the standardization of state incorporation laws, and the use of SOCIOLOGICAL JURISPRUDENCE [4] to expand the vision

and accountability of courts. But these proposals had little impact on the new industrial order. Far more important was the RULE OF LAW [3] itself, for Progressivism was shaped by American values and faith in the American legal process. Most Americans preferred reform through law, a process of constitutional change, rather than revolution. The Progressives' faith in the rationality of man, progress, and the curative powers of law prompted such reforms as the initiative, referendum, recall, and direct elections of United States senators. They did not attack such underlying problems as poverty, racism, discrimination, and the insecurity of labor. Nor was there any major revamping of the legal system itself. Many Progressives argued that judicial review threatened the doctrine of SEPARATION OF POWERS [4], that it was inherently undemocratic, that it might as logically have been exercised by Congress or the President as by the Supreme Court, that most rulings of unconstitutionality had little to do with the language of the Constitution, that the frequency of 5–4 decisions violated the principle that only laws clearly unconstitutional should be invalidated, that split decisions threatened to undermine public faith in the entire justice system, and that judges had little understanding of American society. Yet Congress was unable to adopt major reforms, and most Americans remained wary of tampering with the judicial system.

Although by the 1920s the Interstate Commerce Commission, Federal Trade Commission, and the Federal Reserve Board were the only important national REGULATORY AGENCIES [3], by that time the commission had won out over other options (including antitrust prosecutions, which met with little enthusiasm after the Progressive Era, save for a few years at the end of the 1930s). The commissions served many purposes, including fact-gathering, education, disclosure of illegal practices, encouragement of innovation, the cartelization of industries, and restrictions on monopoly and oligopoly. They combined legislative and judicial functions, or adjudication and planning, and, even more important, they maintained respect for property by following elaborate administrative hearings and procedures similar to regular courts. They built on the assumption that by removing issues from the courts and legislatures, public servants could decide the proper shape and conduct of American business. In short, the commissions fitted comfortably with American views of the legal process.

The regulation of business was one thing; basic reform of the economic system, however, was uncongenial to most Americans. The Progressives agreed that the new industrial order had to be made more predictable, accountable, and responsible; that much was obvious. They also recognized the limits of judicial regulation of business, the judges' lack of knowledge of the economic system, the inability of courts to act unless a complaint was brought to them, and the courts' inability to engage in long-range policy-making. However, while many Progressives feared bigness per se, others looked forward to a new society built on organization, cooperation, and specialization; the competition that had been so valued in the nineteenth century appeared to them as anachronistic and dangerous. The Progressives no less than those who supported the New Deal could not agree on what the structure of business should be, nor could they agree on the form or forms regulation should take. Therefore, many regulatory tools—such as selective corporate taxes (as on companies that used child labor or had interlocking directorates), national incorporation, and an expansion of the NATIONAL POLICE POWER [3]—did not receive the attention they deserved. American values were ambivalent. Most Progressives regarded laissez-faire with disdain, yet they also believed in the sanctity of private property, economic individualism, and a society driven by the harmony of self-interest rather than by the clash of classes.

DONALD J. PISANI

(SEE ALSO: *Child Labor Amendment* [1]; *Child Labor Tax Act* [1]; *Conservatism* [I]; *Federal Trade Commission Act* [2]; *Liberalism* [I]; *Progressive Constitutional Thought* [3].)

Bibliography

BETH, LOREN P. 1971 *The Development of the American Constitution, 1877–1917*. New York: Harper and Row.

SKLAR, MARTIN J. 1988 *The Corporate Reconstruction of American Capitalism, 1890–1916: The Market, The Law, and Politics*. Cambridge: Cambridge University Press.

SWINDLER, WILLIAM F. 1969 *Court and Constitution in the Twentieth Century: The Old Legality, 1889–1932*. Indianapolis and New York: Bobbs-Merrill Co.

PROLIFE MOVEMENT

See: Abortion, II [I]; Anti-Abortion Movement [I]

PROPERTY RIGHTS

In the discourse of American CONSTITUTIONALISM [2], the idea of property has been both primal and protean.

First, there is the text. The DUE PROCESS OF LAW [2] clauses of both the Fifth Amendment and FOURTEENTH AMENDMENT [2,I] rank property by name with life and liberty as a chief human interest to be secured against arbitrary and excessive interference from government. The Fifth Amendment's EMINENT DOMAIN [2], or "taking," clause even adds a special restriction against uncompensated TAKING OF PROPERTY [4,I] for public benefit. Constitutional law perceives various high aims in these general protections for property. Courts dealing with claims of taking without compensation find in property an antiredistributive principle, opposed to imposition on a select few of the costs and burdens of government operations. When the claim is one of deprivation without PROCEDURAL DUE PROCESS [3,I], modern doctrine treats property as primarily a legalistic (or bureaucratic) principle, opposed to subversion of legally warranted expectations by faithless or irregular administration of standing law. Of course, expectations build on constancy in the law itself, as well as on reliable administration. The doctrine of SUBSTANTIVE DUE PROCESS [4,I] arose, in part, out of concern for protecting legally VESTED RIGHTS [4] against retrospective disturbance by changes in law. In a more dramatic form of substantive due process, property has figured as a libertarian principle of independence from state regulation: the right of an owner, as Justice JOHN PAUL STEVENS recently wrote in MOORE V. CITY OF EAST CLEVELAND (1977) [3], "to use her own property as she sees fit."

Second, proprietary norms and notions have inspired and organized constitutional-legal doctrine apparently far removed from the immediate scope of the property-specific clauses. Both the THIRD AMENDMENT [4] and FOURTH AMENDMENT [2,I] obviously tap special values of domestic sanctuary—refuge and privacy—from one prototypical image of property, the home or house. In GRISWOLD V. CONNECTICUT (1965) [2] the Supreme Court marshaled these provisions with others in the BILL OF RIGHTS [1] to construct a constitutional RIGHT OF PRIVACY in the conduct of marital intimacies at home. By the time of ROE V. WADE (1973) [3], the Court had reconceived this as a right to choose for oneself "whether to bear or beget a child." In BUCKLEY V. VALEO (1976) [1] the Court treated deployments of private wealth in electoral politics as exercises of the FREEDOM OF SPEECH [2,I] and the FREEDOM OF ASSEMBLY AND ASSOCIATION [2] protected by the FIRST AMENDMENT [2,I]. In PERRY EDUCATION ASSOCATION V. PERRY LOCAL EDUCATORS' ASSOCIATION (1983) [3], the Court confirmed an old idea that a government acting as a proprietor (rather than as a lawmaker) is unusually free to restrict freedom of speech. In a series of cases including *Reeves, Inc. v. Stake* (1980), the Court similarly relieved states acting as owners from normal duties under the COMMERCE CLAUSE [1] to refrain from commercial discrimination against out-of-state competitors. In contrast, courts adjudicating under the rubric of substantive due process currently treat ECONOMIC LIBERTIES [2] (aspects of self-direction concerned with acquisition, exchanges, and deployment of property) as categorically less resistant to state regulation than more "fundamental" or "personal" aspects, such as control over family formations.

Third, on a broadly ideological level, legal depictions of property have figured strongly in imaginative conceptions of the American constitutional system. Property held a glorified place in the common lawyer's Whig history imbibed by early Americans from WILLIAM BLACKSTONE [1]. With its naturalistic imagery of clearly demarcated "closes," property offered a paradigm of legally sanctioned authority that was supreme within its limits yet firmly delimited by law. Such an image of legal property apparently helped later generations of Americans to represent and confirm to themselves the workings of check-and-balance institutional schemes—FEDERALISM [2,I] and SEPARATION OF POWERS [4]—that depend on jurisdictional boundaries judicially patrolled. More fundamentally, the image has from the beginning helped inspire and sustain a core idea of constitutionalism: a legally LIMITED GOVERNMENT [3] based on a secure bounding of the state's domain from those of the market and private life.

Finally, at the level of practical debate over institutions, the question of property's relation to POLITICS [1] has always been foundational for American constitutionalism. In the strongly influential NATURAL RIGHTS [3] philosophy traced to JOHN LOCKE [3], the relation is oppositional. Property—here meaning acquisition of goods by effort and exchange and retention against force and fraud—is considered a native attribute of humankind, not an artificial contingency of state power and political choice. Accordingly, the state's business is to secure natural property against breakdowns of mutual forbearance that only a supreme civil authority can prevent. For Lockeans, then, the relation of property to politics is that of an a priori external limit and a test of legitimacy.

Yet in an older tradition of civic REPUBLICANISM [I], to which the Founders were also heir, questions of property entitlement and distribution are inseparable from constitutional design and political ministration. By the traditional republican understanding, property, or wealth, is power in politics. Undue concentration of wealth portends either oligarchy or revolution, and warding off those contingencies is very much the business of republican government. Morevoer, in civic republican thought, "corruption" of political motives by preoccupation with private need or advantage (as opposed to public honor and common good) is a chief internal threat to the stability and success of popular governments. Elements of this traditional view, modernized and coupled with Lockean liberal ideas, plainly appear throughout THE FEDERALIST [2] (saliently in JAMES MADISON's [3] famous essay on "faction") and in THOMAS JEFFERSON's [3] political writings. They appear in the Constitution, as well, and in early American constitutional practice. By such devices as indirect election and large constituencies, the Framers avowedly designed the Constitution to ensure that only men of means and

repute would attain national legislative or executive office.

Moreover, it was normal in the early United States for states, which under the Constitution set electoral qualifications even for congressional and presidential elections, to restrict VOTING RIGHTS [4] to persons of independent social status (free adult males) who also held a substantial property endowment or income of a kind not too dependent on governmental machination. In the more egalitarian democratic ethos tracing to the Jacksonian period, RECONSTRUCTION [I], and the Civil War Amendments, WEALTH DISCRIMINATION [4] in the field of voting rights has become constitutionally intolerable. Rather, debate has inevitably arisen over the converse claim that a democratic–republican constitution requires assurance to all, at public expense if necessary, of the material prerequisites of political independence and competence.

In summary, the American constitutional rhetoric of property and property rights is a congested manifold of cross-cutting and contested doctrinal and normative evocations. As might be expected of such an overloaded vocabulary, ambiguity and conflict affect not just normative emanations and doctrinal derivations, but the direct reference of the central terms themselves. In constitutional disputation, "property" and "property right" variously signify holdings, entitlements, and institutions. At one moment, "property" (or "property right") may refer to specific holdings of social wealth that various persons currently claim or practically enjoy; at another, to a set of legal or moral rules and principles supposed to define and condition entitlements to possession and enjoyment of parcels of social wealth; and at still another, to institutional regimes of privatization (the "free market").

This variability of reference would little surprise the generations of Anglo-American theorists—the line runs from David Hume and Jeremy Bentham to Wesley N. Hohfeld, MORRIS R. COHEN [1], Felix S. Cohen, Robert L. Hale, and beyond—who have attempted conceptual analyses and critiques of legal "property." Vagaries in constitutional-legal usage of "property" echo the academic discussions, which have themselves obviously been sensitive to partisan political and constitutional debates. In some respects, however, constitutional-legal usage strays from established jurisprudential positions.

It is common ground, at least, that legal "property" is a relation, not a substance. Property does not consist in parcels of wealth or "stuff." Academic sophisticates have long agreed that it also does not consist in any relation between a person and "his" stuff; neither possessory acts, proprietary intentions, nor both together constitute property. Rather, property is a matter of relations among persons: the social relations and practices that accord to bare, empirical, person-to-parcel connections a measure of public recognition, normative legitimacy, and practical reliability. But that is not all property is, either. Also indispensable to property, say the theorists, is the element of entitlement or legal sanction: there is no true "property" in a casual neighborhood practice of allowing me to farm a field and reap the fruit when we all also know that others may stop me at any time without running afoul any law. The question then becomes whether the law that constitutes property entitlements consists strictly of the "positive" human inventions of legislatures and of courts filling gaps in the common law or, rather, is found in some method of reason or traditional understanding that composes a prelegislative "higher" or "Natural" Law. On this question, JURISPRUDENCE [I] remains deeply divided.

It is easy to find constitutional-legal doctrine officially accepting each step of the jurisprudential consensus so far as it goes. Yet constitutional law seems also often driven to resist the abstract logic of the consensus. According to the theorists, a legal regime that secures the exclusive possession of landowners against unauthorized entry certainly constitutes a property entitlement, but so, by the same reasoning, does a legal regime that permits (and protects against interference) a particular mode of using a parcel—for example, an owner's strip mining of land. Constitutional law, by contrast, differentiates sharply between legal restrictions on use that leave possession undisturbed and laws subjecting owners to "permanent physical occupations" of land. As the Supreme Court recently confirmed in *Keystone Bituminous Coal Association v. DeBenedictis* (1987) and *Nollan v. California Coastal Commission* (1987), new use restrictions, however severe, rarely amount to constitutionally challengeable takings or deprivations of property, but state-sponsored dispossession, however trivial, almost always does. Or consider a law plainly stating that a sheriff may seize goods from a person who bought them on credit whenever the creditor tells the sheriff that the loan is in default. In the sophisticated view, such a law simply defines the extent of the installment buyer's property right and so cannot itself be a constitutionally questionable deprivation of property. Constitutional law on procedural due process officially adopted that view in BOARD OF REGENTS V. ROTH (1972) [I], a case of peremptory unexplained dismissal from a government job expressly held at the supervisor's discretion. Yet at about the same time, in *Fuentes v. Shevin* (1972), the Court found an unconstitutional deprivation of property without procedural due process in the law authorizing unceremonious seizure of goods from an installment buyer's possession. Unlike academic jurisprudence, constitutional law has to mediate practically among demands for proprietary security, sound policy, and popular acceptance, along with the demand for consistent theory. Operating within this field of forces, courts evidently find that governmentally engineered trespasses on extant private possessions are uniquely and unacceptably insulting to property's ideological function as a paradigm of limited government, that is, as private domains secured against governmental intrusion.

A like irresolution appears in constitutional law's response to the theorists' requirement of legal entitlement as essential to property. The Court both expressly avows this requirement and rejects its full implications. Faced in *United States v. Willow River Power Co.* (1945) with a hydroelectric company's claim that the government took its property by damming a river and thereby flooding the tail end of its generating plant, Justice ROBERT H. JACKSON [3] memorably declared that judicial delineation of property rights turns not on any intelligible essence of "property," but on discovery and construal of prior and contemporary law: "We cannot start the process of decision by calling [every existing economic interest or advantage] a 'property right' . . . Such economic uses are property rights only when they are legally protected interests." In short, discoverable legal entitlement is required to qualify an "economic interest" as the "property" mentioned by the Fifth and Fourteenth Amendments. The Court has further perceived that those constitutional mentionings cannot themselves be read (without apparent circularity) to confer the legal status of property on any disputed "interest or advantage." Rather, according to *Regents v. Roth*, the entitlement must be grounded in "an independent source such as state law." The Court has even hitched such a "positivist" approach to the theory of federalism, declaring in PRUNEYARD SHOPPING CENTER V. ROBINS (1980) [3] that "the United States, as opposed to the several states [is not] possessed of . . . authority . . . to define 'property' in the first instance."

Repeatedly, however, the Court has defied this logic and found that the Constitution's property clauses directly demand protection for interests plainly not treated as property by standing subconstitutional law. DRED SCOTT V. SANDFORD (1857) [2] is the earliest instance. The MISSOURI COMPROMISE of 1820 established the northern portion of the Louisiana Territory as "free soil." According to the law of many jurisdictions, a slave taken by a master onto free soil was thereby emancipated. Given that as the standing legal rule, a master's legally grounded entitlement in a slave simply would not extend to retention of title after the master had taken the slave into free territory. At a time when this plainly appeared to be the applicable, governing rule, Scott's "owner" took him from Missouri to north Louisiana Territory. The Supreme Court held that to grant Scott his freedom on that basis would be to deprive Sandford of constitutionally protected property without due process of law.

Although a deservedly infamous decision, *Dred Scott*

is not aberrational in its refusal to allow subconstitutional congressional and state lawmaking to dictate the limits of constitutionally protected property. In *Pennsylvania Coal Company v. Mahon* (1922) the Court granted *arguendo* the public safety justifications for a law forbidding coal-mine owners to remove coal in such a way as to cause the collapse of surface structures, but still found that the law unconstitutionally took the property of mining firms on which it had confiscatory retrospective impact. Justice OLIVER WENDELL HOLMES, JR. [2] wrote that, despite the long-established rule subordinating all property to public-safety regulation, "if regulation goes too far it will be recognized as a taking." The rule's "implied limitation" of property rights "must have its limits, or the contract and due process clauses are gone." In *Kaiser Aetna v. United States* (1979) the Court dealt similarly with the standing rule subordinating all shoreline property holdings to public rights of access to navigable waters. It refused to apply the rule strictly when doing so would have subjected the complaining owners not only to unwelcome "physical invasions," but to loss of their "distinct investment backed expectations" of privacy. Most recently, the Court's opinion in *Nollan v. California Coastal Commission* (1987) strongly implied that a state legal regime expressly subjecting all shoreline land titles to public rights of pedestrian passage would violate a baseline normative standard for property institutions contained in the Fourteenth Amendment.

The Court has thus refused to read the Constitution's property clauses as completely delegating to legislative politics the definition of legal regimes of property rights. It has refused to reduce the judiciary to the ancillary role of protecting persons against retroactive alteration and capricious administration of these subconstitutional legislative regimes. It has done so when the alternative struck it as betrayal of substantive constitutional values linked to property, notably, private sanctuary and limited government. Such cases lie along that contested boundary of JUDICIAL ACTIVISM AND JUDICIAL RESTRAINT [3] where the demand for constitutional vindication confronts the demand for contemporary democratic accountability.

In such cases, the Court is not, however, necessarily rejecting jurisprudential insistence on legal entitlement as a prerequisite to property. It may rather be denying that property-constitutive law can be found only in the "positive" lawmaking acts of legislatures and common-law adjudicators. Not surprisingly (considering the conflicting normative pressures for both a rule of law and government of the people by the people), this choice between an exclusively "positive" and a "natural" provenance for property-constitutive law is just where the jurisprudential consensus on legal property falls apart. We can see the Court in these cases as allying the Framers with those theorists who appeal to "natural" criteria of reason or tradition for a higher-law conception of property entitlement. The Court, in effect, conceives the Framers to have been referring to such criteria when they prescribed constitutional protection for "property."

Thereby, the Court also, and to a like extent, apparently aligns itself (or the Framers) with the Lockean liberal (as opposed to civic republican) antecedents of American constitutionalism. Rather than treat the design and adjustment of property regimes as a central legitimate concern of republican government, the Court to this extent treats property rights as prior and external to state and politics. But the civic heritage may not yet be entirely expunged from American constitutional doctrine or disputation. This heritage may help explain the Court's unshakable tolerance for legislative schemes of property-use regulation that plainly and grossly exceed the bounds of any plausibly Lockean notion of POLICE POWER [3]. More pointedly, it may help explain the settled acceptance of statutory income transfer schemes that appear to "take property from A and give it to B" in defiance of an oft-cited first principle of Lockean higher law. Commentators have argued vigorously, and vainly, that such schemes are both constitutionally obligatory and constitutionally forbidden. The modern Court's refusal of commitment to either view may be its mediation between the civic and the libertarian underpinnings of American constitutionalism.

FRANK I. MICHELMAN

(SEE ALSO: *Economic Due Process* [I]; *Economic Equal Protection* [I]; *Economy* [I].)

Bibliography

ACKERMAN, BRUCE A.   1975   *Private Property and the Constitution.* Cambridge, Mass.: Harvard University Press.

COHEN, FELIX S.   1954   Dialogue on Private Property. *Rutgers Law Review* 9:357–387.

EPSTEIN, DAVID F.   1984   *The Political Theory of the Federalist.* Chicago: University of Chicago Press.

EPSTEIN, RICHARD   1985   *Takings: Private Property and the Law of Eminent Domain.* Cambridge, Mass.: Harvard University Press.

KENNEDY, DUNCAN   1980   Toward a Historical Understanding of Classical Legal Consciousness: The Case of Classical Legal Thought in America, 1850–1940. *Research in Law & Society* 3:3–24.

MICHELMAN, FRANK I.   1987   Possession vs. Distribution in the Constitutional Idea of Property. *Iowa Law Review* 72:1319–1350.

NEDELSKY, JENNIFER   1989   *Private Property and the Limits of American Constitutionalism: A View from the Formation.* Chicago: University of Chicago Press.

SINGER, JOSEPH WILLIAM   1982   The Legal Rights Debate in Analytical Jurisprudence from Bentham to Hohfeld. *Wisconsin Law Review* 1982:975–1059.

SYMPOSIUM 1988 The Jurisprudence of Takings. *Columbia Law Review* 88:1581–1794.

TREANOR, WILLIAM 1985 The Origins and Original Significance of the Just Compensation Clause of the Fifth Amendment. *Yale Law Journal* 94:694–716.

PSYCHIATRY AND CONSTITUTIONAL LAW

New impositions of legal control in the last generation have transformed traditional relationships between providers and consumers of mental health services, cabining the power physicians historically exercised over the insane. Paradoxically, the new legal limits on psychiatrists developed in a period when novel psychotropic medication—veritable wonder drugs—at last provided bases for medical paternalistic authority. Psychiatrists complained that patients would miss out on needed treatment and "rot with their rights on."

The legal developments involve processes for civilly protecting or subduing the mentally impaired, processing them through the CRIMINAL JUSTICE SYSTEM [I], recognizing their rights as psychiatric inpatients, and establishing for them programs of patient advocacy. Patient claims include rights to treatment; to refuse treatment; to the least intrusive alternative form of treatment; and to privacy, autonomy, liberty, information, communication, and protection while undergoing treatment. Mental health lawyers have elevated these claims to new constitutional doctrine, conveniently overlooking that many decisions recognizing them came from lower courts.

The constitutional values underlying these decisions have also found expression in other legal forms: legislative law reform, judicial interpretation of unresisting common law and statutes, and unfolding of state constitutional doctrine. Although not necessarily flying the U.S. constitutional flag, these legal developments are nevertheless based on constitutional values, such as liberty, privacy, due process, equality, and free speech. The principles invoked are not specific to mental health, but common to the modern judicial approach to protecting the vulnerable.

The Supreme Court has been slow to join these trends. In contrast to its behavior in the field of criminal justice, here the Supreme Court has followed reluctantly rather than lead. As with the rights of the criminally accused, the Court has recently retreated, leading to a development of state constitutional law.

A legislative revolution in civil commitment procedures received constitutional underpinnings in *Addington v. Texas* (1979), which mandated a standard of "clear and convincing" evidence for the fact-finding on which commitment is based. Commitment through the criminal process was limited constitutionally by the holding that incompetency to stand trial can justify incarceration only for a reasonable period during which restoration of trial capacity is foreseeable.

The Constitution seems to impose little constraint on changes in the best-known rule in the field of psychiatry and law: the insanity defense to criminal prosecution. The state may redefine the defense and even require the defendant, rather than the prosecution, to bear the burden of proof beyond a reasonable doubt. The "least restrictive alternative" criterion for involuntary treatment, proclaimed by many lower courts, has not been adopted by the Supreme Court.

The Court has also been hesitant about a right to refuse treatment, although recognizing in theory a liberty interest in avoiding unwanted administration of antipsychotic drugs. In WASHINGTON V. HARPER (1990) [I], it refused to hold that a prisoner had the right to refuse such treatment, taking into account that he was confined and determined to be dangerous to himself or others and that the treatment was in his medical interest. Nor was a prior judicial hearing required because the Court believed his interests would be better served by allowing medication decisions to be made by doctors rather than judges. A number of state courts have nevertheless recognized a right to refuse treatment based on common law protection of bodily integrity or state constitutional guarantees of privacy.

The right to treatment and inpatient rights have fared no better in the Supreme Court than has the right to refuse treatment. Ruling on an involuntarily committed, developmentally disabled person, *Youngberg v. Romeo* (1982) held his constitutionally protected liberty interests included minimally adequate training, as well as reasonable safety and freedom from undue bodily restraints. Presumably, the involuntarily committed mentally ill possess similar rights. But the Court eviscerated such rights by declaring that the Constitution requires only that "professional judgment" be exercised, with the courts to show deference to that judgment. "Deliberate indifference" to an inpatient's serious psychiatric needs might perhaps violate the Eighth Amendment by analogy to a holding on prisoners' medical needs.

The new legal limitations on psychiatric power seem confining only by contrast to the vast authority traditionally exercised. The mentally ill are still subject to governmental power not exercised over the healthy, on rationales of paternalism as well as protection of others. The patients' rights movement points out the hypocrisy of claims that governmental power is exercised for the patient's own good if adequate treatment is not guaranteed and if "acquittal" on the ground of insanity can result in loss of liberty for a longer period than conviction. And psychiatrists still are permitted to testify as experts, giving opinions on matters beyond their actual scientific competence, such as predicting dangerousness on the basis of clinical interviews.

The psychiatrist–patient relationship, a central focus for therapists, has been largely overlooked in constitutional case law. When the doctor is double agent for both patient and prosecutor, a *Miranda*-like warning is required before a psychiatrist examines a convicted defendant for a death penalty hearing. Psychiatric assistance itself can be a constitutional right: an indigent defendant must have access to a psychiatrist on a showing of need to prepare his or her insanity defense.

Psychiatric condition is generally not central to an individual's constitutional status. Neither psychiatric patients as a group nor mental illness as a trait has yet been held to invoke specially solicitous judicial protection from elected legislatures, which is labeled heightened scrutiny under the equal protection clause. In *Cleburne v. Cleburne Living Center, Inc.* (1985) the Supreme Court explicitly said it would not extend heightened scrutiny to the developmentally disabled. The Court nevertheless did just what it said it was not doing, on reasoning equally valid for the mentally ill. (Indeed, five Justices repudiated the whole theory of three "tiers" of equal protection scrutiny.) Psychiatric condition nevertheless has some irreducible effect on legal status: the Eighth Amendment prohibits the execution of the mentally incompetent. A finding of initial mental illness is insufficient to justify indefinite confinement; O'CONNOR V. DONALDSON (1975) [3] requires findings of both current mental illness and dangerousness.

Constitutional law has been little affected by psychodynamic perspectives, even though twentieth-century American culture has been heavily influenced by psychoanalysis, whose models of the mind differ significantly from the law's traditions. Some cases contrast "the law's" model of the mind, involving free will and choice, with psychiatry's model, supposedly deterministic; these courts conclude that judges must disregard such psychiatric ideas. A handful of judges openly ask whether a model of the mind must be assumed for constitutional purposes. One of the law's most-cited "unreported" cases, *Kaimowitz v. Dept. of Mental Health* (1973), said that the FIRST AMENDMENT [2,I] must protect the individual's right to generate ideas if it is going to protect the right to communicate those ideas. But in *Mills v. Rogers*, although the Supreme Court cited Michael Shapiro's germinal work on the topic, it declined to rule on this point. Freedom of thought (and implicitly of emotion) was recognized in STANLEY V. GEORGIA (1969) [4], which declared a First Amendment right to personal possession of obscene materials in the home. *Washington v. Harper* (1990) recognized that it is a substantial interference with a person's liberty interest to alter his brain's chemical balance to affect his cognitive process. And Justice LOUIS D. BRANDEIS's famous dissent in OLMSTEAD V. UNITED STATES (1928) [3] had spoken of protecting throughts and emotions as well as beliefs.

In criminal law, the Court early had relied implicitly on a free-will model of the mind to hold a confession involuntary, based on the defendant's insanity at the time he or she confessed rather than on police coercion. This focus on the suspect's state of mind suggested that free will is a constitutional prerequisite for voluntariness. But the Court subsequently retreated from that approach.

A central lesson of psychoanalysis is that much of our mental functioning is largely inaccessible to consciousness, while nevertheless affecting our conscious thoughts, feelings, and behavior. Psychiatrists are therefore used to looking for unconscious intents and unconscious, often symbolic, meanings. The Supreme Court has recognized that actions and institutions can have not only intended but unintended psychological effects with constitutional significance, as in the famous footnote 11 of BROWN V. BOARD OF EDUCATION OF TOPEKA (1954) [1]. But the Court has not yet recognized the argument by scholars that government officials can violate the Constitution by unconscious discrimination, reflecting not overt hatred or contempt but unconscious conflict and ambivalence, aimed not only at ethnic groups and women but also at the poor and the elderly.

Lawyers' theories for interpreting the constitutional text and the motives of constitutional actors are perhaps starting to be more influenced by the experience of that other profession of interpreters, the psychotherapists. The psychoanalytic perspective assumes that multilayered contradictory intentions and symbolic meanings abound; we live lives of poetry, not prose. Speakers do not generally fully comprehend their own purposes, and the intellectual baggage we carry with us distorts our perceptions of current realities. Emotions permeate all that we do, and our rational goals are regularly compromised with dictates of conscience and defense against anxieties. Context, slips, and redundancy are important clues to meaning; useful interpretation requires an ongoing dialogue. By calling our attention to such concepts, psychiatry's chief contribution to constitutional law can be not in dealing with the abnormal but in helping us to understand one another and ourselves.

MARTIN LYON LEVINE

(SEE ALSO: *Patients' Rights* [I]; *Right of Privacy* [3,I].)

Bibliography

KATZ, JAY; GOLDSTEIN, JOSEPH; and DERSHOWITZ, ALAN
    1967 *Psychoanalysis, Psychiatry, and Law.* New York: Free
    Press.
LEVINE, MARTIN LYON 1988 *Age Discrimination and the
    Mandatory Retirement Controversy.* Baltimore: Johns Hop-
    kins University Press.
SHAPIRO, MICHAEL H. and SPECE, ROY G., JR. 1981, 1991
    Bioethics and Law: Cases, Materials and Problems. St. Paul,
    Minn.: West Publishing Co.

PUBLIC FORUM
(Update)

In recent years the Supreme Court has elevated the distinction between public and nonpublic forums into "a
fundamental principle of First Amendment doctrine."
Apart from rules of time, place, and manner, government
regulation of speech within a public forum is usually subject to the STRICT SCRUTINY [4] ordinarily required by
First Amendment jurisprudence. Government regulation
of speech within a nonpublic forum, however, is accorded
wide latitude and presumptive constitutionality. The
Court has increasingly relied upon public forum doctrine
to insulate from JUDICIAL REVIEW [3,I] restrictions on
speech in such settings as schools, prisons, military establishments, and state bureaucracies.

Given the dramatic constitutional difference in the government's power to regulate speech within public and
nonpublic forums, the distinction between the two is a
matter of some importance. The Court has offered two
criteria for this distinction. The first distinguishes public
from nonpublic forums on the basis of whether the government property at issue has "traditionally served as a place
for free public assembly and communication of thoughts
by private citizens." The second turns on whether government has deliberately opened the property at issue for
indiscriminate use by the general public. The Court has
never explained, however, why the exercise of ordinary
First Amendment rights on government property should
depend either upon tradition or upon the permission of
the government. As a consequence, modern public forum
doctrine has justly received nearly universal scholarly condemnation.

The explosive growth of the doctrine is nevertheless
undeniable. The underlying cause of this growth appears
to be that the Court is using public forum doctrine to
distinguish two different kinds of government authority:
management and governance. The government exercises
managerial authority when it acts through institutions to
achieve explicit and fixed ends. The purpose of schools
is to educate the young; the goal of prisons is to punish
and reform convicted criminals; the objective of the military is to safeguard the nation; and so forth. In each of
these settings, the Court has used public forum doctrine
to enable government to regulate speech to achieve these
institutional ends. Thus, for example, the Court has classified schools as nonpublic forums to permit them to censor
student speech inconsistent with the achievement of their
educational mission.

Outside these narrow institutional settings, however,
governmental objectives in a democracy are not fixed and
given, but rather are determined by a process of public
deliberation. For this reason, public speech cannot be
instrumentally regulated in a managerial fashion. In public
forums, therefore, the First Amendment requires that
the state exercise the authority of governance, in which
the regulation of speech is presumptively unconstitutional
unless justified according to strict constitutional tests.
These tests are designed to ensure that governmental
goals and policies be perpetually subject to the evaluation
of democratic deliberation.

Although the Court's doctrine has not explicitly recognized this distinction between management and governance, the pattern of its decisions has served to define
the boundary between these two different forms of authority. Public forum doctrine has thus achieved important
prominence in this age of the activist state, in which the
rapid proliferation of government institutions has both
created a legitimate need for expansive new forms of regulating speech and yet has simultaneously threatened to
strangle public deliberation.

The most controversial aspect of contemporary public
forum doctrine has been the Court's tendency to defer
to institutional authorities on the question of whether
the regulation of speech is truly necessary to achieve institutional objectives. In the 1988 decision HAZELWOOD
SCHOOL DISTRICT V. KUHLMEIER [I], for example, the
Court concluded that determinations of the educational
propriety of speech should properly rest "with the school
board . . . rather than with the federal courts" and that
therefore judges should defer to the decisions of school
officials. But such deference in effect cedes to the states
enormous discretion to regulate speech and sharply raises
the question of the circumstances under which courts
ought to relinquish careful supervision of governmental
curtailments of speech.

ROBERT C. POST

(SEE ALSO: *Bender v. Williamsport* [I]; *Education* [2,I]; *Equal
Access* [I]; *Freedom of Speech* [2,I]; *Military Justice* [3]; *Prisoners' Rights* [3]; *Widmar v. Vincent* [4].)

Bibliography

FARBER, DANIEL A. and NOWAK, JOHN E. 1984 The Misleading Nature of Public Forum Analysis: Content and Context in First Amendment Adjudication. *Virginia Law Review* 70:1219–1266.

POST, ROBERT C. 1987 Between Governance and Management: The History and Theory of the Public Forum. *UCLA Law Review* 34:1713–1835.

PUBLIC INTEREST LAW

Public interest law is the work done by lawyers on behalf of poor individuals, unrepresented interests, and the general good. Public interest law services are usually provided at no cost to the beneficiaries, who are either too poor to pay or are not organized in ways that would allow them to retain lawyers. Public interest lawyers work in the courts, agencies, legislatures, and also through the media and community organizations. Although only a small number of American lawyers participate in these activities, public interest law reflects the American legal profession's commitment to values not fully served by the normal fee-for-service system of legal practice.

There is an intimate relationship betwene public interest law and the Constitution. First, the governmental structure created by the Constitution makes public interest law both necessary and possible. Second, without public interest law, many constitutional protections might be ineffective. Finally, the broader American tradition of CONSTITUTIONALISM [1] depends on institutions like public interest law.

The governmental structure created by the Constitution makes legal advocacy important for the pursuit of many individual and collective interests. United States government is one by representation, not by direct participation. Although, in theory, citizens are supposed to be knowledgeable about public issues and elected representatives are supposed to take account of the interests of all constituents, in fact, most decisions are made in remote arenas and officials often are not aware of all affected interests. As a result, direct advocacy by professionals will make a difference in outcomes. If all such advocacy must be purchased in the marketplace, the system will be skewed toward the interests of the "haves." The presence of public interest advocates, at least to some degree, offsets marketplace bias.

The special role our written Constitution plays in American political life makes subsidized advocacy all the more important. Americans resolve many fundamental issues—from SLAVERY [4] to reproductive freedom—through constitutional litigation. If free legal services are not sometimes available in these struggles, the results can be seriously skewed.

Although the constitutional structure thus makes public interest law necessary, it also helps make it possible. Of course, there is a constitutional RIGHT TO COUNSEL [3] in criminal cases. In addition, several constitutional protections have been given to public interest lawyers. In NAACP V. BUTTON (1963) [3] the Supreme Court ruled that litigation on behalf of a disadvantaged group was constitutionally protected speech and overturned Virginia's efforts to penalize NAACP lawyers. This ruling was extended by *In re Primus* (1978), where the Court made clear that nonprofit groups representing protected interests were exempt from normal bans on solicitation by lawyers.

The rights granted by the Constitution usually are not self-enforcing. Without legal representation, many would remain a dead letter. Protections for criminal defendants remain mere paper promises unless the accused are represented by competent lawyers. Because of the serious consequences of a deprivation of these rights, the Constitution itself guarantees counsel. But there are many other areas in which public interest law, although not constitutionally guaranteed, is equally essential. Many efforts to curb free speech, for example, would have gone unchallenged if public interest groups like the AMERICAN CIVIL LIBERTIES UNION [1] were not available to defend this interest. The guarantee of EQUAL PROTECTION OF THE LAW [2,I] might still sound completely hollow to African Americans if the subsidized services of NAACP lawyers and other public interest advocates were not available.

Public interest law spans the political spectrum. Some of the more notable liberal public interest law groups include the ACLU, the NAACP LEGAL DEFENSE AND EDUCATIONAL FUND [3], and the Commission on Law and Social Action of the AMERICAN JEWISH CONGRESS [1]. Public interest law groups of a conservative persuasion include the Pacific Legal Foundation, which brings suits against governmental regulation; the Rutherford Institute, which litigates cases involving EQUAL ACCESS [I] for religious groups and defends nonviolent protestors in the ANTIABORTION MOVEMENT [I]; and the Washington Legal Foundation, which pursues a grab bag of causes, including JUDICIAL REVIEW [3,I] of redistricting and lawsuits by crime victims.

A major aspect of American political culture is our "constitutionalism": the belief in higher values protected by the Constitution. Often, marginal and subordinated groups have looked to higher law and constitutional values as guides and inspiration for their struggle for inclusion in the American commonwealth. Women, blacks, and other groups have looked beyond existing law and institutions to a penumbra of constitutional values that, they believed, entitled them to fuller participation in economic, social, and political life. Public interest law, as idea and institution, is a reflection of this faith in the redemptive power of law and legal institutions. To be sure, law does not always fulfill the promises Americans put in it. Public interest law is often weak and ineffective; legal solutions may not lead to real gains. But public interest lawyers have won real victories and made some difference for subordinated groups. As long as America's basic political institutions remain unchanged, public interest law will be essential: it ensures that forces of the market and status quo do not overshadow democracy and constitutional values and helps preserve constitutionalism as a real force in our political life.

LOUISE G. TRUBEK

Bibliography

ARON, NAN   1988   *Liberty and Justice for All: Public Interest Law in the 1980s and Beyond.* Boulder, Colo.: Westview Press.
CHAVKIN, DAVID F.   1987   Public Interest Advocacy. In R. Janoskik, ed., *Encyclopedia of the American Judicial System: Studies of the Principle Institutions and Processes of Law,* Vol. 2. New York: Scribners.

PUNISHMENT

See: Sentencing [I]

PUNITIVE DAMAGES

The plaintiff who prevails in a tort case is entitled to compensatory DAMAGES [2], including damages for pain and suffering. In a limited number of cases involving aggravated wrongdoing, the plaintiff can recover punitive damages as well. Sometimes the understanding is that these damages are indeed punitive: that their intent is to punish defendants for their wrongdoing. At other times, punitive damages seem designed to provide a higher level of deterrence than would be occasioned by the mere threat of compensatory damages; at this juncture, the language of "exemplary damages" becomes apt.

Although scholars have long expressed uneasiness with punitive damages, until recently their constitutionality has been taken for granted. In recent years, however, the number of punitive-damage awards has increased, and the size of the average punitive-damage verdict has soared. These changes have encouraged the posing of new questions as to their constitutionality. In *Browning-Ferris Industries, Inc. v. Kelco Disposal, Inc.* (1989), the defendant committed a business tort against the plaintiff

that resulted in $51,146 in actual damages. A jury awarded the plaintiff these damages—and six million dollars in punitive damages as well. An argument advanced by the defendant was that this award constituted an "excessive fine," forbidden by the Eighth Amendment. Amazingly, *Browning-Ferris* was the first case involving the excessive-fines clause that the Supreme Court had ever considered. The Court, divided 7–2, finally decided that punitive damages awarded in private civil actions are not "fines" and are hence unregulated by the clause. The majority opinion, authored by Justice HARRY A. BLACKMUN [1,I], left open the question as to whether the clause pertains only to proceedings that are officially criminal: rather, the rationale adopted by Blackmun was that the clause has no application to a legal proceeding in which the government is no way a party. The dissent, authored by Justice SANDRA DAY O'CONNOR [3,I], would have found the clause applicable to punitive-damage awards and, hence, would have subjected such awards to a "proportionality" analysis that O'Connor drew from the case law under the Eighth Amendment's CRUEL AND UNUSUAL PUNISHMENT [2,I] clause.

Although denying the relevance of the Eighth Amendment, the *Browning-Ferris* majority acknowledged that large punitive-damage awards might raise a problem of DUE PROCESS [2]. A concurring opinion signed by Justices WILLIAM J. BRENNAN [1,I] and THURGOOD MARSHALL [3,I] emphasized the likely relevance of due process. Indeed, the majority and concurring opinions together suggest two different kinds of due process issues. One is an issue of SUBSTANTIVE DUE PROCESS [4,I]: that due process might be violated by punitive-damage awards that are substantively excessive. The other issue relates to PROCEDURAL DUE PROCESS [3,I]; here the concern is for the lack of clarity in the standards that the jury relies on in calculating the amount of punitive damages.

If the vagueness in the standards for calculating punitive damages raise a due process problem, a related problem concerns the amorphousness in the standards relied on in determining whether or not to award punitive damages. Moreover, there are further constitutional issues that punitive-damage practices might be thought to entail. If punitive damages are regarded as sufficiently penal to render at least somewhat relevant the BILL OF RIGHTS [1], then the "preponderance of the evidence" standard of proof that states have traditionally relied on in punitive-damage cases might be inadequate. (Indeed, as part of the tort-reform movement of the late 1980s, several states have raised the punitive-damage standard of proof to clear and convincing evidence.) In so-called "mass-tort" situations involving such products as asbestos and the Dalkon Shield, a large number of punitive-damage verdicts can be entered against a particular defendant on account of a single (although continuing) course of harm-causing conduct. At some point, the cumulation of these awards might suggest an issue of due process or DOUBLE JEOPARDY [2,I]. Indeed, in early 1989, one federal district court judge did find a constitutional violation, although a lack of adequate precedent later persuaded him to withdraw most of his holding.

The Supreme Court further considered the procedural due process issues in *Pacific Mutual Life Insurance Co. v. Haslip* (1991). This case involved an $840,000 punitive damage verdict against an insurance company for the bad faith of its agent. The majority's opinion strongly suggested that a punitive damage award resulting from "unlimited jury discretion" would offend due process. The *Haslip* jury, however, had been given at least minimal standards; and its award had then been reviewed by both the trial judge and the Alabama Supreme Court, under rather elaborate procedures. This combination of protections enabled the *Haslip* majority to conclude that the "punitive damages award in this case" did not violate due process. The majority's case-specific reasoning effectively leaves open the due process status of a large intermediate range of punitive damage practices. Although the Court affirmed Alabama's "preponderance" standard of proof, even this affirmance was tied to Alabama's special set of procedures. And since evidence of defendant's wealth is inadmissible in Alabama punitive damage actions, the Court was in a position to conclude that Alabama procedures are not biased against "a defendant with a deep pocket."

Justices Anthony Kennedy and Antonin Scalia each wrote separate opinions in *Haslip*, concurring only in the majority's result. In their view, the long-standing historical acceptance of punitive damage practices all but eliminates the due process question. Justice Sandra Day O'Connor dissented, arguing that the limited standards applied by the Alabama jury were void for vagueness and also that the Alabama trial procedures entailed a due process violation. In her view, Alabama could satisfy constitutional requirements by allowing the jury to consider the seven substantive factors that the Alabama Supreme Court itself takes into account in the course of appellate review.

GARY T. SCHWARTZ

Bibliography

SYMPOSIUM: PUNITIVE DAMAGES 1989 *Alabama Law Review* 40:687–1261.
——— 1982 *USC Law Review* 56:1–203.

R

RACE-CONSCIOUSNESS

It was once widely believed that BROWN V. BOARD OF EDUCATION OF TOPEKA (1954, 1955) [1] had removed the last vestiges of race-consciousness from the Constitution. Many observers saw the *Brown* decision as a vindication of Justice JOHN MARSHALL HARLAN's [2] lone dissent in PLESSY V. FERGUSON (1896) [3]. Harlan's critique of the majority's SEPARATE-BUT-EQUAL DOCTRINE [4] was summarized in these famous words: "Our Constitution is color-blind, and neither knows nor tolerates classes among citizens. In respect of civil rights, all citizens are equal before the law." In the years between *Plessy* and *Brown*, the ideal of a "color-blind" Constitution served as one of the central tenets of liberal CONSTITUTIONALISM [2].

Today, however, some leading liberal constitutionalists argue that adherence to the ideal of a color-blind Constitution was a mistake. It has been only recently discovered that "color-blindness" was all along a "myth" or, at best, a "misleading metaphor." The principal reason for the volte-face on the part of liberal activists is summarized by Laurence H. Tribe, who writes that "judicial rejection of the 'separate but equal' talisman seems to have been accompanied by a potentially troublesome lack of sympathy for racial separateness as a possible expression of group solidarity." Indeed, it seems to be true that the expression of racial or ethnic group solidarity does require something like the old—and once justly decried—"separate but equal doctrine." Tribe's tergiversations indicate, however, that it is not yet entirely fashionable to speak openly about the desirability of returning to separate but equal. Attacks on the idea of a color-blind Constitution, on the other hand, are legion.

A curious feature of the *Brown* decision is that it did not make a comprehensive condemnation of racial classifications or entirely overrule the *Plessy* decision. Only racial classifications that were said to produce "feelings of inferiority" were deemed to violate EQUAL PROTECTION [2, I], and from the psychological evidence adduced by the Court, this was "proven" to be the case only in the context of grammar school education. Presumably, racial SEGREGATION [4] that did not stigmatize one race or ethnic group as inferior would survive the test adumbrated in *Brown*. Thus, *Brown* did not overrule all racial classifications—or treat them as SUSPECT CLASSIFICATIONS [4]—but left open the possibility that under certain circumstances racial classifications could be "benign" if the classification were designed to produce racial class remedies rather than racial class injuries. Resort to the doctrine of STRICT SCRUTINY [4] in the *Brown* case would probably have effectively foreclosed the future use of race as a legitimate classification.

Perhaps the best expression of the new understanding of "separate but equal" was made by Justice HARRY A. BLACKMUN [1, I] in his separate opinion in REGENTS OF UNIVERSITY OF CALIFORNIA V. BAKKE (1977) [3]: "I suspect that it would be impossible to arrange an affirmative-action program in a racially neutral way and have it successful. . . . In order to get beyond racism, we must first take account of race. There is no other way. And in order to treat some persons equally, we must treat them differently." Justice Blackmun could have used the word "separately" in lieu of "differently" without changing his meaning in the slightest. Indeed, it has been the advent of affirmative action that has generated the greatest controversy about race-consciousness and the Constitution. At

411

its inception, the proponents of affirmative action assured a skeptical world that it was only a temporary measure to be employed in the service of equality of opportunity. But now, some twenty-odd years after its appearance, affirmative action is looked upon unabashedly by its supporters as a means of securing racial class entitlements.

Inevitably, the test of racial class entitlements—and RACIAL DISCRIMINATION [3,I]—is the concept of racial proportionality. This idea assumes that, absent discrimination, the races will freely arrange themselves in the various aspects of political and private life in exact racial proportionality and that when they do not, there is a prima facie evidence of discrimination (or underrepresentation) that eventually must be rectified by any number of coercive remedies. This situation, of course, presents the alarming spectacle of a nation one day looking upon all civil rights as nothing more than racial class entitlements. But any nation with the slightest concern for the lessons of history would never self-consciously allow itself to regard the rights of individuals as nothing more than the by-product of racial class interests. Even though we may be assured that the ultimate ends of such programs as affirmative action are "to get beyond racism," those who advocate such policies simply have not thought out the likely consequences, believing, no doubt, that a means can never become the end itself.

The constitutional doctrine that most contributes to race-consciousness is that of DISCRETE AND INSULAR MINORITY [2]. The underlying premise of this doctrine is that there are certain racial and ethnic minorities that are permanently isolated from the majoritarian political process and therefore cannot vindicate their racial class interests by merely exercising the vote. The concept of the discrete and insular minority assumes that American politics has always been dominated by a monolithic majority that seeks only to aggrandize its own racial class interests at the expense of the various discrete and insular minorities. Thus, the moral authority of the majority—indeed, of majoritarian politics itself—must be questioned, if not undermined. In fact, some legal scholars argue that the only way that the rights of discrete and insular minorities can be absolutely guaranteed is in those instances where legislation disadvantages or injures the majority. Thus, one could argue that the Constitution not only permits affirmative action but requires it. It is only where the majority suffers a positive disadvantage that one can be certain that discrete and insular minorities are not harmed by the operation of the majoritarian political process. Fortunately, the Supreme Court has never accepted this negative version of the categorical imperative.

A bare acquaintance with history shows the impossibility of such a simplistic view of American politics. Could such a monolithic majority bent on the exclusive aggrandizement of its own racial class interests approve the Declaration of Independence and the Constitution? Ratify the Bill of Rights? Fight the Civil War to overturn the DRED SCOTT V. SANDFORD (1857) [2] decision? Ratify the THIRTEENTH AMENDMENT [4], FOURTEENTH AMENDMENT [2,I], and FIFTEENTH AMENDMENT [2]? Pass the CIVIL RIGHTS ACT OF 1964 [1] and the VOTING RIGHTS ACT OF 1965 [4]? These great events (and a host of others) in American constitutional history make it incredible that learned people—including the Justices of the Supreme Court—could believe that the concept of discrete and insular minorities was in any way an accurate reflection of American political life. American life is too subtle and complex to be understood exclusively in terms of racial class interests.

The Framers of the Constitution knew that class politics, in whatever guise it appeared, was incompatible with constitutional democracy. The whole thrust of JAMES MADISON's [3] belief in the "capacity of mankind for self-government" was his conviction that under a properly constructed constitution, majorities could be rendered capable of ruling in the interest of the whole of society rather than in the interest of the part (i.e., in the interest of the majority). The structure of society itself, with its multiplicity of interests and accompanied by a constitutional structure informed by the SEPARATION OF POWERS [4], held the prospect that majorities could act in a manner consistent "with the rules of justice and the rights of the minor party." Madison called these majorities *constitutional* majorities as distinguished from *numerical* majorities. Many legal scholars today, however, simply proclaim that every majority is ipso facto a special-interest group and that majorities cannot therefore be trusted to rule in the interest of the whole. Some even conclude that courts should be cast in the role of virtual representatives of discrete and insular minorities, because judges are isolated from the majoritarian political process and can therefore "rule" in the interest of the whole of society. Others, however, have not forgotten such infamous decisions as *Dred Scott*, *Plessy v. Ferguson*, LOCHNER V. NEW YORK (1905) [3], and *Korematsu v. United States* (1944) and are quick to recognize this scheme as a form of judicial oligarchy. Virtual representation is an idea that is incompatible with republican government.

It has become something of an orthodoxy among legal scholars to ridicule the moral imperative of racial neutrality as the driving force of the Constitution. They retort that race has always been a factor in American political life and it is simply unrealistic to think that it will not be so for the foreseeable future. Because race-consciousness will inevitably be part and parcel of constitutional calculations, it is more honest to advocate them openly than to seek a deceptive refuge in the ideal of a color-blind Constitution. It is true that America's constitutional past is all too replete with race-consciousness. After all, the Constitution itself gave support to SLAVERY [4]. The toleration of slavery in the Constitution was a product of political necessity. The Constitution itself—and thereby any prospects of ending slavery—would never have been accepted without compromise on the issue of slavery. But most of the Framers of the Constitution looked upon that compromise as a necessary (but temporary) departure from the principles of the regime that had been enunciated in the Declaration of Independence. The best they could do under the circumstances was to fix those principles in the Constitution so that the Constitution could one day provide the basis for emancipation. The American founding was incomplete, but the Constitution looked forward to its completion by putting, in ABRAHAM LINCOLN's [3] words, "slavery on the ultimate road to extinction." Lincoln always interpreted the Constitution in light of the principles of the Declaration. In doing this, he was following the lead of the Framers themselves.

In 1857, Lincoln gave an account of the aspirations of the American polity and the role the Declaration played in fixing constitutional aspirations. He noted that the authors of the Declaration "did not mean to assert the obvious untruth, that all were then actually enjoying equality, nor yet, that they were about to confer it immediately upon them." In fact, Lincoln noted, they had no power to "confer such a boon," had they been inclined to do so. Rather, "they meant simply to declare the *right*, so that the *enforcement* of it might follow as fast as circumstances should permit. They meant to set up a standard maxim for free society, which should be familiar to all, and revered by all, constantly looked to, constantly labored for, and even though never perfectly attained, constantly approximated, and thereby constantly spreading and deepening its influence, and augmenting the happiness and value of life to all people of all colors everywhere." With the Constitution viewed as the means of implementing the "standard maxims" of the Declaration, the nation has made tremendous progress since the Civil War and Reconstruction.

Yet, at almost the eleventh hour, liberal constitutionalists want to abandon those principles that have been the source of progress. Surely the progress came too slowly and advanced by fits and starts, according to the political circumstances of the day. But no one can deny that progress occurred and that it resulted directly from our "ancient faith" that the Constitution should be race-neutral. Now we are told that progress in race relations has not gone far enough or fast enough and it is time to return to a race-conscious Constitution to implement a newer, more certain view of racial progress. The return to race-consciousness also means that sooner or later we will have to pronounce the principle of equality "an empty idea." The reason is simple: equality is a principle that is incompatible with group rights and preferential treatment. One prominent author has argued that because it cannot comprehend the "rights of race," "equality is an idea that should be banished from moral and legal discourse." Indeed, group claims—including racial group claims—are not claims of equality, but claims of inequality, and they necessarily rest upon some notion of "separate but equal." Class claims deny the principle of equality because they ascribe to individuals class characteristics that are different—and necessarily unequal—from those of individuals occupying other classes. If there were no inequalities implicit in class distinctions, such distinctions would be superfluous and there would be no need to substitute group rights for individual rights.

Almost the whole of American constitutional history has been a history of the nation's attempt to confine the genie of race by powerful constitutional bonds; yet the most sophisticated constitutional scholars today advocate the release of the racial genie once again, this time to act as a benign, rather than destructive, force. This is dangerous advice because this time the genie will not be restrained by the moral principle that "all men are created equal."

EDWARD J. ERLER

(SEE ALSO: *Racial Preference* [I]; *Racial Quotas* [3].)

Bibliography

ERLER, EDWARD J. 1989 Equal Protection and Regime Principles, Pages 243–283 in Robert L. Utley, Jr., ed., *The Promise of American Politics.* Lanham, Md.: University Press of America.

STRAUSS, DAVID A. 1986 The Myth of Colorblindness. *Supreme Court Review* 1986:99–134.

TRIBE, LAURENCE H. 1988 *American Constitutional Law*, 2nd ed. Pages 1474–1480. Mineola, N.Y.: Foundation Press.

WESTEN, PETER 1982 The Empty Idea of Equality. *Harvard Law Review* 95:537–596.

RACIAL DISCRIMINATION
(Update)

In the mid-1980s, most observers would have said that the Supreme Court's view of racial discrimination was in equipoise. Some of the Justices seemed sympathetic to the aggressive purposeful use of racial criteria to end the legacy of racial subordination; others were skeptical of "benign discrimination" and looked instead to a constitutional principle of colorblindness as the cornerstone of a society free of discrimination. The last several terms have made plain the ascendancy of the latter view. It is now evident that a majority of the Justices are prepared to view with suspicion and hold to the highest standard of constitutional scrutiny governmental efforts to use racial classifications even to assist members of racial minorities. At the same time, governmental actions that disadvantage racial minorities will be sustained absent clear and unambiguous evidence of impermissible racial animus.

AFFIRMATIVE ACTION [1] advocates are particularly concerned about the Court's recent willingness to view benign racial classifications with the same suspicion with which it has traditionally treated classifications intended to oppress. Where this leaves racially conscious programs is unclear, except that as before the stronger the showing that a RACIAL PREFERENCE [I] is related to a bona fide remedial goal, the greater the likelihood the Court will sustain it.

Thus in WYGANT V. JACKSON BOARD OF EDUCATION (1986) [I], the Justices overturned a plan under which a school board extended to minority teachers what a plurality of the Court called "preferential protection against layoffs." The plan was part of the collective-bargaining agreement between the board and the union representing school teachers and was defended before the Court as an effort to alleviate "social discrimination" by providing a diverse set of role models in public schoolrooms. A three-Justice plurality declared that the proper test was STRICT SCRUTINY [4] and held the plan invalid because more specific findings of prior discrimination were necessary before the layoff protection could be said to serve a COMPELLING STATE INTEREST [1].

In contrast, in UNITED STATES V. PARADISE (1987) [I], the Justices voted 5–4 to sustain a federal district court's imposition of a "one-for-one" hiring plan, pursuant to which the Alabama Department of Public Safety was obliged to remedy its past failure to hire black troopers by hiring one black trooper for each white trooper hired. The SOLICITOR GENERAL [4,I] argued that even when a racially conscious remedial program was ordered by a court, strict scrutiny was the proper test, and the program could survive only on a showing of a compelling state interest. Four Justices, in an opinion by Justice WILLIAM J. BRENNAN [1,I], refused to decide this question, ruling that the program could meet any level of scrutiny because it was "justified by a compelling interest in remedying the discrimination that permeated entry-level practices and the promotional process alike." The plurality further noted that the district court had imposed the one-for-one plan only after the department had repeatedly failed to comply with earlier decrees.

Probably the most controversial benign discrimination decision—and the one with the most far-reaching implications—was RICHMOND (CITY OF) V. J. A. CROSON CO. (1989) [I], in which the Justices struck down a program under which the City of Richmond required its prime contractors to subcontract thirty percent of the dollar amount of each contract to minority-owned firms. In *Croson*, a majority of the Justices ruled explicitly that strict scrutiny was the proper level of review for benign discrimination cases. Although there was no majority opinion on the point, six Justices repudiated as insufficiently narrow the city council's defense that the program was needed to eliminate the effects of societal discrimination.

Although it is true that the Justices have always taken the position that even benign classifications are subject to the highest level of constitutional scrutiny, they have not previously applied the rule with quite the strictness used in *Croson*. Indeed, FULLILOVE V. KLUTZNICK (1980) [2], which sustained a federally mandated set-aside program for certain construction projects, is in one sense indistinguishable: in *Fullilove* and in *Croson*, the relevant body (in the first case the Congress, in the other the city council) had before it no record of past discrimination. This aspect of *Fullilove* can be preserved by reference to the special fact-finding competence of the Congress, although this reed is a thin one because the Congress found no facts; in any case, the Justices are noticeably less hospitable to *Fullilove*-style set-asides by state or local governments than they were to Congress's set-asides a decade ago. But at least six Justices seem prepared to pay strong deference to the power of Congress to adopt programs of affirmative action in enforcing the FOURTEENTH AMENDMENT [2,I].

At the same time, the Court has arguably shown increasing sensitivity to certain claims of racial discrimination in the CRIMINAL JUSTICE SYSTEM [I]. Thus in *Hunter v. Underwood* (1985), a unanimous Court struck down a neutrally applied disenfranchisement of persons convicted of misdemeanors involving "moral turpitude" on the ground that it was originally enacted decades earlier for the purpose of discriminating against black citizens. The following term, in BATSON V. KENTUCKY (1986) [I], the Justices eased the burden of a defendant seeking to prove that the prosecution had used its peremptory challenges to exclude jurors on the basis of race. On the same day, the Justices decided in *Turner v. Murray* that a defendant in a capital case has the right to examine prospective jurors about racial bias.

But the trend has gone only so far. In the following term, the Justices made plain their resistance to inferring impermissible discriminatory motivation from circumstantial evidence, especially statistical evidence. In MCCLESKEY V. KEMP (1987) [I], a black convicted of murder argued that Georgia's decision to sentence him to death violated the Eighth and Fourteenth Amendments because statistics demonstrated that black defendants, especially black defendants whose victims were white, were far more likely than white defendants to receive CAPITAL PUNISHMENT [1,I]. The statistics (generally referred to as the Baldus study, after the principal author of the underlying work) were stark indeed; they indicated, among other disparities, that capital juries in Georgia handed down death sentences to black defendants whose victims were white twenty-two times more frequently than they did to black defendants whose victims were black.

The *McCleskey* majority, however, was unimpressed, responding tersely, "We refuse to assume that what is unexplained is invidious." This answer in a sense eluded McCleskey's point, which was that the disparity was great enough to place the burden of explanation on the state. The Court replied that other explanations were plausible, adding that juror discretion should not be condemned or disturbed simply because of an "inherent lack of predictability." As long as forbidden racial animus was not the only possible explanation, the Court would not assume that animus was at work.

As the dissenters pointed out, the result in *McCleskey* seemed to stand as a departure from the BURGER COURT [1] decision in *Arlington Heights v. Metropolitan Housing Development Corp.* (1977). In *Arlington Heights*, the Justices suggested that racial animus might be inferred from "a clear pattern" of official behavior, "unexplainable on grounds other than race." The *McCleskey* majority was correct that other explanations for the Baldus data are conceivable, and some critics have offered them. But in *McCleskey*, the Justices declined even to speculate.

Nevertheless, in important respects, *McCleskey* differed from other racial-discrimination cases. First, as several observers have noted, the Baldus study most strongly supports an argument that the murderers of black people are systematically treated with greater leniency than the murderers of white people. If one believes that the death penalty deters the crime of murder, then the implication is that the state is doing less to protect the lives of black people than to protect the lives of white people. Warren McCleskey, convicted of killing a police officer while committing another felony, was not a particularly attractive candidate to raise this issue. The better case (unfortunately for the Supreme Court's paradoxical ruling in *Linda R.S. v. Richard D.* [1973], which denied standing to raise a claim that the law is inadequately enforced) would be one brought by law-abiding black citizens seeking to protect their lives and property.

A second distinction between *McCleskey* and other cases is that, had it gone the other way, *McCleskey* might have opened up a Pandora's box of claims that blacks in the criminal process—from arrests to sentencing—are treated more harshly than whites, claims that are supported by considerable empirical literature. Even if the literature is accurate (again, there are critics), it is difficult to imagine what practical relief might be fashioned in such cases. For those who are convicted, mandatory resentencing is one possibility, although the continued judicial monitoring of sentencing disparities could produce a procedural nightmare. The fear that this slippery slope lay ahead might well have been a part of the majority's calculus.

The Justices have also worked important changes in the interpretation of one of the keystones of the "Second Reconstruction," Title VII of the CIVIL RIGHTS ACT OF 1964 [1]. In *Ward's Cove v. Antonio* (1989), the Justices reexamined the burden of proof of a plaintiff relying on the Court's decision in GRIGGS V. DUKE POWER CO. (1971) [2]. *Griggs* had read Title VII to prohibit an employment practice with racially identifiable disparate impacts unless the employer was able to show a business necessity for the test. In *Ward's Cove*, the Court ruled 5–4 that the plaintiff must carry the burden of demonstrating the causal link to the composition of the market of people qualified to do the job in question. Critics of *Ward's Cove* argued that the decision had shifted the burden from the employer to the employees and would make employment-discrimination cases more difficult to prove; defenders responded that Title VII plaintiffs should be required to prove all elements of their claims.

Depending on one's point of view, then, the recent work of the Supreme Court in the area of racial-discrimination law has represented either a tragic abandonment of the judiciary's traditional role as protector of the racially oppressed or a return to the shining principles of color-blindness as the fundamental rule for government action. But not all significant changes in the area of racial discrimination require judicial action. In fact, one of the most important developments of recent years involved an attempted legislative correction of a judicial wrong. The WORLD WAR II [I] decisions sustaining the internment of Japanese Americans are widely regarded as among the most horrific judicial decisions of the twentieth century (although it must be said that the programs could never have been approved had the President and Congress not imposed them in the first place). In the mid-1980s, federal courts vacated the convictions of Gordon Hirabayashi, Minoru Yasui, and Fred Korematsu for evading registration for internment. A DAMAGES [2, I] claim by former detainees was rejected by the Federal Circuit in 1988 on statute of limitations grounds, but in August of that year, the Congress adopted legislation apologizing for the internment program and granting to each surviving internee compensation of roughly $20,000—not perhaps the same as justice, but at least an acknowledgment that justice was due.

STEPHEN L. CARTER

(SEE ALSO: *Constitutional Remedies* [I]; *Capital Punishment and Race* [I]; *Japanese American Cases* [3]; *Race-Consciousness* [I]; *Sentencing* [I].)

Bibliography

AREEN, JUDITH, ET AL. 1989 Constitutional Scholars' Statement on Affirmative Action After *City of Richmond v. J.A. Croson Co. Yale Law Journal* 98:1711–1716.

FRIED, CHARLES 1989 Affirmative Action After *City of Richmond v. J.A. Croson Co.*: A Response to the Scholars' Statement. *Yale Law Journal* 99:155–161.

KENNEDY, RANDALL L. 1988 *McCleskey v. Kemp*: Race, Capital Punishment, and the Supreme Court. *Harvard Law Review* 101:1388–1443.

RACIAL PREFERENCE

Debate about racial-preference policies stirs particularly strong passions because it evokes one of the central animating concerns of liberal constitutionalism—its opposition to any system of hereditary castes. But there is little agreement today about what the constitutional principle of equality actually requires.

Some version of racial equality has always been insisted on, at least since the ratification of the FOURTEENTH AMENDMENT [2,I]. Even in the 1890s, when the Supreme Court acquiesced to racial SEGREGATION [4] in the South, it insisted that the separation of the races should not be understood to "imply the inferiority of either race" or be taken as a sign of governmental preference for one race over another. At the same time, however, the Court observed in PLESSY V. FERGUSON (1896) [3] that "in the nature of things," the Fourteenth Amendment "could not have been intended to . . . enforce social as distinguished from political equality. . . ." The Court treated racial bias and inequality among private citizens as equivalent to class antagonisms between rich and poor or to sectarian tensions between rival religious faiths—facts of life that a constitutional government could not expect to suppress.

For a brief period following the modern Supreme Court's ruling against school separation in BROWN V. BOARD OF EDUCATION (1954) [1], there seemed to be an emerging consensus that equality would, after all, be best served by dismantling all racial distinctions in public law. Thus, the historic CIVIL RIGHTS ACT OF 1964 [1] prohibited, in general terms, "discrimination on the basis of race," rather than discrimination against blacks or other racial minorities in particular. But, among other things, the 1964 legislation sought for the first time to prohibit EMPLOYMENT DISCRIMINATION [2] throughout the American economy. Was this done to enforce a new ideal of social indifference to race or to improve the economic condition of depressed minorities?

Legislative history might be cited to support either view, but the latter view largely prevailed in federal enforcement policy. By the early 1970s, federal officials had come to define RACIAL DISCRIMINATION [3,I] as any employment standard that disproportionately excluded minority applicants, regardless of the employer's intent; in this and other ways, government policy, with approval from the courts, pressed employers to redefine their hiring and promotion policies to secure "appropriate" percentages of employees from specified minority groups, even if this required passing over better-qualified whites. (See, for example, GRIGGS V. DUKE POWER (1971) [2] and UNITED STEELWORKERS OF AMERICA V. WEBER (1979) [4].) With federal encouragement, state programs also offered preferences to minority students in admissions to professional schools (REGENTS OF UNIVERSITY OF CALIFORNIA V. BAKKE, 1978 [3]); other programs began to offer preferences to minority businessmen, as, for example, to minority-owned firms bidding for federal construction grants (FULLILOVE V. KLUTZNICK, 1980 [2]).

Court decisions upholding such practices generally invoked the need to "remedy" past discrimination, implying that localized preferences were acceptable only as temporary correctives to offset the effects of particular past abuses. In 1990, however, a five-Justice majority of the Supreme Court upheld a minority-preference policy in the award of broadcast licenses by the Federal Communications Commission (FCC). Noting the small number of minority-owned stations, the Court, in METRO BROADCASTING, INC. V. F.C.C. (1990) [I], endorsed an explicit preference policy as a permissible device for ensuring broadcasting "diversity," disclaiming any need to consider whether there had actually been a history of past discrimination in this particular field.

Critics of such preference policies—including dissenting Justices—have protested that they violate the spirit of constitutional guarantees and the letter of the CIVIL RIGHTS [1,I] laws by prescribing different standards for whites and minorities. Worse, the critics argue, such policies treat minority individuals, not as actual individuals with their own personal merits, but as mere representatives of their racial groups. Defenders of preferential policies insist that civil-rights legislation and constitutional guarantees have been established to help minorities overcome the effects of discrimination and that such help should not be denied for the sake of an entirely abstract and unrealistic doctrine of equal treatment. They argue that guarantees of equality or nondiscrimination should be seen as bulwarks against policies that "stigmatize" or "subjugate" people because of their race, and no AFFIRMATIVE ACTION [1] program, they say, can seriously be regarded as "stigmatizing" or "subjugating" whites as a whole. The critics of preference policies respond that, insofar as preference policies assume that whites would still exclude others without such mandatory preferences, the policies do stigmatize whites—as racist; insofar as preference policies assume that blacks and other minorities could not compete in American society without such governmental preferences, they stigmatize minorities as incapable.

Not surprisingly, critics of preference policies, emphasizing the potential for manipulation and abuse in governmental controls, would place more reliance on the working of private-market decision making; those who defend preference policies tend to take a much more sanguine view of governmental intervention and to regard racially unequal outcomes in the market as inherently suspect. But the debate about racial preference is not simply a special case of a larger argument about the proper scope of government. Neither liberals nor conservatives on the Supreme Court would be likely, for example, to tolerate a policy that sought to enhance broadcasting "diversity" by providing preference to non-Jewish or non-Protestant firms in the award of broadcasting licenses by the FCC.

In fact, the Court has repeatedly struck down governmental financial aid to religious schools, even though such programs might well be seen as efforts to equalize educational opportunity for religious minorities. Such programs, the Court insisted in LEMON V. KURTZMAN (1973) [3], carry too much potential for political divisiveness, setting religious school constituencies against public school constituencies. Yet many of the same Justices and commentators who have most insistently opposed such aid to religious minorities have been quite sympathetic to government preference policies based on race. The difference is not plausibly explained on the grounds that religion is more divisive than race in contemporary American society. If anything, it seems to be the severity of racial divisions in American society that makes proponents of racial-preference policies regard them as necessary.

Recent studies suggest that despite two decades of racial preference policies the gap between whites and blacks in earnings and in educational attainments is scarcely diminished since the 1960s and in some areas is greater than it was. Some critics of racial preference see this as an additional reason for abandoning such programs. Many supporters of these programs regard this fact instead as

an additional reason for redoubling the scale and intensity of preference. This may prove an area of constitutional dispute that is too large to be solved by mere judicial pronouncements.

JEREMY RABKIN

Bibliography

ABRAM, MORRIS B.   1986   Affirmative Action: Fair Shakers and Social Engineers. *Harvard Law Review* 99:1312–1326.

STRAUSS, DAVID A.   1986   The Myth of Colorblindness. *Supreme Court Review* 1986:99–134.

RACKETEER INFLUENCED AND CORRUPT ORGANIZATIONS ACT (RICO)

The Racketeer Influenced and Corrupt Organizations Act (RICO) was enacted by Congress in 1970 to provide federal prosecutors with a powerful tool against organized crime. RICO has been used against the ruling commission of the Mafia in New York City, against corrupt politicians running local government agencies, against Croatian terrorists, against political demonstrators, against the Sicilian Mafia for importing billions of dollars of heroin into the United States in the pizza connection case (the longest criminal trial in federal history), in the largest criminal tax-fraud prosecution in history, and against massive insider-trading securities fraud.

RICO is a complex statute that creates both criminal sanctions and civil remedies, enforceable by the government or by injured private parties. The heart of the statute defines four crimes. First, it is illegal to establish, operate, or acquire an interest in any enterprise affecting either INTERSTATE COMMERCE [2] or FOREIGN COMMERCE [2] with income from a pattern of racketeering activity or collection of an unlawful debt. Second, the act prohibits acquiring or maintaining an interest in any such enterprise through a pattern of racketeering activity or collection of an unlawful debt. Third, it is a crime for any employee or associate of any such enterprise to participate in the enterprise through a pattern of racketeering activity or collection of an unlawful debt. And fourth, it is illegal to conspire to violate any of the first three provisions. A "pattern" of racketeering requires the commission of two or more "predicate offenses" within a ten-year period. These offenses include nine categories of state crimes and twenty-six federal crimes, including murder; drug trafficking; bribery; and mail, wire, and securities fraud. As discussed in *United States v. Turkette* (1981), an "enterprise" includes any individual, partnership, corporation, association, union, or group of individuals associated in fact, whether legitimate or illegitimate. Conviction under RICO carries severe criminal penalties and forfeiture of ill-gotten gains. A person may be liable for triple damages, costs, and attorneys' fees in a private civil RICO action. RICO is unique in its complexity among criminal statutes because of the sheer number of potential predicate offenses and because of the indefinite terms used in defining a violation.

In *H.J. Inc. v. Northwestern Bell Telephone Co.* (1989) the Supreme Court interpreted a "pattern of racketeering activity" to require both "continuity" and "relationship": two or more predicate offenses that are somehow related and that pose a threat of continued criminal activity must be committed within a ten-year period. Four of the more conservative Justices, although concurring in the JUDGMENT [3], suggested that the pattern requirement may be unconstitutionally void for vagueness in both criminal and civil cases. Because it is not clear what RICO requires beyond two predicate offenses, a potential defendant may not know whether his or her conduct is covered by RICO. Lower courts, however, have uniformly held that the pattern requirement is not unconstitutionally vague because the underlying predicate offenses are clearly defined crimes. People of common intelligence, therefore, do not have to guess at what is forbidden, and the discretion of police, prosecutors, juries, and courts in enforcing RICO is constrained. Gerard Lynch has argued that unexpectedly draconian penalties nevertheless may be imposed based on a prosecutor's unrestricted discretion to transform ordinary offenses into a RICO prosecution. This may implicate the principle of legality (penal legislation must describe with precision the conduct it prohibits and the potential punishment) and the related constitutional prohibitions against VAGUENESS [4] and EX POST FACTO LAWS [2].

Among the most powerful applications of RICO has been its use to seek pretrial restraint and forfeiture of illegal proceeds, including assets that a defendant would otherwise use to hire a defense attorney at the very criminal trial where guilt and thus forfeitability will be determined. In *Caplin & Drysdale, Chartered v. United States* (1989) and *United States v. Monsanto* (1989) (construing parallel forfeiture provisions under the continuing criminal-enterprise statute), the Court held, 5–4, that such restraint and forfeiture do not violate the Sixth Amendment RIGHT TO COUNSEL [3] or the Fifth Amendment DUE PROCESS [2] right to a FAIR TRIAL [2]. A defendant who is thus left INDIGENT [2], the majority said, can obtain appointed counsel. The Court left open whether due process requires a fair hearing before a pretrial restraint may be imposed. The Court also construed the forfeiture provisions broadly in *Russello v. United States* (1983) to serve the congressional purpose of creating a potent weapon

to attack the economic roots of organized crime. Lower courts have held that forfeiture may be cruel and unusual, in violation of the Eighth Amendment, if the interest forfeited is grossly disproportionate to the offense committed.

Although the Supreme Court has not yet addressed most constitutional attacks on RICO, in *Sedima, S.P.R.L. v. Imrex Co.* (1985), the Court rejected the circuit court's suggestion that a private civil RICO action in the absence of a prior criminal conviction impermissibly imposes punishment while avoiding the protections of constitutional CRIMINAL PROCEDURE [2].

Lower courts have held that various applications of RICO do not violate the DOUBLE JEOPARDY [2,1] clause. Dual prosecutions—by the state for the predicate offenses and by the federal government for racketeering based on those offenses—are permitted because different sovereigns and separate offenses are involved. Double jeopardy does not bar federal prosecutions for both the underlying federal predicate offenses and RICO offenses based on those predicates, prosecutions for both a RICO conspiracy and substantive RICO offenses, separate sentences for predicate and RICO offenses, or separate sentences for RICO conspiracy and RICO substantive offenses. In *Grady v. Corbin* (1990) the Court held that double jeopardy bars a subsequent prosecution if, to establish an essential element of an offense, the government will prove conduct that constitutes an offense for which the defendant has already been prosecuted. The impact of *Grady* remains to be seen.

Even though a predicate act committed before the statute went into effect may be used to establish a pattern of racketeering, RICO requires that at least one act be committed after its effective date. A person who has committed a prior act is therefore on notice that a subsequent act will subject him or her to liability. Thus, RICO is not unconstitutional as an ex post facto law or BILL OF ATTAINDER [1].

Private civil plaintiffs have expanded civil RICO in dramatic ways against traditional businesses with no ties to organized crime. RICO civil suits have also been employed by both private and government entities in efforts to suppress unpopular political groups, including antinuclear demonstrators in Georgia, an antipornography group in Florida, and anti-abortion protestors across the country. In West Hartford, Connecticut, the city government even sued a local newspaper for covering anti-abortion protests. Such suits raise significant free-speech problems. Many of these expansive uses of RICO were not anticipated by Congress, but nevertheless fall within the plain language of the statute. Claims of abuse have produced repeated efforts with little success to reform RICO through judicial interpretations, legislation, or Justice Department guidelines. It is unlikely that the Courts will reform RICO by applying the BILL OF RIGHTS [1]. The concurring opinion in *H. J. Inc.* notwithstanding, the Supreme Court has not been inclined to find new constitutional protections for the accused. However, at least some federal courts may be unwilling to hear certain kinds of RICO suits. In *Town of West Hartford v. Operation Rescue* (2nd circuit, 1990), the federal appeals court dismissed a civil RICO suit against anti-abortion protestors engaged in CIVIL DISOBEDIENCE [1]. The court labeled the suit's RICO allegations "blatantly implausible" and indicated that the court had no willingness "to countenance fanciful invocations of the draconian RICO weapon in civil litigation."

ROBERT DIDEROT GARCIA

(SEE ALSO: *Federal Criminal Law* [I].)

Bibliography

LYNCH, GERARD E. 1987 RICO: The Crime of Being a Criminal (parts I–IV). *Columbia Law Review* 87:661–764, 920–984.
NOTE 1990 RICO's "Pattern" Requirement: Void for Vagueness? *Columbia Law Review* 90:489–527.

RADIO

See: Broadcasting [I]

RATIFIER INTENT

Ratifier intent is a form of ORIGINAL INTENT [I] or ORIGINALISM [I] that emphasizes the meanings and understandings of the Constitution possessed by those who ratified it. The ratifiers were the members of the state CONSTITUTIONAL CONVENTIONS [1] that ratified the Constitution. The importance of ratifier intent derives from the widely held opinion that the consent of the governed, who alone were sovereign, legitimated the Constitution. The CONSTITUTIONAL CONVENTION OF 1787 [1] had exceeded its instructions: to recommend revisions of the ARTICLES OF CONFEDERATION [1]. Although the Confederation Congress transmitted the Constitution to the states for RATIFICATION [3], thereby implicitly agreeing to the scrapping of the Articles of Confederation, the fact remains that the Convention had violated its commission. Consequently, leading Framers of the Constitution insisted, as JAMES MADISON [3] said, that "the legitimate meaning" of the Constitution should be sought "not in the opinions or intentions of the body which planned and proposed the Constitution, but in the sense attached to it by the people in their respective State Conventions, where it

received all the authority which it possessed." Thus, as its ratification rather than its framing imbued the Constitution with its legitimacy, so ratifier intent rather than original intent (the understandings of the Framers) defined the text. This is the CONSTITUTIONAL THEORY [I] of the matter as transmitted by the Framers.

One should not have to choose between the intent of the Framers and that of the ratifiers. All contemporary expositions should be considered if they illumine a constitutional issue. Moreover, from the broadest perspective, ratifier intent and original intent almost coincided: government by consent of the governed; majority rule under constitutional restraints that limit majorities; guarantees of rights that prevail against the legislative as well as executive branch; a federal system; three branches of government, including a single executive, a BICAMERAL [1] legislature, and an independent judiciary; an elaborate system of CHECKS AND BALANCES [2]; and representative government and elections at fixed intervals. The founding generation also believed in measuring the powers of government, rather than the rights of the people, and they assumed a NATURAL RIGHTS [3] philosophy. They concurred on a great many fundamental matters. Without doubt, the Constitution reflects a coherent and principled POLITICAL PHILOSOPHY [3,I]. All of this consensus bespeaks an enormously important and ascertainable set of original understandings shared by Framers and ratifiers, even by Federalists and ANTI-FEDERALISTS [1]. But none of this history enables judges to reach decisions favoring one side of a constitutional issue rather than another in real cases that come before courts.

More perplexing still is the fact that ratifier intent with respect to the meanings of particular clauses of the Constitution is more often than not unascertainable. The main reason for this is that the historical record is too skimpy to sustain a constitutional JURISPRUDENCE [I] of ratifier intent. In a 1954 report, the National Historical Publications Commission declared that the reporters of the ratification period took notes on the debates "and rephrased those notes for publication. The shorthand in use at that time was too slow to permit verbatim transcription of all speeches, with the result that a reporter, in preparing his copy for the press, frequently relied upon his memory as well as his notes and gave what seemed to him the substance, but not necessarily the actual phraseology, of speeches. Different reportings of the same speech exhibited at times only a general similarity, and details often recorded by one reporter were frequently omitted by another." Reporters used their notes to spur their memories, and their reports were no better than their understandings.

When Jonathan Elliot began publication of his *Debates* in 1827, he collected the previously published records of the state ratifying conventions. He misleadingly called his collection *The Debates in the Several State Conventions, on the Adoption of the Federal Constitution*. In fact, Elliot unreliably reported the proceedings of only five states plus some fragments of others. He acknowledged that the debates may have been "inaccurately taken down" and "too faintly sketched." ELBRIDGE GERRY [2], a member of the Constitutional Convention who became an Anti-Federalist leader, complained that the "debates of the State Conventions, as published by the short-hand writers, were generally partial and mutilated."

For Pennsylvania, Elliot published only the speeches of two advocates of ratification. The editor of the debates for Massachusetts apologized for his inaccuracies and omissions deriving from his inexperience. He also doctored some speeches and provided a few spurious ones. The reporter for New York made similar remarks and recorded only the debates for the first half of convention's proceedings, reverting to a skeletal journal of motions for the remainder. In Virginia, where the debates were most fully reported and by a reporter sympathetic to ratification, James Madison and JOHN MARSHALL [3] expressed dissatisfaction with the results. Madison informed Elliot that he found passages that were "defective," "obscure," "unintelligible," and "more or less erroneous." Marshall complained that if he had not seen his name prefixed to his speeches he would not have recognized them as his own. He further declared that the speeches of PATRICK HENRY [2], the leader of the opposition, were reported worst of all. Similar criticisms apply to the proceedings of North Carolina, whose first convention rejected the Constitution and whose second was wholly unreported.

These are the five states (Pennsylvania, Massachusetts, New York, Virginia, and North Carolina) whose records provide a basis, however inadequate, for determining ratifier intent. We have only scraps of material for the other states, with the exception of Rhode Island, which ratified so late as to count for nearly nothing. Although the people acting through state ratifying conventions gave the Constitution its authority, the ratifiers' intent should not be confused or conflated with legitimacy. Ratification legitimated the text that the Constitutional Convention recommended; the Convention did not recommend its intention, only the text, and the ratifying conventions only ratified the text, without providing a basis for a constitutional jurisprudence based on ratifier intent or understanding. Justice JOSEPH STORY [4] made the definitive rejection of ratifier intent in his *Commentaries on the Constitution*: "In different states and in different conventions, different and very opposite objections are known to have prevailed. Opposite interpretations, and different explanations of different provisions, may well be presumed to have been presented in different bodies, to remove local objections,

or to win local favor. And there can be no certainty, either that the different state conventions in ratifying the constitution, gave the same uniform interpretation to its language, or that even in a single state convention, the same reasoning prevailed with a majority" (1st ed. 1833, I, pp. 388–389).

Story continued by noting that the terms of the Constitution impressed different people differently. Some drew conclusions that others repudiated; some understood its provisions strictly, others broadly. Ratifiers in different conventions revealed a diversity of interpretations. To THOMAS JEFFERSON's [3] demand that ratifier intent be honored as much as possible, Story retorted that it was not possible; he ridiculed "the utter looseness, and incoherence of this canon." No way existed to determine "what was thought of particular clauses" of the Constitution when it was ratified. "In many cases no printed debates give any account of any construction; and where any is given, different persons held different doctrines. Whose is to prevail?" Story concluded that determining ratifier intent is hopeless because "of all the state conventions, the debates of five only are preserved, and these very imperfectly. What is to be done, as to other eight states?" Ratifier intent, despite its present support by some constitutional scholars, including Robert Bork and Charles Lofgren, is as lacking in historical basis or practical application as it may be theoretically attractive.

LEONARD W. LEVY

(SEE ALSO: *Bork Nomination Constitutional Interpretation* [1]; [I].)

Bibliography

BORK, ROBERT H.   1989   *The Tempting of America: the Political Seduction of the Law*. New York: Free Press.

HUTSON, JAMES H.   1986   The Creation of the Constitution: The Integrity of the Documentary Record. *Texas Law Review* 65:1–39.

LEVY, LEONARD W.   1988   *Original Intent and the Framers' Constitution*. New York: Macmillan.

LOFGREN, CHARLES A.   1988   The Original Understanding of Original Intent. *Constitutional Commentary* 5:77–113.

REAGAN, RONALD
(1911–   )
(Update)

No President since FRANKLIN D. ROOSEVELT [3] devoted as much of his administration's attention to the courts and the Constitution as did Ronald Reagan. After a career as an actor and spokesman for General Electric, Reagan was catapulted into politics by a famous televised speech on behalf of Barry Goldwater's presidential campaign.

Twice elected governor of California, Reagan was hailed as the conservative standard-bearer in his unsuccessful race for the Republican presidential nomination in 1976. He came to office in 1980 pledging to reinvigorate the idea of LIMITED GOVERNMENT [3]—to restore what he saw as the constitutional foundations of American politics. In part, this restoration would involve restricting the federal government's encroachments on individual freedom and on the prerogatives of state governments. But more important, it would require that the doctrines stimulating the federal government's inordinate growth be publicly discredited and supplanted.

Reagan won the 1980 presidential election by a large margin and set to work to lower federal tax rates and shore up America's defenses. These tasks absorbed most of his and his administration's attention even after his still more massive electoral victory in 1984; but Reagan wished always to make the "Reagan Revolution" something broader and deeper—what he called in his 1985 State of the Union Address "a Second American Revolution." The changes in economic and defense policy won in the great legislative battles of his first term had therefore to be parlayed into a general rethinking of the purposes of American politics and, especially, of the functions served by the courts.

Large changes in American electoral politics, particularly in the wake of so-called critical or realigning elections, do eventually register on the judiciary (as in 1937, with the "switch in time" that "saves nine") and sometimes on the Constitution itself (for example, the Civil War amendments). Indeed, in Reagan's view, the LIBERALISM [I] that he attacked had always put a high premium on control of the judiciary, from F.D.R.'s COURT-PACKING PLAN [I] to the activism of Chief Justice EARL WARREN [4] to President JIMMY CARTER's [1] efforts to apply strict AFFIRMATIVE ACTION [1] standards to judicial appointments. But Reagan faced the novel circumstance of trying to undo a series of divisive liberal measures that the Supreme Court itself had directed—the legalization of ABORTION [1,I], the expulsion of prayer from the public schools, the promulgation of the EXCLUSIONARY RULE [2], and so forth.

These issues were particularly important to the social conservatives who had joined with traditional Republicans and anticommunists in the 1960s and 1970s to form the coalition that would eventually sweep Reagan into office. Although Reagan campaigned both in 1980 and 1984 for the overruling of such Supreme Court decisions, he himself did little to dislodge them, except to call for constitutional amendments to protect the life of the unborn and to allow voluntary SCHOOL PRAYER [I] in public classrooms. To confront the Court more directly would have risked alienating the more libertarian members of his coalition,

which was united more by its common enemies than by common principles. Instead, he concentrated his administration's energies on the selection of judges pledged to exercise "judicial restraint" and, therefore, more likely over time to modify or overturn their predecessors' activist decisions.

It is probably in this way that the Reagan administration will have its great effect on CONSTITUTIONAL INTERPRETATION [1]. In the course of his presidency, Reagan appointed more than 400 federal judges, nearly half the federal bench, as well as three Supreme Court Justices; and he elevated WILLIAM H. REHNQUIST [3,I] to CHIEF JUSTICE [1] of the Supreme Court in 1986. All these appointments were vetted and approved by an elaborate machinery centered in the Justice Department's Office of Legal Policy and overseen by a newly created White House Judicial Selection Committee. Critics objected to the screening procedure, claiming that it politicized the JUDICIAL SELECTION [I] process by subjecting candidates to a "litmus test" on such issues as abortion and CRIMINAL PROCEDURE [2]. But the Reagan administration denied the charge, arguing that the reviews focused not on specific issues, but on the candidates' general approach to legal and constitutional interpretation, which the President was entitled to consider, and that in any event the liberal critics were applying a double standard.

The issue was raised desultorily in some of Reagan's nominations to the Supreme Court—SANDRA DAY O'CONNOR [3,I] in 1981, the first woman ever nominated (pursuant to a 1980 campaign promise by Reagan); ANTONIN SCALIA [I] in 1986, who replaced Rehnquist when the latter was elevated to Chief Justice; and ANTHONY M. KENNEDY [I] in 1988—but it was raised acutely in the confirmation hearings of Rehnquist and above all of Robert H. Bork. The latter was denied confirmation by the Senate after a long, bitter, and very public struggle over the meaning of "judicial restraint" and of what Attorney General Edwin Meese had called "a jurisprudence of original intention." After Bork's defeat, Reagan nominated Douglas H. Ginsburg, who was forced to withdraw on account of disclosures about his personal life and controversy over his conduct as Justice Department attorney. Shortly thereafter, Reagan nominated Kennedy, who finally assumed the seat vacated by Justice LEWIS F. POWELL [2,I] half a year earlier.

The significant question concerned the meaning of "judicial restraint." Did it mean, as its liberal critics claimed, that judges would respect only those laws and PRECEDENTS approved by conservatives and restrain all the others? Or did it entail genuine respect for the language of the Constitution and a principled deference to the rights of legislative majorities, as its defenders maintained? The controversy over "restraint" therefore pointed to the larger question of the meaning of the Constitution itself. Did the Constitution embody an ORIGINAL INTENT [I] that judges must regard as authoritative? Liberals such as Justice WILLIAM J. BRENNAN [1,I] argued, somewhat contradictorily, that judges could not know what the Framers' intentions 200 years ago were; that even if they could, times have changed and interpretation of the Constitution could not be bound by the views of "a world that is dead and gone"; and that what the Framers actually intended was to leave the Constitution open-ended and alive, so that it might be adjusted to changing times and values. To this, conservatives such as Bork and Rehnquist replied that the Framers' intentions were either clearly spelled out in the Constitution or not, and if not, then it was up to Congress or the states to make law as they saw fit.

But this answer begged the question of whether in ascertaining the Framers' intentions a distinction did not have to be made between the spirit and the letter of the Constitution; or, to put it differently, whether precisely in order to understand the Constitution as the Framers understood it, one did not have to distinguish between its principles and the application (or compromise) of those principles, for example, in the so-called three-fifths compromise. The alternative to seeking such principles as a ground of the Constitution's authority was to accept the letter of the law as itself the highest authority, or more exactly, to accept as just and lawful whatever the sovereign majority decreed in the Constitution or in statute law, no matter how irrational or unjust. That is to say, the alternative was a form of legal POSITIVISM [I] or formalism. That Bork's position came close to this became painfully clear in the debate over the RIGHT OF PRIVACY [3,I] during his confirmation hearings. In short, although his JURISPRUDENCE [I] emphatically rejected judicial tyranny, it did not seem to afford a principled defense against majority tyranny. To that extent, it fell short of the NATURAL LAW principles that justified limited government and that had informed the "original intention" of the Constitution's Framers.

As President, Reagan relied on his Justice Department and SOLICITOR GENERAL [3,I] to encourage the narrowing of the liberal precedents left over from the Warren and Burger courts. The administration succeeded in persuading the Supreme Court to enlarge existing exceptions to the exclusionary rule, to create new ones, and to narrow the acceptable occasions for court-ordered affirmative-action remedies. But Reagan refused to issue an EXECUTIVE ORDER [2] forbidding set-asides and other forms of reverse discrimination in executive-branch contracts and was saddled with an amended Voting Rights Act (1982) that went far toward establishing proportional representation (i.e., quotas) for selected minorities as the paramount goal of legislative redistricting. The Reagan administration's reluctance to face a public debate on CIVIL RIGHTS [1,I] and affirmative action left it vulnerable to attack by the advocates of racial and ethnic entitlements who insisted that anyone who was against the "empowerment" of favored minorities through RACIAL QUOTAS [3] (although the dread word was seldom used) was against civil rights.

Although his administration did much to remind the American people that a strong, purposeful President could initiate profound political change, Reagan was often frustrated by Congress. In a remarkable victory that, along with Reagan's landslide electoral win, seemed to promise a fundamental shift in American politics, the Republicans gained control of the SENATE [I] in 1980—only to lose it six years later; they never came close to taking control of the HOUSE OF REPRESENTATIVES [I]. The result was divided government and a long running battle over foreign and domestic policy in which the administration had the upper hand only in its first two years. From these struggles arose at least two interesting lines of constitutional controversy.

The first concerned FOREIGN AFFAIRS [2], specifically, the scope of the President's discretion under statute law and the Constitution to order covert activities abroad. Stung by congressional opposition to its initial program of "covert" aid to the forces seeking to overthrow the Sandinista regime in Nicaragua, the administration turned to a more overt strategy of aid, appealing directly to the Congress and the people for support. Although sometimes endorsing Reagan's commitment to arm resistance fighters in communist-controlled countries (e.g., in Afghanistan), the Congress vacillated on aid to the Contras fighting in Nicaragua. During Reagan's presidency, at least two versions of the BOLAND AMENDMENT [I] were passed, along with two or three later modifications of the amendment, each restricting Contra aid in different and conflicting ways.

Against the background of Reagan's desire to support the Nicaraguan resistance, and his need to exploit the ambiguities of the Boland Amendment in order to do so, arose the IRAN-CONTRA AFFAIR [I]—a tangled enterprise run out of the National Security Council (NSC) and aimed at a deal involving the release of hostages held by pro-Iranian terrorists, arms sales to Iran, and the diversion of profits to the Contras in Nicaragua. Fearing another WATERGATE [4] scandal, the administration discharged the accused parties, launched its own inside and outside investigations, called for an INDEPENDENT COUNSEL [I], and cooperated with two congressional committees appointed to investigate the affair. The larger legal questions turned on whether or not the NSC was covered by the Boland Amendment's ban on aiding the Contras; the constitutional question as to whether or not the President's authority as COMMANDER-IN-CHIEF [1] (or his oath of office) enabled him to act, for the sake of *salus populi*, on the margins of or even against a congressional statute. In the event, the constitutional issue was quickly eclipsed by the debate over the statutory question and by the dramatic testimony and trial of Oliver North, a hitherto obscure NSC staffer.

In other foreign-policy matters, Reagan enjoyed a wide latitude. He committed U.S. forces to Lebanon, to the raid on Libya, to the liberation of Grenada, and to protection of Kuwaiti oil tankers in the Persian Gulf without invoking the War Powers Resolution and indeed with minimal congressional consultation.

The second interesting line of skirmishes between the Reagan administration and Congress concerned the executive's independence on the domestic front. Here, many administration officials were keen to reign in the authority of the SPECIAL PROSECUTORS [I] created by the Ethics in Government Act for the specific purpose of investigating members of the executive branch, and to curtail the proliferating means of congressional influence over the executive agencies. On the former topic, the Reagan administration argued that the law establishing special prosecutors violated the SEPARATION OF POWERS [4] by impinging on the executive's right to initiate, conduct, and terminate criminal prosecutions and led, in many cases, to the criminalizing of policy differences. But the Supreme Court upheld the law by a 7–1 vote in *Morrison v. Olson* (1988).

On the latter question—the extension of congressional power over the executive and independent agencies—Reagan faced even greater opposition. Although the administration convinced the Supreme Court of the unconstitutionality of the LEGISLATIVE VETO [3] in IMMIGRATION AND NATURALIZATION SERVICE V. CHADHA (1983) [2], Congress continued to pass (and Reagan continued to sign) laws containing such provisions, as well as the even more dubious "committee veto," whereby executive branch decisions may be disallowed by the vote of a single congressional committee.

But the legislative veto was only one of a multitude of ways by which the Congress and its swarm of subcommittees harassed the Reagan administration. In particular, Reagan's appointees complained of the "micromanagement" of the executive agencies by subcommittee chairs and individual members of Congress cajoling and threatening on behalf of their constituents and other friendly interest groups. By this tactic, members of Congress could pass broad, vaguely worded laws serving popular causes and then take credit for saving their constituents from the onerous consequences of the very same laws. The use of omnibus continuing resolutions in place of budget bills was yet another tactic to restrict the executive branch's freedom to veto specific budget bills and its right to decide how to execute the programs funded in the bills.

Reagan himself did not take a leading role in protesting what he regarded as these legislative encroachments on the executive, leaving his subordinates to do most of the disputing. He did vehemently object to being presented with the choice of either signing or vetoing at one stroke the entire BUDGET [1] of the federal government, but nevertheless signed the mammoth Continuing Resolution and Fiscal Year 1988 Budget Reconciliation Act. Rather than precipitate a fiscal, political, and constitutional crisis, he chose to reemphasize his call for two constitutional amendments—one creating a LINE ITEM VETO [I] for the President and the other mandating a BALANCED BUDGET [I]—to strengthen the hand of future Presidents.

For a conservative President, Reagan appealed for an unusual number of constitutional amendments. In part, this was a backhanded admission of his reluctance to engage in direct costly political combat over the budget, school prayer, abortion, and other controversial subjects. This reluctance was not so much temperamental as it was a reflection of a strategic political decision he had made before entering office in 1980, a decision to try to control the national political agenda by concentrating on two critical issues: reducing taxes and strengthening America's defenses. Of course, Reagan's decision was also shaped by the internal weaknesses of his own coalition, which he was never sufficiently able to overcome to bring about a thoroughgoing political realignment like the NEW DEAL [I].

Perhaps his greatest constitutional achievement did not have to do with the institutions of government at all. Reagan strove mightily to restore Americans' confidence in themselves as a fundamental force for good in the world, and in his speeches he seldom failed to remind his fellow citizens of a connection with the heroes and statesmen of the American past. In this way, he helped revive their faith in the goodness of the Constitution itself, a faith that had been sorely tried in the dark decades of the 1960s and 1970s.

CHARLES R. KESLER

(SEE ALSO: *Bork Nomination* [I]; *Budget Process* [I]; *Congress and Foreign Policy* [I]; *Congressional War Powers* [I]; *Conservatism* [I]; *Constitutional History* [1]; *Race-Consciousness* [I]; *Racial Discrimination* [I]; *Racial Preference* [I]; *Rehnquist Court* [I]; *Senate and Foreign Policy* [I]; *War Powers* [4,I].)

Bibliography

JONES, CHARLES O., ED. 1988 *The Reagan Legacy: Promise and Performance.* Chatham, N.J.: Chatham House.

JONES, GORDON S. and MARINI, JOHN, EDS. 1988 *The Imperial Congress: Crisis in the Separation of Powers.* New York: Pharos Books.

MAHONEY, DENNIS J. and SCHRAMM, PETER W., EDS. 1987 *The 1984 Election and the Future of American Politics.* Durham, N.C.: Carolina Academic Press.

REAGAN, RONALD 1980–1989 *Presidential Papers.* Washington, D.C.: U.S. Government Printing Office.

REASONABLE EXPECTATION OF PRIVACY

An issue of extraordinary importance in determining the scope of the protection of the FOURTH AMENDMENT [2,1] is the interpretation of the word "searches" in that amendment's proscription of "unreasonable searches and seizures." If certain conduct of state or federal officials is deemed not to constitute either a search or seizure, then Fourth Amendment requirements need not be met. On the other hand, if that activity is a search or seizure, then it is unconstitutional unless those requirements—that the conduct be undertaken only upon a certain quantum of evidence (PROBABLE CAUSE [3]), and in many instances that it be undertaken only upon prior judicial approval—have been met. How this issue comes out is a matter of considerable practical significance in criminal prosecutions, for the Fourth Amendment's EXCLUSIONARY RULE [2] usually dictates suppression of evidence if the amendment's limitations were exceeded in acquiring it.

The Supreme Court has had difficulty in developing a workable definition of the word "searches." At an earlier time, as in *Hale v. Henkel* (1906), the Court was inclined to say that "a search ordinarily implies a quest by an officer of the law," yet it soon became clear that not every instance of seeking evidence was a search. In OLMSTEAD V. UNITED STATES (1928) [3], for example, the Court held that the placing of a tap on telephone wires and thereby eavesdropping on the defendant's conversations was no search. As the Court later explained in SILVERMAN V. UNITED STATES (1961) [4], there was no Fourth Amendment search unless the police had physically intruded into "a constitutionally protected area." These areas were enumerated in the Fourth Amendment itself: "persons," including the bodies and clothing of individuals; "houses," including apartments, hotel rooms, garages, business offices, stores, and warehouses; "papers," such as letters; and "effects," such as automobiles. But then came the landmark decision of KATZ V. UNITED STATES (1967) [3], which overruled the *Silverman* standard and gave birth to the "reasonable expectation of privacy" test.

Katz was convicted in federal court on a charge of transmitting wagering information by telephone in violation of federal law. At trial the government was permitted to introduce, over defendant's objection, evidence of his end of telephone conversations, overheard by FBI agents who had attached an electronic listening and recording device to the exterior of a public telephone booth from which Katz habitually placed long-distance calls. The court of appeals affirmed Katz's conviction, reasoning that the ELECTRONIC EAVESDROPPING [2] did not amount to a Fourth Amendment search because the microphone had not penetrated the wall of the telephone booth. Before the Supreme Court, the parties disputed whether the booth was a "constitutionally protected area," but the Court declined to address that issue, noting that "the Fourth Amendment protects people, not places. What a person knowingly exposes to the public, even in his home or office, is not a subject of Fourth Amendment protection. . . . But what he seeks to preserve as private, even in an area accessible to the public, may be constitutionally protected." The Court then held, "The Government's activities in electronically listening to and recording the petitioner's words violated the privacy upon which he justifiably relied while using the telephone booth and thus constituted a 'search and seizure' within the meaning of the Fourth Amendment."

In his concurring opinion in *Katz*, Justice JOHN M. HARLAN [2] joined the opinion of the Court [3], but then explained what he took this opinion to mean. Lower courts and ultimately the Supreme Court itself came to rely upon the Harlan elaboration of the *Katz* test: "My understanding of the rule that has emerged from prior decisions is that there is a twofold requirement, first that a person have exhibited an actual (subjective) expectation of privacy and, second, that the expectation be one that society is prepared to recognize as 'reasonable.'" Courts and commentators thereafter attempted to ascertain the meaning of each of these two requirements.

The first part of the Harlan formulation arguably finds support in that part of the *Katz* majority opinion which declared that the government conduct directed at Katz "violated the privacy upon which he justifiably relied." However, an actual, subjective expectation of privacy deserves no place in a statement of what the Fourth Amendment protects. By use of a subjective test, it would be possible for the government by edict or known systematic practice to condition the expectations of the populace in such a way that no one would have any real hope of privacy. Harlan later appreciated this point, observing in his dissent in UNITED STATES V. WHITE (1971) [4] that analysis under *Katz* must "transcend the search for subjective expectations," for "our expectations, and the risks we assume, are in large part reflections of laws that translate into rules, the customs and values of the past and present."

Although a majority of the Court acknowledged in *Smith v. Maryland* (1979) that in some situations the subjective expectation of privacy test "would provide an inadequate index of Fourth Amendment protection," the Court sometimes appears to rely on it nevertheless. Illustrative is *California v. Ciraolo* (1986), holding that the Fourth Amendment was not violated by warrantless aerial observation of marijuana plants inside a fenced backyard of a home. Though the state conceded the defendant had a subjective privacy expectation, the Court offered the gratuitous observation that because "a 10-foot fence might not shield these plants from the eyes of a citizen or a policeman perched on the top of a truck or a 2-level bus," it was "not entirely clear" whether the defendant "therefore maintained a subjective expectation of privacy from *all* observations of his backyard, or whether instead he manifested merely a hope that no one would observe his unlawful gardening pursuits." The unfortunate implication of this comment is that a defendant cannot even get by the first *Katz* hurdle unless he has taken steps to ensure against all conceivable efforts at scrutiny.

The second branch of the Harlan elaboration in *Katz*, apparently an attempt to give content to the word "justifiably" in the majority's formation, prompted the Court on later occasions, as in TERRY V. OHIO (1968) [4], to refer to the *Katz* rule as the "reasonable 'expectation of privacy' test." This language is perhaps unfortunate, for it might be read to mean that police activity constitutes a search whenever it uncovers incriminating actions or objects which the law's hypothetical reasonable man would expect to be private—that is, which as a matter of statistical probability were not likely to be discovered. Though the Court has wisely rejected such an interpretation, as in OLIVER V. UNITED STATES (1984) [4], it still leaves the question of precisely what makes a reliance on privacy "justified" in the *Katz* sense.

In his *White* dissent, Harlan asserted that this question must "be answered by assessing the nature of a particular practice and the likely extent of its impact on the individual's sense of security balanced against the utility of a conduct as a technique of law enforcement." Thus, he added, "those more extensive intrusions that significantly jeopardize the sense of security which is the paramount concern of Fourth Amendment liberties" are searches. Anthony Amsterdam has similarly asserted that the "ultimate question" posed by *Katz* "is whether, if the particular form of surveillance practiced by the police is permitted to go unregulated by constitutional restraints, the amount of privacy and freedom remaining to citizens would be diminished to a compass inconsistent with the aims of a free and open society."

But this is unfortunately not how the Court has subsequently interpreted *Katz*, as is apparent from a sampling of more recent cases. In *United States v. Miller* (1976) the Court held that a person has no justified expectation of privacy in the records of his banking transactions kept at financial institutions with which he has done business, because the documents "contain only information voluntarily conveyed to the banks and exposed to their employees in the ordinary course of business." This conclusion overlooks the fact that bank employees examine checks briefly and one at a time, and thus do not construct conclusions about the customer's lifestyle, while police who study the totality of one's banking records can acquire a virtual current biography. The Court's error in *Miller* was compounded in *Smith v. Maryland*, holding that one has no legitimate expectation of privacy in the numbers he dials on his telephone because those numbers are conveyed to the telephone company's switching equipment and, in the case of long-distance calls, end up on the customer's bill. Thus, the defendant in *Smith* could not object to police use of a pen register to determine all numbers he dialed, though once again the more focused police examination of the information revealed much more than the limited and episodic scrutiny that the phone company employees might give the same numbers.

In *United States v. Knotts* (1983) the Court similarly held that it was no search for police to keep track of a person's travels by using a "beeper" because "anyone who wanted to look" could have learned, without such assistance, of the defendant's 100-mile journey from Minneapolis into rural northern Wisconsin. But to learn what the beeper revealed—that the beeper-laden container of chemicals purchased in Minneapolis was now in a particular secluded cabin 100 miles away—would have taken an army of bystanders in ready and willing communication with one another. And then there is *Ciraolo*, holding that it is no search for police to look down from an airplane into one's solid-fenced backyard because "any member of the public flying over this airspace who glanced down could have seen everything that these officers observed." This ignores the fact, as the four dissenters put it, that "the actual risk to privacy from commercial or pleasure aircraft is virtually nonexistent."

In each of these cases, a majority of the Court failed to appreciate that "privacy is not a discrete commodity, possessed absolutely or not at all" (as Justice THURGOOD MARSHALL [3,I] put it in his *Smith* dissent) and that there is a dramatic difference, in privacy terms, between the sporadic disclosure of bits and pieces of information to a small and often select group for a limited purpose and a focused police examination of the totality of that information regarding a particular individual. Such decisions leave the promise of *Katz* unrealized and ignore the teachings of the Supreme Court's germinal search and seizure decision, BOYD V. UNITED STATES (1886) [1]. There, Justice JOSEPH P. BRADLEY [1] wrote that "constitutional provisions for the security of person and property should be liberally construed" in order to forestall even "the obnoxious thing in its mildest and least repulsive form," as "illegitimate and unconstitutional practices get their first footing in that way, namely, by silent approaches and slight deviations from legal modes of procedure."

Some hope—modest, given the outcome of the case—is to be found in *Florida v. Riley* (1989), holding that an officer's naked-eye observation into the defendant's residential greenhouse from a helicopter 400 feet off the ground was no search. Significant for present purposes is the observation of Justice HARRY A. BLACKMUN [1,I], dissenting, that a "majority of the Court" (the four dissenters and one concurring Justice) believe that the reasonableness of the defendant's expectations "depends, in large measure, on the frequency of nonpolice helicopter flights at an altitude of 400 feet." This means, Justice WILLIAM J. BRENNAN [1,I] concluded in his dissent, that a majority of the Court does not accept "the plurality's exceedingly grudging Fourth Amendment theory, [whereunder] the expectation of privacy is defeated if a single member of the public could conceivably position herself to see into the area in question without doing anything illegal." *Riley* thus may signal a rejection of the all-or-nothing approach to privacy, thereby giving the *Katz* reasonable expectation of privacy test new meaning.

WAYNE R. LaFAVE

(SEE ALSO: *Open Fields* [I]; *Plain View Doctrine* [3,I]; *Right of Privacy* [3,I]; *Search and Seizure* [4,I]; *Unreasonable Search* (4,I]; *Warrantless Searches* [4]; *Wiretapping* [4].)

Bibliography

AMSTERDAM, ANTHONY G. 1974 Perspectives on the Fourth Amendment. *Minnesota Law Review* 58:349–477.

GUTTERMAN, MELVIN 1988 A Formulation of the Value and Means Models of the Fourth Amendment in the Age of Technologically Enhanced Surveillance. *Syracuse Law Review* 39:647–735.

JUNKER, JOHN M. 1989 The Structure of the Fourth Amendment: The Scope of the Protection. *Journal of Criminal Law and Criminology* 79:1105–1184.

RECONSTRUCTION

The Framers of the Constitution did not anticipate a civil war or contemplate the constitutional problems in rebuilding the Union after such a conflict. From ABRAHAM LIN-

COLN's [3] first proposal for restoring the Union in 1863 to the withdrawal of the last federal troops from the South in 1877, Reconstruction was at heart a series of constitutional questions involving the power of the federal government vis-à-vis the states and the relations among the various branches of the national government.

The key issue from the very beginning centered on the nature of the Union. The South claimed that as a compact of states, the Union could be dissolved by the single expedient of the sovereign states choosing to withdraw. The North saw the Union as indissoluble. As Chief Justice SALMON P. CHASE [1] later wrote in TEXAS V. WHITE (1869) [4], "The Constitution, in all its provisions, looks to an indestructible Union, composed of indestructible States." The northern view had prevailed by force of arms, and the Union had been preserved. But if the states had never left the Union, as Lincoln had claimed throughout the CIVIL WAR [I], then why would a reconstruction be necessary to put them back in a status they had never left?

Lincoln approached this question in the same common-sense manner he had approached the war. The Constitution did not specifically authorize the federal government to deal with a civil war, but it was inconceivable that the Framers had not intended for the government to have all the adequate powers to preserve and defend itself. Throughout the war, Lincoln relied on the "adequacy of the Constitution" theory to justify actions that could not be grounded on a specific constitutional clause.

Common sense told him that if theoretically the states could not leave the Union, in initiating the war they had at least left their proper role in that Union, and some actions would have to be taken to make theory and reality whole again. The Ten-Percent Plan, whereby one-tenth of a state's 1860 voters would swear support of the Constitution and "reestablish" state government in return for presidential recognition, must be seen not as Lincoln's final word on the subject but as a wartime measure designed to draw the southern states back with the promise of leniency. Moreover, Lincoln wanted to retain his flexibility; if the Ten-Percent Plan worked, well and good, but if not, then he would try something else. The President vetoed the WADE-DAVIS BILL [4] not because he disagreed with its provisions but because it left him too little room for maneuver. The three state governments set up under Lincoln's plan proved failures, and there is evidence that the President and Congress were moving toward agreement on a new plan at the time of his assassination.

Where Lincoln had shown flexibility and open-mindedness in approaching the problem, his successor took a rigid and uncompromising position: the States had never left the Union, and therefore the federal government had no business telling them what they had to do in order to return to the Union. In ANDREW JOHNSON's [3] mind, Reconstruction amounted to little more than a brief period of readjustment, with oversight over this readjustment completely a presidential function. Just as Lincoln, as COMMANDER-IN-CHIEF [1], had the constitutional authority for directing the war, so now he, as commander-in-chief, would have similar power in tidying up the last few problems of that war. In taking this view, Johnson completely misunderstood how Lincoln had worked closely with congressional leaders to have Congress support his policies.

Over the summer of 1865 the southern states, at Johnson's direction, held conventions to revise their constitutions (primarily to abolish SLAVERY [4]) and to elect representatives to Congress. In the President's mind, when these representatives joined the Thirty-ninth Congress in December 1865, the Union would be whole and the readjustment process at an end. He did not believe then or later that Congress had any power to force the southern states to do anything they did not freely choose to do themselves. The former Tennessee senator, unlike many of his southern colleagues, had been a strong defender of the Union, but like them he shared a strong commitment to STATES' RIGHTS [4].

Congress obviously did not share Johnson's view and recognized that if it seated the southern representatives, Reconstruction would be at an end before the legislators could examine the situation or frame their own plan. Moreover, they believed that the people of the North wanted assurances that the fruits of their victory—the preservation of the Union and the abolition of slavery—would be protected in the peace to follow. With congressional refusal to seat the southerners, two conflicts began, one between the national government and the former Confederate states and the other between Congress and the President, both revolving around the question of what powers the national government had over the states.

Congress passed several bills in early 1866 to assist the newly freed blacks and to create legal protections for their rights. Supporters of these measures relied on what they considered the broad mandate of the THIRTEENTH AMENDMENT [4], ratified in December 1865, which included the first enforcement clause in any amendment. Some scholars have suggested that it is the Thirteenth, and not the Fourteenth, Amendment that recast relations between the states and the national government by giving Congress power over what had hitherto been an internal state matter.

When Congress discussed Reconstruction in early 1866, many Republicans believed that the Thirteenth Amendment by itself gave Congress sufficient power to carry out the broad aims of giving the former slaves full rights as citizens of the United States. Freedom, as they saw it, involved not just the formal abolition of slavery but also the eradication of any signs of inferior status. According to this view, Congress had all necessary power to enact whatever LEGISLATION [3] it thought necessary and proper to secure these goals.

Andrew Johnson, however, claimed that the amendment did little more than formally abolish slavery, and although the evidence is strong that its framers meant more than that, the Republican leadership in Congress worried that the Supreme Court might adopt his view. One can therefore see the FOURTEENTH AMENDMENT [2,I] as an effort to clarify the ORIGINAL INTENT [I] of the Thirteenth and as Congress's Reconstruction plan. By making its goals explicit through a constitutional amendment, Congress intended to quiet all concerns about the legitimacy of its plan.

One should also note that aside from invalidation of the Confederate debt and restrictions on some leaders of the rebellion, the Fourteenth Amendment was not punitive. Congress, as well as Johnson, wanted to see the southern states back in their proper role as quickly as possible. This is clear in the June 1866 report of the JOINT COMMITTEE ON RECONSTRUCTION [3], which, while documenting southern intransigence and oppression of the freedom, is moderate in tone. Ratify the Fourteenth Amendment, the report implies, and welcome back. In fact, Tennessee, which had always had a large Unionist faction, promptly ratified and Congress admitted it back into the Union in 1866.

The committee report is also noteworthy for its discussion of the constitutional issues involved in Reconstruction. Aside from repudiating Johnson's view of Reconstruction as solely a presidential function, it examined the constitutional status of the former Confederate states. In talking about "forfeited rights," it struck a position halfway between those who claimed that the states had never left the Union and therefore had retained all their rights and the radical view of "state suicide," in which the states had ceased to exist as legal entities. Rather, the states had as a result of their rebellion forfeited basic political rights as members of the Union and, until restored fully to the Union, could enjoy only those rights granted to them by the Congress. The report relied on the fact that the Constitution assigned the power for creating new states to Congress, not the President; by implication the task of refixing the states in the Union also belonged to Congress.

The report is a commonsensical effort to deal with practical problems, but its theoretical basis is inconsistent. The states had forfeited all rights and existed as states only at the sufferance of Congress, yet they were being asked to exercise one of the most important political powers under the Constitution—changing the organic framework of government through amendment.

At Johnson's urging, the other southern states refused to follow Tennessee's example, and this refusal raised the question of whether ratification of the amendment required three-fourths of those states still in the Union or three-fourths of all the states—including the southern states now in a constitutional limbo. Here again one can only contrast Johnson's rigid adherence to a theoretical premise that flew in the face of the reality and Congress's efforts to reach a workable solution of a problem fraught with constitutional bombshells.

The election of 1866 ought to have made clear to Johnson that the North overwhelmingly favored the congressional Republican position, but he continued his efforts to thwart Congress. The events of 1867, with continuing tensions between President and legislature, led to a political impasse unforeseen by the Framers—a chief executive who, repudiated at the polls, refused to accept that judgment and who did his best, not to execute duly passed laws of Congress, but to thwart their implementation. There is an ongoing debate over what the Framers intended as grounds for IMPEACHMENT [2], but a number of scholars believe that the device serves as an instrument of last resort for resolving a political deadlock that would otherwise paralyze the government. Although the Senate failed to convict by a single vote, the impeachment proceeding had the desired effect: while Johnson still refused to cooperate with Congress, he no longer attempted to obstruct its will. By then, however, the damage had been done; the intransigence of the southern states, encouraged by Johnson, led to a prolonged Reconstruction and a legacy of bitterness.

Hovering in back of much of the congressional debate in 1866 and 1867 was a concern over what the Supreme Court would say in regard to the Reconstruction statutes. By then, no one questioned the power of the Court to declare acts of Congress unconstitutional, and if the Justices should adhere to the traditional view of limiting federal interference in state affairs, then the entire congressional program might be voided. The Court's decision in EX PARTE MILLIGAN (1866) [3] and in two cases striking down LOYALTY OATHS [3] alarmed Congress, which quickly passed a law narrowing the Court's jurisdiction in certain areas. But in the only case in which the Court directly addressed the constitutional question of Reconstruction, *Texas v. White* (1869), the Court confirmed the congressional view that whatever the theoretical relationship of the states to the Union, the war had at least temporarily suspended that relationship and its associated rights.

While Reconstruction was no doubt a political disaster for all concerned, constitutionally it has confirmed the approach taken initially by Lincoln and later by the Congress that in extreme situations one has to interpret the document not in a narrow theoretical light but in a commonsense reponse to real problems. The intransigence of Johnson and the South required Congress to go beyond the Thirteenth Amendment, but one can argue that at least in terms of the freedmen, a liberal reading of the Thirteenth Amendment would have been sufficient to achieve the goals of full equality before the law. The Fourteenth Amendment and FIFTEENTH AMENDMENT [2], passed in response to unnecessary objections, had their greatest constitutional impact not during Reconstruction but in later years.

MELVIN I. UROFSKY

Bibliography

HYMAN, HAROLD M. and WIECEK, WILLIAM M. 1982 *Equal Justice Under Law: Constitutional Development, 1835–1875.* New York: Harper and Row.
KUTLER, STANLEY I. 1968 *Judicial Power and Reconstruction Politics.* Chicago: University of Chicago.
NELSON, WILLIAM E. 1988 *The Fourteenth Amendment: From Political Principle to Judicial Doctrine.* Cambridge, Mass.: Harvard University Press.

REHNQUIST COURT

The Rehnquist Court began its reign in September of 1986 when President RONALD REAGAN [3,I] appointed WILLIAM H. REHNQUIST [3,I] Chief Justice to replace retiring Chief Justice WARREN E. BURGER [1]. This article reviews the first four years of the Rehnquist Court. Before his appointment as Chief Justice, however, Rehnquist had served as an Associate Justice on the BURGER COURT [1] for almost fifteen years. Like Burger, he was originally appointed by President RICHARD M. NIXON [3] to redeem a specific campaign promise to promote law and order through Court appointments that would stem the tide of WARREN COURT [4] decisions protecting the rights of the criminally accused and to pursue his more general philosophical commitment to appoint "strict constructionists . . . to interpret the law, not to make law."

The Burger Court itself made a fairly quick start in redeeming Mr. Nixon's law-and-order pledge, although the Rehnquist Court has continued and in some ways even accelerated this redemption. It seems highly likely that the elevation of Rehnquist, in conjunction with two subsequent appointments by President Reagan and one by President GEORGE BUSH [I], will complete the more general transformation of the Court contemplated by President Nixon's commitment to STRICT CONSTRUCTION [4].

This broader transformation has been steady but slow. It has been steady because Republican Presidents holding the conservative values associated with "strict construction" have controlled the White House continuously since Nixon's election, except for the four-year interlude of President JIMMY CARTER [1], who did not have the opportunity to appoint a single Justice. It has been slow partly because some of the appointees did not turn out as conservative as expected and partly because some of the conservatives replaced other conservatives rather than liberals. Of President Nixon's four appointments, only one, Chief Justice Burger, remained consistently faithful to the conservative cause, whereas Justice LEWIS F. POWELL [3,I] proved to be a moderate and Justice HARRY A. BLACKMUN [1,I] became increasingly liberal. Justice JOHN PAUL STEVENS [4,I], appointed by President GERALD FORD [2], has also proved to be a moderate; one of President Reagan's first two appointments replaced a moderate, Justice SANDRA DAY O'CONNOR [3,I] replacing Justice POTTER J. STEWART [4], and the other, Justice ANTONIN SCALIA [I], replaced conservative Justice Burger.

The key appointment giving the conservatives on the Rehnquist Court a clear majority on most if not all issues did not come until President Reagan's 1988 appointment of Justice ANTHONY M. KENNEDY [I] to replace retiring Justice Powell. Ironically, this appointment was made only after the Senate, following a historic controversy, had rejected Mr. Reagan's first candidate to replace Powell, Judge Robert Bork, on the ground that he was too conservative. Kennedy, during his first two terms in office, has proved to be as conservative as many expected Bork might have been, and the principal effect of the Senate's rejection of Bork appears to have been that President Bush in nominating his first Court appointee, DAVID H. SOUTER [I], to replace liberal stalwart WILLIAM J. BRENNAN [1,I] searched for a conservative who, unlike Bork, had published nothing indicating his views on any important constitutional questions.

"Strict construction" is sometimes equated with a strategy of interpreting the Constitution according to the "plain meaning" of the text or the intention of its Framers. In fact, however, this interpretive strategy had not proved so far to be of great importance, except with regard to the methodology used by the Court to decide whether rights not expressly mentioned in the text are impliedly protected, where a variation of it has gained prominence. The form of strict construction, or CONSERVATISM [I], that has gradually come to dominate the Court, however, has been based more on institutional and political than on historical or textual commitments.

Institutionally, most of the Republican appointees have been inclined to resolve any doubts about how the Constitution should be interpreted by upholding actions of other agencies of government. This inclination probably rests mainly on three interconnected institutional commitments: a vision of democracy that pictures majoritarian-responsive institutions as its centerpiece and the life-tenured Court as antidemocratic; a vision of the management of society as a complex matter best delegated to various experts and professionals, like school boards and other ADMINISTRATIVE AGENCIES [1]; and a vision of FEDERALISM [2,I] that views with suspicion the intrusion of federal power including the JUDICIAL POWER [3,I], into areas of decision making traditionally left to state and local government.

Politically, most of the Republican appointees have been guided or at least disciplined by the values associated with the constituency of the Republican party in late twentieth-century America. The Burger Court sat and the Rehnquist Court is sitting in an era when the historically dispossessed are actively seeking possession: blacks and other racial minorities; the poor and the homeless; women; gays; and other groups, like the handicapped, who have in different ways been marginalized in our society.

The Republican party has sought in a variety of ways to accommodate the interests of these groups, but it has been the party of mainstream America, not the party of the dispossessed. While Republicans and Democrats have vied for the "law and order" vote, the Republican party has been the more consistently and vocally anticriminal. The party has sought a moderate, compromising posture on the matters touching the protection of minority groups, women, and the handicapped. It has generally aligned itself at least rhetorically with traditional and to some extent religiously inspired moral views on controversial social questions such as ABORTION [1,I] and homosexuality. While it has often conformed to the realities of interest-group politics, it has tended to resist governmental redistributive programs that would tax or otherwise interfere with property interests, preferring to rely instead on a relatively unregulated market to provide full employment and thus help the poor.

The behavior of the Rehnquist Court has been quite consistent with these political commitments, although at the same time, it is worthy of emphasis that a consistent and cohesive "Rehnquist Court" does not yet exist in one important sense. Even the conservative Justices sometimes disagree over outcomes and often, in important ways, over the rationale for decisions. As a result, the Court is often at least doctrinally splintered.

The Supreme Court, like the Republican party, has often sought what might be characterized as compromises; but on the whole, it is the Court of mainstream America, not the dispossessed. In a high percentage of important constitutional cases, its institutional and political commitments have pointed in the same direction. When these commitments have conflicted, it has to this point usually refrained from imposing its values, instead deferring to the governmental agencies whose decisions are challenged. There are some important exceptions, most notably in its resistance to AFFIRMATIVE ACTION [1,I] programs, but these have been few and on the whole restrained. For example, although it has sometimes protected PROPERTY RIGHTS [I] against governmental regulation, its rulings to this point do not remotely promise a return to pre-NEW DEAL [I] ideology. Occasionally, chiefly in FREEDOM OF SPEECH [2,I] cases, it has acted in ways that might be interpreted as neither institutionally nor politically conservative, as in upholding against regulation the speech rights of flag burners, but such cases are also rare. The Rehnquist Court has been, largely but not completely, a passively rather than an actively conservative court.

In one view the Court's overall performance shows only that the system is working as it is supposed to work: the presidential appointment power is the main effective check on these nine Justices who are accountable to no electorate, and twenty years of Republican Presidents has had an effect on the Supreme Court.

The Rehnquist Court has continued the Burger Court's contraction of the RIGHTS OF THE CRIMINALLY ACCUSED [I] and convicted, in general subordinating these rights to law-and-order concerns, except in a subclass of cases in which the prosecution behaved outrageously in a way that might have tainted the guilt determination. Both courts have restricted the application of the FOURTH AMENDMENT's [2,I] prohibition of unreasonable SEARCHES AND SEIZURES [4,I] and the Fifth Amendment's prohibition of compulsory self-incrimination, limited the scope of the EXCLUSIONARY RULE [2], interpreted the Eighth Amendment so as to allow the states great discretion in reinstituting and administering CAPITAL PUNISHMENT [1,I], and virtually eliminated the possibility of HABEAS CORPUS [2,I] and other postconviction challenges to final judgments of criminal conviction.

UNITED STATES V. SALERNO (1987) [I], in which the Court upheld against Eighth Amendment attack the pretrial detention of dangerous defendants, exemplifies the Court's law-and-order commitment. *Maryland v. Buie* (1990) is an example of the priority the Court gives to law enforcement goals over Fourth Amendment rights claims. In this case, the Court sanctioned the use of evidence turned up after an arrest in a "protective sweep" of a house, on less than PROBABLE CAUSE [3], that someone dangerous might have been in the areas searched. The Court seems prepared in many contexts to abandon not only the probable cause requirement but any concept of individualized suspicion as a condition to search, as in *Michigan Department of State Police v. Sitz,* (1990) where

it upheld highway-checkpoint sobriety testing. *Teague v. Lane* (1989) made it much more difficult for constitutional claims by prisoners to be heard in the federal courts, holding that federal habeas corpus is unavailable for the assertion of a right not clearly established by precedent unless the right would apply retroactively. For all practical purposes, this ruling requires a prisoner to show that fundamentally unfair governmental practices might have led to the conviction of someone innocent.

The seeds of the Rehnquist Court's more general conservative agenda, also sown during the Burger Court era, include both broad propositions of law that serve to eliminate whole categories of potential constitutional rights and smaller but continuous doctrinal innovations that cumulatively have made ever more difficult the establishment of a violation of rights. The most important developments of the former have been the following: (1) the Court's unwillingness to interpret the Constitution to protect "implied" rights not explicitly mentioned in the text; (2) its limitation of the concept of constitutional rights to negative private rights against governmental interference, rejecting claims of rights to affirmative governmental assistance or subsidy; and (3) its understanding that the government's fundamental constitutional obligation is to refrain from targeting racial, gender, or religious groups for relatively disadvantageous treatment. It rejects any obligation of government to make accommodations in order to protect or benefit any such groups, and to some extent restricts government from making such accommodations for racial (although not for religious) groups.

Illustrative of the Rehnquist Court's narrow approach to defining the rights protected by the Constitution are *Michael H. v. Gerald D.* (1989) and *Burnham v. Superior Court of California* (1990). The former case raised the question as to how the term "liberty" in the due process clause of the FOURTEENTH AMENDMENT [2,I] should be interpreted; and the latter raised the question as to how the term "DUE PROCESS OF LAW" [2] should be interpreted.

In *Michael H.*, state law conclusively presumed that a child born to a married woman living with her husband was a child of the marriage. A genetic father argued that this law infringed on his "liberty" interest in establishing his paternity. In many prior cases, the Court had held that "liberty," in the due process clause, included implied FUNDAMENTAL RIGHTS [2] not expressly mentioned in the Constitution when they were "implicit in the concept of ordered liberty" or "deeply rooted in this Nation's history and tradition." These formulations do not answer the questions of how and at what level of abstractness traditional values should be identified. The *Michael H.* plurality, following the Burger Court's lead in BOWERS V. HARDWICK (1986) [I], chose to conceptualize this question very narrowly, asking not even whether our traditions recognize the rights of natural fathers, but rather whether they recognize those of adulterous natural fathers; on this basis the Court rejected the claim.

This historically concrete way of identifying constitutional rights does not necessarily eliminate implied constitutional rights, first, because the Court might (or might not) let stand previously announced implied rights, and second, because it is always possible that some small number of states might in the future restrict rights that have been traditionally and widely respected by all the other states. But it does very substantially limit the potential category of implied rights. Moreover, it does so in an odd way, given the traditional assumption that the main point of constitutional rights is to protect minorities: after *Bowers* and *Michael H.*, the stronger, more widespread, and more historically entrenched a rights-restrictive majoritarian imposition, the less likely the Court will find a constitutional violation.

The *Bowers* approach was applied by four Justices in *Burnham*, with the concurrence of enough others to constitute a majority, to reject a claim that subjecting an individual to a state's JURISDICTION [3] on the basis of his fleeting presence within the state amounted to a denial of liberty "without due process of law." The opinion of the four by Justice Scalia found that fleeting physical presence, which would have been thought a sufficient predicate for jurisdiction when the Fourteenth Amendment was adopted, had been assumed to be sufficient since then in many state decisions. This "continuing tradition" was sufficient to validate the practice of founding jurisdiction on a fleeting presence, whether or not it might otherwise be thought unfair.

Cruzan v. Director of Missouri Dept. of Health (1990) suggests that the Court is not prepared to scuttle the implied-rights doctrine completely, but is also not disposed to use it aggressively. The Court found a sufficiently concrete tradition recognizing the right of individuals to refuse medical treatment to imply that this choice was a protected liberty that included the RIGHT TO DIE [I] under at least some circumstances. Nonetheless, it held that the state's interest in insisting that the choice be shown by clear and convincing evidence was sufficiently strong in the case at hand to justify disallowing a patient's parents from making the decision, even though the patient herself could not make it because she was in a vegetative state.

The best known and most practically important of the pre-Rehnquist Court's decisions protecting implied constitutional rights is ROE V. WADE (1973) [3], where the Court ruled that the Constitution impliedly protects a woman's right to have an abortion. The Rehnquist Court's general unreceptiveness to implied-rights claims does not bode well for the future of this right, and some of the sitting Justices have already announced their willingness to over-

rule *Roe*. Whether or not the right to abort will survive may depend on the vote of newly appointed Justice Souter, but even if the right survives, smaller but incrementally important shifts in doctrine by the Rehnquist Court have already weakened it significantly.

These shifts had their genesis in Burger Court decisions protecting the implied "privacy" right of individuals to decide their own family living arrangements, but only if the challenged regulation "substantially interfered" with the right. This substantial-interference concept has so far been important mainly in privacy right cases, although it is theoretically transplantable to other areas of constitutional law. Its patent importance at this point is in the abortion rights controversy where, in one or another formulation, it has appeared from time to time in majority and concurring opinions, including those of the Rehnquist Court, and it might prove important if five Justices are not able to agree that *Roe v. Wade* should be overruled. Use of the substantial-interference requirement, which has been endorsed most consistently by Justice O'Connor, would enable the majority even if it is unable to overrule *Roe*, to allow much greater state regulation of abortion than prior decisions have allowed.

For example, although it is not entirely clear what the criteria are for deciding when a regulation substantially interferes with the right to abort, some opinions suggest that only a regulation making abortions illegal qualifies. If so, waiting periods, mandatory antiabortion counseling, spousal and parental consent requirements, and other forms of regulation previously held unconstitutional would become permissible in the future. Even if the requirement were construed to have a lesser meaning, such as "making abortions very much more difficult to obtain," greater regulatory discretion would be available in the future than it has been in the past.

The ancestry of the Court's refusal to recognize positive constitutional rights to governmental assistance are decisions of the Burger Court that effectively terminated enlargement of the "fundamental interest" branch of EQUAL PROTECTION [2,I] jurisprudence bequeathed to it by the Warren Court, along with decisions that rejected the claim that liberties protected against governmental interference are also entitled to affirmative governmental protection.

The Warren Court has held that individuals had an equality-based right to the subsidized provision of "fundamental" services or rights they were too poor to afford, such as counsel and other important defense services in criminal cases. Warren Court decisions had suggested that which rights were "fundamental" for these purposes would depend on the degree to which they were of practical importance to people. The Burger Court did not overturn the particular rulings of the Warren Court, but early in its tenure, did effectively undercut the equal-protection basis of the doctrine and consequently its future growth, ruling that henceforth rights would be regarded as fundamental only if they were constitutional rights, irrespective of their practical importance. These opinions, however, left open the possibility that such "real" constitutional rights might sometimes include subsidy rights.

Burger Court decisions eventually repudiated this suggestion in holding that the right to abort, although a constitutional right, did not include the right to governmental Medicaid payments for abortions for those too poor to afford them. According to these decisions, constitutional rights are negative entitlements available to individuals only to stop governmental interference with the use of private resources.

The Rehnquist Court has perpetuated this jurisprudence of negative rights, holding in the abortion context, for example, that the closing of state hospitals to abortions did not violate the right to abort because the state's action left women who wanted abortions exactly where they would have been had the state never operated public hospitals—that is, dependent on their private resources.

DeShaney v. Winnebago County Department of Social Services (1989) [I] suggests, moreover, that the Rehnquist Court's commitment to the jurisprudence of negative rights is pervasive and extends beyond the abortion issue. In this case, the Court held that governmental social-service officials did not violate the rights of a boy by failing to remove him from a father whom they knew was continuously beating him and whose beatings eventually resulted in severe brain damage to the boy. The Court found no violation of the boy's right not to be deprived of liberty without due process. It ruled that due process protects individuals only against the government's interfering with their liberty and imposes no "affirmative obligation" on government to take action to protect that liberty. Just as the "culprit" in abortion-subsidy cases is not the government, but rather the pregnant woman's poverty, so (in this view) the boy's father, not the state, was the source of his problem.

The Rehnquist Court's pursuit of a "neutrality" concept of the government's basic constitutional obligation arguably has fairly deep roots in constitutional history, but is grounded most immediately in the Burger Court's Washington v. Davis (1976) [4] decision, which held that unless the plaintiff is challenging a law that expressly classifies people on the basis of race, he or she can successfully challenge a governmental action as racially discriminatory only by proving that it was undertaken for a discriminatory purpose. The vision of racial justice that Washington has retrospectively been understood to endorse in subsequent Burger and Rehnquist Court decisions interpreting it is one of neutrality in a double sense: first because the Constitution requires governmental racial neutrality, any use

by government of race as a classifying trait in law is suspect and likely to be struck down. And second, because the Constitution requires nothing more of government than racial neutrality, its actions are immune from attack so long as it does not act for a racially bad purpose.

This vision has substantially constrained attempts on behalf of minority groups to use law and legal institutions to better their lots in two distinct fashions, one by way of constitutional legitimation and the other by way of constitutional restriction. First, a governmental action that produces effects that disadvantage minority groups to a greater extent than other groups is constitutionally legitimate unless a plaintiff can meet the difficult burden of proving that this relative racial disadvantage was a purpose of the action. Second, voluntary attempts by government specifically and expressly to benefit racial minority groups—commonly called benign or reverse discrimination or affirmative action—are seriously vulnerable to constitutional invalidation.

The Rehnquist Court has vigorously confirmed and extended both the legitimation and restriction branches of the neutrality principle bequeathed to it. In McCleskey v. Kemp (1987) [I], for example, it rejected, on the ground of a failure of proof of discriminatory purpose, a claim by a black criminal defendant sentenced to death that the state's death penalty was administered in a racially discriminatory fashion. McCleskey's discrimination claim was based on a statistical study that, controlling for extraneous variables, found that a black defendant charged with killing a white in Georgia was four times more likely to be sentenced to death than someone charged with killing a black. The Court conceded, arguendo, the statistical reliability of the evidence, but found that even this statistical pattern would not prove that McCleskey himself was sentenced to death because of racial considerations. The case evidently shows the depth of the Rehnquist Court's commitment to its neutrality principle. Even conceding the correctness of the Court's criticism of the proof as to this individual defendant, the statistical evidence showed systematic RACIAL DISCRIMINATION [3,I] and therefore proved that *some* (even if nonidentifiable) individual black murderers of whites were being sentenced to death for racial reasons. Even proof of a pattern of purposeful racial discrimination that might well have infected McCleskey's sentence was not sufficient to establish constitutional illegitimacy without evidence linking this nonneutrality to McCleskey himself.

The depth of the Rehnquist Court's commitment to its neutrality principle is also illustrated by its interpretation of the CIVIL RIGHTS ACT OF 1964 [1], which prohibits among other things racial discrimination by employers. Burger Court decisions had held that proof that an employment practice disadvantaged minority group members to a greater extent than others, although insufficient to establish a presumptive constitutional violation by government, *was* sufficient to establish a presumptive violation of the statute by either governmental or private employers. On such a showing, the burden shifted to the employer to establish the business necessity of the challenged practice, failing which the practice would be found illegal.

In *Wards Cove Packing Co., Inc. v. Atonio* (1989), the Rehnquist Court changed this evidentiary framework in a way that requires the plaintiff to prove almost as much as he or she would need to establish intentional discrimination. After *Wards Cove*, the employer, in response to a showing that the challenged practice disproportionately disadvantages minority group members, need only come forward with some evidence of a business justification, after which the plaintiff must prove that the practice does not serve "in a significant way, the legitimate employment goals of the employer." A plaintiff who can meet this difficult burden will have come very close to proving that the discrimination was intentional because he or she would have shown that the putatively innocent purpose for the racial injury was a bogus explanation.

The restrictive branch of the neutrality principle arises in cases involving benign or reverse discrimination, a practice whose constitutionality was left extremely uncertain by a series of Burger Court decisions. The Rehnquist Court's decision in RICHMOND (CITY OF) V. J. A. CROSON CO. (1989) [I] communicates at a minimum that a majority of the Justices (1) see governmental actions that allocate benefits to minority races on the express basis of race as equally or almost as constitutionally troublesome as actions that expressly disadvantage them on the basis of race; (2) believe that few goals are adequate to justify such actions; and (3) will insist that these goals be pursued through race-neutral means whenever possible.

The "degree of troublesomeness" issue is important because it directly affects the "level of scrutiny" or burden of justification that reverse discrimination cases trigger. Under basic principles of constitutional law that have largely been settled for some time, most laws are constitutional so long as they rationally promote legitimate goals of government. One major historical exception to this rule is laws that expressly classify people for burdens or benefits on the basis of race, which are unconstitutional unless the government establishes that they are necessary to serve goals of compelling importance, a justification burden that is very difficult to satisfy.

The special rule for race cases, however, developed in a line of cases involving governments' acting out of racial hostility or prejudice to the detriment of minority groups. Some have argued and some Justices have agreed that reverse discrimination, which does not share this characteristic, is not so constitutionally troublesome and therefore should be judged under a less demanding justification standard. *Croson* is the first reverse-discrimination case in which a majority of Justices were able to agree on the burden of justification applicable in reverse-discrimination cases. They found such cases sufficiently troublesome to invoke the demanding justification standard historically applied in hostile-discrimination cases, effectively adopting a broad rule requiring governmental neutrality with regard to race.

The remaining important question in *Croson* was under what conditions, if any, this demanding justification standard might be met. A variety of claims have been historically made in an attempt to justify governmental programs that expressly allocate benefits like admission to state medical or law schools or governmental contracts to minority racial groups. Some, for example, see such programs as justified by the goal of preventing the perpetuation of racial underclasses or castes, promoting racial integration in the professions or work force, or creating role models for minority youth. Although *Croson* is not the first and will not be the last Supreme Court decision to consider this question, a majority of the Court indicates that such goals will be treated skeptically. The majority apparently endorsed the view that only one goal was of sufficiently "compelling" importance to justify reverse discrimination, namely, remedying the effects of past discrimination. Although the decision is less than clear on this point, it seems to imply that state and local government must meet a quite demanding standard in proving that the minority beneficiaries of reverse discrimination are in fact suffering present disadvantages by reason of former discrimination either against the particular individual beneficiaries themselves or other members of their race.

A year after *Croson*, the Rehnquist Court upheld reverse discrimination authorized by Congress with respect to broadcast-media licensing in METRO BROADCASTING, INC. V. FEDERAL COMMUNICATIONS COMMISSION (1990) [I], applying a less demanding standard of review. Five Justices apparently believed that the Court owes greater deference to Congress in such cases than to state and local legislative bodies, for Congress is a coequal branch of government with a variety of constitutional powers that confer on it some degree of discretion in matters of national racial-commercial policy. One of the five, Justice Brennan, has since been replaced by Justice Souter, and it is therefore difficult to predict whether the *Metro* distinction between state-local and federal reverse discrimination or a uniform application of *Croson* will ultimately prevail.

The neutrality principle that has played such an important role in the development of race law has been equally important in SEX DISCRIMINATION [4,I] cases, where the same basic rule applies: laws that expressly discriminate on gender grounds are suspect (although subject to a less demanding justification than racial classifications), and in the absence of express gender classification, a plaintiff must prove that a challenged action was taken for a gender-discriminatory purpose. The Rehnquist Court has decided no equal protection cases involving gender discrimination, but has given no reason to suspect that it will depart from its neutrality principle. In fact, its recent assimilation of the free exercise of religion clause to the neutrality principle indicates that its commitment to that principle is quite robust.

This assimilation occurred in EMPLOYMENT DIVISION, DEPARTMENT OF HUMAN RESOURCES OF OREGON V. SMITH (1990) [I], which presented the question as to whether Oregon's penalization of the religious use of peyote violated Smith's right to the free exercise of his religion. Before *Smith*, a law that had the effect of burdening a person's ability to follow a religion was unconstitutional unless shown necessary to the accomplishment of a goal of compelling importance. *Smith* holds that with certain very limited exceptions a "*neutral* law of general applicability" cannot be challenged as an interference with the free exercise of religion. The upshot is that, in the future, adjudication under the free exercise clause will parallel racial and gender equal protection adjudication. Laws that expressly require or prohibit religious practices are not religion neutral and will therefore trigger a heavy burden of justification. But laws that are of general applicability, like those prohibiting drug use, are religion neutral and are not subject to successful constitutional attack unless they were adopted or enforced for the purpose of discriminating against a religion, notwithstanding that their effect burdens certain religious practices. Thus, for example, a law prohibiting the serving of alcohol to minors could be enforced against the Catholic use of wine in communion, although the major religions probably have enough political influence to secure accommodating legislation, and the brunt of *Smith* will likely be borne, as in *Smith* itself, by minority religions.

To say that a principle of "neutrality" pervades the Rehnquist Court's jurisprudence of race, gender, and religion is not of course the same as saying that the Court is employing the only tenable, or the right, or even an internally consistent concept of neutrality, for neutrality is no more self-defining than "equality." With regard to race, for example, critics might argue that for the government to act in a truly neutral way its actions should not disproportionately disadvantage members of some racial groups relative to others, irrespective of its purpose, at least when the subject of the disadvantageous treatment is important. They might also say that even if purpose rather than effect is a proper measure of neutrality, the evidence system through which the Court determines

purpose is nonneutral, for it rests implicitly on the assumption that government does not usually engage in racial discrimination, rather than the opposite assumption. Finally, these critics might say that the neutrality of current governmental actions cannot be fairly judged without regard to its past actions and, consequently, that what might appear to be a nonneutral conferral of governmental advantages to racial groups previously purposefully disadvantaged by government is better characterized as the pursuit of racial neutrality over time. The Rehnquist Court's neutrality concept might be seen as an attempt to compromise competing political interests, but the underlying questions of principle and policy certainly cannot be resolved by reference to the unadorned concept of neutrality.

No question in contemporary constitutional law better illustrates this proposition than what constitutes an unconstitutional ESTABLISHMENT OF RELIGION [2]. The Rehnquist Court has addressed this question several times, but has not yet supplied a clear answer. All of the Justices who disagree with its answer appear to believe they are being religiously neutral, yet their answers differ significantly. Three answers have figured prominently: (1) the government may not take actions that in fact benefit religion (a major part of the pre-Rehnquist Court test and one favored by some current Justices); (2) it may not take actions that amount to active proselytizing for a religion (the test favored by four Justices); and (3) it may not take actions that create the appearance that it is endorsing religion (the test favored by two "swing" Justices and therefore likely in the short run to prove determinative of the outcome of many cases).

These competing visions of neutrality were all at work in COUNTY OF ALLEGHENY V. AMERICAN CIVIL LIBERTIES UNION (1989) [I], where the Court was called on to decide whether either of two Christmas displays by the city of Pittsburgh violated the ESTABLISHMENT CLAUSE [I]. One was a crèche in the county courthouse, and the other a side-by-side display of a Christmas tree and a menorah in front of a public building. A majority of the Court, apparently pursuing what appeared to five Justices a neutral principle that would simultaneously assure that government does not help or hurt religion too much, applied the "no appearance of endorsement" test, and held the crèche unconstitutional and the other display constitutional. The Court found that the factual context of the first display created the appearance of an endorsement of religion, whereas that of the second created the appearance of a celebration of a winter holiday season. Those Justices who applied the "no benefit in fact" test would have held both displays unconstitutional for their nonneutral favoring of the Christian and Jewish religions. Those who applied the "no proselytizing" test criticized the other opinions for their nonneutral hostility toward religion and would have upheld both because neither coerced anyone to support or participate in a religion.

The establishment clause cases illustrate not only the elusiveness of the "neutrality" concept but also, when read together with the free exercise cases, an asymmetry in Rehnquist Court jurisprudence between racial and religious neutrality apparently reflective of the Court's "mainstream America" predisposition.

With regard to its legitimation function, the neutrality concept operates similarly in race and religion cases: regulations are legitimate even if they produce nonneutral effects, so long as they are facially and purposively neutral. With regard to its restrictive function, however, Rehnquist Court neutrality presumptively prohibits regulations that specially benefit minority races, but permits those that specially benefit religious groups, so long as they do not appear to endorse a religion (or, perhaps, so long as they do not actually proselytize).

The Rehnquist Court has also pursued its conservative agenda through numerous smaller but cumulatively important doctrinal avenues. One example is the privacy rights doctrine that interferences must be "substantial" before they will be regarded as constitutionally troublesome. Many other examples might be given, but one will suffice: the Court's use in free-speech cases of the threshold PUBLIC FORUM [3,I] concept effectively to foreclose speech rights on most kinds of public property and its related apparent willingness to accept without serious scrutiny governmentally proffered justifications for regulating speech activities in the few public places where individuals do have the right to engage in expressive activities.

In free speech cases, the Rehnquist Court has been reasonably if sporadically protective of traditional constitutional rights. It has struck down many regulations restricting speech, not only in well-publicized cases, such as those involving FLAG DESECRATION [2,I], but in more mundane settings, such as newsrack placements and handbilling. One area in which it has been less protective, however, concerns the right to engage in expressive activities in public places, a right that has historically been particularly important to the dispossessed who lack the resources to project their views through other media.

The Court's tolerance toward restrictions of speech in public places derives from the Burger Court's legacy, but again, it seems fairly clear that the Rehnquist Court enthusiastically subscribes to the intuitions that informed that legacy. The questions as to whether and to what extent the free speech clause entitles individuals to engage in expressive activity on public property has been implicit in constitutional law for along time, but for a variety of reasons went largely unaddressed in early cases. The Court

was not forced to confront it directly until the mid-1960s, when civil rights demonstrators began to use unconventional sites such as libraries and jails as demonstration locations. The early decisions often rested on unclear reasoning, although for at least a time, the dominant trend was to protect the demonstrators' rights unless the government could prove that the demonstration actually interfered with the normal use of the property.

The Burger Court eventually decided on a tripartite classification of public places and hence speech rights. Streets and parks were labeled "public forums," and speech regulation in these places was "sharply circumscribed." In particular, even so-called content-neutral or "time, place, and manner" restrictions were unconstitutional unless, among other things, they were "narrowly tailored to serve a significant government interest." A second type of public forum consisted of places the government had voluntarily opened for speech purposes, and regulations here were subject to the same constitutional limits. All other kinds of public property were not public forums, and speech activity in such places could be prohibited unless, in substance, the government was simply trying to suppress views it opposed.

Because relatively few places were true public forums and therefore available for speech activities as a matter of right, one important question that remained concerned the circumstances in which the Court would find that property had been voluntarily opened for speech. Additionally, because content-neutral regulation of true public forums is far more common than content-based regulation, the practical effect of these rules on access even to streets and parks depended largely on the circumstances in which the Court would find that "time, place, and manner" regulations were adequately "narrowly tailored."

The current answers to these questions come largely from Rehnquist Court decisions and are not very speech protective. With regard to voluntarily opened forums, the main case is HAZELWOOD SCHOOL DISTRICT V. KUHLMEIER (1988) [I], where the Court upheld the authority of public school officials to censor from a student newspaper articles about student pregnancy and the effect of divorce on students. Although the Court might have decided the case as it did on alternative grounds, its decision suggests that the category of voluntarily opened forums is a very small if not an empty one. It held that the newspaper was not such a forum because school officials had retained curricularly based editorial rights; therefore, even though the paper had always been open to the student body at large to submit opinions and articles, it had not been opened for general student speech purposes. The same theory would seem available for a wide variety of public property. Managers of public auditoriums, for example, might make their facilities broadly available, but retain the right to exclude certain subject matters (although perhaps not viewpoints). After *Hazelwood*, the Court, in this same vein, held in *United States v. Kokinda* (1990) that handbilling and fund solicitation on the sidewalk leading from a parking lot to a post office could be banned because the sidewalk was neither a true nor opened public forum, having been built for post office business purposes.

The most important case on the related question of when a content-neutral regulation is sufficiently "narrowly tailored" to survive constitutional attack is *Ward v. Rock Against Racism* (1989), where the Court appeared to hold that this requirement is met so long as the government can accomplish its goal better with the regulation at issue than without it. The Court did say that a regulation may not burden speech more than is necessary to accomplish the government's legitimate goal, but it simultaneously rejected the view that the government must use the means that would accomplish its goal with the least restriction of speech; it is unclear how these two propositions can coexist. For example, a ban on all picketing on a certain sidewalk would be more effective in accomplishing the goal of pedestrian free movement than no ban would. Thus, it would seem to be constitutional under *Ward*, unless it burdens speech more than is necessary; if it does so, it would seem that this is because pedestrian free movement could have been assured by means that are less restrictive of speech. How *Ward* will ultimately be interpreted is uncertain, but if one takes seriously the idea that any contribution toward a goal validates a content-neutral regulation—and related decisions of the Rehnquist Court suggest that it does take this idea seriously—the Court will have given speech rights so little weight in the balance that virtually all non–content-based restrictions on access, even to true public forums, will survive constitutional attack.

                                                                    LARRY G. SIMON

(SEE ALSO: *Capital Punishment and Race* [I]; *Race Consciousness* [I]; *Religious Liberty* [3,I]; *Right Against Self-Incrimination* [3,I].)

Bibliography

ABRAMS, J. MARC AND GOODMAN, S. MARK 1988 End of an Era? The Decline of Student Press Rights in the Wake of *Hazelwood School District v. Kuhlmeier*. *Duke Law Journal* 1988:706–732

Constitutional Scholars' Statement on Affirmative Action After *City of Richmond v. J. A. Croson Co.* 1988 *Yale Law Journal* 98:1711–1716.

ESTRICH, SUSAN R. AND SULLIVAN, KATHLEEN M. 1989 Abortion Politics: Writing for an Audience of One. *University of Pennsylvania Law Review* 138:119–155.

FRIED, CHARLES 1989 Affirmative Action After *City of Rich-*mond *v. J. A. Croson Co.*: A Response to the Scholars' Statement. *Yale Law Journal* 99:155–161.

KARST, KENNETH L. 1989 Private Discrimation and Public Responsibility: *Patterson* in Context. *Supreme Court Review* 1989:1–51.

SOIFER, AVIAM 1989 Moral Ambition, Formalism, and the 'Free World' of *DeShaney*. *George Washington Law Review* 57:1513–1532.

TUSHNET, MARK 1988 The Emerging Principle of Accommodation of Religion (Dubitante). *Georgetown Law Journal* 76:1691–1714.

WERHAN, KEITH 1987 The O'Briening of Free Speech Methodology. *Arizona State Law Review* 19:635–679.

REHNQUIST, WILLIAM H.
(Update)

William H. Rehnquist grew up in Milwaukee and was educated at Stanford, Harvard, and Stanford Law School. He served as a law clerk [1] to Supreme Court Justice ROBERT H. JACKSON [3] and then entered into private practice in Phoenix. In 1969, through his association with Deputy Attorney General Richard Kleindienst and work as a Republican party official in Phoenix, he went to Washington as Assistant Attorney General for the Office of Legal Counsel. On January 7, 1972, he, along with LEWIS F. POWELL [3,I], was sworn in as an Associate Justice of the Supreme Court. On September 26, 1986, he was sworn in as CHIEF JUSTICE [1] of the United States, only the third sitting Justice to be so elevated. Despite widespread disagreement with Rehnquist's views among legal academics, there is little dispute that he is among the ablest Justices who have ever served on the Court.

Justice Rehnquist's vision of the nation's constitutional structure, emphasizing the words and history of that document, is expressed in three doctrines: STRICT CONSTRUCTION [4] (of both the Constitution and of statutes), judicial restraint, and FEDERALISM [2,I]. He summarized this vision in a 1976 speech at the University of Texas:

It is almost impossible . . . to conclude that the [Founding Fathers] intended the Constitution itself to suggest answers to the manifold problems that they knew would confront succeeding generations. The Constitution that they drafted was intended to endure indefinitely, but the reason for this well-founded hope was the general language by which national authority was granted to Congress and the Presidency. These two branches were to furnish the motive power within the federal system, which was in turn to coexist with the state governments; the elements of government having a popular constituency were looked to for the solution of the numerous and varied problems that the future would bring.

In other words, as he stated, dissenting, in TRIMBLE V. GORDON (1977) [4], neither the original Constitution nor the Civil War amendments made "this Court (or the federal courts generally) into a council of revision, and they did not confer on this Court any authority to nullify state laws which were merely felt to be inimical to the Court's notion of the public interest."

During his early years on the Court, despite the presence of three other Republican appointees, Justice Rehnquist was often in lone dissent, espousing a view of STATES' RIGHTS [4] and limited federal judicial power that many regarded as anachronistic. For example, in *Weber v. Aetna Casualty and Surety Company* (1972), SUGARMAN V. DOUGALL (1973), and FRONTIERO V. RICHARDSON (1973) [2], he resisted the view of the other eight members of the Court that the EQUAL PROTECTION [2,I] clause of the FOURTEENTH AMENDMENT [2,I] applied to, and required heightened scrutiny of, state-sponsored discrimination against illegitimate children, resident aliens, and women, respectively. Indeed, he insisted that the equal protection clause had only marginal application beyond cases of RACIAL DISCRIMINATION [3,I]. In the area of CRIMINAL PROCEDURE [2] Rehnquist urged that the Court overrule MAPP V. OHIO (1961) [3], which applied the EXCLUSIONARY RULE [2] to the states. Rehnquist also seemed hostile to MIRANDA V. ARIZONA (1966) [3], though he never directly argued that it should be reversed. Still, even in his early years on the Court, Justice Rehnquist was less likely to be in dissent than the liberal Justices WILLIAM O. DOUGLAS [2], WILLIAM J. BRENNAN [1,I], and THURGOOD MARSHALL [3,I]; and the ideas expressed in some of Rehnquist's early dissents, such as in CLEVELAND BOARD OF EDUCATION V. LAFLEUR (1974) [1] and *Fry v. United States* (1975) were influential in majority opinions in the years to come.

The 1975 term saw Justice Rehnquist come into his own as the leader of the (ever-shifting) conservative wing of the Court. In that term he wrote for the Court in PAUL V. DAVIS (1976) [3], holding that reputation, standing alone, was not a constitutionally protected "liberty" interest subject to vindication under the guarantee of PROCEDURAL DUE PROCESS OF LAW [3,I]; in NATIONAL LEAGUE OF CITIES V. USERY (1976) [3], holding that the TENTH AMENDMENT [4] limited Congress's power under the COMMERCE CLAUSE [1] to regulate the states; and in RIZZO V. GOODE (1976) [3], holding that "principles of federalism" forbade federal courts from ordering a restructuring of a city police force in response to constitutional violations. In *National League of Cities*, Rehnquist used an expansive reading of the Tenth Amendment to strike down a federal statute that regulated the wages and hours of state government employees, although such regulation was otherwise concededly within Congress's commerce power. The opinion showed that when faced with a choice between judicial restraint/strict constructionism and states' rights, Justice

Rehnquist was prepared to defend the latter aggressively. However, the potential significance of the first decision limiting Congress's use of the commerce power since 1936 was eroded by subsequent Court majorities, first refusing to follow, and then overruling, *National League of Cities* in GARCIA V. SAN ANTONIO METROPOLITAN TRANSIT AUTHORITY (1985) [2]. Despite Justice Rehnquist's prediction in dissent that this issue would return to haunt the Court, it seems unlikely that the Court will really disable Congress from establishing national control of virtually any area in which Congress chooses to assert itself. Whatever the political leanings of the other Justices, a majority generally seems to believe that the strong national–weak state governmental system is the proper direction for the country.

When dissenting, Rehnquist makes his most telling points in opposing the majority's efforts to enact "desirable" social policy with little support from the constitutional or statutory provisions that they purport to be interpreting. An example is UNITED STEEL WORKERS OF AMERICA V. WEBER (1979) [4]. In that case, Kaiser Aluminum Company and the United Steelworkers had devised a "voluntary" affirmative action plan under which half of available positions in an on-the-job training plan would be reserved for blacks. Weber, excluded solely because he was white, filed suit based on Title VII of the CIVIL RIGHTS ACT OF 1964 [1]. The statute provides that "it shall be unlawful for an employer . . . to fail or refuse to hire . . . any individual . . . because of such individual's race." The statute goes on to say that its provisions are not to be interpreted "to require any employer . . . to grant preferential treatment to any individual or group." Moreover, as a unanimous Court had recognized only three years before in *McDonald v. Santa Fe Trail Transportation Co.* (1976), the "uncontradicted legislative history" showed that Title VII "prohibited racial discrimination against the white petitioners . . . upon the same standards as would be applicable were they Negroes." Nevertheless, in *Weber*, a 5–2 majority, reversing the lower courts, found that discrimination against whites was not within the "spirit" of Title VII and consequently not prohibited. In a bitter dissent, Justice Rehnquist accused the majority of Orwellian "newspeak" and concluded that "close examination of what the Court proffers as the spirit of the Act reveals it as the spirit of the present majority, not the 88th Congress." Similarly in ROE V. WADE (1973) [3], where the majority based a woman's right to an ABORTION [1,I] on a constitutional RIGHT OF PRIVACY [3,I] that arose not from the terms but from the "penumbras" of the BILL OF RIGHTS [1], Rehnquist wrote, "To reach its result, the Court necessarily has had to find within the scope of the Fourteenth Amendment a right that was apparently completely unknown to the drafters of the

Amendment." Whatever the wisdom of the policies announced in these cases, it is difficult to disagree that Rehnquist's reading of the textual material in question was the more accurate one.

It is ironic that Rehnquist, often condemned as a right-wing ideologue was, in *Weber* and *Roe*, as in many other cases, advocating a view of the Court's role that had previously been vigorously advanced by the progressive members of the Court. In MOREHEAD V. NEW YORK EX REL. TIPALDO (1936) [3], for example, the dissenting opinion of Justice HARLAN F. STONE [4], joined by Justices LOUIS BRANDEIS [1] and BENJAMIN CARDOZO [1], declared: "It is not for the Court to resolve doubts whether the remedy by regulation is as efficacious as many believe, or better than some other, or is better even than blind operation of uncontrolled economic forces. The legislature must be free to choose unless government is rendered impotent. The Fourteenth Amendment has no more imbedded in the Constitution our preference for some particular set of economic beliefs, than it has adopted in the name of liberty the system of theology which we happen to approve."

In criminal procedure, Rehnquist's views are driven by the same narrow view of the role of courts in a tripartite federal system, and he frankly admits that his goal when he came on the Court was to "call a halt to a number of sweeping rulings of the Warren Court in this area." In this objective he generally was joined by the other appointees of RICHARD M. NIXON [3] and by Justice BYRON WHITE [4,I]. Consequently, the 1970s and 1980s saw a series of decisions aimed at making it easier for the police to investigate crimes and harder for defendants to upset their convictions because of police investigatory errors. For example, in *Rakas v. Illinois* (1978) the Court, per Rehnquist, made it more difficult for a defendant to establish STANDING [4] to litigate SEARCH AND SEIZURE [4,I] violations; in UNITED STATES V. ROBINSON (1973) [3] the scope of police SEARCHES INCIDENT TO ARREST [4] was expanded; and in *United States v. Leon* (1984) the Court, per Justice White, established a GOOD FAITH EXCEPTION [2] to the exclusionary rule in search warrant cases. However, neither Rehnquist nor any of his fellow conservatives sought to undercut the FUNDAMENTAL RIGHTS [2] to counsel, appeal, and TRIAL BY JURY [4] that had been applied to the states by the Warren Court. In a 1985 interview, despite the feeling of most Court watchers that the BURGER COURT [1] had not dismantled the major criminal procedure protections of the Warren Court, including the MIRANDA RULES [3,I] and the exclusionary rule, Justice Rehnquist pronounced himself satisfied that the law was "more evenhanded now than when I came on the Court."

If Rehnquist has not been successful in exempting states from congressional control, he has frequently prevailed in his efforts to exempt state courts from federal court interference. To do this, he has taken the 1971 decision in YOUNGER V. HARRIS [4], which counseled restraint by federal courts in enjoining ongoing state criminal proceedings, and extended it greatly. In *Rizzo* and in *Real Estate Association v. McNary* (1981) he held that "principles of federalism" limited a federal court's ability to enjoin not just the judicial branch but the executive branch of state governments as well and that this comity limitation was not confined to criminal proceedings. Nor, as he held in *Doran v. Salem Inn, Inc.* (1975), was it necessary that a state criminal proceeding predate a federal action for the federal action to be barred by principles of comity.

Similarly, in the area of federal HABEAS CORPUS [2,I] for state prisoners, Rehnquist and his conservative colleagues have advanced the dual goals of limiting federal court interference with state court adjudications and enhancing the finality of criminal convictions. The most significant holding in this line of cases is the decision in WAINWRIGHT V. SYKES (1977) [4]. In this case, Rehnquist, writing for a six-Justice majority, held that a defendant's failure to raise an issue at the appropriate stage of a state criminal proceeding barred the federal courts from considering that issue later under habeas corpus, absent a showing by the defendant of good cause for the failure and prejudice to his case. *Sykes* thus largely overruled FAY V. NOIA (1963) [2], which had allowed new issues to be raised on federal habeas corpus unless they had been deliberately bypassed by the defendant in state proceedings. *Sykes* represented a significant diminution of the power of federal courts to interfere with state convictions. The trend continued in 1989 in the significant case of *Teague v. Lane*, authored by Justice SANDRA DAY O'CONNOR [3,I], where the Court held that "new" rules of criminal procedure generally should not apply retroactively on habeas corpus to defendants whose state convictions had become final before the new law was established. In *Butler v. McKellar* (1990), Justice Rehnquist defined "new" broadly so as to make it very difficult for state prisoners to obtain federal habeas relief.

Consistent with his stance on federalism and judicial restraint, Rehnquist is the Court's leading advocate of a restrictive interpretation of the ESTABLISHMENT CLAUSE [I] of the FIRST AMENDMENT [2,I]. He set forth his view in detail in a DISSENTING OPINION [2] in WALLACE V. JAFFREE (1985) [4], where the majority struck down Alabama's statutorily required moment of silence for "meditation or voluntary prayer" in public schools. Rehnquist rejected the "wall of separation between church and state" principle of EVERSON V. BOARD OF EDUCATION (1947)

[2], arguing that history did not support this rigid interpretation of the First Amendment. According to Rehnquist, JAMES MADISON [3] viewed the purpose of the establishment clause as simply "to prohibit the establishment of a national religion, and perhaps to prevent discrimination among sects. He did not see it as requiring neutrality on the part of the government between religion and irreligion." Consequently, Rehnquist would have found no defect in a state statute that openly endorsed prayer, much less a "moment of silence."

In a similar vein, in FIRST NATIONAL BANK V. BELLOTTI (1978) [2], Rehnquist, in a sole dissent, refused to recognize a First Amendment COMMERCIAL SPEECH [1,I] right for corporations, and in VIRGINIA STATE BOARD OF PHARMACY V. VIRGINIA CONSUMER COUNCIL (1976) [4] he refused to recognize a First Amendment right of consumers to receive commercial information. In short, in the First Amendment area, as in all others, he would generally give the legislative branch, whether state or federal, greater freedom to plot its own course than his colleagues would.

When, in June of 1986, WARREN BURGER [1] announced his resignation as Chief Justice and President RONALD REAGAN [3,I] nominated Rehnquist as his replacement, there was a firestorm of protest among liberals. Senator Edward Kennedy denounced Justice Rehnquist as having an "appalling record on race" and liberal columnists branded him a right-wing extremist. A concerted effort was undertaken to find something in his past that might provide a basis for defeating the nomination. Assorted allegations were raised concerning contacts with black voters when he was a Republican party official in Phoenix, the handling of a family trust, a memo he had written to Justice Jackson as a law clerk urging that the SEPARATE-BUT-EQUAL DOCTRINE [4] not be overruled in BROWN V. BOARD OF EDUCATION OF TOPEKA (1954, 1955) [1], and a racially restrictive covenant in the deed to his Phoenix house. The Senate perceived that these allegations were either unproven or, if true, were "ancient history" and irrelevant to his fitness for the post of Chief Justice. Significantly, no serious charge of misconduct was shown as to Rehnquist's fourteen and a half years as an Associate Justice on the Supreme Court. In the end, after much sound and fury, he was confirmed by a vote of 65–13.

If the 1975 term saw Rehnquist "arrive" as a major force on the Court, it was the 1987 term, his second year in the post, that saw him mature as Chief Justice. In a speech given in 1976 he had discussed the role of Chief Justice, citing CHARLES EVANS HUGHES [2] as his model: "Hughes believed that unanimity of decision contributed to public confidence in the Court. . . . Except in cases involving matters of high principle he willingly acquiesced in silence rather than expose his dissenting views. . . . Hughes was also willing to modify his own opinions to hold or increase his majority and if that meant he had to put in disconnected thoughts or sentences, in they went."

Following his own advice, in the 1987 term he achieved a high level of agreement with his fellow Justices (ranging from 57.6 percent with Justice Thurgood Marshall to 83.1 percent with Justice ANTHONY KENNEDY [I]). His administrative abilities in the 1987 term won the praise of Justice HARRY BLACKMUN [1,I], who deemed him a "splendid administrator in conference." For the first time in years, the Court concluded its work prior to July 1. During that term, Rehnquist showed that he could be flexible, joining with the more liberal Justices to subject the dismissal of a homosexual CIA agent to judicial review and to support the First Amendment claims of *Hustler* magazine to direct off-color ridicule at a public figure. Most significantly, in *Morrison v. Olson* (1988) Rehnquist wrote for a 7–1 majority upholding the office of INDEPENDENT COUNSEL [I] against a challenge by the Reagan administration. In a decision termed an "exercise in folly" by the lone dissenter, Justice ANTONIN SCALIA [I], Rehnquist held that the appointments clause was not violated by Congress's vesting the power to appoint a SPECIAL PROSECUTOR [I] in a "Special Division" of three United States Court of Appeals judges. Nor did the act violate SEPARATION OF POWERS [4] principles by impermissibly interfering with the functions of the executive branch. While the act can be shown to have theoretical flaws, Rehnquist could not be faulted if he perceived that a truly independent prosecutor was a necessary check on the many abuses of executive power, including criminal violations, that were occurring during the latter years of the Reagan administration and in upholding a check on those abuses in an opinion that gained the concurrence of a substantial majority of his colleagues. Rehnquist's performance during the 1988 term led the *New York Times*, which had vigorously opposed his elevation to Chief Justice, to praise him with faint damnation. "While he is certainly no liberal, or even a moderate, his positions are not always responsive to the tides of fashionable opinion among his fellow political conservatives."

Indeed, while Rehnquist's judicial philosophy is undoubtedly born of a staunch political conservatism, the principles of federalism and strict construction will frequently prevail even when they lead to a "liberal" result. For example, in PRUNEYARD SHOPPING CENTER V. ROBINS (1980) [3] he wrote the opinion upholding state constitutional provisions that allowed political demonstrators to solicit signatures for a petition in a shopping center.

He recognized "the authority of the state to exercise its POLICE POWER [3] or its sovereign right to adopt in its own Constitution individual liberties more expansive than those conferred by the Federal Constitution." Similarly, in *Hughes v. Oklahoma* (1979) he dissented when the Court invalidated a state's attempt to preserve its wildlife. And, in *Pennell v. City of San Jose* (1988), he upheld the city's rent control ordinance in the face of a due process challenge by landlords. In numerous criminal cases, such as *United States v. Maze* (1974) and *Ball v. United States* (1985), he has voted to reverse criminal convictions on the ground that the government had failed to prove that the defendant's conduct had violated the terms of the (strictly construed) statute.

But if the 1987 term showed that Rehnquist could be flexible as Chief Justice, that term and the 1988 term also had him, in most cases, leading the Court in a conservative direction. In a series of close cases decided in the 1987 term, ranging across the landscape of the BILL OF RIGHTS [1], the Court denied an equal protection challenge to user fees for bus transportation to school, denied a claim by Indians that a Forest Service logging road through a national forest would interfere with their free exercise of religion, denied food stamps to striking workers, allowed censorship of a school newspaper, upheld federal tort immunity for defense contractors, and allowed illegally discovered evidence to be used against a criminal defendant under the "independent source" exception to the exclusionary rule.

The 1988 term demonstrated that Rehnquist was still prepared to be flexible. For example, in *City of Canton v. Harris* he joined an opinion by Justice White that held both that a city could be liable for damages under SECTION 1983, TITLE 42, U.S. CODE [4] for poor training of police officers and that a new trial was not barred; Justices O'Connor, Kennedy, and Scalia, on the other hand, wanted to dismiss the plaintiff's case because the plaintiff could not have met the "deliberate indifference" standard of proof. Such flexibility was rarely called for during the 1988 term, however, and the conservatives stayed together most of the time. The leading case of the term was WEBSTER V. REPRODUCTIVE HEALTH SERVICES (1988) [I]. Here Chief Justice Rehnquist and four others upheld a Missouri statute that forbade public funding and the use of public hospitals for abortions. The decision was consistent with Rehnquist's views of states' rights and strict construction of the federal Bill of Rights. Rehnquist observed that "our cases have recognized that the due process clauses generally confer no affirmative right to government aid, even where such aid may be necessary to some life, liberty or property interests of which the government itself may not deprive the individual." Because a state is under no constitutional obligation to provide public hospitals at all, it is free to condition their use however it wishes. This notion, that beneficiaries of public largess must accept the "bitter [restrictions] with the sweet" has been a hallmark of Rehnquist's jurisprudence since he first expressed it in ARNETT V. KENNEDY [1] in 1974. However, Rehnquist (at least temporarily) was unable to convince Justice O'Connor that it was time to abandon the "rigid" framework of *Roe v. Wade* that gave a woman an absolute right to an abortion during the first trimester of pregnancy. This failure resulted even though he had drafted a compromise opinion that continued to recognize a limited constitutional right to abortion.

Despite the current national debate on abortion, it seems unlikely that the country in the foreseeable future will be confronted with a constitutional problem of the magnitude of the legal discrimination against blacks (and the closely related problem of police abuse of the rights of criminal suspects) that faced the Warren Court. Consequently, it is also unlikely that the judicial activism displayed by the Warren Court to deal with these problems will seem as morally necessary or politically desirable in the future. Thus, while Justice Rehnquist's vision of a vigorous Tenth Amendment checking Congress's power vis-à-vis the states seems unlikely to prevail in the long term, his view of a more limited role for the federal Constitution, and hence for the federal courts, probably will be the wave of the future. Having reached its highest point in the 1960s, the "Rights Revolution"—already dying during the Burger Court years—terminated with the appointment of William Rehnquist as Chief Justice of the United States; it probably will not recur after he steps down.

CRAIG M. BRADLEY

(SEE ALSO: *Conservatism and the Constitution* [I]; *Rehnquist Court* [I].)

Bibliography

BRADLEY, CRAIG M. 1987 Criminal Procedure in the Rehnquist Court: Has the Rehnquisition Begun? *Indiana Law Journal* 62:273–294.

DAVIS, SUE 1989 *Justice Rehnquist and the Constitution.* Princeton, N.J.: Princeton University Press.

POWELL, H. JEFFERSON 1982 The Compleat Jeffersonian: Justice Rehnquist and Federalism. *Yale Law Journal* 91:1317–1370.

REHNQUIST, WILLIAM H. 1976 Chief Justices I Never Knew. *Hastings Constitutional Law Quarterly* 3:637.

———— 1976 The Notion of a Living Constitution. *Texas Law Review* 54:693–706.

———— 1987 *The Supreme Court: How It Was, How It Is.* New York: Morrow.

SHAPIRO, DAVID L. 1976 Mr. Justice Rehnquist: A Preliminary View. *Harvard Law Review* 90:293–357.

RELIGION IN PUBLIC SCHOOLS
(Update)

Despite several Supreme Court decisions on religion in public schools, conflict in this area has proliferated in recent years. One example is the discord that persists over the teaching of evolution. In EPPERSON V. ARKANSAS (1968) [2] the Court struck down a statute prohibiting the teaching of evolution. In *Edwards v. Aguillard* (1987) the Court invalidated a Louisiana statute requiring that "creation science" be given equal exposure in public schools where evolution is taught. (Among other things, creation science teaches that plants and animals were created substantially as they now exist.) The majority reasoned that the statute was intended to promote the biblical version of creation or to hamper the teaching of evolution for religious reasons. However, the Court did not hold that teaching CREATIONISM [I] is unconstitutional.

In several cases, religious parents have tried to turn the Court's expansive interpretation of the ESTABLISHMENT CLAUSE [I] to their advantage by alleging that public schools were unconstitutionally establishing a religion of secular humanism. Although the Supreme Court has not tackled this issue, the lower federal courts have uniformly rejected these claims. These results seem appropriate. The Supreme Court has stated that nontheistic faiths, including secular humanism, can qualify as FIRST AMENDMENT [2,I] religions. However, if secular humanism is defined narrowly enough to be a specific religion, the public schools are not establishing it, for they promote no particular dogma or rituals. In contrast, if secular humanism is defined broadly enough to include the education given in public schools, it ceases to be a religion for First Amendment purposes. A contrary conclusion would impel the untenable result that virtually any secular enthusiasm, such as music, art, or sports, would be considered a religion and thus barred from the public schools.

This conclusion does not end all controversy, however; parents often charge that teaching in public schools is inimical to their religious beliefs and therefore violates their right to free exercise of religion. The Supreme Court has not yet dealt with this issue, and its pronouncements elsewhere offer little guidance. The Court has often stated that a substantial burden of free exercise can be justified only by a COMPELLING STATE INTEREST [1] pursued by the least restrictive means. Public schools have denied that their teaching burdens free exercise at all because their teaching is secular, not religious; children need not

accept what is taught, and children are not compelled to attend public schools, but are free to attend private schools. Dissatisfied parents reply that free exercise is burdened if children are taught that their religion is wrong, although the children do not have to profess acceptance of the schools' teaching, and although others consider the issues in question secular. These parents stress that young impressionable children may not understand that they are free to reject the school's teaching or may be too intimidated to express their disagreement. They also argue that the option of attending private schools is too expensive to remove the burden on free exercise.

Even if the curriculum does burden free exercise, public schools claim a compelling state interest in giving all children this education. Most observers concede that states have an interest in teaching basic skills such as reading and writing. However, it is debatable how important the state's interest is in other areas, including moral values and sex education. If a public school does burden free exercise without compelling justification, some accommodation of the religious students may be necessary as a remedy. Many school systems excuse students from certain programs to which they have religious objections, and some schools provide students with alternative instruction. The latter approach can be expensive and administratively burdensome; the former may prevent the child from obtaining essential skills. Suggestions that children be given VOUCHERS [I] to attend private schools, meanwhile, have been attacked as both violative of the establishment clause and destructive of the objectives of public education.

The legal need for accommodation may no longer be as pressing as it once was, however. The Supreme Court recently indicated in EMPLOYMENT DIV., DEPT. OF HUMAN RES. V. SMITH (1990) [I] that it has abandoned the "compelling state interest" standard. If the Court adheres to this position, public schools would not be constitutionally required to show a compelling reason for subjecting children to teaching that is hostile to their religion.

In addition to controversies over school curriculum, disputes have also multiplied over the use of public school facilities by student religious groups. In WIDMAR V. VINCENT (1981) [4], the Supreme Court insisted that public university facilities generally available to student groups and speakers also be open to student religious groups. In 1984, Congress tried to extend this principle to secondary schools by adopting the Equal Access Act, which forbids public secondary schools from discriminating on the basis of the content of speech when affording student groups access to school facilities outside school hours. However, the school may not sponsor, and school employees may not participate in, student religious groups.

Some critics believed that the act was unconstitutional because of the possibility that school employees would become involved and that students would perceive the provision of facilities to student religious groups as endorsing religion. The Court disagreed in BOARD OF EDUCATION OF WESTSIDE COMMUNITY SCHOOLS V. MERGENS (1990) [I], holding that the act did not violate the establishment clause.

Although the Court has repeatedly struck down daily school prayers, many schools have included prayers or benedictions in special school events. The Supreme Court has upheld the opening of legislative sessions with prayers in MARSH V. CHAMBERS (1983) [3], but the differences in the public school context have persuaded some lower courts that the practice cannot be permitted there.

The Supreme Court has said that public schools may study the Bible as literature and history, but not for devotional purposes. This has required lower courts to decide case by case whether particular programs meet this standard or improperly include religious indoctrination.

Public school teachers occasionally endorse or criticize religious beliefs in the classroom. Courts generally have tried to distinguish between teachers' statements of their own beliefs, which are permissible and protected by the rights of free speech and free exercise, and propagandizing, which infringes on both the students' right of free exercise and the establishment clause. Lower courts have also upheld regulations against teachers' regularly wearing distinctively religious garb.

GEORGE W. DENT

(SEE ALSO: *Equal Access* [I]; *Religious Fundamentalism* [I]; *Religious Liberty* [3,I]; *Separation of Church and State* [4,I].)

Bibliography

DENT, GEORGE W. 1988 Religious Children, Secular Schools. *Southern California Law Review* 61:863–941.
STROSSEN, NADINE 1986 "Secular Humanism" and "Scientific Creationism": Proposed Standards for Reviving Curricular Decisions Affecting Students' Religious Freedom. *Ohio State Law Journal* 47:333–407.

RELIGIOUS FREEDOM

See; Religious Liberty [3, I]

RELIGIOUS FUNDAMENTALISM

Nathaniel Hawthorne perhaps best captured the paradox of religious fundamentalism in America in his stories about the Puritans. Repelled by the Puritans' intolerance, Hawthorne admired their realism and their unswerving devotion to principle. The latter trait he vividly depicted in his short story "The Gray Champion" (1835), where a first-generation Puritan mysteriously returns to Boston in 1689 to thwart the subjugation of the colonies by King James II. Like a fiery Old Testament prophet, the old Puritan—the "Gray Champion" of the story's title—denounces the usurpations of Royal Governor Sir Edmund Andros and urges the people to resistance.

The character of the Gray Champion symbolizes the Puritans' rigid idealism, an idealism that typifies religious fundamentalism in general. In Hawthorne's view, this idealism constituted both a threat and a promise to republican government. It constituted a threat because it fostered religious intolerance, which if enforced by the state, could destroy civil liberty. It represented a promise because it produced a firm commitment to moral principle, which if properly exercised, could help sustain republicanism. Hence the ultimate paradox of fundamentalism: Its intolerance may destroy republican government, but its rigorous attachment to moral principle may be needed to defend it.

One of the greatest achievements of American CONSTITUTIONALISM [1] was the manner in which it resolved this paradox by harnessing the moral idealism of fundamentalism while restraining its potential for bigotry. The Founders harnessed fundamentalism's moral idealism by stressing the importance of morality in civic life and by acknowledging the crucial role churches played in fostering this morality. At the same time, the Founders sought to temper fundamentalism's intolerance by removing theological questions from the political arena, which greatly reduced the consequences of religious intolerance by ensuring that government power would never be used to resolve theological controversies.

The Founders' arrangement produced an institutional separation between church and state even while forging a practical tie between religion and politics on the basis of morality. Religious fundamentalists were discouraged by the nature of the regime from using the government to promote their theological beliefs; but the door was left open for them to enter the political arena as citizens in order to promote government policies in accord with both the principles of the Constitution and the "laws of nature and nature's God" on which those principles are premised.

The political activities of religious fundamentalists in the new nation (primarily evangelical Christians) reflected the Founders' understanding of the role of religion in society. Many evangelicals opposed state funding of churches because they thought it corrupted religion, and gradually even the congregationalists who supported ESTABLISHMENTS OF RELIGION [2] changed their minds. Hence, when evangelicals became involved in politics in the early nation, they generally sought to do so on the basis of principles of civic morality that were held in common by both reason and revelation. In the years before the Civil War, they entered the political arena by the thousands to spearhead crusades against dueling, lotteries, war, poverty, prostitution, alcoholism, and SLAVERY [4]. These political activities on behalf of secular concerns proved that religious fundamentalism could fulfill a vital political function by serving as the political conscience of the nation.

Nowhere can this be seen more clearly than in the controversy over Cherokee removal from Georgia. Federal treaties had guaranteed the Cherokees their lands on the condition that they become both peaceful and "civilized." In 1828 and 1829, the Georgia legislature tried to legislate the Cherokee Nation out of existence, extending its laws over Cherokee lands and demanding that the federal government remove the Indians. The evangelical missionaries who had been working among the Cherokees rose to the Indians' defense. They based their arguments against removal not simply on biblical morality but on the natural right of property, the inviolability of contracts, and the God-given equality of all men proclaimed in the DECLARATION OF INDEPENDENCE [3], which they argued applied to Indians as well as white men.

Unfortunately, both Congress and the President rebuffed the evangelicals' efforts on behalf of the Cherokees, and the government eventually relocated the Indians further west by force. The controversy nevertheless demonstrated that religious fundamentalists could fulfill the role that the Founders had created for them: they could put their idealism to constructive use by intervening in politics on the basis of principles of natural justice rather than doctrines of sectarian theology.

None of this is to suggest that religious fundamentalists completely forswore introducing sectarian theology into politics in the early nation. Before the Civil War, numerous evangelicals claimed that America had been founded as a "Christian nation," and many sought to introduce sectarian religion into public education. After the Civil War, some even wanted to amend the Constitution to recognize the authority of Jesus Christ and Christianity. In the twentieth century, widespread support persisted among evangelicals for state-sponsored prayer and Bible reading in the public schools. Nevertheless, these efforts were more the exception than the rule, and sometimes actions that seemed directed at obtaining state support for religion were actually much more complicated. For instance, evangelicals were vigorously criticized for trying to mix church and state in the early nineteenth century when they sought repeal of a law requiring many post offices to be open on Sunday. Yet one reason evangelicals found this law so offensive was that it compelled church members employed by the post office to break the sabbath in violation of their religious beliefs. Thus, evangelicals sought repeal of the law (at least in part) to protect a person's natural right to RELIGIOUS LIBERTY [3,I] protected by the free exercise clause of the FIRST AMENDMENT [2,I].

The political significance of religious fundamentalism eventually diminished as the number of fundamentalists declined and as most remaining fundamentalists abandoned politics after the repeal of the EIGHTEENTH AMENDMENT [2]. Yet the very forces of secularization that some had thought decimated religious fundamentalism may have spurred its resurgence in the late 1970s and 1980s. As social ills proliferated and many persons became disenchanted with both the political liberalism and the moral permissiveness of mainline Christian denominations, evangelicalism prospered and political action by evangelicals reemerged with a vengeance. Social issues such as ABORTION [1,I], PORNOGRAPHY [3], and EUTHANASIA [2] attracted the new evangelicals' attention, much as dueling, slavery, and intemperance had sparked the actions of their forebears in the nineteenth century.

In one key respect, however, many of the new evangelical activists were different from those who came before. In the past, most conservative Christians had continued to lobby for at least a limited state power to sponsor religious exercises, such as devotional Bible reading and organized prayers in public schools. Although support for these activities did not disappear in the 1980s, it did become much less noticeable, as evangelicals focused more on eliminating the government's power to restrict individual religious expression than on promoting a state power to promote religion.

This new emphasis on individual religious freedom can be ascribed at least in part to the changing nature of church–state conflicts in the 1970s and 1980s. Whereas previous church–state battles had focused on how much the government could do to promote religion while staying within the confines of the ESTABLISHMENT CLAUSE [I], new controversies concerned how far the state could go in restricting individual religious expression. Public high-school students were forbidden by school authorities from meeting on their own during lunch or before school for prayer and Bible study. Churches were prevented from utilizing public facilities readily available for use by other community groups, and zoning laws were invoked to curtail religious activities in private homes. In addition, many parents faced the choice of either removing their children from public schools or allowing their children to be taught the permissibility of behaviors they found morally unacceptable. Some religious parents who tried to teach their children at home were jailed. These new conflicts caused many evangelicals to see government as the problem rather than the solution, and they accordingly sought ways to curb what they regarded as state-sponsored persecution of their religious beliefs and practices.

One result was an attempt to apply the free exercise clause to curriculum objections in the public schools. In 1986, a group of fundamentalist parents in Tennessee petitioned to have their children exempted from a school reading program because they believed the content of the readers disparaged their religious beliefs. The Tennessee parents did not want to change school curriculum; they simply wanted to teach their children reading at home, while allowing the children to participate in the rest of the school's academic program. The district court granted this request, but a three-judge panel on the court of appeals unanimously reversed. However, the judges could not agree on the reasons for reversal. One judge argued that the reading program did not burden the children's free exercise rights because it did not tell them what to believe. A second judge maintained precisely the opposite, arguing that a broader purpose of the reading was to inculcate certain "values"; according to this judge, this purpose gave the school district a COMPELLING STATE INTEREST [1] in not allowing exemptions to the program. The third judge, meanwhile, claimed that the reading program did burden free exercise, but he did not want to issue a new precedent in this area without express guidance from the Supreme Court. This the Supreme court declined to give, although it later made clear in EMPLOYMENT DIVISION, DEPT. OF HUMAN RESOURCES V. SMITH (1990) [I] that it had no intention of broadening free exercise rights. *Smith* suggests that further litigation using the free exercise approach is likely to fail.

In a related area, there have been efforts by evangelicals to have CREATIONISM [I] taught in public schools. Unlike fundamentalists from an earlier era, the new creationists do not argue that evolution should not be taught; they only contend that whenever evolution is taught, "scientific creationism" must also be taught in order to protect the students' right to study different points of view. Hence, they argue their case in terms of ACADEMIC FREEDOM [1]. In *Edwards v. Aguillard* (1987), however, the Supreme Court struck down a Louisiana law that adopted this approach as violative of the establishment clause.

One new rationale that has not been invalidated by the Court is EQUAL ACCESS [I], which calls for religious expression to be protected as speech under the First Amendment. The primary idea behind equal access is that religious individuals and groups should be accorded the same access to public facilities as nonreligious individuals and groups. For example, if a public library rents rooms to community groups for meetings, it should not be able to forbid religious groups from renting the rooms for religious meetings because this would be discriminating against certain groups on the basis of the content of

their speech. Similarly, if high school students have the right to pass out political leaflets to their classmates on school grounds, then they must also have the right to pass out religious leaflets. The equal access rationale has been applied by evangelicals with particular success in the public high school setting, where many schools previously had denied religious student groups the same right to meet on school grounds routinely afforded to other student groups. The Supreme Court sustained federal legislation providing a limited statutory right to equal access in public secondary schools in BOARD OF EDUCATION OF WESTSIDE COMMUNITY SCHOOLS V. MERGENS (1990) [I].

The development of equal access is yet another indication of how successful the Founders were in setting up a system where the political demands of religious fundamentalism would be framed in terms of generally applicable moral principles rather than petitions based on divine right. In America, religious fundamentalists have increasingly recognized that the same laws that protect other citizens also protect them and that they do not need special privileges conferred by the government to prosper.

JOHN G. WEST, JR.

(SEE ALSO: *Bender v. Williamsport* [I]; *Cherokee Indian Cases* [1]; *Government Aid to Religious Institutions* [2,I]; *Religion in Public Schools* [3,I]; *Separation of Church and State* [4,I]; *School Prayer* [I]; *Sunday Closing Laws* [4].)

Bibliography

HAWTHORNE, NATHANIEL 1970 "The Gray Champion," "The Man of Adamant," and "The Maypole of Merrymount." In *Hawthorne: Selected Tales and Sketches.* New York: Holt, Rinehart, and Winston.
JAFFA, HARRY V. 1990 *The American Founding as the Best Regime: The Bonding of Civil and Religious Liberty.* Montclair, Calif.: Claremont Institute for the Study of Political Philosophy and Statesmanship.
STOKES, ANSON PHELPS 1950 Church and State in the United States, 3 vols. New York: Harper and Brothers.
WEST, JOHN G., JR. 1991 The Changing Battle over Religion in the Public Schools. *Wake Forest Law Review* 26:361–401.

RELIGIOUS LIBERTY
(Update)

Religious liberty finds its protection in three provisions of the Constitution: the prohibition of RELIGIOUS TESTS [3,I] for office in Article IV and the FREE EXERCISE and ESTABLISHMENT CLAUSES [I] of the FIRST AMENDMENT [2,I]. Because the first is self-executing and the last is involved mostly with issues of government aid, endorsement, or sponsorship of religious activities, the bulk of constitutional litigation over religious liberty has taken place under the free-exercise clause.

In recent history, there have been two general conceptions of the protections afforded by the free-exercise clause. The broad conception, which prevailed in the Supreme Court from 1963 (and arguably earlier) until 1990, holds that no law or government practice can be allowed to burden the exercise of religion unless it is the least restrictive means of achieving a government purpose of the highest order—a "compelling" governmental purpose. The narrow conception, adopted by a 5–4 vote in 1990, holds that the free-exercise clause prohibits only those laws that are specifically directed to religious practice.

The classic statement of the broad conception is found in SHERBERT V. VERNER (1963) [4]. In this case, the Court required the state of South Carolina to pay unemployment compensation benefits to a Seventh-Day Adventist notwithstanding her refusal to accept available jobs that would have required her to work on Saturday, her Sabbath. According to the Court, denial of benefits was tantamount to a fine for following the tenets of her religion. Since *Sherbert*, the Court has required states to pay unemployment compensation to others whose religious tenets conflicted with the requirements of available employment: to a Jehovah's Witness who would not work on armaments, in THOMAS V. INDIANA REVIEW BOARD (1981) [4]; to a convert to the Seventh-Day Adventist Church, in *Hobbie v. Unemployment Appeals Commission* (1987); and to a Christian who would not work on Sunday, in FRAZEE V. ILLINOIS DEPARTMENT OF EMPLOYMENT SECURITY (1989) [I]. In *Frazee*, the Court unanimously held that the claimant was entitled to benefits, even though his belief was not mandated by the particular religious denomination of which he was a member. The decision thus confirmed that the right of religious liberty extends to all sincerely held religious convictions and not just to those of established denominations.

In years immediately following *Sherbert*, the Court extended free-exercise protection to other conflicts between religious conscience and civil law, including compulsory education above the eighth grade, in WISCONSIN V. YODER (1972) [4], and jury duty, in *In re Jennison* (1963). After 1972, however, the Court turned aside every claim for a free-exercise exemption from a facially neutral law, outside the narrow context of unemployment compensation. Particularly noteworthy examples included GOLDMAN V. WEINBERGER (1986) [I], in which the Court upheld an Air Force uniform requirement that prevented an Orthodox Jew from wearing his skullcap (yarmulke) while on duty indoors; *Tony & Susan Alamo Foundation v. Secretary of Labor* (1985), in which the Court upheld imposition of minimum-wage laws on a religious commu-

nity in which the members worked for no pay; and LYNG V. NORTHWEST INDIAN CEMETERY PROTECTIVE ASSOCIATION (1988) [I], in which the court allowed construction of a logging road through National Forest lands sacred to certain northern Californian Indian tribes, even though the road would "virtually destroy the Indians' ability to practice their religion."

In each of these cases, the Court either held that the "compelling interest" test of *Sherbert* had been satisfied or that there were special circumstances making that test inappropriate to the particular case. Thus, during this period, the formal legal doctrine sounded highly protective of the rights of religious conscience, but in practice, the government almost always prevailed.

In 1990, the Court abandoned the compelling-interest test in EMPLOYMENT DIV., DEPT. OF HUMAN RES. V. SMITH (1990) [I], holding that "the right of free exercise does not relieve an individual of the obligation to comply with a 'valid and neutral law of general applicability on the ground that the law proscribes (or prescribes) conduct that his religion prescribes (or proscribes).'" The *Smith* case involved the sacramental use of peyote by members of the Native American Church. Although twenty-three states and the federal government specifically exempt Native American Church ceremonies from the drug laws, Oregon does not. The Supreme Court held that the free-exercise clause does not require an exemption.

After *Smith*, the only laws or governmental practices that can be challenged under the free-exercise clause are those in which this clause applies "in conjunction with other constitutional protections," such as cases involving free speech or childrearing, or those in which the law is "specifically directed at their religious practice." Thus, laws discriminating against religion as such would be subject to constitutional challenge. Such cases are unusual in the United States. The only example in recent decades was *McDaniel v. Paty* (1978), which involved a Tennessee law barring members of the clergy from service in the state legislature or a state CONSTITUTIONAL CONVENTION [1]. Because Tennessee had singled out a religious class for a special civil disability, its statute was struck down. Another case of discrimination against religion was WIDMAR V. VINCENT (1981) [4], in which a public university attempted to bar student religious groups from campus facilities. *Widmar*, however, was decided under the free-speech clause, not the free-exercise clause. Except for *McDaniel* and *Widmar*, almost every free-exercise case to come before the Supreme Court involved an ostensibly neutral law of general applicability, now resolved under *Smith* without inquiry into the strength of the governmental purpose.

The debate between the broad and narrow readings of the free-exercise clause goes back even before the proposal and ratification of the First Amendment from 1789 to 1791. JOHN LOCKE [3] and THOMAS JEFFERSON [3] both apparently opposed exemptions; JAMES MADISON [3] favored them, at least in some circumstances. The same issue arose under several of the STATE CONSTITUTIONS [I], yielding conflicting results. The majority of the state constitutions adopted before the First Amendment contained language that suggests the broad reading. Georgia, for example, guaranteed that "[a]ll persons whatever shall have the free exercise of their religion; provided it be not repugnant to the peace and safety of the State" (Georgia Constitution of 1777, Article LVI). Although it is perilous to draw firm conclusions from abstract legal language, the "peace and safety" proviso would appear to be unnecessary unless the free-exercise guarantee were understood to entail some exceptions from otherwise valid laws. Moreover, in actual practice, conflicts between minority religious tenets and general law in colonial and preconstitutional America were not infrequently resolved by crafting exemptions. Examples included exemptions from oath requirements and from military conscription. The evidence, however, is thin because eighteenth-century America gave rise to few conflicts between religious and civil dictates.

If the narrow reading of the free-exercise clause announced in *Smith* remains in force, it will cause major changes in the constitutional rights both of religious individuals and of institutions. It is not uncommon for minority religious practices to conflict with "generally applicable" rules or regulations, and henceforth, any relief from such conflicts must come from the legislatures. Some religious groups—those more numerous or politically powerful—will be able to protect their interests in the political process; some will not. The Supreme Court commented in *Smith*, "It may fairly be said that leaving accommodation to the political process will place at a relative disadvantage those religious practices that are not widely engaged in; but that unavoidable consequence of democratic government must be preferred to a system in which each conscience is a law unto itself."

For many years, some Justices maintained that laws or government policies that exempted religious organizations or religiously motivated individuals from laws applied to others were themselves suspect under the establishment clause. For example, Justice JOHN MARSHALL HARLAN [3], in the CONSCIENTIOUS OBJECTION [1] cases during the VIETNAM WAR [4,I], concluded, in *Welsh v. United States* (1970), that it would be unconstitutional to recognize religious objections to military service without also recognizing nonreligious conscientious objection. More recently, the Court, in WALLACE V. JAFFREE (1985) [4], struck down state efforts to accommodate the religious need of some school children for voluntary prayer through

an officially declared moment of silence, and in THORNTON V. CALDOR, INC. (1985) [4], the Court invalidated a statute that required private employers to honor the needs of Sabbath observers in determining days off.

In *Corporation of Presiding Bishop v. Amos* (1987), however, the Court unanimously upheld a federal statute exempting religious organizations from the prohibition on discrimination on the basis of religion in employment. The Court reasoned that it is permissible for the government to remove government-imposed obstacles to the free exercise of religion, even if, in some sense, this gives preferential treatment to religious organizations. And in TEXAS MONTHLY, INC. V. BULLOCK (1989) [I], when a fragmented Court struck down a Texas law exempting religious magazines from sales tax, the plurality was careful to note that benefits conferred exclusively on religious organizations are constitutionally permissible if they "would not impose substantial burdens on nonbeneficiaries" or if they "were designed to alleviate government intrusions that might significantly deter adherents of a particular faith from conduct protected by the Free Exercise Clause."

Thus, although individuals or religious bodies can no longer challenge generally applicable government action under the free-exercise clause, the courts have also become more likely to uphold legislation designed to accommodate religious exercise.

MICHAEL W. MCCONNELL

(SEE ALSO: *Equal Access* [I]; *Lemon Test* [I]; *Religion in Public Schools* [3,I]; *Religious Fundamentalism* [I]; *Separation of Church and State* [4,I]; *Board of Education of Westside Community Schools v. Mergens* [I].)

Bibliography

LAYCOCK, DOUGLAS 1986 A Survey of Religious Liberty in the United States. *Ohio State Law Journal* 47:409–451.
LUPU, IRA C. 1989 Where Rights Begin: The Problem of Burdens on the Free Exercise of Religion. *Harvard Law Review* 102:933–990.
MCCONNELL, MICHAEL W. 1990 The Origins and Historical Understanding of Free Exercise of Religion. *Harvard Law Review* 103:1409–1517.

RELIGIOUS SYMBOLS IN PUBLIC PLACES

In 1984 the Supreme Court, in LYNCH V. DONNELLY [3], rejected a constitutional challenge to the display of a publicly financed nativity scene—a crèche—in a private park in Pawtucket, Rhode Island. Chief Justice WARREN E. BURGER's [1] decision for a 5–4 majority evoked deep resentment in many quarters, particularly among non-

Christians who opposed the use of public funds to depict an event—the birth of Jesus to the Virgin Mary—that is a central tenet of Christianity. Moreover, the decision appeared to be a sharp departure from the Court's establishment clause precedents, particularly LEMON V. KURTZMAN (1971) [3], in which the Court set forth the three "tests" that the ESTABLISHMENT CLAUSE [I] imposes on government actions involving religion: "The statute must have a secular legislative purpose . . . its principal or primary effect must be one that neither advances nor inhibits religion . . . [and] the statute must not foster 'an excessive government entanglement with religion.'"

Conceding that the crèche was a religious symbol, the majority opinion nevertheless perceived the Pawtucket display as essentially a secular recognition of the historical origins of the Christmas season and therefore a permissible accommodation to religion. The Chief Justice's opinion observed that the display contained a Santa Claus, sleigh, candy-striped poles, and some reindeer. Critics chided the Court for creating a "two-reindeer" rule and, more seriously, for demonstrating extreme insensitivity to non-Christians.

As lower courts and local governments addressed the questions that *Lynch v. Donnelly* left unanswered, they were guided in large part by Justice SANDRA DAY O'CONNOR's [3,I] concurring opinion in which she reformulated the three-part LEMON TEST [3,I] by emphasizing that the "purpose" and "effect" prongs of the test are designed to prevent government practices that endorse or disapprove of religion. "Endorsement," she wrote, "sends a message to adherents that they are outsiders, not full members of the political community." Based on this interpretation of *Lemon*, Justice O'Connor concluded that the purpose of the crèche was not to endorse Christianity but to celebrate a public holiday of secular significance, notwithstanding its religious aspect. As for the effect of the crèche, its "overall holiday setting . . . negates any message of endorsement" of the religious aspect of the display. Justice O'Connor's "endorsement" test provided a more focused approach than the open-ended emphasis on "accommodation" in Chief Justice Burger's opinion and has been widely followed in subsequent cases even by Justices who disagreed with her conclusion that the Pawtucket crèche was constitutional.

After five years of extensive litigation and public controversy, the Supreme Court revisited the religious-display issue in 1989 when, in COUNTY OF ALLEGHENY V. AMERICAN CIVIL LIBERTIES UNION [I], it ruled that (1) a privately financed crèche, without holiday trappings and embellished with a banner proclaiming "Gloria in Excelsis Deo," was unconstitutional as displayed in the main staircase of a county courthouse; and (2) an eighteen-foot menorah situated outside a county office building was constitutional

as part of a display that featured the menorah alongside a forty-five-foot Christmas tree and a "Salute to Liberty" sign reminding viewers that "We are the keepers of the flame of liberty and our legacy of freedom." In light of the retirement of Justice WILLIAM J. BRENNAN [1,I] in July of 1990, the division on the Court in the *Allegheny* case was significant. Four Justices (WILLIAM H. REHNQUIST [3,I], BYRON R. WHITE [4,I], ANTONIN SCALIA [I], and ANTHONY M. KENNEDY [I]) would have upheld both displays because there was no governmental effort to coerce or proselytize, and three Justices (Brennan, THURGOOD MARSHALL [3,I], and JOHN PAUL STEVENS [4,I]) found both displays unconstitutional. Thus, the votes of Justices HARRY A. BLACKMUN [1,I] and O'Connor produced majorities upholding one display (the menorah) and invalidating the other (the crèche).

The Pawtucket crèche posed a risk of government endorsement because it was publicly financed. The Allegheny County displays, although privately financed, posed a similar danger because they were located in or near government buildings. By eschewing a clear test that would bar all government-financed displays with religious messages, or privately financed displays adjacent to government buildings, certain Justices on the Court were compelled in both cases to emphasize the design of the display as the key element of constitutionality. It was predictable, therefore, that governments would almost certainly invite litigation if they paid for holiday displays containing religious symbols or placed them in front of or in government buildings. Such displays require a fact-specific evaluation to determine whether the religious message has been sufficiently mixed with the secular holiday observance to avoid the overall impression of governmental endorsement of religion. A subject as intensely personal as religion is likely to evoke strong reactions if religious displays are constructed with public funds or if they are placed in locations that give them some type of official status.

These disputes, and the attendant divisiveness, can be minimized, however, if private groups, rather than the government, pay for holiday displays that contain religious symbols and if such displays are placed in traditional forums, like parks and plazas, that are normally used for speeches, displays, or other expressions of opinion. Indeed, the free-speech provisions of the FIRST AMENDMENT [2,I] probably protect the right of a private group to display a crèche or menorah in a PUBLIC FORUM [3,I], even without holiday trappings, as the symbolic expression of the celebration of the holiday season.

Since the Supreme Court's decision in *Allegheny County*, there is evidence that local communities have indeed adopted policies that avoid the divisiveness that the establishment clause was intended to prevent. They have relied increasingly on private groups to sponsor religious holiday displays and have selected locations that are not adjacent to public buildings such as city halls and courthouses. This development has the salutary effect of compelling governments, private parties, and courts to consider the nature of the forum rather than the numbers of reindeer, the prominence of Santa Claus, or the relative sizes of a menorah and a Christmas tree.

If governments desire to participate more actively in celebrating the Christmas season, the traditional Christmas tree provides a constitutionally acceptable alternative. Christmas trees have acquired a sufficiently secular meaning as a symbol of the holiday season so that their display does not endorse Christianity regardless of who bears the cost or wherever the tree may be located. If communities display understanding and restraint, the Constitution need not prevent the Christmas holiday season from serving as an occasion for uniting Americans rather than dividing them along religious lines.

NORMAN REDLICH

Bibliography

DORSEN, NORMAN and SIMS, CHARLES 1985 The Nativity Scene Case; An Error of Judgment. *University of Illinois Law Review* 1985:837–868.
REDLICH, NORMAN 1984 "Nativity Ruling Insults Jews." *New York Times*, March 26, 1984.
VAN ALSTYNE, WILLIAM 1984 Trends in the Supreme Court: Mr. Jefferson's Crumbling Wall—A Comment on *Lynch v. Donnelly. Duke University Law Journal* 1984:770–787.

REPUBLICANISM

Republicanism was the ideology of the AMERICAN REVOLUTION [I], and as such, it still influences much of what Americans believe; in recent years it has had a renewed importance in American constitutional thought. It is difficult for us today to appreciate the revolutionary character of this republican ideology. We live in a world in which almost all nations purport to be republican; even those few countries that remain monarchies, such as Britain and Sweden, are more republican in fact than some others that claim to be republican in theory. But to the monarchy-dominated world of the eighteenth century, republicanism was a radical ideology; indeed, it was to the eighteenth century what Marxism was to be for the nineteenth century. Republicanism was a countercultural ideology of protest, an intellectual means by which dissatisfied people could criticize the luxury, selfishness, and corruption of eighteenth-century monarchical culture.

Yet it would be a mistake to think of republicanism, in the English-speaking world at least, as a distinct and coherent body of thought set in opposition to monarchy or to the English COMMON LAW [1] tradition of rights and liberties. In the greater British world, republican thinking blended with monarchy to create the mixed and LIMITED GOVERNMENT [3] of the English constitution that was celebrated everywhere by enlightened theorists like MONTESQUIEU [3]. Britons regarded the republican part of their constitution, the House of Commons, as the principal bulwark protecting their individual rights and liberties from encroachment by monarchical power. Thus, the sharp distinction drawn by some historians and political theorists today between the civic tradition of republicanism, often identified with James Harrington, and the common law tradition of personal and property rights, often identified with JOHN LOCKE [3], would not have been clear to eighteenth-century Englishmen.

Republicanism, however, was more than a form of government; it was also a form of life—a set of beliefs that infused the cultures of the Atlantic world in the age of Enlightenment. Its deepest origins were in ancient Rome and the great era of the Roman republic. The enlightened world of the eighteenth century found most of what it wanted to know about the Roman republic from the writings of the golden age of Latin literature, between the breakdown of the republic in the middle of the first century B.C. to the establishment of the empire in the middle of the second century A.D. The celebrated Latin writers of this time—Cicero, Sallust, Tacitus, and Plutarch, among others—lived when the greatest days of the republic had passed, and thus, they contrasted the growing stratification, corruption, and disorder they saw around them with an imagined earlier world of rustic simplicity and pastoral virtue. Roman farmers had once been hardy soldiers devoted to their country. But they had become selfish, corrupted by luxury, torn by struggles between rich and poor, and devoid of their capacity to serve the public good. In their pessimistic explanations of the republic's decline, these Latin writers left a legacy of beliefs and ideals—about the good life, about citizenship, about political health, about social morality—that have had an enduring effect on Western culture.

This great body of classical literature was revived and updated during the Renaissance and blended into a tradition of what has been called "civic humanism." This classical republican tradition stressed the moral character of the independent citizen as the prerequisite of good politics and disinterested service to the country. To be good citizens, men had to be free of control by other men and free of the influence of selfish interests.

The classical republican tradition passed into the culture of northern Europe. In England it inspired the writings of the great seventeenth-century republicans John Milton, James Harrington, and Algernon Sidney. And it was carried into the eighteenth century by scores of popularizers and translators. By the late eighteenth century, being enlightened was nearly equivalent to believing in republican principles; many Englishmen even described the English monarchy as being a republic in fact. This republican tradition had a decisive effect on the thinking of the American revolutionary leaders.

Republicanism meant for the American revolutionaries in 1776 more than eliminating a king and instituting an elective system of government; it meant setting forth moral and social goals as well. Republics required a particular sort of independent, egalitarian, and virtuous people, a simple people who scorned luxury and superfluous private expenditure, who possessed sufficient property to be free from patronage and dependency on others, and who were willing to sacrifice many of their selfish interests for the res publica, the good of the whole community. Republican equality meant a society whose distinctions were based only on merit. No longer would one's position rest on whom one knew or married or on who one's father was.

Such dependence on a relatively equal, uncorrupted, and virtuous populace that had a single perceived public good made republics very fragile and often short-lived. Monarchies were long-lasting; they could maintain order from the top down over large, diverse, and even corrupt populations through their use of patronage, hereditary privilege, executive authority, standing armies, and an ESTABLISHMENT OF RELIGION [2]. But republics, such as the American states, had to be held together from below, from virtue, from the consent and sacrifice of the people themselves. Consequently, as Montesquieu and other theorists had warned, republics necessarily had to be small in territory and homogeneous and moral in character. The only republics existing in the eighteenth century—the Netherlands and the city-states of Italy and Switzerland—were small and compact. Large heterogeneous states that had tried to establish republics—as England had in the seventeenth century—were bound to end up in chaos, resulting in some sort of military dictatorship, like that of Oliver Cromwell. If it was too large and composed of too many diverse interests, a republic would fly apart.

It was little wonder, then, that the Americans in 1776 embarked on their experiment in republicanism in a spirit of great risk and high adventure. Nothing resembling their confederation of thirteen independent republican states had existed since the fall of Rome.

By 1787, however, American leaders had lost some of their earlier confidence in the American people's capacity for republicanism. Experience with popular government in the 1770s and 1780s, especially in the democratic state legislatures, had increasingly cast doubt on the people's virtue and disinterestedness. Selfish and local interests had captured majority control of the popularly elected legislatures and had used their lawmaking authority to promote their partial interests at the expense of the general good and minority rights. Such abuses of power by democratic state legislatures, wrote a concerned JAMES MADISON [3] in 1787, had brought "into question the fundamental principle of republican government, that the majority who rule in such governments are the safest guardians both of public good and of private rights." Suddenly the people's civic liberty, their participation in government, which lay at the heart of republicanism, seemed incompatible with their personal rights and liberties.

Such a conflict between majoritarian republicanism and minority rights had not been anticipated by the revolutionaries. The Americans of 1776 had thought that the people's republican participation in government was the best guarantee of the people's personal rights. They had assumed, said Madison in a series of 1780s letters, speeches, and working papers, culminating in his essays in THE FEDERALIST [2], that the people composing a republic "enjoy not only an equality of political rights, but that they have all precisely the same interests and the same feelings in every respect," which was why republics were supposed to be small in size. They had thought that in such small republics "the interest of the majority would be that of the minority also; the decisions could only turn on mere opinion concerning the good of the whole of which the major voice would be the safest criterion; and within a small sphere, this voice could be most easily collected and the public affairs most accurately managed."

Now, however, to Madison and other national leaders, with a decade's experience behind them, these assumptions about republicanism seemed "altogether fictitious." No society, no matter how small, "ever did or can consist of so homogeneous a mass of citizens." All "civilized societies" were made up of "various and unavoidable" economic distinctions and marketplace interests: rich and poor, creditors and debtors, farmers and manufacturers, merchants and bankers, and so on.

In a small republic, such as each of the thirteen states, it was sometimes possible for one of these competing factions or partial interests to exploit the popular electoral process and gain majority control of the legislature and pass laws oppressive of other groups and interests and contrary to the common interest of the community. This problem of tyrannical and factious legislative majorities, the contradiction between public and private liberty, was precisely what had troubled most of the states since 1776, and it was the principal cause of the crisis that had led to the formation of the new national Constitution. "To secure the public good and private rights against the danger of such a faction, and at the same time to preserve the spirit and the form of popular government," wrote

Madison, was "the great object to which our inquiries are directed."

Madison and other Framers solved the problem in 1787 by standing the body of conventional assumptions about the size of the republics on its head. Instead of trying to keep the republic small and homogeneous, Madison seized on, and ingeniously developed, David Hume's radical suggestion that a republican government operated better in a large territory than in a small one. The republic, said Madison, had to be so enlarged, "without departing from the elective basis of it," that "the propensity in small republics to rash measures and the facility of forming and executing them" would be stifled. In a large republican society "the people are broken into so many interests and parties, that a common sentiment is less likely to be felt, and the requisite concert less likely to be formed, by a majority of the whole." Madison and the other Framers, in other words, accepted the reality of diverse competing partial interests in American society and were quite willing to allow them free play in the society.

But not, it was hoped, in the new national government. Madison was not a modern-day pluralist. He did not expect the new federal government to be neutralized into inactivity by the competition of these numerous diverse interests. Nor did he see public policy or the common good emerging naturally from the give-and-take of these clashing interests. He did not expect the new national government to be an integrator and harmonizer of the different interests in the society; instead, he expected it to be a "disinterested and dispassionate umpire in disputes between different passions and interests in the State." And it would be able to play that role because the men holding office in the new central government would by their fewness of number and the largeness of the electoral districts most likely be "men who possess the most attractive merit, and the most diffusive and established characters." Thus, the Founding Fathers hoped that the new extended national republic would be led by enlightened men who were free of local constituent pressures and selfish marketplace concerns and who would deliberate in a disinterested manner and promote the general good. To this extent, the Framers clung to the tenets of classical republicanism.

But they clung even more firmly to the tenets of their belief in personal rights and liberties, whether defined as common law protections like HABEAS CORPUS [2,I] and TRIAL BY JURY [4] or as natural rights like a free conscience in matters of religion. Indeed, protecting these personal rights, including the individual's right to pursue happiness and property, was increasingly regarded as the principal end of government, to which republicanism was only a means, and not a very adequate one at that. Hence, SEPARATION OF POWER [4], CHECKS AND BALANCES [1], BILLS OF RIGHTS [1], the independent judiciary, and JUDICIAL REVIEW [3,I] all worked to limit the power of government and to undermine the classical republican reliance on the general will of a united people.

The democratic revolution of the decades following the creation of the Constitution further transformed the tradition of classical republicanism. In the North at least, it virtually destroyed the classical republican dream of an enlightened aristocracy acting as disinterested umpires over the economic and political struggles of the society. POLITICAL PARTIES [3] emerged to reestablish patronage and to promote the partisan local interests of people, and countless individuals took off in pursuit of their private happiness. By the middle of the nineteenth century, America gave as free a rein to commercial activity and the self-interestedness of people as any society in history.

But much of the republican tradition has remained alive, even to this day. Republicanism tempers the scramble for private wealth and happiness, and accounts for many of the Americans' ideals and aspirations: for their belief in equality and their dislike of pretension and privilege; for their relentless yearning for individual autonomy and freedom from all ties of dependency; for their periodic hopes that some political leaders might rise above parties and become truly disinterested umpires and deliberative representatives, hopes expressed, for example, in the election of military heroes and in the mugwump and Progressive movements; for their long-held conviction that farming is morally healthier and freer of selfish marketplace concerns than other activities; for their preoccupation with the fragility of the Republic and its liability to corruption; and, finally, for their remarkable obsession with their own national virtue—an obsession that still bewilders the rest of the world.

GORDON S. WOOD

(SEE ALSO: *Constitutional History Before 1776* [1]; *Constitutional History, 1776–1789* [1]; *Natural Rights and the Constitution* [3]; *Political Philosophy of the Constitution* [3,I]; *Republican Form of Government* [3]; *Social Compact Theory* [4].)

Bibliography
POCOCK, J. G. A.   1975   *The Machiavellian Moment: Florentine Political Thought and the Atlantic Republican Tradition.* Princeton, N.J.: Princeton University Press.

WOOD, GORDON S.   1969   *The Creation of the American Republic, 1776–1787.* Chapel Hill: University of North Carolina Press.

REPUBLICANISM AND MODERN CONSTITUTIONAL THEORY

Recent historical scholarship has traced a linkage between the civic tradition of republicanism and the Constitution devised by the Framers. The histories have turned academic American constitutional thought toward a renewed interest in traditional republican ideas about politics. Neorepublican scholarship seeks to adapt such ideas to various contemporary issues of constitutional-legal doctrine and practice.

Characteristically figuring in this neorepublican "revival" is a cluster of normative notions. As construed by contemporary legal scholars, republicanism demands strong accountability of the government to "the people" considered as their own ultimate rulers. It promotes active citizenship—participation in politics—as partially constitutive of the good life for all. It aims at public regarding laws that define rights in accord with consensually accepted values and set policies in accord with the general good. It urges sincerely deliberative, multivocal, independent-minded political debate ("dialogue") as the way to identify such values, rights, policies, and goods. It demands unrestricted access to political debate and influence for people from all sectors of society regardless of private means; looks askance at social hierarchies, material deprivations, and conflicts of interests that may compromise independent-minded, energetic, or public-spirited citizenship and governance; and seeks protection of cultural diversity and personal self-formation against undue governmental and social encroachment.

In moments of detached contemplation, all these aims and impulses may perhaps cohere as aspects of one aspirational vision of CONSTITUTIONALISM [2] or even as steps in an argument about how constitutionalism ought ideally to work. Set in the field of actual, contemporary American constitutional-legal disputation, however, republicanism figures not as a stock set of answers, but as an agenda of questions. In live contexts of dispute already framed by the past development of American constitutional-legal doctrine and practice, the various "republican" impulses have uncertain, controversial, and sometimes arguably inconsistent implications.

Consider how various "republican" aims have actually been invoked to generate positions in contemporary constitutional-legal debates. For example, republicanism insists strongly on the nonidentity of the sovereign people with the government and on the government's subservience to the people's will. From such insistence stems support for the idea judicially championed by Justice WILLIAM J. BRENNAN [1] and credited by him to ALEXANDER MEIKLEJOHN [3]: the "central meaning" of the FIRST AMENDMENT [2,I] is to secure the public forum of debate among citizens against governmental machination and control. Another republican precept, however, is that opportunity for access to this forum and influence in it should be equal for all regardless of wealth and other forms of social power. These two republican antipathies—to government control over the public forum and to socially

unequal access to the forum—have carried seemingly contradictory implications for constitutional-legal doctrine. In BUCKLEY V. VALEO [1], for example, the Supreme Court condemned legislative attempts to cap political campaign expenditures—professedly as a way of controlling domination of politics by the wealthy—as a departure from constitutionally required state neutrality.

Somewhat similarly, republican concern for the independent-minded public regarding quality of people's political motivations has produced diametrically opposed stances toward governmentally directed redistributions of wealth. From one side, it is argued that redistributions are required to assure the material prerequisites of political competence and independence to all who may participate, as voters or activists, in America's sweepingly democratic political system. From the other side, it is argued that by allowing governments to tamper with distribution we invite exactly the kind of self-serving political motivation that republicanism decries.

Out of regard for protecting cultural diversity and personal self-direction against potentially totalitarian control by the state, scholarship in the neorepublican vein has called for strong judicial enforcement of constitutional barriers (including UNENUMERATED RIGHTS [I]) against governmental encroachments on conscience, privacy, and association. At the same time, however, republican-style regard for the polity's underlying sense of solidarity has been cited by scholars and judges as justification for government restraint of arguably self-formative expression or conduct—a Nazi street march, a sexually explicit publication, homosexual sex in private—when construed as offensive or destructive to an enveloping political "community" or "tradition."

Out of regard for the public directedness of laws and for the deliberative quality of law making, some neorepublican scholarship has drawn a broader defense of wide-ranging JUDICIAL ACTIVISM [3]: Against partisan laws, such scholarship sets vigorous judicial scrutiny of the public justifications for statutes challenged under the equal protection and due process guaranties as "irrationally" discriminatory or injurious to liberty or property. Against narrowly strategic and self-serving legislative politics, such scholarship pictures appellate courts—actual or potential—as sites of open-minded deliberative dialogue. At the same time, however, republican encomia to active citizenship and popular self-government have put new energy into JAMES BRADLEY THAYER's [4] old objection to the habitually court-privileging character of American constitutional practice: It saps the people's determination to govern themselves.

A number of difficulties confront transplantation of historical republican thought to the contemporary American constitutional scene. First, the normative elements in republican thought depend on descriptive ones that are not fully true to contemporary American experience. Second, republicanism's valorization of political activity for its own sake, as an aspect of the good life, does not match prevailing American understanding. Third, republican thought is not easily reconcilable with the fixture of JUDICIAL SUPREMACY [3] in the American practice of constitutionalism.

When historians say that the Framers envisioned a constitutional scheme in which competent representatives deliberate and act in the common interest, this means that the Framers not only desired such a competent deliberative institution, but supposed they had successfully designed one in the Congress their charter constituted. But then, presumably, this supposition would have governed the Framers' conception of the judiciary's role, leaving little room for censorious JUDICIAL REVIEW [3,I] of the "rationality" of congressional action. Today, however, few Americans believe that Congress will or can be relied on to perform consistently up to the standard of the Madisonian deliberative model. How, in these circumstances, do we go about redeeming the Framers' design?

One answer offered by neorepublican scholarship is that reviewing courts should aggressively engage in "after the fact" evaluations of both the public merits of congressional enactments and the deliberative quality of congressional processes. The aim is to prevent, by deterrence and nullification, partisan or ill-conceived legislation that presumably would not have issued from a Congress actually functioning in accordance with Madisonian expectations. Leaving aside the difficulties of execution of this judicial commission, it is questionable republican doctrine. It does not speak to republicanism's attribution of value to direct personal engagement in the political process.

In the republican tradition, realization of the putative common good is not the whole point of broad-based political activity. A person's engagement, as an equal, in joint pursuit with others of the common good is republically valued as a vital aspect of personal freedom. It is far from clear how this personally emancipatory value of civic participation can at all be realized at two removes: first, from the people to the Congress and, then, from the Congress to the Court. It may be true that a person's ulterior interests can be represented in a functional sense, more or less accurately, by delegates. The experience of citizenship as public freedom, however, is a different matter. Freedom is representable, if at all, only pictorially, not functionally. Representation of interests may conceivably, if things go well, succeed in effectuating people's interests fairly. But representations—dramatizations—of freedom do not realize people's freedom.

Here, historical republicanism may seem to offer assistance. Traditional republican thought articulates political activity into distinct and complementary roles—including those of electors as well as of officials—and professes to see the juice of political freedom flowing through all the circuits. This idea occurs not only in canonical republican writings, such as those of James Harrington; it is apparent as well in the thought of American Framers such as JAMES WILSON [4]. The idea supposes that everyone can be politically active, in the freedom-conferring way, in public encounters by which we elect, instruct, and evaluate political representatives. It depends, however, on what today seems an unacceptably inegalitarian assignment of a good—"positive" (participatory) political freedom—that by republicanism's own account is humanly fundamental. Moreover, it attributes to electoral politics a liveliness, immediacy, and accessibility that contemporary American experience cannot easily credit.

In view of contemporary realities in the political life of the continental republic, some observers conclude that the best that can now be done on behalf of the republican strain in constitutional thought is to protect and nurture civic dialogic engagement not within the national constitutional setup, but beyond it. Such observers see local associations, both governmental and nongovernmental, as the realms that in modern life remain for the "positive" freedom of political action. With varying emphases, they accordingly suggest that constitutional law best serves this freedom through judicial specification and enforcement of supportive legal rights respecting municipal and associational autonomy, political expression, cultural and ideological diversity, personal self-formation through associations both intimate and civic, and personal independence construed as "liberty" and "property." In effect, the suggestion is to pump content from civic-republican wellsprings into the liberal doctrine of LIMITED GOVERNMENT [3]; it is to direct a participatory-communitarian ideology of politics to the purposes of a judicially administered, libertarian HIGHER LAW [2].

This makes for a troubled, diluted republicanism. In quintessential republican thought, a right against the government is strictly a matter of here-and-now popular political will. Such a right can exert no force against the political resolutions that alone confer its existence. In quintessential republican thought, if there are constitutional rights, this is only because and insofar as the people politically engaged have so resolved. This is rather a far cry from the judge-led constitutionalism on which Americans have come to rely for assurance of their liberties. The republican premise that the polity, with good fortune, can lead itself by unconstrained political deliberation to a duly libertarian general will is one for which modern political wisdom does not easily allow. Political modernism not only denies the existence of any publicly demonstrable and compelling moral reality; it further doubts the possibility on which quintessential republican thought is grounded: that political conversation, unconstrained by an externally enforced higher law of rights, can itself sustain the social conditions of a true dialogic concourse of free persons.

FRANK I. MICHELMAN

(SEE ALSO: *Republicanism and Constitutional History* [I].)

Bibliography

EPSTEIN, RICHARD A. 1987 Beyond the Rule of Law: Civic Virtue and Constitutional Structure. *George Washington Law Review* 56:149–171.

FALLON, RICHARD H., JR. 1981 What Is Republicanism, and Is It Worth Reviving? *Harvard Law Review* 102:1695–1735.

MICHELMAN, FRANK I. 1986 The Supreme Court, 1985 Term—Foreward: Traces of Self-Government. *Harvard Law Review* 100:4–77.

——— 1990 Tutelary Jurisprudence and Constitutional Property. In Ellen Paul and Howard Dickman, eds., *Liberty, Property, and the Future of Constitutional Development*, pages 127–171. Albany: State University of New York Press.

SYMPOSIUM 1987 Republicanism and Liberalism in American Constitutional Thought. *William and Mary Law Review* 29:57–112.

SYMPOSIUM 1989 The Civic Republican Tradition. *Yale Law Journal* 97:1493–1723.

REPUBLICAN PARTY

The Republican party was organized in response to the KANSAS-NEBRASKA ACT (1854) [3], which allowed SLAVERY [4] in the Kansas and Nebraska territories. This was a repudiation of the MISSOURI COMPROMISE (1820) [3], which had prohibited all SLAVERY IN THE TERRITORIES [4] west and north of Missouri and for a generation had served as the basis of all sectional accommodation on slavery and territorial settlement. This new political organization was initially known as the Anti-Nebraska party.

As a coalition of former Whigs, antislavery Democrats, former Know-Nothings, and abolitionists who had been in the Liberty and Free-Soil parties, Republicans differed among themselves on such issues as currency, banking, and tariffs. But they all agreed on the need to stop the extension of slavery in the territories. In his "House Divided" speech of 1858 ABRAHAM LINCOLN [3] expressed this view, noting that he wanted to "arrest the further spread of it [slavery], and place it where the public mind shall rest in the belief that it is in the course of ultimate extinction." Republicans were also motivated by the fear that freedom was actually on the defensive and that a "slave-power conspiracy" threatened the liberty of all Americans.

Especially after the decision in DRED SCOTT V. SANDFORD (1857) [2], Republicans feared a nationalization of slavery. Lincoln worried there might soon be "another Supreme Court decision, declaring that the Constitution of the United States does not permit a *state* to exclude slavery from its limits. . . . We shall lie down pleasantly dreaming that the people of Missouri are on the verge of making their State free; and we shall awake to the reality, instead, that the Supreme Court has made Illinois a slave state." The implications of *Dred Scott* were clear to Republican leaders. Lincoln argued that "the logical conclusion" from Chief Justice ROGER BROOKE TANEY's [4] opinion was "that what Dred Scott's master might lawfully do with Dred Scott, in the free State of Illinois, every other master might lawfully do with any other one, or one thousand slaves, in Illinois, or in any other free State." In 1856, Senator Henry Wilson, a future vice-president, stated that the party's "object is to overthrow the Slave Power of the country."

This battle with the slave-power conspiracy did not mean an all-out assault on slavery wherever it existed. Most Republicans agreed, however reluctantly, that the Constitution did not permit the federal government to interfere with slavery in the states. Some Republicans, including Lincoln, even acknowledged the constitutional obligation to return fugitive slaves, although many other leading Republicans, including SALMON P. CHASE [1], WILLIAM SEWARD [4], and THADDEUS STEVENS [4], were active in defending fugitive slaves and their white allies.

Whatever their differences over the fugitive slave laws, Republicans agreed that the Constitution was fundamentally antislavery. This interpretation was at odds with both the southern view and the abolitionist view of WILLIAM LLOYD GARRISON [2] that the Constitution was a proslavery compact and thus a "covenant with death." Republicans tied their CONSTITUTIONAL THEORY [I] to the DECLARATION OF INDEPENDENCE [2] to argue that the thrust of the Constitution—the intent of the Framers—was against slavery.

The constitutional principles of the antebellum Republican party can be organized around the party's election slogan—Free Soil, Free Labor, Free Speech, Free Men—and by the party's endorsement of the principles of the Declaration of Independence.

"Free Soil" had two meanings for the Republicans. First, it meant closing the territories to slave settlement. Until the Civil War mooted the issue, Republicans consistently opposed allowing any new slave states into the Union and fought against allowing masters to bring their slaves into any of the territories. They argued that Congress had full authority to prohibit all slavery in the territories. This left the party in a constitutional quandary after the ruling in *Dred Scott v. Sandford*. Republicans could not maintain their Free Soil position without opposing the Supreme Court. They tried to extricate themselves from this dilemma by asserting that Taney's rulings on the power of Congress over slavery in the territories and on the status of free blacks to sue in federal courts were OBITER DICTA [3] that had no legitimate constitutional authority. The Republican editor Horace Greeley declared in the *New York Tribune* that Taney's opinion was "atrocious," "wicked," "abominable," and had no more constitutional authority than what might be heard in any "Washington bar-room."

Republicans also believed that "Free Soil" should dictate national policy on western lands. Thus, the party supported the HOMESTEAD ACT [2] and the MORRILL ACT [3] as ways of stimulating western settlement.

The Republican commitment to "Free Labor" centered on the dignity of labor, the importance of individual enterprise in nineteenth-century northern society, and a middle class culture of hard work. One Iowa Republican proclaimed that America's greatness was based on the fact that "even the poorest and humblest in the land, may, by industry and application, attain a position which will entitle him to the respect and confidence of his fellowmen." Free labor was also the opposite of slave labor. Free labor meant "Free Men" to Republicans. While the party opposed the extension of slavery, Republicans acknowledged that the national government had no power to end slavery in the states. But, wherever the national government had power over slavery, Republicans wanted to exercise that power.

Tied to the free-labor and free-men beliefs of Republicans was strong support, at least for the era, for black rights. Republicans were horrified by Chief Justice Taney's assertion in *Dred Scott* that blacks could not be citizens of the United States or sue in federal courts. In states like Massachusetts, where blacks could vote, Republicans worked for full integration. In states like Iowa, Wisconsin, and Connecticut, where blacks could not vote, Republicans worked to remove race as a criterion for suffrage. Not all Republicans were racial egalitarians, but most believed in minimal equality for blacks, even if they opposed full social and political equality. The connection between some racial fairness and free labor was articulated by Lincoln in his debate with STEPHEN A. DOUGLAS [2] at Quincy, Illinois: "There is no reason in the world why the negro is not entitled to all the rights enumerated in the Declaration of Independence—the right of life, liberty and the pursuit of happiness. I hold that he is as much entitled to these as the white man. I agree with Judge Douglas that he is not my equal in many respects, certainly not in color—perhaps not in intellectual and moral endowments; but in the right to eat the bread without leave of anybody else which his own hand earns, he is my equal and the equal of Judge Douglas, and the equal of every other man."

The party was also committed to "Free Speech" and other basic CIVIL LIBERTIES [1,I]. Republicans believed that the South had violated the BILL OF RIGHTS [1] by suppressing freedom of expression and that the South and slavery stood for the suppression of FREEDOM OF SPEECH [2,I] and violence against any who dared to oppose slavery. This belief was given credence by the banning of *Uncle Tom's Cabin* in most of the South and such incidents as the caning of Senator CHARLES SUMNER [4] by Congressman Preston Brooks of South Carolina and the expulsion from South Carolina and Louisiana of two Massachusetts commissioners who were attempting to negotiate an end to the arrest of free black sailors entering those states. Republicans believed that the Bill of Rights restricted the states, as well as the federal government, and that BARRON V. CITY OF BALTIMORE (1833) [1], the leading precedent on this issue (which reached the opposite conclusion), had been wrongly decided.

The greatest test of Republican constitutional theory was SECESSION [4] and the Civil War. Republicans firmly believed that the Union was "perpetual" and could not be broken by any state or group of states. Republicans rejected the radical Garrisonian view that there should be "no union with slaveholders." The Republicans likewise rejected the southern notion that secession was permissible. Lincoln declared in his inaugural, "I hold that, in contemplation of universal law and of the Constitution, the Union of these States is perpetual."

In the Civil War era Republicans constitutionalized much of their thought and theory. The THIRTEENTH AMENDMENT [4] ended slavery, the FOURTEENTH AMENDMENT [2,I] overturned the doctrine of *Dred Scott* on black CITIZENSHIP [1,I], and the FIFTEENTH AMENDMENT [2] enfranchised blacks on the same basis as whites. Through the PRIVILEGES AND IMMUNITIES [3] and DUE PROCESS [2] clauses of the Fourteenth Amendment, Republicans appeared to apply the Bill of Rights to the states, thus overturning *Barron v. Baltimore*. Finally, through the EQUAL PROTECTION [2] and due process clauses of the Fourteenth Amendment, Republicans seemed to guarantee substantive equality to blacks all over the nation. Supreme Court decisions in the SLAUGHTERHOUSE CASES (1873) [4], CIVIL RIGHTS CASES (1883) [1], and PLESSY V. FERGUSON (1896) [3] undermined the Republican goals of a nationalization of CIVIL RIGHTS [1,I] and civil liberties. The late-nineteenth-century Supreme Court, although dominated by Republicans, failed to interpret the new amendments in light of the party's antebellum constitutional theory.

PAUL FINKELMAN

Bibliography

FEHRENBACHER, DON E. 1978 *The Dred Scott Case*. New York: Oxford University Press.

FINKELMAN, PAUL 1981 *An Imperfect Union: Slavery, Federalism, and Comity*. Chapel Hill: University of North Carolina Press.

FONER, ERIC 1970 *Free Soil, Free Labor, Free Men: The Ideology of the Republican Party*. New York: Oxford University Press.

HYMAN, HAROLD M. and WIECEK, WILLIAM M. 1982 *Equal Justice Under Law: Constitutional Developments, 1837–1877*. New York: Harper and Row.

RESIDENTIAL SEGREGATION

Residential segregation refers to the physical or spatial separation of groups. While residential segregation along racial and ethnic lines affects various groups, its most persistent and pervasive manifestations primarily disadvantage African Americans. SEGREGATION [4] is both a condition of life and a process of group differentiation and distinction. As condition and process, it is closely related to INVIDIOUS DISCRIMINATION [2]. The condition of segregation is primarily that of social and territorial isolation and containment. Now, as in the past, the basis of segregation is the actual or perceived incompatibility of groups due to conflicts in values, interests, behavior, and associational preferences. As a legacy of SLAVERY [4,], black–white racial segregation has served in significant part as a substitute for caste. Segregation continues today as a part of the ideology of the color line, implicitly defining the African American's place, role, and status.

Racial segregation in American cities and metropolitan areas is marked both by the large extent of racial separation of blacks from whites within and between given neighborhoods and by the pattern of blacks concentrated in central cities and whites dispersed throughout the suburbs. African Americans are now an urban people, with eighty percent of them residing in cities. The high degree of segregation tends to isolate African Americans—and, to a lesser degree, Hispanics and Asians—from amenities, opportunities, and resources that benefit social and economic well-being.

During the first half of this century, the "Great Migration" of the southern black population primarily to the urban North and Midwest was a significant factor in creating a national presence and elevating the so-called Negro problem into one of national dimensions. This change inspired blacks to press their unfulfilled claims not only on the nation's moral sense but also on its lawmaking institutions, including the courts. National principles, supported by constitutional law, became a principal means of attacking inequality of fact and opportunity.

Although the Supreme Court decision in BROWN V. BOARD OF EDUCATION (1954) [1] is more celebrated, challenges to residential segregation preceded attacks on segregation in public schools. These residential segregation cases focused on two segregation props, racially zoned municipal areas and RESTRICTIVE COVENANTS [3] related to transferring property. In BUCHANAN V. WARLEY (1917) [1], fifty years after the FOURTEENTH AMENDMENT [2,I] was ratified, the Supreme Court relied on the amendment's due process clause to invalidate a municipal ordinance that prohibited blacks from purchasing or occupying a dwelling located on any block where a majority of the dwellings were white-occupied. The Supreme Court struck down similar acts of de jure segregation in *Harmon v. Taylor* (1927) and in *City of Richmond v. Deans* (1930).

One white reaction to the *Buchanan* decision was the restrictive covenant, a contractual devise by which purchasers of real property assume an obligation not to dispose of the property to certain designated classes (i.e., blacks particularly and non-Caucasians generally). In 1948, as part of the black campaign against residential segregation, the Supreme Court held in SHELLEY V. KRAEMER (1948) [4] that state court enforcement of the restrictive covenants was unconstitutional STATE ACTION [4,I] that violated the Fourteenth Amendment's EQUAL PROTECTION [2,I] clause.

During the 1950s the federal government began to take steps toward weakening the de jure basis of racial segregation. Simultaneously, however, across the land racial homogeneity was being established by white surburbanization. This movement solidified the de facto basis of racial segregation in housing and therefore in schools as well. As historian Richard Polenberg has observed, "Suburbanization encouraged the growth of a racially segmented society, offering a classic example of how demographic trends would work at cross purposes with constitutional, political, and social change." Suburbanization, however, was not simply a matter of demographics, family settlement, and economic opportunity. Political decisions at the state, local, and federal levels not only contributed heavily to suburbanization but also to its virtually all-white nature.

The city–suburbs segregation has become a subject of special importance because arguably the exclusion of blacks from the suburbs denies them access to newer, better-quality housing, less crime-ridden neighborhoods, public schools with higher-achieving students, new and viable job opportunities, and local governments with adequate tax bases to support appropriate municipal services delivery. For many blacks, however, there are certain drawbacks to suburban integration, because it may dilute central-city black voting strength and rob central-city black communities of potential leadership and representation.

Moreover, stable integration that depends on relatively low numbers of blacks to avoid neighborhood tipping, white flight, and resegregation preempts the potential for social cohesiveness and the maintenance of black identity.

Although the legacy of racism directed toward African Americans had virtually frozen in the effects of past residential discrimination and segregation by the 1960s, the modern era of OPEN HOUSING LAWS [3] did not begin until 1968. Four significant events occurred that year within months of each other: first, on March 1, the Kerner Commission released the *Report of the National Advisory Commission on Civil Disorders;* second, on April 4, MARTIN LUTHER KING, JR. [3], was assassinated; third, on April 11, President LYNDON B. JOHNSON [3] signed into law Title VIII of the CIVIL RIGHTS ACT OF 1968 (the Fair Housing Act) [1]; and fourth, on June 17, the Supreme Court revitalized the CIVIL RIGHTS ACT OF 1866 [1] when it decided JONES V. ALFRED H. MAYER CO. (1968) [1], making it clear that this statute, enforcing the THIRTEENTH AMENDMENT [4], prohibited both public and private acts of RACIAL DISCRIMINATION [3,I] in the sale or leasing of housing.

The Kerner Commission report recognized that the nation was rapidly moving toward two separate Americas and that within two decades, "this division could be so deep that it would be almost impossible to unite." The societies described were blacks concentrated within large central cities and whites located in the suburbs, in smaller cities, and on the periphery of large central cities. The report also recognized that community enrichment had to be an important adjunct to integration, "for no matter how ambitious or energetic the program, few Negroes now living in central cities can be quickly integrated. In the meantime, large-scale improvement in the quality of ghetto life is essential." Many commentators see the Kerner Commission report and Dr. King's assassination as precipitating passage of the Fair Housing Act, similar legislation having failed to pass in 1966 and 1967.

Title VIII, the nation's primary open housing law, contains broad prohibitions against public and private housing discrimination, including lending and brokering practices. The act prohibits discrimination on the basis of race, national origin, religion, or sex. As amended in 1988, the law now also includes as protected classes the handicapped and families with children. The act provides for independent enforcement by private lawsuits or Justice Department lawsuits, as well as enforcement through the administrative channels of the Department of Housing and Urban Development (HUD). Prior to the 1988 amendments, federal administrative enforcement power was largely ineffective, restricted to conciliation.

In the late 1960s and early 1970s, fair housing advocates focused heavily on integrating suburbs. A primary target was economic-racial exclusionary land use practices. Although exclusionary ZONING [4,I] was seen as the principal device for maintaining the race- and class-based segregation of inner-city residents, other local government exclusionary devices often worked in combination with zoning. Those devices included voter initiatives and referenda, as in JAMES V. VALTIERRA (1971) [3], HUNTER V. ERICKSON (1969) [2], and REITMAN V. MULKEY (1967) [3]; withdrawal from, or nonparticipation in, housing and community development programs designed to benefit the poor; tactics of delay and obstruction of private efforts to develop low-income housing; privately caused displacement; publicly supported urban revitalization or gentrification that displaced nonwhite residents; and HUD's sale of formerly subsidized properties acquired through foreclosure, without protecting the low-income character of those properties.

In the area of exclusionary zoning on the basis of race, two significant Supreme Court equal protection cases were decided in the 1970s, *Warth v. Seldin* (1975) and ARLINGTON HEIGHTS V. METROPOLITAN HOUSING DEVELOPMENT CORPORATION (1977) [1]. In *Warth* a 5–4 majority held that plaintiffs, who included low-income housing developers, prospective tenants, and local tax-paying residents, all lacked STANDING [4] to challenge the town's zoning ordinance that prevented the construction of low- or moderate-income housing. According to the Court, plaintiffs' allegations were insufficient to demonstrate "an actionable causal relationship between Penfield's zoning practices and petitioners' asserted injury." The Court found, among other facts, that no specific project was ready for development and likely occupancy by the poor and nonwhite plaintiffs. Moreover, the townspeople's "right to live" in an integrated community was seen by the Court as an "indirect harm" that resulted from the exclusion of others and thus violated the prudential standing rule that prohibits the assertion of rights on behalf of third parties.

The *Arlington Heights* opinion reaffirmed the WASHINGTON V. DAVIS (1976) [4] holding that violation of the equal protection clause required evidence of discriminatory purpose, and held that even evidence of such a purpose would not necessarily invalidate state action; it would merely shift to defendant the burden of showing that "the same decision would have resulted even had the impermissible purpose not been considered."

Title VIII claims, on the other hand, aside from applying to PRIVATE DISCRIMINATION [I], revealed two clear advantages to claimants over equal protection claims: (1) standing was broadly defined, as even the rights of third parties could be asserted (*Trafficante v. Metropolitan Life Insurance Company*, 1972, and *Havens Realty Corporation v. Coleman*, 1982), and (2) discriminatory effects would establish a claim for relief.

The protracted institutional litigation associated with the *Gautreaux* case—begun in 1967 and producing thirty-four opinions, including one Supreme Court opinion, HILLS V. GAUTREAUX (1976) [2]—successfully challenged the Chicago Housing Authority's site selection and tenant assignment as violations of the equal protection clause and the Fair Housing Act. The Supreme Court opinion in *Gautreaux* distinguished the case from MILLIKEN V. BRADLEY (1974) [3], which had overturned a lower court decision ordering interdistrict busing of public school children in Detroit and its suburbs as a desegregation remedy. In *Gautreaux* the Court granted such metropolitan relief, obligating HUD to act beyond Chicago's boundaries in effectuating desegregation of the housing authority buildings. The Court distinguished *Gautreaux* from *Milliken* by emphasizing that the federal government had violated its constitutional equal protection obligations; the interdistrict remedy was commensurate with the constitutional violation. Although *Gautreaux* was hailed as a doctrinal success, its remedial results were, at best, mixed. For many years no public housing was produced in Chicago or in the metropolitan areas, and many intended beneficiaries chose not to avail themselves of the limited access to housing beyond Chicago.

During the 1980s the Supreme Court diluted the effectiveness of the 1866 Civil Rights Act. In MEMPHIS V. GREENE (1981) [3] the Supreme Court upheld a white neighborhood's street closure that blocked black access to the city through the white neighborhood. The Court held that this closure did not sufficiently implicate black property rights and therefore the act was not violated. Moreover, the Court concluded that the facts indicated an inconvenience to blacks, but not a BADGE OF SERVITUDE [1] that could violate the Thirteenth Amendment.

A year after *Greene*, in *General Building Contractors Association v. Pennsylvania* (1982), the Supreme Court found that a related provision of the 1866 act required intentional discrimination to constitute a violation. In light of *General Building Contractors* most lower federal courts are requiring intent as part of all fair-housing claims under the 1866 act. Thus, Title VIII now virtually stands alone as a viable basis for challenging private action that causes racially discriminatory effects. In *Huntington Branch NAACP v. Town of Huntington* (1988) the Supreme Court endorsed the discriminatory-effect theory for Title VIII claims in a limited per curiam affirmance.

Housing segregation is often closely related to de facto public school segregation. In the highly publicized case of *United States v. Yonkers Board of Education* (1987), a Second Circuit opinion affirmed the trial court's finding that the city had confined its subsidized housing to areas of concentrated nonwhite population and that this action had contributed to the segregation of the city's public schools. As a remedy the district court ordered the city to permit construction of subsidized housing in white, nonpoor residential areas and to implement a magnet-school program. When the city council refused to implement the housing plan, the court held both the city and the council members in contempt, levying substantial fines. The Supreme Court in *Spallone v. United States* (1990) upheld the fines against the city, but disapproved the fines against individual council members.

There is growing black skepticism and loss of faith in integration, particularly in light of the disproportionately high poverty rate of blacks and the continuously high rates of housing segregation for blacks of all socioeconomic classes. At the time of Title VIII's enactment, its sponsors thought that the statute's emphasis on antidiscrimination would lead to residential integration. Congress perceived antisegregation and antidiscrimination as complementary remedies. Often, however, in the name of integration or desegregation, racial discrimination against individuals has occurred and housing opportunities actually have been decreased. In the principal "integration maintenance" decision, *United States v. Starret City Associates* (1988), the Supreme Court denied certiorari, leaving intact a Second Circuit decision holding that Title VIII was violated by a RACIAL QUOTA [3] limiting black access to an apartment complex in order to maintain integration. Interestingly, the NAACP supported the Justice Department's challenge to the integration maintenance scheme at issue.

Housing persists as one of black America's most intractable social issues. For most of white America, on the other hand, home ownership in a supportive neighborhood of choice represents the highest achievement in terms of status and material acquisition, while simultaneously serving to validate the incentives associated with equality of opportunity. This vision of the American dream, however, is sullied and distorted by racism and economic subjugation. Even accepting the moral imperative and the practical necessity of integrated housing for the national commonwealth, it is difficult to escape the conclusion of Derrick Bell: "Discrimination in housing, with its vices of segregated housing patterns and inadequate and overpriced housing for minorities, continues to be one of those areas where the law is unable or unwilling to keep up with conditions in the real world."

JOHN O. CALMORE

Bibliography

CALMORE, JOHN O. 1989 To Make Wrong Right: The Necessary and Proper Aspirations of Fair Housing. Pages 77–110 in Janet Dewart, ed., *The State of Black America 1989.* New York: National Urban League.

GOERING, JOHN, ED., 1986 *Housing Desegregation and Federal Policy.* Chapel Hill: University of North Carolina Press.

KUSHNER, JAMES A. 1983 *Fair Housing: Discrimination in Real Estate, Community Development and Revitalization.* Colorado Springs, Colo.: Shepards/McGraw-Hill.

SCHWEMM, ROBERT 1990 *Housing Discrimination Law and Litigation.* New York: Clark Boardman Company, Ltd.

REVERSE DISCRIMINATION

See: Race Consciousness [I]; Racial Preference [I] Racial Quotas [3]

RICHMOND (CITY OF) v. J. A. CROSON CO.
488 U.S. 469 (1989)

In FULLILOVE V. KLUTZNICK (1980) [2] the Supreme Court upheld an act of Congress requiring that ten percent of certain federal subsidies to local governments be set aside for contractors that were minority-owned business enterprises (MBE). In *Croson* the Court invalidated a similar AFFIRMATIVE ACTION [1,I] ordinance adopted by a city. The ordinance, adopted for a five-year term, required a prime contractor to allocate thirty percent of the dollar amount of the contract to MBE subcontractors. A waiver was authorized in the event that MBE were not available. The Court held, 6–3, that this scheme denied nonminority businesses the EQUAL PROTECTION OF THE LAWS [2,I].

Justice SANDRA DAY O'CONNOR [3,I] wrote an opinion that was in part the OPINION OF THE COURT [3] and in part a PLURALITY OPINION [3]. A majority concurred in the opinion's basic building blocks: that the appropriate standard of review for a state and local affirmative action program was STRICT SCRUTINY [4]; that the city had not offered sufficient evidence of "identified discrimination" that could justify a race-conscious remedy; and that the city's program, even if it were remedial, was not sufficiently narrowly tailored to such discrimination. In addition, she spoke for a plurality in concluding that Congress's remedial powers, unlike those of the states, could extend to remedying past societal discrimination. (See FOURTEENTH AMENDMENT AND SECTION 5 [JUDICIAL CONSTRUCTION] [I].) Justice ANTHONY M. KENNEDY [I], concurring, dissociated himself from the latter position, and Justice ANTONIN SCALIA [I], also concurring, argued that the city had power to use race-conscious remedies only for its own discrimination. Justice JOHN PAUL STEVENS [4,I] concurred only in the view that Richmond's plan was not justified by sufficient evidence of past discrimination and was not narrowly tailored.

Justice O'Connor concluded that Richmond could constitutionally provide a race-conscious remedy not only for its own past discrimination but also for past discrimination by private contractors or trade associations in the Richmond area. She also concluded that such discrimination might be proved by statistics showing a serious disparity between the percentage of qualified MBE in the area and the percentage of contracts awarded to MBE. Here, however, the city had shown only that the MBE contracts were extremely low in comparison with the percentage of minorities in Richmond's general population. To achieve a "narrowly tailored" program, she said, Richmond would have to show that race-neutral alternatives were unworkable, and to peg its MBE set-aside percentage at a figure that bore a clearly stated relation to the percentage of qualified MBE.

Justice THURGOOD MARSHALL [3,I] wrote a sharply worded opinion for the three dissenters. He argued that strict scrutiny was inappropriate and that Richmond's ordinance served the important purposes of remedying the effects of a pattern of past discrimination and keeping the city from reinforcing that pattern. He found the Richmond council's conclusions about past discrimination, both by the city and by private contractors, to be soundly based. Justice HARRY A. BLACKMUN [1,I] also dissented.

Although many civil rights advocates regarded *Croson* as a serious setback for affirmative action, it may turn out, like REGENTS OF UNIVERSITY OF CALIFORNIA V. BAKKE (1978) [4], to be a blessing in disguise for their cause. Certainly, *Croson*'s standards for affirmative action in state and local government contracting will, in some communities, prevent any effective affirmative action. One of the legacies of RACIAL DISCRIMINATION [3,I] is the paucity of minority businesses in many of the fields in which governments offer contracts. However, Justice O'Connor's explicit approval of statistical proof of past discrimination offers considerable opportunity, particularly for states and for large cities, to satisfy the Court's requirements. More important, six Justices not only reaffirmed the *Fullilove* precedent, which had seemed vulnerable, but also issued to Congress a sweeping invitation to engage in broad-scale affirmative action of its own aimed at remedying the effects of past societal discrimination.

KENNETH L. KARST

(SEE ALSO: *Race-Consciousness* [I]; *Racial Preference* [I].)

Bibliography

Constitutional Scholars' Statement on Affirmative Action After City of Richmond v. J. A. Croson Co. 1989 *Yale Law Journal* 98:1711–1716.

FRIED, CHARLES 1989 Affirmative Action After City of Richmond v. J. A. Croson Co., A Response to the Scholars' Statement. *Yale Law Journal* 99:155–161.

Scholars' Reply to Professor Fried 1989 *Yale Law Journal* 99:163–168.

RIGHT AGAINST SELF-INCRIMINATION
(Update)

In the original edition of this *Encyclopedia*, Leonard W. Levy characterized the right against self-incrimination as "the most misunderstood, unrespected, and controversial of all constitutional rights," yet stressed that the Supreme Court "has tended to give it an ever widening meaning" unconfined by textual literalism. Recent Fifth Amendment jurisprudence has brought an end to this expansion of scope without clarifying the theoretical underpinnings of the right. While scholars propose and criticize alternative conceptual foundations for this right, the Supreme Court has been content to point to a grab bag of motivations, including humaneness to suspects, commitment to "accusatorial" procedures and a fair state-individual balance, distrust of confessions, concern for privacy, and respect for the human personality. The Court has made little effort to assign different weights or distinct roles to these concerns or to link them explicitly to the outcomes of particular cases. Current law indeed suggests that the Court's primary aim is to prevent the right against self-incrimination from interfering unduly with the paramount truth-finding function of the CRIMINAL JUSTICE SYSTEM [I].

Achieving this aim is particularly difficult because the Fifth Amendment, unlike the FOURTH AMENDMENT [2,I], does not prohibit only "unreasonable" intrusions on the right that it protects; thus, the Court is at least officially reluctant to "balance" the Fifth Amendment right against competing government interests. Moreover, the Fifth Amendment appears on its face to forbid admission of EVIDENCE [2] compelled from the defendant, leaving no room to argue—as with the Fourth Amendment—that exclusion of improperly obtained evidence is a judicially created remedy to which courts may freely create exceptions. The Fifth Amendment right must instead be limited by the manner in which it is defined and by the explanations given to the key terms in that definition.

The right against self-incrimination forbids the government to compel an individual to provide testimonial or communicative evidence that could be used to incriminate that individual. Only a natural person, not an organization, can claim this right, but not with regard to items a person holds as custodian for an organization. However, it may be claimed in any forum in which government seeks to compel a response, whether by legal process or through the informal coercive pressures of police interrogation, and with regard to any item that could potentially furnish a link in a chain of incriminating evidence, even though not sufficient in itself to convict. In most contexts, this right is deemed waived unless actively claimed by the right holder, and it is inapplicable to evidence for whose disclosure the government grants the right holder IMMUNITY [2] (against any use, direct or indirect, to convict the right holder of crime).

MIRANDA V. ARIZONA (1966) [3], which extended the right against self-incrimination to the POLICE INTERROGATION [3,I] context, established special rules for this setting, elaborated in subsequent opinions. Statements by a person interrogated while in custody are presumed compelled, and hence, are inadmissible at trial to prove guilt, unless the suspect is told before the interrogation that he or she has the right to remain silent, to consult a lawyer before any questioning, and to have the lawyer present during questioning; that a lawyer will be provided if the suspect wants but cannot afford one; and that anything the suspect says can be used against him or her in court. If the suspect requests a lawyer, no questioning is permitted until one is provided, unless the suspect initiates further discussion with the police. If the suspect consents to questioning but subsequently indicates a desire to remain silent, the interrogation must cease.

The principal recent developments have arisen in two quite different contexts. One is the police-interrogation setting—unique because (as will be discussed) the detailed rules of *Miranda* and its progeny are only tenuously related to the constitutional ban on compelled self-incrimination. The other development, which unequivocally implicates the constitutional right itself, comprises efforts by investigatory targets to resist official demands for the production of evidence that could potentially lead to criminal charges. Opinions in both areas exhibit the Court's efforts to minimize interference with the truth-finding process.

The recent police-interrogation decisions preserve the *Miranda* doctrine while restricting its scope. The Court's reluctance to overrule *Miranda* outright is surprising in light of opinions strikingly eroding the doctrine's legitimacy. These opinions, culminating in OREGON V. ELSTAD (1985) [3], view the *Miranda* doctrine not as commanded or entailed by the Fifth Amendment, but as a set of "prophylactic rules" devised by the Court to forestall genuine constitutional violations. Breach of *Miranda*'s requirements need not, therefore, violate the constitutional right against self-incrimination. This view leaves the Court free (as in *Elstad*) to hold certain evidence derived from such a breach admissible in circumstances in which the fruits of a constitutional violation must be suppressed. But it also undermines the very foundation of *Miranda*: why may the Court require police to obey rules that the Court itself concedes are neither required by the Constitution nor imposed to remedy constitutional violations? Both friends and critics of *Miranda* suggested that the Court was preparing to discard the doctrine altogether.

This has not happened, however, nor have opinions since *Elstad* crucially exploited the nonconstitutional status of *Miranda*. Rather, the Court has simply narrowed *Miranda*'s reach in various ways. "Interrogation," which triggers the warning requirement, includes conduct the police should know is likely to prompt incriminating admissions. Yet *Arizona v. Mauro* (1987) held that allowing (and recording) a meeting between an arrestee and his wife was not "interrogation," despite police awareness that such admissions might occur. Telling an unsophisticated suspect that a lawyer would be appointed "if and when you go to court" could cast doubt on the required notice that the lawyer would be provided "before any questioning." Yet *Duckworth v. Eagan* (1989) found no ambiguity, analyzing the amended warnings from a legally knowledgeable standpoint.

Most notably, the Court has repudiated suggestions—arguably latent in *Miranda* itself—that the *Miranda* doctrine guarantees a "rational," "responsible," or "fully informed" choice between silence and speech. Instead, the Court treats the doctrine solely as forestalling coercion and has found WAIVERS OF THE CONSTITUTIONAL RIGHT [4] to silence valid in a variety of situations where the suspect's decision was less than "rational" or "fully informed." In *Moran v. Burbine* (1986), the police did not tell the suspect that a lawyer hired by his sister was trying to reach him. In *Colorado v. Barrett* (1987) the suspect apparently thought only written statements could be used against him. In *Colorado v. Spring* (1987) a suspect arrested for a firearms violation agreed to talk without knowing he would be questioned about an earlier murder in a different jurisdiction. Most strikingly, COLORADO V. CONNELLY (1986) [I] found voluntary a *Miranda* waiver by a MENTALLY ILL [3,I] suspect in the grip of paranoid delusions, reasoning that only official coercion would render a waiver "involuntary."

In its *Miranda* jurisprudence the Court is dealing with what it views as a judge-made supplement to the right against self-incrimination. Its desire to keep the doctrine within narrow bounds may thus say little about the Court's commitment to the core concerns animating this right. The recent decisions concerning production of evidence, however, evince a readiness to limit the Fifth Amendment right itself.

In *Fisher v. United States* (1976) the Court distinguished the contents of items sought by the government and the act of producing those items. Each requires separate analysis, and the Fifth Amendment is violated only if either the contents or act of production is, by itself, compelled, testimonial, and incriminating. (In effect, as Peter Arenella has observed, a Fifth Amendment violation occurs only when the government's compulsion creates incriminating testimonial evidence that did not previously exist.) One result was to make the self-incrimination right harder to invoke; documents whose contents were created voluntarily are shielded only if the compelled act of producing them is itself both testimonial and incriminating. In contrast, by acknowledging that production itself could implicitly communicate incriminating information, *Fisher* opened a novel route for Fifth Amendment arguments. The REHNQUIST COURT's [I] decisions in this area narrow that route in three ways.

First, the criterion for "testimonial" or "communicative" evidence was tightened in *Doe v. United States* (1988) to permit compelling a suspect to sign a directive authorizing foreign banks to release information about any accounts he might have. Although executing the directive would communicate directions to the banks, the Court insisted that only the communication of factual assertions or information counts as "testimonial." The Court left unexplained how informing a bank that it is authorized to make specified disclosures does not count as conveying "information."

More significantly, the "collective entity rule" precluding self-incrimination claims with respect to documents held as custodian for an organization was found applicable to the custodian's act of production, not merely the documents' contents. The collective-entity rule reflected the Court's view that the personal nature of the Fifth Amendment right was inconsistent with the impersonal representative capacity in which the custodian holds organizational records. After *Fisher*, the Court could have reinterpreted the rule as existing because the contents of such records were not created under compulsion—implying nothing about an act that was compelled. But BRASWELL V. UNITED STATES (1988) [I] rejected this harmonization of the collective-entity and *Fisher* doctrines. The Court instead extended its pre-*Fisher* explanation of the collective entity rule by insisting that the representative capacity in which custodians hold documents makes even their individual acts of production not "personal." This strained "sleight of hand" insistence that a natural individual's overt behavior is somehow not that individual's "personal" act allowed the Court to escape an implication of its own act/content distinction that it feared would eviscerate the investigation of white-collar crimes.

Finally, in *Baltimore City Department of Social Services v. Bouknight* (1990), the Court combined *Braswell*'s custodial rationale with an amorphous expansive exception to the self-incrimination right for noncriminal regulatory schemes to reject the self-incrimination claim of a suspected child abuser ordered to produce her son in court. Although the mother's act of production would testify to her control over the child and could thereby assist her prosecution, the Court appealed to cases rejecting Fifth Amendment challenges to civil regulatory requirements not confined to groups inherently suspect of criminal activities. Reliance on this exception is troubling, however, because of its extraordinary manipulability. (Why, for example, regard as "civil" and "regulatory" a state juvenile-protection scheme intimately related to criminal laws against child abuse?) Doubts are scarcely dispelled by the Court's additional argument that Bouknight's status as custodian for her son under a prior court order was analogous to that of a custodian of corporate records. The "custodian" argument had never before extended beyond agents of collective entities, and it entailed ignoring this "custodian's" prior and continuing status as mother.

OBITER DICTUM [3] in *Bouknight* suggests that if the state should later seek to prosecute the mother, it may be prohibited from using the testimonial aspects of her act of production. Similarly, *Braswell* stated that although the government could compel a custodian to produce organizational records, it could not in a subsequent prosecution of the custodian divulge that he or she produced those records. There is a tension between these obiter dicta and the HOLDING [3] in each case that compelled production does not violate the Fifth Amendment. This tension suggests that the Court may be uneasy with the extent to which its decisions have in fact cut into the core area of the right against self-incrimination. In an unacknowledged fashion, the Court may be balancing the individual's self-incrimination right and the social goal of truth finding in an effort to accommodate both concerns.

DAVID DOLINKO

Bibliography

ARENELLA, PETER 1982 Schmerber and the Privilege Against Self-Incrimination: A Reappraisal. *American Criminal Law Review* 20:31–61.

DOLINKO, DAVID 1986 Is There a Rationale for the Privilege Against Self-Incrimination? *UCLA Law Review* 33:1063–1148.

SCHULHOFER, STEPHEN 1987 Reconsidering *Miranda*. *University of Chicago Law Review* 54:435–461.

SEIDMAN, LOUIS MICHAEL 1990 Rubashov's Question: Self-Incrimination and the Problem of Coerced Preferences. *Yale Journal of Law and the Humanities* 2:149–180.

STUNTZ, WILLIAM 1988 Self-Incrimination and Excuse. *Columbia Law Review* 88:1227–1296.

WHITE, WELSH 1986 Defending Miranda: A Reply to Professor Caplan. *Vanderbilt Law Review* 39:1–22.

RIGHT OF PRIVACY
(Update)

Despite extensive litigation and commentary, the right of privacy has remained uncertain in constitutional law since it was first established in GRISWOLD V. CONNECTI-CUT (1965) [2]. The ABORTION [1,I] decision in ROE V. WADE (1973) [3] raised the level of controversy about the right of privacy without clarifying the scope or nature of the rights understood under this concept. Sharp criticism of the vagueness of the concept of privacy and persistent doubts about its supporting constitutional text and traditions have not hampered the vitality of the right of privacy. In some areas, such as the RIGHT TO DIE [I], privacy and related concepts have made notable advances in constitutional law. Senate hearings on recent Supreme Court nominees, notably those leading to the rejection of Robert H. Bork and the confirmation of DAVID H. SOUTER [I] seem to confirm these advances as political achievements. We cannot be sure, however, whether or not particular rights (such as the right to abortion) will survive changes in the personnel of the Court.

Recent majorities on the Supreme Court have generally identified the FOURTEENTH AMENDMENT's [2,I] guarantee of "liberty" as the source of privacy rights. This is a notable shift for two reasons. First, it signals the willingness on the part of recent Justices to accept SUBSTANTIVE DUE PROCESS [4,I] as a legitimate concept in constitutional law, so long as it does not touch on economic or labor matters. To Justices of the generation of WILLIAM O. DOUGLAS [2] and HUGO L. BLACK [1], adjudication under such a general rubric was perilous. It encouraged judicial excess. Douglas went to great, perhaps absurd, lengths in *Griswold* to find textual sources for a right to privacy in the First, Third, Fourth, Fifth and Eighth Amendments. ARTHUR GOLDBERG [2] sought to find privacy in the NINTH AMENDMENT [3]. This is now widely understood as a fool's errand.

Second, the preference for a more general source of rights reflects continuing uncertainty about definition of the right of privacy together with an unwillingness to surrender its advantages. Whatever its source, Justice HARRY A. BLACKMUN [1,I] wrote in *Roe v. Wade*, "[t]his right of privacy . . . is broad enough to encompass a woman's decision whether or not to terminate her pregnancy." Justices in more recent decisions have sometimes altogether avoided the term privacy, with conservatives often speaking of "liberty interests" and liberals of personal or "intimate" decisions. In *Cruzan v. Missouri Department of Health* (1990), the "right to die" case, Chief Justice WILLIAM H. REHNQUIST [3,I] made this avoidance explicit: "Although many state courts have held that a right to refuse treatment is encompassed by a generalized constitutional right of privacy, we have never so held." The issue, he added, "is more properly analyzed in terms of a 14th Amendment liberty interest."

Outside of the law of SEARCH AND SEIZURE [4,I], privacy has proven extremely hard to define. Scholars have been unable to agree on the elements of ordinary usage, CONSTITUTIONAL HISTORY [1,I], or moral philosophy from which to construct a normative concept. The concept itself has been of little but rhetorical help in deciding particular cases in which, typically, regulation is seen to invade an individual's preference for seclusion or immunity. All this has made the precedents of *Griswold* and *Roe* hard to confine by ordinary arguments. The steps from privacy in marital sexuality to privacy in abortion and from heterosexuality to homosexuality have not been easy to resist when arguments are made in terms of a right to privacy possessed by all persons.

However disappointing to those awaiting clarification, the turn from privacy to liberty may nonetheless make good legal and political sense. Privacy as a term has no plain reference or meaning for most of us. "The right to be let alone," as EARL WARREN [4] and LOUIS BRANDEIS [1] called it, covered many situations and many abuses. In CRIMINAL PROCEDURE [2], the protection of "persons, papers, and effects" refers to those things (including one's own body) over which we normally exercise complete control. But the transportation from one context to another—search and seizure, for example, to sexuality—leaves much of the force of argument, as well as PRECEDENT [3] and tradition, behind. We are left then with an argument for immunity unaided by the concept under which immunity is claimed. Obviously, private life—*la vie privée*—must shelter information, decisions, and behaviors of many different kinds. The question is, which ones are to be protected against regulation or governmental intrusion?

Liberty is not much more helpful in this regard than is privacy. Yet liberty offers a plainer inquiry with less confusion and less of a temptation to believe that we will find our rights by simply defining a concept. Moreover, liberty, unlike privacy, is a concept with a long constitutional history.

The inquiry that now seems to govern adjudication is whether or not fundamental liberties extend to certain aspects of private life, including sexuality, reproduction, and perhaps dying. Often, regulations have reached these matters in connection with medical treatment. Thus, the right to die is the right to refuse medical treatment where it might prolong life. The right to abortion is the right to choose whether or not to terminate a pregnancy before the fetus is viable outside the womb. We may generalize from these instances to a concept of privacy in intimate associations or intimate decisions, but the Supreme Court's response to this generalization remains equivocal: Sexuality between consenting adults of the opposite sexes seems at this point effectively protected. Although *Griswold* relied on the context of MARRIAGE [3] for its extension of protection to information about the use of BIRTH CONTROL [I], EISENSTADT V. BAIRD (1972) [2] seemed to make clear that this context was unnecessary. We should note,

however, that the effective protection for disapproved behavior lies in a conjunction of privacy decisions from the Supreme Court and, of equal or greater importance, regulatory reforms from the various state legislatures that permit a greater range of behaviors than heretofore. Sodomy statutes remain on the books in many states, and it is not yet clear that unmarried heterosexual sodomy would be held to be protected by the Supreme Court.

In BOWERS V. HARDWICK (1986) [I] the Court upheld a Georgia statute that made sodomy a felony in a case in which charges had been filed and then withdrawn against two consenting adult males. The 5–4 decision sharply divided the Court. "The issue presented," wrote Justice BYRON R. WHITE [4,I], for the majority, "is whether the Federal constitution confers a fundamental right upon homosexuals to engage in sodomy. . . ." Justices Blackmun, WILLIAM J. BRENNAN [1,I], THURGOOD MARSHALL [3,I], and JOHN PAUL STEVENS [4,I] dissented. "This case is no more about a fundamental right to engage in homosexual sodomy," Justice Blackmun wrote, "than STANLEY V. GEORGIA (1969) [4] was about a fundamental right to watch obscene movies, or KATZ V. UNITED STATES (1967) [3] was about a fundamental right to place interstate bets from a telephone booth." For the dissenters, Brandeis's dissent in OLMSTEAD V. UNITED STATES (1928) [3] provided the applicable concept, "the right to be let alone," as Warren and Brandeis had described it (without any reference to sexuality) in their famous *Harvard Law Review* article on the "Right to Privacy." Thus, Blackmun insisted on a certain understanding of the concept of privacy: "I believe we must analyze respondent's claim in the light of the values that underlie the constitutional right to privacy. If that right means anything, it means that, before Georgia can prosecute its citizens for making choices about the most intimate aspects of their lives, it must do more than assert that the choice they have made is an 'abominable crime not fit to be named among Christians.'"

The incommensurability of these points of view may be understood from at least three angles. First, and most obvious to students of the concepts of privacy and liberty, there is a difference over the level of abstraction at which the argument will be joined. The majority refused to accept the claim that adult homosexuals might shelter their consensual sexual practices under the same general liberty as adult heterosexuals. To the majority, the assertion is of an immunity to engage in a homosexual act consistently condemned in our tradition. The dissenters argue that this act must be understood in relation to other sexual intimacies protected by the Fourteenth Amendment. It is, after all, an expression of sexuality between consenting adults in the bedroom of a private apartment. (A houseguest had admitted the policeman into the apartment and directed him to Hardwick's bedroom.) Neither position is refutable as illogical or inconsistent. The choice of a level of abstraction will often decide a dispute over rights; yet there seems to be no conclusive argument that one level of abstraction is the appropriate one for a given case. What makes one level preferable to another is the sense of coherence and completeness at that level of whatever issues are understood as pertinent. This is inevitably a circular process of reasoning. Intimacy and sexuality seem the relevant terms to the dissenters, but not to the majority, which focuses on homosexuality. A simpler way to understand this difference is to note that, as always, each side in legal argument denies the applicability of the other side's precedents. In this case, the majority will not accept the force and bearing of *Griswold, Eisenstadt,* and *Roe v. Wade.* For the dissenters, however, these are the relevant precedents, pointing the way to a different result.

Finally, there is an important line of argument, going back to the younger Justice JOHN MARSHALL HARLAN [2] in *Poe v. Ullman* (1961), that tradition should inform our understanding of the concept of liberty. Constitutional traditions, like others, are notoriously inexact. Moreover, there are good traditions and bad ones. Yet it is undeniable that legal and institutional traditions give us a context in which to understand the terms and arrangements provided for in the Constitution. DUE PROCESS [2] is one example, JUDICIAL REVIEW [3,I] is another, and privacy may be a third.

Harlan, in *Poe* and *Griswold,* relied on a specific tradition, namely, marriage. The various measures of restriction and permission attached to it by law suggested to him that the concept of privacy had constitutional standing in protecting the uses of sexuality—including contraception—by husband and wife. He never went beyond this point, however, retiring from the Court in 1971, one year before the *Eisenstadt* decision and two years before *Roe v. Wade.*

Eisenstadt's majority opinions had relied on an EQUAL PROTECTION [2,I] argument that left the factual question of the marital status of the recipient of a contraceptive unresolved. Justice Brennan's language, however, was unambiguous: "If the right of privacy means anything, it is the right of the *individual,* married or single, to be free from unwarranted governmental intrusion into matters so fundamentally affecting a person as the decision whether to bear or beget a child." This language may be said either to disregard tradition or to generalize it, raising it to a more abstract level. Only in MOORE V. CITY OF EAST CLEVELAND (1977) [3] has the Court openly pursued Harlan's approach. In this case, the Court invalidated a ZONING [4,I] ordiance disallowing residence in the same house of a grandmother and two grandchildren who were cousins

rather than siblings. Justice LEWIS F. POWELL [3,I] cited Harlan's reasoning in *Poe* in a plurality opinion insisting on "the sanctity of the family." "Ours is by means a tradition limited to respect for the bonds uniting the members of the nuclear family," he wrote.

Predictions about the future of the right to privacy must rely in part on assumptions about appointments to the Court. The Bork hearings seemed to suggest that a consensus now exists—in the Senate and in public opinion—on the importance of the right to privacy in constitutional law. This consensus does not mean, however, that the right to an abortion is secure. With the departure of Justice Brennan, *Roe v. Wade* is vulnerable to reversal. Justices ANTHONY M. KENNEDY [I], ANTONIN SCALIA [I], and Byron White, along with the Chief Justice, have all suggested an eagerness to reverse. Justice SANDRA DAY O'CONNOR [3,I] has also indicated her preference for a new and less restrictive standard of review in abortion cases, although without clarifying its implications. Regulation that does not "unduly" burden abortion will survive judicial scrutiny, she wrote in HODGSON V. MINNESOTA (1990) [I]. This may well be the last decision to leave *Roe's* holding in place. What seems unlikely is that *Griswold* or *Eisenstadt* will be reversed. Indeed, many would foresee the likelihood of an extension of privacy protections to homosexuals as inescapable, however conservative the Court. If so, cultural acceptance may ultimately prove more crucial in constitutional debate than the conclusions of scholarship or formal argument.

Similarly, the right to die as an aspect of privacy, liberty, or both, seems at this point to have secured its toehold in constitutional law. Like sexual privacy at the time of *Griswold,* this right remains uncertain in scope and definition, and the concept at work—once we move beyond a narrow statement of the right to refuse treatment—is both elastic and ambiguous. But these are not fatal intellectual flaws in constitutional law. Privacy, like many legal concepts, is not so much a philosophical conception as a practical one, more readily identified by its messy precedents than by its tidy definition.

TOM GERETY

Bibliography

BAKER, RICHARD ALLAN 1989 The Senate of the United States: "Supreme Executive Council of the Nation," 1787–1800. *Prologue* 21:299–313.

BICKFORD, CHARLENE BANGS and BOWLING, KENNETH R. 1989 *Birth of the Nation: The First Federal Congress 1789–1791.* Madison, Wis.: Madison House.

BOWLING, KENNETH R. 1968 Politics in the First Congress 1789–1791. Ph.D. diss., University of Wisconsin.

SILBEY, JOEL H. 1987 "Our Successors Will Have an Easier Task": The First Congress Under the Constitution, 1789–1791. *This Constitution* 17:4–10.

SMOCK, RAYMOND W.   1989   The House of Representatives: First Branch of the New Government. *Prologue* 21:287–297.

RIGHT OF PROPERTY

See: Property Rights [I]

RIGHTS OF THE CRIMINALLY ACCUSED

In criminal prosecutions, the state can bring its authority, organizational power, and resources to bear against individuals. History, particularly precolonial and early colonial English history, demonstrated to the American Revolutionaries that governments could and did use their prosecution powers abusively—to imprison or destroy political enemies, tyrannize or cow populations, and preserve or advance unpopular regimes or policies. For such reasons, the Constitution and BILL OF RIGHTS [1] included provisions restricting governmental use of prosecution powers and granting the criminally accused procedural protection.

Among these are specific denials of governmental authority to take certain kinds of actions, such as constitutional proscriptions on EX POST FACTO LAWS [2], BILLS OF ATTAINDER [1], and suspension of HABEAS CORPUS [2,I]. The Fifth, Sixth, and Eighth Amendments accord the criminally accused specific criminal process rights. In addition, there are criminal process rights and protections mentioned neither in the Constitution nor the Bill of Rights, such as the right of proof of guilt beyond a REASONABLE DOUBT [3], which the Supreme Court has concluded are necessarily implied from the Constitution, history, and American practice. Finally, the FOURTH AMENDMENT [2,I] right against unreasonable SEARCHES AND SEIZURES [4,I], a right accorded to all persons in the United States, has particular significance and impact in criminal proceedings.

Of principal importance are the criminal defendant's inferred and specifically listed constitutional trial rights. Although not expressly mentioned in the Constitution, first and foremost among these is the right of trial under an *adversary* system of trial. Adversary trial, as opposed to inquisitorial trial, was the established form of trial at COMMON LAW [1], and has always been the American practice—so much so that it has been deemed an essential feature of the Sixth Amendment right to a fair trial. In an inquisitorial system of trial, judicial officials take an active role in advancing a prosecution and eliciting facts, and lawyers, or party representatives, play a rather passive role. In contrast, in the adversarial system, the parties to a prosecution, through their attorneys, control the pre-

sentation of EVIDENCE [2], and the judge plays the more passive role of umpire, attempting to insure both a fair contest between the parties and a fair fact determination. Party control of the presentation of evidence significantly enhances its ability to shape evidence to its advantage or to influence the fact finder, particularly in jury trials, where laypersons determine facts and decide questions of criminal responsibility.

Although criminal adversary trial is grounded in a rhetoric of a fair contest between equals as a way to accord both fairness to defendants and to discover truth, adversary trial actually has an asymmetric structure in which the prosecution has greater burdens and obligations than the defense. In particular, the prosecution has the burden of presenting a prima facie case against a defendant—the burden of proving guilt beyond a reasonable doubt—and an obligation to disclose to the defense evidence favorable to the defendant and material relevant to issues of guilt or punishment.

Although rarely considered to be a right of the accused, the government's burden of first presentation of evidence does confer potential strategic or tactical advantages on the defense in a criminal case. Knowing the specific nature of the prosecution's case, the defense can shape its own proofs for greatest benefit. Similarly, the prosecution's burden of proving guilt beyond a reasonable doubt, which the Supreme Court held in *In re Winship* (1970) to be a constitutional requirement, is, in effect, a defendant's right to require the government to prove guilt to a substantial certainty. This high burden inhibits the government from bringing or winning prosecutions based on weak evidence, and precludes the use of evidentiary presumptions that might favor it.

The prosecution also has a duty to disclose evidence. This requirement, which is derived from DUE PROCESS [2] fairness considerations, insures there is no miscarriage of justice through failure to disclose evidence bearing on guilt. There is, however, no reciprocal, counterpart defense duty to disclose evidence favorable to the prosecution. With narrow exception, the Court has interpreted the requirements of adversary trial and the Fifth Amendment RIGHT AGAINST SELF-INCRIMINATION [3,I] to prohibit the government from requiring the defense to provide evidence to the prosecution or otherwise to assist it in its case.

Adversary trial, as now understood, also assumes attorney representatives for each party, and the Court has interpreted the Sixth Amendment RIGHT TO COUNSEL [3] to guarantee criminal defendants the right to be represented by an attorney at all "critical stages" of a criminal proceeding. This right applies in any case, FELONY [2] or MISDEMEANOR [3], in which an accused, if convicted, will suffer incarceration as a punishment. A "critical stage" is any occasion, once a criminal prosecution has been initiated, where the state takes action (usually in a proceeding where the defendant is present) that can be adverse to the defendant's interests in not being incarcerated or convicted. In addition, in the famous case of MIRANDA V. ARIZONA (1966) [3], the Supreme Court held that criminal suspects in custody have a right to consult with counsel, if they wish, before speaking with police.

Criminal defendants have a right to representation by counsel of their choice if they can afford it or to appointed counsel if they cannot. The Sixth Amendment, however, also implies a right of self-representation, and the criminally accused may represent themselves if they knowingly and intelligently choose to do so.

The right to counsel when there is attorney representation also entails a right to "effective" assistance of counsel, that is, counsel generally competent to handle a criminal case, actually making decisions of a kind that competent criminal-trial attorneys would make, and not suffering from any conflict of interest that would impair or bias the representation. Finally, in the case of the INDIGENT [2], the right to effective assistance of counsel combined with the more general right to a FAIR TRIAL [2] may also require some state financial assistance in investigating or presenting a case, for example, payment of expert-witness fees.

The Sixth Amendment also accords a criminally accused the right to an impartial jury. TRIAL BY JURY [4] is of particular importance because jurors are laypersons from the community, not governmental functionaries, and independent jury decision making in criminal cases can provide further protection against possible governmental overreaching. The Court has interpreted the jury-trial right to apply in prosecutions for all crimes except petty offenses, the latter defined as those punishable by no more than six months in prison and a $500 fine. This right includes the right to a PETIT JURY [3] selected from a larger group of persons, called the jury venire, which is cross-sectionally representative of the community.

Federal criminal juries must be composed of twelve persons and return unanimous verdicts. The Court has, however, interpreted the jury-trial requirement as applied to the states through FOURTEENTH AMENDMENT [2,I] due process to permit state criminal trial juries with as few as six members, but no fewer, that number being thought sufficiently large to provide the benefits of representativeness and of group deliberation. Similarly, the Court has concluded that state criminal trial juries, at least where there is a twelve-person jury, require only a substantial majority, rather than unanimity, to convict.

Criminal defendants have Sixth Amendment rights to confront and cross-examine witnesses. The right to CONFRONTATION [1,I] is essentially a right to have the witnesses against the accused to appear in open court to make a face-to-face accusation, a requirement thought to enhance the reliability of witness statements. The associated right of cross-examination is in effect the right to test both the witness and his or her testimony in open court before the fact finder. With few exceptions, these rights entail that where a witness against the defendant is available, the government must produce that witness in court, rather than use previously recorded statements of the witness. In addition, the state may not impose rules restricting the defense's relevant cross-examination of a testifying witness.

The Sixth Amendment also gives criminal defendants the right to COMPULSORY PROCESS [1] to require the attendance at trial of witnesses in their behalf. This right is obviously important where a defendant has witnesses who could testify favorably, but are unwilling to appear in court. The right, however, is also read as a general right to present evidence in one's behalf and thus operates to prohibit states from restricting the defendant's presentation of relevant and generally reliable evidence. For example, when a state rule of HEARSAY [2] evidence operates to exclude from a criminal trial trustworthy evidence that may be favorable to the defendant, the right to present evidence would override this rule.

Finally, the Sixth Amendment confers on criminal defendants rights to a SPEEDY TRIAL [4,I] and a PUBLIC TRIAL [3]. Defendants may desire speedy trials so they do not languish in jail or to quickly resolve the criminal accusation. Yet criminal defendants often seek to delay a criminal trial, either because they are not prepared or because they perceive some advantage in delay, such as the fading of witnesses' memories. For such reasons, the Court has held that delay in coming to trial does not of itself violate the speedy-trial right. Instead, the Court uses a multifactor BALANCING TEST [1] to determine when the right was violated. This test considers the length of delay, the government's reasons for it, the defendant's assertion or waiver of his or her speedy-trial right, and the actual prejudice to the defendant. This test obviously gives little guidance, and it is apparent that even quite long delays of years may not trigger the right. In contrast, it is necessary to note that the government also has an interest in speedy trials and that both state and federal governments have statutes regulating trial delay. Because of such statutes, the speedy-trial right as a control over the timing of trials has receded far into the background.

The public-trial right protects defendants from unfair or abusive trials by ensuring that trials are open to public scrutiny. However, although defendants may demand that their trial be open to the public, they do not have a right to close their trial without a showing of real necessity. The Court has concluded that the FIRST AMENDMENT [2,I] free-speech and free-press guarantees entail public and press access to criminal trials so that the public can remain informed regarding the administration of criminal justice. Because criminal trials are presumptively open and only a weighty justification can justify closure, a defendant's public-trial right no longer retains much practical importance.

The Fifth Amendment provides three additional rights for the criminally accused: the right to INDICTMENT [2] by GRAND JURY [2], the right against self-incrimination, and the protection against DOUBLE JEOPARDY [2]. In theory, the grand jury acts as a check on governmental prosecution by committing the decision to indict a person of a crime to a group of ordinary citizens rather than vesting it in state officials. In practice, however, grand juries rarely operate independently of the prosecutors' offices providing them with information and guidance. Consequently, grand juries do not in fact constitute any significant check on criminal charging. Furthermore, the Supreme Court has not required the states to indict by grand jury. Although many states nonetheless use grand juries, state prosecutors generally are also free to charge persons by information, that is, a charging paper issuing solely from the prosecutor's office rather than from the grand jury.

The right against self-incrimination, which is the right to refuse to give evidence against oneself, however, does play an important role in criminal justice. The right protects a criminal defendant from governmental compulsion to speak, an abusive practice common in England in precolonial and early colonial history. In a criminal trial it amounts to a defendant's right to remain silent and not to take the stand to testify. Because comment by the prosecution on a defendant's refusal to testify—by claiming the refusal evidences guilt—might bring pressure on a defendant to testify, the Court has also held that prosecution comment on a defendant's silence violates the privilege.

More important, the right against self-incrimination now plays a critical role in analyzing and resolving issues regarding POLICE INTERROGATIONS [3,I] of suspects, which results in confessions or inculpatory statements. Originally, the Court viewed Fifth and Fourteenth Amendment due process as requiring the state accord a suspect "fundamental fairness." The Court found police coercion of confessions or incriminating statements inhumane and unfair, forbade such practices, and barred the prosecution's use of such material in criminal trials whenever the defendant's statements were deemed involuntary. For various reasons, the voluntariness test proved unsatisfactory and unworkable. Police forces continued to use questionable techniques in seeking confessions and resorted to deceptive or progressively more subtle, yet nonetheless manipulative or abusive, interrogation practices. Finally, the Court took a major step to solve the general police-interrogation problem, and in *Miranda v. Arizona* held the right against self-incrimination applicable outside the context of a trial. Specifically, the Court held that when police conduct a custodial interrogation of a suspect they must respect the suspect's right to remain silent and cannot interrogate him or her if he or she does not knowingly, intelligently, and voluntarily agree to the interrogation. In *Miranda* the Court also concluded that the right of a criminal suspect to consult with counsel before speaking to police was essential to protect the suspect's right to remain silent if he or she chose to exercise it. Consequently, *Miranda* also held that when a suspect asks to speak with an attorney, all interrogation must cease until the suspect has consulted with an attorney or appropriately waived his or her right to do so. To insure that suspects understood their rights and could invoke them, *Miranda* further required police to give suspects they arrest or hold a set of "*Miranda*" warnings. These advise suspects of their right to silence, that their statements may be used against them, and that they have a right to an attorney appointed free of charge if necessary.

The Fifth Amendment further protects criminal defendants from double jeopardy, that is, from multiple prosecutions for the same offense by the same jurisdiction or for reprosecutions for the same offense after acquittal or conviction. Disallowing multiple or successive prosecutions, this clause prevents the government from rehearsing its proofs to perfect them and from persecuting or exhausting individuals through repeated efforts to convict. The double-jeopardy clause applies once the state places the accused in "jeopardy," which occurs in a jury trial when the jury is empaneled and sworn and in a trial to a judge when the first witness is sworn. Before these events, although the state may be advancing a criminal case against an individual, jeopardy is not thought to "have attached," and dismissals during this period do not bar the refiling of charges or a subsequent prosecution. The clause also does not bar reprosecutions where a convicted person has had his or her conviction overturned on grounds other than the insufficiency of the evidence to convict.

The double-jeopardy clause does not prohibit different "sovereigns" from prosecuting for the same offense. As many criminal offenses violate both state and federal law—for example, bank robbery—multiple prosecutions for the same offense are possible. As a matter of policy, however, federal and state prosecutors usually decline to prosecute an individual for the same offense when the other sovereign has prosecuted.

The Fourth Amendment protects all persons, not just the criminally accused, from UNREASONABLE SEARCHES [4,I] and seizures. As a practical matter, however, it has special application in criminal prosecutions because, when the government unlawfully searches or seizes from one whom it criminally charges, the remedy that the courts apply is the exclusion of the evidence unlawfully taken from that person's criminal trial.

In general, exclusion of evidence is the remedy courts apply to governmental violations of a defendant's Fourth, Fifth, or Sixth Amendment rights that result in evidence that the government seeks to use against the defendant at trial. This might occur when the government unlawfully searches and seizes, coerces a confession or statement from a person or obtains statements in violation of the MIRANDA RULES [3,I], or improperly obtains evidence through violation of a suspect's or accused's Sixth Amendment right to counsel. There has been considerable debate as to whether an accused in any of these situations has a *constitutional right* to have such evidence excluded or exclusion of evidence is simply a default remedy applied in the absence of any other effective sanction for the violation of constitutional rights. If there is no constitutional right to exclusion, the government could avoid the exclusion of evidence by providing other remedies for rights violations, at least where the remedies were thought to constitute sanctions as effective as exclusion. As a practical matter, however, neither the federal nor state governments have provided equally effective remedies, and courts and commentators continue to speak of an accused's "right" to have unlawfully obtained evidence excluded.

The Eighth Amendment proscribes excessive BAIL [I] and CRUEL AND UNUSUAL PUNISHMENT [2,I]. Under Supreme Court decisions applying the bail clause, an accused does not necessarily have the right to be released on bail. The Court has held that the excessive-bail provision prohibits bails set at a figure higher than an amount reasonably calculated to insure that the accused will make his or her necessary appearances in criminal proceedings and will submit to sentence if found guilty. However, the Court has also upheld PREVENTIVE DETENTION [3,I] statutes under which persons shown to be dangerous to others if released may be denied bail.

The Eighth Amendment's cruel and unusual punishment clause applies both to capital and noncapital punishments. Strictly speaking, the clause protects the convicted, not the accused, but its importance to an accused's prospects of punishment warrants its inclusion here. The Court has held CAPITAL PUNISHMENT [1,I] cruel and unusual when it is applied arbitrarily, irrationally, or discriminatorily or when it is seriously disproportionate to the offense committed. With regard to noncapital punishments, the Court has held that the clause prohibits punishments that involve torture or the unjustifiable infliction of involuntary pain. It has also applied the clause to strike down confinements whose length or conditions are disproportionate to the crime or that involve serious deprivations

of a prisoner's basic human needs (such as failure to provide medical care) and punishments involving loss of CITIZENSHIP [1,I] for status.

GARY GOODPASTER

Bibliography

DAMASKA, MIRJAN 1975 Presentation of Evidence and Fact-finding Precision. *University of Pennsylvania Law Review* 123:1038–1106.
——— 1983 The Adversary System. In Kadish, Sanford, ed. *Encyclopedia of Crime and Justice.* Vol. 1, pages 24–29. New York: Macmillan and Free Press.
LAFAVE, WAYNE R. and ISRAEL, JEROLD H. 1984 *Criminal Procedure.* 4 Vols. St. Paul, Minn.: West Publishing Co.

RIGHT TO DIE

The "right to die" is an ambiguous, and therefore expansive, phrase. It can encompass the right to refuse life-sustaining medical treatment, the right to commit suicide, the right to have a doctor assist a person in suicide, and the right of third parties to kill legally incompetent patients by administering lethal doses of drugs or by removing food, water, respirators and/or other medical care.

The constitutional arguments for the right to die are premised on either the RIGHT OF PRIVACY [3,I] or on the right to liberty guaranteed by the DUE PROCESS [2] clause of the FOURTEENTH AMENDMENT [2,I]. Several lower federal courts, as well as state supreme courts, have held that the right of privacy includes at least a limited right to die. In *Cruzan v. Director, Missouri Department of Health* (1990), however, the Supreme Court suggested that right-to-die cases fit more appropriately within the due process framework.

Cruzan involved the tragic plight of Nancy Cruzan, who sustained severe head injuries in a car accident in 1983. After three weeks in a coma, she improved sufficiently that she could chew and swallow food. A feeding tube was nevertheless inserted into her stomach in order to make long-term care easier. Subsequent efforts to rehabilitate her failed.

In 1987 Nancy's parents sought to stop the food and hydration provided through the tube, arguing that their daughter was in a "persistent vegetative state," manifesting no awareness of herself or her environment. They further said that previous to her accident Nancy had indicated that she would not want to be kept alive in such a condition. The trial court granted the Cruzans' request, but the Missouri state supreme court reversed, ruling that not enough evidence had been presented to demonstrate that Ms. Cruzan would in fact choose to forgo food and liquids if she were competent to make the choice.

The U.S. Supreme Court narrowly upheld the constitutionality of this determination by a vote of 5–4.

Writing for the majority, Chief Justice WILLIAM H. REHNQUIST [3,I] said that according to previous decisions of the Court, "a competent person has a constitutionally protected liberty interest in refusing unwanted medical treatment" based on the due process clause. This liberty interest is not inviolable, however. It must be weighed against various state interests, including the state's commitment to the preservation of human life. According to Rehnquist, this commitment justifies prohibitions against both homicide and assistance to commit suicide. It also justifies state measures to prevent suicide. In Rehnquist's words, "we do not think a State is required to remain neutral in the face of an informed and voluntary decision by a physically-able adult to starve to death."

Nancy Cruzan, of course, was not physically able; and for the purpose of this case, Rehnquist assumed that while competent able persons may not have the constitutional right to starve themselves to death, competent persons requiring artificially administered food and fluids do. The question was how this right could be applied to an incompetent individual like Nancy Cruzan. Concerned about the possible abuse of the power to remove life-sustaining treatment from others, Missouri had stipulated that food and hydration can be removed from an incompetent patient only when there is clear and convincing evidence that this is what the patient would have wanted under the circumstances. In the case of Nancy Cruzan, the Missouri supreme court held that insufficient evidence had been presented to make this determination. Rehnquist and the majority concluded that in this particular case this was a permissible way to safeguard the state's interest in protecting human life.

However, the Court also hinted that a different result might be required in a situation where a person had duly appointed a third party to make decisions in the case of the person's incompetency. In other words, had Nancy Cruzan made clear prior to her accident that she wanted her parents to make medical decisions for her if she ever became incompetent, the Court might have compelled the state to carry out the parents' wishes. Justice SANDRA DAY O'CONNOR [3,I] emphasized this point in her concurring opinion.

Dissenting, Justice WILLIAM J. BRENNAN [1,I] claimed that more than enough evidence existed to show that Nancy Cruzan did not want to be kept alive in her present condition. Even if there had not been sufficient evidence to determine Cruzan's wishes, however, the state still had no right to maintain her life according to Brennan. Instead, it was obligated by the due process clause to leave the decision over whether or not to remove medical treatment to "the person whom the patient himself would most likely have chosen as proxy or . . . to the patient's family."

Justice JOHN PAUL STEVENS [4,I], in a separate dissent, adopted a different approach. He articulated an objective "best interests" test whereby the courts would determine if it is in the best interests of the patient to continue to receive life support. Reviewing Nancy Cruzan's tragic condition, Stevens concluded that her "best interests" unquestionably dictated that food and fluids be shut off. Some might find chilling Stevens's expansive definition of "best interests," however, for it apparently included a patient's interest in not being a burden to others. At the end of his opinion, Stevens spoke of Nancy's "interest in minimizing the burden that her own illness imposes on others . . . [and] in having their memories of her filled predominantly with thoughts about her past vitality rather than her current condition."

Several aspects of the right to die raise difficult questions. Many oppose physician-assisted suicide, for example, because suicide wishes are often fleeting and irrational. They add that if society makes suicide too easy, efforts to prevent suicide may be undermined. Advocates for persons with disability claim this is already happening, pointing to a case in California where a court sanctioned the request of a disabled woman to starve herself to death in a hospital—despite clear evidence that the woman was severely depressed because of recent personal tragedies.

The power of third parties to deny life-sustaining measures to incompetent patients is equally problematic. Underlying much of the discussion over incompetent patients is the assumption that these persons are not fully human. This came out with force in the dissents in *Cruzan*, where Justices Brennan and Stevens both claimed that Nancy existed in a state "devoid of thought, emotion and sensation." This contention was fundamental to their arguments, because it allowed them to claim that the state could have no legitimate interest in preserving Nancy's life, because no human life in fact existed for the state to protect.

There are serious problems, however, with premising the right to die on judgments about someone else's humanity. Such judgments are not nearly so clear or so objective as many presume. Nancy Cruzan, for example, was supposed to be oblivious to her environment. Yet the trial court heard testimony from nurses who testified that Nancy tracked with her eyes, smiled after being told stories, and cried after family visits. Even in cases where a patient cannot respond at all, one may question whether this alone is a sufficient indicator of a person's loss of cognitive faculties. Research on coma victims who have recovered shows that the mere fact that they could not respond outwardly while comatose did not mean they had lost their humanity. They could hear what others said about them in their hospital room. They experienced emotions. They dreamt. But if persons in a persistent vegetative state retain their humanity in some fundamental sense, the assumption that the state has *no* interest in protecting their lives becomes much less persuasive.

The application of the right to die to incompetent patients other than those in persistent vegetative states is even more problematic. The right to die has been used to justify withholding food, fluids, and basic medical treatment from a wide array of incompetent individuals, from conscious stroke victims to infants with Down's Syndrome or treatable physical disabilities such as spina bifida. Disability rights groups complain that in these cases the right to die is nothing more than the right to discriminate against the physically and mentally handicapped. They argue that not only is such discrimination not constitutionally protected, it is constitutionally proscribed by guarantees of due process and EQUAL PROTECTION [2,I].

Like ABORTION [1,I], the right to die implicates some of the most fundamental beliefs humans hold about the nature of human life. Right-to-die cases often require judges to be physicians and philosophers as well as jurists, and few would pretend that a judge's role in such cases is either enviable or easy.

JOHN G. WEST, JR.

(SEE ALSO : *Euthanasia* [2]; *Patient's Rights* [3,I].)

Bibliography

ARKES, HADLEY 1987 "Autonomy" and the "Quality of Life": The Dismantling of Moral Terms. *Issues in Law and Medicine* 2:421–433.

BARRY, ROBERT 1988 *Protecting the Medically Dependent: Social Challenge and Ethical Imperative.* Stafford, Va.: Castello Institute.

BOPP, JR., JAMES 1987 Is Assisted Suicide Constitutionally Protected? *Issues in Law and Medicine* 3:113–140.

LONGMORE, PAUL K. 1987 Elizabeth Bouvia, Assisted Suicide and Social Prejudice. *Issues in Law and Medicine* 3:141–168.

RIGHT TO REMAIN SILENT

See: Right Against Self-Incrimination [3,I]

ROBERTS v. UNITED STATES JAYCEES (1984)

See: Freedom of Association [I]

RUTAN v. REPUBLICAN PARTY OF ILLINOIS
110 S.Ct. 2729 (1990)

The governor of Illinois prohibited state entities under his control from hiring any employees without his express consent. Because more than 5,000 state positions become vacant in Illinois each year, this policy allowed the governor to make several thousand additional appointments. Evidence suggested that the governor's hiring policy operated as a patronage system, with the governor restricting appointments to people who belonged to his political party. Persons alleging that they had been denied jobs, promotions, transfers, or recall after layoffs because of their party affiliation filed suit, claiming that these employment practices violated their rights of speech and association guaranteed by the FIRST AMENDMENT [2,I]. The challenge was based on previous cases such as ELROD V. BURNS (1976) [2], where the Court had held that the First Amendment barred political affiliation from being used as a reason for dismissal from most governmental jobs. In *Rutan*, the Court ruled 5–4 to extend the doctrine of *Elrod v. Burns* to promotions, transfers, recall from layoffs, and hiring decisions.

Writing for the majority, Justice WILLIAM J. BRENNAN [2,I] applied the COMPELLING STATE INTEREST [I] test used by the Court in many other types of cases, arguing that patronage clearly violates the First Amendment unless it is "narrowly tailored to further vital government interests." In Brennan's view, a general patronage system manifestly fails this test because it is not necessary to maintain either strong political parties or employee loyalty; these goals can be achieved by other means, such as having a handful of senior positions filled by political appointees.

Justice ANTONIN SCALIA [I], writing for the dissenters, argued that the compelling-interest standard was inappropriate for this case because the government was acting in the role of employer. Numerous decisions have upheld the idea that the government has more leeway in regulating the conduct of its employees than it does in regulating the behavior of ordinary citizens. According to Scalia, as long as the benefits of an employment practice can "reasonably be deemed to outweigh its 'coercive' effects," the practice should pass constitutional muster. In this case, Scalia believed that the perceived benefits clearly outweighed the coercive effects, because patronage has long been regarded as a cornerstone of our party system, "promoting political stability and facilitating the social and political integration of previously powerless groups." Scalia disputed the majority's contention that "parties have already survived" the demise of patronage. Saying the Court's assessment had "a positively whistling-in-the-graveyard character to it," Scalia noted recent evidence of party decline, including the substantial decrease in party competition for congressional seats. Reasonable men and women can differ about the appropriateness of patronage in various contexts, said Scalia; but this is precisely why the Court should respect the federal system and not impose its own will in the matter.

JOHN G. WEST, JR.

SABLE COMMUNICATIONS OF CALIFORNIA v. FCC (1989)

See: Dial-a-Porn [I]

SALERNO, UNITED STATES v.
481 U.S. 739 (1987)

In many nations of the world, governments imprison people believed to be dangerous because of their opinions. This does not happen in a free society. However, since the Bail Reform Act, passed by Congress in 1984, persons arrested for a specific category of serious offenses, those violating the RACKETEER INFLUENCES AND CORRUPT ORGANIZATIONS ACT (RICO) [I], may be imprisoned while awaiting trial. This is PREVENTIVE DETENTION [3,I], which is based on the supposition that the prisoner will likely commit other crimes if let out on BAIL [1,I]. When the Court sustained the constitutionality of the 1984 statute, Justice THURGOOD MARSHALL [3,I], dissenting, joined only by Justice WILLIAM J. BRENNAN [1,I], made the following remarkable statement:

This case brings before the Court for the first time a statute in which Congress declares that a person innocent of any crime may be jailed indefinitely, pending the trial of allegations which are legally presumed to be untrue, if the Government shows to the satisfaction of a judge that the accused is likely to commit crimes, unrelated to the pending charges, at any time in the future. Such statutes, consistent with the usages of tyranny and the excesses of what bitter experience teaches us to call the police state, have long been thought incompatible with the fundamental human rights protected by our Constitution. Today a majority of this Court holds otherwise. Its decision disregards basic principles of justice established centuries ago and enshrined beyond the reach of governmental interference in the Bill of Rights.

Justice JOHN PAUL STEVENS [4,I], dissenting separately, agreed with Marshall that the statute violated both the presumption of innocence and the Eighth Amendment's excessive-bail clause.

Chief Justice WILLIAM H. REHNQUIST [3,I], for the majority, first rejected the contention that the statute conflicted with the Fifth Amendment's DUE PROCESS [2] clause. No conflict existed, he held, because Congress's purpose in authorizing pretrial detention was not penal, but merely regulatory. So construed, the statute did not authorize impermissible punishment without trial; it merely employed pretrial detention to protect the community against danger. Not only was SUBSTANTIVE DUE PROCESS [4,I] not violated; the statute conformed with PROCEDURAL DUE PROCESS [3,I] as well, because it provided for a full adversary hearing before a judge. The government had the burden of proving that to offer bail to the prisoner endangered society and that the prisoner had the RIGHT TO COUNSEL [3] and all other trial rights.

Rehnquist also rejected the argument based on the Eighth Amendment's excessive-bail clause. It did not guarantee a right to bail, only that, when available, bail should not be excessive. In murder cases, bail can be denied. Moreover, in SCHALL V. MARTIN (1984) [4], the Court had permitted pretrial detention of juveniles following a showing before a judge that the person might commit crimes if bailed. Finally, the bail clause bound courts, not Congress. Given the Court's extraordinary deference to Congress on an important Bill of Rights issue, *Salerno* may deserve a good part of Justice Marshall's denunciation and show the risks of judicial faineance. However, the risk comes from Congress, not an acquiescent Court, and Congress is controllable by the people.

LEONARD W. LEVY

SCALIA, ANTONIN
(1936–)

Associate Justice Antonin "Nino" Scalia became the 103rd Justice of the United States Supreme Court on September 27, 1986. Justice Scalia came to the Court after a distinguished career in law, teaching, government, and as a federal appellate judge. He is the first Italian-American to be appointed to the Court and was second of three conservative Supreme Court Justices appointed by President RONALD REAGAN [3,I]. Scalia has established himself as an outspoken proponent of a jurisprudence that is profoundly at odds with the jurisprudence of later twentieth-century LIBERALISM [I] (i.e., the liberalism of the WARREN COURT [4]) and differs in significant detail from current judicial conservatism of the role it assigns the judiciary. Before analyzing this jurisprudence, it is important to place it in the context of Scalia's life and professional career, both of which had revealed him as an articulate exponent of political CONSERVATIVE opinions.

Scalia was born in Trenton, New Jersey, on March 11, 1936, the only child of Italian immigrant parents. The family moved later to Queens, New York, where Scalia's father, S. Eugene Scalia, was a college professor, and his mother, Catherine Louise Panaro Scalia, was an elementary school teacher. S. Eugene Scalia was a scholar of romance language and literature who wrote several monographs on Italian literary history and criticism and translated Italian works into English. Antonin Scalia was a brilliant student. He graduated first in his class at a Manhattan Jesuit military academy, Xavier High School, and then repeated that accomplishment at Georgetown University, from which he graduated in 1957. He attended Harvard Law School, where he again excelled scholastically and was elected Note Editor of the *Harvard Law Review*. After graduation he entered practice with Jones, Day, Cockley & Reavis in Cleveland. He practiced corporate law with the firm until 1967, when he declined a partnership offer. Instead, he accepted a position on the faculty of the University of Virginia Law School.

At Virginia, Scalia began, both through his teaching and research, to develop a specialty in ADMINISTRATIVE LAW [1]. He published several articles critical of procedural aspects of federal agencies before leaving Virginia to work in Washington, D.C. Scalia's conservative political orien-tation, which friends and colleagues identify as having been held by him consistently since college, led him to leave teaching to accept several positions in the administration of President RICHARD M. NIXON [3]. He first served as general counsel in the executive office of telecommunications policy and then was appointed chairman of the Administrative Conference of the United States. The conference is responsible for studying common legal and management issues affecting federal executive branch agencies and for recommending improvements in administrative procedures. Scalia next became embroiled in the political battles of WATERGATE [4] when he moved to the Department of Justice in the summer of 1974 as assistant attorney general in charge of the Office of Legal Counsel, the office that provides legal advice to the President. Among Scalia's first duties was drafting a defense of the President's claim that the tapes and records that Congress sought were his property, not the government's, and that they were protected from congressional subpoena by EXECUTIVE PRIVILEGE [2]. After Nixon's resignation, following the Supreme Court's rejection of his argument, Scalia remained at the Justice Department until January 1977 when President GERALD R. FORD left office [2]. He subsequently spent six months at the American Enterprise Institute, a conservative research organization, and then accepted a position as a professor at the University of Chicago School of Law.

Scalia taught at Chicago until his appointment to the federal appellate court bench in 1982. (He served one year as a visiting professor at Stanford Law School.) During his time at Chicago, Scalia established himself as a leading voice among conservative academics. He continued to write and teach in the area of administrative law, and he edited the American Enterprise Institute's journal *Regulation*, which was largely devoted to attacking regulatory excesses and advocating deregulation. Scalia also attacked judicial inattention to the provisions of the Administrative Procedure Act—most notably, the U.S. Court of Appeals for the District of Columbia's review of the work of the Nuclear Regulatory Commission in the *Vermont Yankee Nuclear Power Corp.* case (1978). From 1981 to 1982 Scalia served as chair of the administrative law section of the American Bar Association, and he used his office to call for lawyers to become involved in reforming administrative procedure to make it fit the new environment of deregulation.

Scalia's writings addressed other items on the conservative political agenda as well. He attacked AFFIRMATIVE ACTION [1,I] in a 1979 article in the *Washington University Law Quarterly* both on principle and because he believed that it could not effectively overcome discrimination. He ridiculed white Anglo-Saxon judges such as Justice LEWIS F. POWELL [3,I] and Judge John Minor Wisdom for justifying affirmative action as "restorative justice" when the members of white ethnic groups—such as Scalia's own Italian family—most often bore the cost of compensating blacks for the WASPs' prior treatment of blacks. Scalia further denounced the FREEDOM OF INFORMATION ACT [2] for imposing prohibitive costs on the government and promoting openness at the cost of law enforcement, privacy, and national security, and at an American Enterprise Institute conference in 1978, he blasted the Supreme Court's 1973 ruling in ROE V. WADE [5] for being an illegitimate exercise in judicial lawmaking.

Hence, by the early 1980s, when President Reagan was showing propensity to fill federal court positions with conservative legal academics, Nino Scalia was a prime candidate. He was first offered a position on the United States Court of Appeals for the Seventh Circuit in Chicago, but he turned it down, preferring instead the Court of Appeals for the District of Columbia. A vacancy on that court occurred in 1982, and he resigned his professorship at the University of Chicago to move his wife Maureen and their nine children to Washington, D.C.

Judge Scalia's tenure on the federal appellate bench was marked by the political conservatism of his opinions and by his ability to maintain strong personal working relationships on a court that had been politically and socially divided for many years. Among Scalia's notable opinions on the D.C. Circuit were those that supported the executive branch over both the legislative branch and independent federal agencies. For example, Scalia wrote an opinion striking down the GRAMM-RUDMAN-HOLLINGS ACT [2] on SEPARATION OF POWERS [4] grounds. According to Scalia, the act impermissibly delegated executive branch functions to an official who was subject to removal by Congress. Scalia further gained attention by narrowing press protection from LIBEL [3] suits in two opinions: one against the *Washington Post* and one in which his dissent would have allowed a suit against two political columnists. He also narrowly read Title VII contending in a dissent that sexual harassment on the job did not violate the provisions of the act.

Judge Scalia's conservative politics and his performance as a judge made him the choice of the Reagan administration in 1986 for the Supreme Court seat of Associate Justice WILLIAM H. REHNQUIST [3,I] when the President elevated Rehnquist to the position of Chief Justice. The American Bar Association endorsed Scalia without qualification, and only a few feminist and civil rights groups opposed him at his confirmation hearings. He was subjected to far less criticism and hostile questioning than Rehnquist, and he avoided the political battle his fellow circuit judge, Robert Bork, experienced two years later when he was nominated to the court. The Senate approved Justice Scalia's nomination unanimously on September 16, 1986.

As a Supreme Court Justice, Scalia has received attention for the intellectual tenacity of his positions and for his jurisprudential methodology. Not unexpectedly, he voted most often with the Court's conservatives: Chief Justice Rehnquist, Justice ANTHONY M. KENNEDY [I], Justice SANDRA DAY O'CONNOR [3,I], and Justice BYRON R. WHITE [4,I]. Over the years he has been on the Court, Scalia and the Chief Justice have agreed in about eighty-five percent of the Court's cases, which is similar to his rate of agreement with Justice Kennedy and only slightly higher than the rate with Justice O'Connor. He has agreed with Justice White at a slightly lower rate (seventy-five percent), whereas his agreement rates with Justices WILLIAM J. BRENNAN [1,I], THURGOOD MARSHALL [3,I], HARRY A. BLACKMUN [1,I], and JOHN PAUL STEVENS [4,I] have been closer to fifty percent. That he has voted in support of conservative policies is not surprising. For example, Justice Scalia's dissent in WEBSTER V. REPRODUCTIVE HEALTH SERVICES (1989) [I] argued that ROE V. WADE should be overturned. He joined the majority in striking down affirmative action plans in (CITY OF) RICHMOND V. J. A. CROSON CO. (1989) [I], and he has rejected challenges to the constitutionality of CAPITAL PUNISHMENT [1,I].

What has been noted by commentators, however, is the jurisprudential vision that Justice Scalia has forcefully constructed through his opinions. The cornerstone of his jurisprudence is the limited role of the judge and the judiciary in the American constitutional system. In Scalia's understanding of American democracy, the Constitution granted the legislature and (by delegation) the executive the power to define rights and to determine the wisdom of specific policies designed or executed within their respective constitutional spheres. This may sound similar to the familiar criticism judicial conservatives have made to "judicial legislation" engaged in by liberal justices since the Warren Court. However, Scalia has taken the position further by advancing the argument for judicial restraint across all areas of judging, building on the critiques of JUDICIAL ACTIVISM [3] offered by liberals such as Justices LOUIS D. BRANDEIS [1] and FELIX FRANKFURTER [2] and later elaborated by professors such as Harvard's HENRY HART [2] and Herbert Wechsler. This position must be contrasted to the post-New Deal liberals as well as to many twentieth-century conservatives. Both have had at the core of their jurisprudence an active role for the judiciary as the balancers of society's interests. The liberals have envisioned the judge as the protector of individuals against majoritarian legislatures and thus have used concepts such as DUE PROCESS [2] and EQUAL PROTECTION [2,I] to create rights and strike down both federal and state legislation. Conservatives, typified by Chief Justice WILLIAM HOWARD TAFT [4], have believed that judges should ensure that the majority's legislative actions (which generally have taken the form of increased regulation of social and economic activities) are gradual and that property interests are protected.

Justice Scalia's differences with such conservatives can be illustrated through both his writings and his opinions. Perhaps the most striking comparison that can be made is between his article "The Rule of Law as a Law of Rules" and the writings of Chief Justice Taft. Taft celebrated the creation of "the rule of reasonableness" in determining violations of the provisions of the SHERMAN ANTITRUST ACT [4] precisely because it left the federal judiciary as the arbiter of which monopolies were unlawful. Also, for Taft the glory of the COMMON LAW [1] process was that judges made law incrementally and directed change through their opinions by the elaboration of rules and the application of facts to those rules. Scalia's article directly challenges both these points. He argues that judges should attempt to formulate general rules rather than gradually developing standards through common law case-by-case determinations. He maintains that cases decided by such standards are determined by the weight individual judges place on particular facts, thus allowing the individual to decide outcomes by his or her individual preferences. An example of what Justice Scalia means, as well as how his approach differs from both liberals and conservatives on the Supreme Court, can be found in a recent PUNITIVE DAMAGES [I] case decided by the Court, *Pacific Mutual Life Insurance Co. v. Haslip* (1991). In this opinion, the majority (Justices Blackmun, Rehnquist, White, Marshall, and Stevens) considered the constitutionality of an award of punitive damages by an Alabama jury. The Court held in an opinion by Blackmun that punitive damages were not per se unconstitutional but that due process considerations required that both the process for instructing the jury as well as the amount awarded must be "reasonable" in order to be constitutional. The majority then discussed the factors that should be considered in testing the reasonableness of the award. Justice O'Connor in dissent argued that the Alabama punitive-damages scheme did not meet due process standards as it was impermissibly vague. Justice Scalia concurred in the result reached by the majority, but rejected both its reasoning and that of Justice O'Connor. He rejected the inquiry into the reasonableness or fairness of the procedures because "this jury-like verdict provides no guidance as to whether any *other* procedures are sufficiently 'reasonable,' and thus perpetuates the uncertainty that . . . this case was intended to resolve." Justice Scalia instead derived a per se rule that these damages were constitutional by broadly canvassing this history of their use and concluding that, since they had been "a part of our living tradition that dates back prior to 1868, I would end the suspense

and categorically affirm their validity." He stated that "it is not for the Members of this Court to decide from time to time whether a process approved by the legal traditions of our people is 'due' process, nor do I believe such a rootless analysis to be dictated by our precedents."

As this example reveals, Justice Scalia's attempt to implement judicial restraint requires an interpretive methodology that can derive categorical rules that are founded on something other than the judges' individual sense of what is right. He does not totally embrace ORIGINALISM [I] as do other conservatives such as Robert Bork, although he acknowledges that the intent of the Framers is where analysis must begin. Instead, Justice Scalia has adopted a literalistic approach in which the plain and ordinary meaning of the language of texts—whether they be the U.S. Constitution, statutes, or regulations—must govern the judge's decision. For example, in *Morrison v. Olson* (1989), Justice Scalia issued the only dissent in the case that upheld the federal law governing the appointment of SPECIAL PROSECUTORS [I]. His strongly worded attack on the majority's opinion centered on the wording of Article I. All EXECUTIVE POWER [I] was vested in the President by the wording of Article I, and this law removed some of this power and thus was unconstitutional. He rejected any idea that the Court could balance the interests of the two branches to decide the reasonableness of this statutory scheme. Similarly, in *Cruzan v. Missouri Department of Health* (1990), Scalia concurred in the majority's decision to refuse to create a constitutional RIGHT TO DIE [I]. He differed from the majority in that he would have forthrightly declared that no such right existed because to do so would be "to create out of nothing (for it exists neither in text nor tradition)."

This methodology requires several subsidiary rules. Because the ordinary meaning of the words are to govern, the intent of the drafters of legislation have no place in judicial analysis. Thus, Justice Scalia refused to resort to an inquiry into the legislative history of statutes. If the plain meaning of a law creates a hardship that was unintended or if enforcement of a law as written is unworkable, it is for the legislative branch to redraft the act rather than for judges to amend it through their interpretations. Scalia outlined this position in his first term on the Court in a concurrence in *Immigration & Naturalization Service v. Cardoza Fonseca* (1987). He stated that the Court's result was correct, but that it could reach the result through the plain meaning of the statute. Not only was the majority's inquiry into the legislative history unnecessary, it was also irrelevant. He thus rejected a technique not only used consistently by the Warren Court but also accepted by conservative Justices. Second, when the ordinary meaning of a text is not determinative, the judge should look to "objective" standards, such as the history and tradition of a particular practice. These would require consultation of historical sources and monographs, as well as judicial PRECEDENTS [3]. An example of this approach was *Pacific Mutual*, where Justice Scalia relied on American common law history of punitive damages to determine what due process meant in this context. Similarly, in STANFORD V. KENTUCKY (1989) [I] Justice Scalia determined that executing a juvenile was not "cruel and unusual" under the Eighth Amendment because, in part, a canvass of state laws showed that a majority allowed execution of sixteen-year-olds. Thus, he reasoned, the practice could not be considered unusual.

Two points should be made in concluding a review of Justice Scalia's strikingly innovative jurisprudential methodology. As most of the examples reveal, his approach is most often made in concurrences or individual dissents. At the Supreme Court he has not played the role of a consensus builder, and in fact, his sharp attacks on other Justices in dissent (most notably against Justice O'Connor in *Webster*) have received critical comment. Although there is some evidence that the Court has moved toward him on some issues, such as ignoring legislative history, he has yet to emerge as the intellectual leader of the Court, as opposed to a single highly intelligent voice. Second, his jurisprudence has been developed at a time when political conservatives have enjoyed considerable success in both legislative and executive branches on the state and federal levels. Although there is certainly some evidence that he has followed his methodology even when it has surprisingly resulted in liberal outcomes (he voted to strike down the FLAG DESECRATION [2,I] statute in *Johnson v. Texas* [1989] and has reached prodefendant positions in several CRIMINAL PROCEDURE [2] cases, it remains to be seen what might happen if the future were to bring a strongly liberal executive and legislature intent on expanding federal social and economic reform.

RAYMAN L. SOLOMAN

(SEE ALSO: *Coy v. Iowa* [I]; *Johnson v. Transportation Agency* [I]; *Lemon Test* [I]; *Rutan v. Republican Party of Illinois* [I].)

Bibliography

COMMENT 1987 The Appellate Jurisprudence of Justice Antonin Scalia. *University of Chicago Law Review* 54:705–739.

ESKRIDGE, WILLIAM N., JR. 1990 The New Textualism. *University of California at Los Angeles Law Review* 37:621–691.

KANNAR, GEORGE 1990 The Constitutional Catechism of Antonin Scalia. *The Yale Law Journal* 99:849–865.

SCALIA, ANTONIN 1989 Originalism; The Lesser Evil. *University of Cincinnati Law Review* 57:849–865.

———— 1989 The Rule of Law as a Law of Rules. *University of Chicago Law Review* 56:1175–1188.

SCIENTIFIC CREATIONISM

See: Creationism

SCHOOL PRAYERS

Few constitutional issues have generated as much public controversy, and as much confusion, as the question of prayer in public schools. The Supreme Court's 1962 decision in ENGEL V. VITALE [2] concerned an official prayer that had been composed by a group of politically appointed officials, the New York State Board of Regents. The defendant school district required every school principal to direct that the Regents' prayer be recited in unison in every classroom at the beginning of each school day. The Court held that even though individual students were permitted to abstain from participating in the recitation, the program violated the ESTABLISHMENT CLAUSE [I] because it "officially establishe[d] the religious beliefs embodied in the Regents' prayer."

One year later the Court applied the principle of *Engel* to religious readings selected by public officials. Laws in Pennsylvania and Baltimore required every public school to begin each day with the reading of verses from the Holy Bible and group recital of the Lord's Prayer. Students were permitted to be excused from participation upon written request of a parent or guardian. In ABINGTON TOWNSHIP SCHOOL DISTRICT V. SCHEMPP [I], the Court held that these programs also violated the establishment clause, which the Court interpreted to preclude actions by state or federal governments that had the purpose or primary effect of either advancing or inhibiting religion. The Court noted that while the FIRST AMENDMENT [2,I] permitted the study of the Bible or religion as part of its program of education, it did not permit government to organize devotional religious exercises. The fact that the particular devotionals had been selected by government officials, rather than composed by them as in *Engel*, was not a difference of constitutional import.

The school prayer and Bible reading decisions sparked a substantial public outcry, and repeated, unsuccessful efforts were made to overturn the decisions by amending the Constitution. The decisions were misinterpreted by some to mean that even the utterance of a private prayer by an individual student while at school was unconstitutional. What the establishment clause actually prohibited was action by government officials that endorsed or inhibited religion, and not religious activity initiated by students and not encouraged or promoted by school officials.

As subsequent decisions would make clear, the Court had never held that prayer itself was necessarily precluded in public schools or other public buildings, as long as the prayer resulted wholly from the private choice of individual citizens. Although the Court in WALLACE V. JAFFREE (1985) [4] invalidated an Alabama law providing for a moment of silence "for meditation or voluntary prayer," a majority of the Court strongly suggested that some laws providing for a moment of silence would be constitutional. Alabama had previously enacted a statute, sustained by the lower court and not challenged before the Supreme Court, which authorized a one-minute period of silence for meditation. The new statute before the Court in *Jaffree* added "prayer" as an expressly approved activity. Because students were provided an opportunity to pray under the earlier moment-of-silence statute, the new law's only additional purpose appeared to be "the State's endorsement and promotion of religion and a particular religious practice." This, the Court held, crossed the line into impermissible endorsement by the government. A majority of the Justices indicated, however, that they would sustain moment-of-silence laws that did not expressly single out prayer as one of the officially preferred activities.

When a statute creates an open, undesignated silent time, government itself has not undertaken to favor or disfavor religion. The seemingly trivial addition of the words "for prayer" to a moment-of-silence law crosses the line of constitutionality precisely because it is unnecessary to the goal of creating an opportunity for students to choose to pray. If a simple moment of silence is created at school, parents and religious leaders may, if they wish, suggest to their children or parishioners that they use the moment of silence for prayer. Expressly providing in the state's code of laws that "prayer" is a designated activity unnecessarily takes the state itself into the improper business of official endorsement and promotion of a religious exercise.

Ideally, a simple moment of silence is functionally a one-minute open forum which each student can fill as she chooses. Implementation of such a policy in a truly neutral fashion is, however, difficult in practice. The facts of some lower court cases suggest that teachers and school officials in some districts have encouraged or coerced students to pray during the silent moment. Teachers may appropriately ask students to remain quiet for the moment of silence; if teachers suggest or insist that students pray or adopt a prayerful attitude, they have invoked the authority of the state for an impermissible end.

The Court has also used the concept of the open forum to permit students at school to engage in spoken, group prayers as long as the religious activities are not encouraged, endorsed, or promoted by government or school officials. In WIDMAR V. VINCENT (1981) [4], the Court held that a state university that allowed a wide range of voluntary student activity groups to meet in university facilities was not required by the establishment clause

to deny access to student-initiated religious clubs whose meetings on school property included prayer and other devotionals. Indeed, such clubs had a free speech right of EQUAL ACCESS [I] to the school's facilities on the same basis as volunteer student groups engaged in other speech activities. In BOARD OF EDUCATION OF WESTSIDE COMMUNITY SCHOOLS V. MERGENS (1990) [I] the Court sustained the federal Equal Access Act that extended this principle to public secondary schools. The act provides that when a public school creates a "limited open forum" by allowing student-initiated, noncurriculum groups to meet at the school, it may not deny access to the school for meetings of other student-initiated groups on the basis of the "religious, political, philosophical, or other content of the speech at such meetings." One effect of the act is to give student religious clubs (whose meetings may include prayer) the same right to meet on campus as other noncurricular, student-initiated organizations like the chess club or the Young Democrats.

Even though many in the public remain unreconciled to the original school prayer and Bible reading decisions, and even though some recent decisions suggest that the Supreme Court is becoming more tolerant of some governmental promotion of religion, it seems unlikely that the Court's original decisions will soon be overturned either by the Court or by constitutional amendment. The constitutional principle remains for now, as it was when Justice HUGO BLACK [1] wrote for the Court in *Engel*: "it is no part of the business of government to compose official prayers for any group of the American people to recite as part of a religious program carried on by government."

WALTER DELLINGER

(SEE ALSO: *Bender v. Williamsport* [I]; *Lemon Test* [I]; *Religion in Public Schools* [3,I]; *Separation of Church and State* [4,I].)

Bibliography

DELLINGER, WALTER 1986 The Sound of Silence: An Epistle on Prayer and the Constitution. *Yale Law Journal* 95:1631–1646.

LAYCOCK, DOUGLAS 1986 Equal Access and Moments of Silence: The Equal Status of Religious Speech by Private Speakers. *Northwestern University Law Review* 81:1–67.

SCIENCE, TECHNOLOGY, AND THE CONSTITUTION

The Constitution's only reference to science occurs in Article I, section 8, which grants, among other congressional powers, the authority to "promote Science and useful Arts" by establishing nationwide protection of PATENTS [3,I] and COPYRIGHTS [2]. Despite the document's otherwise silence on the subject, a constitutional law of science may be evolving—an inevitable and, to some extent, auspicious development in our technological age. Indeed, cases involving some aspect of the constitutional status of science form a burgeoning part of constitutional law, principally, but not exclusively, under the FIRST AMENDMENT [2,1].

Perhaps the most obvious question about the status of science is whether scientific speech falls within the First Amendment's protection of FREEDOM OF SPEECH [2,1]. Some critics, notably Robert Bork, have challenged the idea that scientific speech is fully protected, and no court has reached the question explicitly. The most likely answer, should a case arise, is that scientific communication is entitled to the same degree of First Amendment protection as other speech. A number of decided cases, including the Supreme Court's opinion in GRISWOLD V. CONNECTICUT (1965) [2], contain OBITER DICTA [3] referring to scientific speech as though it were in no way different from other First Amendment activity. If one sees the First Amendment's protection of speech as a means of enabling self-actualization or of discovering truth through the free interplay of ideas, the case for including scientific speech is straightforward. But even if one considers political debate as the core of the constitutional guarantee, in our society the use and regulation of technology form a central part of governmental activity. Debate concerning the scope and efficacy of these efforts will necessarily include a scientific component.

Scientific researchers insist that absolute freedom to communicate their ideas is necessary to the scientific enterprise. Constitutional protection, however, is rarely absolute, and to say that scientific speech is protected is only a part of the answer. Like other speech, scientific speech may be subject to regulation in certain circumstances. In particular, the federal government has increasingly sought to regulate the flow of scientific information in the name of NATIONAL SECURITY [3].

National security regulations on scientific speech fall into two broad categories. First, there are restrictions through which the government seeks ownership of the information in question. For example, under the "born classified" provisions of the ATOMIC ENERGY ACT [1], inventions or discoveries that are "useful solely in the utilization of special nuclear material or atomic energy in an atomic weapon" are not patentable and, in many cases, are from their inception property of the federal government. The constitutionality of this restriction apparently has never been challenged, but given the plenary nature of congressional authority over the patent system, it is difficult to imagine that it would be struck down.

Second, there are restrictions through which the government, without regard to ownership, seeks to regulate the transmittal of the information in question. For example, a number of federal regulations seek to treat certain scientific information, especially information on "military critical technologies," as a commodity, subject to export restrictions. Another example is the consistent effort by the National Security Agency to discourage American researchers from publicly revealing (even in the United States) the fruits of any work with important implications for the field of encryption.

What the government must show to sustain its regulation is unclear because the constitutionality of national security restrictions on the communication of scientific information has been rarely tested. An exception is *United States v. The Progressive* (1979), in which the federal government sought to enjoin the publication of a magazine article that purportedly revealed how to construct a hydrogen bomb. A federal district court granted the INJUNCTION [2], holding that the publication of the article might do infinite damage to the nation's (and the world's) security, and therefore, the test of NEAR V. MINNESOTA EX. REL. OLSON (1931) [3] and NEW YORK TIMES V. UNITED STATES (1971) [3] was easily met. Before an APPEAL [1] could be decided, however, the article was published elsewhere and the trial court's judgment was vacated as moot.

Critics mocked the court's reasoning, arguing that it would enable government to enjoin publication of many scientific ideas; all the court required was a showing of a minuscule possibility of infinite harm. As has subsequently become clear, moreover, the article involved in *The Progressive*, although setting out some of the theory behind the hydrogen bomb, did not actually reveal the critical model necessary to make the bomb explode. The trial judge undertook no close scrutiny of the article, however, resting his decision on the government's affidavits. In so doing, the judge showed far greater deference to the government's assertion of harm to the nation's national security than have courts confronted with similar claims when the speech in question has lacked a scientific component. The one lesson of *The Progressive* is that courts may view an argument that scientific speech will harm the nation's security with considerably greater sympathy than they have displayed for the same argument concerning other kinds of speech.

Not all attempted restrictions on scientific speech rest on a national security foundation. Perhaps the most controversial attempt has been the effort by some believers in the Genesis account of creation to prohibit or limit the teaching of the theory of evolution in public school classrooms. *Scopes v. State* (1927), in which Clarence Darrow battled eloquently, but in vain to prevent the conviction of a teacher for violating a ban on teaching the Darwinian theory of evolution in the public schools, is a part of our popular legal mythology, but the *Scopes* case was the zenith of judicial deference to creationism. In recent decades, the federal courts have been unwavering in their refusal to allow restrictions on the teaching of evolution in public schools. Thus in EPPERSON V. ARKANSAS (1968) [2], the Supreme Court struck down a state prohibition on teaching evolution. In *Daniel v. Waters* (1975), a federal appeals court overturned a state law requiring that students be told that evolution is a theory, not a fact. In *Edwards v. Aguillard* (1987) the Supreme Court held UNCONSTITUTIONAL "balanced treatment" legislation that mandated the teaching of CREATIONISM [I] alongside the theory of evolution.

Some commentators have argued that such decisions as these are most readily defensible on the ground that children in a public school classroom are a captive audience lacking the ability to draw some of the critical distinctions that adults might draw. The courts, however, have in each case rested squarely on the ESTABLISHMENT CLAUSE [I]. The courts have viewed the entire effort at restricting the teaching of evolution as a religiously motivated assault on modern science. (Even in *Scopes*, the state supreme court sustained Tennessee's antievolution statute only after the state argued that deleting evolution from the curriculum was the only way to get the public to accept modern science instruction in the schools.) So, whatever may be the constitutional status of national security–based restrictions on scientific speech, the courts seem disinclined to permit restrictions that appear to be based on religious belief.

A chorus of critics has suggested that by striking down balanced-treatment statutes the courts are in effect granting science itself a special constitutional status. Justice ANTONIN SCALIA [I], in his dissent in *Edwards,* did not embrace this broad-scale criticism, but he did raise a related objection to the Court's decision. He argued that the Louisiana legislature had determined, on the advice of people they considered scientists, that creation science was not just religious dogma but a scientific theory founded on evidence and subjected to testing. As yet, the Court had before it no interpretation by the Louisiana Supreme Court of the law's meaning and no evidence of its actual application in the schools. Thus, he argued, it was premature for the Court to conclude that the legislature's purpose was merely to promote a religious belief.

The more far-reaching criticism, that the courts are giving science a special status under the Constitution, is met head on by some critics who assert that the courts should do precisely that. Proponents of this view typically point to the views of the Founders, many of whom accepted a contemporaneous, philosophical, commonplace holding of scientific progress to be an essential component of human happiness. A few scholars, perhaps stretching

an otherwise interesting historical point, have even tried to demonstrate that the Founders intended to write this doctrine into the Constitution itself.

This is an argumentative turn that matters because the more important problem for scientific researchers may not be potential restrictions on communication, but the possibility of limits on experiments. In this situation, the difficulty is not religious belief but public fear and skepticism. The use of bona fide health and safety arguments to justify the regulation of the use of technology is nothing new and raises no significant constitutional questions. Scientific experiment, however, lies somewhere between pure scientific speech and pure application of technology, and recent efforts at its regulation have led to constitutional controversy.

A particular focus of debate is the effort in recent years to restrict experimentation on recombinant deoxyribonucleic acid (rDNA) techniques and other aspects of the "new biology" because of popular concern over the results and the implications. Several years ago, for example, Cambridge, Massachusetts, the home of two of the nation's leading research universities, was urged to adopt an ordinance banning rDNA experiments. Cambridge finally settled for requiring compliance with certain federal guidelines, but for a time, the matter seemed to hang in the balance. Experts argued that the techniques were relatively safe, but many members of the public simply disbelieved the experts' claims.

In response to the wave of public fear in the 1970s and 1980s, several commentators urged a form of First Amendment protection for scientific experiment. The difficulty these theorists have faced is overcoming the distinction between speech and conduct that has long governed First Amendment jurisprudence; scientific experiment would seem to fall plainly on the conduct side of the divide. But theorists have challenged the application of this neat dichotomy to the distinction between scientific speech and scientific experiment. Some supporters of protection for experiment have claimed to find support in the original understanding of free speech, others have contended that experiment is as important as communication for self-actualization, and still others have argued that experimentation is protected because it is a prerequisite to the protected activity of scientific speech. Critics have responded that the First Amendment argument for protection of experiments is clever, but far-fetched. As the critics note, the Supreme court rejected an analogous claim, in *Houchins v. KQED* (1978), that the activity of news gathering is protected as a prerequisite to the protected activity of news reporting. No court has yet accepted the claim of a constitutional right to experiment; on the contrary, courts have occasionally granted injunctions against controversial scientific experiments.

Although freedom of scientific speech has been a central part of the scholarly debate on the constitutional status of science, most Americans are more directly concerned with the technologies that scientific research makes possible, not science itself. This concern has generated arguments for two quite different rights: the right to use technology without governmental interference and the right to be free of governmental use of technology. As a practical matter, courts have dealt with claims of both these kinds in much the same way as they have treated the arguments of scientific creationists: they have tried to follow the experts.

The claim of a right to use technology has been most prominent in debates over medical treatment. For example, in *Andrews v. Ballard* (1980), a federal district court upheld a claim to a constitutional right to choose acupuncture therapy. To reach this result, the court was forced to reconceptualize the Supreme Court's decisions in *Griswold v. Connecticut* and ROE V. WADE (1973) [3] as involving not the RIGHT OF PRIVACY [3,I] *simpliciter*, but rather the right to make a private choice whether to use medically approved BIRTH CONTROL [1] technologies. The requirement of medical approval enabled the court to distinguish acupuncture, which a considerable number of researchers believe to hold genuine benefits, from such exotic drugs as laetrile, which the medical profession generally rejects as a cancer treatment. (The courts have rejected arguments for a constitutional right to use laetrile.)

The idea of a constitutional right to be free from governmental use of technology was rejected at the turn of the century in JACOBSON V. MASSACHUSETTS (1904) [3]. In this case, the Supreme Court rejected a constitutional challenge to a mandatory vaccination against smallpox. The Court cited the right of the state to protect itself, and faced with the argument that vaccination was unnecessary or dangerous, or both, responded that it was the responsibility of the legislature, not the Court, to choose among competing medical theories. More recently, courts have employed similarly deferential reasoning to sustain such regulations as forced medical care for children whose parents raise religious objections and mandatory AIDS testing of some federal employees.

Perhaps the most controversial among recent governmental uses of technology, however, is mandatory DRUG TESTING [2] of employees. In NATIONAL TREASURY EMPLOYEES UNION V. VON RAAB (1989) [I] and SKINNER V. RAILWAY LABOR EXECUTIVES ASSOCIATION (1989) [I] the Supreme Court rejected FOURTH AMENDMENT [2,I] privacy challenges to two very different programs of drug testing. In *Skinner*, the Justices voted 7–2 to sustain federal regulations allowing railroads to require breath and urine tests to determine whether employees committing

safety infractions had used alcohol or drugs. In *National Treasury Employees Union*, the Court voted 5–4 to uphold a program mandating urine tests for employees seeking transfer or promotion to positions in drug-interdiction programs.

Both cases were decided on technical Fourth Amendment arguments not relevant to this discussion. In each case, however, the majority found it necessary to make reference to the accuracy of the tests. Thus in *Skinner*, the Court stated that the breath and urine tests, "if properly conducted, identify the presence of alcohol and drugs in the biological samples tested with great accuracy." In *National Treasury Employees Union*, the Court took care to note that the test "is highly accurate, assuming proper storage, handling, and measurement techniques." In neither opinion did the Justices explicitly hold that the accuracy of the tests was a factor in their decision. Nevertheless, the fact that they mentioned the point at all and with such confidence raises the possibility that they might have reached a different result had serious expert challenges to the tests been available.

None of this suggests that expert agreement on a sufficiently accurate result is itself a decisive argument in favor of constitutionality. But these and other opinions plainly raise the possibility that the Supreme Court will defer to scientific expertise in answering constitutional questions. This judicial deference, if it exists, might reflect a recognition by the courts of their limited capacity to decide scientific questions. The difficulties that courts and legislatures alike have with science have led a number of commentators, notably Arthur Kantrowitz, to suggest the creation of a special science Court to decide the scientific components of complex policy and legal questions. Critics of the Science Court proposal call it undemocratic. Defenders argue that democracy would be better served if courts and other decisionmakers made no pretense of scientific expertise.

The possibility that the courts really do defer to scientific judgments in resolving constitutional questions has led not only to scientific creationism but to such legislative initiatives as the Human Life Bill advocated by the ANTI-ABORTION MOVEMENT [I]. That bill, had the Congress enacted it, would have tried to overturn *Roe v. Wade* by finding as a scientific fact that life begins at conception. That a Human Life Bill would even be offered, or that creationists would think their views more acceptable if dressed up as natural science might, after all hold a special constitutional status.

STEPHEN L. CARTER

Bibliography

CARTER, STEPHEN L. 1987 Evolutionism, Creationism, and Treating Religion as a Hobby. *Duke Law Journal* 1987:977.

CARTER, STEPHEN L. 1985 The Bellman, the Snark, and the Biohazard Debate. *Yale Law and Policy Review* 3:358.

DELGADO, RICHARD 1978 God, Galileo, & Government: Toward Constitutional Protection for Scientific Inquiry. *Washington Law Review* 53:349–404.

FERGUSON, JAMES R. 1979 Scientific Inquiry and the First Amendment. *Cornell Law Review* 64:639–665.

GOLDBERG, STEVEN 1979 The Constitutional Status of American Science. *University of Illinois Law Forum* 1979:1–33.

REDISH, MARTIN H. 1985 Limits on Scientific Expression and the Scope of First Amendment Analysis. *William and Mary Law Review* 26:863–907.

ROBERTSON, JOHN A. 1978 The Scientist's Right to Research: A Constitutional Analysis. *Southern California Law Review* 51:1203–1279.

SEARCH AND SEIZURE

Since 1985 the Supreme Court has refined and expanded upon previously articulated exceptions to the SEARCH WARRANT [4] requirement, the PROBABLE CAUSE [3] requirement, and the EXCLUSIONARY RULE [3]. Few decisions have addressed novel issues or fashioned new approaches to the FOURTH AMENDMENT [2,I].

Earlier cases, beginning with CAMARA V. MUNICIPAL COURT (1967) [1] and TERRY V. OHIO (1968) [4], established that a warrant and probable cause may not be needed when a search is undertaken primarily for noncriminal purposes or is limited in scope. Rather, the essential criterion of the Fourth Amendment is "reasonableness," which requires balancing the intrusiveness of a particular category of search against the special law enforcement needs served by the search. In recent years, the Court has increasingly applied a BALANCING TEST [1] to permit the government to conduct WARRANTLESS SEARCHES [4] and searches with less than probable cause, in pursuit of special law enforcement interests aimed at particular groups, including government employees, schoolchildren, probationers, prisoners, and automobile owners.

Two recent decisions upholding government employee DRUG TESTING [I] programs illustrate both the advantages and the difficulties of a balancing approach to the Fourth Amendment. Balancing is attractive because it permits the Court to give a full account of competing interests and to adjust constitutional limitations accordingly. In SKINNER V. RAILWAY LABOR EXECUTIVES ASSOCIATION (1989) [I], which upheld mandatory blood and urine testing of all railroad workers involved in train accidents or certain safety violations, the Court engaged in a two-stage analysis. First, the pervasively regulated nature of the railroad industry and railroad employees' awareness of the testing regime lessened the employees' REASONABLE EXPECTATION OF PRIVACY [I] concerning their bodily fluids. Second, the government's interest in deterrence and detection of drug use by railroad workers, in order to ensure safety on the railroads, was sufficiently compelling to outweigh any residue of legitimate privacy expectations with respect to testing of bodily fluids.

The limitations of balancing analysis become apparent in a companion case, NATIONAL TREASURY EMPLOYEES V. VON RAAB (1989) [I]. At issue in *Von Raab* was a more sweeping program that required drug testing of all Customs Service employees hired or promoted into positions in which they would carry guns or come into contact with drugs. Yet *Skinner*—which, like all balancing opinions, was inherently fact-specific and conclusory—shed little light on how *Von Raab* should be resolved. Ultimately, a bare majority upheld the Customs Service program, concluding that the government's special need for honest "frontline offices" in the midst of a national illicit drug crisis outweighed any individual Customs Service employee's expectation of privacy. For Justice ANTONIN SCALIA [I] in dissent, the balance came out differently in *Von Raab* because there was no record of a history of substance abuse in the Customs Service, as there had been in the railroad industry of *Skinner*. Yet others might strike the opposite balance, upholding the program in *Von Raab* but not that in *Skinner*, on the ground that the Customs Service program contained a significant internal limitation not present in the railroad program: that the government could not use drug test results in criminal prosecutions.

The Customs Service program is almost unique in actually prohibiting introduction of acquired evidence in criminal trials, but in several other recent search cases the Court has invoked government interests other than criminal prosecution. Noncriminal motivation was critical in the school search case NEW JERSEY V. T.L.O. (1984) [3]. In the Court's view, the special interest of school authorities in maintaining order permits them to search a student when there are "reasonable" grounds for believing the search will yield evidence of a violation of a law or a school rule and the search is not especially intrusive. *T.L.O.* expressly withheld judgment as to whether the police, as opposed to school officials, could likewise conduct school searches without a warrant and on less than probable cause. Yet, in *New York v. Burger* (1987), the Court permitted evidence seized from automobile junkyards in warrantless ADMINISTRATIVE SEARCHES [1,I] conducted by police officers to be used for penal, as well as administrative, purposes because the two purposes were sufficiently related.

The government's interest in effective supervision of particular groups was also determinative in *Griffin v. Wisconsin* (1987), which held that probation officers may search probationers' homes if there are "reasonable grounds" to suspect a probation violation, and in *O'Connor v. Ortega* (1987), which held that government supervisors may search employee offices for "work-related purposes" (in this case, to investigate alleged misconduct). The Court has declined to establish an explicit middle-tier cause standard somewhere between probable cause and the *Terry* "reasonable suspicion" standard. Nevertheless, the "reasonable scope" test of *T.L.O.* may implicitly create such an intermediate standard governing focused searches for primarily noncriminal purposes.

In several other recent cases, the Court has refused to impose Fourth Amendment limitations on particular categories of investigative activity on the basis that the activities at issue were not "searches" at all under the Fourth Amendment. In *California v. Ciraolo* (1985) and *Florida v. Riley* (1989), the Court concluded that there are no Fourth Amendment restrictions on aerial surveillance from publicly navigable airspace (by plane and by helicopter, respectively). In *California v. Greenwood* (1988) the Court agreed with the great majority of lower courts in holding that police need neither particularized suspicion nor a warrant to seize trash placed for roadside pickup. In each of these cases, the Court applied the two-pronged test set forth in KATZ V. UNITED STATES (1967) [3] for determining when government action invades privacy protected by the Fourth Amendment: first, whether the individual has an actual expectation of privacy and, second, whether any such expectation of privacy is reasonable or legitimate. The majority in each case concluded that any expectation of privacy was not one "the society" at large was prepared to accept as reasonable. The Court made clear that state law is not controlling either as to the creation of privacy expectations or as to their reasonableness, although FAA regulations apparently are highly relevant to both prongs of the test. Despite the invocation of *Katz*, each decision is more persuasive by analogy to the pre-*Katz* test for determining what constitutes a search under the Fourth Amendment: whether there has been a trespass upon traditionally recognized property interests.

The Supreme Court has continued to cast an unfavorable eye on the exclusionary rule, which precludes admission at trial of evidence obtained through an illegal search or seizure. Previously, in NIX V. WILLIAMS (1984) [3], the Court had ruled that illegally seized evidence is admissible if it would have been "inevitably discovered" through an "independent source." In *Murray v. United States* (1988), a four-Justice majority (Justices WILLIAM J. BRENNAN [1,I] and ANTHONY KENNEDY [I] not participating) applied the logic of the INEVITABLE DISCOVERY [I] and "independent source" exceptions to permit admission of evidence first viewed in an illegal search as long as the evidence was subsequently seized pursuant to an indepen-

dently valid search warrant. The moral hazard of these two exceptions to the exclusionary rule is especially apparent in *Murray*, which may be read to provide an incentive to make an illegal search to determine whether obtaining a search warrant later would be worthwhile. Yet the Court is intent upon reminding us that there is also hazard—to society at large and to the integrity of criminal trials—in suppressing probative evidence, especially where probable cause existed apart from any illegal search.

The Court has also expanded the exclusionary rule's GOOD FAITH EXCEPTION [2], first developed in *United States v. Leon* (1984), to include warrantless administrative searches authorized by statutes later held to be unconstitutional; *Illinois v. Krull* (1987) held that the exception applies whenever the police officer acts "in good-faith reliance on an apparently valid statute." *Krull* thus signals a departure from *Leon*, which had given much weight to institutional considerations justifying reliance on search warrants issued by neutral, independent judicial officers. As Justice SANDRA DAY O'CONNOR [3,I] indicated in dissent for herself and three others, legislative schemes authorizing warrantless searches do not invite such reliance, because legislators are not expected to operate as independent, politically detached interpreters of the Constitution.

Some recent cases have articulated new Fourth Amendment standards. In *Winston v. Lee* (1984) the Court recognized that the Fourth Amendment may prohibit as unreasonable certain forms of search and seizure (in this case, surgically extracting a bullet from the body) even where there is probable cause. Similarly, TENNESSEE V. GARNER (1984) [4] held that the shooting death of a fleeing felon is an unreasonable form of seizure, even though there was probable cause to believe the individual had just been engaged in burglary, because the police lacked probable cause to believe that the burglary involved violence or that the felon otherwise presented a threat to someone's physical safety.

It was unclear after *Garner* whether successful termination of freedom of movement is a sine qua non for a "seizure" under the Fourth Amendment. The majority in *Michigan v. Chesternut* (1988) rejected both the state's argument that no seizure occurs "until an individual stops in response" to a show of authority and the defendant's contention that a seizure occurs as soon as the police "pursue" an individual; rather, the Court appeared to reaffirm the test of *Florida v. Royer* (1983) and *Immigration and Naturalization Service v. Delgado* (1984): there is a seizure when the police's actions would cause a reasonable person to believe she is not free to leave. During the term after *Chesternut*, however, in *Brower v. County of Inyo* (1989), a bare majority of the Court concluded that a seizure under the Fourth Amendment does not occur until there is an actual "termination of freedom through intentionally applied means."

In other cases, the Court has refused to develop new Fourth Amendment principles. *United States v. Sokolow* (1989) declined to hold a stop unconstitutional merely because it was based on a drug-courier profile; as long as there is *Terry's* "reasonable suspicion" in the particular case, the police may stop the suspect. In *United States v. Verdugo-Urquidez* (1990), the Court refused to apply Fourth Amendment limitations to U.S. law enforcement agents operating against aliens in foreign jurisdictions.

KATE STITH

(SEE ALSO: *Fourth Amendment* [I].)

Bibliography

GOLDSTEIN, ABRAHAM S. 1987 The Search Warrant, the Magistrate, and Judicial Review. *New York University Law Review* 62:1173–1217.

GRANO, JOSEPH 1984 Probable Cause and Common Sense: A Reply to the Critics of *Illinois v. Gates. University of Michigan Journal of Law Reform* 17:465–521.

KAMISAR, YALE 1987 Comparative Reprehensibility and the Fourth Amendment Exclusionary Rule. *University of Michigan Law Review* 86:1–50.

SECOND WORLD WAR

See: World War II and the Constitution

SENATE

The United States Senate resulted from the decision of the CONSTITUTIONAL CONVENTION OF 1787 [1] to replace the unicameral legislature that had functioned under the ARTICLES OF CONFEDERATION [1] with a bicameral Congress. BICAMERALISM [1] reflected the existing structure of the British Parliament and most of the state legislatures. The VIRGINIA PLAN [4] originally proposed that the larger, popularly elected HOUSE OF REPRESENTATIVES [I] elect the smaller "second house," but the convention ultimately assigned the election of senators to the state legislatures. On the issue of representation, the Convention reached an impasse between delegates from larger states, who wanted both houses of Congress apportioned according to population, and those from smaller states, who demanded equal status. The GREAT COMPROMISE [2] satisfied these conflicting demands by giving each state two seats in the Senate and assigning seats in the House by population. Equality was so essential for the smaller states that the Constitution further specified that "no State without

its Consent, shall be deprived of its equal Suffrage in the Senate" (Article V).

The Senate (from the Latin *senatus*, council of elders) was expected to provide a check on the popularly elected House. Envisioning an American House of Lords, some delegates to the Constitutional Convention proposed that senators serve for life, at no salary. The convention rejected these strictures, but the Constitution assigns senators six-year terms and requires them to be at least thirty years of age and citizens for nine years (compared with two-year terms, a twenty-five-year age minimum, and seven years of citizenship for representatives). Although the federal Constitution sets no property-holding qualifications for senators, delegates depicted a Senate that would represent landed and commercial interests. "This checking branch must have great personal property," GOUVERNEUR MORRIS [3] insisted, "it must have the aristocratic spirit; it must love to lord it through pride." "A good Senate," said EDMUND RANDOLPH [3], would serve as a cure for the "turbulence and follies of democracy" under which the Congress of the Articles of Confederation had labored. JAMES MADISON [3] observed that while the House might err out of fickleness and passion, the Senate would provide "a necessary fence against this danger."

The delegates first considered assigning appointment of judges and making of treaties to the Senate, but eventually divided these powers between the chief executive and the Senate. The Senate would advise and consent— or withhold consent—on presidential nominations and treaties negotiated by the executive branch. The Senate would share all powers of Congress and participate in all legislative functions. Senators could introduce and amend bills and resolutions without restriction, except that revenue bills must originate in the House, because "the people should hold the purse strings."

Despite their shared legislative powers, the Senate and House from the beginning have acted independently. The Senate sets its own rules, elects its own officers, judges the credentials of its members, and decides any contested elections (first by state legislatures and later by direct election after ratification of the SEVENTEENTH AMENDMENT [4] in 1913). The Senate may also discipline its members through censure and expulsion. During its first two centuries the Senate censured eight senators for conduct ranging from violating Senate secrecy to financial misconduct. Most notably, in 1954 the Senate censured Senator Joseph R. McCarthy of Wisconsin for conduct "contrary to senatorial traditions," relating to his treatment of committee witnesses and other senators. Censure has not led to expulsion, except by the voters in the next election. The Senate has expelled only WILLIAM BLOUNT [1], charged with treasonous conspiracy in 1797, and fourteen senators who supported the Confederacy during the CIVIL WAR. Every other expulsion proceeding has ended either with the senator's vindication or with his resignation to avoid an expulsion vote.

Unlike the House, whose membership stands for election every two years, senators are divided into three classes elected at two-year intervals. Because at least two-thirds of the Senate continues in office from one Congress to the next, the Senate has defined itself as a continuing body that does not need to reestablish its rules at the start of each Congress. Although the House elects its own presiding officer, the vice-president of the United States serves as the president of the Senate. To preside in the vice-president's absence, the Senate elects a president pro tempore, generally the most senior member of the majority party. As the presiding officer, the vice-president has to play an essentially neutral role, voting only to break ties, speaking only with the permission of the Senate, and having his rulings subject to reversal by vote of the Senate.

The Constitution requires each house of Congress to publish a journal of its proceedings. Since 1789, the Senate has produced legislative and executive journals, which consist of short minutes of official actions taken on all bills, resolutions, treaties, and nominations. Separately from these journals, the *Congressional Record* evolved from stenographic notes published in private newspapers. Prior to the *Congressional Record*, these notes were compiled in the *Annals of Congress* (1789–1824), the *Register of Debates in Congress* (1824–1837), and the *Congressional Globe* (1833–1873).

For its first years the Senate met entirely in secret session, while the House immediately opened its doors. Seeing their role as a council to revise LEGISLATION [3] drafted in the House and to advise the President on nominations and treaties, and having no need to appeal to their constituents, senators believed they could debate more freely and productively without a public gallery. In 1795, after much criticism in the press, the Senate regularly admitted the public to view legislative sessions, but continued to conduct most executive business—treaties and nominations—in closed session until 1929. Persistent leaks of executive sessions to the press steadily diminished their "secret" nature, and the Senate abandoned closed sessions, except for rare instances concerning highly classified information. Even after opening its doors, the Senate received minimal public attention. "Henceforth you will read little of me in the Gazettes," one representative notified his wife after his election to the Senate in 1804. "Senators are less exposed to public view than Representatives." House leadership in national affairs predominated through the War of 1812; but subsequently legislators of the stature of HENRY CLAY [1], DANIEL WEBSTER [4], and JOHN C. CALHOUN [1] found the Senate a better forum for their sectional appeals and national aspirations. While Senate debate flourished, the House in 1847 established a "five-minute rule" for members' speeches. The smaller Senate clung to the tradition of unlimited debate, which took its most extreme form in the filibuster. This stalling devise gave the minority the opportunity to stop objectionable measures by occupying the floor with lengthy speeches and procedural delays. Not until 1917 did the Senate establish the first cloture rule, to provide a mechanism for cutting off debate.

Filibusters proved especially potent during the short second sessions of Congress. The Constitution originally set the opening date of Congress on the first Monday in December, more than a year after the elections. These first sessions generally met through the following spring. The second session again convened on the first Monday in December in the even-numbered years, but automatically expired on March 4. With the Senate facing an absolute deadline and with many of its members having retired or been defeated in the intervening election but not yet out of office, filibusters more easily prevailed. In 1933 the TWENTIETH AMENDMENT [4] moved the opening of each session to January 3, which eliminated the long interregnum after elections and reduced the lame-duck filibusters. However, individual senators, no matter how junior, retain great capacity to defeat or delay legislation through amendments, objections to unanimous-consent requests, filibusters, and other parliamentary maneuvers generally not available to rank-and-file members of the House.

The Constitution grants members immunity from prosecution for their remarks in Congress. Judicial interpretations have extended the SPEECH OR DEBATE CLAUSE (Article I, Section 6) [4] to cover a variety of congressional activity. In GRAVEL V. UNITED STATES (1972) [2], the Supreme Court declared Senator Mike Gravel of Alaska and his staff immune from prosecution for making public classified portions of the *Pentagon Papers*. By contrast, the Court ruled in HUTCHINSON V. PROXMIRE (1979) [2] that Senator William Proxmire of Wisconsin had immunity for statements made on the floor but not for information in his press releases and newsletters.

Exercising its ADVICE AND CONSENT [1,I] power, the Senate in 1789 rejected President GEORGE WASHINGTON's [4] nomination of Benjamin Fishbourn as naval officer of the port of Savannah, because of opposition from the senators from Georgia. Fishbourn's rejection was the first instance of "senatorial courtesy," by which the Senate deferred to the objections of senators from a nominee's home state. This practice has given senators great influence over the nominations of federal judges and attorneys from their states. In 1795 the Senate rejected Washington's nomination of JOHN RUTLEDGE [3] as CHIEF JUSTICE [1] of the United States, citing Rutledge's intemperate speeches on political issues. Over the next two centuries, the Senate rejected nearly twenty percent of all Supreme Court nominees, while it turned down only three percent of all Cabinet nominees. The disparity reflected senatorial attitudes that cabinet members should reflect the President's choices, but the Supreme Court is an independent branch not responsible to the President. The Senate has also tended to reject judicial appointments made during the President's last months in office.

Similarly, the Senate asserted its authority to advise and consent on the ratification of treaties. In 1789, at the urging of members, President Washington personally appeared in the Senate chamber to receive the Senate's advice on questions relating to the negotiation of treaties with several Indian nations. When the Senate deferred debate until the questions had been studied in committee, Washington determined not to repeat the experiment. Succeeding Presidents have generally limited themselves to seeking the Senate's consent rather than its advice.

In offering consent, the Senate has revised treaties through amendments, reservations, and understandings. In 1795 the Senate approved JAY'S TREATY [3] with Great Britain only with the understanding that certain trade provisions would be renegotiated. In 1824 advocates of SLAVERY [4] deliberately amended a treaty regarding suppression of the slave trade to cause Great Britain to reject the agreement. The following year, the Senate defeated a similar treaty with Colombia, marking its first formal rejection of a treaty. The Supreme Court consistently upheld the Senate's right to alter treaties, noting in *Haver v. Yaker* (1869) that "a treaty is more than a contract, for the Federal Constitution declares it to be the law of the land. If so, before it can become law, the Senate in whom rests authority to ratify it, must agree to it. But the Senate are not required to adopt or reject it as a whole, but may modify or amend it." Such revisions often provide the basis for consensus needed to achieve the constitutional two-thirds vote in favor of ratification. Most notably, the Senate's failure to agree on reservations to the Treaty of Versailles in 1919 and 1920 caused the treaty to fall short of a two-thirds vote of approval.

The division of power on foreign policy has been "an invitation to struggle" between the President and Congress. Through its influence over treaties and diplomatic nominations, the Senate Foreign Relations Committee exerted considerable influence over foreign policy. By contrast, only through the passage of appropriations bills, largely dealing with foreign aid, has the House exerted comparable authority. Influential chairs of the Foreign Relations Committee, from CHARLES SUMNER [4] and

HENRY CABOT LODGE, SR. [3], to J. William Fulbright, have strongly opposed and frustrated presidential policy. During the 1930s the Senate took the lead in enacting neutrality legislation. After American entry into World War II and particularly during the cold war that followed, the Senate adopted a generally bipartisan approach to foreign policy and accepted presidential leadership. Neither the KOREAN WAR [3] nor the VIETNAM WAR [4,I] was launched with a congressional DECLARATION OF WAR [2]. Between 1955 and 1964, Congress enacted a series of resolutions to support presidential initiatives in Formosa (Taiwan), the Middle East, Berlin, Cuba, and the Tonkin Gulf. While often compared to blank checks, these resolutions were enacted to demonstrate national unity. Congressional consensus collapsed during the Vietnam War, with increasing numbers of senators protesting unilateral presidential actions. In 1973, Congress overturned a presidential veto and enacted the War Powers Resolution, requiring the President to report the use of American troops in combat and to withdraw troops unless authorized by Congress.

Exercising quasi-judicial powers, the Senate also sits as a court of IMPEACHMENT [2] whenever the House of Representatives votes to impeach a federal official. Two-thirds of the senators must vote to convict. "Where else, than in the Senate should have been found a tribunal sufficiently dignified, or sufficiently independent?" asked ALEXANDER HAMILTON [2] in *The Federalist* [2] #65. Between 1789 and 1989 the House impeached sixteen federal officers—among them, a President, a senator, a cabinet member, and thirteen federal judges—on charges ranging from treason to intoxication. Three resigned voluntarily. The Senate found seven guilty and removed them from office. In 1868, by a single vote, the Senate declined to remove President ANDREW JOHNSON [3].

The Senate elects its own officers, sets its own rules, and appoints it own committees. Since 1789 the Senate has elected a secretary of the Senate, a sergeant at arms (originally called the doorkeeper), and a chaplain. Within its first week of business, a special committee proposed nineteen rules, which the Senate adopted with a single addition. There have been few general revisions of these rules. At first, the Senate operated chiefly as a committee of the whole, electing an array of ad hoc committees to deal with specific bills. In 1816, concerned with improving continuity and permitting more specialization, the Senate established sixteen standing committees. After the creation of standing committees, senators no longer needed to give a day's notice or receive permission from a majority of members to introduce bills and resolutions. They have since introduced legislation at will, to be referred to the appropriate committee for initial consideration. For a time, the presiding officer appointed committee membership. Throughout the nineteenth century senators could be appointed to chair committees on which they had never served, based upon their seniority in the Senate as a whole. After reforms established in 1921, members advanced solely on the basis of seniority within a committee.

The committee system came to dominate the legislative process. By 1885, WOODROW WILSON [4] described the federal system as "a government by chairmen of the Standing Committees of Congress." From time to time, the proliferation of committees has stimulated reforms leading to reductions in the number of committees and subcommittees. Most significant among these was the Legislative Reorganization Act of 1946, which revised committee jurisdiction and permitted the hiring of professional staffs. A series of reforms in the 1970s opened executive sessions of the committees to public view, provided for hiring minority staff members, and gave senators staff on each of their committees.

Committees have been the prime shapers of legislation and the vehicles for senatorial oversight and investigation. In the twentieth century the Senate increasingly played the role of investigator. Beginning with the 1924 Teapot Dome investigation of corruption in the WARREN G. HARDING [2] administration and continuing through the investigation of banking and stock exchange practices after the 1929 stock market crash, the investigation of the national defense program during World War II, the crime investigations and the anticommunist hearings of the 1950s, and the WATERGATE [4] hearings of 1973, Senate investigations have focused national attention on malfeasance and laid the groundwork for reform legislation. In a few investigations—those on the conduct of the Civil War, the attack on Pearl Harbor, and the IRAN-CONTRA AFFAIR [I]—joint Senate and House committees conducted the proceedings. Senate committees also maintain regular oversight of the executive agencies. Although witnesses have raised objections regarding their rights while testifying, the Supreme Court in MCGRAIN V. DAUGHERTY (1927) [3] and *Sinclair v. United States* (1929) has upheld the Senate's ability to subpoena private citizens and to hold recalcitrant witnesses in CONTEMPT OF CONGRESS [I], citing investigations as legitimate means to remedy social, political, and economic defects or to expose corruption and waste.

An important twentieth-century innovation has been the emergence of the majority and minority leaders and whips as party leaders, legislative floor managers, and presidential spokesmen. During the nineteenth century, Senate leadership divided among the chairmen of the party caucuses and influential committees. Not until the 1920s did the parties designate official floor leaders and station them prominently in the chamber, giving them responsibility to manage their party's agenda and the legislative schedule. Rarely able to rely on party discipline in voting, Senate leaders gained influence through their ability to make committee appointments and schedule floor business and through the "power to recognition," by which the presiding officer calls first upon the majority and minority leaders before recognizing other senators. The post of Senate majority leader evolved to equal stature with the Speaker of the House. "The minority leader speaks for his party," Senator Robert C. Byrd noted. "But the majority leader, whether he be a Democrat or Republican, is the leader of the Senate."

Just as the United States Senate has preserved the polite parliamentary language, snuffboxes, and spittoons from centuries past, it has retained its original constitutional shape and functions. Yet the Senate has grown from a small council meeting in secret to a powerful legislative body, with more authority, independence, and media attention than the upper house of any other national legislature. Senators have jealously guarded and exercised the powers that the Constitution assigned to them, while developing the modern leadership, staff support, and rule changes necessary to meet vastly expanded legislative demands.

DONALD A. RITCHIE

(SEE ALSO: *Appointment of Supreme Court Justices* [1]; *Appointments Clause* [I]; *Congressional Membership* [1]; *Congressional Powers* [I]; *Congressional Privileges and Immunities* [1]; *Gulf of Tonkin Resolution* [2]; *Legislative Investigations* [3]; *McCarthyism* [3]; *Senate and Foreign Policy* [I]; *Senate Judiciary Committee* [I]; *Senate Subcommittee on Constitutional Rights* [I]; *Treaty Power* [4].)

Bibliography

BAKER, RICHARD A. 1988 *The Senate of the United States: A Bicentennial History.* Malabar, Fla.: Robert E. Krieger.

BYRD, ROBERT C. 1989 *The Senate, 1789–1989: Addresses on the History of the United States Senate.* Washington, D.C.: Government Printing Office.

HAYNES, GEORGE H. 1938 *The Senate of the United States: Its History and Practice,* 2 vols. Boston: Houghton Mifflin.

ROTHMAN, DAVID J. 1966 *Politics and Power: The United States Senate, 1869–1901.* Cambridge, Mass.: Harvard University Press.

SWANSTROM, ROY 1988 *The United States Senate, 1787–1801: A Dissertation upon the First Fourteen Years of the Upper Legislative Body,* Senate Document 100–31. Washington, D.C.: Government Printing Office.

SENATE AND FOREIGN POLICY

The text of the Constitution creates a special role for the United States Senate in two key aspects of foreign policymaking, the approval of treaties and appointments. Article II, section 2, clause 2, provides that the President "shall have power, by and with the advice and consent of the Senate, to make treaties, provided two-thirds of the Senators present concur; and he shall nominate, and by and with the advice and consent of the Senate, shall appoint ambassadors and other public ministers and consuls." In addition to these explicitly conferred powers, the Senate, by practice and tradition, participates in JOINT RESOLUTIONS [3] dealing with foreign policy; it takes part informally in other foreign policy activities as well.

Although the Senate in early years exercised an "advice" role in connection with treaty-making, that function has atrophied. The Senate can, and occasionally does, express its opinion concerning the desirability of concluding a certain treaty or concerning what outcome negotiations should produce. But it is the President who determines whether to commence negotiations and what topics those negotiations comprise. The President's responsibility for the conduct of international negotiations is plenary, and he may decline to transmit to the Senate a treaty he has signed.

Strictly speaking, the Senate does not "ratify" a treaty: the President does so after the Senate gives its advice and consent by a two-thirds majority of Senators present. This may seem like a steep requirement, but the Senate from the outset has rejected only about a dozen treaties. More frequently it approves a treaty subject to conditions that the President opposes, in which case he may decline to proceed with ratification. These conditions have been called "amendments," "reservations," "understandings," "statements," "declarations," and a variety of other terms, but the terminology is secondary to their substance. All are conditions to the Senate's approval, and if the Senate does condition its consent, the President, in bringing the treaty into effect, is required to honor the Senate's intent and modify the treaty accordingly.

The role of the Senate ends after the treaty takes effect. The President is responsible for its implementation and interpretation. A treaty is a law, and under the Constitution the President is charged with its faithful execution. During a well-publicized dispute between the Senate and the administration of RONALD REAGAN [3,I] over the proper construction of the ABM Treaty, executive officials accused the Senate of meddling in the process of interpretation, while certain Senators charged that putative United States action based on the President's interpretation would have departed from the meaning of the treaty to the point of breaching the constitutional requirement that the law be faithfully executed.

The text of the Constitution makes no reference to the making of other international agreements on behalf of the United States, but Presidents have long concluded EXECUTIVE AGREEMENTS [2]. These agreements have been concluded by Presidents with and without statutory au-

thority. Either route obviates the requirement of two-thirds approval of the Senate—which explains both their popularity with Presidents and their unpopularity with some senators. The courts have provided no conclusive guidance as to when the treaty instrument is constitutionally required.

It has been argued that Senate participation also is required in ending a treaty. In GOLDWATER V. CARTER (1979) [2], however, the Supreme Court declined to decide a challenge to the validity of the termination of the mutual security treaty with the Republic of China on Taiwan by President JIMMY CARTER [1]. In light of the President's determinative role in initiating treaty relations and given past Senate acquiescence to presidential termination of several treaties in accordance with their terms, it is hard to see how a claim of Senate authority over treaty termination can be sustained. Treaty abrogation, however, is another matter. A president who ends a treaty in violation of its terms seemingly violates the presidential duty of faithful execution. Whether the Senate and President, acting together, can approve treaty abrogation and thereby end the treaty's status as the LAW OF THE LAND [3] is an open question.

These constitutional matters are almost entirely a function of what the Senate Foreign Relations Committee has called "customary constitutional law"—practice acquiesced in by both political branches over many decades that has taken on the weight of a constitutional norm. Custom assumes particular significance in foreign affairs because so few judicial opinions mark the constitutional terrain. No court, for example, has upheld the power of the Senate to condition its consent to a treaty, but the practice has been unchallenged since the earliest days of the Republic and is now widely accepted as constitutionally permissible.

By contrast the Senate has not conditioned its consent to appointments, and it would be clearly impermissible today for the Senate to approve the appointment of a certain ambassador on the condition, say, that he resign and be reconfirmed after two years. Custom surrounding the APPOINTMENTS CLAUSE [I] is different from that pertinent to the treaty clause.

In sheer numbers, the Senate's appointments work load is far heavier than its treaty work load. During the 96th Congress, for example, 2,728 nominations were referred to the Committee on Foreign Relations. By contrast, in a typical year no more than a dozen or so treaties are transmitted to the Senate for approval.

Many of these nominations are ambassadors, consuls, or other public ministers whose confirmation by the Senate is required by the Constitution. Others, however, are Foreign Service officers, whose appointment and promotion must be confirmed by the Senate under the Foreign Service Act of 1980. Other statutes require Senate confirmation of various United States representatives to international organizations and of executive-branch officials dealing with foreign affairs. These officials include the secretary of state and twenty-five other officials of the Department of State, as well as top appointees in the Arms Control and Disarmament Agency, the Peace Corps, and the United States Information Agency.

One notable exception to the requirement of Senate confirmation is the President's assistant for national security affairs, who heads the National Security Council. This exception has caused Senate critics concerned about "two secretaries of state" to argue for the enactment of a statute requiring Senate confirmation for this office. Executive officials have responded that such a requirement would impinge upon the President's constitutional foreign relations powers.

In fact, a variety of foreign affairs appointments have been made without Senate advice and consent. Delegates to international conferences and representatives in international negotiations often do not receive Senate approval. Presidents have on occasion given such persons the "personal rank" of ambassador or minister. But as the Foreign Relations Committee's onetime chairman Senator J. William Fulbright has pointed out, such designations are not appointments in the Article II sense and thus cannot confer additional legal powers or compensation upon the recipient.

On occasion, members of the Senate have themselves served as representatives to international negotiations. Some have not been appointed with the Senate's advice and consent; others have. The practice is in any event long-standing. In 1813, for example, Senator James A. Bayard of Delaware served as envoy extraordinary and minister plenipotentiary in negotiating and signing a commerce treaty with Russia. Bayard's appointment was accorded Senate advice and consent. Without Senate confirmation Senators Arthur Vandenberg and THOMAS T. CONNALLY [1] served as members of the United States delegation to the San Francisco conference that drafted the UNITED NATIONS CHARTER [4]. The United Nations Participation Act, enacted after the conference, expressly provides for the participation of members of Congress in the United States delegation to the United Nations. They are subject to Senate confirmation, but Vandenberg himself expressed reservations about the constitutionality of the arrangement. "I am increasingly impressed," he said, "with the difficulties confronted by 'congressional' representatives because of their dual nature . . . it will always be true that a man cannot serve two masters. Yet that is precisely what I attempt to do . . . when I,

as a Senator, sit in the United Nations as a delegate."

The mingling of executive and senatorial functions also occurs at less formal levels. During visits to the United States, foreign dignitaries often are invited for "tea" with the Foreign Relations Committee. The meetings are not open to the public, and although some time is consumed by social chitchat, it would be naive to think that substantive policy matters are not also reviewed. Ambassadors from foreign countries also meet on occasion with members of the Foreign Relations Committee and Senate leaders on legislative matters, as occurred in the 1970s during the normalization of relations with the People's Republic of China. And indirect contacts often occur during the consideration of treaties because the approval of conditions by the other signatory is required under international law and because Senate sponsors may not wish to render the treaty unacceptable by adding conditions that are unpalatable.

There is thus no airtight division between the foreign policy roles of the Senate and the executive. The Constitution, as reflected in custom deriving from two centuries of conflict and cooperation between Presidents and senators, reflects political accommodations reached by many different individuals representing many different philosophies over many different eras. It is not reducible to tidy "black-letter" formulas by which functions might be assigned neatly to one branch or the other. Yet it is perhaps the Constitution's very rejection of mechanical construction techniques that has given it the "play at the joints" necessary to adapt and survive.

MICHAEL J. GLENNON

(SEE ALSO: *Congress and Foreign Policy* [I]; *Congressional War Powers* [I]; *Foreign Affairs* [2]; *President and the Treaty Power* [I]; *Treaty Power* [4]; *War Powers* [4,I]; *War Powers Acts* [4].)

Bibliography

American Journal of International Law October 1989 Volume 83, Number 4.

FRANK, THOMAS M. and GLENNON, MICHAEL J. 1987 *Foreign Relations and National Security Law*. St. Paul, Minn.: West Publishing Co.

GLENNON, MICHAEL J. 1990 *Constitutional Diplomacy*. Princeton, N.J.: Princeton University Press.

SENATE JUDICIARY COMMITTEE

The Senate Judiciary Committee, created as a standing committee in 1816, is responsible for a vast array of constitutional and legislative issues. The subcommittee structure reveals the broad substantive areas covered by the committee.

The Subcommittee on Immigration and Refugee Affairs responds to illegal immigration, the admission and resettlement of refugees, NATURALIZATION [3], private relief bills, and international migration. The Simpson-Mazzoli Act in 1986 represented the first comprehensive overhaul of immigration laws since the McCarren-Walter Act of 1952. The Subcommittee on Antitrust, Monopolies, and Business Rights is responsible for such statutes as the SHERMAN ANTITRUST ACT [4] of 1890 and the CLAYTON ACT [1] of 1914. The Subcommittee on Patents, Copyrights, and Trademarks monitors traditional statutes in its area and such emerging issues as home video recording and intellectual property rights. The Subcommittee on Technology and the Law oversees all laws relating to information policy, electronic privacy, and security of computer information. These issues frequently involve complex interpretations of SEARCH AND SEIZURE [4,I] law.

The Subcommittee on Courts and Administrative Practice reports legislation dealing with new courts and judgeships, bankruptcy, court administration and management, judicial rules and procedures, administrative practices and procedures, tort reform and liability issues, and private relief bills other than immigration. One of the controversial bills to emerge from this subcommittee was the Judicial Councils Reform and Judicial Conduct and Disability Act of 1980, which created a procedure for disciplining federal judges in addition to the impeachment process. The constitutionality of this statute has been upheld by a number of appellate courts.

The Subcommittee on the Constitution has jurisdiction over all constitutional amendments. Amendments examined in recent years have dealt with ABORTION [1,I], a BALANCED BUDGET [I], EQUAL RIGHTS [2] for women, SCHOOL BUSING [4], and SCHOOL PRAYER [I]. The subcommittee is also responsible for legislation needed for CIVIL RIGHTS [1,I] enforcement, including the VOTING RIGHTS ACT OF 1965 [4], AFFIRMATIVE ACTION [1], and fair housing. Other duties involve CIVIL LIBERTIES [1,I], INTERSTATE COMPACTS [2], and criminal legislation related to constitutional issues, such as HABEAS CORPUS [2,I], CAPITAL PUNISHMENT [1,I], and the EXCLUSIONARY RULE [2].

The Senate Judiciary Committee reviews nominations for the Supreme Court, appellate courts, UNITED STATES DISTRICT COURTS [4], the ATTORNEY GENERAL [1], the SOLICITOR GENERAL [4,I], U.S. attorneys, marshals, and many other federal officials with duties to the courts. Some of the major controversies over Supreme Court appointments in recent years include the refusal in 1968 to advance Justice ABE FORTAS [2] to the position of CHIEF JUSTICE [1], the rejection of Clement F. Haynsworth, Jr., and G. Harrold Carswell in 1969 and 1970, and the rejection of ROBERT H. BORK [I] in 1987.

Hearings by the committee have helped clarify the boundaries of presidential powers in a number of areas, including the impoundment of appropriated funds, the use of EXECUTIVE PRIVILEGE [2] to deny information to Congress, reliance on EXECUTIVE AGREEMENTS [2] as a substitute for the treaty process, POCKET VETOES [3], and ELECTRONIC EAVESDROPPING [2] conducted by administration officials without judicial warrant.

The committee has been tested under fire many times. A variety of court-stripping bills come before it for analysis, including such emotional subjects as abortion, school prayer, and school busing. Perhaps the committee's most enduring contribution to an independent judiciary came in 1937, when it voted against the Court-packing bill submitted by President FRANKLIN D. ROOSEVELT [3]. In a report that contained probably the most stinging repudiation ever of a presidential proposal, the committee shredded the bill's premises, structure, content, and motivation. The authors of the report, using language scathing in tone, hoped that their emphatic rejection would help guarantee that "its parallel will never again be presented to the free representatives of the free people of America."

Until 1981 the Senate Judiciary Committee consistently selected only lawyers to serve as members. That practice ceased in 1981 when the committee added two nonlawyers, Jeremiah Denton of Alabama and Charles E. Grassley of Iowa. Another nonlawyer, Paul Simon of Illinois, joined the committee in 1985.

LOUIS FISHER

Bibliography

SCHUCK, PETER H.   1975   *The Judiciary Committees: A Study of the House and Senate Committees.* New York: Grossman.
UNITED STATES SENATE   1982   *History of the Committee on the Judiciary, United States Senate, 1816–1981.* 97th Cong., 1st Sess., Senate Document No. 97-18.

SENATE SUBCOMMITTEE ON CONSTITUTIONAL RIGHTS

In 1955 the Civil Rights Subcommittee of the SENATE JUDICIARY COMMITTEE [I] became the Subcommittee on Constitutional Rights. Subcommittee chair Thomas Hennings, a Missouri Democrat, urged the change because of the exclusive identification of CIVIL RIGHTS [1,I] with race relations. He wanted the subcommittee to assert jurisdiction over a wider range of issues, particularly in response to the anticommunist assault on CIVIL LIBERTIES [1,I].

The subcommittee's first hearings explored the denial of DUE PROCESS [2] in the loyalty-security programs of the DWIGHT D. EISENHOWER [2] administration. Members also investigated passport suspensions, WIRETAPPING [4], ELECTRONIC EAVESDROPPING [2], government secrecy, and EXECUTIVE PRIVILEGE [2]. Senator Hennings sponsored the first "freedom of information act" in 1958, but otherwise the subcommittee produced little legislation during the 1950s. Its main contribution was the obstruction of bills threatening to infringe on civil liberties or restrict the Supreme Court.

The Senate regularly referred civil rights bills to the subcommittee, which held hearings on the civil rights bill of 1957. When the southern-dominated Judiciary Committee, chaired by Mississippi Democrat James O. Eastland, refused to report the subcommittee's bill to the floor, the Senate bypassed the committee entirely and debated the House of Representatives' bill instead.

Following Hennings's death in 1960, North Carolina Democrat SAMUEL J. ERVIN [2] became subcommittee chair. Because Ervin viewed civil rights legislation as an erosion of civil liberties, the subcommittee played no role in the enactment of the CIVIL RIGHTS ACT OF 1964 [1] and helped to derail the omnibus civil rights bill of 1967. Yet under Ervin the subcommittee remained committed to civil liberties and reported out a "bill of rights" for mental patients in 1965, the Bail Reform Act of 1966, the Military Justice Act of 1968, and the Indian Bill of Rights in 1968. Over the chair's objections, the Senate ordered the subcommittee to report bills to extend the VOTING RIGHTS ACT [4] in 1970 and the CIVIL RIGHTS COMMISSION [1] in 1972.

Having consistently addressed matters of PROCEDURAL DUE PROCESS [3,I], privacy, FREEDOM OF SPEECH [2,I], FREEDOM OF THE PRESS [2,I], and SEARCH AND SEIZURE [4,I], subcommittee members became alarmed over alleged intrusions upon those rights by the administration of RICHARD M. NIXON [3]. In 1971 the subcommittee focused attention on the violation of the RIGHT OF PRIVACY [3,I] through government data banks and military spying. Senator Ervin strongly opposed administration proposals for PREVENTIVE DETENTION [3,I] and fought for repeal of laws allowing NO-KNOCK ENTRY [3]. The subcommittee proposed granting reporters protection against compulsory disclosure of sources, heard testimony relating to FBI surveillance of journalists, and conducted what Ervin called "a thorough and unprecedented series of hearings on the free press of America."

Given the conservatism of its parent committee, the subcommittee operated under considerable limitations. Not until Ervin became chair of the Government Operations Committee could he successfully guide to the floor the PRIVACY ACT [3] of 1974. In part because of his long association with the subcommittee, Ervin became chair of the Select Committee on Presidential Campaign Activities that investigated the WATERGATE [4] scandal.

Lacking Ervin's influence after his retirement, the Subcommittee of Constitutional Rights was abolished during a committee reorganization in 1977. For two decades, however, it had established a creditable record in defense of American rights and liberties.

DONALD A. RITCHIE

(SEE ALSO: *Bail* [1]; *Mental Illness* [3,I]; *Military Justice* [3].)

Bibliography
KEMPER, DONALD J. 1965 *Decade of Fear: Senator Hennings and Civil Liberties.* Columbia: University of Missouri Press.

SENTENCING

Anomalously, the constitutional law of criminal sentencing is a thinly developed field. Detailed procedural protections and an elaborate body of constitutional doctrine govern the investigation and adjudication of guilt in the pretrial and trial phases of a criminal case. The sentencing phase is just as important; indeed, for most defendants (who plead guilty without trial), the sentencing phase is even more important. Yet, outside the area of CAPITAL PUNISHMENT [1,I], sentencing is characterized by the almost complete absence of governing standards of substantive law, an extreme informality in prevailing procedures, and few constitutional restraints.

Although we ordinarily think of sentencing as a decision made by the judge after trial, the judge in reality shares sentencing authority with the legislature, the prosecutor, the jury, and the parole board or correctional agency. The division of authority varies widely from one jurisdiction to another and can have great impact upon the questions of constitutionality and fairness that arise.

The most important alternatives for the organization of sentencing authority are the mandatory, discretionary, and indeterminate systems. In a mandatory sentencing system, the sentence to be served upon conviction for a given crime is specified in the penal statute as a fixed term of years. Although the legislature ostensibly controls the sentence by defining it in advance, sentencing authority in a mandatory system tends in practice to become centered in the hands of the prosecutor, who decides which charges to file and, in effect, which mandatory sentences to seek. This prosecutorial decision is regarded as a discretionary one and is made without any hearing or other procedural formalities, without any governing standards, and without any opportunities for independent judicial review.

In the indeterminate sentencing system, neither the statute nor the judge limits the term to be served. The offender is sent to prison, potentially for life, and the time actually served is determined by the parole board. Usually that decision is based primarily on a judgment about whether an offender's progress toward rehabilitation makes him a good prospect for release. The parole board's decision is subject to few constitutional restraints. *Connecticut Board of Pardons v. Dumschat* (1981) holds that when a state's statutory regime treats parole as a privilege and creates no expectation of a right to early release, PROCEDURAL DUE PROCESS [3,I] requirements do not apply at all. When statutes do create an expectation of release, procedural due process requirements apply, but in *Greenholtz v. Inmates* (1979) the Supreme Court held that DUE PROCESS [2] was satisfied by an opportunity to be heard and some indication of the reasons for denying parole. There is no RIGHT TO COUNSEL [3] or right to confront or cross-examine witnesses in this context.

In a discretionary sentencing system, the penal statute sets only the boundaries within which the sentence must fall—a maximum sentence and sometimes a minimum sentence. These legislative boundaries typically leave a broad range of choice to the judge, who can choose the time to be served (or the fine or terms of probation) within the applicable limits. In some jurisdictions the judge's discretionary sentencing authority is qualified by legislative or administrative guidelines that require the sentence to fall within a narrow range unless the judge identifies unusual aggravating or mitigating circumstances. But many jurisdictions permit the judge to select any sentence within the broad legislatively authorized range without giving reasons and without facing appellate review.

In both mandatory and discretionary systems, sentencing authority is qualified by PLEA BARGAINING [3]. The prosecutor may agree either to recommend a sentence or to fix a sentence that the judge must impose if the plea is accepted. The Constitution places few limits on the boundaries of plea negotiation. For example, the Supreme Court held in *Brady v. United States* (1970) that a guilty plea remains valid even if induced by the defendant's fear of facing the death penalty if he stands trial. On the other hand, the Constitution requires that plea agreements be respected by the government and by the courts. The Supreme Court held in *Santobello v. New York* (1971) that if a plea agreement is not honored, then the defendant has a constitutional right to withdraw the plea. In many jurisdictions, plea bargaining (with few constitutional restrictions) is in practice the principal mechanism for the determination of sentence.

In noncapital cases the Eighth Amendment's prohibition against CRUEL AND UNUSUAL PUNISHMENT [2,I] has not been vigorously enforced. A punishment must be proportionate to the severity of the offense, but normally courts hold that any sentence within statutory limits satisfies this requirement. In SOLEM V. HELM (1983) [4] the Court held that a sentence of life imprisonment without possibility of parole was cruelly disproportionate to an offense of issuing a bad $100 check, committeed by an offender with a record of six prior nonviolent felonies. The Court said that disproportionality should be determined by considering the gravity of the offense and the harshness of the penalty, sentences imposed for other crimes within the same jurisdiction, and sentences imposed for the same crime in other jurisdictions. Although this analysis could cast doubt on the severity of many sentences imposed on nonviolent offenders, in practice courts seldom strike down sentences that are less severe than life without possibility of parole.

Procedural due process requirements in noncapital cases are also slender. Under *Mempa v. Rhay* (1976) the defendant must be afforded the right to be heard at sentencing and the assistance of counsel. But there are only limited contexts in which the courts will recognize other trial-type safeguards.

The starting point for analysis of the procedural due process questions is *Williams v. New York* (1949). In *Williams* the Court upheld a death sentence imposed by a judge who had relied on a confidential presentence report. Emphasizing that "most of the information now relied upon by judges to guide them in the intelligent imposition of sentences would be unavailable if information were restricted to that given in open court by witnesses subject to cross-examination," the *Williams* Court held that the defendant had no right even to disclosure of the report.

Although courts continue to rely on *Williams* for the broad proposition that trial-type guarantees are inapplicable at the sentencing stage, subsequent decisions have qualified *Williams*. The case of *Garner v. Florida* (1977) makes clear that nondisclosure is impermissible in the capital sentencing context and suggests, though in general terms, a greater sensitivity to due process concerns even for noncapital sentencing. More important, *United States v. Tucker* (1972) invalidated a sentence based in part on prior convictions obtained without the assistance of counsel. The premise of *Tucker*, quite inconsistent with that of *Williams*, is that procedural due process is violated when a sentence is imposed on the basis of unreliable information.

Courts continue to have difficulty identifying the proper sphere of the *Tucker* principle. If given its full scope, it would swallow *Williams* and imply full rights to disclosure, confrontation, and cross-examination. Instead, most courts have limited *Tucker* narrowly. There is still no right to full disclosure of the presentence report, though the defense is normally made aware, at least in general terms, of its content. With respect to contested facts, there is no general right to cross-examination or to a formal evidentiary hearing. Instead, cases like *United States v. Weston* (1971) and *United States v. Fatico* (1978) hold that when factual claims are based on hearsay or other evidence that is difficult to challenge, reliability must be established either by cross-examination or by some form of sufficient corroboration. And there is no requirement that facts relevant to sentencing be proved beyond a REASONABLE DOUBT [3], even when such facts require that a substantially more severe punishment be imposed. Under *McMillan v. Pennsylvania* (1986) facts relied upon to support an aggravated sentence need be proved only by a preponderance of the evidence.

In capital cases, sentencing is governed by elaborate constitutional doctrines based primarily on the Eighth Amendment's prohibition against "cruel and unusual punishments." This prohibition has been held to embody both substantive and procedural requirements. In addition both the Eighth Amendment and the FOURTEENTH AMENDMENT [2,I] EQUAL PROTECTION [2,I] clause require evenhandedness in capital sentencing.

Sentencing procedure in capital cases typically involves a TRIAL BY JURY [4] on the question of guilt, followed by a separate hearing (usually before the same jury) to determine sentence. The Supreme Court has not explicitly held that such a bifurcated trial is constitutionally mandated, but it has implied that bifurcation is necessary when the death penalty is set by a jury. In some states, the jury's role is merely advisory and the judge may impose a death sentence, despite the jury's contrary recommendation.

Furman v. Georgia (1972), the first decision in the modern era of capital punishment precedent, held unconstitutional the then-common procedure of leaving the death penalty decision to the unguided discretion of the sentencing jury. The crucial opinions stressed that the pattern of death sentences imposed under such a system was so wanton and freakish as to violate the Eighth Amendment. *Furman* and its sequel, *Gregg v. Georgia* (1976), require guidance to the jury about aggravating and mitigating factors so that choice between life and death will not be made on a wholly arbitrary basis. Critics continue to wonder, however, whether jury instructions specifying standards in "boilerplate" terms will effect any real change in the rationality of the sentencing process.

Under *Furman* and *Gregg* the legislature must provide guidelines identifying relevant aggravating and mitigating circumstances. The guidelines may not be too rigid, however. The Court held in *Sumner v. Shuman* (1987) that the legislature may never make the death penalty mandatory, even for a narrowly specified class of offenses, such as murder by a prisoner already serving a life sentence without possibility of parole. Similarly, the Court held in *Lockett v. Ohio* (1976) and *Skipper v. South Carolina* (1986) that the states may not preclude the sentencing authority from considering as a mitigating factor any arguably extenuating aspect of the defendant's character or the offense.

There is a basic tension beneath these lines of authority. *Furman* requires guidelines to ensure that the death penalty is imposed predictably and uniformly, but *Sumner, Lockett,* and *Skipper* require that the sentencer retain discretion to respond to the circumstances of the individual case. In effect, the Supreme Court has interpreted the Eighth Amendment to require both evenhandedness through rules and individualization through case-by-case discretion. Recent emphasis on the latter consideration can leave the sentencing process open to the disparities and irrationalities that *Furman* intended to eliminate.

The dilemma may be inescapable so long as capital punishment is retained. The dramatic severity and finality of the ultimate penalty demand especially high degrees of both consistency and humanity. But human institutions are fallible. The conflicting dimensions of fairness are thus inherently difficult to realize in capital sentencing procedure.

The demand for evenhandedness should be heightened against the background of concern about racial bias in death penalty decisions. Many studies suggest that black defendants are more likely to suffer the death penalty than white defendants similarly situated and that the death penalty is more likely to be exacted for white than for black victims. For example, MCCLESKEY V. KEMP (1987) [I] involved an empirical study showing that the death penalty is four times more likely in the case of defendants charged with killing whites than in the case of defendants charged with killing blacks. But the Court held that such a study, even if statistically valid, did not render the death penalty unconstitutional, in the absence of evidence that the jury in the particular case had been racially motivated. *McCleskey* is especially important to concerns about race bias because the evidence seemed to meet the usual burden of persuasion: the statistics showed that racial motivation was more likely than not. Yet, somewhat inconsistently with precedent in related areas, the Court held such a likelihood insufficient to "prove" RACIAL DISCRIMINATION [3,I].

In its substantive dimension the Eighth Amendment requires that the death penalty be proportional to culpability. Culpability has at least two aspects, one concerned with the nature of the crime and another concerned with the character of the offender. With respect to the former, the Supreme Court held in COKER V. GEORGIA (1977) [1] that the death penalty may not be inflicted on a rapist who has neither taken nor endangered human life. Similarly, *Enmund v. Florida* (1982) and *Tison v. Arizona* (1987) held that an accomplice in murder may not be executed if he neither intended to kill nor acted with reckless indifference to life.

The Supreme Court has not yet decided whether the death penalty is permissible in the case of a person who kills unintentionally. In most states, a person who accidentally kills in the course of a robbery, burglary, or rape is guilty of first-degree murder, and in some states, such a person would be eligible for the death penalty. The Court's recent emphasis on the harm one causes suggests that the Court might view death as a proportionate penalty, despite the lack of intent to kill. Yet, viewed as a matter of culpability, *Enmund* teaches that it is "fundamental that causing harm intentionally must be [punished] more severely than causing the same harm unintentionally."

The second dimension of culpability concerns the character of the offender. The Court held in THOMPSON V. OKLAHOMA (1988) [I] that to execute an offender who was under the age of sixteen at the time of the offense is impermissible. But STANFORD V. KENTUCKY (1989) [I] upheld the constitutionality of executing a minor who had turned sixteen at the time of the offense, so long as the jury was permitted to consider the offender's youth as a mitigating factor. Similarly, PENRY V. LYNAUGH (1989) [I] holds that a retarded offender may be executed, even if his "mental age" is equivalent to that of a seven-year-old child, provided that the jury is permitted to consider the mental impairment as a mitigating factor.

As a corollary of the principle that capital punishment must be proportionate to culpability, the sentencer must not give weight to facts that are irrelevant to blameworthiness. For example, BOOTH V. MARYLAND (1987) [I] holds that the sentencing jury may not consider a "victim impact statement" that details unforeseeable harms suffered by the family of a murder victim.

The *Booth* principle, which requires that culpability be assessed in terms of acts and circumstances within the offender's knowledge or control, has recently come under criticism from members of the Court who believe that criminal justice responds inadequately to the interests of the victims. *South Carolina v. Gathers* (1989) indicates that a substantial minority of the Justices is prepared to overrule *Booth*. That step would not only permit the use of victim impact statements in capital sentencing but would also cut the proportionality requirement loose from its anchor in moral culpability. In effect, it would hold the

defendant "responsible" for unforeseeable harms and events over which he had no control.

STEPHEN J. SCHULHOFER

(SEE ALSO: *Capital Punishment and Race* [I]; *Capital Punishment Cases of 1972* [1]; *Capital Punishment Cases of 1976* [I].)

Bibliography

AMERICAN BAR ASSOCIATION 1980 *Standards for Criminal Justice 18–5.1 et seq.*, 2nd ed. Boston: Little, Brown.

KADISH, SANFORD H. 1962 Legal Norm and Discretion in the Police and Sentencing Process. *Harvard Law Review* 75:904–931.

NOTE 1968 Procedural Due Process at Judicial Sentencing for Felony. *Harvard Law Review* 81:821–846.

NOTE 1978 A Hidden Issue of Sentencing: Burdens of Proof for Disputed Allegations in Presentence Reports. *Georgetown Law Journal* 66:1515–1535.

SCHULHOFER, STEPHEN J. 1980 Due Process of Sentencing. *University of Pennsylvania Law Review* 128:733–828.

WHITE, WELSH S. 1987 *The Death Penalty in the Eighties*. Ann Arbor: University of Michigan Press.

SEPARATION OF CHURCH AND STATE
(Update)

In the law concerning religion and the Constitution, the period from the end of World War II until the mid-1980s can be best characterized as the separationist period. Since 1985, however, two major developments have altered the face of the constitutional landscape. The first concerns interpretation of the ESTABLISHMENT CLAUSE [I] of the FIRST AMENDMENT [2,I], upon which much separationist history and law is based. Although some establishment clause principles have been reaffirmed, others have been strongly questioned and several are in flux. Second, the free exercise clause of the First Amendment has become a significant springboard for litigation. Although the number of free exercise precedents has dramatically increased, the direction in which that body of law is heading remains difficult to discern.

Establishment clause problems generally fall into three categories—GOVERNMENT AID TO RELIGIOUS INSTITUTIONS [2,I], the role of RELIGION IN PUBLIC SCHOOLS [3,I], and government support of RELIGIOUS SYMBOLS IN PUBLIC PLACES [I] or activities. In all three categories, a crucial and overarching question is whether the clause demands maximum separation of government and religious institutions (separationism) or, alternatively, whether government support of religion is acceptable so long as sectarian discrimination is avoided (accommodationism).

These competing themes remained submerged when

an important principle related to the provision of aid to religious institutions was reinforced in the Supreme Court [4,I] decision in WITTERS V. WASHINGTON DEPARTMENT OF SERVICES FOR THE BLIND (1986) [I]. In *Witters* the Court built upon MUELLER V. ALLEN (1983) [3] in ruling that the establishment clause did not require a state to deny aid to a blind applicant who would use the grant to pay tuition in a program of preparation for the Christian ministry. Though the Justices differed among themselves on the rationale, all seemed to agree that the individual, not the state, was responsible for selecting the program in which the funds would be spent. Such a private choice creates no risk of forbidden church-state interaction and, when viewed in the aggregate with other individual choices of how to spend such grants, creates quantitatively little religious consequences.

This distinction between grants to individuals, which may be "spent" in religious institutions, and grants to the institutions themselves, which the state may not make, may be in danger of collapsing. Only a narrow and shaky majority on the Court reaffirmed the legal principles governing financial aid to religious institutions in the 1985 cases of *Grand Rapids School District v. Ball* and *Aguilar v. Felton*. Each case produced another in the line of dissents complaining of the "catch-22" of school aid law: categorical grants of benefits to parochial schools are impermissible aid to religion unless the benefits are monitored to eliminate the possibility of their use to promote religion, but the acts required to monitor restrictions on benefits produce forbidden interaction between church and state.

By 1988 these dissents had ripened into what may well signal a major change in the law governing aid programs. In BOWEN V. KENDRICK (1988) [I] a 5–4 majority upheld portions of the Adolescent Family Life Act, which provides federal funds to religious as well as secular institutions for counseling teenagers on matters of sexuality and pregnancy. Despite the obvious dangers of religious indoctrination built into any program that enlists religiously affiliated institutions in counseling on such theologically charged matters, the Court shifted the basic focus of establishment clause analysis by asking whether such indoctrination had occurred in fact. Under its prior cases, the risk of such indoctrination would have been enough to doom the program. Although it is possible that litigants can prove in an individual case that government money is subsidizing religious counsel, the process of judicial decision making in aid to religion cases will be profoundly altered if the *Bowen* approach is extended to aid to schools and other kinds of church-supported programs. Such proof may be difficult to obtain, and the consequences of such proof will be to condemn isolated instances of abuse rather than to invalidate entire programs of state assistance.

The establishment clause principle that has changed least and seems strongest is that which prohibits the introduction of religious worship or sectarian theology into the public schools. Such an effort was handed a ringing defeat in *Edwards v. Aguillard* (1987), which invalidated a Louisiana statute requiring public schools to teach "creation science" whenever they teach biological theories of evolution. Despite the state's defense of the requirement as a protection of the ACADEMIC FREEDOM [1] of those interested in pursuing CREATIONISM [I], the Court found this scheme to be a deliberate attempt to introduce sectarian religious teachings (in particular, the teaching of the Book of Genesis that God created the universe and all its life forms in six days) into the public schools. As such, the law ran afoul of the principle enunciated in the various school prayer cases that the public school must remain free of efforts at religious indoctrination. While teaching about religion may be permissible, teaching designed to inculcate or reinforce religious beliefs is not.

A third context for establishment clause litigation—government involvement with the display or production of religious symbols—has been the most volatile over the past several years. LYNCH V. DONNELLY (1984) [3], discussed briefly in the original Encyclopedia entry for this topic, upheld the validity of a city's sponsorship of a Christmastime display that included a Nativity scene at its center. The uncertain scope of *Lynch* as authority for government support of displays with some religious significance led to a flurry of litigation in the lower courts involving both Christmas displays and other symbols with religious origins. One lower court, for example, found an establishment clause violation in the adornment of San Bernardino, California, police cars with a shield bearing a Latin cross and Spanish words translating to "With This We Conquer."

In 1989 the Supreme Court tried again to draw lines concerning government sponsorship of such symbols and displays. In COUNTY OF ALLEGHENY V. ACLU (1989) [I], a case arising from the celebration of winter holidays in Pittsburgh, Pennsylvania, the Court reached mixed results: a Nativity scene displayed on the grand staircase of the Allegheny County Courthouse was held to constitute a violation of the establishment clause, while an eighteen-foot Hanukkah menorah displayed near a larger Christmas tree outside the city-county building was held not to violate the Constitution. This pair of results is explicable only by reference to the three main groupings on the Court that the *County of Allegheny* case produced. One group of four Justices—ANTHONY M. KENNEDY [I], WILLIAM H. REHNQUIST [3,I], ANTONIN SCALIA [I], and BYRON R. WHITE [4,I]—would have upheld both displays on the ground that they were temporary and noncoercive, and therefore did not threaten to establish Christianity or Judaism or any combination of the two. Another group of three Justices—WILLIAM J. BRENNAN [1,I], THURGOOD MARSHALL [3,I], and JOHN PAUL STEVENS [4,I]—would have invalidated both displays on the grounds that they included objects "which retain a specifically (religious) meaning" and therefore may not be supported by the government. The deciding votes in the cases were cast by Justices HARRY A. BLACKMUN [1,I] and SANDRA DAY O'CONNOR [3,I], who adopted the view that government may display, but may not endorse, symbols that have religious meaning for some. Viewing both displays in their seasonal context, these two Justices found that the county had endorsed Christianity with its crèche display but was simply recognizing the secular aspects of the season's holidays with its Christmas tree and menorah combination.

These cases are troubling, and the problems they represent are difficult to solve. Atheists feel offended by any government acknowledgment of the existence of God; many religious people are deeply disturbed by the state's embrace or exploitation of religious symbols; and a line of cases that permits government to display menorahs and crèches next to Christmas trees, but not crèches standing alone, does not inspire confidence in the Court's judgment about law or religion. Solutions at the extreme—eliminating practices such as imprinting "In God We Trust" on coins and currency, on the one hand, or tolerating blatant endorsement by government of sectarian religious symbols, on the other—appear inconsistent with America's national traditions and values. A principled middle ground is hard to articulate and defend, however, as the Allegheny County case reveals.

The symbols cases may reflect a movement away from separationism and toward accommodationism. Though the latter takes many forms, the narrowest and most defensible version involves exemptions for religious activity from legislative burdens otherwise imposed on comparable activity. In Corporation of Presiding Bishop v. Amos (1987), for example, the Supreme Court upheld as an accommodation the exemption for religious institutions from the federal statutory ban on religious discrimination in employment.

Yet not all legislative efforts at accommodation survive establishment clause attack. In TEXAS MONTHLY, INC. V. BULLOCK (1989) [I] a closely divided Court held it impermissible for a state to exempt only religious publications from the state's sales tax. Such an exemption involves the state in distinguishing religious from nonreligious activity and preferring the former. Accommodationism permits such a preference; separationism does not.

The provision protecting the "free exercise of religion" provoked substantial litigation after 1985, but dominant themes are yet to emerge from this body of law. The 1980s were a time of revival among fundamentalist religions in the United States and a time of decline for mainstream religions. One consequence of this was an increase in constitutional attacks under the free exercise clause upon laws that were not intentionally hostile to religion but nevertheless interfered with its practice.

The recent free exercise cases have produced mixed results. The Court's earlier holdings that conditions on unemployment compensation benefits must not, absent an unusually strong reason, interfere with religious practice were reaffirmed and extended in Hobbie v. Florida Unemployment Appeals Commission (1987) and FRAZEE V. ILLINOIS DIVISION OF EMPLOYMENT SECURITY (1989) [I]. But in a number of other cases, the Supreme Court rejected free exercise claims. Some of these were relatively uncontroversial; for example, in Hernandez v. Commissioner of Internal Revenue and Graham v. Commissioner of Internal Revenue (1989) the Court ruled against a claim by members of the Church of Scientology that they were constitutionally entitled to income tax deductions, as charitable contributions, for payment they had made to the church in direct exchange for "auditing" or "training" sessions. Suspicion about whether Scientology was a bona fide religion or an elaborate money-making scheme for its founder may have influenced the outcome of those cases. In Tony and Susan Alamo Foundation v. United States (1985) a unanimous Court—perhaps operating on similar suspicions—rejected a religious foundation's claim to be constitutionally exempt from the wage and hour restrictions of the federal FAIR LABOR STANDARDS ACT [2] with respect to employees engaged in commercial activities. And in JIMMY SWAGGART MINISTRIES V. BOARD OF EQUALIZATION OF CALIFORNIA (1990) [I] the Court built logically upon Texas Monthly by holding that the free exercise clause did not compel what the establishment clause forbade—an exemption for the distribution of religious material from the state's generally applicable sales and use tax.

In other free exercise cases, however, claims that appeared meritorious under the Court's announced standards fared equally poorly. In GOLDMAN V. WEINBERGER (1986) [I] the Court held that the air force need not accommodate the religious concern of an Orthodox Jewish captain to wear a skullcap while on duty. Deferring to what seemed decidedly trivial objectives on the part of the military to preserve uniformity of appearance, the Court's majority treated the free exercise claim as deserving little respect. O'LONE V. ESTATE OF SHABAZZ (1987) [I] extended this approach by granting wide authority to prison officials to refuse to accommodate the religious concerns of prison inmates through any prison regulations that are "reasonably related to legitimate penological interests." And, in what may be the most disturbing of this trio of cases about government enclaves, LYNG V. NORTHWEST INDIAN CEMETERY (1988) [I], a 5–4 majority concluded that the free exercise clause was not even implicated, much less violated, when the United States government proposed to build in a national forest a road that would disturb, by sight and sound, places of religious significance to several Native American tribes. Despite the use of open lands by the tribes for spiritual purposes over many centuries, the *Lyng* result effectively forecloses any and all free exercise litigation by Indian tribes against government land-use decisions that may despoil Indian holy places. Earlier, in *Bowen v. Roy* (1986), the Court had also rejected a free exercise claim by a Native American concerning the use of SOCIAL SECURITY [4] numbers on government files pertaining to his family.

Fundamentalist Christians have fared little better in free exercise cases than have the Native American tribes. State courts have been unreceptive to attempts by parents to educate their children at home without state approval. And in a celebrated 1987 case that reached the United States Court of Appeals for the Sixth Circuit, *Mozert v. Hawkins County School Board*, a group of fundamentalist parents unsuccessfully sought to have their children exempted from a reading program in the public schools that they found objectionable to their religious beliefs. In the battle over education generally, and the public schools in particular, the separationists continue to prevail.

Characterized most generally, the trend in the Supreme Court has been toward easing some of the restrictions imposed on government by the establishment clause while maintaining or increasing the hurdles for free exercise claims. In such a world of deference to legislative judgment, accommodation is far more likely to emerge from the legislative branch than from the judicial branch. Accommodationism, so practiced, presents a substantial risk of favoritism for majority religions—that is, of replicating the evils that the religion clauses of the First Amendment were intended to combat.

IRA C. LUPU

(SEE ALSO: *Religious Fundamentalism* [I]; *Religious Liberty* [3,I].)

Bibliography

LEVY, LEONARD W. 1986 *The Establishment Clause: Religion and the First Amendment*. New York: Macmillan.
LUPU, I. C. 1989 Where Rights Begin: The Problem of Burdens on the Free Exercise of Religion. *Harvard Law Review* 102:933–989.
MCCONNELL, MICHAEL W. 1985 Accommodation of Religion. *Supreme Court Review* 1985:1–59.

SEPARATION OF POWERS

See: *Bowsher v. Synar* [I]

SEVENTH AMENDMENT

See: Trial by Jury [3]

SEX DISCRIMINATION

During the 1980s and early 1990s intense disagreement has arisen over the appropriate strategy for eliminating sex discrimination. Some courts and commentators argue for gender-neutral rules that define categories in purely functional terms. Others, who point out that gender-neutral rules promise equality only for women who can meet a "male standard," think that legal distinctions between the sexes are not only appropriate but necessary, at least in cases involving perceived biological differences. Still others refuse to think in terms of sameness and difference. They analyze each issue by asking whether the disputed rule furthers the domination of men and the subordination of women.

Those who favor gender-neutral rules argue that the equality and liberty of women is best furthered by treating women, like men, as autonomous individuals capable of exercising free choice. Their opponents believe that legal rules ought to acknowledge the degree to which many women are actually constrained in ways men are not— by direct and indirect pressures to engage in intercourse, to become pregnant, and to assume parenting and nurturing responsibilities. The disagreement is most painfully joined over laws, such as those granting unique benefits to pregnant women or mothers, that seem intended to help women but resemble earlier, unconstitutional "protective" legislation in assuming difference and dependency between men and women.

In the latter half of the 1980s, the Supreme Court was not asked to resolve this dispute in constitutional terms. No case presented an EQUAL PROTECTION [2,I] challenge to a governmental distinction based on sex. The basic structure of intermediate review of gender-based rules was reaffirmed in passing in nongender cases such as *City of Cleburne v. Cleburne Living Center* (1985) and *Kadrmas v. Dickinson Public Schools* (1988). In OBITER DICTA [3] in a race case, MCCLESKEY V. KEMP (1987) [I], the Court reaffirmed its earlier ruling that unconstitutional discrimination could not be established by unexplained statistical disparities that correlate with sex. This latter principle effectively eliminated use of the Constitution in suits such as those arguing theories of COMPARABLE WORTH [I], which challenged structural and economic disparities between the sexes.

The equal protection cases that touched on family relationships and gender roles did not involve classifications between men and women and thus did not call for "heightened scrutiny." For example, in *Bowen v. Owens* (1986) the Court ruled on an equal protection challenge to a distinction drawn by the SOCIAL SECURITY ACT [4]. For a four-year period widowed spouses of deceased wage earners who remarried after the age of sixty continued to receive survivor's benefits, while divorced widowed spouses who remarried were not so treated. In this context, where the distinction was drawn within, rather than between, gender groups, the Court held that Congress could make presumptions about dependence: "Because divorced widowed spouses did not enter into marriage with the same level of dependency on the wage earner's account as widows or widowers, it was rational for Congress to treat these groups differently after remarriage."

Although no case directly raised the constitutional question, several Title VII cases gave the Court an opportunity to respond to the debate among advocates of women's rights. The question was posed most starkly by *California Federal Savings & Loan v. Guerra* (1987), a challenge to a California statutory requirement that employers provide unpaid pregnancy disability leave. As amended by the Pregnancy Disability Act, Title VII of the CIVIL RIGHTS ACT OF 1964 specifies that discrimination on the basis of pregnancy is sex discrimination. Opponents of the California law argued that it was preempted by federal law because it required benefits for pregnant women that were not required for temporarily disabled men. The Court, in an opinion by Justice THURGOOD MARSHALL [3,I], found no conflict with Title VII. Earlier protective legislation that had been held invalid under the equal protection clause and Title VII was distinguished on the ground that it "reflected archaic or stereotypical notions about pregnancy and the abilities of pregnant workers." Justice Marshall found that Title VII and the state law shared a common goal of equal employment opportunity for women: "By taking pregnancy into account, California's . . . statute allows women, as well as men, to have families without losing their jobs."

Because the Court has not modified its holding in *Geduldig v. Aiello* (1974) that discrimination on the basis of pregnancy is not unconstitutional because it is not gender-based, *Guerra* raised no equal protection questions. But the decision indicates that the Court is willing to permit governmental distinctions between men and women when those distinctions appear to benefit women without perpetuating pernicious sex-role stereotypes. The

decision leaves ambiguous exactly how the Court will determine whether such stereotyping exists. Justice Marshall described the statute as "narrowly drawn to cover only the period of *actual physical disability.*" Yet "disability" seems an odd description for a common human condition like reproduction. The term suggests that mandatory pregnancy leave is necessary only because of real biological differences between men and women, and not as a remedy for the problem of inequality caused by the allocation of child-rearing responsibilities to women. Some commentators fear that in the long run mandatory pregnancy leave, like earlier forms of protective legislation, will decrease the actual employment opportunities of women by increasing the cost of hiring them.

A related question is whether the law ought to recognize a practice as discriminatory when it is said to harm women though it presents no threat to men who seem, at least superficially, to be similarly situated. Just as it has been difficult for the court to see pregnancy discrimination as sex discrimination, some lower courts refused to characterize sexual harassment claims as sex discrimination claims, especially when both men and women worked in an environment that only women perceived as hostile. In another Title VII case, MERITOR SAVINGS BANK V. VINSON (1986), [I] the Supreme Court emphatically affirmed that claims of a hostile work environment are actionable under the statute as sex discrimination. Again, the Court was willing to look beyond formal equality of treatment to determine whether practices have different social meanings for, and thus different impacts on, men and women.

Many of the earliest constitutional sex discrimination cases decided by the Court involved challenges by men to "benign" gender distinctions that could be eliminated by simply extending the challenged benefit to men as well as women. In this respect, sex discrimination law differed from cases involving race; few racial classifications benefited blacks at the expense of whites. However, in challenges brought by men to AFFIRMATIVE ACTION [1] programs, the claim is the same as in race cases: the preference ought to be eliminated, not simply be available without reference to gender or race. This similarity may explain why the Court's approach to gender-based affirmative action has tended to merge with its approach to race-based affirmative action, even though racial classifications are theoretically subject to a stricter level of scrutiny. In JOHNSON V. TRANSPORTATION AGENCY (1987) [I] the Court found no violation of Title VII in a public employer's voluntary affirmative action plan that permitted the sex of an employee to be considered as one factor in promotion decisions for jobs in which women historically had been underrepresented. The Court approved the plan as a "moderate, flexible, case-by-case approach to effecting a gradual improvement in the representation of minorities and women in the Agency's work force." Title VII imposes identical restrictions on gender-based and race-based affirmative action plans, but the Court also cited WYGANT V. JACKSON BOARD OF EDUCATION (1986) [I], a racial affirmative action case decided under the equal protection clause, as if it would provide the standards for evaluating a constitutional challenge to the *Johnson* plan. Thus, the Court, although reserving the question, suggested that the constitutional approach, like the Title VII approach, may be identical for both kinds of affirmative action.

Two years later, in RICHMOND V. J. A. CROSON CO. (1989) [I], a constitutional case in which STRICT SCRUTINY [4] was applied to overturn a municipal set-aside plan for racial minorities, the Court signaled a new reluctance to approve government affirmative action plans that could not be justified by evidence of identified past discrimination. Whether the constitutional approach in *Richmond* will be applied to gender-based governmental affirmative action plans depends on whether gender classifications will be distinguished as calling for less searching scrutiny. Since intermediate review has been the standard in other gender-preference cases, governmental affirmative action designed to benefit women may, if the suggestion in *Johnson* is not followed, be found to raise no constitutional problems, even where identical plans benefiting racial minorities are unconstitutional.

Some efforts by LOCAL GOVERNMENTS [I] to further sex equality have been challenged as unconstitutional under the FIRST AMENDMENT [2,I]. Those that further women's claims for equal access to all-male institutions have proved most resistant to constitutional attack. In *Board of Directors of Rotary International v. Rotary Club* (1987) and NEW YORK STATE CLUB ASSOCIATION V. NEW YORK CITY (1988) [I], the Supreme Court upheld state and local requirements that women not be excluded from membership in certain private organizations, despite the claim that the local laws infringed upon male members' First Amendment right to FREEDOM OF ASSEMBLY AND ASSOCIATION [2, I]. The effort to impose local restrictions on PORNOGRAPHY [3] as a step toward the elimination of the subordinate status of women has proved more vulnerable to constitutional challenge. In *Hudnut v. American Booksellers Association* (1986), a divided Supreme Court summarily affirmed a lower federal court's conclusion that a municipally created CIVIL RIGHTS [1,I] action for women injured by pornography impermissibly burdened protected speech.

CHRISTINA BROOKS WHITMAN

(SEE ALSO: *Feminist Theory and Constitutional Law* [I]; *Gender Rights* [I].)

Bibliography

BECKER, MARY 1987 Prince Charming: Abstract Equality. *Supreme Court Review* 1987:201–247.

FINLEY, LUCINDA M. 1986 Transcending Equality Theory: A Way Out of the Maternity and the Workplace Debate. *Columbia Law Review* 86:1118–1182.

MACKINNON, CATHARINE A. 1987 *Feminism Unmodified: Discourses on Life and Law.* Cambridge, Mass.: Harvard University Press.

———— 1989 *Toward a Feminist Theory of the State.* Cambridge, Mass.: Harvard University Press.

OLSEN, FRANCES 1986 Statutory Rape: A Feminist Critique of Rights Analysis. *Texas Law Review* 63:387–432.

RHODE, DEBORAH 1989 *Justice and Gender.* Cambridge, Mass.: Harvard University Press.

WEST, ROBIN 1988 Jurisprudence and Gender. *University of Chicago Law Review* 55:1–72.

WILLIAMS, JOAN C. 1989 Deconstructing Gender. *Michigan Law Review* 1989:797–845.

SEXUAL ORIENTATION
(Update to *Sexual Preference and the Constitution*)

Today government officially and systematically stigmatizes persons of homosexual orientation in two principal ways. The first is embodied in the sodomy laws that remain in about half of the states, and the second is embodied in laws and regulations restricting government employment to persons who are heterosexual. Most prominent among the employment restrictions are the federal government's regulations barring gay men and lesbians from serving in the ARMED FORCES [I].

In BOWERS V. HARDWICK (1986) [I] the Supreme Court, 5–4, upheld the application to homosexual sex of a Georgia law making sodomy a crime punishable by imprisonment up to twenty years. The majority rejected a claim that the law violated the RIGHT OF PRIVACY [3,I] that had been recognized within the doctrine of SUBSTANTIVE DUE PROCESS [4]. Justice LEWIS F. POWELL [3,I], who provided the crucial fifth vote for the majority, originally voted with the dissenters, but after the Court's CONFERENCE [1] switched his vote to uphold the law. In a CONCURRING OPINION [1], however, he noted that the case would be different for him if the state actually enforced the law by putting someone in prison.

Justice Powell's effort at accommodation leaves wholly untouched the most serious harm caused to gay and lesbian Americans by the sodomy laws. Although such a law played a role in the harassment of Michael Hardwick, the sodomy laws are rarely enforced by prosecution. Their mission today is to symbolize society's disapproval of persons who are gay or lesbian, legitimizing the identification of homosexuals as outsiders and thus encouraging not only police harassment but privately inflicted harm, from insults to trashing to violence. Stigma, in other words, is not just a by-product of the sodomy laws; it is their main function.

The *Hardwick* majority not only failed to deal with this problem of stigmatic harm but evaded the whole question of inequality. The Court noted that the Georgia law, despite its general language, was never applied to heterosexual sodomy; accordingly, the Court would not pronounce on the constitutionality of any such application. Having thus raised a serious issue of discrimination, the majority ignored the question whether the discrimination violated the guarantee of EQUAL PROTECTION OF THE LAWS [2,I].

A similar equal protection issue has been presented to a number of lower courts in the years since *Hardwick*, most frequently in contexts involving exclusion of persons identified as lesbians and gay men from government employment, notably service in the armed forces. Some judges have been sympathetic to these equal protection claims; but to date the prevailing view has rejected them, and thus far the Supreme Court has declined to review these decisions. The military exclusion policy, which seems likely to confront the Court with the equality issues in antigay discrimination, illustrates those issues as they may arise in other contexts as well.

The judges who conclude that heightened judicial scrutiny is appropriate for discriminations based on the status of homosexual orientation make a number of persuasive arguments. Gay men and lesbians have historically suffered from pervasive discrimination, both governmental and private. Despite some recent improvement in the lot of persons of homosexual orientation, this historic pattern continues today, seriously impairing the ability of lesbians and gay men to end discrimination through the political process. Sexual orientation bears little relation to the capacity to perform military tasks or any other tasks. Although a person's behavior and self-identification are subject to his or her control, the sexual orientation of persons who are exclusively homosexual is immutable. The usual indicia of SUSPECT CLASSIFICATIONS [4], in other words, are present in these cases.

Furthermore, discriminations against lesbians and gay men reinforce traditional stereotypes of gender; indeed, this reinforcement appears to be the main point of the military services' policy of exclusion. Putting the preservation of military secrets to one side, the main arguments of the Department of Defense are that ending the policy of exclusion would harm discipline, morale, and mutual trust; would invade the privacy of servicemembers; and would prejudice recruiting and "the public acceptability of military service." These arguments rest on the assumption that the existence of discrimination justifies government's imposition of further discrimination—an argument soundly rejected by the Supreme Court in the context of RACIAL DISCRIMINATION [3,I], as PALMORE V. SIDOTI (1984) [3] made clear. If the services' arguments supporting the exclusion policy seem familiar, the reason is that during World War II the leaders of the armed forces offered the same arguments—all of them—as reasons why racial integration of the services would impede the military mission.

The proposition that gay orientation increases security risk has no factual support. The concern expressed by the military services rests on the idea that homosexual orientation implies susceptibility to blackmail. In considerable measure, any such risk to security would be created by the policy of exclusion itself, which punishes disclosure of homosexuality with discharge. In any case, the risk disappears in the case of servicemembers known to be homosexual—who are the only ones excluded by these policy directives. The circularity of reasoning here is so obvious that even the Department of Defense has stopped barring civilians who are openly homosexual from receiving security clearances.

During World War II the military induction system examined eighteen million men and women and routinely (but perfunctorily) inquired into their sexual orientation. Eventually, sixteen million of the examinees served in the armed forces. The number of gay and lesbian servicemembers during the war is estimated between 650,000 and 1,600,000; the induction examiners excluded between 4,000 and 5,000 persons on grounds of homosexual orientation, and the services discharged another 10,000 on these grounds. Today, too, scores, and perhaps hundreds, of thousands of gay and lesbian servicemembers are performing their jobs without incident. Despite several well-publicized group investigations of lesbians (called "witchhunts" by proponents and victims alike), the services generally deal with the exclusion policy in a reactive way, taking action in individual cases when they are directly confronted with the issue.

It was the military exclusion that introduced the American public, during World War II, to the idea that one's personal identity could focus on sexual orientation. Today, the service regulations require dismissal of a member who acknowledges being "a homosexual," provided that the relevant decision makers believe that statement. In such a case no conduct need be proved; the status of "homosexual" requires discharge even if the member is celibate. The regulations also require dismissal for a "homosexual act" (a category that includes not only sodomy but also touching and kissing), but make an exception for the case in which such an act is found to be out of line with the servicemember's general sexual behavior in the past and his or her desires or intentions for the future. If the decision makers conclude that the act is unlikely to recur, and the member declares his or her heterosexuality, then the member can be retained if his or her retention is for the good of the service. Thus, it is the member's public identity as "a homosexual" that requires discharge. The perceived harm in this situation is not that the member is unqualified to perform his or her assigned tasks—the records in these cases are replete with praise from commanders and other work associates—but that the image of the services will be tarnished. The focus of concern is the gender line, the maintenance of what a Marine general once called "the manliness of war."

The crucial question for the services in determining whether to exclude a member on this ground is the member's sexual identity. Although the regulations require a yes-or-no answer to the question of whether the member is "a homosexual," the question of identity is far more complex than can be comprehended in so simple a categorization. Humans are distributed over a considerable range of modes of sexual behavior and over an even greater range of thoughts and feelings about their sexual orientations. The result is that the exclusion regulations are a powerful inducement for servicemembers to resolve private ambivalence by suppressing the parts of themselves that are homosexual, or, even if they privately consider themselves to be gay, to adopt public identities that are unambiguously heterosexual. Whatever degree of self-betrayal one might find in either of these responses, undeniably both kinds of behavior serve the regulations' main purpose of maintaining the armed forces' public image.

The centrality of questions about public identity—for individual servicemembers and for the services themselves—naturally suggests a role for the FIRST AMENDMENT [2,I] in challenges to the military's exclusion policy. One of the values protected by the FREEDOM OF INTIMATE ASSOCIATION [2] is the power to shape one's own public identity by reference to one's intimate associations. The experience of the "gay liberation" movement shows that an individual's public avowal of homosexual orientation is not merely a self-defining statement; it is also a political act. Several recently litigated cases have involved discharges of servicemembers with sterling records in direct response to their "coming out," that is, publicly expressing their homosexual identity. Although some judges have found merit in First Amendment attacks on these discharges, most lower courts have rejected these claims. Ultimately, First Amendment doctrine in this context will surely follow the Supreme Court's disposition of parallel equal protection claims. Just as Bowers v. Hardwick is this generation's version of PLESSY V. FERGUSON (1896) [3], a generous protection of the freedom to express one's gay or lesbian identity probably must await another gen-

eration's version of BROWN V. BOARD OF EDUCATION (1954) [1].

KENNETH L. KARST

Bibliography
BENECKE, MICHELLE M. and DODGE, KIRSTIN S.   1990 Recent Developments—Military Women in Nontraditional Job Fields: Casualties of the Armed Forces' War on Homosexuals. Harvard Women's Law Journal 13:215–250.
BÉRUBÉ, ALLAN   1990 Coming Out Under Fire: The History of Gay Men and Women in World War Two. New York: Free Press/Macmillan.
Developments in the Law—Sexual Orientation and the Law. 1989 Harvard Law Review 102:1508–1671.
HALLEY, JANET E.   1989 The Politics of the Closet: Towards Equal Protection for Gay, Lesbian, and Bisexual Identity. UCLA Law Review 36:915–976.
HARRIS, SETH   1989–1990 Permitting Prejudice to Govern: Equal Protection, Military Deference, and the Exclusion of Lesbians and Gay Men from the Military. New York University Review of Law and Social Change 17:171–223.
LAW, SYLVIA A.   1988 Homosexuality and the Social Meaning of Gender. Wisconsin Law Review 1988:187–235.
MOHR, RICHARD D.   1988 Gays/Justice: A Study of Ethics, Society, and Law. New York: Columbia University Press.
SUNSTEIN, CASS R.   1988 Sexual Orientation and the Constitution: A Note on the Relationship Between Due Process and Equal Protection. University of Chicago Law Review 55:1161–1179.

SIXTH AMENDMENT

See: Compulsory Process, Right of [1]; Confrontation, Right of [1, I]; Right of Counsel [3]; Speedy Trial [4,II] Trial by Jury [4,II]

SKINNER v. RAILWAY LABOR EXECUTIVES ASSOCIATION
489 U.S. 602 (1989)

In this case, the Supreme Court significantly restricted the protections of the FOURTH AMENDMENT [2,I]. The Court had never before sustained a BODY SEARCH [I] apart from ARREST [1] and without suspicion of individual wrongdoing, except with respect to prison inmates. In Skinner the Court sustained the constitutionality of government regulations requiring blood and urine tests by railroad employees involved in train accidents and by those who violated certain safety rules.

Employee abuse of alcohol and drugs resulting in jeopardy to the public explains the regulations and the decision. Drunken employees had caused accidents from the beginning of railroad history, and employees drugged by use of other substances were responsible for dozens of accidents killing and maiming passengers and inflicting damages amounting to millions of dollars.

A 7–2 Court, speaking through Justice ANTHONY M. KENNEDY [I], upheld both the compulsory and discretionary DRUG TESTING [I] as well as the alcohol testing. Kennedy recognized that the urine and blood tests were searches within the meaning of the Fourth Amendment, but held that PROBABLE CAUSE [3] was an irrelevant consideration. Searches had to be reasonable, but did not have to satisfy the SEARCH WARRANT [4] requirement. Accordingly, the mandatory searches of employees involved in an accident did not violate the amendment because specificity or individualized suspicion was not necessary. (Reasonable suspicion based on individual conduct was necessary, according to the federal regulations, when an employee had violated safety requirements but had not been involved in an accident.) Kennedy asserted, rather than explained, that the warrant requirement was irrelevant because it might stymie governmental objectives of promoting safety.

Similarly, he asserted that privacy interests implicated in the blood and urine testing were "minimal." Blood and breath tests were commonplace, safe, and painless. Urine testing, by contrast, was intrusive, but the expectations of privacy on the part of employees were diminished by their knowledge that their industry was severely regulated to promote safety and that their fitness was related to safety. The government interest in requiring the tests was simply compelling, overriding any privacy or Fourth Amendment rights that might prevail in a criminal case.

Justice THURGOOD MARSHALL [3,I], joined by Justice WILLIAM J. BRENNAN [1,I], shrilly dissented. The tests, which the majority thought to be minor invasions of privacy, were "draconian," exacted from employees who had personally given no basis for belief that they were guilty of working under the influence of drugs or alcohol. "The majority's acceptance of dragnet blood and urine testing ensures that the first, and worst, casualty of war on drugs will be the precious liberties of our citizens." All PRECEDENTS [3] required individualized suspicion before warrantless blood testing could be sustained. Privacy interests offended by compulsory and supervised urine testing could not be dismissed as "minimal." The chemical analysis of blood and urine specimens also conflicted with privacy interests. Such analysis could reveal a variety of medical disorders that were none of the government's business. Marshall believed that railroad workers did not relinquish their constitutional rights by taking employment in a regulated industry; furthering the public safety had to be subordinated to constitutional rights.

If the entire public, not just airline employees, must submit to WARRANTLESS SEARCH [4] without probable cause or individual suspicion to enter passenger areas in airports, promoting public safety in railroads seem an adequate reason for the testing of railroad employees who break safety rules or are involved in an accident. A consideration of that sort did not, however, obtain in the companion case of NATIONAL TREASURY EMPLOYEES UNION V. VON RAAB (1989) [I].

LEONARD W. LEVY

SOBELOFF, SIMON E.
(1894–1973)

Born in Baltimore, Maryland, to immigrant parents, Simon Sobeloff began his long and distinguished public career at the age of fourteen as a congressional page. After graduation from the University of Maryland School of Law in 1915, Sobeloff alternated private practice with public service, including a term as United States attorney for the District of Maryland, until 1952. In that year, he was appointed chief judge of the Maryland Court of Appeals, and in 1954 President DWIGHT D. EISENHOWER [2] named him SOLICITOR GENERAL [4,I] of the United States.

While solicitor general, Sobeloff argued the government's case in the implementation phase of BROWN V. BOARD OF EDUCATION (1955) [1] and also declined as a matter of conscience to sign the government's BRIEF [1] in Peters v. Hobby (1955), a LOYALTY OATH [3] case.

In 1955, President Eisenhower nominated Sobeloff to the United States Court of Appeals for the Fourth Circuit, but his confirmation was delayed for a year by southern Democrats who distrusted his views on school DESEGREGATION [2]. Sobeloff served on the Fourth Circuit from 1956 until his death and was chief judge from 1958 to 1964.

As chief judge, Sobeloff wrote numerous majority opinions affirming school board attempts to comply with Brown v. Board of Education. He grew increasingly impatient with school board progress, however, and after retiring as chief judge, he dissented frequently in the numerous school desegregation cases heard EN BANC [2] by the Fourth Circuit. Several of his dissents led to Supreme Court review and reversal of Fourth Circuit HOLDINGS [2] that approved school board actions, as Sobeloff consistently argued for the complete dismantling of the desegregated school systems in the face of continued school board recalcitrance and delay.

Other Sobeloff dissents led to Supreme Court majority opinions, including Davis v. North Carolina (1966), which invalidated a confession given in coercive circumstances.

In other cases, Soboloff went further than the Supreme Court was prepared to go, holding, for example, that a harsher sentence on retrial following reversal of a conviction unconstitutionally conditioned the right to a FAIR TRIAL [2].

Frequently described by Maryland Governor Theodore R. McKeldin as a "champion of the underdog," Soboloff reflected in his judicial opinions a consistent concern both for meticulous DUE PROCESS [2] and for the rights of minorities, the underprivileged, the dissenter, and the prisoner.

ALISON GREY ANDERSON

Bibliography

TRIBUTE ISSUE 1974 *Maryland Law Review* 34, no. 4:483–540.

SOCIAL PROGRAMS

See: Entitlements [I]

SODOMY

See: *Bowers v. Hardwick* [I]; Sexual Orientation [I]; Sexual Preference and the Constitution [4].

SOLICITOR GENERAL
(Update)

The solicitor general is the chief advocate in the Supreme Court for the United States government, its officers, and its agencies, but he is also known as the Tenth Justice. By tradition rather than constitutional mandate, the solicitor has a "dual responsibility" to the judicial and the executive branches, as Justice LEWIS F. POWELL [3,I] observed. For generations (the solicitor's post was established in 1870), Supreme Court Justices have counted on the solicitor to look beyond the government's narrow interests and help guide them to the "right" result in the case at hand; they also expect him to pay close attention to the case's impact on the law. The solicitor's reach extends to the lower federal courts, as well: although the executive branch is usually represented there by other lawyers from the Justice Department, the solicitor approves all appeals taken by the government. After the Supreme Court issued its landmark ONE PERSON, ONE VOTE [3] ruling in BAKER V. CARR (1962) [1], which Chief Justice EARL WARREN [4] called the most important decision of his tenure, an AMICUS CURIAE [1] brief filed by Solicitor General Archibald Cox was credited with having persuaded at least two members of the Court's majority to treat REAPPORTIONMENT [3] of electoral districts as a justiciable issue.

Without those votes, the Court would have reaffirmed a lower court decision to leave the issue to the legislature as a POLITICAL QUESTION [3,I].

The Court's explicit reliance on the solicitor in its interpretation of the Constitution and development of a new legal doctrine in the *Baker* case fits larger patterns. The solicitor general plays a major role in determining which cases the government will contest in the Supreme Court. As a result of this screening, in recent years the Supreme Court has granted approximately eighty percent of the petitions for a writ of CERTIORARI [1] submitted by the solicitor, as opposed to only three percent of those submitted by other lawyers across the country. Furthermore, the solicitor has won approximately eighty percent of his cases. In cases dealing with the Constitution in particular, the Court has shown special interest in the views of the SG, as he is informally called. The Justices have regularly invited him to file amicus briefs even in cases to which the United States is not a party.

In 1977 an executive-branch controversy about the solicitor general's amicus filings led to the first official statement about the solicitor's role in the century-old history of the office. Offering then-conventional wisdom among constitutional lawyers, a Justice Department memorandum stated that the solicitor general should be relatively "independent" within the department and the executive branch. The memorandum gave four reasons for this view: "The Solicitor General must coordinate conflicting views within the Executive Branch; he must protect the Court by presenting meritorious claims in a straightforward and professional manner and by screening out unmeritorious ones; he must assist in the orderly development of decisional law; and he must 'do justice'—that is, he must discharge his office in accordance with law and ensure that improper concerns do not influence the presentation of the Government's case in the Supreme Court."

The transformation of the Supreme Court's docket during the years of both the WARREN COURT [4] and the BURGER COURT [1] led to a serious reconsideration of the solicitor general's role, however, and to a basic disagreement about the propriety of such "independence." The discussion was prompted by actions within, affecting, and officially taken by the solicitor's office during the administration of RONALD REAGAN [3,I], as the administration sought to enact a vision of the Constitution largely at odds with views that had evolved in the legal mainstream since midcentury. Within the solicitor's office, for the first time, a deputy was hired to ensure that the government's filings conformed to the ideological views of the administration. The administration tolerated scant dissent from those views, and during a period of turmoil, it drove away a notable share of the office's nonpartisan career lawyers: the office suffered a fifty percent turnover in one year, or twice the normal rate. The first Reagan solicitor general, Rex E. Lee, a conservative whose advocacy was not aggressive enough to satisfy more influential administration officials, was forced out with this group. After leaving office, he said, "There has been this notion that my job is to press the Administration's policies at every turn and announce true conservative principles through the pages of my briefs. It is not. I'm the Solicitor General, not the Pamphleteer General."

In the Justice Department, in key cases like THORN-BURGH V. AMERICAN COLLEGE OF OBSTETRICIANS AND GYNECOLOGISTS (1986) [I], dealing with the right to ABORTION [1,I], the solicitor general played only an academic role in determining whether the government would file a brief; the decision was essentially made by other officials in the department and the White House. Monitored by a Justice Department official who amounted to a "shadow solicitor" (William Bradford Reynolds, the assistant attorney general for civil rights as well as counselor to Attorney General Edwin Meese), the SG was changed from the legal conscience of the government into a partisan spokesman for the President.

At the height of this period, during the 1985 term of the Supreme Court, the solicitor general's advocacy drew explicit criticism in opinions written by Justices from across the legal spectrum on the moderately conservative Burger Court. In at least a dozen and a half cases, the Supreme Court cited instances of overstatements or inaccurate representations in SG briefs about legislative history, court holdings, and other basic tools of legal reasoning. In a televised interview not long after, Justice THURGOOD MARSHALL [3,I] commented, "They can't separate the political from the legal. They write political speeches and put the word 'brief' on them." He added, "The solicitor general is the government's spokesman in this Court. It's always been true until the past decade or so. Now it seems as though he speaks only for the President, and not for the rest of the government."

The Reagan administration's explanation of these shifts was that its approach to the solicitor general's role and his aggressive conservative advocacy were required in order to persuade the Court to overturn a range of flawed liberal precedents. Eventually it seemed that forces at large in the rest of the legal culture, which were later especially apparent on the REHNQUIST COURT [4] at the close of the divisive 1988 term, had also affected the solicitor's approach.

In particular, a breakdown in consensus about constitutional law, represented by the high percentage of Supreme Court cases decided by a bare one-vote majority (in the 1988 term, twenty-four percent of the total cases decided), seemed to some to challenge the notion that any expert could have a "clear vision of what the law requires," as

the 1977 Justice Department memorandum claimed for the solicitor. This breakdown seemed to reemphasize the solicitor's primary duty of advocacy for the executive branch and of carrying to the Court the positions of the administration he serves.

To observers of the solicitor general's office who hold to the belief that the law can have a reassuring sense of continuity despite its contradictions, a measure of stability that contributes to social order, and an integrity provided by, among other things, the careful practice of legal reasoning, a significant way to work toward maintaining those qualities is by preserving an appropriate measure of independence for the solicitor general. Such independence represents an expression of faith in the idealized political neutrality of his office.

Still, as controversy about the nature of law has played out most dramatically in disagreements over how to interpret the Constitution, even to scholars the solicitor general's role has recently become heavily layered with political choices.

LINCOLN CAPLAN

(SEE ALSO: *Attorney General and Department of Justice* [1].)

Bibliography

CAPLAN, LINCOLN 1988 *The Tenth Justice: The Solicitor General and the Rule of Law.* New York: Vintage Books.
SYMPOSIUM 1988 The Role and Function of the United States Solicitor General. *Loyola Law Review* 21:1047–1271.

SOUTER, DAVID H.
(1939–)

David Hackett Souter, who became Associate Justice of the Supreme Court of the United States in 1990, was born on September 17, 1939, in Melrose, Massachusetts. He was graduated from Harvard College in 1961 and was awarded a Rhodes Scholarship. From 1961 to 1963 he studied at Oxford University. He then returned to Harvard for his legal education and graduated from Harvard Law School in 1966.

Following law school, Justice Souter practiced law at a private firm in Concord, New Hampshire, for two years. This is the only time that Justice Souter spent in the private sector. In 1968, he accepted a position as assistant attorney general for the State of New Hampshire. During the next ten years he rose to the top of the state attorney general's office, becoming deputy attorney general in 1971 and attorney general in 1976.

In 1978, Justice Souter was appointed to the Superior Court of New Hampshire. Five years later, he was elevated to the New Hampshire Supreme Court, where he served until 1990. In early 1990 he was appointed by president GEORGE BUSH [I] to the United States Court of Appeals for the First Circuit. He served on that court for only five months, participating in only one week of oral arguments and writing no opinions.

On July 20, 1990, Justice WILLIAM J. BRENNAN JR. [1,I] resigned from the Supreme Court of the United States after thirty-four years of service. Five days later, President Bush nominated Justice Souter to be Associate Justice of the Supreme Court. Justice Souter's nomination was perceived by both supporters and opponents to be historically significant. This was true for several reasons, few of them related to Justice Souter himself.

First, during Justice Brennan's long and distinguished tenure, Brennan became the leading symbol of the "liberal" approach identified with the Supreme Court under Chief Justice EARL WARREN [4]—an approach concerned with promoting equality and protecting individual rights against the government. Supporters of that approach viewed with alarm the prospect that Justice Brennan would be replaced by the appointee of a Republican President who had made a campaign issue of Supreme Court decisions supported by the liberal wing of the Court.

Second, Justice Souter was the ninth consecutive Justice to have been appointed by a Republican President; no Democratic President had made an appointment to the Supreme Court for twenty-three years, since President LYNDON B. JOHNSON [3] appointed Justice THURGOOD MARSHALL [3,I] in 1967. While there had been comparable periods in history—Democratic Presidents FRANKLIN D. ROOSEVELT [3] and HARRY S. TRUMAN [4], for example, appointed thirteen consecutive Justices—those were periods in which one party thoroughly dominated national politics. By contrast, Justice Souter was appointed at a time when Democrats held a majority in the Senate, as they had for all but six of the previous thirty-two years. This long-standing division of power in Washington, combined with the perception among Democratic senators that President Bush and President RONALD REAGAN [3,I] consciously sought to make judicial appointments that would change the political orientation of the federal courts, made partisan controversy over Justice Brennan's replacement almost inevitable no matter who the replacement was.

Third, both supporters and opponents perceived Justice Souter to be a crucial appointment in determining the direction of the Court. Senate Judiciary Committee Chair Joseph Biden, for example, asserted that no nomination had been so significant to the future of the Court since the 1930s. In particular, both supporters and opponents of the nomination expected that Justice Souter would cast the decisive vote on whether the Constitution permits the states to outlaw ABORTION [1,I]. After the Supreme Court's 1989 decision in WEBSTER V. REPRODUCTIVE HEALTH SERVICES [I], which upheld significant state restrictions on abortion, supporters of the right to an abortion believed that four Justices were prepared to overrule ROE V. WADE (1973) [3], the decision that first established that right. Partly in response to *Webster*, abortion was an important issue in several closely watched political campaigns in 1989. Justice Souter had made few significant public statements about *Roe v. Wade* or the constitutional right to an abortion, and his views on abortion were the subject of intense investigation, and speculation, in the period between his nomination and his eventual confirmation by the Senate in October 1990.

Finally, Souter's nomination to the Court occurred in the shadow of the rejection of President Ronald Reagan's nomination of Judge Robert Bork to the Supreme Court, in 1987. The nationally televised hearings on the BORK NOMINATION [I] were the longest confirmation hearings on any Supreme Court nomination in history, and during the confirmation battle Bork's fate became a major national political issue. Bork had made extensive public statements on many issues of constitutional law and philosophy and was a nationally known, highly controversial figure in legal circles. Justice Souter, by contrast, had made virtually no public statements on broad issues of constitutional law and was unknown outside of New Hampshire. Those inclined to be suspicious of Justice Souter suggested that President Bush had deliberately sought out an unknown candidate who would pursue the President's agenda but who did not have the record that made Bork vulnerable. Others, including supporters of Bork, argued that the Souter nomination confirmed their fears that the treatment of Bork made it impossible for anyone except an undistinguished anonymity to be confirmed to the Supreme Court.

Souter's record was revealing in certain respects. Even among his opponents, few criticized the overall quality of the more than 100 opinions he wrote while a justice of the New Hampshire Supreme Court. Few questioned his general intellectual ability. His opinions as a state supreme court justice showed a tendency to favor the interests of the government over those of criminal suspects. Apart from that, however, his New Hampshire opinions revealed few clear patterns. Accordingly, reporters and investigators for concerned interest groups made extraordinary efforts to uncover information that might shed light on Souter's views, particularly on the abortion issue. Ultimately little such material was uncovered.

Souter's confirmation hearings were the third longest in history (after those of Bork and Justice LOUIS D. BRANDEIS [1]). Justice Souter himself testified for almost twenty hours, the second longest time for any Supreme Court nominee (after Bork). The hearings were notable in several respects.

Perhaps most significant, senators asked, and Souter answered, numerous substantive questions about the nominee's views on specific issues of constitutional law. Justice Souter made specific statements about his views on RACIAL DISCRIMINATION [3,I]; AFFIRMATIVE ACTION [1,I] to aid racial minorities; SEX DISCRIMINATION [4,I]; legislative REAPPORTIONMENT [3] and the principle of ONE PERSON, ONE VOTE [3]; congressional power to enforce the FOURTEENTH AMENDMENT's [2,I] guarantees of DUE PROCESS [2] and EQUAL PROTECTION [2,I] against the states; the enforcement of the BILL OF RIGHTS [1] against the states through the Fourteenth Amendment's due process clause; the free speech clause, free exercise clause, and ESTABLISHMENT CLAUSE [I] of the FIRST AMENDMENT [2,I]; and the decision in MIRANDA V. ARIZONA (1966) [3], which required police officers to warn suspects in custody before interrogating them. Souter commented specifically on several Supreme Court decisions—endorsing, for example, the landmark expansions of free speech rights in NEW YORK TIMES V. SULLIVAN (1964) [3] and BRANDENBURG V. OHIO (1969) [1], but criticizing the standard for judging establishment clause issues specified in the LEMON TEST [I] and the approach that Justice ANTONIN SCALIA [I] took to the role of tradition in determining the rights protected by the due process clause. Justice Souter also engaged in broad-ranging discussions with members of the SENATE JUDICIARY COMMITTEE [I] on the significance of the intentions of the Framers of the Constitution and on a Supreme Court Justice's obligation to follow precedent.

Souter's extensive substantive answers were significant principally because, before the Senate hearings, there had been considerable controversy over whether it was proper for Senators to ask Supreme Court nominees their views on specific issues, and whether it was obligatory, or even appropriate, for the nominee to answer. Some recent nominees (notably Justice Scalia) had refused to answer substantive questions about constitutional issues, and many thought that Bork's uninhibited willingness to answer contributed to his downfall. Souter's extensive answers buttressed the position of those who maintained that nominees should be expected to give their views on constitutional issues in detail to the Senate committee.

Souter's hearings were also significant for what he did not disclose. Despite repeated questioning, he declined to state his views on whether the Constitution protected the right to an abortion and on whether Roe v. Wade should be overruled. Ultimately, many senators who believed that this issue was of the first importance, and that a Supreme Court nominee was obligated to disclose his views on it, voted to confirm Justice Souter despite his reticence.

Another conspicuous aspect of Souter's confirmation process was the role of groups of private citizens interested in specific issues. Those groups had played a significant role in mobilizing public opinion against the Bork nomination, and many—especially groups concerned about the possible overruling of Roe v. Wade—testified against Justice Souter and attempted, unsuccessfully, to rally public opinion against him. In this respect as well, the Souter nomination confirmed the trend toward the increased politicization of the Supreme Court nomination process.

Finally, Souter's confirmation hearings were significant because of the extraordinary degree of preparation that preceded them and the increasing tendency of confirmation hearings to take on the aspect of choreographed productions. The Bush administration assigned several officials to help Souter prepare for the Senate hearings, and Souter spent most of the period between his nomination and the hearings studying intensely and practicing his responses to anticipated questions from the senators. His preparation was manifestly successful: most observers considered his testimony at the hearings to be a virtuoso performance in which he demonstrated careful thought on a wide range of constitutional issues to which he had not been greatly exposed while on the New Hampshire Supreme Court. Justice Souter was confirmed by an overwhelming vote in the Senate despite the salience of the abortion issue and his refusal to indicate his views on that issue. This emphasis on careful preparation to defuse political difficulties is another respect in which it seems likely that Justice Souter's confirmation process established a lasting pattern.

The cases decided through April 1991 of Justice Souter's first Term on the Supreme Court revealed little about his orientation, and what they did reveal was not surprising. The most important cases during that period dealt with CRIMINAL PROCEDURE [2], and in each of them Justice Souter voted in favor of the government. Perhaps the most significant single vote was in Arizona v. Fulminante (1991), where a 5–4 majority of the Court (in an opinion by Chief Justice WILLIAM H. REHNQUIST [3,I]) ruled that the admission of a coerced confession in a criminal trial can be harmless error. Observers speculated, plausibly, that Justice Brennan would have reached the opposite conclusion and that Justice Souter's appointment determined the result on this issue. In McClesky v. Zant (1991), Justice Souter joined a six-Justice majority (in an opinion by Justice Kennedy) in adopting a rule that sharply limited the ability of prisoners to bring successive federal habeas corpus petitions. The ruling was issued in a capital case, and its most marked effect will be to cut off the avenues of federal judicial review available to defendants who have been sentenced to death. Finally, in California v. Hodari D. (1991), Justice Souter, with six of his colleagues, joined an opinion (written by Justice Scalia) that adopted a narrow construction of the term "seizure" in the Fourth Amendment: The Court ruled that a suspect who ran away when a police officer ordered him to stop was seized not at the time the order was given but only when he was finally restrained. In all of these cases, Justice Souter's votes confirmed the strong tendency he had shown in his opinions on the New Hampshire Supreme Court to favor the government in criminal cases.

DAVID A. STRAUSS

Bibliography

Nomination of David H. Souter to Be an Associate Justice of the United States Supreme Court, Senate Executive Report No. 101–32, 101st Cong., 2d Sess. (October 1, 1990).

SOUTH DAKOTA v. DOLE

See: Conditional Spending Power [I]

SPECIAL INTEREST GROUPS

See: Interest Groups and the Constitution [I]

SPECIAL PROSECUTOR

Special prosecutors, also known as INDEPENDENT COUNSEL [I], are private attorneys appointed to investigate and, if need be, to prosecute government officials accused of criminal wrongdoing. In 1978 Congress enacted a law providing for the appointment of special prosecutors investigating executive branch officials as part of the Ethics in Government Act. The law was revised and reenacted in 1983 and 1987. It has come under heavy attack by some as violative of the SEPARATION OF POWERS [I], but the Supreme Court sustained the law in *Morrison v. Olson* in 1988.

As currently codified in 28 U.S.C. §§ 591–599, the independent counsel statute provides that a majority of members of Congress of either party sitting on the judiciary committee of either house may request an independent counsel to investigate allegations against a wide array of executive branch officials. Once the members have requested a special prosecutor under the law, the ATTORNEY GENERAL [1] must initiate a preliminary investigation into the allegations, and unless the attorney general can certify that "there are no reasonable grounds to believe that further investigation is warranted . . ." he or she must subsequently apply to a special panel of federal judges for appointment of a special prosecutor. The panel, rather than the attorney general, chooses the special prosecutor and determines the scope of the counsel's investigation. Once

appointed, the counsel may be fired by the attorney general only for "good cause, physical disability, mental incapacity, or any other condition that substantially impairs the performance of such independent counsel's duties"— determinations that are all subject to review by the federal courts.

Defenders of the law cite the WATERGATE [4] scandal and argue that the law is necessary to curtail executive branch corruption in cases that the executive branch would rather not prosecute. Critics, however, claim that the statute violates the principle of equality because its provisions apply solely to the executive branch and not to Congress or the judiciary. They also charge that it places an unfair burden on those being investigated. The "no reasonable grounds" standard practically assures that the attorney general will appoint an independent counsel once requested by Congress; and unlike ordinary prosecutors, independent counsels command virtually unlimited financial resources and may extend their investigations for years.

Most important critics contend that the law undermines the separation of powers established by the Constitution. It does this most explicitly by appearing to violate the Constitution's appointments clause, which grants the President alone the power to nominate all executive branch officials except "inferior officers." More subtly, the law seems to shift the balance of power in political battles between the executive and legislative branches. According to the Constitution, the proper congressional remedy for executive branch wrongdoing is IMPEACHMENT [2] by the House and trial by the Senate. This process safeguards the executive branch from unwarranted attacks by the legislature because it requires Congress to lay its own prestige on the line whenever it prosecutes executive officials. Congress is less likely to impeach executive officials on purely partisan grounds because in so doing it risks losing public support. The independent counsel law, however, insulates Congress from these political costs. Because an independent counsel is ostensibly separate from Congress, it allows members of Congress to cloak partisan attacks behind a façade of impartiality. In short, critics allege, the independent-counsel law almost invites use as a political weapon.

The law's potential for abuse is well illustrated by the case of Theodore Olson, an attorney who served in the Office of Legal Counsel in the Reagan Justice Department. Olson provided legal advice to the administration during its dispute with Congress over the release of documents held by the Environmental Protection Agency (EPA). The administration invoked EXECUTIVE PRIVILEGE [2] and refused to hand over some of the documents requested by Congress; a rancorous political battle ensued. After it was over, Democratic staff members to the House Judiciary

Committee produced a 3,000-page report critical of the Justice Department's role in advising the administration in the controversy. Republicans on the committee strenuously objected to the report as an exercise in partisanship, noting among other facts that no committee or subcommittee meetings were ever held to authorize the report. Nevertheless, House Democrats used the report as the basis for requesting an independent counsel investigation of Justice Department officials.

An independent counsel was subsequently appointed to determine whether Olson gave false and misleading testimony to Congress with regard to the executive privilege controversy. After a six-month investigation, independent counsel Alexia Morrison acknowledged that Olson's testimony "probably d[id] not constitute a prosecutable violation of any federal law." But instead of ending the investigation, Morrison sought permission to expand it. When both the attorney general and the judicial panel that appointed her rebuffed this request, Morrison nevertheless continued the inquiry. All told, Morrison investigated Olson for nearly three years, spending about a million dollars in the process—and forcing Olson to spend roughly the same amount of money defending himself. While still under investigation, Olson challenged the constitutionality of the independent counsel law, and in *Morrison v. Olson*, a federal appeals court struck down the statute, holding that it violated not only the appointments clause but also Article III of the Constitution and the principle of the separation of powers. The Supreme Court reversed by a vote of 7–1.

Writing for the majority, Chief Justice WILLIAM H. REHNQUIST [3,I] maintained that the independent counsel law does not violate the appointments clause because the independent counsel is an "inferior officer" under the clause and hence requires no presidential nomination. Neither does the law violate Article III of the Constitution by giving the judiciary executive powers because the power to appoint the independent counsel derives from the appointments clause rather than Article III. Finally, the law does not violate the separation of powers because (according to Rehnquist) it does not compel the attorney general to ask for an independent counsel and because the executive branch retains some power to remove an independent counsel from office. Moreover, the law "does not involve an attempt by Congress to increase its own powers at the expense of the Executive Branch."

The lone dissenter, Justice ANTONIN SCALIA [I], scoffed at this last statement, accusing the majority of ignoring the political realities that clearly underlay the case. He further criticized the majority for its circumscribed reading of the separation of powers. According to Scalia, the question before the Court was simple and unambiguous. The Court had to determine whether the prosecutorial function

is a purely executive power. If it is, then the independent counsel law had to be struck down unless it granted the executive branch complete control over the independent counsel. Because no one disputed the fact that the prosecutorial function had always been considered the sole prerogative of the executive branch, the independent counsel provisions as currently constituted were clearly unconstitutional in Scalia's view. "It is not for us to determine, and we have never presumed to determine, how much of the purely executive powers of government must be within the full control of the President. The Constitution prescribes that they *all* are." The fact that the statute gave the executive branch *some* authority over an independent counsel (extremely limited authority in Scalia's view) did nothing to alter the significance of the constitutional violation.

Morrison v. Olson seems to foreclose future court challenges to the independent counsel law. Nevertheless, the majority in *Morrison* did indicate that it would give a narrow reading to certain of the act's provisions. For example, Rehnquist granted greater leeway to the executive branch when he stated that the decision of the attorney general not to appoint an independent counsel is unreviewable by the courts, even though this is nowhere stated in the statute.

JOHN G. WEST, JR.

(SEE ALSO: *Constitutional History, 1980–1990* [I].)

Bibliography

CARTER, STEPHEN L. 1988 The Independent Counsel Mess. *Harvard Law Review* 102:105–141.
CROVITZ, GORDON 1988 The Criminalization of Politics. In Gordon S. Jones and John A. Marini, eds., *The Imperial Congress.* New York: Pharos Books.
EASTLAND, TERRY 1989 *Ethics, Politics and the Independent Counsel: Executive Power, Executive Vice, 1789–1989.* Washington, D.C.: National Legal Center for the Public Interest.

SPEEDY TRIAL

Since the original publication of this *Encyclopedia*, the Supreme Court has decided only one case of note regarding the constitutional right to a speedy trial. In *United States v. Loud Hawk* (1986) the Court concluded that a delay of ninety months did not entitle the defendant to relief. The Court analyzed the case under the four-factor analysis of BARKER V. WINGO (1972) [1]—length of delay, reason for delay, defendant's assertion of the right, and prejudice to the defendant. The Court concentrated on the first two of these factors in concluding that the right to a speedy trial had not been violated.

Beginning with the length of delay, the Court concluded

that a substantial period during which the INDICTMENT [2] was dismissed should be excluded when considering the speedy trial claim. It followed the reasoning used in UNITED STATES V. MacDONALD (1982) [3] that once an indictment has been dismissed the defendant is no longer subject to public accusation; thus, a major concern of the speedy trial right is eliminated. The government's publicly expressed desire to prosecute Loud Hawk if successful on its appeal of the dismissal did not constitute public accusation for purposes of triggering the protection of the right to a speedy trial. Additionally, Loud Hawk had been unconditionally released, and during the ninety-month period, he was without any restraint on his liberty.

The Court concluded that the reason for most of the delay—an interlocutory appeal by the government—contributed little weight to the defendant's claim. Given the important public interest in appellate review, delay for this purpose is generally justified. Moreover, both the strength of the government's legal position and the importance of the issue further justified the delay. Finally, the Court concluded that the portion of the delay caused by the defendant's own interlocutory appeals did not count toward substantiating a violation of the speedy trial right. Typically, the defense would be required to show either unreasonable or unjustifiable delay by the prosecution or appellate courts before delays occasioned by its own appeals would count in the balance. No reason existed to count such delay in Loud Hawk's case because his appeals were frivolous.

The scarcity of constitutional decisions on the right to speedy trial reflects the fact that the federal Speedy Trial Act of 1974 and similar legislation in many states provide far more protection than does the Constitution. Dismissals for violation of the Sixth Amendment right to a speedy trial are also rare. *Loud Hawk* illustrates the major reasons for this result. The test fashioned by the Supreme Court is entirely too indeterminate and manipulable. The four *Barker* factors will rarely cut in the same direction. Often the defendant cannot show that he sought a speedy trial; defendants, especially those at liberty pending trial, usually have an interest in delay. When the factors are mixed, the courts generally avoid the draconian result of dismissal of the prosecution with prejudice, which is the only permissible remedy under the Sixth Amendment. Probably for the same reason, courts have resolved many of the subsidiary issues under the four-part test in favor of the government, as the Court did in *Loud Hawk*, by concluding that lengthy delay during appellate review should not be given any effective weight.

Occasionally a case is dismissed where a defendant has suffered substantial prejudice because of delay or where the government has acted in bad faith. However, for the vast bulk of the cases, the speedy trial statutes, despite their weaknesses, remain the primary guardians of the defendant's and the public's right to speedy justice.

ROBERT P. MOSTELLER

(SEE ALSO: *Criminal Justice System* [1]; *Criminal Procedure* [2].)

Bibliography
LaFave, Wayne R. and Israel, Jerold H. 1985 *Criminal Procedure*. St. Paul, Minn.: West Publishing Co.
Misner, Robert L. 1983 *Speedy Trial: Federal and State Practice*. Charlottesville, Va.: Michie.

SPENDING POWER

The power to spend public funds is so much a sine qua non of government that ordinarily it needs no express authorization in constitutions, including those of the several states. However, because the U.S. Constitution was designed to give the federal government specified powers, particularly the fiscal power lacking under the ARTICLES OF CONFEDERATION [1], Article I, section 8, begins its enumeration of powers of Congress with the power to "lay and collect taxes, duties, IMPOSTS [2], and excises, to pay the debts and provide for the common defense and general welfare of the United States." The list continues with specified objects of lawmaking, such as commerce, bankruptcy, coinage, war and military and naval forces, and (in Article IV, section 3) the territory or other property of the United States. From the start, there was controversy whether the implicit power to spend revenues for the "general welfare of the United States" extended beyond the enumerated objects of congressional law-making powers.

JAMES MADISON [3], in THE FEDERALIST #41 [2] and later as President, maintained the restrictive view of the spending power. ALEXANDER HAMILTON [2], in his influential Report on Manufactures, argued for broad national power to appropriate funds in pursuit of whatever Congress determines to be in the "general welfare," such as subsidies for chosen forms of economic activity; and as President, GEORGE WASHINGTON [4] took Hamilton's view. But the appropriation of national funds for purposes not otherwise within Congress's law-making powers, particularly for construction of INTERNAL IMPROVEMENTS [2], remained debatable; President JAMES MONROE [3], for instance, first maintained Madison's view, but later changed his position.

Congress, however, early induced the construction of state agricultural colleges and private railroads by subsidies other than tax revenues, such as grants of public lands, followed in 1900 by supplemental appropriations from general funds. In the 1923 cases of *Massachusetts v. Mellon* and FROTHINGHAM V. MELLON [2], the Supreme

Court declined to review the constitutionality of federal funds for state maternity programs in suits by a state and a taxpayer. But in UNITED STATES V. BUTLER (1935) [1], the Court adopted Hamilton's broad reading of the GENERAL WELFARE CLAUSE [2] even while striking down a program that tied agricultural subsidies to crop reduction on grounds that it invaded regulatory powers reserved to the states.

A broader understanding of Congress's regulatory powers soon undermined concerns about state powers as a limitation on the spending power, and this understanding has persisted to this day. Thus, the Supreme Court has let Congress condition federal funds for state highways on a state's restructuring its highway commission (*Oklahoma v. Civil Service Commission* [1947]) or on raising the minimum age for purchasing alcoholic beverages, as long as such conditions are not unrelated to the federal interest in the funded program (*South Dakota v. Dole* [1987]). STATE CONSTITUTIONS [I], in contrast, commonly dedicate some tax revenues to specified purposes, such as roads, and entirely forbid spending for certain purposes, for instance, to invest in private enterprises. State constitutions also forbid deficit spending, and some have adopted spending ceilings. The FIRST AMENDMENT [2,I] and many state constitutions forbid public spending for support of religion, with different results; purchasing secular textbooks for parochial school students, for instance, has been permitted under the First Amendment (BOARD OF EDUCATION V. ALLEN [1968] [1]), but forbidden under some state constitutions.

The national and state executive and legislative branches often contend over control of spending. Article I, section 9, prohibits spending without a congressional appropriation and mandates an accounting to the public. Unlike many governors, the President cannot veto individual items in an appropriation bill, but some Presidents have asserted power not to spend—to "impound"—unwanted appropriations; Congress in turn has countered by steps such as creating enforceable contract claims to carry out its programs.

Difficult issues arise mainly in applying constitutional guarantees of individual rights to state and federal spending programs. For instance, a person facing potential loss of essential government benefits, such as welfare payments, is entitled to procedures satisfying DUE PROCESS OF LAW [2] (GOLDBERG V. KELLY, 1971 [2]), but may have to submit to home visits for which officers otherwise would have to meet FOURTH AMENDMENT [2,I] standards (WYMAN V. JAMES, 1971 [4]). The Supreme Court has found denials of EQUAL PROTECTION [2,I] when states deny benefits to resident aliens (GRAHAM V. RICHARDSON, 1971 [2]) or to recent residents (SHAPIRO V. THOMPSON, 1969 [4]), but not when Congress does so (*Mathews v. Diaz*,

1976). As of 1989, the Court remained fragmented as to the effects of the equal-protection clause in limiting preferences in public contracting for members of racial or ethnic minorities (RICHMOND [CITY OF] V. J. A. CROSON CO. [1989] [I]). The Court's formula that Article IV's PRIVILEGES AND IMMUNITIES clause requires any state preference in favor of its own residents against those of other states to rest on nonresidency as a "peculiar source of [the] evil" may not govern most direct spending of state funds, but the Court has applied it to public contracting (*United Building & Construction Trades Council v. Camden*, 1984).

The First Amendment and its state equivalents are crucial but complex constraints on government programs pursued with public funds rather than regulatory sanctions. A national controversy in 1990 concerned standards for denying grants by the National Endowment for the Arts on grounds of OBSCENITY [3], provisions ultimately repealed by Congress. In principle, government may not require otherwise qualified beneficiaries of spending programs to abandon constitutionally privileged views or conduct; the problem is what may legitimately constitute a qualification. The Court held in SHERBERT V. VERNER (1963) [4] that a state could not constitutionally deny unemployment compensation to one who had religious scruples against working on Saturdays. However, in the central arena of political expression, which government may not restrict directly, the Court in BUCKLEY V. VALEO (1976) [1] held not only that Congress could offer widely supported candidates public-election campaign funds and exclude others with less preexisting support but also that this public funding could be conditioned on limiting campaign expenditures from private funds. In *Federal Communications Commission v. League of Women Voters* (1984) a statutory ban on editorializing by noncommercial broadcasters receiving federal funds was found to exceed First Amendment bounds. Yet public libraries, public theaters, public museums, and public broadcasters necessarily must select on what to spend public funds, and selection is not always easily distinguishable from disqualification.

Denying the use of the spending power to "coerce" or to "penalize" what government could not directly command or forbid does not clearly distinguish UNCONSTITUTIONAL CONDITIONS [4] from required performance or from valid preconditions and limits of a governmental program. A distinction between an impermissible sanction and a permissible refusal to subsidize depends on the choice of the assumed baseline, as does a distinction between denying support by public funds and by tax exemptions. Analysis also is colored by whether a constitutional claim starts from a vocabulary of rights, which focuses attention on the impact on individuals, or from a vocabulary of constitutional limitations, which focuses on forbidden governmental choices of ends or of means. In cases of the latter type, inquiry into the policy goals and motivations of governmental actors may be unavoidable.

HANS A. LINDE

Bibliography

ADVISORY COMMISSION ON INTERGOVERNMENTAL RELATIONS 1987 *Fiscal Discipline in the Federal System: National Reform and the Experience of the States.* Washington, D.C.: U.S. Government Printing Office.

CORWIN, EDWARD S. 1923 The Spending Power of Congress Apropos the Maternity Act. *Harvard Law Review* 36:548–582.

KREIMER, SETH 1984 Allocational Sanctions: The Problem of Negative Rights in a Positive State. *University of Pennsylvania Law Review* 132:1293–1397.

LINDE, HANS A. 1965 Constitutional Rights in the Public Sector: Justice Douglas on Liberty in the Welfare State. *Washington Law Review* 39:4–46.

McGUIRE, O. M. 1935 The New Deal and the Public Money. *Georgetown University Law Review* 23:155–195.

ROSENTHAL, ALBERT J. 1987 Conditional Federal Spending and the Constitution. *Stanford Law Review* 39:1103–1164.

STANFORD v. KENTUCKY
492 U.S. 361 (1989)

By a 5–4 vote, the Court held that the infliction of CAPITAL PUNISHMENT [1,I] on juveniles who committed their crimes at sixteen or seventeen years of age did not violate the CRUEL AND UNUSUAL PUNISHMENT [2,I] clause of the Eighth Amendment, applied to the states by the FOURTEENTH AMENDMENT [2,I].

Justice ANTONIN SCALIA [I], for the majority, acknowledged that whether a punishment conflicts with evolving standards of decency depends on public opinion. But in examining the laws of the country, Scalia found that a majority of the states permit the execution of juvenile offenders. He refused to consider indicia of society's opinion other than by examination of jury verdicts and statutory law. Public opinion polls and the views of professional associations seemed to invite constitutional law to rest on "uncertain foundations." The Court also ruled that the imposition of death on juvenile offenders did not conflict with the legitimate goals of penology.

The four dissenters, led by Justice WILLIAM J. BRENNAN [1,I], argued that the Eighth Amendment prohibits the punishment of death for a person who committed a crime when under eighteen years of age. The dissenters relied on a far wider range of indicia of public opinion than did the majority to reach their conclusion that evolving standards of decency required a different holding.

They argued too that the death penalty is disproportionate when applied to young offenders and significantly fails to serve the goals of capital punishment.

LEONARD W. LEVY

STATE ACTION DOCTRINE
(Update)

America's federal constitutional system generally protects individual rights only against violation by the national and state governments, their agencies, and officials. State action doctrine limits the scope of constitutional rights guarantees. If a state police officer arrests a criminal suspect without an ARREST WARRANT [1], for example, state action is clearly present and the Constitution's Fourth Amendment and Fourteenth Amendment SEARCH AND SEIZURE [4,I] prohibitions apply. By contrast, if a private individual or organization infringes on another private person's constitutional liberties, the courts may well not find state action, and the federal Constitution will not provide a remedy. The more controversial extensions of the state action doctrine involve cases where constitutional injuries are caused in part by ostensibly private actors. At its furthest reaches, then, the doctrine depends on workable and principled standards for attributing the constitutionally harmful conduct of a private person to the public sector.

In *Lugar v. Edmonson Oil Co.* (1982) Edmonson had obtained an invalid attachment order from a state court clerk to sequester Lugar's property. Lugar contended that Edmonson had acted jointly with the state to deprive him of property in an unconstitutional manner. Justice BYRON R. WHITE's [4,I] opinion in *Lugar* explained that in order for any constitutional rights claimant to attribute a private defendant's wrongful conduct to the federal or state government, the claimant must satisfy two independent inquiries. First, the private defendant must be sufficiently identified with the government to be fairly labeled a state actor. This might be called the "identity" inquiry. Second, the defendant's wrongful conduct must have been the direct and affirmative cause of a constitutional injury; the government will not be held liable for an error of omission or a failure to prevent constitutional injury. This might be called the "causality" inquiry. Because the state court official had assisted Edmonson in using the state's constitutionally defective procedures to sequester Lugar's property, the Court held that the identity and causality requirements were met.

Two critical decisions in the 1970s, JACKSON V. METROPOLITAN EDISON COMPANY (1974) [2] and FLAGG BROTHERS, INC. V. BROOKS (1978) [2], set extremely narrow terms for the current identity and causality standards. Even if a government delegates general law enforcement powers to a private individual (as in state self-help repossession statutes) or heavily regulates a private industry (as in state utility rate regulation), the private party will be identified with the government only if these powers and operations had been exercised traditionally and exclusively by the government. Even if the government knew, or should have known, of the private party's wrongdoing, causality now requires evidence that the government affirmatively compelled or specifically approved the practice that harmed a constitutional liberty.

Today the Supreme Court guards these narrow boundaries of the state action doctrine with a rigorous and sterile formalism. In two unusual cases emerging from the arena of amateur sports, the Court recently shielded private organizations from constitutional liability by discounting their functional relationships with the government. After the United States Olympic Committee refused to license use of the name Gay Olympic Games for a homosexual international athletic event, a Fifth Amendment challenge for discrimination in *San Francisco Arts & Athletics v. United States Olympic Committee* (1987) failed on the basis that the committee was not a governmental actor to whom constitutional prohibitions apply. Because the committee coordinated activities that were not traditional government functions, even Congress's unprecedented grant to the committee of exclusive regulatory authority over American athletic organizations and of unlimited trademark rights in the name Olympic did not satisfy the identity tests. Furthermore, because the committee's trademark enforcement decisions went unsupervised by any federal official, causality could not be attributed to the national government.

In *National Collegiate Athletic Association v. Tarkanian* (1988) the Court insulated the NCAA from liability for violation of a state university basketball coach's CIVIL RIGHTS [1,I], ruling that the university's voluntary compliance with NCAA disciplinary recommendations did not transform the NCAA's private conduct into state action. Although the NCAA's findings made at NCAA hearings of NCAA rules violations had influenced the university's decision to suspend Tarkanian in accord with its NCAA membership agreement, the Court reasoned that NCAA had neither imposed the sanction directly nor compelled the university to act within the meaning of the causality standards.

Theoretically, the state action doctrine may serve two important purposes. Jurists defend the doctrine as a safeguard of FEDERALISM [2,I]: by preventing the federal judiciary from enforcing constitutional rights guarantees against private violators, the doctrine preserves the traditional realm of STATE POLICE POWER [4] to regulate private

civil rights. Additionally, the doctrine may promote liberal legal values: to the extent that it limits the Constitution's interference with private exercise of federal and state statutory or COMMON LAW [1] rights, the doctrine fosters a realm of individual freedom of action.

To serve federalism and liberalism meaningfully, however, state action requires a dichotomy between public and private action that is both definite and defensible. The current standards for identity and causality could be challenged on both accounts. Given the highly bureaucratic state of modern America, characterized by government penetration into most private economic and social dealings, the integrated public and private venture is a commonplace. Yet, identity and causality demand the conceptual division of integrated operations into discrete practices that are traditionally governmental, governmentally compelled, and injury-causative. Practical rules for this division will be difficult for courts to formulate and apply; reliance on criteria such as tradition and government compulsion will result in line-drawing of the most arbitrary and unprincipled sort.

Moreover, the doctrine undermines its own raison d' être: with its narrow focus, it will not rip the veil away from nominally private actors who wield governmentally delegated powers to destroy individual rights. Although the Constitution permits government to "privatize" the functions that it otherwise would perform, the state action doctrine ought not to immunize the government from liability for private violations of its constitutional obligations.

However appropriate for federal constitutional purposes, the state action doctrine is often an anomaly in state constitutional law interpretation. The texts of many state bill of rights provisions do not explicitly target state action for their prohibitions; indeed, a number of state constitutions directly regulate specific transactions among private individuals and corporations. Because the states do not recognize county and municipal governments as coordinate sovereigns, state action need not reinforce federalism interests. State high courts might reject the conceptual limitations of the federal state action doctrine to provide stronger protection of CIVIL LIBERTIES [1,I] under their state constitutions against private infringements.

DAVID M. SKOVER

(SEE ALSO: *Private Discrimination* [I].)

Bibliography

ALEXANDER, LARRY A. and HORTON, PAUL 1988 *Whom Does the Constitution Control?* Westport, Conn.: Greenwood Press.

CHEMERINSKY, ERWIN 1985 Rethinking State Action. *Northwestern University Law Review* 80:503–557.

SKOVER, DAVID M. 1992 State Action Doctrine. In Collins,

Skover, Cogan, and Schuman, *State Constitutional Law and Individual Rights: Cases & Commentary.* Durham, N.C.: Carolina Academic Press.

SYMPOSIUM 1982 The Public/Private Distinction. *University of Pennsylvania Law Review* 130:1289–1608.

VAN ALSTYNE, WILLIAM and KARST, KENNETH L. 1961 State Action. *Stanford Law Review* 14:3–58.

STATE CONSTITUTIONS

When the American colonies broke with the mother country, several traditions led to the drafting of constitutions for the newly independent states. Steeped in the writings of JOHN LOCKE [3], Americans might have viewed themselves as being in a kind of state of nature; writing state constitutions would therefore be the adoption of social compacts. British constitutionalism offered a precedent; although Britain had, of course, no written constitution, the colonists, during the years up to the American Revolution, had become accustomed to relying upon "liberty documents" such as MAGNA CARTA [3]. Americans could look as well to the example of their COLONIAL CHARTERS [1], whose guarantee of the "privileges, franchises, and immunities" of Englishmen they had invoked against British policies on revenue and other subjects during the 1760s and 1770s.

In 1775, Massachusetts proposed that Congress draft a model constitution for all the states. Congress chose not to take this step. In May 1776, Virginia's convention, meeting in Williamsburg, instructed its delegates in Congress to introduce a resolution declaring the colonies to be free and independent states. The Virginia resolves viewed the drafting of state constitutions as best left to the several states.

The drafting of a constitution was, in 1776, a new art, but drafters did not want for advice. As early as November 1775, JOHN ADAMS [1] had offered his ideas on a constitution for Virginia in a letter to RICHARD HENRY LEE [3]; Adams's plan was of a distinctly democratic flavor. Others, like Carter Braxton, looked to the British constitution, in the form it took after the Glorious Revolution of 1688–1689, as the best model for Americans. THOMAS JEFFERSON [3], then in Philadelphia, thought that the people ought to have a say if a state constitution was to be written. As early as 1776, work on, and thinking about, state constitutions foretold the emergence of comparative CONSTITUTIONALISM [2].

Virginia's convention set to work on two documents: a "declaration of rights" and a "plan of government." GEORGE MASON [3] of Fairfax County had a central role in the drafting of both documents. The VIRGINIA DECLARATION OF RIGHTS [4] became especially influential. It served as a model for the bill of rights subsequently adopted in other states, and it foreshadowed the BILL OF RIGHTS [1] added to the United States Constitution in 1791. Indeed, French scholars have traced the influence of Mason's draft on their declaration of Rights of Man and Citizen, adopted in 1789.

In the 1770s the distinction between a constitution and ordinary laws was still imperfectly perceived. One thinks of a constitution as the ultimate act of the people, yet the first state constitutions were commonly drafted by revolutionary conventions or legislative assemblies and then enacted by the same bodies, without referendum. This pattern of enactment presented something of the paradox found in British notions of Magna Carta as a superstatute, yet, like other acts of the realm, subject to alteration or repeal by Parliament. Both Thomas Jefferson and JAMES MADISON [3] argued that Virginia's 1776 convention had no authority to enact anything but ordinary legislation; by such reasoning, the 1776 constitution was only an ordinance. Jefferson called for a constitution resting "on a bottom which none will dispute."

It fell to Massachusetts to perfect the idea of a constitution based upon popular consent. In western Massachusetts, the Berkshire constitutionalists called for a "social Compact" so that there would be a clear distinction between FUNDAMENTAL LAW [2] and the acts of the legislature. There must be, as an address from Pittsfield to the General Court put it, a foundation "from which the Legislature derives its authority." When the Commonwealth's leaders sought in 1779 to produce a constitution without full popular participation, western Massachusetts resisted. In 1780 a CONSTITUTIONAL CONVENTION [1] was elected specifically to draft a constitution, which was then submitted to the voters for their approval. The political theory underlying the MASSACHUSETTS CONSTITUTION [3] of 1780 is explicit in the document's declaration that it is "a social compact, by which the whole people covenants with each citizen, and each citizen with the whole people, that all shall be governed by certain laws for the common good."

The early state constitutions varied in important particulars. For example, in some states, legislatures were to be bicameral, and in others, unicameral. Notwithstanding such variations, however, the early state constitutions reflected certain shared assumptions. There was common ground, not simply in the tenets of political theory but more immediately in Americans' political and social experience during the colonial period, a gestation period for what became the framework of American constitutionalism. The first state constitutions bespoke a belief in LIMITED GOVERNMENT [3], the consent of the governed, and frequent elections. They were based, by and large, on a Whig tradition emphasizing direct, active, continuing popular control over the legislature in particular and of government in general.

In these constitutions, professions of theory sometimes conflicted with reality. A commitment to the SEPARATION OF POWERS [4] was common, yet the early state constitutions in fact made the legislature the dominant branch of government. State governors were, by contrast, virtual ciphers. Only in New York and Massachusetts was the governor elected by the people. In the other states, he was elected by the legislature, lacked the power of veto, and executed the laws with the advice of a council of state chosen by the legislature. Jefferson criticized Virginia's 1776 constitution for disregarding its own proclamation of the separation of powers: "All the powers of government, legislative and judicial, result to the legislative body. The concentrating of these in the same hands is precisely the definition of despotic government."

State courts at the outset had little power or stature. The principle of JUDICIAL REVIEW [3]—the power of a court to declare a legislative act unconstitutional—was not spelled out in the first state constitutions (just as it was not made explicit in the United States Constitution). After 1776, state judges gradually began to declare the power of judicial review. In a famous OBITER DICTUM [3] in COMMONWEALTH V. CATON (1782) [1], GEORGE WYTHE [4] declared that should the legislature "attempt to overleap the bounds, prescribed to them by the people," he would be obliged to point to the Virginia constitution and say that "here is the limit of your authority; and hither, shall you go, but no further."

The states' experience with their constitutions between 1776 and 1787 was an important proving ground for constitutional principles and structure. The idea of a bill of rights proved especially powerful. The same George Mason who drafted Virginia's Declaration of Rights saw the CONSTITUTIONAL CONVENTION OF 1787 [1] defeat his call for a bill of rights in the proposed federal Constitution. He and his fellow ANTIFEDERALISTS [1] came so close to thwarting ratification of the constitution, however, that the Federalists undertook to add a bill of rights as soon as the new federal government came into being—a pledge James Madison redeemed in drafting proposed amendments in 1789.

As to the frames of government created by the first state constituions, draftsmen of national constitutions were able to point to the states' documents as models to be imitated or avoided. The members of France's National Assembly, debating in 1789 what that nation's new constitution should look like, found the American precedents relevant. One faction, led by J. J. Mounier, argued for a bicameral legislature and an executive veto. The other faction, led by the Abbé Sieyès, saw such devices as being impediments to the popular will. The latter group, which ultimately prevailed, depended on POPULAR SOVEREIGNTY [3] for a constitution's enforcement—rather like the path taken by the drafters of the first American state constitutions.

The delegates at the Convention of 1787 in Philadelphia read the state experience quite differently. Concerned that there were too few fetters on state legislative majorities, James Madison and others at Philadelphia looked to institutional safeguards to protect the constitutional order. Thus, the Madisonian constitution, relying on such devices as the separation of powers and CHECKS AND BALANCES [1], stands in striking contrast to the Whig constitutions found in the states.

In the two centuries since the founding era, the federal Constitution has only occasionally been amended (sixteen times since 1791). Most of what the Framers of 1787 wrote endures. State constitutions, by contrast, have seen frequent amendment and, in many states, periodic overhaul. Indeed, the people of most states seem to have honored Jefferson's advice that each generation ought to examine and revise the constitution so that laws and institutions will "go hand in hand with the progress of the human mind."

The evolution of the states' constitutions has mirrored the great movements and controversies of American history. The early years of the nineteenth century saw the rise of JEFFERSONIANISM [I] and JACKSONIANISM [I]. Growth and migration of population brought rising pressures to rewrite state constitutions that, in the older states, tended to insulate the existing order from change: reform brought the progressive abolition of property qualifications for voting, representation in state legislatures became more nearly equalized, governors gained power and status, limits began to be placed on LEGISLATIVE POWER [3] (to protect against abuses by members of that branch), and explicit provisions were made for the revision and amendment of constitutions.

The era of CIVIL WAR [I] and RECONSTRUCTION [I] brought another period of great activity in the writing and rewriting of state constitutions. Between 1860 and 1875, eighteen states adopted new or revised constitutions. Reconstruction resulted in constitutions obliging the former Confederate states to respect the rights of the newly freed slaves. After federal troops left the South, Bourbon democracy emerged and southern states rewrote their constitutions yet again. This time the thrust was to institutionalize Jim Crow and to achieve widespread disenfranchisement of blacks through the POLL TAX [3], discriminatory registration requirements, and other devices.

The proponents of populism and progressivism used state constitutions to battle what they saw as the excessive power of corporations and other economic interests. Drafters sought to bypass legislatures by writing detailed provisions regarding the regulation of railroads and corporations. Oklahoma's 1907 constitution concerned itself with enumerating who would be permitted to ride on railroad passes and with legislating the eight-hour day in public employment. Opinions on such state constitutions varied. WILLIAM HOWARD TAFT [4] called Oklahoma's constitution a blend of "Bourbonism and despotism, flavored with socialism." William Jennings Bryan declared that Oklahoma had "the best constitution today of any state in this Union, and a better constitution than the Constitution of the United States." The resemblance of such constitutions to codes of law struck JAMES BRYCE [1], who concluded, "We find a great deal of matter which is in no distinctive sense constitutional law . . . matter which seems out of place in a constitution because [it is] fit to deal with in ordinary statutes."

Progressives pressed for forms of direct government—the initiative, the referendum, and recall, with Oregon leading the way. By the mid-1920s, nineteen states had adopted constitutional provisions providing for initiatives to enact legislation, fourteen states had provided for initiatives to approve constitutional amendments, twenty-one states had adopted the use of the referendum, and ten states had provided for recall measures.

As notions of the role of government expanded, including the delivery of services, some observers sought to recast state constitutions in a managerial mode. "Good government" groups sought to streamline state government. Emphasizing efficiency and rational administration, they argued that state constitutions should be revised to give more power to the government, make fewer offices elective (by way of the "short ballot," thus concentrating more power in the executive branch), and create a civil service. The paradigm of this kind of state charter is the National Municipal League's Model State Constitution (first drafted in 1921 and periodically updated).

Much of the mid-twentieth century was marked by a decline of interest in state constitutions. Several factors were at work. Too often state courts showed little interest in enforcing their own state charters. Moreover, state constitutional law tended to be eclipsed by the activism of the WARREN COURT [4]. During those years of JUDICIAL ACTIVISM [3] on the High Court, state judges could do little more than try to keep pace with advances in federal constitutional law. There seemed little time or opportunity for state courts to develop doctrine under state constitutions.

The passage of time brought a renaissance of interest in state constitutions. The BURGER COURT [1] continued to plough new ground, but in some areas—notably in CRIMINAL JUSTICE [1] opinions—a more conservative note was sounded. As the Supreme Court trimmed back earlier efforts to impose national standards on state criminal proceedings, litigants began to turn to state courts, asking them to use state constitutions to impose higher standards than those required by federal decisions.

After RONALD REAGAN [3,I] became President in 1981, his efforts to cut back the role of the federal government was paralleled by the states' acceptance of enhanced responsibility. Indeed, partly because of federal mandates (ONE PERSON, ONE VOTE [3], decisions of the courts, and the operation of the VOTING RIGHTS ACT OF 1965 [4]), the states were healthier entities, better able to function as the social and political "laboratories" proclaimed by Justice LOUIS D. BRANDEIS [1].

There is ample evidence of state courts' taking state constitutions seriously. Leading state judges—Oregon's Hans Linde and New Jersey's Stewart Pollock, for example—have called for more reliance by lawyers and judges on state constitutions. Even Supreme Court Justice WILLIAM J. BRENNAN [1,I], a leading architect of the Warren Court's activism, joined the chorus of those urging greater use of state constitutions.

One key to understanding the independent role that state constitutions play in shaping American constitutional law is to recognize that the state and federal documents are separate documents, each to be enforced in its own right, independently of the other. A state judge is of course obliged to enforce the United States Constitution, just as is a federal judge. But, while a state court cannot do less than the federal Constitution requires, the court is free to look to the state constitution for imperatives quite beyond anything found in federal constitutional law. If a state court decides that a state law or other action violates the state constitution, the ruling in itself raises no FEDERAL QUESTION [2] and the Supreme Court will decline review of the case (citing the "adequate and independent state ground" doctrine).

The Supreme Court has explicitly recognized the terrain thus left to state courts. The Supreme Court of California held that its state constitution gave right of access, for purposes of expression, to a privately owned shopping center, even though the United States Supreme Court had previously held that the FIRST AMENDMENT [2,I] conferred no such right. Upholding California's action, Justice WILLIAM H. REHNQUIST [3,I] saw nothing in the federal Supreme Court's prior rulings that would limit the state's authority "to adopt in its own constitution individual liberties more expansive than those conferred by the Federal Constitution."

State courts have sometimes used constitutions where the United States Constitution has little or nothing to say about the issue at hand. In other instances, a state court will use the state charter in areas in which federal doctrine exists but there is room for additional state interpretation. Examples include the following:

1. Economic regulation. Since the so-called constitutional revolution of 1937, the Supreme Court has abdicated the earlier practice of using the Fourteenth Amendment due process clause to second-guess state social or economic legislation. State courts, however, often use state constitutions to review economic measures. For example, a state court might invalidate a law restricting entry into a given trade (such as hairdressing) where it is evident that the purpose of the law is not to protect the public interest but to give special advantages to a favored group.

2. Environment. The federal courts have refused to recognize a federal constitutional right to a decent environment. State constitutions, however, often have provisions protecting the environment. State courts may, for example, give force to a "public trust" in state resources such as rivers and wetlands.

3. Education. The Supreme Court has refused to use the Fourteenth Amendment to require that states equalize expenditures for wealthy and poor school districts. Education is, however, dealt with at length in state constitutions. Courts in some states have used various state constitutional grounds to require more-equal funding of schools throughout the state.

4. Criminal justice. Through the INCORPORATION DOCTRINE [2], the Supreme Court has applied most of the provisions of the Bill of Rights to the states. Thus, federal constitutional standards regarding police practices (such as POLICE INTERROGATION AND CONFESSIONS [3,I] and SEARCH AND SEIZURE [4,I]) and criminal trials (such as the RIGHT TO COUNSEL [3]) bind the states, as they do the federal government. Even in this highly federalized area of constitutional law, state constitutions play a role. For example, courts in some states have read the state constitutional ban on UNREASONABLE SEARCH [4,I] and seizure as forbidding police actions that might be upheld under the Supreme Court's FOURTH AMENDMENT [2,I] decisions.

If one were to review these and other uses state courts make of state constitutions, it would be difficult to label such decisions as being, in sum, liberal or conservative. Those who may benefit from a state court's decision may be as diverse as business enterprises, criminal defendants, or environmentalists.

State court interpretation of state constitutions raise questions about judicial role. The familiar debate over the legitimate bounds of judicial review by the federal courts applies in somewhat altered form to the state courts' displacement of judgments made by state legislatures or by other political forums.

State judges, no less than their federal counterparts, should be aware of the way that judicial review, state and federal, triggers a tension between two principles. One is the principle that in a democracy decisions are made by agents ultimately accountable to the people. The other principle, embodied in judicial review, is that the commands of the Constitution should be enforced, even in the face of a legislative or popular majority.

At the federal level, there are some potential checks on judicial power, for example, the President's power to fill vacancies on the bench or Congress's Article III power to alter the Supreme Court's APPELLATE JURISDICTION [1]. Practice among the states offers more opportunities for popular discontent with judicial decisions to be manifested. In particular, it is far easier to amend state constitutions than to amend the federal Constitution. Voters have used the amendment process to curb state courts' ability to decide when there had been illegal search and seizure (California and Florida) and to overturn court decisions invalidating CAPITAL PUNISHMENT [1,I] on state constitutional grounds (Massachusetts and California).

No function of a constitution, state or federal, is more important than its use in defining a people's aspirations and fundamental values. The federal Constitution is, however, more concerned on its face with structure and process than with substantive outcomes. State constitutions, in the American tradition, tell us more of a people's values. It is in their state constitutions that the people of a state have recorded their definitions of justice, their moral values, and their hopes for the common good. A state constitution, in short, defines a way of life. In so doing, these state charters derive from the tradition given in George Mason's precept (in Virginia's Declaration of Rights) that "no free government, nor blessings of liberty, can be preserved to any people" but by a "frequent recurrence to fundamental principles."

A. E. DICK HOWARD

Bibliography

ADAMS, WILLI PAUL 1980 *The First American Constitutions: Republican Ideology and the Making of the State Constitutions in the Revolutionary Era.* Chapel Hill: University of North Carolina Press.

HOWARD, A. E. DICK 1976 State Courts and Constitutional Rights in the Day of the Burger Court. *Virginia Law Review* 62:873–944.

MCGRAW, BRADLEY D., ED. 1985 *Developments in State Constitutional Law: The Williamsburg Conference.* St. Paul, Minn.: West Publishing Co.

PETERSON, MERRILL D. 1966 *Democracy, Liberty, and Property: The State Constitutional Conventions of the 1820s.* Indianapolis: Bobbs-Merrill.

SYMPOSIUM 1985 The Emergence of State Constitutional Law. *Texas Law Review* 63:959–976.

SYMPOSIUM 1987 New Developments in State Constitutional Law. *Publius: The Journal of Federalism* 17:1–179.

SYMPOSIUM 1988 State Constitutions in a Federal System. *Annals of the American Academy of Political and Social Science* 496:1–191.

WILLIAMS, ROBERT F. 1988 *Understanding State Constitutional Law: Cases and Commentaries.* Washington, D.C.: United States Advisory Commission on Intergovernmental Relations.

STATE AND LOCAL GOVERNMENT TAXATION

The Constitution contains only one provision explicitly restricting the general scope of state and local tax power. The IMPORT-EXPORT CLAUSE [2] provides that "no State shall, without the Consent of Congress, lay any Imposts or Duties on Imports or Exports, except what may be absolutely necessary for executing its inspection laws." For most of America's constitutional history, the Supreme Court construed this clause as forbidding any state tax on imports and exports, a question the Court resolved by asking whether the imported goods subject to tax were in their ORIGINAL PACKAGE [3] and whether the exported goods subject to tax were within the "stream" of exportation. In MICHELIN TIRE COMPANY V. ADMINISTRATOR OF WAGES (1976) [3], however, the Court dramatically revised its approach to import-export clause analysis by refocusing the constitutional inquiry on the question of whether the levy at issue was an "impost" or "duty," which the Court in essence defined as a tax discriminating against imports and exports. Hence, nondiscriminatory taxes, even though imposed on imports or exports, are constitutionally tolerable under contemporary doctrine.

Other restraints on state and local taxation derive from constitutional provisions directed at concerns much broader than the subject of taxation. The Court has construed the COMMERCE CLAUSE [1,I] as requiring that any tax affecting interstate commerce must satisfy four criteria: First, the tax must be applied to an activity that has a substantial nexus with the state. Second, the tax must be fairly apportioned to the activities carried on by the taxpayer in the taxing state. Third, the tax must not discriminate against INTERSTATE COMMERCE [2]. Fourth, the tax must be fairly related to services provided by the state. The commerce clause has been by far the most significant source for judicially developed restraints on state taxation of interstate business. The Court has decided hundreds of such cases delineating commerce clause restraints on state taxation.

The Court has interpreted the DUE PROCESS [2] clause of the FOURTEENTH AMENDMENT [2,I] as restraining the territorial reach of the states' taxing powers. It has declared that there must be a minimum link between the state and the person, property, or transaction it seeks to tax. Furthermore, the due process clause requires a state, in taxing the property or income of an interstate enterprise, to include within the tax base only that portion of the taxpayer's property or income that is fairly apportioned to the taxpayer's activities in the state. Thus, there is considerable overlap between the restraints imposed by the commerce and due process clauses. However, the due process clause restrains state tax power under circumstances in which the commerce clause is inapplicable, either because the tax does not affect interstate commerce or because Congress has consented to state taxation under its power to regulate commerce.

The Court has interpreted the EQUAL PROTECTION [2,I] clause of the Fourteenth Amendment as prohibiting the states from making unreasonable classifications. The Court, however, has generally accorded the states considerable leeway in drawing classifications for tax purposes. Under current doctrine, a state tax classification will be sustained if the tax has a legitimate state purpose and if it was reasonable for state legislators to believe that the use of the challenged classification would promote that purpose.

The Supreme Court has relied on the PRIVILEGES AND IMMUNITIES [3] clause of Article IV to invalidate state taxes that discriminate against residents of other states. Thus, the Court has struck down license and other taxes that impose heavier burdens on nonresidents than on residents, and it has invalidated a taxing scheme that denied personal income tax exemptions to nonresidents. The scope of the privileges and immunities clause was significantly limited, however, by the Court's determination in the mid-nineteenth century that the clause, which technically protects only "citizens" of other states, did not apply to corporations.

In MCCULLOCH V. MARYLAND (1819) [3] the Court held that the states are forbidden from taxing the federal government or its instrumentalities. Rooted in both the SUPREMACY CLAUSE [4] and the underlying structure of the federal system, this INTERGOVERNMENTAL IMMUNITY [2] doctrine was for many years interpreted broadly to exempt from state taxation not only the federal government itself but also private contractors who dealt with the government. Beginning in the late 1930s, however, the Court substantially cut back on the scope of the federal government's immunity from state taxation. Broadly speaking, modern case law has narrowed the immunity to a proscription against taxes whose legal incidence falls on the United States and to levies that discriminate against the federal government.

WALTER HELLERSTEIN

(SEE ALSO: *Economic Due Process* [I]; *Economic Equal Protection* [I]; *Intergovernmental Tax Immunities* [I]; *State Regulation of Commerce* [4,I].)

Bibliography

HELLERSTEIN, JEROME R.   1983   *State Taxation, I: Corporate Franchise and Income Taxes*. Boston, Mass.: Warren, Gorham & Lamont.

———— and HELLERSTEIN, WALTER   1988   *State and Local Taxation*, 5th ed. St. Paul, Minn.: West Publishing Co.

————   1989   *Cumulative Supplement to State Taxation, I: Corporate Franchise and Income Taxes*. Boston, Mass.: Warren, Gorham & Lamont.

STATE REGULATION OF COMMERCE
(Update)

In the period covered by this supplementary article, the Supreme Court has decided a case or two a year on state regulation of commerce. Considered individually, none of the cases through mid-1989 seems destined to become a landmark in DORMANT COMMERCE CLAUSE [I] doctrine. Collectively, however, the cases may indicate a decreasing emphasis on "balancing" and an increasing focus on preventing states from intentionally discriminating against out-of-state interests.

As Edward Barrett pointed out in the original article on this topic for this Encyclopedia, the Court has always recognized that state regulations discriminating against INTERSTATE COMMERCE [2] are unconstitutional. But in 1970, in *Pike v. Bruce Church, Inc.*, the Court stated a BALANCING TEST [1], under which even a nondiscriminatory state regulation is unconstitutional if it affects interstate commerce and if the burdens imposed on such commerce by the regulation outweigh the local benefits. For the next fifteen years, balancing was treated as the central element in dormant commerce clause analysis, both by the Court and by scholars, who had taken up the cause of balancing long before the Court endorsed it explicitly.

Similarly, the first expressions of disaffection with balancing appeared, not in judicial opinions, but in the scholarly literature. Starting around 1980, some scholars began to question whether there was any warrant in the Constitution for judicial balancing of economic interests and to suggest that such balancing was a task courts were not well qualified for. These commentators suggested that courts would be more faithful to the Constitution—and would be doing something they were better qualified for—if they concentrated on identifying and overturning state regulations that discriminated against out-of-state interests.

Unfortunately, discrimination is a chameleon among concepts. The first proponents of the new antidiscrimination theory tended to think that a regulation was discriminatory if it would not have been adopted had all affected out-of-state interests been represented in the state legislature equally with the affected in-state interests. In application, this test leads right back to balancing. Furthermore, the test is theoretically suspect because it presupposes that out-of-state interests are entitled to virtual representation in the state's legislature, a notion that seems at odds with the genius of a federal system.

If we look for a narrower definition of discrimination, we are naturally led to a choice between defining it in terms of the effects of a regulation and defining it in terms of the regulation's purpose. Both possibilities have their advocates. It may seem at first that discriminatory effects are easier to identify than discriminatory purpose, so we should focus on effects. But it is clear that we cannot hold unconstitutional every state regulation that has any effect, however unintended, of (for example) moving business from out-of-state companies to their in-state competitors. Such a rule would plainly invalidate too much regulation. Thus, if we set out to focus on discriminatory effect, treating it as significant in itself and not just as evidence of discriminatory purpose, then whenever we find such an effect, we are led back to a version of balancing, as we try to decide whether the benefits of the regulation justify the discriminatory effect we have found.

The only test that does not lead back to balancing is a test that focuses on discriminatory purpose, invalidating a regulation when the legislature's motive was to prefer in-state over out-of-state interests. There is, of course, a long-standing debate, not limited to the dormant commerce clause, about whether the courts should review legislative motivation. The Court has spoken out of both sides of its mouth on this issue for two hundred years: on many occasions, the Court has said it would not engage in motive review, but on many others, it has engaged in it, covertly or openly. Motive review is now firmly ensconced in the SUSPECT CLASSIFICATIONS [4] branch of equal protection doctrine and in the doctrine of the ESTABLISHMENT CLAUSE [I], and almost as firmly in the law on FREEDOM OF SPEECH [2,I]. With regard to the dormant commerce clause, the Court explicitly reaffirmed the propriety, if not yet the centrality, of motive review in *Amerada Hess Corp. v. New Jersey* (1989).

To illustrate that there may be a trend away from balancing in the Court's opinions, one can compare the two most widely discussed recent cases, both involving statutes regulating corporate takeovers. In *Edgar v. MITE Corp.* (1982) the Court struck down an Illinois antitakeover statue. The statute applied only to corporations with significant Illinois connections, but even so, it covered some corporations that were incorporated outside Illinois and had mostly non-Illinois shareholders. Six Justices voted to overturn the statute, relying on three different theories (most of them relying on more than one of these theories). The theories were (1) that the statute was preempted by federal statutory law; (2) that the statute amounted to constitutionally forbidden extraterritorial regulation; and (3) that the statute failed the balancing test of *Pike v. Bruce Church, Inc.* (1970). Technically, the only theory supported by a majority of the Justices, and therefore the theory of the Court, was the *Pike* balancing theory, and *MITE* was widely read as a balancing case. Close reading would have cast doubt on this interpretation (as indeed close reading of the Court's other decisions, including *Pike* itself, raises doubt about whether the Court, whatever it has said, has ever actually engaged in balancing, except in cases involving regulation of the transportation system). In *MITE* the fifth vote for balancing, which made balancing the official theory of the Court, came from a Justice who seemingly disagreed with the result in the case and was voting with the sole object of making the holding of the case as little restrictive of state power as possible.

Five years later, in *CTS Corp. v. Dynamics Corp. of America* (1987), the Court reviewed an Indiana antitakeover statute. The most significant difference between it and the Illinois statute was that the Indiana statute was limited to businesses incorporated in Indiana. This difference is highly relevant to the extraterritoriality issue and arguably relevant to the preemption issue, but it is essentially irrelevant to the balancing approach. Therefore, the standard reading of *MITE* as a balancing case suggested the Indiana statute should be struck down. Instead, the Court upheld it. Writing for the Court, Justice LEWIS F. POWELL [3,I] began his commerce clause analysis with the statement that "the principal objects of dormant Commerce Clause scrutiny are statutes that discriminate against interstate commerce." In his analysis of the case, Powell never cited *Pike*, the standard citation for the balancing approach since 1970. Justice ANTONIN SCALIA [I], concurring in the result in *CTS*, vehemently attacked balancing under the dormant commerce clause, as he has in many cases since.

Justice Scalia has not yet carried the day. He wrote for a unanimous Court in *New Energy Co. of Indiana v. Limbach* (1988) when he relied on "the cardinal requirement of nondiscrimination." But then, in *Bendix Autolite Corp. v. Midwesco Enterprises, Inc.* (1988), seven Justices reaffirmed the propriety of balancing and purported to invalidate the statute before them by balancing. The Court may have been right when it chose not to rely on a finding

of discrimination in *Bendix Autolite*, but even so, it need not have claimed to balance. *Bendix Autolite* was one of those rare nontaxation cases like *Allenberg Cotton Co. v. Pittman* (1974), involving what we might categorize roughly as administrative requirements on businesses, that probably should be decided by a "multiple burdens" analysis similar to that used in state taxation cases.

As late as 1989, in *Northwest Central Pipeline Corp. v. State Corporation Commission of Kansas*, a unanimous Court cited *Pike* as authority for balancing. But many considerations suggest that this citation of *Pike* means little: the Court upheld the statute, the supposed balancing was a perfunctory coda to a long and complex discussion of statutory preemption, and even Justice Scalia did not bother to register disagreement. The Court as a body still seems much less confident about the role of balancing than it seemed ten years ago.

One other possible trend deserves mention. Since 1974, the Court has decided four cases under the dormant commerce clause that centrally involved EXTRATERRITORIALITY [2] issues (the two cases on antitakeover statutes and two others on beer price-affirmation statutes). Extraterritoriality is a problem that has lurked in the background of many dormant commerce clause cases, but has rarely taken center stage. The Court has never produced anything like an adequate theory of when a regulation is impermissibly extraterritorial, and it is doubtful whether extraterritoriality should be viewed as a commerce clause problem at all. On the other hand, the Constitution undoubtedly prohibits extraterritorial state regulation, and this prohibition is not easily assignable to any particular clause of the Constitution. There is no harm in the Court's sometimes treating the prohibition as grounded in the commerce clause, provided the Court does not confuse extraterritoriality with other commerce clause issues. For the most part, the Court has treated extraterritoriality as a distinct issue, even when assigning it to the commerce clause. The Court may have taken a step down a dangerous path in *Healy v. The Beer Institute, Inc.* (1989), when it emphasized that the Connecticut price-affirmation statute would make it economically necessary for beer distributors setting a price for one state to consider market conditions in various states. In a multistate economy most state regulations have effects of this kind, and to treat such an effect as establishing a presumptive violation of the extraterritoriality prohibition would require some further step, presumably balancing, to decide when the presumptive violation was an actual violation. On the other hand, the Court also said in *Healy* that price-affirmation statutes "facially" violate the commerce clause, which means balancing is not required to identify the violation. There is work to be done here to develop a doctrine.

DONALD H. REGAN

(SEE ALSO: *Economic Due Process* [I]; *Economic Equal Protection* [I]; *Economic Regulation* [2]; *Legislative Intent* [3]; *Legislative Purposes and Motives* [I].)

Bibliography

EULE, JULIAN N. 1982 Laying the Dormant Commerce Clause to Rest. *Yale Law Journal* 91:425–485.

REGAN, DONALD H. 1986 The Supreme Court and State Protectionism: Making Sense of the Dormant Commerce Clause. *Michigan Law Review* 84:1091–1287.

STEVENS, JOHN PAUL
(1920–)
(Update)

In 1975, President GERALD R. FORD [2] sought a "moderate conservative" of unimpeachable professional qualifications to fill the Supreme Court seat vacated by WILLIAM O. DOUGLAS [2]. John Paul Stevens of Chicago, an intellectually gifted antitrust lawyer, former law clerk to Justice WILEY B. RUTLEDGE [3], occasional law professor, and federal court of appeals judge for the preceding five years, seemed to fit the bill. Justice Stevens in fact has more often been described as a "moderate liberal" of sometimes unpredictable or even idiosyncratic bent or as a "moderate pragmatist." A prolific writer of separate opinions frequently offering a different perspective, he generally is not a coalition builder. Even the common term "moderate" reflects his agreement in result with sometimes one and sometimes another more readily identifiable group of Justices on the Court or his balanced accommodation of community rights to govern and individual freedoms rather than his judicial substance or style.

Such labels usually mislead more than instruct, and in Justice Stevens's case conservative, moderate, and liberal strands of constitutional thought blend in a singular combination. He shares the judicial conservatism of Douglas's (and thus his) predecessor, Justice LOUIS D. BRANDEIS [1], who frequently urged the Court to reach constitutional questions only when necessary and to resolve constitutional disputes as narrowly as possible. He shares the moderate rationalist's antipathy to excessive generalization that Nathaniel Nathanson, Brandeis's law clerk and Stevens's admired constitutional law teacher, abhorred. He also shares the liberal substantive vision of Justice Rutledge, whom Stevens once admiringly described as a Justice who "exhibited great respect for experience and practical considerations," whose "concern with the importance of procedural safeguards was frequently expressed in separate opinions," and most importantly, who believed that "the securing and maintaining of individual freedom is the main end of society." Each of these

elements of his intellectual lineage appear centrally in Justice Stevens's own constitutional writings.

His particular mixture of judicial restraint and vigorous judicial enforcement of individual liberty, although akin to those of Brandeis and Rutledge, sets Stevens apart from his contemporaries on both the BURGER COURT [1] and the REHNQUIST COURT [I]. His is not the judicial restraint of extreme deference to government authority, but the judicial restraint of limiting the occasions and the breadth of Supreme Court rulings, particularly when he concludes that a ruling is unnecessary to protect liberty. His adjudicative approach is to balance all the relevant factors in a particular context with thorough reasoning whose ultimate aim is resolving the particular dispute, not declaring broad propositions of law. Yet, because Stevens sees protection of liberty as a peculiarly judicial obligation, there is no conflict for him between judicial restraint and liberty-protecting judicial intervention, however narrow the basis of that intervention might be. Thus, his frequent criticism of "unnecessary judicial lawmaking" by his colleagues, although it extends to reliance on any intermediate doctrinal standard of review that is a judicial gloss on constitutional text, is most bitterly voiced when judge-made doctrines stand in the way of vindicating individual freedom. In *Rose v. Lundy* (1982), for example, his dissent objected to several judicially imposed procedural obstacles to federal HABEAS CORPUS [2,I] review of claims of fundamental constitutional error in the conviction of state criminal defendants. In contrast, Stevens, always sensitive to matters of degree, expressed his inclination to address constitutional claims more readily the more fundamental they are and to husband scarce judicial resources for the occasions when judicial action is most acutely needed. Accordingly, he urged the Court to confine "habeas corpus relief to cases that truly involve fundamental fairness."

The same preference for employing JUDICIAL POWER [3] to secure and maintain individual freedom, rather than to vindicate government authority, appears in other positions he has taken on the proper scope of the Court's institutional role. He has waged a lengthy, but largely unsuccessful, battle to convince the court to curtail its use of discretionary certiorari jurisdiction to review cases in which the claim of individual liberty prevailed in lower courts. In NEW JERSEY V. T.L.O. (1984) [3] he inveighed against the Court's "voracious appetite for judicial activism in its Fourth Amendment jurisprudence, at least when it comes to restricting the constitutional rights of the citizen." To Stevens, the Court should not be concerned with legitimating prosecution practices or other governmental controls that lower courts have erroneously restricted through overly generous interpretations of federal law. In general, he sees dispersal of judicial power as a positive good, especially when state courts restrain state officials from interfering with individuals, even when those courts have applied the federal Constitution more stringently than the Supreme Court might. He has argued with respect to STARE DECISIS [4] that the Court should adhere more readily to prior rulings that recognized a liberty claim than to those that rejected one. Similarly, he appears more likely to find a "case or controversy" calling for decision on the merits in an individual challenge to government action than in review of a claim that the government's prerogatives have been unreasonably limited. This distinction can be seen in a comparison of his dissents on the issue of standing in ALLEN V. WRIGHT (1984) [1] and *Duke Power Co. v. Carolina Environmental Study Group* (1978). Similarly, he has argued for reduction in the Court's reliance on the doctrine of "HARMLESS ERROR" [2], which allows convictions to be affirmed where arguably nonprejudicial error has occurred; in his view, saving convictions should have a low priority.

His substantive conception of the source and content of constitutional liberty is as distinctive as his view of the systemic judicial role in protecting it. Unlike protections for PROPERTY RIGHTS [I], which Stevens agrees originate in positive law, he believes liberty stems from NATURAL LAW [I]. His dissents in *Hewitt v. Helms* (1983) and *Meachum v. Fano* (1976) illustrate his belief that even justifiably confined inmates retain claims to liberty, including the right to be treated with dignity and impartiality. The source of that liberty "is not state law, nor even the Constitution itself." Rather, drawing on the DECLARATION OF INDEPENDENCE [2], he found it "self-evident that all men were endowed by their Creator with liberty as one of the cardinal inalienable rights." Not surprisingly, given this view, he has embraced judicial recognition of a wide spectrum of textually unenumerated fundamental liberties that cannot be infringed without strong justification, including those implicated by criminal and civil commitment proceedings, termination of parental rights, loss of CITIZENSHIP [1,I], restrictions on ABORTION [I,1] and consensual sex, and laws limiting prisoners' rights to refuse antipsychotic drugs and terminal patients' rights to refuse unwanted, life-prolonging medical intervention. As to the last, his dissent in *Cruzan v. Missouri Department of Health* (1990) opined that "choices about death touch the core of liberty" and are "essential incidents of the unalienable rights to life and liberty endowed us by our Creator" and that the "Constitution presupposes respect for the personhood of every individual, and nowhere is strict adherence to that principle more essential than in the Judicial Branch." Stevens has been particularly distressed by the Court's rejection of a wide liberty to retain counsel in government-benefit disputes and the right to government-provided counsel in proceedings to terminate parental

status, because he thinks these rulings substantially undervalue the fundamental liberty of legal representation. Of his general approach, he has written that judges are to use the common-law method of adjudication to ascertain the content of liberty: "The task of giving concrete meaning to the term 'liberty,' like the task of defining other concepts such as 'commerce among the States,' 'due process of law,' and 'unreasonable searches and seizures,' was a part of the work assigned to future generations of judges."

Contained in his conception of liberty are government obligations of impartiality, rational decision making, and procedural fairness. These obligations are tempered, however, by two factors. First, Justice Stevens is willing to search broadly for acceptable regulatory justifications, especially the justification that a particular regulation enhances rather than diminishes liberty. Second, he is a candid, interest balancer, willing to distinguish among degrees of liberty and degrees of regulatory interference, as well as among degrees of strength of governmental interests to be served. The result is to give government at least some leeway. Moreover, he would hold judges to at least the same level of obligation, a fact that sometimes enlarges the regulatory freedom of political actors. Thus, although Justice Stevens starts from the presumption that government must justify its interference with liberty, rather than a presumption of judicial deference to regulation, he can be quite generous in accepting certain forms of regulation.

For Stevens, government treatment of individuals as equals with dignity and respect is a portion of their liberty, not just a derivation of the EQUAL PROTECTION [2,I] clause of the FOURTEENTH AMENDMENT [2,I]. His particular brand of equality analysis would eschew judicial searching for biased subjective motivations of decision makers in favor of an inquiry into whether a law's objectively identifiable purposes are legitimate and sufficiently served. His aversion to motive inquiry is founded largely on two concerns: judges lack capacity to assess motivation accurately and reliance on motive might mean that identical laws would be valid in one JURISDICTION [3] and invalid in another, depending on their sponsors' motives. Lack of nationwide uniformity of federal constitutional restraints on regulatory power is anathema to Stevens because it tends to undermine the judicial obligation of evenhandedness.

Justice Stevens opposes the Court's longstanding articulation of different tiers of equal-protection review depending on the nature of the group disadvantaged. He also opposes sharply differentiating between discriminatory intent and disproportionate impact as the dividing line between permissible and impermissible laws. Sacrificing guidance to others for sensitive analysis—an easy accommodation for one who sees the judicial role as dispute resolution, not pronouncement of law—he would consider such factors relevant, but not determinative. Instead of categories, he insisted in CRAIG V. BOREN (1976) [2] that there is "only one Equal Protection Clause" and that its requirement is "to govern impartially." To be impartial, classifications may not be based on insulting assumptions or allow "punishment of only one of two equally guilty wrongdoers," as he wrote in dissent in MICHAEL M. V. SUPERIOR COURT (1981) [3]. His version of impartiality requires that people be treated as equals in dignity and moral respect, not that they necessarily receive equal treatment; so that unlike the "insulting" law held invalid in *Craig*, which forbade young men, but not young women, from buying beer, and the statutory rape law that he would have invalidated in *Michael M.*, which punished only males, he voted in ROSTKER V. GOLDBERG (1981) [3] to uphold Congress's male-only draft law—a law that did not assume greater moral culpability of males than females.

When assessing impartiality, Justice Stevens would also consider whether persons other than the complainants are disadvantaged and whether members of the complaining group could rationally support the disadvantaging classification. Thus, he refused to invalidate a veterans' preference for jobs in PERSONNEL ADMINISTRATOR OF MASSACHUSETTS V. FEENEY (1979) [3], despite its disproportionately disadvantageous effect on women, because the law also disadvantaged nonveteran men in large numbers. And in *Cleburne v. Cleburne Living Center, Inc.* (1985) he left open the possibility that some restrictive regulations based on MENTAL RETARDATION [3] might be permissible because a mentally retarded person, like an impartial lawmaker, could accept some regulation to protect himself or herself, or others.

Attention to the full composition of the disadvantaged group and to their views is related to political limits on discrimination and treatment with moral respect. In particular, adjusting judicial aggressiveness to the level of political protection that a constitutional challenger might otherwise have available pervades Justice Stevens's jurisprudence. Most obviously, this view of the judicial function underlies his preference for reserving judicial power for vindicating the constitutional claims of individuals, not government. Less obviously, it is also reflected in his fervor for addressing the substance of unpopular claims, especially those raised by prisoners, to whose conditions politicians are seldom responsive. Conversely, Justice Stevens is unlikely to overturn arrangements that disadvantage those with considerable political clout. His majority opinion in *Lyng v. Castillo* (1986) upholding a food-stamp policy that disfavored close relatives in contrast to more distant relatives noted that families are hardly politically powerless. Outside the equal-protection arena, similar

considerations explain his support of the current Court position that judicial enforcement of TENTH AMENDMENT [4] limits on Congress's power to regulate the States is generally inappropriate given the states' ability to apply political pressure in Congress. On a similar ground, he agreed in GOLDWATER V. CARTER (1979) [2] that, given congressional power to protect its prerogatives, whether the President may terminate a treaty with a foreign power without Senate consent is a nonjusticiable "political question." Likewise, in *United States v. Munoz-Flores* (1990) he argued unsuccessfully that the Court should not address a claimed violation of the constitutional provision requiring revenue bills to originate in the House of Representatives. It is the "weakest imaginable justification for judicial invalidation of a statute" to contend "that the judiciary must intervene in order to protect a power of the most majoritarian body in the Federal Government, even though that body has an absolute veto over any effort to usurp that power." In yet another sphere, he was the sole dissenter from the ruling in *Davis v. Michigan Department of Treasury* (1989) that a state may not extend a tax on employee retirement benefits to retired federal employees if state and local retirees are exempt. So long as the state taxed retirement benefits of private sector employees—"the vast majority of voters in the State"—he thought the tax on federal retirees was allowable.

The obligation of impartiality also embraces another theme that extends beyond the realm of equal protection: judges should not adopt constitutional standards that themselves risk arbitrary or uneven treatment. Evenhandedness does not mean equal concern for governmental power and individual liberty, but equal liberty for all. This is a judicial obligation that sometimes has led Justice Stevens to limit, and sometimes to approve, governmental regulation. For example, unlike his colleagues, who tend either to favor or disfavor *both* ESTABLISHMENT OF RELIGION [2] and "free exercise of religion" arguments, he is simultaneously receptive to claims of strict SEPARATION OF CHURCH AND STATE [4,I], but unreceptive to claims that the free-exercise clause requires exemption from generally applicable laws for religiously motivated conduct. His singular stance appears grounded in an emphasis on evenhandedness. To Justice Stevens, preference for one religion over another or seeming endorsement of a limited set of religions that would offend others, violates the government's obligation of religious neutrality imposed by the ESTABLISHMENT CLAUSE [I]. In contrast, neutral laws that apply generally do not impugn governmental evenhandedness, and religion-based claims to a selective exemption would reintroduce this problem. Accordingly, he concurred in decisions refusing to exempt the Amish from paying social-security taxes, an Orthodox Jew from an Air Force regulation barring headgear indoors, and members of the Native American Church from a ban on drug use, including peyote, which they smoked as part of a religious ceremony.

A similar emphasis on evenhandedness surfaces in his PUBLIC FORUM [3,I] and other free-speech opinions, with alternately restrictive and permissive results. As with equal-protection standards of review, Justice Stevens doubts the value of public forum doctrine to resolve FIRST AMENDMENT [2,I] issues of access to public property for free speech. But he is simultaneously intolerant of viewpoint discrimination and tolerant of broad but neutral exclusions of expression from public property. His majority opinion in *Los Angeles v. Taxpayers for Vincent* (1984) upheld an ordinance broadly banning posting of signs on public property after noting its viewpoint neutrality and its evenhanded enforcement. He rejected a claim for exemption of political signs because such an exemption "might create a risk of engaging in constitutionally forbidden content discrimination." Similarly, although he has adamantly opposed prohibitions on speech when the government's justification rests solely on the offensiveness of the message, he accepts restrictions designed to maintain government neutrality in the marketplace of ideas, even though the restrictions significantly lessen speech. This distinction is explained in *FCC v. League of Women Voters* (1984), where he dissented from the Court's invalidation of Congress's ban on all editorializing by publicly funded broadcasters. Finally, he is particularly critical of the Court's judge-made standards for defining OBSCENITY [3] unprotected by the First Amendment. As he wrote in his separate opinion in *Marks v. United States* (1977), those standards "are so intolerably vague that evenhanded enforcement of the law is a virtual impossibility," and "grossly disparate treatment of similar offenders is a characteristic of the criminal enforcement of obscenity law."

Justice Stevens's evenhandedness standard does not completely reject qualitative assessments of the comparative value of different kinds of speech. In particular, if speech is of limited social value, and its form, rather than its viewpoint, is found offensive—a distinction he, but not others, can perceive as viable—he would acknowledge government's right to regulate its nuisance effects, although probably not to ban it altogether. In accepting ZONING [4,I] laws restricting the location of businesses offering "almost but not quite obscene" materials, and in permitting the Federal Communications Commission to declare that a profane radio broadcast during the day might be disciplined, Justice Stevens took explicit account of the low value of the speech, as well as of the limited nature of the governmental restriction. He concluded that the justification for both restrictions was offensiveness of the form of communication, not the message. In the profanity case, FEDERAL COMMUNICATIONS COMMIS-

SION V. PACIFICA FOUNDATION (1978) [2], he reasoned that it is "a characteristic of speech such as this that both its capacity to offend and its 'social value' . . . vary with the circumstances."

The moderating tendency of accepting regulation of limited intrusiveness into liberty of lesser dimension so long as discernible, nonrepressive governmental puposes are present has often led Justice Stevens to emphasize the validity of civil nuisance-type regulations where he might find criminalization unacceptable. Indeed, there is evidence that he would uphold innovative moderate forms of regulation as a means of accommodating the tension between individual freedom and the right of communities to protect against the harm that exercising such freedom may do to others. There is much of John Stuart Mill in Justice Stevens's severely limited view of government power to restrain individual liberty that does no tangible harm to others, but his more generous view of government's power to protect against the nuisance effects of unrestrained freedom. This view is evident not only in his obscenity opinions and opinions regarding civil DAMAGES [1] for recovery for LIBEL [3] such as *Philadelphia Newspapers, Inc. v. Hepps* (1986), but also in opinions addressing whether regulation of private property constitutes a deprivation of property without DUE PROCESS [2] or a "TAKING OF PROPERTY" [4,I] requiring payment of JUST COMPENSATION [3]. In MOORE V. EAST CLEVELAND (1977) [3], for example, he separately concurred in the Court's judgment invalidating the city's single-family zoning ordinance, which defined a family to exclude a grandmother and two grandsons who were cousins to each other. In that opinion he located the ordinance's constitutional defect in its interference with the grandmother's "right to use her own property as she sees fit" with respect to the "relationship of the occupants." He distinguished zoning ordinances forbidding unrelated individuals from living together as legitimately based on controlling transient living arrangements that arguably might impair a sense of permanence in the community. Stevens generously approaches zoning ordinances based on arguable external effects, but is unsympathetic to those that fail to accord the reciprocal advantages to all in the community that zoning regulations normally create. These views are reflected in his majority opinion allowing an uncompensated prohibition on coal mining that would cause subsidence of others' property in *Keystone Bituminous Coal Association v. DeBenedictis* (1987), from which Chief Justice WILLIAM H. REHNQUIST [3,I] dissented. The same views surely explain his joining of Rehnquist's dissent in PENN CENTRAL TRANSPORTATION CO. V. NEW YORK CITY (1978) [3], which upheld a historic landmarks-preservation law as applied to prevent development in the airspace above Grand Central Terminal. Moreover, Stevens's tendency to allow moderate regulation of the use of property that affects others and his openness to a wide scope of legitimate, potentially innovative forms of regulation, underlies his dissenting view in *First English Evangelical Lutheran Church v. Los Angeles* (1987). He believed that the government should not be obligated to pay for the loss of property use during the temporary period that a land-use regulation is challenged as a compensable "taking." He was concerned that if government was required not only to lift its regulation, but also to pay for the loss during the period of the constitutional challenge, officials would be deterred from acting, and "the public interest in having important governmental decisions made in an orderly informed way" would be sacrificed.

A final distinctive theme of Justice Stevens—one he admired in Justice Rutledge—is that, even if government decision makers have broad latitude in choosing what goals to pursue and considerable discretion in choosing the means to achieve them, judges should carefully review the decision-making process to assure that the responsible officials sufficiently considered the rights of those whose constitutional interests are sacrificed. Moreover, his version of this "due process of lawmaking," which sometimes provides procedural safeguards in lieu of substantive limitations, tailors the intensity of the required process to the magnitude of the liberty and equality interests implicated by the decision or policy. His CAPITAL PUNISHMENT [1,I] opinions illustrate this concern, as well as his reluctance to narrow government goals and his deep attachment to impartiality. He would not prohibit imposition of the death penalty altogether, but he supports a variety of significant limitations on the process of its administration to limit arbitrariness. He insists on narrowing the category of those eligible for capital punishment, policing against its racially disproportionate infliction, and limiting, through defined and acceptable criteria, discretion of the prosecution to seek death sentences and discretion of the jury to impose them. He would not permit any death sentence not approved by a jury—in his view, the only acceptable voice for so irrevocable an expression of the community's sense of moral outrage. Furthermore, although he finds individualized guided jury discretion essential in all cases, he would preserve the jury's absolute discretion to spare life, as his powerful dissents in *Spaziano v. Florida* (1984) and *Walton v. Arizona* (1990) demonstrate.

Justice Stevens has expressed this preference for a calibrated review of process in a variety of circumstances. He readily protects the foundational rights of free and equal political participation against governmental action that would distort a fair political regime, just as he would broadly uphold governmental efforts to protect the purity of the political process. Not only do his influential and forceful opinions favoring constitutional limits on partisan gerrymandering and political patronage in cases like *Karcher v. Daggett* (1983), *Davis v. Bandemer* (1986), and BRANTI V. FINKEL (1980) [I] reflect this; so do his concurring opinion favorable to government-imposed anti-corruption limits on corporate expenditures to support candidates in *Austin v. Michigan Chamber of Commerce* (1990), his dissent from the Court's refusal to extend the federal mail-fraud statute to cover deprivation of rights to honest government in *McNally v. United States* (1987), and his unwillingness in dissent in BROWN V. SOCIALIST WORKERS '74 CAMPAIGN COMMITTEE (1982) [1] to require a First Amendment exemption for the Socialist Workers Party from a law mandating that political parties disclose their contributors. Not consistent judicial deference, but an overriding concern for a properly functioning political system, underlies his alternately restrictive or generous view of political efforts at domination or reform.

As many of these opinions suggest, he would require fair process for application as well as formulation of law, process whose demands increase the more fundamental the interest at issue. His dissent in BETHEL SCHOOL DISTRICT V. FRASER (1986) [I] acknowledged that school officials could consider the content of vulgar speech in setting rules of student conduct, but especially since speech was involved, he would not have allowed a student who made sexually suggestive remarks at a school assembly to be suspended without sufficient warning that his speech would provoke punishment. He would also distinguish between the process fit for legislation and that suited for adjudication. Dissenting in *City of Eastlake v. Forest City Enterprises* (1976), he would have found "manifestly unreasonable" a requirement that zoning changes be approved by fifty-five percent of the vote in a city-wide referendum. He insisted that "[t]he essence of fair procedure is that the interested parties be given a reasonable opportunity to have their dispute decided on the merits by reference to articulable rules." Although he had "no doubt about the validity of the initiative or the referendum as an appropriate method of deciding questions of community policy," he thought it "equally clear that the popular vote is not an acceptable method of adjudicating the rights of individual litigants."

A distinctive element of Stevens's expectation of a rational decision-making process is found in his oft-noted inventive opinion in HAMPTON V. MOW SUN WONG (1976) [2], which insisted that if questionable policies are to be implemented, at least the appropriate authority must adopt them. His plurality opinion invalidated a rule barring employment of aliens in the federal civil service, not because it violated equal protection, but because it was adopted by the Civil Service Commission to serve governmental interests that only the President or Congress could assert. More generally, he adheres closely to a constitutional vision in which all government officials, including judges, carry out the responsibilities particularly assigned to them. Several opinions aim to prevent Congress from abdicating its policymaking responsibilities. One is his separate concurrence in BOWSHER V. SYNAR (1986) [I], arguing that although "Congress may delegate legislative power to independent agencies or to the Executive," if it elects to exercise lawmaking power itself, it cannot "authorize a lesser representative of the Legislative Branch to act on its behalf," but must follow the normal process of enactment by both Houses of Congress and presentment to the President. In that case, Congress had inappropriately given power under the GRAMM-RUDMAN-HOLLINGS ACT [2] to the comptroller general, one of its own agents, to make important economic policy that binds the nation. Similarly, in his plurality opinion in *Industrial Union Department v. American Petroleum Institute* (1980), Stevens interpreted the Occupational Health and Safety Act to prohibit the secretary of labor from adopting standards for controlling potentially hazardous substances unless reasonably necessary to prevent significant harm in the workplace, rather than to achieve absolute safety. Construing Congress's intent more broadly would assume a delegation of "unprecedented power over American industry" that might constitute an unconstitutional transfer of legislative power—a conclusion that Justice Rehnquist's concurrence embraced.

Finally, Justice Stevens's vision of the minimal elements of an acceptably rational decision-making process builds on his presumption that government must justify its actions and entails a realistic appraisal of whether an identifiable and legitimate public purpose supports the challenged act, even if that purpose is not identified by the decision maker itself. Although broadly defining the legitimate goals that government may pursue—particularly including latitudinous conceptions of environmental or aesthetic improvements in the quality of community life and programs providing veterans benefits—he will not strain his imagination to prop up conduct that realistically could not have been aimed at legitimate objectives. Thus, he is not loath to ferret out protectionist state purposes that are invalid under the DORMANT COMMERCE CLAUSE [I] or the absence of secular purposes for religion-connected decisions that are invalid under the establishment clause. Moreover, he condemns harmful classifications adopted out of "habit, rather than analysis," as he shows in several of his opinions involving sex discrimination and distinctions based on legitimacy of birth. Although he will not impose on legislative bodies a duty to articulate their "actual purposes"

for legislation, he will not accept, as a majority of the Court does, any "plausible" or "conceivable" purpose. Rather, as he wrote in his separate concurrence in *United States Railroad Retirement Board v. Fritz* (1980), he demands "a correlation between the classification and either the actual purpose of the statute or a legitimate purpose that we may reasonably presume to have motivated an impartial legislature." As his lone dissenting opinion in *Delaware Tribal Business Committee v. Weeks* (1977) demonstrates, it is not enough for him that a disadvantaging classification is not invidious; it cannot be neglectful, purposeless, or unthinking.

Several of these themes coalesce in his otherwise seemingly inconsistent pattern of positions in the Court's AFFIRMATIVE ACTION [1,I] cases. He dissented in FULLILOVE V. KLUTZNICK (1980) [2] from the Court's sustaining of Congress's setting aside ten percent of public works employment funds for minority business enterprises, largely because Congress gave only "perfunctory consideration" to a racial classification of "profound constitutional importance." He detected a decision illegitimately based on pure racial politics, generally urged that "the procedural character of the decisionmaking process" should affect any constitutional assessment, and specifically insisted that "because classifications based on race are potentially so harmful to the entire body politic, it is especially important that the reasons for any such classification be clearly identified and unquestionably legitimate." He did not assume that all race classifications were impermissible, however, and in WYGANT V. JACKSON BOARD OF EDUCATION (1986) [I] he dissented from the invalidation of a race-based preference for minority teachers contained in a lay-off provision of a COLLECTIVE BARGAINING [1] agreement. Here he thought the interests of the disadvantaged white teachers were adequately represented and considered in the collective-bargaining process. He also urged that the validity of racial classifications must not be evaluated solely in relation to the justification of compensating for past discrimination, but also by considering their relevance to any valid public purposes, including achievement of the benefits of future diversity—a position subsequently adopted by the Court in METRO BROADCASTING, INC. V. FEDERAL COMMUNICATIONS COMMISSION (1990) [I]. In fact, he suggested in his concurring opinion in RICHMOND (CITY OF) V. J.A. CROSON COMPANY (1989) [I], where he voted to nullify the city's *Fullilove*-style setaside program, that "identifying past wrongdoers" and fashioning remedies for past discrimination is better suited to judicial than to legislative bodies.

Matching purposes to appropriate decision makers and requiring deliberation adequate to the liberty affected, yet remaining open to a multiplicity of valid governmental objectives, are essential characteristics of this rational, liberty-devoted and open-minded judge.

                                        JONATHAN D. VARAT

Bibliography

BURRIS, SCOTT 1987 Death and a Rational Justice: A Conversation on the Capital Jurisprudence of Justice John Paul Stevens. *Yale Law Journal* 96:521–546.

CARLSON, JONATHAN C. and SMITH, ALAN D. 1976 The One Hundred and First Justice: An Analysis of the Opinions of Justice John Paul Stevens, Sitting as a Judge on the Seventh Circuit Court of Appeals. *Vanderbilt Law Review* 29:125–209.

——— 1978 The Emerging Constitutional Jurisprudence of Justice Stevens. *University of Chicago Law Review* 46:155–213.

——— 1987 Justice Stevens' Equal Protection Jurisprudence. *Harvard Law Review* 100:1146–1165.

O'BRIEN, DAVID M. 1989 Filling Justice William O. Douglas's Seat: President Gerald R. Ford's Appointment of Justice John Paul Stevens. *Supreme Court Historical Society Yearbook* 1989:20–39.

SICKELS, ROBERT JUDD 1988 *John Paul Stevens and the Constitution: The Search for Balance.* University Park and London: The Pennsylvania State University Press.

STEVENS, JOHN PAUL 1983 The Life Span of a Judge-Made Rule. *New York University Law Review* 58:1–21.

——— 1986 The Third Branch of Liberty. *San Diego Law Review* 22:437–452.

SUBSTANTIVE DUE PROCESS
(Update)

In the period preceding the NEW DEAL [1], DUE PROCESS OF LAW [2] meant more than a guaranty of procedural regularity; it also embodied a substantive dimension that curtailed the role of the state in altering the outcomes of private marketplace decisions. This was the era of LOCHNER V. NEW YORK (1905) [3], in which the Supreme Court decreed that government could intervene only to aid parties deemed in special need of paternalistic measures, such as minors and women, or to address externalities (where private bargains impose uncompensated costs on third parties). During a time of considerable social unrest, Lochnerian jurisprudence imposed sharp limits on the domain of ordinary politics while, in many quarters, also placing in question the very legitimacy of JUDICIAL REVIEW [3,I].

With the onset of the Great Depression, the growing political demands on government to curb instability in markets, to reduce widespread unemployment, and to bolster consumer demand forced the Court to alter its conception of the role of the state. Thus, in NEBBIA V. NEW YORK (1934) [3] and WEST COAST HOTEL CO. V. PARRISH (1937) [4], the Court rejected *Lochner's* narrow definition of permissible governmental goals. Legislative efforts to redistribute wealth through social programs or enhance the bargaining positions of weaker parties were now legitimate exercises of power. With the permissible ends of government thus broadened, the Court soon indicated in UNITED STATES V. CAROLENE PRODUCTS CO. (1938) [1] that *Lochner's* rigorous insistence on a close fit of "ends" and "means" in ECONOMIC REGULATION [2] had to yield to a policy of judicial deference to reasonably debatable economic measures. The hands-off approach to economic regulations with a RATIONAL BASIS [3] also extended to decisions narrowly construing the reach of the CONTRACT CLAUSE [2] and the takings clause.

This policy of judicial deference would not necessarily extend beyond the economic sphere, however. Justice HARLAN FISKE STONE [4], in his famous footnote four to *Carolene Products,* explained that regulations interfering with fundamental personal liberties and burdening disadvantaged minority groups would be subjected to a more demanding level of scrutiny. This dual standard for review allowed the Court in a number of decisions that culminated in ROE V. WADE (1973) [4] to apply STRICT SCRUTINY [4] to government action interfering with private decisions within a "zone of privacy" that included the intimate realms of marriage, reproduction, and child rearing.

In the years since 1985, without rejecting this dual framework, the Court has confined the privacy interests protected by substantive due process to those that reflect deeply entrenched, widely held traditional values. In *Michael H. v. Gerald D.* (1989) the state's traditional interest in the "unitary family" prevailed over a natural father's paternity claim where the child was born into an extant marital family. Most prominently, in BOWERS V. HARDWICK (1986) [I] the Court held that Georgia could criminalize the act of homosexual sodomy between consenting adults committed in the privacy of the home. Justice BYRON R. WHITE's [4,I] opinion for the majority explained that the right to engage in such conduct had no textual support in the constitutional language. Moreover, he said, the claimed right could not be deemed fundamental, given the long-standing proscription of such conduct in state law and the Court's policy of "great resistance to expand[ing] the substantive reach of [the due process clauses of the Fifth Amendment and FOURTEENTH AMENDMENT (2,I)], particularly if it requires redefining the category of rights deemed to be fundamental."

As critical commentators like Ronald Dworkin have shown, the Court's position in *Bowers* that prohibition of private sexual conduct may be based solely on the moral preferences of majorities is difficult to reconcile with the principle of cases like *Roe v. Wade* (1973). Indeed, in WEBSTER V. REPRODUCTIVE HEALTH SERVICES (1989) [I], the PLURALITY OPINION [3] of Chief Justice WILLIAM H. REHNQUIST [3,I] openly stated that the Court was prepared "to revisit the holding of *Roe*" in an appropriate case. In the meantime, he suggested, the Court would sustain state laws barring the use of public facilities for the performance of ABORTIONS [1,I] and requiring non-medically indicated tests for the purpose of determining fetal viability. Proponents and opponents of abortion alike have viewed *Webster* as a remand of the abortion controversy to the political arena.

In *De Shaney v. Winnebago County Department of Social Services* (1989), the Court held that states were not constitutionally accountable for failure to intervene effectively to curb family domestic violence. "In the substantive due process analysis," Chief Justice Rehnquist wrote, "it is the State's affirmative act of restraining the individual's freedom to act on his own behalf . . . which is the 'deprivation of liberty' triggering the protections of the Due Process Clause, not its failure to act to protect his liberty interests against harms inflicted by other means."

Along with this partial constriction of the "zone of privacy," there have been some stirrings toward greater judicial protection of ECONOMIC LIBERTIES [2]. The Court's COMMERCIAL SPEECH [1,I] decisions have extended FIRST AMENDMENT [2,I] protections to individual professionals facing regulatory restrictions arguably put in place by professional associations to protect established interests from new forms of competition. The Court also has indicated a willingness to depart from traditional deferential review of land use regulation. In *Nollan v. California Coastal Commission* (1987), the Court used the doctrine of UNCONSTITUTIONAL CONDITIONS [4] to find a regulatory TAKING OF PROPERTY [4,I] under the Fifth Amendment. At issue was a zoning board's decision to permit construction of a larger house on a beachfront lot on condition that the owners allow the public an easement to pass across their beach. Some writers have argued that the unconstitutional conditions doctrine should be widely deployed to accomplish a resurrection of ECONOMIC DUE PROCESS [I] protections.

As a general matter, the post–New Deal resistance to substantive due process now appears to be on the wane in the academy. Critics from both the Left and the Right have advocated theories of aggressive CONSTITUTIONALISM [2] at variance with the judicial deference to economic regulations typified by *Carolene Products*. Richard Epstein, among others, has argued that the retreat from *Lochner* after the Great Depression was an unprincipled abandonment of economic liberties thought fundamental by the Constitution's Framers; in his view, the Court properly may confine government intervention to true instances of market failure, such as externalities. Such writers as Frank Michelman and Cass Sustein reject *Lochner*'s facile reliance on laissez-faire economic principles, but they nevertheless agree that the Court properly may, in the service of reconstructed "republican" values, proscribe the use of governmental power simply to further the self-interest of established economic groups.

These academic commentaries derive support in part from JUDICIAL ACTIVISM [3] on behalf of racial equality and voting rights. Social acceptance of the Supreme Court's active role in the latter areas has diluted the concerns over "government by judiciary" that led Harlan Fiske Stone, FELIX FRANKFURTER [2], and others to seek to limit judicial interference with political outcomes. It remains to be seen, however, whether these new versions of substantive due process can be implemented free of a crisis of legitimacy similar to the one that marked the Court's handiwork during the *Lochner* era.

SAMUEL ESTREICHER

(SEE ALSO: *Constitutional History 1877–1901, 1901–1921, 1921–1933, 1933–1945* [1]; *Economic Equal Protection* [I]; *Economic Freedom* [I]; *Economy* [I]; *Reproductive Autonomy* [3].)

Bibliography

EPSTEIN, RICHARD A. 1985 *Takings: Private Property and the Power of Eminent Domain.* Cambridge, Mass.: Harvard University Press.

ESTREICHER, SAMUEL 1981 Platonic Guardians of Democracy: John Hart Ely's Role for the Supreme Court in the Constitution's Open Texture. *New York University Law Review* 56:547–582.

MICHELMAN, FRANK 1986 The Supreme Court Term—Foreword: Traces of Self-Government. *Harvard Law Review* 100:4–77.

POSNER, RICHARD A. 1987 The Constitution as an Economic Document. *George Washington Law Review* 59:4–38.

SUNSTEIN, CASS 1987 *Lochner*'s Legacy. *Columbia Law Review* 87:873–919.

SUPREME COURT AT WORK

In its first decade, the Supreme Court had little business, frequent turnover in personnel, no chambers or staff, no fixed customs, and no institutional identity. When the Court initially convened on February 1, 1790, only Chief Justice JOHN JAY [3] and two other Justices arrived at the Exchange Building in New York City. They adjourned until the next day, when Justice JOHN BLAIR [1] arrived.

With little to do other than admit attorneys to practice before its bar, the Court concluded its first sessions in less than two weeks. When the capital moved from New York City to Philadelphia in the winter of 1790, the Court met in Independence Hall and in the Old City Hall for ten years, until the capital again moved to Washington, D.C. Most of the first Justices' time, however, was spent riding circuit. Under the JUDICIARY ACT OF 1789 [3], they were required twice a year to hold CIRCUIT COURT [1], in the company of district judges, to try some types of cases and to hear appeals from the federal district courts. Hence, the Justices resided primarily in their circuits rather than in Washington and often felt a greater allegiance to their circuits than to the Supreme Court.

The Supreme Court is a human institution that has adapted to changing conditions. The Justices no longer ride circuit and the caseload now keeps them in Washington most of the year. As the caseload increased, sessions became longer, and an annual TERM [4] was established. Throughout the nineteenth century, Congress moved the beginning of each term back in stages to the present opening day on the first Monday in October; the term now runs through to the following June or July. These and other changes in the Court's conduct of its business have been shaped by American society and politics. The Justices' chambers have come to resemble "nine little law firms," and the Court has become a more bureaucratic institution.

When the capital moved to Washington, D.C., in 1800, no courtroom was provided. Between 1801 and 1809, the Justices convened in various rooms in the basement of the Capitol. In 1810, they shared a room in the capitol with the Orphans' Court of the DISTRICT OF COLUMBIA [2]. This room was destroyed when the British burned the Capitol on August 24, 1814, and for two years, the Court met in the Bell Tavern. In 1817, the Court moved back into the Capitol, holding sessions in a small dungeon-like room for two years. In 1819, it returned to its restored courtroom, where it met for almost half a century.

For most of the nineteenth century, the Justices resided in their circuits and stayed in boardinghouses during the Court's terms. Chief Justice ROGER BROOKE TANEY (1836–1864) [4] was the first to reside in the Federal City, and as late as the 1880s most Justices did not maintain homes there. Lacking offices and sharing the law library of Congress, the Justices relied on a single clerk to answer correspondence, collect fees, and to locate boardinghouse rooms for them.

Coincident with the 1801 move into the Capitol, JOHN MARSHALL [3] assumed the Chief Justiceship. During his thirty-four years on the Court, Marshall established regularized procedures and a tradition of collegiality. He saw to it that the Justices roomed in the same boardinghouse and, thereby, turned the disadvantage of transiency into strategic opportunity for achieving unanimity in decision making. After a day of hearing ORAL ARGUMENTS [3], the Justices would dine together, and around 7:00 PM they would discuss cases.

After 1860, the Court met upstairs in the old Senate Chamber, between the new chambers of the Senate and those of the House of Representatives. The Justices still had no offices or staff of their own. After the CIVIL WAR [I], however, the caseload steadily grew, the Court's terms lengthened, and the Justices deserted boardinghouses for fashionable hotels along Pennsylvania Avenue. Instead of dining together and discussing cases after dinner, they held CONFERENCES [1] on Saturdays and announced decisions on Monday.

By the turn of the century, the Justices resided in the capitol and for the most part worked at home, where each had a library and employed a messenger and a secretary. The Court's collegial procedures had evolved into institutional norms based on majority rule. The CHIEF JUSTICE [1] assumed a special role in scheduling and presiding over conferences and oral arguments. But the Court's deliberative process was firmly rooted in the Justices' interaction as equals. Each Justice was considered a sovereign in his or her own right, even though the Justices decided cases together and strove for institutional opinions.

After becoming Chief Justice in 1921, WILLIAM HOWARD TAFT [4] persuaded four Justices to support his lobbying Congress for the construction of a building for the Court. Taft envisioned a marble temple symbolizing the modern Court's prestige and independence. Yet, when the building that houses the Court was completed in 1935, none of the sitting Justices moved in, although sessions and conferences were held there in the later years of the HUGHES COURT (1930–1941) [2]. Upon his appointment in 1937, HUGO L. BLACK [1] was the first to move in, leading the way for President FRANKLIN D. ROOSEVELT's [3] other appointees. Even when HARLAN FISKE STONE [4] was elevated from Associate to Chief Justice, he still worked at home. The VINSON COURT (1946–1953) [4] was the first to see all nine Justices regularly working in the Supreme Court building.

The marble temple stands for more than a symbol of the modern Court. Once again, the institutional life of the Court changed. As Taft hoped, the building buttressed the Court's prestige and reinforced the basic norms of secrecy, tradition, and collegiality that condition the Court's work. The Justices continued to function independently, but the work of the Court grew more bureaucratic. Along with the rising caseload in the decades following

WORLD WAR II [I], the number of law clerks more than tripled and the number of other employees dramatically increased as well. The Justices in turn delegated more and incorporated modern office technology and managerial practices into their work. The WARREN COURT (1953–1969) [4] started delivering opinions on any day of open session, and the BURGER COURT (1969–1986) [1] moved conferences back to Fridays.

When POTTER STEWART [4] joined the Court in 1958, he expected to find "one law firm with nine partners, if you will, the law clerks being the associates." But Justice JOHN MARSHALL HARLAN [2] told him, "No, you will find here it is like nine firms, sometimes practicing law against one another." Even today, each Justice and his or her staff works in rather secluded chambers with little of the direct daily interaction that occurs in some appellate courts. Nor do recent Justices follow FELIX FRANKFURTER's [2] practice of sending clerks ("Felix's happy hotdogs") scurrying around the building to lobby other clerks and Justices.

A number of factors isolate the Justices, but most important is the caseload. The Justices, in Justice BYRON R. WHITE's [4,I] view, "stay at arm's length" and rely on formal printed communications because the workload discourages them "from going from chamber to chamber to work things out." Each chamber averages about seven: the Justice, three to four law clerks, two secretaries, and a messenger. As managing chambers and supervising paperwork consumes more time, the Justices talk less to each other and read and write more memoranda and opinions. Each chamber now has a photocopying machine and four to five terminals for word processing and legal research.

Law CLERKS [1] became central to the work of the Court. In 1882, Justice HORACE GRAY [2] initiated the practice of hiring a "secretary" or law clerk. When OLIVER WENDELL HOLMES, JR. [2] succeeded Gray, he continued the practice, and other Justices gradually followed. By Chief Justice Stone's time it was well established for each Justice to have one clerk. During the chief justiceships of FRED M. VINSON [4] and EARL WARREN [4], the number increased to two. In the 1970s, the number grew to three and to four. The number of secretaries likewise increased—initially, in place of adding clerks and, later, to assist the growing number of clerks. A Legal Office, staffed by two attorneys, was created in 1975 to assist with cases in the Court's ORIGINAL JURISDICTION [3] and with expedited appeals.

Although the duties and functions of clerks vary with each chamber, all share certain commonly assigned responsibilities. Most notably, Justices have delegated to them the task of initially screening all filings for writs of certiorari [1]. This practice originated with the handling of INDIGENTS' [2] petitions by Chief Justice CHARLES EVANS HUGHES [2] and his clerks. Unlike the "paid" petitions that are filed in multiple copies, an indigent's petition is typically a handwritten statement. Except when an unpaid petition raised important legal issues or involved a capital case, Hughes neither circulated the petitions to the other Justices nor discussed them at conference. Stone, Vinson, and Warren, however, circulated to the chambers their clerks' memoranda, which summarized the facts and questions presented, and recommended whether the case should be denied, dismissed, or granted a review. But Chief Justice WARREN E. BURGER [1] refused to have his clerks shoulder the entire burden of screening these petitions. And in 1972, a majority of the Justices began to pool their clerks, dividing up all paid and unpaid filings and having a single clerk's certiorari memo circulate to those Justices participating in what is called "the cert. pool." With more than a hundred filings each week, even those Justices who objected to the "cert. pool" have found it necessary to give their clerks considerable responsibility for screening petitions. Justice JOHN PAUL STEVENS [4,I] describes his practice: "[The clerks] examine them all and select a small minority that they believe I should read myself. As a result, I do not even look at the papers in over 80 percent of the cases that are filed."

Law clerks have also assumed responsibility for the preliminary drafting of the Justices' opinions. Chief Justice WILLIAM H. REHNQUIST's [3,I] practice, for instance, is to have one of his clerks do a first draft, without bothering about style, in about ten days. Before beginning work on an opinion, Rehnquist goes over the conference discussion with the clerk and explains how he thinks "an opinion can be written supporting the result reached by the majority." Once the clerk finishes a draft and Rehnquist works the draft into his own opinion, it circulates three or four times among the other clerks in the chambers before it circulates to the other chambers.

In addition to law clerks, five officers and their staffs also assist the Justices. Central to the Court's work is the Office of the Clerk. For most of the Court's history, the clerk earned no salary, but this changed in 1921 when Taft lobbied for legislation making the clerk a salaried employee. The clerk's office collects filing and admission fees; receives and records all motions, petitions, BRIEFS [1], and other documents; and circulates those necessary items to each chamber. The clerk also establishes the oral-argument calendar and maintains the order list of cases granted or denied review and final judgments. In 1975, the office acquired a computer system that automatically notifies counsel in over ninety-five percent of all cases of the disposition of their filings.

There was no official reporter of decisions during the first quarter-century of the Court, and not until 1835 were the Justices' opinions given to the clerk. Early reporters worked at their own expense and for their own profit. In 1922, Congress established the present arrangement (at Chief Justice Taft's request): the reporter's salary is fixed by the Justices and paid by the government, and the Government Printing Office publishes the *United States Reports*. The reporter has primary responsibility for supervising the publication of the Court's opinions, writing headnotes or syllabi that accompany each opinion, and for making editorial suggestions subject to the Justices' approval.

Order in the courtroom was preserved by U.S. marshals until 1867, when Congress created the Office of Marshal of the Supreme Court. The Marshal not only maintains order in the courtroom and times oral arguments but also oversees building maintenance and serves as business manager for the more than two hundred Court employees, including messengers, carpenters, police and workmen, a nurse, physiotherapist, barber, seamstress, and cafeteria workers.

The Justices acquired their first small library in 1832. It was run by the clerk until the marshal's office took over in 1884. In 1948, Congress created the Office of the Librarian, which employs several research librarians to assist the Justice.

Unlike other members of the Court, the Chief Justice has special administrative duties. Over fifty statutes confer duties ranging from chairing the JUDICIAL CONFERENCE [1] and the Federal Judicial Center to supervising the Administrative Office of the U.S. Courts and serving as chancellor of the Smithsonian Institution. Unlike Taft and Hughes, Stone felt overwhelmed by these duties. His successor, Vinson, appointed a special assistant to deal with administrative matters, whereas Warren delegated such matters to his secretary. By contrast, Burger became preoccupied with administrative matters and pushed for judicial reforms. In historical perspective, he brought Taft's marble temple into the world of modern technology and managerial practices. Burger also lobbied Congress to create a fifth legal officer of the Court, the administrative assistant to the Chief Justice. While also employing an administrative assistant, Chief Justice Rehnquist has less interest in judicial administration, and his assistant is less occupied with liaison work with organizations outside the Court.

The caseload remains the driving force behind the Court's work; its increase has changed the Court's operations. After Taft campaigned for relief for the Court, Congress passed the JUDICIARY ACT OF 1925 [3], which enlarged the Court's discretionary JURISDICTION [3] and enabled it to deny cases review. Subsequently, on a piece-meal basis, the Court's discretion over its jurisdiction was further expanded, and in 1988, virtually all mandatory appeals were eliminated. As a result, the Court has the power to manage its docket and set its agenda for decision making.

The cornerstone of the modern Court's operation, in Justice John Harlan's words, "is the control it possesses over the amount and character of its business." The overwhelming majority of all cases are denied review; less than three percent of the more than 5,000 cases on the Court's annual docket are granted and decided by fully written opinion.

When a petition is filed at the Court, the clerk's staff determines whether it satisfies the rules as to form, length, and fees. After receiving opposing papers from respondents, the clerk circulates to the chambers a list of cases ready for consideration and a set of papers for each case. For much of the Court's history, every Justice reviewed every case, but this practice no longer prevails. Since the creation of the "cert. pool" in 1972, most of the Justices have delegated to their clerks much of this initial screening task. Moreover, the Court has found it necessary to hold its initial conference in the last week of September, before the formal opening of its term. At this conference, the Justices dispose of more than 1,000 cases, discussing less than two hundred. Before the start of the term, the Court has thus disposed of approximately one-fifth of its entire docket, with more than four-fifths of those cases effectively screened out by law clerks and never collectively considered by the Justices.

In conference, attended only by the Justices, the Court decides which cases to accept and discusses the merits of argued cases. During the weeks in which the Court hears oral arguments, conferences are held on Wednesday afternoons to take up the four cases argued on Monday, and then on Fridays to discuss new filings and the eight cases argued on Tuesday and Wednesday. In May and June, when oral arguments are not heard, conferences are held on Thursdays, from 10:00 AM to 4:00 PM, with a forty-five-minute lunch break around 12:30 PM.

Summoned by a buzzer five minutes before the hour, the Justices meet in their conference room, located directly behind the courtroom itself. Two conference lists circulate to each chamber by noon on the Wednesday before a conference. On the first list are those cases deemed worth discussing; typically, the discuss list includes about fifty cases. Attached is a second list, the "Dead List," containing those cases considered unworthy of discussion. Any Justice may request that a case be discussed, but over seventy percent of the cases on the conference lists are denied review without discussion.

Since the Chief Justice presides over conferences, he has significant opportunities for structuring and influencing the Court's work. Chief Justices, however, vary widely in their skills, style, and ideological orientations. Hughes is widely considered to be the greatest Chief Justice in this century because of his photographic memory and ability to state concisely the relative importance of each case. "Warren was closer to Hughes than any others," in Justice WILLIAM O. DOUGLAS's [2] view, and "Burger was closer to Vinson. Stone was somewhere in between." Rehnquist, by all accounts, is an effective Chief Justice because he moves conferences along quickly and has the intellectual and temperamental wherewithal to be a leader.

For a case to be heard by the Court, at least four Justices must agree that it warrants consideration. This informal RULE OF FOUR [3] was adopted when the Justices were trying to persuade Congress that important cases would still be decided after the Court was given discretionary control over much of its jurisdiction under the Judiciary Act of 1925. Unanimity in case selection, nevertheless, remains remarkably high because the Justices agree that only a limited number of cases may be taken. "As a rule of thumb," Justice White explains, "the Court should not be expected to produce more than 150 opinions per term in argued cases." The rule of four, however, also permits an ideological bloc to grant review in cases it wants to hear and, thus, to influence the Court's agenda.

Immediately after conference, the Chief Justice traditionally had the task of reporting to the clerk which cases were granted review, which were denied review, and which were ready to come down. Burger, however, delegated this task to the junior Justice. The clerk then notifies both sides in a case granted review that they have thirty days to file briefs on merits and supporting documents. Once all briefs (forty copies of each) are submitted, cases are scheduled for oral argument.

The importance of oral argument, Chief Justice Charles Evans Hughes observed, lies in the fact that often "the impression that a judge has at the close of a full oral argument accords with the conviction which controls his final vote." Because the Justices vote in conference within a day or two of hearing arguments, oral arguments come at a crucial time. Still, oral arguments were more prominent in the work of the Court in the nineteenth century. Unlimited time was allowed, until the Court began cutting back on oral argument in 1848, allowing eight hours per case. The time has been reduced periodically, and since 1970, arguments have been limited to thirty minutes per side. The argument calendar permits hearing no more than 180 cases a year. For fourteen weeks each term, from the first Monday in October until the end of April, the Court hears arguments from 10:00 to 12:00 and 1:00 to 3:00 on Monday, Tuesday, and Wednesday about every two weeks.

Justices differ in their preparation for oral arguments. Douglas insisted that "oral arguments win or lose a case," but Chief Justice Earl Warren claimed that they were "not highly persuasive." Most Justices come prepared with "bench memos" drafted by their law clerks, identifying the central facts, issues, and possible questions. On the bench, they also vary in their style and approach toward questioning attorneys. Justices SANDRA DAY O'CONNOR [3,I] and ANTONIN SCALIA [I], for example, are aggressive and relentless in the questioning of attorneys, while Justices WILLIAM J. BRENNAN [1,I] and HARRY A. BLACKMUN [1,I] tend to sit back and listen.

Conference discussions following oral arguments no longer play the role they once did. When the docket was smaller, conferences were integral to the Court's work. Cases were discussed in detail, differences hammered out, and the Justices strove to reach agreement on an institutional opinion for the Court. As the caseload grew, conferences became largely symbolic of past collective deliberations. They currently serve only to discover consensus. "In fact," Justice Scalia points out, "to call our discussion of a case a conference is really something of a misnomer. It's much more a statement of the views of each of the nine Justices."

Most of the time spent in conference is consumed by the Justices deciding which cases should be granted review. Moreover, less time is spent in conference (now about 108 hours) each term. The caseload and conference schedule permits on average only about six minutes for each case on the discuss list and about twenty-nine minutes for those granted full consideration. Perhaps as a result, the Justices agree less often on the opinion announcing the Court's decision and file a greater number of separate opinions. In short, the combination of more cases and less collective deliberation discourages the compromises necessary for institutional opinions and reinforces the tendency of the Justices to function independently.

All votes at conference are tentative until the final opinion comes down. Voting thus presents each Justice with opportunities to negotiate which issues are to be decided and how they are to be resolved. Before, during, and after conference, Justices may use their votes in strategic ways to influence the outcome of a case. At conference, a Justice may vote with others who appear to constitute a majority, even though the Justice may disagree with their reasoning. The Justice may then suggest changes in draft opinions to try to minimize the damage, from his or her perspective, of the Court's decision.

Because conference votes are tentative, the assignment, drafting, and circulation of opinions is crucial to the Court's work. Opinions justify or explain votes at conference. The OPINION OF THE COURT [3] is the most important and most difficult to write because it represents a collective judgment. Writing the Court's opinion, as Justice Holmes put it, requires that a "judge can dance the sword dance; that is he can justify an obvious result without stepping on either blade of opposing fallacies." Because Justices remain free to switch votes and to write separate opinions, concurring in or dissenting from the Court's decision, they continue after conference to compete for influence on the final decision and opinion.

The power of opinion assignment is the Chief Justice's "single most influential function," observed Justice TOM C. CLARK [1], and an exercise in "judicial-political discretion." By tradition, when the Chief Justice votes with the majority, he assigns the Court's opinion. If the Chief Justice is not with the majority, then the senior Associate Justice in the majority either writes the opinion or assigns it to another Justice.

Chief Justices may keep the Court's opinion for themselves, especially when a case is unanimously decided. Since Vinson, however, Chief Justices have generally sought parity in their opinion assignments. Opinions may be assigned to pivotal Justices to ensure or expand the size of the majority joining the opinion for the Court. But the Chief Justice may also take other factors into account, such as a Justice's expertise or what kind of reaction a ruling may engender. Hughes, for example, was inclined to assign the opinions in "liberal" decisions to "conservative" Justices.

The circulation of draft opinions among the chambers has added to the Supreme Court's workload and changed its deliberative process. The practice of circulating draft opinions began around 1900 and soon became pivotal in the Court's decision-making process, especially with the Justices spending less time in conference discussing and reconciling their differences. Occasionally, proposed changes in a draft opinion will lead to a complete recasting or to having the opinion reassigned to another Justice. To accommodate the views of others, the author of an opinion for the Court must negotiate language and bargain over substance. At times, however, Justices may not feel that a case is worth fighting over; as Justice GEORGE SUTH-ERLAND [4] noted on the back of one of Stone's drafts, "probably bad—but only a small baby. Let it go."

Final published opinions for the Court are the residue of compromises among the Justices. But they also reflect changing norms in the work of the Court. Up until the 1930s, there were few concurring or dissenting OPINIONS [3]. But individual opinions now predominate over opinions for the Court. When the Court's practice in the 1980s is compared with that of forty years ago, there are roughly ten times the number of CONCURRING OPINIONS [1], four times more DISSENTING OPINIONS [2], and seven times the number of separate opinions in which the Justices explain their views and why they concur and dissent from

parts of the Court's opinion. Even though the business of the Court is to give institutional opinions, as Justice Stewart observed, "that view has come to be that of a minority of the Justices."

The Justices are more interested in merely the tally of votes at conference than in arriving at a consensus on an institutional decision and opinion. As a result, whereas unanimity remains high on case selection (around eighty percent), unanimous opinions for the Court count for only about thirty percent of the Court's written opinions. The number of cases decided by a bare majority also sharply grew in the 1970s and 1980s, and frequently, no majority could agree on an opinion announcing the Court's rulings.

A Justice writing separate concurring or dissenting opinions carries no burden of massing other Justices. Concurring opinions explain how the Court's decision could have been otherwise rationalized. A concurring opinion surely is defensible when a compromised opinion might be meaningless or impossible to achieve. The cost of concurring opinions is that they add to the workload and may create confusion over the Court's rulings.

A dissenting opinion, in the words of Chief Justice Hughes, appeals "to the brooding spirit of the law, to the intelligence of a future day, when a later decision may possibly correct the error into which the dissenting judge believes the Court to have been betrayed." Even the threat of a dissent may be useful in persuading the majority to narrow its holding or tone down the language of its opinion.

The struggles over the work of the Court (and among the Justices) continue after the writing of opinions and final votes. Opinion days, when the Court announces its decisions, may reveal something of these struggles and mark the beginning of larger political struggles for influence within the country.

Decisions are announced in the courtroom, typically crowded with reporters, attorneys, and spectators. Before 1857, decisions came down on any day of the week, but thereafter they were announced only on Mondays. In 1965, the Court reverted to its earlier practice, and in 1971, the Justices further broke with the tradition of "Decision Mondays." On Mondays, the Court generally releases memorandum orders and admits new attorneys to its bar. In weeks when the Justices hear oral arguments, opinions are announced on Tuesdays and Wednesdays and then on any day of the week during the rest of the term. By tradition, there is no prior announcement of the decisions to be handed down. In 1971, the practice of reading full opinions was abandoned; typically, only the ruling and the line-up of the Justices is stated.

Media coverage of the Court's work has grown since the 1930s, when fewer than a half-dozen reporters covered the Court and shared six small cubicles on the ground floor, just below the courtroom, where they received copies of opinions sent down through pneumatic tube. In 1970, the Court established a Public Information Office, which provides space for a "press room" and makes available all filings and briefs for cases on the docket, as well as the Court's conference lists and final opinions. More than fifty reporters and all major television networks currently cover the Court, although cameras are still not allowed in the courtroom.

When deciding major issues of public law and policy, Justices may consider strategies for winning public acceptance of their rulings. When holding "separate but equal" schools unconstitutional in 1954 in BROWN V. BOARD OF EDUCATION [1], for instance, the Court waited a year before issuing its mandate for "all deliberate speed" in ending school SEGREGATION [4]. Some of the Justices sacrificed their preference for a more precise guideline in order to achieve a unanimous ruling, and the Court tolerated lengthy delays in the implementation of *Brown*, in recognition of the likelihood of open defiance.

Although the Justices are less concerned about public opinion than are elected public officials, they are sensitive to the attitudes of their immediate "constituents": the SOLICITOR GENERAL [4,I], the ATTORNEY GENERAL AND DEPARTMENT OF JUSTICE [1], counsel for federal agencies, states' attorneys general, and the legal profession. These professionals' responses to the Court's rulings help determine the extent of compliance. With such concerns in mind, Chief Justice Warren sought to establish an objective bright-line rule that police could not evade, when holding, in MIRANDA V. ARIZONA (1966) [3], that police must inform criminal suspects of their Fifth Amendment RIGHT AGAINST SELF-INCRIMINATION [3,I] and their Sixth Amendment RIGHT TO COUNSEL [3], which included the right to consult and have the presence of an attorney during POLICE INTERROGATION [3,I]. The potential costs of securing compliance may also convince the Justices to limit the scope or application of their decisions.

Compliance with the Court's decisions by lower courts is uneven. They may extend or limit decisions in anticipation of later rulings. Ambiguities created by PLURALITY OPINIONS [3], or 5–4 decisions invite lower courts to pursue their own policy goals. Differences between the facts on which the Court ruled and the circumstances of a case at hand may be emphasized so as to reach a different conclusion.

Major confrontations between Congress and the Court have occurred a number of times, and Congress has tried to pressure the Court in a variety of ways. The Senate may try to influence the APPOINTMENT OF SUPREME COURT JUSTICES [1], and Justices may be impeached. More frequently, Congress has tried to pressure the Court when setting its terms and size and when authorizing

appropriations for salaries, law clerks, secretaries, and office technology. Only once, in 1802, when repealing the JUDICIARY ACT OF 1801 [3] and abolishing a session for a year, did Congress actually set the Court's term in order to delay and influence a particular decision. The size of the Court is not preordained, and changes generally reflect attempts to control the Court. The Jeffersonian Republicans' quick repeal of the act passed by the FEDERALISTS [I] in 1801, reducing the number of Justices, was the first of several attempts to influence the Court. Presidents JAMES MADISON [3], JAMES MONROE [3], and JOHN ADAMS [1] all claimed that the country's geographical expansion warranted increasing the number of Justices. Congress, however, refused to do so until the last day of ANDREW JACKSON's [3] term in 1837. During the Civil War, the number of Justices increased to ten. This was ostensibly due to the creation of a circuit in the West, but it also gave ABRAHAM LINCOLN [3] his fourth appointment and a chance to secure a pro-Union majority on the bench. Antagonism toward ANDREW JOHNSON's [3] RECONSTRUCTION [I] policies, then, led to a reduction from ten to seven Justices. After General ULYSSES S. GRANT's [2] election, Congress again authorized nine Justices. In the nineteenth century at least, Congress rather successfully denied Presidents additional appointments in order to preserve the Court's policies, and increased the number of Justices so as to change the ideological composition of the Court.

More direct attacks are possible. Under Article III, Congress is authorized "to make exceptions" to the Court's APPELLATE JURISDICTION [1]. This has been viewed as a way of denying the Court review of certain kinds of cases. But Congress succeeded only once in affecting the Court's work in this way; an 1868 repeal of jurisdiction over writs of HABEAS CORPUS [2,I] was upheld in *Ex Parte McCardle* (1869).

Court-curbing legislation is not a very viable weapon. Congress has greater success in reversing the Court by constitutional amendment, which three-fourths of the states must ratify. The process is cumbersome, and thousands of amendments to overrule the Court have failed. But four rulings have been overturned by constitutional amendment. CHISHOLM V. GEORGIA (1793) [I], holding that citizens of one state could sue another state in federal courts, was reversed by the ELEVENTH AMENDMENT [2,I], guaranteeing SOVEREIGN IMMUNITY [4] for states from suits by citizens of other states. The THIRTEENTH AMENDMENT [4] and FOURTEENTH AMENDMENT [2,I], abolishing SLAVERY [4] and making blacks citizens of the United States, technically overturned DRED SCOTT V. SANDFORD (1857) [2]. With the ratification in 1913 of the SIXTEENTH AMENDMENT [4], Congress reversed POLLOCK V. FARMERS' LOAN AND TRUST COMPANY (1895) [3], which had invalidated a federal income tax. In 1970, an amendment to the VOTING RIGHTS ACT OF 1965 [4] lowered the voting age to eighteen years for all elections. Although signing the act into law, President RICHARD M. NIXON [3] had his attorney general challenge the validity of lowering the voting age in state and local elections. Within six months, in OREGON V. MITCHELL (1970) [3], a bare majority held that Congress had exceeded its power. Less than a year later, the TWENTY-SIXTH AMENDMENT [4] was ratified, thereby overriding the Court's ruling and extending the franchise to eighteen-year-olds in all elections.

Even more successful are congressional enactments and rewriting of legislation in response to the Court's rulings. Congress, of course, cannot overturn the Court's interpretations of the Constitution by mere legislation. But Congress may enhance or thwart compliance with its rulings. After the landmark ruling in GIDEON V. WAINWRIGHT (1963) [2] that indigents have a right to counsel, for instance, Congress provided attorneys for indigents charged with federal offenses. By contrast, in the Crime Control and Safe Streets Act of 1968, Congress permitted federal courts to use evidence obtained from suspects who had not been read their *Miranda* rights if their testimony appeared voluntary based on the "totality of the circumstances" surrounding their interrogation.

Congress may also openly defy the Court's rulings. When holding in IMMIGRATION AND NATURALIZATION SERVICE V. CHADHA (1983) [2] that Congress may not delegate decision-making authority to federal agencies and still retain the power of vetoing decisions with which it disagrees, the Court invalidated over two hundred provisions for congressional vetoes of administrative actions. Congress largely responded by deleting or substituting joint resolutions for one-House veto provisions. However, in the year following *Chadha*, Congress passed no less than thirty new provisions for LEGISLATIVE VETOES [3].

Congress indubitably has the power to delay and undercut implementation of the Court's rulings. On major issues of public policy, Congress is likely to prevail or at least temper the impact of the Court's rulings.

The Court has often been the focus of presidential campaigns and power struggles as well. Presidents rarely openly defy particular decisions by the Court, and in major confrontations, they have tended to yield. Still, presidential reluctance to enforce rulings may thwart implementation of the Court's rulings. In the short and long run, Presidents may undercut the Court's work by issuing contradictory directives to federal agencies and assigning low priority for enforcement by the Department of Justice. Presidents may also make broad moral appeals in response to the Court's rulings, and those appeals may transcend their limited time in office. The Court put school DESEGRE-GATION [2] and ABORTION [1,I] on the national political agenda. Yet JOHN F. KENNEDY's [2] appeal for CIVIL RIGHTS [1,I] captivated a generation and encouraged public acceptance of the Court's ruling in *Brown v. Board of Education*. Similarly, RONALD REAGAN's [3,I] opposition to abortion focused attention on "traditional family values" and served to legitimate resistance to the Court's decisions.

Presidential influence over the Court in the long run remains contingent on appointments to the Court. Vacancies occur on the average of one every twenty-two months, and there is no guarantee as to how a Justice will vote or whether that vote will prove the key to limiting or reversing past rulings with which a President disagrees. Yet through their appointments, Presidents leave their mark on the Court and possibly align it and the country or precipitate later confrontations.

The Supreme Court at work is unlike any other. It has virtually complete discretion to select which cases are reviewed, to control its work load, and to set its own substantive agenda. From the thousands of cases arriving each year, less than two hundred are accepted and decided. The Court thus functions like a superlegislature. But the Justices' chambers also work like nine separate law offices, competing for influence when selecting and deciding those cases. The Justices no longer spend time collectively deliberating cases at conference. Instead, they simply tally votes and then hammer out differences, negotiating and compromising on the language of their opinions during the postconference period when drafts are circulated among the chambers. When the final opinions come down, the Court remains dependent on the cooperation of other political branches and public acceptance for compliance with its rulings. The work of the Court, in Chief Justice EDWARD D. WHITE's [4] words, "rests solely upon the approval of a free people."

DAVID M. O'BRIEN

(SEE ALSO: *Jeffersonianism and the Constitution* [1].)

Bibliography

ABRAHAM, HENRY J. 1986 *The Judicial Process*, 5th ed. New York: Oxford University Press.

CHOPER, JESSE 1980 *Judicial Review and the National Democratic Process*. Chicago: University of Chicago Press.

CONGRESSIONAL QUARTERLY 1989 *Guide to the U.S. Supreme Court*, 2nd ed. Washington, D.C.: Congressional Quarterly Press.

DIAMOND, PAUL 1989 *The Supreme Court & Judicial Choice: The Role of Provisional Judicial Review*. Ann Arbor: University of Michigan Press.

FISHER, LOUIS 1988 *Constitutional Dialogues*. Princeton, N.J.: Princeton University Press.

JOHNSON, CHARLES and CANNON, BRADLEY 1984 *Judicial Policies: Implementation and Impact.* Washington, D.C.: Congressional Quarterly Press.

O'BRIEN, DAVID M. 1990 *Storm Center: The Supreme Court in American Politics*, 2nd ed. New York: W. W. Norton.

STERN, ROBERT and GRESSMAN, EUGENE 1987 *Supreme Court Practice*, 6th ed. Washington, D.C.: Bureau of National Affairs.

SUPREME COURT BAR

The bar of the Supreme Court is not cohesive, and it is not active in any organizational sense. The number of lawyers admitted to practice before the Supreme Court is greatly in excess of the number who actually appear there.

The first rule of the Supreme Court with respect to admissions was adopted on February 5, 1790, three days after the Court opened in New York. The Court then made the provision, which continues to this day, that applicants for admission shall have been admitted "for three years past in the Supreme Courts of the State to which they respectively belong." The formula also provided, then and throughout the nineteenth century, that the private and professional character of the applicants "shall appear to be fair." As the American language evolved, the word "fair" acquired a dual meaning, and the use of the phrase in oral motions sometimes produced a laugh in the courtroom. So the wording was changed, and for most of the twentieth century the sponsor was required to say that he "vouched" for the applicant. Under the rule as it stands now, he affirms "that the applicant is of good moral and professional character." All motions for admissions were made in open court until about 1970. Now the whole procedure can be done by mail.

Under the first rule for admission, the applicant was required to elect whether he would practice as an attorney (office lawyer) or as a counselor (appearing in court), and he could not practice as both. If this rule had remained in effect (it was eliminated in 1801), the long-established division in England between solicitors and barristers would have been perpetuated in the United States and the bar of the Supreme Court would have been drawn from a much narrower group.

There is no published list of the members of the bar of the Supreme Court. Indeed, no one knows how many members there are. The clerk of the Supreme Court maintains a list of those admitted since October 1925. In early 1990 the number of those who had been admitted was about 185,000. But there is no record of those who have died or retired from active practice (though the list does record 800 names of lawyers who have been disbarred). By an estimate there are now 75,000 lawyers in the United States who have been admitted to practice before the Supreme Court and thus are members of its bar. No more than 300 of these actually present arguments before the Supreme Court in any year, and there are probably fewer than 5,000 living lawyers in the country (out of a total of close to 700,000 lawyers altogether) who have ever made a personal appearance before the Court.

The first member of the bar of the Supreme Court was Elias Boudinot of New Jersey, who was admitted to practice in February 1790. There was, of course, no one to move his admission. No procedure had yet been established for the filing of credentials. After a short interval, the Court turned to the attorney general, EDMUND RANDOLPH [3]. Though he was never admitted to practice before the Court, he was treated as an officer of the Court. Before long, the practice was established of admission to the bar on motions of persons already admitted.

During the first ten years of its existence, the Supreme Court heard very few cases. ALEXANDER HAMILTON [2] made his sole appearance before the Court in the case of HYLTON V. UNITED STATES [2] in 1796. JOHN MARSHALL [3] made his sole appearance before the Court in WARE V. HYLTON (1796) [4]. This was the famous British debts case, and Marshall was unsuccessful.

As time passed, and the country developed, the number of cases before the Court steadily increased. Thomas A. Emmet arrived in New York from Ireland in 1804 and was soon established as a leading lawyer. He appeared before the Supreme Court for the first time in 1815. The culmination of his career was his argument in the famous steamboat case of GIBBONS V. OGDEN (1824) [2]. Another of the early leaders was Littleton W. Tazewell of Virginia, who specialized in criminal law and admiralty. DANIEL WEBSTER [4] wrote of him, "He is a correct, fluent, easy & handsome speaker and a learned, ingenuous & *subtle* lawyer"—a standard to which any Supreme Court lawyer might aspire. Others who appeared during the early years of the nineteenth century were LUTHER MARTIN [3], WILLIAM PINKNEY [3], and Francis Scott Key of Maryland; Roger Griswold of Connecticut; Edmund J. Lee and WILLIAM WIRT [4] of Virginia; JOHN QUINCY ADAMS [1], Samuel Dexter, LEVI LINCOLN [3], and Rufus G. Amory of Massachusetts; JARED INGERSOLL [2] and HORACE BINNEY [1] of Pennsylvania; and Edward Livingston of New York and Louisiana.

Daniel Webster made his first appearance in 1814. Early in his career he argued DARTMOUTH COLLEGE V. WOODWARD (1818) [2]. The decision of the Court in this case, announced in 1819, relied on the OBLIGATION OF CONTRACTS [3] clause in the Constitution to uphold the charter of Dartmouth College against efforts of the legislature of New Hampshire to change it. The argument in *Dartmouth College* lasted for three days and was a great social event in Washington. Webster concluded with an emotional peroration that has become part of American folklore. He is supposed to have said, "It is . . . a small college. And yet *there are those who love it.*" But there is no contemporaneous record of this passage. It first appeared in a eulogy on Webster spoken by Rufus Choate in July 1853, thirty-five years after the argument. Choate's source was a letter written to him in 1852 by Chauncey Goodrich, a professor at Yale University, who attended the March 1818 argument.

Webster (perhaps aided by geography and travel limitations of the times) was for more than thirty years the acknowledged leader of the Supreme Court bar. Indeed, he still holds the record for arguing the most cases before the Court—more than three hundred of them. The second largest total of cases argued was also achieved at this time by a little-known figure, Walter Jones, a District of Columbia lawyer. He appeared in more than two hundred cases before the Court. The next highest total of arguments, and the highest total in the twentieth century, was made by JOHN W. DAVIS [2], who was active from about 1910 to 1954. He argued a total of 141 cases. Davis was SOLICITOR GENERAL [4,I] of the United States from 1913 to 1918 and in 1924 was the Democratic presidential candidate. Today no one makes such a high number of arguments unless he is a solicitor general or a member of the staff of the solicitor general's office.

The first black lawyer to be admitted to the bar of the Supreme Court was Dr. John S. Rock, who was born of free parents in New Jersey in 1825. He was admitted on February 1, 1865, just short of his fortieth birthday. Before then, he had been a teacher, a dentist, and a doctor. He had moved to Boston in 1853 and was one of the founders of the Republican party in Massachusetts. In 1858 he wanted to go to France for medical treatment, but he was refused a passport on the ground that he was not a citizen. The Massachusetts legislature then passed a law providing for state passports, and this was accepted in France.

A year or so later, Dr. Rock returned to Boston where he read law. He was admitted to practice in Massachusetts in September 1861 and in the Supreme Court in 1865, shortly after the appointment of SALMON P. CHASE [1] as Chief Justice. It is interesting to note that this came before the termination of the Civil War and before the adoption of the Thirteenth, Fourteenth and Fifteenth amendments—and with DRED SCOTT V. SANDFORD (1857) [2] still on the books. As the *New York Times* reported, "By Jupiter the sight was good." Rock's admission was moved by Senator CHARLES SUMNER [4]. The newspaper reporter observed that the "assenting nod" of the Chief Justice "dug . . . the grave to bury the Dred Scott decision."

The next of these significant events was the admission of the first woman to the Supreme Court bar. In BRADWELL V. ILLINOIS (1873) [1] the Supreme Court refused to interfere with the action of the supreme court of Illinois, which denied admission to Myra Bradwell, publisher of a successful legal newspaper in Chicago. Bradwell relied in the Supreme Court on the PRIVILEGES AND IMMUNITIES [3,I] clause of the recently adopted Fourteenth Amendment, but persuaded only Chief Justice Chase.

Less than seven years later, however, Belva A. Lockwood became the first woman admitted to practice before the Supreme Court. This was on March 3, 1879. So quick was the change of view that this action evoked no opinion from any member of the Court. Indeed, Myra Bradwell herself, who had been denied admission in 1872, was finally admitted when she applied again in 1892.

Despite this opening of the door, it took fifty years, or until 1929, before the number of women admitted to the bar of the Supreme Court reached a total of one hundred. Some of the early admittees had distinguished careers in the law. These included Florence Allen, who became the first woman judge of a constitutional federal court; Mabel Walker Willebrandt, who was assistant attorney general under President HERBERT C. HOOVER [2]; and Helen Carloss, who had a long and distinguished career in the Tax Division of the Department of Justice. The great increase in the number of women lawyers, however, has occurred in the past fifteen years. In another fiteen years, if present trends continue, they will constitute perhaps thirty percent of the members of the bar of the Supreme Court.

There have been periods when relatively few lawyers were widely recognized as leaders of the bar practicing before the Supreme Court. There were the orators of the nineteenth century, starting with Daniel Webster and continuing through John G. Johnson of Pennsylvania. There was such a bar in the 1920s and the 1930s, when CHARLES EVANS HUGHES [2], Owen D. Roberts, John W. Davis, George Wharton Pepper, and William D. Mitchell made frequent appearances before the Court. By this time, oratory had become passé. The presentations were less flowery, but they were mellifluous. Davis showed great skill in persuasion, though his record of wins over losses was not especially high, reflecting the fact that the cases in which he was retained were often especially difficult. There is one case that brought together three of these giants. In *United States v. George Otis Smith* (1932) the question was whether the Senate could reconsider its confirmation of a presidential nomination after the President had acted on it by making the appointment.

The Senate retained Davis as its counsel. Attorney General William D. Mitchell appeared for the United States, essentially representing the President, and George Wharton Pepper represented Smith, the nominee. That argument was one of the high points of advocacy in this century.

One group has long provided the backbone of the Supreme Court bar: the solicitor general and his staff, and his associates in the Department of Justice. This office has long maintained a high standard and a great tradition. It appears, in one way or another, in nearly half the cases heard on the merits by the Court and in a high percentage of all applications for review.

A considerable number of cases are now brought to the Supreme Court by parties representing particular interests. The National Association for the Advancement of Colored People was first represented by one of the country's great lawyers, CHARLES H. HOUSTON [2]—work carried on with great ability by THURGOOD MARSHALL [1,I]. Other similar work has been done by lawyers representing groups interested in the rights of women, in other civil rights, in the environment, and in other causes.

The bar of the Supreme Court can never be assembled, nor is it possible to take a consensus of the bar. It is clear that it plays an important role in the work of the Court. Yet the demands on the Court are such that the bar has difficulty in making its full contribution. In 1935, arguments were heard five days a week for a total of about seventy-five days a year. Now the Court hears arguments on about forty-five days during the year. Fifty years ago, the time made available for oral argument was an hour on each side, and there were frequent substantial allowances of additional time. Now the time allotted is thirty minutes on a side, and additional time is rarely granted. This inevitably presents problems for oral arguments and requires a wholly different type of argument from that customary even fifty years ago. The advocate today can rarely present his case as a case. He has to pick out certain salient points and hope that with questioning by the justices he will still have time to deal with the matters he regards as vital. The printed briefs filed by counsel today appear to be much better than they were fifty years ago, probably more greatly improved than is commonly recognized. But oral argument remains a difficult and tantalizing field.

The Supreme Court moved into its new building in 1935. According to newspaper articles, the first words spoken by Chief Justice Hughes in the new courtroom were "Are there any admissions?" Thus was the bar recognized, and thus has it been recognized at every session since.

The bar of the Supreme Court, diverse and divided as it is, plays an important part in the work of the third branch of American constitutional government. Though Alexander Hamilton called the judiciary "the least dangerous branch," its role is central to the effective operation of our federal system. If the work of the Court is central to American government, the efforts of the Supreme Court bar may well be regarded as an essential buttress to the Court.

ERWIN N. GRISWOLD

(SEE ALSO: *Supreme Court's Work Load* [I]; *Women in Constitutional History* [I].)

Bibliography

CONTEE, CLARENCE G. 1976 The Supreme Court Bar's First Black Member. Pages 82–85 in *Supreme Court Historical Society Year Book, 1976.* Washington, D.C.: Supreme Court Historical Society.

HARBAUGH, WILLIAM H. 1973 *Lawyer's Lawyer.* New York: Oxford University Press.

O'DONNELL, ALICE L. 1977 Women and Other Strangers Before the Bar. Pages 59–62 in *Supreme Court Historical Society Year Book, 1977.* Washington, D.C.: Supreme Court Historical Society.

WARREN, CHARLES (1908) 1970 *History of the Harvard Law School and of Early Legal Conditions in America.* New York: DaCapo.

——— (1911) 1980 *A History of the American Bar.* Boston: Longwood.

WHITE, EDWARD G. 1988 *The Marshall Court and Cultural Change, 1815–34.* New York: Macmillan.

SUPREME COURT'S WORK LOAD

With the growth of population and the enormous expansion of federal law in the post–NEW DEAL [I] period, the business of the federal courts has mushroomed. This increase is most striking in the first two tiers of the federal judicial pyramid. In the years 1960–1983, cases filed in UNITED STATES DISTRICT COURTS [4] more than tripled, from 80,000 to 280,000, but cases docketed in the UNITED STATES COURTS OF APPEALS [4] during the same period increased eightfold, from 3,765 to 25,580. To cope with this rise in appeals, Congress more than doubled the number of appellate judgeships. Not surprisingly, a similar growth can be found in Supreme Court filings: decade averages have increased in units of a thousand, from 1,516 per term in the 1950s to 2,639 in the 1960s, to 3,683 in the 1970s, to 4,422 in the 1981 term and 4,806 in the 1988 term.

The contrast between this explosion in federal judicial business and the fixed decisional capacity of the Supreme Court—the nine Justices sitting as a full bench hear an average of 150 argued cases per year—has led to persistent calls for enhancing the appellate capacity of the federal system. A number of proposals have emerged since 1970, none resulting in legislation. In 1971 the Study Commission on the Caseload of the Supreme Court, chaired by Paul A. Freund of the Harvard Law School, recommended creation of a National Court of Appeals (NCA) that would assume the Supreme Court's task of selecting cases for review. The Freund committee believed that the selection process consumed time and energy the Justices might better spend in deliberation and opinion writing. This proposal died at birth. In 1972, Congress created the Commission on Revision of the Federal Court Appellate System, chaired by Senator Roman Hruska. The Hruska commission envisioned a mechanism for national resolution of open intercircuit conflicts, recommending an NCA that would hear cases referred to it by the Supreme Court or the United States Courts of Appeals. This NCA was to be a permanent tribunal, with its own institutional identity and personnel. In 1983, Chief Justice WARREN E. BURGER [1] publicly endorsed proposed legislation to create on an experimental basis an Intercircuit Tribunal of the United State Courts of Appeals (ICT), which would decide cases referred to it by the Supreme Court. The ICT would be comprised of judges drawn from the current courts of appeals who would sit for a specified number of years. This proposal drew faint support.

Other proposals have sought to enhance national appellate capacity without establishing new tribunals. The most recent recommendation of this type can be found in the 1990 report of the Federal Courts Study Committee, chaired by Judge Joseph F. Weis, Jr. The report urges Congress to give the Supreme Court authority, for an experimental period, to refer cases presenting unresolved intercircuit conflicts to a randomly selected court of appeals for a ruling by that court's full bench. These EN BANC [2] determinations would be binding on all other courts, save the Supreme Court.

Many of these proposals are conceived as measures to alleviate the Supreme Court's work load. The work load problem is, however, not one of obligatory jurisdiction; the Court's APPELLATE JURISDICTION [1] has been largely discretionary as far back as the JUDICIARY ACT OF 1925 [3], but even more so after 1988 legislation repealing virtually all mandatory appeals. The Justices do have to screen all of the petitions filed. It is doubtful, though, that any of the recent proposals promise much relief on this score. The Freund committee's NCA did, but received widespread criticism for suggesting delegation of the selection function. It is hard to believe referral to an NCA or a randomly selected court of appeals would reduce the Court's screening burden, for the losing party would still be free to appeal to the High Court. Moreover, the Justices will not likely tolerate nationally binding resolutions with which they disagree. Indeed, the Court's case selection

process may be significantly complicated by adoption of any of these proposals.

If the Court's overload is not a function of its mandatory jurisdiction and if its selection burden cannot be alleviated (under current proposals), what function is the Court failing to perform that it ought to perform?

Critics claim that the Court is unable to ensure uniformity in federal law, because 150 appeals a year must leave unresolved an intolerable number of intercircuit conflicts. The evidence for this contention is largely anecdotal, and what little empirical work exists is sharply contested in the literature. Significant disagreement exists as to what constitutes a "conflict." Are conflicts clear disagreements over a governing issue of law or simply different approaches to a legal issue that are capable ultimately of being reconciled? Much also depends on one's view of the costs and benefits of leaving particular conflicts unresolved for a time. Does the absence of a rule of intercircuit STARE DECISIS [4] in the federal system reflect a deliberate policy of allowing disagreements to percolate? The continuing conflicts may aid the Court's selection process by highlighting legal issues requiring national resolution. Through the process of multicourt consideration, the conflicts may improve the final decision of the Supreme Court when it does intervene. Moreover, some conflicts do not require immediate resolution, because they involve questions of local procedure, or do not frustrate planning concerns of multicircuit actors, or are not capable of being exploited by litigant forum shopping.

A broader claim, one not dependent upon the incidence of intercircuit conflict, is also made: that the problem is fundamentally one of insufficient supervision of the panel rulings of the courts of appeals. That conflicts are appropriately left unresolved does not matter, the argument goes. Given the sheer number of appeals, the practical inability of many of the circuits to engage in en banc review, and the infinitesimal probability of Supreme Court review, the panels operate as a law unto themselves. This version of the case for enhancing appellate capacity does have some force. It is undeniable that the Court can no longer engage in the kind of direct oversight of the courts of appeals that was possible in the 1920s, when it reviewed one in ten appellate rulings.

Whether this inability to supervise creates a problem requiring new institutional arrangements is, however, debatable. At present the Supreme Court appears not to have on its docket enough cases warranting plenary review to fill its argument calendar. Moreover, whether the panels operate as such wayward institutions is not clear. Many a circuit has, for example, adopted a "mini" en banc procedure to ensure uniformity of law within the circuit and to promote reconciliation of intercircuit splits. Even if one concedes that the Supreme Court has a work load problem (or that there is a need for additional appellate capacity), will the oversight benefits of an additional layer of review in, say, another 150 cases outweigh the attendant costs? Or will these otherwise nationally binding rulings be irresistible candidates for immediate plenary review by the Supreme Court—and hence a new category of practically mandatory jurisdiction?

The expansion of federal judicial business is the result of an explosion in federal law. Creating new layers of appeals creates more law, but not law enjoying the peculiar finality of a Supreme Court resolution. Improvements can be made. They are more likely to be found, however, in legislation reducing forum choice in federal statutes and imposing sanctions for unwarranted appeals; better management by the courts of appeals of panel disagreements and a greater willingness to reconsider circuit law in light of developments elsewhere; and strategic deployment by the High Court of its scarce decisional resources.

SAMUEL ESTREICHER

Bibliography

BAKER, THOMAS E. and MCFARLAND, DOUGLAS D.   1987   The Need for a New National Court. *Harvard Law Review* 100:1401–1416.

ESTREICHER, SAMUEL and SEXTON, JOHN E.   1986   *Redefining the Supreme Court's Role: A Theory of Managing the Federal Judicial Process.* New Haven, Conn.: Yale University Press.

GINSBURG, RUTH BADER and HUBER, PETER W.   1987   The Intercircuit Committee. *Harvard Law Review* 100:1417–1435.

POSNER, RICHARD   1985   *The Federal Courts: Crisis and Reform.* Cambridge, Mass.: Harvard University Press.

STRAUSS, PETER L.   1987   One Hundred Fifty Cases per Year: Some Implications of the Supreme Court's Limited Resources for Judicial Review of Agency Action. *Columbia Law Review* 87:1093–1136.

TAKING OF PROPERTY
(Update)

Recent historical scholarship indicates that the taking clause was something of an innovation. Only two of the state constitutions adopted between 1776 and 1780 required the government to pay compensation when private property was taken for a public use. The lack of constitutional protection for property rights was consistent with the republican ethos of the period. BENJAMIN FRANKLIN [2], for example, once said that "Private Property . . . is a Creature of Society, and is subject to the Calls of that Society, whenever its Necessities shall require it, even to its last Farthing; its contributions therefore to the public Exigencies are . . . to be considered . . . the Return of an obligation previously received, or the Payment of a just Debt." The taking clause seems to represent a victory of Lockean liberalism over this earlier republican philosophy.

The Supreme Court has recently used the taking clause to strike down a variety of government regulations. In one case, the federal government claimed that the public had the right to use a marina that a private developer had connected with a public waterway. The Court held that giving the public access to the marina would be an unconstitutional taking of the developer's property. In another case, Congress was concerned because certain lands belonging to American Indians had so many owners that managing the lands had become impractical. As a way of consolidating landholdings, a federal statute mandated that some of the tiniest interests would revert to the tribe on the owners' deaths. This, too, was an unconsti-

tutional taking. The Court also found a taking when New York required landlords to give their tenants access to cable television. The reason was that the cable box would "take" some of the space on the building's roof.

A 1987 case, *Nollan v. California Coastal Commission*, exemplifies the Court's revived interest in protecting property rights. The case involved a couple who wanted to build a larger beach house. As a condition for receiving a permit, the California Coastal Commission required them to allow the public to walk along the beach. The majority opinion was written by Justice ANTONIN SCALIA [I], who had quickly emerged as the strongest guardian of PROPERTY RIGHTS [I] on the REHNQUIST COURT [I]. Scalia was willing to concede, at least for the purposes of argument, that California could have banned the construction entirely as a means of preserving the public's right to see the ocean from the street. Alternatively, he conceded, the Nollans could have been required to allow the public to walk from the street around to the back of their house. But because the government had chosen to give the public direct access laterally along the beach, rather than from the street, Justice Scalia held the permit condition unconstitutional.

The Court's rationale in *Nollan* was that lateral access was not closely enough related to the government's right to protect the view of the ocean. Justice Scalia seemed suspicious of the government's motives in imposing the permit condition, at one point referring to similar permit conditions as a form of "extortion."

In contrast to *Nollan*, another 1987 case rather surprisingly failed to find a taking. *Keystone Bituminous Coal Association v. DeBenedictus* was a replay of *Pennsylvania Coal Co. v. Mahon* (1922), the classic decision of Justice

539

OLIVER WENDELL HOLMES, JR. [2]. Holmes had struck down a Pennsylvania statute that required underground coal mines to maintain adequate support for surface structures. The *DeBenedictus* Court, however, found a similar but more recently enacted Pennsylvania statute to be constitutional. The Court distinguished *Mahon* on the ground that the newer statute had a broader public purpose. No taking was found, because the statute required mining companies to leave only a small fraction of their coal in the ground.

It is often difficult to predict whether a given government regulation will be found to be a taking, but two factors seem particularly significant. First, if the regulation takes away the owner's right to control physical access to the property, it is much more likely to be found a taking—and almost sure to be found a taking if there is a permanent physical occupation of the property. Second, unless physical access is involved, the owner probably will not be able to claim a taking unless the regulation virtually destroys the value of the property.

At present, takings doctrine is in flux. Under Chief Justices HARLAN F. STONE [4] and EARL WARREN [4], the Court took little interest in the taking clause. The BURGER COURT [1] began to take a renewed interest in the area, but did not aggressively use the taking clause as a means of attacking important government regulations. It remains to be seen whether the Rehnquist Court will introduce a greater degree of activism.

Most of the current scholarship on the taking clause may be divided into three camps. One group argues for minimal judicial scrutiny of economic regulations, so that very few government actions would be held a taking. In contrast, a second group argues for vigorous scrutiny under the auspices of the taking clause—reminiscent of the era of LOCHNER V. NEW YORK (1905) [3]. A third group argues for renewed judicial protection, but limited to a particular category of property, that of peculiar personal significance to individuals, as opposed to ordinary business interests. It is uncertain whether any of these groups of scholars will succeed in influencing the Justices. At present, the Court seems content to muddle through taking cases without the benefit of a broad theoretical perspective.

DANIEL A. FARBER

(SEE ALSO: *Economic Analysis* [1]; *Economic Liberties* [1]; *Eminent Domain* [2,I]; *Land Use* [I]; *Law and Economics Theory* [I].)

Bibliography

EPSTEIN, RICHARD A. 1985 *Takings: Private Property and the Power of Eminent Domain*. Cambridge, Mass.: Harvard University Press.
LEVY, LEONARD W. 1988 Property as a Human Right. *Constitutional Commentary* 5:169–184.
NOTE 1985 The Origins and Original Significance of the Just Compensation Clause of the Fifth Amendment. *Yale Law Journal* 94:694–716.

TAXATION

See: State and Local Government Taxation [I]

TELEVISION

See: Broadcasting [I]

TEMPORAL LIMITS ON LAWMAKING POWERS

A republic derives its power from the people, and as JAMES MADISON [3] declared in *The Federalist* #39 and #53, the persons elected to administer it hold office only "for a limited period" and enjoy no license to extend the length of their terms. Although in contemporary America such a concept seems almost beyond dispute, Madison's pronouncement marked a radical departure from English tradition.

By the Triennial Act of 1694 the English Parliament limited the term of Parliament to three years. In 1716, however, the members of Parliament, in their final year of service and concerned that elections might be perilous to the ruling party, repealed the Triennial Act. In its place they enacted the Septennial Act, by which the legal duration of the sitting Parliament was immediately extended to seven years. The powers of the incumbent members of the House of Commons were thus prolonged by four years. Although the English might have regarded this exercise of legislative authority as contemptuous or extravagant, they did not consider it ULTRA VIRES [4] in a system constructed on the concept of parliamentary supremacy.

The United States Constitution rejects the cornerstone of legislative supremacy. The recognition of the citizenry as an external force from which all power originates severed the umbilical connection with English tradition. The Preamble's opening phrase, "We the people," is more than flashy prose. The legislators were transformed from the masters of the electorate to their servants. The people are the source of all power; the legislators are merely designated agents.

There is, as ALEXANDER HAMILTON [2] pronounced in *The Federalist* #78, "no position which depends on clearer principles, than that every act of a delegated authority, contrary to the tenor of the commission under which it is exercised, is void." Agency may be limited in duration as well as scope. The Framers devoted considerable attention to the appropriate length of a representative's term of office. The decision to limit the terms of the members of the HOUSE OF REPRESENTATIVES [I] to two years was prompted by a recognition that in order to ensure liberty, government must have an immediate dependence on, and intimate sympathy with, the people. Frequent elections, warned Madison in *The Federalist* #53, are "the only policy by which this dependence and sympathy can be effectively secured." Although the longer six-year term for senators was a concession to the need for some continuity and stability in government, the expiration of the terms of one-third of the body every two years provides a reminder of accountability (the dependence factor) and permits infusions of new directions from the electorate (the sympathy factor) at more frequent intervals.

Just as American legislatures lack the power to extend their terms beyond those set by their constitutive documents, they may not undermine the spirit of that document by "entrenching" their legislative efforts. Each election furnishes the electorate with an opportunity to provide new directions for its representatives. The process would be reduced to an exercise in futility were newly elected representatives bound by the policy choices of a prior generation of voters. The fundamental, although often debatable, assumption of American political life—that legislative action reflects current majoritarian preferences—could be finally laid to rest if shifting majorities were unable to alter prior majoritarian preferences.

Instances of legislative entrenchment rarely are the subjects of judicial decision. To begin with, most legislators share an understanding of the temporal limits of their authority. Of equal import, successor legislators usually find ways to outflank entrenched restrictions, but if they cannot, they may simply choose to ignore their predecessors' directives, safe in the knowledge that courts are unlikely to void their efforts. Nonetheless, the prohibition against entrenchment has been at the heart of numerous congressional debates.

The CLOTURE [1] rule of the Senate requires the assent of a supermajority (sixty members) to terminate a filibuster. On more than eighty occasions since this rule's adoption, a majority of senators have unsuccessfully attempted to cut off debate and bring an issue to a vote. Such failures have often been followed by efforts to amend the cloture rule; but the supermajority requirement has been entrenched. Rule 32(2) of the Senate's Standing Rules explicitly mandates, "The rules of the Senate shall continue from one Congress to the next Congress unless they are changed *as provided in these rules*." Thus, any effort to change the cloture rule may itself be blocked by a filibuster. The defenders of this entrenchment argue that because each biennial election only affects one-third of the Senate's membership, the Senate is a continuing body capable of binding itself. Periodically, senators mount constitutional attacks against Rule 32(2) on the ground that no legislative body can so limit its successors. In 1957, Vice-President RICHARD M. NIXON [3], the Senate's presiding officer, announced his personal opinion that a rule limiting the right of the Senate's current majority to promulgate its own rules was unconstitutional. In the end, however, Nixon and his successors have left the ultimate issue of constitutionality with the membership of the Senate itself. Numerous votes of that body have rejected Nixon's constitutional assessment. Today an overwhelming majority of the senators are of the view that the "continuous" nature of the Senate permits this narrow exception to the rule against entrenchment.

Entrenchment issues also surround much of the constitutional AMENDING PROCESS [1]. Thus, the binding power of legislative bodies has been at the heart of debates about (1) the power of Congress to extend time limits for RATIFICATION [3] placed on a proposed constitutional amendment by a prior Congress; (2) the right of a state legislature to rescind its predecessor's ratification vote; and (3) Congress's ability, by legislation, to establish the rules of operation for future constitutional conventions that might occur.

One of the few entrenchment issues to have received a judicial airing concerns the extent to which contractual commitments made by legislatures bind subsequent legislatures. The CONTRACT CLAUSE [2] of the Constitution prohibits states from impairing the OBLIGATION OF CONTRACTS [3]. There exists no evidence, however, that the Framers intended or expected the contract clause to be applied to obligations involving the state itself. In spite of this unequivocal history, Chief Justice JOHN MARSHALL [3], in FLETCHER V. PECK (1810) [2], extended the reach of the contract clause to legislatively created obligations, finding it sufficient that the words of the Constitution drew no distinction between private and public contracts. The tension between *Fletcher's* extension of the contract clause and the temporal nature of lawmaking power was first clearly articulated by ROGER BROOKE TANEY [4] during his tenure as ATTORNEY GENERAL [1]. Legislatures, said Taney, "cannot bind the state by contract . . . beyond the scope of the authority granted them by their constituents." The power to limit contractually the legislative powers of successors, Taney asserted, is one that the agent cannot enjoy consistent with "the principles upon which our political institutions are founded." Even Marshall was mindful of the entrenchment implications of his interpretation. Recognizing that his reading potentially allowed legislatures to limit the power of their successors, he endeavored to draw a distinction between "general legislation" (which could not bind successor legislators) and "contracts" (which could). Marshall therefore concluded that when a law is in its nature a contract, vesting absolute rights, "a repeal of the law cannot devest those rights."

The dichotomy Marshall posited between general legislation and contracts matured in later years into a judicial understanding that at least some state action was beyond the reach of the contracting power. No body of representatives can bargain away the so-called POLICE POWER [3] of the state. Thus, in STONE V. MISSISSIPPI (1880) [4], the Supreme Court sustained a legislative revocation of its predecessor's grant of a twenty-five-year charter to operate a lottery, noting that the police power must remain a continuing power to be exercised "as the special exigencies of the moment may require." This limitation ultimately proved the contract clause's undoing as the exception swallowed the rule, and the contract clause faded from the judicial scene following the 1930s.

In the 1970s the Supreme Court temporarily resurrected the specter of contractual entrenchment. New Jersey and New York issued bonds in 1962 to construct bridges and tunnels, and promised bondholders that none of the tolls pledged to secure such bonds would be used for "any railroad purpose." By 1974, the public call for increased mass transit made such a commitment unwieldy. Massive toll increases were announced. A reserve fund was established for the bondholders, but in 1974 the commitment not to spend any surplus toll money for mass transit was repealed. There was no evidence of a diminution in the value of the bonds as a result of this broken promise. Nonetheless, the Court, in UNITED STATES TRUST CO. OF NEW YORK V. NEW JERSEY (1977) [4], ruled that the state legislature had impaired the bondholders' contractual rights. Justice WILLIAM J. BRENNAN [1,I], in dissent, reminded his colleagues that "one of the fundamental premises of our popular democracy is that each generation of representatives can and will remain responsive to the needs and desires of those whom they represent." Nothing, he summed up, so jeopardized the "legitimacy of a system of government that relies on the ebbs and flow of politics to clean out the rascals than the possibility that those same rascals might perpetuate their polices simply by locking them into binding contracts." Justice Brennan may have struck a resonant chord. Since *United States Trust*, no legislative commitment has been enforced against a recalcitrant successor legislature. It is ordinarily in a legislature's best interest to maintain a reputation for honoring its word. On those occasions, however, when the public interest leads a legislature to abandon a

prior commitment, it will be rare for courts to enforce the promise.

JULIAN N. EULE

(SEE ALSO: *Vested Rights* [4].)

Bibliography

EULE, JULIAN N. 1987 Temporal Limits on the Legislative Mandate: Entrenchment and Retroactivity. *American Bar Foundation Research Journal* 1987:379–459.

HOCHMAN, CHARLES B. 1960 The Supreme Court and the Constitutionality of Retroactive Legislation. *Harvard Law Review* 73:692–727.

KAHN, PAUL W. 1987 Gramm-Rudman and the Capacity of Congress to Control the Future. *Hastings Constitutional Law Quarterly* 13:185–231.

TEXAS v. JOHNSON

See: Flag Desecration

TEXAS MONTHLY, INC. v. BULLOCK
489 U.S. 1 (1989)

The decision in this case affected the fifteen states whose statutes on sales and use taxes exempted religious publications. Texas exempted periodicals that consisted entirely of writings promulgating a religious faith. Voting 6–3, the Court held the act unconstitutional. Justice BYRON R. WHITE [4,I] believed that because the statute discriminated on the basis of the content of publication, it violated the free-press clause. A bare majority believed that the statute violated the ESTABLISHMENT CLAUSE [I]. Justice WILLIAM J. BRENNAN [1,I], for the Court, concluded that the statute failed to serve the secular purpose of maintaining the SEPARATION OF CHURCH AND STATE [4,I], but rather, had the purpose of advancing the religious mission of a particular faith. The exemption of the religious periodical in effect subsidized its teachings at the expense of taxpayers who were not exempt from the tax.

Brennan went further, thereby losing Justices HARRY A. BLACKMUN [1,I] and SANDRA DAY O'CONNOR [3,I], when he also declared the statute violative of the free-exercise clause. Blackmun and O'Connor preferred to rest exclusively on the establishment clause, believing that Brennan's free-exercise argument subordinated RELIGIOUS LIBERTY [3,I] to the establishment clause. In dissent, Justices ANTONIN SCALIA [I], WILLIAM H. REHNQUIST [3,I], and ANTHONY M. KENNEDY [I] protested that the Court had mangled its own PRECEDENTS [3] and diminished the free-exercise clause. Their views, however,

would have altered the constitutional law of the subject.
LEONARD W. LEVY

TEXTUALISM

Textualism denotes the opinion that whenever possible, judges resolving questions of constitutional law should rely primarily on the language of the Constitution itself. The text should guide decision and the text itself, rather than other considerations such as ORIGINAL INTENT [I], ratifier intent, history, principles inferred from the text, altered circumstances, judicial readings of societal values, or even judicial precedents. Justice OWEN J. ROBERTS [3], for the Court in UNITED STATES V. BUTLER (1936) [1], manifested an allegiance to textualism when he declared that the constitutionality of a contested statute should be squared against the appropriate language of the text to see if they match.

This view of the best way to determine constitutionality was the most prevalent one at the time of the making of the Constitution. THOMAS JEFFERSON [3] and ALEXANDER HAMILTON [2] differed on the question as to whether an act of Congress incorporating a bank was constitutional; but, as Hamilton said, Jefferson would agree "that whatever may have been the intention of the framers of a constitution, or of a law, that intention is to be sought for in the instrument itself, according to the usual & established rules of construction." Hamilton accurately stated the truth of the matter to the founding generation.

Despite near unanimity on the propriety of interpreting the Constitution according to established rules of construction, the Framers arrived at contradictory results when applying those rules to numerous important constitutional issues. Their belief in textualism did not prevent them from dividing on the removal power, the power to charter a corporation, the power to declare neutrality, the scope of executive powers, the power to enact excise and use taxes without apportioning them on population, the power of a treaty to obligate the House to appropriate money, the power of JUDICIAL REVIEW [3], the power to deport aliens, the power to pass an act against SEDITIOUS LIBEL [4], the power to abolish judicial offices of life tenure, and the jurisdiction of the Supreme Court to decide suits against states without their consent or to issue writs of MANDAMUS [3] against executive officers.

Rules of constitutional construction by which to construe the text are comparable to those of statutory construction, which a current federal judge, Frank Easterbrook, called "a total jumble." For every rule, as Karl Llewellyn demonstrated in his *Common Law Tradition,* "there is an equal and opposite rule." A master commentator, Justice JOSEPH STORY [4], discoursed on the rules of construction for some sixty pages in his *Commentaries on the Constitution,* yet he failed completely to convince his Jacksonian colleagues on the bench. Rules of construction in effect free, rather than fetter, judicial discretion. The fact remains, however, that textualism should be the bedrock of judicial review; as Story said, "Nothing but the text itself was adopted by the whole people." Whenever the fair or plain meaning of the Constitution can be ascertained, it should guide judgment.

The problem is that the Constitution is a brief elliptical document framed by common lawyers trained to believe that a few comprehensive and expansive principles supplementing a structural description will be infinitely adaptable and will provide guides that can serve to answer virtually any question that might arise on a case-to-case basis. In some crucial respects, the Constitution resembles Martin Chuzzlewit's grandnephew, who, Dickens said, "had no more than the first idea and sketchy notion of a face." The Framers had a genius for studied imprecision and calculated ambiguity. They relied on many general terms because common lawyers expressed themselves that way out of conviction and because politics required compromise, and compromise required ambiguity and vagueness.

The text, even with twenty-six amendments that have been added in two centuries, is scarcely 7,000 words long, and only about two percent of the verbiage possesses any significance in constitutional law. Almost without exception, these are the purposefully or unavoidably general terms: commerce among the states, OBLIGATION OF CONTRACTS [3], NECESSARY AND PROPER [3], BILLS OF CREDIT [1], REPUBLICAN FORM OF GOVERNMENT [3], DUE PROCESS OF LAW [2], PRIVILEGES AND IMMUNITIES [3], direct taxes, GENERAL WELFARE [2], liberty, UNREASONABLE SEARCHES [4,I], EQUAL PROTECTION [2,I], and the like.

For the most part, the CONSTITUTIONAL CONVENTION OF 1787 [1] designed the Constitution with the utmost diligence and attention to detail. The Convention usually chose words with craft and craftsmanship. This is the reason that constitutional law does not involve the bulk of the Constitution. It does not have to be litigated because it is clear and understandable. Consequently, the vagueness and ambiguities found in the Constitution were probably deliberate. In THE FEDERALIST #37, JAMES MADISON [3] replied to the Anti-Federalist criticism that the Constitution's lack of clarity on some matters threatened the states and liberty. Obscure and equivocal language was inevitable, he contended, but its meaning would be clarified in time by adjudications. ABRAHAM BALDWIN [1] of Georgia, another Framer, declared that some subjects were left "a little ambiguous and uncertain" for political reasons and would be settled in time by practice or by amendments. Some textual language remained open-ended to avoid giving offense by explicitness. Treaty powers, judicial powers, and rival powers of legislation fell into these categories, according to Baldwin.

Ambiguity and vagueness arise in the nonstructural sections. Ambiguous words permit different understandings; vague words do not allow for much understanding. The exceptions clause of Article III is a good example of ambiguity. It might mean that Congress may switch APPELLATE JURISDICTION [1] to ORIGINAL JURISDICTION [3], thereby adding to the Supreme Court's original jurisdiction, as counsel in MARBURY V. MADISON (1803) [3] argued, or it might mean that the original jurisdiction of the Court is fixed, as JOHN MARSHALL [3] held. If the exceptions clause means that Congress may make exceptions to the Court's jurisdiction by diminishing its appellate jurisdiction, how far can Congress go? And how can the Court exercise the jurisdiction specified in Article III as belonging to the JUDICIAL POWER OF THE UNITED STATES [3] if it is dependent on Congress's will?

The text of Article I, section 8, poses problems too. Congress may pass no capitation or "other direct tax" unless apportioned among the states on the basis of population. Although the Framers probably regarded direct taxes as only taxes imposed on people per capita and on land, they did not say so. They left "other direct taxes" open to interpretation. Article I, section 8, on the tax power is all the more puzzling because it is not known whether the tax power connotes an equally expansive power to spend, and the meaning of the "general welfare" is equally mystifying. Constitutional government as the Framers understood it cannot survive a national power to legislate for the general welfare, nor can the federal system survive a national power authorized to spend for the general welfare, yet the text gives credibility to these views.

The term "in pursuance of" in Article VI (the SUPREMACY CLAUSE [4]) is also ambiguous. Usually this term is taken to mean that in order for acts of Congress to be constitutional, they must be consistent with the Constitution. The "in pursuance of" clause is a mainstay of the argument that the Supreme Court may exercise judicial review over acts of Congress. Yet at the time of the framing, the text of the ARTICLES OF CONFEDERATION [1] showed that "in pursuance of" meant "under authority of" or "done in prosecution of."

The EXECUTIVE POWER [I] with which the President is endowed is ambiguous too. It is not known what is meant by the executive power, apart from an obligation to execute the laws faithfully. Moreover, the text indicates that the President can call on the armed forces to suppress rebellions or repel attacks, but not whether he can engage in military hostilities without either congressional support or a congressional DECLARATION OF WAR [2]. In the case of EXECUTIVE AGREEMENTS [2], there is not even a vague provision of the Constitution to construe. Nothing in the document authorizes treaty-making by the President without the ADVICE AND CONSENT [1] of the Senate. Nothing in the document authorizes the Congress to empower the President to make international agreements that have the force of the supreme law of the land or authorizes such agreements to have this force when both branches of Congress retroactively or subsequently approve of an international agreement made by the President on the President's own initiative. Nevertheless, Presidents have been making executive agreements with foreign nations throughout U.S. history and on major matters, without successful constitutional challenge. Moreover, the text of the Constitution does not provide for the device of the JOINT CONGRESSIONAL RESULTION [3]. By this device, Congress has considerably augmented its powers in foreign affairs, as when it annexed Texas and then Hawaii to circumvent the requirement of a two-thirds vote of the Senate to approve treaties.

Three major provisions of the Constitution are among the vaguest: Congress has the power to regulate commerce among the states; neither the national government nor a state may take life, liberty, or property without due process of law; and no state may deny to any person the equal protection of the laws. These are the most litigated clauses in U.S. constitutional history because they are among the muddiest and most important.

Even the seemingly specific injunctions and provisions of the BILL OF RIGHTS [1] are vague or ambiguous, offering little guidance for interpretation. A good example of such ambiguity is the term ESTABLISHMENT OF RELIGION [2] in the FIRST AMENDMENT [2,I]. James Madison, its author, mistakenly used the term interchangeably with "religious establishment," which denotes an institution of religion such as a church or sectarian school. "Religious establishment" carries no implication of government aid to religion or government involvement with it, as does "establishment of religion." When Madison misquoted the clause as if it outlawed religious establishment, he meant that the government had no authority to legislate on religion or its institutions. Nevertheless, the term itself has no self-evident meaning. History supplies that meaning, and historians differ.

The term FREEDOM OF THE PRESS [2,I] constitutes another ambiguity. In Anglo-American thought and law, it meant an exemption from PRIOR RESTRAINT [3]; it did not exclude liability under the criminal law for seditious, obscene, or blasphemous LIBEL [3]. In contrast, the Framers, who did not adopt or reject the definition of a free press under the COMMON LAW [1], knew only a rasping, corrosive, and licentious press. They did not likely use the term "freedom of the press" without intending to protect the freedom that in fact existed and that they knew. The text itself surely lacks clarity. It declares in absolute terms that Congress shall make no law abridging the freedom of speech or press, but the COPYRIGHT [2] clause of the Constitution authorizes Congress to make laws that do abridge the freedom of speech and press of those who would infringe copyrights.

This same clause, in Article I, section 8, refers only to "authors and inventors," making a literal interpretation of it fail to protect artists, sculptors, composers, computer-software designers, television programmers, and many others who come under its protection. If only authors and inventors benefited from the clause, they could not even assign a copyright to others. The problem with the copyright clause is not that it is ambiguous or vague; it is utterly clear. But, it possesses inappropriate specificity and therefore cannot mean what it says.

The First Amendment exhibits the same problem. Assuming that its framers chose their language carefully, the fact that they failed to give adequate protection to the free exercise of religion must be confronted. The text declares that the freedom of the press may not be abridged, but by contrast, only says that freedom of religion may not be prohibited. This is a comparatively diminished protection because freedom of religion may be abridged in many ways without being prohibited. The same amendment also suffers from terminological exactitude: Congress shall make "no law" abridging freedom of the press. A reliance on textualism would mean that neither PORNOGRA-PHY [3,I] nor direct and successful verbal incitements to crime can be abridged. Yet the absolute of "no law" cannot apply to copyright laws, which can constitute abridgments.

The Fifth Amendment's self-incrimination clause cannot be taken literally either. If the text meant what it says, it meant little when framed because defendants then had no right to give sworn testimony for or against themselves. Moreover, the clause protected the right only in criminal cases, but the right existed in civil as well as criminal cases and in nonjudicial proceedings such as grand jury and legislative investigations. Finally, a person may be compelled to be a witness against himself or herself in noncriminal ways; at the time of the adoption of the Bill of Rights, the Fifth Amendment right protected persons from being forced to expose themselves to public infamy. In 1892, the Supreme Court acknowledged that the text does not mean what it says; the Court declared, "It is impossible that the meaning of the constitutional provision can only be that a person shall not be compelled to be a witness against himself in a criminal prosecution against himself."

Other examples of the text not meaning what it says appear in the Sixth Amendment, which enumerates a variety of RIGHTS OF THE CRIMINALLY ACCUSED [I] available to them "in all criminal prosecutions." "All" is an absolute that admits of no exceptions. Yet the Framers did not intend to extend the right of TRIAL BY JURY [4] to misdemeanants; persons accused of petty crimes were tried in a more summary manner than trial by jury. In this regard, the Sixth Amendment reinforced the provision in Article III, section 2: "The trial of all crimes, except in cases of impeachment, shall be by jury. . . ." "All crimes" here means merely all felonies; the exception for impeachments really extended to misdemeanors also. Misdemeanants are still not entitled to trial by jury unless they can be imprisoned for more than six months. The text misleads.

Similarly, the right to the assistance of counsel in all criminal prosecutions does not mean what it says: "In all criminal prosecutions, the accused . . . shall have the assistance of counsel." "Shall" conveys an imperative; but the amendment merely meant that one might have counsel if he or she could afford it. Not until 1932 did indigents receive the benefit of court-appointed counsel in capital cases in state courts; not until 1938 did all federal defendants receive the right to court-appointed counsel in any criminal prosecution. Juveniles have long been deprived of the right to trial by jury, and no one is entitled to be represented by counsel before a GRAND JURY [2,I], which initiates a criminal prosecution. Furthermore, the text does not mean what it says in the provision that in all criminal prosecutions the accused shall be confronted with the witnesses against them; the exceptions to this, in fact, are numerous.

The problem of inappropriate specificity appears in the DOUBLE JEOPARDY [2,I] clause of the Fifth Amendment: "Nor shall any person be subject for the same offense to be twice put in jeopardy of life or limb." Here the Constitution neither means what it says, nor says what it means. It means "life or liberty," not "life or limb." The reference to "limb" is meaningless because we have long ceased to tear people apart or crop their ears. One cannot be put in jeopardy of loss of limb even if convicted by due process of law at a single trial. The double jeopardy clause implies, however, that a conviction can result in loss of limb. This would surely constitute a violation of the Eighth Amendment's guarantee against CRUEL AND UNUSUAL PUNISHMENT [2,I]. The text also leads to a logical puzzle. Life may be taken if one receives due process and is not exposed to double jeopardy. But if limb may not be taken, why may life be taken?

The SECOND AMENDMENT [4] is both vague and ambiguous. Some think it upholds the collective right of state militias to bear arms, while others argue that it protects the right of individuals to bear arms. But this right existed only to maintain militias. If a standing army, even in peacetime, has succeeded militias, and if the armed forces provides weapons to those in the service, the reason for the right to bear arms may no longer be as apparent as it once was. "Arms" once meant a flintlock rifle. Does the right to bear arms include a right to bear a Saturday-night special, an assault rifle, or a bazooka?

Vagueness, not ambiguity, saturates the FOURTH AMENDMENT [2,I], which prohibits "unreasonable" SEARCH AND SEIZURE [4,I] and provides that no warrants shall issue "but on probable cause." "Unreasonable" and "probable" rank high on any list of indefinite terms. It is possible, similarly, to parse every provision of the Bill of Rights and be bewildered by the meaning of the text. Terms such as SPEEDY TRIAL [4,I], JUST COMPENSATION [3], PUBLIC USE [3], "impartial jury," "excessive bail," "excessive fines," and "cruel and unusual" simply do not permit a constitutional jurisprudence to be based securely on textualism. To speak of STRICT CONSTRUCTION [4] is faintly ridiculous given the imprecision of the provisions of the Bill of Rights and of the FOURTEENTH AMENDMENT [2,I]. Ambiguity cannot be strictly construed. Strictly construing vagueness as well as inappropriately specific terms can equally lead to ludicrous, tragic, or unjust results.

The Constitution is, indeed, as Jefferson once said in exasperation, "a thing of wax that the Judiciary may twist and shape into any form they please." Unlike Humpty Dumpty, the Framers of the Constitution were unable to make words mean what they wanted them to mean. Perhaps they sensed that America would change beyond their grasp, and they did not think they could master the future. Perhaps they understood, with JAMES WILSON [4], that they were representatives "not merely of the present age, but of future times; not merely of the territory along the sea-coast, but of regions immensely extended westward." This is the reason the Constitutional Convention accepted the advice of EDMUND RANDOLPH [3] to keep the Constitution focused on "essential principles" so it can "be accomodated [sic] to times and events." The text is merely a point of departure; textualism as constitutional gospel is as impractical as original intent. Like original intent, however, textualism is entitled to serious attention, within its distinct limits, because Story was right: the people of the United States ratified the text, only the text, and it is the fundamental and supreme law of the land.

LEONARD W. LEVY

Bibliography

LAYCOCK, DOUGLAS. 1984 Taking Constitutions Seriously: A Theory of Judicial Review. *Texas Law Review* 59:343–394.
LEVY, LEONARD W. 1988 *Original Intent and the Framers' Constitution.* New York: Macmillan.
SCHAUER, FREDERICK 1985 Easy Cases. *Southern California Law Review* 58:399–440.

TUSHNET, MARK V. 1985 A Note on the Revival of Textualism in Constitutional Theory. *Southern California Law Review* 58:683–700.

THIRD-PARTY CONSENT

When someone invites the police into his or her home, the police need neither PROBABLE CAUSE [3,I] nor a warrant to accept the invitation. Acting on one person's invitation or consent to search, however, the police may uncover evidence that incriminates some other person. For example, a spouse or child may consent to a search that uncovers evidence against another spouse or a parent; a landlord may permit a search that reveals evidence useful in prosecuting the landlord's tenant; a common carrier may authorize the police to open a package shipped by a suspected drug dealer; or a school principal may authorize the police to search a student's locker. In litigation under the FOURTH AMENDMENT [2,I], the issues raised by cases of this sort have been treated under the rubric "third-party consent." Courts have held that the consent of someone other than the person against whom evidence is offered can sometimes justify seizure of this evidence despite the lack of probable cause or a SEARCH WARRANT [4].

Some courts and commentators have objected to upholding searches on the basis of third-party consent, noting that one person may not waive another's constitutional rights. This objection, however, begs a critical question—whether the person claiming a violation of the Fourth Amendment had a right to be free of a search to which some other person had consented. The search of a family home with the consent of a child's parents, for example, may not invade the child's REASONABLE EXPECTATION OF PRIVACY [I]. This search may not violate his or her rights.

No unitary theory explains when third-party consent justifies a search under the Fourth Amendment. In some cases, courts have invoked concepts of agency. In an extreme and unlikely case, the agency might be express; a person might execute a document authorizing an agent to admit the police to his or her premises at the agent's unfettered discretion. In these circumstances, a court could easily conclude that the principal himself or herself had authorized the search. Agency principles appear to justify both holdings that a manager of business premises may consent to a search that uncovers evidence against the owner of the business and rulings that the consent of a secretary or maintenance worker to a search of areas not open to casual visitors is ordinarily insufficient.

Courts also have upheld third-party consent searches that could not have been justified on agency principles. For example, a husband may assault his wife, and the wife may admit the police to the home that she owns with her husband to reveal the location of the assault weapon. In this case, the husband may be present and may inform the police that his wife has no authority to waive his Fourth Amendment rights. When the wife admits the police, however, she does not act as the agent of her husband, and she does not waive his rights. Instead, she exercises her own PROPERTY RIGHTS [I]. As in other cases of third-party consent, the husband's Fourth Amendment rights are limited by the authority of others to control premises in which he otherwise would have a reasonable expectation of privacy. Whether the authority of others is grounded in agency, property, license, contract, or something else does not matter.

The general rule articulated in *United States v. Matlock* (1974) is that when two or more people have joint access to or control over premises that the police wish to search, "any of the co-inhabitants has the right to permit inspection." The Supreme Court cautioned that "the authority which justifies third-party consent does not rest upon the law of property, with its attendant historical and legal refinements." In practice, the consenting party's authority is determined largely by general cultural understandings, and as in other situations in which courts consider expectations of privacy, these understandings may be ad hoc, changing, and difficult to assess.

For example, an inhabitant ordinarily may invite a guest to enter the house that he or she shares with another, but the inhabitant may not invite his or her guest surreptitiously to observe the inhabitant's housemate in the shower. Even sole ownership of a house does not confer a privilege to invade the privacy of a guest or to permit others to do so. Similarly, a lease may give a landlord authority to inspect the leased premises, but the landlord would exceed his or her authority if he or she invited the television crew of "Lifestyles of the Rich and Famous" to participate in the inspection. (Courts have in fact held the consent of a landlord insufficient to justify a police search of leased premises.) In *Stoner v. California* (1964), although a hotel clerk had authorized the search of a hotel room, the Supreme Court held the search invalid. Maids and other hotel employees might legitimately have entered the room, but they could not properly have brought along their friends, their relatives, or the police.

Whether a person should have greater or lesser authority to permit the police to search than he or she would have to authorize a search by someone other than a police officer may be a difficult question. A wife whose husband has permitted a police search might protest, "I have no reasonable expectation that my husband will not invite guests to our home; but in most situations I do expect that he will not invite the police to enter for reasons hostile to my interests." On this view, a person's consent to a search by a police officer might be invalid, although consent to a similar inspection by a nonpolice officer would be permissible.

A person is likely to have stronger legitimate reasons to cooperate with the police than to permit inspection by others, however, and courts have upheld police searches based on third-party consent when consent to inspection by anyone else—even by a close friend—probably would have been unauthorized. For example, a husband probably would violate customary norms of privacy by permitting a friend to rummage through a dresser used not only by him but by his wife. In *Matlock* and in *Frazier v. Cupp* (1969), however, the Supreme Court upheld searches in which the police had opened closets and luggage used in common by consenting and nonconsenting parties. To consider what authority a consenting party would have had to permit inspection by someone other than a police officer may be helpful as a starting point, but courts cannot avoid fact-specific assessments of expectations of privacy in particular situations. Because most police searches lack close analogues in everyday experience, this task is often difficult.

Under the Supreme Court's decision in *Illinois v. Rodriguez* (1990), courts judge the authority of a third party to consent to a search from the perspective of a reasonable police officer; they do not require that the consenting party have authority in fact. This approach may seem harsh when a thief who pretends to be the owner of luggage that he or she has stolen gives the police permission to open it—with the result that the police uncover evidence against the owner. This owner may be incriminated by evidence that the police obtained without his or her consent and without probable cause.

Nevertheless, the Constitution guards almost exclusively against governmental abuse, and the Fourth Amendment proscribes only UNREASONABLE SEARCHES [4,I] and seizures. When the police act on the basis of reasonable appearances, the objectives of the amendment seem satisfied. These objections do not include protection against all unjustified invasions of privacy but only against improper invasions of privacy by the government. Permitting the police to rely on a consenting party's apparent authority seems especially appropriate when the police might have conducted their search with a warrant had a seemingly valid consent not been given.

The third party's consent must reasonably appear to the police to be voluntary. When the police coerce a person to consent to a search that reveals evidence against another, the incriminated person has the same power to object to the search that he or she would have had if the police had not obtained the third party's consent at all.

This principle applies to cases of ELECTRONIC EAVESDROPPING [2] just as it does to cases in which the police have seized tangible evidence. Although state statutes sometimes forbid electronic monitoring even when one party to a conversation has consented to it, the Fourth Amendment as construed by the Supreme Court permits electronic monitoring so long as any party to a conversation has agreed to it. The Court has concluded that this monitoring is indistinguishable from the disclosure of a conversation by one of the participants after it has occurred.

If consensual electronic monitoring is indistinguishable from a participant's later disclosure of a conversation, however, any party who could assert that another's consent to electronic monitoring was involuntary also should be allowed to object to an informant's involuntary disclosure of a conversation after the fact. Yet he or she is not. Although the question has been litigated rarely, no one other than the informant himself or herself has been permitted to challenge the voluntariness of the informant's disclosure. The rule that a person lacks STANDING [4] to object to the violation of another person's rights has been thought to foreclose a challenge to the voluntariness of an informant's statements by a person other than the informant.

The principles that courts have developed in cases of third-party consent thus have not been consistently applied, and these principles might work important changes in the police informant system. Permitting others to challenge the use of coercive tactics against informants would subject some common police practices to new judicial scrutiny (for example, the practice of threatening to charge potential informants with crimes and to hold them on high bond). The coercion of third-party informants may invade the reasonable expectations of privacy of people whom the informants incriminate. This coercion can violate the rights of these people along with the rights of the informants themselves.

ALBERT W. ALSCHULER

(SEE ALSO: *Consent Search* [1]; *Exclusionary Rule* [2,I]; *Search and Seizure* [4,I].)

Bibliography

ALSCHULER, ALBERT W.   1983   Interpersonal Privacy and the Fourth Amendment. *Northern Illinois University Law Review* 4:1–57.
LAFAVE, WAYNE R.   1987   *Search and Seizure: A Treatise on the Fourth Amendment*, 2nd ed, Vol. 3, pp. 235–331.

THOMPSON v. OKLAHOMA
487 US 815 (1988)

The Court held that the CRUEL AND UNUSUAL PUNISHMENT [2,I] clause of the Eighth Amendment, applicable to the states by the INCORPORATION DOCTRINE [2,I], pro-

hibited the death sentence against a first-degree murderer who committed the offense at the age of fifteen. Justice JOHN PAUL STEVENS [4,I] spoke for a four-member plurality in whose JUDGMENT [3] Justice SANDRA DAY O'CONNOR [3,I] joined. Stevens asserted that the execution of the juvenile would "offend civilized standards of decency" and be "abhorrent to the conscience of the community."

O'Connor discerned no such consensus from the EVIDENCE [2] adduced by the plurality. Indeed, the Court divided 4–4 on the question as to whether such a consensus existed. O'Connor believed that the sentence must be set aside because of the risk that the state did not realize that its CAPITAL PUNISHMENT [1,I] statute might apply to fifteen-year-olds.

Stevens had a second string to his bow. He declared that the execution of the minor did not contribute to the purposes underlying the death penalty. O'Connor and the dissenters believed that the plurality Justices failed to understand that some fifteen-year-olds were as blameworthy as adults.

Justice ANTONIN SCALIA [I], for the three dissenters (Justice ANTHONY M. KENNEDY [3] did not participate), believed that a consensus existed showing that the execution of juveniles under fifteen years of age did not offend community standards and therefore did not violate the Eighth Amendment. In STANFORD V. PENRY (1988) [I] the Court ruled that the execution of juveniles who murdered at sixteen years of age was constitutional.

LEONARD W. LEVY

THORNBURGH v. AMERICAN COLLEGE OF OBSTETRICIANS AND GYNECOLOGISTS
476 U.S. 747 (1986)

Although this 5–4 decision struck down a series of Pennsylvania laws restricting ABORTION [1,I], it also showed that support within the Supreme Court for the principles of ROE V. WADE (1973) [3] had eroded. The invalidated restrictions covered a wide range: (1) a twenty-four-hour waiting period; (2) a requirement that a doctor provide a woman seeking an abortion with literature and oral statements, including warnings about medical risks, an estimate of the fetus's gestational age, a description of the probable physical characteristics of the fetus at two-week gestational increments, information about possible medical benefits for childbirth, and a reminder of a father's responsibility for child support; (3) detailed reporting requirements for doctors, including a statement of the basis for the doctor's finding that the fetus was not viable; and (4) a second-physician requirement. Justice HARRY A. BLACKMUN [1,I] wrote for the Court, reaffirming *Roe v. Wade* and concluding that all of the challenged requirements subordinated women's interest in privacy "in an effort to deter a woman from a decision that, along with her physician, is hers to make."

Chief Justice WARREN E. BURGER [1] dissented, noting his willingness to "reexamine *Roe.*" Justice BYRON R. WHITE [4,I], joined by Justice WILLIAM H. REHNQUIST [3,I], filed a lengthy and vigorous dissent that called for *Roe* to be overruled and specifically challenged the majority's rulings on each of the provisions invalidated here. Justice SANDRA DAY O'CONNOR [3,I], the fourth dissenter, reasserted what she had said in an earlier opinion, that the three-trimester analysis demanded by *Roe v. Wade* was unworkable and should be replaced by a principle that would uphold a law unless it were "unduly burdensome" on a woman's decision to have an abortion. Justice JOHN PAUL STEVENS [4,I] concurred in a long opinion, taking issue with Justice White's attack on *Roe.* The White–Stevens debate encapsulates many of the main points made in the debate over the proper role of the judiciary in the field of abortion.

KENNETH L. KARST

TORTS

The Constitution intersects with tort law, broadly conceived, in various ways. Most basically, the DUE PROCESS clauses [2] of the Fifth Amendment and FOURTEENTH AMENDMENT [2,I] require that in any legal proceeding enforced by public authority in which a property interest is at stake, as it almost invariably is in a tort suit, the parties must be accorded PROCEDURAL DUE PROCESS [3,I] and the EQUAL PROTECTION OF THE LAWS [2,I]. These requirements, however, are not cumbersome. As the Supreme Court said in *Snyder v. Massachusetts* (1934), a state remains "free to regulate procedure of [its] courts in accordance with [its] own conception of policy and fairness unless in so doing it offends some principle of justice so rooted in the traditions and conscience of our peoples as to be ranked as fundamental." Moreover, due process of law does not always require a proceeding in court. The states are free, for example, to replace the traditional COMMON LAW [1] approach to employee injuries with an administrative workers' compensation system, as all states have now done.

Beyond these rudimentary requirements of procedural due process, which apply to all state-enforced proceedings, the interactions between the Constitution and tort law become considerably more complex. To begin with, the Constitution sometimes functions as a sword, that is, as a source of rights that may be protected by tortlike civil action and damage remedies, and sometimes functions as a shield, that is, as an obstacle to civil actions and remedies that would otherwise be available under state or federal law. Moreover, the Constitution interacts with tort law as a sword and as a shield both directly and obliquely. We begin with the Constitution's more indirect interactions.

By virtue of the SUPREMACY CLAUSE (Article VI, clause 2) [4], the Constitution is the ultimate source of congressional authority. Thus, the Constitution is indirectly the source of all tortlike civil causes of action created by federal statutes. Where a statute explicitly creates a private cause of action, this area of law raises few problems. However, many federal regulatory and criminal statutes specify standards of conduct without expressly authorizing suits for money DAMAGES [2]. Not surprisingly, individuals injured by violations of these laws often ask the federal courts to create private causes of action with damages as a remedy. All agree that the issue of whether the federal courts should infer such a cause of action is a matter of statutory construction and that what must ultimately be determined is whether Congress intended to create the private remedy asserted. Yet, the question of what constitutes sufficient evidence of congressional intent and how restrictive or liberal the Court should be in finding implied private causes of action is highly controversial and has sharply divided the Court. It is clear, however, that during the twenty-five years since its 1964 decision in *J. I. Case Co. v. Borak,* where the Court seemed willing to create a private right of action wherever doing so would help effectuate the purpose of the statute, the Court has generally grown increasingly hostile toward implied causes of action. The prevailing view on the Court now seems to be that first expressed by Justice LEWIS F. POWELL [3,I] in his dissent in *Cannon v. University of Chicago* (1979): "absent the most compelling evidence of affirmative congressional intent, a federal court should not infer a private cause of action."

The Constitution is also the ultimate source of authority for the FEDERAL TORT CLAIMS ACT [2], which provides that the "United States shall be liable . . . to tort claims in the same manner and to the same extent as a private individual under like circumstances" (28 U.S.C. 2674). The act does not create new causes of action. Rather, it constitutes a waiver of SOVEREIGN IMMUNITY [4] by the United States for negligent acts by its employees that would constitute torts in states where the conduct occurs. The act has many important express exceptions (such as an exception for intentional acts and for "discretionary functions") and the Supreme Court has inferred additional exceptions (such as the bar to suits by members of the ARMED FORCES [I] for injuries they incur while in the military). Nevertheless, the act, which was not passed until 1946, remains the only basis for recovery of damages from the United States for the torts of its employees.

Not only is the Constitution the ultimate source of authority for federal statutes that create or permit tortlike causes of action, but it is also the ultimate source of authority for federal statutes that preclude state tort remedies that would otherwise be available. In this case, too, the issue is one of statutory interpretation (did Congress intend to displace state laws dealing with the same subject matter as the federal statute?), and here, also, the issue is easily resolved where Congress made it clear that the federal statute is intended to preempt the relevant state law. For example, in *Duke Power Co. v. Carolina Environmental Study Group*, the Court upheld the Price-Anderson Act, which expressly limited aggregate liability for a single nuclear power plant accident to $560 million, thereby limiting the tort remedies that might otherwise be available to plaintiffs in state courts. The Court rejected the claim that the statute resulted in an unconstitutional deprivation of the property rights of potential accident victims.

More difficult issues arise where Congress's intent with respect to state law is unclear. For example, the Federal Cigarette Label and Advertising Act requires that cigarette packages be marked with certain specified warning labels. Although the act forbids states to require additional warnings of any kind, the act does not make it clear whether, or to what extent, state courts are precluded from allowing tort actions by smokers who claim to have been harmed by smoking cigarettes sold with the requisite federal warnings. This issue is now being widely litigated in state and lower federal courts.

Although there are limits to generalizations that can be drawn, it seems that the Supreme Court has been unwilling to find PREEMPTION [3] of state tort remedies in the absence of clear legislative intent to displace state law. For example, in *Silkwood v. Kerr-McGee Corp.* (1984), the Court held that state laws awarding punitive damages for injuries resulting from the escape of plutonium from a nuclear plant were not preempted by the extensive federal regulatory scheme governing the safety of nuclear plants.

Both the implied-cause-of-action cases and the preemption cases raise issues of statutory interpretation. Unquestionably, Congress has broad constitutional power to create new tortlike causes of action or, instead, to abolish or replace existing causes of action. In recent years, however, the Supreme Court has tended to construe federal statutes narrowly, leaving things as they are in the absence of a clear indication of an intent by Congress to change them. Thus, the Court has been reluctant either to infer private causes of action from federal statutes or to find that state law has been preempted by federal statutes.

The Constitution not only affects tort law indirectly through the commands of federal statutes, but bears directly on tort law as a source of tortlike causes of action against governmental officials and entities and as an obstacle to tort actions and remedies that would otherwise be available. We begin with the constitution as a sword.

The idea that compensatory and punitive-damage actions could be premised on the Constitution itself took some time to develop, particularly where the defendant was an official of the federal government. The common-law courts tended to treat an official who invaded the protected interests of another without legal authority simply as a private individual who had committed a tort. The BILL OF RIGHTS [1], which originally applied only to the federal government, incorporated some common-law norms against unjustified official invasions of person and property. For example, it forbids federal officials from making unreasonable SEARCHES AND SEIZURES [4,I], forbids issuance of SEARCH WARRANTS [4] without probable cause, and forbids deprivations of life, liberty, or property without due process of law.

Until the CIVIL WAR [I], the Constitution played only an indirect role in tort actions against federal officials. A person who believed that his or her person or property had been wrongfully invaded by a federal officer would bring a common-law trespass action against him. The official pleaded justification—that he or she had been acting within his or her constitutional and statutory authority, so the action was not tortious. For example, an official might argue that a seizure of the plaintiff's property was reasonable. The issue of reasonableness could have been characterized as a question of whether the plaintiff's FOURTH AMENDMENT [2,I] rights had been violated. But neither the parties, nor the courts it seems, perceived the action as different from an ordinary tort action because the constitutional and preexisting common-law standards were largely coextensive.

The constitutional amendments and legislation of the RECONSTRUCTION [I] era increased the interplay of tort law and the Constitution, particularly in actions against state and local officials. With the Fourteenth Amendment, the common-law protections against unjustified invasions of liberty or property were now constitutionalized as against state and local officials rather than only against federal officials. And new rights that were not recognized at common law, such as the right to equal protection of the laws, were added to the Constitution.

In addition, the 1871 Civil Rights Act recognized under COLOR OF STATE LAW [1] a cause of action for invasion of rights secured by the Constitution, and the JUDICIARY ACT OF 1875 [3] extended FEDERAL COURT JURISDICTION [I] to FEDERAL QUESTION [2] cases generally. Before the Civil War, plaintiffs had brought suits against government officers as tort claims, and the constitutional issues arose by way of answer and reply. The Reconstruction legislation, however, offered the plaintiffs a federal forum if they pleaded a constitutional violation in their complaints. Over time these "constitutional" torts came to be viewed as separate from the common-law tort actions from which they derived. This separation occurred in part because constitutional rights came to include some rights that had not received protection in common-law actions, such as rights to free speech. In addition, the demise of the concept of a general nationwide common law made lawyers look for federal or state positive-law sources for interests that the courts would protect and look to the source of constitutional tort actions as the Constitution rather than general tort law.

Today federal court actions against state and local officials for constitutional invasions are primarily brought under SECTION 1983 [4] of the 1871 Civil Rights Act. Suits against LOCAL GOVERNMENT [I] entities—although not states, which are usually shielded from federal court liability by the ELEVENTH AMENDMENT [3,I]—can also be brought in federal courts under section 1983. (Local governments are liable, however, only for their own unconstitutional policies, not for the unauthorized tortious acts of their employees.) There is no counterpart to section 1983 for suits against federal officials. Therefore, a claim against a federal official, such as the claim that an FBI agent violated the plaintiff's Fourth Amendment rights, must be rooted in the Constitution itself. Although the general federal-question statute empowers federal courts to adjudicate cases arising under the Constitution, neither that statute nor the Constitution itself expressly creates a cause of action for money damages. It was not until 1971, in the landmark case of BIVENS V. SIX UNKNOWN NAMED AGENTS [1], that the Supreme Court ruled that a federal official can be sued for money damages as a cause of action implied from the Constitution itself—in this case, from the Fourth Amendment. *Bivens* made clear that the constitutional claim was not tied to the niceties of state tort law: "The federal question becomes not merely a possible defense to the State Law action, but an independent claim both necessary and sufficient to make out the . . . cause of action."

Since *Bivens*, the Court has recognized other constitutional provisions, such as the Eighth Amendment's proscription on CRUEL AND UNUSUAL PUNISHMENT [2,I], as bases for damage actions. *Bivens*, however, leaves many open questions, most crucially, whether the availability of a cause of action against federal officers for money damages is required by the Constitution itself or is federal common law that Congress could abolish by statute. In recent years the Court has rejected a variety of constitutional damage claims either because, in the Court's view,

Congress had provided an alternative remedy or, more broadly, because the Court perceived "special factors" counseling caution in inferring a constitutional cause of action for damages. Moreover, the Supreme Court has ruled that both state officials sued under section 1983 and federal officials sued in a *Bivens* action possess some degree of immunity from liability (municipalities sued under section 1983 do not). Some officials, such as judges and prosecutors performing their official duties, enjoy absolute immunity from suit, but most officials are accorded only a "qualified," or "good faith," immunity. This form of immunity, which has little support in the common law and is not mentioned either in section 1983 or in the Constitution itself, must be claimed as an affirmative defense. Although this partial immunity is often called good-faith immunity, the Supreme Court's most recent formulation in *Harlan v. Fitzgerald* (1982) makes clear that the test is an objective one: "[G]overnment officials performing discretionary functions generally are shielded from liability for civil damages insofar as their conduct does not violate clearly established statutory or constitutional rights of which a reasonable person would have known."

Although the rights litigated in these "section 1983" and *Bivens* suits are rights secured by the Constitution and the various immunity doctrines are peculiar to suits against governmental officials, these actions are still seen in some respects as in the nature of tort actions, as shown by the borrowing of state-tort statutes of limitation. In addition, many such constitutional actions, for example, those seeking damages for illegal searches or arrests, resemble common-law actions that may be brought under state tort law or, in limited cases, under the Federal Tort Claims Act if the violator is a federal law enforcement official. Other "constitutional tort" actions go beyond the common law—for example, an action under the 1871 Act claiming that one was dismissed from public employment for exercising one's FIRST AMENDMENT [2,I] rights. Actions for official negligence typically are relegated to traditional tort remedies, as are some intentional torts, such as libel.

If it took a surprisingly long time for the Court to rule that the Constitution could itself be the source for tortlike causes of action for damages, it took almost as long for it to rule that the Constitution could be an obstacle to tort remedies otherwise available. The primary constitutional limit on common-law private tort actions is the First Amendment's prohibition against "law[s] . . . abridging the freedom of speech or of the press." Originally, this prohibition applied only to Congress, but with the INCORPORATION [2,I] of the Bill of Rights into the Fourteenth Amendment, it became applicable to state governments as well. Nevertheless, it was not until NEW YORK TIMES V. SULLIVAN (1964) [3] that the Supreme

Court interpreted the First Amendment as a limitation on damage remedies in private suits brought under the states' common law of libel. Although it might seem anomalous that constitutional language securing rights against the government would also come into play in legal actions between private parties, by the time of *Sullivan* it had become clear that a state could infringe constitutionally protected interests by enforcing a legal judgment as well as by enacting a statute.

In *Sullivan*, a city commissioner of Montgomery, Alabama, brought a libel action in state court against the *New York Times* and four black ministers who had advertised in the *Times*, appealing for contributions to a legal-defense fund for Martin Luther King, Jr., who had recently been arrested in Alabama on a perjury charge. The ad, which had not mentioned Sullivan, made several assertions about the conduct of the Montgomery police that were largely, though not entirely, accurate. Sullivan claimed that because his duties included supervision of the Montgomery police, the allegations against the police defamed him personally. An Alabama jury awarded him $500,000. By the time the case reached the Supreme Court, it was but one of eleven LIBEL [3] claims totaling $5,600,000 pending against the *Times* in Alabama; it was obvious that the *Sullivan* litigation was part of a concerted effort to discourage the press from supporting the CIVIL RIGHTS MOVEMENT [I] in the South and to silence the movement's leaders. This effort, moreover, seemed likely to succeed, for under the common law of Alabama and most other states it was difficult to defeat these libel claims. Under standard common-law rules governing libel actions, truth was an affirmative defense, but the evident inability of civil rights advocates to prove to hostile juries the "truth" of statements criticizing popularly elected officials posed the clear danger that speech would be stifled by the threat of crushing civil liability. And in most states the common-law rule of strict liability for defamation recognized no privilege of "fair comment" for statements of fact that were false. To combat this danger to First Amendment values, the Court in *Sullivan* ruled that a statement criticizing a public official and relating to matters of public concern could be actionable under state libel law only if the statement were defamatory, false, and made with " 'actual malice'—that is, with knowledge that it was false or with reckless disregard of whether it was false or not."

In subsequent years, the Court recognized that "the establishment" against which caustic political speech was often addressed encompassed more individuals than merely those who actually held public office. Indeed, there are many people, such as labor leaders or prominent business leaders, who may be so powerful or influential that their actions clearly affect the outcome of political controversies. Acknowledging this reality, the Court, in the cases

of *Associated Press v. Walker* and *Curtis Publishing Company v. Butts* (1967), extended the *Sullivan* rules to libel actions brought by PUBLIC FIGURES [3]. However, in GERTZ V. ROBERT WELCH, INC. (1974) [2], the Court recognized that there are other people who, although perhaps well known, have not so injected themselves into public controversy as to become public figures for purposes of the First Amendment's limitations on libel actions. Where such a nonpublic figure brings a libel suit, there is much less likelihood that a libel action is a state-supported attempt to silence unpopular speech. Moreover, such private individuals have a correspondingly lesser opportunity than public figures or public officials to obtain access to the media to rebut the allegedly defamatory statements. Thus, the Court ruled in *Gertz* that private plaintiffs in such cases need only to show whatever standard of fault the state requires, although some level of fault (at the least negligence) is a constitutional requirement for recovery.

First Amendment concerns ebb as the public status of the plaintiff decreases, but the status of the plaintiff is not the only factor that determines whether the challenged speech is entitled to special constitutional protection. In DUN & BRADSTREET V. GREENMOSS BUILDERS, INC. (1985) [2] the Supreme Court ruled that special First Amendment protection extends only to speech relating to matters of public concern. If the challenged statement touches only matters of private concern, there is little danger that state libel law is being used to silence unpopular political speech, and so the states are free to apply whatever libel law they choose. It is possible, in theory, that public officials or public figures might thus succeed in silencing the speech of unpopular critics. But it is clear that a given topic of interest may change categories as the social status of the plaintiff changes, so that matters that are "private" in the context of statements about private citizens may be of public concern in the context of statements about public officials or public figures.

The Court's First Amendment libel jurisprudence has become extremely—some would say unduly—complex and has required extensive revamping of not only substantive libel law, but procedural and remedial libel law as well. For example, in a "public concern" case the defendant no longer bears the burden of persuasion on the issue of the truth of the alleged defamation. Now, in a departure from the common law, it is the plaintiff who must prove that the challenged statement contains an untrue assertion before any liability will exist. And although falsehood may be established by the common-law standard of a preponderance of the evidence, "actual malice" (in the case of a "public official" or "public figure" plaintiff) or negligence (in the case of a "private individual" plaintiff) must now be established by clear and convincing evidence. In addition to these changes in trial procedure, the Court has effected a change in appellate procedure in libel actions, ruling in *Bose Corporation v. Consumers Union of United States, Inc.* (1984) that a reviewing court is not to accord trial court findings the normal "clearly erroneous" standard of deference. Instead, said the Court, the First Amendment requires that an appellate court independently evaluate the evidence in the record to determine whether there is clear and convincing evidence of "actual malice" or the appropriate level of fault.

With respect to remedies for libel and defamation, the law is also complex and, perhaps, in a state of flux. But in essence, the current rule is the following: where the speech relates to matters of public concern, regardless of the social status of the target of the speech, presumed and punitive damages may be awarded only upon a showing of actual malice (of course, where the plaintiff is a public official or public figure, no damages at all will lie, absent a showing of actual malice); but where the subject matter of the speech is purely private, the First Amendment places no limitation on any type of damages.

Many libel plaintiffs also allege that they are entitled to recover on some other basis, such as invasion of privacy or intentional infliction of emotional distress. Like libel, these other causes of action also present the risk of state-supported attempts to silence controversial or unpopular speech. Not surprisingly, when the Court in HUSTLER MAGAZINE V. FALWELL (1988) [I] considered whether the First Amendment places any limitations on actions for intentional infliction of emotional distress, it held that a public official or a public-figure plaintiff in such an action must prove that the statement at issue contains a false assertion made with actual malice. The Court did not discuss the public concern/private concern distinction of *Dun & Bradstreet*, but its reasoning suggests that emotional distress actions, as well as other tort actions based on defendant's speech, must be analyzed in light of the same First Amendment principles as libel actions.

Until now, the First Amendment has been by far the most important source of constitutionally based limitations on tort law. But the Court will soon consider whether the due-process clause of the Fourteenth Amendment places some limits on the award of punitive damages under state law, not only for speech related torts, such as libel and slander, but for all torts. As punitive-damage awards have skyrocketed in recent years, business interests have argued for some constitutionally based limits on the size of punitive awards. In *Browning-Ferris Industries of Vermont Inc. v. Kelco Disposal Inc.* (1989) the Court ruled that the Eighth Amendment's EXCESSIVE FINES [I] clause applies only to criminal cases and not to awards of punitive damages in civil suits between private parties. However, the Court expressly left open the possibility that the due-process clause regulates in some way the imposition of punitive damages in such suits.

SILAS WASSERSTROM
ANNE WOOLHANDLER

Bibliography

JEFFRIES, JOHN C. 1989 Compensation for Constitutional Torts: Reflections on the Significance of Fault. *Michigan Law Review* 88:82–103.

NICHOLS, GENE 1989 *Bivens, Chilicky,* and Constitutional Damages Claims. *Virginia Law Review* 75:1117–1154.

SMOLLA, RODNEY 1987 *Dun & Bradstreet, Hepps,* and *Liberty Lobby:* A New Analytic Primer on the Future Course of Defamation. *Georgetown Law Journal* 75:1519–1573.

U

UNENUMERATED RIGHTS

The starting point for interpreting the NINTH AMENDMENT [3] is its text: "The enumeration in the Constitution of certain rights shall not be construed to deny or disparage others retained by the people." The text and the rule of construction that requires plain meaning to be followed clearly establishes the existence of unenumerated rights. Why would the Framers have included an amendment that protects such rights in the midst of the BILL OF RIGHTS [1], which specifies rights in the first eight amendments?

The Framers scarcely had an alternative after they botched an explanation for their failure to have included a bill of rights as part of the original Constitution. They protected a few rights in it, but ignored most; and they subsequently made several frail and foolish explanations instead of confessing misjudgment and promising subsequent amendments. As a result they placed RATIFICATION [3] in serious jeopardy. The Constitution was finally ratified only because crucial states, where ratification had been in doubt, accepted a pledge that a bill of rights would be added to the Constitution in the form of amendments.

THE FEDERALIST #84 [2] presented a commonplace ratificationist argument that boomeranged and made necessary a provision safeguarding unspecified rights. According to ALEXANDER HAMILTON [2], a bill of rights was unnecessary and even dangerous, because by containing exceptions to powers not granted, it would provide a basis for repressive LEGISLATION [3]. For example, to say that liberty of the press ought not be restricted furnished "a plausible pretense" for the very power feared, a power to legislate on the press, because a provision "against

restraining the liberty of the press afforded a clear implication that a power to prescribe proper regulations concerning it was intended to be vested in the national government." Equally dangerous, the omission of some right in a catalogue of rights allowed the assumption that it was meant to be unguarded. JAMES MADISON [3], OLIVER ELLSWORTH [2], and JAMES WILSON [4], among other leading Framers, made the same damaging argument.

Their logic, which nearly undid their cause, surely merited public rejection. They proved that the particular rights that the unamended Constitution protected—no RELIGIOUS TESTS [3], bans on BILLS OF ATTAINDER [1] and EX POST FACTO LAWS [2], and TRIALS BY JURY [4] in criminal cases, among other rights—stood in grave jeopardy because to specify a right implied a power to violate it. Moreover, the inclusion of some rights in the Constitution implied, contradictorily, that all unenumerated ones were relinquished. The unsatisfactory arguments by ratificationists imperiled their cause and obliged them to reconsider.

Madison switched to the cause of amending the Constitution with a bill of rights in order to appease the fears of the people. When he rose in Congress to propose constitutional amendments, he asserted that the Constitution must "expressly declare the great rights of mankind." He acknowledged that a major objection to a bill of rights consisted of the argument that "by enumerating particular exceptions to the grant of power, it would disparage those rights which were not placed in that enumeration; and it might follow, by implication, that those rights which were not singled out, were intended to be assigned into the hands of the General Government, and were consequently insecure." This claim had become a ratificationist cliché that self-destructed because the Constitution explicitly protected several rights exposing all those omitted, including "the great rights of mankind" to governmental violation. Madison's solution was the simple proposal that became the Ninth Amendment. It was, he said, meant to guard against the possibility that unenumerated rights might be at risk as a result of the enumeration of some. By excepting enumerated rights from the grant of powers, no implication was intended and no inference should be drawn that rights not excepted from the grant of powers were at risk. As Madison phrased his proposal, it read as follows: "The exceptions [to power] here or elsewhere in the constitution made in favor of particular rights, shall not be so construed as to diminish the just importance of other rights retained by the people. . . ."

What were the unenumerated rights retained by the people? They had to be either "natural rights" or "positive rights," to use Madison's own terms. He distinguished "the preexistent rights of nature" from those "resulting from a SOCIAL COMPACT [4]." He mentioned freedom of "speach" (sic) as a natural right, but failed to include it in his recommendations. (A committee rectified this oversight.) His omission illustrates his acknowledgment of an important right that briefly fell within the unenumerated category. In Madison's thinking, this category also included the natural right of the people to govern themselves and to alter their government when it was inadequate to its purposes. Those purposes embodied another unenumerated natural right: governments are instituted to secure the people "in the enjoyment of life and liberty, with the right of acquiring and using property and generally of pursuing and obtaining happiness and safety." Madison had borrowed from the preamble of the DECLARATION OF INDEPENDENCE [2], which expressed opinions on natural rights that were shared by virtually all Americans and were central to the meaning of the Ninth Amendment.

Its text meant what it said; its context consists of the widespread endorsement of natural rights at the time of the framing of the Bill of Rights. STATE CONSTITUTIONS [I] referred to natural rights. Virginia's 1788 recommendations for amendments to the Constitution did so also, as had New York's and North Carolina's. At the Pennsylvania ratifying convention, James Wilson, second only to Madison as an architect of the Constitution, quoted the preamble of the Declaration of Independence and added, "This is the broad basis on which our independence was placed; on the same certain and solid foundation this system [the Constitution] is erected."

The Framers also believed that all people had a right to equal justice and to equality of rights before the law. That slaveholders subscribed to such opinions proves the inconsistency of some of the Framers and their inability to transform their societies. But ABRAHAM LINCOLN [3] understood when he described the creation of a new nation "conceived in liberty and dedicated to the proposition that all men are created equal." The Ninth Amendment embodied the principle of equality as well as that of liberty. Madison himself, when presenting his recommended amendments, spoke of "the perfect equality of mankind." Other natural rights that were unenumerated included the right, then important, to hunt and fish; the RIGHT TO TRAVEL [3]; the right to associate freely with others; and the right to intimate association or privacy in matters concerning family and sex, at least within the bounds of marriage. Such rights were fundamental to the pursuit of happiness.

In addition to natural rights, the unenumerated rights included some that were positive, deriving not from "Nature's God," but from social compacts that created governments. What positive rights were familiar when the Ninth Amendment became part of the Constitution, yet were not enumerated in the original text or the first eight amendments? The right to vote and hold office, the right of free elections, the right not to be taxed except by consent through representatives of one's choice, the right to be free from monopolies, the right to be free from standing armies in time of peace, the right to refuse military service on grounds of religious conscience, the right to choose a profession, and the right of an accused person to an initial presumption of innocence and to have the prosecution shoulder the responsibility of proving guilt beyond a REASONABLE DOUBT [3]—all these were among existing positive rights protected by various state laws, state constitutions, and the COMMON LAW [1]; and all were unenumerated. Any of these rights, among others, could legitimately be regarded as rights of the people before which the powers of government must be exercised in subordination.

In addition to rights then known, the Ninth Amendment probably had the purpose of providing the basis for unknown rights that time alone might disclose. Nothing in the thinking of the Framers foreclosed the possibility that new rights might claim the loyalties of succeeding generations. As EDMUND PENDLETON [3], Virginia's chief justice and a leading ratificationist, mused when the Bill of Rights was being framed, "May we not in the progress of things, discover some great and important [right], which we don't now think of?"

Without doubt, to read the Ninth Amendment as a cornucopia of unenumerated rights is an invitation to JUDICIAL ACTIVISM [3]. As Professor John Hart Ely has written, if natural rights in particular are read into the amendment, it does not lend itself "to principled judicial enforcement." But neither do enumerated rights—natural or positive. FREEDOM OF SPEECH [2,I] and DUE PROCESS OF LAW [2], to mention one of each kind of right, have resulted in some of the most subjective result-oriented constitutional

JURISPRUDENCE [I] in our history. The fact that judicial decisions can be unprincipled or biased does not detract from the principle expressed in a right, whether or not it is enumerated.

If the Ninth Amendment instructs us to look beyond its four corners for unenumerated rights of the people, as it does, it must have some content. To read it as if it is merely the converse side of the TENTH AMENDMENT [4] is to confuse the two amendments, as did Professor Raoul Berger. He spoke of "the ninth's retention of rights by the states or the people." It is the Tenth Amendment that reserves powers, not rights, to the states or to the people. The Ninth Amendment, according to Berger, "was merely declaratory of a basic presupposition: all powers not 'positively' granted are reserved to the people. It added no unspecified rights to the Bill of Rights." In fact, however, an explicit declaration of the existence of unenumerated rights is an addition of unspecified rights to the Bill of Rights. Confusion between the Ninth and Tenth amendments originated with proposals for amendments by Virginia in 1788. Moreover, Madison himself argued that the line between a power granted and a right retained by the people amounted to the same thing if a right were named. Unenumerated rights, however, are not named, and no affirmative power has been delegated to regulate or abridge them.

Without doubt, the Ninth Amendment and its problem of identifying unenumerated rights continue to bedevil interpreters, on and off the bench. Courts do continue to discover rights that have no textual existence and might be considered unenumerated, but for the judicial propensity to ignore the Ninth Amendment and make believe that some unspecified right under discussion derives from a right that is enumerated. Opponents of such rights howl their denunciation of judicial activism. Court-invented rights exceed in number the rights enumerated. Judges have composed rights great and small, including the MIRANDA RULES [3,I], the right to engage in nude dancing with pasties and G-string, the right to engage in FLAG DESECRATION [2,I], the right to secure an ABORTION [1,I], or the right against the invasion of an expectation of privacy.

So long as we continue to believe that government is instituted for the sake of securing the rights of the people and must exercise its powers in subordination to those rights, the Ninth Amendment should have the vitality intended for it. The problem is not so much whether the rights it guarantees are as worthy of enforcement as are the enumerated rights; the problem, rather, is whether our courts should read out of the amendment rights worthy of our respect, which the Framers might conceivably have meant to safeguard, at least in principle.

LEONARD W. LEVY

(SEE ALSO: *Freedom of Assembly and Association* [2]; *Freedom of Intimate Association* [2]; *Right of Privacy* [3,I].)

Bibliography
BARNETT, RANDY E., ED. 1988 Symposium on Interpreting the Ninth Amendment. *Chicago-Kent Law Review* 64:37–268.
BERGER, RAOUL 1980 The Ninth Amendment. *Cornell Law Review* 61:1–26.
CAPLAN, RUSSELL L. 1983 The History and Meaning of the Ninth Amendment. *Virginia Law Review* 69:223–268.
REDLICH, NORMAN 1989 The Ninth Amendment as a Constitutional Prism. *Harvard Journal of Law and Public Policy* 12:23–28.

UNREASONABLE SEARCH
(Update)

"Unreasonable search and seizure" is a technical phrase that refers to any governmental SEARCH AND SEIZURE [4,I] deemed to violate the FOURTH AMENDMENT [2,I] of the Constitution. In general, searches and seizures are unreasonable if the government undertakes them without properly authorizing SEARCH WARRANTS [4] or, in exceptional circumstances not requiring warrants, in violation of the rules laid down for those exceptions. The Fourth Amendment provides, "The right of the people to be secure in their persons, houses, papers, and effects, against unreasonable searches and seizures, shall not be violated, and no Warrants shall issue, but upon probable cause, supported by Oath or affirmation, and particularly describing the place to be searched, and the persons or things to be seized." The amendment defines neither "unreasonable" nor "searches and seizures," and the judiciary has taken on the task of definition. The Supreme Court has concluded that particularized searches and seizures with a warrant, as called for by the amendment's warrant clause, establish the norm for reasonableness. It is the neutral, detached, judicial determination of good reason or "probable cause" to search for/or seize particular persons or things in particular places that makes such acts presumptively "reasonable." Unauthorized searches and seizures, unless specially justified, are generally thought unreasonable.

Although searches and seizures based on proper warrants are the accepted constitutional norm, not all WARRANTLESS SEARCHES [4] and seizures violate the Fourth Amendment. They do not if they are directed at objects or interests the amendment does not protect, if they do not constitute "searches" or "seizures" in the legal sense, or if they fall within one of the recognized exceptions to the warrant or probable cause requirements.

In KATZ V. UNITED STATES (1967) [3], the Supreme Court stated that the Fourth Amendment, among other things, protected certain individual interests in privacy from unreasonable government search and seizure. Subsequent opinions have said the amendment protects an individual's REASONABLE EXPECTATION OF PRIVACY [I], a test involving both a subjective expectation of privacy and one that society is prepared to recognize as "reasonable." Where an individual has no reasonable expectation of privacy, the government may search and seize without a warrant and even without probable cause. Consequently, the government may search and seize things or matters that an individual of necessity or willingly exposes to the public. For example, the government may photograph one's features, lift one's fingerprints, tape public lectures, or place tracking devices on cars.

The second part of the *Katz* test requires that the expectation of privacy be one that society—here represented by the Supreme Court—is prepared to recognize as reasonable. One consequence of the Court's "reasonable expectation" definitions has been that police may freely examine some places where people might actually expect some privacy, at least in the sense of not contemplating that the government would seek evidence against them there. For example, the Court has held that persons have no reasonable expectation of privacy in trash placed out for collection. The Court has also held, in effect, that persons have no expectation that items hidden from ordinary view on real property will be free from aerial surveillance. Finally, it has held that an occupant of real property has an expectation of privacy only with regard to his or her home and its "curtilage," or the area immediately surrounding it and associated with intimate home uses. Consequently, even were one to hide something in dense, secluded woods on one's private property, the government could legitimately search the woods without a warrant or probable cause.

There are a number of recognized exceptions to the warrant requirement and even some to the probable cause requirement. These exceptions are made in situations in which, while the police have probable cause to search for and seize particular evidence or persons in particular places, some other circumstance—usually referred to as an "exigent" or emergency circumstance—makes it impossible, impracticable, self-defeating, or unwise to obtain a warrant. In situations in which the government demonstrates a special and important need for a limited search, the reasonableness of the search depends upon a balancing of the need to search against the intrusion the search entails. For such reasons, the Court has held several kinds of warrantless searches reasonable: SEARCHES INCIDENT TO ARREST [4]; investigative STOPS-AND-FRISKS [4]; AUTOMOBILE SEARCHES [1,I] and searches of other mobile vehi-

cles; inspection and regulatory searches, including BORDER SEARCHES [1]; some employer drug-testing searches; and CONSENT SEARCHES [1].

An ARREST [1] is a seizure of a person. Under COMMON LAW [1] and constitutional rule, when police see a crime being committed or have probable cause to think that a specific person has committed a FELONY [2] and may escape unless arrested, they may arrest without a warrant. Arrest may place police officers at risk if the person arrested has a weapon, and one arrested may wish to dispose of incriminating evidence. To protect themselves and others and to prevent destruction of evidence, officers arresting on probable cause may conduct a full BODY SEARCH [1] of the arrestee and the area within his or her ready reach.

In contrast, warrantless searches and seizures within a home are presumptively unreasonable. Consequently, when police have probable cause to arrest someone who is at home and unlikely to flee while a warrant is sought, they must obtain an ARREST WARRANT [1].

There are police-civilian encounters short of arrest, usually called "investigative detentions" or "stops-and-frisks." Police rightly investigate suspicious circumstances or characters, and good police work may entail stopping and questioning persons on some reasonable suspicion. If police do stop someone to investigate, however, they may place themselves at risk if the person carries a weapon. On the other hand, a general police authority to stop and question anyone for any reason opens possibilities of police harassment. The Court has held therefore that although the procedure entails a seizure and a search, it is reasonable for officers to stop persons they reasonably suspect of criminal activity and of being armed and dangerous, for the purpose of questioning them and searching for weapons. Under this authority, when police have reasonable suspicion to think that luggage, parcels, or other containers contain contraband or EVIDENCE [2] of a crime, they may detain them for a limited, unintrusive inspection, such as sniffing by a trained narcotics-detection dog.

Mobile vehicles present a special problem. Were police to seek a warrant for a vehicle they have probable cause to suspect contains evidence of a crime, the vehicle might leave the JURISDICTION [3] in the interim. In addition, as the Court has held, because of extensive regulation of vehicles and the character of their public uses, there is a lesser expectation of privacy in vehicles than there is in homes or offices. Consequently, the Court has laid down the rule that when police have probable cause regarding a mobile vehicle, they may undertake a warrantless search of it. The authority remains even if the vehicle is unlikely to be moved or the police have immobilized it.

Governments undertake inspection or regulatory searches for a variety of purposes. Fire inspection codes often require home and building safety inspection. Airline safety dictates some inspection of luggage and persons flying. Entry into an agricultural pest quarantine zone calls for inspection for designated pests. Crossing an international border calls for inspection to ensure right of entry and search to ensure against smuggling of contraband or dutiable goods. In these situations, the need to inspect or search is great, any inconvenience is small, and the scope and the extent of associated interrogation and search is limited. Similarly, public safety or security may require mandatory drug testing for railway or airline employees where their inattention or dereliction of duty would involve an immediate risk of serious harm. In general, the combination of an overriding public interest and the relatively limited character of the search are thought to make such searches reasonable.

Consent searches constitute the final major exception to the warrant and probable cause requirements. Individuals may voluntarily waive their constitutional rights. One can therefore give up the search and seizure protections the Fourth Amendment accords by agreeing to a search. The major questions in such a case are whether there was voluntary consent to the search and whether the party consenting had authority to do so. Whether consent was voluntary or coerced is a factual question, but the state need not show that the person who allegedly gave consent knew that he or she had a right to refuse to give consent. The Court has also indicated that anyone who has common authority over premises or effects can consent to a search of them and that such consent holds against an absent nonconsenting person who shares the authority. In other words, third parties, who are not the targets of a search, can sometimes consent to searches aimed at securing evidence against a target.

GARY GOODPASTER

(SEE ALSO: *Exigent Circumstances Search* [2]; *Open Fields Doctrine* [1]; *Plain View Doctrine* [3,1].)

Bibliography

AMSTERDAM, ANTHONY 1974 Perspectives on the Fourth Amendment. *Minnesota Law Review* 58:349–477.

LaFAVE, WAYNE 1987 *Search and Seizure: A Treatise on the Fourth Amendment*, 3 vols. St. Paul, Minn.: West Publishing Co.

LANDYNSKI, J. 1966 Search and Seizure and the Supreme Court. *Johns Hopkins University Studies in Historical and Political Science*, ser. 84, No. 1.

TAYLOR, TELFORD 1969 *Two Studies in Constitutional Interpretation*. Columbus: Ohio State University Press.

VIETNAM WAR
(Update)

The Vietnam War, more accurately labeled America's Indochina War, claimed 46,400 American lives. During its most active phase, from 1964 to 1973, it cost over $107 billion. American troop strength in the conflict reached a peak of 536,100 in March 1969. Yet the war was never formally declared.

Direct American involvement in Indochina began in 1949–1950 when Congress provided for financial and material assistance in "the general area of China" and for the use of noncombatant military advisers. Using this authority, President HARRY S. TRUMAN [4] began sending aid to the associated states comprising French Indochina. When the KOREAN WAR [3] heightened America's commitment in the Far East, Congress anticipated the pattern of coming years by approving additional aid. Following the end of France's military involvement in Indochina in 1954, the United States took the initiative in negotiating the Southeast Asia Collective Defense Treaty, which committed each of its adherents to meet "armed attack in the treaty area . . . in accordance with its constitutional processes." Prior to the treaty's approval by the Senate in 1955, Secretary of State John Foster Dulles interpreted this provision as meaning the President would seek congressional support before launching major military moves, but others hedged on whether such action was constitutionally required. Between 1954 and 1964, the United States provided more than $1 billion in military aid to South Vietnam and by late 1963 the American Military Assistance Advisory Group there had grown to 16,300.

In 1964 the war took on a new constitutional cast. South Vietnam's position having deteriorated, President LYNDON B. JOHNSON [3] sought to continue a policy of measured firmness. In May and June he directed the State Department to begin drafting possible congressional resolutions to affirm the American commitment in Vietnam. This approach drew partly on the experience of the 1950s and early 1960s, when the United States response to crises involving the Formosa Straits, the Middle East, Berlin, and Cuba included congressional resolutions of support in 1955, 1957, 1961, and 1962. Although temporarily shelved, the project soon became urgent. On August 2, perhaps provoked by American-supported commando raids along the North Vietnamese coast, North Vietnam torpedo boats attacked an American destroyer on an intelligence mission in the Gulf of Tonkin. Two days later, another attack may have occurred. Johnson reported the attacks to the American people, but refrained from mentioning either the intelligence mission or doubts about whether the second attack had actually occurred. Congressional leaders received a fuller briefing but not a complete account. Giving them a draft resolution, Johnson asked for its prompt passage even as he ordered retaliatory air strikes against North Vietnam.

Following a perfunctory hearing and almost no floor debate, the House of Representatives passed the GULF OF TONKIN RESOLUTION [2] by a vote of 416–0. In the Senate, owing especially to questions raised by Wayne Morse about the events in the Tonkin Gulf and about the problem of unconstitutionally delegating Congress's WAR POWERS [4,I], the hearing process and floor debate took slightly longer, but the measure won approval by 88 to 2, and Johnson signed it into law on August 10.

After stating Congress's support for the President's determination "to take all necessary measures to repel any armed attack against the armed forces of the United States and to prevent further aggression," the resolution declared that peace in Asia was a vital American interest and that "the United States is, therefore, prepared, as the President determines, to take all necessary steps, including use of armed force, to assist any member or protocol state of the Southeast Asia Collective Defense Treaty requesting assistance in defense of its freedom."

In February 1965 the United States escalated its air war in Vietnam and soon began sending ground combat troops (as opposed to "advisers"). When voting in 1964, most congressmen had not contemplated this turn of events, yet Senator J. William Fulbright, chairman of the Foreign Relations Committee, had admitted during debate that the resolution could undergird major military action. In 1967, Under Secretary of State (and former Attorney General) Nicholas Katzenbach explained that the Tonkin Gulf Resolution was "as broad an authorization for the use of armed forces . . . as any declaration of war so-called could be in terms of our internal constitutional process." Significantly, however, its State Department drafters had carefully avoided any language conceding that congressional authorization was a requirement for escalating the American presence in Vietnam. This allowed continuing reliance on the President's own authority, as illustrated in February 1966 when a State Department legal memorandum argued that the President's direct powers under Article II covered the commitment in Vietnam. That being the case, the Southeast Asia Collective Defense Treaty's provision for action in accordance with American "constitutional processes" further authorized the war in Vietnam. But, explained the memorandum, the existence of the Tonkin Gulf Resolution and congressional appropriations for the conflict obviated the need to delineate precise constitutional boundaries.

Despite growing public and congressional criticism of the war, Congress enacted at least twenty-four laws supporting it between 1964 and 1969. Senator Morse's 1966 call for repeal of the Tonkin Gulf Resolution met defeat, as, for example, did antibombing amendments to appropriations bills in 1968. In 1967 the Senate Foreign Relations Committee began to consider a "National Commitments Resolution," after Fulbright, its chairman, switched to an antiwar stance. But the resulting measure, as adopted in June 1969, merely expressed "the sense of the Senate" that the commitment of troops abroad should result only from affirmative and explicit joint action by the President and Congress. Finally, in December 1970, Congress included repeal of the Tonkin Gulf Resolution as a rider to the Foreign Military Sales Act, which President RICHARD M. NIXON [3] signed in January 1971.

By this time, Nixon and his backers had accepted the argument of the Johnson administration that the resolution was constitutionally unnecessary—but with a twist. Whatever the constitutional basis for the war under Johnson, as Assistant Attorney General WILLIAM H. REHNQUIST [3,I] explained after the Cambodian "incursion" in April 1970, Nixon inherited a conflict in progress and had "an obligation as commander-in-chief to take what steps he deems necessary to assure the safety of American forces in the field."

Such claims did not prevent senators of both parties and growing numbers of House Democrats from proposing limits on the war. Between late 1969 and mid-1973, ten restrictive measures became law. One barred use of combat troops in Thailand and Laos; another forbade further expenditures for ground operations in Cambodia. Still another, an amendment to a defense procurement act, stated that United States policy was to cease all military operations "at a date certain," but when Nixon signed the act, he denied that the policy declaration had "binding effect." In actuality, prior to the Vietnam cease-fire in January 1973, congressional "doves" were unable to pass ironclad restrictions.

Finally, after the Vietnam cease-fire, but while air attacks on Cambodia continued, Congress voted that no funds "may be expended to support directly or indirectly combat activities in, over, or from off the shores of Cambodia, or in or over Laos by United States forces." When Nixon vetoed the appropriations bill containing the cutoff and its supporters threatened to add similar language to all appropriations measures, a compromise emerged, signed by Nixon on July 1. The Second Supplemental Appropriations Act for 1973 forbade use of any funds in the act itself for military operations in Indochina and added that "after August 15, 1973, no other funds heretofore appropriated under any other Act may be expended for such purpose."

Doubtful of congressional action, opponents of the war had already turned to the judiciary in efforts to enjoin Johnson's warmaking and then Nixon's. Here the need for STANDING [4] proved an initial barrier. At one time or another, federal district courts and courts of appeal held that taxpayers, citizens qua citizens, reservists, draft registrants, inductees, members of Congress, and probably states lacked the required immediate and concrete stake in the controversy. In some later cases, however, the barrier was relaxed, particularly for servicemen under orders to go to Vietnam, and in a few instances, courts finessed the problem of standing by first examining other issues.

Ultimately the POLITICAL QUESTION [3,I] doctrine proved insuperable. In *Orlando v. Laird* (1971), for example, lower federal courts held that once a conflict reached the magnitude and duration of the war in Vietnam, the Constitution imposed the duty of some joint action by the President and Congress. This requirement established a manageable test that allowed judicial determination without running up against the political questions doctrine. The courts found, however, that the Tonkin Gulf Resolution, wartime extension of the SELECTIVE SERVCE ACT [4], and continuing appropriations satisfied the joint-action requirement. The issue raised by the decision of Congress and the President to use these means for collaboration rather than a DECLARATION OF WAR [2] *was* a nonjusticiable political question. In *Mitchell v. Laird* (1973), which arose after repeal of the Gulf of Tonkin Resolution, a court of appeals went further, declaring that it could "not be unmindful of what every schoolboy knows"—that appropriations and draft extensions did not necessarily indicate congressional approval of the war. Yet the court would not substitute its judgment for the President's regarding the appropriate military means for concluding the conflict.

The closest the federal judiciary came to blocking American involvement in Indochina occurred after the Vietnam cease-fire itself. In *Holtzman v. Schlesinger* (1973) a member of Congress and three Air Force officers sought to enjoin further bombing of Cambodia. Federal District Judge Orin Judd in New York found that all existing legislative authorization for operations anywhere in Indochina had ceased with the end of the war in Vietnam. Moreover, as Judd interpreted it, the compromise specifying a funding cutoff on August 15 conferred no new authority. Accordingly, on July 25, 1973, he ordered the secretary of defense to stop the bombing, but the United States Court of Appeals for the Second Circuit promptly stayed his order. Lawyers for the plaintiffs next asked THURGOOD MARSHALL [3,I], the circuit's Justice on the Supreme Court, to vacate the stay, and when he declined, they tracked down Justice WILLIAM O. DOUGLAS [2], then vacationing in Washington State. Douglas issued the necessary order, but at the request of the government, Marshall polled the full Court by telephone and proceeded to reinstitute the stay.

On August 8 the court of appeals reversed Judd, holding that the relation of the continued bombing to implementation of the peace agreement did constitute a political question. In OBITER DICTA [3], it opined further that Judd had incorrectly interpreted the compromise on the funding cutoff and had erred in granting standing to Congresswoman Elizabeth Holtzman and the Air Force officers. The court's reliance in *Holtzman* on the political questions doctrine was consistent with the sweeping recognition of the doctrine in *Atlee v. Laird* (1972), the only lower court decision involving the constitutionality of the war that the Supreme Court affirmed (although without opinion) rather than sidestep by denying CERTIORARI [1].

Three years earlier, Congress had begun to consider general war-powers legislation. By 1973 the House had passed a version imposing strict consulting and reporting requirements on the President, whereas the Senate's bill sought to define precisely the circumstances in which the President could use force without congressional authorization. In October 1973 both houses acccepted a compromise measure. Its detailed mandatory sections stressed requirements for consultation and reporting and provided that if the President did not receive congressional approval within sixty days of committing forces to hostilities or situations of imminent hostilities, he had to withdraw them. (The President had another thirty days for withdrawal if he certified that the safety of the troops required the additional period.) Claiming the War Powers Resolution infringed on the constitutional authority of the President, Nixon vetoed it, but Congress overrode the veto. A clear legacy of the Indochina War, the law triggered ongoing debate in subsequent years regarding its constitutionality, wisdom, and effectiveness.

Throughout the war CIVIL LIBERTIES [1] issues arose. Beginning in 1965–1966 growing numbers of opponents publicly demonstrated against American participation and its escalation and mounted focused protests against recruiting, the draft, and even military training. Ensuing criminal prosecutions (which war resisters often invited) included well-publicized and sometimes chaotic conspiracy trials that swept in prominent antiwar figures like pediatrician Benjamin Spock (of the "Boston Five") and social activist Tom Hayden (of the "Chicago Eight"). In addition, federal and some local agencies responded with domestic intelligence operations involving both surveillance and use of agents provocateurs. In part, the prosecutions and intelligence activities reflected the firm belief of both Johnson and Nixon that the domestic protest movement had connections to communism abroad.

In contrast to its largely hands-off approach to issues of external warmaking, the judiciary supported the antiwar position in key cases. Where juries convicted war resisters, appellate courts often proved receptive to FIRST AMENDMENT [2] arguments and procedural challenges. In COHEN V. CALIFORNIA (1971) [1], for example, the United States Supreme Court held that the words "Fuck the Draft" sewn on a jacket fell within the limits of protected expression. In UNITED STATES V. SEEGER (1965) [4] and *Welsh v. United States* (1970) the Court in effect rewrote the Selective Service Act in order to broaden permissible grounds for conscientious objection. *Oestereich v. Selective Service Board* (1968) and *Breen v. Selective Service Board* (1970) disallowed use of selective service reclassification as a means of punishing opposition to the draft. But UNITED STATES V. O'BRIEN (1968) [3] upheld legislation outlawing draft card destruction. In NEW YORK TIMES

v. UNITED STATES (1971) [3], although the Court allowed publication of the so-called Pentagon Papers, a majority of Justices eschewed an absolutist position, revealing instead an openness to some forms of censorship. And in LAIRD V. TATUM (1972) [3] an attempt to stop the United States Army's domestic surveillance program failed when the Court found that the plaintiffs had suffered no personal injury.

Overall, the Vietnam War significantly broadened the range of constitutional debate in America. Although hardly an unambiguous example of executive warmaking, the war helped stigmatize further accretions to an "imperial presidency." Although not blocked by the judiciary, it drew judges partway into defining the external warmaking authority. And although far from the only source of domestic unrest and reaction in the 1960s and early 1970s, the conflict triggered a wide enough spectrum of opposition to give renewed respectability to dissent.

CHARLES A. LOFGREN

(SEE ALSO: *Congress and Foreign Policy* [I]; *Congressional War Powers* [I]; *Executive Power* [I]; *Executive Prerogative* [I]; *Foreign Affairs* [I]; *Senate and Foreign Policy* [I]; *War, Foreign Affairs, and the Constitution* [4].)

Bibliography

BANNAN, JOHN F. and BANNAN, ROSEMARY S.   1974   *Law, Morality and Vietnam: The Peace Militants and the Courts.* Bloomington: Indiana University Press.

GIBBONS, WILLIAM C.   1986–1989   *The U.S. Government and the Vietnam War: Executive and Legislative Roles and Relationships*, 3 vols., series in progress. Princeton: Princeton University Press.

KEYNES, EDWARD   1982   *Undeclared War: The Twilight Zone of Constitutional Power.* Chaps. 5–7. University Park: Pennsylvania State University Press.

STRUM, PHILIPPA   1976   The Supreme Court and the Vietnamese War. In Richard A. Falk, ed., *The Vietnam War and International Law: The Concluding Phase.* Vol. 4, pages 535–572. Princeton, N.J.: Princeton University Press.

VISAS

Although the Constitution does not directly mention the power to control and regulate IMMIGRATION [2,I], the Supreme Court, in CHAE CHAN PING V. UNITED STATES (1889) [1], held that immigration control was an implied power inherent in national sovereignty. The Court has subsequently held that Congress has virtual plenary power to regulate or condition immigration and NATURALIZATION [3], and can admit noncitizens to the United States, regulate their presence within the country, and expel, deport,

or exclude them. Congress may also accord resident ALIENS [1] and citizens different treatment, but because aliens are persons within the meaning of the Fifth Amendment protection of persons, they are entitled to some PROCEDURAL DUE PROCESS [3,I] rights. With that exception, the regulation of immigration and other admission of aliens to the United States is a matter of statutory law.

Congress, through various immigration and naturalization statutes, has created an elaborate system and set of rules and procedures governing the admission of foreigners to the United States and regulating their stay within the country. American law, like the law in other countries, requires most persons seeking to enter the United States to obtain visas from United States consular offices abroad. A visa is an official document indicating that the party to whom it was issued appears to qualify for legal entry into the United States in accordance with the immigration laws. As aliens enter the United States for many varied reasons (e.g., to transit, to visit, to study, to work, to conduct business, to join a relative, to become a resident), the visa also designates the purpose or type of entry. The latter factor governs the length of stay and the alien's lawful activities while in the United States. A visa is consequently a preliminary determination of admissibility, a designation of entry category, and a permission to apply for admission at the border. The issuance of a visa, while necessary, does not guarantee admission into the United States, for immigration officers, disagreeing with a consul's determination, may refuse to admit persons with valid visas. Such refusals occur infrequently, however, and in most cases a visa is tantamount to a permission to enter.

There are two broad classes of visas: immigrant visas, issued to those seeking permanent admission into the United States, and nonimmigrant visas, issued to those seeking only temporary admission for business or pleasure. The United States limits the number of those who may seek permanent admission, with the exception of immediate relatives of citizens—defined as spouses, children under twenty-one, and parents of American citizens over twenty-one. A complicated system of seven preferences sets priorities among immigration seekers according to statutory criteria of desirability. For example, this scheme assigns the first preference among immigration applicants to adult unmarried sons and daughters of American citizens. The statute assigns twenty percent of the total number of available immigrant visas to this category. Consequently, in passing on immigrant visa applications, consular officers must prefer unmarried sons and daughters over other applicants for up to twenty percent of immigrant visas.

There are thirty-two statutory grounds for denying immigrant visa applications, including ill health, homosexuality, poverty, criminal convictions, insanity, narcotic addiction, entry for purposes of prostitution, subversive affiliations, and participation in Nazi persecution.

Many classes of persons are eligible for nonimmigrant visas, including visitors for business or pleasure, foreign officials and international representatives, intracompany transferees, exchange visitors, students, temporary workers and trainees, transit aliens, treaty traders and investors, foreign media representatives, fiancés or fiancées of U.S. citizens, and spouses and children of persons in some of these categories. Each class has its own type of visa, and entry periods and other restrictions depend on the type of visa issued.

As the consular decision whether to issue a visa depends on factual determinations and judgments, consuls exercise considerable discretion. Because the immigration statutes do not provide for JUDICIAL REVIEW [3,I] of visa denials, the issue arises whether the Constitution, at least in some cases, requires such review. In *Kleindienst v. Mandel* (1972) the American government excluded a Belgian Marxist seeking to enter the United States to attend lectures. Asserting a FIRST AMENDMENT [2,I] right to receive information and ideas, persons who wished to hear, speak, and debate with Mandel claimed that the Constitution required the government to waive his excludability—in effect to issue him a nonimmigrant visa. Relying on Congress's plenary power over the admission of aliens, the Supreme Court held that the First Amendment did not override the ostensibly legitimate exclusion. Lower courts have read *Mandel* to preclude judicial review of consular visa denials. Consequently, short of administrative relief or statutory change, applicants denied visas have no remedy and cannot gain admission to the United States.

GARY GOODPASTER

Bibliography
GORDON, CHARLES and ROSENFIELD, HARRY 1959 *Immigration Law and Procedure.* Albany N.Y.: Banks Publishing Co.

VOUCHERS

Widespread discontent with public schools has precipitated demands that parents be given some choice about which school their children will attend. Several states have adopted laws affording parents some choice among public schools in their area. These laws have attracted few constitutional attacks. Many people argue that choice plans should be broadened to offer parents government vouchers redeemable at any accredited school, public or private, including religious, or parochial, schools. Supporters of this approach cite as a model the GI Bill, under which the federal government pays certain expenses of military veterans to attend any accredited college.

Proponents contend that vouchers will produce better education, especially for poor and minority students who often fare poorly in public schools. They cite the superior performance of private-school students. They also believe that public schools would be shaken out of the complacency induced by their monopoly on state funding and prodded to do better by competition from private schools. Further, proponents want parents to be able to choose for their children an education consistent with their values, whether religiously based or not. Opponents of vouchers deny that private schools generally provide a better education; they ascribe any superior performance to private schools' "skimming the cream" by taking better students. They also question whether public schools would benefit from increased competition. They feel that vouchers would lead to further skimming of the cream, leaving public schools to handle the most difficult students.

Critics further assert that voucher plans would be unconstitutional. They fear that vouchers would exacerbate racial segregation in violation of EQUAL PROTECTION [2,I] as interpreted in BROWN V. BOARD OF EDUCATION (1954, 1955) [1]. They also argue that vouchers redeemed at parochial schools would constitute GOVERNMENT AID TO RELIGIOUS INSTITUTIONS [2,I] and an unconstitutional ESTABLISHMENT OF RELIGION [2].

Defenders respond that vouchers would not worsen school segregation, which is already widespread, but that if they did, this effect would result from individual choices, not from STATE ACTION [4,I], which is necessary to invoke the FOURTEENTH AMENDMENT [2,I]. Moreover, segregative effects could be avoided by requiring participating schools to meet certain standards of racial composition in admissions procedures. Defenders also deny that vouchers would establish religion. Pointing again to the GI Bill, they see vouchers merely giving parents a choice in obtaining a service that the government subsidizes for secular reasons; any benefit to religious institutions is incidental and thus of no constitutional concern. Critics reply that even an indirect benefit is an unlawful establishment.

No state has yet adopted a true voucher program, although a few have proposed limited programs for low-income children. Confused and conflicting Supreme Court pronouncements on aid to religious schools preclude any prediction of how the Court would handle the issue. Quite possibly, vouchers could be upheld for the same reasons that the GI Bill is considered constitutional, especially if steps were taken to avoid racial segregation. Some kind of voucher program might even be necessary to accommodate children with religious objections to what is taught in public schools.

GEORGE W. DENT

(SEE ALSO: *Establishment Clause* [I]; *Religion in Public Schools* [3,I]; *Religious Fundamentalism* [I].)

Bibliography

NOWAK, JOHN E. 1976 The Supreme Court, the Religion Clauses, and the Nationalization of Education. *Northwestern University Law Review* 70:883–909.

WAR POWERS
(Update)

The phrase "war powers" does not appear in the Constitution. By the mid-1980s a complex of specific grants in the document nonetheless provided the federal government broad authority to protect national security through military action abroad and domestic mobilization. Court decisions and practice had established that when Congress and the President acted in concert, hardly any barriers existed, except on those rare occasions involving violations of the BILL OF RIGHTS [1]. Executive action lacking congressional endorsement had proved more debatable, although less litigated. Courts had not effectively challenged presidential ventures abroad, nor had Congress itself institutionally challenged the President, save when the VIETNAM WAR [4,I] was nearly over.

In the late 1980s little changed. Because of the absence of foreign conflicts sufficient to require domestic mobilization and controls, existing case law pertaining to the home front in wartime remained undisturbed, encapsulated in an earlier era. Indeed, this situation seemed likely to continue, because by the end of the decade shifts within the former "Communist bloc" significantly lessened the chance that the nation would again see massive domestic build-ups like those of WORLD WAR I [I] and WORLD WAR II [I]. (Reserve call-ups during the American confrontation and war with Iraq in 1990–1991 proved, however, that lesser mobilizations could still occur.)

Even the JAPANESE AMERICAN CASES [3] sat untouched. To be sure, Congress offered its tardy amends

for the World War II relocation program, providing modest compensation for surviving internees; and with an assist from academic researchers who uncovered evidentiary deficiencies and procedural irregularities in the wartime prosecutions, the original federal trial courts used the old writ of error *coram nobis* to vacate the convictions of Gordon Hirabayashi, Fred Korematsu, and Minoru Yasui. But the major Supreme Court decisions from 1943 and 1944 now served amazingly as authority for viewing race as a SUSPECT CLASSIFICATION [4].

Abroad, presidential war making continued. Following his popular intervention in Grenada in 1983 and his more controversial use of marines in Lebanon during the same period (which Congress finally authorized), President RONALD REAGAN [3,I] sent naval forces to the Persian Gulf in 1987–1988 to protect oil shipments during the Iran-Iraq War. In December 1989 his successor, GEORGE BUSH [I], committed troops to combat in Panama, after failing to dislodge Panamanian dictator Manuel Noriega by other means. Then, beginning in August 1990, Iraq's invasion and occupation of Kuwait triggered an escalating response by Bush that recalled memories of both the KOREAN WAR [3] and the VIETNAM WAR [4,I]. Both Presidents skirted the reporting requirements of the 1973 War Powers Resolution. By late 1990 some twenty-one instances of presidential war making had arguably fallen under the coverage of the law since its passage, but in only one (during GERALD R. FORD's [2] tenure) had a President explicitly reported to Congress that he had sent forces into hostilities or situations of imminent hostility.

The Panamanian episode typified the practice. Bush informed Congress, but stated that his report was "consistent with" the War Powers Resolution, not pursuant to it. In particular, he carefully avoided mention of section 4(a)(1), the provision defining the commitment of forces that triggers the law's requirement for troop withdrawal after sixty days unless Congress authorizes continuation. The military operations, Bush said, "were ordered pursuant to my constitutional authority with respect to the conduct of foreign relations and as Commander in Chief."

Such actions did not go entirely unchallenged. After Reagan ordered naval forces to the Persian Gulf, just as in 1982 after he sent military advisers into El Salvador, individual members of Congress asked the federal District Court for the District of Columbia to enjoin the President to file the report required to start the War Powers Resolution's sixty-day "clock." In *Lowry v. Reagan* (D.D.C. 1987) the court declined, invoking the D.C. Circuit's doctrine of "remedial discretion" by finding that the members' dispute was not with the President, but with their legislative colleagues who refused to pass legislation starting the clock. The court added that the POLITICAL QUESTIONS [3,I] doctrine also barred the suit in its present form, because a court injunction could endanger diplomatic initiatives through multiple pronouncements on a sensitive matter.

The demonstrated ineffectiveness of the War Powers Resolution in turn led to proposals to amend it. This step became more urgent because most authorities viewed IMMIGRATION AND NATURALIZATION SERVICE V. CHADHA (1983) [2] as invalidating the law's provision for use of a CONCURRENT RESOLUTION [1] to terminate a military action prior to the sixty-day deadline. Suggested changes included tightening key definitions within the law, substituting joint resolutions for concurrent resolutions as the disallowance mechanism, specifying which members of Congress the President was to consult under the act's consultation requirement, eliminating the sixty-day limit on the use of force without congressional approval, and granting individual members of Congress standing in court challenges under the War Powers Resolution. By mid-1991, none of the proposals had passed.

These disputes, along with covert arms-for-hostages deals in the Middle East and support for the Contra rebels in Nicaragua, produced renewed debate over the constitutional locus of the external war-making power. Defenders of presidential initiatives predictably trotted out arguments for inherent EXECUTIVE POWER [I] that dated back to ALEXANDER HAMILTON's [2] "Pacificus" essays in 1793 and had received apparent endorsement in UNITED STATES V. CURTISS-WRIGHT EXPORT CORP. (1936) [2]. Critics again quickly pointed out the egregious historical errors in such defenses. Talk of an "imperial Congress" also missed the point, they argued, because the constitutional framework contemplated congressional control of

foreign commitments and policy decisions relating to military force. In December 1990, while the Iraqi crisis heightened, U.S. District Judge Harold H. Greene agreed in *Dellums v. Bush* (D.D.C. 1990) that the Constitution gives Congress authority over offensive warfare. At the same time, relying on the doctrine of RIPENESS [3], he declined to enjoin President Bush from acting without congressional authorization. Although denying he needed it before ordering an attack on Iraq, Bush requested congressional approval anyway in January 1991, and received it with votes of 52–47 in the Senate and 250–183 in the House of Representatives.

Overall, neither side clearly prevailed in the recurring constitutional disputes over warmaking. The subject remained largely within the "zone of twilight" identified during the Korean War by Justice ROBERT H. JACKSON [3] in YOUNGSTOWN SHEET & TUBE CO. V. SAWYER (1952) [4].

CHARLES A. LOFGREN

(SEE ALSO: *Congress and Foreign Policy* [I]; *Congressional War Powers* [I]; *Foreign Affairs and the Constitution* [2]; *Senate and Foreign Policy* [I]; *War, Foreign Affairs, and the Constitution* [4].)

Bibliography

ELY, JOHN HART 1988 Suppose Congress Wanted a War Powers Act That Worked. *Columbia Law Review* 88:1379–1431.

HENKIN, LOUIS et al. 1989 The Constitution in Its Third Century: Foreign Affairs. *American Journal of International Law* 83:713–900. Symposium Issue.

WORMUTH, FRANCIS D. and FIRMAGE, EDWIN B. 1989 *To Chain the Dog of War: The War Power of Congress in History and Law*, 2nd ed. Urbana: University of Illinois Press.

WASHINGTON v. HARPER
110 S.Ct. 1028   (1990)

A Washington state prison policy authorized the treatment of a prisoner with antipsychotic drugs against his or her will, provided that the prisoner be (1) mentally ill, and (2) either gravely disabled or likely to do serious harm to others. These two findings were to be made by a committee consisting of a psychiatrist, a psychologist, and an official of the institution in which mentally ill prisoners were held. The state supreme court held that this procedure, which lacked fully adversarial procedural guarantees such as those available in a court proceeding, denied a mentally ill prisoner PROCEDURAL DUE PROCESS OF LAW [3,I]. The Supreme Court reversed, 6–3.

Justice ANTHONY M. KENNEDY [I] wrote for the Court. The prisoner had a "liberty interest" in being free from arbitrary administration of a psychotropic drug; however, the procedure provided by the state was sufficient to satisfy the demands of due process. A court in a single proceeding cannot adequately evaluate the intentions or likely behavior of a medically ill person; such an evaluation requires ongoing observation of the kind available to the members of the committee given responsibility for the decisions here. The risks of an antipsychotic drug are mainly medical risks, which can best be evaluated by professionals. Although the state's policy does not allow representation by counsel, it does provide for a lay adviser who understands the psychiatric issues; this assistance is sufficient to satisfy due process.

Justice JOHN PAUL STEVENS [4,I] wrote for the dissenters. In his view, the state policy violated both SUBSTANTIVE DUE PROCESS [4,I] and procedural due process. In support of the first objection, he argued that the policy authorized invasion of the prisoner's liberty not only for his own medical interest but also to maintain order in the institution. The second objection was that, considering the seriousness of the invasion of the prisoner's liberty interest, the committee was insufficiently independent of the institution's administration to satisfy the requirements of a fair hearing.

KENNETH L. KARST

WEBSTER v. REPRODUCTIVE HEALTH SERVICES
492 U.S.   (1989)

The *Webster* case had been advertised as the one in which the Supreme Court might overrule ROE V. WADE (1973) [3], but in the event the decision offered only minor adjustments at the margins of the constitutional doctrine governing a woman's right to have an ABORTION [1,I]. The decision's political consequences, however, were anything but minor.

From the time of the *Roe* decision, Missouri has produced a steady stream of legislation designed to restrict women who seek abortions and the doctors who attend them. In this case the Court considered several provisions of a 1986 Missouri law: (1) the preamble, containing the legislature's "findings" that human life begins at conception and that "unborn children have protectable interests in life, health, and well-being"; (2) a prohibition on the use of public facilities or employees to perform abortions; (3) a prohibition against public funding of abortion counseling; and (4) a requirement that a doctor conduct a fetal viability test before performing an abortion. Chief Justice WILLIAM H. REHNQUIST [3,I] wrote for the Court.

The Court refused to pass on the preamble, saying

that, for all the Justices knew, the "findings" had no effect beyond the expression of the legislature's value judgment. The Court upheld the prohibition on using public facilities or public employees in performing abortions, reaffirming the holdings of MAHER V. ROE (1977) [3] and HARRIS V. MCRAE (1980) [2] that the state has no constitutional duty to provide assistance to women who cannot afford abortions. The controversy over the prohibition on using public money for abortion counseling was dismissed for MOOTNESS [3] because the plaintiffs agreed that this part of law did not affect them.

On the validity of the viability-testing provision there was no OPINION OF THE COURT [3]. Chief Justice Rehnquist, for three Justices, interpreted this requirement to conflict with the analysis in *Roe v. Wade* and concluded that, to the extent of the conflict, *Roe* must give way. The testing requirement might make abortions more costly, but it "permissibly further[ed] the State's interest in protecting potential human life" and was constitutional. Justice SANDRA DAY O'CONNOR [3,I] agreed that the testing requirement was valid, but thought it was consistent with the Court's prior decisions. She thus resisted the invitation to address the question of *Roe*'s continuing force and reaffirmed her earlier position that a law should not be invalidated unless it "unduly burdens" the right to seek an abortion. Justice ANTONIN SCALIA [I], concurring in upholding the testing requirement, agreed with the dissenters that the Chief Justice's opinion on this issue would effectively overrule *Roe*. He thought, however, that the Court should perform its overruling of *Roe* more explicitly and criticized the majority for failing to do so. In an especially scornful footnote, he rejected Justice O'Connor's position and lectured her on the vocabulary of "viability."

Justice HARRY A. BLACKMUN [1,I], for three Justices, dissented, strongly reaffirming the correctness of *Roe v. Wade* and its successor decisions. He saw the Chief Justice's opinion on Missouri's requirement of viability testing as, in effect, calling for *Roe* to be overruled and added his gloomy prediction of a piecemeal process of overruling "until sometime, a new regime of old dissenters and new appointees will declare what the plurality intends: that *Roe* is no longer good law."

The most important result of *Webster* was political: the mobilization of nationwide support for reproductive freedom. In the year following *Webster*, forty-four legislatures met, and about two-thirds of them considered proposals to restrict abortions; only four adopted restrictions. If *Roe* was a catalyst for the "prolife" movement, *Webster* was a catalyst for the "prochoice" movement. Governors, legislators, and even the President seemed to recognize that two strong views now demanded a hearing.

KENNETH L. KARST

WELFARE PROGRAMS

See: Entitlements [I]

WELFARE RIGHTS

Is there a constitutional right of indigent people to basic survival assistance from the state? The current Supreme Court says no, but there is a strong argument that a future Supreme Court should recognize a positive constitutional right to basic subsistence.

The current Court's view was essentially settled in DAN-DRIDGE V. WILLIAMS (1971) [2], when the Court ruled that a state law setting a maximum grant of WELFARE BENEFITS [4] to any one family, regardless of family size, was to be categorized as ECONOMIC REGULATION [2]. On this assumption the law should be upheld if it were supported by a RATIONAL BASIS [3], which the Court found to be present.

For a decade and a half prior to that time, the Court had tantalized scholars and advocates with a series of holdings requiring provision of transcripts to indigent criminal defendants in GRIFFIN V. ILLINOIS (1956) [2], outlawing the POLL TAX [3] because of its impact in barring indigent people from voting in HARPER V. VIRGINIA STATE BOARD OF ELECTIONS (1966) [3], mandating a face-to-face hearing before welfare benefits could be terminated in GOLDBERG V. KELLY (1970) [2], and invalidating durational RESIDENCE REQUIREMENTS [3] for welfare in SHAPIRO V. THOMPSON (1969) [4].

These opinions suggested there was something particularly unacceptable or vulnerable about indigence that required special treatment of indigent people by the state. Some welfare advocates thought the Court might strike down America's patchwork income-maintenance system, in which there was no statutory obligation to help two-parent families and states could set payment levels as they chose.

Dandridge was the Court's response, followed as the decade wore on by declarations, in *Lindsey v. Normet* (1972), that there is no constitutional right to any minimum level of housing and, in MAHER V. ROE (1977) [3], that there is no right to any minimum level of health care.

Yet a kernel of doctrine remains to support the notion of a right to subsistence help. Indigence does require the state to take steps it would not otherwise have to take, at least when some other liberty or property interest is also at stake. The state, for example, has no obligation to provide a transcript to the rich, and it can impose durational residential requirements or differential fees for nonresidents applicable to a number of state benefits. But when indigence is involved, the liberty or property interests concerned become vital enough to require a different response from the state.

The Court's handling of public education provides a particularly important clue. In SAN ANTONIO INDEPEN-DENT SCHOOL DISTRICT V. RODRIQUEZ (1973) [4], the Court, while upholding Texas's system of school finance, noted that a refusal to provide public education altogether would present a different case, a point it reiterated in *Papasan v. Allain* (1986). Considering that the wealthy can purchase education for their children, these references imply some obligation to provide education for those who cannot afford it. One argument supporting such a claim is that it is difficult to exercise one's political rights effectively without education. The same commonsense argument applies more generally to the status of indigence. Lack of food and shelter impedes political participation, among other things. Insofar as families with children are involved, indigence interferes gravely with the liberty interest in family relations recognized in MEYER V. NE-BRASKA (1923) [3]. The door left open in *Rodriguez* has important implications.

If the state has a special obligation to protect some liberty and property interests when indigence is also present, it is arguable that there is an analogous liberty interest in not being indigent. Because indigence in an extreme form represents a threat to life itself, it is arguable that the state has an obligation to provide basic subsistence.

The Supreme Court has been reluctant throughout American history to declare any positive constitutional rights—rights creating affirmative obligations for the state to act, even though it has committed no legal wrong. Nonetheless, an alternative stream of doctrine, more muted and episodic, has permitted the Court to impose on the states affirmative obligations to act. For example, the Court's strained efforts to find state action in SHELLEY V. KRAEMER (1948) [4] and MARSH V. ALABAMA (1946) [3] might be characterized as imposing constitutional obligations on states to intervene to nullify unacceptable private arrangements or outcomes of private activities. The claim of a right to a subsistence, or "survival," income can well be said to rest on a similar state obligation to intervene to alter unacceptable market outcomes and vindicate individual liberty interests.

The argument for a right to subsistence does not need to rest solely on the idea of a positive right. For the nonelderly the current welfare system, in terms of cash and cash-equivalent assistance, consists primarily of Aid to Families with Dependent Children (AFDC) and food stamps. Because the states set payment levels for AFDC benefits, combined payment levels under the two programs vary from less than half the poverty level up to a point near the poverty level ($9,435 for a family of three in 1988). The states do not seek to justify this variation by reference to any regional difference in the cost of living—or, indeed, by reference to any other factor. The median state's benefits approximate two-thirds of the poverty-level income. In other words, in half the states welfare assistance brings a family with children up to less than two-thirds of what the government itself says is required to achieve a bare minimum standard of living. No substantial cash or cash-equivalent federal assistance other than food stamps is available to nondisabled nonelderly individuals or to couples without children.

It is not excessive to argue that this system lacks a rational basis. If any degree of heightened scrutiny were attached to legislation affecting the indigent, it is hard to see how the current welfare system could be justified in the face of an EQUAL PROTECTION [2,I] challenge. Surely the current Supreme Court would not respond positively to these arguments. Yet similar arguments might be taken seriously by Justices of the future.

PETER B. EDELMAN

(SEE ALSO: *Economic Equal Protection* [I]; *Economic Freedom* [I]; *Welfare State and the Constitution* [I].)

Bibliography

BLACK, CHARLES L., JR. 1985 Further Reflections on the Consitutional Justice of Livelihood. *Columbia Law Review* 86:1103–1117.
EDELMAN, PETER B. 1987 The Next Century of Our Constitution: Rethinking Our Duty to the Poor. *Hastings Law Journal* 39:1–61.

WELFARE STATE

The United States Constitution, unlike many constitutions in the world, does not mandate WELFARE RIGHTS [I]. For example, the Soviet Constitution of 1977 provided for "guaranteed work, health protection, [and] education." In contrast, our Constitution guarantees FREEDOM OF SPEECH [2,I], FREEDOM OF THE PRESS, [2,I], and VOTING RIGHTS [4] that cannot be denied because of race or sex. The people can then use the right to vote and the right of free speech and other such rights to persuade legislators to enact laws providing for welfare rights such as WORKERS' COMPENSATION [4], public education, aid to dependent children, Social Security benefits, medicare, and so forth. The United States Constitution, in short, guarantees democracy, and with democracy the people can choose to have as much or as little of a welfare state as they wish.

Such is the modern view of the American Constitution, but it was not always so. To understand the modern view we must first look briefly at the historical background. Toward the end of the last century and during the first part of this century until President FRANKLIN D. ROOSE-

VELT's [3] 1937 Court-packing plan, the Supreme Court was antagonistic toward the early efforts of the state and federal governments leading to the modern welfare state. The Court, often over biting dissents, invalidated efforts to enact a progressive federal income tax, minimum-wage legislation, maximum-hour laws, child labor laws, and so forth.

Justice OLIVER WENDELL HOLMES, JR. [2], was one who dissented from the Court's efforts (through the use of the DUE PROCESS [2] clause, a belief in "liberty of contract," and a narrow interpretation of federal commerce powers) to limit the power of the government to engage in social welfare legislation. Holmes's dissent in LOCHNER V. NEW YORK (1905) [3] objected to the majority's decision invalidating a state law setting sixty hours as the maximum workweek for bakers. "The liberty of the citizen to do as he likes so long as he does not interfere with the liberty of others to do the same, which has been a shibboleth for some well-known writers, is interfered with by school laws, by the Post Office, by every state or municipal institution which takes his money for purposes thought desirable, whether he likes it or not. The Fourteenth Amendment does not enact Mr. Herbert Spencer's Social Statics." Later, in ADKINS V. CHILDREN'S HOSPITAL (1923) [1], when the Court invalidated a federal law setting minimum wages for women and children in the DISTRICT OF COLUMBIA [2], Holmes said in dissent, "Pretty much all law consists in forbidding men to do some things that they want to do, and contract is no more exempt from law than other acts."

Within five years of Holmes's leaving the Court (after FDR's Court-packing plan of 1937 failed), the Court effectively overruled more than a quarter-century of opinions and recognized the power of the state and federal governments to engage in a wide range of activities that promoted various aspects of a modern welfare state. Although the constitutional power of government to provide welfare benefits does not constitutionally obligate it to do so, the Constitution does place important limits on the government's discretion.

The Constitution assures that once the state grants welfare rights, those benefits are not distributed in a way that violates substantive guarantees. For example, there is no constitutional requirement that a state enact legislation providing public housing for poor people. However, the Fourteenth Amendment forbids the state, once it has provided for public housing, to pass out such benefits in a way that violates the EQUAL PROTECTION OF THE LAW [2,I]. Thus, if a state builds public housing, it cannot then exclude poor people who are black, for to do so would constitute RACIAL DISCRIMINATION [3,I] in violation of the equal protection clause. Similarly, if the state provides for medical services as part of its welfare program, the state cannot deny those medical services to Democrats or Socialists, because that would unconstitutionally deprive someone of a governmental benefit because of that person's beliefs, in violation of the FIRST AMENDMENT [2,1] as applied to the states through the INCORPORATION DOCTRINE [2].

Implied constitutional rights, like explicit ones, limit the states when they distribute welfare benefits. For example, the Constitution does not explicitly grant a RIGHT TO TRAVEL [3] within the United States, and yet the right certainly exists. As Justice POTTER J. STEWART [4] noted in UNITED STATES V. GUEST (1966) [2], although the right to travel "finds no explicit mention in the Constitution," the explanation may be that "a right so elementary was conceived from the beginning to be a necessary concomitant of the stronger Union the Constitution created. In any event, freedom to travel throughout the United States has long been recognized as a basic right under the Constitution."

Thus, in EDWARDS V. CALIFORNIA (1941) [2] the Court invalidated, under the commerce clause, a California statute that made it a misdemeanor to assist in bringing into that state any indigent person who was not already a resident of California and was known to be an indigent. The Court rejected the state's argument that the migration of poor persons brought severe health and financial problems to the state. The concurring opinion of Justice ROBERT H. JACKSON [3] noted that " 'indigence' itself is neither a source of rights nor a basis for denying them." Otherwise, the heritage of our constitutional privileges and immunities "is only a promise to the ear to be broken to the hope, a teasing illusion like a munificent bequest in a pauper's will."

Later, in SHAPIRO V. THOMPSON (1969) [4], the Court invalidated several state statutes and a District of Columbia statute that denied welfare benefits to persons who had not resided within the jurisdiction for at least one year. The Court struck these durational RESIDENCE REQUIREMENTS [3] because the state laws violated the equal protection clause of the Fourteenth Amendment and because the law of the District of Columbia (which is not governed by the Fourteenth Amendment because it is not a state) violated the equal protection component that has been found within the due process clause of the Fifth Amendment (which restricts the federal government).

The Court argued that the effect of the residence requirements was to deter the entry of indigents into jurisdictions with durational residence requirements, thus burdening the indigents' right to interstate travel. Because this right to travel is "fundamental," the Court would invalidate the statutory classification unless the state could show that it was "necessary to promote a *compelling* gov-

ernmental interest" (emphasis in original). The majority rejected the argument that the durational residence requirement was necessary to deter indigents who migrated solely to obtain another jurisdiction's more favorable welfare benefits, holding that no state has the right to exclude poor persons from its borders. Nor may a state distinguish between new and old residents when that distinction burdens the fundamental right to travel. The states (and the District of Columbia), said the Court, may not create subclasses of citizens based on the length of time that persons have been residents. The states, in short, may require that indigents be residents of the state at the time they apply for welfare benefits, but the states may not impose durational residence requirements.

Similarly, in *Memorial Hospital v. Maricopa County* (1974) the Court invalidated an Arizona statute requiring a one-year durational residence in a county as a condition for receiving nonemergency medical care at the county's expense. The Court said that medical care, like welfare assistance, is "a basic necessity of life"; hence, the case was governed by *Shapiro v. Thompson*.

However, in *Starns v. Malkerson* (1971) the Court upheld a University of Minnesota regulation providing that no student could qualify as a resident for purposes of lower in-state tuition unless the student had been a resident of Minnesota for a year. College tuition, unlike food, clothing, or shelter, is not one of the basic necessities of life.

In HARPER V. VIRGINIA STATE BOARD OF ELECTIONS (1966) [2] the Court invalidated a Virginia law conditioning voting on payment of an annual POLL TAX [3] of $1.50. Voting, said the Court, is a FUNDAMENTAL RIGHT [2] preservative of our other rights, and hence, a state violates the equal protection clause whenever it makes the affluence of the voter or payment of any fee a requirement for voting. The state has the power to fix qualifications for voting, such as requiring residence and voting registration. But "wealth, like race, creed, or color, is not germane to one's ability to participate intelligently in the electoral process."

The Court has also held that indigents must be granted equal access to various aspects of the criminal process that are basic to the fair determination of their guilt or innocence. Once the state has fulfilled this duty by giving indigents the opportunity for a FAIR TRIAL [2] and access to the initial appellate process, there is no requirement that the state go further and level all economic distinctions by continuing to provide free counsel throughout successive appeals and collateral attacks.

These cases illustrate an important aspect of Supreme Court jurisprudence involving welfare rights and the Constitution. When the Court reviews certain classifications under the equal protection clause—for example, a classification based on race or color—the Court treats the classification as "suspect" and unlikely to be approved unless the state can demonstrate that the SUSPECT CLASSIFICATION [4] is necessary to promote a COMPELLING STATE INTEREST [1]. Thus, in cases like BROWN V. BOARD OF EDUCATION OF TOPEKA (1954) [1], the Court invalidated state laws requiring school SEGREGATION [4] according to race. Similarly, the Court engages in active review under the equal protection clause of state laws that classify "fundamental" rights (like the right to travel or the right to vote) on the basis of poverty.

Modern Supreme Court Justices have concluded that where suspect classes or fundamental rights are not at issue there is nothing in the Constitution that authorizes judges to decide economic policy regarding the allocation of income and wealth through the review of legislative classifications. Poverty, unlike race, is not a suspect classification. And there is no fundamental constitutional right to be free of poverty. As a general matter, the state constitutionally may engage in legislative classifications that pass out benefits or burdens in ways that disadvantage poorer people so long as the law has a RATIONAL BASIS [3]. Thus, a state may enact a progressive income tax, even though such a law requires richer persons to pay a greater percentage of their income to the states than poorer persons. Or a state may enact a sales tax on food, although such a regressive tax requires poorer persons to pay a greater percentage of their income to the states than do richer persons.

For example, the Court rejected the challenge to the welfare law involved in DANDRIDGE V. WILLIAMS (1970) [2]. In that case, the Court upheld state legislation that set a maximum amount for welfare aid to any one family; the law, in effect, offered lessened benefits for children born to families over a certain size. The appellees in that case argued that the law violated the equal protection clause by discriminating against them because of their larger families. The majority rejected the claim: "In the area of economics and social welfare, a State does not violate the Equal Protection Clause merely because the classifications made by its laws are imperfect. If the classification has some 'reasonable basis,' it does not offend the Constitution simply because the classification 'is not made with mathematical nicety or because in practice it results in some inequality.'" There is a fundamental right to travel; there is no fundamental right to welfare.

Similarly, although a woman may have a constitutional right to an ABORTION [1,I] under certain circumstances, it is constitutional for the state to deny state funding for medically necessary abortions, even when it is providing funds for childbirth. The state need not provide affirmative assistance to a poor woman to procure an abortion any more than the state must provide subsidized airfare to protect an indigent's right to travel.

SAN ANTONIO INDEPENDENT SCHOOL DISTRICT V. RODRIGUEZ (1973) [4] upheld the constitutionality of a state property tax system that financed primary and secondary education in such a way as to create different districts with large variations in the amount of money spent on the education of children, depending on where the children lived. Some districts were much richer than others, with the poorer districts having much less taxable wealth subject to the property tax. The majority found nothing in the allocation of education opportunities based on district wealth that furnished a constitutional justification for active and close judicial supervision of the legislative policy. The Court emphasized that it had never adopted an active standard of review solely because the law burdened poor persons in the allocation of benefits, unless those benefits were deemed to be fundamental constitutional rights.

However, in a footnote to the majority opinion in *Rodriguez*, Justice LEWIS F. POWELL [3,I] suggested that if a state set up an educational system that absolutely deprived poor children of the opportunity for any education, legislative choice might raise problems under the equal protection clause: "If elementary and secondary education were made available by the State only to those able to pay a tuition assessed against each pupil, there would be a clearly defined class of 'poor' people—definable in terms of their inability to pay the prescribed sum—who would be absolutely precluded from receiving an education. That case would present a far more compelling set of circumstances for judicial assistance than the case before us today."

In short, the issue in fundamental rights cases is whether the statute in question limits the fundamental right in a way that violates the Constitution, and not whether the statute is fair or unfair to poor people. In fact, the law in question may be unconstitutional, even though it seeks to level wealth distinctions in the exercise of the fundamental right rather than to create wealth distinctions. In BUCKLEY V. VALEO (1976) [1], for example, the Court invalidated limits on campaign spending by candidates for public office as an unconstitutional burden on the fundamental right to free speech, guaranteed by the First Amendment. Although Congress designed the legislation in part to equalize the ability to run for office between persons of differing wealth, the Court found no interest of a sufficiently compelling magnitude to justify the limitation on free speech rights.

In addition to these substantive guarantees, the Constitution also provides procedural protections for persons entitled to welfare benefits under state or federal law. The due process clause of the Fourteenth Amendment forbids a state to deprive any person of life, liberty, or property without due process of law. The Fifth Amendment similarly restricts the federal government. Since 1970, the Supreme Court has recognized that government welfare benefits may constitute statutory ENTITLE-MENTS [I], a new type of "property" that the government may not take away without offering basic procedural protections.

In GOLDBERG V. KELLY (1970) [2] the Court held that a state could not constitutionally terminate public assistance payments for a recipient without affording her the opportunity for an evidentiary hearing prior to the termination. As the Court later explained in BOARD OF REGENTS V. ROTH (1972) [I]:

To have a property interest in a benefit, a person clearly must have more than an abstract need or desire for it. . . . He must have a legitimate claim of entitlement to it. It is a purpose of the ancient institution of property to protect those claims upon which people rely in their daily lives, reliance that must not be arbitrarily undermined. It is a purpose of the constitutional right to a hearing to provide an opportunity for a person to vindicate those claims.

Property interests, of course, are not created by the Constitution. Rather, they are created and their dimensions are defined by existing rules or understandings that secure certain benefits and that support claims of entitlements to those benefits. Thus, the welfare recipients in *Goldberg v. Kelly* had a claim of entitlement to welfare benefits that was grounded in the statute defining eligibility for them.

Government need not offer welfare or other such benefits to its citizens. But once government decides to offer such benefits and establishes standards that define when a person is eligible, the government has created an entitlement and cannot arbitrarily deny those benefits. It must provide PROCEDURAL DUE PROCESS [3,I]. The government may provide benefits in cash, such as social security benefits or farm subsidies; it may offer benefits in kind, such as free housing in a publicly-owned building; it may offer benefits in hybrid forms, such as food stamps, which can only be redeemed for particular items. In all cases, once the government establishes such benefits as entitlements, the government can withdraw them from particular individuals only after it offers procedural protections such as fair notice and an opportunity to be heard.

The U.S. Constitution does not demand a welfare state. Yet the Constitution is flexible and adaptable enough to allow it. The Constitution guarantees that if the state does provide for welfare protection, the state's largess will be subject to various substantive and procedural limitations.

RONALD D. ROTUNDA

(SEE ALSO: *Campaign Finance* [1,I]; *Economic Due Process* [I]; *Economic Equal Protection* [I]; *Economic Regulation* [2]; *Poverty Law and the Constitution* [I]; *Substantive Due Process of Law* [4,I].)

Bibliography

NOWAK, JOHN E. and ROTUNDA, RONALD D.   1991   *Constitutional Law,* 4th ed. St. Paul, Minn.: West Publishing Co.

REICH, CHARLES   1964   The New Property. *Yale Law Journal* 73:733–787.

ROTUNDA, RONALD D.; NOWAK, JOHN E.; and YOUNG, J. NELSON   1986   *Treatise on Constitutional Law: Substance and Procedure.* 3 vols., St. Paul, Minn.: West Publishing Co.

VAN ALYSTYNE, WILLIAM   1968   The Demise of the Right-Privilege Distinction in Constitutional Law. *Harvard Law Review* 81:1439–1464.

WINTER, RALPH   1972   Poverty, Economic Equality, and the Equal Protection Clause. *Supreme Court Review* 1972:41–102.

WHIG PARTY

The Whig party emerged as a coalition of politicians opposed to ANDREW JACKSON [3] and Jacksonian Democracy. Some prominent Whigs, like DANIEL WEBSTER [4], traced their political roots to the old FEDERALIST [I] party, while others, like HENRY CLAY [1], had been Jeffersonian Democrats. Most had also been National Republicans and, as such, supported the presidencies of JAMES MONROE [3] and JOHN QUINCY ADAMS [1]. When the Anti-Masonic party collapsed, most of its members became Whigs. Some extreme STATES' RIGHTS [4] southerners briefly affiliated with the Whigs in reaction to Jackson's heavy-handed response to South Carolina in the NULLIFICATION [3] controversy. A few Democrats joined the Whigs because they disagreed with Jackson over the BANK OF THE UNITED STATES [1] or because they were disillusioned with Old Hickory's successor, MARTIN VAN BUREN [4]. In the 1850s the Whig party collapsed. Most northern Whigs joined the REPUBLICAN PARTY [I], while southern Whigs became Know-Nothings or Democrats.

Whigs favored high tariffs, federally funded INTERNAL IMPROVEMENTS [2], a national banking system, a relatively weak presidency, and deference to Supreme Court rulings on constitutional questions. In 1832 the Young Men's National Republican Convention, which nominated Henry Clay for President, resolved "that the Supreme Court of the United States is the only tribunal recognized by the constitution for deciding, in the last resort, all questions arising under the constitution and laws of the United States, and that, upon the preservation of the authority and jurisdiction of that court inviolate, depends the existence of the Union."

The Whig party avoided taking any position on SLAVERY [4], seeking northern compromise on the issue in return for southern support for northern economic interests. Northern Whigs, like Daniel Webster, ABRAHAM LINCOLN [3], and WILLIAM H. SEWARD [4], opposed slavery with differing degrees of passion. In the 1830s some Whig congressmen, led by John Quincy Adams and Joshua Giddings, fought for the right to petition Congress on slavery. Adams viewed this as a constitutional right guaranteed by the petition clause of the FIRST AMENDMENT [2,I]. However, when Whigs controlled Congress and the White House in the early 1840s, they, too, adopted gag rules to prevent the reading of abolitionist petitions. Southern Whigs supported slavery, but they never supported southern extremists. Indeed, southern Whigs opposed states' rights, southern nationalism, and SECESSION [4]; however, in 1861 southern ex-Whigs, like ALEXANDER STEPHENS [4], ROBERT TOOMBS [4], and Judah P. Benjamin, became confederate leaders.

Whigs from both sections opposed the ANNEXATION OF TEXAS [1], the Mexican War, and other aggressions of Manifest Destiny. During the Mexican War they argued that President JAMES K. POLK [3] had exceeded his constitutional authority by sending troops into southern Texas and Mexico to provoke war.

The Whigs won only two presidential elections. General WILLIAM HENRY HARRISON [2], elected in 1840, died a month after taking office and was succeeded by JOHN TYLER [4], a former states' rights Democrat who had little sympathy for many Whig positions. Under Tyler the Whigs passed a major but short-lived BANKRUPTCY [1] law and a higher tariff. President Tyler vetoed two Whig-sponsored bills to reestablish a national banking system.

In 1848 the Whigs captured the White House with another war hero, General ZACHARY TAYLOR [4], by avoiding taking a stand on any major issues. Whigs generally supported the COMPROMISE OF 1850 [1], which was passed as individual pieces of legislation and signed into law by the deceased Taylor's vice-president, MILLARD FILLMORE [2], a moderate Whig from New York. By 1852, however, the party was deeply divided over the compromise and slavery in general. After 1850 the Whig party collapsed in the South, as southerners abandoned the party that appeared to be dominated by staunch antislavery men such as Senator William Seward of New York. After 1854 most northern Whigs also abandoned the party, either for the nativist American (Know-Nothing) party or the Republican party.

Constitutionally the Whigs stood for a strong Union and federal intervention in the economy. Whigs argued for a broad reading of federal power under the COMMERCE CLAUSE [1,I] and an expansive JUDICIAL POWER [3]. Although neither was appointed by a Whig President, Justices JOSEPH STORY [3] and JOHN MCLEAN [3] came to symbolize Whig views of the Constitution. The greatest symbol of the party's constitutional position was not, however, a judge, but the attorney and politician Daniel Webster.

Even before the Whig party was formed, Webster presented "Whig-like" arguments in the DARTMOUTH COLLEGE V. WOODWARD (1819) and GIBBONS V. OGDEN (1824) [2], in which he argued for a strict interpretation of the CONTRACT CLAUSE [2] and a reading of the Constitution that gave Congress exclusive jurisdiction over INTERSTATE COMMERCE [2]. He made similar arguments in GROVES V. SLAUGHTER (1841) [2], the LICENSE CASES (1847) [3], and the PASSENGER CASES (1849) [3]. The bedrock of Whig constitutional nationalism was best stated by Webster's 1830 reply to Senator ROBERT YOUNG HAYNE's [2] argument in favor of nullification and Webster's speech supporting the Compromise of 1850. In answering Hayne, Webster declared, "I go for the Constitution as it is, and for the Union as it is." Webster argued, "It is, sir, the people's Constitution, the people's government, made for the people, made by the people, and answerable to the people." He concluded with the ringing plea for "Liberty *and* Union, now and for ever, one and inseparable." In his March 7, 1850, speech Webster supported the compromise measures, declaring, "I wish to speak today, not as a Massachusetts man, nor as a Northern man, but as an American, and a member of the Senate of the United States." He told his colleagues, "I speak today for the preservation of the Union." These measures, introduced by the Whig Clay and supported by Webster, symbolize the constitutional principles of the Whigs—support for the Union and compromise above all else—and the reason for their collapse. By the mid-1850s, compromise based on blind fidelity to the Union was no longer possible in a nation torn by sectional strife and about to go to war over slavery. Significantly, perhaps, the last Whig President, Millard Fillmore, opposed secession but also opposed all of Lincoln's policies to stop secession. By this time, however, the supporters of Whig nationalism and CONSTITUTIONALISM [2] had followed such Whigs as Seward and Lincoln into the Republican party.

PAUL FINKELMAN

Bibliography

BARTLETT, IRVING H. 1978 *Daniel Webster*. New York: Norton.

McCORMICK, RICHARD P. 1966 *The Second American Party System*. Chapel Hill: University of North Carolina Press.

VAN DEUSEN, GLYNDON G. 1973 The Whig Party. In Arthur M. Schlesinger, Jr., ed., *History of U.S. Political Parties*. Vol. 1, pages 332–493. New York: Chelsea House.

WHITE, BYRON R.
(Update)

When he was appointed to the Supreme Court in 1962, Byron White, at the age of forty-four, was a symbol of the vigor, youth, and intellectual power of the JOHN F. KENNEDY [3] administration. From a poor rural background, he had ranked first in the class of 1938 at the University of Colorado, becoming a football All-American and winning a Rhodes Scholarship. By the time he graduated from Yale Law School in 1946, he had briefly studied at Oxford, played two seasons of professional football, served as a naval intelligence officer in the Pacific, and twice encountered John Kennedy (once at Oxford, once in the Pacific). After clerking for Chief Justice FRED M. VINSON [4], White joined a law practice in Denver where he remained for fourteen years. When Kennedy won the Democratic nomination for President in 1960, White chaired the nationwide volunteer group Citizens for Kennedy. His service as deputy attorney general under ROBERT KENNEDY [3,I] included screening candidates for judicial appointments and supervising federal marshals protecting workers in the CIVIL RIGHTS MOVEMENT [I] in the South. He had been at the job only fourteen months when the President nominated him to fill the vacancy created by the resignation of CHARLES WHITTAKER [4].

During his nearly thirty years on the Court, White has generally reflected the commitments of the President who appointed him: to equal opportunity, to effective law enforcement, and to enablement of government as it responds to new challenges—with less concern for individual rights, group rights, and STATES' RIGHTS [4]. To the distress of those who would prefer greater elaboration of a philosophical vision, he has approached the judicial task in a lawyerly and pragmatic fashion, although sometimes in excessively cryptic opinions. His independence and analytic bent of mind have often isolated him from more ideological colleagues. As he has served with twenty other Justices during times of great ferment on the Court, his role has changed considerably. He was in the majority in fewer than half of the 5–4 decisions during the 1960s, in more than sixty percent of the 5–4 decisions during the 1970s, and in nearly three-fourths of the 5–4 decisions during the 1980s—more frequently than any other Justice during that decade. Although profound changes in American society (often shaped by the Court itself) have significantly affected the issues before him and, to a lesser extent, his resolution of particular issues, a review of his work on the Court reveals significant consistency in perspective, method, and conviction.

White knows that judges make law. His time at Yale Law School was the heyday of that school's celebration of LEGAL REALISM [3]. As he explained in dissent in MIRANDA V. ARIZONA (1966) [3], "[T]he Court has not discovered or found the law in making today's decision; what it has done is to make new law and new public policy in much the same way that it has in the course of interpreting other great clauses of the Constitution. . . . [I]t is wholly legitimate . . . to inquire into the advisability of its end product in terms of the long-range interest of the country."

White also understands that the triumph of the administrative state, marked especially by an affirmative and vigorous federal government, has forever altered the shape of American political institutions, including the Court. For White, however, neither legal realism nor expanding concepts of national political authority and responsibility justify the exercise of "raw judicial power." A recurring theme of his opinions is that the judiciary undermines its own legitimacy when it seeks to achieve political objectives not sanctioned by the other branches of government or when it promotes social transformation resisted by the democratic institutions of society.

White's confidence in the good faith and capabilities of democratic institutions—Congress especially, but also the executive, state legislatures, and juries—exceeds that of other justices of the "left" or of the "right." For White, the powers of government are limited neither by abstract conceptions of individual autonomy, nor by any extrademocratic mandate for perfection in human affairs. Rather, government power is limited by the very forces that legitimate it: the people acting through fair and free elections and a Constitution that both authorizes and specifically checks government actors.

In the spirit of the NEW DEAL [I] and of President Kennedy, White gives great weight to securing and preserving federal authority, especially Congress's authority. Where Congress has legislated (or federal agencies have acted pursuant to delegated power), he is disposed to find federal PREEMPTION [3] of state law. Where Congress has not legislated, he gives wide berth to the DORMANT COMMERCE CLAUSE [2]. Where states seek to regulate federal entities, he is disposed to place limits on state power. He does not view the TENTH AMENDMENT [4] as a limitation on Congress's regulatory power; he would permit Congress to abrogate state SOVEREIGN IMMUNITY [4] under the ELEVENTH AMENDMENT [2,I]; and he recognizes significant legislative power to implement the FOURTEENTH AMENDMENT [2,I]. Where Congress has delegated interpretative authority to ADMINISTRATIVE AGENCIES [I], he is strongly disposed to defer to agency interpretations of statutes. In many ways, he has been the preeminent nationalist on the Court in the modern era. For instance, White was the only dissenter to the Court's 1978 decision upholding the multistate tax compact, which had not been approved by

Congress, because of its *"potential* encroachment on federal supremacy."

White's understanding of the SEPARATION OF POWERS [4] in our national government, as set forth in a series of powerful dissents, is similarly rooted in his recognition that Congress needs latitude to solve economic problems and to reallocate governance authorities in response to the growing demands on national institutions in the post–New Deal era. Thus, he urged in BUCKLEY V. VALEO (1976) [1] that "Congress was entitled to determine that personal wealth ought to play a less important role in political campaigns than it has in the past." He lamented in NORTHERN PIPELINE CO. V. MARATHON PIPE LINE CO. (1982) [3] that "at this point in the history of constitutional law" the Court should not have "looked[ed] only to the constitutional text" to determine Congress's power "to create adjudicatory institutions designed to carry out federal policy." He explained in IMMIGRATION NATURALIZATION SERVICE V. CHADHA (1983) [2] that the LEGISLATIVE VETO [3] "is an indispensable political invention that . . . assures the accountability of independent regulatory agencies and preserves Congress' control on lawmaking." And the budget-balancing legislation of BOWSHER V. SYNAR (1986) [1] was "one of the most novel and far reaching legislative responses to a national crisis since the New Deal."

White conceives of a more limited role for the federal courts, not to supplement or second-guess Congress's policies, but to ensure their implementation by state and federal actors. His concurrence in *Chapman v. Houston Welfare Rights Organization* (1979)—urging that in the CIVIL RIGHTS [1,I] legislation of the RECONSTRUCTION [I] Congress had provided a remedy for denial not only of constitutional rights but also of rights created by federal statutes—was subsequently adopted by a majority of the Court. White would also more narrowly construe EXECUTIVE IMMUNITY [2] than would a majority of his colleagues. He is less willing than many others on the Court, however, to infer a private cause of action to enforce federal rights where Congress has lodged responsibility for enforcement with a federal agency or has provided for administrative remedies. Nor is he uniformly activist on issues of POLITICAL QUESTION [3,I], STANDING [4], and other prudential limitations on JUDICIAL REVIEW [3,I]. Although he has sometimes resisted efforts to restrict HABEAS CORPUS [2,I] jurisdiction, he has joined in limiting the bases on which habeas review may upset a criminal conviction.

To achieve consistency in CONSTITUTIONAL INTERPRETATION [1], White has taken an expansive view of the Supreme Court's JURISDICTION [3] over state court decisions. Moreover, often dissenting from denial of CERTIORARI [1], he has regularly urged the Court to use its discretionary jurisdiction to review apparent inconsistencies in the lower courts. His longstanding extrajudicial campaign for creation of a national court of appeals or similar structure to ensure uniformity in federal law may finally have run its course in view of the reduction in the Supreme Court's workload in recent terms.

White's clear sense of the primacy of democratic institutions is reflected in his commitment to the protection of rights to participate in the electoral process. From AVERY V. MIDLAND COUNTY (1968) [1] to *Board of Estimate of the City of New York v. Morris* (1989), he has led the Court in expansively interpreting the principle of ONE PERSON, ONE VOTE [3] to subject varieties of political apportionment and GERRYMANDERING [2] to judicial review, even as he has taken a relatively permissive and pragmatic approach to apportionment disparities. His dissent in MOBILE V. BOLDEN (1980) [3] effectively became the majority position two terms later in ROGERS V. LODGE (1982) [3], which eased the burden of minority challenges to electoral districting schemes that perpetuate purposeful RACIAL DISCRIMINATION [3,I]. As indicated in *Buckley* and subsequent cases, White would go further than other Justices in permitting Congress to regulate the electoral processes to root out potential corruption and inequality, even at the cost of some inhibition of free speech.

More generally, his FIRST AMENDMENT [2,I] jurisprudence permits significant intrusions on the media, whether in the form of the FAIRNESS DOCTRINE [2] as in RED LION BROADCASTING CO. V. F.C.C. (1969) [3]; SEARCH WARRANTS [4], as in ZURCHER V. STANFORD DAILY (1978) [4]; SUBPOENAS [4], as in BRANZBURG V. HAYES (1972) [1]; or LIBEL [3] law, as in HERBERT V. LANDO (1979) [2] and his dissent in GERTZ V. ROBERT WELCH, INC. (1974) [2]. White is likewise deferential toward regulation and prosecution of OBSCENITY [3], CHILD PORNOGRAPHY [I], and SUBVERSIVE ADVOCACY [4]. He has been a leading opponent of a strict, separatist conception of the ESTABLISHMENT OF RELIGION [2] and would, for instance, permit state aid for secular activities in parochial schools.

Although White gives broad scope to LEGISLATIVE POWER [3], he has usually subjected the legislative product to close scrutiny for invidious purpose or for insufficient relationship to a legitimate purpose. For a time, White's purpose analysis produced a more activist Fourteenth Amendment jurisprudence than the majority of the Court was willing to embrace; for example, he argued in dissent in PALMER V. THOMPSON (1971) [3] that a Mississippi town should not be permitted to close its swimming pool where its purpose was to prevent implementation of a DESEGREGATION [2] order. White's scrutiny of purpose is decidedly nonactivist, however, in the face of minority challenges to government programs that have disparate racial impact without discriminatory intent. In the seminal case of WASHINGTON V. DAVIS (1976) [4], he held for a

7–2 majority that disparate impact alone does not constitute the kind of racial discrimination that presumptively violates the constitutional principle of EQUAL PROTECTION OF THE LAWS [2,I]. White has not adopted the view that the Constitution prohibits all "reverse discrimination" to counteract diffuse societal discrimination. His joint opinion in REGENTS OF UNIVERSITY OF CALIFORNIA V. BAKKE (1978) [3], permitting government to take race into account in university admissions, reflects his oft-demonstrated concern for equal educational opportunity. His votes, in FULLILOVE V. KLUTZNICK (1980) [2] and METRO BROADCASTING, INC. V. FEDERAL COMMUNICATIONS COMMISSION (1990) [I], to uphold federal minority "set-aside" and race-preference requirements underscore his deference to Congress even as he voted, in RICHMOND (CITY OF) V. J.A. CROSON CO. (1989) [I], to strike down a LOCAL GOVERNMENT'S [I] "set-aside" scheme.

For a decade after he joined the majority opinion in GRIGGS V. DUKE POWER CO. (1971) [2], White appeared content with permitting disparate impact alone to be sufficient for broad RACE-CONSCIOUS [I] remedies in EMPLOYMENT DISCRIMINATION [2] cases brought under Title VII of the CIVIL RIGHTS ACT OF 1964 [1]. In 1979, he even joined in endorsing a private employer's use of RACIAL QUOTAS [3] intended to eliminate the effects of societal discrimination. White began to express significant dissatisfaction with aspects of the prevailing Title VII jurisprudence in a series of opinions, mostly dissenting, in the mid-1980s. By the end of the decade, amid indications that the disparate-impact test invited use of racial quotas, White commanded a majority in *Wards Cove Packing Co. v. Antonio* (1989) to shift the BURDEN OF PROOF [1] in disparate-impact cases.

In school desegregation cases, however, White has been as ready as any member of the Court to find evidence of past purposeful discrimination and to approve broad remedies. His majority opinion in COLUMBUS BOARD OF EDUCATION V. PENICK (1979) [1] permitted inference of purposeful discrimination from evidence of long-past misconduct and a continued discriminatory effect, and placed the burden on the defendant school system to prove that it had not caused any current racial SECREGATION [4] in its schools. In addition, he would hold the state, not the defendant school district, ultimately responsible for removing the effects of purposeful discrimination; in this view, neither the happenstance of school-district boundaries nor state laws impeding school funding may stand in the way of remedial decrees. Thus he was in a minority in MILLIKEN V. BRADLEY (1974) [3] in arguing and a remedy of interdistrict SCHOOL BUSING [4], and he wrote the 5–4 decision in *Jenkins v. Missouri* (1990) upholding the power of the federal district court to order a defendant school board to impose tax increases in violation of fiscally restrictive state law.

One may infer several reasons for White's different stances in school desegregation cases and employment discrimination cases. Even outside the race-discrimination context, White has adopted an ethic of group equality in EDUCATION [2], as demonstrated in his dissent in SAN ANTONIO INDEPENDENT SCHOOL DISTRICT V. RODRIGUEZ (1973) [4], where he would have struck down school-financing schemes that leave the poorest school districts with the most impoverished schools. Moreover, the proof of purposeful racial discrimination by school districts is often palpable, but it is difficult to trace disparate racial impact in the job market to purposeful discrimination by a defendant employer. In addition, although busing does not deny schooling to any child, White has expressed particular unhappiness with quota systems that take jobs away from nondiscriminating white workers. Finally, judicial imposition of systems of RACIAL PREFERENCE [I] in employment would cause upheavals in collective bargaining, seniority systems, and other underpinnings of industrial society.

White's belief in the legitimacy of the law in ordering our social life, along with his confidence in the institutions of government, have made him reluctant to impose "decriminalization," either directly (by limiting legislative power to punish) or indirectly (by insisting on perfection from police, prosecutors, and others charged with achieving criminal justice). Even as he joined the holding in *Furman v. Georgia* (1972), striking down a scheme of CAPITAL PUNISHMENT [1,I] that provided no guidance for the sentencing authority, White noted the good faith of Georgia in granting discretion to sentencing juries out of a "desire to mitigate the harshness" of capital punishment laws. Subsequently, he has voted to uphold carefully structured death penalty laws, rejecting the arguments that juries "disobey or nullify their instructions" and that others who retain discretion, such as prosecutors, inevitably wield it arbitrarily. Invoking the Court's ill-famed journey earlier in this century into the realm of SUBSTANTIVE DUE PROCESS [4,I], he has refused to make the judgment that the death penalty cannot comport with the Constitution. White has, however, recognized substantive limitations on the types of crimes for which this penalty may be imposed; he wrote the Court's opinion in COKER V. GEORGIA (1977) [1], holding the death penalty disproportionate for the rape of an adult, and the Court's opinion in ENMUND V. FLORIDA (1982) [2], holding capital punishment improper where a murder conviction was based solely on a theory of felony murder.

The criteria of "reasonableness" and "good faith," at the core of much of White's JURISPRUDENCE [I], are especially prominent in his approach to the FOURTH AMEND-MENT [2,I]—which has largely become the law of the land. He has been the leading proponent of clear and simple rules governing police SEARCH AND SEIZURE [4,I]. He understands the Constitution's requirement that searches and seizures be "reasonable" to have broad applicability, if shallow in depth; he wrote the opinion in CAMARA V. MUNICIPAL COURT (1967) [1], which spawned a new jurisprudence upholding an array of regulatory searches on less than PROBABLE CAUSE [3], but he also wrote TENNESSEE V. GARNER (1985) [4], which prohibited use of deadly force against fleeing felons, and he has recognized the Fourth Amendment's applicability to subpoenas issued by GRAND JURIES [2]. His oft-stated antipathy to the EXCLUSIONARY RULE as a remedy for Fourth Amendment violations finally led to adoption of the GOOD FAITH EXCEPTION [2] to this rule in *United States v. Leon* (1984). White has likewise taken a functional and pragmatic approach to the Sixth Amendment's right to TRIAL BY JURY [4]. He has resisted efforts to limit criminal investigations and forfeitures through broad application of the RIGHT TO COUNSEL [3]; he has dissented from interpretations of the Fifth Amendment RIGHT AGAINST SELF-INCRIMINATION [3,I] that depart from historical practice and impede reliable administration of justice; and he has been at the forefront of the Court in permitting great leeway in PLEA BARGAINING [3], as in *Brady v. United States* (1970).

White's opinions on CRIMINAL PROCEDURE [2] reveal not only his perspective on issues of criminal justice but also his unusual commitment to the rule of STARE DECISIS [4] in constitutional adjudication, which has sometimes led to the perception that he is "unpredictable." Like many Justices, White is ready to overrule previous decisions that prove unworkable or ill-advised. For instance, he joined BATSON V. KENTUCKY (1986) [1], which, overruling his own SWAIN V. ALABAMA (1965) [4], subjected preemptory jury challenges to judicial review for racial discrimination; *Batson* acknowledged that *Swain's* confidence in state prosecutors had not been vindicated. Yet White, more than other Justices and regardless of ideological inclination, has on most issues sought to adhere to constitutional PRECEDENT [3] not yet overruled. Thus, although he dissented forcefully in *Miranda*, he has clearly accepted the major contours of that decision. Indeed, he wrote EDWARDS V. ARIZONA (1981) [2], which went beyond the core of *Miranda* in prohibiting all questioning once the suspect in custody has requested an attorney. Similarly, despite his long, carefully composed dissent in PAYTON V. NEW YORK (1980) [3], which required an ARREST WARRANT [1] to arrest persons in their homes, White ten years later wrote the majority opinion applying *Payton* to the arrest of someone hiding out overnight in

a friend's home. Even where he would vote to overrule a precedent, White has sometimes exasperated observers by refusing to cast the fifth vote for simply narrowing the reach of the precedent, insisting he is bound until it is expressly overruled.

The most controversial decision by White upholding government power to invoke the criminal process is BOWERS V. HARDWICK (1986) [I], which refused to strike down a Georgia law forbidding consensual sodomy between men. White conceived the issue much as he had the issue in the death penalty cases: whether the Supreme Court should bypass political institutions to establish a new social order. White had long objected to the Court's discovery of new constitutional rights deriving from the concept of "privacy." His concurrence in GRISWOLD V. CONNECTICUT (1965) [2] declined to find a general RIGHT OF PRIVACY [3,I], emphasizing instead the lack of a rational relationship between the statute's ban on distributing BIRTH CONTROL [1] information to married persons and the purported purpose of the statute. ROE V. WADE (1973) [3], the decision establishing a broad right to ABORTION [1] throughout pregnancy, evoked a response reminiscent of his *Miranda* dissent: "The Court simply fashions and announces a new constitutional right . . . with scarcely any reason or authority." In dissents in subsequent privacy rights cases during the 1970s and early 1980s, including MOORE V. CITY OF EAST CLEVELAND (1977) [3], which struck down a ZONING [4,I] ordinance that narrowly defined "single family," White even more explicitly compared the Court's "new" substantive due process with the efforts of the Court in LOCHNER V. NEW YORK (1905) [3] to impose its will on a divided polity. By 1986, in THORNBURGH V. AMERICAN COLLEGE OF OBSTETRICIANS AND GYNECOLOGISTS [I], he advocated overruling *Roe*, urging that the right it recognized was neither "implicit in the concept of ordered liberty," nor "deeply rooted in the nation's history and traditions." For White, *Bowers* was a replay of *Thornburgh*, with the important difference that he was writing the majority opinion. As White must have anticipated, once the majority had adopted his approach to enunciation of a FUNDAMENTAL RIGHT [2], it was only a matter of time before *Roe* itself would begin to collapse, as indeed it did in WEBSTER V. REPRODUCTIVE HEALTH SERVICES (1989) [I].

Yet White himself had recognized certain fundamental liberty interests that may be subsumed under the label substantive due process—including, in *Griswold*, "the right to be free of regulation of the intimacies of the marriage relationship" and, in a long series of cases (continuing even after *Bowers*) dealing with ILLEGITIMACY [2], the rights of natural parents "in the companionship . . . of their children." White's purpose-based jurisprudence might have considered proscriptions of sodomy as different from anti-abortion laws. In the latter, the organized community may have the purpose of protecting human life, whereas in the former, its motiviation may simply be antipathy towards homosexuals—a purpose that could be recognized (but that White in 1986 declined to recognize) as invidious. Here as elsewhere, White's jurisprudence seldom puts the Court ahead of the country. For him, the Court's primary role in constitutional lawmaking is not to pioneer or even to lead, but rather to secure for the whole nation the democratic consensus that has already been reached.

KATE STITH

Bibliography
HUTTON, MARY CHRISTINE   1986   The Unique Perspective of Justice White: Separation of Powers, Standing and Section 1983 Cases. *Administrative Law Review* 40:377–414.
LIEBMAN, LANCE   1987   Justice White and Affirmative Action. *University of Colorado Law Review* 58:471–496.
NELSON, WILLIAM E.   1987   Deference and the Limits to Deference in the Constitutional Jurisprudence of Justice Byron R. White. *University of Colorado Law Review* 58:347–364.
O'DONNELL, PIERCE   1987   Common Sense and the Constitution: Justice White and the Egalitarian Ideal. *University of Colorado Law Review* 58:433–470.
STUDENT NOTE   1987   The Intercircuit Tribunal and Perceived Conflicts: An Analysis of Justice White's Dissents from Denial of Certiorari During the 1985 Term. *New York University Law Review* 62:610–650.
VARAT, JONATHAN D.   1987   Justice White and the Breadth and Allocation of Federal Authority. *University of Colorado Law Review* 58:371–428.

WITTERS v. WASHINGTON DEPARTMENT OF SERVICES FOR THE BLIND
474 U.S. 481 (1986)

Suffering from a progressive eye condition, Witters sought state financial assistance to attend a Bible college to prepare himself for a career as a minister. Washington State generally provided aid to visually handicapped persons seeking education or training for careers so they could be self-supporting. Nevertheless, the state denied Witters aid, citing the Washington State constitution's prohibition of public aid to religion. The state supreme court upheld the denial, but on ESTABLISHMENT CLAUSE [I] grounds, holding that aid to Witters would advance religion as its primary effect and thus violate the second prong of the LEMON TEST [I]. The U.S. Supreme Court unanimously reversed.

Writing the opinion of the Court, Justice THURGOOD MARSHALL [3,I] said it would be inappropriate to view the funds ultimately flowing to the Bible college in this case as the result of state action to aid religion. Marshall noted that the financial assistance "is paid directly to the student, who transmits it to the educational institution of his or her choice. Any aid provided under Washington's program that ultimately flows to religious institutions does so only as a result of the genuinely independent and private choices of aid recipients." Marshall further emphasized that the program "is in no way skewed toward religion" and "creates no financial incentive for students to undertake sectarian education." Finally, Marshall stressed that nothing indicated any significant proportion of state money provided under the program would flow to religious institutions if Witters's claim was granted.

That last reason was not dispositive for a majority of Justices, five of whom joined concurring opinions that noted the applicability of MUELLER V. ALLEN (1983) [3] to *Witters*. In *Mueller* the Court had upheld general tax deductions for certain school expenses, despite the fact that over ninety percent of these tax benefits went to those who sent their children to religious schools.

JOHN G. WEST, JR.

WOMAN SUFFRAGE

When American women voted in the election of 1920, they did so for the first time as a constitutional right protected by the NINETEENTH AMENDMENT [3]. The amendment's ratification marked the end of a long struggle that was bound up with both the shifting status of the ballot and the political development of a women's movement.

The struggle, which began formally at the women's rights convention at Seneca Falls, New York, in 1848, emerged when most states had already dropped their property qualifications for white male voters. "Resolved," averred Elizabeth Cady Stanton, "that it is the duty of the women of this country to secure to themselves the sacred right to elective franchise." Yet in the context of the mid-nineteenth century the right to elective franchise still was not a national, constitutional issue. Moreover, voting embodied so powerful a symbol of personal autonomy that granting it to women was profoundly controversial. In fact, woman suffrage, as contemporaries called it, barely won the support of the delegates at Seneca Falls.

Reconstruction transformed woman suffrage into a compelling constitutional issue. The second clause of the FOURTEENTH AMENDMENT [2,1] introduced the word "male" into the Constitution, and the FIFTEENTH AMENDMENT [2], which prohibited abridging the VOTING RIGHTS [4] of black males, was silent on the disfranchisement of females. Inasmuch as the two amendments seemed at once essential to the rights of freedmen and inimical to the cause of woman suffrage, the women's movement divided over their ratification.

The spacious terms of the first clause of the Fourteenth Amendment, however, sparked numerous challenges to women's disfranchisement. Susan B. Anthony created a dramatic test in the election of 1872 by registering and voting with fifteen other New York women, thereby violating a federal election statute, but her case did not reach the Supreme Court. The case that did was launched by Virginia Minor, who with her attorney-husband, Francis, sued the state of Missouri for restricting suffrage to males. The plaintiff's brief in MINOR V. HAPPERSETT (1875) [3] argued that women had been empowered to vote in federal elections from the inception of the Constitution, had actually voted for a time in New Jersey, and were simply reaffirmed in their right to vote by the terms of the Fourteenth Amendment. The disfranchisement of women, the brief asserted, was a BILL OF ATTAINDER [I], an infringement on FREEDOM OF SPEECH [2,1], a form of involuntary servitude, and a violation not only of DUE PROCESS [2] but of the constitutional guarantee that every state shall have a REPUBLICAN FORM OF GOVERNMENT [3]. In a unanimous decision drafted by Chief Justice MORRISON R. WAITE [4], the Court ruled that suffrage was neither protected in the original text of the Constitution nor incorporated in the PRIVILEGES AND IMMUNITIES [3] of CITIZENSHIP [1] guaranteed by the Fourteenth Amendment.

By the 1890s, the drive for suffrage had stalled, despite the unification of the two wings of the women's movement. State-by-state campaigns yielded disappointing results, and after *Minor* a constitutional amendment was needed to ensure suffrage nationwide. Headway came with the bold campaigns of the Congressional Union (later called the Woman's party), an organization founded in 1913 by Alice Paul and Lucy Burns to replicate the militant tactics of English feminists. Picketing, arrests, and hunger strikes generated attention at a time when resistance to women voting was ebbing. Giving women the vote was regarded increasingly as a way of bringing their domestic concerns into the political arena and therefore as a potential instrument of Progressive reform. The final strategy for victory came from the lobbying efforts of Carrie Chapman Catt, president of the National American Woman Suffrage Association, who not only pulled a recalcitrant WOODROW WILSON [4] into the suffrage camp but also capitalized on the temporary gratitude of the nation for the wartime service of its women.

NORMA BASCH

(SEE ALSO: *Constitutional History, 1865–1877, 1877–1901, 1901– 1921* [1]; *Feminist Theory and Constitutional Law* [I]; *Gender Rights* [I]; *Progressive Constitutional Thought* [3]; *Progressivism* [I]; *Women in Constitutional History* [I].)

Bibliography

DUBOIS, ELLEN CAROL   1987   Outgrowing the Compact of the Fathers: Equal Rights, Woman Suffrage, and the United States Constitution, 1820–1878. *Journal of American History* 74:836–862.

FLEXNOR, ELEANOR   (1959) 1968   *Century of Struggle: The Woman's Rights Movement in the United States.* Cambridge, Mass.: Harvard University Press.

WOMEN IN CONSTITUTIONAL HISTORY

At first glance, women seem missing from much of the historical landscape of the Constitution, and in the few instances where they do appear, they suffer negative consequences for their legal status. Before the Civil War sex did not even figure as a contested constitutional classification, and for a century after the war virtually every effort to eradicate its discriminatory aspects met with defeat at the hands of the Supreme Court. Indeed, until the 1970s, when the Court began to apply closer scrutiny to sex as a discriminatory category, the Constitution seems to have treated women as women with either casual indifference or zealous paternalism. Yet, on closer inspection, the role of gender in the life of the Constitution has been longer, larger, and more subtle than this first impression suggests. The constitutional status of gender, moreover, has been shaped by shifting conceptions of legal equality, the evolving relationship between the states and the federal government, and the changing circumstances in women's day-to-day lives.

FEDERALISM [2,I] goes a long way toward illuminating the constitutional role of gender in the first stage of its development. Given the sharp delineation between the appropriate rights and duties of men and women in both the life and the law of the early Republic, the original text of the Constitution, which employs terms such as "persons," is remarkably gender-neutral. The Framers could afford to be gender-neutral in their language precisely because state laws were gender-specific. The Framers were hardly indifferent, then, to gender as a legal classification; rather, federalism obviated the need to frame it in national constitutional terms.

State statutes and constitutions spelled out the exclusion of women from the political process, while COMMON LAW [1] assumptions and precedents informed their legal disabilities. The principles of coverture, which placed a married woman under the tutelage of her husband, influenced legal attitudes toward women in general. Of course, single women, unlike their married counterparts, could enter into contracts, sue, and be sued. However, the tendency of the law to define all women as wives and mothers rather than as citizens, property owners, or wage earners, or as dependent and relative rather than as independent and autonomous, was pervasive in constitutional approaches to gender. But reform efforts to define the role of women more broadly were also pervasive. They began officially in the 1840s when women's rights advocates organized to demand both legal and political equality at the state level, and these efforts have animated new conceptions of constitutional equality from the antebellum era to the present day.

After the Civil War, gender entered into formal constitutional discourse largely as a corollary of race. Although the second section of the FOURTEENTH AMENDMENT [2,I] incorporated the word "male" into the Constitution, the DUE PROCESS [2] and EQUAL PROTECTION [2,I] clauses of the first section held the potential to apply to gender as well as to race. The consequences for women were ambiguous. On the one hand, SEX DISCRIMINATION [4,I] acquired a new legitimacy as a result of constitutional tests of the RECONSTRUCTION [I] amendments; on the other hand, it became a legal issue that was suffused with constitutional import.

Nonetheless, postbellum efforts to enhance the constitutional status of women via judicial decision failed miserably. In BRADWELL V. ILLINOIS (1873) [1], the Supreme Court denied Myra Bradwell's claim that her right to practice law was among the PRIVILEGES AND IMMUNITIES [3] of citizenship protected under the Fourteenth Amendment. In MINOR V. HAPPERSETT (1875) [3], the Court denied that Missouri's restriction of suffrage to males violated the privileges and immunities of Virginia Minor's citizenship. And despite admitting Belva Lockwood to practice before its bar, the Court in In re Lockwood (1894) held that states could apply the word "person" in the Fourteenth Amendment to men only.

However, legal equality between women and men was not a consistent goal of the women's movement, and by the turn of the century, female reformers were clearly selective in their support of it. They backed special protective labor legislation for women workers not only in the hope that such legislation would be extended to all workers but also in the belief that long hours and hazardous working conditions were particularly injurious to women as potential mothers. If in hindsight their arguments seem oblivious to the constitutional risks of protecting women exclusively and to the disadvantages created for women in the labor market, in their own day they evoked a powerful appeal.

That appeal was perhaps best encapsulated in the voluminous BRANDEIS BRIEF [1], written for MULLER V. OREGON (1908) [3], a case in which the Court upheld maximum-hour laws for women and thereby exempted them from a laissez-faire commitment to the principle of FREEDOM OF CONTRACT [2]. The rationale in the brief remained popular among progressive reformers long after *Muller*. Indeed, by the 1920s the vast majority of women who had worked for women's political equality by supporting the NINETEENTH AMENDMENT [3] were against the proposed EQUAL RIGHTS AMENDMENT [2] largely because they feared its effects on special health and labor legislation for women. The Supreme Court, however, was now prepared to view women as the complete equals of men, at least with regard to their capacity to contract for wages. In ADKINS V. CHILDREN'S HOSPITAL (1923) [1], the Court undermined statutory attempts to put a floor under women's wages by invalidating a DISTRICT OF COLUMBIA MINIMUM WAGE LAW [2]. Underscoring the equality women enjoyed as a result of the Nineteenth Amendment, the *Adkins* opinion applied the principle of freedom of contract to women workers without overtly overturning *Muller*, and *Adkins* itself was not overruled until WEST COAST HOTEL CO. V. PARRISH (1938) [4].

Efforts to apply the equal protection clause to sex as a discriminatory classification met with further defeats in the post–World War II era. In GOESAERT V. CLEARY (1948) [2], for example, adjudicated at a time when men were returning to jobs that had been filled temporarily by women, the Court upheld a Michigan statute prohibiting a woman from selling or serving liquor unless she was the wife or daughter of the tavernkeeper. Equal protection, the decision averred, did not require perfect symmetry, and in *Hoyt v. Florida* (1961) the Court relied on similar reasoning to reject an effort to block sex discrimination in the jury selection process.

Yet as women entered the work force in unprecedented numbers after World War II and as the divorce rate soared, it became even harder to sustain the old legal prototype of protection and dependence. As a result of a burgeoning CIVIL RIGHTS MOVEMENT [I] and a revitalized women's movement, the analogies between sex and race as discriminatory categories came to the forefront of constitutional discourse in the 1960s, and they were applied in turn to a host of new federal CIVIL RIGHTS [1] statutes. Significant breakthroughs in the constitutional status of women came in the 1970s not only with the heightened judicial scrutiny of sex discrimination but also with the growing legitimation of REPRODUCTIVE AUTONOMY [3]. No less important symbolically was the 1981 appointment of SANDRA DAY O'CONNOR [3,I], the first woman to serve as a Justice of the Supreme Court.

The change in constitutional attitudes toward gender was heralded by *Reed v. Reed* (1971), a decision that invalidated a statutory preference for males in appointing the administrators of intestate estates on the ground of the law's inherent irrationality. Inasmuch as the state's purposes were "as well served by a gender-neutral classification as one that gender-classifies and therefore carries with it the baggage of sexual stereotypes," the Court determined that the state "cannot be permitted to classify on the basis of sex." FRONTIERO V. RICHARDSON (1973) [2], the closest the Court came to regarding sex as a suspect classification, struck down a rule that disadvantaged the dependents of servicewomen, relative to the dependents of servicemen, in calculating dependency benefits. A series of subsequent cases equalized Social Security payments, welfare benefits, and workers' compensation. *Stanton v. Stanton* (1975) ruled that girls were entitled to child support up to the same age as boys; *Orr v. Orr* (1979) held that a state law could not exempt women of means from paying alimony on the same basis as men; and CRAIG V. BOREN (1976) [2] invalidated a law that differentiated between the sexes in setting the statutory age for buying 3.2 percent beer.

Clearly the decision that most dramatically altered both the lives and the status of women in this blizzard of judicial reinterpretation was ROE V. WADE (1973) [3], which followed the rationale the Court had used in GRISWOLD V. CONNECTICUT (1965) [2] to prohibit a state ban on BIRTH CONTROL [1]. The *Roe* decision, which struck down a Texas statute defining ABORTION [1,I] as a criminal offense, did so not on the equality-based theory that it was a violation of women's rights but rather on the ground that it violated an implied constitutional RIGHT OF PRIVACY [3,I]. Nonetheless, except for the last trimester of pregnancy, the *Roe* opinion significantly subordinated the power of the state to that of a woman and her doctor.

However, ambivalence toward scrutinizing sex discrimination strictly was evident in many quarters. Even as the Court moved toward upholding equal rights for women through its reinterpretations of the equal protection clause, it never subjected its scrutiny of sex to the same rigorous standards that it applied to race, and there were some indications in the 1980s of a retreat from the stance it had taken in the 1970s. Because the issues were by no means simple, to cite rules on pregnancy leave as one example, there were radical feminists as well as conservative women who continued to support preferential or differential treatment for women. Furthermore, the right of reproductive autonomy, a hotly contested issue that right-to-life adherents elevated into a political litmus test for candidates at all levels of government, became especially vulnerable to inroads by the end of the 1980s. Finally, the political campaign for women's constitutional rights stalled on a distinct note of defeat. The failure of the EQUAL RIGHTS AMENDMENT [2] to be ratified by three-

quarters of the states after it had passed Congress meant that the Constitution still stood without a discrete provision on which to ground the eradication of the remaining sex inequalities in state law, much less to prevent new ones from emerging.

NORMA BASCH

(SEE ALSO: *Feminist Theory and Constitutional Law* [I]; *Gender Rights* [I]; *Labor and the Constitution* [3,I]; *Labor Movement* [I]; *Racial Discrimination* [3,I]; *Woman Suffrage* [I].)

Bibliography

BAER, JUDITH 1986 *The Chains of Protection: The Judicial Response to Women's Labor Legislation.* Westport, Conn.: Greenwood Press.

BERRY, MARY FRANCES 1986 *Why ERA Failed: Politics, Women's Rights, and the Amending Process of the Constitution.* Bloomington: Indiana University Press.

GINSBURG, RUTH BADER 1978 Sex Equality and the Constitution. *Tulane Law Review* 52:451–475.

WORLD WAR I

The United States entered World War I on a note of Wilsonian idealism, but the shattering experience of wartime mobilization ended the era of PROGRESSIVISM [I]. Broad federal powers, previously used to further domestic reforms, were expanded to meet the demands of international conflict. These changes accelerated the trends toward national centralization and executive authority. Thus, ironically, WOODROW WILSON [4], who had been elected on a platform of firm but limited government control, brought Leviathan to the nation.

With little in the way of precedents, Congress and the President were pressed to extend national government control to a vast new range of complex subjects. The result was multitudinous delegations of power to President Wilson, designed to allow the executive branch to develop programs to meet the changing requirements of a fluid war situation. The breadth of this legislation was startling. Acts to achieve wartime economic mobilization and efficient use of natural resources were augmented by a SELECTIVE SERVICE ACT [4] vesting the President with authority to raise an army by conscription. Espionage and sedition legislation afforded power to punish dissenting expression that might impede the war effort. The Trading with the Enemy Act gave the government power to control trade with enemy nations and to become an alien-property custodian for the duration of the war. The same measure authorized censorship of all communications by mail, cable, radio, or otherwise with foreign countries, and gave the postmaster general almost absolute censorship powers over the American foreign-language press. More sweepingly, the act empowered the chief executive to take over and operate the rail and water transportation systems of the country, along with the telegraph and telephone systems. In creating a modified executive dictatorship for the war period, these actions also raised complex constitutional questions, the answers to which reflected crisis pressures.

The LEVER FOOD AND DRUG CONTROL ACT [3] of 1917 is a case in point. One of the most important war measures, it authorized broad federal control of the domestic economy, a sphere of regulation traditionally reserved to the states. The law gave the President virtually unlimited discretionary power to license the manufacture and distribution of food and related commodities, to take over and operate mines and factories, to regulate exchanges, and to fix commodity prices. The measures precipitated a bitter debate in Congress. Critics called it a violation of the TENTH AMENDMENT [4] and thus of STATES' RIGHTS [4], but Congress enacted it on a theory of the WAR POWERS [4] and on the argument that the industries controlled were affected with a public interest. During the war, the act was not challenged in court. In *United States v. L. Cohen Grocery Co.* (1921) the Supreme Court voided the price-fixing provision, which failed to specify what constituted unjust process. By concentrating on the detailed phrasing of only one section, the Court implicitly accepted the broad grant of power. Indeed, it did not reach the issue of the government's authority to regulate prices under the war power. The Court thus recognized that the requirements of modern war left little FEDERALISM [2,1] in wartime.

Another example of expanding federal power and increased executive authority was presidential seizure and governmental operation of the nation's rail networks. As early as 1916, the Army Appropriations Act had authorized the President "in time of war . . . to take possession and assume control of any system of transportation." After Wilson took over the railroads in 1917, Congress passed the Railway Administration Act of 1918, providing for government operation of the rails and compensation of their owners. The Court upheld this executive seizure in *Northern Pacific Railway Co. v. North Dakota* (1919), Chief Justice EDWARD D. WHITE [4] invoking Congress's war powers, which, he argued, reach as far as necessary to meet the emergency. The Court also approved the government's takeover of telephone and telegraph lines in a series of cases argued with the railroad suit, notably *Dakota Central Telephone Co. v. South Dakota* (1919).

The wartime period also brought the long crusade for PROHIBITION [3] to a successful conclusion. The Lever Act, under the mandate of preserving scarce food resources, authorized the President to limit or forbid the use of foodstuffs for production of alcoholic beverages.

Beginning in December 1917, Wilson issued a series of war proclamations that in effect established near total prohibition. Congress joined in, passing the Wartime Prohibition Act in November 1918, prohibiting the manufacture or distribution of alcoholic beverages until the war came to a formal end and demobilization had been completed.

In the meantime, Congress had approved the EIGHTEENTH AMENDMENT [2], which the states ratified in January 1919, although not without an attack on the constitutionality of the amendment, the first time such action had taken place. Subsequently, a case reached the Supreme Court, *Rhode Island v. Palmer* (1920), where a large number of "wet" attorneys submitted briefs against the measure. The Constitution, they contended, had not created an unlimited amendment power, and ordinary legislation should not be made part of it. Thus, the Eighteenth Amendment had exceeded legitimate amending limits. Second, they argued that Section 2 altered traditional lines of authority by giving both Congress and the states concurrent enforcement powers, thereby undermining the federal system. The Court brushed aside these and other arguments, seeing no radical invasion of the original POLICE POWER [3] of the states.

The Overman bill came before Congress in early 1918 and provoked substantial resistance to further expansion of presidential authority. The measure was inspired by a desire to introduce some order and flexibility into the chaotic welter of wartime bureaus, commissions, and other special agencies, and to straighten out overlapping jurisdictions that were creating administrative confusion. The measure gave the President a blank check to reorganize the executive agencies "as he may deem necessary, including any functions, duties, and powers hitherto by law conferred on any executive department." The act was to remain in force until a year after the close of the war. By its terms the President could reassign any function, no matter where it had been lodged previously, even if Congress had specifically given that responsibility to a particular agency. The bill imposed no checks on presidential discretion and provided no standards for evaluating the executive's conduct.

The constitutionality of the measure elicited vigorous debate. Supporting senators argued that the bill was a necessity and that it was limited, for the President could create no new functions but merely transfer those already in existence. But critics argued that the bill could not be justified by the war power, for many departments and functions unrelated to the war might be affected by its terms. Republican Senator Frank Brandagee of Connecticut denounced the bill as an attempt to force Congress to "abdicate completely its legislative power and confer it upon the executive branch of the government." The measure passed in the SENATE [1] in late April, with the majority senators overlooking constitutional doubts. A bitter Brandagee then offered an ironic amendment, providing that "if any power, constitutional or not, has been inadvertently omitted from this bill, it is hereby granted in full." The Overman Act, like the Lever Act, demonstrated that ordinary restraints upon delegation of legislative power to the President had been shelved for the duration of the war. The Supreme Court was not afforded an opportunity to pass on the act's constitutionality.

President Wilson wisely did not exercise the tremendous authority delegated to him by this measure and previous ones. Instead, he used ordinance-making powers to establish a series of commissions, boards, bureaus, and government-owned corporations to carry on wartime functions. These agencies included the Office of Food Administration; the Office of Fuel Administration; the National War Labor Board, for handling labor disputes during the war; and other agencies to deal solely with aspects of wartime transportation. The War Industries Board had complete authority over all war purchases and eventually came to exercise almost total control over all industry.

Wilson also created, by EXECUTIVE ORDER [2], the Committee on Public Information, whose principal responsibility was to "manufacture" public sentiment favorable to measures necessary to the conduct of the war. Run by a flamboyant journalist, George Creel, the committee operated as a loosely knit, ever-changing, but always powerful organization spreading information and propagating beliefs for the American people. With no authority beyond the executive order that created it, the committee worked alongside the Food Administration, the Fuel Administration, and many other agencies, pouring out publicity and propaganda to promote the war effort. It also worked with the Post Office Department to restrict circulation of news and propaganda, in the process imposing a type of informal censorship.

The CIVIL LIBERTIES [1,I] implications of the Committee on Public Information were troubling to a number of liberal Americans, yet it faced no court challenge to its actions. Other governmental restrictions on individual freedoms, however, did elicit legal challenges. The Selective Service Act was the first. As opponents of the war questioned its constitutionality, lower courts expedited various draft cases, permitting an early test case in the Supreme Court. In the SELECTIVE DRAFT LAW CASES [4] of January 1918, a unanimous Court found the constitutional authority to impose compulsory military service in Congress's powers to declare war and to "raise and support armies." Pushing aside states' rights challenges and a charge that conscription was "involuntary servitude," forbidden by the THIRTEENTH AMENDMENT [4], the Court also shrugged off a challenge that the measure's conscientious-objection exception violated the FIRST AMENDMENT

[2,I] because it amounted to an ESTABLISHMENT OF RELIGION [2]. Thus sustained, the act was administered at the local level through "neighborhood" civilian draft boards, the government hoping thereby to create the illusion that the process was democratic and free of national control.

While conscription curtailed the freedom of those drafted, the freedom of critics of the war was constrained through other legislation. Although Congress adopted no general censorship law, it did enact two statutes limiting press and speech freedoms. The ESPIONAGE ACT [2] of 1917 drafted to "outlaw spies and subversive activites by foreign agents," drew fire from critics who complained that the measure was far too destructive to basic American liberties. Softened, the measure focused on expression that might disrupt the war effort by causing disobedience in the armed forces or by obstructing recruitment and enlistment. The Justice Department prosecuted more than 2,000 cases under the 1917 act, and a comparable number of prosecutions were brought under similar state laws. Congress's SEDITION ACT [4] amendment (1918) broadened the scope of punishable criticism, providing criminal penalties for eight offenses, coming generally under the concept of SEDITIOUS LIBEL [4], or unjustifiably criticizing the government, its officials, and its policies. Again the act was enforced broadly to silence public criticism.

Test cases on the two measures had to await the postwar period. In SCHENCK V. UNITED STATES (1919) [4], OLIVER WENDELL HOLMES, JR. [2], spoke for the Court in sustaining the Espionage Act, finding the expression of a Socialist party leader presented a CLEAR AND PRESENT DANGER [1] to recruitment. However, in ABRAMS V. UNITED STATES (1919) [1], when the Court sustained the amended Sedition Act, Holmes dissented, contending that the defendant's expression had not met that standard. The Court sustained all federal and state curtailment of unpopular expression, leaving a restrictive set of precedents to govern interpretation of the First Amendment. But criticism of this behavior and of the Palmer raids spawned a civil liberties movement, which in subsequent years became a central feature of American constitutional development.

PAUL L. MURPHY

(SEE ALSO: *Executive Power* [I]; *Executive Prerogative* [I]; *Presidential Ordinance-Making Power* [3]; *Presidential Powers* [3]; *War, Foreign Affairs, and the Constitution* [4].)

Bibliography

CUFF, ROBERT D. 1973 *The War Industries Board: Business-Government Relations During World War I.* Baltimore, Md.: Johns Hopkins University Press.

KENNEDY, DAVID M. 1980 *Over Here: The First World War and American Society.* New York: Oxford University Press.

MURPHY, PAUL L. 1979 *World War I and the Origin of Civil Liberties in the United States.* New York: Norton.

WORLD WAR II

The inherent conflict between the organizational needs of a nation at war and individual rights raised several constitutional questions during World War II. Although the Roosevelt administration showed far greater sensitivity to the protection of CIVIL LIBERTIES [1,I] than did the administration of WOODROW WILSON [4], restrictions on individual rights did take place, most notably the incarceration of thousands of Japanese American citizens.

As the nation prepared for war even before Pearl Harbor, FRANKLIN D. ROOSEVELT [3] adopted the view that the Constitution allowed the President great flexibility in meeting his obligations as COMMANDER-IN-CHIEF [1]. With Congress reluctant to act, Roosevelt expanded his foreign policy prerogatives by negotiating secret EXECUTIVE AGREEMENTS [2]. In October 1939 the United States and nineteen Latin American states established a "neutrality belt" through the Declaration of Panama. In August 1941, Roosevelt and Winston Churchill defined the war aims of the free world in the Atlantic Charter. The most famous executive agreement involved a swap of fifty over-age American destroyers in exchange for British naval bases in the Caribbean. Although conservatives attacked the President's alleged dictatorial behavior, a majority in Congress and of the American people supported the agreements.

In May 1941 the President proclaimed an "unlimited" emergency to justify various defensive measures for the western hemisphere. What this meant, and on what constitutional authority it relied, remained uncertain. Attorney General FRANK MURPHY [3] declared that "the constitutional duties of the Executive carry with them the constitutional powers necessary for their proper performance." Like ABRAHAM LINCOLN [3] and Woodrow Wilson before him, Roosevelt believed in "the adequacy of the Constitution"—that whether or not specific powers were spelled out, the Constitution granted the President and Congress sufficient authority to meet any crisis.

Roosevelt's use of executive agreements and EXECUTIVE ORDERS [2], revolutionary in themselves, masked the fact that more often than not he sought—and received—legislative authorization. The Neutrality Act of 1939, the Draft Act of 1940, the Lend-Lease Act of 1941 all gave the President broad discretion; following Pearl Harbor, Congress passed a series of measures giving the chief executive extensive powers over the economy and the government. Roosevelt not only fully utilized these powers but told the nation that he would exercise whatever authority he thought necessary for the successful prosecution of the war. At one point, Roosevelt warned that if Congress failed to repeal a portion of the 1942 Price Control Act, "I shall accept the responsibility and I will act. . . . The President has the power, under the Constitution, and under Congressional acts, to take measures necessary to avert a disaster." But, he assured the people, he would always act with due regard to the Constitution, and "when the war is won, the powers under which I act automatically revert to the people—where they belong."

Although wartime measures are often challenged in the courts, unless there is an egregious violation of a specific constitutional prohibition the courts will affirm the law or delay a decision until the end of hostilities. The Supreme Court heard several challenges to the sweeping price-fixing provisions in the Emergency Price Control Act of 1942. Although Congress had set few limitations on presidential discretion and although these delegations of authority far exceeded the scope of those struck down in SCHECHTER POULTRY CORPORATION V. UNITED STATES (1935) [4], the Court rejected all challenges to the law; the judiciary would not second-guess the executive and legislative branches on what had to be done to win the war.

The seizure of property to avert labor disputes, the freezing of wages and prices, and even executive agreements with the force of law are less troubling in wartime than restrictions placed on individual liberties. In World War I the Justice Department and the postal authorities had shown little regard for constitutional protection of dissident speech and publication. Because no pro-German or antiwar sentiment existed between 1941 and 1945 comparable to that of the earlier war, the Roosevelt administration expressed—and, for the most part, maintained—a firmer commitment to civil liberties. The wartime Justice Department, headed successively by Frank Murphy, ROBERT H. JACKSON [3], and FRANCIS BIDDLE [1], showed itself unwilling to stifle expression in the name of national unity.

Many of the worst abuses during World War I had resulted from prosecutions under state criminal laws, but the Roosevelt administration avoided a repetition of those abuses. It asserted sole federal control over internal security through the ALIEN REGISTRATION ACT [I] of 1940, and a few months later the Supreme Court affirmed federal supremacy. In HINES V. DAVIDOWITZ (1941) [2] the Court overturned a Pennsylvania alien registration statute on the ground that the federal law had preempted the field.

The administration did, however, seek to revoke the citizenship of allegedly disloyal naturalized citizens of German and Italian origin, on the supposition that current disloyal or even dissident behavior proved they had earlier secured citizenship under false pretenses. The case testing this policy happened to involve neither a Nazi nor a Fascist sympathizer but a communist. The government based its case on the claim that membership in the Communist party proved the defendant did not have the "true faith and allegiance to the United States" that citizenship demanded. The Court, by a 6–3 majority, rejected the government's claim in *Schneiderman v. United States* (1943). Although citizenship constituted a privilege granted by Congress, Justice Frank Murphy explained, once a person became a citizen he or she enjoyed all the rights guaranteed by the Constitution, especially freedom of thought and expression. This and other cases reversing denaturalization orders indicated how far the nation had moved from its anti-alien hysteria of World War I, at least in terms of freedom to express unpopular ideas.

The country did, however, deprive one group of basic constitutional rights in what has remained the greatest civil liberties stain on the Roosevelt administration's record—the incarceration of more than 110,000 men, women, and children of Japanese origin, two-thirds of them native-born American citizens, solely on the basis of race. Anti-Japanese sentiment, especially on the West Coast, long predated the war, but the attack on Pearl Harbor whipped it up to hysterical proportions. Fears of fifth-column attacks and sabotage, reinforced by Japanese military victories, led to demands that both Japanese aliens (Issei) and American citizens of Japanese ancestry (Nisei) be removed from the coastal areas and relocated inland.

On February 19, 1942, President Roosevelt signed EXECUTIVE ORDER 9066 [2] authorizing military officials to designate parts of the country as "military areas" from which any and all persons might be excluded. Roosevelt issued the order on his authority as commander-in-chief, but army lawyers feared that so slender a constitutional reed might not support evacuating large numbers of citizens solely on the basis of their race. So they asked for, and received, congressional affirmation of 9066 on March 21.

Three days later, the army declared a curfew along the coastal plain for German and Italian nationals and for all persons of Japanese ancestry. Three days after that, both Issei and Nisei were prohibited from leaving the military areas, and then on May 9, they were excluded from West Coast military zones. Japanese Americans could comply with these contradictory orders only by reporting to central depots, from which they would be transferred to relocation centers in the interior. Although families could stay together, they had to leave homes and jobs and dispose of their property within a matter of days, often sustaining severe losses in the process. Amazingly, the Japanese and Japanese Americans responded cooperatively, and a number of younger Nisei volunteered to serve in the army, where their units turned out to be among the most highly decorated in the European theater of operations.

A race-based policy of such striking dimensions could hardly avoid constitutional challenge, and within a short time the nation's High Court had placed its imprimatur on relocation. In *Hirabayashi v. United States* (1943), a native-born citizen had been arrested for failing to report to a control center and for violating the curfew. The Court, speaking through Chief Justice HARLAN F. STONE [4], unanimously affirmed the curfew as lying within the presidential WAR POWERS [4,I] as well as congressional authority. Although any RACIAL DISCRIMINATION [3,I] was "odious to a free people," the Court would not challenge the discretion of the military in its interpretation of the war powers.

Justices Murphy, WILLIAM O. DOUGLAS [2], and WILEY B. RUTLEDGE [3] entered concurring opinions that practically amounted to dissents; Murphy in particular noted the "melancholy resemblance" between American treatment of the Japanese and the incarceration of Jews in Nazi-dominated Europe. But the three reluctantly consented to what they perceived as an unconstitutional program because of the supposedly critical military situation.

The Justices heard two other relocation cases in 1944, and in both they shied away from the central question of constitutional authority for the detention of peaceful American citizens. In *Korematsu v. United States*, an American citizen, turned down for voluntary army service because of ulcers, had refused to leave the military zone. Justice HUGO L. BLACK's [1] majority opinion tried to separate the issue of exclusion from that of detention and found the war powers of Congress and the President sufficient to sustain an order excluding certain persons, for whatever reason, from designated military zones. Black rather ingenuously said that race had nothing to do with the case; Fred Korematsu had been ordered to leave the area not merely because he was Japanese, but because of military necessity. This time Justices Murphy, Jackson, and OWEN J. ROBERTS [3] entered strenuous dissents, with Roberts bluntly declaring that Korematsu had been convicted "for not submitting to imprisonment in a concentration camp."

The same day, in *Ex parte Endo*, the Court unanimously authorized a writ of HABEAS CORPUS [2,I] to free Mitsuye Endo, a citizen whose loyalty had been clearly established. Although the AMERICAN CIVIL LIBERTIES UNION [1] had hoped to make this case a challenge to the entire relocation program, Justice Douglas carefully skirted that issue. He confined his ruling to the narrow question of whether the government could detain persons whose loyalty had been confirmed. There is evidence that Douglas wanted to go further, but that even this late in the war, other members of the Court still did not feel free to challenge the relocation program.

There has been general condemnation of the relocation program and of the Court's decisions affirming it from that day forward, and the judgment of history has clearly been that the Roosevelt administration and the Court erred badly. In later years, Congress took several steps to apologize to the Japanese Americans and, at least partially, to indemnify them for their suffering and losses. Gordon Hirabayashi, Fred Korematsu, and others also succeeded in overturning their convictions on the basis of the misconduct of government attorneys in misleading the Supreme Court.

The Court also considered constitutional issues involving treason and espionage. Ever since Aaron Burr's trial (1807), the Court had held to a restricted definition of treason, from which it did not depart during World War II. It drew a sharp distinction between civilian trials for treason and military trials for espionage, in which different criteria for evidence and guilt prevailed.

The first case arose from the arrest of eight Germans put ashore from submarines with orders to sabotage American defense plants. Quickly arrested and tried by military tribunals, which sentenced six of them to death, they appealed to the Supreme Court. In *Ex parte Quirin* (1942) a unanimous Court affirmed the powers of the President to establish military commissions with appropriate jurisdiction to try such cases. Chief Justice Stone's elaborate opinion, however, also implied that even spies and prisoners of war had some rights under the Constitution; that implication had no basis in either American or English law, and the Court soon backed down. In *Ex parte Yamashita* (1946) Stone conceded that a Japanese general tried for war crimes had no constitutional rights and could appeal his conviction only to military authorities.

In two treason cases involving American citizens arising from the German saboteur incident, the Court adhered to a strict interpretation of treason, "levying War against [the United States], or in adhering to their Enemies, giving them Aid and Comfort." In CRAMER V. UNITED STATES (1945) [2], Justice Jackson held for a 5–4 Court that the overt act had to be traitorous in intent by itself, and not merely appear so because of surrounding circumstances. In HAUPT V. UNITED STATES (1947) [2], however, the Court moved away from this rigorous intent standard to sustain the conviction of the father of one of the Germans, whose activities were "steps essential to his design for treason."

The government then prosecuted other Americans who had aided the enemy during the war, such as Douglas Chandler, who had broadcast English-language programs from Berlin during the war. The Chandler case raised the issue of whether treason could take place only within the territorial limits of the United States. In *Kawakita v. United States* (1952) the Court ruled that treason encompassed activities by American citizens anywhere.

MELVIN I. UROFSKY

(SEE ALSO: *Executive Power* [I]; *Executive Prerogative* [I]; *Japanese American Cases* [3]; *Naturalization* [3]; *Stone Court* [4]; *War, Foreign Affairs, and the Constitution* [4].)

Bibliography

HURST, J. WILLARD   1971   *The Law of Treason in the United States.* Westport, Conn.: Greenwood Press.
IRONS, PETER   1983   *Justice at War.* New York: Oxford University Press.
ROSSITER, CLINTON L.   1976   *The Supreme Court and the Commander-in-Chief.* Ithaca, N.Y.: Cornell University Press.

WRIGHT, J. SKELLY
(1911–1988)

J. Skelly Wright was serving as the U.S. attorney for New Orleans when he was appointed to the Federal District Court bench by President HARRY S. TRUMAN [4] in 1948. At the time of his appointment, Wright, at thirty-seven, was the youngest judge on the federal bench. From 1956 to 1962, he presided over the DESEGREGATION [2] of the New Orleans school district, becoming in the process "the most hated man in New Orleans." Displaying real boldness, he ruled unconstitutional various state statutes adopted with the apparent goal of thwarting desegregation. In 1962, President JOHN F. KENNEDY [3] wanted to appoint Wright to the Fifth Circuit Court of Appeals (whose jurisdiction then covered much of the South). This appointment, however, was blocked by Senator Russell Long, for reasons of Louisiana politics. Instead, the President ended up appointing Wright to the District of Columbia Circuit. Wright sat on this court for twenty-five years, eventually becoming its Chief Judge.

On the D.C. Circuit, Wright proved to be a liberal activist; indeed, his career is one of the purest examples of this genre of judging. A genuinely humble man, he was distinctly gratified by a judicial position that enabled him, in his words, to "make a contribution." He was the author of a large number of noteworthy opinions, dealing with such issues as the unconscionability defense in contract law, the implied warranty of habitability in residential leases, the broad rule-making powers of the Federal Trade Commission, the impermissibility of ex parte contracts in the course of informal rule making, and the proper scope of the National Environmental Protection Act. Designated in one instance to sit as a district court judge, Wright issued an opinion that required the D.C. school system to equalize spending between schools that were de facto white and those that were black, to cure problems of teacher segregation, and to end a rigid system of student ability grouping. In its time, the Wright opinion was a leader in the development of what was then called the "new equal protection."

Judge Wright's interests in public law were also reflected in his authorship of a significant number of major law review articles, including one advocating the revival of the antidelegation doctrine. In his articles and his opinions as well, Wright was a remarkable stylist, writing with a directness and sense of purpose that gave his work a distinctive voice.

Having retired from the court a year before, Wright died in 1988.

GARY T. SCHWARTZ

Bibliography

MILLER, ARTHUR SELWYNE 1984 A "Capacity for Outrage": The Judicial Odyssey of J. Skelly Wright. Westport, Conn.: Greenwood Press.
SYMPOSIUM, JUDGE J. SKELLY WRIGHT 1980 Hastings Constitutional Quarterly:857–999.

WYGANT v. JACKSON BOARD OF EDUCATION
476 U.S. 267 (1986)

Although the Wygant decision did not produce a majority opinion, it advanced the growth of constitutional doctrine governing AFFIRMATIVE ACTION [1,I]. A school board and a teachers' union had approved an affirmative action plan as a response to complaints of past RACIAL DISCRIMINATION [3,I] in the hiring of teachers. To maintain minority-hiring gains in the event of a contraction in teacher employment, the plan protected some minority teachers against layoffs. When some minority teachers were retained while some nonminority teachers with greater seniority were laid off, the laid-off teachers challenged the layoff provision in federal court. By a 5–4 vote, the Supreme Court held the provision a violation of the EQUAL PROTECTION OF THE LAWS [2,I].

Justice LEWIS F. POWELL [3,I], for four Justices, concluded that the appropriate STANDARD OF REVIEW [4] was STRICT SCRUTINY [4]. Using this standard, he rejected the lower courts' two justifications for the layoff provision: as a means of keeping minority teachers to serve as role models for students and as a remedy for past societal discrimination. He agreed that past discrimination by the school board itself was a COMPELLING STATE INTEREST [1] that would justify some RACE-CONSCIOUS [I] remedies, assuming that the board had evidentiary support for deter-

mining that remedial action was warranted. Here no such determination had been made, but Justice Powell was unwilling to remand the case for exploration of this issue. Even if the purpose were remedial, he concluded, the layoff provision was an impermissible remedy because it was too burdensome on innocent nonminority teachers. Preferential hiring, he intimated, would be acceptable; layoffs, however, placed the whole burden on particular individuals.

Justice SANDRA DAY O'CONNOR [3,I] concurred separately to emphasize that a public employer that wished to adopt an affirmative action plan need not make a contemporaneous finding of past wrongdoing. Such a requirement would undermine the employer's incentive to meet its civil rights obligations. Rather, the employer could show "a disparity between the percentage of qualified blacks on a school's teaching staff and the percentage of qualified minorities in the relevant labor pool" that would support a prima facie case of EMPLOYMENT DISCRIMINATION [2,I] under Title VII of the CIVIL RIGHTS ACT OF 1964 [I]. Justice BYRON R. WHITE [1,I] added a brief concurrence emphasizing the difference between a hiring preference and a preference in avoiding layoffs.

Justice THURGOOD MARSHALL [3,I] dissented, joined by Justices WILLIAM J. BRENNAN, JR. [1,I] and HARRY A. BLACKMUN [1,I]. Marshall argued that the case should be remanded to the trial court for further findings about the board's past discrimination, but also disagreed with the majority Justices' disposition on the merits. The board's interest in preserving a valid policy for affirmative action in hiring, he argued, was a sufficient state purpose, and the layoff provision was sufficiently narrowly tailored to pass the test of constitutionality. Justice JOHN PAUL STEVENS [4,I] also dissented, arguing that the board's interest in educating children justified measures to assure a racially integrated faculty, irrespective of any showing of past discrimination.

Wygant was a way station on the road to RICHMOND v. J. A. CROSON CO. (1989) [I], in which a majority of the Supreme Court explicitly adopted the rhetoric of strict scrutiny for reviewing state-sponsored affirmative action programs. Justice Powell's and Justice O'Connor's opinions, taken together, also provided a "how to do it" manual for public employers that want to adopt affirmative-action plans for achieving integrated work forces.

KENNETH L. KARST

Bibliography

KARST, KENNETH L. 1989 Belonging to America: Equal Citizenship and the Constitution, pages 158–167. New Haven, Conn.: Yale University Press.
SULLIVAN, KATHLEEN 1986 Sins of Discrimination: Last Term's Affirmative Action Cases. Harvard Law Review 100:78–98.

WYZANSKI, CHARLES E., JR.
·(1906–1986)

Charles E. Wyzanski, Jr., contributed to constitutional law both as a barrister and as a federal judge. He was the son of a Boston real estate developer and graduated with distinction from Phillips Exeter Academy, Harvard College, and Harvard Law School. He had been attracted to law by a reading of *Freedom of Speech*, by ZECHARIAH CHAFEE, JR. [1]. On the recommendation of Professor FELIX FRANKFURTER [2], he served successively as law clerk to Judges AUGUSTUS N. HAND [2] and LEARNED HAND [2], whose broad cultivation, legal acumen, and largeness of spirit became the greatest influence on his professional life.

After a brief association with the Boston law firm of Ropes and Gray, and not yet thirty years old, he was called to Washington to be solicitor of the Labor Department under Secretary Frances Perkins. There he drafted the public works provisions of the Industrial Recovery Act and the Charter of the International Labor Organization. For the Immigration and Naturalization Service, then within the Labor Department, he drew up a plan for collective private guarantees of the welfare of immigrants, which unblocked entry into the United States; this remained his proudest achievement.

He was brought to the Office of the SOLICITOR GENERAL [4,I] in 1935 to strengthen the presentation of crucial New Deal cases in the Supreme Court. He had a central role in the government's victories in the National Labor Relations Act and the Social Security cases in 1937, although when congratulated on his success he would reply that the cases were won "not by Mr. Wyzanski but by Mr. Zeitgeist." He had been on the point of resigning because of his opposition to the Court-packing plan, but was persuaded by Judge A. N. Hand to remain until he could present the government's arguments in these cases.

After returning to Ropes and Gray, he was appointed by President FRANKLIN D. ROOSEVELT [3] in 1941 to the UNITED STATES DISTRICT COURT [4] in Massachusetts, where he served for forty-five years. As a judge he was morally demanding, bold, and courageous, sometimes testing the limits of judicial power, whether on the side of severity, as in municipal corruption cases, or of leniency, as in cases of draft resistance. Notable among the latter was *United States v. Sisson* (1969), where he rejected the defendant's argument that the VIETNAM WAR [4,I] was an undeclared war and therefore unconstitutional, holding that this claim presented a POLITICAL QUESTION [3,I]. Wyzanski then set aside the guilty verdict on the ground, barely advanced by counsel, that the defendant's CONSCIENTIOUS OBJECTION [1] to the conflict, though not strictly satisfying the statutory religious standard for an exemption, nevertheless warranted acquittal under American moral traditions. In his judicial opinions, as in his probing essays and speeches, Wyzanski's search was for enduring, historically attested values.

PAUL A. FREUND

(SEE ALSO: *Immigration* [2]; *Immigration Law and the Constitution* [I].)

Bibliography

IN MEMORIAM 1987 In Memoriam: Charles E. Wyzanski, Jr. *Harvard Law Review* 100:705–727.

WYZANSKI, C. E., JR. 1965 *Whereas: A Judge's Premises.* Boston: Little, Brown.

ZONING
(Update)

Zoning—the public allocation into use categories of privately held land and the subsequent regulation of land development—is by and large a legislative act undertaken by thousands of local governments. As a legislative exercise of the POLICE POWER [3], zoning determinations have long been presumed to be constitutionally and statutorily valid by the courts. This acceptance has not prevented the leveling of strong criticism at the zoning process. The criticism occurs on two levels: first, there is the belief that expanded social welfare conceptions of the police power are uneasily reconciled with private property and the constitutional protection thereof, and second, even if a particular zoning measure is constitutional, its effects may be economically inefficient or socially exclusionary.

The constitutional concern over modern zoning practice is often raised in terms of the Fifth Amendment's prohibition against the TAKING OF PROPERTY [4,I] for public use without the payment of JUST COMPENSATION [3]. This constraint against the federal government has been judicially incorporated into the Fourteenth Amendment's due process limitations upon state power. Influenced by WILLIAM BLACKSTONE [1] and JOHN LOCKE [3], the founding generation understood the taking clause as protecting the liberty engendered by private property. The most significant—perhaps only—qualifications of this liberty was that property not be used to injure one's neighbor. The principal drafter of the Fifth Amendment, JAMES MADISON [3], affirmed this conception by excluding from the idea of private property uses that harmed others by not "leav[ing] to everyone else the like advantage."

Had modern applications of zoning been similarly confined to the prevention of harms or nuisances, such public control would have triggered little controversy. It is scarcely surprising, though now often overlooked, that the initial case favoring zoning's general constitutionality, EUCLID V. AMBLER REALTY (1926) [2], stressed a nuisance-prevention rationale for public land use control. The highly influential AMICUS CURIAE [1] brief filed in favor of the ordinance for the National Conference of City Planning stated that "the Police Power endeavors to prevent evil by checking the tendency toward it and seeks to place a margin of safety between that which is permitted and that which is sure to lend to injury or loss." Fifty years later, however, conceptions of the police power had grown dramatically, and as a consequence, governmental control of land use had become far more intrusive. The opinion of the Supreme Court in PENN CENTRAL TRANSPORTATION CO. V. NEW YORK CITY (1978) [3] boldly asserted that valid exercises of the police power do not depend upon the "noxious' quality of the prohibited uses but rather on the ground that the restrictions were reasonably related to the implementation of a policy . . . expected to produce a widespread public benefit."

Recent Supreme Court decisions may curb somewhat this accelerated growth of the police power. Rejecting as constitutionally infirm prior state doctrines that had limited relief for overzealous zoning exercises to invalidation, the Court has now clearly held that the compensation clause of the Fifth Amendment is self-executing; moreover, the Court held in *First English Evangelical Lutheran*

Church v. County of Los Angeles (1987) that just compensation is required for either temporary or permanent regulatory takings—that is, substantial deprivations of economic value by regulation. In actual fact, the Court seldom finds a taking based on a single factor of economic loss; generally, the Court also considers the investment expectations of the landowner and the relations between the zoning objective and both the regulatory means chosen to advance it and the landowner's contribution to the land use "problem" to be solved. One closely divided opinion of the Court, *Nollan v. California Coastal Commission* (1987), held that zoning regulations are to be judged by a higher level of judicial scrutiny than that applied in the review of other economic legislation.

Other cases such as LORETTO V. TELEPROMPTER, INC. (1982) [3] make clear that any regulation accompanied by physical invasion or use by the public merits compensation. The total destruction of a "core" PROPERTY RIGHT [I], such as the ability to transfer property interests at death, is also constitutionally improper, as the Court stated in *Hodel v. Irving* (1987). Overall, the Court's recent decisions in the zoning area have established a constitutional outer limit premised upon the distinction between regulatory burdens that can be fairly placed on an individual property owner and those that more properly should be borne by the community at large through a general tax system. This principle may mean that exotic uses of the zoning power—say, withholding permits until an office developer makes a substantial contribution to the community housing or cultural fund—will be increasingly suspect.

While the Supreme Court has recently addressed the more egregious abuses of zoning, there remains substantial dissatisfaction with zoning in practice. Zoning measures continue to be presumed valid in state and federal courts, notwithstanding the Supreme Court's suggestion of heightened scrutiny, with the frequent result that physically and locationally indistinguishable property may be arbitrarily classed in very different use categories. Because the resulting value differences are profound, zoning measures are under the constant pressure of amendment or variance without meaningful standards. Regrettably, in some communities the wide-ranging discretion exercised by zoning authorities has invited serious corruption.

Zoning is also heavily reliant upon "specification standards" to accomplish land use objectives indirectly. For example, a typical zoning ordinance employs height, minimum lot, and setback limits to encourage open space and reduce or disperse density. Meeting these limits produces a monotony of design and often is not the most efficient method for accomplishing the open space objective. The advance specification of use requirements also introduces a highly static impediment to change, not to

mention the consequent administrative cost and delay. These costs are most often borne by the housing consumer, and recent studies suggest that the regulatory cost burden can be as high as twenty-five percent of the finished price of a home.

The costly administrative burdens of zoning are most strongly felt by the least-affluent. To the extent that the lower economic stratum of society in a given locality is predominantly composed of members of racial or ethnic minorities, this cost obviously worsens racial SEGREGATION [4] in housing. Absent a racially discriminatory intent, this effect does not constitute a denial of federal EQUAL PROTECTION [2,I], as the Court held in ARLINGTON HEIGHTS V. METROPOLITAN HOUSING DEVELOPMENT CORPORATION (1977) [1]. However, zoning practices that exclude low-income, multi-family structures and have a discriminatory impact may constitute a violation of the federal Fair Housing Act, as was the case in *Huntington Branch, NAACP v. Town of Huntington* (2nd Cir. 1988).

A variety of alternatives have been proposed to overcome these undesirable zoning effects. To supply greater procedural and distributional fairness, some JURISDICTIONS [3] have more closely tied zoning decisions to comprehensive land use planning and have recharacterized zoning as an administrative or quasi-judicial decision. Such reforms not only supply more specific standards but also supply greater judicial supervision of abuse. To enhance the efficiency of zoning, other communities are experimenting with performance zoning systems, which articulate overall community objectives but leave the actual accomplishment of land use goals to plans submitted by individual landowners. Finally, as a general matter, modern subdivisions with detailed private covenants restricting use are less affected by zoning than are land areas within older central cities. Arguably, private controls are more sensitive to market demand and less apt to be applied uniformly over an entire community, and are therefore less exclusionary.

                                          DOUGLAS W. KMIEC

Bibliography

BLAESSER, BRIEN; FOREST, CLYDE; KMIEC, DOUGLAS; MANDELKER, DANIEL; WEINSTEIN, ALAN; and WILLIAMS, NORMAN JR., EDS. 1989 *Land Use and the Constitution*. Chicago: Planners Press, American Planning Association.

ELLICKSON, ROBERT C. and TARLOCK, A. DAN, EDS. 1981 *Land Use-Controls*. Boston: Little, Brown.

HAAR, CHARLES M. and KAYDEN, JERROLD S., EDS. 1989 *Zoning and the American Dream*. Chicago: Planners Press, American Planning Association.

KMIEC, DOUGLAS W. 1986 *Zoning and Planning Deskbook* (with 1991 Supplement). New York: Clark Boardman.

SYMPOSIUM 1988 The Jurisprudence of Takings. *Columbia Law Review* 88:1581–1794.

Case Index

HOW TO READ A CASE CITATION

A case citation tells the reader where the decision and opinion in a case have been reported. It gives, in shorthand form, all the information necessary to find a copy of the report.

The elements of a typical citation are: the volume number, the name of the reporter or of the compilation, (the series number,) the page number of the first page of the report, (the court or jurisdiction,) and the year in which the case was decided. Any information that is unnecessary or inapplicable is omitted. Thus,

384 U.S. 346 (1966)

is the citation to the case reported in volume 384 of the United States Reports, beginning on page 346; the case (*Miranda v. Arizona*) was decided in 1966 by the Supreme Court of the United States. So far, there is only one series of volumes in the United States Reports, and all cases in the United States Reports are Supreme Court cases or matters disposed of by Supreme Court Justices. And

13 N.Y. 378 (1858)

is the citation to the case reported in volume 13 of the New York Reports beginning on page 378; the case (*Wynehamer v. People*) was decided in 1858 by the New York Court of Appeals (the highest court of New York).

Many volumes of reports, especially reports of older cases, bear the name of the reporter rather than of the jurisdiction. Some volumes of reports, especially specialized volumes, have names indicating neither the reporter nor the jurisdiction. The table that follows lists the reports in which cases cited in this *Encyclopedia* are to be found:

U.S.	United States Reports
Dall.	Dallas (= United States Reports, vols. 1–4)
Cranch	Cranch (= U.S. Reports vols. 5–13)
Wheat.	Wheaton (= U.S. Reports vols. 14–25)
Pet.	Peters (= U.S. Reports vols. 26–41)
How.	Howard (= U.S. Reports vols. 42–65)
Black	Black (= U.S. Reports vols. 66–67)
Wall.	Wallace (= U.S. Reports vols. 68–90)
S.Ct.	West's Supreme Court Reporter (cited only when the citation to U.S. Reports was unavailable at the time of compilation)
F.	Federal Reporter (F. 2d = Federal Reporter, 2d series)

F.Supp.	Federal Supplement
F.Cas.	Federal Cases
Ct.Cl.	U.S. Court of Claims Reports
Dane Abr.	Dane's Abridgment of American Law
Gill & J.	Gill & Johnson (Maryland)
Pick.	Pickering (= Massachusetts Reports vols. 18–41)
Metc.	Metcalf (= Massachusetts Reports vols. 42–54)
Cush.	Cushing (= Massachusetts Reports vols. 55–66)
Gray	Gray (= Massachusetts Reports vols. 67–82)
Quincy	Quincy's Reports (Massachusetts)
Hals.	Halsted's New Jersey Reports
N.J. Super.	New Jersey Superior Court Reports
Abb. Prac.	Abbott's New York Practice Reports
Hill	Hill's New York Reports
Johns.	Johnson's New York Reports
Johns. Cas.	Johnson's New York Cases
N.Y.S.	New York Supplement (N.Y.S. 2d = N.Y. Supplement, 2d series)
Martin	Martin's North Carolina Reports
Serg. & R.	Sergeant & Rawles's Pennsylvania Reports
Whart.	Wharton's Pennsylvania Reports
Bay	Bay's South Carolina Reports
P.	West's Pacific Reporter (P. 2d = Pacific Reporter, 2d series)
State Abbreviations	Reports of the state's highest court
A.C.	Appeal Cases (English)
E.R.	East's King's Bench Reports (English)
Eng. Rep.	English Reports
How. St. Tr.	Howell's State Trials (English)
Mod.	Modern English Cases

Numbers in **boldface** refer to the main entry on the subject.

A

Abbate v. United States 359 U.S. 187 (1959), 102–103

Abington Township School District v. Schempp 374 U.S. 203 (1963), **1**, 105, 293, 609, 855, 1139–40, 1538, 1651, 1652, 1653, 1658, 1769, 2006, 2029, Supp.I:168, 307, 475

Ableman v. Booth 21 How. 506 (1859), **1–2**, 4, 237, 288, 302, 812, 1694, 1860, 1865

Abood v. Detroit Board of Education 431 U.S. 209 (1977), **4**, 1118, 1119, Supp.I:297–98

Abrams v. United States 250 U.S. 616 (1919), **7–8**, 225, 294, 299, 732, 791, 896, 922–23, 1203, 1439, 1493, 1623, 1624, 1643, 1645, 1805, 2015, 2059, 2060, Supp.I:385, 585

Adair v. United States 208 U.S. 161 (1908), **15–16**, 325, 504, 650, 778, 814, 816, 828, 900, 1113, 1131, 1178, 1239, 1392, 1596, 1799, 1800, 2054, 2083, Supp.I:161

Adams v. New York 192 U.S. 585 (1904), 1633

Adams v. Storey 1 F.Cas. 141, No. 66 (C.C.D. N.Y. 1817), 1174

Adams v. Tanner 244 U.S. 590 (1917), **23**

Adams v. Williams 407 U.S. 143 (1972), 73, 1780

Adamson v. California 332 U.S. 46 (1947), **23–24**, 120, 580–81, 592, 759, 765, 868, 871, 899, 903, 972, 1198, 1287, 1377, 1474, 1475, 1476, 1477, 1618, 1930, 1973, Supp.I:204–205

Adderley v. Florida 385 U.S. 39 (1966), **24**, 582, 756, 2027, Supp.I:242

Addington v. Texas 441 U.S. 418 (1979), 1248, Supp.I:356, 404

Addyston Pipe & Steel Co. v. United States 175 U.S. 211 (1899), 62, 302, 815, 1241

Adickes v. S. H. Kress & Co. 348 U.S. 144 (1970), 313

Adkins v. Children's Hospital 261 U.S. 525 (1923), **25–27**, 187, 536, 570, 604, 779, 934, 1230, 1239, 1245, 1279, 1280, 1284, 1356, 1599, 1620, 1748, 1764, 1772, 1799, 1838, 1848, 1851, 1936, 2045, 2046, Supp.I:161, 571, 582

Adler v. Board of Education 342 U.S. 485 (1952), 13, **27**, 1102, 1971

Aetna Life Insurance Co. v. Haworth 300 U.S. 227 (1937), 31

Aetna Life Insurance Co. v. Kennedy 301 U.S. 389 (1937), 2004

Afroyim v. Rusk 387 U.S. 253 (1967), **36**, 675, 754

Agins v. Tiburon 447 U.S. 255 (1980), 631, 1750

Agnello v. United States 269 U.S. 20 (1925), **37**, 250, 1636

Aguilar v. Felton 473 U.S. 402 (1985), **39**, Supp.I:493

Aguilar v. Texas 378 U.S. 108 (1964), **39**, 948, 979, 1464, 1629–30, 1719

Agurs, United States v. 427 U.S. 97 (1976), 566, 685, 1449–50

Air Pollution Variance Board v. Western Alfalfa Corp. 416 U.S. 861 (1974), 639

Ake v. Oklahoma 470 U.S. 68 (1985), **40**, 1248, Supp.I:323, 397

Akron v. Akron Center for Reproductive Health 462 U.S. 416 (1983), 828, 1338, 1356, 1555, 1556, 1557, Supp.I:5, 38, 347

Alabama v. King & Boozer 314 U.S. 1 (1941), Supp.I:266

Alabama v. White 110 S.Ct. 2412 (1990), Supp.I:226

Alabama Public Service Commission v. Southern Railway 341 U.S. 341 (1951), 11

Alberts v. California 354 U.S. 476 (1957), 1105, 1335, 1612–13

Albertson v. Subversive Activities Control Board 382 U.S. 70 (1965), **40**, 953, 992, 1803, 1807

Alderman v. United States 394 U.S. 165 (1969), **40–41**, 757, 1348, 1635

Alexander v. Holmes County Board of Education 396 U.S. 19 (1669), **41**, 44, 559, 2026

Alfred Dunhill of London, Inc. v. Republic of Cuba 425 U.S. 682 (1976), 15

Allegheny Pittsburgh Coal Co. v. County Commission of Webster County 488 U.S. 336 (1989), Supp.I:163

Allen v. Illinois 478 U.S. 364 (1986), Supp.I:327

Allen v. McCurry 449 U.S. 90 (1980), Supp.I:38–39

Allen v. State Board of Elections 393 U.S. 544 (1969), 1987

Allen v. Wright 468 U.S. 737 (1984), 45, 1723, Supp.I:347, 519

Allen Bradley Co. v. Local Union #3 325 U.S. 797 (1945), **45**, 1111

Allenberg Cotton Co. v. Pittman 419 U.S. 20 (1974), Supp.I:517

Allgeyer v. Louisiana 165 U.S. 578 (1897), 23, **45**, 153, 604, 778, 828, 1080, 1371, 1578, 1798, 1800

Allied Structural Steel Co. v. Spannaus 438 U.S. 234 (1978), **45–46**, 498–99, 1334

Allstate Insurance Co. v. Hague 450 U.S. 971 (1981), 252

Almeida-Sanchez v. United States 413 U.S. 266 (1973), **46**, 135

Amalgamated Food Employees Union v. Logan Valley Plaza 391 U.S. 308 (1968), 1211, 1219, 1388, 1681, 1734, 1735

Ambach v. Norwick 441 U.S. 68 (1979), 42, **46**, 1808, Supp.I:168

Amerada Hess Corp. v. Director, New Jersey Division of Taxation 490 U.S. 66 (1989), Supp.I:516

American Banana Co. v. United Fruit Co. 213 U.S. 347 (1909), 677

American Booksellers Association v. Hadnut 771 F.2d 323 (7th Circuit, 1985), Supp.I:214, 375, 376

American Communications Association v. Douds 339 U.S. 382 (1950), **50–51**, 122, 184, 772, 877, 1855, 1969, 1971

American Federation of Labor v. American Sash & Door Co. 335 U.S. 538 (1949), 1040, 1596

American Insurance Company v. Canter 26 U.S. (1 Pet.) 511 (1828), **52–53**, 405, 410–11, 1144, 1179, 1217, 1877, 1878, Supp.I:200, 309

American Party of Texas v. White 415 U.S. 767 (1974), 1415

American Power & Light Co. v. Securities and Exchange Commission 329 U.S. 90 (1947), 1286, 1495, Supp.I:339

American Publishing Company v. Fisher 166 U.S. 464 (1897), 1087

American Steel Foundries v. Tri-City Labor Council 257 U.S. 184 (1921), 1850–51

American Tobacco Co., United States v. 221 U.S. 106 (1911), 425, 542, 719, 818

Amistad, The 40 U.S. (15 Pet.) 518 (1841), 1866

Anderson, United States v. 76 U.S. (9 Wall.) 56 (1870), 1744

Anderson v. Celebrezze 460 U.S. 780 (1983), 1415

Anderson v. Dunn 19 U.S. 204 (1821), 1026

Anderson v. Mt. Clemens Pottery Co. 328 U.S. 680 (1946), 681

Andrews v. Ballard 498 F. Supp. 1038 (S.D. Tex. 1980), Supp.I:479

Antelope, The 23 U.S. (10 Wheat.) 66 (1825), 230, 1710

Anthony, United States v. 24 F.Cas. 833 (C.C. N.Y. 1877) No., 14, 460 254

Apex Hosiery Company v. Leader 310 U.S. 469 (1940), **63–64**

Apodaca v. Oregon 406 U.S. 404 (1972), 170, 592, **1027**, 1084, 1087

Appalachian Electric Power Co., United States v. 311 U.S. 377 (1940), **64**, 2038

Aptheker v. Secretary of State 378 U.S. 500 (1959), **70–71**, 122, 849, 998, 1354, 1421, 1595, 1802, 2017

Argersinger v. Hamlin 407 U.S. 25 (1972), 14, **71**, 685, 1266, 1588

Arguello v. United States 444 U.S. 860 (1855), 1864

Arizona v. Fulminante (1991), Supp.I:504

Arizona v. Hicks 480 U.S. 321 (1987), Supp.I:360

Arizona v. Mauro 481 U.S. 520 (1987), Supp.I:330, 460

Arizona v. Robertson 486 U.S. 675 (1988), Supp.I:330, 331

Arizona v. Rumsey 104 S.Ct. 2305 (1984), 1355

Arizona v. Youngblood 488 U.S. 51 (1988), Supp.I:392

Arkansas v. Sanders 442 U.S. 753 (1979), 1631

Arkansas Writers' Project, Inc. v. Ragland 481 U.S. 221 (1987), Supp.I:215

Arlington Heights v. Metropolitan Housing Development Corporation 429 U.S. 252 (1977), 57, **71**, 1140, 1148, 1361, 2036, 2089, Supp.I:415, 456, 592

Armour & Co. v. Wantock 323 U.S. 126 (1944), 681

Arnett v. Kennedy 416 U.S. 134 (1974), **71**, 119, 854, 1465, 1468, Supp.I:177, 393, 440

Arnold, Schwinn & Co., United States v. 388 U.S. 365 (1967), 1770

Arredondo, United States v. 31 U.S. (6 Pet.) 691 (1832), 95

Ash, United States v. 413 U.S. 300 (1973), 78, 1591

Ashcraft v. Tennessee 320 U.S. 728 (1944), 1402, 1404

Ashton v. Cameron County Water Improvement District 298 U.S. 513 (1937), **78**, 100, 1285

Ashwander v. Tennessee Valley Authority 297 U.S. 288 (1936), **78–79**, 143, 1033, 1244

Associated Press v. NLRB 301 U.S. 103 (1937), 651, 1990–92

Associated Press v. Walker 388 U.S. 130 (1967), 1159, 1313, 2027, Supp.I:552

Atascadero State Hospital v. Scanlon 473 U.S. 234 (1985), **79–80**, Supp.I:39

Atchison, Topeka & Santa Fe Railway Co., U.S. v. 233 U.S. 173 (1914), 1178, 1199

Atchison, Topeka & Santa Fe Railway Co. v. Robinson 219 U.S. 219 (1914), 547

Atlas Roofing Co. v. Occupational Safety and Health Administration 430 U.S. 442 (1976), 639, 1919

Atlee v. Laird 347 F. Supp. 689 (E.D. Pa 1972), Supp.I:563

Attorney General of New York v. Soto-Lopez 476 U.S. 898 (1986), Supp.I:29–30, 179

Austin v. Michigan Chamber of Commerce 110 S.Ct. 1391 (1990), Supp.I:64, 522

Avery v. Midland County 390 U.S. 474 (1968), **85**, Supp.I:577

Ayers, In re 123 U.S. 443 (1887), 623

B

Babbitt v. United Farm Workers 442 U.S. 360 (1964), 1358

Badham v. Eu 488 U.S. 1024 (1989), Supp.I:236

Baggett v. Bullitt 377 U.S. 360 (1964), 1353, 1957

Bailey, United States v. 444 U.S. 394 (1980), Supp.I:38, 40

Bailey v. Alabama 219 U.S. 219 (1911), **91–92**, 931, 1378, 2059

Bailey v. Drexel Furniture Co. 259 U.S. 20 (1922), **92**, 246, 893, 1139, 1234, 1297, 1710, 1847

Bailey v. Richardson 341 U.S. 918 (1951), 184, 670, 1969, 1971

Baker v. Carr 369 U.S. 186 (1962), **92–93**, 149, 309, 349, 729, 839, 852, 866, 875, 1041, 1053, 1058, 1066, 1068, 1421, 1422, 1437, 1520, 1521, 1551, 1559, 1565–66, 1662, 1819, 1946, 1986, 2021, 2026, 2029, 2030, 2045, Supp.I:51, 310, 367, 501

Bakery Drivers v. Wohl 315 U.S. 769 (1942), 1116

Baldwin v. Fish & Game Commission 436 U.S. 371 (1978), **96**, 1459, 1460

Baldwin v. Franks 120 U.S. 678 (1887), 712

Baldwin v. G.A.F. Seelig, Inc. 294 U.S. 511 (1935), 211, 1350, 1754

Baldwin v. New York 399 U.S. 66 (1970), **97**, 1085, 1266, 1588, 1919

Ball v. United States 470 U.S. 856 (1985), Supp.I:440

Ballard, United States v. 322 U.S. 78 (1944), 528, 732, 1537, 1543–44

Ballew v. Georgia 435 U.S. 223 (1978), **97**, 170, 1085, 1087, 1703, 1916

Baltimore and Carolina Line v. Redman 295 U.S. 654 (1935), 1918

Baltimore City Department of Social Services v. Bouknight 110 S.Ct. 900 (1990), Supp.I:460–61

Balzac v. Porto Rico 258 U.S. 398 (1922), 987

Banco Nacional de Cuba v. Sabbatino 376 U.S. 398 (1964), 15, 753, 1052

Bancroft, United States v. 260 U.S. 706 (1922), 1744

Bank of Augusta v. Earle 38 U.S. (13 Pet.) 519 (1829), 96, **98**, 222, 1240, 1858, 1864

C

D

Dairy Queen, Inc. v. Wood 369 U.S. 469 (1962), **533**, 1665, 1919

Dakota Central Telephone Co. v. South Dakota 250 U.S. 163 (1919), Supp.I:584

Dames & Moore v. Regan 453 U.S. 654 (1981), 461, **534**, 752, 1444, Supp.I:188, 189, 386

Dandridge v. Williams 397 U.S. 471 (1970), 268, **534**, 784, 1210, 1620, 2041, 2045, Supp.I:378, 570, 573

Daniel v. Waters 515 F.2d 485 (6th Cir. 1975), Supp.I:478

Daniel Ball, The 27 U.S. (10 Wall.) 557 (1871), 237

Daniels v. Williams 474 U.S. 327 (1986), Supp.I:392

Darby Lumber Co., United States v. 312 U.S. 100 (1941), 246, 328–29, 444, 503, 508, **536–37**, 604, 680, 894, 1098, 1114, 1230, 1296, 1330, 1480, 1794, 1876, 1992, 2062, Supp.I:207, 208, 339, 343

Darnel's Case (Five Knights Case) 3 How.St.Tr. 1 (English) (1627), 90, 880, 1383

Dartmouth College v. Woodward 17 U.S. (4 Wheat.) 518 (1819), 101, 255–56, 397, 494–95, 497, 500, 507, **537–39**, 574, 594, 1206, 1217, 1391, 1598, 1785, 1864, 1901, 1962, 2032, 2043, 2072, 2074, Supp.I:533–34, 575

Davidson v. New Orleans 96 U.S. 97 (1878), 139, 917, 1256, 1258, 1269

Davis v. Alaska 415 U.S. 308 (1974), 341, Supp.I:91

Davis v. Bandemer 478 U.S. 109 (1986), Supp.I:236, 367, 522

Davis v. Beason 133 U.S. 333 (1890), **541–42**, 1425, 1539

Davis v. Board of School Commissioners 402 U.S. 33 (1971), 1840

Davis v. Massachusetts 167 U.S. 43 (1897), Supp.I:241

Davis v. Michigan Department of Treasury 489 U.S. 803 (1989), Supp.I:266, 520

Davis v. Mississippi 394 U.S. 721 (1969), Supp.I:53

Davis v. North Carolina 384 U.S. 737 (1966), Supp.I:500

Davis v. Passman 442 U.S. 228 (1979), 120, 533, **542**, 961, Supp.I:144

Day-Brite Lighting, Inc. v. Missouri 342 U.S. 421 (1952), 1230

Dayton Board of Education v. Brinkman 433 U.S. 406 (1977) and 443 U.S. 526 (1979), **314–15**

Dayton-Goose Creek Railroad Co. v. United States 263 U.S. 456 (1924), **543**, 652, 1681

Dean Milk Company v. Madison 340 U.S. 349 (1951), 292, 544, 866, 1132, 1754

DeBartolo Corp. v. Florida Gulf Coast Building Trades 485 U.S. 568 (1988), Supp.I:297

Debs, In re 158 U.S. 564 (1895), 152, 302, 316, 427, **544**, 1006, 1343, 1816, 1924, 2059, Supp.I:184

Debs v. United States 249 U.S. 211 (1919), **544–45**, 653, 1805

De Chastellux v. Fairchild 15 Penn. State 18 (1850), 595, 844

Decoster, United States v. 487 F.2d 1197 (1979), 1591

DeFunis v. Odegaard 416 U.S. 312 (1974), 34, **551**, 1278, 1506, 1529

DeGeofroy v. Riggs 133 U.S. 258 (1890), 1911

DeGregory v. New Hampshire Attorney General 383 U.S. 825 (1966), 1151

De Jonge v. Oregon 299 U.S. 353 (1937), 523, **551**, 770, 806, 877, 932, 1818

Delaware v. Fensterer 474 U.S. 15 (1985), Supp.I:91

Delaware v. New York 385 U.S. 895 (1966), 618, 1284

Delaware v. Prouse 440 U.S. 648 (1979), 73, 1630

Delaware v. Van Arsdall 475 U.S. 673 (1986), Supp.I:91

Delaware, Lackawanna & Western Railroad Co. v. Yurkonis 238 U.S. 439 (1915), 542

Delaware Tribal Business Committee v. Weeks 430 U.S. 73 (1977), 52, Supp.I:523

DeLima v. Bidwell 182 U.S. 1 (1901), 986

Dellinger, United States v. 472 F.2d 340 (1972), 515, 1942

Dellums v. Bush (D.D.C.) (1990), Supp.I:568

De Lovio v. Boit 7 F.Cas. 418, No. 3, 776 (C.C.D. Ma. 1815), 254

Democratic Party v. LaFollette 448 U.S. 909 (1981), 1416, 1417, 1452

Dennis, United States v. 183 F.2d 201 (1950), 1942

Dennis v. United States 341 U.S. 494 (1951), 44, 88, 94, 122, 145–46, 184, 299–300, 515, **555–56**, 792, 847, 896, 970, 1007, 1305, 1774, 1806, 1807, 1930, 1969, 1970–71, 2082–83, Supp.I:370

Dent v. West Virginia 129 U.S. 114 (1889), 2001

Department of Agriculture v. Moreno 413 U.S. 528 (1973), **556**, 788

Department of Justice v. Reporters' Committee for Freedom of the Press 489 U.S. 749 (1989), Supp.I:87

Department of Revenue v. Association of Washington Stevedoring Companies 434 U.S. 815 (1978), 966, Supp.I:40

Derby v. Blake 2 Dane Abr. 649 (Mass. 1799), 494

DeShaney v. Winnebago County Department of Social Services 489 U.S. 189 (1989), Supp.I:**148–49**, 293, 432, 525

Desist v. United States 394 U.S. 244 (1969), 757

DeSylva v. Ballentine 350 U.S. 931 (1955), 691

DeWitt, United States v. 9 Wall. 41 (1869), 232, 237

Di Re, United States v. 332 U.S. 581 (1948), 1463

Diamond v. Chakrabarty 447 U.S. 303 (1980), 1367

DiFrancesco, United States v. 449 U.S. 17 (1980), **563**, 577

Dillon v. Gloss 256 U.S. 368 (1920), 48, 1511, 1512

Dionisio, United States v. 410 U.S. 1 (1973), **564**, 1632

DiSanto v. Pennsylvania 273 U.S. 34 (1927), **565**, 1365

Dobbins v. Commissioners of Erie County 41 U.S. 435 (1842), 311, 2039, Supp.I:266

Dodge v. Woolsey 59 U.S. (18 How.) 331 (1856), 200, 222, **573–74**, 1859, 2039

Doe, John, Inc. (1987), *see* John Doe, Inc., United States v.

Doe v. Bolton 410 U.S. 179 (1973), 1459, 1553, 1555, 1602–1604, 1671

Doe v. Commonwealth's Attorney 403 F.Supp. 1199 (1976), 686, 788, 1674

Doe v. McMillan 412 U.S. 306 (1972), 1716

Doe v. United States 487 U.S. 201 (1988), Supp.I:460

D'Oench Duhme & Co. v. F.D.I.C. 314 U.S. 592 (1942), 690

Dombrowski v. Pfister 380 U.S. 479 (1965), **575**, 1353, 1354, 2085

Donaldson v. O'Connor 422 U.S. 563 (1974), Supp.I:152

Donovan v. Dewey 452 U.S. 594 (1981), 30, Supp.I:9

Dooley v. United States 182 U.S. 222 (1901), 986

Doran v. Salem Inn, Inc. 422 U.S. 922 (1975), Supp.I:438

Dorchy v. Kansas 272 U.S. 306 (1926), Supp.I:297

Doremus, United States v. 249 U.S. 86 (1919), 246, **575**, 906, 1297, 1306, 1870, 2053

Doremus v. Board of Education 342 U.S. 429 (1952), **575**, 1872, 1972

Dorr v. United States 195 U.S. 138 (1904), 986

Dorsey v. Stuyvesant Town Corporation 299 N.Y. 512 (1949–1950), 1731

Dothard v. Rawlinson 433 U.S. 321 (1977), 286

Dougherty County Board of Education v. White 439 U.S. 32 (1978), 1987

Douglas v. California 368 U.S. 815 (1963), 14, 534, **583**, 662, 870, 975, 1010, 1588, 1611, 1619, 1620, 2041

Douglas v. Seacoast Products 431 U.S. 265 (1977), 1210

Douglass v. Pike County 101 U.S. 677 (1880), 497

Dow Chemical Company v. United States 476 U.S. 227 (1986), Supp.I:137–38

Dowd Box Co. v. Courtney 369 U.S. 502 (1962), Supp.I:298

Dowdell v. United States 221 U.S. 325 (1911), 987

Dowling v. United States (1990), Supp.I:156

Downes v. Bidwell 182 U.S. 244 (1901), 986

Draper v. United States 358 U.S. 307 (1959), **584**, 974, 1629

Dred Scott v. Sandford 60 U.S. (19 How.) 393 (1857), 4, 88, 103, 107, 125, 166, 200, 212, 222, 231, 234, 258, 265, 274, 281, 344, 347, 408–12, 426, 528–29, 535, 548, 568, 579, **584–87**, 590, 626–27, 641–42, 805, 828, 868, 916, 919, 1025, 1057, 1131, 1136, 1162, 1165, 1166, 1201, 1208, 1242, 1269, 1307, 1381, 1397, 1423, 1460, 1500, 1606, 1666, 1688, 1693, 1697, 1699, 1786, 1789, 1809, 1816, 1823, 1843, 1857, 1858, 1860, 1861, 1864, 1866–67, 1878, 1979, 1982, 2030, 2040, Supp.I:79, 105, 119, 260, 342, 343, 364, 402–403, 412, 453–54, 531, 534

Dronenburg v. Zech 741 F.2d 1388 (D.C. Cir. 1984), Supp.I:46

Drummond, United States v. 38 U.S. (13 Pet.) 84 (1835), 1908

Duckworth v. Arkansas 314 U.S. 390 (1941), 767

Duckworth v. Eagan 109 S.Ct. 2875 (1989), Supp.I:250, 330, 331, 361, 460

Duke Power Co. v. Carolina Environmental Study Group 438 U.S. 51 (1978), 1597, 1723, Supp.I:519, 550

Dun & Bradstreet, Inc. v. Greenmoss Builders, Inc. 472 U.S. 749 (1985), **591–92**, Supp.I:552

Dunaway v. New York 442 U.S. 200 (1979), 73, 1630

E

F

G

H

I

J

M

Madden v. Kentucky 309 U.S. 83 (1940), 310, **1189**, 1461

Mahan v. Howell 410 U.S. 315 (1973), **1197**, 1523

Maher v. Roe 432 U.S. 464 (1977), 6, 904, **1197**, 1554, 1671, 2041–42, Supp.I:323, 357–58, 569, 570

Maine v. Thiboutot 448 U.S. 1 (1980), 1641

Mallory v. United States 354 U.S. 449 (1957), 717, 1242, 1243, 1343, 2028

Malloy v. Hogan 378 U.S. 1 (1964), 521, **1197–98**, 1401, 1478, 1575, 1605, 1930, 1931, 2028

Manson v. Brathwaite 432 U.S. 98 (1977), 342, Supp.I:191

Maple Flooring Manufacturers Association v. United States 268 U.S. 563 (1925), 1621

Mapp v. Ohio 367 U.S. 643 (1961), 72, 121, 178, 293, 521, 624, 663, 765, 766, 955, 973, 1045, 1102, **1199**, 1356, 1476, 1563–64, 1634, 1949, 1973, 2022, 2028, 2061, 2073, Supp.I:223, 396, 437

Marbury v. Madison 5 U.S. (1 Cranch) 137 (1803), 66, 135, 172, 219, 235, 269, 306, 333, 345, 347, 357, 383, 393, 464, 479, 503, 595, 844, 915, 919, 1033, 1041, 1049, 1052–53, 1054–60, 1067, 1069, 1076, 1079, 1088, 1137, 1172, 1196, 1198, **1199–1202**, 1206, 1208, 1213, 1214, 1215, 1221, 1349, 1368, 1420, 1436, 1437, 1550, 1574, 1614, 1662, 1764, 1789, 1814, 1828, 1877, 1936, 1960, 2030, Supp.I:98, 104, 109, 119, 127, 143, 144, 266, 276, 282, 342, 351, 366–67, 368, 370, 544

Marchetti v. United States 390 U.S. 39 (1968), 40, **1202–1203**, 1298, 1710, 1870, 2022

Marion, United States v. 404 U.S. 307 (1971), 1718

Marks v. United States 430 U.S. 188 (1977), Supp.I:521

Marron v. United States 275 U.S. 192 (1927), 1636, 1638

Marsh v. Alabama 326 U.S. 501 (1946), 276, 507, 929, **1205**, 1681, 1732, 1734, 1735, 1737, Supp.I:390, 570

Marsh v. Chambers 103 S.Ct. 3335 (1983), **1205**, 1657

Marshall v. Baltimore and Ohio Railroad 57 U.S. (16 How.) 314 (1853), 200, 867

Marshall v. Barlow's Inc. 436 U.S. 307 (1978), **1211**, 1633, Supp.I:9

Marshall v. United States 360 U.S. 310 (1959), 693

Marshfield Family Skateland, Inc. v. Town of Marshfield 464 U.S. 987 (1983), Supp.I:87

Marston v. Lewis 410 U.S. 679 (1973), 592, 1594

Martin v. City of Struthers 319 U.S. 157 (1943), 1007, 1543, Supp.I:302

Martin v. Hunter's Lessee 14 U.S. (1 Wheat.) 304 (1816), 65, 305, 397, 594, 884, 1049, 1076, 1212, 1216, **1219–22**, 1598, 1783, 1784, 1815, Supp.I:287

Martin v. Mott 25 U.S. (12 Wheat.) 19 (1827), 418, 1217, **1222**, 1783, Supp.I:82

Martinez-Fuerte, United States v. 428 U.S. 543 (1976), 135

Martino v. Michigan Window Cleaning Co. 327 U.S. 173 (1946), 1106

Maryland v. Baltimore Radio Show 38 U.S. 912 (1950), 1493

Maryland v. Buie, Supp.I:430

Maryland v. Craig 110 S.Ct. 3157 (1990), Supp.I:91, 130, **324**

Maryland v. Wirtz 392 U.S. 183 (1967), 681, 833, 1294, Supp.I:208, 240

Maryland Committee for Fair Representation v. Tawes 377 U.S. 656 (1964), 1566

Massachusetts v. Laird 400 U.S. 886 (1970), **1223–24**

Massachusetts v. Mellon 262 U.S. 447 (1923), 503, 809, 1756, 1838, 1870, Supp.I:507–508

Massachusetts Board of Retirement v. Murgia 427 U.S. 307 (1976), 36, 37, **1225**

Masses Publishing Co. v. Patten 244 Fed. 535 (1917), 145–46, 895, **1227–28**, 1623

Massiah v. United States 377 U.S. 201 (1964), **1228**, 1403, 1407–1408, 1590–91

Mastro Plastics v. NLRB 348 U.S. 910 (1956), 1116

Mathews v. DeCastro 429 U.S. 181 (1976), 1705

Mathews v. Diaz 426 U.S. 67 (1976), 42, Supp.I:259, 508

Mathews v. Eldridge 424 U.S. 319 (1976), 599, 679, 981, **1228**, 1364, 1467, 1468, 1704, Supp.I:302, 382, 393, 394

Mathews v. Lucas 427 U.S. 495 (1976), 947, 1921

Matilda's Case (Birney v. Ohio) 80 Ohio 230 (1838), 402

Matlock, United States v. 415 U.S. 164 (1974), 1633, Supp.I:547

Matsushita Electric Industrial Co. v. Zenith Radio Corp. 631 F.2d 1069 (1980), 1918

Maxwell v. Dow 176 U.S. 581 (1900), 971, **1231**, 1360, 1475, 1929

Mayor of New York v. Miln 36 U.S. (11 Pet.) 102 (1837), 101, 1217, **1231**, 1241, 1784, 1785, 1859, 1863, 1865, 1896, 1954, 2067

Maze, United States v. 414 U.S. 395 (1974), Supp.I:440

Mazer v. Stein 347 U.S. 201 (1954), 504

Mazurie, United States v. 419 U.S. 544 (1975), 552

McAllister v. United States 141 U.S. 174 (1891), 301

McAuliffe v. Mayor of New Bedford 155 Mass. 216 (1892), 1486, 1487, 1935

McCabe v. Atchison, Topeka & Santa Fe Railroad 235 U.S. 151 (1914), 931, 2059

McCardle, Ex parte 74 U.S. (7 Wall.) 506 (1869), 65, 215, 231, 235–36, 347, 422, 539, 888, 1053, 1075, **1232**, 1256, 1816, 1924, Supp.I:285, 286, 531–32

McCarthy v. Arndstein 262 U.S. 355 (1924), 1574

McClesky v. Kemp 481 U.S. 279 (1987), Supp.I:23, 64, 67, 68, 77, 180, **324–25**, 383, 414–15, 432, 491, 495

McClesky v. Zant (1991), Supp.I:504

McCollum v. Board of Education 333 U.S. 203 (1948), 123, 766, **1233–34**, 1527, 1535, 1536–37, 1538, 1547, 1652, 1658, 1972, 2090

McCormick v. Talcott 61 U.S. (20 How.) 402 (1858), 868

McCracken v. Hayward 43 U.S. (2 How.) 608 (1844), 96

McCray v. Illinois 386 U.S. 300 (1967), 980

McCray v. United States 195 U.S. 27 (1904), 92, 246, 1234, 1306, 1869, 2053

McCulloch v. Maryland 17 U.S. 316 (1819), 98, 158, 166, 214, 266, 289, 305, 311, 328, 343, 347–48, 397, 401, 465, 468, 507, 508, 537, 636, 699, 709, 856, 864, 891, 963, 990, 1008, 1035, 1044, 1057, 1067, 1136, 1138, 1139, 1141, 1206, 1213, 1216, 1219, 1221, **1234–37**, 1270, 1271, 1272, 1306, 1346, 1350, 1351, 1355, 1391, 1430, 1598, 1772, 1783, 1789, 1811, 1812, 1864, 1873, 1875, 1887, 2030, 2043, 2046, 2072, 2074, Supp.I:104, 203, 207, 209, 265, 276, 309, 342, 515

McDaniel v. Paty 435 U.S. 887 (1978), 1546, Supp.I:445

McDermott v. Wisconsin 228 U.S. 115 (1913), 1808

McDonald v. Santa Fe Trail Transportation Co. 427 U.S. 273 (1976), 1893, Supp.I:437

McDonnell Douglas Corp. v. Green 411 U.S. 792 (1973), 285

McElvane v. Brush 142 U.S. 155 (1891), 1099

McGautha v. California 402 U.S. 183 (1971), 201, 207–208

McGill v. Brown Federal, Supreme Court (1833), 95

McGowan v. Maryland 366 U.S. 420 (1961), 1515, 1544–45, 1653, 1810, 2029

McGrain v. Daugherty 273 U.S. 135 (1927), 1103, 1150, **1237–38**, 1959, Supp.I:485

McKeiver v. Pennsylvania 403 U.S. 528 (1971), 836, 1092, **1238**, 1919

McLaughlin v. Florida 379 U.S. 184 (1964), 1181, 1266

McLaughlin v. Tilendis 398 F.2d 298 (7th Cir. 1968), Supp.I:297

McLaurin v. Oklahoma State Regents 339 U.S. 637 (1950), 275, **1241**, 1266, 1841, 1946, 1969

McLean v. Arkansas Board of Education 211 U.S. 539 (1909), 153, 543, 1945

McLemore, United States v. 1714 45 U.S. (4 How.) 286 (1846), 1714

McMann v. Richardson 397 U.S. 759 (1970), 810, 2004

McMillan v. Pennsylvania 477 U.S. 79 (1986), Supp.I:491

McNabb v. United States 318 U.S. 332 (1943), 717, 766

McNally v. United States 483 U.S. 350 (1987), Supp.I:522

Meachum v. Fano 427 U.S. 215 (1976), Supp.I:519

Mechanik, United States v. 475 U.S. 66 (1986), Supp.I:246, 247

Meech v. Hillhaven West, Inc. 776 F.2d 488 (Mont. 1989), Supp.I:298

Meek v. Pittenger 421 U.S. 349 (1975), 245, 1655, 1656

Memoirs v. Massachusetts 383 U.S. 413 (1966), 846, 1009, **1246**, 1259

Memorial Hospital v. Maricopa County 415 U.S. 250 (1974), 1210, 1561, Supp.I:572

Mempa v. Rhay 389 U.S. 128 (1967), 1589, Supp.I:490

Memphis v. Greene 451 U.S. 100 (1981), **1247**, 1894, Supp.I:322, 457

Memphis Fire Department v. Stotts see Firefighters Local Union No. 1784 v. Stotts

Mendenhall, United States v. 446 U.S. 544 (1980), 73

Meritor Savings Bank, FSB v. Vinson 477 U.S. 57 (1986), Supp.I:**327–28**, 347, 496

Merryman, Ex parte 17 F.Cas 144 (C.C. Ma. 1861) (No. 9, 486), 103, 629, 1025, 1861, 2013, 2014

N

O

P

S

T

U

V

Virginia, Ex parte 100 U.S. 339 (1880), 56, **1786–87**
Virginia v. Rives 100 U.S. 313 (1880), 282, 1303, **1786–87**, 1792
Virginia v. Tennessee 148 U.S. 503 (1893), 749, 996
Virginia v. West Virginia 78 U.S. (11 Wall.) 39 (1870), 236, 540, 623
Virginia State Board of Pharmacy v. Virginia Citizens' Consumer Council 425 U.S. 748 (1976), 104, 125, 380, 598, 739, 1168, 1642, **1976–77**, Supp.I:39, 40, 84, 85, 439
Vitek v. Jones 445 U.S. 480 (1980), Supp.I:92
Von Moltke v. Gillies 332 U.S. 708 (1948), 1028
Von's Grocery Co., United States v. 384 U.S. 270 (1966), 1770

W

Wabash, St. Louis & Pacific Railway v. Illinois 118 U.S. 557 (1886), 139, 324, 604, 854, 865, 994, 1229, **1984**
Wade, United States v. 388 U.S. 218 (1967), 757, 1105, 1167, 1343, 1591, **1990**, Supp.I:53, 91, 191
Wainwright v. Sykes 433 U.S. 72 (1977), 10, 689, 764, 1278, 1993, 2004, Supp.I:438
Wainwright v. Witt 469 U.S. 412 (1985), 1978
Walder v. United States 347 U.S. 62 (1954), 950, 1634, Supp.I:397
Wales v. Statson 2 Mass. 143 (1806), 494
Waley v. Johnston 316 U.S. 101 (1942), 883
Walker v. Birmingham 388 U.S. 307 (1967), **2005**
Walker v. Jennison Mass., unreported (1781), 334
Walker v. Sauvinet 92 U.S. 90 (1876), **2005–2006**
Wallace & Tiernan Company, United States v. 336 U.S. 793 (1949), 121, 1338, 1538, 1653, 2006
Wallace v. Jaffree 472 U.S. 38 (1985), 1338, 1538, 1653, **2006**, Supp.I:169, 182, 307, 346, 438–39, 446, 476
Wallace v. Van Riswick 92 U.S. 202 (1872), 80
Waller v. Florida 397 U.S. 387 (1970), 577
Walter v. United States 447 U.S. 649 (1980), 1631
Walters v. National Association of Radiation Survivors 473 U.S. 305 (1985), Supp.I:393
Walton v. Arizona 110 S.Ct. 3047 (1990), Supp.I:522
Walz v. Tax Commission 397 U.S. 664 (1970), 331, 855–56, 1545, 1654, 1656, 1657, **2006**
Ward, United States v. 449 U.S. 851 (1980), 639
Ward v. Illinois 431 U.S. 767 (1977), **2006**
Ward v. Rock Against Racism 109 S.Ct. 2746 (1989), Supp.I:294, 436
Ward v. Texas 316 U.S. 547 (1942), 1402
Warden v. Hayden 387 U.S. 294 (1967), 674, 1251, 1393, 1636, 1638, 1948, 1949, **2007**
Warder v. La Belle Creole 1 Pet. Adm. 31, 29 F.Cas. 215 (No. 17, 165) (1792), 1383
Wardius v. Oregon 412 U.S. 470 (1973), 684
Wards Cove Packing Co. v. Antonio 490 U.S. 642 (1989), Supp.I:77, 415, 433, 578
Ware v. Hylton 3 U.S. (3 Dallas) 199 (1796), 233, 531, 1001, 1013, 1368, 1827, 1829, **2007**, Supp.I:533
Waring v. Clarke 46 U.S. (5 How.) 441 (1847), 2039, 2074
Warth v. Seldin 422 U.S. 490 (1975), 45, 180, 1048, 1432, 1684, 1793, Supp.I:380, 456
Washington v. Davis 426 U.S. 229 (1976), 57, 71, 315, 645, 870, 999, 1083, 1270, 1361, 1382, 1503, 1504, 1670, **2035–36**, 2040, 2050, Supp.I:76, 432, 456, 577–78
Washington v. Harper 494 U.S. (1990), Supp.I:152, 294, 327, 357, 404, 405, **568–69**
Washington v. Seattle School District No. 1 454 U.S. 890 (1982), 514, 1626, Supp.I:151, 316
Washington v. Texas 388 U.S. 14 (1967), 340, 660, 1477
Washington State Apple Advertising Commission v. Hunt (1977), Supp.I:264
Watkins v. United States 354 U.S. 178 (1957), 101, 293, 928, 1150, 1233, 1574, 1662, **2038**
Watson, United States v. 423 U.S. 411 (1976), 72, 74, 1631, 1632
Watson v. Jones 80 U.S. (13 Wall.) 679 (1872), 1544
Waugh v. Board of Trustees of the University of Mississippi 237 U.S. 589 (1915), 773

Wayman v. Southard 23 U.S. (10 Wheat.) 1 (1825), 552
Wayte v. United States 105 S.Ct. 1524 (1985), **2040–41**
Weatherford v. Bursey 429 U.S. 545 (1977), 566
Weaver v. Graham 450 U.S. 24 (1981), 676
Weaver v. Palmer Bros. Co. 270 U.S. 402 (1924), 187
Weber v. Aetna Casualty and Surety Company 406 U.S. 164 (1972), Supp.I:437
Webster v. Reproductive Health Services 492 U.S. (1989), Supp.I:1–3, 4–6, 21, 38, 73–74, 294, 347, 440, 473, 503, 525, **569**, 579
Weeks v. United States 232 U.S. 383 (1914), 37, 250, 624, 663, 674, 1199, 1633, 1634, 1636, 1682, 1683, 1948, 1949, **2044**, Supp.I:223
Weems v. United States 217 U.S. 349 (1910), 525, 987, **2044**, Supp.I:141
Weinberger v. Salfi 422 U.S. 749 (1975), 1001, 1705, 1978
Weinberger v. Wiesenfeld 420 U.S. 636 (1975), 1141, 1669, 1670, 1705
Welsh v. United States 398 U.S. 333 (1970), 353, Supp.I:446, 563
Welsh v. Wisconsin 104 S.Ct. 2091 (1984), 2045
Welton v. Missouri 91 U.S. 275 (1876), 1757
Wengler v. Druggists Mutual Insurance Co. 446 U.S. 142 (1980), 1669, **2045**
Wesberry v. Sanders 376 U.S. 1 (1964), 121, 310, 349, 616, 866, 1045, 1521, 1522, **2045**, Supp.I:253
West Coast Hotel Company v. Parrish 300 U.S. 379 (1937), 214, 507, 536, 570, 604, 720, 779, 922, 932, 935, 1114, 1230, 1244, 1280, 1356, 1599, 1606, 1800, 1936, **2045–46**, Supp.I:128, 162, 524, 582
West Hartford (Town of) v. Operation Rescue (1990), Supp.I:419
West River Bridge Co. v. Dix 47 U.S. (6 How.) 507 (1848), 496, 535, 680, 1490, 1864, 1963, 2039, **2046–47**
West Virginia State Board of Education v. Barnette 319 U.S. 624 (1943), 210, 299, 609, **741–43**, 1540, 1542, 1543, 1618, 1774, 1802, Supp.I:168
Western Air Lines, Inc. v. Criswell 105 S.Ct. 2743 (1985), 37
Western Livestock v. Bureau of Revenue 303 U.S. 250 (1938), 1758–59
Weston, United States v. 448 F.2d 626 (9th Cir. 1971), Supp.I:491
Weston v. City Council of Charleston 27 U.S. (2 Pet.) 449 (1829), 1217, **2046**, Supp.I:266
Westside Community Schools v. Mergens (1990), *see* Board of Education of the Westside Community Schools v. Mergens
Whalen v. Roe 429 U.S. 589 (1977), 1578, 1579, 1580, 1581, 1802, **2047**, Supp.I:86–87
Wheeler, United States v. 434 U.S. 313 (1978), 52
Wheeler v. Greene 280 U.S. 49 (1979), 1741
Wheeler et al., United States v. 254 F.611 (1912), 1282
Whitcomb v. Chavis 403 U.S. 124 (1971), 1284, 2035
White, United States v. 401 U.S. 745 (1971), 619, 621, 1345, 1574, 1633, **2054–55**, Supp.I:137, 424–25
White v. Hart 80 U.S. (13 Wall.) 646 (1872), 236
White v. Massachusetts Council of Construction Employers 460 U.S. 204 (1983), 257
White v. Regester 412 U.S. 755 (1973), 1197, 1284, 1523, 2035
White v. Texas 310 U.S. 530 (1940), 1402
White v. Weiser 412 U.S. 783 (1973), 1197
Whiteley v. Warden 401 U.S. 560 (1971), 1463
Whitney v. California 274 U.S. 357 (1927), 143, 146, 299, 300, 523, 735, 771, 1423, 1620, 1624, 1805–1806, 1807, **2060**
Wickard v. Filburn 317 U.S. 111 (1942), 38, 328–29, 446, 537, 597, 606, 613–14, 843, 963, 994, 997, 1006, 1115, 1245, 1296, 1481, 1682, 1728, 1777, **2061–62**
Widmar v. Vincent 454 U.S. 263 (1981), 1538, 1546, 1547, 1652, **2062–63**, Supp.I:37, 42, 178, 441, 445, 476
Wieman v. Updegraff 344 U.S. 183 (1952), 122, 293, 1182, 1184, 1486, 1935, **2063**
Wiener v. United States 357 U.S. 249 (1958), 941
Wilkes v. Wood 19 St.Tr. 1153 (1763), 762, 2064
Wilkes Cases 19 How.St.Tr. (1763–1770), 618, 837, 1288, 1299, 1393, 1434, 1574, 1948, **2063–64**
Wilkinson v. Leland 27 U.S. (2 Pet.) 627 (1829), 1860, 1962
Wilkinson v. United States 365 U.S. 399 (1961), 928
Will v. Michigan Department of State Police 109 S.Ct. 2304 (1989), Supp.I:293
William, The, United States v. 28 F. Cas. 614 (C.C.D.C. Ma. 1808) (No. 16, 700), 627, 1215

Y

Z

Name Index

*Numbers in **boldface** refer to the main entry on the subject.*

A

Abraham, Kenneth, 465
Acheson, Dean, 1108, 2056
Ackerman, Bruce, Supp.I:16
Acton, John, 267
Adair, Douglas, 892
Adams, Charles Francis, 4
Adams, Henry, **16**, Supp.I:103
Adams, John, **16–21**, 41, 43, 75, 76, 148, 233,
    359, 390, 391, 513, 531, 549, 598, 626, 808,
    827, 889, 978, 1012, 1014, 1015, 1200, 1205,
    1211, 1226, 1276, 1352, 1369, 1409, 1427,
    1614, 1804, 1825, 1965, 1973, 1981, 2011,
    2032, 2033, 2035, Supp.I:127, 188, 210, 216,
    217, 275, 308, 511, 531
Adams, John Quincy, **20–22**, 192, 193, 195, 271,
    297, 398, 401, 405, 406, 523, 617, 1004,
    1215, 1241, 1273, 1274, 1448, 1513, 1519,
    1782, 1784, 1815, 1867, 1888, 1897, 1920,
    1981, 2072, Supp.I:82, 108, 273, 277, 533,
    574, 575
Adams, Samuel, 7, **22–23**, 913, 1196, 1226, 1639,
    Supp.I:18
Addams, Jane, 50
Agee, Philip, 888
Agresto, John, 1042
Akerman, Ames T., 81, 863
Alexander, James, 2088
Allen, Florence, Supp.I:534
Allen, William B., Supp.I:22
Althusias, Johannes, 475
Amar, Akhil, Supp.I:289
Ambrose, Spenser, 1379
Ames, Fisher, **23**, 53, 54

Ames, James Barr, 764
Amory, Rufus G., Supp.I:533
Amsterdam, Anthony, Supp.I:224, 425
Andros, Sir Edmund, Supp.I:442
Anthony, Susan B., 261, 1982, Supp.I:581
Aquinas, Thomas, 260
Archer, Sir John, 959
Arenella, Peter, Supp.I:460
Aristotle, 239, 1420, 1613, 1639, Supp.I:105
Armstrong, Scott, Supp.I:98
Arnold, Thurman, **72**, 304, 322, Supp.I:103
Arthur, Chester A., **74**, 152, 351, 817, 834, 1448,
    1965
Ashley, James, 1767
Attucks, Crispus, 1693
Augustine, Saint, 264
Austin, John, 1716

B

Bache, Benjamin, 693
Backus, Isaac, **87**
Bacon, Augustus O., 656
Bailyn, Bernard, 943
Baker, George F., 1149
Baker, Howard, Supp.I:271
Bakke, Allan, 34, Supp.I:381
Baldridge, Homer, 1923
Baldwin, Abraham, **95**, Supp.I:309, 543–44
Baldwin, Henry, **95–96**, 241, 254, 874, 1217,
    1783, 1862, Supp.I:274
Baldwin, Roger, 50, **96**, 651, 1627
Ballah, Robert, 105, Supp.I:103
Bancroft, George, 97–98, 312

Barber, Benjamin, Supp.I:364
Barbour, Philip P., **100**, 399, 1231, 1963,
    Supp.I:274
Barker, Ernest, 1125
Barrett, Edward, Supp.I:516
Bassett, Richard, **103**
Bates, Edward, **103**, 629
Bator, Paul, Supp.I:286
Batson, James, Supp.I:36
Bayard, James A., Supp.I:487
Beard, Charles A., 97, **104–05**, 321, 386, 548,
    596, 1241, 1481, 2019, Supp.I:111, 263
Beck, James M., 321
Becker, Frank J., 105
Beckley, John, Supp.I:216
Bedford, Gunning, Jr., **106**, 384, Supp.I:11
Begin, Menachem, 217
Belknap, William, 215
Bell, Derrick, Supp.I:457
Bell, Griffin B., 82, Supp.I:262
Bell, John, 541
Benjamin, Judah P., Supp.I:575
Bentham, Jeremy, 645, Supp.I:109, 401
Benton, Thomas Hart, **107**, 813, Supp.I:273
Berger, Raoul, 469, 671, 760, 961, Supp.I:351,
    352, 557
Berkely, John, 1309
Berle, Adolph, 436
Berns, Walter, Supp.I:175
Beveridge, Albert J., **108**, 600, 1202, 1234,
    1237
Bickel, Alexander M., 70, **111**, 259, 322, 470,
    646, 760, 1059, 1061, 1142, 1736, 1847,
    Supp.I:101–02, 121
Biddle, Francis, 41, **111**, 1010, 1608, Supp.I:586

Subject Index

*Numbers in **boldface** refer to the main entry on the subject.*

631

C

First Amendment—*Continued*
  free exercise of religion, Supp.I:236–37
  as fundamental law, 113, 829
  grand jury secrecy limits, Supp.I:247
  incorporated into Fourteenth Amendment, 731, 734
  obscenity, 733
  overbreath, 158
  penumbras, 871, 872, 1377, 1388
  preferred freedoms theory, 737
  proprietary prerogatives of government, Supp.I:239, 242
  protection of motion pictures, 183, 1105
  protection of picketing, Supp.I:299–300
  protection of right to generate ideas, Supp.I:405
  protection of scientific experiments, Supp.I:478
  and public employment, 27
  rights protected by, 730, 732, Supp.I:51–53
  spending power, Supp.I:508
  state monopoly over education, Supp.I:168
  Sunday closing laws, 734
  Uniform Code of Military Justice, Supp.I:27
  and visa denials, Supp.I:565
  zoning for adult theaters, Supp.I:71–72
First Congress, Supp.I:**215–17**
First Continental Congress, Declarations and Resolves of (October 1, 1774), **739**
  British Constitution as model, 155, 156
  colonial charters as model, 1312, 1313
  federalism grasped, 704–708
  see also Pennsylvania Constitution; Virginia Constitution
First World War, *see* World War I
Flag burning, *see* Flag desecration
Flag desecration, **740–41**, Supp.I:**217–20**
  First Amendment applied to, 741, Supp.I:213–14, 229–30
  as symbolic speech, 1843, 1844
Flag salute cases, **741–43**
  and Jehovah's Witnesses, 728, 1453, 1540
Food and Drug Administration (FDA), 27
Food, Drug, and Cosmetic Act (1938), **746**
  revision of Pure Food and Drug Act, 1496
Force Act (1833), 727, **746**
  enforce federal laws, 1008
  nullification and secession, 746
  response to South Carolina Ordinance of Nullification, 1712
Force Acts (1870, 1871), **746–47**
  civil rights conspiracies outlawed, 875
  Colfax Massacre of 1873, 527
  invoked by Nixon, 1430
  and Ku Klux Klan, 527, 746
  military as law enforcement, 1430
  not applicable to individuals, 904
Foreign affairs, **747–55**
  Boland Amendment, Supp.I:44
  Congress and foreign policy, Supp.I:92–95
  constitutional interpretation, 464–71
  executive prerogative, Supp.I:187–89
  implied powers, 962–66
  Marshall Plan, 1218
  Monroe Doctrine, 1274
  original intent, Supp.I:349
  president's exclusive powers, 1390, 2007, Supp.I:209–10, 270–71
  president and treaty power, Supp.I:385–88
  Reagan administration, Supp.I:422–23
  Senate and foreign policy, Supp.I:485–87

Foreign affairs—*Continued*
  war powers, 2007–16, Supp.I:567–68
  see also Treaty power
Foreign commerce, **755–56**
  definitions of, 39
  discrimination against, 164
  interference with, 565
  original package doctrine confined to, 2075
  regulation of, 749
  RICO Act and, Supp.I:417
Foreign Intelligence Surveillance Act, 1300
Foreign policy, *see* Congress and foreign policy; Congressional war powers; Foreign affairs; Senate and foreign policy; War powers
Foreign Sovereign Immunities Act, 15
Fourteenth Amendment, **757–61**
  in abortion decision, 5, Supp.I:437–38
  in affirmative action, 34–36
  antidiscrimination legislation, 55–58
  arrest, 72
  basis for abolition of slavery, 2, 757
  and citizenship, 36, 88
  civil rights protection, 757, Supp.I:204–05
  due process clause, Supp.I:395
  equal protection of the law, 92, 640
  incorporation doctrine and original intent, Supp.I:260–61
  just compensation, 32
  private discrimination, Supp.I:389, 390
  protection of unenumerated rights, 24
  right against self-incrimination, 23
  right to counsel, 40
  Section 5, Supp.I:220–23
  segregation violating, 161
  Slaughterhouse cases, 57
  as source of privacy rights, Supp.I:461
  trial by jury, 97
Fourteenth Amendment and Section 5 (framing), Supp.I:**220–21**
Fourteenth Amendment and Section 5 (judicial construction), Supp.I:**221–23**
Fourth Amendment, **761–63**, Supp.I:**223–27**
  administrative search, Supp.I:8
  arrest, 72
  arrest warrant, 73
  body search, Supp.I:43–44
  damages claims, Supp.I:143, 144
  drug-testing programs, Supp.I:158–60
  exclusionary rule of Burger Court, 182
  historical origins, 761–63, Supp.I:223
  home visits by social workers not violating, 2078
  made applicable to states by Fourteenth Amendment, 1371
  most creative decision under, 2044
  probable cause, 46, 761
  right of privacy, 5, 29, 30
  and rights of criminally accused, Supp.I:466–67
  scope of, Supp.I:424–26
  searches for mere evidence, 2090
  search warrants, 29, 79, Supp.I:480–82
  shoot-to-kill orders as unreasonable seizure, 1874
  third-party consent, Supp.I:546–48
  unreasonable search, Supp.I:557–58
  vagueness of text, Supp.I:546
  wiretapping, 108
Frazier-Lemke Acts, **769**
  revised version upheld, 2077

Freedmen's Bureau, **770**
  Black Codes, 124
  civil rights enforcement, 712
  and Justice Department, 81
Freedom of . . . , *see also* Right of . . .
Freedom of assembly and association, **770–74**, Supp.I:**228–29**
  due process and Fourteenth Amendment, 589–91
  First Amendment, 732, 770, 772, 1292
  First Amendment and PACs, Supp.I:361–62
  fundamental rights, 829, 830
  infringed, 844
  labor unions, Supp.I:297–98
  picketing, 1387, 1388
  and political parties, 1408–13, Supp.I:362–63
  prior restraint against, 1453–56
  and private discrimination, Supp.I:391
  public forums, 1488, 1489
  in state constitutions, 770
  see also Freedom of intimate association; Subversive activities and the Constitution
Freedom of contract, **774–81**
  Adamson Act, 24
  Allgeyer v. Louisiana, 45
  Bunting v. Oregon, 169, 170
  due process in minimum wage laws, 25, 26, 1259
  economic liberties, 601
  invalidation of minimum wage law, 736
  maximum hour law upheld, 920
  in public interest, 32
  and sixty-hour work week, 1175
  see also Antitrust and the Constitution; Commerce Clause
Freedom of Information Act (1966), **781**
  executive privilege exemptions, 671–73
  and First Amendment, 738
  government secrecy, Supp.I:244
  and Ninth Amendment, 1316–20
  Privacy Act of 1974, 1457
Freedom of intimate association, **782–89**
  Bowers v. Hardwick, Supp.I:48
  choice of public or private schools, 1389
  compelling state interest, 337
  divorce, 572, 573
  Griswold v. Connecticut, 870, 871
  in illegitimacy, 948
  and miscegenation, 1266
  reaffirmed, 1252
  reproductive choice, 870, 871, 1552–58
  zoning, 788
Freedom of petition, **789–90**
  abolitionists' right to, 3
  English Bill of Rights, 113
  and First Amendment, 732
  Magna Carta, 1196
Freedom of religion, *see* Religious liberty
Freedom of speech, **790–97**, Supp.I:**229–31**
  absolutism, 8, 9
  academic freedom, 12, 13
  access to press, 1252
  balancing tests, 8, 94
  Barenblatt v. United States, 101
  Bethel School District v. Fraser, Supp.I:37
  Board of Education of the Westside Community Schools v. Mergens, Supp.I:42
  in broadcasting, 157
  children and the First Amendment, Supp.I:69–70
  clear and present danger test, 7, 8

Military justice, **1253–55**
  Court of Military Appeals, 510, 511
  governed by Uniform Code of Military Justice, 1253, 1254
  and habeas corpus, 881, 1255
  mandamus, 1198
  Uniform Code, 1365, 1937
Military Reconstruction Acts, **1255**
  constitutionality upheld, 1235
  and racial discrimination, 888
Minimum wages, *see* Maximum hours and minimum wages legislation
Ministerial act, **1261**
Minnesota rate cases, **1261–62**
  distinguished in Shreveport Doctrine, 929
  federal regulation of intrastate commerce, 997
Minors, *see* Child benefit theory; Child labor amendment; Child pornography; Children and the First Amendment; Children's rights; Juvenile proceedings
Miranda rules, **1264–65**, Supp.I:**330–31**
  Brewer v. Williams, 153
  and Burger Court, 177
  deception, Supp.I:257
  differing warnings, Supp.I:396
  evidence, 658
  exceptions, 1347
  in police interrogation, 613, 1264, 1404, 1405, Supp.I:361, 459–60
  for psychiatrist-patient relationship, Supp.I:405
  public safety exception, 1311
  right against self-incrimination, 655, 1350
  right to counsel, 905, 1265
  waiver, 2003–2005
Miscegenation, **1265–66**
  Black Codes, 124
  and Constitution, 1204
  justiciability, 1090
  and racial discrimination, 1181, 1204
  Virginia's Racial Integrity Act reversed, 1181
Misdemeanor, **1266–67**
  and arrest warrants, 72
  Bill of Rights guarantees, 1266
  jury trial for, 97
  right to counsel, 71
Missouri Compromise of 1820, **1268–69**
  Dred Scott decision, 584, 585, 1269
  slavery in the territories, 1696
  voided, 1095, 1096
Monetary power, **1270–73**
  gold clause cases, 850, 851, 1270
  and implied powers, 862–66
  legal tender cases, 1270–73
  necessary and proper clause, 1305–1307
Monroe Doctrine, **1274**
  foreign affairs, 747–55
  unwritten constitution, 1949–51
Mootness, **1278–79**
  in affirmative action case, 34, 551, 1278
  justiciability, 1089, 1279
  relaxed in class actions, 1047, 1279
Morrill Act, land-grant college system establishment, 1280
Multimember districts, **1284**
  and reapportionment, 93
  in state legislations, 110
Mundt-Nixon Bill, **1284–85**
  House Committee on Un-American Activities, 927

Municipal Bankruptcy Act (1934), **1285**
  invalidated in 1936, 1285
Municipal immunity, **1285–86**
  in common law, 1285
  none in deprivation of constitutional rights, 1357
  not conferred by Eleventh Amendment, 1285

N

NAACP Legal Defense and Education Fund, 1292
  adequate state grounds, 25
  Brown v. Board of Education, 161–64
  Buchanan v. Warley, 167
  and civil liberties, 270, 1292
  and civil rights movement, Supp.I:79–80
  equal protection arguments, 642
  freedom of association case, 771, 844
  interest group litigation, 987–89, Supp.I:321
  legislative investigation of, 1151
  opposed by Justice Department, 714
Narcotics, *see* Controlled-substance abuse; Drug regulation; Drug testing
Nashville Convention, **1293**
  and Jefferson Davis, 541
  and Missouri Compromise, 1268, 1269
  secession and lack of unity, 1293
National Association for the Advancement of Colored People, *see* NAACP Legal Defense and Educational Fund
National Court of Appeals, Supp.I:536
National Emergencies Act (1976), 2016
  see also Emergency powers
National Environmental Policy Act, *see* Environmental regulations
National Firearms Act, 1203
  excise tax on manufacturers and dealers in firearms, 1710
National Industrial Recovery Act, **1293–94**
  as administrative law, 27
  general welfare clause authority, 837, 838
  invalidation of, 28, 1622, 1623
  "little" NIRA, 217
  petroleum quotas held unconstitutional, 1363
  unauthorized by commerce clause, 1622
  unconstitutional delegation of powers, 552, 553, 1294, 1622
  unfair competition proscribed, 1293, 1622
National Labor Relations Acts, *see* Taft–Hartley Act; Wagner Act
National minimum drinking age, Supp.I:89, 90
National police power, **1295–99**
  law enforcement and federal-state relations, 1126–30
  and mislabeled drugs, 1808
  over interstate shipment of lottery tickets, 226, 1295
  registration of narcotics dealers, 575
  in state-federal law enforcement, 1126–30
  taxing power, 1297
  vitiated in *Hammer v. Dagenhart*, 893
National Prohibition Cases, *see* Amending process; Eighteenth Amendment
National Security Act (1947), **1299**
  creation of Central Intelligence Agency, 1299
  and foreign affairs powers of the President, 1299

National security and the Fourth Amendment, **1299–1300**
  balancing test, 94
  freedom of association, 337
  freedom of speech, 793, 888
  freedom of the press, Supp.I:232
  procedural due process, 888
  right to travel, 888
  scientific information, Supp.I:477
  wiretapping in cases of, 619
National Security Council, *see* National Security Act
Native Americans, *see* American Indians
Natural gas regulation, *see* Economic regulation
Naturalization, **1300–1301**
  and common law, 198
  defined by Supreme Court, 1300
  denied in oath case, 1627
  expatriation and, 675
  of group, 1301
  see also Denaturalization
Natural law, *see* Higher law; Natural rights and the Constitution
Natural rights and the Constitution, **1301–1303**
  Americans with Disabilities Act, Supp.I:20
  Declaration of Independence, 545–48, 1301
  Federalist, The, 708–711
  fundamental interests, 825
  and higher law, 914
  and Magna Carta, 1196
  political philosophy, Supp.I:364
  relation of property to politics, Supp.I:401
  unenumerated rights, Supp.I:556
Navigable waters, *see* Subjects of commerce
Necessary and proper clause, **1305–1307**
  broad construction, 158, 1306
  Embargo Acts, 627
  full faith and credit, 824
  implied powers, 962–66, Supp.I:216
  judicial policymaking, 1044
  legislation authorized as, 824
  limits on, 1306
  national police power, 1295–99, 1306
Neutrality concept of the Rehnquist Court, Supp.I:432–36
New Christian right, *see* Religious fundamentalism
New Deal, Supp.I:**335–39**
  court-packing plan, Supp.I:127
  liberalism of, Supp.I:312–13
  Charles E. Wyzanski, Jr., Supp.I:590
New Jersey Colonial Charters, **1309**
  evidence of constitutionalism, 1309
New Jersey Plan, **1309–10**
  at Constitutional Convention of 1787, 360–67
New Right, Supp.I:**339–40**
Newsman's privilege, *see* Reporter's privilege
New York Charter of Liberties and Privileges (1683), **1311–12**
  based on Magna Carta, 1195–97
Nineteenth Amendment, **1315–16**
  woman suffrage, 42, Supp.I:580–81
Ninth Amendment, **1316–20**
  Justice Burger's opinion in *Richmond Newspapers, Inc. v. Virginia*, 1319
  originalism, Supp.I:353
  protection of homosexual activity, Supp.I:48
  protection of individual liberty, 1318
  unenumerated rights, Supp.I:555–57
Noise, *see* Sound trucks

Poverty law, **Supp.I:377–80**
  welfare rights, Supp.I:570–71
  welfare state, Supp.I:571–74
  see also Indigent
Pragmatism, **Supp.I:384–85**
  deconstruction, Supp.I:144
Prayer, school, *see* Religion in public schools;
    School prayers
Preamble, **1435–36**
  authorship attributed to Gouverneur Morris,
    1435
  objection by Patrick Henry, 1435
Precedent, **1436–38**
  adherence to, Supp.I:353–54
  constitutional theories, Supp.I:122
  interpretivism, Supp.I:269
  memorandum orders, 1246
  in right to counsel, 40
  weight of, 1437
Preemption, **1438–39**
  and civil rights, 42
  exceptions to doctrine, Supp.I:298
  regulation of navigable airspace, 170
  of state authority by federal, 1148, 1438,
    Supp.I:177
  state registration of aliens barred, 918
  of state tort remedies, Supp.I:550
Preferred freedoms, **1439–40**
  First Amendment, 1439
  and fundamental rights, 829
  incorporation doctrine, 970–73
  strict scrutiny of, 829
  undermining *Gitlow* decision, 847
Presentment, **1440**
  by grand jury, 859–61
President and the treaty power, **Supp.I:385–
    88**
  and Congress, Supp.I:94
  and Senate, Supp.I:486
Presidential Election Campaign Fund Act, *see*
    Federal Election Campaign Acts
Presidential ordinance-making power, **1440–41**
  executive orders, 669
Presidential powers, **1441–47**
  Boland Amendment, Supp.I:44
  budget process, 168, 169, Supp.I:56–58
  checks and balances diminished, 1441
  as commander-in-chief, 316, 317
  executive agreements, 666, 668
  executive orders, 669
  foreign affairs, 747–55, Supp.I:92–93, 96, 270–
    71
  and inherent powers, 982
  and limited government, 1160–62
  ordinance-making, 1440–41
  separation of powers erosion, 1441
  spending, 1447
  treaty-making, Supp.I:94, 385–88
  war powers, 1444
  World War I, Supp.I:583–85
  World War II, Supp.I:586–88
  see also Executive power; Executive preroga-
    tive; Executive privilege
Presidential Recordings and Materials Preserva-
    tion Act, 1324
  Nixon's claims rejected by Court, 1324
Presidential spending power, **1447**
Presidential succession, **1448–49**
  Twenty-Fifth amendment, 1927
Presumption of constitutionality, *see* Rational ba-
    sis; Standard of review

Pretrial disclosure, **1449–50**
  discovery, 565, 566
  fair trial, 684
  Federal Rules of Criminal Procedure, 717,
    718
Preventive detention, **1450–51**
  and bail, 91
  and bill of attainder, 111–12, 1451
  and Burger Court, 177
  Internal Security Act, 992
  Japanese American Cases, 1010
  for juveniles, 91, 1622
  RICO offenders, Supp.I:471
Price-Anderson Act, Supp.I:550
Price-fixing, *see* Antitrust law and the Constitu-
    tion; Economic regulation
Primary elections, **1452–53**
  all-white, 727
  all-white invalidated, 1324, 1325, 1698
  all-white upheld, 874
  and equal protection, 642
  one person, one vote principle, 1344
  selection of political party nominees, 1408–13
Prior inconsistent testimony, *see* Confrontation,
    right of
Prior restraint and censorship, **1453–56**
  enjoining obscene materials, 1105
  Espionage Act of 1917, 652
  fair trial, 807
  and First Amendment, 735, 1109, 1700
  of free press, 798, 1303, Supp.I:232
  of free speech, 794
  gag order on pretrial publicity, 1305, 1455
  and Hughes Court, 938, 1303
  Pentagon Papers case, 1313
Prisoners' rights, **1456, Supp.I:388–89**
  access to the courts, 1480
  body search, Supp.I:43–44
  cruel and unusual punishment, Supp.I:141–42
  forced medication, Supp.I:327
  freedom of the press, 1372
  freedom of speech, 1372, 1480
  religious rights, Supp.I:348
  to refuse medical treatment, Supp.I:404
  Washington v. Harper, Supp.I:568–69
Privacy Act (1974), **1457**
Privacy and the First Amendment, **1457–58**
  freedom of speech, 790–97
  freedom of the press, 797–804
  see also Reasonable expectation of privacy;
    Right of privacy
Private discrimination, Supp.I:389–92
  and Fourteenth Amendment, Supp.I:221–22
  freedom of association, Supp.I:228
  Patterson v. McLean Credit Union, Supp.I:358
  state action doctrine, Supp.I:509–10
Privileges and immunities, **1458–61**
  of citizens, 505
  congressional, 350, 351
  economic regulation, 603, Supp.I:155
  Fourteenth Amendment, 757, 1262
  in hiring Alaska residents, 914
  presidential, 671–73
  proprietary concepts, Supp.I:240
  in racial discrimination, 3
  right against self-incrimination, 137
  sex discrimination, 140
  state discrimination, Supp.I:30
  woman suffrage denied, 1262
Privy council, **1461–62**
  Senate's powers, 31

Prize Cases, **1462**
  blockade of Confederacy as political question,
    1420–22
  need for declaration of war, Supp.I:82
Probable cause, **1462–65**
  administrative search, Supp.I:8
  in arrest, 73
  exclusionary role, 664
  and flight from an officer, 2074
  informant's tip not contributing to, 1719
  standard for search, 29, 40, 46, Supp.I:480
  and stop-and-frisk rule, 2083
  to detain occupants during search, 1253
  for urine testing, Supp.I:157–58
  for warrantless search, 155, 216, Supp.I:359
  for warrants, 73
Procedural due process of law, civil, **1465–72,**
    Supp.I:392–95
  Bishop v. Wood, 119
  Board of Regents v. Roth, 131, 132
  in bureaucracy, 172
  and computers, Supp.I:87
  confrontation, 346, Supp.I:92
  Goldberg v. Kelly, 849, 850
  for indigent defendants, 40, Supp.I:379
  right to treatment for mentally disabled,
    Supp.I:152, 153
  security against corporal punishment, 981
  social compact view, 1700, 1701
  standards for calculating punitive damages,
    Supp.I:408
  torts, Supp.I:549–53
  for welfare benefits, 849, 850, Supp.I:176–
    77
Procedural due process of law, criminal, **1472–**
    80, Supp.I:395–98
  bail, Supp.I:33–34
  and computers, Supp.I:87
  and confrontation, right of, Supp.I:90–92
  criminal procedure, 516–22
  Fifth Amendment, 1472, 1477
  Fourteenth Amendment, 757–61
  Fourth Amendment rights, 761–63
  habeas corpus, Supp.I:249–50
  incorporation doctrine, 970–73
  indigent defendants, Supp.I:377–78
  Miranda rules, Supp.I:330–31
  narrow view by Court, 1930
  ordered liberty, 1346, 1347
  prison inmates, Supp.I:389
  rights of criminally accused, Supp.I:464–67
  sentencing, Supp.I:490
Process-oriented constitutional theories,
    Supp.I:123
Prochoice movement, *see* Abortion; Reproduc-
    tive autonomy
Proclamation of Neutrality (1793), **1480**
  advisory opinion sought from Supreme Court,
    192
  concurrence of Washington's cabinet, 192
Production, **1480–81**
  and child labor, 1098
  distinguished from interstate commerce,
    1103
  regulation reserved to states, 36, 893
Progressive constitutional thought, **1481–82**
  amending process reforms, 1482
  assumptions challenged, 1481
  budget process, Supp.I:57–58
  criticism of the Constitution, 1481
  motives behind ratification, 1481

Q

R

T

U

V

W